THE RANGER IDEAL VOLUME 3

Texas Rangers in the Hall of Fame, 1898–1987

by
Darren L. Ivey

University of North Texas Press
Denton, Texas

Printed in the United States of America.

10 9 8 7 6 5 4 3 2 1

Permissions:
University of North Texas Press
1155 Union Circle #311336
Denton, TX 76203-5017

The paper used in this book meets the minimum requirements of the American National Standard for Permanence of Paper for Printed Library Materials, z39.48.1984. Binding materials have been chosen for durability.

Library of Congress Cataloging-in-Publication Data

Ivey, Darren L., 1970— author.
The Ranger ideal / Darren L. Ivey.
pages cm
Includes bibliographical references and index.
ISBN-13 978-1-57441-843-9 (cloth : alk. paper)
ISBN-13 978-1-57441-853-8 (ebook)
1. Texas Rangers in the Hall of Fame, 1898–1987 2. Texas Rangers—Biography. 3. Texas—History, Military.

F385.I94 2017
363.209764–dc23
2017027901

Cover image: Jim Riddles' Colt M1911 .45 automatic and gun belt, gift of Mrs. Jim Riddles. Stan Guffey's Texas Ranger Badge, loaned by Josefina Guffey Jennings. Courtesy Texas Ranger Hall of Fame and Museum, Waco, Texas.

Cover photographs: William L. Wright, Wilson County Historical Society; Captain Bob Crowder, #1983/112_R-316-1, Texas State Library & Archives Commission; Bobby Paul Doherty, Texas Ranger Hall of Fame and Museum, Waco, Texas.

The electronic edition of this book was made possible by the support of the Vick Family Foundation. Typeset by vPrompt eServices.

For Dusti

The Texas Ranger Song
Also known as “They Took It Up”

Many stories have been written of the Rangers and their deeds
Some are true, some are legends
All of justice and its needs
There were Mexicans, and Indians around
There were Texans and they sought a common ground
There are outlaws in every breed of us
For justice and for freedom, the Rangers took it up.

They took it up, with men who didn’t care about the law
They took it up, with men who wanted everything they saw
They envisioned all proud men as drinking from a common cup
It was freedom, it was justice
And the Rangers took it up.

—Lyrics by Tom T. Hall and Allen Pace
Performed by Johnny Rodriguez

Contents

Preface and Acknowledgments

The esteemed historian Robert M. Utley observed that "the twentieth century featured two breeds of Texas Rangers, the old and the new. But the new kept the name of the old and clung to the history, the traditions, and even the legendry that had gained pride and renown for the old. Like other states, Texas has a criminal investigative arm of the state government. In deference to the past, it is made up of officers called Texas Rangers, a term and probably an organization destined to endure for the foreseeable future."

Byron Johnson, executive director of the Texas Ranger Hall of Fame and Museum in Waco, is responsible for preserving the organization's history and traditions. In the course of his many years at the repository, he has observed qualities that have benefitted Rangers over their nearly two hundred years of serving the Lone Star State. Dubbed "The Ranger Ideal," these traits include respecting one's sense of right and wrong, spending a lifetime dedicated to the common good rather than to self, and knowing that one man (or woman) can make a difference in the world, even in the face of fierce opposition. Johnson noted, "The outstanding Rangers of the 20th century honored this code. Like the Lone Ranger of fiction, most avoided publicity and acclaim. They faced off against mobs and prison riots, gave their lives rescuing children, defused armed standoffs and trained those who would follow. In those few instances when political action degraded their ranks, or took away their right to use the title of Texas Ranger, many continued to serve the common good in the Ranger tradition."

Now, at last, with Volume 3, we bring the Texas Rangers into the modern age. The men in these pages will continue the service's march toward modernity. They will change from gunfighters and manhunters, although aspects of these attributes will remain, to professional criminal investigators. As we will see, the Rangers survived some "dark days" and emerged on the other side determined to be and do better, even if they did not put this sentiment into words. However, actions speak plainly.

The first two and a half decades of the twentieth century were, as journalist Paul I. Wellman commented, "a sort of a bridge between the 'classic' era, when outlaws used horses, six-shooters, and Winchesters, and the new age, when they employed automobiles, automatic pistols, and submachine guns in their crimes." Characteristically, the Rangers adapted to their better-equipped adversaries, except when hindered by parsimonious legislatures and paltry appropriations.

Rather than strictly trailing desperadoes by their hoofprints, the Rangers of the twentieth century became equipped to follow clues using modern techniques. While a detective might correctly observe that talking to people, suspects and witnesses alike, is still the most important practice in a criminal investigation, the Rangers of the Texas Department of Public Safety (DPS) came to be supported by a state laboratory that offered a variety of forensic methods, including fingerprints and blood typing. Instead of begging railroads for transportation, twentieth-century Rangers were issued state vehicles, which increased their responsiveness and efficiency. Telephones and two-way radios would enhance communications and the transmission of information.

Eventually, through much toil and some missteps, the Rangers would become a division of the DPS, a new state-level organization designed to remove politics from law enforcement. While not entirely successful, the department offered Rangers a career path that was not determined by gubernatorial elections and political whim. Turnover, once the bane of the Frontier Battalion and the Ranger Force, became a thing of the past, and a modern Ranger could be assured he would work cases for the foreseeable future, if he met the exacting standards expected of him.

Colonel Homer Garrison, Jr. was the source of those benchmarks, and he would loom large over the service for thirty years. Many a man was proud to call himself a "Garrison Ranger." Indeed, years after his passing, the colonel's stamp can still be found throughout the organization.

The twelve men featured in this last volume served the people of Texas from 1898 to 1987. "The Big Four" captains—Will Wright, Frank Hamer,

Tom Hickman, and Manual Gonzaullas—set the standards of physical courage, personal integrity, and dedication to duty for Garrison to maintain and for twentieth-century Rangers to emulate. Coming from the same generation, Charlie Miller and Marvin Burton spent the 1920s and 1930s upholding the traditions of the service. Those who followed after the establishment of the DPS—Bob Crowder, Johnny Klevenhagen, Jim Riddles, Clint Peoples—continued in the footsteps of those who came before them. Embodying these principles, Bob Doherty and Stan Guffey gave their lives in the service of others.

Elsewhere, I have made the observation that certain men in the Hall of Fame have been underserved by history. Frank Hamer, Manual Gonzaullas, John Klevenhagen, and Clint Peoples have been the subjects of at least one full-length biography. At the time of this writing, Professor Richard B. McCaslin is finalizing a work on the life of Will Wright. The remainder, while not completely ignored, have not had their tales fully explored and conveyed to an audience. Additionally, while John Boessenecker has recently written an exceptional biography of Hamer, the existing books on Gonzaullas, Klevenhagen, and Peoples were published decades ago. A man's story is never complete, and the potential for new information or interpretation always remains.

In chronicling the lives of these twelve men, I was assisted by an immense number of generous people. Even during the global pandemic of 2020, they freely gave of their time and expertise to make this book a reality. To them all, I wish to express a heartfelt "thank you": Christina Stopka, Christina Smith Clariday, Amanda Crowley, and Rusty Bloxom, Texas Ranger Research Center, Texas Ranger Hall of Fame and Museum, Waco, Texas; Sergeant Joe B. Davis, Texas Rangers (Ret.), Jean Eckstein, and James M. McCrae, Former Texas Rangers Foundation and Association, Fredericksburg, Texas; Sharon Yglecias, Texas Ranger Foundation Association, Waco, Texas; Sergio Velasco, Tonia Wood, Caitlin Burhans, and Richard Gilreath, Texas State Library and Archives Commission, Austin, Texas; David S. Turk, U.S. Marshals Service, Washington, DC; Annette Amerman, Historical Reference Branch, U.S. Marine Corps History Division, Arlington, Virginia; Jennifer L. Hall, Human Resources Bureau, Texas Department of Public Safety, Austin, Texas;

Catherine Wusterhausen, Texas Legislative Reference Library, Austin, Texas; the reference staffs at Kansas State University, Manhattan, Kansas, and Emporia State University, Emporia, Kansas; Aryn Glaizer, Briscoe Center for American History, Austin, Texas; Travis Goode, Eugene McDermott Library, University of Texas at Dallas; Caroline Byrne, Southern Methodist University, Dallas, Texas; Karen Oliver, Austin College, Sherman, Texas; Melleta R. Bell, Archives of the Big Bend, Sul Ross State University, Alpine, Texas; William D. Short, Lamar University, Beaumont, Texas; Mary H. Perez, University of Texas at Brownsville; Yvonne Realivasquez, Sul Ross State University; Charles David Grear, Killeen, Texas; Maurine Liles, Wilson County Historical Society, Floresville, Texas; Sophia Franco, Pecos County Clerk's Office, Fort Stockton, Texas; Kristina Kidd, Denton County Criminal District Attorney's Office, Denton, Texas; Pat Nichols, Genealogy Department, Montgomery County Public Library, Conroe, Texas; Clay Renick, Hutchinson County Historical Museum, Borger, Texas; Anita Vanklaveren, Kerr County Clerk's Office, Kerrville, Texas; Maria Cristina Coke, Edwards County and District Clerk's Office, Rocksprings, Texas; Carol Kysar, Bastrop County Historical Society Museum, Bastrop, Texas; Linda Merryman and Hannah Kubacak, West Waco Library and Genealogy Center, Waco, Texas; Rita Wilson, Ector County Library, Odessa, Texas; James Bales, Chisholm Trail Museum, Wellington, Kansas; Sarah Ganderup, Western History and Genealogy Department, Denver Public Library, Denver, Colorado; Maria Carter and Veronica Martinez, Local History Department, Corpus Christi Public Library, Corpus Christi, Texas; Allison Ehrlich, *Corpus Christi Caller-Times*, Corpus Christi, Texas; Betsy Thomas, Sid Richardson Museum, Fort Worth, Texas; Kevin Kinney, Galveston and Texas History Center, Rosenberg Library, Galveston, Texas; Susan Chandler, Nesbitt Memorial Library, Columbus, Texas; Janet Shapiro, San Antonio Genealogical and Historical Society, San Antonio, Texas; Betty Thompson, Taylor Public Library, Taylor, Texas; Susie M. Homeyer, City Secretary, Navasota, Texas; Mike Wilfong, Restland of Dallas, Dallas, Texas; Richard Lane, Huntsville Public Library, Huntsville, Texas; Chuck Parsons, Luling, Texas; Dr. Richard B. McCaslin, Denton, Texas; John Boessenecker, San Francisco, California; Randy Lish, Salt Lake City, Utah; Taronda Schulz, Giddings, Texas; Patterson Smith, Montclair,

New Jersey; Dr. Charles H. Harris III, Betty Harris, and Dr. Louis R. Sadler, Albuquerque, New Mexico; Connie Rodriguez, San Antonio, Texas; Marlene Seaton, Albuquerque, New Mexico (in memory of Raymond L. Seaton, Louisville, Kentucky); Kirby Franklin Warnock, Pecos, Texas; Ernest Woodward, Fort Stockton, Texas; Alfredo Aguilar, Texas Tech University; Dr. Donald E. Green, Orlando, Florida; Janith Johnson, Crestline, California; Jim Causey, Annetta, Texas; Michael H. Ivey, Manhattan, Kansas; Evan S. Ivey, St. Charles, Missouri; Joel Hutchcroft, Peoria, Illinois; Kristen Voss and Maureen A. Denfeld, Fairfax, Virginia; Jane Lawson Hammonds, Charlotte, North Carolina; Cameron Woodall, Cedar Hill, Texas; Robert Nichols, Conroe, Texas; David Parsons, Brownsville, Texas; and Paul Miller, therailroadpolice.com. If I failed to mention anyone, please know your contributions are appreciated.

One of the more enjoyable tasks I had was the opportunity to talk with the families and friends of some of the Rangers featured in this book. My gratitude for their patience, kindness, and enthusiasm cannot be overstated. I owe a warm thanks to Captain Bob G. Prince, Texas Rangers (Ret.); Carolyn Doherty, Buster W. Doherty, and Kelly L. McIlveene; David B. Hickman; Mike Gault; James E. Riddles, Carolyn Anne Riddles, and the late James B. Riddles; Andrew Miller, Rex A. Miller and the late Roger H. Miller; James T. Crowder, Jr., Catherine McGuire, and Carol Rodat; Josie Guffey Jennings, Stacy Guffey, Travis Guffey-Jennings, and Brenda Perrin; Senior Captain H. R. "Lefty" Block, Texas Rangers (Ret.); and Barbara Klevenhagen Gann. I sincerely hope I have given their loved ones the honor and respect they deserve.

For the third time, I thank the dedicated team at the University of North Texas Press in Denton: Ronald Chrisman and Elizabeth "Bess" Whitby.

Special thanks to Bob Alexander, Bellville, Texas, and Doug Dukes, Austin, Texas, for reviewing the manuscript and for their insightful advice. My profound appreciation goes to Byron Johnson for his continued generosity and support, and for loaning me the phrase that ended up on this book's cover.

My lovely and gracious bride, Dusti, continues to make each book better with her perceptiveness, strict adherence to good grammar, and formidable proofreading abilities. She has not only my gratitude but also my heart.

Introduction

The Homer Garrison Texas Ranger Museum, located at historic Fort Fisher on the banks of the Brazos River, officially opened to the public on October 25, 1968. The fulfillment of a desire to honor Texas Rangers, past and present, took years, and its guiding force was Senior Captain, and later U.S. Marshal, Clint Peoples. While the project was his brainchild, Peoples had the assistance of the Fort Fisher Committee, the Fort Fisher Ranger Museum Committee, the Texas Ranger Commemorative Commission, the Texas Ranger Commemorative Foundation, and scores of other dedicated and civic-minded individuals. As part of the agreements the project required, the museum's management was turned over to the City of Waco. At the same time, the facility was certified by the Texas Department of Public Safety as the Official Museum of the Texas Rangers. Presently, the museum showcases exhibits related to the Rangers and pioneer history of Texas, and has grown to include, but is not limited to, firearms, badges, clothing, saddles, equipment, and an extensive art collection. Starting in 1978 and continuing through the 1980s, several additions were built to expand the museum space.

The Texas Ranger Commemorative Commission, established by the legislature in June 1971, was appointed to oversee the celebration of the famed service's sesquicentennial anniversary in 1973. A subsidiary organization, the Texas Ranger Commemorative Foundation, chaired by Captain Peoples, became responsible for building and financing a Texas Ranger Hall of Fame. During a banquet that followed the groundbreaking ceremony at Fort Fisher on August 4, 1973, a film, entitled *The Texas Rangers: A Certain Kind of Man*, was shown to the audience. The program portrayed several historical events involving the Texas Ranger service, including the deaths of outlaws Sam Bass and Bonnie and Clyde. Country western singer Johnny Rodriguez, a good friend of the late Ranger Joaquin Jackson, sang "They Took It Up," which had been composed specifically for the occasion by Tom T. Hall and Allan Pace. In addition, the future facility was named the

Official Hall of Fame of the Texas Rangers by the Texas Ranger Commemorative Commission. After months of construction that cost the taxpayers not one cent, the Hall of Fame was dedicated at high noon on February 7, 1976. An integral component of the Hall of Fame and Museum, the Moody Texas Ranger Memorial Library was established to house an ever-growing collection of service records, case files, correspondence, photographs, microfilm, periodicals, and books.

Twenty Texas Rangers were initially inducted, and the remaining eleven have been added in the years since. The inclusion of some men has later stirred debate, but as Byron Johnson commented to me in an email, "The serving Rangers who make induction decisions for the Texas Ranger Hall of Fame have a unique perspective on the service—at their point in the continuum … We have urged them to consider candidates based on criteria: who made major contributions to the development of the service, displayed exceptional valor—outside that normally expected of their contemporaries, or gave their lives in the line of duty under extraordinary circumstances. We think these adapt well to changing times, mores and mindsets."

On May 29, 1997, the Seventy-fifth Legislature passed House Concurrent Resolution No. 55, which designated the Texas Ranger Hall of Fame and Museum as the official state repository, library, and archives for the service. As well, the Moody Library was renamed the Texas Ranger Research Center. Governor George W. Bush, later to become the nation's forty-third president, signed the measure into law. With the archival collection growing too immense for the available space by the mid-2000s, the family of the late Tobin and Anne Armstrong, descendants of Texas Ranger John B. Armstrong, headed a fundraising campaign for the renovation and expansion of the Research Center. The facility was dedicated on June 7, 2012, as the Tobin and Anne Armstrong Texas Ranger Research Center.

Timeline of Texas Ranger History (1898–1987)

1898	Wright enlists in the Frontier Battalion.
1901	The Frontier Battalion reorganizes as the Ranger Force.
1906	Hamer enlists in the Ranger Force.
1919	The Ranger Force is the subject of a legislative probe; Hickman and Miller first join the Rangers.
1920–1921	Gonzaullas enlists in the Ranger Force; Hickman, Miller, and Gonzaullas enforce the law in the North Texas oil fields.
1920	Hickman and Miller keep order in Galveston.
1920–1924	Wright battles *tequileros* in several noted encounters.
1922	Hamer, Hickman, and Gonzaullas tames Mexia.
1922–1923	Burton and Hamer investigate a series of murders in Waco.
1922	Wright, Hamer, and Hickman keep the peace at a labor strike in Denison; Burton receives appointment as Texas Ranger.
1923	Burton leads raids in the "Glen Rose Liquor War."
1923–1924	Miller enforces Prohibition in San Antonio.
1926	Hickman ends a bank robbery in Clarksville.
1927–1930	Hamer, Hickman, Gonzaullas, and Burton are active in Borger.
1927–1931	Hamer tackles the Texas Bankers Association's scandal.
1927	Hickman closes the "Santa Claus Bank Robbery" case.
1929–1930	Burton investigates the Johnny Holmes murder case.
1930	Hamer and his men fail to protect George Hughes in Sherman.
1931	Hickman enforces a court order at the Red River bridge near Denison.

1931–1933	Hickman, Gonzaullas, and Burton active in the East Texas oil fields.
1939	Crowder is appointed into the Texas Rangers.
1941	Klevenhagen receives Texas Ranger commission.
1946	Gonzaullas works the "Phantom Slayer" case in Texarkana; Peoples is promoted to Texas Ranger.
1951	Peoples goes undercover in George Parr's Duval County and works the John Douglas Kinser murder in Austin.
1952	Miller and Klevenhagen involved in the investigations that would ultimately bring down George Parr; Riddles is appointed to the Texas Ranger.
1955	Crowder resolves the Rusk State Hospital prison riot.
1957	Klevenhagen involved in gunfight with Gene Paul Norris; Klevenhagen leads his Rangers in dismantling the Maceo gambling empire in Galveston.
1961–1962	Peoples works the Henry Marshall homicide near Franklin.
1963–1968	Peoples begins the process that will result in the establishment of a Texas Ranger museum.
1963	Riddles works the murder of Elgin Police Chief James M. Mumford.
1965	Peoples and Jim Riddles solve the murders of Susan Rigsby and Shirley Stark in Austin.
1969	Crowder works the Lone Star Steel labor strike.
1970–1974	Riddles investigates the murder of Nancy Mitchell, which leads to the apprehension of two serial killers.
1971–1973	Peoples involved in Texas Rangers' sesquicentennial and the creation of the Hall of Fame.
1976	Doherty is appointed a Texas Ranger.
1978	Doherty is killed in the line of duty during a narcotics raid in Denison.
1979	Guffey is commissioned into the Texas Rangers.
1985	Guffey participates in the rescue of Amy McNeil.
1987	Guffey loses his life while saving Kara-Leigh Whitehead.

William L. Wright. *Courtesy Wilson County Historical Commission Archives, Floresville, TX.*

Chapter 1

William L. Wright: "A Well-Deserved Reputation"

William Leonidas Wright was the first of the "Big Four" Texas Ranger captains. In over forty years as a peace officer, he developed a well-deserved reputation for fearlessness, personal integrity, and dedication to duty. Like the captains who came before, Wright led from the front, and his long scouts through the brush country in pursuit of smugglers are comparable to the forays of the nineteenth-century Rangers. However traditional his approach, he utilized the latest technology available to him. Historian Robert Utley remarked: "William L. Wright embodied probity, ideals, and professionalism acquired as a young Ranger … [he] would serve long, successfully, and honorably, but without the dash and glamour of his fellow captains."

He was born on February 19, 1868, in Lockhart, Caldwell County, Texas.[1] Little Berry "L. B." Wright, his father, had been born in Perry County, Alabama, on December 4, 1830, and immigrated to Texas from Panola County, Mississippi, in 1851. William's mother, Mary Elizabeth "Ann" Wright, came from the illustrious Tumlinson clan that figured so extensively in early Texas history. She was born on January 5, 1842, in Eagle Lake, Colorado County. L. B. and Ann were married on November 4, 1858, in DeWitt County. After farming in Karnes County, they returned to Yorktown. Their union produced, in addition to Will, Robert Wright, born in 1858;

Cornelia Elizabeth "Neelie" Wright, born on August 26, 1861; Zora Lee Wright, born in 1866; Mary H. Wright, born in 1872; Joseph T. Wright, born in 1875; and Milam Harper Wright, born on September 6, 1878.[2]

As the nation fell into civil war, L. B. was occasionally absent from home while serving as a corporal in Captain Charles A. Russell's company of mounted riflemen ("Helena Guards") in Karnes County on May 6, 1861. The company was assigned to the Twenty-ninth Brigade, Texas State Troops. Beginning on September 26, 1863, L. B. enlisted in his father-in-law's company of mounted minutemen in DeWitt County.[3]

After the war ended, the Wright family returned to Caldwell County but moved back to DeWitt when William was an infant. In the latter county, the elder Wright served as justice of the peace for Precinct No. 3, operator of a mercantile business, and farmer. In 1868, his merchandise was valued at twenty-five hundred dollars. By the following year, he was the owner of two hundred acres, three horses, and ten head of cattle. In the course of his official duties, L. B. held inquests on the bodies of James W. Cox, John W. S. "Jake" Christman, and John Jackson Marshall "Jack" Helm, all casualties of the Sutton-Taylor feud. In addition to being a concerned citizen, as one related to the Tumlinson clan, L. B. was "pained" to send a report to Governor Edmund Jackson Davis on the "verry [*sic*] bad State of affairs in our County." L. B. died on June 15, 1882 and was buried in the Upper Yorktown Cemetery.[4]

As a youngster, William attended the public schools of Yorktown and Cuero. Lieutenant William L. Rudd's detachment of Company F, Frontier Battalion made its headquarters camp behind L. B.'s store in Yorktown. According to his daughter, William, or "Bud" as he was known, often visited the Ranger camp. He confided to one of Rudd's men he was going to join that same organization when he came of age. Regardless of the tale's veracity, Wright rode as a cowboy for the ranches of Robert Christian Eckhardt in DeWitt County, and John Locke Rutledge in Karnes County. In addition, he worked a cattle drive as far as San Angelo for rancher John Rufus Blocker, and another from Tom Green County to Cheyenne, Wyoming, in 1889. Wright joined his widowed mother in Sutherland Springs, Wilson County, in 1891. Their new home was a farming community engaged in raising, among other products, cotton, corn, and livestock, but the mineral waters also attracted resort development. Wright married Mary Ann "Mollie" Brown on December 22, 1892. She had been born on March 25, 1871. Their oldest son, Charles Hays, nicknamed "Pat," was born on February 25, 1894. A second boy, Maurice Humphrie, known to the family as "Jack," entered the world on March 17, 1895. With a growing family, Wright dutifully worked his farm, "but I quit," he later told the *San Antonio Express*. "I didn't like it. It didn't rain enough."[5]

Soon after he won the election on November 6, 1894, Sheriff John Sutherland Craighead of Wilson County appointed the well-respected Wright his chief deputy. Upon receiving the appointment, Wright moved to Floresville and served in the position for four years.[6]

In the summer of 1897, Wright made "the most important arrest I … ever had a hand in." On June 5, Maximo Martinez was suspected of stabbing to death Juanita Acosta, the eighteen-year-old girl with whom he was infatuated. Juanita's grandparents also fell victim to the vicious killer. For five days, Wright, Karnes County Sheriff William Taylor "Brack" Morris, and several deputies tracked the fugitive to the Osborn Ranch near San Diego in Duval County. After an "exciting chase," the fugitive was captured when Wilson County Deputy Sheriff Juan Garza spotted him hiding in the brush. While Garza held him at gunpoint, Wright searched Martinez for weapons. Loading their prisoner into a borrowed buggy, the officers arrived in Karnes City on June 11. The next morning, Martinez was transported to Floresville to face a murder indictment. The strong evidence of his guilt convinced the suspect to confess to the murders, although he denied raping the girl. In order to give the accused a fair and impartial hearing, the Twenty-fifth District Court appointed attorneys John Edward Canfield and West Reagan Wiseman as defense counsel. The trial in Floresville concluded on June 22, and the jury returned a guilty verdict the next morning. Judge Munford Kennon immediately sentenced Martinez to death. Strangely, the condemned man requested a twelve-piece brass band play music during his hanging, but later rescinded his wish. While Sheriff Craighead and his deputies kept order around the gallows, five thousand people flocked to town to witness the execution on July 30.[7]

Zora Belle Wright, the only daughter born to Will and Mollie, entered the world on September 1, 1898, in Sutherland Springs.[8] Resigning from the sheriff's office that same year, Wright enlisted in Company E, Frontier Battalion at Cotulla on February 20, 1899, as a private. Serving under the famed captain John H. Rogers, Wright's first year as a state officer was eventful. While enforcing state health guidelines during a smallpox outbreak in Laredo, Rogers was wounded in a shooting on March 20, while Private Augustus Yardley "Augie" Old and Special Ranger Thomas Ragland narrowly escaped injury. Earlier the same day, Wright had accompanied Sergeant Henry Gilpin "Harry" DuBose, and Rangers Thomas Carney "Creed" Taylor, William Anthony "Billy" Old, and James Moore to Laredo to assist the captain. Notified of the shooting, DuBose led his men to the scene in the eastern portion of town. Upon arrival, they found a large crowd of *Mexicanos* numbering from sixty to one hundred, although only some twenty-five were armed. As the Rangers rounded the street corner, they were fired upon, which was immediately returned. The state officers steadily advanced and wounded at least seven assailants, one possibly mortally, in the thirty-minute gun battle. During the fight, Wright narrowly avoided a painful death when a bullet ricocheted off his belt buckle.[9]

Wright's first recorded arrest as a Ranger took place on April 24, 1899, when he and Private Billy Old apprehended an escapee from the La Salle County jail. In the midst of the Reese-Townsend feud in Colorado County, Wright and Creed Taylor were assigned to keep the peace in Columbus. The former arrested Albert Bushy and Fritz Hasty on charges of assault to murder at the end of May, and delivered the prisoners to Sheriff William Thomas Burford. From June 4 to 8, Wright arrested Duff Hines for cattle theft, and J. T. Reese for unlawfully carrying a pistol; recovered nine head of stolen cattle; and apprehended Hines and Sumpter Joiner for rustling, and Walter Reese for using abusive language. The Ranger returned to town on the eighth and discovered a riot had narrowly been avoided thanks to the efforts of Taylor and Deputy Sheriff Robert Wood Westmoreland. The following day, Wright requested the presence of one more Ranger, as Burford had "turned off" his deputies and was allowing Wright and Taylor to do all the work. On June 10, the two Rangers arrested Marcus Harvey Townsend, James Gaither "Jim" Townsend, Marion Hope, James "Jim" Clements, and Steph Yates for carrying firearms. The feud threatened to explode once more, as twenty-four armed men gathered at the Reese home on June 11. General Scurry, Sergeant DuBose, and Augie Old arrived the next day, and the crowd was dispersed.[10]

On July 14, Wright arrested Jack Stallion in Columbus for intent to rape. Two days later, while in Richmond, the Ranger witnessed a desperate street battle with ex-sheriff and former state senator Walter Moses Burton and his daughter, Hattie, opposing Doctor A. S. Stephenson. Wounding his two assailants in front of the post office, the physician died of his injuries within five minutes. The Burtons were apprehended and charged with murder. Stemming from another altercation, Wright arrested Arthur McDow on the twenty-fourth for assault with intent to murder. On July 27, Wright and Taylor were ordered to return to Cotulla. Wright arrested Ross Roebuck and George Evetts on August 7 on a charge of cattle theft. The following day, the Ranger took the pair to Carrizo Springs to appear before the grand jury. Roebuck was killed before the grand jurors met, then they failed to indict Evetts.[11]

White capping had been occurring in Texas for approximately ten years, and Wright would observe its effects firsthand. The practice began as "a movement of violent moral regulation by local masked bands." Likely influenced by the Reconstruction-era Ku Klux Klan, these vigilantes combined their supposedly high-minded ideals with a racist hostility.[12] In the town of Orange, a mob of white cappers sent threatening messages to local blacks working in the sawmills. On August 12, a mob of approximately twenty men shot into a house, killing one black man, and wounding another two. Captain Rogers and Augie Old were ordered to entrain to Orange on August 18. Wright and Taylor departed Cotulla, DuBose and James Moore made their way from Laredo, and the quartet united in San Antonio on the nineteenth. The state officers arrived in Orange on the twentieth to assist Rogers, and they reported to Sheriff Jefferson Davis Bland as directed. With the scene calmed, the captain investigated the recent shooting, but he could make little progress. The same day, the battalion was reorganized into four companies, each consisting of one captain, one sergeant, and eight privates.[13]

On September 1, Wright and Taylor returned to Columbus by order of General Scurry. The former arrested Frank Seveir on the seventh on a charge of cattle theft, and D. M. Horn on the eleventh for the same crime.

The following day, Wright once more took Arthur McDow into custody for murder. The Ranger and Sheriff Burford scouted for Tom Chappel, Harroll Chappel, and James Chappel on September 29. Once the trio were found, they were apprehended for murder and transported to the county jail.[14]

On December 17, Wright and Curren Lee "Kid" Rogers, the captain's brother, were ordered to report to Scurry in Hempstead. The Rangers arrested four men between the nineteenth and the twenty-third on charges ranging from disturbing the peace, to unlawfully carrying a pistol, to fighting. Wright returned to Cotulla, then welcomed his brother, Milam, into the company on the twenty-ninth.[15] Wright and Ranger Gratz D. Brown, also stationed at Cotulla, and Private Eugene Bell of Palestine, left on February 6, 1900, for Groveton. Their assignment was to assist Captain Rogers and Ranger Dabney White of Company B in keeping order in the midst of the ongoing feud in Columbus. On February 12, Rogers and Wright went to Bastrop to watch over the bail hearing for Walter Reese, James "Jim" Coleman, Thomas Barnette "Tom" Daniels, and Les Reese. Prior to the beginning of the proceedings three days later, local lawmen searched individuals who entered the courthouse for weapons, and the two state officers escorted Townsend partisans from the courtroom to their hotels. Ensuring violence was avoided, the Rangers guarded the faction's members on the sixteenth for their return trip to Columbus. Rogers and his men were back in Cotulla on the eighteenth.[16]

Wright, C. L. Rogers, Gratz Brown, A. Y. Old, and Levie Old, Augie's other brother, returned to Orange on February 22 at the request of State Representative Clarence Albert Teagle. Reporting to Sheriff Bland and Acting Mayor Benjamin H. Norsworthy, the Rangers found residents troubled by the attempted murder of clerk George W. Tate on the sixteenth, and by the posted notices threatening the lives of would-be assassins. The Rangers denounced the circulars and removed them while succeeding in "restoring peace and confidence" to the public. Norsworthy authorized a one-thousand-dollar reward for evidence that led to the arrest and conviction of the guilty party. Will Wright took charge of the detachment, and Milam was assigned to reinforce the Rangers in Orange. They made a number of arrests for disturbing the peace, carrying a pistol, theft, robbery, aggravated assault, assault and battery, and assault to murder. Wright was ordered to travel to Ducktown,

Tennessee, on April 4, and identify a man potentially wanted in Karnes County for murder. The suspect was not the right individual, and the Ranger returned to Orange on the ninth. Wright, Milam, and Levie Old left Orange for their respective stations on April 21.[17]

As the Frontier Battalion underwent a period of reorganization, each of the captains was ordered on February 28 to reduce his company to number one sergeant and nine privates. In accordance with the directive, Gratz Brown was discharged. In order to maintain the battalion within the appropriation, each company commander was ordered to discharge two privates on May 15. Furthermore, Rogers was directed to discharge an additional Ranger.[18]

Wright and DuBose were promoted to the rank of first lieutenant on June 1, 1900, and the latter was placed in command of Company A. Wright remained with Company E. On the twenty-eighth of the following month, Rogers dispatched Wright and Constable ____ Petty to scout Frio County for cattle thieves. Unfortunately, the pair were unable to secure any evidence, and they returned to Cotulla on July 30. The next day, the lieutenant was sent to Pearsall to locate a suspect wanted for murder. On August 20, Wright and Deputy Sheriff ____ Trammell scouted Dimmit County for stolen stock and recovered three head of cattle.[19]

After arresting one individual for swindling and three more for livestock theft in September, Wright made arrests for murder, cattle rustling, forgery, and unlawfully carrying a pistol the following month. On October 24, he was at home in Cotulla with his wife and his mother who was visiting the couple. Their family time was interrupted at six o'clock in the evening when a woman appeared at the front door and reported James Richard Devenport was intoxicated and firing his pistol in front of Pease & Jay's saloon. Having served five years in prison on a manslaughter charge, Devenport had been arrested for being drunk and disorderly several times in the past. Indeed, Wright had jailed Devenport on November 23, 1899, for unlawfully carrying a pistol. Having already encountered the inebriated man that afternoon, the Ranger left his house and, hurrying to the scene, attempted to make another arrest. Unlike previous occasions, though, Devenport resisted and attempted to shoot Wright twice at point-blank range. The bullets whipped through the lieutenant's coat, then Wright knocked Devenport's gun aside and fired his own weapon five times. The .45-caliber bullets slammed into the outlaw's chest, and Devenport slumped to the ground dead. The range was so close that the dead man's vest briefly caught fire from the muzzle blast of Wright's pistol. John Guy Smith, the editor of the *Isonomy*, had accompanied Devenport, and the newspaperman was arrested by Wright inside the saloon. Three pistols, two daggers, and a pair of brass knuckles were removed from his person.[20]

Sheriff William Merrill Burwell noted Devenport was a "desperate character." William Warren "Bill" Sterling would later say of the incident: "It closed the stormy career of an outlaw and firmly established the reputation of Will Wright as a man among men. Wright's trial by fire proved to the hard cases around Cotulla that he was more than a match for any of them, and he had no further trouble there."[21]

Plagued with cattle rustlers, the stockmen of Atascosa and Wilson Counties requested assistance from Rogers, and the Wright brothers were sent to the affected area on November 20. Two days later, the Rangers arrived at the Ellis Ranch between Pleasanton and Floresville. On November 24, they scouted the counties of McMullin, Wilson, and Atascosa, and gave special attention to the town of Campbellton. The same day, Rogers was instructed to transfer company headquarters to Laredo "as early as practicable." Despite a week of scouring the countryside, Will and Milam were unable to find any suspicious activity that required their attention. They returned to the Ellis spread on the thirty-first, then to Pleasanton on December 1. The two Rangers assisted Sheriff Abner Mathew Avant in escorting two murder suspects to the Floresville jail. They then scouted Karnes County at the request of local cattle raisers. Avant telephoned Wright on the tenth, and requested assistance in apprehending Joe Newman. The fugitive had fatally shot Jim Walker in Atascosa County, but, strangely, the crime received little attention in the newspapers. Furthermore, the exact identity of the killer is unclear. Since Joseph Eli Newman and Joseph D. Newman, both of whom were living in Atascosa County at the time, had connections to Karnes, DeWitt, and Wilson Counties, either man could potentially be the culprit. Wright visited Joe's father in Floresville and convinced him to give up his son who was hiding in DeWitt County. The younger Newman surrendered to a deputy sheriff at Runge on December 11, and was turned over to Wright at Floresville. The state officer then transported his prisoner to Pleasanton.[22]

Accompanied by Taylor, Wright assisted Deputy U.S. Marshal William Martin Hanson on January 20, 1901, in arresting one man for smuggling. The following day, the two Rangers and mounted Customs inspector Samuel Vaughn "Pete" Edwards scoured Zapata County for stolen horses and smugglers. They made no arrests, and returned to camp on the twenty-seventh.[23]

On March 11, Rogers sent Wright to Austin to secure permission from General Scurry to investigate the murder of William Early Jones, the former sheriff of Gonzales County. Jones, who had owned a ranch eight miles north of Medina, was killed on March 1, 1900, in a private altercation with the Reverend William David Robinson, his neighbor. Even though the killing had occurred the previous year, Wright proceeded to work up the case. He met with the victim's brother in San Antonio, then traveled to Bandera on the fifteenth to interview witnesses. While he was the state's witness in several forgery cases in Pleasanton on April 1, Wright made an arrest for perjury, and another the next day for cattle rustling. On the sixth, he returned to Bandera. Robinson, a Methodist minister, had been taken to the county jail and granted an examining trial on April 3. The state's principal witness was too intimidated to testify, and the prosecution did not otherwise possess sufficient evidence for a conviction. Wright provided protection to the witness, who agreed to appear in court. On April 17, Robinson was convicted of murder in the second degree, and received ten years in prison; the sentence was affirmed on June 22. He entered Huntsville on July 9, and was granted a pardon on August 27, 1904.[24]

Sought for the murders of Sheriffs Brack Morris on June 12, and Richard Martin "Dick" Glover two days later, Gregorio Cortéz y Lira rode into Wilson County on a worn-out horse. He stopped at the farm of James M. Allen, four miles south of Floresville, and helped himself to an eight-year-old Quarter Horse, soon to known as the "little brown mare." Having been in Bandera County for the last month chasing stock thieves, Wright left Medina city on June 15, and joined the massive manhunt that followed the fugitive through Atascosa County. There he united with Sheriff Avant and rancher and noted tracker Emanuel Tom. Tom quickly discovered the trail south of Twohig, but following Cortéz's tracks proved difficult, as the wily fugitive was familiar with the ways to throw off pursuers and knew the prickly-pear and mesquite country well. Soon, the chase moved toward the border beyond their reach. Despite the enormous number of law officers involved in the search, Captain Rogers was the one who took Cortéz into custody. Wright returned home to Laredo, and discovered his third son had been born on April 25. He named the boy Emanuel Avant after his two companions on the recent manhunt.[25]

During the month of September, Wright arrested two men for murder, one for burglary and another for hog theft. He apprehended another killer in October, then seemingly remained inactive until March 1902, when he took another hog thief into custody in Kimble County. Originally, Wright had been ordered there to keep order during a murder trial. The case had been transferred to Junction on a change of venue from Menard. Accompanied by Ranger Charles Sandherr, and later Oscar Latta, Wright watched over the proceedings. He noticed two armed men loitering around the courthouse, but thought nothing of their presence, assuming them to be guards. On March 30, after going to sleep in his hotel room, Wright was awakened by a call to respond to the courthouse. Dispatching Sandherr and Latta, Wright was shortly summoned by his two subordinates to come to the scene. Arriving, the lieutenant found a large crowd standing in the corridor outside of the county clerk's office. Pushing his way through the throng, he found a man lying on the hall floor with a head wound, and blood spattered over every surface. A second man, battered and bloodied, was sitting in a chair with his back to the office door. Upon being informed the seated individual had killed the first, Wright placed him under arrest. The crowd became agitated, and the numerous raised voices incoherent. Finally, after he was to able question the onlookers, Wright learned six sections of state-owned land were to be opened to settlement on April 1. Stockman Leslie Beasley, who was using the properties for pasturage, was determined to be the first to file on them. Thirty days prior to the filing date, he had arranged for four men in two 12-hour shifts to position themselves day and night in front of the courthouse and prevent others from submitting their applications for the allotment. Two of Beasley's men—George Clements and Alvin Capp—had laid down on the hallway floor to sleep, and Jim McAtee had simply stepped over them and sat down in the chair with his back to the door.[26]

Upon awaking, Capp and Clements were furious when they realized what had happened. Although angry, Capp did not want trouble, but Clements attempted to violently eject McAtee from the chair. In the ensuing brawl, all three men used their pistols as clubs, and McAtee finally struck Clements across the forehead, fracturing his skull. Capp apparently fled, and McAtee resumed his seat to await the authorities. Wright charged McAtee with assault to murder and placed him into the custody of Sheriff (and future Ranger captain) William Walter Taylor and Justice of the Peace Thomas Jefferson Meredith, while Clements was discovered to be seriously injured rather than dead. Capp was placed under arrest on a charge of aggravated assault and Clements for assault to murder; the latter presumably before he was taken to Kerrville for medical treatment. Meanwhile, the commissioners' court arranged for the General Land Office to change the time of filing, and the courthouse was closed. At the appointed time, two more of Beasley's men were present to file his application, and Wright and other lawmen were on hand at the clerk's office to prevent trouble. At 7:00 a.m., the sheriff unlocked the front door of the courthouse, and the assembled crowd swarmed, swearing and shoving, into the building. With McAtee in the lead, fights broke out all through the corridor to the clerk's office. Finally, a man named Fairchild was able to push his way through the mob and slide his papers into the slot on the door. He was judged the first and awarded the best portions of the allotment.[27]

In April, Wright arrested an accused horse thief and an additional man for illegally carrying a pistol, two men for assault to murder in May, and another in June for burglary and theft. On July 13, Juan Acosta, the leader of a burglary gang in Gonzales County, opened fire on Seguin City Marshal George Holloman during an arrest attempt at the Southern Pacific depot. He was spotted seven days later north of town in the company of other armed Mexicans. Wright assisted local officers in attempting to apprehend the fugitive, but the outlaw escaped into the dense brush. Expecting a fight, the lawmen trailed the robber to no avail.[28]

Wright's conduct as a member of Rogers's company prompted a number of Wilson County citizens to petition him to return and run for the office of sheriff in the upcoming election. Apparently, Sheriff James J. Heathcock's lackluster performance during the Gregorio Cortéz pursuit had cost him the support of his constituents. After a considerable amount of persuasion, Wright agreed, and resigned from the Ranger Force on August 31, 1902, in San Antonio.[29]

The contest was heated, and Wright's health apparently suffered to some extent, but he was nevertheless elected sheriff on November 4. He moved his family into a four-room apartment in the county jail, and chose his jailer to be the only full-time deputy. For some time, Wright was assisted by "pistol deputies," authorized volunteers who would keep the peace in their respective towns on Saturday nights. Later, he would increase his staff of assistants to include his brother Milam. Further utilizing family members, Sheriff Wright placed Mollie and their two oldest sons in charge of managing the jail.[30]

To the east of the sheriff's living quarters was a corral for his horses and buggies, and a barn. The Wrights kept a milk cow, chickens, pigs, and various family pets. Later, as the boys grew older, Mollie would send them on horseback to deliver messages to the sheriff or his deputies, to serve subpoenas to grand jury members, and to deliver election boxes to county polling places. Once he was of age, and since the adults could not drive, E. A., known to everyone as "Dogie," chauffeured his father and the deputies around the county in the departmental-issue Ford Model T. From the time they were small boys, the sheriff instructed his sons they must "obey the law, and be honest and upright, and tell the truth no matter what."[31]

Wright proved to be a well-regarded and popular lawman who easily turned his constituents into friends. Throughout his stint in Wilson County, he became known for his truthfulness and integrity. Shortly after the election, Captain Rogers reportedly wired his former lieutenant: "Make the people a Ranger sheriff, acting impartially without regard to nationality, color, or wealth." Sheriff Wright was said to have made this guidance his creed. The basic duties of the county sheriff in Texas remained much the same as they had for decades. Wright was the chief law enforcement officer in Wilson County, and sworn to "protect citizens' lives and property, to keep public order, to prevent crime, and to arrest lawbreakers." Additional duties included maintaining the county courthouse, managing the county jail and any prisoners who might be detained therein, and functioning as the executive officer of the county and district courts by serving writs, subpoenas, summonses, and other articles of criminal and civil process.[32]

Wright traveled into San Antonio where he and Deputy Sheriff ____ Kincaid took John Taylor into custody on the evening of June 8, 1904. Taylor was wanted in Wilson County for criminal assault on a fourteen-year-old girl. The sheriff returned the suspect to Floresville the same night.[33] Wright's effective tenure secured him a unanimous vote from the delegates of the county Democratic convention on July 17, 1904. As a result, he was handily reelected on November 8.[34]

While in San Antonio on business in 1906, Wright told the *Daily Light* that Wilson County was in "pretty fair condition." With increasing prosperity and population, the sheriff hoped the county would become the most populous in that portion of the state. Wright observed Germans, who comprised a significant portion of new arrivals, made "good citizens and taxpayers." The newspaper noted the sheriff was a candidate for reelection, and that Wright had no worries regarding the results.[35] His faith was rewarded on November 6, 1906, when the voters retained him in office.[36] However, not all his professional aspirations were fulfilled. Along with William J. "Billy" McCauley, Wright applied for the Ranger captaincy vacated by William J. McDonald, but the appointment instead went to Tom Ross.[37]

Wright worked up a case in late June 1907 that identified San Antonio as a clearinghouse for the trafficking of stolen cowhides from South Texas to Travis and Williamson Counties. The high prices paid by hide buyers in the Alamo City, and inconsistent local and state inspection laws in various other counties contributed to the highly competitive illegal trade. The sheriff believed the thieves had been operating for over two years. His breakthrough in the case had been a raid on an encampment of cattle thieves along the San Antonio River near the line between Wilson and Bexar Counties. The arrest of five Mexicans, and the excavated remains of scores of slaughtered cattle, brought to light the system for disposing of the contraband commodities in San Antonio. Due to a complete lack of inspection and fees, Wilson County was a waystation where stolen hides were purchased by a trader, or a "fence," prior to their movement to Bexar for sale to local buyers. With an absence of recorded brands or a bill of sale, the latter were ignorant of the hides' origins, and the fences were near impossible to detect. Once some members of the gang were jailed, Wright followed the trail of twenty others into Bexar County. Taking a room at the Southern Hotel, he worked in conjunction with Bexar County Constable (and future Ranger captain) Charles Francis Stevens in searching the hide stores in town. They found that fewer than half of the transactions had been accompanied by a bill of sale, contrary to state law, making tracking the thieves extremely difficult. However, alerted to the situation, lawmen were better able to enforce compliance and reduce future thefts.[38]

Following a family quarrel in the town of Lavernia on November 29, Louis Gibson, a thirty-six-year-old black man, brutally murdered Betty Taylor, his wife's mother, and Cora Taylor, his sixteen-year-old sister-in-law. The older woman's head was nearly severed from her body with an ax, while the young girl's throat had been slashed from ear to ear with a pen knife; her head was repeatedly smashed with a rock postmortem. The second homicide occurred at the segregated schoolhouse, and was witnessed by a teacher and several terrified students. Accompanied by two deputies, Wright directed a posse comprised of both white and black citizens. Gibson fled about five miles from Lavernia, then his trail doubled back and disappeared. Law officers believed he was hiding in cabins owned by family members near town. On December 2, Gibson was shot to death by Joe Morgan, who was leading an all-black posse, three miles east of Lavernia.[39]

While Wright was diligently enforcing the law in his jurisdiction, William Berry "Bill," his fourth son, was born in Floresville on April 20, 1905. The joy of this occasion was contrasted by the passing of his fifth son, who died in infancy possibly on December 27, 1907.[40]

Doubtless still grieving the family's loss, Wright was nevertheless compelled to perform his duty. During the night of February 27, 1908, professional robbers used nitroglycerine to blow open safes at the Kott, Linne & Riega store in Lavernia, as well as the Wells, Fargo office. Both buildings suffered damage from the explosions, but, strangely, no town residents were awakened. The perpetrators stole ninety dollars from the first establishment, and took only the cash drawer from the second; the contents of which included checks, business papers, and three hundred dollars in cash. The drawer was recovered in a culvert under the railroad tracks one hundred yards from the road to San Antonio. The papers were intact, and only the money was missing. Having few clues with which to work, Wright, Ranger Oscar Latta, and Captain Henry Scott Sisk of the Southern Pacific Railroad's police force followed the trail to San Antonio to no avail. The pursuit seemed fruitless, and Wright returned to Floresville to receive seven prisoners from Latta on charges of fighting and disturbing the peace. Once more in the Alamo City, Wright attended the Cattlemen's Association meeting on March 18. Happily, the aforementioned thieves did not entirely escape justice, as the sheriff returned to San Antonio on May 21 to identify two men being held in the county jail on suspicion of the Lavernia robbery.[41]

On the night of July 2, twenty-five-year-old Refugio Jaureque sexually assaulted Alvina Olenik, a Polish girl of fifteen, while she was walking home from the post office in Sutherland Springs. In the process, he beat her, stomped on her face, and stabbed her twice in the neck before leaving her to die with the knife buried in her chest. However, she survived the attack and, covered in blood, managed to crawl to her home. Alerted to the crime, Wright arrived at the victim's house at one o'clock in the morning, and secured her statement. She named Jaureque, a laborer working in the area, as her assailant, and the sheriff arrested him three hours later. The next afternoon, Wright, three deputies, and the prosecuting attorney took the prisoner to the Olenik home so Alvina could make a positive identification. Returning for Floresville, Wright's party was followed by a gang of twenty-five to thirty men. When they passed the scene of the crime, the mob attempted to take Jaureque away. The lawmen encircled the suspect and drove the crowd back with their rifle butts. No shots were fired, and the officers successfully returned to the county seat. Securely lodged in the jail, Jaureque was later convicted of the crime and sentenced to hang.[42]

Doctor John D. Becton of Almus shot and killed Albert Toombs, his son-in-law, on September 3, while the twenty-year-old was picking cotton on a farm near Hedwig, located five miles north of Lavernia. Witnessed by the victim's wife, who was also Becton's stepdaughter, the murder was said to have been caused by family troubles. Wright arrested the physician the same evening at his home, and took him to Lavernia for a preliminary hearing the next day. However, the proceedings were postponed, and Wright secured the prisoner in the Bexar County jail overnight before taking him back to the Floresville lockup on the fifth. The examining trial, scheduled for September 18, was delayed due to bad weather. While still under indictment, Becton died of sepsis from a urinary infection on December 4 at Surgeons' and Physicians' Hospital. In the midst of a divorce, the doctor had no blood relatives to claim his body.[43]

Wright was reelected November 3, 1908, and, later in the year, he pursued Joe Allen, the alleged leader of a dangerous safe-blowing gang that had struck several Texas towns. Regrettably, the sheriff lost the trail. However, Sheriff Dave Leftwich Hemsell of Hunt County, where the thief was wanted, alerted Bexar County Sheriff Benjamin Dennis Lindsey by telegram that Allen was reportedly in San Antonio. On December 4, Allen narrowly escaped capture by Lindsey, Wright, and Sheriff Eli Calloway Seale of Karnes County, as they scoured the city. Lindsey sent telegrams to multiple jurisdictions requesting them to be on the lookout for the fugitive. Having taken the northbound Missouri, Kansas & Texas (Katy) train, the safecracker and his female companion were nabbed by the sheriff in Hillsboro and held for Hemsell.[44]

The San Antonio law offices of Thomas Henry Ridgeway, in the Kampman Building on Commerce and Soledad Streets, was the scene of a remarkable confrontation on May 15, 1909. The attorney was speaking with a client, Doctor Charles H. Dewey, a dentist residing in Wilson County, when Ms. Frances Riddle entered the room. After an unspecified remark, the doctor pulled a pistol and pointed the weapon at Riddle. She screamed, retreated into the hallway, and prepared to jump from the fourth-floor window. The commotion attracted the attention of other lawyers in neighboring offices, and the hysterical woman was escorted from the building to the courthouse. There she filed a complaint before Justice of the Peace Benjamin Sappington "Ben" Fisk for assault with intent to murder. Dewey saw the crowd in the corridor and slammed the door. He remained in his attorney's office for several minutes before making his way outside to the street. Constable John Edgar Trainer and Deputy Constable Feliciana Flores were given an arrest warrant for Dewey, and joined in the search being conducted by city policemen and sheriff's deputies. The dentist evaded his pursuers, and Trainer and Flores visited Sheriff Wright, who was in town on official business, at the Southern Hotel. The constable hoped Wright would be able to find Dewey at home and serve the warrant. The three lawmen departed the hotel, and Trainer spotted the fugitive coming down the stairway of the Elliott Flats. The dentist spied Trainer and immediately turned around, but he was nabbed by the swift-running Flores. Dewey was placed under arrest and taken to Justice Fisk's courtroom, where he waived examination and was released on a five-hundred-dollar bond.[45]

Rapist and attempted murderer Refugio Jaureque's appointment with the hangman finally occurred on June 18, 1909. As Wright escorted him to the gallows, the doomed man began to struggle against his bindings. Jaureque called to his brother who approached from out of the crowd, shook hands with his condemned sibling, and moved away. Jaureque suddenly spun around and stabbed the sheriff in the chest with a sharpened spoon handle. With the wound two inches above his heart, Wright was rushed to the jail where he received medical attention from Doctor John Vaughan Blake before being taken home. Meanwhile, Milam, who was employed as a State Ranger, Sheriff Seale, Sheriff Jesse B. Farris of DeWitt County, Constables Albert Alexander Lyons and Marcus Walton Hines of Karnes County, Constable William Henry Adams of Comal County, and Constable Trainer of Bexar County restrained the prisoner and wrestled him to the trap door. Even then, Jaureque continued to thrash as he fell downward, delaying his death by thirty minutes of strangulation, rather than the immediacy of a broken neck. Trainer commented: "I never saw a man die so hard in all my career as an officer." The injured sheriff was in stable condition the next day, and consulted a physician in San Antonio on the nineteenth.[46]

Wright recovered and was soon involved in another homicide case. On the morning of June 2, Justo Morales, labeled "The Mex with the Evil Eye" by the newspapers, killed George Schuler at his farm twelve miles east of San Antonio. The victim's fourteen-year-old son witnessed the murder. Morales, a tenant of Schuler, fled in a southerly direction, and local officers from town were soon on his trail. Sheriff Lindsey led the posse, which stayed in the saddle for over sixty hours. When the pursuit crossed over into Wilson County, Wright lent the assistance of his office, and the fugitive was thought to be cornered near Lavernia. Unfortunately, by the ninth, Morales slipped through the net, and headed for the Mexican border. Lindsey and Wright broke off the pursuit, and Morales's description was sent to Eagle Pass, Hondo, Uvalde, Pearsall, Divine, Losoya, and Lavaca. Lindsey offered a reward, which Governor Thomas Mitchell Campbell quickly matched. The trail seemingly went cold until a man matching Morales's description was seen near Pearsall on July 12. The tip, though, proved to be worthless.[47]

On the night of July 31, 1910, Rangers Quirl Bailey Carnes and James Patterson Nelson "Pat" Craighead were leading a posse comprised of Special Deputy Sheriff Henry Boomer Lawrence, Constable Larkin Earl West, and six employees of the San Benito Land and Water Company to intercept murder suspect Jacinto Treviño as he returned to Texas from Mexico. Treviño had been accused of killing James Samuel "Jim" Darwin, an engineer of the San Benito headgates, on May 27, although the former's real target had been Chief Engineer Samuel Arthur "Sam" Robertson. While lying in wait near the Rio Grande, the officers heard someone approaching, and one of them called out in Spanish. A reply, also in Spanish, was heard, then the night exploded in gunfire. Carnes was mortally wounded by rifle bullets, one of them entering behind his right ear and exiting his right eye; Lawrence was killed by a shotgun blast in the side of his head. Craighead and West, who had been positioned nearby, ran to their comrades' aid. They came under rifle fire, and West was hit by a bullet that entered his right arm, passed through his shoulder, and exited his back. The only member of the opposing party left at the scene was Pablo Treviño, a relative of Jacinto who had informed on him for the reward.[48]

The gunfire ceased, and Craighead decided to seek aid for his fallen partners. Reaching the road and hearing an approaching automobile, he loosed a shot into the air, which was a predetermined signal to alert the relief party. Not knowing Craighead was the one firing, the car's occupants opened up on him. The Ranger was struck in the right leg by buckshot and his left thigh by a rifle bullet. The reinforcements quickly realized their mistake and hurried to give assistance to the wounded Craighead. Carnes, West, and Craighead were driven back to San Benito for medical treatment, but the former died from his wounds at nine o'clock the next morning.[49]

As news of the ambush spread, enraged citizens began to gather in San Benito. Two Ranger captains and three of their men, thirty-five members of the Second Texas Infantry, the Cameron County sheriff and two deputies, and the Brownsville city marshal were on hand by August 1. The following day, Wright arrived on the noon train from Floresville with seven deputies. Carnes, West, and Craighead had each hailed from Wilson County, and among Wright's posse were several of the three officers' kinsmen. All of them wanted retribution for their fallen relatives. In addition to the lawmen and the national guardsmen, numerous armed vigilantes swarmed into the area from nearby towns.[50]

Sheriff Wright's posse, the guard troops, and civilian volunteers searched along the Rio Grande. They knew they were wasting their time, but doing nothing was worse. Wright headed home on the fifth before departing for the Sheriffs'Association of Texas convention in El Paso. Conversely, the five Rangers had a definite plan. They rode to the Las Rusias *rancho* near town on August 1, and arrested seven of Treviño's relatives who lived there. The prisoners were herded to the pumping plant and interrogated overnight. They were freed early the following morning. Treviño's kin were detained for, as the *Brownsville Daily Herald* reported the same day, "no reason … beyond the fact that they are cousins of Jacinto Treviño … who appears to be the black sheep of a very respectable flock." Such a flagrant violation of their constitutional rights did the state officers no favors.[51]

Despite the best efforts of the various law officers in the San Benito area, Brownsville City Marshal Joseph Laulom "Joe" Crixell was the only one to accomplish anything worthwhile. As the Rangers were detaining Treviño's kinfolk, Crixell quietly crossed the river to conduct an independent investigation. Interviewing some witnesses at a *baile* (open air dance) in the tiny hamlet of Tahuachalito, he discovered that Treviño, Benjamin Estrada, and a man named Loya were seen near the Rio Grande the night of the ambush. Estrada was already wanted in Duval County for the murder of a prominent cattleman. At Crixell's bidding, the Cameron County authorities requested the Mexican government issue arrest warrants for Treviño and Estrada.

Despite the international cooperation and the sizeable reward offered for the fugitive pair, they were never captured, instead disappearing into the chaos of the Mexican Revolution.[52]

Dennis Bangs Chapin, former Hidalgo County judge, legislator, and owner of the Chapin townsite, had become embroiled in a business dispute with Edward Roos, a real estate dealer from Houston. On August 18, 1910, Chapin fatally shot ex-Ranger Oscar James Rountree in Dan Breen's saloon in San Antonio. Rountree had admirably served in Captain John R. Hughes's company between 1907 and 1910. At the time of death, he was said to have been a Cameron County deputy sheriff and acting as Roos's bodyguard. Although shot through the head, Rountree retained sufficient consciousness to offer a deathbed statement before expiring on the nineteenth. Eyewitnesses differed on details of the incident, such as the number of shots fired or who fired first. Present in the area that night, Wright testified at the *habeas corpus* hearing in Thirty-seventh District Court on August 23. On the witness stand, the sheriff stated he had been talking with Tom Moore and Albert Sammons in John Dolan's bar, opposite the Southern Hotel, the day of the killing. Rountree entered the room and left with one of the men. Later in the evening, Wright had been walking near the intersection of Houston and Losoya Streets when he heard pistol shots. Following the sounds, Wright entered Breen's establishment and observed Chapin standing behind the bar, and Rountree on the floor. Chapin told Wright that Rountree had tried to kill him, and Sammons, also present, confirmed Rountree had fired his weapon twice. Police Captain Charles William McCabe later testified Rountree's pistol had not been discharged, while Chapin's recently fired weapon possessed five spent cartridge casings. The prosecution argued for a denial of bail, as the charge was a capital offense punishable by hanging. However, Chapin was released on a bond of fifteen thousand dollars to await the grand jury in the fall term of district court. He received a change of venue to Victoria.[53]

Wright's son Dogie remembered his father "always wore a coat, collar, tie, and a gun." Indeed, grateful citizens had presented the sheriff with an engraved pearl-handled and silver-plated Colt .45 pistol on July 4, 1910. Reelected on November 3, Wright was personally involved in a number of apprehensions. Accompanied by several deputies on January 7, 1911, he went into the "negro part" of Floresville, where several black men were reported as being disorderly. Arriving at the house in question, the lawmen encountered Lee Roberts, who was intoxicated. The sheriff instructed him to raise his hands, but Roberts resisted arrest and attempted to flee. He ignored orders to halt, and Wright shot him in the leg below the knee. Six days later, Wright returned from Houston with a man accused of sexually assaulting his fourteen-year-old sister-in-law near Stockdale. The prisoner was given an examining trial the following day.[54]

The sheriff traveled to Aguilares in Webb County and returned on February 11, 1911, with Nasario Palacios. In 1905, at the age of eighteen, Palacios had fatally stabbed another youth to death, and immediately fled to Guerrero. The murder charge remained on the books in Wilson County. Only a short time before his capture, Palacios had emerged at a ranch near Aguilares. Constable Roque Gonzalez of San Ignacio had sent his brother to watch Palacios until Wright's arrival. The sheriff and the constable, accompanied by Pete Edwards and Robert Stuart "Bob" Rumsey, Jr., rode to the ranch. When he saw Wright, Palacios attempted to run into the house, but Gonzalez's sibling seized him, and the fugitive was manacled. A search revealed a dagger on the killer's person, and firearms inside the residence.[55]

Chapin's jury trial was scheduled to begin in Twenty-fourth District Court in Victoria on May 22. More than two hundred people were on hand to offer testimony, and numerous prominent men were in attendance to support Chapin, including former Ranger John B. Armstrong, and political bosses James Babbage Wells, Jr. of Brownsville, and Archer "Archie" Parr of San Diego. The defendant was present with his co-counsels, Carlos Bee and Walter Courtney Linden. Along with Edward Roos and Augustus Weyman Houston, Jr. of San Antonio, Wright was a material witness for the prosecution. However, the trial had to be delayed for two days when the three men did not appear. For his part, despite being served with a subpoena on May 17, the sheriff was unable to attend since the district court in Floresville had convened two days previously, and his presence as a witness in three or four murder trials there was likewise required. Wright was fined fifty dollars, but the penalty was later remitted once the court in Victoria was made aware of the circumstances. Upon District Attorney Guy

Mitchell's motion, Judge John Middleton Green granted a continuance in Chapin's case to December 7. The defendant expressed "great disappointment" with the delay.[56]

Jury selection for the Chapin case began on schedule, and resulted in eleven preemptory challenges each from the defense and the state. Once the jury was impaneled on the eighth, the trial began with Mitchell and Samuel Green Tayloe acting for the people. The courtroom was surprised on December 9, when the prosecution asked for a two-day postponement so a missing witness could be located. Once the trial resumed, legal sparring consumed much of the day before testimony was heard. The prosecution rested its case the same day, and the defense pursued the strategy of portraying Rountree as a dangerous man who had made threats against Chapin's life. Joseph Verlinde Vandenberg, Jr., who had joined Bee, Linden, and William Madden Fly on the defense team, rested on December 13. District Attorney Mitchell introduced five rebuttal witnesses, including Wright, followed by one more for the defense. The following day, after closing remarks, the jury retired to deliberate, and was out only twenty minutes before they returned a verdict of not guilty. Wright returned home on the seventeenth.[57]

Even while caught up in a trial in which he played such a minor role, Wright dealt with more dangerous lawbreakers. Dionicio Martinez was under indictment in Texas for seven counts of homicide by 1909, including the murder of Placido Garza in Wilson County. A known border country renegade for over twenty-five years, the killer fled to Mexico, despite being wanted in that country for nine murders. Determined to close the case in his own jurisdiction, Sheriff Wright spent a great deal of time and money trying to bring Martinez to justice. On October 7, 1905, he had obtained a requisition from Governor Samuel Willis Tucker Lanham for Martinez's extradition. A subsequent request from Governor Oscar Branch Colquitt was finally granted by outgoing Mexican *presidente* Porfírio Díaz as one of his last official acts. However, when Wright appeared in Nuevo Laredo on June 17, 1911, to take charge of the prisoner, the municipal authorities refused to honor the agreement. They claimed the sheriff could not have Martinez, as the latter had applied for a writ of *amparo*. The outlaw's case ultimately went before the Mexican Supreme Court, but the justices refused the application and returned the matter to the court of origin. Undaunted, Martinez and seven other prisoners managed to escape, and killed a Nuevo Laredo policeman in the process. Martinez was recaptured and returned to the jail from which he had absconded. On January 21, 1914, he was placed on a work detail with Mexican federal soldiers to extend the trenches of the city. Despite being guarded by a squad of troops, the wily criminal once more bolted, and he found sanctuary in the ranks of the *huertista* and *carrancista* guerrillas.[58]

The town of Poth, seven miles from Floresville, was the scene of a bloody saloon brawl on July 29, 1911. When Deputy Sheriff Love Allen disarmed a knife-wielding Mexican in front of a saloon, he was attacked by the latter's friends. Anglos in the vicinity rushed to the deputy's assistance; saloonkeeper Joe Ludwig was fatally slashed across the stomach, farmer Rudolph Joseph Woellert was badly cut, and Allen suffered two broken bones in his right arm while being repeatedly struck with a club. A stout traveling photographer and several more bystanders waded into the fight to assist the beaten lawman, and the Mexicans fled the scene. Sheriff Wright, accompanied by deputies and Doctor John Blake, made the trip by automobile in nine minutes. At eleven o'clock that night, Ludwig's killer was captured as he crawled through the brush toward his home. The following morning, five more Mexicans were taken into custody, while one remained at large.[59]

On November 12, 1911, and again on the sixteenth, James Henry Bain, Sr., president of the First State Bank of Stockdale, received alarming letters in the mail. The two notes ordered Bain to leave four thousand dollars under the Cibolo River bridge on the eighteenth at a certain time, and threatened the lives of his family if he failed to comply. Notified of the warning, Wright and five men, including "pistol deputies" Thad Reese and Will Clemens, were on hand to surreptitiously watch Bain leave a sack of fake money in the designated spot while carrying a red lantern as instructed by the extortionist. They observed an unknown man approach and retrieve the cash, but the suspect failed to obey commands to surrender. The blackmailer attempted to flee, and the lawmen fired seven to ten shots, striking his horse. The suspect, later identified as Twing Wheeler, Jr., fled on foot to his home in Stockdale. Wright and his men took him into custody there without further incident. The sheriff obtained an arrest warrant from Justice of the Peace

James Frank Henson. Wheeler, aged twenty-four, was placed into the county jail, while claiming he had been forced to commit the blackmail after a third party threatened his own family. Given the case involved the post office, Wright notified U.S. Marshal Eugene Nolte, who sent deputy John Lee Dibrell to transport the prisoner to San Antonio. Wheeler was arraigned before U.S. Commissioner Richard Lee Edwards on a charge of using the mails to defraud. The defendant waived a preliminary hearing and posted a one-thousand-dollar bond to appear at the next term of the federal district court. On January 5, 1912, he was indicted by the federal grand jury, and Wheeler immediately entered a plea of guilty. He was sentenced to one year and one day in the federal penitentiary at Leavenworth, Kansas.[60]

Frank Schmidt, his son, and William Rehfeldt, all well-known farmers, were robbed by a single armed individual while walking home on the Camp ranch on September 25, 1913. The highwayman was identified as a Mexican who claimed to be working for Francisco Ignacio Madero González, even though the *presidente* had been assassinated months prior. Sheriff Wright and Deputy John Joseph Edds investigated, and arrested Faustino de Vara on a farm near Floresville on the twenty-seventh. The charge was robbery by force of arms. The two officers submitted into evidence papers taken from the prisoner, which were identified as belonging to the elder Schmidt. Vara was refused bail at his examining trial and remanded to the county jail.[61]

Wright had been retained in office on November 5, 1912, and was elected the following year to the vice presidency of the Sheriffs' Association while attending the organization's annual meeting in Austin.[62] As a county sheriff, Wright had to perform the role of a politician as well as a lawman. Thus he was on hand when Sam Sparks, former state treasurer and ex-president of the Sheriff's Association, came to Floresville for a political event in support of gubernatorial candidate Thomas H. Ball. Wright headed a delegation of approximately twenty prominent citizens that greeted Sparks at the train station on July 8, 1914. The contender himself arrived in Floresville ten days later. Wright was again involved as a member of the reception committee. Ball was subsequently defeated in the election. The victor was James Edward "Farmer Jim" Ferguson, whose corrupt practices would impact Will Wright and the Ranger Force for years to come. The only Texas governor to be impeached, he would be removed from office on September 25, 1917. That lay several years in the future, though. In the Democratic primary in July 1914, Wright ran unopposed, and he was reelected on November 3.[63]

During the annual convention of the Sheriff's Association, held in Corpus Christi in August 1914, the assembled members elected Wright president of the organization for a one-year term. The following year, he went to Waco on July 13, and presided over the convention. The event was lightly attended by South Texas sheriffs, but those from North Texas were well represented.[64]

On September 30, 1914, wealthy rancher and landowner "Colonel" George Washington Parks was found dead near his home, three miles southeast of Nixon. The stockman had left his home to go into town on business at about eight o'clock in the morning, and his body was later discovered on the roadside by his pasture gate. An autopsy revealed he had been shot behind the left ear, the bullet exiting at the base of his skull. Sheriff Wright investigated the murder with the assistance of Houston Blair "Hugh" Hanley, a representative of Solomon Parks (the victim's brother), and Gonzales City Marshal Norman Dudley Cone. Wright arrested Lonnie Leon Parks, the colonel's son, who confessed his role in the crime to Justice of the Peace Fisk. The twenty-year-old Lonnie implicated John "Johnnie" Jones and George Dawson, as well as Chris House, a former deputy marshal of Nixon.[65]

"About six weeks ago I took some cattle belonging to my father and sold them," Lonnie stated in his confession. "Afterwards I heard that my father was going to prosecute me for stealing cattle. I went to Chris House … and told him about it. House told me that a negro named George Dawson would kill my father, that he would do the work."[66]

George Dawson was arrested on October 19, and made his own confession to Justice of the Peace Gus Harris DeWitt in Gonzales. He stated he had been hired to commit the murder for one thousand dollars, and had been given a note for $325 and promised the remainder after the deed was done. Following his confession, he remained in the Gonzales jail. Dawson had subcontracted the killing to Johnnie Jones, who was captured in Columbus after a letter he had written to Dawson alerted Wright to his location. In the message, Jones said he had only received four dollars and fare to San Antonio, and he demanded more money. Wright and the mayor of Nixon, who knew Jones by sight, went to Columbus. The mayor pointed out the accused killer, and Wright returned Jones to Seguin. The suspect confessed to District Attorney Lester Holt. Jones, Dawson, and Lonnie Parks were lodged in the Bexar County jail, while House was released on a bond of three thousand dollars. The grand jury returned felony indictments on January 11, 1915, charging Jones with Parks's murder, and the other three as accomplices. In Lonnie's trial, the jury deliberated for ninety minutes before returning a verdict of not guilty on February 10, 1915. Jones and Dawson entered guilty pleas in their trial, which convened on July 23. The following day, the former drew a sentence of twenty-five years in prison while the latter received five years.[67]

Two changes in Wright's life occurred in 1915. The first was an occasion for rejoicing when his sixth son, Houston Tom, was born on January 14.[68] The second, less welcome, adjustment was the resignation of Chief Deputy John Edds, and his departure for Harlingen to enlist in Company D of the Ranger Force.[69]

Two armed robbers struck the bank at Marble Falls on October 26, 1915, and killed cashier Robert Hamilton "Robbie" Heinatz II. For over a week, a heavily armed posse of Wright, Sheriff John Wallace Tobin and Chief Deputy James W. Galbreath of Bexar County, Sheriff Albert Ramos Mace of Lampasas County, Sheriff James Cannon Wall of McCulloch County, Sheriff Hugh Miller of San Saba County, Sheriff George Matthews of Travis County, and Sheriff Horace Faulkner Pirtle of Hays County conducted a search in the San Marcos and Boerne area. Two suspects were apprehended by Sheriff Pirtle, and Ranger Captains James Monroe Fox and Edward Hume Smith, on October 30 near San Marcos. The arrest proved fruitless, then word was received by telephone that another two suspects were last seen in Castroville. However, further investigation revealed the pair were wood haulers who could prove they had not left Kendall County for months.[70]

During the night of November 29, the post office in Sutherland Springs was robbed when unknown burglars blew open the safe with high explosives. The yeggs, likely professionals, stole three canvas bags containing

$1,185 in cash, currency, and stamps. The crime attracted no attention, and was discovered the next morning once Postmaster George Briggs Everts opened the office. Two strangers had been spotted in town the day of the robbery and were thought to have headed for San Antonio. Wright informed that city's police force of the heist by telephone, but the case seems to have gone unsolved.[71]

On December 1, Wright arrested Enrique Mata, who was wanted on a murder charge in Webb County, and informed Forty-ninth Judicial District Attorney John Anthony Valls of the apprehension the same day. Mata had already been indicted two years previously for the death of his sweetheart, and for a charge of assault with intent to murder. Deputy Sheriff Joe Herrera left Laredo and traveled to Floresville to extradite the prisoner.[72]

On the night of Saturday, January 8, 1916, three prisoners, all sentenced at the recent term of district court, made an escape from the county jail. Two days before the getaway, two Mexicans and a black man began using the iron pieces from the sides of their cots to widen a small hole on the floor of their second-floor steel cell. They then dug through the concrete and cut into the sheet iron ceiling of the ground floor. About eight o'clock, at the same time as a tent show performance across the street, the escapees slipped through the hole and strolled out the front door. Mollie heard the prisoners creep across the first floor, but, thinking it was just someone moving through the office, paid no mind.[73]

Local lawmen were alerted, and several citizens were appointed as special deputies. The sheriff and Deputy Robert Graves Seale were returning home from Austin at the time and arrived about midnight. Within minutes, Wright and Bexar County Deputy Antonio Diaz were in pursuit of the felons. At 2:00 a.m., one of the Mexicans, who was named Morales, was recaptured at the railroad bridge near Calaveras, and the hunt for the other two fugitives lasted into Sunday and Monday. Officers in adjacent counties were notified, and the black escapee, a man named Roberson, was apprehended on a freight train at Rosenburg. Sheriff Wright retrieved Roberson and brought him back on Wednesday afternoon. The recaptured fugitive talked and stated he had left the last runaway, a notorious Mexican bandit named Emilio Soforo, in San Antonio. The captured prisoners were taken to the state penitentiary, while Soforo was believed to have escaped into Mexico. Officers on the border kept watch for him to no avail.[74]

On March 25, Mexican laborer Petronilo Romulo murdered his wife while working in the fields of J. D. Gray's farm west of Fairview. The homicidal husband committed his brutal act by spearing her in the stomach with a pitchfork, then stabbing her in the back five times with a pocketknife. The Mexican fled, and officers in Wilson and neighboring counties combed the woods for the fugitive. Wright offered a reward of fifty dollars for Romulo's capture.[75]

The killer was finally apprehended on April 4 near Canada Verde by Adolfo Flores. Assisted by Deputy Sheriff Alfred Burton Carnes, Flores transported the prisoner to the county jail. At the same time, Wright had been contacted by the Bexar County chief deputy, who thought the guilty man was on the Medina River, and the sheriff was driving to San Antonio to meet with authorities there. Romulo confessed to the murder, and stated his wife had slapped him across the face for an unknown reason. Enraged, he had stabbed her. He fled to Atascosa County and worked for a Mexican farmer near Leming. Thinking perhaps his wife was still alive, Romulo returned to his old camp near Canada Verde early on the fourth and was identified by a neighbor, and subsequently taken into custody by Flores. An examining trial was scheduled for April 10.[76]

Shortly after midnight on May 11, Wright boarded a San Antonio & Aransas Pass train at Floresville and assisted William M. Hanson, chief special agent of the San Antonio, Uvalde & Gulf Railroad, and Howard P. Wright, a Justice Department Bureau of Investigation agent, in transporting José María Morín to Kleberg County. Agent Wright and Hanson had apprehended Morín, a former colonel in Francisco "Pancho" Villa's *División del Norte*, at Saspamco. While being taken into custody, the revolutionary attempted to pull a .45-caliber semiautomatic pistol, but he was overpowered and securely shackled. With the sheriff aboard the sleeper car, the *villista* was taken to the Kingsville jail and charged with conspiracy and sedition. An uprising in South Texas, New Mexico, and Arizona had been scheduled for May 5, then postponed to the tenth before being suspended indefinitely due to lack of funds. At the same time, other federal agents and Kleberg

County deputies raided the Mexican quarter of Kingsville, noted to be the center of the conspiracy, and arrested newsman Eulario Vasquez and baker Victoriana Ponce on the same charges as Morín. The following morning, Vasquez was released, but four additional suspects were taken into custody and several others remained under surveillance. Agent Wright directed the investigation, and seven county sheriffs, several U.S. marshals, and "scores of service men" converged on the town. By the fifteenth, fifteen Mexicans were being held in the county lockup.[77]

Willacy County Sheriff Joel Clinton Adkins arrived in town on May 22, and identified Morín as being the leader of the *guerrillero* attack on the Norias Ranch on August 8, 1915. Two Anglos had died in the raid, and another two were wounded. The same day, Ponce was identified by a railroad brakeman as being one of the bandits that derailed and robbed the St. Louis, Brownsville & Mexico train on October 18, 1915; three Americans were killed. Following these revelations, Ranger Joe B. Brooks of Company A, and Special Ranger William Thomas "Tom" Moseley, attached to Company C, bypassed the Cameron County jail, and took Morín and Ponce north for the supposed purpose of securing further identifications. Seventy-five miles from Brownsville, the prisoners reportedly escaped, and a posse later failed to locate any trace of them. In all likelihood, Morín and Ponce were executed in the brush with their bodies buried deep. As Professors Charles H. Harris III and Louis R. Sadler observed, the Rangers used a variation of the *ley fuga*—"the prisoner wasn't shot while trying to escape, he did escape, and we have no idea where he is." This and other instances in the border country would become known as "evaporations." Although pressed for details, the Adjutant General's Department maintained its official version regarding the episode, and Brooks and Moseley never discussed the matter. Perhaps due to the ominous and mysterious nature of the episode, further rumors of an insurrection ceased.[78]

Having no role in the questionable conclusion, Sheriff Wright returned to his county. He was summoned to the Weinert ranch near Nixon early on October 5, 1916, in response to the report of a body found in a shallow grave. Although originally reported to have been a Mexican woman, the remains were those of a man later confirmed to have been murdered four days prior.

The deceased victim was found because his hands were protruding from the earth. Wright and his deputies investigated, and the murdered man was identified as horse trader Catarino Flores. By the eighth, the sheriff had returned from Lockhart with the wife of a Mexican named Florencio Compian. Both Compian and his spouse were implicated in the killing. Last seen in Lockhart on October 7, Compian remained at large despite a one-hundred-dollar reward offered by Governor Ferguson.[79] The outcome of the case had little effect on Wright, as he was reelected on November 7.[80]

On May 5, 1917, at three o'clock in the morning, burglars used nitroglycerin to break into a safe in Ernest E. Perry's drug store in Sutherland Springs. Even as the blast awoke the sleeping residents, the thieves stole between $150 and two hundred dollars before making their getaway. Two strangers who had been earlier seen in town were sought by Sheriff Wright, and he contacted the authorities in San Antonio to be on the lookout. The use of explosives was the first to be reported in the area since three robberies had been committed in early April.[81]

Anti-American sentiment in Mexico and a large number of draft dodgers (known as "slackers") and deserters taking refuge south of the border coupled to produce chaotic conditions. These fugitives were without much food or money, or sources of employment to acquire them. In order to survive, they turned to raiding into the Lone Star State for livestock and loot, or guiding bandits to ripe targets. Additionally, the revolutionary turmoil and Mexican depredations continued across the Rio Grande, while various factions used Texas as a base of operations.[82]

In late 1917, Adjutant General James Aloysius Harley requested Wright raise a new Ranger company and serve as its commander. The sheriff submitted his resignation to the commissioner's court on December 31, and Company K was ordered into service on January 1, 1918. Wright's old deputy, J. J. Edds, was appointed company sergeant. Two months short of his fiftieth birthday, the new captain's bearing and mode of dress more resembled that of a minister than a career lawman. He stood five feet, ten inches and wore glasses. A lover of good stories, he possessed a charming personality and an infectious laugh. In stark contrast to the previous decade, eleven Ranger companies were now in existence, eight of them on the border. Wright and

Captain William Matthew Ryan of Company I were assigned to Laredo, the former choosing the Lecea house on the Heights as his headquarters. While Ryan would patrol along the river north to Eagle Pass, Wright's area of operations was south toward Sam Fordyce in Hidalgo County as he scouted for draft evaders, horse thieves, and bandits. Before he left Wilson County, Wright's friends in Stockdale had presented him with "Jack," a magnificent bay Quarter Horse, as a Christmas present. The new captain prized this gift immensely.[83]

When Wright ended his tenure as sheriff, the family was required to vacate the living quarters in the county jail, and Mollie and the minor children moved into a two-story rented house. The change in employment was part of a major adjustment for the Wrights. Since two sons had recently enlisted in the army for war duty, and another was preparing for his own service in the Rangers, Mollie decided to remain in Floresville until the family situation stabilized, then rejoin her husband in Laredo.[84] Attorney and author Cyril Leone Patterson praised Mollie in the pages of the *Chronicle-Journal*:

> Mrs. Wright, Captain Wright's better half, was the best Sheriff Wilson County ever had and we regret to see her retire to other fields. For fifteen years she saw to it that the county prisoners in jail were fed while caring for her family of children and keeping track of Sheriff Wright's whereabouts as no other could have done. Let us all join in one full and unreserved acknowledgement of our indebtedness to her for her faithful discharge of her official duties that she, like Captain Wright, may know that our appreciation extends to both of them.[85]

Once he assumed command of Company K, Wright refused to participate in the well-established practice of claiming subsistence and forage allowances for the men when appreciative ranchers were in fact providing some of the supplies. The integrity and moral courage Wright displayed in repudiating such petty graft soon ended the practice. The one sergeant and fourteen Rangers under Wright's leadership came to respect their captain, but, more importantly, they also liked him. One example of Wright's thoughtfulness was that the company stationary not only bore the company's designation, station location, his name, and the name of his sergeant as was customary, but also the names of every man in the command.[86]

Captain William Hanson, onetime federal marshal and now the Ranger Force's inspector and "special operative," wrote to the adjutant general on February 20, 1918: "Capt. Wright has been down the River as far as Rio Grande City and has stationed his force at the most advantageous points. He has a fine lot of men, the best I have seen, and they are under perfect control, and discipline, and I believe will prove a great honor to our force. Such men are hard to get and but for his personality think it would be impossible to get together such a force of men. He is in full accord in everything with your ideas as to the management of the border and her people."[87]

Wright and Rangers Thomas Connolly, Sidney Sill Hutchinson, James Paul Perkins, Thomas Nolan "Tom" Pullin, Wright C. Wells, and Monroe Madison Wells departed Laredo on a scout on March 3, and arrived in Hebbronville the evening of the next day. On March 7, the captain was awakened shortly after 4:00 a.m. with the news that thirty *bandidos* had raided the ranch of Thomas Timmons "Tom" East, Sr., a highly successful cattleman. Wright quickly assembled a posse and informed the recently elected Sheriff Pat Craighead of Jim Hogg County. In a sign of the modern times, Wright and his men mounted automobiles rather than horses and set out for the East ranch thirty-five miles south of Hebbronville. They were accompanied by a truck that hauled their saddles, and Wright Wells was ordered to follow with the company's horses and mules.[88]

After reaching the East Ranch, approximately thirty-five miles from Hebbronville, Wright and his five Rangers were joined by Special Ranger William Thomas "Tom" Moseley, a cattleman's association brand inspector, and two East employees who also held appointments as Special Rangers. Tom East offered to follow the posse with fresh horses. Setting out after the bandits, the reinforced party was forced to acquire nearly worn-out mounts at East's San Antonio Viejo Ranch. The trail led toward the village of Roma, some fifteen miles upriver from Rio Grande City, but the raiders soon left the road and dived into the thick *brasada*; the brush was so dense the lawmen had to follow in single file.[89]

Near the El Javali Ranch, the posse suddenly spotted fourteen marauders, who had dismounted to rest their horses, at a distance of only twenty feet. "They were all on the ground, their horses standing by them," the captain wrote. "They commenced shooting at us as they got on their horses, and before you could snap your finger they were all running and we after them. After they ran a short distance they scattered in bunches and the men also scattered to follow them." Wright, Pullin, Moseley, and two other men chased a band of eight Mexicans for about three miles. During the pursuit, the bandits fired over their shoulders, and the officers shot back. Wright estimated his men killed at least two and wounded several more, judging by the blood trails. "We crowded them so close that they threw away everything. They lost pistols, Winchesters, five of them lost their hats, and also their booty they had taken from the stores on East Ranch," he reported. An additional three were killed later that night at Salineno. Four of the bandits, including the leader, escaped across the Rio Grande.[90]

The posse's horses were worn out, but East failed to deliver on his promise of fresh remounts. While the Rangers were risking their lives to find those who had stolen from him and recover his property, the rancher ordered his employees to dip several hundred head of cattle before they set out with the horses. The following morning, the posse rode on to the river and along the way recovered seven horses and two mules, an equal number of saddles, bridles, spurs, the stolen foodstuffs, and seven rifles and pistols. The manhunters returned on the tenth, and Sergeant Lon Willis of Ryan's company reported "five to ten bandits were killed."[91]

According to authorities in Guerrero, one of the escaping bandits was captured by Mexican customs guards and soldiers on March 11. The brigand confessed he and his partners in crime were not Mexican nationals, but rather Texas Hispanics. Their band had organized north of the Rio Grande and equipped themselves with American-made goods. Apparently, the raid on the East Ranch had been their first foray. Melquiades Garcia, the Mexican consul in Laredo, and military officers from Nuevo Laredo presented a report with their findings to American officials. Captain Hanson was able to confirm some, but not all, of the bandit's information.[92]

Accompanied by Hanson, Adjutant General Harley traveled to Laredo on April 13 to acquaint himself on border conditions and confer with Wright and Ryan. Following the inspection, Harley declared "Mexico is seething with German intrigue and propaganda." Along with Captains Jerry D. Gray at Marfa and Charles Stevens at Brownsville, Wright pursued German provocateurs working the *frontera*. Throughout the remainder of the year, the officers arrested a man for stealing government munitions stored at Ruidosa, broke up an espionage ring in Laredo, and captured a German entomologist and his three coconspirators.[93]

Wright and his men assisted Secret Service agents in August with a federal investigation into a counterfeiting ring operating out of Laredo. Posing as managers for cotton pickers, the gang passed bogus coinage in San Antonio, Victoria, Corpus Christi, and other South Texas towns. Two counterfeiters were apprehended in Tivoli and Laredo respectively, but the gang's leader remained at large until Wright found him in Rio Grande City. The captain had received information as to the fugitive's whereabouts from mounted Customs inspector Robert S. Rumsey, and Edds was dispatched to make the arrest. Rumsey took the fourth gang member into custody in Laredo on August 17. Between the four arrests, authorities recovered a considerable sum of counterfeit money, and the machine and materials with which the specie was made. The suspects were brought before the U.S. commissioner in Victoria, and bond was set at $2,500 each.[94]

Company K was posted to Santa María, about thirty miles upriver from Brownsville, in October 1918 to support Captain William W. Taylor's Company F. Wright and some of his men went into Brownsville on October 13, and "received a warm welcome from old friends who reside [there]." The army allowed both Wright and Taylor to tap into the military telephone network so they could stay in contact with their various detachments. This spirit of cooperation between the soldiers and the Rangers was vital, since the level of depredations had recently increased. Following a raid on ranches thirty miles south of Hebbronville in Jim Hogg County, Sheriff Craighead and a detachment of Company K trailed the *bandidos*. Wright mounted a joint effort with troops from Fort Ringgold to intercept the brigands before they crossed the river above Rio Grande City.[95]

However, threats to law and order in South Texas did not always originate from beyond the border. For a decade, Archer Parr had exercised absolute power over Duval County's political offices. While serving as county commissioner and state senator, he acted as *patrón* to the largely illiterate Hispanic community, which comprised 80 percent of the electorate. Known as the "Duke of Duval," Parr used his influence to dispense patronage and siphon county funds for his own usage.[96] Professor Evans Anders noted Parr's unique level of immorality:

> The types of abuses that Archie Parr engaged in were no different from the practices of the other South Texas power brokers, but the Duval Democrat exhibited no sense of restraint, whether he was rigging an election, gerrymandering a new county, or stealing money from the county treasury ... progressives across the state came to regard Parr as the symbol of the worst qualities in Texas politics: corruption, violence, and intransigent opposition to reform.[97]

In mid-1918, David William Glasscock challenged incumbent Parr for the Twenty-third Senatorial District seat. In the July 27 primary election, Glasscock maintained a slight lead over his opponent. However, the crafty Parr's supporters convinced the Democratic executive committee on August 24 to disallow some decisive results that favored Glasscock. As a result, the "Duke" was certified as the party's candidate. After an unsuccessful write-in run in the general elections on November 5, Glasscock persuaded the legislature to probe the whole matter. Wright's men had watched over polling places at Falfurrias and the Santa Rita schoolhouse during the vote, while Rangers from Ryan's and Captain John Jesse Sanders's companies did the same at Benavides and the San Jose Ranch. Before the state Senate Committee on Elections and Privileges convened, the captain went into Hidalgo County and obtained signed affidavits concerning election methods. Once the legislators met on February 13, 1919, the candidates' attorneys argued whether the statements could be entered into the record. Although the challenger had presented himself as an upright, moral alternative to Parr's corruption, Marshall Hicks, the state senator's lawyer, was able to demonstrate Glasscock did not possess a higher ethical standing, and the race was nothing more than a dirty political fight. The investigative committee accepted Hicks's argument, and the majority report sustained the election results. The Senate narrowly returned Parr to his seat.[98]

Even while Wright was gathering evidence in one legislative probe, Representative José Tomás Canales initiated another inquiry in January 1919, to investigate nineteen charges of alleged Ranger Force misconduct. Wright's involvement began when he assisted the investigating committee by subpoenaing witnesses in the Twenty-third District. On February 12, John H. Rogers, now a U.S. marshal, appeared before the joint committee. The day after his venerable old captain's appearance, Wright testified on the actions of Sergeant Edds, who was named in the second, third, and fourth charges brought by Canales. The second charge involved the alleged abuse of a prisoner in the custody of Edds and other Rangers. Wright was not involved in the purported incident or any investigation afterward.[99]

Canales's third charge concerned a shooting incident that had occurred in Rio Grande City on October 6, 1918. Early in the morning, Edds and Rangers Monroe Wells and Royal Wade Lorenz had gone after Alonzo Sanchez at Los Saenz Ranch near Rio Grande City. Their quarry has been described as either a deserter or a "slacker," and the sergeant incorrectly believed he did not need an arrest warrant or military order to detain Sanchez. Leaving his men to cover the outside of the house while he went into the fenced backyard, Edds mistakenly identified the sleeping Lisandros Muñoz as the man he sought, and woke him. The suspect reached for the barrel of Edds's rifle and attempted to take it away. In the scuffle, Edds fatally shot Muñoz in the groin, the bullet having severed the femoral artery. Wright and the justice of the peace arrived at the scene approximately an hour after the shooting. The justice and a deputy sheriff investigated the same morning at Wright's insistence, and ruled the Ranger sergeant had acted in self-defense. However, the grand jury met on February 2, 1919, and indicted Edds. Three days later, he was suspended from the force pending the outcome of the committee's investigation. Canales believed Edds guilty of second-degree murder and spent a good deal of time on this charge throughout the proceedings. He did his best to cast Edds in a negative light, but could never prove any illegal behavior. In the end, Edds's legal case was given a change of venue to Alice, and the trial opened in district court on January 29, 1920. The defendant was acquitted of the charges the same evening, after the jury deliberated for ten minutes.[100]

The fourth charge referred to the killing of Jose Maria Gomez Salinas, an alleged horse thief who had been captured by the crew of the Izaguirre Ranch in Jim Hogg County. Edds was called to Agua Nueva on September 1, 1918, to take the suspect into custody. Instead, the following morning, he instructed Sabas Ozuna and Federico Lopez, two Mexican cowboys, to transport the prisoner to the Hebbronville jail. Edds later stated he could not see to Gomez himself as he had to attend district court in Rio Grande City later in the day. The trip to Hebbronville was quiet until, within four miles of their destination, Ozuna and Lopez fatally shot the handcuffed Gomez. Contacted at Torrecillas (present Oilton), Wright ordered the killers be arrested and taken to the Hebbronville jail. They were soon released by the justice of the peace under bond of five hundred dollars each to await the grand jury. Both men assumed responsibility for shooting Gomez, who they claimed had been attempting to escape, and denied Edds had ordered them to murder the prisoner. Edds did, however, admit to Canales that he had instructed the authorities in Hebbronville to deny Salinas bail, giving the Ranger more time to collect evidence. In the end, neither Ozuna nor Lopez were indicted for the shooting, and Canales supported his charge with nothing but hearsay evidence. While Edds's decision was negligent and denied Salinas his constitutional right to due process, any suggestion he was criminally responsible for Salinas's death cannot be taken seriously. In addition, Wright resolutely supported his sergeant, and the captain's prestige in the service and the public was sufficient for Edds to be declared innocent of any wrongdoing.[101]

Wright emerged from the Canales episode with his integrity unquestioned. His stalwart defense of his embattled sergeant demonstrated his moral courage, and Cameron County Sheriff William Thomas Vann, no supporter of the Ranger Force, testified the captain was "a prince" and "a good man." Canales did not cease in his efforts to see Edds dismissed from the service, and eventually Wright would be forced to part ways with the troublesome Ranger.[102]

The wartime emergency ended, and the Ranger Force was reduced to meet existing conditions. The term of Captain Sanders expired, and his Company A was disbanded. Wright was ordered to take charge of the territory and personnel for which Sanders had been responsible. By virtue of the law enacted by the Thirty-sixth Legislature, the Ranger Force was reorganized effective June 20, 1919, and Company K was redesignated as Company D. The authorized strength of the outfit was one captain, one sergeant, and twelve privates. Edds remained as his sergeant, and eight men transferred from Company K to the new command. Three moved from Sanders's old company. Wright reenlisted as captain of Company D, effective June 29, 1919. Assigned to the Brownsville district, he and five of his men arrived in town on August 21.[103]

On November 21, the captain was on the streets of Brownsville when he was hailed by a soldier and a military policeman from the fort. They were looking for a city police officer to apprehend an allegedly drink-crazed Mexican who had thrown a bottle at the soldier's vehicle. Wright agreed to go with them and take the drunk into custody until a Brownsville officer could be located. The Ranger captain, with a cigar in his mouth, was not anticipating trouble when he approached the man, later identified as Jose Corona, in front of the Federal Building. Suddenly the Mexican thrust at him with a knife, but the blade was stopped by a bag of tobacco in the captain's left vest pocket. Wright pulled his sidearm and wounded his attacker in the leg. The intoxicated Corona again attempted to stab him, and Wright fired once more. The bullet struck the knife wielder in the head, and he died on the sidewalk within five minutes. An inquest was held the following day, and Justice of the Peace Henry J. Kirk cleared Captain Wright of any wrongdoing. The matter of jurisdiction arose since the shooting happened on the sidewalk in front of the Federal Building, but attorneys concluded Wright was within his authority to act as a state officer.[104]

Legalized Prohibition was enacted in Texas with the Dean Law on October 21, 1919. Following the passage of this state-level statute, and the national Volstead Act two months later, the smuggling of liquor grew from an effort to simply avoid import tariffs to a major and lucrative criminal enterprise. Many distilleries and breweries simply transported their entire operations to Mexico or the Caribbean where the manufacture of alcohol was legal. One favorite spirit was *mescal.* Made from the maguey plant, the strong, smoky liquor cost two to three dollars per gallon in Mexico, but brought up to ten dollars per quart in Texas. Each packhorse brought over the border could carry up to fifty bottles of liquor, and trains averaged between twenty and forty animals guarded by ten to twelve heavily armed Mexicans. Unlike his colleague Captain Ryan, who spent much of his time in Laredo, Wright pursued *tequileros* (liquor smugglers) relentlessly by horse, car, or truck. His efforts earned him the nickname *el capitan diablo* ("the devil captain"). The major border crossings used by *tequileros* were between the towns of Zapata in Zapata County and Los Ebanos in Hidalgo County. The multiple *senderos* (cleared trails) then led through the thinly populated brush country of Zapata, Starr, and Jim Hogg Counties before reaching San Diego in Duval County. The town was a haunt for smugglers, gamblers, and prostitutes, and there the "horsebackers" sold their wares to bootleggers. The latter drove the merchandise in automobiles to San Antonio, Houston, Corpus Christi, Dallas, and Fort Worth. Most of the time the state officers confronted the offenders well inside the United States where sympathizers along the Rio Grande could not inform the smugglers on the whereabouts of lawmen.[105]

"Apprehending violators of the eighteenth amendment was always a distasteful duty to the Rangers," a veteran Ranger remembered. "They were never interested in the cargoes of pack trains, as such. Other serious factors were involved in the movement of this illicit liquor." The incursions of the well-equipped and well-armed *tequileros* equated to an "armed invasion of the United States," and the majority of them were prepared to commit murder to protect their investments. Additionally, smugglers sometimes cut barbed wires fences that blocked their path, and their horses and pack animals introduced fever ticks into the state, which could prove hazardous to cattle herds.[106]

On New Year's Day, 1920, Wright, Sergeant Edds, and Rangers Stanley Morton, Desiderio "Jesse" Pérez, and William Sanders Peterson were returning from a scout along the river when they encountered three Customs inspectors. The federal officers, one of whom was Wright's son, Charles, requested

Two Rangers crossing Rio Grande on horseback, ca. 1919. J. R. Hunnicutt Collection. *Courtesy Texas State Library and Archives Commission, Austin, TX.*

assistance with a liquor raid. Later that evening, the Rangers and the Customs men stopped a wagon on the road from Hidalgo to Donna. In addition to five cases containing three hundred quarts of whiskey, tequila, *mescal*, aguardiente, and wine, the lawmen seized five military-issue .45 pistols, one .32-caliber pistol, and the team of horses. Five men were arrested on charges of smuggling, and detained in the old Hidalgo jail before being transferred to the county lockup in Edinburg. Authorities also intended to file charges of illegal possession of government property. Indeed, other Ranger captains on the river had noted an ongoing trend of Mexican smugglers carrying army handguns. Wright informed a newspaper reporter that one of the suspects had been wearing the uniform of a Mexican Army officer. The alcohol was stored in the vault of the Hidalgo County courthouse, along with other seizures, and surprisingly survived a fire that destroyed the building on January 11. Wright commented to the *Brownsville Herald*, "We had hoped that the fire destroyed the liquor so that we would not have to bother with it any more [*sic*].” He noted that immigration and customs documents had been removed from the vault to make room for the alcohol. The captain ruefully concluded, “Of course, the valuable records were lost, while the liquor that might as well have been destroyed is still intact.”[107]

Later in the month, Wright and Morton joined forces with Customs inspectors James Campbell “Doc” White and William Shears, and Department of Justice agent Louis Frank Shelton, to conduct a series of raids in the San Juan and Swallow area of Hidalgo County. The lawmen seized ninety-seven quarts of liquor and arrested two men. Upon their return to Brownsville, the Customs officers swore out complaints before U.S. Commissioner Emmette Knepp Goodrich. Even though Wright’s Rangers were kept busy enforcing the state’s prohibition laws, other crimes were undertaken in the lower valley. In the early weeks of 1920, a large number of ranches were experiencing a severe loss in livestock. Based on information gathered by army scout Hugh Eugene Barnes, the State Rangers were able to arrest three men, one of whom confessed.[108]

Throughout the rest of the year, Mexican *insurrectos* and *contrabandistas* continued to plague the border county. As the interlopers were violating federal and state laws, Rangers stationed on the Rio Grande worked in cooperation with Customs, Immigration, and Prohibition officers. All of them, regardless of government affiliation, were known as *los Rinches* (Rangers) or *empleados*. On September 21, Wright and a detachment intercepted a band of twelve horsebackers, sixty miles east of Laredo near Concepion. Four Mexicans were seriously wounded, another quartet was captured, the remainder escaped, and their liquor haul was seized. Although hundreds of gunshots were fired, none of the state officers were injured.[109]

In late 1920, Louis Clarence McDuff, deputy collector of customs at Hidalgo, became aware of a Mexican and several cohorts who had come to Pharr with the funds to purchase 522 bottles of tequila, Scotch, and rye whiskey. The liquor was then concealed within loose alfalfa hay, which was baled around the contraband, four bottles to the bale. The rumrunners intended to smuggle their goods aboard a train back to Gonzales, but McDuff, assisted by Wright and mounted Customs inspector Marcus W. Hines, discovered the load on the tracks. The hay was sold for one hundred dollars, and the alcohol was taken to Hidalgo for later disposal.[110]

During a reorganization of the Ranger Force in February 1921, Wright was placed in charge of the Rio Grande district stretching from Brownsville to Eagle Pass. Captain Ryan was relieved of his command in Laredo, and Wright stationed a number of his men in the town. He established base camps at San Antonio Viejo, *Agua Dulce*, and *Los Ojuelos* ranches, and at Mission and Hebbronville, which allowed the Rangers to conduct mounted patrols through "the center of the horsebacker country." As one example of the cooperation Wright enjoyed from private citizens, Don Eusebio Garcia, owner of the *Los Ojuelos* ranch forty miles east of Laredo, had offered the Rangers the use of his twenty-thousand-acre property at no cost along with a spacious rock ranch house, a large corral, and a barn. For the next several years, the Rangers of Company D utilized an assortment of equipment while working the *brasada*. In accordance with the service's historical trend, Wright's men took advantage of modern technology by acquiring one Thompson submachine gun, but the "Tumlinson Carbines" proved to be far more effective in the thick *chaparral*. Modified in Jacob Henry "Jake" Petmecky's sporting goods store in Austin, the latter weapons were either Winchester Model 1894 .30-30 or Model 1895 .30-06 rifles with their barrels shortened to fifteen or sixteen inches for easier handling. Professor Walter Webb visited Wright's camp south of Mirando City in 1924, and he noted: "Every ranger is mounted. They travel horseback all the time, carrying their provisions by packhorse. The bootleggers are usually mounted also so that it is necessary for the rangers to be on horse in arresting them." The year previous, Wright's son Bill observed the company possessed three "large missouri [*sic*] mules"—Lizzie, Monk, and Poly—and two smaller "mexican [*sic*] mules"—Spider and Rat. However, the captain supplemented his pack train with automobiles when necessary, and Wright gladly took possession of a one-ton truck in March 1922.[111]

Throughout 1921, Wright's men battled *tequileros* on eight occasions, captured ninety-five head of horses, and confiscated ten thousand quarts of liquor. In one of their first forays, the state officers intercepted a heavily armed band of *contrabandistas* on February 25, thirty-five miles northwest of San Diego. In the encounter, the Rangers captured eight Mexicans, eight Winchesters, a quantity of horses, saddles, and ammunition, and six hundred quarts of whiskey without a shot being fired. Wright and his men made several other apprehensions during the same foray, including seven hundred quarts of liquor. In time, the activities of Wright, Jerry Gray in the Big Bend, and Aaron Washington Cunningham at Del Rio forced the horsebackers into the desperate act of attacking law officers. During the month of March, Gray reported: "Mexicans opened fire on rangers without cause. There were about 30 shots fired. One Mexican was seen to fall headfirst through a wire fence. I'm convinced bad Mexicans from across the river plan to kill rangers, and the boys have to look out." Wright and his men apprehended another six smugglers in Duval County on May 20, and seized eight horses and several hundred quarts of tequila. The prisoners were taken to Corpus Christi for an appearance before the U.S. commissioner. On August 6, Wright, along with Ranger Hubert Patrick Brady, arrested two men on the old San Antonio–Laredo road near Callahan, north of Laredo. The officers seized the prisoners' Ford and 141 one-quart bottles of tequila. On September 10, Wright, Edds, Pérez, three other Rangers, Bob Rumsey, La Salle County Deputy Sheriff John Wildenthal, and folklorist James Frank Dobie left the latter's ranch to track a heavily armed gang of smugglers on the Nueces River. They found their quarry two days later in a camp on the Withers Ranch, forty miles south of Cotulla. Taken by surprise, seven of the *tequileros* were captured, but Ygnacio Serna, the leader, chose to resist, and was slain by Edds. The sergeant later commented on the killing: "One of them thought he would learn us how to shoot so I naturalized him (made an American Citizen out of him you know)." The lawmen seized 564 quarts of tequila and six Winchesters and recovered eleven stolen horses. Dobie later remarked to his wife, "I've never enjoyed two days so much in my life."[112]

The month of November brought Wright and his men into contact three times with what was believed to be a well-organized *tequilero* ring. On the seventeenth, Wright, Edds, Brady, Pérez, Rangers Juan Candelario González, William L. Miller, and David Cornelius "Jack" Webb, and three Customs inspectors—Charles Wright, Roy Lee Hearn, and Walter Frank Smith—encountered a gang of armed smugglers at Colorado Chiquita, sixty miles south of Hebbronville. The seven Mexicans immediately opened fire at the lawmen, and one dismounted and deliberately shot at Wright with a rifle. The captain was unhurt. The Texans responded with their rifles and revolvers causing the rumrunners to flee, shooting over their shoulders as they rode. The state and federal officers pursued the horsebackers for five miles through the brush before overtaking them. Frank Smith was described as "chained lightning" with a gun or rope, and, during the chase, he was said to have lassoed three Mexicans from their saddles one by one. In addition to the trio of captives, the Rangers confiscated eleven horses and saddles and eight hundred quarts of tequila.[113]

Captain Wright, four Rangers, and Customs inspectors Smith and Charles Wright faced a band of six *tequileros* the following day at Bruni, forty-five miles east of Laredo. The lawmen wounded two smugglers and took three into custody, but the remainder escaped across the Rio Grande. The captain's party also seized eighteen horses, six saddles, and eight hundred bottles of tequila. Wright, Edds, Brady, González, Miller, Webb, and Inspectors Smith and Wright made their largest seizure on November 22, when they engaged sixteen *contradbandistas* on the Barronena Ranch fifteen miles northwest of Realitos in Duval County. Having followed a fresh trail, the captain's party came across a man armed with a rifle and leading a packhorse from a thicket. When he spotted the law officers, the individual immediately opened fire, and more shots rang out from the brush. The state officers charged the thicket, holding their fire until they dismounted at the edge. Although the Rangers wounded two of the *tequileros*, the Mexicans all managed to escape into the thick brush after a sustained chase of several miles. The state officers did, however, confiscate thirty-three horses, sixteen saddles, and more than three thousand quarts of prohibited spirits, as well as the smugglers' pack saddles, bridles, rations, and camp equipage. The monetary value of the contraband seized throughout the month was estimated at more than seven thousand dollars.[114]

Despite the demands imposed on law officers by Prohibition-related smuggling, Wright and his men worked up other cases in 1922. On January 13, J. W. Minner was mortally wounded at 10:00 p.m. on his farm three miles northwest of Mercedes. The victim had been roused from his sleep by the noise of hoofbeats in his back yard. Minner went outside with a pistol to investigate, and confronted two Mexicans who shot him in the head, left hand, and abdomen. Taken into the house, the dying man was able to describe his murderers before expiring an hour later. Wright and four Rangers were in Mercedes at the time of the killing, and they set out in pursuit at daybreak accompanied by Deputy Marshals Perry Warren Perkins and Arthur Simmons, Hidalgo County Chief Deputy Sheriff Alexander "Alec" Champion, Marcus Hines, other county officers, U.S. soldiers, and local civilians. Two posse members from Weslaco encountered a pair of "suspicious characters" at Llano Grande early in the morning. A brief flurry of gunfire was exchanged before the fugitives escaped into the underbrush. After an exhaustive search, Wright, Perkins, and Hines determined the two suspects had fled into Mexico. Sheriff Anderson Yancey "Ancey" Baker requested the cooperation of the Mexican authorities in capturing the pair and extraditing them to the United States. No indications were found that Minner's killers ever faced American justice.[115]

On March 18, Wright and Company D went into the Mirando oil field in Zapata County. The Rangers seized eight hundred quart bottles of Mexican liquor, and arrested ten men. The prisoners were taken to the Carrizo jail pending preliminary hearings and the fixing of bail. The state officers scouted approximately seventy-seven miles below Laredo in early April, and "ran into numerous bandits." Wright was conferring with Edward "Ed" Cotulla, deputy collector of customs in San Antonio, on May 29, when he noted the recent decreasing rate of cross-border smuggling. "Business has been slack for the last six months on the border," he informed the *Express*, "and the smugglers are just as scary as coyotes when they do come across." The captain blamed the trend on the abundance of cheap moonshine whiskey and the flooding affecting the Rio Grande and the Nueces River, all of which hindered the *tequileros'* business.[116]

On July 22, Wright and one man were on duty in Corpus Christi to keep the peace during the primary election season. Three days later, nineteen Rangers under Wright and Captain Roy Carlisle Nichols left San Antonio and arrived in Denison the next morning. Uniting with Tom R. Hickman and his twelve men, all of whom had been in town for several days, their mission was to provide protection to Katy Railroad shop workers during an on-going labor strike. Ordered to bring a machine gun, Jerry Gray's company was similarly en route from the Rio Grande Valley. The Rangers were encamped in Forest Park, several hundred yards from the Katy shops. On the twenty-eighth, Wright and two Rangers were in Fort Worth to confer with authorities regarding the labor troubles. Police and Fire Commissioner John Alderman declined the assistance of the state officers, and the Rangers were instead sent to Cleburne to enforce the Open Port Law enacted in the wake of the Galveston dockworkers' strike two years prior. Reaching Cleburne the same day, Wright and thirteen men joined the force already assembled in town to protect railroad property and employees. The captain's detachment was prepared for trouble, as Jack Webb was packing a Thompson submachine gun. Despite the heavy armament, the Rangers of Company D had an easy time and especially enjoyed the Pullman car the Santa Fe Railroad had provided for their use. However, they did make a number of arrests.[117]

On August 3, Wright received a letter from a detachment in Temple that the Rangers there had arrested five men in connection with a whipping that had occurred on July 24. More tales of floggings administered to seven employees of the Santa Fe Railroad shops in Gainesville prompted official action. Five days later, Governor Pat Morris Neff ordered the town be placed under the provisions of the Open Port Law. Every violation committed within the act's stipulations was automatically a felony, and the offender was empowered to change the venue for a trial to an adjacent county. Wright was instructed to take charge of a detachment in Gainesville, and the entire company, save one man, was dispersed to other troubled locales. In addition to Cleburne and Gainesville, forty-four regular Rangers and 132 Special Rangers were assigned to strike duty in Texline, Dalhart, Amarillo, Childress, Big Springs, Quanah, Stanford, Smithville, Lufkin, Waco, Palestine, Marshall, Greenville, Longview, Baird, Sherman, Denison, Texarkana, Kingsville, Sanderson, Uvalde, and De Leon. The state officers in Gainesville arrested a total of nine men and charged each of them with seven counts of flouting the Open Port Law. The suspects were released on bonds of five hundred dollars for each case, and their day in court was scheduled for the October term.[118]

In the meantime, Edds had resigned on December 10, 1921, and Jack Webb was promoted to sergeant on August 1, 1922. The drawing of so many Rangers from the still-turbulent Rio Grande country for strike duty had repercussions. Anxious to return to South Texas, Wright noted in a letter to Barton that bandits and *tequileros* were "getting bold since we left." The law enforcement community on the border was dismayed when Wright's old friend Bob Rumsey was murdered by smugglers near Torrecillas on August 19. The captain later wrote to Rumsey's family: "The customs service lost its best inspector." Reflecting on the current state of affairs, Aldrich informed Wright: "We'll probably buy a couple of machine guns for your use down there. You're going to need them."[119]

A return to the border would have to wait, though. The following October, the general elections in Corpus Christi were plagued with a series of shootings and bombings. The minority Catholic faction in the city was headed by Judge Walter Francis Timon of the Twenty-eighth Judicial District, while the larger Protestant clique was led by real estate developer and businessman Samuel Johnson "Fred" Roberts. Timon's organization, known as the "Old Gang," courted the working-class Irish and Hispanic vote and dominated that portion of South Texas through its control of industry, commerce, and the press. As both blocs of the Democratic Party struggled for dominance, Roberts's group was backed by the local Ku Klux Klan and vied for the support of white middle-class Anglos. On October 14, two of the judge's gunmen fatally shot Roberts as he sat in his automobile in front of Gustavus Ericson Warren's store. Shortly afterward, Chief of Police (and disgraced ex-Ranger captain) James Monroe Fox took County Sheriff Frank Gravis Robinson, Constable Tilford Lee Petzel, Special Officer Joseph Arnold "Joe" Acebo, and Cleve Goff, a farmer, into custody in connection with the murder. The prisoners were transferred into the care of Chief Deputy William James Cody at the county jail.[120]

At the request of County Judge Hugh R. Sutherland and Mayor Peter Gray Lovenskiold, Wright returned to Corpus Christi with Captains Frank Hamer and Roy Wilkinson Aldrich on October 15 and investigated for fifteen days. Rangers Pérez and John Edward Hensley came from Kingsville to assist. Acting as the lead investigator, Hamer described the conditions in town as "deplorable" and "tense." He went before Justice of the Peace William Wellington Sharp to swear out warrants charging the suspects with murder. Robinson resigned on the seventeenth, and Cody replaced him the next day. Working the case, Wright interviewed Howard Grant, a deputy constable and eyewitness to the shooting, and received one of the fatal bullets from the undertaker who performed the autopsy on Roberts. The captain testified at the examining trial on October 23, and the grand jury indicted all four men. Robinson and the others made bail on November 3, with the sheriff and Acebo posting bonds of ten thousand dollars cash each and Goff and Petzel $2,500 each. Judge Timon, who did not recuse himself, granted a change of venue to Laredo. Before a Texas jury decided justice, the grateful residents of Corpus Christi presented each of the captains with an engraved, silver-plated Colt Single-Action Army .45 revolver.[121]

While the homicide investigation was unfolding, Wright and Prohibition agent Edwin Morgan DuBose, Sr. led a "clean-up" drive on the town's vice dens. Aided by Webb, Benjamin Thomas Tumlinson, Jr., Pérez, Ranger Grenade Donaldson "Don" Gilliland, Prohibition agent ____ Frye, and Customs inspectors Charles Wright and T. W. Richardson, they commenced the sweep on October 27. Wright left Corpus Christi on November 9 and returned to Cleburne to assess the situation in the open port. With conditions peaceful, he was back in the "Sparkling City by the Sea" by the seventeenth when he led a raid on a gambling den. Six men, including Joe Acebo, and one woman were apprehended and charged with gambling; the female suspect was additionally charged with maintaining a gaming house and possession of liquor. During their raids in Corpus Christi, the lawmen arrested a total of forty-six individuals and seized several hundred gallons of whiskey, beer, fine wines, and Mexican liquors.[122]

On November 9, Elias Villarreal Zárate, a Mexican national engaged in erecting a creamery in Weslaco, had broken the arm of coworker J. Frank Sullivan in a street fight. Zárate was jailed on charges of assault, but was removed later that night from his cell by approximately eight men. The general consensus was that he had been lynched, and his bullet-riddled body was found on the eleventh on an abandoned road five miles from Weslaco. Subsequently, threats were hurled at Francisco Pérez, the Mexican consul in Hidalgo. With similar violence occurring in Breckenridge, Don Manuel C. Téllez, the consul in San Antonio, protested to the State Department and demanded guarantees regarding the safety of his countrymen in Texas. The murder was widely reported across the country and quickly became an international incident. Sheriff Baker arrested City Marshal Thomas Jefferson Buckow, Deputy Marshal George Tollie "Tol" Humphries, and area farmers S. L. Henson and Jim Davidson in connection with the case. The quartet posted bond and were released the same day. Meanwhile, Wright was ordered to make a "thorough investigation" and submit a report to the governor and adjutant general. Assisted by Jesse Pérez and County Attorney John Cleveland Epperson, the captain presented his findings into the "cold blooded affair," complete with eyewitness testimony, on December 5, but the murder suspects were never brought to trial.[123]

While he was engaged in demanding assignments elsewhere, Wright remained "mighty anxious" to pursue the horsebackers who were "running the country in the Valley since the rangers left." He got his wish in November, and the state officers began patrolling the pastures of the Jennings Ranch in Zapata County on December 1. On the evening of the eighteenth, east of Mirando City, Wright, six of his Rangers, and Customs inspector Frank Smith, the latter noted for his "special ability to track horses and men," were following a band of twenty Mexicans leading a pack train of fifteen horses through the rocky ground and thick *chaparral* of Jim Hogg County. Two dissimilar versions of this episode exist. In *Horsebackers of the Brush Country*, Don Gilliland described how Wright spotted their quarry encamped in an arroyo on the Las Animas ranch. The captain dismounted and led Webb, Gilliland, and Pérez to the north of the gulch. Likewise afoot, William Peterson, Hubert Brady, and Smith went to the south. Also present, Tumlinson was not mentioned. Gilliland later maintained the lawmen moved to within fifty yards of the smugglers before shouting "*ríndanse!*" (give up). The Mexicans seized their .30-30 rifles and opened fire. Leandro Villareal, Gerónimo Gracia, and Silvando Gracios were killed in the subsequent thirty-minute running gunfight. The surviving Mexicans fled into the brush, and Wright and his party seized 650 bottles of liquor and seven horses.[124]

According to Walter Webb, who was given a tour of the scene by Wright in August 1924, the captain posted two men to the east side of the wash, took one with him to the west side, and dispatched one or two south to drive the *tequileros* out from cover and onto the open ground to the north. Half an hour later, the blocking force pushed their foes toward the waiting Rangers; the three *tequileros* were killed, and the rest scattered. Struck by rock fragments from a ricocheting slug, Wright killed one smuggler with a carbine shot to the neck. The rifle stock of another dead *tequilero* had been split in half by a bullet. The engagement has come to be known as the "Las Animas fight." Writing in *The Texas Rangers*, Webb did not specifically state whether the Rangers had called for the smugglers' surrender before firing. Seizing upon the professor's oversight, some historians have looked askance on Texas law officers supposedly shooting first, and not giving "liquor runners on the border" a chance to give up. However, the *San Antonio Evening News* reported at the time, "The smugglers showed fight, and both sides spread into skirmish lines," which seems to refute the notion of an ambuscade in this particular instance. In an interview with the *Express*, Wright explained his experience in dealing with *tequileros*: "They will fight and shoot to kill unless good luck is in your favor and you get the drop on them. But they are a wary lot, and while many of them get a running start, they will shoot it out with you when cornered."[125]

President Warren Gamaliel Harding called on the nation's governors to support the efforts of the federal government in enforcing the Eighteenth Amendment. Governor Neff summoned the entire forty-five-man Ranger Force to Austin on December 28, 1922, for a conference to discuss the state's response to Prohibition. While thirty-five of "the boys," as Neff called the rank and file Rangers, waited in the reception room outside the governor's office, Adjutant General Thomas Dickson Barton and the five captains met for one hour with the executive; five Rangers had been unable to attend for various reasons. Wright disclosed he did not know exactly the total quantity of liquor his men had seized in the last year, but he reckoned "the amount sufficient to fill a deep well and then overflow some."[126]

With the murder trial of Frank Robinson and his codefendants set to begin in Judge John Francis Mullally's Laredo courtroom, a special venire of one hundred men was summoned on January 3, 1923, but only three jurors were accepted. Fifteen were peremptorily challenged, a few more were excused for cause, while the majority expressed conscientious objections to imposing capital punishment. Another list of 227 special veniremen was utilized to secure the remaining six jurors. The trial convened on the sixth with John Valls, John M. Mathis of Houston, and Champe Goodwyn Carter of San Antonio prosecuting. James M. Taylor of Corpus Christi and Manuel John Raymond and John Adam Pope of Laredo represented the defendants. Wright's role in the trial was brief as he testified on his thorough investigative activities. The state rested its case on January 6 after calling eleven witnesses, and the defense declined to present rebuttal testimony. The defense presented its case on the eighth and called Chief Fox as a witness. Valls created a sensation when he attacked Fox's credibility and questioned him on the massacre that had occurred at Porvenir in 1917. The Klan issue was introduced with all the defendants going on record as opposing the organization and its ties to the party in power in Nueces County. Having once been under indictment for several killings near San Diego, Robinson admitted on the stand to the Roberts killing, but claimed he had acted in self-defense. The defense rested on January 9, and closing arguments were heard the following day. The case was given to the jury on the eleventh, and the defendants were acquitted of all charges after fifty hours of deliberation.[127]

Wright and Hamer returned to Corpus Christi four months later when the county sheriff's election was contested in court. Hamer left on April 5, while the other captain remained with five Rangers until the conclusion of the hearing. One raid on a house on Leopard Street netted the state officers a twenty-five-gallon still and a number of arrests.[128] Later in the month, Jim Hogg County Sheriff Pelton Bruce "Pell" Harbison warned Wright that Aristeo "*El Pajaro*" Gracia, brother of one of the *tequileros* slain at Las Animas, was attempting to assemble twenty men for an attack on Company D. According to Harbison, Gracia, wanted on federal liquor charges, was operating in South Texas and had cached a supply of booze along the border. Thus far, he had recruited ten men in his search for *la revancha* (revenge). Wright remained undisturbed and proposed to capture the smuggler between Zapata and Starr Counties if he moved north from the river. The Ranger apparently did not need to concern himself further as Gracia never followed through on his threats.[129]

Sheriff Walter Malone of Bee County planned to raid into Refugio County and apprehend bootleggers. Having been tipped to the presence of a still along the Mission River on the Bar B Ranch, he invited along Captain Wright, who brought his Customs inspector son, Charles, and two Rangers. Wright's party arrived in Beeville on August 22, and left immediately for the ranch, ten miles below Refugio. Leveling a half-dozen .30-30 rifles at the surprised lone operator, the officers arrested him and seized a still judged to be the best they had seen thus far, several fruit jars of liquor, and two or three barrels of prunes. Charged with violation of Prohibition laws, Adolph P. Jurek, the still operator, was taken to Beeville to await a federal officer from Corpus Christi. Two days later, Charles and Roy Hearne seized a large still, four hundred gallons of mash, and twenty-five bottles of moonshine on the Aransas River. On September 5, Wright, William Peterson, Ranger Asa Light Townsend, and Sheriff Frank Hunt of Refugio County assisted Customs officers in seizing a twenty-gallon still located in the brush along the Blanco River near Woodsboro. The owner of the still was not located, and no arrests were made.[130] The next three months were quiet, as the Rio Grande ran at flood stage. In the final week of November, *tequileros* became more active.[131]

In January 1924, Wright was ordered to proceed to Corpus Christi and investigate charges involving Ranger Duncan Sylvester "Dunk" Wright (no relation) of Captain Tom Hickman's company. According to the criminal complaint, D. S. Wright had gone to the Metropolitan Café on Chaparral Street with fellow private Richard Ross Bledsoe on January 7. Inside the establishment, they disarmed and assailed police officer M. T. "Mike" Pena. The lawmen under investigation were each charged with aggravated assault and assault upon a peace officer and arraigned in county court the following day. They were freed on $250 bonds. Duncan Wright was suspended from the service, and Captain Wright was further instructed to present his findings directly to the governor. The captain submitted the report, and Privates Wright and Bledsoe were both transferred to Company E the following month. Their legal cases were continued and seem to have been dismissed.[132]

Beginning in May, Wright increased the pace of his already vigorous efforts and reported: "I've cleaned this country from top to bottom. Mexicans are leaving by the dozen. We've been raiding day and night. People are tickled to death." However, the peace he had provided did not last long. By the summer, Wright noted to newspaper reporters that cattle and horse thieves were active along the Rio Grande from the Maverick County line to Brownsville. Wright traveled to Hebbronville at the end of August and later recalled being in the brush nearly the entire time, except for one or two trips to town. He emphasized, "I gave the State my whole time and brains." He and his Rangers arrested two men and seized nine horses and six hundred quarts of tequila near Hebbronville on September 1. Additionally, Wright and Captain Gray met with Governor Neff on September 4 to discuss the smuggling of cotton into Texas from Mexico. In a brief interlude four days later, Wright addressed high school students in the district courtroom in Hebbronville during opening exercises for the new scholastic year.[133]

Wright, his son Bill, Rangers James Warren Smith and John W. Sadler, and Customs inspectors Hearn, Frank Smith, Creed Taylor, and Jack Webb embarked on a two-week scout, and raided a "Mexican farm" near Hebbronville. The officers captured nine hundred quarts of tequila. Wright had a stroke of good fortune on September 17 when his party caught up to a band of horsebackers fifteen miles southwest of Hebbronville. The Rangers captured one man, five horses, all of the smugglers' equipage, and three hundred quarts of tequila. None of the lawbreakers were killed, and each lawman remained uninjured.[134]

Wright's detachment received word on September 22 of a large liquor shipment crossing the river en route to San Diego. The law officers surrounded and stopped a covered wagon being drawn by six mules on a sandy trail between Starr and Hidalgo Counties. Two of the three Mexicans inside were captured while the third, thought to be the leader, escaped. The officers found within the wagon six hundred quarts of tequila, and a richly decorated saddle, as well as three head of stock hitched to the back. A jury later sentenced the wagon driver to one year and a day in Leavenworth, while the other received ninety days in the county jail.[135]

On November 14, Wright, five Rangers of Company D, and four Customs officers struck the trail of *tequileros* near the Cabeza Toro ranch in Duval County. The lawmen followed the tracks one hundred miles to a large thicket near the Santa Cruz ranch. They approached the horsebackers' camp on the fifteenth, but a picket spotted them and opened fire. Killing the guard, the law officers rushed the camp, and the remainder of the outlaws fled into the sand dunes. None of the lawmen were injured, and twelve horses and one mule, a large quantity of Mexican liquor, and a number of saddles were captured. While the local justice of the peace held an inquest over the picket's body, Frank Smith and Ranger Eugene H. Tumlinson tracked the *tequileros* who were overtaken in Starr County.[136]

From September 1, 1923, to December 1, 1924, the members of the Ranger Force made over five thousand apprehensions, destroyed more than five hundred stills, recovered five hundred head of rustled cattle, horses, and sheep, and recouped $32,964 worth of stolen federal property. Additionally, they kept order at a number of ballot boxes and protected prisoners from mob violence. Governor Neff asserted that "the mere presence of a Texas Ranger creates regard for the law," but some actively worked to thwart their actions.[137]

In 1899 and 1900, separate rulings by Orange County Judge George Franklin Poole and Hall County Judge William Merritt Purdue, Jr. had led to the abolishment of the Frontier Battalion and the creation of the Ranger Force. Twenty-four years later, the Rangers would face another, perhaps greater, challenge to the service's existence.[138] Acting for a San Antonio client, Dennis Chapin brought a lawsuit on August 1, 1924, challenging the constitutionality of Articles 6754 and 6757, Title 116, Chapter 144 of the state's Revised Civil Statutes, which authorized the organization of the Ranger Force and the position of quartermaster. The case was heard by Judge Robert Berkeley Minor of the Fifty-seventh Judicial District in San Antonio on October 20. Three months later, the jurist ruled the legislative enactment of 1919 was unconstitutional, and issued an injunction that ordered the service to cease operations. Once the ruling went into effect, the Ranger Force was forced into inactivity. Chapin predicted the state would save half a million dollars in reduced annual appropriations. The attorney general's office filed a motion in district court to suspend judgment and prepared to argue before the Fourth Court of Civil Appeals for setting aside the injunction. Attorney General Daniel James Moody was ready to take the case to the state supreme court and test the ruling of the trial court, if necessary. Denied any funding, Wright and his fellow captains waited at the adjutant general's office for the situation to be resolved, while lawbreakers along the border learned of the suspension from duty and grew bolder. Wright notified Adjutant General William Mark McGee that a gang of fifteen heavily armed *bandidos*, led by Pantaleon "Leon" Villers, had reportedly crossed the border with twenty pack mules and at least three thousand quarts of tequila. Villers was described in the *Mexia Daily News* as "one of the worst bandit leaders along the border." Wright, mindful of the court order, requested instructions from McGee. Fearing local ranches would fall prey to the Mexicans, the adjutant general responded by saying the Laredo station had not been enjoined and ordered Wright to "take whatever steps are necessary" to protect the stockmen. The captain took six men to a ranch fifty miles east of Laredo from which they watched the trails from the border. Fortunately, the Fourth Court reversed the earlier decision on February 25, and the Rangers were free to resume their activities.[139]

After Miriam Amanda "Ma" Ferguson was inaugurated as Texas's twenty-ninth governor, she undertook a policy of retrenchment in the state government. At the same time, the Senate passed a departmental appropriations bill that cut the Ranger Force's budget of $234,000 by 50 percent. In order to save $2,500 a month, General McGee recommended to the executive a reduction of the service from fifty-one men to twenty-eight. He also planned to assign the bulk of the Rangers to the border, while retaining only a handful in Austin for emergencies. Rather than continue under these conditions, Wright tendered his resignation, effective March 31, 1925.[140]

In presenting his letter of resignation to the adjutant general, he summarized his career and declared his pride in his record as a law officer. Wright then expressed his desire to not jeopardize the latter since "the Rangers, curtailed as to numbers and liberty of action against the lawless element as they have been, can be but figureheads, therefore useless … It is a well-known fact … that since the World War a wave of crime is sweeping our country, and especially our own state, and in my humble opinion, if there

Miriam Amanda Ferguson. #1/102-155. *Courtesy Texas State Library and Archives Commission, Austin, TX.*

ever was a time in the history of Texas when this force was necessary, it is now." He went on to call for an increase of the Ranger Force and full authority for its members to operate in every county in the state. He further advocated for the service to be an independent, nonpolitical organization. Before he concluded with a personal message to McGee, Wright stated,

"I am proud that I have served my beloved state as Captain of Company D, Texas Rangers. I am proud that I have served with some of the best men in Texas on the border."[141]

In mid-November 1925, Wright was offered employment as deputy city marshal of Robstown in Nueces County. After considering the matter for several days, the former Ranger accepted the position from Marshal James Galbreath on a trial basis. Wright soon decided to take the job permanently, as his proposed official duties and the compensation were appealing. His family joined him one week later, and the townspeople gave them a warm welcome.[142]

His first day on duty, Wright arrested Juan Recio of Premont, who had acted suspiciously upon entering town. The new city officer followed the new arrival and arrested him while in possession of nineteen bottles of French brandy. Recio was tried in the justice court in Robstown, then remanded to the county jail in Corpus Christi. From there, he awaited the decisions of the federal grand jury which would convene on November 21. On the eighteenth, Wright, Officer Bob Riser, and Marshal Galbreath arrested a man for burglarizing a home and stealing a diamond ring. The stolen merchandise was recovered, and the suspect was placed in jail to await grand jury action. Also found in his possession were several pocketbooks and a deputy sheriff's badge from Travis County.[143]

On February 18, 1926, Wright announced his candidacy for sheriff of Nueces County in the upcoming Democratic primaries. He told the *Robstown Record* he had been encouraged to run for the office by a number of friends. Wright doubtless welcomed an endorsement in the press from Wilson County residents attesting to his fitness for the position. As Wright's personal character and professional record were impeccable, the incumbent, Sheriff Ben Dechard Lee, Sr., dwelled on the fact the challenger had been a resident of Nueces County for only nine months, whereas he, Lee, had already served one term in office. He also condescendingly advised Wright's Wilson County supporters to mind their own business and called into question whether Nueces County needed a "ranger sort" of sheriff, alluding to the dark days of the last decade. The sheriff's strategy was apparently successful. In the primaries held on July 24, Wright received 2,422 votes while Lee won 2,764.

Although disappointing, the narrow margin was nevertheless impressive considering Wright's relevant newcomer status.[144]

Once Governor Daniel Moody entered office, Wright applied for reappointment to the Ranger service. According to the *San Antonio Light*, rumors of Wright's return were being whispered in border country *jacales* and among the brush thickets. "'*El Capitán Diablo cabalga otra res.*' The Devil Captain rides again," as the newspaper commented with an imperfect translation. He was appointed captain of Company C at Del Rio on April 13, 1927, to take effect on May 15. On May 14, he was ordered to instead take command of Company A at Marfa, while Captain John H. Rogers was assigned to Company C. The appointments met with the approval of District Attorney John Valls, who wrote: "I have known Will Wright, John Rogers, and Frank Hamer for many years. I know their superb courage and their integrity. In my opinion, loyalty to the law and undoubted honesty are the chief characteristics of a peace officer. Will Wright has discretion and judgment and will arrest any guilty person regardless of rank or station."[145]

In early September, Wright sent Sergeant William W. Taylor and Ranger J. C. Parker to investigate cattle rustling in Hudspeth County, while he answered calls for assistance in McCamey. Conditions in the developing oil fields of Upton, Pecos, and neighboring counties were growing worse as the lawless element rushed to exploit opportunities. Indeed, Upton County Attorney William Moore Davis had reported being threatened by the sheriff, the postmaster, the town's mayor, and city councilmen. Wright and his men followed a pattern in which "the Rangers … moved into town quickly, raided gambling dens, roughed up a few of the local toughs, and intimidated the more intractable operator before moving out, leaving the sheriff's deputy to keep a lid on things as best he could." Through the month of October, the captain, Taylor, and Robert W. Sumrall assisted the sheriff to keep the peace in Marfa; Pinkney F. Dyches and Sumrall hunted cattle thieves before going to Presidio; and Wright traveled to Winkler County with two brand inspectors. The following month, Wright and Taylor received orders to make a general survey of the oil fields. They raided the vice dens of Wink, Pyote, and Grube, arresting 105 gamblers and four speakeasy operators. On December 7,

Wright worked with federal agents in launching raids in the Yates oil field in Pecos County. The lawmen seized forty-six gallons of liquor and arrested one man; the alcohol was subsequently destroyed. District Attorney Joe Montague of Fort Stockton went to Austin in January 1928 and requested Governor Moody provide a Ranger company to his troubled section. Two of Wright's Rangers and two from Captain Rogers's contingent combined forces in a sweep of the oil fields of Pecos and Crockett counties. They raided several gambling joints and illegal saloons, arrested twenty-four gamblers and seven peddlers, and destroyed several slot machines and gambling tables. Wright left the four men to guard particularly troublesome locales: two in Grube in Crockett County and two in Iraan in Pecos County.[146]

Following the opening of new oil fields, the headquarters of Company A was transferred from Marfa to McCamey on February 1. The move upset many of the former community's residents, but Moody was compelled to address the latter town's deplorable conditions. Later in the month, Wright was working in Wink, a Winkler County boomtown that had been born in a cow pasture and quickly grew to a population of ten thousand oil field workers, speculators, merchants, gamblers, and prostitutes. Rather than an organized syndicate, Wink's underworld was a loose collection of vice peddlers and colluding local politicians. Making a one-night raid on the twenty-fourth, the captain was accompanied by Sergeant Taylor and Rangers James W. Smith, Con Cecil Wren, and Samuel Cloud "Sam" Mayes from Company A, and Henry Doyle Glasscock and Sergeant James Thomas Laughlin from Company C. Together with Sheriff William Patrick Rooney, Deputy Sheriff Hugh Gillespie, and Prohibition agent Jay D. Reeder, they closed vice dens and confiscated seven thousand dollars in cash, gambling equipment, a large quantity of liquor, and a fifteen hundred-gallon still. One hundred and forty-eight gamblers were arrested; most pleaded guilty and paid fines of $19.75 each. Four owners were transported to the county jail in Pecos. The law officers also ordered five hundred undesirables to leave town by sundown. On March 6, the captain and several of his men were riding through the streets when they became aware of the smell of liquor emanating from a suspicious house. After obtaining a search warrant, the officers raided the domicile and seized fifteen hundred gallons of whiskey, three 50-gallon tanks of mash, and assorted kegs and barrels.[147]

As lawbreakers departed Wink, a great many fled thirty-one miles west into New Mexico where they settled in the hamlet of Jal in southeastern Lea County. The Rangers soon became aware of the illegal liquor being trafficked in Jal, but they lacked the authority to go into another jurisdiction. Wangling positions as deputy sheriff and town mayor, Emerald Allen "Two Gun Dick" Herwig, once a feared enforcer for the dominant criminal syndicate in Borger, partnered with Clyde Woolworth and Wilbur Floyd Stuart in founding the Jal Townsite Company. Doubtless bitter over being unceremoniously evicted from Borger and Wink, Herwig established a saloon that mockingly bore the sign "Eight miles from Texas Rangers." He would not have the last laugh. On March 17, those engaged in the vice trades were again disconcerted when Will Wright came to town. In order to allow the captain to cross state lines, the chief Prohibition official for West Texas and New Mexico had temporarily sworn Company A's personnel into federal service. Toting pistols, sawed-off shotguns, and a "machine gun," Wright; Rangers Taylor, Smith, Wren, and Mayes; Prohibition officers Van Zandt and Wright; Reeves County Sheriff Edgar Bertham Kiser; and eight other lawmen then scoured Jal. They closed the saloons and gambling dens, stripped residents standing in the streets of their firearms, and took four men into custody. Among those disarmed, Herwig protested, "I'm deputy sheriff here." The reply was curt and dismissive: "You ain't nothing." Having surreptitiously watched the bootleggers for several weeks, the federal officers drove approximately ten miles out of town to the Mont Beckham Ranch where they confiscated a three hundred-gallon still, 640 gallons of whiskey mash, sixty gallons of whiskey, and one truck-load each of rye and sugar. The prisoners were placed in the Wink jail before being taken to Pecos for a preliminary hearing. They were freed on bonds of $750 each. Herwig was held for three hours, then released.[148]

On March 24, 1928, Wright and three Rangers were in Reeves County, where they, along with two Prohibition agents and the county sheriff, raided the largest still found west of Fort Worth up to that point. Moreover, the lawman captured six Oklahoma residents, six thousand gallons of mash, five hundred gallons of whiskey, a truckload of sugar, and another of rye. The moonshiners were heavily armed, but they offered no resistance to being arrested.[149]

While headquartered in McCamey, the majority of Company A's activities were spent in the Permian Basin oil fields; although Wright kept Private Sumrall posted at Presidio. Unsanitary conditions and an outbreak of smallpox prompted Wright's move into Winkler County to enforce health laws. Additionally, the company guarded a city charter election in Wink on May 28. They also raided gambling houses in Upton, Crane, and Winkler Counties, and seized 135 men and eight thousand dollars. The Rangers closed the Pastime Club in McCamey, the Club House in Crane City, and the Yellowfront in Wink. Seventieth Judicial District Attorney Roy Biggs informed Wright the Winkler County officers were unreliable, and, indeed, Sheriff William Allen "Pecos Bill" Priest had applied a "live and let live" philosophy to enforcing the law. The captain had previously informed the adjutant general he was unable to get anyone to testify on the stand concerning the sheriff's behavior. Similarly, city government officials were abusing their authority and making money from public utility franchises, fines exacted in municipal court, bribes, and graft. During the night of July 14 and into the next day, the Rangers conducted raids on "liquor and dope nuisances" in Wink and made numerous arrests, including those of prominent bootleggers Joe Wells and C. E. Rose. As conditions in the oil field worsened, Company A's headquarters was transferred to Fort Stockton on August 1. Sheriff Priest told the newspapers the state officers had not been invited by him, but he and Deputies Otis Morehead, Ross DeRacy, and Ray Ballard soon faced lawsuits alleging official misconduct. The sheriff's case was called for trial in federal court in Pecos on September 28, and Judge Charles Boynton dismissed the charges. Admitting he was not "too sympathetic" with Prohibition laws, Judge Charles Klapproth of the Seventh District Court in Kermit did likewise on October 8. However, the federal grand jury in El Paso indicted Priest and all his deputies for conspiracy to violate the national Prohibition law.[150]

On November 2, the captain arrested four men on charges of cattle rustling in Pecos County and jailed them in Fort Stockton. One of the suspects was Garza County rancher James William "Dutch" Luman, who was due to be tried for the murder of Marvin Breeding. After several continuances, the trial opened on December 3 in Lamesa, and the defendant was found guilty three days later. While the case was ongoing, Luman and his wife were indicted in

Pecos County for cattle rustling on December 5. Wright and federal officers conducted raids in the Yates oil field that resulted in the seizure of forty-six gallons of liquor and one arrest. A liquor shipment smuggled from Mexico and worth $500,000 was stolen outside Wink, and the rumrunners responded by kidnapping P. C. "Denver Blackie" Burcham, the hijackers' leader, and leaving him for dead in the desert. Sheriff Priest made a dozen arrests, but the feud threatened to escalate into an all-out gang war. Forestalling the anticipated violence, more than twenty Rangers, county officers, and federal agents swept through Wink on the night of December 18, armed with warrants for violations of the Mann, Harrison, Dyer, and Volstead Acts. They raided and closed thirty gambling resorts and arrested scores of citizens and transients alike. Others scoured the Hendrick, Leck, and Sid Richardson-Frank Kelsey oil patches, serving warrants and forcing lawbreakers to flee. Two days later, the lawmen patrolled the quiet streets and endeavored to locate the source of liquor proliferation. They also attempted to ascertain the ownership of automobiles and trucks abandoned in the wake of the crackdown. Twelve prisoners, five of them women, were charged with illegal possession and sale of liquor and appeared before U.S. Commissioner William Walters Dean in Pecos. Most pled not guilty and waived preliminary hearings, and bond was set at $750 each.[151]

The town of San Angelo was the source of troubling reports, and the county's top law enforcement officers were implicated in the protection of a local liquor ring. Ranger Dott Edward Smith, Sr. went undercover on December 11, visited a number of wide-open drinking and gambling establishments, and reported his findings to Tom Green County Attorney Robert B. Brown. Based on his investigation, Smith was certain Sheriff Joseph Robert Hewitt and Police Chief (and former Ranger captain) James Carroll Bates were protecting lawbreakers. Beginning on December 20, eleven Rangers of Companies A and B, and federal agents descended on San Angelo where they raided thirty "whiskey resorts" and confiscated one still and bonded liquor worth ten thousand dollars. They arrested thirty-five violators. On January 10, 1929, Smith, deputized as a federal marshal, and Prohibition officers arrested Bates on a charge of conspiracy to violate the Volstead Act. He waived a preliminary hearing before U.S. Commissioner Jesse Thomas Couch the next day and was released on a three-thousand-dollar bond. Bates resigned his office on the thirteenth. On April 26, twenty-nine men and women, including Bates and former assistant police chief A. W. Brown, were charged in federal court with conspiracy in a blanket indictment.[152]

While Bates's case moved through the courts, Wright visited Wink on January 7, and he arrested twelve gamblers and seized three hundred dollars. After visiting Fort Stockton on the twelfth, he was once more in Wink on January 17, where he and officers discovered a warehouse containing twenty-five quarts of sugar and twenty gallons of whiskey. Leaving for Fort Stockton that same night, Wright was at Iraan on February 4 where he destroyed forty-five gallons of whiskey. He arrested several suspects in McCamey the next day and raided gambling houses in Fort Stockton and Wink on the seventh. Wright returned to Wink on February 14 and began yet another cleanup campaign. He seized a number of slot machines and obtained an injunction from the district attorney to close all vice dens as soon as a new judge was appointed and sworn into office. The captain informed General Robertson, "I'm tired of fooling with them. I'm coming after them with blood in my eyes." However, by February 1929, the depleted Ranger Force numbered only thirty men covering the entire state. The lawmen rode exclusively in automobiles as not a single horse remained in the service. Traveling to Wink and Kermit on April 7, the undaunted Wright effected numerous arrests and testified before the grand jury.[153]

During the well-attended trial of Bates and nineteen others in U.S. district court, one prosecution witness testified he personally paid the defendant $125 weekly for protection against raids. Two San Angelo bankers revealed Bates's deposits between May 1, 1926, and April 22, 1929, totaled more than $54,000. The former police chief's salary had been $225 per month, but Bates insisted the money represented earnings from a farm sale and gambling winnings. Nonetheless, all the defendants were convicted on May 3. Bates was sentenced to eighteen months in Leavenworth and assessed a fine of $7,500.[154]

On March 25, 1930, two fishermen were standing on the banks of the Pecos River near the bridge located four miles from Imperial. While casting for catfish, they noticed the bare shoulder of a man appear out of the water.

They immediately alerted the authorities in Imperial, and Wright and Sheriff Rooney soon arrived on the scene. The naked bodies of a thirty-year-old woman and a ten-year-old girl had been discovered in the river near Grandfalls on February 21. The officers were anxious to know if they were dealing with the same perpetrator. The male's body was brought out of the river by means of a rope, placed on a tarpaulin, and photographed. Upon examination, the lawmen observed the victim had been shot in the back, and the justice of the peace later ruled death to be the result of a homicide. William Leonard Zent, San Angelo chief of police, brought Ruby Taggart to Fort Stockton a few hours later, and she identified the deceased as Henry M. Poland, a small-time gambler from Plentywood, Montana. The victim's clothing was found burned on the riverbank. An informant led the officers to convicted felon Fred Leroy Moutray, who was present in San Angelo on March 22, and in McCamey the next day. He was further seen riding in a car similar to Poland's Ford coupe. An Ector County grand jury indicted Moutray, but the man had already left the state. Two years after the crime, Moutray was picked up in Chicago, returned to Texas, and taken to the Pecos where Poland's corpse had been stripped and thrown into the water. "Take me away from this river and I will tell all," the suspect reportedly cried. Moutray was lodged in the Pecos County jail, where he revealed details of the murder in forty-three hours of questioning. Wright, District Attorney Weaver Baker of Junction, and Special Ranger James G. Rooney of Iraan were among those in the room. According to Moutray, Roger Thompson, a man he had known in prison, and an unnamed woman planned to rob Poland, but the crime had gone awry, and the gambler was killed in Sterling County. The victim's body was transported to San Angelo in the trunk compartment of his own car before Moutray and Thompson drove to the Pecos to dispose of the remains. Poland was said to have been carrying a large sum of money distributed in secret pockets throughout his clothing, and the cash was likely destroyed when the culprits burned the evidence.[155]

Thompson was indicted by the grand jury, and Governor Ross Shaw Sterling issued a requisition for his return from the state of Washington. Wright and Rooney traveled to Walla Walla to extradite the fugitive. Both Moutray and Thompson were indicted in Sterling County, but held in the

Tom Green County jail awaiting trial. The two men were tried separately in the Fifty-first District Court, and Thompson's hearing began on May 8, 1933. With Moutray acting as the state's chief witness, the trial ended the next day with a conviction and a fifty-year prison sentence. On June 8, Rangers arrested Ruby Taggart in Longview, and she was charged in Sterling County with Poland's murder. Authorities believed her to have been the woman who assisted Thompson in the robbery attempt. However, Taggart was released, as investigators could not secure sufficient evidence to corroborate Moutray's testimony. Tried in Tom Green County, the latter pled guilty to acting as an accomplice on June 23, and was given a sentence of four years. In August 1933, Thompson's attorney filed an appeal to his murder conviction in the court of criminal appeals in Austin. The lower court's decision was reversed in December, and the murder charges were dismissed in January 1934.[156]

While Wright was working up the Poland murder, the case involving the two females found in the Pecos in February 1930 remained active. Hundreds of inquiries poured into Pecos and Tom Green Counties regarding missing women and children, but few clues developed. Wright believed he had experienced a breakthrough the following year when Topeka, Kansas, police officers advised a suspect was in custody. The man had lived in San Angelo with a woman and girl, and they were missing. A complaint charging him with murder was filed. Armed with legal papers, Wright and Pecos County Deputy Sheriff Claude Isiah Miller were preparing to leave Fort Stockton when they received word the missing females had been located.[157]

Howard County was the center of an automobile theft ring. Pursuing the case, Sheriff Jess Slaughter and two of his deputies were able to recover a car several weeks after it was stolen. One suspect, W. E. Gore, was arrested on a charge of auto theft. Wright, Rangers William Early "Earl" Young and Theodore Arthur "Ted" Lewis, and Edward A. Gromley of the National Automobile Theft Bureau were invited into the investigation that extended into Midland and Winkler Counties. In Wink, the law officers uncovered a "mass of stolen cars," which had been stolen from Vernon, Pampa, Fort Worth, Midland, and other Texas towns, taken to Wink, and sold to buyers. One car was found in Kilgore, and another out of state.[158]

In late June, Wright and Rangers Young, D. E. Smith, and Thad George Tarver traveled to Crane County while a murder trial was in session. Rancher Jack Hall had shot and killed Thomas Carwin Barnsley, Sr., manager of the V Rocker Ranch, on April 9. The murder marked the end of a dispute over ranch interests and land leases. The Rangers had taken no part in the investigation, but they did come to town to assist Sheriff Bud Blair in keeping the peace. Hall was convicted on June 26 and sentenced to thirty years in prison.[159]

On May 5, 1932, Wright, Sergeant Taylor, three other Rangers, and a Ward County deputy raided a dance hall and gambling house three miles from McCamey. The structure was actually fifty feet over the line in Crane County. Gaming was occurring inside at a brisk rate, including a large craps game. Observing approximately seventy cars in the parking lot, the officers knocked down the rear door at 12:20 a.m. and arrested everyone on the premises. The suspects were held until dawn when the county attorney filed charges. Twenty-seven gamblers were freed on bond, and Sheriff Fowler took the establishment's owner to Pecos to face federal charges.[160]

The First State Bank at Seagraves in Gaines County was robbed on May 28 of more than three thousand dollars after a lone, masked gunman forced the assistant cashier to open the vault, then scooped up the loose cash in the tills. Oscar Herring, former Palo Pinto County attorney, was tracked to a private sanitarium in Wichita Falls on June 8, and arrested by Wright, Ranger Robert E. Poole, and Sheriff Frank Kuykendall of Gaines County. Twenty-two dollars in small coins were found in the suspect's room, and more was subsequently discovered at his home in Seagraves. He was booked into the Archer County jail overnight. James W. Baker, a schoolteacher, and two other men were held for questioning in connection to the crime. Appearing before Gaines County Judge John Jones Kendrick, District Attorney Thomas L. Price of the 106th Judicial District filed complaints charging the four suspects with bank robbery and accessory to commit bank robbery. Officers sought the identity of a fifth man, possibly a professional who was imported to perpetrate the holdup. Further investigation led them to Jodie Edwards, believed to be the triggerman, and all five men were indicted by the grand jury. However, Edwards remained at large.

Baker led lawmen to two separate caches where they recovered more than five hundred dollars.[161]

Desiring to get inside the notorious Goodman Roadhouse near McCamey, Wright and Taylor hatched a clever scheme and recruited three cowboys from Grandfalls. The trio went to the water hole located on the Girvin road and gained entry. Suddenly, they whipped out weapons and held up the 123 patrons. None of the roadhouse's staff were able to sound the warning buzzers. One of them answered a knock on the door and admitted Wright and Taylor to whom the three cowpunchers promptly "surrendered." The other occupants were doubtless thankful in thinking they would not have to turn out their pockets. That relief was short-lived when the captain convened a justice court that lasted through the night. Thirty men were fined for gambling, and three were charged with violating the Volstead Act.[162]

With the election of Miriam Ferguson to the governorship in November 1932, Wright looked elsewhere for employment. He went to Robstown and conferred with Sheriff-elect James Galbreath about an appointment. The talks were successful, and Wright was named a Nueces County deputy sheriff on January 1, 1933. With the exception of two men, the entire Ranger Force—forty-eight in all—resigned before the gubernatorial inauguration. Wright separated from state service effective on February 15. Albert R. Mace, former sheriff of Lampasas County and captain of Company D at Falfurrias, was also attached to Galbreath's office.[163]

Wright, Mace, Deputy N. A. Kennedy, and Captain Boone Choate conducted two raids on Staples Street on March 25. They arrested two men and confiscated fifty gallons of apricot mash and over seventy pints of beer. Sheriff Galbreath died suddenly in San Antonio four days later. His successor, former county tax collector Paul Cox, was sworn into office the following day. The change in administration had no effect on Wright's employment, as he continued with the sheriff's department for another two years.[164]

Controversy followed a raid on the pleasure boat *Jacopin* on July 28. Possessing search warrants from the Justice Court of Precinct No. 2, and authorization from the attorney general's office, Sheriff Cox, Chief Deputy Leonidas Lipscomb Nusom, and Wright boarded the boat while it lay grounded in three feet of water adjacent to Bird Island. The lawmen placed the crew under arrest for violations of the Dean Law, and Cox took several of the prisoners ashore. As the two deputies were transferring beer cases to their boat, George Roberts, the *Jacopin's* captain, offered to move to the nearby City Pleasure pier. Instead, he sailed to the floating filling station where he took on Maxwell P. Dunne, charter-owner of the *Jacopin*, and headed toward Port Aransas. Wright demanded the *Jacopin* reverse course and head to the pier. He was initially rebuffed before Dunne agreed. Returning from the pilot's cabin, Roberts informed Wright he was under arrest and ordered him at gunpoint to relinquish his sidearm. The deputy refused and, at the shipmaster's command, several crewmen rushed from the rear cabin and covered Wright and Nusom with guns. Two or three seized Wright and took his pistol, and Nusom was similarly disarmed. In the subsequent days, Dunne charged the sheriff and his men had violated his maritime rights and argued he had been in compliance with federal law allowing the sale of 3.2 beer. An attempt was made on the twenty-ninth to file a complaint against Wright for assaulting Chief Engineer Francis French, but Commissioner Julius Allen Mount advised the plaintiffs to see U.S. Attorney Henry M. Holden in Houston first.[165]

District Attorney De Valson Sellers Purl filed a suit for permanent injunction against the operation of the *Jacopin* in 117th District Court. Cox, Wright, and Mace were the complaintants. The application sought to enjoin the pleasure boat's operation for one year, and declared Dunne, Roberts and Harry Cockhill were operating within the confines of Nueces County and, thus, subject to state law. Ruling on August 10, Judge Birge Holt refused to grant the injunction, declaring 3.2 beer was "not intoxicating in fact."[166]

On February 14, 1935, Wright was once again appointed to the Ranger Force and Company D. In a move that suggests politics were a motivating factor, he was not named a captain, despite forty-one years of effective law enforcement experience. As a private reporting to Captain William "Bill" McMurrey, he was initially assigned to Harlingen. The sorry way Wright was treated illustrates the vulnerability of the Ranger Force to the vagaries of politics. William Sterling observed, "The Ranger captains were always greatly concerned over the change of administration, and were particularly interested in knowing as soon as possible the identity of the new [adjutant] general."[167]

While stationed in Harlingen, Wright's assignments were more or less routine and failed to compare to his earlier rip-roaring adventures on the border. Governor James Burr V. Allred initiated a campaign to stamp out liquor sellers and gambling dens throughout the state. He called on all "law-abiding citizens of Texas to back me up and to demand that their local officers stop this wholesale flaunting of the law." Throughout the year and beyond, Rangers, federal agents, and city and county officers raided establishments that were in violation of alcohol and gaming statutes. In March 1935, Captain McMurrey, Wright, other Rangers, and Border Patrolmen raided a club in Rio Grande City, and seized a quantity of liquor and smashed two gambling tables. Allred ordered the Rangers to cease enforcing statewide prohibition on August 27, 1935, as the law had been repealed three days prior. However, gambling remained illegal. Taking a respite from the governor's crusade, McMurrey next led twelve Rangers, including Wright, to Corpus Christi in October to keep the peace during a labor strike. While violence had broken out in Houston, the waterfront at Corpus Christi was quiet. Wright and Ranger Alfred Young Allee returned after members of the International Longshoremen's Association tangled with nonunion dock workers on November 2; one man was shot, and seven others were beaten. McMurrey, along with Privates Everard Meade Davenport, Jr. and W. M. Wheatley, arrived on the fourth as reinforcements, and four ILA workers were arrested for disturbing the peace on the sixth. On the twenty-third, McMurrey, Wright, and Ranger Zeno Smith worked with Highway Patrol Captain Hill Foreman and four Border Patrolmen in raiding gambling houses in McAllen and Mercedes. Thirty-eight individuals were arrested, and felony charges were prepared against two of the operators.[168]

Members of an armed robbery gang struck a ranch house near Falfurrias on December 24, 1935. Two residents were bound, while the thieves stole $5,600 in cash and property. Captain McMurrey, Wright, Ranger Luckett Pemberton "Leo" Bishop, Sheriff Jack Ballard and Deputy Jess Grimes of Brooks County, and Customs officers David Allison Blackwell and William Wallen Musgrave worked up the case. The lawmen followed the trail of clues from Falfurrias to Corpus Christi and arrived in the latter town on the twenty-seventh. McMurrey's party was joined by Police Chief Leo Petzel, Sheriff William Shely, and members of both departments. The captain, Petzel, and city officers ____ Murdock, ____ Brown, and Matt Pellegrino located the homes of two suspects on the twenty-eighth, placed them under arrest, and searched the residences. The lawmen recovered $138 in currency and approximately forty dollars' worth of jewelry from one of the homes. The two men subsequently confessed in interviews. Two more were apprehended, and one of those admitted to the crime, while the fourth was held for further questioning. Two more suspects were believed to have escaped into Mexico with most of the loot. Charges of robbery with firearms were filed in Brooks County.[169]

Wright resumed his assignment to curtail illegal gaming in Harlingen on February 22, 1936, when he, Captain Foreman, and Highway Patrolman Dan Abbott raided a gambling hall on West Tyler Street. The state officers seized paraphernalia, including a roulette wheel and a dice table, and arrested nine men. Brought before Justice of the Peace Will Glenn Fields, the prisoners were charged with gambling and operating the establishment, and each fined one dollar and costs.[170]

On October 31, Wright and Trooper Abbott confiscated and subsequently destroyed three slot machines found in Combes and at the Arroyo Colorado bridge in Harlingen. Three men were charged with operating gaming devices on November 2 in Justice of the Peace Frank Dunn Nance's court, and each fined twenty-five dollars and court costs. Several days later, Wright, Abbott, and State Patrolman Gerald Wood Modesette seized another two machines at Barreda.[171]

Luther Blanton, fifty-seven, and his son, John, twenty-four, went missing on November 18, 1936, on the King Ranch adjacent to their San Perlita farm. They had crossed through the barbwire fence separating the two properties with the intent of hunting ducks on a lagoon five hundred yards from their front door. The disappearance of the pair bore resemblance to that of local farmhands Jesus Rivera and Reyes Ramirez who had vanished without a trace the previous year. Several gunshots were heard shortly after each set of men went onto the ranch. Mrs. Blanton reported she had seen a Mexican horseman riding the fence line thirty minutes prior to noticing the sound of the shots. Fifteen-year-old George Halton had been found brutally beaten and unconscious the year before while hunting in the same densely brushed section. On November 20, Patrolman Modesette led a seventy-five-man search party near where the Blantons had last been seen. McMurrey and Wright conducted another search the following day with a posse of one hundred San Perlita and Raymondville citizens, Rangers, county deputies, and highway patrolmen. Sheriff Howard Cragg of Willacy County expressed hope that the Blantons had merely become lost, but relatives stressed how the two knew well the country near their home, and feared foul play. The searchers returned on the twenty-first without having found the missing farmers. An article in *Life* magazine noted, "Plain Texans hate the King Ranch and its owners, the Klebergs. The Klebergs refuse to let hunters into their game-abounding land, refuse to let main highways go through their vast acres and are politically a law unto themselves." Feelings were running high, and McMurrey asked for three days in which he and his men could investigate without interference. Rangers Joe Bridges and Powers Fenner, who were stationed in Hebbronville, arrived the same day to assist, while Wright was reassigned to other cases. Manuel T. Gonzaullas, chief of the DPS crime lab, analyzed bloodstains on a man's coat and a scrap of canvas found at the scene to determine whether they belonged to an animal or a human being. The owner of the coat, a Mexican ranch hand, was believed by Patrolman Abbott to have known too much about the Blanton's disappearance or been made a scapegoat in the case.[172]

McMurrey's three days turned into weeks and months. In July 1937, the captain laconically asserted: "The Blanton case is solved. When it's ironclad we'll have another announcement." He never discussed the Blanton's ultimate fate or the whereabouts of their bodies, and the promised statement never came, perhaps due to political pressure. Indeed, the Blanton case became a scandal for the King Ranch, and rumors and accusations that ranch game wardens or armed fence riders had murdered Luther and John for poaching or trespassing continue to swirl. Ranger Bridge came to believe "the disappearance of these two men may have been of their own volition. At any rate, the case was never solved."[173]

On December 1, 1936, Wright, Captain Foreman, and city detective Rufe Oliver raided a store on Marguerite Street in Corpus Christi and seized three slot machines. The proprietor was assessed a twenty-five-dollar fine and costs in Justice of the Peace Joe D. Browning's court. The owner of the machines signed a wavier, and the devices were destroyed. The coins contained within the devices amounted to fifteen dollars in silver and $1.40 in pennies, and were donated to the local chapter of the American Red Cross. The previous week, Wright and Foreman had seized a slot machine from an establishment at Seventh and Laredo Streets. The nine dollars confiscated was also given to the Red Cross.[174]

Thirty-two men were charged with misdemeanor complaints on February 15 as a result of raids conducted by Wright, Foremen, and Modesette in Corpus Christi over the previous two days. Meeting with Nueces County Attorney Linton Savage, Wright signed complaints against thirteen men taken into custody at the Sundown Night Club, eleven at an establishment on Laredo Street, five at the Wayside Club, and four at the Paradise Club. The charges were filed before Justice Browning, and fines ranged between twelve and thirty-six dollars.[175]

At the request of District Attorney Joseph Proctor "Joe" Hatchitt, Wright was directed to make his permanent station in Corpus Christi in April 1937.[176] Wright and Foreman continued their drive on illegal gambling along the "Texas Riviera" with more raids on May 14. Four individuals were arrested in the Rendezvous nightclub on Mesquite Street. The two lawmen seized from an establishment on Waco Street several large dice tables, a blackjack table, and a number of chairs. Thirteen men were apprehended and fined in Justice of the Peace Jack Sutherland's court. Sixteen more were arrested on Winnebago Street. The confiscated gaming equipment was broken and burned by Wright on the nineteenth. Wright, Foreman, and three highway patrolmen raided the Turf Grill in Port Aransas on June 26. Among the patrons were fifteen state senators who were the guests of Representative Walker Elmer Pope of Corpus Christi, and Senator Morris Roberts of Beeville. Eight men were fined by Justice of the Peace Bill Ellis, and one gaming table was destroyed. Pope asserted to the press that Governor Allred had ordered the raid since the legislators had voted against repealing the horseracing law.

On July 15, Wright, Foreman, and Rufe Oliver, now a special investigator for the district attorney's office, raided the Oasis and Sundown nightclubs, and arrested nine men at the former establishment and two at the latter. Gambling equipment was seized, including a quantity of dice, poker chips, a small table, nine chairs, several drink and cigarette trays, fifty dollars in cash, and a light projector and slides that displayed an image of a dice board onto a tabletop. The prisoners were assessed ten-dollar fines in Justice Sutherland's court on gaming charges. The tables and chairs were given to the county welfare agent, while the Red Cross received another cash donation. Gaming paraphernalia was discovered behind an electrically operated secret panel at the Oasis Dinner Club during the course of a raid spearheaded by Wright and Foreman on July 27. The equipment was seized, and the owner signed a waiver forfeiting his claim. Wright single-handedly raided another establishment on August 29 and arrested six men on gambling charges. He seized dice and a dice table, the latter of which was subsequently destroyed.[177]

Wright and Hugh E. Barnes, an agent for the Texas Liquor Control Board, seized a forty-gallon still on Mussett Street, and arrested the operator. Charges were filed in federal court, and the case was transferred to the alcohol tax unit for further investigation and prosecution. On October 13, the captain (as he was still publicly known) and Liquor Control Board agent John McKay confiscated a forty-gallon still and two hundred gallons of mash from a house on Josephine Street.[178]

On January 10, 1938, Wright, Ranger Walter Everette "Ebb" Riggs of Alice, and Barnes and McKay arrested four operators and twelve players on gambling charges. Two poker and two dice tables and approximately thirty dollars were also confiscated, and the cash was donated to the Red Cross. The defendants appeared before Justice Sutherland, who ordered the operators to pay fourteen dollars in fines and the gamblers ten dollars. Six days later, Wright accompanied Barnes and McKay on several raids that resulted in the filing of three cases in county court. A bartender at the Marine Bar on Water Street and the owner of Joe's Place at Sam Rankin and Winnebago Streets were charged with selling alcohol on a Sunday. A private citizen on Antelope Street was charged with possession of unstamped whiskey.[179]

District Attorney Hatchitt launched a campaign to eliminate gaming devices in his jurisdiction. He was successful in Nueces County, but less so in Kleberg. His efforts were rewarded when Governor Allred ordered the removal of marble tables and slot machines from stores. Pursuant to this directive, Wright instructed store owners in Nueces and surrounding counties to do away with all these devices. Two machines were seized at the Trot Inn and Bohemian Village. However, a revision to his orders arrived from Colonel Horace Henry Carmichael, director of the Texas Department of Public Safety. The colonel advised the captain to only require the elimination of those machines that paid the winnings in cash or tokens.[180]

Evidently, there were some who failed to heed the warning. On June 16, Wright and Rangers Quincy Joseph Lowman and Hugh Jack Pharies raided a gambling room on Agnes Street. Departing from the customary procedure, Wright ordered the captured gamblers to destroy the seized paraphernalia, including two dice tables, two poker tables, and a three-gallon bucket of playing cards. Seven men appeared before Justice Sutherland to face charges of gambling.[181]

Diagnosed with gastroenterocolitis on May 5, 1938, Wright's son, Charles, died of mitral stenosis and coronary occlusion at Eagle Pass on June 27. He had worked for the Floresville Mercantile Company in 1912, and purchased the City Tailor Shop the next year. He served in his father's Ranger company in Alice from May 11 to November 30, 1916. By the time he registered for the draft, he was employed by the San Antonio & Aransas Pass Railroad as a bridge guard in Calaveras. With the United States' entry into World War I, Charles enlisted in the army on June 25, 1917, and served as a sergeant in Battery D, 131st Field Artillery Regiment, 61st Field Artillery Brigade, 36th Division at Camp Bowie. Battery D sailed from Hoboken, New Jersey, aboard the USS *Siboney* on July 31, 1918. Upon their arrival in Brest, France, the men of the 61st Brigade were separated from the division and billeted in Redon. Unlike the balance of the division, the brigade saw no action. Departing from St. Nazaire, Charles and his comrades sailed to Newport News, Virginia, on the USS *Aeolus* on February 25, 1919. The brigade was demobilized at Camp Travis on April 2. Following in the footsteps of his father and other family members, he pursued a law enforcement career by entering the U.S. Customs Service on July 1, 1919, as a mounted inspector. As already noted, he frequently served alongside the Rangers, and his duty stations included Harlingen, McAllen, Falfurrias, Del Rio, San Diego, Mission, Laredo, Corpus Christi, and Eagle Pass. He married Arline Masters on January 1, 1932, in Brownsville. Receiving word of their son's death, Wright and Mollie traveled to Eagle Pass. Charles's body was taken to Floresville, where he was buried in the City Cemetery on the twenty-eighth.[182]

Wright, Lowman, and an unnamed Ranger (likely Pharies) confiscated three slot machines from the Star Novelty Company on July 14, 1939. After extracting approximately seventeen dollars, which was earmarked for the Red Cross, the machines were destroyed at the highway patrol barracks. Wright filed a complaint with Justice Sutherland and charged J. E. Loyd with displaying the devices.[183]

"Damnedest thing ever happened in Texas," Wright declared. "Sending the Rangers out to guard a little old table nobody would bother to run off with anyhow." The piece of furniture to which he referred was a ten-thousand-dollar trick table owned by local painter George J. Fulton and on display in the lobby of the Corpus Christi National Bank. Perplexed as to why he was assigned to this needless task, yet obedient to orders from Austin, Wright was provided a chair, plenty of cigars, and a spittoon to guard the valuable article.[184]

Bill Sterling remarked, "While counterfeit Rangers who were not worthy of blacking his boots were basking in the favors of those in charge, Captain William Lee Wright terminated his service patrolling the docks in Corpus Christi." Doubtless still shaken by his son's untimely death, Wright was discharged at the end of August 1939.[185]

Sheriff John Ball Harney of Nueces County sent Governor Wilbert Lee "Pappy" O'Daniel a telegram on the captain's behalf:

> I am addressing you as one sheriff in Texas who does not resent the presence and invaluable assistance of old-time Texas Rangers. Capt. W. L. Wright of Corpus Christi just notified of his dismissal from the service effective September 1 removes from active duty one of the

> most courageous, honorable, and outstanding peace officers that ever served this state … From personal knowledge I know him to be still very active, and his dismissal will be a severe blow to law enforcement in this section of Texas. Such a record of service without one blemish as to his honor, integrity, and fearlessness certainly should not go without a reward. I appeal to you to have this reconsidered and Captain Wright retained in the service for the good of law and order.[186]

The plea was to no avail, and the venerable Ranger returned to Floresville in early November.[187]

On February 28, 1940, Wright became the sixth candidate for the office of Wilson County sheriff. At the behest of his many friends, he had reportedly spent several weeks considering the run before he made the official announcement. He posted a statement that acknowledged he was seventy-two years of age, but he reminded the voters of his many decades of service. He also pledged his "loyalty, friendship, and devotion to duty to serve [the county] with the best that's in me in this important office." The next month, though, Wright regretfully announced his withdrawal from the race citing his declining health and that his general physical condition did not allow for a vigorous campaign. He expressed his gratitude to the many men and women in the county who had pledged their active support.[188]

Although his health had begun to fail, Wright still remained active. Several days before his death, he developed what he believed was a case of influenza, but he failed to respond to medical treatment. Just before midnight on March 6, 1942, he suffered a sudden coronary occlusion and died on March 7 at 12:35 a.m. A note written on his death certificate stated his heart attack was brought on by worrying about his son Houston who was serving overseas. The funeral services were held the following day in the auditorium of the Floresville High School. The venue was chosen to accommodate the massive crowd of neighbors, friends, sheriffs, Texas Rangers, police chiefs, highway patrolmen, judges, and state officials (including Colonel Homer Garrison, Jr.) that came to pay their respects. Doctor Pierre Bernard Hill, former chaplain of the Texas Rangers and an old friend of the captain, and the Reverend Charles Benjamin Diltz, pastor of the Floresville Methodist

Church, officiated at the service. The deceased's body was escorted to the Floresville City Cemetery by members of Floresville Lodge No. 515 A. F. & A. M.[189]

On June 17, 1967, the Wilson County Historical Survey Committee held a dedication ceremony for the state marker honoring Captain Wright on the courthouse square. Dogie, Zora, Colonel Garrison, various friends and family, and the general public were in attendance.[190]

Mollie spent two months following her husband's death with Dogie's family in Tucson and Bill's in Seattle. She returned to Floresville in June 1942, and made her home with Zora's family in Corpus Christi. On July 2, 1950, Mollie suffered a heart attack while visiting friends near Falls City and underwent medical treatment at the Floresville Hospital. She recovered and returned to Corpus Christi. Dying at Hearth Rest Home on April 18, 1958, Mollie was buried in the Floresville City Cemetery.[191]

Maurice also served overseas in Battery D with his brother as a mechanic. He was discharged on November 11, 1918. He married Helen Maria Gordon, a nurse, on June 23, 1919, in San Antonio, and fathered two daughters. He and Helen later divorced. Maurice worked as a well digger, automobile repairman, and laundry mechanic and engineer. Diagnosed with arteriosclerotic cardiovascular disease, he suffered a myocardial infarction on February 27, 1960. Pronounced dead on arrival at Robert B. Green Memorial Hospital, he was buried in the Floresville City Cemetery.[192]

As a young girl, Zora worked as a salesclerk for the Palace Drug Company in Floresville. She married Blake Davidson Fore on March 10, 1921, at her parents' home. She later bore her husband two sons, one of whom died in 1949. Blake worked as a druggist in Floresville and Kenedy from 1926 to 1936. He was then appointed to the State Liquor Control Board and posted to the Gateway bridge in Brownsville. After a brief time in Harlingen, the Fores moved to Corpus Christi in 1937. Blake then spent twenty-five years in the oil and gas division of the Texas Railroad Commission. He suffered a heart attack and died on May 1, 1963. Zora was employed by the U.S. Postal Service and by the Nueces County Tax Assessor/Collector Office until her retirement in 1970. She moved to Brownsville in 1992. Zora died on May 31, 1996, and was buried in the Floresville City Cemetery.[193]

Dogie enlisted in his father's Company K on June 10, 1918, and served for four months. He joined Company C under Captain Aaron W. Cunningham on March 25, 1921, then transferred to Company A on August 1. He was discharged at the end of the same month on account of a reduction in the force; he then performed undercover work for Captain Hamer in Austin. Dogie joined the El Paso District of the U.S. Border Patrol on September 18, 1924, as a patrol inspector and served during "one of the most vicious times in the history of the border." The *Corpus Christi Caller-Times* observed "many of the border patrol men have been trained in that strict school for officers—the Ranger service with Captain W. L. Wright of Fort Stockton, perhaps producing more men for the border patrol than any one [*sic*] else in Texas." This was certainly true in Dogie's case. For much of his career, he was stationed in Sierra Blanca, except for the six years he was in charge of the Tucson station. He married Mabel Beulah "Tiny" Love on July 21, 1928, and fathered two daughters. Holding the rank of assistant district chief, Dogie retired on May 5, 1951, to devote time to his sheep ranch near Sierra Blanca. He served as sheriff of Hudspeth County from 1953 to 1957, and was once more from 1960 to January 1, 1969. He told an Associated Press correspondent of his time as a border lawman: "It was the kind of life with a lot of freedom. I liked chasing people. And I caught a lot of them. It was dangerous, but I was lucky and never got shot." Dogie died on December 19, 1989, and was buried in the Sierra Blanca Cemetery.[194]

Following high school, Bill enlisted in the Civilian Military Training Corps in June 1922, then he served short stints as a deputy U.S. marshal in Kenedy and as a deputy sheriff of Webb County. He was appointed a Special Ranger in his father's company from September 1923 to October 1924, then as a U.S. public health inspector at the International Bridge in Laredo. Choosing a career in business rather than law enforcement, Bill began working for Standard Oil Company of California in 1925; his positions included station salesman, development specialist in Albuquerque and El Paso, assistant district manager in Los Angles, and regional vice president in Arizona and New Mexico. He married Mildred Pearl Edgar on September 1, 1928, and fathered one son. He and his family also lived in Tucson, Phoenix, and Denver. Bill was appointed president of the Signal Oil Company in Los

Angeles in August 1962, and retired five years later. He died on July 25, 1993, in El Cajon, San Diego County.[195]

Tom attended high school in Floresville before going to work for Standard Stations, Inc. as a service station attendant in Douglas, Arizona. He enlisted in the U.S. Army at Fort Sam Houston on January 24, 1941. After basic training, he was assigned to Battery F, 2nd Battalion, 131st Field Artillery, 36th Infantry Division. Tom was aboard the USS *Republic* bound for Brisbane, Australia, when the naval base at Pearl Harbor, Hawaii, was attacked. Nicknamed "Slug" by his fellow soldiers of "The Lost Battalion," he was captured on March 8, 1942, when Java fell to the Japanese. Nearly six hundred Texans, including Tom, were among the thousands of American, British Commonwealth, and Dutch prisoners forced to build the infamous railroad between Bangkok and Rangoon. After forty-two months of inhumane captivity, an emaciated Tom was released to U.S. military custody and returned home. He moved to Oceanside, California, and opened Wright's Service Station at 1806 Mission Road; his business was affiliated with Standard Oil Company of California. On August 18, 1947, he was installed as commander of Joseph G. McComb Post 146 of the American Legion for the 1947–1948 year. He had befriended fellow veteran Gertrude Veronica Grunert at American Legion meetings and married her on August 29, 1947, in St. Mary's Star of the Sea Catholic Church. In addition to his business, Tom also served as a city councilman from 1948 to 1952, mayor from 1952 to 1953, and councilman once more from 1962 to 1970. Gertrude died on December 16, 1961, at Sharp Memorial Community Hospital after a long illness. She was interred at Fort Rosecrans National Cemetery in San Diego. Tom married Louise Bayley (Vance) Purcell on March 29, 1963, and retired in 1971. In failing health, he died on October 4, 1996, in San Diego, California, and was buried in the Fort Rosecrans cemetery.[196]

Will Wright spent a lifetime enforcing the law. In performing his duty over four decades, he established an unblemished record of personal integrity and physical courage. As one of the "Big Four" Ranger captains, he led and mentored the next generation of Texas lawmen who continued his tradition of principled peacekeeping.

Frank A. Hamer. *Courtesy Taronda Schulz.*

Chapter 2

Frank A. Hamer: "A Living Legend"

Francis Augustus "Frank" Hamer was a living legend. Although his most publicized feat occurred after he had left the Rangers, he built a lengthy record of effective law enforcement. Mentored by one of the "Four Great Captains," he began his career pursuing criminals on horseback, and ended doing the same in an automobile. As he grew in experience, he became a skilled criminal investigator and manhunter. He was an impassive man of few words who was more inclined to action. A physically imposing man, he engaged armed lawbreakers in a number of shooting incidents that added to his reputation as a modern-day gunfighter. His good friend, Professor Walter Prescott Webb, said: "If all criminals in Texas were asked to name the man that they would most dread to have on their trail, they would probably name Captain Frank Hamer without hesitation. There is not a criminal in Texas who does not fear and respect him."

He was born on March 17, 1884, in Fairview, Wilson County, Texas. His father, Franklin Augustus Hamer, had been born on February 19, 1853, in St. Louis, Missouri. After living in Ohio and Pennsboro, West Virginia, Franklin enlisted in Company B, Fourth U.S. Cavalry on January 13, 1874, and was assigned to Fort Clark, Texas. He received a medical discharge five months later, and settled in Fairview where he worked as a blacksmith and farmer. He married Lou Emma Francis on September 26, 1881. She had been born on February 17, 1860, in Parker County. In addition to Frank, they welcomed into the world Dennis Estill Hamer, born July 12, 1882; Sanford Clinton "Sant" Hamer, born July 4, 1886; Harrison Lester Hamer, born August 15, 1888; Mary Grace Hamer, born August 16, 1891; Emma Patience Hamer, born February 23, 1894; Alma Dell Hamer, born October 8, 1898; and Flavious Letherage Hamer, born February 21, 1900.[1]

Franklin was a restless and hard-drinking man who moved his family to, first, a tenant house on the Linn-Pérez Ranch near the Medina River and Leon Creek in southwestern Bexar County, then Bend in San Saba County in 1890, and Oxford in Llano County four years later. Young Frank spent a great deal of time working in his father's blacksmith shops. "As a youth he had put in many hours ... at the anvil, swinging a sledge hammer [*sic*], and working with other heavy tools. This was where Frank Hamer got his brawny arms," recalled Adjutant General William Warren "Bill" Sterling.[2]

In addition to a robust work ethic, he acquired a minimal formal education at the rural school in Oxford. He was said to have been influenced by Josiah Wilbarger's *Indian Depredations in Texas*. Rather than emulate the Texas Rangers portrayed in Wilbarger's book, "I made up my mind to be as much like an Indian as I could." Throughout his childhood, Hamer trained himself in marksmanship, horsemanship, and all aspects of field craft. As Hamer grew into adulthood, faith became a cornerstone of his life; he "had long, confidential talks with God instead of uttering a prayer only."[3]

As they matured, Hamer and his brothers learned the skills of handling cattle, including riding, roping, and branding. He began working the ranches throughout the county as a cowboy before his seventeenth birthday. He appeared older than his age, and possessed a strong personality that impressed the straw bosses.[4]

In 1900, Franklin moved the family once more, this time to Regency in Mills County. He and his sons worked as sharecroppers on Daniel McSween's 340-acre farm along Spring Creek. The census taken that summer indicates Franklin was renting the farmhouse in which they lived. Purportedly, McSween, a known troublemaker, offered Frank two hundred dollars on June 10 or 12, in exchange for murdering a prominent local rancher. Hamer refused, and informed the intended victim of the proposal. Consequently, McSween bushwhacked the youth two days later with a double-barreled shotgun. Frank was struck in the back and on the left side of his head. He and Harrison, who was present, fled into the countryside. Recovering in West Texas, he allegedly returned and killed McSween in a fair fight. Often recounted as part of the Frank Hamer legend, the only source for this tale was Harrison, who shared his account with H. Gordon Frost and John Holmes Jenkins, Frank's first biographers, in 1967. The story is problematic at best. As attorney and author John Boessenecker, Hamer's most recent profiler, has noted, neither of the alleged shootings were mentioned in the *San Saba News* or court records; a review of other Texas newspapers in this period likewise failed to produce any references. Furthermore, McSween, a long-time resident of Kaufman County, sold his Spring Creek property in 1904, and died five years later. Lastly, the notion ex-cavalryman Franklin would have meekly accepted the attempted murder of his teenage son, without responding by either lawful or extralegal means, seems doubtful.[5]

In 1901, Frank and Harrison were hired as wranglers on Green Berry Ketchum, Jr.'s ranch on Independence Creek, a tributary of the Pecos River, nine miles west of Sheffield in Pecos County. Operating another ranch in Tom Green County, Berry, as he was known, was the elder brother of notorious outlaw Thomas Edward "Black Jack" Ketchum. Still working on the Independence Creek ranch on April 26, the Hamer brothers doubtless heard the news when the desperado dropped through the trapdoor of a gallows in Clayton, New Mexico.[6]

Two years later, the Hamer brothers worked cattle on James Franklin McKenzie's ranch headquartered on Escondido Creek. When he was nineteen, Frank narrowly escaped following a different path, that of the outlaw. He had been hired to help drive a herd of horses to a buyer in San Angelo. One of his fellow cowboys was a career criminal who made use of his mature age and personality to manipulate the younger men in the crew. While the drovers held the remuda near town and the business arrangements were finalized, the crook proposed robbing the local bank and using the loot to start a ranch in Mexico. Hamer was among those who agreed to the suggestion, and plans were hurriedly formed. On the edge of changing their lives forever, the men walked to the top of the street near the bank. They were about to put their scheme into motion when their foreman suddenly appeared and instructed them to move the herd to the buyer's corral. The spell was broken, and the foreman's unwitting intervention benefited both Texas and the future lawman. "It was the adventure, and not the money, that appealed to me," Hamer said. "Had I gone into it, things would have been different."[7]

Professor Walter P. Webb's book, *The Texas Rangers*, first described how Hamer went to work for the "Carr Ranch," which was reportedly located between Fort Stockton and Sheffield. In the eighty-odd years since the publication of Webb's landmark work, though, additional details on the cattle spread have not surfaced. The reason for this dearth of information may be due to the fact a large number of Pecos County ranches did and do occupy leased lands, sometimes for decades. Additionally, these outfits have often been operated by absentee ranch owners. Documents, such as land abstracts and patents or county tax rolls, only recorded deeded properties' owners. For example, the University of Texas's Permanent University Fund, with 2.1 million acres of land under ownership, has issued grazing leases to numerous individual ranches for over one hundred years, including some in Pecos County. However, copies of the agreements that might bear the names of past lessees are not readily available. According to Ernest Woodward, longtime Pecos County cattleman and president of the Pecos County Historical Society, Hamer was actually working on a pair of tracts that Carr had leased from the massive ranch owned by George Rollie White and John Thomas Baker. The two properties, known today as the "north Carr pasture" and the "south Carr pasture," were situated on either side of the old Tunis Creek stage station and the short-lived Adams post office, both of which sat adjacent to the junction of the San Angelo–Fort Stockton and San Antonio–El Paso stage routes. Unfortunately, Carr's first name remains unknown, although a R. J. Carr registered the CAR brand in the county on April 4, 1900, as did a H. W. Carr for the VC brand.[8]

In Webb's retelling of the story, Hamer was alone at the Carr headquarters in October 1905, and overheard a conversation on the telephone party line between Sheriff Dudley Snyder "Dud" Barker and a former deputy. The sheriff was discussing a horse thief heading in the direction of the

Carr spread. Hamer figured the thief would stop at the ranch windmill to water his horse, the only spot to do so for miles around. Interrupting the conversation, Hamer offered his services to the sheriff, and Barker deputized him over the telephone. When the criminal arrived at the windmill, he found himself looking down the barrel of Hamer's Winchester rifle. The young cowhand disarmed the fugitive and took him back toward Fort Stockton. Hamer and the thief encountered the sheriff driving a buckboard from town at breakneck speed.[9]

Impressed with the young cowhand, Barker later recommended Hamer to Ranger Captain John H. Rogers, whose Company C held jurisdiction for that section of the state. Hamer enlisted in the company on April 21, 1906, in Alpine as a private. His first recorded arrest occurred on June 18 when he and Private Wallace N. Howell apprehended three men in Brewster County for the theft of ore. In the coming years, he accumulated the necessary abilities to function as a manhunter and detective. While he declined to call himself a gunfighter, Hamer became highly skilled with firearms, and possessed the cool nerve required to face a desperate criminal in an armed confrontation.[10]

Years later, he explained his approach to law enforcement and life in general:

> I know more criminals and characters of the underworld in the southwest than any other man living. Every man and woman of them knows that I never betrayed a criminal who put his confidence in me. And I never will. I never played unfair with a criminal in my life. I kept every promise I ever made. And I never let a criminal be framed … I don't say this boastfully. It is just a plain fact.[11]

Estill, Harrison, and Flavious in time pursued their own careers in law enforcement, as would one of Frank's sons. Hamer would interact professionally with Estill and Harrison, but Flavious would serve as a Ranger and Special Ranger in companies other than Frank's. One characteristic all the brothers shared was that they were exceedingly private men. While they were amiable, and liked people, they were nevertheless remote loners. Another was their absolute commitment to their personal integrity and honesty.[12]

With reports of Mexican revolutionary activity threatening Nuevo Laredo and Ciudad Porfirio Díaz (present Piedras Negras), Governor Samuel Willis Tucker Lanham ordered Company C and Captain William J. McDonald and two of his men to the Rio Grande. Arriving in Del Rio on September 29, Captain Rogers's seventeen Rangers assisted army garrisons in watching the border downriver to Eagle Pass. The rumors proved unfounded, but Company C remained to keep the peace.[13]

On November 30, the body of Blake Morris Cauthorn, a wealthy Val Verde County sheep rancher, was discovered in his buggy four miles north of Del Rio between the Sonora and Devil's River Roads. The dead man had been shot in the back. Additionally, John W. Ralston, a stockman from Rocksprings, had been missing for eleven days and was presumed to be the victim of foul play. Suspicion quickly fell on Ed Putnam, a former convict who was using the alias of A. R. Sibley. Gradually, lawmen learned the killer had committed the crimes while trying to separately defraud each murdered man out of a sheep herd. On December 1, Rogers, Hamer, Private Robert Marmaduke "Duke" Hudson, Sheriff John Robinson, and a posse pursued him to Del Rio, where he took hostage the women of the Glass Sharp brothel. The captives were able to escape, but Putnam held off the Rangers for approximately one hour. The killer moved swiftly from window to window and shot at the state officers, while they returned fire. Both murderer and lawmen discharged some three hundred rounds of ammunition until Hamer ended the exchange with a carefully aimed bullet to Putnam's head. Dumped into a ravine, Ralston's remains were found on the third.[14]

Company C was transferred to Austin in May 1907, to replace Captain John R. Hughes' men who had been assigned to Marfa. On the eighth, Hamer was in town when he arrested an individual for maliciously poisoning livestock. Some months later, the Ranger was assigned to Groveton in Trinity County, which was wracked with potentially violent racial tensions. The trouble had begun when the Trinity Lumber Company hired black laborers to build a logging railroad, and white workers had objected. The company suspended operations and requested assistance from the Rangers. Hamer and Sergeant John Lee Dibrell were sent to the troubled town on September 14 and investigated the case. One week later, they served an arrest warrant for

Charles Mossenton, a white ruffian who was charged with intimidating the railway workers.[15]

The Groveton matter ended peacefully, but more racial strife awaited Hamer and the Rangers of Company C. In Nacogdoches County, Dock Bailey, a black man, was charged with the September 4, 1907, murder of white farmer D. G. "Dee" Owens. The day of his wedding, the victim had been shot once, brutally beaten until his skull fractured, and dragged to death behind a horse. Bailey was apprehended in Rusk, and physical evidence recovered at the murder scene convinced local officers he was the guilty party. Their notion was confirmed when the suspect confessed. Rather than take him back to Nacogdoches, where a lynching was likely, Bailey was lodged in the penitentiary for safekeeping. On September 18, the grand jury indicted him on a charge of murder in the first degree. The prisoner was transported to the jail in Nacogdoches on October 3, in preparation for his trial the following day. Three weeks prior, leading citizens held a public meeting in Nacogdoches, and the participants adopted a course of nonviolence throughout the proceedings. Nevertheless, three county sheriffs and their deputies, state guardsmen, Adjutant General James Oscar Newton, Captain Rogers, and six Rangers, including Hamer, were on hand as a precautionary measure. The Rangers guarded the entrances to the courthouse, and only those with written permission from Rogers or the adjutant general would be allowed admittance. While the crowd, estimated at twenty-five thousand, was angry and loud, none of them made any attempt to storm the building. Former sheriff Andrew Jackson "John" Spradley was particularly troublesome, and resisted arrest for inciting a riot. The captain was forced to pistol-whip the one-time lawman into compliance and arrest him for obscene language and disturbing the peace. The trial lasted only one day, and Bailey entered a plea of not guilty, claiming the homicide was the result of a gambling dispute. Once the case was given to the jury, the members deliberated for thirty minutes before returning a guilty verdict. Waiving his right to an appeal, the convicted man dropped through the gallows' trapdoor on November 7 in front of four to five thousand spectators.[16]

Rogers, Hamer, and Private James Thomas Laughlin traveled to San Augustine on October 25 to investigate three killings. Henry A. "Harry" Head, a bootlegger with a known violent streak, his brother Lewis, Charlie Alvis, and Jack Davis had been gambling with six black railroad section hands on the nineteenth. The ten men were in the section house on the Santa Fe Railroad tracks when Davis began quarreling with the railroaders and pulled a pistol. Monroe King, one of the section hands, took the gun away and used it as a club to beat Davis. Harry Head intervened, and King opened fire, killing Lewis, mortally wounding Davis, and injuring Harry slightly. The six black men fled the scene on foot into the piney woods. After his wounds were treated, Harry assembled five friends and relatives, who armed themselves with shotguns, and pursued the fugitives on horseback. The posse encountered a pair of innocent black men two days later and, after questioning them as to King's whereabouts, murdered them in cold blood. Head and his followers then went on a rampage of intimidation and arson that threatened to incite a race riot. Meanwhile, Davis died of his wounds on October 22. Once the three Rangers arrived on the twenty-seventh, Hamer tracked the murdered men and their killers, and quickly determined Head and his men were responsible for the two homicides. When interrogated, two of Head's friends swore the other members of their party had pulled the triggers. Rogers swore out arrest warrants, and Hamer and Laughlin were sent in pursuit. Three white killers were soon apprehended and lodged in the more secure Beaumont jail. Warrants for the six section hands were likewise issued, but they remained at large. While Rogers, Hamer, and Laughlin returned to company headquarters on November 4, Sergeant Dibrell and Rangers Duke Hudson and Goff White remained in San Augustine to maintain order. The three lawmen arrested another four suspects in connection with the recent tragedies, including Alvis and Head. Three of the prisoners were transferred to the Nacogdoches jail.[17]

On January 12, 1908, Hamer, Rogers, Hudson, and Private James Campbell "Doc" White extradited Head and his friends to San Augustine for trial. While the suspects were closely guarded, their defense counsels obtained a change of venue to Beaumont. Hamer was stationed in Navasota, assisting local officers, when he was ordered back to San Augustine in April. He and the other Rangers protected witnesses until Judge William Henry Pope of the Fifty-eighth Judicial District granted a continuance until June; Head and the other defendants were released on bond. On May 25, Hamer and Ranger

Oscar Latta were in San Augustine County to keep the peace. During their stint in town, the pair arrested Head for whitecapping and carrying a pistol, another man for whitecapping, five for gambling, and one for being drunk and disorderly. Head's murder trial began on June 23, and lasted six days, but three perjured witnesses and a deadlocked jury resulted in a mistrial on July 2. Rogers arrested the perjurers on June 24, and they were charged and released on five-hundred-dollar bonds to await the grand jury.[18]

While maintaining order during the trial, Hamer and Latta also arrested nineteen-year-old black man Perry Price on June 21 in connection with the murder of Aron Martin "Artie" Johnson at Geneva. The victim was a twenty-four-year-old white farmer who had been killed in his Sabine County home the previous day. Price implicated Robert Wright, the victim's brother-in-law, in the homicide by claiming the latter had paid him five dollars to kill Johnson. Wright was taken into custody by Sheriff William S. "Sneed" Noble a few hours after Price. Hugh Dean, another white local, had recently been murdered by black men, and enraged white citizens of the county responded to the two killings with their own murderous violence. The six suspects in Dean's death were removed from the jail in Hemphill by a mob of 150 vigilantes; five were lynched and one was shot. Additionally, the bodies of two unknown black men were discovered in a creek bottom near Hemphill on the morning of the twenty-second. Despite having no connection to the Johnson killing, William "Rabbit" McCoy was found shot to death the same day at the farmer's gate, a loaded pistol at his side. The murders were followed by a general exodus of black residents from the county. Amidst the racially charged atmosphere, Hamer and Latta transferred their prisoners from San Augustine to Beaumont for safekeeping.[19]

On July 14, Hamer arrested four men for gambling in San Augustine. The next day, he returned to Beaumont where racially motivated mob violence was threatening the local black community despite—or due to—the efforts of municipal law officers. The previous day, Ada Bell Hopkins, a thirteen-year-old white girl who had been cruelly beaten and raped, was discovered by a black youth; an African American male was seen fleeing the scene. Two other black men pursued the fugitive into the woods. Despite the fact men of color had given assistance to the victim and chased the alleged culprit, a mob of three hundred enraged whites rampaged through the neighborhood where the girl had been attacked, and burned several black-owned homes and businesses. While the police force conducted a dragnet and arrested ten "suspicious" black men on the basis of little to no evidence, Sheriff Ras Landry conducted a more effective investigation. He soon had two black men—Claude Golden and Matthew Fennell—in jail, but a growing lynch mob was gathering in the town's streets. When Hamer met with the sheriff, he learned the officer had secretly released the two prisoners from their cells and hidden them in a nearby barn. Hamer slipped into the barn under the cover of night, while a deputy attempted to bring a buggy to the Ranger. Some of the vigilantes haphazardly searched the barn, but Hamer, Golden, and Fennell remained unnoticed. After a night spent hiding in the swamps, Hamer and the other law officers were able to get their prisoners aboard the Gulf International train and safely to the Galveston jail. Ada identified Golden as her assailant, and, following his indictment and rape conviction, he was executed by hanging in Jasper on February 12, 1909.[20]

The town of Navasota in Grimes County was a wild and woolly place, and gunfights were a common occurrence. On November 4, 1908, City Marshal William Burrell Loftin resigned effective the nineteenth. By that time, Hamer had acquired such a sufficient reputation that the city council sought to hire him as Loftin's replacement. The council members warned Hamer the position would be difficult. The previous marshal had been warned by the town's powerful political clique that "we don't allow our kind to be arrested." Undeterred by the dangers, Hamer resigned from the Ranger Force on November 30, and pinned on the marshal's badge on December 3. His monthly salary was set at eighty-five dollars.[21]

On his first day on the job, Hamer was challenged by the bearded leader of a gang of rowdies who boasted he would teach the new lawman a lesson. The older man strutted along the streets, shouting a deafening rebel yell. The marshal approached the braggart and requested he stop making so much noise, whereupon the man bellowed louder. Hamer's hand streaked out and seized a handful of whiskers, then he threw the gang leader into the mud. He coolly gazed at the watching crowd and said, "I told him what was going to happen. He's going to jail."[22]

Days later Hamer was compelled to arrest one of the town's political leaders who was becoming drunk and disorderly. The marshal cornered the carouser in front of his friends. As he took the man into custody, Hamer looked at the increasingly hostile crowd and said, "I understand you don't allow 'your kind' to be arrested." He then waited for one of them to make a move. They wisely declined, and he escorted the offender to jail. With those two challenges to his authority crushed, Hamer was truly The Law in Navasota.[23]

Early in his tenure, Hamer befriended Mance Lipscomb a fourteen-year-old black youth who, decades later, would become a distinguished blues musician. The son of a former slave and sharecropper, Lipscomb grew to idolize the notable lawman and often drove Hamer's buggy. Judging by the future bluesman's reminisces, Hamer's particular biases toward African Americans were paternalistic rather than malignant. Future actions involving Hamer's significant interactions with black people would tend to support this interpretation. Based on his own formative years during the Jim Crow Era, Lipscomb was cautious in later discussing the white Hamer and referred to him as "Charlie Hayman."[24]

Hamer closed his first significant case as city marshal (or "special police officer," as he was sometimes termed) on January 8, 1909. On the seventh, $110 was discovered to have been stolen from the Throop Saloon's safe by manager Sol Meyers. Hamer was notified, and the "indefatigable officer spent all night on the case and worked so successfully" that the missing money was discovered by 10.00 a.m.[25]

Word spread of Navasota's bold new marshal, and many of the gambling element, involved in dice games, poker, horse races, and cockfights, quietly began to leave town. Occurrences grew less for the next several months until Hamer was called upon to eliminate a dog that was acting strangely aggressive. The owner of Navasota's most prominent hotel kept a bulldog that terrorized the town. After the animal killed several pets and attacked passersby, the city council passed an ordinance requiring the dog's owner to either confine or muzzle it. Shortly after, Hamer caught the bulldog with his jaws around on the throat of another pet that was tied to a wagon wheel. Hamer slapped the dog with his pistol barrel which infuriated its owner.

The marshal reminded the man of the dog's past aggression and warned him if the behavior continued, he would have to shoot it. The owner laughed and walked away. Several days later, Hamer was informed the bulldog had killed again. The marshal immediately went to the hotel, pulled his pistol, and shot the offending canine. Holstering his weapon, he told the stunned bystanders, "Maybe now you'll believe that when I say I'm going to uphold the law, I mean what I say." The issue of killing the dog divided the community into two camps: one that supported the marshal and the other that opposed him. The hotel owner became the leader of the anti-Hamer faction comprised of saloon keepers and the toughs who had already encountered the marshal's iron hand.[26]

Even while he clamped down on the lawlessness in Navasota, Hamer met public school teacher Mollie Bobadillo Cameron in 1908, and soon became smitten with the cultured and attractive brunette. She had been born on February 16, 1887, in Waller County. After a two-year courtship, they would marry on March 19, 1911, in Hempstead.[27]

On April 28, 1909, boys passing by Long's grocery store heard strange noises at the rear of the closed business, and interrupted a robbery in progress. The suspect escaped before Hamer could be summoned. Investigating, the marshal gave "the case considerable attention today arresting as a suspect, one Ernest Neblett, a colored boy." The *Navasota Examiner* commented, "Officer Hamer deserves special attention for the quick work he did on the case which is remarkable on account of the flimsy clue he had to work on." A black man working for a circus "got on the warpath," likely a euphemism for being drunk, and cut a black woman on October 6. Hamer was summoned and attempted to arrest the assailant. The suspect bolted and ran down the nearby railroad tracks. Due to the surrounding crowd, Hamer declined to use his pistol, choosing, instead, to chase the man on foot. Overtaking the runner, Hamer relieved him of a pistol and a pair of brass knuckles and took him into custody.[28]

On April 13, 1910, Hamer had to shoot another mad dog, then broke up a gambling ring the same day. The marshal and his deputy, John E. Cuthrell, were informed of the game and infiltrated an old barn in the Fourth Ward at 2:00 a.m., catching fourteen craps shooters and confiscating two revolvers.

All the gamblers entered guilty pleas and paid their fines. The city council heartily approved of the marshal's endeavors and raised his salary from eighty-five to one hundred dollars per month. County Attorney Conlaw Michael Spann was equally impressed and presented Hamer with a four and three-quarter-inch Colt Single-Action Army .45 pistol that bore Type C (near full coverage) engraving. Appreciative of the thoughtful gesture, Hamer christened the weapon "Old Lucky" and carried it on his hip for much of his career.[29]

Hamer took a short leave of absence on July 14, 1910, to visit relatives in Mason County, and Ranger Edmund Ledbetter "Ed" Avriett of Company C temporarily assumed the duties of town marshal. Navasota remained a tough town, as Avriett quickly discovered. In his first five days, he was involved in two shooting incidents: one during an attempt on his life, and the other while trying to take two horse thieves into custody.[30]

Returning from his vacation, Hamer decided to enact a policy of banning firearms in town. Related in Lipscomb's vernacular, Hamer purportedly told townspeople, "I'm the only man—me an my deputy—sposed ta wear a pistol in the broad open day or night. We gittin paid fur it. Now if I catch y'all wit a pistol on, I'm gonna put you in jail." He approached those with concealed weapons and told the offender to take his gun home. If the man lied, he seized the hidden gun, then literally kicked them to the jail. Indeed, W. W. Sterling likened Hamer's foot fighting technique to the French martial art style known as *savate*. He noted Hamer utilized his feet with great skill.[31]

On February 28, 1911, at about 10:00 p.m., Eugene N. Simmons, a section foreman for the International & Great Northern, reported to Hamer that his home had been burglarized. That same night, the marshal observed a stranger emerging from the darkness and going into the train depot's waiting room. Entering the same building, Hamer confronted the man and began to question him. His suspicions raised by inconsistent answers, the law officer led the suspect outside, ordered him to raise his hands, conducted a search, and found a pocket watch. Summoning Simmons, Hamer asked him to identify the timepiece whereupon the stranger bolted down the train tracks. The marshal fired two warning shots, but the fleeing man refused to halt. Consequently, Hamer shot him through the right arm and through the middle of his back, the second bullet exiting his abdomen. The suspect managed a few further steps, then fell. The thief was identified as Granville Johnson (alias Manny "Kid" Jackson), a thirty-year-old career criminal. Before expiring from his wounds on March 1, Jackson confessed to burgling five homes in Brenham on February 25, seven more the following day, and two more in Courtney on the twenty-seventh. Before the shooting, Jackson had robbed two houses, including Simmons, in Navasota. Also found on Jackson's person were the railroad employee's wedding ring, knife, wrench, and pocket change. According to routine procedure, Hamer was arrested, and appeared for an examining trial the next morning, where the judge placed him under a two-hundred-dollar bond. Under common law, a peace officer was justified in using any means necessary, even deadly force, to apprehend a fleeing felony suspect, and the marshal was acquitted of any wrongdoing in the ensuing inquest.[32]

For months, Mayor Horace Baldwin Rice of Houston had been trying to persuade Hamer to come work for him as a special officer in the crime-ridden Bayou City. Hamer refused to leave until a suitable replacement could be hired. Fortunately for the mayor, Marvin Eugene Bailey, who had served with Hamer in Company C, arrived in town on April 30 to accept the position. Hamer's resignation took effect on May 1, and Bailey took the oath of office the same day.[33]

Houston had benefitted greatly from the Spindletop oil discovery ten years earlier. Indeed, that particular location had produced over seventeen million barrels of black gold in 1902 alone, and other finds soon followed along the Gulf Coast. In 1905, the Texas Company's headquarters was established in Houston, which soon became the world's oil capital. However, amid the booming population and expanding economy, the city had long been plagued by a series of killings. Twenty-six homicides and 131 assaults with intent to kill were recorded for the years 1906 and 1907. Additionally, the police department had suffered nine line-of-duty deaths in recent years, including the murder of Deputy Chief William E. Murphy on April 1, 1910. Mayor Rice, a reformer, had publicly expressed his distrust of the historically underfunded and undermanned city police force, and Chief George Ellis abruptly resigned on August 22. Night Chief James Maurice Ray succeeded

Ellis, but an additional thirteen officers were discharged. The following year, former deputy sheriff Duff Voss replaced Ray as police chief. Operating alongside the police, the position of special officer had been in existence since the 1840s, originally as an informant on the city's slave population. Following the Civil War, special officers gathered intelligence on the criminal element, including possibly corrupt policemen. As time went on, their responsibilities became more ambiguous, with the exact nature depending on the particular mayors and their requirements.[34]

To clean up the town, Rice hired Hamer, as well as former Rangers Henry Lee Ransom, Jules Joseph Baker, and Joseph Lee Anders; all of them answered directly to the mayor. Sworn in on April 21, 1911, Hamer possessed the same authority bestowed upon Houston's Finest to carry a firearm and to detain. His chief duties included arresting gamblers and individuals carrying firearms inside the municipal limits in violation of the city ordinance. According to Mance Lipscomb, the special officer was instructed to ignore whites gambling at the Rice Hotel and other posh resorts and concentrate on black bettors. The order aggravated Hamer's sense of fair play, though, and he refused to obey. Perhaps to underscore the point, he and Anders raided a sizeable poker game in one of the rooms of the Planters' Hotel on Preston Avenue on November 7. Seven players were taken into custody and a large quantity of chips and decks of cards confiscated. The prisoners all expressed a willingness to pay the minimum fine of $17.45 each.[35]

Despite his status as a troubleshooter for the mayor's office, Hamer cooperated well with the police department's detective bureau. He and Detective George Peyton received a tip that Owen Matthews, a jailbreaker from Brazos County, was holed up at his father's house in the Fourth Ward. On February 6, 1912, the two lawmen stealthily entered the house at 1:30 a.m. and found a sleeping man in the front room. However, he was not their prey, and, while Hamer watched the slumbering individual, Peyton continued into the back sleeping quarters. As he entered one room, the detective was fired on by Matthews. Slightly wounded, Peyton retreated into the hallway and fatally shot Matthews as the fugitive charged out of the bedroom. Peyton requested he be placed under arrest and indicted on a charge of murder. However, Justice of the Peace John Henry Crooker, Sr. later ruled the detective had acted in self-defense.[36]

Master Scott, a black man, was shot and killed while walking along the streetcar tracks on Heights Boulevard on May 15. Sheriff Archie Rolander Anderson immediately initiated an investigation, and, two days later, he, deputies John Smith and ____ Reed, Hamer, and Justice Crooker arrested two white men, Clarence Safford and Ulysses Theriot, for the crime. Both suspects were charged in Crooker's court, and they flatly denied any involvement in the murder.[37]

On February 28, Mayor Rice had named Henry Ransom to head the police department. The new chief was a man comfortable with violence and death. In 1899, he deployed to the Philippines with the Thirty-third U.S. Volunteer Infantry and saw heavy combat. After becoming a career lawman, he twice faced indictments for murder, but was exonerated on both occasions. Whether his stint in the war accounted for his temperament, Ransom was undoubtedly a brutal killer with a badge. The mayor's choice proved to be unfortunate.[38]

Hamer had little regard for Ransom, and his low opinion was vindicated after a police officer and a jeweler were involved in a physical altercation that resulted in an arrest. Ransom defended his officer, while each side blamed the other in court. When the patrolman was shown to be drunk on duty at the time of the altercation, the chief fired him. However, Ransom's bellicose comments to a newspaper reporter produced indignation among some of the town's citizens. Deluged with complaints, Mayor Rice announced the city commission would conduct a public probe into the police department's activities, beginning on June 17. However, few witnesses appeared before the commissioners, and Rice adjourned the proceedings on the twentieth. Ransom tendered his resignation on June 28 and planned to return to his old position as a special officer. In his final days, though, the chief severely beat a boorish citizen who had insulted the force, and Ransom personally. He was indicted for aggravated assault and battery the following month. Working outside the police department's purview, Hamer and his colleagues were not involved in any of these events. However, the ex-Ranger would, in the future, find Ransom once more a source of trouble.[39]

While Ransom dealt with his own issues, Hamer was bringing to justice a cop killer. On June 14, 1911, Constable Edgar Eugene Isgitt of the Harrisburg Precinct had been mortally wounded while attempting to arrest alleged wifebeater Mat "Mississippi Red" Young at a craps game near town. Although a tough gambler, Young, a black man, was defended by the local African American community, who insisted he had acted in self-defense. The killer had fled the scene and remained at large, despite a $250 state reward. In November 1912, newly elected Harris County Sheriff Marion Franklin "Frank" Hammond decided to make Young's apprehension a priority for his department. Although he had opposed the use of special officers in the past, the sheriff enlisted Hamer's assistance in closing the case.[40]

Beginning the investigation in his customary relentless style, Hamer pursued leads for the next few weeks and obtained information Young had been gambling in Opelousas, Louisiana, under the alias of "Poor Boy Taylor." The special officer and Sheriff Hammond entrained to Opelousas, where they discovered the fugitive had moved on to Baton Rouge. The two lawmen followed their quarry to the state capital, and learned Mississippi Red was working on a levee near Melville. Arriving at Melville on January 3, 1913, Hamer disguised himself as a Baptist preacher and secured lodging at the boarding house where Young was staying. He learned Young was located on the Atchafalaya River near the village of Red Cross. Together with Hammond, he traveled into the river bottoms and met with a local constable and a guide. The quartet struggled through the marsh and brakes toward a spot where they could observe Young as he passed by. When the guide signaled their prey was approaching, the officers sprang out of their concealment, rifles at the ready. The fugitive was taken without incident. The following day, Hamer and Hammond returned to Houston with their prisoner. The two lawmen took equal shares in the reward, but the sheriff related to the media how their expenses exceeded their returns. Young pled guilty of second-degree murder and received a twenty-year sentence. He entered Huntsville penitentiary on May 1, 1913, but, rather than serve his full sentence, he was discharged on August 13, 1922.[41]

Charles Smith had broken out of Huntsville in November 1912 and remained at large. At the time of his escape, he had been twenty days into a seven-year sentence for being an accessory to the February 21, 1911, killing of a brakeman at the Houston Belt and Terminal Yards, and the shooting of the yardmaster. Based on a tip from a confidential informant, Hamer, and Special Officers Anders and Matthews, went to the First Ward and peacefully took Smith into custody on January 16, 1913. Smith was returned to prison to serve out the remainder of his sentence.[42]

In a months-long effort, Hamer and Sheriff Hammond had been tracking the individual suspected of murdering Houston policeman John Morris Cain on August 4, 1911. On the day of his death, Officer Cain attempted to arrest a freighthopping man who had dropped down from a slowing International & Great Northern train on the North Side. Cain called on the suspect to stop, and the latter turned and fired twice, killing the officer. "Mississippi Red" Young was a suspect in the officer's slaying for a time. In mid-February 1913, Hamer and Hammond located J. M. Torrence, who had "bummed" the same train, and took him to the Imperial State prison farm. There, Torrence identified H. A. Tatnell as the man he had seen minutes before the killing. Tatnell, later imprisoned for burglarizing a store in Montgomery, had been carrying the stolen items on his person when he stepped down from the railcar. In the end, though, while he was charged, the case was not prosecuted due to insufficient evidence.[43]

Despite the setback in the case, Hamer continued to work effectively with local officers in apprehending lawbreakers. On February 19, he accompanied Detective Yancy Quitman Brizendine and two other city plainclothesmen in driving nineteen miles and walking several more through woods and creek bottoms near Duke Station to apprehend Andy Spears for murder. The suspect was charged with the stabbing death of Arthur Lyles in a restaurant on Commerce Avenue on October 6 of the previous year. On March 4, Hamer and Brizendine traveled to Victoria and arrested Ike Simpson, who was wanted in Leesville, Louisiana, on a murder charge. Simpson was held in the Houston city jail awaiting action by the Louisiana authorities.[44]

For more than five months, Hamer had been at odds with the *Houston Press* over a damaging misquote. Next, an article appeared in the April 14, 1913, issue implying the special officers were protecting vice rings in the city, Two days later, Hamer encountered Henry Clay Waters, Jr., the reporter responsible for the story, on Fannin Street. Losing his temper, he slapped the journalist across the face. Eyewitnesses later claimed the special officer then pistol-whipped the fallen Waters. The same day, Hamer encountered George Bailey Waters, Henry's brother and also a *Press* reporter, at the local police station, struck him, and literally kicked him out of the building. Arrested for aggravated assault, Hamer submitted a bond of twenty-five dollars. He resigned on April 17, but remained in Houston awaiting his court appearance. Pleading guilty to the misdemeanor charge on June 10, he paid the fine of $88.70 and departed town.[45]

Moving back to Navasota with Mollie, Hamer endured an excruciating seven months of idleness. Perhaps indicating he would not remain unemployed for long, he was named an honorary member of the Texas Sheriffs' Association at their annual meeting in July. After the Brazos River overflowed its banks in one of the worst floods in the state's history, he accepted employment from Marvin Bailey as a temporary policeman in town. When he was offered a position as a special officer with the Kimble County Angora Goat Raisers and Breeders Association, Hamer quickly accepted and traveled to Junction; Mollie remained home. Given legal sanction by virtue of a deputy sheriff's commission, his salary was paid by the association. True to form, Hamer aggressively acted to intimidate the livestock thieves threatening his employers' livelihood. He found a ready ally and friend in County Attorney Coke Robert Stevenson, who accompanied Hamer night after night into the hills after lawbreakers. Dayton Moses, former district attorney of Kimball County, testified before a House investigating committee in 1919 that Hamer was known in the community either as a first-class officer or as one too harsh in the discharge of his duties.[46]

The period of unemployment, their dire financial situation, and the separation might have placed a great deal of strain on Hamer and Mollie's marriage. They divorced sometime between late 1914 and early 1915. In an interview Ranger aficionado Robert Neiman conducted with several members of the Hamer family, they stated she had drowned six months after the wedding at a Sunday school picnic. As shown, this is incorrect, but only partially. After the breakup of her marriage, Mollie was employed as a stenographer at a bank. Later she worked for an oil company as a secretary, then married Raymond Elwood Ford. Mollie died on August 22, 1937, when she unsuccessfully attempted to rescue two children from drowning at her summer camp near Union.[47]

While Hamer's marriage dissolved, the ongoing Mexican Revolution, and the bloodshed that spilled over the Rio Grande into Texas, alarmed lawmakers in the statehouse. Indeed, as Professors Charles H. Harris III and Louis R. Sadler observed, "The supreme irony is that the Mexican Revolution saved the Texas Rangers." For the last several years, the service had been increasingly considered an anachronism. With the outbreak of yet more border violence, the Thirty-fourth Legislature approved an act on March 22, 1915, to appropriate ten thousand dollars for the purpose of adding additional men to the Ranger Force. By the end of fiscal year 1916, the adjutant general calculated that one thousand dollars were required annually to maintain each ranger. Consequently, legislative appropriations limited the force to thirty men.[48]

Eager for border service, Hamer reenlisted in Company C on March 29, 1915. The company commander, headquartered in Austin, was Captain Edward Hume Smith. Joining the company on the same day were James Dallas Dunaway, Winfred Finis Bates, and Eugene B. Hulen. William Lee Barler enrolled in the outfit on April 9, and Nat B. "Kiowa" Jones on the twenty-fourth. Although his duty station was ostensibly Del Rio, Hamer was ordered to return to Junction and complete his work there. Kerrville banker and rancher Charles Schreiner had written the governor on April 19 detailing goat, sheep, and cattle thefts in Kimble County by bandits crossing the Rio Grande. He further requested Hamer and Oscar Lata be assigned to halt the depredations. Hamer believed much of the rustling occurring in the county was due to John Fletcher Gardner, Jr. and William Harrison "Buck" Gardner, two sons of prominent rancher John Fletcher Gardner, Sr. With the assistance of County Attorney Stevenson, Hamer was able to amass sufficient evidence to arrest Fletcher, Jr. on April 22, and an accomplice, part-time court bailiff Willis Cross, two days later. Hamer also swore out a complaint against Buck for the four-year-old murder of a Mexican sheepherder. The dead man would be denied his justice when a jury acquitted Gardner. Additionally, following another trial and an appeal, the defendant's conviction for goat theft and two-year sentence was reversed on February 19, 1919.[49]

Despite any disappointment or bitterness over his inability to see the Gardner brothers convicted, Hamer continued to pursue and arrest rustlers. However, his desire was to serve on the border, and he was finally attached to Captain James Monroe Fox's Company B in the Big Bend from August to October. For five years, Mexico had been racked with violence as the republic underwent a bloody series of interconnected revolutions. The associated banditry, arms trafficking, and smuggling plagued the upper Rio Grande Valley, and two Rangers had paid the ultimate price in 1915: Eugene Hulen, on May 24, and Robert Lee Burdett of Company B, on June 8.[50]

The *Plan de San Diego*, which had been scheduled to commence on February 20, 1915, was a revolutionary manifesto that called for an uprising of Mexicans, blacks, and Indians to kill all white males over the age of sixteen and seize control of Texas, Colorado, New Mexico, Arizona, and California. The conquered states were then to establish an independent republic with the possibility of future annexation by Mexico. Harris and Sadler have thoroughly outlined the covert involvement of "First Chief" Venustiano Carranza in the plot. While February 20 passed peaceably, throughout the following summer, bands of armed Hispanic *sediciosos* (Seditionists) raided ranches, irrigation works, and railroads, and stole livestock, burned bridges, murdered Anglos, and robbed post offices and stores. Local and state law officers, and federal troops responded, and South Texas became a combat zone of attacks and reprisals. Throughout its course, the Revolution disrupted socioeconomic conditions on both sides of the border. Mexican towns were depopulated by depredations and property destruction, crop shortages, hunger, and disease. Connected economically to their sister communities across the river, American towns, filled with refugees, were only marginally better. On August 10, a cavalry detachment skirmished with bandits and captured documents indicating Mexican authorities were behind the raids. Appointed to the Ranger Force, Harry Ransom was tasked by Governor James Edward "Farmer Jim" Ferguson with recruiting a new Company D and stamping out the *insurrectos* by whatever means deemed necessary. All too often, Anglo lawmen and vigilantes resorted to "evaporations," as these unlawful executions were euphemistically termed. The death toll of *mexicanos*, both *sediciosos* and innocent bystanders, in this "Bandit War" ranges from a ludicrous number of five thousand to Major-General Frederick Funston's more reasonable yet still uncorroborated estimate of three hundred. Hamer was never directly involved in the ongoing evaporations, but he would be affected by their consequences.[51]

In early August 1915, a sizable band of *bandidos* rode onto the Sauz division of the King Ranch. Caesar Kleberg alerted the Rangers in Brownsville and the military at Fort Brown, and requested assistance. Adjutant General Henry Hutchings, Ransom, and Sheriff William Thomas Vann led a posse from San Benito on the fifth. The next day, they engaged the brigands at a ranch thirty miles northeast of Brownsville at El Paso Real. Three Mexicans were killed in the gun battle, and three were apprehended. In light of the continuing depredations, Fox's Company B was assigned to Raymondville and Ransom's company to Harlingen. On August 8, a special train carrying a captain and twelve troopers of the Twelfth U.S. Cavalry, Rangers from Ransom's and Fox's commands (including Hamer), and a posse of local lawmen headed to Norias. Arriving at the ranch, they found King horses already saddled and waiting. Accompanied by foreman Tom Tate and several cowhands, the party mounted up and rode southeast to the Sauz pastures. After supper, two ranch hands, eight soldiers, two Customs inspectors, one deputy sheriff, and an Immigration officer were lounging at the ranch headquarters when they noticed riders approaching. Thinking they were the Rangers returning, the men were shocked to realize these were bandits. Under the leadership of Antonio Roche and Dario Morada, the Mexican horsemen charged, and the defenders opened fire with rifles and shotguns. The fight ended at eight-thirty that same evening, with seventeen *bandidos* dead on the ground. About an hour later, the posse of soldiers and Rangers returned without having found the Mexicans they had sought.[52]

The following month, Hamer told a San Antonio reporter, "The Rangers did much better and more effective work in fighting Mexican bandits than the soldiers."[53] John R. Peavey, reflecting on thirty-plus years' service as a border lawman, later agreed:

> The Rangers had a decided advantage over the military in the men that made up the personnel of the Rangers were men who were reared in frontier cattle country and could speak Spanish fluently. They were never known to ride into a bandit trap. They were good riders, trailers, and excellent rifle and pistol shots; whenever they made contact with a bandit gang, they wiped it out. They did much and talked little. Their methods were criticized by the military, and the military were controlled by the swivel-chair boys in Washington who knew very little about the border or its people.[54]

However, the extralegal and immoral activities of Ransom and Fox disgusted Hamer, and he resigned effective November 8, 1915. Looking for better opportunities, he became a brand inspector for the Cattle Raisers' Association of Texas the same day. Since the 1890s, association detectives and inspectors had obtained Special Ranger warrants in order to legally carry firearms and make arrests. Receiving his commission, Hamer was attached to Company C and worked from the fashionable Landon Hotel in San Angelo. Within weeks, he was able to report: "We are dealing the cow thieves misery here."[55]

Working in Big Spring, Hamer became embroiled in the last great blood feud in the state's history. On December 16, 1916, twenty-six-year-old Ida Gladys (Johnson) Sims and her brother, Sidney Arthur Johnson, were involved in a fatal altercation with Edward Caldwell Sims, a leading rancher and Gladys's ex-husband. Sims had reportedly attempted to take his two daughters, Helen Trix and Mildred Beverly, away from their mother, and Gladys responded by shooting him with a small-caliber revolver, inflicting two flesh wounds. Her brother then ended the confrontation, and Sims's life, with a shotgun. After surrendering to the county sheriff, the two appeared at an examining trial and were released on bond, twenty thousand dollars for Sidney and eight thousand for Gladys.[56]

The Johnsons were influential and wealthy ranchers in Scurry County, while the Sims family was equally powerful in neighboring Garza County.

The earlier, bitter divorce had heightened tensions between the two clans and, with a corpse on hand, the area was faced with the commencement of a feud. At the same time, Harrison Hamer, a deputy game warden, was in town acting as an armed bodyguard for the Johnson family. Frank Hamer and a fellow brand inspector, Eben M. Holman, were drawn into the affair when Sims partisan Isaiah George "Gee" McMeans threatened Harrison. A former Ranger of Company C and ex-tax collector of Ector County, McMeans had spent five months in Huntsville for assault with intent to murder before being pardoned in January 1902. Hamer arrived in Snyder and "informed the bunch, which was headed by a man by the name of McMeans, that if anyone murdered my brother that they would pay dearly for it." Sheriff Wilson Alexander Merrell reported to the adjutant general the Hamers and Holman were causing a great deal of trouble and were openly hostile to the local officials. The county attorney requested the presence of regular Rangers who would act in a fair and impartial manner. The governor and adjutant general sent John Dudley White, Sr. and Alexander Glenn Beard with orders to keep the peace between the two factions.[57]

Hamer temporarily resigned from the cattlemen's association, and General Hutchings revoked his Special Ranger authority on January 10, 1917. Three days later, Hamer wrote to the adjutant general, expressing his regrets that he was not able to retain his warrant and enclosed the same. Harrison's state commission with the Game and Fish Commissioner was also canceled.[58]

No further trouble occurred, and White and Beard stayed in Snyder until after the conclusion of the March 1917 term of district court. Stung by the rescinding of their official status, the Hamer brothers remained as well and worked full-time as bodyguards for the Johnson family. "He was daring and handsome," Gladys recalled fondly of Frank. "The sort of man a suspect was afraid to answer and afraid not to. The Lord seemed always to be tapping him on his shoulder." Hamer was similarly attracted to Gladys, and they married in New Orleans on May 12, 1917. In time, he adopted Gladys's daughters. Helen had been born on July 15, 1907, and Beverly on November 7, 1909.[59]

Hamer's connection to his Johnson in-laws further involved him in the ongoing feud with the Sims family. Samuel David Sims, Sr., father of the slain Ed, had allegedly hired gunmen to kill the Hamer brothers, Sheriff Merrell, and Glady's father, William A. "Bill" Johnson. Apprehensive of directly confronting Hamer, McMeans served as the intermediary. Later, after an abortive murder attempt, Sims offered a four-thousand-dollar bounty for the elder Johnson's death. Felix Robert Jones, a paid assassin, was interested, but he had already contracted to murder New Mexico cattle baron Thomas Lyons for two thousand dollars. Instead, W. G. Clark, his partner, took on the task. Once Jones killed Lyons, and the slain man's widow posted a ten-thousand-dollar reward for her husband's killer, Clark chose the easier and more substantial payday and informed on his partner. Jones was arrested and tried in El Paso. During the proceedings, Clark detailed the complete plan to murder Lyons, and also revealed McMeans's efforts to kill Bill Johnson and Frank Hamer. During the trial, Jones spotted Hamer, who was on hand to listen to testimony, and asked to speak with the lawman. The assassin offered his hand in greeting, but then cowered under Hamer's baleful stare. Since Jones and Clark were both in custody, the former sentenced to twenty-five years in prison for murder, and the latter jailed as a material witness, Dave Sims was forced to once more approach McMeans, who decided he needed backup.[60]

In the matter of Ed Sims's killing, Scurry County prosecutors had obtained a change of venue to Lemesa for Gladys's trial, and to Baird for Sidney's hearing. Gladys's court case began on September 17, 1917. Almost immediately, the judge dismissed the case after the defense argued she had not fired the fatal gunshots, and she had acted as a mother defending her children. The questionable verdict enraged the Sims family.[61]

Hamer was scheduled to testify in Sidney's trial in Eighty-eighth District Court on October 1. However, with the attorneys' agreement, Judge Joseph Washington "Joe" Burkett continued the case until the spring court term. As Hamer prepared to take Gladys, Harrison, and Emmett, Gladys's brother, and his wife to Snyder, he was informed of a plot to permanently silence him and cautioned not to go through Sweetwater. Hamer replied, "I [have] always gone where I pleased and … I [am] going through Sweetwater." Old Lucky was shoved into his waistband, and the tough lawman emphasized his pronouncement by packing an extra gun, a Smith & Wesson Triple-Lock .44 pistol, in a shoulder holster. Hamer drove his Cadillac Eight into Sweetwater about two o'clock in the afternoon. Needing to fill up the fuel tank and fix a punctured tire, he stopped at the City Garage on the corner of Locust and Broadway.[62]

Hamer and his party decided to go uptown, and were heading to the office adjacent to the south entrance to stow their shotguns. Suddenly, Gee McMeans and H. E. "Red" Phillips drove through the exterior door. Bounding from his car, McMeans pulled a Colt Government Model .45-caliber pistol and pointed it at Hamer from a distance of three feet. Leaping forward, the latter slapped the weapon down as it fired, the bullet hitting the lawman in the right thigh. As Hamer grappled with his assailant, the pistol fired again. The bullet struck the watch chain hanging from his breast pocket, driving metal fragments into his left shoulder. Although shot twice, Hamer continued to hold onto his would-be killer until McMeans wrenched himself loose. In the next instant, Phillips, having dodged gunfire from Gladys, fired at Hamer with a shotgun; the blast tore the brim off his hat. The concussive force of the discharge also knocked Hamer off his feet. McMeans raced for his nearby automobile, while Phillips, realizing Hamer was still alive, fled.[63]

As McMeans reached his car, he grabbed up a shotgun and ran back toward the downed law officer. Hamer pulled his Smith & Wesson revolver and carefully shot his attacker through the heart, killing him instantly. The garage attendant, the only witness not affiliated with either faction, later claimed a total of fifteen to twenty shots were fired during the fracas. Likely, the majority of these came from Gladys's pistol as she attempted to shoot Phillips. Police Chief William Robert "Buck" Johnson arrived on the scene and placed Hamer and his companions under arrest. Additionally, Johnson confiscated seven revolvers, two semiautomatic pistols, one riot gun, one semiautomatic shotgun, and three repeating rifles from those present at the fight. Every person involved was confined in the jail except for the wounded Hamer, who was taken into the courthouse to receive medical attention from Doctor Charles Asher Rosebrough, Sr. After his wounds were treated, he joined the rest in the cells. Hamer claimed he did not know the dead man, but he had confronted McMeans and other Sims men following the threats to Harrison's life. Contrary to popular legend, the Hamer party and Phillips remained behind bars for five days while the grand jury gathered evidence. Phillips asserted the meeting was accidental rather than a planned assassination attempt. On October 6, the jurors declined to return any indictments and adjourned. Released from jail, Hamer was taken to the Johnson ranch to recuperate.[64]

The confrontation in Sweetwater was the first of Hamer's shooting incidents in which he faced armed men in a classic gunfight. William Barclay "Bat" Masterson, the lawman and gambler-turned-sportswriter, famously said three qualities were necessary for a successful gunfighter: courage, ability with firearms, and deliberation at the crucial moment. The latter he defined as possessing a cool nerve while under pressure. Echoing Masterson's belief seventeen years after Sweetwater, Hamer explained to a newspaper reporter his tried-and-true practice for winning gun battles: "When you've got to fight it out with a six shooter the only sure way is to make the first shot count. Just one shot, and that the first one. Take it slow and cool. Don't get excited." More than his own skills, though, Hamer credited God with his continued survival: "They say I am a good shot. I know I am. But as long as I'm doing what is right—and I'm always trying to cut it square—there's something of Higher Help that looked down the gun barrel with me and told me when to pull the trigger." In addition to nerves of steel and divine assistance, Webb noted Hamer's eyesight: "He can see the bullet, which looks like a bee, enveloped in a tiny cloud of heat waves produced by friction between lead and air. The discharge from a shotgun 'looks like a swarm of gnats.'" Whether his vision was that acute, Hamer was indeed an expert marksman with firearms, and practiced using a handgun at long-range. An avid hunter, he was highly accomplished with a rifle, a weapon he preferred to use in a fight.[65]

Regardless of his physical gifts, Hamer consistently refused to label himself as a "gunfighter." He told *Dallas Dispatch* managing editor Frank Clarke Newlon in an interview: "I don't like to be pointed out as a killer. The men I have shot down have all been criminals in the act of committing a crime or resisting arrest. I'm hired to do that work. It's my job. I do it because I have to. I don't like to talk about it or think about it. It's something to be forgotten." Despite his unwillingness to accept the moniker, Hamer survived numerous deadly encounters in his long career, and rightfully earned his reputation as a skilled and deadly shooter.[66]

Within two weeks, Frank was sufficiently recovered to visit downtown Snyder. Using crutches to move around, the wounded man and his family went on a much-needed vacation to California. They spent time in Hollywood, where Hamer became good friends with cowboy-actor Thomas Edwin "Tom" Mix. While there, Frank and Gladys welcomed Francis Augustus, Jr. on April 11, 1918, in Pasadena. However, legal matters stemming from the dispute between the Johnson and the Sims families back in Texas had not yet been resolved. Sydney's trial in Baird convened on September 23. As a precaution, every person entering Judge Burkett's courtroom was searched for weapons, even the women. The state rested on direct examination of witnesses later the same day, and the defense presented its case beginning on the twenty-fourth. Having returned home, Gladys testified on her brother's behalf. The defense rested the next day, and the jury rendered a verdict of not guilty on September 26.[67]

Fully healed, Hamer decided to rejoin the Ranger Force, and enlisted as a private in Company F on October 1, 1918. Headquartered in Brownsville, Captain William Walter Taylor, Hamer's new company commander, was working closely with Sheriff W. T. Vann to end the activities of one Encarnación Delgado and his "band of dangerous smugglers." In addition to smuggling opium, *mescal*, and other goods from Matamoros into Brownsville, Delgado was known as a murderer and a "very bad and dangerous character."[68]

From an informant, the lawmen discovered the Mexicans were planning to cross the Rio Grande below Fort Brown near Tomate Bend with a load of *mescal*. On the night of October 10, Sheriff Vann, Deputy Fred Winn, Captain Taylor, Sergeant Delbert "Tim" Timberlake, Hamer, and Customs inspectors Benjamin Thomas Tumlinson, Sr. and Joel Clinton Adkins made ready to ambush the *contrabandistas* along two possible routes from the river. In a discussion before the law officers settled into their positions, Hamer advocated, should anyone cross the border, shooting first and calling on them to surrender afterward. The sheriff balked at opening fire before the targets could be identified as friend or foe. Although only a private, Hamer argued that innocent citizens would not be traveling the river at night. He was overruled by the captain and the sheriff, with tragic consequences.[69]

After a wait of several hours, Vann and Hamer spied a figure creeping up the path. They allowed the man to continue past for another thirty feet, then the officers rose from concealment and ordered him to halt. The man, who turned out to be Delgado, whipped around and opened fire with a pistol. Vann immediately responded with a shotgun, but the smuggler was out of range. Shouldering his Remington Model 8 .25 Remington rifle, Hamer coolly hit the outlaw five times. The mortally wounded Delgado staggered several feet and dropped dead, a weapon in one hand and spare shells in the other. Unfortunately, the one bullet he had been able to fire hit Timberlake over his left hip, traveled through his abdomen, and halted against his watch in his right-hand trouser packet. The stricken timepiece stopped at exactly 9:27 p.m. Timberlake was rushed to the hospital in Brownsville, but as usual with such wounds in that era, there was nothing the surgeons could do except keep him comfortable. The Ranger sergeant remained conscious until he expired at seven o'clock the next morning. While Captain Taylor escorted Timberlake's body home to his parents, Hamer was promoted to sergeant on October 12. The following month brought more tragedy as Ranger T. Ellzey Paul Perkins of Company L was killed on November 17.[70]

State Representative José Tomás Canales of Brownsville had come to regard the Rangers as part of the problem rather than the solution. In addition to the number of Mexicans who were "shot while trying to escape," the legislator was certain his cousin Santiago Tijerina had been verbally abused by a posse of federal, state, and local officers near Brownsville on October 15. Tijerina insisted he was mistreated in the hopes he would respond and give the lawmen an excuse to kill him. The lawmen had been lying in wait for *tequileros*, and their position had been exposed by Tijerina. His actions led them to suspect him of being part of the gang they were pursuing. Tijerina was probably the target of profanity, but no independent evidence exists to suggest he was ever physically harmed. Additionally, Tijerina's stated reason for being in the area, which was that he was trailing stolen cattle, was equally unsubstantiated. However, Canales's criticisms did produce a discernable reaction. Hamer had been involved in the incident with Tijerina, and the

Ranger sergeant angrily confronted the representative in downtown Brownsville on December 11. "You are hot-footing it here, between here and Austin and complaining to the governor and the adjutant general about the Rangers, and I am going to tell you if you don't stop that you are going to get hurt," he informed the legislator. Amazingly, Hamer even repeated his ill-considered threat later in the presence of a witness.[71]

Canales reported the Ranger's warning to Sheriff Vann. The sheriff was no admirer of the Ranger Force and advised the lawmaker to "take a double-barreled shotgun … and kill that man … No jury would ever convict you." Canales, writing Governor William Pettus Hobby, labeled the Rangers in Brownsville a "gang of ruffians." The governor wired back, assuring Canales he would investigate, and referred the matter to the adjutant general.[72]

Adjutant General James Aloysius Harley expressed his regrets to Canales in writing, and assured him the alleged threat would be investigated; he went on to imply the entire episode might be nothing more than a misunderstanding. The representative replied Hamer's words could not have been clearer. Harley advised Canales on December 23 that Hamer had been ordered to desist from any future threats. Indeed, the Ranger was directed to protect the lawmaker.[73]

Canales was not inclined to trust Hamer, so he penned Congressman John Nance Garner requesting federal intervention to remove the Rangers from the lower valley. Garner passed the letter to the White House, which forwarded it to the War Department. Orders were sent to a military intelligence officer at Fort Brown directing him to investigate the controversial situation. His conclusions were dispatched through his chain of command to Washington, where the adjutant general prepared a report. The senior officer had found that the Rangers, despite some deviations from recognized procedure, were an effective force for law and order. He concluded, "The complaint of Mr. Canales appears to have been inspired to some extent by personal animosity and political differences."[74]

Meanwhile, Hamer was assigned to detached service on December 31, 1918, and operated from Austin. He was at the Driskill Hotel on January 12, 1919, where Canales, who was in town for the start of the legislative session, saw him "and his presence was made known to me very marked by passing in front of me, as though he simply wanted me to know he was there and on the force." Canales was later at the Avenue Hotel, and Hamer was also there. "He wanted me to know it and I know it, of course … I took his action as a challenge that I would be intimidated if I make any charges against those rangers or introduced any law attempting to regulate them." During later cross-examination, the adjutant general's attorney derisively asked, "Hamer didn't go into hiding because you were in town?" Canales apparently missed the mockery and replied, "No, but he showed himself very markedly, as much as to tell me he was here in Austin."[75]

Hamer's baiting of Canales made the representative even more determined to restrain the Ranger Force. He introduced House Bill No. 5 on January 14, 1919, which called for the reduction of the service to twenty-four men. The act required each applicant to possess at least two years' experience in law enforcement and to have no convictions on their record. He also wanted each Ranger to post a bond ranging from five thousand to fifteen thousand dollars to guarantee they maintained a high level of conduct. The measure provided that each Ranger would deliver his prisoners to the resident sheriff and could be forced to leave a particular county if the local officials demanded it.[76]

As Professor John Busby McClung wrote, "[Once] the suspicion and fear of foreign intrigue abated and … the danger of border bandit raids lessened, the excitement and terror of the past nine years gave way to calmer and more rational judgment." The governor and adjutant general were publicly willing to take steps to improve the quality of the individual Ranger, but they were opposed to undermining the force. Canales and his allies in the legislature fought for the bill, but the measure failed to advance to a vote. Stymied in his effort, Canales did succeed in pushing through a resolution on January 24 requesting the Adjutant General's Department provide the chief clerk of the House all records concerning Ranger-involved shootings from 1917 to 1918. Two days later, General Harley countered by calling for a full investigation of the Rangers "and all its activities with reference to its conduct and efficiency, the good that it does, and the forces of evil that it must necessarily encounter."

The strategy of Governor Hobby and General Harley was to frame the Ranger Force debate as one of "for or against its existence" rather than a narrow probe into allegations of misconduct.[77]

The debate in the House was impassioned, and Canales nearly lost his fight to a combination of amendments and motions to delay discussion. Finally, the legislators passed Concurrent Resolution No. 20 on January 27, which authorized a joint investigating committee of four House members and three senators. Hamer received orders to make himself available to the committee "for the purpose of summoning and witnesses in the twenty-third Senatorial District."[78]

The inquiry convened at 10:00 a.m. on January 30 in the Railroad Commission hearing room of the state capitol, and the members heard opening statements from Harley and Canales. The adjutant general had earlier requested the committee examine eleven areas extending from the Ranger Force's stated mission to Canales's contention that a Ranger had threatened him with bodily harm. The committee accepted Harley's proposal and directed Canales to present specific charges in writing. Throughout the hearings, Canales would read into the record additional charges, and Harley filed exceptions to them on one occasion.[79]

Eighty witnesses were ultimately called, but their statements often proved to be more hearsay than actual testimony. The lawmakers themselves were somewhat arbitrary in applying rules of evidence. Allegations included extralegal executions, drunkenness, cursing in public, assault, and torture. Canales contrived to have a place in the proceedings and, indeed, was labeled a "prosecuting witness." While questioning witnesses, he often attempted to lead them into giving testimony unfavorable to the Rangers. At other times, he employed innuendo and *ad hominem* attacks to discredit those supporting the status quo. The attorneys representing the Adjutant General's Department were equally contemptuous and depicted the legislator as a delusional, unpatriotic hypocrite working for interests other than his constituents. Canales' sixteenth charge stated that citizens in his district refused to bring complaints against the Rangers, as they were convinced the Adjutant General's Department would merely excuse the officer's actions. Taking the stand on February 10 to support his assertion, the legislator offered testimony regarding his earlier confrontation with Hamer and his correspondence with the governor and adjutant general.[80]

The inquiry phase ended on February 13, and the joint committee submitted a report to the lower chamber six days later. Among the findings of the committee was their belief that Harley was a "conscientious, efficient and faithful officer;" that the situation on the border required the Ranger Force be maintained, and that "gross violation of both civil and criminal law" did occur in years past. They concluded with a recommendation that the service be reorganized. Over Canales's objections, the House adopted the report by an overwhelming vote of eighty-seven to ten. The legislators referenced the fact that Harley had discharged for cause more than one hundred Rangers out of a total 108 during the time span in question. They also publicly declared that, in their opinion, Canales had not been prompted by improper motives.[81]

Representative William Harrison Bledsoe, chairman of the investigating committee, offered a substitute version of Canales's bill that was passed by the lawmakers on March 8 by a vote of ninety-five to five. With the House's consent, the Senate added several amendments and approved the measure twenty-seven to one on March 17. The governor signed the bill into law on March 31, which became effective on July 1. The reordered Ranger Force was decreased to four mounted companies of one captain, one sergeant, and fifteen privates, but still retained the quartermaster. The headquarters company was comprised of a senior captain and six privates. Pay scales were fixed at $150 for captains, one hundred dollars for sergeants, and ninety dollars for privates, with longevity raises after two years of continuous service. The act also created a formal procedure for handling citizen complaints. However, Professor Harold J. Weiss, Jr. noted that "although it helped to restore public confidence, the new law failed to address the issue of political influence and patronage in Ranger affairs. The next generation of political leaders could follow the policies of those, like Gov. James E. Ferguson and James B. Wells of Cameron County, who had hampered Ranger attempts to administer even-handed justice."[82]

A popular misconception of the Canales investigation is that it single-handedly imposed fundamental reformation on the Ranger Force.

Even the official histories of the Department of Public Safety, written by James W. Robinson and Mitchel P. Roth, implied a connection. Although Canales's efforts were an important step, additional factors influenced the reorganization. By the beginning of 1919, the Hobby administration was already contemplating reforms, such as a budget committee and a civil service commission, designed to bring efficiency and professionalism to state agencies. The end of World War I contributed to the reduction in the Rangers' numbers as the existing manpower was no longer needed nor financially viable. For instance, the Loyalty Rangers, created to thwart subversive activities, was certainly superfluous in a postwar Texas. The U.S. military was undergoing similar reductions in troop strength following the signing of the Armistice. Likewise, the Mexican Revolution more or less ended in 1920, and, with chaotic border conditions subsiding in the last year of the conflict, Rangers could be utilized to enforce the law in counties far from the Rio Grande. While little of Canales' original bill can be found in the final measure enthusiastically supported by the legislature, the reformer's crusade provided an impetus for the Ranger service to modify its practices and take yet another institutional step toward modernity.[83]

The adjutant general distributed copies of a fourteen-page booklet detailing the new rules and regulations by which the force would operate. Here the influence of the legislative inquiry and Canales's bill can be observed, including the requirement that Rangers refrain from shooting escaping prisoners, the proper procedure for transporting prisoners, and the guidelines for acquiring arrest warrants.[84] In the preamble, Harley defined the mission of the organization:

> The Texas Ranger Force was created … for the purpose of protecting all good citizens against depredation upon their property and their rights. A Ranger who is appointed under this law is a creature of the law, and any authority he may have, or any power he may exercise, is given and received by virtue of the law under which he operates ... There is one thing always to be remembered by a peace officer, particularly a Ranger, and that is, that the constitutional rights of the citizens are inviolable and are superior to any personal opinion or desire on

> the part of an officer, and when an officer so disregards his duty as to forget the constitutional rights of citizens he puts himself without the pale of the law, and must, therefore, be deprived of all authority which has been given him.[85]

As Mexico's internal conflict headed toward its conclusion, arms smuggling across the Rio Grande continued unabated. Hamer became aware of a large shipment being prepared by the Bering-Coates Hardware Company in Houston in December 1918. Their prospective customer was Francisco "Pancho" Villa, the *revolucionario* leader who had broken with *presidente* Carranza. Hamer notified General Harley of the plan and assured his superior he would capture the shipment. Over dinner in Brownsville several days later, Captain William Martin Hanson instructed Hamer to turn a blind eye to Villa's consignment. Stunned, Hamer indignantly refused to ignore the law, even when Hanson assured him those were the adjutant general's orders. The sergeant continued to protest and angrily accused Hanson of corruption. Hamer later demanded orders in writing instructing him to ignore the embargo, but none were forthcoming. Instead, when Company F was disbanded at the end of the month, the immovable Hamer was placed on detached duty on the border, which he patrolled alone. He stubbornly refused to comply, as "the law was the law, and he intended to keep right on enforcing it." He promptly crossed the river and met with Lieutenant-Colonel Manual Bernea, commander of the Tamaulipas state police. By the end of the conference, Hamer was the unofficial leader of a large squad of Mexican soldiers who patrolled the border between Matamoros and Nuevo Laredo. For two months, Hamer kept Bernea informed of *bandido* gangs intent on crossing back into Mexico, whereupon at least twenty-eight outlaws were summarily executed. The stolen loot or livestock was placed into the Ranger's custody. After Percy Aubrey Cardwell, sergeant of Company G, was granted a discharge effective March 31, 1919, Hamer was transferred on paper to the company's headquarters at Marathon, but he remained on detached service in Brownsville.[86]

Once the new Ranger law went into effect, all Rangers were required to request reappointment or face the cancellation of their enlistments. Still in exile, Hamer claimed he was never informed of this requirement, although he was supposedly written on the matter two or three times. Consequently, his warrant of authority expired on June 19, 1919. Unfriendly individuals, such as new quartermaster Captain Roy Wilkinson Aldrich, noted in Hamer's service records that he had "resigned."[87]

Hamer lived in Snyder while he applied for a new warrant in the Ranger Force, but General Harley and Captain Hanson continued to block him. Finally, after Harley resigned and Hanson traveled to Washington, DC, Hamer's application was approved by the new adjutant general, William Dade Cope. He reenlisted in Company B, now under Captain Charles Francis Stevens, at Ysleta as a private on November 25, 1919. His welcome return to the service on December 7 was enriched with a promotion to sergeant eight days later. On the last day of the month, Hamer accompanied his captain across the border to Ciudad Juárez to meet with Mexican authorities.[88]

For decades, Texas and Oklahoma had disagreed over whether the middle of the Red River or its south bank constituted the exact line between the two states. The origins of the argument lay in the vague language of the Adams-Onís Treaty of 1819 that had established the border between the possessions of the Spanish crown and the lands belonging to the United States. The resulting mess proved to be one of the most complex boundary disputes in American history. Complicating matters, the Burkburnett oil boom had commenced in 1918, and wells were soon being drilled in the Red River's floodplain. Interest centered on a 480-acre tract in the riverbed known as the Burk Divide, which was estimated to be worth over five million dollars. Texas and Oklahoma claimed ownership of portions of the riverbed. Texas claimants responded on August 16, 1919, by petitioning Judge George Calhoun of the Fifty-third District Court for a temporary injunction halting drilling in the disputed area. Calhoun and a counterpart in Oklahoma each appointed receivers to manage the contested properties until the legal cases were adjudicated.[89]

On March 16, 1920, verbal orders from the adjutant general, and written orders from the governor instructed Captain Joseph B. "Joe" Brooks and Hamer, and Ranger George W. Robinson of Company F, to the Burk Divide property. After the captain assumed command of the detachment already in place at that location, their assignment was to assist James Lynn Hunt, the receiver appointed by Judge Calhoun, in enforcing the court's order. Brooks was to also "preserve peace and order, enforce the laws of Texas, protect the lives and property of citizens from unlawful depredations by outside armed bands, and … disarm every individual found armed who is not a duly qualified or acting Peace Officer under the laws of Texas." Hamer had already visited the oil field in northern Wichita County two months previously when the governor had ordered the Rangers to enforce an injunction issued by Calhoun. However, the U.S. Supreme Court, not a state judge, had constitutional authority to render judgement in a boundary dispute between two states. On March 10, six days before the Rangers' arrival, Federal Judge Frank Abijah Youmans, temporarily presiding over the Western District of Oklahoma in Enid, had granted a temporary injunction against Texas claimants. However, motivated by the potential taxation from oil revenues, Governor Hobby ordered the Rangers to arrest Tillman County, Oklahoma, deputy sheriffs, the only armed men from that state in the Burk Divide, and to openly oppose Deputy U.S. Marshal Frank Morgan, who had served the federal court order. While Judge Youmans considered contempt of court charges, the Supreme Court issued an injunction on April 1, halting Texas's control of the oil wells, and appointed Frederick A. Delano as receiver over the entire disputed territory. On April 11 of the following year, the High Court ruled that the cut bank on the south side of the Red River constituted the true boundary. Throughout his time in Wichita County, Hamer dutifully obeyed his superiors, and his true feelings on the legal and ethical aspects of the matter are unknown. The episode does, however, present another example of gubernatorial misuse of the Ranger Force as a political instrument.[90]

On April 10, 1920, Hamer was ordered to his new station at Austin. Perhaps disenchanted by the Burk Divide incident or motivated by a fifteen-hundred-dollar annual salary, he was honorably discharged on May 11, and became a federal Prohibition agent the same day. He was assigned to the San Antonio office managed by Chief Prohibition Officer Thomas Ralph Stevic, although he worked with his old captain, John H. Rogers, now a U.S. marshal, in closing two cases in Austin. Indeed, Clifford G. Beckham, Stevic's superior in Austin, was short of investigators in the state capital, so Hamer was detailed there the following month. The increased income allowed Hamer to finally purchase his own home. Since April, the family had stayed in a hotel in town until they purchased a house at 1007 Riverside Drive in Travis Heights from Johnson Brent Hewey for $5,500. The deed was transferred to Gladys on July 1, and the Hamers moved into their new residence four days later. Hamer took a deep pride in his home and, no matter his later assignments, lived there the rest of his life.[91]

Getting immediately to work, he conducted a raid on a residence immediately outside the city limits where he seized six barrels of wine and an additional vessel of mash. The home's occupant was arrested and charged with "manufacturing and the illegal possession of intoxicating liquor." The offender was released on a five-hundred-dollar bond. On August 30, Hamer raided a house in the eastern part of the city, where he seized eighty-eight pints of liquor and arrested two men and one woman. The female and one of the males escaped before they could be brought before the U.S. commissioner. While in Austin, Hamer was one of approximately twenty-five state and federal law officers who took part in a three-day conference to discuss better enforcement methods for the national prohibition laws. Marshal Rogers and former Ranger James C. White, a federal Prohibition agent in San Antonio, were also in attendance.[92]

Hamer's direct supervisor, Thomas Stevic, was a former army captain who had served in France during the war. He was appointed to his position through the influence of his uncle, Doctor Charles Elmer Sawyer, close friend and personal physician of President Warren Gamaliel Harding. No career lawman, Stevic was personally corrupt and was said to have connections to the Black Hand in Chicago. Completely misjudging the man, he approached Hamer and offered the ex-Ranger a percentage of his crooked transactions. Notifying the Department of Justice, Hamer was instructed to feign acceptance and gather evidence of Stevic's malfeasance. Finally, the chief agent and three of his cronies were arrested on August 10 and charged with conspiring to import, transport, and sell liquor. Stevic waived examination and was bound over for the grand jury. His bond was fixed at a total of two thousand dollars. Two more coconspirators were arrested the next day. The six men were indicted by the federal grand jury in December, due in part to Hamer's investigation. On January 19, 1921, Stevic pled guilty and was sentenced to 366 days in the federal penitentiary at Leavenworth, Kansas, and a fifty-dollar fine. Going behind the prison's walls on February 3, he served only two months before being released on a writ of *habeas corpus* arranged by his pretty French war bride. She might have been aided by his uncle's connections to the president, while Federal District Judge John Pollock ordered Stevic to be freed due to a flawed indictment. Although Hamer was disgusted with the entire episode, Stevic's temporary successor was, happily, Charles Stevens, ex-captain of Rangers and Frank's old boss.[93]

Throughout its existence, the Prohibition Bureau was perpetually understaffed, underfunded, and otherwise insufficient to enforce laws that did not possess widespread popular support. Approximately 8 percent of the unit's agents were dismissed for cause. The exposure of Stevic's nefarious activities, and rumors of other corruption in the bureau, resulted in a reorganization. James Shevlin, the respected chief agent for New York, was promoted in October to head the new Border Department consisting of Texas, New Mexico, and Arizona. Hamer's experience and abilities were sorely needed in El Paso, which had become a center for liquor smuggling. By early January 1921, he was assigned to the border city.[94]

On the morning of January 9, the recently arrived Hamer and several agents were sitting in an automobile, watching the border at Cordova Island. In the darkness, they observed two suspicious individuals crossing the river and ordered them to halt. The suspects piled into a waiting vehicle, loosed a few gunshots at the lawmen, and raced down the road. Hamer and the other agents pursued the pair north into the center of El Paso, reaching a speed of sixty miles per hour. When the fugitives approached the intersection of Copia Street and Alameda Avenue, the lawmen opened fire, their bullets puncturing the gas tank and the left front tire. The vehicle crashed into the curb, and the passengers bailed out. One of them was identified as Manuel Osollo, a taxi driver and suspected smuggler, who was apprehended a few hours later. The lawmen seized ninety quarts of tequila from the automobile. Osollo was charged with receiving smuggled property and concealing and transporting illegal liquor. Appearing before U.S. Commissioner

Albert Jacob William Schmid, he smiled widely while pleading not guilty, and his bond was set at two thousand dollars.[95]

Working from the San Antonio office on February 24, Hamer arrested Mastin Burgess Ussery and Eugene Morgan for possession of a thirty-five-gallon still and 150 gallons of mash near their Luling home. The pair were charged with the manufacture of liquor and property intended for the production of liquor. The Prohibition agent took them before U.S. Commissioner Roy C. Archer later that afternoon, but their cases in federal district court were repeatedly continued until June 12, 1922. The defendants pled guilty at their trial, and Morgan paid of a fine of one hundred dollars and Ussery fifty dollars.[96]

The day after Hamer had arrested Ussery and Morgan, Customs inspector Joseph Eugene "Joe" Davenport halted a pack train of potential *tequileros* eight miles to the west of El Paso. Davenport was wounded in the subsequent gun battle, but Customs officers seized 407 quarts of tequila and twenty-two pints of whiskey. Hamer and other federal agents rushed to the scene, but the smugglers had already fled across the border. Agent Jonathan Dansby "Jay" Reeder led a party of Customs men across the state line into New Mexico and arrested five men in connection with the Davenport shooting. The prisoners were taken before the U.S. commissioner in Las Cruces for arraignment.[97]

On March 2, Hamer was informed a farmer and an El Paso policeman were fired upon by two *contrabandistas* guarding a cache of liquor on Cordova Island at the end of Second Street. Along with Agent Ernest Walter Walker, the former Ranger swiftly drove to the scene. Fellow agent Stafford E. Beckett and narcotics inspector Charles Archibold "Arch" Wood quickly arrived, and they all began to search the brush. Suddenly, the four federal officers encountered twenty-five armed smugglers who were moving toward the twenty-one cases of hidden alcohol. The Mexicans opened fire, and Hamer and Walker rushed to cover, firing as they ran. Walker was struck in the abdomen by a steel-jacketed bullet, and Hamer covered his colleague with a fusillade of fire from his Remington rifle. The smugglers were driven back to shelter in the trenches and adobe houses. Reinforcements rushed from El Paso, and the federal agents, provost guards, and policemen battled the fortified Mexicans for two hours; more than one thousand rounds of ammunition were expended. The Mexicans slipped away, and the Americans were unaware of that fact until Rafael D. Davila, chief of the customs guards in Juárez, crossed the border and informed them. The critically wounded Walker was taken to the Hotel Dieu Hospital, and the other Prohibition agents returned to the scene the next day to search for the fallen officer's lost pistol. As they searched through the brush, another band of smugglers opened fire, and the two sides traded gunshots until the Mexicans once more disappeared. Walker died of his wounds on March 5, but he was not the only El Paso-based Prohibition agent to be slain that year.[98]

According to Albert Lawrence Raithel, Sr., a one-time federal narcotics agent in El Paso, Hamer steadfastly opposed the standard practice of standing and calling out "*manos arriba*" (hands up) when confronting *contradbandistas*. Too many times these encounters ended in a firefight and, all too often, at least one dead lawman. His attitude had been doubtless reinforced by the violent deaths of four Texas Rangers and five federal officers along the border in the last five years, Delbert Timberlake and Ernest Walker among them. Instead, on one particular night, Hamer demonstrated his preferred technique. Accompanied by agents Raithel, Arch Wood, and Elmer Birdie McClure, Hamer settled into position atop a sand dune overlooking the international boundary. They soon observed six armed Mexicans bearing liquor cases cross the river in the moonlight. Raithel recounted that Hamer whispered, "Don't do anything until I give the word. When I give the word, do as exactly as I do." Hamer waited patiently until the *tequileros* had reached American soil, then shouted, "OK!" As he spoke, he and McClure unleashed a barrage of lead, killing all six. The shooting was so swift that Raithel was only able to fire once, while Wood did not have the chance to use his weapon at all. Hamer indicated the smugglers' bodies and commented, "Now holler *manos arriba* at these sons of bitches and see how many of them shoot you." This practice obviously denied the smugglers access to due process and would never be considered acceptable by modern standards, but, in those deadly times on the border, Hamer was determined to offer violent lawbreakers few options. His resolve was likely further strengthened by the fate of Arch Wood and Stafford Beckett, both of whom were killed on March 22 by bootleggers at a hog ranch located five miles east of El Paso. Additionally, Prohibition agent John Watson was mortally wounded in a fight with rumrunners, and died at Hotel Dieu Hospital on May 2.[99]

Hamer was transferred to San Antonio on March 16, but his stint in the Alamo City proved brief. His efforts in El Paso had brought him recognition from his superiors, and, in early May, he was promoted to chief agent for the district encompassing Austin.[100] Despite the promotion, Hamer continued to lead in the field. On May 9, he filed a complaint on Joe Malisch, a farmer who lived seven miles south of Taylor. The actual arrest was carried out by Deputy U.S. Marshal Arley Vance Knight, and a search of Malisch's property uncovered a working still and five gallons of corn whiskey. Appearing before Commissioner Archer, the suspect's bond was fixed at five hundred dollars. The next day, Hamer assisted Austin police detectives James Newell Littlepage and Edward Lafayette "Lafe" Young, and Officer Adolphus Love Bugg, in raiding a back room at the Avenue Hotel on Congress Avenue. The lawmen arrested twenty men who had been engaged in a craps game. The prisoners were taken to police headquarters where the majority each paid $19.80 in fines and costs, and the remainder posted bail. Austin police officers raided a home at Fourteenth and Red River Streets on May 11, and discovered a hidden cache of forty-five one-pint bottles of corn whiskey. The house's occupants, a married couple, were arrested, and subsequent investigation by Travis County and Austin officers led to a still in the Bee Cave country west of town the following morning. They seized fifty gallons of "alleged perfectly good" corn whiskey and poured the liquor into the Colorado River. An additional five-gallon keg of whiskey, five barrels of mash, and a large still were uncovered. The two cases were turned over to Hamer, who filed complaints in federal court. On May 28, Hamer directed the largest liquor raid in Central Texas since the passage of the Eighteenth Amendment. Armed with warrants issued by Commissioner Archer, and supported by Prohibition agent Coley White and four Rangers, Hamer traveled to two farms near Thorndale, fifty miles northeast of Austin. The law officers seized eight large whiskey stills, six hundred gallons of corn mash, several gallons of whiskey, and large amounts of sugar and cornmeal. The moonshining farmers were lodged in the Williamson and Milam County jails.[101]

In the midst of his numerous investigations, Hamer was the subject of a complaint for assault with intent to kill. The Prohibition agent, Police Sergeant Robert Edward Nitschke, Sr., and Officer Bugg had apprehended Tom W. Hamby and Leon Koch on the night of June 7 for possession of intoxicating liquor. Hamer had apparently been forced to pistol-whip Hamby while making the arrest on East Sixth Street. In addition to Volstead Act violations, Hamer entered a charge of forcibly resisting an officer against Hamby before Commissioner Archer. Freed on a one-thousand-dollar bond, Hamby filed his own suit on Hamer in George Washington Mendell, Sr.'s justice court the next morning, and claimed the agent had shot at him with a pistol. The liquor cases were set for trial on the seventeenth. On June 8, a foray to a farm three miles south of Taylor on the Rice's Crossing road netted Hamer, Constable Louis Lowe, and Deputy W. P. McConnell a still, 125 gallons of mash, wine, corn whiskey, and Joe Volney, the operator. Volney was arraigned before Commissioner Archer and released on a bond of one thousand dollars. More arrests followed on June 13. Four days later, in Judge Duval West's federal courtroom, Hamer described how Hamby had struck him with a fist and attempted to flee in an automobile that contained three 1-quart bottles of tequila. The defendant was found guilty on all counts and assessed a sentence of three months in the county jail and a one-dollar fine; charges against Koch were dismissed.[102]

Hamer was once more able to exercise his distaste for corrupt politicians and government officials on August 25, when he arrested two state legislators who were subsequently charged with the transportation and possession of alcohol. In the same week, Hamer arrested Edgar Louis "Ed" Moeller, city marshal of New Braunfels, for bootlegging. On August 27, Prohibition Director David H. Morris supervised a raid on a residence on Rainey Street and two grocery stores on Sixth. Morris, Hamer, Agents Bassett Miles and Morris Arnold Moore, and Deputy U.S. Marshal Paul Alvin Lockhart seized a total of 415 gallons of wine and a sizeable quantity of flavoring extract. Three suspects were arrested, and one was charged with possession of intoxicating liquors and the other two with selling extract for beverage purposes in violation of the prohibition laws.[103]

By an act of the Thirty-seventh Legislature, the Ranger Force was reduced to fifty officers and men. Meanwhile, Hamer was interested in obtaining a captaincy in the reorganized service, but he possessed few friends amongst Austin's political elite. Hence, his application was ignored until Governor Pat Morris Neff personally offered him the position. Neff was a staunch supporter of the Prohibition experiment, and of law enforcement, and he desired a professional Ranger service. Hamer resigned from the Prohibition Unit on August 29, 1921, effective September 15. Replacing Aaron Washington Cunningham, he was appointed captain of Company C at Del Rio on September 1, and scheduled to assume his new duties exactly one month later.[104]

A friend and admirer of Hamer, Professor Walter Prescott Webb once wrote of the new captain:

> He is respected by the rangers, by the citizens and even by the crooks. The rangers respect him, and acknowledge him as a leader, because of his sublime courage, because of his willingness to face any danger in the performance of his duty, and because he has never been known to show the white feather … The citizens respect Hamer because they know that he is a terror to the criminal and the crook. And strange to say, the crooks and criminals respect him too. Captain Hamer is what the crooks call a "square shooter," that is to say, he fights the criminal fairly, though with terrible vigor. He is noted for the fact that he will not take an unfair advantage of anyone, gunman or bootlegger.[105]

Reaching his station early, Hamer reported to Aldrich on September 9: "Arrived in Del Rio and took charge of the company. Things have been running mighty loose. Nothing's being done at all. I'll make a more definitive report later." Cunningham had declined as a leader and administrator, but the quartermaster expressed his confidence in the new captain: "The Del Rio territory is where we had most of the 'kick' from, and Frank will have plenty to do to get things straightened out … I believe that he can straighten out that mess out there if anybody can." Acting swiftly, Hamer discharged every man in the company, except for Charles E. Miller, and recruited a new slate of Rangers.[106]

Shortly after taking over the company, Hamer helped to end the career of a murderous outlaw who had left a trail of corpses from Utah to Texas. Years earlier, on November 21, 1913, Rafael Lopez had killed fellow miner Juan Valdez in the Highland Boy camp adjoining Bingham, Utah, over a family dispute. In the subsequent chase, Lopez, a man with a history of violent assaults, killed from ambush five law officers—Police Chief John William "Billy" Grant, Deputy Sheriffs Otto Witbeck and Nephi Stannard Jensen, and posse members James Douglas Hulsey and Thomas Manderich—at a ranch

Company C, Ranger Force, ca. 1921. Front (L-R): E. B. McClure, F. A. Hamer, J. A. Gillon, M. T. Gonzaullas; Middle (L-R): W. L. Barler, C. Darlington, C. E. Miller; Rear (L-R): H. D. Glasscock, N. B. Jones, C. A. Carta, O. Latta. *Courtesy Randy Lish.*

house nine miles west of Lehi, and at the Minnie claim in the Utah-Apex diggings near Bingham. Escaping through the mine's labyrinth of tunnels and exits, Lopez then fled the state, while a reward of one thousand dollars was posted for his capture. In later months, he was reportedly spotted in Chicago and Los Angeles.[107]

According to legend, the following year, Lopez and a gang of bandits robbed a train traveling along the Mexican border and killed nineteen American passengers. The massacre supposedly sparked a massive manhunt, and Lopez remained at large for another eight years. This tale is undoubtedly false. Instead, Colonel Pablo López, said to be Rafael's uncle, and one hundred *villaistas* ambushed a train carrying nineteen American mining engineers at Santa Ysabel on January 10, 1916. All but one of the mining men were executed; the lone survivor managed to escape. While Rafael may have fought in the revolution, no evidence has been discovered placing him at the scene of this particular bloodbath. To complicate matters, he has also been confused with *maderista* leader Arturo "Red" López whose *insurrectos* commandeered a train and held the town of Agua Prieta for several days in April 1911.[108]

Nevertheless, Rafael Lopez was wanted in Texas for a series of felonies, and Hamer, commanding the Rangers at Del Rio, knew of the killings in Utah. In October 1921, the captain was alerted by an informant that Lopez was riding with a gang of smugglers operating between Coahuila and Del Rio. The mole also provided the fugitive's pending location near Quemado at a particular date and time. Hamer organized a posse, including Charles Miller and possibly Ranger Manuel T. Gonzaullas, and placed them in an irrigation ditch from which to take the outlaw gang when they arrived. Soon after, some sense of intuition prompted Hamer to shift his squad to another ambush site thirty yards away. Just as the posse members settled into their new position, they observed twenty heavily armed men stealthily approaching the irrigation ditch from behind. The snitch's information had been a trap. Seemingly violating his own rule, Hamer called in Spanish for the outlaws to surrender. The startled bandits instead started shooting. As a bullet from the first shot grazed the captain's cheek, the posse returned fire. Hamer triggered his Remington Model 8 autoloading rifle as swiftly as possible. Moments after the gunfire began, eleven bandits were lying dead, and the rest were fleeing. The first outlaw to die was Lopez, who had been killed by a bullet from Hamer's rifle. The slug had pierced a gold watch Lopez had been carrying in the pocket of his bib overalls and lodged in his heart. Hamer gave the watch to his brother Harrison, a Customs officer at that time. Harrison displayed the timepiece in the window of the Customs House in Laredo for ten years as a warning to other evildoers. The treacherous informant apparently fell from his horse the day after the shooting, and died of a broken neck.[109]

The family of Deputy Jensen first learned that the outlaw had been slain in Texas in November 2002. Due to the limited telephone system and decentralized nature of law enforcement at the time, authorities in Utah were never informed of the killer's death. Only after Jensen's grandson read of the gun battle in a copy of "*I'm Frank Hamer*" did the family finally suspect the truth. Their suspicions were confirmed by Randy Lish, a court services officer with the Salt Lake County Sheriff's Department. The deputy had read Lynn Bailey's book *The Search for Lopez* in 1994, and *Manhunter*, Gene Shelton's novelized biography of Frank Hamer, in 1998. Making the connection, Lish proceeded to conduct an exhaustive investigation into the decades-old deaths of his brother officers. While officially authorized in March 2001, he pursued the many leads at his own expense, including securing an interview with the then-eighty-four-year-old Frank, Jr. By November 2002, Lish had conclusively established that the Rafael Lopez who murdered six men in Utah was the same individual who died by Frank Hamer's hand in Texas. As a result, the Salt Lake County district attorney declared the eighty-nine-year-old homicide case to be officially closed on January 24, 2003.[110]

Hamer's first six months as a Ranger captain had been a success. While he would reap the rewards of a fruitful tenure in Del Rio, he and Gladys were overjoyed to welcome their second son, Billy Beckham, born on December 3, 1921. Later in the month, Frank was ordered to switch places with Captain Roy Carlisle Nichols and assume command of Headquarters Company in Austin, effective January 1, 1922. By virtue of his new position in the service's chain of command, Hamer was now the senior captain of the Ranger Force.[111]

Professor Webb later described the role Headquarters Company played:

> The duties of this company differ somewhat from those of the other companies, either border or interior. Whereas the other companies operate in a particular section, the headquarters men operate all over the state. One week they make a raid in the Panhandle of north Texas; the next week we may hear of them investigating a murder case in the Rio Grande Valley of the Mexican border. All the members of this company are stalwart men, physically strong and of proved courage.[112]

Hamer, Adjutant General Thomas Dickson Barton, Captain Tom R. Hickman, eleven Rangers, and seven federal Prohibition agents, including Manuel Gonzaullas, traveled to the oil boomtown of Mexia to crack down on the lawlessness in the area. The once-quiet Limestone County seat of 2,500 residents, situated forty-one miles east of Waco, had exploded into a wild hellhole of 55,000 by year's end. Captain Aldrich was informed the town was "tougher than Breckenridge in its palmiest days. Gambling rooms are wide open, high-jackers galore, women running gambling joints and boot legging outfits, liquor sold in the open." Indeed, liquor, narcotics, and games of chance were peddled overtly in the red-light district known as "Juarez," while murder and robbery flourished. Illicit distilleries were erected along the streams outside the city. Working undercover, Ranger Horace C. Greathouse of Company C and an unnamed federal agent were able to compile maps displaying the liquor operations in Mexia, including distribution depots and retail sellers. On January 7, 1922, fifteen well-armed state and federal officers launched raids on two notorious illegal establishments situated just across the line in Freestone County—the Winter Garden, located four miles from Mexia on the Teague highway, and the Chicken Farm, near the oil town of Wortham. Hamer, his Headquarters Rangers, and Prohibition agents under Group Head William Ware Edwards of Houston descended on the Winter Garden at eleven o'clock at night, while Hickman, his detachment, and Prohibition Inspector Morris A. Moore simultaneously struck the Chicken Farm. Altogether, the raiders seized gambling paraphernalia, three automobiles, and 165 gallons of bootleg whiskey and corn liquor worth over ten thousand dollars.

Twenty-two managers and employees were arrested. The upscale Chicken Farm had operated a brisk trade just two hundred yards from the home of a Limestone County deputy sheriff. He had sold the four acres on which the drinking joint stood for $750 per acre, but the deputy later feigned ignorance of what transpired literally next door. Other local officials expressed amazement that the dives had even existed. Eight of the men arrested appeared before U.S. Commissioner Andrew Phelps McCormick in Waco for a preliminary hearing.[113]

The lawmen followed up on their initial success with raids on the Bowie, Commercial, and Derrick Hotels on January 9. They seized liquor and gaming devices and apprehended thirty suspects. They also accumulated evidence implicating five Limestone County deputies. More troubling, the state and federal officers noted a series of obstructions from judges who refused to sign search warrants, citizens who feared to come forward, and city and county law enforcement personnel who failed to act.[114]

Dissatisfied with the paltry amount of assistance from local officials, Governor Neff declared martial law on January 11, to take effect the next day in Precinct No. 4 in Limestone County, including the city of Mexia, and Precinct Nos. 5 and 6 in Freestone County.[115] Among the reasons he cited were the:

> … open and flagrant violation of the law, in this, that highway robbery is of frequent occurrence accompanied in some cases by the murder of peaceful and law-abiding citizens; gambling houses are in full operation day and night protected by armed men; intoxicating liquor is being openly sold … a multitude of unfortunate women ply their nefarious business in houses of ill fame, and the local officers are either unable or unwilling to maintain and enforce the law.[116]

On the twelfth, Brigadier-General Jacob Franklin Wolters arrived to assume command of the martial law zone, with headquarters at City Hall. Seven officers and forty-seven National Guardsmen from the Fifty-sixth Cavalry Brigade marched into Mexia the next day and encamped at the Winter Garden. Approximately three thousand people promptly left town for easier locales. Hamer and Hickman remained on the scene with thirteen Rangers. Assistant Attorney General Clifford L. Stone and Major Chester H. Machen, Judge Advocate of the Texas National Guard, were on hand to act as legal advisors. Fire raged through the business district on the fourteenth, and a mob of approximately fifteen thousand formed. State troops dispersed the crowd as Rangers walked the streets to thwart any looting. With martial law in effect, certain civil liberties were suspended, including Fourth Amendment guarantees, and the state lawmen were free to conduct searches without the need for probable cause or warrants. As Wolters informed a reporter, "The Rangers made the arrests, aided in some raids by a detail of soldiers, and the soldiers transported the prisoners to camp and guarded them." The jail in Mexia was not large enough to house the number of persons arrested, so the Rangers transferred their prisoners to nearby counties. The suspects were then taken to Groesbeck where the grand jury was in session. Those charged under federal law were transported from there to Waco. In all, the Rangers and the Guardsmen made 602 arrests on such charges as bootlegging, highway robbery, theft, gambling, possession of stolen property, carrying prohibited weapons, and the sale and use of narcotics. The law officers seized twenty-seven distilleries, five thousand dollars in gaming equipment, and four thousand dollars' worth of narcotics. In the process, they destroyed 215 barrels of corn mash and 2,270 gallons of liquor. They also recovered fifty-three stolen automobiles and impounded thirteen vehicles under federal forfeiture laws.[117]

As conditions improved, the Reverend Pitser Duff Tucker, Sr. of the First Southern Presbyterian Church announced on January 21 he would hold Sunday afternoon services the next day at Camp Winter Garden; other pastors and church elders followed his example. By January 28, County Attorney Lon Eubanks, the chief deputy sheriff, four deputies, one police officer, and a number of former peace officers were among the seventy violators of the national Prohibition laws arraigned before Commissioner McCormick and bound over for the next federal grand jury. Eubanks was released on a one-thousand-dollar cash bond, and his trial was scheduled for January 20, 1923. Embarrassed by the criminality in their community, law-abiding Mexiaites took a renewed interest in local government. They held public meetings, and the various law enforcement agencies in the county—the county attorney, sheriff, and city police—were reorganized. The governor formally lifted martial law on March 1, even though the majority of the soldiers had departed the previous day. Speaking before the state convention of the Anti-Saloon League, Neff vowed, "While I am Governor of Texas, no band of criminals will ever take charge of a community as long as a Texas Ranger can pull a trigger."[118]

On January 13, Hamer had displayed his shooting prowess in an impromptu exhibition behind the Winter Garden. Using his Remington .25, he smashed butter dishes out of the air and greatly captivated a watching Remington Arms Company salesman. The representative contacted his superiors, and the equally impressed company officials shipped an engraved, gold-inlaid Remington Model 8F in .30-caliber to Frederick Frank "Fred" Petmecky's sporting goods store in Austin. The rifle was later presented to the surprised Ranger.[119]

In his special report on martial law activities, General Barton reported that the Rangers commanded by Hamer and Hickman had "proved themselves to be gentlemen in the broadest sense of that often misused term. Courageous and impersonal in the performance of duty, they exemplified on every occasion the highest ideals and the best traditions of the Ranger Force that constitutes so great a part of the glorious history of Texas."[120]

In mid-October, Hamer was assigned to take charge of the Rangers on strike duty in Amarillo, Texline, and Dalhart. On the thirteenth, he met with officials of the adjutant general's department and reported on the tranquil conditions in the Panhandle. Five days later, Hamer reiterated Amarillo, Childress, and Texline were quiet, and by the following month peaceful conditions would be observed all along the railroad. Late in October, Hamer was in conference with Chief Deputy Collector of Customs Edward "Ed" Cotulla and Bureau of Investigation (BOI) agent-in-charge Gus Tiner "Buster" Jones in San Antonio. The three officials were discussing the more than $200,000 in automobiles stolen in the Panhandle region of Texas, Oklahoma, and New Mexico in the previous three years. Hamer suspected a gang of car thieves and rumrunners who, while operating from a base in Northern Mexico, stole expensive vehicles from the United States and transported them across the border. Once south of the Rio Grande, the automobiles, including

Cadillacs and Packards, were stripped of any means of identification, remodeled, and repainted. They were then sold in Mexico or shipped back north. Hamer identified one point of entry into Mexico as a seldom-used bridge near a smelter one hundred miles below El Paso.[121]

The Ku Klux Klan had emerged in Texas by October 1920, ostensibly to correct the social problems affecting the state. The Klansmen portrayed themselves as a law-and-order league, and actively recruited men of good standing. Indeed, they may have even enjoyed the support of the adjutant general. However, the KKK's violent, racist impulses soon became apparent, as they were responsible for some eighty floggings by July 1921. When a young Tenaha woman suspected of bigamy was kidnapped, beaten with a wet rope, and tarred and feathered, public opinion began turning against the Klan in Texas.[122] A letter from a private citizen to the editor of the *Dallas Morning News* stated:

> When a mob of masked men take a lash, a kettle of tar and a bag of feathers, go forth under cover of darkness, overpower a man or woman, carry him or her to some lonely spot, and carry out their nefarious intentions, and still proclaim that they are for upholding the Constitution, can any one [*sic*] believe them? When in this manner they trample the law under their feet, are they 100 per cent American?[123]

Despite the growing opposition, the "Invisible Empire" of over one hundred chapters in the state continued to act. Among its estimated seventy-five to ninety thousand members were numerous legislators, prosecutors, jurists, federal marshals, police officials and sheriffs, and journalists. The Anti-Klan League demanded the governor produce the names of any Klan members in the Rangers or the National Guard. On May 10, 1922, Neff ordered Barton to investigate. The adjutant general reported that his inquiries had failed to produce anyone who admitted to Klan membership. Neff called attention to the fact the majority of Rangers were stationed in West Texas where the Klan had a minimal presence.[124]

On November 16, a mob of approximately three hundred armed white supremacists stalked through the streets of Breckenridge, demanding local Mexicans and blacks leave the city within twenty-four hours. Even after they pleaded for official protection, local Hispanic leaders were told by the mayor he could not guarantee their safety. Scores of those who were at risk left town. Don Enrique D. Ruíz, the Mexican consul general in San Antonio, requested the State Department intervene, but the latter lacked jurisdiction. Secretary of State Charles Evans Hughes, Sr. did, however, convince Governor Neff to dispatch Rangers over the objections of Breckenridge officials. The state officers arrived on the seventeenth. Encountering local opposition, Hamer and three of his men nevertheless sought to uncover the identities of those who had made threats and committed violence. At his behest, BOI Agent James Porter "J. P." Huddleston was assigned to the case. Huddleston had just completed an investigation into a Ku Klux Klan murder of two men in Mer Rouge, Louisiana. Hamer and Huddleston determined the "White Owls," a racist vigilante organization, were responsible for the move to expel the Mexicans from Breckenridge. Beyond this revelation, the state and federal lawmen were unable to bring any of the culprits to justice. They left town within two weeks of their arrival, but their presence had been enough to restore order and curtail further acts of intimidation and violence. Interestingly, a mere three years after the Canales hearings and the service's reorganization, the Rangers were now publicly perceived as protectors of Mexican rights rather than oppressors.[125]

Even while Hamer warred with violent white supremacist groups, the enforcement of Prohibition was still a concern. Austin authorities were alerted to a high-powered automobile en route to San Antonio with a load of illegal liquor. Hamer and Travis County officers attempted to interdict the car near Elgin on March 16, 1923, but the rumrunners opened fire on the law officers and broke through the gauntlet. As deputies in Hays and Comal unsuccessfully attempted to halt the vehicle, twenty gallons of alcohol were poured out on the road in its wake; nine quarts were recovered intact. Two men visited the Prohibition service headquarters in San Antonio and confessed to owning the suspected automobile, but they claimed they had rented it to another man. However, the pair were unable to furnish either his name or address. Disbelieving their story, the Travis County grand jury indicted the two suspects for violation of the Dean Law. Hamer left for San Antonio the next day to extradite them to Austin.[126]

Klansmen whipped and tarred Robert W. Burleson, a traveling sock salesman and reputed Lothario, in Taylor on April 1. Neff abstained from ordering the Rangers to investigate, which has led some to believe he harbored pro-Klan sentiments. Regardless of the governor's true opinions on the matter, his hesitancy emboldened white supremacists into committing other acts of violence. Railroad worker Otto Lange was shot by a party of masked men while sitting on his porch approximately two miles from Somerville on July 2. As he fell mortally wounded, his three-year-old daughter was likewise hit, "having part of her hand shot off." A motive for the murder was not readily apparent. Captain Aldrich initially worked the case, but he was unable to make any headway. Acting in Neff's stead while the executive was out of the country, Lieutenant Governor Thomas Whitfield Davidson was not satisfied with Aldrich's report, and Captain Roy Nichols made a point of assuring him the quartermaster was no Klansman. Four days after the killing, Davidson, keenly opposed to the Klan, assigned Hamer and Ranger Ollie Burnett Chesshir to the investigation. The state officers cooperated with District Judge Richard Julius Alexander, Burleson County Attorney Albert Benjamin Gerland, Sheriff Clint DeWitt Lewis, and Washington County Sheriff Burney Parker, Sr.[127]

The Rangers discovered that masked vigilantes had previously committed approximately six acts of violence. However, they were informed by Constable William Sledge Houston, Sr. of Somerville, a leader in the local klavern, that the Klan had not been involved in the Lange homicide. Despite an exhaustive investigation, neither Hamer nor Aldrich could secure any conclusive evidence implicating the secret order. Aldrich relayed to reporters an alternate theory that the killing had been the result of "family difficulties." The lawmen nevertheless developed evidence that a pair of workers at the Santa Fe roundhouse in town were responsible for the murder. Additionally, the two suspects, Kinch Milam Shelburne and Charles Herman Balke, Jr., were believed to be former Klansmen. Hamer and Sheriff Lewis provided a special session of the grand jury with the information that had been gathered. No arrests or indictments ensued, but the sheriff continued to work the case, and he, two Rangers, and District Attorney Merton Leonard Harris slowly accumulated proof of Shelburne and Balke's involvement. Lange's death had been "an outgrowth of the bitter klan fight that was waged in [the] county." The suspects were finally indicted on June 11, 1926, and taken into custody the next day. Rangers transported Shelburne to Belton for safekeeping, while Balke was taken to Caldwell. In a *habeas corpus* hearing, Judge Joseph Burton "J. B." Price of the Twenty-first District Court set bail at five thousand dollars each. However, the case against Balke was dismissed on November 30. After a postponement and a continuance, Shelburne's murder trial ended with a conviction on June 11, 1927, and the defendant was given five years in prison.[128]

General Barton, Hamer, and three Rangers were ordered to San Antonio to enforce Prohibition. The Alamo City had been particularly lax in adhering to the law, and the staunch Baptist in the governor's mansion wanted to make an example. On July 24, 1923, the Rangers raided the Pastime Club at 103 South Flores Street and arrested twenty-six employees and patrons. The suspects, several of whom were prominent citizens, were charged at the county jail. The state officers swooped down on other speakeasies and gambling dens. While District Attorney Duncan Alexander McAskill publicly approved of their work, Fire and Police Commissioner Phil Lee Wright, Mayor John Wallace Tobin, and Chamber of Commerce President Claude Vivian Birkhead all opposed the Rangers' presence. Ironically, the Pastime had been on the second story of a building located across the street from City Hall. Hamer and his men raided other vice dens on Pecan and Losoya Streets and arrested a number of bootleggers. Unfortunately, witnesses proved reluctant to testify, local authorities failed to prosecute, and the grand jury returned only twenty indictments, mostly for misdemeanors. As Hamer was needed elsewhere, Neff authorized an additional Ranger company under Captain Berkhead Clarence Baldwin to take over.[129]

On August 15, members of the Klan flogged, and subsequently tarred and feathered, Fort Worth & Denver Railroad worker Elijah Thomas McDonald, an alleged bootlegger, in Amarillo. At the same time, more Klansmen flogged a suspected lawbreaker at Iowa Park in Wichita County. The next day, Acting Governor Davidson ordered Hamer to Amarillo to investigate the group's misdeeds. Additionally, two brothers suspected of killing Port Arthur Police Detective Ben A. Harris were kidnapped from the front door of city hall and whipped on the seventeenth. After Neff returned to Austin on August 19, he continued to employ the Rangers to quell the Klan's activities. Once Hamer left Canyon, where he had maintained order during an important murder trial, the captain was expected to submit his report on the Somerville and Amarillo investigations. On August 20 the appointed day, Hamer was not in the state capital, nor were Aldrich or Sergeant James Walter McCormick able to deliver their reports on the Port Arthur and Iowa Park floggings. Barton believed Hamer was en route from Amarillo to Austin. The senior captain was also due to testify in the first trials resulting from the Pastime Club raid in San Antonio the previous month.[130]

Despite the amount of evidence provided to them, local prosecutors failed to gain convictions in Wichita Falls and Port Arthur. In Amarillo, Hamer was able, by August 17, to gather sufficient proof implicating five Klan members for the cases to be taken to the grand jury. Potter County Sheriff Less Whitaker and County Attorney Henry L. Ford were indicted on September 12 for misconduct in office, and Thomas W. Stanford, George O. Gall, W. L. Honeycutt, and Andy Knox were charged with whitecapping and assault with a prohibited weapon. Local Klan leader Stanford was convicted on October 12 and sentenced to two years in prison, but the charges against the county attorney were dismissed on November 22. The sheriff was acquitted on January 5, 1924. Hamer testified in Whitaker's trial and believed Ford, a Klansman, had botched the prosecution to shield his fellow white supremacists.[131]

With the investigations and trials highlighting their transgressions, and with the resulting bad publicity, the Klan abandoned its campaign of violent terror in favor of political action. However, even that avenue proved short-lived. District Attorney Daniel James Moody prosecuted four Klansmen for the assault on Robert Burleson in Williamson County. On September 25, 1923, Moody gave closing arguments to an all-white jury that lasted over two hours. When the first defendant was found guilty after only fifteen minutes of deliberation, the days of the Klan as a serious political force in Texas became numbered, especially after the Klan-backed candidate, Felix D. Robertson, was defeated in the Democratic primaries for governor in August 1924.[132]

Officials standing in front of City Hall in Austin had a moment of surprise on May 1, 1924. That morning, Hamer drove up to the curb in a Studebaker, and he and Ranger Walter Ernest Mayberry climbed out of the automobile carrying shotguns. Private William Mackinnon Molesworth remained in the back seat with a thirty-five-gallon copper still, a sack of copper coils, and forty one-quart jars of "white lightning" whiskey. The captain informed his astonished audience that his party had left Austin the previous evening and drove to a residence in the Yegua Creek bottoms, twelve miles northeast of Giddings in Lee County. The property owners had fled before the Rangers raided at sunrise, but the contraband was abandoned for the lawmen to seize. Hamer stated his intention to file charges in federal court.[133]

On June 11, Hamer, Mayberry, Austin Police Commissioner Harry Nolen, and Prohibition agent Lee Shannon conducted a raid on the Gander Slu district of the Luling oil field in Guadalupe County. The Rangers suspected local law enforcement of being in collusion with the bootleggers, and Hamer was well known for his loathing of crooked peace officers. Ben H. Hare, a store proprietor and possibly a county deputy, and Ballard Julien Miles, a garage owner, were arrested and charged with peddling intoxicating liquors. The Ranger captain also confiscated 889 pints of beer, a fifty-gallon still, eleven gallons of whiskey, and a complete set of saloon equipment. The Rangers took their prisoners back to Austin and lodged them in the county jail. Later the same evening, in an unrelated raid, Hamer struck the new Stephen F. Austin Hotel where Texas druggists were holding their annual convention. The Ranger arrested one bellhop and seized twenty-five quarts of whiskey and gin. The next day, Guadalupe County Sheriff Walter Marvin McGee and Deputy Ferrell Exum "Ex" Hollamon came to town to obtain the release of Hare and Miles. One of Hamer's men arrested Hollamon, but the deputy secured a writ of *habeas corpus* and was soon released. Sheriff McGee and Hollamon left for home only to find Hamer waiting as they crossed the Colorado River bridge. The captain placed both law officers under arrest. He took them back to town and brought Hollamon before U.S. Commissioner Paul A. Lockhart. Before the deputy could acquire his release, he had to furnish a one-thousand-dollar bond. That night, Miles was transferred to the custody of the federal marshal in San Antonio. On the sixteenth, Hare appeared before Lockhart and was remanded to a jail cell after defaulting on his own bond.[134]

One month after Governor Miriam Amanda "Ma" Ferguson, wife of the disgraced former executive, took office in January 1925, Adjutant General William Mark McGee altered policy in that Rangers would only operate in a county if the local officers requested their presence "except in unusual cases where the adjutant general and the governor believe the situation demands the initiative be taken by them." On March 30, the Thirty-ninth Legislature enacted a law relating to unlawful searches and seizures by peace officers and State Rangers. The act prohibited officers from searching private residences, places of business, persons, or personal possessions without first obtaining a search warrant.[135]

Rumors spread that oil tankers entering the Port of Houston were in danger from radical members of the Industrial Workers of the World. Officials of the Humble Oil and Refining Company and other petroleum concerns met in Houston with Sheriff Robert E. Kirk and Ranger officers. As a precautionary measure, state lawmen were assigned to board tankers moving up the Houston ship channel to their berth, then return to Bolivar to wait for the next ship. Hamer, Privates William Molesworth and Arthur Parrish "Sug" Cummings of Headquarters Company, Captain Hickman and Private Stewart Stanley of Company B, and Private James Lemuel "Lem" Lamkin of Company C were all ordered to proceed to Houston on April 28 and report to Major John C. Townes. Neither Jim Ferguson, speaking on his spouse's behalf, nor the local authorities knew of any trouble on the wharves. The rumors proved false, and the Rangers returned to their duty stations on May 11. They reported the presence of wide-open saloons in Galveston, including a four-block area "where liquor is dispensed without fear of interference."[136]

With the return of the Fergusons to the statehouse, Hamer, as senior captain, was certain to oppose their attempts to use the Ranger Force for political patronage. As Walter P. Webb rightfully noted, "The Rangers can not [*sic*] be effective when made the tool of politics and the plaything of the courts." The practice had started under Governor Oscar Branch Colquitt in 1911, and continued during Jim Ferguson's first term and through the Hobby administration. Another time Webb observed: "The Ranger service was … affected by the fact that the state was split politically into Ferguson and anti-Ferguson factions. Both factions used the Rangers for political purposes at a time when the force really had a great opportunity for distinguished service." Hamer was offered the option to be summarily discharged or resign. Hamer chose the more dignified alternative and left the service effective June 30, 1925.[137]

Ever the politicians, the Fergusons never publicly criticized Hamer, even though he despised them professionally and personally. Although she had removed him from his influential position, Ma Ferguson did not want to lose an asset completely, so the former senior captain received a warrant of Special Ranger on July 1, 1925. From an office at Camp Mabry, he worked directly for General McGee on special assignments. On October 13, undercover federal agents and Texas Rangers, including Hamer, swept through the town of Best in Reagan County, closing thirteen saloons, dance halls, and gambling parlors, arresting enough men to fill the Reagan and Pecos County jails to capacity, and seizing 2,500 gallons of illegal liquor. With local lawmen unable or unwilling to act, honest citizens of the former county, tiring of the blatant disregard for the prohibition laws, had called on the Prohibition and Customs officers, and the state authorities, to intervene. Major Herbert Hamlin White, Prohibition administrator for Oklahoma and Texas, directed the crackdown. By the twenty-third, the grand jury had returned more than two hundred indictments. District Court Judge Claude Sutton insisted on rigid bond securities, and only three of the suspects were able to make bail.[138]

Hamer and William W. Taylor traveled to Del Rio in November 1925 and met with Harrison. The younger Hamer brother was still employed by the Customs service on the border and accompanied the two Rangers to the Rio Grande. As their car halted near Jiminez, the three lawmen came under fire from gunmen situated across the river. The officers took cover and engaged their assailants. After a few minutes of shooting, the gunmen fled into the night. Newspapers observed this incident was the third time Americans had been fired upon recently.[139]

As a special investigator, Hamer was called upon to handle open and unsolved homicides. On the evening of May 20, 1926, Doctor James A.

Ramsey disappeared from his Mathis home in San Patricio County. By the following morning, the community was alarmed, and Sheriff Samuel Franklin "Frank" Hunt arrived from Sinton to conduct a search. While hundreds of men combed the countryside, no sign of Ramsey could be found. After a week had passed, Governor Ferguson sent Rangers Asa Light Townsend and Jules Wakeman "Tod" Aldrich (brother of the quartermaster) to assist in the baffling investigation; they would concentrate on finding Ramsey's automobile. Several days later, the sheriff requested the presence of Hamer. Arriving in Mathis, the captain's inquiry took him to San Antonio in search of missing papers that many believed would shed light on the doctor's disappearance. The aged physician had been at odds with lawyer and rancher Harry J. Leahy after he purchased fifteen hundred acres of foreclosed land that had once belonged to Leahy's parents. Within a short time, Hamer advocated for the arrest of ex-Ranger and San Patricio County Deputy Edwin Morgan DuBose, Sr., Harry Leahy, and Edgar Leahy. Hunt, Hamer, Townsend, Aldrich, and Deputy Sam Bell took the trio into custody on June 17, and Harry was charged with murder. Producing an iron-clad alibi, Ed Leahy was freed. On June 22, the charges against DuBose were dismissed due to insufficient evidence. In the examining trial, Justice of the Peace Andrew Jackson Custer set Harry Leahy's bond at a surprisingly high $66,500. The defendant was granted a *habeas corpus* hearing before Judge Thomas Marion Cox of the Thirty-sixth District Court in Beeville, and his bond was reduced to twenty thousand.[140]

After Leahy was released, he was placed under constant surveillance. Roberto Martínez, the key to breaking the case, was lured back from Nuevo Laredo by Webb County Constable Eduardo "Ed" Villarreal and Laredo Night Marshal Candelario Mendiola. Once he set foot on American soil, Martínez was arrested and transported to Mathis on August 25. He confessed to have aided Leahy in deceiving Ramsey to leave his home and offered to lead officers to the doctor's grave located near the Old Spanish Trail, six miles from Mathis in Live Oak County. Disinterred on the twenty-sixth, the recovered body bore marks of torture, blunt force trauma, and a slit throat. Since the homicide had occurred in Live Oak County, the trial was held in George West, the county seat. Amid reports the defendant was under physical threat, Hamer, Live Oak County Sheriff Christopher Eugene Key and his deputies, and Bexar County officers escorted Leahy from San Antonio to George West on September 3. The rumors proved unfounded, and the trial began twenty days later. On the twenty-fifth, Judge Cox granted a continuance to Leahy, who was acting as his own counsel. After a number of defense motions and jury selection, the prosecution began presenting its case on November 18. Turning state's evidence, Martínez took the witness stand the first day and described in detail the murder and subsequent burial of the victim. Through testimony, DuBose was revealed to have been a private detective working for Mrs. Ramsey. Playing a dangerous game of gaining Leahy's confidence, he had kept Sheriff Hunt aware of his movements. His fate sealed, Leahy was convicted on November 26 and sentenced to fifty years. The guilty man appealed and was granted a change of venue to Williamson County for a new trial. This second jury found him guilty on February 9, 1927, and Leahy received the death penalty.[141]

The doomed man received one last chance to escape his fate when Miss Amanda Davidson, a telephone operator in Taylor, signed an affidavit stating that she had visited Leahy in Huntsville and believed he had become mad since his conviction. State law prevented a potentially insane man from being executed, no matter when the psychological break occurred, until his illness could be confirmed. The insanity hearing was held in Georgetown, and Hamer was among the one hundred witnesses who testified on Leahy's mental stability. The captain attested he thought the defendant was completely sane. The last gambit failed, and the death sentence was carried out at Huntsville shortly after midnight on August 2, 1929. Fifty-five minutes before he paid for his crimes in the electric chair, Leahy was said to have called for Hamer and told him, "All my life things have broken my way, but this time the cards were stacked against me." Hamer replied, "Who stacked them, Harry? None but yourself."[142]

Temple Police Chief Wiley Vick Fisher, Sr. was shot down in the streets of Belton on August 20, 1926. Having earlier sued the slain officer for libel, Albert W. Bonds, former sheriff of Bell County, was an early suspect. He had also left town at about the same time as the shooting. Bonds was indicted for the murder, but his whereabouts remained unknown. Fisher's nephew personally appealed to Tom Hickman for assistance, but a representative of the governor's office revealed county authorities had made no official request for Ranger assistance. Then, suddenly, on November 13, Bonds appeared at Hamer's home and informed the captain, "I want to surrender. I am your prisoner. I want to surrender where I'll be safe." Taking Bonds into custody, Hamer, Benjamin Maney Gault, his best friend and neighbor, and Captain Taylor accompanied the ex-lawman to Belton the following day. The latter returned to his hometown apparently expecting to die there. "You'll get an invitation to my funeral in two or three weeks," Bonds reportedly told Hamer. He was released by Judge Lewis Henry Jones of the Twenty-seventh District Court after posting bail in the amount of ten thousand dollars. Bonds sought a change of venue when his case was called for trial, but he was shot and seriously wounded on December 2. Twenty-three-year-old Monroe Fisher, son of the slain police chief, was taken into custody and charged with assault to murder. Young Fisher made a second, more successful, attempt on May 11, 1927, in front of the Belton National Bank. Monroe and his younger brother Johnnie were charged with murder.[143]

One particularly difficult case involved the 1923 murders of Jesse Addison Barnes, Sr. and his seven-year-old namesake. Barnes, a real estate investor, had been instantly killed on November 14 by a package bomb inside his Corpus Christi home; the boy lived a few additional minutes before succumbing to his injuries. Hickman, Police Chief Monroe Fox, Sheriff George Peters, and an investigator for the American Railway Express Company had followed the trail of evidence to San Antonio, from where the bomber was thought to have sent the package. Two males were arrested, one of whom was sixteen-year-old newsboy Juan Morales, who claimed to have been given the parcel marked "magazines" by a crippled man. The youth was instructed to deliver the box to the International & Great Northern Railroad's express office for shipment to the Barnes residence. Hickman worked the case "day and night," but, although the pair were indicted, their cases never went to trial. Once Hamer took over the investigation, the primary suspect became Frank Hubert Bonner, Barnes's twenty-eight-year-old son-in-law. Arrested in San Antonio on December 8, 1926, Bonner was indicted by the Nueces County grand jury the same day, and arraigned before District Court Judge Abner Webster Cunningham on the thirteenth. Hamer appeared before the grand jury as the state's sole witness. With Bonner's arrest, Hamer and Hickman ceased their statewide search for a culprit. The accused's trial in Corpus Christi, which began on January 17, 1927, ended in a hung jury, and the circumstantial case was transferred to San Antonio on a change of venue. On May 2, the prosecution moved the charges be dismissed, as new evidence had arisen contradicting testimony given at trial. However, Hamer and his colleagues remained convinced of Bonner's guilt, and persuaded the Nueces County grand jury to re-indict him on November 2, 1931. The centerpiece of the new effort was a witness who had failed to testify at the Corpus Christi trial. Nevertheless, the case was never introduced in a courtroom.[144]

Unsuccessful convictions were not Hamer's only dilemma. The Fergusons were profoundly corrupt individuals and working in their administration caused the morally upright Ranger no end of concern. The one act he personally found contemptible was the pardon of Felix Jones, the assassin hired to kill the Ranger and his father-in-law nearly a decade prior. Apparently, the convicted murderer was entitled to a "full pardon because of long service with a clear record."[145]

Dan Moody was elected governor based in part on a campaign promise to restore effective law and order to the state. Reorganizing the Ranger Force, Moody retained Roy Aldrich and Tom Hickman, and fired the remainder of the captains. To replace the Ferguson appointees, he selected William W. Sterling and recalled William L. Wright and John H. Rogers, the last of the "Four Great Captains." As his Special Ranger warrant expired on February 1, 1927, Hamer was immediately named captain of Company D in Laredo on the twenty-second. He transferred to Headquarters Company on May 1 as senior captain.[146]

In the month of October, Hamer apprehended Oklahoma desperado Asa Omer "Ace" Pendleton and bank robbers Curtis T. Black (also identified as "Blackie" Cole) and William Jennings "Whitey" Walker in Marlin; the trio was wanted for the robbery of the Stockyards National Bank in Fort Worth. The following month, Hamer discovered a cache of automobiles concealed in the wooded hills around Llano by a Central Texas ring of car thieves. The gang had been active for several years, and had grown so bold as to operate in the open. Stolen from all over the state, the fleet of seventy vehicles was valued in the thousands of dollars. Forty-eight indictments were returned by the grand jury, and Hamer arrested the ringleaders, including fugitive W. C. McBride.[147]

Although Ranger Marvin Burton had tirelessly worked to end their enterprise, the moonshiners of Somervell County resumed operations by the end of 1925. Charles Stevens led fellow Prohibition agents and county officers in a series of raids along the Paluxy River on January 29, 1926. The lawmen seized four complete stills and fifty gallons of corn whiskey. Four men were arrested. Sixty-nine-year-old Sheriff Joe Dotson, Constable Clyde Hawkins, and Deputy Sheriff Lee Taylor killed one moonshiner and captured another in a pitched battle six miles south of Glen Rose on November 30, 1927; a third bootlegger escaped into the brush. The dead man was identified as farmer Tom Whitt. Threats were made to "get officers," and Adjutant General Robert Lamar Robertson ordered the Rangers to investigate. Captain Hamer assigned several of his men to assist the sheriff in seizing stills and arresting prohibition violators. Sergeant Jerome B. Wheatley investigated the shooting and confirmed Whitt had been slain by Hawkins. Based upon the Ranger's finding, the constable was charged in justice court on December 1 with murder. He waived an examining trial, and was released on a one-thousand-dollar bond while awaiting the grand jury.[148]

"Reward. Five Thousand Dollars for Dead Bank Robbers and Not One Cent for Live Ones" was prominently displayed on posters in every depository in the Lone Star State. The Texas Bankers' Association had offered the bounty to curb a flood of bank robberies and remedy the failure of the courts to convict the thieves. Captain Hickman, the service's bank robbery expert, noted the rewards' obvious flaw: "It may provide a more profitable field of endeavor for some of those bank robbers. It is easy to see how a member of a bank robbery gang would double-cross his pals tip off a scheduled bank robbery let officers shoot them down and then share a part of the reward money." At the captain's urging, the Northern Texas and Southern Oklahoma Peace Officers' Association voted on whether to endorse the bankers' actions. Doubtless to his disappointment, the lawmen voted to support the reward forty-one to eleven. Over the subsequent months, Hickman was proven correct as Hamer detected an ominous trend, in that a number of robbers were killed after dark while the banks were closed. He investigated and satisfied himself that unscrupulous individuals had lured eight drunks or gullible youths to banks in Odessa on November 25, 1927, Stanton on December 23, and Rankin on January 11, 1928, where they were executed by parties lying in wait. The conspirators then collected a combined twenty thousand dollars in blood money from the association. Referring to a failed yet daring heist at a Cisco bank, Hamer charged only one professional robber had been killed as a result of the reward offer. The Ranger captain attempted to take legal action against the men instigating the premeditated killings, but he could not gain the support of local officers who refused to believe his allegations, nor that of grand juries dominated by these lawmen. He also went to the bankers' association to have the reward rescinded or altered, but its president, William Munford Massie, refused. The position of his organization was that any man who agreed to rob banks deserved to die. Hamer certainly did not approve of theft, but he could also not subscribe to the entrapment and murder of nonviolent offenders.[149]

Fortunately, the day after the alleged robbery attempt in Stanton, Judge Charles Louis Klapproth of the Seventieth District Court instructed a grand jury to investigate the events that occurred in front of the Home National Bank. Glasscock County deputy Calvin Cidney "Cal" Baze and former cowboy Lee L. Smith of Wink claimed they had killed Norberto Díaz and J. Hilario Núñez while foiling a theft, but they only wounded the third participant. Victor Ramos, the survivor, had a different story to tell at the preliminary hearing, one in which he and his companions, all unarmed, had been "planted" at the bank. Baze and Smith then appeared and abruptly opened fire. The accused killers appeared before Justice of the Peace James Houston Watson for an examining trial, and were charged with murder. Witnessed by Midland County Judge Melvin Rufus Hill, Sheriff Audie Cecil Francis, and Deputy Doney Ernest Covington, Baze voluntarily signed a confession admitting to entrapping the three Mexicans for the reward money, although he implicated Smith as entirely responsible for the cold-blooded killings. The two suspects were denied bail and remained behind bars while waiting for the grand jury to convene on March 26. With the assistance of two fellow prisoners, Baze overpowered Deputy Covington and escaped from the Midland County jail on March 18. Rangers and sheriffs throughout West Texas joined in the manhunt. While his accomplices were quickly recaptured, Baze was never again seen in Texas. Despite his absence, the grand jury assembled and called on Hamer to present his evidence. In his charge to the grand jurors, Judge Klapproth upbraided the bankers' association for their reward policy. The following day, Baze and Smith were indicted for murder and assault to murder. With Ramos the chief prosecution witness, Smith was tried in Forty-second District Court at Baird, convicted of Núñez's murder, and sentenced to life imprisonment.[150]

Even while the Baze-Lee case was unfolding, the normally taciturn Hamer decided to take his allegations to the media. On March 12, 1928, his press release cited three specific cases to support his charge. In conclusion, he stated: "Here is as perfect a murder machine as can be devised, supported by the Bankers' Association, operated by the officers of the state and directed by the small group of greedy men who furnish the victims and take their cut of the money." He also asserted the culprits were planning two more robberies for the express purpose of gaining the reward. Hamer declared the practice was a disgrace to Texas, and he called on the association to commission a panel to review his evidence. The story was front-page news in every major daily in the state, and quickly spread across the country. Editorial pages demanded his charges be investigated, and the resulting public outrage led Moody to suggest Hamer present his findings to the Upton County grand jury. The captain was subpoenaed by telephone on the twenty-eighth to appear, and Hamer announced himself "willing, anxious, and rarin' to go."[151]

Apparently convinced by the Ranger's testimony, the grand jury served Massie with a summons to appear on April 4. Upton County deputies Carl Fred "Red" Wood and James Houston "Bill" Dumas were indicted on April 7 on charges of murder and conspiracy to commit murder in the deaths of W. M. "Blackie" Miller and a man identified only as "Whitey" in Rankin. Hamer was on hand to arrest them both: Wood in Springfield, Missouri, and Dumas at Lubbock. With the assistance of Special Ranger Graves Peeler, Hamer was soon able to secure written confessions. On April 18, Dumas appeared for an examining trial in Rankin, and the cases were transferred to Travis County on a change of venue. On November 12, Dumas's bond of $2,500 in each of his two cases was forfeited due to a failure to appear for trial, while Wood remained in custody. Thus, their cases were continued to December 3 in Criminal District Court in Austin. Furthermore, on November 19, officers and members of the bankers' association, Ector County Sheriff Reeder Webb, Sheriff A. C. Francis, Upton County Sheriff John Oscar "Bud" Barfield, and cattle inspector J. W. B. Hogan were named in a $100,000 damage lawsuit brought by Mary Hansen, widow of William Carl Hansen, who was slain in Odessa. Regrettably, the Ector County grand jury took no action in the suit. The trial of Dumas and Wood convened at the appointed time, and District Judge James Robert Hamilton ordered them returned to Upton County as his court was without jurisdiction. Their cases were instead transferred to San Marcos. Dumas was freed on bond, but Wood continued his stay in jail. The bankers of the association escaped legal consequences, but the reward was revised to read "dead or alive," and only during daylight hours.[152]

However, Hamer's investigation continued for another two years, and he testified before the Upton County grand jury on June 19, 1931. The panel returned four bills of indictment against former Sheriff Barfield and two ex-deputies, Clarence Shannon and Hugh Gillespie, for the murder of Miller and Whitey. Their cases became ensnared in a limbo of delays and continuances. Dumas and Wood were re-indicted on conspiracy charges. However, since three grand jurors had been unqualified to sit on the jury, the charges against Barfield, Shannon, and Gillespie were quashed in 112th District Court on September 29. The cases against Dumas and Wood seem to have never gone to trial, but the former was convicted of horse theft in Seventy-second District Court on February 23, 1934. Based on two previous property crime convictions, the jury ruled Dumas a habitual criminal, and sentenced him to life imprisonment. However paltry, Miller and Whitey had been accorded some measure of justice.[153]

While Hamer was dealing with the bankers' association, he assisted officers in Burnet County in the search for thieves who had struck the Farmers' State Bank in Bertram on March 17. Citizens of Freestone County had joined with Special Rangers in enforcing liquor laws. A "Committee of One

Thousand" was formed under Judge Robert Lee Williford, and more than fifty stills were seized. However, Special Ranger Timothy Samuel Willard was killed in a whiskey raid on April 19. Hamer and a squad of five Rangers were dispatched to Freestone to augment the force already there. In early May, the captain and Tom Hickman went into Fort Bend County to close several roadhouses, and brought back two roulette wheels as souvenirs. Continuing the governor's anti-liquor campaign, Headquarters Company made two raids in the environs of Austin. Hamer personally directed one, while Rangers Tod Aldrich and James Edward "Jim" McCoy made the other. The state officers arrested two men, one of them a former policeman, and confiscated and destroyed one thousand bottles of beer.[154]

Armand Alexander, a twenty-seven-year-old former porter in the state land office building, was involved in a domestic dispute-turned-spree-killing in South Austin that left four people dead, including Police Chief James N. Littlepage. Earlier on the day of October 9, the killer had reportedly said, "I'm bound for hell and I'm going to take white folks and colored people with me." Following a violent argument with his wife at 2121 South Congress Avenue, he went to 303 Elizabeth Street, the home of relatives whom he blamed for his troubles, and killed Catherine Pyburn, his aunt, and his cousin Ethel. After failing to murder his uncle and another cousin, Alexander fled west on foot along Elizabeth Street, then down East Bouldin Creek. Chief Littlepage confronted him on the 2400 block of Wilson Street, where the fugitive mortally wounded the lawman in the face and abdomen. Racing to the home of a friend at 1800 Newton Street, Alexander murdered innocent bystander Joseph "Joe" Blunn, who was merely a carpenter working on the structure. He then ran one block west to South First Street and invaded the home of Mrs. Leatha Arnold, who fled with her one-month-old daughter Dolores. The murderous rampage had taken place only two miles from Hamer's residence, and he and Sergeant William "Bull" Stewart, Chief of Detectives Adolphus Love Bugg, and Officers Harvey Maddox, Rex Fowler, and James Franklin "Jim" Parker quickly traced Alexander to the Arnold home. The suspect fired at the officers, then retreated into the bathroom as the small house was riddled with the city detectives' bullets. Hamer kicked in the rear door while the policemen went through the front. As they entered the structure, a shot was heard, and the lawmen found Alexander on the bathroom floor dead from a self-inflicted gunshot wound. Chief Littlepage's pearl-handled .45 pistol was next to the body.[155]

Comprised of Republicans and disaffected Democrats, the Good Government League of Hidalgo County stood in opposition to Anderson Yancey "Ancey" Baker, the "millionaire sheriff" who had dominated local politics for a decade. Formerly a member of Captain James A. Brooks's Ranger company, Baker had been allied to political boss James Babbage Wells, Jr., and controlled an "administration ring" enabled by the Hispanic voting bloc. Two thousand telegrams had been sent to President Calvin Coolidge and the Department of Justice protesting the sheriff's alleged violations of election laws. Traveling to Houston, Mayor Frank Byron Freeland of McAllen, and D. E. Worley of Harlingen submitted to U.S. Attorney Henry Matthews Holden, Sr. affidavits asserting that, among other irregularities, three hundred ineligible Mexicans were on the county's poll tax list. Holden requested the Bureau of Investigation conduct a "preliminary investigation" and ascertain whether a formal probe was necessary. Agent Gus T. Jones, a former Ranger, was dispatched from San Antonio to "begin the investigation as soon as possible."[156]

On November 6, Hamer, Jim McCoy, Tod Aldrich, and Bill Sterling and the five men of Company D were sent to Hidalgo County to monitor the local elections. Although the proceedings were peaceful, Hamer stopped three men who had crawled under the voting booth in Edinburg and bored holes in the floor. Once the polling was complete, supporters of the Citizens' Republican, or Independent, ticket criticized county voting judges who had thrown out twelve hundred ballots and permitted alleged fraudulent voting by Mexican nationals. Hamer went to the town of Mercedes, seized the ballot box, and secured it inside the courthouse in Edinburg. With an Independent victory in the balance, subsequent vote counting consumed several days, while Rangers and deputies stood watch in a light rain. The sheriff and his cronies captured every county office save two. Company D remained in Hidalgo County, while Hamer and his two men were withdrawn on the ninth. Opponents of the Baker machine launched a legal and political campaign that initiated a federal grand jury investigation. Baker and seven henchmen were indicted for voter fraud, but the sheriff's stroke and death in November 1930 was the event that put an end to his organization. However, boss rule would endure in South Texas for several more decades.[157]

Hamer's good friend, Maney Gault, lived at 1606 Nickerson in the Riverside section of Austin. The Ranger captain had known the former dairy farmer and Woodward Manufacturing Corporation foreman for several years, and their wives were close companions. The two men spent much time together with other associates, including Walter Webb, playing poker. Appreciating his qualities of fearlessness, loyalty, and integrity, Hamer recruited Gault for undercover work in investigating bootlegging, gambling, and other illegality. When his factory job ended, Gault accepted the invitation to enlist on January 1, 1929, in Headquarters Company where he replaced Ranger Edgar B. "Ed" McMordie.[158]

Hamer and Gault hurried to Mason County after Sheriff Allen Thomas Murray was murdered on a country road on February 28. The two state lawmen offered their assistance in the considerable manhunt. Armed with a description of the suspects' vehicle, local officers persuaded radio station WOAI in San Antonio to deliver a public service announcement of the information. County residents contributed to a reward fund that exceeded seventeen hundred dollars, while Governor Moody offered an additional $250. After Offilio Herrera and Antonio Chavez were apprehended, the state lacked the means to recover physical evidence, including bloodstains in an automobile. The services of a forensically trained Sutton County deputy were instead used to fingerprint and photograph the accused men. Officers took two pistols off the suspects after their arrests; one of which was identified as belonging to Sheriff Murray. Herrera was identified by four eyewitnesses, and could not account for the weapons or the bloody clothing and forty-five gallons of whiskey in his possession. Chavez turned state's evidence and revealed the details of Murray's murder. In order to strengthen the circumstantial case, the deputy processed the weapons for fingerprints and found several. He compared them to the fingerprints taken from the jailed suspects. Herrera's right thumbprint was found on Sheriff Murray's handgun. After his conviction for murder on March 21, Herrera was executed in an electric chair later in the year.[159]

Benjamin Maney Gault. *Courtesy Mike Gault.*

Hamer went undercover in Austin on March 23 and 25, and purchased liquor from the occupant of 2512 Montopolis Road. Using the booze as evidence, he secured a search warrant and the services of Deputy Sheriffs James H. "Jim" Ables and Bob Ayres. Upon arriving at the house in question, Hamer went to the front door, while the deputies covered the rear. Looking through the screen door, the Ranger captain saw five men drinking beer, and Tom Hamby, the speakeasy's operator, opening pint bottles; five empties were on the table. Hamer informed the men he and the deputies were executing a search warrant, and placed them under arrest. The officers seized and destroyed the bootlegger's wares, including twenty-nine pints of beer and eighteen gallons of beer mash. The five prisoners at the table later admitted they had purchased pint bottles from Hamby, and all were transported to jail. Elnora Hamby, Tom's wife, was also taken into custody, and she claimed ownership of the entire illegal inventory. The customers paid fines on vagrancy charges and were released. On March 26, Hamer, Sergeant Wheatley, and Deputies Ables, Joe Oscar Bratton, and Tony Lock raided two downtown hotels and a "beer joint" on Red River Street. Six men and women were jailed, and several cases of beer were destroyed.[160]

On April 6, Hamer raided a shack near the Colorado River in Austin and seized a gallon of whiskey. A manual training instructor and an athletic coach from Austin High School were arrested and charged with violating prohibition laws. They were released on their own recognizance pending the arrival of a federal agent from San Antonio. In addition to the two suspects, a young woman and a married couple were taken into custody.[161]

Believing Hamer had not acquired valid search warrants before conducting raids on suspected bootleggers, Judge George Calhoun charged the Travis County grand jury and referenced the U.S. Constitution as a guarantee against illegal searches. Hamer took issue with the jurist's remarks and said, "I don't see why he did not say 'turn the bootleggers out of jail, pat them on the back, and indict the officers,' and be done with it." When asked if he planned to continue his raids, the captain defiantly replied, "If he doesn't like the raids I'm making he can assemble his grand jury and indict me and my bunch of rangers." Prohibition officials in Austin refused to accept evidence from several of Hamer's bootlegging cases, and "a jail full of bootleggers" was released as a result.[162]

Similar to his predecessor, Governor Charles Allen Culberson, Moody opposed prizefighting, and compelled the cancellation of bouts in Houston, Donna, and Galveston on June 3. However, the American Legion card in Waco featuring bantamweights Hilo "Hill" Hernandez and Kid Gambino was held as scheduled. Hamer traveled to Galveston to enforce the executive's order.[163]

He returned to the Island on June 19 with William Hale Kirby and Jim McCoy, several other Rangers, and a Prohibition agent. Executing previously obtained search warrants, the law officers divided into squads and proceeded to raid establishments along the beachfront and downtown. Thirty-five people were arrested and turned over to the sheriff. Bond for those charged with vagrancy and gambling was set at two hundred dollars each, while the ten men and two women charged with violations of liquor laws were arraigned before U.S. Commissioner Brantly Callaway Harris, Sr.[164]

On September 13, John A. Holmes, the forty-three-year-old district attorney of the Eighty-fourth Judicial District, was shot to death in front of his wife and mother-in-law. The murderer had been hiding in the bushes situated outside the victim's Borger home, and his identity and the motive were not readily known. Taking the Fort Worth & Denver train from the "Queen City of the Prairie," Captains Hamer and Hickman, Sergeant J. B. Wheatley, and Rangers Maney Gault and Chesley Omer Moore arrived around midnight to investigate. Governor Moody posted the next day a five-hundred-dollar reward for the capture and conviction of the perpetrator. After searching Holmes's office and home, the state officers determined documents that were to be used in the prosecution of twelve men and two women in federal court for liquor violations had gone missing. The fourteen defendants had been apprehended in a Ranger sweep of the city the previous July. In addition, Holmes was to have presented evidence to the federal grand jury in Amarillo regarding five Borger residents facing indictments. Once he examined the crime, Hamer informed journalists he knew the motive behind the Holmes murder, but did not go into details. Furthermore, on September 18, the Rangers recovered the signed confessions of two men believed to have murdered two deputy sheriffs in 1927; once more Hamer and Hickman refused to reveal specifics. Later, the former reported he had found "the worst bit of organized crime" he had ever seen in all his years in law enforcement. In a front-page editorial, the *Borger Daily Herald* called on the Ranger to prove his assertion, and Police Chief John William Crabtree dismissively replied the statement "sounded just like Hamer." Sheriff Joseph Monroe "Joe" Ownbey characterized the captain's allegation as a lie. On September 24, the sheriff declared he had been misquoted, and claimed his statement had been in relation to Hamer's assertion that local officials were involved in a criminal conspiracy.[165]

On the twenty-eighth, the governor declared martial law in the crime-ridden town would commence at 3:00 a.m. the following day. Clem Calhoun, the hard-drinking 104th District Attorney, was appointed to succeed Holmes and handle the anticipated court cases. Sergeant Manuel T. Gonzaullas and Rangers William Hale Kirby and J. P Huddleston, the latter formerly of the BOI, were dispatched to Borger to bolster the investigative force. On September 29, the governor suspended from office Mayor Glenn A. Pace, Chief Crabtree and the entire police force, Constable ____ Mitchell and his deputies, and Sheriff Ownbey and county jailer Burt Bryan. The order was to remain in effect until martial law was lifted. Once he too was relieved of his civil duties, Justice of the Peace Walter Broomhall resigned. Wheatley assumed the role of sheriff, and Tod Aldrich acted as police chief. Hamer and fourteen Rangers, Highway Patrolmen Martin Nickolas Koonsman and John Keller, Brigadier-General Wolters, and fourteen officers and eighty-four enlisted men of the Fifty-sixth Cavalry Brigade occupied the city, disarmed the local officers, closed the sheriff's office at Stinnett, and quickly began making arrests. Hamer apprehended Borger police officer Clint Millholon, Gault detained Deputy Constable Sam Jones, and Gault and Aldrich took Pace into custody for allegedly enabling the escape of a murder suspect.[166]

Similar to earlier visits to Borger, the state officers raided the speakeasies and harried the criminal element. The largest raid occurred on October 5, when Hamer, Hickman, Gonzaullas, Gault, Moore, Huddleston, Kirby, and a National Guard detachment seized two 250-gallon stills and apprehended three bootleggers. Those arrested for misdemeanors were fined by the adjutant general's provost marshal, while those detained on felony charges were brought before a grand jury. In addition, many wrongdoers were "invited" to leave the state and never return. General Wolters also convened a military court of inquiry to "investigate all matters pertaining to crime and law enforcement in Hutchinson County." The panel's members were Colonel Oscar Edgar Roberts, Colonel Louis Scott Davidson, Major Harry Hubert Johnson, Assistant Attorney General Paul DeWitt Page, Jr., District Attorney Calhoun, County Judge Henry Matthew Hood, Sr., County Attorney Henry D.

Meyers, and Captains Hamer and Hickman. After twelve days of activity, the testimony of one hundred witnesses was assembled into a one-thousand-page report which was then submitted to the grand jury. The document "nearly established the existence of a criminal ring in Borger and Hutchinson County, involving many persons and Peace Officers." Wolters issued General Order No. 6, which stated all prisoners identified as part of the criminal conspiracy and detained would be denied bail until order was restored.[167]

On October 14, the sheriff resigned his office, and Mayor Pace stepped down two days later. Moore was granted a one-year leave of absence on the seventeenth, in order to replace Ownbey, and Wheatley became acting deputy sheriff. Albert Ramos Mace, an experienced and capable lawman, was hired as the new police chief. Indeed, a completely new slate of law enforcement officials from district judge to city policeman was appointed. Additionally, civic-minded citizens were installed as city commissioners. With local government stabilized, the Guardsmen departed on October 18, while the Rangers remained until the twenty-first to see the police and sheriff's departments become operational. By the end of nineteen days of occupation by state troops, Calhoun had received the resignations of seven municipal and county officials, and jailed six former law officers and scores of bootleggers and other offenders. The governor formally lifted martial law on October 29.[168]

Adjutant General Robertson later described the Ranger detachment's activities:

> A thorough-going clean-up was put underway. The liquor traffic was broken up, many stills being seized and destroyed, and several thousand gallons of whiskey being captured and poured out. Two hundred and three gambling slot machines were seized and destroyed. Numerous gambling resorts were placed under surveillance and forced to clean up, and in a period of twenty-four hours it is assumed that no less than twelve hundred prostitutes left the town of Borger. As the result of a demand on the part of the citizens of Borger for administration of the law, the Mayor, City Commissioners, Chief of Police, and practically all of the Police Force of Borger resigned and were replaced by citizens pledged to enforce the laws.[169]

By the end of the decade, the Rangers were badly in need of overhaul. Continued involvement in politics meant the turnover in personnel disrupted any continuity. Furthermore, the miserly pay induced many qualified officers to seek employment elsewhere. The lack of state-funded transportation hampered Rangers in getting on the trail of automobile-driving criminals. The Winchester lever-action rifles and Colt .45 six-shooters issued by the adjutant general's department were outclassed by the Thompson submachine guns and Browning Automatic Rifles (BAR) favored by high-profile robbers. Hickman's Company B had been the only one adequately armed. Due to private donations, they were equipped with four submachine guns, and fifty tear gas grenades and a gas mask for each Ranger. Finally, the service's affiliation with the adjutant general's department meant their supervisor was an individual unfamiliar with the realities of law enforcement. Working with Governor Moody, the Forty-first Legislature increased the annual appropriation to $94,600 and authorized a salary increase effective September 1. Captains, such as Hamer, received $225 per month, sergeants $175, and privates $150. Longevity pay was also approved so each Ranger would be eligible for a 5 percent raise after two years' continuous service, with another 5 percent each additional year, not to exceed 20 percent.[170]

The mutilated body of an unidentified, twelve-year-old girl had been discovered in a shallow grave along the highway near Fredericksburg on September 20, 1927. On the twenty-eighth, Hamer brought to headquarters garments and a ring found with the remains. He stated publicly he had little hope of establishing her identity. The case mystified local authorities for three years. Hamer, Gault, McCoy, and Tod Aldrich arrived in town on February 18, 1930, to assist in a new grand jury investigation. However, the grand jurors adjourned on March 3 without resolving the case. Tragically, while they intended to revive the matter in the August term, the homicide went unsolved, and the girl's name was never learned.[171]

On May 3, Sheriff Arthur Vaughn of Grayson County arrested forty-one-year-old field hand George Hughes for the sexual assault of Mrs. Pearl Ines Farlow, his employer's wife. Besides the vile nature of the crime, the fact Hughes was a black man and the victim was white only added to the public furor. Heretofore, race relations in Sherman, the "Athens of Texas," were relatively harmonious, especially for the Jim Crow Era. Unusual among other Southern locales, blacks and whites in Grayson County had lived together peacefully, albeit within clearly established boundaries. The alleged rape shattered this delicate sense of communal goodwill. Goaded by inflammatory newspaper reports, a wrathful mob of white citizens amassed outside the county courthouse two days after the attack, but they were dispersed without incident. The next morning, Judge Roger Mills Carter of the Fifteenth District Court requested Governor Moody send two Rangers. The judge desired to avoid any trouble from the rabble, so he expedited the case through the court system. The grand jury indicted Hughes on May 5 on three counts of criminal assault and two counts of attempt to murder. The examining trial was scheduled for Thursday, May 8, but, by Tuesday, a crowd had again gathered on the town square. Unlike the last instance, deputies had to fire a number of shots into the air to scatter the mob.[172]

Hamer, Sergeant Wheatley, and Privates Tod Aldrich and Jim McCoy arrived in town on the eighth. Hughes pled guilty at his arraignment, and Judge Carter ordered that the case be heard the following day. The jurist opened the proceedings at nine o'clock the morning of Friday, May 9, in a second-floor courtroom closed to everyone but the trial participants. Meanwhile, a mob once more gathered outside the courthouse, and the roads leading into town became choked with automobiles. As the jury heard the first witness, Hamer and two Rangers confronted infuriated citizens inside the building who were determined to exact their own brand of justice on the accused. Several members of the mob started toward the three Rangers, and Hamer and his men struck the citizens over the head with their pistol barrels. They then threw tear gas grenades and the crowd withdrew; the state officers shoved the dazed men away. Meanwhile, Judge Carter ordered the defendant be secured inside a forty-square-foot walk-in vault in the county clerk's office on the same floor. Newspaper reporters erroneously claimed the governor was informed of the trouble, and he had sent Hamer the message: "Hold them if you can, but do not shoot anybody." When Moody's purported instructions became known, the mob was further emboldened.[173]

Thirty minutes later, the frustrated crowd again rushed the staircase leading to the courtroom, without success, then followed up with another futile attempt using dynamite. The fourth charge occurred at two-thirty in the afternoon. Prior to this latest attempt, Hamer had armed himself with a shotgun loaded with birdshot, which he proceeded to fire low into the throng. With several of their leaders wounded, the mob again pulled back. Hamer informed the mob the defendant would not be turned over them. "Well we are coming up and get him!" a would-be vigilante shouted. "Any time you feel lucky," the Ranger captain replied, "come on up, but if you start up the stairway once more, there is going to be many funerals in Sherman tomorrow."[174]

On the fifth and last effort, two youths in the crowd threw a rock, a five-gallon can of gasoline, and an ignition source through a glass window into the county tax collector's basement office on the east side of the structure. The resulting fire spread quickly within the fifty-year-old courthouse. Hamer vainly tried to find someone who could open the locked vault where Hughes was trapped. Unsuccessful, he took his men out of the building through a second-floor window before they perished in the enveloping flames. In a move that would generate decades of controversy, Hamer and his men left town for a short time to utilize a secure telephone connection to the governor. They returned to Sherman later that night. As the blaze gutted the courthouse, the rabid mob restrained the responding firemen and even cut the water hoses. Buildings on the north side of the square were threatened, and firefighters struggled to protect the exposures. Hughes perished in the vault from either the blistering heat or a lack of oxygen. However, the bloodthirsty crowd of approximately four thousand demanded confirmation. Later in the evening, they used a stolen acetylene torch and dynamite to open the vault. Finding Hughes's remains, they seized the corpse and dragged it through the streets to the black neighborhood of North Sherman. There they hanged him from a cottonwood tree on the corner of Mulberry and Branch with a chain, looted furniture from a nearby drugstore, and built a fire under the body. The rioters went on to burn or pillage the two-story Andrews Building, the Smith Hotel, two cafes, two physician's offices, a beauty parlor, a mortuary, and other establishments for three blocks. As Doctor Arthur F. Raper commented, "Negro property was at the mob's mercy." When the latter descended on the county jail to seize some black prisoners, though, they found a recently arrived and heavily armed Manuel Gonzaullas in the front entrance. The mob wisely decided to refrain from attacking the formidable Ranger.[175]

Moody deployed Colonel Lawrence Ebenezer McGee and contingents of National Guardsmen—forty-two officers and 375 enlisted men in total—to Sherman throughout the night. Confronted with thousands of crazed rioters, Hamer's detachment and the reinforcements struggled to take control of the scene. The colonel later reported the guardsmen fired forty to fifty shots over the crowd's heads, even after they were pelted with soda water bottles, bricks, and timbers. Nine soldiers and six mob members were injured. Three of the latter had been shot, one of them with birdshot at the courthouse. Order was reestablished by dawn, but the entire black business district on East Mulberry lay in smoking ruins. Captain Hickman and Sergeant Kirby arrived from Abilene on May 10; they were later joined by Huddleston, Robert Gray "Bob" Goss, and H. B. Purvis. Nineteen law officers from Dallas and Tarrant Counties also made the trip. Declaring martial law, the governor tackled the media's story of the alleged message to Hamer by categorically denying to the Associated Press he had sent any communication. A search among the records of telegraph and telephone companies failed to disclose any communiqué from the governor to Hamer until after the courthouse was on fire. Colonel McGee convened a military court of inquiry on May 11, and martial law was finally lifted on the twenty-fourth. In the meantime, the Rangers under Hamer and Hickman had investigated and arrested sixty-six people on charges ranging from inciting to riot to attempted murder. They were able to see fourteen indicted by the grand jury on the twentieth, but only J. B. "Screw" McCasland, a seventeen-year-old troublemaker, was convicted. He had been seen by several eyewitnesses carrying a gas can near the courthouse, and received a thirteen-year prison sentence for arson and rioting. McCasland entered Huntsville on November 22, 1931, and received a pardon on December 30, 1934.[176]

Historian Robert Utley correctly called the Sherman rampage "one of the most brutish and shameful episodes in the history of Texas."[177] Despite

Hamer's inability to defend Hughes or prevent the riot, some admirers continued to insist the captain had

> adhered to the principles he had followed since first joining the Rangers. His obvious courage remained unquestioned after successfully defying the mob, fearlessly standing his ground with less than a dozen men against hundreds of half-crazed lynchers. No matter what his personal feelings about African Americans, Hamer attempted to protect Hughes—as well as law and order—even after the rapist had pled guilty and his fate was all but inevitable … Clearly, Captain Hamer and his men rose to the highest standards of Ranger conduct in their actions at Sherman.[178]

Hamer's physical bravery was indeed beyond question, but he had utterly failed in his assignment, and the Sherman riot represents the lowest point in his lengthy career. As Boessenecker noted, "Ranger traditions were extremely important [to Hamer], and he felt shame and embarrassment to be the only Ranger who ever lost a prisoner to lynchers. It was a direct affront to his personal honor."[179]

The death of Hughes while under their protection stung, and the Rangers of Headquarters Company endeavored to atone for their inability to protect their prisoner. On March 15, 1931, Sergeant Wheatley and Rangers Oscar Thomas Martin, Sr., Maney Gault, James McCormick, Jim McCoy, and George Martin Allen, Sr., struck the exclusive Loma Linda nightclub, which had recently reopened in Richmond, Fort Bend County. Seventy-eight individuals were arrested and fined. Seven days later, Hamer led five Rangers and a party of Bexar County officers in a raid on the Shadowland roadhouse near San Antonio. The lawmen found five hundred to six hundred people dancing and dining in the café section of the building but left them undisturbed. However, the Rangers and deputies did destroy gaming equipment valued between two thousand and five thousand dollars, and arrested seven men on charges of loitering. The captain's standard practice was to use monies seized from gambling tables to purchase food and clothing for needy children. The suspects were later released on bond. Bill Cohen, a proprietor of the establishment, claimed no one was gambling at the time of the raid, and the equipment was merely in storage. Appearing before Justice of the Peace John Read Shook on April 3, Hamer filed a motion to dismiss the cases against five of the defendants, stating he did not want to jeopardize an ongoing conspiracy case involving them. Returning to the San Antonio area in late July, Hamer, McCoy, and Allen raided the Boerne home of Lloyd Whitehead and found the suspect with nearly twenty gallons of whiskey. They took Whitehead to Llano, where he was already wanted, and filed a liquor charge against him before U.S. Commissioner Tillman Smith in San Antonio. Whitehead was also the subject of a federal warrant.[180]

On November 23, 1931, the body of nineteen-year-old Aubrey Burnett was found in a San Antonio hotel room. There were no signs of struggle, and the young man had been injured with a knife sometime prior to his death. Justice of the Peace John Franklin "Pete" Onion held an inquest and returned a verdict of death by unknown natural causes. Captain Aubrey Hopkins of the city's detective bureau received a telephone call from a mysterious tipster in St. Louis, who suggested Burnett had been strangled in his sleep. The informant also revealed that a hypodermic needle and a spoon were secreted in the wall telephone box in the room where Burnett was drugged and killed. Based on the information, Hamer brought Sebe Stephenson, an Austin man, to San Antonio on January 10, 1932, for questioning. Captain Hopkins appeared before Justice Onion and filed a complaint charging Stephenson with Burnett's murder. On the twenty-ninth, Stephenson was no-billed by the grand jury.[181]

Hamer and the rest of the Ranger Force were often, if not always, working more than one case at the same time. In the midst of the Burnett investigation, Hamer, assisted by Rangers Oscar Martin and George Allen, solved the robbery of the Lexington State Bank in Lee County that had occurred on February 10. The thieves stole from the safe over ten thousand dollars, with $550 in Liberty bonds. On December 5, Hamer arrested former cashier Milton MacGregor in Houston, William Dungan in Brenham, Louis Grant in San Marcos, and Earl Riggs in Lexington. Questioning the prisoners, the captain learned the time lock on the vault had been reset to open at three-thirty in the morning, and two of the suspects entered the bank to claim the loot. Three burglars revealed the bonds had been burned in a tourist camp near Temple, while the currency and coinage were divided among the foursome. Ranger James Spurgeon Scarborough, Sr., ex-county sheriff, had relentlessly worked the crime, and Hamer credited him with the case's successful closure.[182]

Unfinished business arose in the Rio Grande Valley, and Hamer returned to Hidalgo County. Three years prior, *Collier's* magazine had published an exposé which laid bare the corruption overseen by Ancey Baker. Even though the millionaire sheriff's empire had crumbled with his subsequent death, several of his cronies were elected to the Donna irrigation district. Leaders of the Good Government League were determined to eradicate all vestiges of Baker's machine, and offered a Mexican *pistolero* five hundred dollars to kill up to six notable Democrats in the Donna area. However, the murder plot frightened one of the conspirators, and he informed Adjutant General William Sterling. The general dispatched Hamer, Captain Albert Mace, and a detachment of Rangers to Edinburg. Hamer and Mace apprehended eight plotters on February 19, 1932. They also seized a pistol and fifty dollars thought to be a partial payment for the scheduled killings. Three of the men arrested immediately signed written confessions. The prisoners were released on bonds of fifteen hundred dollars each, and appeared before Justice of the Peace Daniel A. Salinas in Rio Grande City for an examining trial on March 4. The grand jury indicted the eight on April 8 on charges of conspiracy to commit murder. Four of the schemers were convicted and each received a two-year prison sentence. On November 29, 1933, the court of criminal appeals reversed the lower court's decision and remanded the defendants for a new trial. The appellate judges were reluctant to let the convictions stand due to a lack of corroborating testimony.[183]

In the hills north of San Marcos, the two sons of millionaire rancher and newsman Arthur Hunter Morton were found dead in a small stone house near their parents' home. The body of fifteen-year-old Arthur lay inside the dwelling with a gunshot wound to the head, while his brother, fourteen-year-old Henry, was discovered twenty-five yards away. Having been shot three times, Henry was taken to a local hospital, but he died within minutes of arrival. Investigators discovered a revolver that had been fired four times near Arthur's body, and blood spatter on the walls of the sleeping porch, the floor, and a cot. They also noted the three bullet holes in the screen wire surrounding the porch, and a bloodstained hand ax inside the house. Justice of the Peace Armistead Mason Ramsay returned a verdict of accidental death, citing his belief the boys had received their wounds while struggling for possession of the revolver. Hamer and Ranger Allen arrived from Austin to investigate and were able to confirm Ramsay's findings.[184]

The Ranger Force had made a grave mistake in July 1932, when the entire service openly backed Governor Ross Shaw Sterling in the Democratic primary against Miriam Ferguson. The Fergusons promptly accused the Rangers of ballot stuffing and voter intimidation. The charge was supremely ironic as 132 counties supporting Ferguson, especially those comprising the East Texas oil fields, reported higher vote counts than the numbers indicated by poll tax records. In point of fact, though, the Rangers' interference with the election was ethically inappropriate and a complete violation of their rules and regulations. However, they had already seen the results of a Ferguson administration and fully expected more of the same. Sterling's frequent use of martial law in East Texas oil fields, the deteriorating economy, and the Fergusons' machinations undermined his efforts. He failed in his bid on August 27, and Mrs. Ferguson was sure to take her revenge. She easily triumphed in the November general election and would be sworn into office on January 17, 1933.[185]

Walter Webb and other authors have asserted the captain "resigned before the Fergusons returned to the governor's chair in 1933." In a 1934 interview with the professor, Hamer acknowledged he separated from state service on November 1, 1932. Boessenecker stated the captain took an indefinite leave of absence to lobby for the soon-to-be vacant position of U.S. Marshal for the Western District of Texas. Harris and Sadler declared Hamer quit the following year. In actuality, these views all share degrees of accuracy and error. The *San Antonio Light* reported Hamer resigned "effective November 1, but … remained on duty at the instance of General Sterling, as an acting captain." Additional newspaper stories confirm Hamer continued to discharge his duties as a Ranger in the interim period between the general elections and inauguration day. On November 18, he and Hidalgo County deputy sheriffs arrested a man wanted for burglarizing a home in Mission and stealing one thousand dollars' worth of diamonds and other jewelry. The suspect was placed in the jail in Edinburg. Still in charge of Headquarters Company, the captain dispatched Sergeant Richmond Earl McWilliams on December 22 to assist Milam County Sheriff Leonidas Leonard Blaylock in investigating the brutal murder of a grocery merchant in Cameron. Finally, on January 9, Hamer publicly announced "he [would] not remain in the service after the change of administration," an odd comment to make if he had completely left two months prior. In the interlude before the Fergusons returned to power, Hamer was able to preserve his pride by resigning, rather than being fired, while also remaining in the job he loved most.[186]

His days on the state payroll were numbered, though, and Hamer was sought for other positions in the law enforcement field. Prominent citizens wrote letters to the Texas Senatorial delegation in Washington recommending Hamer for the job of federal marshal.[187] Amarillo attorney and former prosecutor Clem Calhoun penned one such:

> Time and again in the performance of his duty he has had to resort to the use of fire arms, but he never yet fired the first shot in any such encounter. His body bears several scars nobly and honorably received in the performance of his duty as a peace officer. He has always been my ideal as a peace officer in that he had never craved publicity, but is as eager to avoid the same as the usual run of officer are to secure the same. He is the type that 'saws wood' and says nothing.[188]

Additionally, Dallas City Manager John N. Eddy offered to make a provision to the civil service rules, so the captain could apply to the police department's detective bureau.[189]

The day after she entered the governor's mansion, Governor Ferguson discharged the entire Ranger Force, including Hamer. Perhaps spitefully, she then appointed Hamer's brother, Estill, as the new captain of Headquarters Company on January 19. Nearly coming to blows over the matter, Estill's acceptance drove a wedge between the two brothers for a time.[190]

Hamer's warrant of authority expired on February 1, 1933, and he traveled to Washington, DC early the next month to lobby the Franklin Delano Roosevelt administration for the open post of U.S. marshal. He also met with Senators Tom Connally and Morris Shepherd. While none of the other aspirants possessed Hamer's experience, the president appointed Guy James McNamara. The new marshal had been police chief during the Waco Horror of 1916, and his performance proved decidedly subpar. Roosevelt's choice engendered much bitterness in Hamer's mind, and he harbored a lifelong grudge toward the president. Politically conservative, he came to oppose the New Deal and joined the Republican Party. Meanwhile, Hamer lobbied for positions as a federal Customs officer and a Prohibition agent, but neither effort bore fruit.[191]

However, Hamer, when given the opportunity, continued to chase outlaws. On May 22, three armed bandits and a red-haired female accomplice robbed the First National Bank of San Marcos of $7,040 in cash. They escaped in a black Buick into the hill country of western Hays County. The pursuit of the thieves spread throughout Central Texas, and military policemen at Fort Sam Houston engaged in a running gun battle with the occupants of a Buick sedan that was traveling though the post at sixty miles per hour. The suspicious vehicle escaped. While the confrontation occurred, Hamer accompanied Austin police detective Wade Stubbs in an all-night search of Travis, Hays, Blanco, Gillespie, Mason, Llano, and Williamson Counties. The two lawmen traveled five hundred miles and spotted abundant wild game but no robbers. In late June, Hamer traced a suspected bank robber and killer from Del Rio to Laredo. Information he provided to Laredo officers led to the man's arrest.[192]

While Hamer searched for employment and assisted in manhunts, the Ranger Force under the Ferguson administration was limited to thirty-two men, while the budget was slashed to $82,765 annually. The new members of the service were sometimes unsuited to the position they held, either because of inexperience or questionable character. One of the first orders newly appointed Adjutant General Henry Hutchings issued was to subordinate the Rangers' authority in favor of the county sheriffs. The state officers could only operate in a particular county with the approval of the sheriff and, if they were not wanted, the Rangers could also be removed. As Harris and Sadler noted, "the 'Ferguson Rangers' did manifest some ability as investigators, continuing the transition to a modern law enforcement agency." Unfortunately, their best was not enough.[193]

Indeed, these factors resulted in state officers unable to counter the crime wave sweeping the state in 1934. One such notorious episode began on January 16 at the Eastham prison farm in the Trinity River bottom near Weldon. Early that morning, Clyde Chestnut Barrow, a West Dallas hoodlum and killer, freed convicted felons Raymond Hamilton, Henry Methvin, Joseph Conger "Joe" Palmer, and Hilton Bybee. Barrow was accompanied by his lover, Bonnie Elizabeth Parker Thornton, and James Mullen, a friend of Hamilton who had been released from Eastham on the tenth. Two days previously, Mullen and Floyd Hamilton, Raymond's brother, had concealed two .45 pistols under a bridge near the farm's wood yard. After the prisoners were marched to the field to begin clearing brush, Methvin, Bybee, and Palmer seized the hidden handguns and mortally wounded Major Joseph "Joe" Crowson. Concealed in the brush, Barrow covered the escape with a machine-gun. The four inmates then ran to Barrow's waiting car, which raced away followed by a hail of gunfire from the other guards. Crowson died of his injuries on January 27.[194]

Glamorized in the press and idolized by a citizenry who had felt the pain of bank foreclosures, the duo popularly known as Bonnie and Clyde were a thoroughly dangerous pair of desperadoes. Since 1932, they and a revolving array of accomplices had committed store and gas station robberies, auto thefts, and kidnappings in Texas, Indiana, Minnesota, and Louisiana. More troubling than their relatively petty thefts, though, was their willingness, perhaps eagerness, to resort to cold-blooded murder. Either during hold-ups, chance encounters, and attempts to flee, gang members had killed jeweler John Napoleon Bucher in Hillsboro, Texas, on April 30, 1932; Atoka County Deputy Sheriff Eugene Clyde Moore in Stringtown, Oklahoma, on August 5, 1932; innocent bystander Doyle Johnson in Temple, Texas, on December 25, 1932; Tarrant County Deputy Sheriff Malcolm Davis on January 6, 1933, in Dallas; Detective Harry Leonard McGinnis and Newton County Constable John Wesley Harryman in Joplin, Missouri, on April 13, 1933; and City Marshal Henry Dallas Humphrey in Alma, Arkansas, on June 26, 1933. After their fiercest escape from the law, rolls of camera film discovered at the gang's hideout in Joplin were developed by the *Joplin Globe*. The photographs, including the famous images of Bonnie, holding a cigar in her mouth and a pistol in her hand, were published in newspapers across the country.[195]

With Ferguson Rangers and local officers unable to corner the outlaws, Texas prison system director Lee Simmons personally hired Hamer on February 1 to join the pursuit as a special investigator. The former Ranger captain was given *carte blanche* to ramrod the manhunt in any manner he chose, and to pick whomever he needed to assist him. In order to possess arrest powers, he received a commission of state highway patrolman with a monthly salary of $180. Before setting out, Hamer carefully considered the weapons he would need in this chase. While he naturally packed Old Lucky, the captain knew he might have to contend with the heavy gauge steel body of Barrow's preferred V-8 Fords, so he acquired a Colt Government Model .38 Super pistol. Various primary and secondary sources have established Hamer did not favor semiautomatic handguns. However, as a well-informed firearms expert, Hamer recognized the 130-grain .38 Super bullet had excellent penetration capabilities. In addition, numerous secondary sources have claimed he traded his Remington .30 autoloader for another of the same model in .35 Remington, but firsthand accounts do not identify the exact long guns he may have later used.[196]

Before he left town, Hamer assisted in pursuing bank robbers closer to home. The First National Bank of Coleman was robbed of $24,000 on February 2, and nine employees were temporarily kidnapped during the escape. Texas Rangers and officers of Travis, Blanco, and Bexar Counties joined in the massive manhunt for three suspects. An early rumor, later dispelled, theorized Raymond Hamilton and Clyde Barrow were involved. Captain James Robbins and Rangers Albert West and Vollie Campbell chased a suspicious car south along Highway 20 into the small town of Blanco later that night, but the two occupants escaped in a hail of gunfire. Sheriff John Summerfield Casparis at Johnson City was asked to watch for the vehicle, and he blocked the west end of the highway. Travis County Sheriff Lee O. Allen and Hamer took a squad of men to Oak Hill, but the car vanished somewhere between Dripping Springs and the "Y" on Highway 20. On the morning of February 3, John "Snake" Newton of Fort Worth and his wife Marie were arrested near Sandy by Ranger Captain Eldred Herman Hammond, Sr.

After being booked at city hall, Newton was brought into the office of Austin Police Chief Raymond Thorp, where he talked with Hammond and Estill and Frank Hamer. Newton confessed he had been present in Coleman two days before, but insisted he was innocent of the robbery. His story was contradicted by eyewitnesses and the nearly $7,800 that was found on the Newtons' persons. The money was both new currency issued by the Coleman bank and old that was bound in the institution's wrappers. Complaints were made in A. N. Brewer's justice court charging both Newtons with robbery with firearms, and Marie for concealing stolen property and as an accomplice after the fact. The couple was indicted on February 6. A third suspect was arrested the same day, and a fourth evaded apprehension. John Newton's case was called for trial on June 18 in 119th District Court in Coleman. Later the same night, he was convicted and sentenced to fifteen years' imprisonment.[197]

Hamer set out on Barrow and Parker's trail on February 10, and stayed on it for 102 days through Texas, New Mexico, Oklahoma, Arkansas, Missouri, Kansas, Iowa, Mississippi, and Louisiana. In total, he covered approximately sixteen thousand miles in his car. He used informants to acquire all available information on the fugitives. He learned of Clyde's inclination to steal cars, switch the license plates, and drive hundreds of miles over country roads in a single night. He studied numerous photographs of Barrow and Parker, memorizing their physical details. He interviewed people who knew Barrow, and accumulated an encyclopedic knowledge of the outlaw's habits and behaviors, including the brands of cigarettes and whiskey they preferred. He plotted their volatile *modus operandi* in order to predict their future actions. Hamer's intelligence-gathering was improved when Dallas County Sheriff Richard Allen "Smoot" Schmid loaned the captain the services of Deputy Robert F. "Bob" Alcorn. Having previously arrested Barrow, and knowing Bonnie since she was a girl, the deputy would be able to easily recognize them. Indeed, Schmid, Alcorn, and Deputy Ted Cass Hinton had engaged in a wild shootout with the outlaw duo the previous November.[198]

Time and again, the Barrow gang traveled throughout the Midwest, but the trail always returned to Louisiana. Hamer and Alcorn followed a series of leads to Texarkana, Longansport, Keachi, and Shreveport, arriving in the latter town on February 15. Traveling to Arcadia, they met with Sheriff Henderson Jordan of Bienville Parish on the nineteenth, and found him to be "discreet and reliable." On the twenty-third, the Texas lawmen returned to Dallas, and Alcorn resumed his normal duties with the sheriff's department. Working alone, Hamer checked into the downtown Sanger Hotel, on the corner of Ervay and Canton Streets. Barrow's sister and brother-in-law managed the hotel's beauty shop, and Hamer observed their movements while gathering information on the gang.[199]

With Alcorn busy investigating a bank robbery, Hamer teamed with veteran agent Edward J. Dowd of the Division of Investigation (renamed from the BOI the previous year). Early in March, the pair visited Huntsville prison and interviewed Hilton Bybee, who had been recaptured in Amarillo. The convict was able to give details on the gang's movements, including the fact they had abandoned a vehicle near Electra, twenty-seven miles west of Wichita Falls. Hamer and Dowd traveled to Grapevine in Denton County to speak with an informant, but the lead proved useless. They then went to Wichita Falls, where they met with the county sheriff, the police chief, and other local officers on March 7. Based on Bybee's information, Hamer discovered the gang's hideout near the Tenth Street Bridge, south of the Wichita River and west of town. The only items left were spent shell casings and a bullet-riddled automobile. Expanding their search, the officers found the abandoned car Bybee had described, and discovered, inside, shotgun shells and a receipt for two dresses from Lord's department store in Dallas.[200]

Even while Hamer was following the trail of clues, Barrow, Parker, and their cohorts were continuing their outlaw ways. On February 16, they burglarized the National Guard armory in the town of Ranger and accumulated four .30-caliber BARs, thirteen Colt Model 1911 .45 semiautomatic pistols, and a quantity of ammunition. Eleven days later, they robbed the Henry Bank in Lancaster of more than four thousand dollars. After this theft, bickering arose within the gang, and Hamilton and his girlfriend struck out alone. Joe Palmer followed suit. However, Hamilton was apprehended in Howe, Grayson County, on April 25 after robbing the First National Bank of Lewisville.[201]

On Easter Sunday, April 1, Barrow and Parker gunned down state troopers Holloway Daniel "H. D." Murphy and Edward Bryant Wheeler on West Dove Road, just off Highway 114 near Grapevine. Methvin was asleep in the car at the time of the murders. The next day, law officers swarmed the area to collect physical evidence, which included three 16-gauge shotgun shells, three 12-gauge shells, five .45-caliber cartridge casings, and one .30-06 shell. Examining a whiskey bottle left at the crime scene, a Bertillon expert from the Tarrant County Sheriff's office found latent fingerprints and, over time, positively identified them as belonging to Barrow's right ring finger and Methvin's right index finger. The manhunt grew exponentially to include hundreds of county and municipal lawmen in Iowa, Nebraska, Colorado, Wyoming, Kansas, Missouri, Arkansas, Oklahoma, and Texas, who pursued a variety of leads in their individual jurisdictions; most proved to be false. Yet, even while authorities sought the gang, Barrow, Parker, and Methvin murdered Constable William Calvin Campbell of the Commerce, Oklahoma, Police Department on April 6. The outlaws also wounded and kidnapped Police Chief Percy Boyd, but released him alive the next day near Fort Scott, Kansas. On May 18, Clyde and Bonnie were indicted by the Tarrant County grand jury for the murders of Wheeler and Murphy.[202]

The same day the two patrolmen were murdered, Hamer was appointed a special grand jury bailiff by Judge Noland G. Williams of Dallas County Criminal District Court No. 2. Deputies Bob Alcorn and Ted Hinton were detailed to accompany the captain. Nine days later, Hamer was instructed by Highway Patrol Chief Louis Graham Phares to secure the services of one more man. The captain's single choice was his trusted friend Maney Gault, who joined the pursuit in Dallas on April 14.[203]

On May 21, Sheriff Henderson Jordan received a tip that the First National Bank of Arcadia was going to be robbed in the next two or three days. He immediately notified Hamer. Indeed, the sheriff proved to be the one who most facilitated the coming events. The manhunters had already received a break in the case when Ivy Terrell Methvin, Henry's father, met with Jordan and agreed to give up the outlaw duo if his family was not prosecuted for harboring fugitives, and if his son received a pardon. Governor Ferguson gave her approval, and, through intermediaries, the deal was struck.

Methvin would place himself at a predetermined rural site near Gibsland, Louisiana, which Barrow and Parker, leaving their Black Lake hideout, were sure to pass in their automobile. Hamer, Gault, Alcorn, Hinton, Jordan, and Chief Deputy Prentiss Morel Oakley of Bienville Parish traveled to the location on the side of Highway 154. Despite the grand-sounding name, the road was a graveled secondary lane. The six lawmen arrived at about 2:30 a.m. on May 23 and waited for the two outlaws to show. None of the Texans held legal powers in Louisiana, so the team cooperated under the sheriff's authority. They positioned themselves north to south in the tall grass at intervals of ten feet along the road as it swept around a curve and through a patch of pine trees. Although later narratives contradict one another, Hamer was likely on the right of the line with a Remington Model 11 semiautomatic shotgun; next to him was Gault with another Remington shotgun; then Jordan and Alcorn with two Remington Model 8s of indeterminate caliber; and Oakley with a .35 Remington Model 8. Hinton was on the extreme left with a BAR. Hamer, Gault, and Jordan were tasked with firing into the front seat, and Alcorn and Oakley into the rear in the event it was occupied. If the outlaws looked to be escaping the trap, Hinton was prepared to step in front of the vehicle and "bust the engine." Additional shotguns may have been ready at hand, and each man also carried a personal sidearm. In Hamer's case, he packed "Old Lucky" and his Colt .38 Super. The countryside surrounding the ambush site was later described as a "hazed vista across a valley of piney woodlands and cornfields and patches of cotton in bloom, with the red clay hills shimmering beyond." All too soon, though, nature's splendor would be spoiled by bullets and spilled blood.[204]

Due to Barrow's and Parker's penchant for murdering law officers, Hamer was of two minds in apprehending them peacefully. He held no regard for Clyde, and resolved to kill him without hesitation, if the need arose. However, Hamer, a product of the Old West, was naturally inclined to honor and respect women, especially one who was the same age as his cherished stepdaughter Beverly. Further increasing his wish to avoid bloodshed, Bonnie was rumored to be in a "delicate condition," a genteel euphemism for a pregnancy. Thus, he had little desire to be forced into shooting her. Nevertheless, Hamer knew the choice was not his to make.[205]

The posse waited through the mosquito-infested night. Beginning at dawn, Methvin pretended to be fixing a flat tire on his logging truck. Barrow and Parker appeared in a new tan-colored Ford V-8 "Deluxe Fordor" sedan at 9:15 a.m. Their identity was confirmed by Alcorn and Hinton before Barrow stopped the car at Methvin's truck, pressing the clutch and downshifting the transmission to low gear. At a range of less than fifteen yards, events then unfolded swiftly. Clyde inched forward to allow two approaching logging trucks, one driven by eyewitness William Lyons, to pass on the narrow road. Alcorn and Hinton each asserted that several of the lawmen called on the bandits to halt, while Lyons claimed there was no warning. Thinking the outlaw pair were escaping, Oakley opened fire, which prompted the other officers to begin shooting. Bonnie and Clyde died almost instantly in a hail of 167 bullets and buckshot. Barrow's lifeless foot slipped off the clutch, and the car, still in gear, rolled forward downhill into the embankment on the left. Alcorn rushed onto the road and delivered a *coup de grace* to Clyde through the back window, then another into Bonnie via the rear passenger's window. As he approached the bullet-riddled Ford, Hinton's immediate thought was reportedly, "I hope we haven't just blown an innocent farmer and his wife all to hell." However, his fears were allayed when they observed the bodies. Clyde, clutching a revolver, had been struck seventeen times. Due to the angles of the shooters' positions, Bonnie, doubled over a .45 pistol and a half-eaten sandwich, was hit by twenty-six bullets. Her sister, Billie Jean Mace, later commented from a jail cell: "I have been expecting it to end this way."[206]

Hamer telephoned Phares and informed him, "the job is done." News of the infamous outlaws' demise quickly spread, and curious spectators were soon surrounding the "death car," stealing small items from the interior as souvenirs, and prying spent slugs from nearby trees. The Ford, with Bonnie and Clyde still inside, was towed into Arcadia eighteen miles to the east. Thousands of interested sightseers flooded the town. Telephone and telegraph news services, and radio stations, blasted the event nationwide. Reporters raced to the area to capture the story. Inundated with interview requests, Hamer told a *St. Louis Post-Dispatch* reporter over the telephone: "We shot the devil out of them … We just laid a trap for them. A steel trap." Doctor

James L. Wade's autopsy and the coroner's inquest did not confirm the account Bonnie was carrying a child at the time of her death. In an interview with Texarkana newsman Charles H. Newell, Hamer dispelled many of the myths that had sprung up regarding Bonnie and Clyde. At the same time, he was careful to conceal Ivy Methvin's role in the affair, and, in speaking with Newell, first mentioned the story of Barrow collecting messages deposited in a tree stump at the ambush site. However, newspapers reported Henry Methvin had received a conditional pardon from Ma Ferguson, and speculated on whether he had provided information to authorities. Phares denied Methvin was the informant and declared that only "Providence" had saved him from accompanying his two compatriots into death.[207]

While Bonnie and Clyde never attained the gangland stature of John Harvey Bailey or John Dillinger, their readiness to murder police officers and innocent civilians had made them extremely dangerous. "I never knew another outlaw like Barrow. He was a wanton killer and steered pretty clear of underworld associates except for Bonnie Parker," Hamer told the United Press. "I hate to bust a cap on a woman," he said in another interview, "especially when she was sitting down. However, if it wouldn't have been her, it would have been us." The act of killing a woman, no matter how homicidal, troubled the ex-captain, and he mentioned his uneasiness on several occasions. Indeed, Gibsland was the last time Frank Hamer fired a weapon at another human being. Shortly afterward, he sat down in Austin and gave a lengthy interview to *Kansas City Star* investigative reporter Alexander Black "A. B." MacDonald. When the Pulitzer Prize winning journalist asked him directly the number of people he had killed, the former Ranger refused to answer: "I won't discuss it. All my killings were in the line of duty. It was an unpleasant duty." He did, however, disclose that he had been involved in fifty-two gunfights, which included numerous skirmishes with bandits and smugglers along the Rio Grande. Then and now, armed encounters with violent offenders is hazardous work, and Hamer revealed he had been shot twenty-three times; some bullets he carried to his dying day.[208]

In spite of the discussions Hamer would have with reporters, though, the manhunter consistently refused offers to profit from the killing of Bonnie and Clyde. He reportedly treated a tendered ten thousand dollars from a book publisher as something worth "no more than a Mexican dime." During the pursuit, Hamer received a wage of $180 per month and a promise of reimbursement for expenses. When he submitted his fifteen-hundred-dollar expense account, the state disallowed fourteen dollars for telephone calls because he had not acquired receipts. The fact he was essentially undercover and unable to ask for chits seemed to have escaped the auditors' notice. However, the four Texans present at Gibsland received equal shares of the one-thousand-dollar reward offered by Phares; Jordan and Oakley opted not to apply for payment. Additionally, two private contributors designated Hamer and Gault were to receive an additional two hundred dollars.[209]

Among the arsenal found in Bonnie and Clyde's car were three BARs, two riot shotguns, seven Colt Model 1911 .45 pistols, two other handguns, over one hundred 20-round magazines for the BARs, and three thousand rounds of ammunition. Also recovered were road maps, romance and detective magazines, a saxophone, varied canned goods, and more than a dozen license plates. Hamer later received several letters from the families of the slain outlaws, mostly concerning the four pistols and one sawed-off shotgun he had taken from the car and kept as a legacy for his family. He declined to respond. Following Hamer's death, all the firearms in his collection were bequeathed to Robert Richard "Bobby" Shelton, a senior executive of the King Ranch and an avid gun collector. They were later donated or loaned to the Texas A&M University Museum in College Station. The firearms were subsequently lent to the Texas Ranger Hall of Fame, but the provenance records were lost sometime before 1989.[210]

With the bandit duo safely in the ground, speculation arose that Hamer and Gault would be hired by the FBI to hunt down Dillinger, but Director John Edgar Hoover's innate jealousy prompted him to forgo retaining the manhunters' services. The Bureau publicly insisted Hamer did not meet the requirement that every agent be either a lawyer or an accountant, ignoring the fact that Gus T. Jones, Charles Bastell Winstead, and James "Doc" White, all capable Texas lawmen on the federal payroll, were neither of those things. However, Hamer continued to be identified with the Texas Rangers, and the dispatching of Bonnie and Clyde had a positive effect on the fortunes of the beleaguered service. With the final ouster of the Fergusons from the statehouse, and the election of James Burr V. Allred, many had talked of disbanding the organization as tarnished and outdated. The successful manhunt still fresh in the public's mind made such a decision unlikely. As Boessenecker observed, "It was a great irony that Hamer, although his career as a Ranger Captain was over, had saved the Texas Rangers."[211]

The Barrow-Parker episode was not his last case, though. On July 22, 1934, Ray Hamilton, Joe Palmer, and Irvin Newton "Blackie" Thompson successfully escaped from death row at Huntsville, and scaled the prison walls. Whitey Walker was killed by guards in the attempt, and convicts Roy Alvin Johnson, Hub Stanley, and Charles Frazier (real name Eldridge Roy Johnson) were recaptured. The surviving trio became the subjects of a massive manhunt, and Palmer was apprehended in Paducah, Kentucky, on August 11. Rumors spread that Hamer would become involved, but an altercation at the Travis County relief headquarters sent two men to the hospital. In response, the ex-Ranger was employed as special investigator for the state relief commission. The state relief administrator announced, "Hamer will remain at the county relief headquarters as long as necessary." The matter was soon resolved. While Hamer waited to be called upon, Thompson died in a December 6 shootout with police on Highway 66 near Amarillo. More trouble kept the former Ranger close to home. Clara Grohman, wife of County Commissioner Adolph C. Grohman, was sitting in the living room of her Bastrop home on December 30, when an unknown assailant fired a shotgun through a window. Although she was struck in the forehead, face, and neck, Grohman recovered. Meanwhile, Hamer and Gault joined Sheriff Edward Duvall Cartwright in a fruitless search for the gunman. Likewise, Hamilton remained at large, and Hamer, who was still a bailiff for the Dallas County grand jury, was finally assigned on March 13, 1935, to track down the fugitive. However, Hamilton was captured by Sheriff Schmid and five deputies, including Ted Hinton, on April 6 in Grapevine, and Hamer was removed from the county payroll. Both Hamilton and Palmer were executed on May 10, 1935.[212]

Hamer had one last moment of police work on April 24, 1935. That evening, Texas Supreme Court Associate Justice William A. Pierson and his wife Lena were fatally shot on the Bull Creek Road approximately fifteen miles west of Austin. Apprised of the homicides, Hamer immediately initiated an investigation and assisted the authorities in the early stages. Investigators determined the victims' twenty-year-old son Howard had committed the killings and attempted to conceal his crime by concocting a story of murderous highwaymen. By then, Hamer's involvement in the case had ended, and Howard was declared criminally insane and committed to an asylum. After being diagnosed as medically competent, he was tried for the murders in November 1963, and found not guilty by reason of insanity.[213]

With the conclusion of his public career, Hamer passed the next few years in the private sector. In October 1935, during an International Longshoremen's Association strike in Houston, he was deputized by the Port Commission to lead a special squad in policing the waterfront. The retired captain employed a force of twenty former lawmen. Two years later, he partnered with Roy T. Rogers, ex-Houston police chief, in establishing a private security guard firm. Protecting oil fields, refineries, wharves, shipping operations, bottling plants, and building projects, the company scored lucrative contracts with Gulf Oil, the Texas Company (known today as Texaco), Coca-Cola, and the A. J. Rife Construction Company of Dallas. In November 1936, Hamer's and Rogers's guards protected the property of shipping and trucking interests during a seamen's strike. Hamer shuttled back and forth from Austin to Houston, but his work initially earned him five hundred dollars per month, substantially more than he had ever made wearing a badge. Working more and more exclusively for the Texas Company, Hamer carried the title of special investigator by 1940, and the company's annual report for 1944 stated the former Ranger had received $67,507 in compensation for his protection services.[214]

Hamer continued to provide security on the docks, and earned the enmity of the labor unions. A firm supporter of democracy and free market capitalism, he loathed totalitarianism in all its forms—communism, socialism, and fascism—and distrusted the expansion of government power under President Roosevelt's New Deal. Following the German invasion of Poland on September 1, 1939, and the commencement of World War II, Hamer closely monitored the situation in Europe. In March 1941, he proposed the establishment of a one-thousand-man volunteer defense force composed of former lawmen and veterans, each one with "a pistol and an inclination." The offer seems to have never been accepted. Once the United States and Japan were at war, Hamer spent $260 in long-distance phone calls in an unsuccessful attempt to raise a company of men for jungle and guerrilla warfare.[215]

Although Frank would not take an active role in the war effort, the Hamer family, like countless other American households, made its own sacrifices. Billy, the Hamer's oldest son, had attended the Allen Military Academy in Bryan and the San Marcos Academy. He married Joy Ann Stubblefield in 1941, and they had one daughter the following year. Billy spent the majority of the conflict as a guard captain at the Pennsylvania Shipworks in Beaumont. In 1944, the couple divorced, and Billy enlisted in the U.S. Marine Corps on June 24. He trained at the San Diego Marine Base, and served with the 9th Marine Regiment, 3rd Marine Division as a private. Participating in the invasion of Iwo Jima, he was killed in action on March 7, 1945, while evacuating wounded personnel. The ship *Burning Knot* was dedicated to Billy's memory upon its launch at the Pennsylvania Shipworks' yards on June 30. His body was shipped home to his parents four years later, and he was buried in Austin's Memorial Park Cemetery with full military honors. Billy's death was a shattering blow to his father, and one from which the normally resilient captain never fully recovered.[216]

In 1948, Coke Stevenson, the former governor, was running against Lyndon Baines Johnson for an open seat in the U.S. Senate. The contest would prove to be the narrowest Senate primary race in the nation's history. Following a close election in July, the run-off occurred on August 28. As the final count was tallied, Stevenson began emerging as the victor by September 2, with a margin of just 362 votes. However, the following day, late returns from Precinct No. 13 in Jim Wells County increased Johnson's statewide lead by eighty-seven votes, making him the declared winner. As Jim Wells was dominated by corrupt political boss George Berham Parr, Stevenson suspected voter fraud, and called on his old friend and hunting buddy Frank Hamer to investigate. Once Hamer, Stevenson, and former FBI agent T. Kellis Dibrell, the candidate's campaign manager, arrived in Alice on September 10, the old Ranger advised them to remove their suit jackets. Having revealed the other two as unarmed, Hamer removed his coat and exposed Old Lucky tucked into his waistband. He had received a warrant of Special Ranger on February 1, 1946, which authorized him to carry a sidearm.[217]

Ordering the *pistoleros* guarding the door to the Parr-owned South Texas State Bank to stand aside, Hamer and his companions entered the building and confronted Deputy Sheriff Luis Salas, the election judge for Precinct No. 13. Stevenson demanded to see the poll list and tally sheets, which were stored in the bank's vault. As part of the records of Clarence Martens, who had recently retired as chairman of the Jim Wells County Democratic Executive Committee, the tallies had been the basis for the certification of the official returns in the primary. Before Benjamin Franklin "Tom" Donald, Jr., the secretary of the county committee, changed his mind, the lawyers were able to verify 203 votes were fraudulent. Tellingly, the names had been added to the poll list in alphabetical order and in a different color of ink than the others. Donald snatched the list away before all of them could be copied. Armed with only a partial list of eleven names, Hamer interviewed purported voters and was able to obtain signed and notarized affidavits from some Hispanics testifying they had not voted. Stevenson's lawyers confirmed another man on the list had been out of the county on Election Day, and another three had been deceased for years. Playing offense, the Johnson camp pointed to alleged voting irregularities benefitting Stevenson in Brown, Jack, Dallas, Gregg, and Cameron Counties. However, demographics played a larger role in these locales than chicanery. Johnson biographer Robert Dallek argued both candidates participated in the switching of votes in places where they enjoyed strong support. Law professor Edward B. Foley observed that Johnson never refuted Stevenson's claims, and only the former governor produced credible evidence of fraud. Johnson's campaign manager, future governor John Bowden Connally, later observed vote switching was simple while creating new votes was more difficult.[218]

Before he and Hamer left Alice on the tenth, Stevenson filed a petition with the county clerk requesting the Jim Wells County Democratic Executive Committee undergo a recertification of a new and accurate count of the county's votes for the State Democratic Executive Committee. Recently elected chairman Harry Lee Adams and ten reform-minded county committee members met and discussed Stevenson's affidavit and the additional evidence of voter fraud that had been uncovered in Precinct 13. They agreed to draw up a new certification for the state committee by either removing the two hundred names from the tally sheet or, in the face of rampant corruption, disqualify all votes from the precinct.[219]

Johnson's lawyers responded the same day by filing a civil suit in 126th District Court in Austin, seeking to prevent Jim Wells County from certifying new election returns. They charged that Stevenson, Hamer, Dibrell, Harry Adams, and eighteen members of the Jim Wells County committee were engaged in a conspiracy to steal the election. The attorneys further claimed Stevenson and Hamer had used threats and intimidation to force the committee into participating in the scheme. With no basis in legal precedent, Judge Roy Coleman Archer granted a temporary restraining order halting the recount of votes, and ordered a hearing in Seventy-ninth District Court in Alice. Stevenson was not given notice prior to the ruling. Appearing before Judge Lorenz Broeter, a Parr ally, in Alice on September 13, Johnson's attorneys argued only the Travis County court had jurisdiction over the case, while Stevenson's lawyers countered by questioning the jurisdiction of any court to restrain the recounting of votes. Broeter ruled for Johnson, and Stevenson's counsel gave notice of appeal. Stevenson challenged the election results before the state party's central committee, but his claim was rejected by a vote of twenty-nine to twenty-eight. Stevenson then filed an election contest in federal court, and obtained a preliminary injunction on September 22 that allowed for a hearing into the balloting in Jim Wells County. Evidence of fraud in Jim Wells, Zapata, and Duval Counties was persuasive, but Johnson's attorneys obtained a ruling from Supreme Court Justice Hugo Lafayette Black that asserted the federal courts had no jurisdiction over state elections. The justice set aside the injunction on the twenty-eighth. Stevenson appealed the decision to the entire Supreme Court, which refused on October 5 to hear the petition. Emerging victorious from the episode, "Landslide Lyndon," as he became known, appeared on the general ballot in November and quashed his Republican opponent.

Courtesy of widespread voter fraud, the new senator's path to the White House was made possible.[220]

Indignant over the bogus charges Johnson had leveled, Hamer appeared before Justice of the Peace Preston Leon Nairn, Sr. on October 20, 1949, and filed a felony complaint, charging Johnson with "false swearing in an affidavit." The Travis County grand jury heard the evidence, but refused to indict Senator Johnson. The official fiction that the election had been honest lasted until July 1977, when Luis Salas, allegedly suffering from a guilty conscience, made a full confession of the whole matter. He told the Associated Press that George Parr had ordered him to add two hundred additional voters to the tally list.[221]

Meanwhile, in 1948, Hamer had turned the day-to-day operation of the security company over to Rogers. He sold his interest to his partner the following year and retired to his Austin home. He was suggested for a place on the Texas Public Safety Commission that became vacant in 1951, but Governor Robert Allan Shivers declined to appoint him. Hamer stumped for Dwight David Eisenhower's presidential campaign, and, after the general's victory, lobbied for appointment for U.S. Marshal of the Western District of Texas. This endeavor was also unsuccessful.[222]

Hamer's Special Ranger commission expired on January 1, 1955, and he chose to not apply for a renewal. Having suffered from arteriosclerotic heart disease for the previous fifteen years, he died on July 10, 1955, in Austin of congenital heart failure. He was buried two days later next to Billy. Among the eight active and five honorary pallbearers were W. W. Sterling, Colonel Lee Simmons, Captain Tom Hickman, and Ranger Charlie Miller. His funeral was officiated by Doctor Pierre Bernard Hill, longtime chaplain of the Texas Rangers. During the service, the reverend said of Frank Hamer, "Here lies before us the remains of one of the greatest men I ever knew … a man who feared Almighty God, but never feared the face of any man."[223]

Hamer remained well-known in Texas, even while his national fame diminished. Then, two Hollywood screenwriters read biographer John Toland's 1963 *Dillinger Days* and learned of Parker and Barrow's misdeeds. Their subsequent work led the public to rediscover the outlaw pair when the motion picture *Bonnie and Clyde* appeared in theaters in 1967. Directed by

Arthur Penn, and starring Warren Beatty and Faye Dunaway, the film was a historically inaccurate, violent blockbuster that tapped into contemporary themes of youth rebellion, women's liberation, and distrust of authority. As portrayed by Denver Pyle, the Frank Hamer of the movie was the spiteful villain, while Beatty and Dunaway were the charismatic and sexually vibrant heroes. As author and journalist Bryan Burrough commented, "Art had now done for Bonnie Parker and Clyde Barrow something they could never achieve in life: it had taken a shark-eyed multiple murderer and his deluded girlfriend and transformed them into sympathetic characters, imbuing them with a cuddly likeability they did not possess, and a cultural significance they do not deserve." On the other hand, the late Ranger captain's reputation was besmirched by the movie, and the slanderous interpretation would remain in the public consciousness for decades. Gladys was outraged and retained Joseph Dahr "Joe" Jamail, a leading trial lawyer in Texas. Jamail filed a lawsuit charging defamation, invasion of privacy, and the unauthorized use of Hamer's name. Warner Brothers fought the suit, but, when Jamail swore to take Beatty's deposition, the studio conceded the case. In an out-of-court settlement, Gladys received twenty thousand dollars in damages.[224]

Gladys moved to San Marcos in 1973 to be closer to her son. She died there on May 17, 1976, of cancer of the pancreas. She was buried next to Frank and Billy in Austin's Oakwood Cemetery.[225]

Helen married stock raiser Benton Vernon McMullan on September 16, 1924, in Snyder. They had a son and a daughter, and lived in Scurry and Garza Counties. The couple participated in another marriage ceremony in Mitchell County on September 16, 1942, but seem to have separated or divorced by March 1950. Helen died on April 12, 1966, in a fire that completely consumed her historic ranch house.[226]

Beverly attended the Orton School for Girls in Pasadena, California. Returning to Texas, she attended high school in Austin, then studied with well-known vocal instructor Ralph Leo at the University Conservatory of Music. She married Benton's brother, Rudolph L. "Rudy" McMullan, in her parents' Riverside Drive home on July 26, 1928. She and Rudolph brought one son into the world. They divorced, and Beverly married architect Albert

Baldwin Benson and gave birth to another son. Albert had worked with the design team headed by Paul Philippe Cret and Robert Leon White for the Main Building ("The Tower") on the campus of the University of Texas in Austin. The Benson family lived in Springhill, Alabama, where Albert was the president of his own architecture firm. He died in Mobile on June 17, 1968, and was buried in Austin Memorial Park Cemetery. Beverly died in Snyder on March 9, 2011.[227]

Frank, Jr. married Dorothy Elinor "Dottie" Bissell on November 4, 1939, and they had one son. Already an experienced officer with the Civil Air Patrol, he joined the U.S. Marine Corps on June 26, 1944, and served as a pilot and a pilot instructor. He was discharged from service on April 24, 1945. In 1948, Frank, Jr. received a Special Ranger commission, and worked as a bodyguard for governors Beauford Jester and Allen Shivers. He then spent thirty years as a warden-pilot with the Texas Fish and Game Commission, which became the Texas Parks and Wildlife Department in 1963. He was appointed to the Texas Ranger Commemorative Commission by Senior Captain Clint Peoples in 1973. His last assignment for Parks and Wildlife was as game warden for Hays County. Retiring in 1980, he lived in San Marcos. Dorothy died on November 13, 1996, in San Marcos, and Frank, Jr. followed her in death on September 19, 2006, in Wimberley.[228]

Frank Hamer was one of the greatest Texas lawmen of the twentieth century. As a detective, manhunter, and gunfighter, he contended with desperadoes, smugglers, Klansmen, bootleggers, bank robbers, corrupt politicians, arrogant bankers, and a future president. He accumulated a remarkable score of accomplishments and earned a reputation as an incorruptible and relentless enforcer of the law.

Tom R. Hickman. *Courtesy Texas Ranger Hall of Fame and Museum, Waco, TX.*

Chapter 3

Thomas R. Hickman: "A Daring and Honorable Lawman"

Thomas Rufus Hickman emulated the Hollywood stereotype of the Texas Rangers in the early twentieth century. Always wearing a wide-brimmed Stetson, and immaculately dressed in western attire, he was tall, wiry, and handsome. His broad smile and extroverted nature revealed a flair for courting publicity and an eagerness to speak to reporters, although he was described as sometimes alternating between depression and elation. An accomplished horseman, he delighted in rodeos, either as a participant or a judge. However, as author Mike Cox commented, "Despite his ready smile and a propensity for showmanship, Hickman could be as serious as a train wreck when necessary." He refrained from gambling or imbibing liquor and ordered his men to do the same. Throughout a long career as a daring and honorable lawman, he confronted bank robbers, tamed oil boomtowns, and kept the peace during labor strikes.

He was born on February 21, 1886, on the family farm near Gainesville, Cooke County, Texas. His parents, Walker Broadhead and Mary Ann "Mollie" (McCormick) Hickman, had been born in Nelson County, Kentucky, on July 20, 1849, and October 17, 1855, respectively. They married on September 19, 1880. Prior to 1884, the couple moved to Cooke County where

Walker partnered with his older brother, Rufus Henry Hickman, in farm properties. Tom's siblings were Willett J. Hickman, born on December 23, 1884, and Nancy "Nannie" Hickman, born on June 20, 1887. Beginning in 1902, Walker and Mollie acquired a three-acre homestead in the northern section of Gainesville and over time a cattle spread of fifteen hundred acres in the northwest portion of the county. In addition, Walker and Mollie dealt in a number of land transactions, both together and separately.[1]

Tom played for the Gainesville Athletic Club's football team in 1905 and 1906; the team was undefeated both seasons. After graduating from Gainesville Business College in 1907, he was a member of the Miller Brothers' 101 Ranch Wild West Show for one year. While traveling with the ensemble, he befriended imminent silent-film star Thomas Edwin "Tom" Mix and future national treasure William Penn Adair "Will" Rogers. Throughout his life, Hickman, an outgoing extrovert, demonstrated a showman's flair that might have been honed as a member of the troupe. "I always got by with a sense of humor, I guess," he later stated. "If you just keep smiling, usually you won't need to draw." However, he did possess a temper when provoked. According to Hickman's son, the captain loved horses and cows, but hated small animals such as dogs and cats. Family tradition holds that Hickman was chased by wolves as a schoolboy.[2]

Returning home, he became a deputy constable in Gainesville in 1908. The town boasted a population of ten to eleven thousand residents, with twenty-three retail liquor stores and seven wholesale houses. The liquor retailers used "spring wagons" to haul packaged alcohol to the express office at the railroad depot. Once the Santa Fe Company train arrived, the liquor was placed aboard the express cars and transported into Oklahoma, bound for the Indian agencies. While this traffic was prohibited on the federal reservations, the shipments were legal in Texas. However, Oklahoma outlaws periodically crossed the Red River into Cooke County with the intention of visiting Gainesville's red-light district. Hickman and fellow constable N. M. Burch were compelled to visit the saloons and corral rowdy drunks. In 1912, he was hired as a deputy by Sheriff Louis Bringham. Five years later, Bringham chose to not seek another term, and Hickman threw his hat into the electoral ring. The contest was a close-run thing, and Hickman was narrowly defeated at the polls.[3]

On August 24, 1918, the Texas rifle team that would participate in the National Match at Camp Perry, Ohio, on September 1 was announced to the public. Hickman was among the fifteen members who all belonged to rifle clubs affiliated with the National Rifle Association. Considered the crack shots of Texas, each man was qualified as a marksman or expert rifleman.[4]

Following the death of Henry Lee Ransom, Hickman petitioned Adjutant General James Aloysius Harley on April 2, 1918, for a commission as Ranger captain. However, his time had not yet arrived.[5] Instead, he enlisted in Company A of the Ranger Force in Marfa on June 16, 1919, as a private. Under Captain Jerry Gray, Hickman was equipped with a saddlehorse and a packhorse, and assigned to patrol the international boundary.[6] The declared emergency prompted the Thirty-sixth Legislature to approve an appropriation of thirty thousand dollars for the maintenance of the Ranger Force.[7]

Hickman transferred to Headquarters Company on August 8. Sergeant Joseph B. "Joe" Brooks was acting as company commander while Captain William Martin Hanson was in Austin attending the legislative inquiry into the Ranger Force.[8] As a member of Headquarters Company, Hickman carried out a number of special assignments for which there are few details. On September 16, he was ordered to report to Governor William Pettus Hobby for duty. On completion of his task, he was to return to his home station.[9] On October 21, Hickman was ordered to proceed to Henrietta by the first train and report to District Attorney Fletcher Samuel Jones of the Thirtieth Judicial District.[10]

Even though the U.S. Supreme Court had ruled in 1896 the boundary between Texas and Oklahoma was the south banks of the Red River and its main tributary, the Prairie Dog Town Fork (or South Fork), the two states became embroiled in a dispute over the exact verbiage of the decision. The oil bonanza occurring in the Burkburnett oil fields north of Wichita Falls had only exacerbated the ongoing issue. Petitioning Judge George Calhoun of the Fifty-third District Court in Austin, Texas, claimants to the Burk-Bet and Burk-Senator plots requested a receiver be appointed to manage the properties until the courts resolved the matter. Before Calhoun made his ruling on October 7, 1919, though, Judge William Chamberlayne "Cham" Jones of the Fifteenth Judicial District in Lawton issued a court order authorizing

Oklahoma parties to seize the contested properties. Judge John William Hornsby, the receiver appointed by Judge Calhoun, secured possession from his counterpart by means of a ruse and deployed forty men armed with rifles and a machine gun around the wells. On November 13, Hickman, Captain Roy Wilkinson Aldrich, and Harrison Hamer were ordered to proceed to Wichita Falls. Two days later, they accompanied Hornsby to the oil wells along the Red River where the lawmen held the property and kept the peace.[11]

Once known as "Hogtown," Desdemona in Eastland County was a quiet village known for its socialists, peanut industry, and baseball field. Then, in September 1918, Tom Moore Dees's Hog Creek Oil Company struck black gold on the Joe Duke farm south of Desdemona in Comanche County. On November 26, 1919, the recently promoted Captain Joe Brooks, Hickman, and Private Fred Marks received orders to proceed to Desdemona.[12] Eleven days later, Brooks and Hickman were ordered to Eastland to comply with verbal instructions.[13]

Privates Samuel "Sam" McKenzie and Sterling Orlando Durst, Company E, and Hickman and James Taylor Martin, Headquarters Company, received verbal orders on December 19 to proceed by the first available train to Desdemona. In total, six Rangers would be dispatched to the troubled oil town to replace the two sheriff's deputies who had stepped down. Sheriff Elmer Lawrence denied that he had quit, and signaled his intention to serve out the remainder of his term. The mass resignations had been the result of a citizens' committee demanding an end to vice trades, and a justice of the peace was left as the only law officer in the city of fifteen thousand. Within a few days, the sheriff appointed deputies to police Desdemona, but Judge Edward Alvin Hill of the Eighty-eighth Judicial District requested one or two Rangers remain in town. McKenzie and Ranger Hardy Burl Purvis stayed while Hickman, Martin, and Durst were ordered to report to the captain.[14]

The boundary dispute along the Red River continued, and ownership of the oil-rich Burk Divide, worth some $100 million, remained at stake. The State of Oklahoma filed an original suit against Texas in the U.S. Supreme Court on December 8, 1919, to determine the true boundary. Additionally, the U.S. government, representing the riparian claims of Comanche, Kiowa, and Apache allottees, intervened in the case asserting oil was being pumped from Indian lands north of the river, and demanded royalty payments. On behalf of the State of Texas, Attorney General Calvin Maples Cureton filed suit in Fifty-third District Court on January 10, 1920, against three Oklahoma-based companies seeking to recover nearly five hundred acres of riverbed. The court granted a temporary injunction restraining those operators holding federal placer mining claims or permits issued by the Oklahoma state government. However, claimants began issuing threats of violence against those interfering in their operations, and fears of an armed clash grew.[15]

On January 20, Captains Brooks and William Matthew Ryan of Company C were sent to Wichita Falls with fifteen Rangers. Arriving four days later, they met Company B under the command of Captain Charles Francis Stevens and Sergeant Frank A. Hamer. The twenty-eight well-armed Rangers were supposedly present to put a halt to gambling, bootlegging, and other felonies, but their camp was on land claimed by both Texas and Oklahoma. Six days later, General Cope and a detachment of Rangers, including Hickman and Hamer, served an injunction on the Burk Divide Oil Company's wells. Hamer dared the Oklahoman guards to force the Texans off the property, but the latter declined and retreated. Sam Sparks, a Texas claimant to the land, warned Cope that an Oklahoma deputy sheriff had reportedly cached arms and ammunition in a bunkhouse south of the Red River. As the governor's orders made the Rangers publicly paid gunmen in the service of private oil concerns, Stevens had refused to obey since "such action was not sanctioned by the courts." He resigned his commission effective February 3. While the matter was ended for the Rangers two months later, the legal arguments would continue until 1926.[16]

On March 19, 1920, sixteen hundred dockworkers belonging to Locals 385 and 807 of the International Longshoremen's Association in Galveston left their jobs in a nationwide walkout over high prices and low wages. Their actions effectively closed the port, and hundreds of tons of merchandise was left unloaded. Tension grew between the city commission, who championed working-class needs and interests, and local capitalists, who felt their livelihood was being threatened by labor groups and city officials. The Morgan and Mallory steamship lines brought in nonunion workers on

May 10, and violence threatened to erupt. Three privates under Captain Aldrich were sent to support the local authorities. Unfortunately, while the situation appeared calm by the twentieth, even a Ranger presence was not enough to ensure the unimpeded movement of cargo at the port.[17]

Accompanied by Captain Brooks, Adjutant General William Dade Cope was dispatched by the governor on June 3 to the island city to investigate the situation. After inspecting conditions, Cope advised Hobby to declare martial law in Galveston, and the governor issued the proclamation directing Brigadier-General Jacob Franklin Wolters to assume supreme command of the island, effective June 7. Eighteen cavalry troops, three machine-gun companies, and two medical detachments of the Texas National Guard—seventeen officers and 947 enlisted men—proceeded to Galveston. While the soldiers implemented the governor's edict the port be kept open, they also enforced laws regarding prohibition, gambling, and prostitution. With military police patrolling the streets, the Rangers departed the city.[18] While his captain was dealing with an explosive situation, Hickman was ordered on June 5 to proceed by the first available train to Mount Pleasant and comply with verbal instructions.[19]

On July 2, Hickman was designated to represent the Adjutant General's Department in the State Rifle and Pistol Shoot in San Antonio that was already underway. He left for the Alamo City the same day. With the competition completed, he was ordered on July 13 to Breckenridge under verbal instructions of the Adjutant General. He returned to Camp Perry as a member of the Texas civilian rifle team on August 1, and competed through the twenty-eighth. Unfortunately, Hickman was not among the twelve highest-scoring individuals who would represent the state in the National team matches. The team placed tenth place in Class B, or twentieth overall, and returned home with silver medals.[20]

The situation in Galveston continued to be troubling. Cope reported to Governor Hobby that the city commission, the city attorney, and the unionized police department were reluctant to cooperate with the military authorities. Hobby responded on July 14 by suspending the aforementioned officials and the mayor from office until the end of martial law. The following day, the provost marshal of the Military District of Galveston

Jacob F. Wolters. *Courtesy Nesbitt Memorial Library Archives, Columbus, TX.*

was ordered to take charge of the police department, the city jail, and the city judge's office. Under Wolters's supervision, Galveston's police officers were disarmed, but the shipping company's private guards were allowed to continue as "special marine policemen" under military authority. The apparent display of bias infuriated the city's officials, which was exacerbated by a series of accidental deaths attributed to the state troops. On September 16, a citizen's committee and the board of city commissioners reached an agreement with Hobby in which martial law would be lifted, and Texas Rangers would assume the enforcement duties carried out by the National Guard.[21]

Hickman was ordered to proceed to Gainesville under the verbal instructions of the Adjutant General.[22] After he rejoined the company, Captain Brooks was directed to return to Galveston and make the necessary arrangements to assume control of the police department by September 30. Hickman, Sergeant Charles Jourdan Blackwell, and Ranger William Mackinnon Molesworth from Headquarters Company; Dee W. Cox, John Crow, T. J. Jackman, and William T. Miles from Company A; and Larry Hall, Pelton Bruce Harbison, and W. L. Miller from Company C were ordered to meet Captain Brooks in the city. In addition, Roy Lee Hearn, John Edward Hensley, Sidney Sill Hutchinson, Benjamin Thomas Tumlinson, Jr., and David Cornelius "Jack" Webb from Company D, and Charles Arthur Carta, Henry Doyle Glasscock, and Marcus Lafayette Langford from Company F traveled to the Island. General Order No. 25 ended martial law on October 1, and civil law enforcement, under the auspices of Brooks, once more took precedence. Blackwell was assigned to command Emergency Company No. 1, and Hickman became his sergeant the same day. At the end of the month, Rangers Samuel Clay Blackwell and James Audley Hyde acted on a tip and went to a seemingly deserted house on the west end of the island. There they arrested two men and confiscated a still and eight hundred gallons of red and white wine. Notified of the seizure, Captains Brooks and Blackwell, and two Prohibition agents, left for the scene. Arraigned before U.S. Commissioner Charles Grainger Dibrell, the two prisoners each posted a bond of one thousand dollars and were bound over for the grand jury. On the same day, Rangers Glasscock, Martin, and Thomas Jefferson Cole raided a house on Avenue D within half a block of police headquarters. The lawmen arrested a man and woman and seized a still and five gallons of corn whiskey. The pair of suspects were turned over to a deputy U.S. marshal. The Rangers remained in Galveston until January 19, 1921, when the governor returned authority to city officials.[23]

In the aftermath of the Galveston strike, Hobby pushed for an Open Port Bill, which would sanction the state's chief executive in declaring martial law when labor strikes disrupted the free traffic of goods. The bill was overwhelmingly approved by the legislature in October 1920 and signed into law on January 1, 1921. The Open Port Act authorized the state government to use its law enforcement powers in the event common carriers—railways, streetcar and wharf companies, and pipelines—found their commercial activities being obstructed by union organizations. This new law would soon be utilized throughout the state in the continuing struggle between capital and labor.[24]

In the meantime, Hickman was appointed captain of Emergency Company No. 2 on November 22, 1920, and all Rangers not part of other companies were assigned to him. Four days later, he and Privates Caleb Thomas Williams, William Lee Lesueur, and Martin Nickolas Koonsman traveled to Stephens County and made their headquarters in Breckenridge. On November 29, Lesueur and Private James A. Bracewell raided the Crystal gambling hall in Desdemona. Assisted by Police Chief J. W. Wiley, Assistant Chief J. E. Perry, Officer A. E. Coggin, and Captain Horace Soule of the American Legion, they arrested Mayor H. W. Elliot and five other men on complaints of illegal gaming; four were additionally charged with operating a gaming house. Furthermore, 123 suspects were taken into custody in other raids, scores of prostitutes were ordered to leave town, and ten quarts of Canadian Club whiskey and a quantity of beer was seized. The same night, state officers worked with sheriff's deputies in the town of Ranger in raiding gambling houses and apprehending four individuals. After delivering the prisoners to the city jail, deputies piled the seized gaming tables in the street and set them on fire. Hickman noted that "city and [county] officers don't seem to be cooperating with rangers." Indeed, Sheriff Clarence Bennett Sears was indicted by the grand jury for bribery on November 30, just hours before he was scheduled to leave office; he was subsequently freed on $2,500 bail. Deputies James Marion "Jim May" Ellis and Brett Harte "Angelo" Hughes were similarly arrested on murder and bribery charges, and each was released after posting a ten-thousand-dollar bond. Ellis, Hughes, and taxi driver W. F. "Cadillac Bill" Ramsey were indicted in connection with the November 16 deaths of Herman Stevens and A. E. Lockhart. Hickman escorted the two victims' widows from Gainesville to Eastland on December 16. The women were slated to be witnesses for the state in the upcoming trial.[25]

On December 18, Hughes's attorneys were granted a continuance to January 3 on account of two defense witnesses being absent. For their safety, the prosecution's witnesses were kept in seclusion. Ellis's case was scheduled for January 6, but the trial opened in Ranger on the fourth. Three days later, the jury rendered a verdict of not guilty. Granted a change of venue, Hughes was tried for Lockhart's murder beginning on February 7 in Judge Charles A. Pippen's district court in Dallas, and he was likewise acquitted on the tenth. In the latter trial, Texas Rangers, "in picturesque sombreros and cowboy boots," were assigned to guard the courtroom.[26]

The sporting crowd was poised to resume their activities in Desdemona, and Justice of the Peace William Henry Whitworth wrote a confidential letter to Aldrich requesting Ranger assistance. Sent to clean up the oil fields in Eastland and Wichita Counties, Hickman and four Rangers arrived in Wichita Falls on January 25, 1921, in answer to a summons from District Attorney Fletcher Jones. Two men had been arrested three days before in an apparent attempt on the prosecutor's life. Hickman reported to Barton: "In my opinion, Jones is excited, but not in any danger whatsoever." However, for a time, Jones was provided with Ranger Thaddeus Pulaski "Tip" Robinson, then Sergeant James Walter McCormick, as bodyguards. Hickman returned to Breckenridge on the twenty-seventh.[27]

Representative Joseph Washington "Joe" Burkett, Sr. of Eastland complained about the presence of Rangers in his hometown, and alleged misconduct on their part. He specifically claimed state officers had fired into an automobile. General Barton denied the lawmaker's broader allegations and presented Hickman as an example of the service's good conduct. The captain replied to Burkett's particular accusation by relaying how Rangers had heard shooting near a Mexican camp north of town. Rangers Lesueur, McCormick, Joseph "Joe" Orberg, John Harrison "Johnnie" Asher, Sr., and Sam T. Walker drove out to investigate. Special Officer Tom Pigg of the Harmon railroad informed them parties had fired into the camp from separate directions, and he had, in turn, shot into suspicious automobiles. Two deputy sheriffs were identified as the shooters. While heading back to town, the Rangers encountered the pair of deputies in the road and drove closer to investigate. According to McCormick and his comrades, the two men cursed the lawmen and attacked Asher and Walker with flashlights and pliers. The assailants were pistol-whipped into submission, searched for firearms, and, upon finding none, released. All the offending parties appeared before the grand jury the next day. Barton informed Burkett in no uncertain terms, "In view of all the above facts, I wish to inform you that I am prepared to put fifty Rangers in Eastland County within twenty-four hours, and I have the moral, political, and physical courage to do so, if it becomes necessary."[28]

Recently elected Governor Pat Morris Neff disbanded Emergency Company No. 2 on February 15 as part of a general shakeup of the Ranger Force. The same day, Hickman's command was reorganized as Company B, and he was placed in charge of one sergeant and nine men. Their headquarters was transferred to Fort Worth. On the twenty-fifth, Lesueur, McCormick, Orberg, and Walker were indicted by the Eastland County grand jury on charges of aggravated assault resulting from the earlier altercation with the two deputies. A letter signed by forty-two citizens was presented to the mayor demanding Hickman discharge the accused. If the captain refused, they were prepared to raise the matter with the governor and the adjutant general. The matter was resolved after an assistant attorney general traveled to Ranger, and Hickman paid minor fines for two of his men. The cases of the other pair were dismissed. The public dispute between Barton and Burkett intensified after the adjutant general assigned three additional Rangers to Eastland County. Hickman accompanied the reinforcements to the town.[29]

The captain and four of his men entrained to Paris on April 15 to keep the peace during a murder trial in the Sixth District Court. Two days previously, Virgil Sampson, a black man, had been indicted for raping a fourteen-year-old white girl near Honey Grove. Taken to Bonham, the accused nearly lost his life to a lynch mob, and only the heroic actions of Fannin County Deputy Sheriff William Barnett Leeman, Sr. saved him. The presence of Rangers was requested by Lamar County officials, and Hickman, Sergeant Jerome B. Wheatley, and Privates Warren William

"Billy" Belcher, Claremore McKelvey "Buck" Weaver, and James T. Eads escorted Sampson to the county jail for safekeeping. A local citizen's committee pledged to assist the sheriff's department in maintaining order. The state officers remained for the trial, which opened on the twentieth, and the accused was convicted after just nine minutes of jury deliberation. Paris citizens requested Hickman leave his four men in town until the twenty-third when the death sentence was passed. While awaiting execution in the Dallas County jail, Sampson confessed on April 25 to killing Mrs. Neomi Blanch Wadford and her three-year-old daughter Mildred near Bairdstown the previous year. Luther Thomas Wadford, the victims' husband and father respectively, had been charged with double homicide, and Sampson had testified against him at the examining trial and before the grand jury. Scheduled to begin on April 28, Wadford's trial was postponed, and the murder charge was subsequently dismissed. Sampson paid the price for his crimes on May 27 when he was hanged in the Lamar County jail.[30]

Hickman and the entire detachment were withdrawn from the oil fields on April 26, except for three Rangers assigned to Wichita Falls. On June 1, a riot broke out in the town of Dublin when the "unlawful element of the laboring class tried to run Mexicans out of town." Hickman dispatched Eads and Weaver, and the Rangers' presence calmed the passions of the community. The captain traveled to Denton on July 22 to assist Prohibition agents in seizing one still and arresting three men. Reductions in the annual appropriations compelled Hickman to reduce his company to himself, Sergeant McCormick, and nine privates by the end of August. The citizens of Wichita Falls had been reluctant to part with Hickman's full company, and offered to cover the rental expenses of a headquarters in town. The proposal proved persuasive, and Hickman ordered his Rangers to begin transferring their station back to Wichita Falls on December 5. After four Rangers arrived in town in automobiles packed with equipment, they established themselves in a building west of the Call Field hospital. There they joined Sergeant McCormick and Private Roy Wesley Hardesty, who had been stationed in the city for months. The captain and the remaining Rangers reached Wichita Falls the following day. Their first breakfast of locally provided buffalo meat was a convincing demonstration of the community's appreciation. The Rangers quickly went to work, and McCormick and Koonsman cooperated with Prohibition agents ____ Tyler and Manual T. Gonzaullas in raiding a residence on North Sixth Street. The lawmen confiscated seventy-five quarts of whiskey they had discovered hidden in a cowshed and other caches around the house. One man was arrested and pled guilty in Judge William Irwin Grubb's federal court; the defendant was fined twenty-five dollars and costs.[31]

In the wake of the clean-up in Mexia, Waco proved to be a popular destination for legal proceedings, and up to fifteen Rangers were soon quartered in the courthouse. Hickman and Rangers Koonsman, Hardesty, and John Alexander Gillon were serving as bailiffs in Seventy-fourth District court as the lawsuit of Inez L. Crow against Sheriff Robert Caldwell "Bob" Buchanan was brought to trial. Jury selection began on February 23, 1922. Mrs. Crow's late husband had perished during a riot in Lorena the previous October, and she sought fifty thousand dollars in damages. The other Rangers—Wheatley, Molesworth, Orberg, Alonzo B. "Jack" Barnett, James Lemuel "Lem" Lamkin, Thomas Isaac "Tom" Laymance, Stewart Stanley, Edgar B. "Ed" McMordie, Rudolph Daniel Shumate, Charles Miller, and Charles Corta—were in town to act as witnesses before the federal grand jury that was impaneled on the twenty-seventh. The Buchanan-Crow case was transferred to Bell County on March 6 due to a failure to seat a jury. Before recessing court, Judge Harvey MacGaughey Richey, Sr. stated, "I desire to personally thank and compliment Captain Hickman and his men for the high grade service they have rendered in this trial."[32]

Throughout his adulthood, Hickman served as a judge of rodeo events in Texas and all over the nation. He performed this role in March 1922 at the Southwestern Exposition and Fat Show in Fort Worth. On the sixth of the following month, the captain was honored by his men with the presentation of two gold- and silver-plated Colt .45 revolvers inscribed with his name and "Company B, Texas State Rangers." The butts of the pistols were pearl, and engraved with the likeness of a Texas longhorn. Hickman had a chance to flaunt his fancy handguns when he was selected as one of the judges at a rodeo at the Wichita Falls ballpark beginning on May 3.[33]

He reenlisted on May 10, 1922, as captain of Company B in Wichita Falls.[34] On June 3, the company was ordered to transfer to Waco. Two days later, Hickman and four men made their headquarters in a house at 1515 Austin Avenue that was leased from Judge Charles Albert Boynton, Sr.[35]

On July 1, approximately 400,000 railroad workers across the country walked off the job over a wage disagreement. About 3,800 members of six Federated Shop Craft Union locals in Texas participated in the strike. The walkout particularly affected the Denison freight yards of the Texas & Pacific and the Missouri, Kansas, & Texas (Katy) Railroads. Strikebreakers were imported on the sixth and deployed around the Katy property as private guards. Taking a violent tact on July 11, several hundred striking workers kidnapped twenty-four strikebreakers in front of local officers and conveyed them to the Red River bridge. There the guards were beaten and expelled north into Oklahoma. The strikers then intercepted all trains, captured any newly arriving "scab" workers, and warned trainmasters to stop work previously performed by union members. The railroad companies pleaded with Governor Neff to protect their property.[36]

Joined by U.S. Attorney Randolph Bryant, Marshal Phil E. Baer arrived from Paris, and a force of sixty-eight federal deputies, including former Ranger C. J. Blackwell, took station in town by July 13. Governor Neff ordered Hickman and General Barton to the scene the next day to evaluate the worsening situation. Indeed, by this time, at least one hundred had been flogged. Railroad officials opined the crisis would require hundreds more men to defuse the situation, but Neff declined to call out state troops, though he did not completely rule out that option. Concerned about the far-reaching economic effects of the strike, the federal government advised the governor to take appropriate action or regular troops from Fort Sam Houston would be dispatched. Hickman rushed into a demonstration on July 17 and single-handedly saved two deputy marshals from being kidnapped. In the aftermath, strikers complained that Hickman had "sworn at them." Four days later, the governor himself traveled to the North Texas town for a personal inspection. Mayor William Franklin "Bill" Weaver saw no need for the deployment of the National Guard, but reluctantly acknowledged the prerogative of the executive. Convinced he needed to act, Neff directed forty-five Rangers to Grayson County on the twenty-third, leaving only Captain Aldrich at headquarters, another Ranger at Presidio with a broken leg, and a third at Mission caring for Company D's horses. They were assigned to the Katy roundhouse, the depot, and Denison's main street. On July 26, the governor reluctantly declared martial law in Denison and all of Grayson County's Precinct No. 2. Deploying swiftly, five companies—sixteen officers and 257 National Guardsmen—of the Third Battalion, 142nd Infantry Regiment assembled in the town under the command of Colonel Charles William Nimon. Two days later, Hickman and four men traveled from their Waco headquarters to Sherman and relieved Captain Roy Carlisle Nichols in policing the local train yards. They arrested six men for threatening a railroad employee. Hamer was given responsibility for Childress and Amarillo where an undercover operative kept him informed of the strikers' plans. Barton raised a 789-man contingent of "Railroad Rangers" to supplement the regular force. The railroads covered the expense incurred by this emergency force, which was distributed to Cleburne, Temple, Amarillo, Marshall, Lufkin, Kingsville, De Leon, Waco, Childress, Greenville, and Sherman.[37]

Barton took personal command of the state forces on August 8, and the number of National Guardsmen in Denison was increased to more than five hundred. Hickman was commanding eight regular Rangers and twenty-three Special Rangers on October 1. The governor ordered the state troops to depart town by the twenty-first, and martial law was discontinued in Denison the following day. The Railroad Rangers were discharged, and most of the regular Rangers were returned to their home stations. Approximately three hundred arrests had been made, largely for assault or vagrancy, but few were convicted. Similarly, several shootings, occurring at the Katy terminal yards and the Missouri, Oklahoma & Gulf railyards, went unsolved. Once the soldiers departed, Neff substituted military rule with the Open Port Law, which banned any act impeding free trade in the state. Hickman arrested two men for threatening shop workers and for fighting, took them to the U.S. marshal, and filed complaints in federal court in Sherman. Due to continuing unrest, the Ranger camp in Denison was made a permanent fixture on December 1. In support of their assignment, Hickman's men received a shipment of horses early that same month. The new mounts had recently been running wild and needed to be broken to city life before they could be used downtown. Twice in December, Hickman foiled plans to bomb the Santa Fe roundhouse in town. By January 1, 1923, the Open Port Law had been lifted from the last six of the affected towns.[38]

Although the situation in Denison was not quite calmed, Neff sent Hickman and Company B to Corpus Christi in late May 1923 to maintain order following the recent grand jury session. Numerous indictments involving political corruption had been returned against local residents. The captain closed vice centers through mid-June. The Rangers then seized stills in Robstown and Kingsville and, in conjunction with federal agents, intercepted liquor shipments coming into Corpus Christi.[39]

Hickman's father, Walker, died on August 25, 1923, and his death led his son's impending nuptials, scheduled for October 20, to be postponed. Instead, Tom married Mayme Katherine Arterberry on January 5, 1924. Born in Munroe County, Kentucky, on August 4, 1895, she was a resident of Whitewright in Grayson County. One month after the wedding, Hickman was ordered to transfer his company headquarters from Corpus Christi to the Cora-Lina Ranch near Fort McKavett. Cattle and sheep theft in the San Angelo area had become a serious dilemma, which the captain and his men quickly solved through regular patrols.[40]

Hickman and his bride were described by friends as "passionately devoted to each other." Tragically, however, their union proved brief. The captain was granted a leave of absence to travel abroad. On April 18, Mayme was packing a trunk in their Fort McKavett home when she accidentally shot and killed herself with her husband's rifle.[41]

After burying his wife in Fairview Cemetery in Gainesville three days later, Hickman maintained his plans and journeyed to Wembley Park, London, England, to judge rodeo promoter John Van "Tex" Austin's International Stock Show. Part of the British Empire Exposition, the opening of the rodeo on June 15 was marred when a steer's leg was accidentally broken while being roped and thrown by an American cowboy. The forty thousand Britons in attendance were displeased, and many indulged in several minutes of booing and hissing. The following day, the Royal Society for the Prevention of Cruelty to Animals unsuccessfully appealed to Prime Minister James Ramsay

MacDonald to ban the steer roping and wrestling competitions. The society also applied for and received five court summonses against Austin and his fellow promoters. The hearing was scheduled for June 27, three days before the cowboy contests ended. Opponents of the rodeo grew further indignant after two steers suffered broken necks while being roped and another had a horn broken. At the close of the performance, Hickman presented a pony named "Tejana" to Edward, Prince of Wales on behalf of the Texas Rangers. The prince was delighted with the animal. However, British law barred a member of the royal family from receiving lavish gifts, so Edward remunerated Hickman thirty pounds for the horse. The outrage exhibited at the rodeo did not extend to the entire island kingdom. Hickman reported being inundated with invitations, and Harry Gordon Selfridge, founder of the London-based department store bearing his name, invited the Ranger and 124 other guests to his home for Sunday dinner and two suppers that evening. Following the show, the British police court at Waeldstone heard the alleged animal cruelty case. Hickman was regarded as the most important witness for the defense, and the charges were dismissed on July 7.[42]

After he returned to Fort McKavett, Hickman observed an abundance of stills and drinking in the surrounding counties. While the Menard County sheriff and the majority of his constituents were indifferent to Prohibition, Sheriff D. R. "Dee" Gibbs of Kimble County informed the captain he planned to employ an undercover man to secure evidence. Hickman indicated he was willing to assist in recruiting an operative. However, he and Rangers Stewart Stanley and Koonsman were transferred to Waco on October 7. Beginning on November 3, Hickman and Stanley conducted an undercover investigation of Prohibition violations in Thurber, Strawn, and Mingus. Three days later, the captain met with Erath County Sheriff John William Wright and the dean of Tarleton State College to discuss the arrest of individuals selling liquor to members of the college cadet corps. He also conferred with Edwin Asby Turner, head of the Prohibition group in Fort Worth, and arranged for assistance in raids in Thurber. In order to save living expenses, Hickman closed his headquarters in Waco on January 31, 1925, and moved to Fort Worth. He obtained a room in the house of William B. and Ola Beatrice Knight, old friends who lived at 425 South Adams Street. As he informed Aldrich,

Hickman expected to work up the six bank robberies that had occurred since December 19.[43]

For several years, Denton County had been under the sway of a criminal ring headed by brothers Nathan Andrew and Henry Yancy Story. Headquartered on the family ranch seven miles south of Argyle, the Story Gang had started out as petty thieves and matured into professional bank robbers and burglars. Their fortunes began to change when William Steadman "Bill" Fry became county sheriff in November 1924. A complaint was filed against Nathan for the January 29 murder of Fred Crane, and he surrendered that evening. The defendant waived an examination trial, and bail was set at $6,500. Yancy, as he was known, was wanted on a charge of auto theft in Fort Worth. On February 2, he and Wilburn A. Martin, a member of the gang, were trailed home from Fort Worth by three law officers. The policemen were gathered on the courthouse lawn when the two suspects drove by and opened fire. Eight men were involved in the subsequent gun battle, and Fort Worth Detective Edward Newton Smith was lightly wounded in the shoulder. Plate glass windows along the block were not so fortunate. The outlaws escaped and took refuge in Martin's two-story frame home at 1001 Oakland Street. Fry unsuccessfully tried to obtain their surrender. Resolved to capture the fugitives peacefully, the sheriff requested assistance from law enforcement agencies throughout Northeast Texas. Approximately fifty answered the call, including deputized National Guardsmen, special deputy sheriffs, Fort Worth policemen, and a Fort Worth riot squad.[44]

Hickman was also summoned, but Fifty-seventh District Court Judge Robert Berkeley Minor had recently issued an injunction that forced the entire Ranger Force to cease operations. Having received the appeal from Denton on February 3, Adjutant General William Mark McGhee and Attorney General Daniel James Moody constructed a temporary response to the writ that called on Rangers to serve without pay until the courts decided the matter. Hickman was ordered to assist Fry, and found Martin's neighborhood evacuated, even while three machine guns were deployed on the lawn of the nearby College of Industrial Arts (presently the Texas Woman's University campus). Martin's wife and two children were inside the house, and Fry refused to allow Fort Worth officers, irate over the shooting of one of their own, to force entry. Instead, negotiations were held over the telephone, and the pair finally agreed to surrender shortly after noon. Hickman and Tarrant County Sheriff Carl Smith entered the barricaded structure unarmed and took Martin and Yancy by car to the courthouse. The prisoners were charged in justice court with three counts of assault with intent to murder, pending the action of the grand jury. Each man was released on a bond of ten thousand dollars. Story was then taken into custody by Sheriff Smith and driven to Fort Worth to make bail on the auto theft charge.[45]

By March, Hickman was quietly investigating the activities of the Story mob, including the recruitment of an undercover operative. On February 14, he spent two days in Red River County inspecting a burgled bank vault. The method of using a cutting torch to gain entry was remarkedly similar to that employed in robberies in Valley View and Reisel. The captain and Ranger Stanley suspected the Story's involvement in the robbery of the Sanger National Bank on March 11. The gang was also thought to be responsible for the June 9 holdup of the Farmers and Merchants State Bank in Krum. In the latter theft, the thieves escaped with $3,200 in cash and $1,550 in negotiable paper. Hickman likewise investigated the robbery at the First National Bank of Holland in Bell County on March 19. Five armed men entered the depository, but they only made off with forty dollars. On August 6, Deputy Sheriff Robert Bruce Parsons was shot to death on Hickory Street, two blocks east of the courthouse. Martin was positively identified as the killer. The deputy's murder spelled the end of the Story Gang's grip on Denton County. Investigators obtained a search warrant for the Story ranch, and Hickman, Stanley, Molesworth, and Ranger Charles Nimrod Davis; Sheriff Fry and other Denton County officers; and Dallas County Sheriff Schuyler Bailey Marshall, Jr. and Deputies John Rowland, Manuel Gonzaullas, Sheppard Franklin "Shep" Pickens, Reuben Sherman Little, Phillip Osborne Towers, and J. L. Rowland seized the property. They unearthed a stolen car, masks, bank sacks, an acetylene torch, a fifty-pound box of dynamite, a bag of household silver, and more than two thousand dollars in Treasury certificates. The brothers and twenty-one others were soon arrested. The grand jury of the Sixteenth District Court convened on August 13 to probe Parsons's slaying. Martin was indicted for homicide, as well as for attempted murder and participation in four bank robberies. His case was transferred from Denton to Criminal District Court No. 2 in Dallas on August 27. Yancy eventually faced thirty charges, including two for robbery with firearms of the Sanger and Krum banks. By September 5, the Denton grand jury had returned eighty-one indictments against the gang's nine members. Hickman and Stanley extradited Louise Ross from Texarkana on September 10. Believed to have taken part in the two bank heists, she nevertheless denied involvement. The following day, Ross was indicted by the grand jury as being an accessory to the Parsons homicide; she was also charged with two counts of attempted murder. On September 23, Martin and Yancy Story, and three other men, were charged in Belton for the Holland bank job.[46]

On October 5, Martin was tried on the homicide charge, found guilty six days later, and received a ninety-nine-year prison term from Judge Charles A. Pippen. The conviction was appealed, and the prosecution rested on January 15, 1926. Yancy's case was also transferred to Judge Pippen's court, and his trial was set for January 25. Hickman took the stand as a prosecution witness. The case was given to the jury at 9:00 p.m. on the thirtieth. He was convicted and sentenced to ninety-nine years in prison, but the ruling was reversed by the court of criminal appeals. Yancy was retried on November 21, 1927, in Sherman, but the case ended in a mistrial. His case was transferred to Marlin on a change of venue, and the trial was scheduled for January 14, 1929. Following his conviction, he appealed, and a hearing was scheduled for January 27, 1930. Instead, on the twenty-sixth, he agreed to a plea bargain of a five-year sentence for the Krum robbery in exchange for the other charges being dropped. He dropped from sight on April 14, and remained at large until he appeared at the Huntsville penitentiary door ready to "do the fair and square thing." After a change of venue to Gainesville and two continuances, Nathan was tried for Fred Crane's murder in the Sixteenth District Court. Following his conviction, he was sentenced to ninety-nine years in prison.[47]

On May 15, 1925, Coleman County Sheriff Richard Allen "Dick" Pauley was critically wounded in a gun battle with John Smith and Arthur Tebo, two transient black men. The altercation occurred atop a boxcar at the Santa Fe Railroad depot. When he was shot in the neck, Pauley fell from the car and suffered a severe laceration. The bullet was lodged near his spine, leaving the sheriff paralyzed. Tebo was quickly apprehended in an abandoned house, but Smith escaped. From his bed in Overall Memorial Hospital, Pauley identified Smith as the shooter. Along with Brownwood city officers, Runnels County Sheriff Richmond Earl MacWilliams and his deputies gathered to join in the pursuit. Within three hours, a posse of several hundred men captured the fugitive and lodged him in the county jail next to his accomplice. Sheriff Pauley died the next afternoon, and District Judge Jesse Owen Woodward requested Ranger assistance in keeping the peace during the examining trial.[48]

The accused were later taken to the Tarrant County jail for safekeeping, and a Ranger detachment under Hickman was held in readiness in Coleman on May 21. Hickman reported to Aldrich that conditions were quiet, and he did not think mob violence likely. The case was called for trial on the twenty-second. Hickman and two Rangers assisted local officers in controlling the spectators, and searching everyone who entered the courtroom for weapons. After seating only one juror out of seventy-three examined veniremen, Judge Woodward transferred the case to Brown County. Smith and Tebo were escorted by Brown County Sheriff Bert Hise and a Tarrant County deputy from Fort Worth to Brownwood on May 28. Trouble seemed likely, and Pauley's sixteen-year-old son was determined to avenge his father. At 1:00 a.m. on the thirty-first, a mob of one hundred Coleman County citizens attempted to take the two prisoners from the Brown County jail. Sheriff Hise and eight deputies stopped them in the jail yard until District Attorney Walter Early and Brownwood Mayor Fred Abney arrived to convince the would-be vigilantes to let the law run its course. The trial began in Thirty-first District Court on June 1 and lasted one day. Once the jury deliberated for eighteen minutes, Smith was convicted and sentenced to death. Governor Miriam Amanda "Ma" Ferguson declined to commute the sentence after the pardons board recommended against clemency. Smith met his end in the electric chair at Huntsville on April 16, 1926.[49]

During the same time the Pauley case was unfolding, similar unrest was occurring in Dallas County. The county jail was surrounded on May 20 by a mob of five thousand intent on seeing justice done in a rape case. The suspects inside the cells, brothers Frank and Lorenzo Noel, had been apprehended for robbing and killing Ryan Adkins and Walter LaTour Milstead, and sexually assaulting the murder victims' girlfriends, in two separate incidents in April. While much of the crowd was composed of curious observers, a single-minded cadre of vigilantes was also present. As the horde grew wild, the police cracked down with fire hoses, but a lynch mob of three hundred men stormed the jail at 1:30 a.m., throwing bottles, bricks, and rocks. Forty lawmen and firefighters were injured, including Sheriff Marshall. Two rioters loosed gunshots, and sixteen city and county officers returned fire, wounding five men, one mortally, and dispersing the crowd. Joining forty-six National Guardsmen, deputy U.S. marshals, and city and county officers, Hamer and Wheatley arrived in town the next day with a machine gun, and Hickman and Stanley were on scene on the twenty-third. The rape trials convened on May 28 in Judge Pippen's court, and Hickman, Hamer, and their men were on hand to keep the peace. The brothers were tried one after the other on the same day, and both admitted to raping the women; the jury was out less than five minutes. Sentenced to death by electric chair, the two convicted murderers were escorted to Huntsville by Hickman, Stanley, Sheriff Marshall, and a party of deputies. Believing the condemned men possessed knowledge of several unsolved crimes in Dallas, District Attorney Shelby Shepard Cox wrote a letter to Marshall expressing frustration he had not been allowed to question them. The Noels were executed on July 3, right after confessing to the killings and rapes in front of Hickman and the prison chaplain.[50]

On June 16, 1925, the governor reassigned Hickman to Headquarters Company in Austin as senior captain. The transfer was part of Governor Ferguson's reshuffling of the Ranger Force. Companies A, B, and D were dispatched to the border, while Company C remained in Marshall to investigate bootlegging. The four captains were ordered to report to Adjutant General William Mark McGee on October 15 for a general conference.[51]

On August 8, 1925, Charles E. "Charley" Engler, his wife Augusta, and their twenty-five-year-old adopted daughter Emma were murdered in their farmhouse at Moore's Crossing, nine miles southeast of Austin. The couple had been shot in their sleep, while Emma was tortured to death. Raymond D. Thorp, identification superintendent for the Austin police, and Detective James Elmer McClain were assigned to assist Sheriff Winston D. Miller in solving the brutal homicides. Six suspects—two Anglos, two blacks, and two

Mexicans—were taken into custody on suspicion, but eventually released for lack of evidence. On the thirteenth, the sheriff requested Ranger assistance. Hickman, Stanley, and two other Rangers arrived at the crime scene and assisted county officers. One possible motive investigators pursued was the alleged presence of a home safe containing confidential plans and specifications for cotton-chopping machinery reportedly worth thousands of dollars. John Baptiste Johnson, a suspect in the homicides, was wounded by Special Deputy Sheriff Manual Gonzaullas in an unrelated altercation. A revolver matching the murder weapon was found in his possession, but no connection could be found between him and the Englers. Other strong suspects included Link Bookman, a gambler who had a previous conviction for a killing, and John Sternnadl, Jr. and Willie Giese, two of Emma's suitors. Hickman was reassigned to other cases, but Thorp and McClain continued to work up the homicide. They were assisted by Deputy Sheriff and Special Ranger Edward Lafayette "Lafe" Young. In an attempt to make a breakthrough, Doctor Robert Ernest House was summoned to administer scopolamine to Bookman. The answers the gambler provided under the drug's influence cleared him of any involvement. Through the efforts of Colonel Calvin Hooker Good, the inventor of the comparison microscope, and the emerging science of ballistics, the investigators were able to conclusively prove Giese's Spanish-made .38-caliber handgun was the murder weapon. However, the grand jury remained unconvinced of his guilt and refused to indict. The case went unsolved.[52]

General McGee announced his resignation on November 9, to take effect on December 5. Due in part to his role in closing notable cases, Hickman was the subject of a rumor emanating from Austin that he was interested in replacing McGee. Responding to press queries, the captain denied the report on November 16: "I have never been an applicant for the office of adjutant general." He then added he would not be making such a bid in the future, and Dallas Jefferson Matthews, Sr. was soon appointed to the post. The new adjutant general continued the guidelines of his predecessor: "It is the policy of this Department not to send Rangers to any community without the request of the local authorities, and never without the request of the sheriff of the county."[53]

The discovery of a severed human head in an abandoned Erath County farmhouse on December 9 led to another homicide investigation. Two days later, the victim was identified as eighteen-year-old Bernard D. "Bernie" Connally, and Sheriff David Medicus "Med" Hassler interviewed Francis Marion Snow, Connally's stepfather, at his farmhouse near Seldon. Snow claimed his wife, Maggie May Snow, her mother, Samantha Ann Olds, and Bernie were visiting Waco for a few days, and professed to have no knowledge of his stepson's demise. That night, the sheriff contacted the Rangers, and Stanley was assigned to the investigation. The state officer arrived the next morning and "began work on what proved to be the most amazing and horrible case [he had] ever encountered." Inconsistencies in Snow's statements quickly made him a person of interest, and Stanley and Hassler took him into custody for more questioning. In order to forestall an anticipated lynching, the lawmen took the prisoner to Fort Worth where he was placed into the custody of Hickman. The captain lodged Snow in the Tarrant County jail for safekeeping. Returning to Stephenville, Stanley and Hassler secured a search warrant and reexamined Snow's farm where they found traces of blood on an ax. Suspiciously, the bed of the suspect's wagon had been scoured clean, but the underside was still clotted with dried gore. Most damning was evidence that bodies had been burned in the fireplace, and human bones were quickly found in ash piles in the backyard. While Stanley was working the case in Erath County, Hickman obtained a written confession from Snow on December 11 that he had shot his stepson during a domestic quarrel on November 27, then beheaded the body. Snow led the two Rangers, Hassler, Deputy Ross Pearcy, District Attorney Samuel Morris Russell, and Fort Worth officers to the site atop Cedar Point, sixteen miles from Stephenville, where he had discarded Connally's headless corpse. Standing over the body of his victim, the killer also admitted to shooting to death Maggie Snow and Samantha Olds, witnesses to the initial murder, and burning their bodies.[54]

The State of Texas vs. F. M. Snow was gaveled to order on January 18, 1926, in the courtroom of Twenty-ninth District Judge John Buckner "J. B." Keith. An attempt at an insanity defense was quickly thwarted, and the jury was impaneled on the twenty-second, after three separate venires totaling three hundred men had been exhausted. Called to the witness stand on the second day of trial, Hickman recounted his involvement in the case and confirmed Hassler's earlier testimony that Snow had voluntarily signed the confession before multiple witnesses. Given the case on December 27, the members deliberated only briefly before returning a verdict of guilty. Snow was denied an appeal and went to Huntsville's "death house" on August 12, 1927. An identical murder complete with decapitation had occurred in Mineral Wells in November 1912, and Snow was living in the area at the time. Prior to witnessing his execution, Hickman attempted to learn whether Snow had been responsible, but the condemned man refused to comment as he was strapped into the electric chair.[55]

Following the Story Gang case, Hickman began acting on his own initiative in offering assistance to the sheriffs within his jurisdiction whenever a bank robbery occurred. Throughout the summer of 1926, Hickman worked from Fort Worth and Dallas while searching for a gang of ex-convicts who had committed a string of North Texas bank holdups beginning in Lipan on January 8. Hickman pursued the thieves for three days. More heists followed at Venus, on February 3; Valera, on April 5; and Oak Cliff, on June 2. In the midst of this spree, Stanley resigned, and the captain was reportedly not pleased to lose his trusted subordinate. On August 25, three men struck the bank in Irving. While a wheelman waited outside in an automobile, the other two young robbers forced a pair of cashiers and a customer into the vault. After tossing seven thousand dollars in cash into a sack, they escaped in the getaway vehicle. Hickman arrived in town the following day and took over the pursuit. The thieves were originally thought to have been headed for Dallas, but investigators speculated whether they had instead gone to Fort Worth.[56]

Weeks later, the captain received information that robbers would strike the Red River National Bank at Clarksville on September 9, 1926. He drove to the town which lay 125 miles northeast of Dallas. Once there, Hickman, former Ranger Stewart Stanley, his father Samuel Beauregard Stanley, and Constable Ervin Q. Ivy waited across the street from the bank. As noon drew near, a car approached and stopped in front of the bank with the engine still running. Two armed men, one carrying a suitcase, exited the vehicle and entered the building. Inside, the bandits herded five bank employees and two customers in front of the vault and forced them to lie on the floor. While one man covered the victims, the other scooped up all the cash in sight and stuffed it into the suitcase. The thieves then stepped back outside. In contrast to modern practices, Hickman and his men did not identify themselves as peace officers or command the thieves to surrender. Instead, they ran into the street and began firing. Both suspects were quickly cut down. The suitcase was opened to reveal $33,150 in stolen money. The slain robbers were later identified as D. L. Smallwood and A. M. Slaton. Sheriff Schuyler escorted bank officials from Irving to Clarksville, where they could hopefully identify the dead men as the same thieves who held up their institution. On September 10, Hickman traveled to a camp fifteen miles outside Clarksville, took a red-haired woman into custody, and lodged her in the Dallas jail. She and two other women also arrested were linked to the Irving and Clarksville robberies. Adjutant General Dallas Matthews declared Hickman's handling of the case "good law enforcement."[57]

In the aftermath of the shooting, the *Brownwood Bulletin* published an editorial that discussed a common viewpoint regarding bank robbers:

> Some peace officers, including some state Rangers, probably act too hastily, some times [*sic*], in shooting men apprehended in crime. In recent weeks, however, a number of officers in various states have been murdered because they did not shoot quickly enough, and dozens of people have been shot down in cold blood by bank robbers and other criminals. The modern bank robber has none of the traits of the gentleman. He never gives his victim a fighting chance.[58]

On September 14, the legislature resolved "that the courageousness of [Hickman's] action, together with his fidelity to duty, warrants the public commendation by the Senate of Texas, and we express to him our appreciation for his services." In a more practical gesture, the Maryland-based insurance company that covered the bank presented Hickman with a check for five hundred dollars in appreciation for his services. Furthermore, the Red River National Bank and the First National Bank of Clarksville bestowed upon the lawmen a reward totaling one thousand dollars. The Texas Bankers

Association matched the payment, and each of the one thousand-member institutions subsequently decided to offer five dollars for every dead bank robber. While Hickman claimed the rewards had decreased bank heists, the incentive contributed to several questionable killings. The solution to that controversy would fall to another Ranger captain.[59]

In 1927, Representative Harbin Hansbrow Moore of Cooper introduced House Bill 270 recommending a fifty-dollar state tax on optometrist practices. Doctor Willis W. Chamberlin, a highly regarded Houston optometrist and also a representative of the Optometry Association, was in the state capital to lobby for the bill's defeat. He believed the proposed legislation was nothing more than a way to exhort a sizable amount of money from law-abiding citizens. Chamberlin hosted members of the legislature to dinner several times and found that Representative Francis Aaron Dale of Bonham was the facilitator for Moore's scheme. Dale offered to encourage the committee to issue an unfavorable report on the bill in exchange for one thousand dollars in cash. Chamberlin went to Speaker of the House Robert Lee Bobbitt, Sr. to discuss the matter. The Speaker spoke to Governor Dan Moody, and the executive authorized Captains Hickman and Hamer to open an investigation and, if the allegation was true, to arrest the two legislators.[60]

Assured of the Rangers' assistance, Chamberlin met with Moore and Dale in a hotel room on February 1. Chamberlin and Dale left the room and walked out of the hotel. As they passed an alley, Chamberlin handed the other man the money, which had been marked by a bank cashier the previous day. Hamer and Hickman appeared and prevented Dale from reentering the hotel. Hamer accused the lawmaker of taking a bribe, but Dale denied the charge, saying he had received the currency as a fee to represent someone. Hamer searched the suspect and found the one thousand dollars, which he handed to Hickman. Dale offered to sort the whole matter out in Moore's room upstairs. The two captains went to the room and Hamer entered while Hickman stayed in the hallway with Dale.[61]

Hamer asked Moore if any kind of deal had just been made for a one-thousand-dollar fee for representation. Moore denied the allegation and hesitated before admitting he knew Dale, although he gave conflicting statements about when he had last seen his fellow legislator. Hickman and Dale entered the room, and Hamer arrested Moore. The two politicians were taken to Justice of the Peace Frank Richardson Tannehill's court where the Rangers signed complaints against them for bribery. Moore and Dale were released on a bond of two thousand dollars each. While the case was waiting to go before the Travis County grand jury, the House established a nine-member investigating committee. On February 4, Hickman and Hamer testified regarding their activities in the case. The next day, Moore denied the charge and insisted he had been framed. Chamberlin was exonerated, but the committee recommended the two lawmakers be ejected from the body. On February 7, the entire House met and voted to hear a full reading of the committee's record of testimony, a process that consumed eight hours. The two defendants were expelled from the House the same day.[62]

Moore and Dale were indicted on February 23, and their cases were severed for the trials. The state subpoenaed Hamer and Hickman as witnesses, the latter having recently broken a record in steer-roping at a Laredo rodeo. The two Rangers were in Borger by then and had to be excused from their duties there. Other individuals testifying included *Houston Chronicle* correspondent Cudellas Dent Waide, who had earlier appeared before the House inquiry, and Charles Pickle, the stenographer who was present for the investigating testimony. Moore's trial opened on April 27 in the Travis County Criminal District Court, but his case was continued on July 11 until November 7 on the state's motion. Dale's case was continued from November 7 until January 9, 1928. The state unexpectedly rested its case against Dale on April 18, 1928, after Hamer took the stand earlier that morning. The captain's testimony was limited by the defense who argued he had arrested Dale without a warrant and without firsthand knowledge of the alleged bribe.[63]

The city of Borger, established by developer Asa Philip "Ace" Borger and attorney John R. Miller in Hutchinson County in March 1926, was part of the oil bonanza in the Panhandle. Hickman arrived in Borger on February 27, 1927, and, interestingly, reported the town "not such a bad place." On March 2, he arrived in Amarillo to confer with Hamer. The two captains traveled to Borger the next day where they compiled a list of the ninety-two slot machines they found operating. Hickman commented: "It is my opinion that Borger is the cleanest largest oil town that we have ever had." However, having grown to a population of more than forty thousand in the first three months, the boomtown of tents and shacks was truly lawless by April. An organized crime ring known as "The Line" was suspected of controlling vice in the county. Honky-tonks, speakeasies, brothels, and more than twenty gambling clubs operated openly. Sheriff Joseph Monroe "Joe" Ownbey turned a blind eye and may have taken payments to allow the underworld to flourish. His chief deputy, Emerald Allen "Two Gun Dick" Herwig, oversaw whiskey and beer sales and prostitution in town, and served as the Line's chief enforcer and collector. Appealing an Oklahoma murder conviction, Herwig hired other deputies, including John Waltine "Shine" Popejoy, the so-called "king of the bootleggers."[64]

However, Borger's underworld was not entirely united, as six hoodlums beat Deputy Sheriff Tom Wilson nearly to death and shot Popejoy in the forehead; both men survived their injuries. Bill Parks and Bob Hanna, dance hall managers in Electric City and Pantex, were arrested by a sheriff's posse. Four other suspects remained at large. Additionally, the gangsters murdered night policeman Richard Coke Buchanan on March 19, 1927, and Deputy Sheriffs Daniel Pat Kenyon and Almer L. Terry on April 1. County and city officers scoured the brakes outside Borger and the seedy portions of town in a search for Oklahoma outlaws Ray Terrill and Matthew Edward Kimes, who were wanted in connection with the deputies' murders. The suspects were also accused of robbing the First National Bank at Pampa, and lawmen had orders to shoot on sight. District Judge Newton Willis contacted Governor Moody about the desperate situation, and citizens implored the executive to declare martial law. Believing that an unneeded and drastic step, Moody instead ordered Hickman and Hamer, with McCormick, Molesworth, Ray R. Ballard, Jules Wakeman "Tod" Aldrich, Arthur Parrish "Sug" Cummings, Charles M. Davis, James Edward "Jim" McCoy, and William Walter Taylor, to stay in town "until the lawless unconditionally surrender." Commenting on the search for Kimes and his companion, Davis reported to Robertson that they were likely being protected and that local officers were uncooperative. William Jennings Bryan "Whitey" Walker, his brother John Hugh Walker, and Ed Bailey were indicted on charges of complicity in murdering the three law officers. Held in the county jail at Stinnett, they were refused bail. Attorney Walter Campbell Witcher arranged for a *habeas corpus* hearing in Austin, and the three suspects were released on bonds of fifty thousand dollars, thirty thousand dollars, and $35,000, respectively.[65]

"Borger … was the roughest town ever created by an oil boom," Hickman later recalled. "More citizens were killed, more peace officers were killed, and more men were slain in hijackings. It was a gunplay town."[66] Twenty Rangers smashed the criminal syndicate in three weeks. They destroyed 203 slot machines and numerous stills, seized thousands of gallons of whiskey, padlocked gambling joints, ordered prostitutes to leave before sundown (twelve hundred departed in twenty-four hours), and arrested 124 men. The local jail was inadequate to house the numerous prisoners, so the Rangers shackled them to a "trotline" which was fastened to the central floor beam. From there the offenders were transferred to the county jail at Stinnett. Assistant Attorney General Charles Galloway Calhoun arrived in town to file legal cases.[67]

Joined by Captain William Warren "Bill" Sterling, who arrived on Easter Sunday, Hickman and Hamer also tackled the corruption in the city and county governments. The municipal elections were held on April 5, and, amid voter fraud and disturbances at the polls, all four incumbents were returned to office. Under the threat of *quo warranto* proceedings, Mayor John R. Miller fired Police Chief Fred Williams and much of the police force on April 9, and placed the department under the supervision of Hamer and Hickman. Sheriff Ownbey likewise discharged many of his deputies. Twenty-two municipal and county officials resigned by the eighteenth, including two justices of the peace, a city commissioner, the city attorney, and the city clerk. Richer than when he had arrived, Dick Herwig left town for Wink. Despite pledging to cooperate with state officers, Miller was indicted on April 22 for accepting a two-hundred-dollar bribe to allow a gambling house to operate. Appearing in Eighty-fourth District Court, the mayor was freed on a five-thousand-dollar bond. Finally, Miller and his remaining cronies in city hall left office in early May. Not all the suspected local officials, including the sheriff, were rooted out, but Hickman and Hamer submitted reports in August describing conditions in Borger as satisfactory. The last of the Rangers left Borger on the twentieth, but, unfortunately, the captains' assertion proved to be only temporary.[68]

Many of the miscreants who fled the Rangers' sweep through Borger settled in Winkler County. District Attorney Roy I. Biggs noted thieves, gamblers, and bootleggers were responsible for nightly drunken brawls, gun battles, and robberies. In the meantime, as part of the normal shakeup caused by incoming gubernatorial administrations, Hickman was transferred from Headquarters Company to Company B at Fort Worth on May 1. Fifteen days later, he and Privates Robert William Sumrall and Pinkney F. Dyches were dispatched to restore order to the crime-ridden oil fields. On May 27, Hickman, Will Sterling, and other Rangers arrested Roy "Blackie" Wilson and Owen Edwards in Borger in connection with two bank heists in Beggs, Oklahoma, on the eighteenth. While escaping with eighteen thousand dollars, the robbers had killed Police Chief William James "Will" McAnally and wounded a female bystander. Deputy sheriffs from Okmulgee were dispatched to extradite the prisoners to the Sooner State.[69]

On June 25, 1927, Hickman was elected third vice president of the Chiefs of Police and City Marshals' Association of Texas at the twenty-ninth annual convention in Fort Worth. He was chosen as first vice president on June 5, 1928, in Houston, and selected to be president of the organization the following year while attending the meeting in San Antonio. Beaumont was chosen as the venue for the 1930 meeting.[70]

During the Moody administration, Texas saw a rise in the number of bank robberies. The Panhandle Bankers' Association opted to take drastic measures. On June 9, 1927, during the twenty-third annual meeting in Plainview, the attendees approved a motion to offer five hundred dollars for every bank robber killed in the act, and $250 each for those arrested and convicted. The obvious flaw in the plan was that individuals could gain a greater financial benefit while avoiding the vagaries of the court system by simply killing holdup men. Six months later, the Texas Bankers' Association escalated their stance on bank robbing in a much more radical fashion.[71]

Recognized as a bank robbery specialist since the Clarksville heist, Hickman worked numerous such cases in North Texas over the next few years. On August 23, three armed and unmasked men walked into the University

Bank in Austin, and, within three minutes, forced four patrons to the floor, and snatched $26,000 in cash, bonds, and bankers' checks before escaping in a stolen Buick sedan. Obvious amateurs, the young-looking thieves were described as "nervous and highly excited." The ten thousand dollars in bonds they stole were non-negotiable. Alerted to the first bank robbery in town in twenty years, law enforcement officers rushed to the scene within minutes and began canvassing the vicinity. Dactylography specialist Raymond Thorp arrived to process the scene, but he was unable to recover any usable fingerprints. Hamer and Roy Aldrich reached the bank and assisted the local officers. The getaway car was found abandoned with a flat tire in the underbrush at Hooper's Switch near the Missouri Pacific tracks. Footprints indicated the trio had gone into cedar brakes in the Bull Creek section five miles northwest of town. With two airplanes circling overhead, Hickman, Wheatley, Rangers Joseph "Joe" Osoba, Sr. and Tod Aldrich, county and city officers, and National Guardsman scoured dense tangles of cedars, chaparral, and thorns, and the troops stood watch through the night at Spicewood Springs and nearby thickets. The next day, investigators discovered the three gunmen had met an unknown individual on the old Burnet road west of town. One of the robbers left in the fourth person's gray roadster, while the other two either caught a northbound freight train or walked back to Sixth Street. No money, guns, or clothing were left in the Buick; no additional clues were developed after a fruitless forty-hour search. Rewards of five hundred dollars were offered by the bank, the local clearinghouse association, and the Texas Bankers' Association. Travis County Sheriff Horace E. Burleson continued to work the case, and one suspect was in custody by September 3.[72]

Two unmasked youths robbed the East Grand Avenue State Bank of fifteen hundred dollars in cash on November 17. One of the bank employees was struck with the butt of a pistol when he resisted. After failing to lock the staff in the vault, the bandits fled in a light roadster in the direction of Garland. The getaway car was later found burned near the Forney Avenue Road. Hickman and Ranger Gonzaullas arrived in Dallas the following day to assist local officers in locating the perpetrators. The state officers believed the holdup men were part of a gang of career criminals operating from Oklahoma, and the search extended toward the Sooner State. However, a week of searching failed to locate the robbers, and many officers believed they had escaped into Oklahoma or Arkansas. A tip led lawmen to Chet Fowler and Jack Long, who were said to be hiding in the Pecos Valley oil fields. The pair were not apprehended, but they were indicted by the grand jury on November 29 with robbery with firearms. They were also persons of interest in a bank robbery in Plano, and another in Jefferson.[73]

While the East Grand Avenue bank job investigation was still underway, Hickman was involved in stopping the most remarkable heist in Texas history. On December 23, 1927, four men entered the First National Bank in Cisco, a railroad town in Eastland County, and robbed the institution at gunpoint. The thieves were later identified as Marshall Ratliff, Henry Helms, and Robert Hill, all ex-convicts, and Louis E. "Lonnie" Davis. Ratliff wore a Santa Claus costume during the crime, and this led the media to dub the caper the "Santa Claus Bank Robbery."[74]

Chief of Police George Emory "Bit" Bedford and Officer George W. Carmichael were alerted by Mrs. Maybell Blasingame and her six-year-old daughter Frances, both of whom had managed to escape as the robbers pulled their weapons out of concealment. The two officers grabbed shotguns and raced to the bank. Carmichael took up a post behind the institution in the alley, while Bedford positioned himself in front on busy Avenue D (present-day Conrad Hilton Avenue). From his post, Carmichael peered into a window and observed Ratcliff stuffing twelve thousand dollars in cash and negotiable securities valued at $150,000 into money bags, while one of the bandits herded the hostages into the bookkeeping room. The policeman loosed a shotgun blast through the glass, and the thieves returned fire. Helms had been positioned by the side door, and he fired blindly up and down the alley. Hearing the gunshots, nearby civilians grabbed their guns and hurried to assist the officers.[75]

As they exited the side door into the alley, the thieves seized five customers to use as human shields. While making for their waiting dark blue Buick, they encountered Officer Carmichael and shot him in the head and body; he would die of his injuries on January 7, 1928. Lonnie Davis was wounded four times, but his partners in crime pulled him and two of the hostages into the getaway car. In an exchange of approximately one hundred gunshots, two hostages and six citizens were wounded. The thieves pulled out of the alley and left Chief Bedford dying in the middle of Avenue D as they made their escape. They led their pursuers on a high-speed chase on two flat tires, and failed to steal another vehicle, thanks to the quick thinking of fourteen-year-old Woodrow Wilson Harris. The gang abandoned their loot, the hostages, and Davis before fleeing on foot. The mortally wounded thief was taken to the Tarrant County jail, while charges of murder and robbery by firearms were filed against him.[76]

Goaded by the bankers' association reward, more than five hundred law officers and possemen flooded the post oak sections of Eastland County. Alerted by the governor, Hickman took the train from Austin to Fort Worth where he interviewed Davis in the county jail. However, the dying outlaw refused to reveal any details of his confederates. The captain arrived in Cisco the next morning, but the swarm of people had obliterated any trace of the robbers. Hickman asked, "the members of the posse to take these men alive if possible, but if anyone was killed to make sure it was a bandit and not another peace officer." The surviving bank robbers stole more vehicles and attempted to drive to Wichita Falls. Instead, they met a sheriff's posse near South Bend in Young County and traded gunfire with the lawmen. In particular, Eastland County Deputy Sheriff Daniel Silas "Si" Bradford, Sr., a seasoned lawman, used his double-barreled shotgun to good effect. Ratliff was shot and captured, while Helms and Hill, both seriously wounded in the fight, escaped into the dense cedar brakes in the Goose Neck of the Brazos River. Hickman and Gonzaullas departed Wichita Falls for South Bend in a high-powered automobile equipped with a Thompson submachine gun. The Rangers arrived on the scene the following day and found the possemen had been so anxious to collect the reward on Ratliff, who survived his wounds, that they had allowed the other fugitives to get away.[77]

Buffeted by sleet and a cold northern wind, the captain led the pursuit on the ground with bloodhounds and arranged for a plane from Fort Worth to conduct an airborne search. In a surplus World War I-era biplane, Sergeant Gonzaullas, armed with the Thompson, cast an eye over the river bottoms where Hill and a fevered Helms frantically attempted to stay concealed. The Lone Wolf spotted one of the outlaws out in the open, and his plane returned to Graham to report to Hickman. The two exhausted and starving fugitives staggered into Graham on December 30 and surrendered. Hickman reported to Aldrich the pursuit's successful conclusion: "It was better than a deer hunt." He expressed his gladness the pair were taken alive, even if they were worth ten thousand dollars dead. The captain also noted the Bankers' Association had requested he be assigned exclusively to bank robberies and offered to furnish transportation.[78]

Ratliff, Helms, and Hill were indicted on January 2, 1928. Ratliff was convicted in Ninety-first District Court on the twenty-seventh and sentenced to ninety years in prison. The trial of Helms convened on February 20, and, six days later, he was sentenced to die in the electric chair. Hill pled guilty to a charge of robbery with firearms on March 21, and District Judge George L. Davenport pronounced a sentence of ninety-nine years. Subsequently tried for the murder of Chief Bedford, Ratliff was found guilty and sentenced to death on March 30. To escape his fate, Helms attempted an insanity defense at a hearing in Eastland on August 28. Hickman testified and stated his belief that Helms was sane. The jury agreed and declared the defendant competent; the death sentence was carried out on September 6. On October 24, Ratliff's mother filed a petition claiming the wait for his execution had driven him insane. The next day, the condemned man was brought to the Eastland County lockup on a bench warrant prior to a sanity hearing. On November 19, Ratliff mortally wounded Deputy Sheriff Thomas Alexander "Tom" Jones while trying to escape, but his efforts were thwarted. A mob of two hundred outraged citizens marched on the jail, dragged Ratliff from his cell, and lynched him from a telephone pole on the corner of West White and North Mulberry Streets.[79]

Fifteen people barely escaped with their lives on April 24, 1928, when a fire destroyed the farmhouse of Jim Marchman, southwest of Cisco. Ominously, the blaze occurred only a quarter-mile from the home of Robert Nicholas "Boss" Jackson, where he, his wife, and their six young daughters had been killed on April 6, and the structure was set alight. Charles Jackson, brother to Robert, was visiting the Marchman home with his family at the time of the arson. With the assistance of District Attorney Frank Sparks, Hickman opened an investigation. One day after the second fire, Sheriff John S. Hart and the county attorney questioned and arrested laborer Bill Sluder, but the suspect was no-billed by the grand jury and released. Hickman traveled to Baylor County on April 26 in an unsuccessful attempt to locate a former friend of Sluder. An examination of the crime scene revealed footprints leading from the destroyed home to a point a quarter-mile distant where an automobile had turned around. On May 8, Hickman conferred with former neighbors of Boss Jackson in Dallas and Rockwall Counties. Combining the information he gleaned, the captain drove to Texarkana and spoke with Mr. and Mrs. Charles Gregory regarding the threats Boss Jackson had made to kill his entire family. Hickman confirmed the threats and discovered the dead man had caught Sluder having intercourse with the oldest Jackson daughter, who was only twelve years old. The latter man had been involved in a rape case three years earlier. The Ranger believed the distraught Jackson had slain his family, set the fire, and cut his own throat. Most of the Eastland County authorities concurred with his opinion of murder-suicide.[80]

Authorities investigating the Grand Avenue bank robbery caught a break when Jack Long was detained on May 5 while trying to cross the border into El Paso from Ciudad Juárez. Three days later, Judge Grover C. Adams of the Criminal District Court in Dallas issued a bench warrant for his delivery to Dallas. The suspect applied for *habeas corpus*, but his efforts were in vain. District Attorney William McCraw announced he would seek the death penalty. Returned to Dallas on May 10, Long's day in court on the eighteenth lasted less than ten minutes, as he pleaded guilty to the robbery charge without the firearms qualifier and was sentenced to ninety-nine years in prison. Chet Fowler, Long's brother-in-law, was believed to be residing in Mexico.[81]

On June 20, weeks before the start of the 1928 Democratic National Convention in Houston, Robert Powell, a twenty-four-year-old black man, was kidnapped by eight armed and unmasked white men from his bed at Jefferson Davis Hospital in the Fourth Ward. Harris County Deputy Sheriff Yancy Quitman Brizendine proved unable to stop the abduction. Powell's body was later found hanging from the Post Oak Road bridge six miles from downtown. Sheriff Thomas Abner Binford noticed the rope around the victim's neck was knotted in a double hitch rather than a hangman's noose. Undertakers discovered Powell had been shot in the head and hanged postmortem. Justice of the Peace James Maurice Ray ordered an immediate autopsy to recover the slug. Claiming a bullet wound in his abdomen came from a dice game, Powell had earlier been charged with the murder of city detective Albert Worth Davis. The policeman had been killed on the seventeenth while attempting to arrest a black man. His sidearm had been discharged. While Governor Moody offered a reward of $250, Judge Langston King ordered the grand jury to concentrate on the Powell homicide. In preparation for the convention, the city fathers had been promoting Houston as a growing metropolis of industry and progress, and the lynching was a stark contrast to their publicized image. Citizens across racial lines were appalled and angered, and the NAACP and the city council offered rewards of one thousand and ten thousand dollars respectively. Tensions heightened among civic leaders, especially between the pro-growth white and black business communities and the segregationists who favored extrajudicial violence as a means of social control. Hickman, Hamer, and three Rangers already in Houston were placed at the disposal of the local authorities. Having once been infected by elements of the Ku Klux Klan, the ranks of the Houston Police Department were filled with persons of interest. Fifty officers who had been on duty between the hours of three and 11:00 p.m. were questioned. Six suspects, purportedly friends of the slain detective, were indicted on June 22 and held without bond until August 1. In trials that stretched more than two years, none were convicted.[82]

While they ably assisted in the Powell case, the picked detachment of twelve Rangers, including Gonzaullas, Wheatley, Roy Aldrich, and Ed McMordie, was actually assembling in Houston to keep order during the Democratic convention. To that end, the state officers stopped poker and dice games taking place in adjoining rooms on the thirteenth floor of the Rice Hotel on June 26. Fourteen individuals were taken into custody, and their fines promptly paid. The same day, the Rangers were appointed assistant sergeants-at-arms for the duration of the convention.[83]

The American Legion convention of 1928 in San Antonio also afforded the Rangers an opportunity to arrest lawbreakers. On October 9, while the conference was underway, Hickman, accompanied by Adjutant General Robert Lamar Robertson, Captain Sterling, and Private Dott Edward Smith, Sr., burst into a room at the St. Anthony Hotel. The law officers shut down four dice tables, four "do and don't" layouts, a roulette wheel, and a chuck-a-luck cage. The assistant hotel manager was ordered to sign a receipt for the gaming equipment that remained locked in the room. The Rangers had been after professional gamblers, and those playing the "friendly" craps games were released.[84]

In the early hours of December 19, an attempt was made to burglarize the First State Bank of Jarrell in Williamson County. The would-be thieves entered the building by tunneling through the eighteen-inch wall into the vault with a pickaxe. They then knocked the combination lock's knob off the safe and, using an acetylene torch, burned a five-inch hole in the steel door before quitting the endeavor. Stymied in obtaining the $4,500 in currency and coinage, the robbers rifled the safety deposit boxes and took much of the contents. As the town possessed no marshal or watchman, the attempted burglary was not discovered until employees arrived in the morning. Sheriff Louis Lowe, Hickman, Hamer, and a fingerprint expert from the Austin Police Department worked the case. Since the bandits wore gloves, no fingerprints could be processed.[85]

Larry Meinert, a long-time Dallas boxing promoter, arranged for a bout to take place between Al "Kid" Kober and Marvin Irby "Duke" Tramel on April 8, 1929. Under orders from the governor, Hickman traveled to Dallas to halt the fight. Meinert obtained an injunction from Seventy-seventh District Judge Hardy Fountain Kirby in Fairfield to keep the captain and Sheriff Howell Alexander "Hal" Hood from intervening. Despite the court order, the two lawmen, together with District Attorney William "Bill" McGraw, stopped the proceedings and later faced a contempt of court citation. The trio planned to argue in court that they had obtained another writ from Judge Towne Young of Dallas that dissolved Kirby's earlier decree. All three were arraigned before Judge Kirby on August 29, who granted a continuance when the court papers went missing. The documents were later found in the district clerk's office. Arguments in the case were heard beginning on September 6, although Hickman was not present, as he had been subpoenaed to appear in the Henry Helms insanity hearing. Judge Kirby dismissed the charges on the ninth.[86]

Borger—"the Sodom of the Prairie"—remained a problem for the Ranger Force. State officers had swept through the town in September and November of 1927, and August of 1928, in an attempt to keep the town's vice rackets incapacitated. By the end of the latter month, a group of reformers had won all the county offices except sheriff, which was still held by the shady Joe Ownbey. Hickman and Hamer were on hand to keep the peace during the elections. The newly elected district attorney for the Eighty-fourth District, John A. Holmes, had once defended criminals in court, but now he was on the other side. Publicly possessing a reputation for honesty and persistence, he declared his desire to prosecute lawbreakers as vigorously as he had once represented them. In spite of this, one month before Holmes's death, Representative John Herron White of Borger claimed the district attorney's "main thought is for the dollar" and he "gets a part of this money paid by these bootleggers to get their cases either dismissed or set over to later terms of court." With ambiguous motivations, Holmes requested the presence of an undercover officer, and Dott Smith was ordered to report to the prosecutor. Despite their efforts, Borger was still run by the corrupt mayor Glen Pace and the equally dishonest police chief John William Crabtree, both of whom protected the town's underworld. In April 1929, Pace and his cohorts arranged for nonresidents to vote in the city elections, paid the required poll taxes, and saw the reform party crushed.[87]

That same month, Holmes informed the governor he could only do his job if Rangers were on hand indefinitely. In the past, as soon as the state officers departed, the vice rackets resumed business until the next time the Rangers were called in. The district attorney added that the cycle would continue as long as Sheriff Ownbey remained in office.[88]

On June 28, Hickman, Gonzaullas, Privates Jim McCoy, James Porter "J. P." Huddleston, Hardy Burl Purvis, Chesley Omer Moore, Dott Smith, and William Hale Kirby, and eight federal agents thundered through fifteen of Borger's dives, destroying gambling equipment and liquor, and arresting thirty-six men and women. The prisoners were held in a vacant storeroom until charges could be filed in federal court in Amarillo. Thirteen suspected bootleggers were arraigned the following day and made bonds of two thousand dollars each. Their trials were scheduled for September. Unfortunately, the Ranger Force possessed only thirty men to cover the entire state, and Hickman's detachment was needed elsewhere. Thus, the familiar routine continued, and the closed joints reopened. The police chief and the sheriff refused to cooperate with Holmes. The unscrupulous pair went on to tamper with jury lists and hesitant witnesses. Tragic events involving the district attorney would soon cause the Rangers to return with different results.[89]

An earlier arrest in Borger presented Hickman with a welcome return on March 13, 1930, when he finally received a reward for the apprehension of "Blackie" Wilson. Over the previous two years, the captain had been compelled to make four trips to Oklahoma City to press his claim, as well as expend funds for notary fees, three telegrams, one telephone call, and seventy-six letters. The State of Oklahoma paid the Ranger $1,090, which he split equally between Sterling, Gonzaullas, Purvis, Tod Aldrich, former Ranger William P. McConnell, ex-Special Ranger John Taylor "Jack" deGraffenreid and himself.[90]

Taking a break from the pressing needs of his occupation, Hickman married Tina Martha Knight in her Fort Worth home on June 4, 1930. The ceremony was officiated by the Reverend Pierre Bernard Hill, chaplain of the Ranger Force, and witnessed by Gonzaullas. The couple was long acquainted, as Hickman had been a lodger in her parents' boarding house for the past six years. Born on January 29, 1905, Tina attended high school in Denton, where she was judged the most beautiful girl. The family moved to Fort Worth in 1922, and Tina attended the business college. Hickman's new bride was later described as a gracious and caring woman who had an appreciation for art and music. The couple honeymooned in Mineral Wells, then made ready to travel overseas.[91]

Teaming with Knox K. "Hoss Fly" Kelly of Post in a lariat-twirling duet, Hickman appeared with the Cowboy Band of Simmons University at the Hippodrome Theater in New York City on June 11. Sailing with his wife the next day on the SS *Leviathan*, and landing at Southampton on the seventeenth, Hickman accompanied twenty-six members of the band on a concert and educational tour of Europe. The captain and Kelly were assisted in their rope act by ten-year-old William Wilkes "Wild Bill" Kelly, Knox's younger brother, and twelve-year-old Tom Bryant, Jr. of Cross Plains. Young Tom had been commissioned by Governor Moody into Hickman's company, making him the youngest Ranger in the history of the service. During the band's engagement at the Palladium in London, Hickman toured Scotland Yard and visited with detectives of that famed department. He took the opportunity to correct editors of the London *Evening Standard* on some of their erroneous reporting concerning the riot at Sherman. Additionally, while touring the Continent, the captain had the occasion to speak to police officers in Holland, Belgium, and France, and study their systems and procedures. When he and Tina boarded the *Leviathan* for the return trip to the United States on August 10, the captain was sporting a Van Dyke beard of "manly proportions." Tina declined to publicly comment on her husband's facial hair, but Hickman remarked to reporters he had heard from "family headquarters" that he should promptly shave. With his wife's wishes satisfied, Hickman was selected to be one of the judges for the Second Annual World Championship Rodeo at the State Fair.[92]

On December 2, a delegation of Fort Worth citizens called on Governor Moody to order Hickman to make investigation of conditions in the city. The captain devised a strategy for raiding gambling dens, and obtained the necessary search warrants. He began the drive by assisting Sheriff James Robert "Red" Wright in raiding an enormous whiskey still located in the eastern portion of the county. On January 27, Hickman, Gonzaullas, Huddleston, and Captain Albert Ramos Mace of Company A secured search warrants and raided the farm of W. D. May, north of Hadley. In searching the houses and barns, the officer discovered and seized two complete three-hundred-gallon copper stills and associated equipment. Assembling in Fort Worth on March 13, Hickman, Gonzaullas, Mace, Huddleston, Kirby, McCoy, Thomas Lee Heard, Walter Everette "Ebb" Riggs, Benjamin Maney Gault, Robert Gray "Bob" Goss, Marvin Burton, and George Martin Allen, Sr., and the sheriff and his deputies, struck a number of houses, but they all were empty. Hickman and Gonzaullas suspected a county official had leaked information to the gamblers.[93]

The Ranger Force had prospered under the Moody administration, and the state officers enjoyed another champion in the governor's mansion when

Ross Shaw Sterling took office in 1931. One of his first appointments was to choose William W. Sterling as adjutant general, thus ensuring the Rangers were commanded by one of their own. Sterling's selection was the first such advancement for a Ranger since John B. Jones in 1879. The general retained Hickman, Hamer, Mace, and William L. Wright as captains, and appointed Asa Light Townsend to a company command. Chesley Moore was named quartermaster. Sterling moved almost immediately to remove politics from the Force by empowering the five captains to personally recruit their men. He did, however, reserve the right to approve the appointments and carefully considered each for personal experience, a good record, and seniority.[94] In the new administration, Hickman spent a good deal of time investigating bank robberies in Fort Worth, Mineral Wells, Petrolia, Pilot Point, Cedar Hill, Sherman, Paris, Tyler, and Boyd.[95]

Rather than as a law enforcement officer, Hickman found himself before a justice of the peace as a defendant on March 18, 1931. Earlier in the day, he had engaged in a physical altercation on the courthouse lawn in Gainesville with former sheriff Ate T. Reece. The county attorney prepared a complaint for simple assault, and Hickman was fined one dollar and court costs, the total amount being $14.65.[96]

His obligation to the court completed, Hickman returned to work. The governor had ordered the state's police forces to intervene and halt boxing matches. Obeying instructions from the adjutant general, Hickman prevented a bout in Fort Worth. On April 10, promoter Dick Griffith cancelled the event after the captain informed him the show would be stopped if attempted. Hickman was then ordered to Galveston to stop any prizefights before going to Kilgore on April 12.[97]

Captains Hickman and Hamer found themselves to be the victims of a con artist who had assumed their identities to cash checks in Chicago and St. Louis. The impostor traveled to Texas and passed bad checks at the Brazos Hotel in Houston on July 13, 1926, the American Express office in Austin the next day, and the Kaufman Dry Goods store in San Antonio on the fifteenth. The suspect bore a Ranger's badge and several identification cards. He was apprehended and lodged in the Bexar County jail. Curious, Hickman and Hamer came to town to see the prisoner. Following the swindler's capture,

Ross S. Sterling. William Deming Hornaday Collection. *Courtesy Texas State Library and Archives Commission, Austin, TX.*

the Forty-sixth Legislature passed an act on May 28, 1931, prohibiting the impersonation of Texas Rangers. The law made falsely assuming the identity of a Ranger guilty of a misdemeanor, punishable by six months in prison and a fine of five hundred dollars. Time behind bars did not convince the impersonator to change his ways. By early February 1934, he had shifted his transgressions to Oregon and Washington.[98]

Hickman was next involved in a legal dispute concerning Texas and the Sooner State. The nearly finished Red River bridge between Denison and Durant, Oklahoma, had been a joint project between the highway departments of both states. The crossing had been built next to a privately-owned toll bridge that had charged a seventy-five-cent fee. Since travelers would now be able to cross the river for free, the owners of the private span, the Red River Bridge Company, had negotiated a sixty-thousand-dollar compensation arrangement with the Texas Highway Commission. As the free bridge approached completion, though, the toll operators had still not been reimbursed, and they applied for a federal injunction to keep the public bridge closed until the solution could be determined. Judge Thomas Martin Kennerly of the Eastern District of Texas issued the restraining order on June 25, 1931.[99]

William Henry David "Alfalfa Bill" Murray, governor of Oklahoma, insisted the ruling only affected Texas and not his state. On July 16, he ordered his highway department to dismantle a barricade that had been built on the Texas side of the free bridge. Governor Sterling responded by ordering Adjutant General Bill Sterling to ensure the next barrier remained in place. Sterling, accompanied by Hickman, Huddleston, and Kirby, was on the scene at daybreak on July 18. "This time," the adjutant general subsequently recounted, "the bridge stayed closed."[100]

Newspaper reporters from Dallas and Fort Worth learned of the confrontation and hurried to the bridge. They overstated the argument between the two states as a kind of civil war. Governor Murray, a flamboyant character, assisted the media in presenting their depiction. Gonzaullas, Bob Goss, and Alfred Young Allee were sent to reinforce Hickman. After the Rangers had replaced the barricade, Murray ordered his highway department to tear up two hundred yards of U.S. Highway 75 leading to the toll bridge on July 17. He also declared martial law six days later and mobilized National Guard troops. General Sterling publicly embodied the popular image of the Texas Rangers as he directed six Rangers in opposing thirty-two Guardsmen. There were no hostilities at the scene, and the only thing spilled was newspaper ink. The injunction barred automobile traffic over the free bridge, and Hickman similarly stopped a drunken pedestrian from Durant and compelled him to return to the Oklahoma side of the river. As legislators and lawyers dealt with the frustrating situation in the statehouse and the courtroom, the Rangers entertained the press and onlookers with exhibitions of their shooting prowess. Goss held his pistol upside down and split a playing card turned edgeways at twenty yards, while *Time* magazine reported the captain hit eighteen out of twenty matches while firing from the hip at fifty feet. After the chief physicist of the Peters Cartridge Company wrote a letter to the periodical's editor questioning the "shooting yarn" involving Hickman, the Ranger wrote his response several weeks later. He confirmed the impossibility of the reported gun handling and, tongue in cheek, revealed, "I am such a poor marksman that I never shoot until the other fellow has shot at me."[101]

On July 23, the Texas legislature passed a bill that permitted the Red River Bridge Company to bring suit against the Texas Highway Commission for damages. Two days later, Judge Kennerly temporarily suspended the injunction. Governor Sterling immediately issued an executive order instructing the Rangers to remove the wooden barricades, and Hickman delayed taking down the obstruction long enough to obtain confirmation. Waiting in a line that stretched for over a mile, more than two thousand automobiles and pedestrians crossed the free bridge. Thereafter, Hickman received orders to go to Gainesville and investigate the murder of Fire Marshal Walter Clements. Meanwhile, Kirby returned to Fort Worth, Gonzaullas to the East Texas oil fields, Goss to Honey Grove, and Allee to Del Rio. Once Judge Kennerly permanently rescinded the order on August 6, the Oklahoma Guardsmen also departed.[102]

Even as the "war" with Oklahoma was winding down, tensions in the East Texas oil field were ratcheting up. While the Great Depression continued its crushing effects, crude oil prices dropped to less than ten cents a barrel despite the sixteen hundred wells in the East Texas field that were pumping out one million barrels per day—or one-third of the country's total production. Indeed, the wells in that region were producing more oil than the market could handle. Earlier, on August 27, 1930, the Texas Railroad Commission had established the maximum allowable production at 750,000 barrels per day, but the decision resulted in legal challenges in the state courts. The commission, the large oil corporations, and the governor were all alarmed at this flouting of the basic tenets of supply and demand and urged the independent operators to slow down their drilling. The governor responded by calling the legislature into special session on July 14, 1931, in order to write a new law enforcing the portion of the state constitution that asserted the "conservation and development of all natural resources" of Texas to be "public rights and duties." Exercising his authority to its limits, Sterling declared martial law in Gregg, Rusk, Smith, and Upshur Counties on August 16, on the basis that specific independent oil companies were "in a state of insurrection" by continuing to produce oil in spite of the clear economic imperatives. General Jacob F. Wolters, commanding the Fifty-sixth Cavalry Brigade, arrived in Kilgore and deployed his troopers throughout the area. Hickman, Gonzaullas, Goss, Stanley, Purvis, Kirby, Huddleston, Burton, and Chaplain Pierre Hill were on hand to greet them.[103]

On August 17, twelve hundred National Guardsmen, Hickman's men already on the scene, and Rangers Thad George Tarver and Louis Young from Falfurrias and Captain Mace and Private Ebb Riggs from Fort Stockton proceeded to close the entire oil field. Hickman assigned one of his men to accompany every twenty-man cavalry detachment and carry out any necessary arrests. Within twenty hours, the state forces had secured the field without incident. While scouring the oil field, the Rangers also descended on dance halls and beer joints, recovered stolen autos and other property, seized liquor and firearms, and apprehended twenty-one gamblers, bootleggers, and prostitutes. Some of the offenders were ordered to leave the county the following day. Two waves of arson swept through Kilgore in the month of August, with two churches being destroyed and a number of buildings damaged. Over the next several days, National Guardsman patrolled the streets looking for suspicious characters while Rangers and police officers kept a close watch on well-known underworld figures in the oil fields. Anxious citizens armed themselves and placed heavy guards around oil company properties and local businesses. The volunteer fire department recruited additional manpower in preparation of more incendiarism. By August 24, though, the field had quieted to the point where Wolters could release from active duty half of the rank and file and several of the officers. However, there still remained work to be done.[104]

On August 29, Hickman, Gonzaullas, Goss, Stanley, and Burton, and William Early "Earl" Young of Company A, raided dance halls, beer joints, and tourist camps in Willow Springs. Twenty individuals were arrested, and a quantity of liquor was seized. A number of people were advised to leave the region or face going to jail. Hickman ordered every dance hall to close at midnight on the weekdays and all day on Sundays. The Rangers closed another four dance halls on the Longview–Gladewater road on the thirtieth. The next day, General Wolters ordered the thirty-six Guardsmen patrolling Kilgore: "Don't shoot unless you must. If you must shoot, shoot at the waist line [*sic*] but don't come back and tell me you missed."[105]

Eighteen hundred wells were allowed to resume production on September 2, but the Railroad Commission imposed a new proration amount of 400,000 barrels per day. Reductions were maintained through October, which drove up crude prices. As before, the regulation proved to be difficult, if not impossible, to enforce for long. Operators merely drilled additional wells or blatantly disregarded the rule; the illicit product became known as "hot oil" and was smuggled nightly into Louisiana and Oklahoma. The production of thirteen hundred wells in the field soon totaled 1,400,000 barrels per day, which markedly surpassed the quantity mandated by the commission. Moreover, the operators of five independent wells were successful in obtaining a federal injunction against the state's directive on October 31.[106]

Even while the hot oil controversy raged, Hickman's detachment continued to deal with the criminal element in their district. Ranger Tarver, accompanied by Rusk County Deputies Homer Gary and Edwin Holt, was surveilling a tent camp near New London on the morning of September 2 and waiting for Oklahoma desperado Joe R. Rochat (also known as Bob Williams) to arrive. Their quarry, wanted for a bank robbery in Pelican, Louisiana, spotted the posse and fled into the woods, pistol in hand. When Williams emerged from the other side of the trees, the deputies fired at him, and one bullet struck the bandit in the neck, killing him. On September 17, Hardy Purvis and Ranger Lockhart Valentine Hightower, Sr. apprehended Bige Harrell, another wanted fugitive from the Sooner State. Hickman traveled to Gainesville on October 7 to assist in the trial of Frank Bracken, who had killed Police Officers John Walter Clements and William Edward Johns on July 24. On October 19,

Hickman and his men were directed to Wichita Falls to keep order during a potentially volatile murder and rape trial. They performed the same duty the following month in Daingerfield for a trial of a black man accused of sexually assaulting a white woman. "Determined to dry up Fort Worth by Christmas," Hickman seized 325 gallons of whiskey and two thousand gallons of mash at a nearby farm on December 10 and arrested two men. The liquor had been hidden in a subterranean network so intricate additional inspection had to be performed the next day.[107]

On January 15, 1932, Hickman, Stanley, and Kirby raided an elaborate gambling hall in the Palace Hotel at Longview. Twenty-two gamblers and five alleged casino operators were arrested. The customers were fined, while Hickman filed felony charges against the owner and the dealers. With their prisoners in custody, the Rangers summoned a justice of the peace, then destroyed the gaming equipment.[108]

The captain, Stanley, Kirby, and Customs inspectors Walter Ernest Mayberry and Fred Egbert Edwards trailed a freight car originating in Laredo across the state before seizing it in Fort Worth on February 10. Although the car was labeled "cabbage," the cargo was actually fifteen hundred gallons of alcohol. Once the liquor was delivered to a trio of different residences, the lawmen moved in and arrested three men. Mayberry filed complaints of violating the federal liquor laws before U.S. Commissioner Lois Newam.[109]

On February 18, a three-judge federal panel ruled that the governor had overstepped his authority in using martial law to halt the production of hot oil. In their decision, the jurists determined Sterling had infringed upon the powers legislated to the Railroad Commission. Nevertheless, the National Guardsmen and the Rangers remained to enforce the commission's proration orders. Civil and military authorities conducted a forty-five-day investigation into the unlawful movement of one million barrels of product. Professional "hot oil artists" were believed to have used by-passes or cut-off valves on pipelines running from at least five Gladewater wells. Additionally, experts who did not even own an interest in a well profited by tapping into the lines of others, bleeding off a certain amount, and selling the stolen crude to the black market they had helped ethically pliable producers to create. Based on the recommendations of District Attorney John E. Taylor, Justice of the Peace

Eugene Bryant Penick issued arrest warrants, and Hickman, Hamer, Gonzaullas, Hightower, George Allen, and Oscar Thomas Martin, Sr. were directed to serve them. The Rangers were supported by seven military officers. Eighteen men were apprehended on May 1 and charged with 213 separate counts of felony theft and conspiracy to commit felony theft. In addition to three oil operators and seven field workers, the suspects included a deputy supervisor of the Railroad Commission, a brother-in-law of an assistant state attorney general, and a Texas & Pacific Railway agent in Gladewater. General Sterling directed an additional thirty-six Rangers to the area on August 23, but the governor countermanded the order. Even without the reinforcements, Hickman and his ten men quietly arrested sixty men in Gladewater and Kilgore, including two wanted bank robbers. While proration would eventually become an acknowledged method of conservation, the governor's policy cost him at the Democratic primary later that year, even though voter fraud in East Texas played a significant role. Furthermore, Sterling's defeat to Miriam Ferguson meant the Rangers had lost their greatest ally.[110]

The Forty-third Legislature would pass an act on May 22, 1933, "prohibiting certain practices in production of oil and gas, providing for accurate measurement and recording." The law basically proscribed oil produced by a private entity from passing out of its possession or control without first measuring and documenting the amount yielded. The measure also empowered certain state governmental agencies, including the Railroad Commission and the Texas Rangers, to inspect records and property held by production companies. Commission agents and Rangers were also given authority to serve civil and judicial process in enforcement of the state's conservation laws. A federal court upheld the legality of the legislation in January 1934.[111]

Returning to Fort Worth on March 9, 1932, Hickman and Gonzaullas obtained search warrants, then led Huddleston, Kirby, Stanley, and Ranger Arthur B. Ham in raiding the Imperial Hotel at 1006 Main Street three days later. They arrested ten men and filed felony charges. While city and county officers made their own forays, Hickman, Gonzaullas, and Stanley next raided the Siebold Hotel on Seventh and Commerce Streets. Interrupting a craps game on the fourth floor, they arrested nine men, confiscated over seven hundred dollars in cash, and destroyed elaborate gambling equipment in two rooms. An anonymous informant had written General Sterling and accused Hickman of protecting the game, a charge the captain mocked as he destroyed the large table, wicker furniture, and water cooler found in the rooms.[112]

Hickman returned to the East Texas oil field and led a squad of Rangers in raids in Gladewater and Kilgore on August 21 and 23. While arresting sixty men, including two bank robbery suspects, the state officers worked so quietly that few knew of their presence until several prisoners were delivered to the Longview jail.[113]

Unlike many of his colleagues, Hickman chose not to resign when Mrs. Ferguson took office. According to newspaper reports, Hickman was reportedly seeking a deputy U.S. marshal's commission, if one were offered. He responded to the rumors by asserting he was not interested in leaving an organization he had served for fourteen years. Albeit reluctantly, he and Sergeant Gonzaullas escorted the new executive to her swearing-in ceremony at the State Capitol on January 17, 1933. The governor returned the favor the following day by discharging both Rangers—and the rest of the force still in service. In the aftermath of his dismissal, Hickman went to work for the state comptroller's office as a special investigator headquartered in Fort Worth.[114]

Once the Fergusons regained power, the Ranger Force entered a "dark period." In the wake of the recent discharges, the co-governors chose thirty-nine appointees who were often substandard; some were later accused and convicted of felonies, including theft, embezzlement, and murder. The disastrous policies became readily apparent as Texas became the sixth most crime-ridden state in the nation. The annual rate for 1933 was 27,533 offenses per one million of urban population. Murder, bank robberies, kidnappings, and illegal gambling became rampant. Two years after Repeal, state law banning hard liquors continued to be ignored. Moreover, the Forty-third Legislature drastically lowered Ranger salaries, slashed manpower to thirty-two men, and abolished longevity pay. In total, the force's budget was cut by 45 percent. To balance out the reduced organization, Ferguson issued 2,245 Special Ranger commissions to political patrons. Among the occupations held by those Special Rangers were undertaker, barber, druggist, hardware clerk, retail liquor dealer, night club bouncer, guard at gambling houses or dog and horse tracks, cement worker, and veterinarian. Highlighting the Fergusons' rampant abuse of the commissions during their two-year administration, a search of the Texas State Library's digitized Adjutant General Service Records revealed a total of 4,160 Special Rangers from the early 1880s to 1935.[115]

In light of the rise in crime, Hickman became an advocate for a new state police force. He wrote letters to the editor calling for an experienced and nonpolitical superintendent to take charge, assisted by ballistics and fingerprint bureaus. As he had in September 1930, he introduced a resolution for a strong state police in May 1934 at the annual meeting of the Chiefs of Police and City Marshals' Association meeting in Austin. The proposal was narrowly defeated due to its lack of a definite plan. Having already inspected the operations of Scotland Yard in 1924 and 1930, Hickman was granted an extended leave of absence to undertake a three-month, fact-finding tour of police systems in the Midwest and Northeast. He and Tina began the trip on August 20, 1934, and called on state police headquarters and substations in Michigan, Kentucky, Indiana, Ohio, Maryland, Delaware, Pennsylvania, New Jersey, New York, and Massachusetts. He took copious notes which he compiled into a series of seven articles for the *Dallas Morning News*. Hickman also obtained copies of relevant laws, annual reports, and special investigations in the visited states and provided them to the Texas legislature.[116]

Months earlier, Griffenhagen and Associates, a public administration research firm in Chicago, had been commissioned by the Joint Legislative Committee on Organization and Economy to review the efficiency of the state government and offer recommendations. In the report submitted to the Forty-third Legislature, a broad overview of local law enforcement in Texas revealed essential flaws, including lack of organization and the fee system utilized by some sheriffs and constables. Griffenhagen analysts emphasized the need for a strong state constabulary and noted the Rangers acted without legislative support and were too undermanned and under-equipped to be truly effective.[117]

When James Burr V. Allred was inaugurated as governor on January 15, 1935, he set about fulfilling his campaign promise to reform the state's law enforcement efforts. One of the governor's first steps was to discharge, on January 23, twenty-nine regular Rangers and all two thousand-plus Special Rangers in service. Only three of the former—Quartermaster Roy W. Aldrich, Sergeant Sidney Nolan "Sid" Kelso, and Private Fred D. Holland—were retained. The same day, the new adjutant general, Carl Nesbitt, recalled Hickman to resume command of Company B. While the thirty-six recent appointees were an overall improvement over the Ferguson Rangers, Allred allowed patronage politics to enter into the equation. Eleven experienced men had served prior to the last Ferguson administration, but some others were unqualified and appointed for purely political reasons.[118]

Days after receiving his commission in Austin, the captain was in Leon County investigating a bank robbery. Inside of a week, Hickman, a posse of Texas and Oklahoma police officers, and several federal agents had captured two suspects, Cory Hudson and Arthur Whitten, thirty-five miles northwest of Smith Paul's Valley in Oklahoma. Both suspects confessed in the presence of newspapermen to holding up the Citizens State Bank of Buffalo. The bandits had escaped with seven thousand dollars in stolen money, but lawmen recovered only thirteen hundred dollars. Fugitive thief Raymond Hamilton was identified as being one of the heist gang, but neither Hudson nor Whitten implicated him. As part of a statewide sweep, the captain directed raids on two Fort Worth nightclubs on March 17. Hickman and Private Isaac Troy Rackley seized a case of liquor at the Ringside Club and placed one man under technical custody, while Rangers Stewart Stanley and Finis O. Goen visited the Sylvan Club but made no seizures or arrests. Two days later, Hickman, Captains Richard Crews "Red" Hawkins and Fred McDaniel, Sergeant Sid Kelso, and Rangers Stanley, Goen, Dick Odom, and Zeno A. Smith raided the Texas and the Siebold Hotels and confiscated several thousand dollars' worth of gambling equipment and fixtures. On April 9, Hickman and five Rangers raided three speakeasies and one sportsbook in Kilgore; they arrested six people. Two days later, the captain led two Rangers and two Gregg County deputies in raiding "every disreputable place on the [Gladewater] highway" between Lake Lamond and Longview. Forty men and women were arrested and charged with vagrancy. On October 2, Hickman attended a conference of law officers from sixteen Southwest Texas counties in Beeville. Called by Sheriff James Brennon Arnold, the meeting was a planning session for combating the area's criminal element, especially cattle rustlers.[119]

Even before the election, candidate Allred had appointed his personal friend Albert Sidney Johnson, a Dallas attorney and National Guard veteran of the 1930 Sherman riot, to draft a bill establishing a new state law enforcement agency. Johnson studied the state police departments of Illinois, Michigan, New York, and Pennsylvania, as well as the findings of the Griffenhagen report and Hickman's inspection tour. On January 24, 1935, Senator John W. E. H. Beck of DeKalb introduced Johnson's measure as Senate Bill No. 146, "An Act to create the Department of Public Safety of the State of Texas." The bill passed the Senate with only one dissenting vote. The Senate's Investigating Committee on Crime recommended in its February 2 report that "it would be for the best interest of all people of Texas to create a State Department of Safety, to be known as the Department of Public Safety." State Representative Alfred Petsch of Fredericksburg sponsored SB 146 in the House, but after it moved out of the House Committee on State Affairs, the measure bogged down in behind-the-scenes disputes. Petsch was able to defeat various floor amendments that would have effectively killed the proposal.[120]

The Senate committee compiled incomplete crime statistics that revealed in 226 counties, from June 1, 1933 to October 1, 1934, there were 3,016 indictments for violations of the Dean Law. Three hundred and eighty defendants received prison sentences, 609 obtained suspended sentences, 104 were found not guilty, 862 had their cases dismissed, and 1,061 were awaiting trial at the time of the study. There were 3,785 indictments for burglary for which 2,157 defendants were convicted, seventy-seven were acquitted, 614 were exonerated, and 966 had their prosecutions pending. In robbery cases, there were 829 indictments, 373 convictions, twenty acquittals, 121 dismissals, and 315 were pending. Out of 716 indictments for murder, 306 defendants were convicted, 58 were cleared, sixty-four had their cases dismissed, and 288 were awaiting trial.[121]

The revised Senate Bill No. 146, a compromise proposal written by a conference committee, was adopted by the Senate on May 3 in a twenty-nine to one vote. Four days later, the measure passed the House eighty-three to forty-four. According to the legislature's rules, since the bill did not pass by a two-thirds majority, the new law would not go into effect until ninety days after the session ended. The governor signed the legislation into law on May 8. The Texas Rangers were slated for transfer from the adjutant general's department to a new agency, the Department of Public Safety. The original plan called for them to be organized into a headquarters company of one captain, one sergeant, and four privates, and two mounted companies of one captain, one sergeant, and fifteen privates each. In actual practice, regardless of the law specifying three companies, the Rangers' organization and staffing survived the move. Two years later, the act was amended to provide for six captains and one headquarters sergeant. The authorized number of privates was subject to the discretion of the legislature, except in cases of emergency when the Commission could temporarily increase the size of the force. Long a mainstay of the service, the number of Special Rangers was capped at three hundred. The Rangers were tasked with keeping the peace during labor disputes, and investigating major crimes that crossed county and state lines.[122]

On May 14, General Nesbitt named Hickman as captain of Headquarters Company in Austin. Based on the appointment, he was mentioned as a possible director of the new Department of Public Safety. Comprised of Chairman Albert Johnson, George Wallace Cottingham, and Ernest Sherman Goens, the Public Safety Commission was to provide oversight to the divisions of the department, which would commence operations on August 10. The following day, the commission met for the first time and, among other business, designated Hickman as senior captain. He transferred to Headquarters Company on September 1, 1935. In time, the Rangers were organized into five administrative districts with each commanded by a captain, and the privates scattered throughout their particular territories. At the time of their respective appointments, Hickman and Johnson were close personal friends, but, as time went on, their relationship grew less cordial.[123]

While one of Governor Allred's top priorities was the clampdown of illegal gambling, Hickman and many of his Rangers believed the handling of misdemeanor gaming offenses to be the responsibility of local law enforcement. The executive's chief nemesis was Top O'Hill Terrace, an elite gambling house near Arlington owned and operated by Charles Frederick "Fred" Browning. In an October 31 meeting with Allred and Acting DPS Director Louis Graham Phares, the senior captain informed them Top O'Hill was a private residence and that he would need a search warrant. His preferred option, he later testified, was to put an informant inside the nightclub and gather evidence that would stand up in court. Allred was not impressed with his arguments. Obeying a direct order from the governor, Hickman reluctantly planned a raid on the establishment. The captain was familiar with the basement casino, having visited once with his good friend Tom Mix. He was also reportedly well-acquainted with Fred Browning.[124]

On November 2, under Hickman's supervision, Highway Patrolman Eugene M. Wells, his wife Aurora, and Doris Wheeler, the widow of an officer murdered by the Barrow gang on Easter Sunday 1934, drove to Top O'Hill in an unmarked state car. The license plates of their vehicle had been switched prior to leaving. Dressed in civilian clothing, the patrolman and the two women infiltrated the well-guarded gambling house with one hundred dollars personally contributed by the governor. The belief was that their activities would provide the evidence needed to convict Browning.[125]

The trio was unsuccessful in entering the casino that night, and they subsequently stated the bouncer seemed to have been unusually suspicious, giving specific notice to the license plates on the car. Hickman and Captain Fred McDaniel, commander of Company B, raided the nightclub later the same night, but they did not observe any evidence of gambling in plain sight. What they did find present, though, were some of Fort Worth's pillars of society, including friends of the governor. Apparently, the portable gaming equipment was hidden behind a door by the staircase. Witnesses later reported that the roulette, dice, and blackjack tables were rolled out after the Rangers departed. Allred would later accuse Hickman of tipping off Browning about the raid.[126]

On November 6, Captain James McCormick, a favorite of the governor, led another raid on Top O'Hill. He and Sid Kelso, who had recently been demoted to private, crawled a half-mile through dense woods and underbrush behind the building, cut an opening in the wire fence, and evaded lookouts. The two Rangers then slipped through a rear window and discovered forty men and women in the underground gambling room. The two Rangers arrested Fred Browning and four employees on charges of keeping and exhibiting premises for the purpose of gambling. Transported to the Tarrant County jail, they made bonds of $750 each in the early morning hours. An estimated ten thousand dollars' worth of gambling paraphernalia, including three roulette wheels and tables, four dice tables, two blackjack tables, one "chuckaluck" layout, fifteen decks of cards, five thousand poker chips, and a half-bushel of dice, were confiscated. A court order was sought for the destruction of the seized equipment. Although the state officers seized plenty of evidence, the grand jury returned a no-bill on November 19, and the five defendants went free. Browning's release was due in part to the fact that McCormick had not secured a search warrant.[127]

The three public safety commissioners interviewed Wells and his companions on November 7 about the events at Top O'Hill, then they questioned Hickman. Once the senior captain had finished and departed, the commissioners and Phares conferred on Hickman's past performance and the botched raid. The deliberations ended with the decision to demand Hickman's resignation effective December 1.[128]

The senior captain later testified he privately met with commission chairman Johnson in Dallas on November 9. The commissioner allegedly told his old friend, "Tom, you know if we don't run this the Governor's way we won't be reappointed next January. We've been having hell, captain, your commission doesn't censure you, no man questions your honesty, but if you don't resign it will blow the whole thing up."

Hickman stated, "I told him I had nothing to resign for and that I didn't care if the whole roof went off."

Johnson answered him, "You just don't fit in the picture."[129]

The captain was suspended on November 11 until further notice. Phares defended the announcement by remarking that every DPS employee had been placed on a six-month probation the previous August and the decision was in-line with departmental policy. Unfortunately, Hickman then sabotaged himself by speaking with a reporter. While taking the train back to Austin, he gave his side of the controversy, and the story printed the next day created a firestorm of epic proportions. The commissioners discussed the matter in a three-way telephone conference call and decided to fire Hickman immediately "for the good of the service." McCormick was appointed the new senior captain on the twelfth. The discharged Ranger pinned his hopes on his friends in the legislature, and left town for a hunting trip to the ranch of Longview oilman Walter Ruben Nicholson, fifteen miles east of Junction.[130]

On November 14, the House adopted, by a vote of sixty-seven to sixty-one, a resolution that authorized a special committee to investigate the Public Safety Commission and the role of politics in law enforcement. Convening in the Texas Hotel in Fort Worth on December 3, Representative Sam Chester Hanna of Dallas served as chairman, and he was joined by John Arthur Atchison, Jr. of Gainesville, and James Bert Ford of McGregor. Hickman was the first witness to take the stand. The former captain testified that Phares had opposed consolidation of the Highway Patrol and the Rangers from the beginning. He quoted the director's intention to "smother the Rangers as much as possible." He further asserted that the creation of the DPS had "failed to take law enforcement in Texas out of politics" and hinted that his dismissal had occurred for partisan reasons. Hickman delved into personnel matters by relating how he had wanted to sack Sid Kelso for destroying equipment taken in raids without authority, but Phares had only reduced him in rank. The captain addressed the issue of someone apprising Fred Browning of the November 1 raid as something "done intentionally or unintentionally by someone talking." Only four people were initially privy to the raid plan—Governor Allred, Director Phares, Hickman, and Edward Aubrey Clark, the governor's private secretary. The captain denied he had informed Browning, and Stephen W. Schuster asserted in his master's thesis that Kelso was the source of the leak. In speaking with his biographer, Clint Peoples concurred with this assessment, calling the former Ranger a "good con man." During his own testimony, Kelso made plain his dislike for Hickman, and referred to Frank Hamer and Maney Gault as "his enemies." When Atchison questioned the appropriateness of Rangers engaging in intraservice feuds, Kelso retorted, "Do you representatives always get along with each other?" The committee adjourned on the fourth and planned to reconvene in a few days.[131]

The next session of the inquiry was held in San Antonio's Gunter Hotel on December 13. Appearing before the committee in the Oriental Room,

Chairman Johnson, Director Phares, and Ed Clark were questioned about the circumstances of Hickman's dismissal. According to Johnson, Hickman refused to relocate from Fort Worth to Austin, and was often out of town without explanation. Furthermore, the captain failed to effectively organize the companies and submitted reports that were insufficient. Hickman also expressed discontent after the commission denied his request to participate in a Hollywood film about the Texas Rangers. Hanna and Atchison interviewed local officials and casino owners about Ranger activities in the Alamo City; an unwanted presence considered by Sheriff Albert Washington West, Jr. to be a political move. Governor Allred believed the hearings were designed to "besmirch and besmear" him politically. He called on the legislators to hold a session in Austin so officials who had been "slurred" could have a chance to respond to allegations. On December 14, he angrily burst into the capitol press room in Austin where the three committee members were conferring, and demanded to testify. After Atchison demurred, Allred insisted a court reporter be summoned and the legislators ask him any question they desired. Going on the record in a nearby hearing room, the furious governor presented a written statement listing thirteen reasons he supported the Public Safety Commission in discharging Hickman, including the senior captain procrastinated in performing his duties; he issued orders to the Ranger captains to only raid gambling establishments with his express permission; in establishing the companies' areas of responsibility, Hickman gave his company a "shoestring" district encompassing gambling centers from Fort Worth, Dallas, and Austin to Houston and Galveston to San Antonio; gambling had increased after the reorganization; and Hickman had tipped off Fred Browning. Following the governor's impassioned testimony, the committee took no further action, and Hickman's dismissal stood. The three legislators had shown little interest in determining the truth of the captain's situation and used the opportunity to instead attack Allred and the DPS. With their budget expended, the trio recessed permanently on April 1, 1936.[132]

Although the entire episode was embarrassing to all concerned, Hickman had been appointed a deputy sheriff of Cooke County on December 11, 1935. He served for six years under Sheriffs Luther Francis McCollum and Carl Wilson. On December 14, 1941, he was employed by the security department of Gulf Oil Company and received a warrant of Special Ranger. His responsibilities included protecting plants, pipelines, and pump stations in the Gulf region from sabotage. He recruited a force of former Rangers, and they patrolled an area covering Texas, Oklahoma, New Mexico, Arkansas, and Louisiana.[133]

When not engaged in security work, Hickman returned to his family's 1,500-acre ranch in the northern part of Cooke County, where he conducted breeding experiments with his small cattle herd. A talented horse trader, he purchased horses in South Texas and brought them north to Gainesville for auction. Settling into a "quiet, peaceful life," he and Tina were overjoyed by the births of Thomas Rufus, Jr., on August 24, 1937, and David Benton, on September 2, 1942. The Gainesville Community Circus, a three-ring attraction, took part in the Texas Centennial Exposition in Dallas in late June 1936, and Hickman was on hand to perform his trick roping act. Later in the year, he signed a contract to judge rodeos at state and district fairs in the northern and eastern portions of the country. Affiliated with the Texas Cowboy Reunion Association since 1931, he continued to attend the annual rodeo in Stamford. In addition to his rope act and working as a judge of riding events, he served on the board of directors as range boss and later first vice president. On July 2, 1951, Hickman was elected president of the organization for a one-year term.[134]

Continuing to be involved in show business, Hickman conceived the plan to ride the entire length of the old Chisholm Trail without the use of modern conveniences. To that end, he traveled on horseback from Caldwell, Kansas, to Nacona, Texas, a distance of some three hundred miles. In January 1955, amid sleet and freezing rain, Hickman rode 125 miles from Gaines Crossing of the Red River to Fort Worth. He timed his arrival so as to participate in the opening parade of the Sixtieth Southwestern Exposition and Fat Stock Show on January 27. After completing this leg, Hickman remarked, "I had a great trip. The women all waved at me, the dogs all barked at me, and the men—they all laughed at me." Between September 20 and 28, 1956, he rode from Fort Worth to Waco as part of a promotion for Heart O' Texas fair, which opened on the twenty-seventh.[135]

Additionally, Hickman was involved in various political matters. Gubernatorial candidate Beauford Halbert Jester recommended the former captain be appointed sergeant-at-arms of the state Democratic convention held in San Antonio on September 10, 1946. The meeting was peaceful until the state-level committee on party elections decided to reject any county committee members who were unacceptable to Jester. Instead, they substituted persons who had supported the candidate in the primaries. Amid cries of "dictatorship" and "home rule," thirty-five county delegations initiated a minority protest, and several speakers took to the floor to object. Hickman and a squad of policemen attempted to calm passions, while the aggrieved demonstrators started a parade that ultimately stormed the platform. The protestors demanded a roll call vote, and the convention chairman finally acquiesced, provided order was restored. However, those opposing the state committee's action lost 1,184 to 524 votes.[136]

On May 1, 1952, Hickman testified in the trial of Rebecca Doswell, who was accused of murdering her husband, Dallas oilman Thomas W. Doswell, on August 20 of the previous year. The victim had been shot in the left side of the chest and was dead on arrival at Parkland Hospital. During the trial, the state argued the murder weapon, a snub-nosed revolver, could not have been accidentally fired twice in quick succession, as Mrs. Doswell's lawyers claimed. Taking the stand, Hickman acted as an expert witness for the defense and relayed how he had always distrusted that particular type of pistol since they "go off so easy."[137]

Hickman was appointed to the Public Safety Commission on December 31, 1956, the first former Ranger to be chosen. Still believing his dismissal in 1935 to have been politically motivated, the gray-haired veteran lawman found his selection to be extremely pleasing. His satisfaction was likely deepened when he was nominated to become the commission's chairman on February 17, 1961. "Captain Tom Hickman is a living symbol of law enforcement in Texas," Commissioner Clarence Thurston McLaughlin of Snyder commented after nominating the former captain for the chairmanship. "His colorful career as a peace officer covers a span of more than fifty years during which Texas has seen some of its most turbulent periods. We consider him one of the outstanding Texas Rangers of all time."[138]

At a party held at his Cooke County ranch celebrating his seventy-fifth birthday, Hickman reminisced about his Ranger days. "We operated on a shoestring. The state didn't even furnish us a car." When asked if the Rangers were necessary in the 1960s, he replied, "As long as there are men who break the law, there is a need for officers like the Texas Rangers to uphold it."[139]

Suffering from carcinoma of the prostate for the previous three years, Tom Hickman died at his ranch on January 29, 1962. He was buried in Fairview Cemetery in Gainesville.[140]

Tina never remarried, and she continued to reside in Gainesville. She died at Gainesville Convalescent Center on December 26, 1979, of a cerebrovascular accident brought on by arteriosclerosis. She was buried next to her husband.[141]

Tom, Jr. attended Rice University, then moved west to attend the University of California's Los Angeles and Berkley campuses. He was employed as a woodworker for a custom door company in Santa Rosa. He married Karla M. McGee on October 10, 1963, in Contra Costa, and fathered one son. They divorced on March 8, 1983. Tom died of a heart attack in Sonoma on November 6, 1984.[142]

David served in the U.S. Navy, then attended Cooke County Junior College and the University of Texas at Arlington majoring in electrical engineering. He was involved in motorcycle racing for ten years and owned a motorcycle shop. He married Barbara Elaine Pruitt in Sherman on August 22, 1960, but they divorced on March 28, 1979. David studied under Mexican-born artist and sculptor Octavio Medellin from 1967 to 1979; he also assisted Medellin with several large-scale projects between 1975 and 1980. He remarried in October 1982. After working for Surgikos, Inc. (a division of Johnson & Johnson) for fifteen years, he became a professional sculptor in 1987, specializing in wind-driven, kinetic elements.[143]

Tom Hickman enforced the law with great panache. His colorful style and talent for showmanship was an outward pose for a serious and steely nerved peace officer. The willingness with which he tackled armed robbers and gangsters contributed toward a greater law-abiding and peaceful society in his time. His contributions to the creation of the Texas Department of Public Safety have given more efficient and effective policing methods to succeeding generations of Texans.

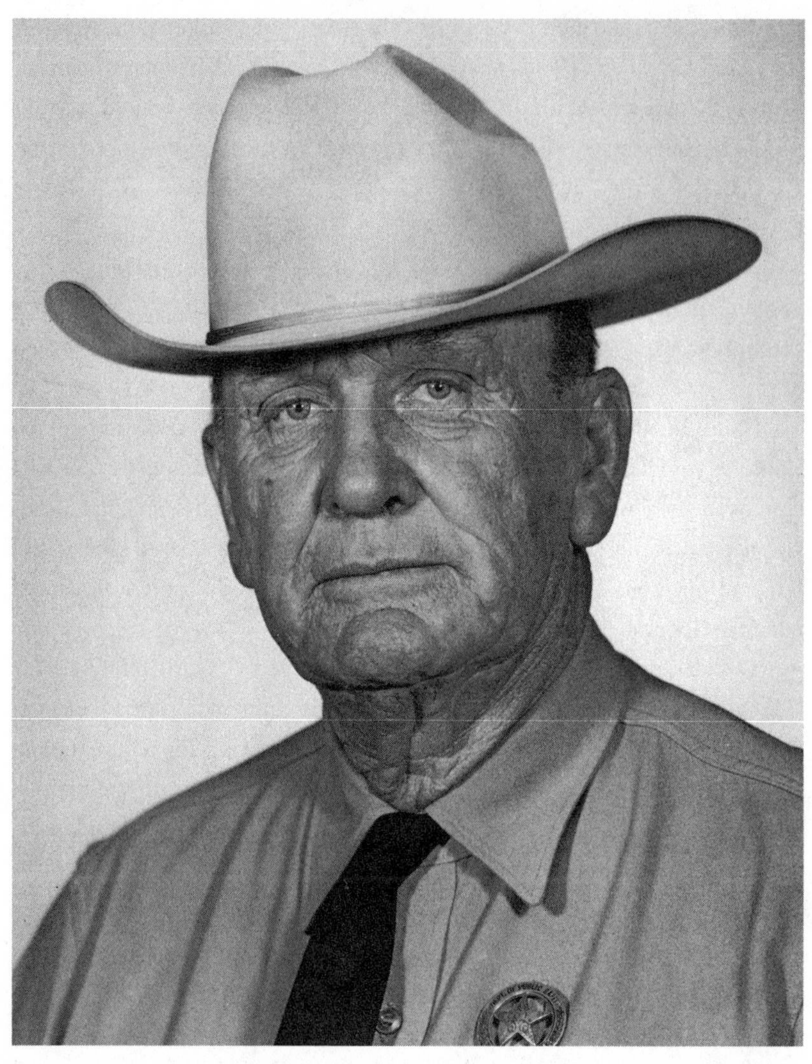

Charles E. Miller. *Courtesy Texas Ranger Hall of Fame and Museum, Waco, TX.*

Chapter 4

Charles E. Miller: "A Most Formidable Ranger"

Charles Edward "Charlie" Miller, Jr. was a most formidable Ranger. Entering the service in a time of exceedingly violent bandits and bootleggers, he was educated in a hard school that offered nothing for second place except death or injury. Yet he was more than a thug with a gun and badge. He served the state of Texas intermittently for fifty years. He was a successful rancher who enjoyed a wide circle of friends, both inside and outside of law enforcement. Former Crockett County Sheriff Jim Wilson commented, "According to those who knew him, Miller represented the best of the entire Texas Ranger force. Dan Westbrook, Lee Trimble, A. Y. Allee, and Bob Favor all remember him as a great Ranger who was a great officer and tougher than the toughest outlaws ever thought about being."

He was born in Miguel, Frio County, Texas, on June 9, 1898. His parents were Charles Edward Miller, Sr. and Hattie (Steinmetz) Miller. The elder Miller was born Charles Mueller on February 6, 1864, in Buffalo, New York. Hattie was born on January 22, 1880, in San Antonio. They married on March 20, 1897, at Travis Park Methodist Episcopal Church South in San Antonio. Hattie came from a family of some wealth, but the fortune was lost in the Crash of 1929.[1]

By 1900, Miller, then two years old, and Hattie were living in Atascosa County at his maternal grandfather's farm. His father had pled guilty to a charge of cattle and horse theft on October 13, 1898, and entered the state penitentiary at Huntsville on January 3, 1899. By 1900, he was incarcerated in Convict Camp No. 2 in Colorado County. The family was reunited when Charles was released on April 25, 1902, and they moved to San Antonio. Apparently having decided to go straight, the elder Miller worked as a carpenter and building contractor. The younger attended Main Avenue High School in San Antonio.[2]

Charles and Hattie divorced, and she was living at 920 South Cherry Street by May 1914. The elder Miller married Kathryn "Katie" Binz on December 12, 1914. She had been born in Bexar County on April 8, 1886. To the new union was born Henry Herman Miller, on September 22, 1915; Wilhelmina Anna Miller, on January 9, 1917; Dorothy Mary Miller, on July 14, 1918; and Lydia Katherine Miller, in 1921.[3]

Making his own way in the world, Miller married Marie J. (Stamp) Minica on March 17, 1917, in Bexar County. Born on March 6, 1891, in Waelder, she had two children from a previous union: Myrtle, born on August 15, 1910, and Thomas Louis, born on December 17, 1911. The Millers lived at 331 East Cincinnati and later at 410 West Evergreen. Miller's World War I draft card indicates he was employed by the Praeger Hardware Company as a chauffeur. A review of San Antonio newspapers from this period reveals the term "chauffeur" was synonymous with delivery driver. By 1918, he was employed by the San Antonio Public Service Company as a trainman. Charles's marriage to Marie proved brief, as they divorced in 1920 or 1921.[4]

He enlisted in Company F on December 10, 1919, at Del Rio and served under Captain William W. Davis. The company was comprised of one sergeant and eight privates.[5] With the final gasps of the Mexican Revolution and the commencement of Prohibition, the Rio Grande country was a demanding and dangerous place for a lawman. In his annual report, Adjutant General William Dade Cope commented:

> The companies stationed along the border have, in addition to protecting the lives and property of the citizens in that district, assisted the

> local peace officers, the United States military officers in command of Posts along the River, the U. S. Custom officials, U. S. Immigration officers, Federal Prohibition enforcing officers and United States Government Scouts when it was possible to permit them to leave their regular duty.[6]

On January 20, 1920, Miller received orders to report to the adjutant general at Wichita Falls. Additional Rangers directed to the beleaguered town included Sergeant Claude "Pudge" Franklin, Privates Larry Livingston Hall, William L. "Bill" Miller, Henry C. Keene, and Amzy Darius Putman, Company C; and Privates John Grosson, Henry Doyle Glasscock, Troy Randolph Owens, James Lovett Seale, Jesse Gray Osgood, James Lawrence Dial, and George Washington Robinson, Company F.[7] Miller and Seale, and Samuel "Sam" McKenzie, John Monroe Rooney, James M. "Jim" Ellis, Company E, were ordered to report to Captain Joseph "Joe" Brooks of Headquarters Company at Wichita Falls on March 23. Upon their arrival, the Rangers found themselves embroiled in the boundary dispute between Texas and Oklahoma.[8] On April 10, 1920, Captain Brooks was ordered to send the detached Rangers, including Miller, to Austin to report to the adjutant general.[9]

From there, Miller was assigned to Galveston. On December 5, he and Ranger Samuel Clay Blackwell visited a gambling house in the west part of town and arrested eleven men on gaming charges. Later in the evening, Captain Brooks, Miller, Blackwell, Police Sergeant William Zuber, and Rangers Claude Darlington, John Furman Crow, and Benjamin Thomas Tumlinson, Jr. entered a house on West Avenue One and arrested fourteen men for gambling. The defendants in both raids were later each fined ten dollars and court costs in the corporation court. The following afternoon, Miller, Blackwell, Darlington, and Crow raided a residence near Thirty-third and Winnie Streets that resulted in captured distillery equipment, sixty gallons of mash, and several bottles of liquor. The officers had been seeking the still operator who was out on bail for earlier prohibition violations, but the suspect was absent from the house. Miller was ordered to Del Rio where, on December 12, he and mounted Customs inspector Nathaniel

Beryl "Nat" Malone encountered an automobile near Uvalde driven by Antonio Munoz. As the car was moving away from the border toward San Antonio, Miller ordered Munoz to halt. Instead, the vehicle accelerated, and the passengers, Joe Slavin and Deodata Flores, began shooting. Miller and Malone returned fire, killing Munoz and seriously wounding the other two. Two hundred and thirty bottles of smuggled liquor were found in the car. Once the procedures were completed, Miller returned to Galveston. He, Sergeant Edward "Ed" McCarthy, Jr., and Rangers James Taylor Martin and Thomas J. Jackman received a tip on the twenty-first concerning a cache of liquor. Within fifteen minutes, they enacted a raid that uncovered nine quarts of brandy, three quarts of raisin wine, and seventy bottles of homemade beer. Two men were arrested and arraigned before U.S. Commissioner Charles Grainger Dibrell. Upon payment of a two-hundred-dollar bond, each suspect was released.[10]

Miller married Lora La Ray Clark in 1921. Born on October 28, 1895, in Caldwell County, she and her family were ranching near Spofford in Kinney County by January 1920. Miller's new bride was described as "hot-headed." She gave birth to Roger Hamer Miller on January 9, 1923. Miller had named his first son after Captains John H. Rogers and Frank A. Hamer, two men he admired tremendously. Unfortunately, his marriage to La Ray ended in 1923.[11]

Miller was transferred from Company F to Company C at Del Rio on February 15, 1921. While driving across town on June 20, he and Emanuel Avant "Dogie" Wright heard gunshots and saw a large crowd in front of the St. Charles Hotel. Stopping their Model T Ford in the middle of Main Street, the two lawmen pushed through the bystanders and found rancher William Tompkins Ochiltree Holman dead on the sidewalk, pistol in hand. Eighty-Third District Judge James Cornell was standing thirty feet away. Miller disarmed the jurist as the friends of Holman and Cornell in the crowd grew unruly. While Wright delayed the onlookers, Miller escorted the judge into the hotel and out the back, then took him to Sheriff Whistler. Cornell was arrested and charged with murder. Later the same night, Miller drove the prisoner to Brackettville and placed him in the jail for safekeeping. The examining trial was waived, and Cornell was freed on a five-thousand-dollar bond; he was indicted on June 25. The trial convened on November 14, with the defendant pleading self-defense. He was acquitted by the jury on the nineteenth.[12]

Miller was discharged on September 8 in a reorganization of Company C. His son's namesake, Frank Hamer, was placed in charge, and Miller reenlisted on October 1. In the first week of May 1922, Miller, Sutton County Sheriff Benjamin Willer Hutcherson, and Deputy Jesse Lott Cook discovered a large whiskey still in a canyon in Terrell County, fifteen miles from Sheffield. They determined that, if at full production, the still was capable of wholesale volume. Additionally, the law officers seized several jugs of whiskey, two barrels of mash, and 135 pounds of sugar. Three men were arrested and taken to Del Rio, where they were arraigned before U.S. Commissioner William Wiley Freeman. Their bonds were set at one thousand dollars each.[13]

On May 11, 1922, Miller was transferred to Headquarters Company in Austin, remaining under Hamer, as the famed Ranger had recently assumed command. Two days later, Miller advised the Adjutant General's Department that Rangers had recovered 131 sheep stolen from a Pecos County ranch. He also seized a fifty-five-gallon still and arrested three men on the Pecos River. On the nineteenth, he accompanied his captain, Prohibition Agent Elmer Birdie McClure, and three other federal officers in raiding the Dallas Street home of Joe Hermann in San Antonio. Brandishing high-powered rifles, the lawmen surprised Hermann while he was standing in his back yard. Executing a search warrant, the raiders discovered and seized between fifty and one hundred gallons of bonded liquor in the cellar and behind the wash house. Hermann and his adult son were arrested on charges of possessing and selling intoxicating liquor. The elder Hermann was already facing a charge of assault to murder. The two appeared before U.S. Commissioner Richard Lee Edwards and were released on bonds of five hundred dollars each.[14]

Miller and Edgar B. "Ed" McMordie travelled to San Antonio on May 22 and recovered a Paige automobile that was part of an extradition case; they took the vehicle to Austin. The following day, Governor Neff honored a request from his counterpart in Oklahoma to return two men to Oklahoma City. Held in San Antonio, the pair were wanted for moving the vehicle, which was mortgaged property, to Texas. They remained in the custody of local authorities awaiting the arrival of Fort Worth police officers. Three days later, Miller, Ranger William Mackinnon Molesworth, and police officers Edward Lafayette "Lafe" Young and James Newell Littlepage raided the Austin home of a barber. The lawmen arrested the suspect on charges of possessing, manufacturing, and selling intoxicating liquor, and seized three gallons of alcohol and assorted equipment. The defendant was released on a one-thousand-dollar bond set by U.S. Commissioner Paul Alvin Lockhart. On June 3, Miller and McClure arrested four men on the Bull Creek Road outside Austin after the quartet's unruly behavior aroused the officer's suspicions. Two bottles of an intoxicating "preparation" were found in the suspects' vehicle.[15]

As enforcement of the national Prohibition experiment became a central focus of American police agencies, Miller received an appointment as a federal Prohibition agent in San Antonio on August 24, 1922. Discharged from the Rangers on September 30, he took his federal oath of office the same day. Getting quickly to work, he and Agent George C. Ray raided a farm one mile north of Boerne and seized five gallons of whiskey, a five-gallon still, and forty gallons of mash. The property's owner was arraigned before Commissioner Edwards on October 5 on charges of manufacture, sale, and possession of liquor. Bond was fixed at five hundred dollars. The same day, Miller and fellow agent James D. Plumb dispersed a waiting line of fifteen men at a cold drink stand on San Pedro Avenue, confiscated a five-gallon keg of beer, and arrested the proprietor. The federal agents were assisted by George W. Robinson, and George J. Stendebach, special investigators for the mayor's office Along with Plumb, and Special Officers James Lyons and Joe Lozano, Miller signed a complaint charging farmer Mateo Castillo with violating federal liquor laws. Deputy U.S. Marshal ____ Bacon served a warrant and found Castillo to be in possession of more than a quart of whiskey. The defendant appeared in Edwards's courtroom and was released on a five-hundred-dollar bond. Just after midnight on November 3, Miller accompanied Lyons, Robinson, and Stendebach in raiding the Arthur Hotel. The law officers searched every room, breaking the locks or kicking in the doors of a few, and arrested a couple for violating the vice ordinances and a soldier for being drunk and disorderly. The manager was likewise taken into custody. The four were taken to the police station in the patrol wagon. Arraigned before the Corporation Court later in the day, the two men were each fined ten dollars and the woman's case was continued. The manager's case was dismissed. Miller and Agent J. H. McKay approached a vehicle parked on West Commerce Street between the International & Great Northern station and the San Antonio & Aransas Pass tracks on November 17. As they neared, the car's occupant dropped a gallon jug of moonshine whiskey onto the ground, then agreed to lead the agents to a cache containing four more gallons. Arraigned before Commissioner Edwards on charges of possession and transportation, the suspect was released on a bond of five hundred dollars.[16]

On January 10, 1923, Miller and Agent Ray raided the residence of Charles Westenberg, located some fifteen miles southeast of town. Searching the barn, they seized a fifteen-gallon still, two ten-gallon stills, and one five-gallon still. The officers also confiscated seven fifty-gallon barrels of mash, two stoves with gas burners, a high-pressure tank, and several empty containers. The *San Antonio Evening News* labeled Westenberg's operation "almost unequaled in the history of dry law enforcement in San Antonio." Miller and Ray charged the moonshiner with possessing and transporting illegal liquor and transporting and manufacturing same. Commissioner Edwards set the required bond at three hundred dollars for each charge. Westenberg's two accomplices posted bonds of three hundred dollars each. Later in the afternoon, Miller, Ray, and Agent ____ Thomason uncovered another large moonshining concern at 950 Essex Street and seized a twenty-five-gallon still and two hundred gallons of mash. One suspect was charged with possession of the equipment and taken before Edwards the next day. On March 15, Miller and Ray raided a distillery plant near Blue Wing Lake. They seized twenty-four barrels of premium rye mash, two double-lined copper stills and other equipment, and 120 gallons of high-grade rye whiskey aging in charred barrels. The distillery's operator was arrested and arraigned before Edwards; he waived examination and posted a bond of one thousand dollars.[17]

On May 5, Miller and Agent R. G. Pfeffer searched a dugout on a hillside near Losoya, eighteen miles outside San Antonio on the Corpus

Christi road. Accompanying them was a motorcycle officer who had earlier attempted to stop their vehicle for speeding. Once they identified themselves as federal agents, the policeman joined in the raid. No finished liquor was discovered, but the lawmen did uncover a fifty-gallon still and fifty gallons of mash. One suspect was arrested for the possession and the sale and manufacture of liquor. Appearing before Commissioner Edwards, the defendant waived preliminary examination and was placed under a five-hundred-dollar bond. In the middle of the month, Miller opined to the *San Antonio Light* that approximately two-thirds of the liquor smuggled across the border and transported to San Antonio came through the Del Rio district. He informed the correspondent, "Citizens of Del Rio are complaining that the cattle and sheep thieves are exceedingly active in the country covered by the Del Rio district." Charles Francis Stevens, supervisor of Customs inspectors in San Antonio, reported in the same article that "the bootlegger has practically driven the rum-runner out of business. Prohibition agents report very few seizures of smuggled liquors. Practically all of their seizures consist of moonshine liquor. Bootleggers, themselves, say that tequila is now difficult to obtain."[18]

While engaged in a liquor investigation, Miller shot and killed rooming house operator Zaragosa de Leon on May 16. According to his later statement, the Prohibition agent and Ranger Noland G. Williams had gone to the dead man's Gilbeau Street residence to ascertain whether liquor was being illegally manufactured on the premises. While Williams stayed on the porch, Miller pretended to be a prospective tenant and secured a room on the first floor. Walking back out into the front yard, he told the landlord the room was too hot and asked whether there were any available upstairs. Upon being denied the chance to see the second floor, Miller identified himself as a federal officer. De Leon ordered his daughter in Spanish to retrieve his rifle and pistol; Miller revealed he had understood the command. De Leon suddenly whipped out a knife and slashed the agent's coat. Miller pulled his Colt 1911 .45 pistol and fired four times, fatally striking his assailant in the chest and abdomen. De Leon fell onto the porch and died before the arrival of a police ambulance. Miller remained on the scene and surrendered to responding sheriff's deputies. The knife was recovered, and a later search of the house's upper floor revealed a disassembled still and 250 gallons of peach mash. Placed under arrest, Miller was charged with murder in Justice of the Peace Robert Neil Campbell's court, waived a preliminary hearing, and submitted an appearance bond of five hundred dollars. His pistol was immediately returned to him by Chief Deputy Sheriff Alphonse Newton, Jr. The Thirty-seventh District grand jury investigated the shooting, while federal prosecutors examined the question of Miller not possessing a search warrant when he entered de Leon's building. U.S. Attorney John Daniel Hartman and Assistant Attorney William Clinton Williams declared they were satisfied with Miller's self-defense plea. Moreover, the warrant matter was moot since de Leon's rooming house was a public place, not a private dwelling. The grand jury no-billed Miller on May 23.[19]

J. C. Dillworth, another Prohibition officer, was charged with the June 13 murder of Galveston city detective Fredius Wilson. Held on June 16, the preliminary hearing was postponed at the request of the state until the nineteenth. While Miller had witnessed the shooting, he was unable to attend the inquiry. When the hearing was convened, Dillworth was bound over for the grand jury and released on a ten-thousand-dollar bond. Miller was once more unavailable to the court that afternoon as he and George Ray slipped away to wait for an anticipated liquor shipment from Del Rio. Regrettably, the driver turned out to be a former Ranger whom Miller had known in Wichita Falls. The agents stopped a touring car belonging to James L. Dial, once of Company B, three miles west of Leon Springs. Searching the rear of the vehicle, they found 215 quarts of Jose Cuervo tequila and twenty-five bottles of cognac packed into straw baskets and placed in twelve burlap sacks. Dial was charged with possession and transportation of smuggled liquor and arraigned before Edwards. Waiving preliminary examination, the defendant was released on a one-thousand-dollar bond.[20]

Leaving federal service, Miller returned to the Rangers and enlisted in Headquarters Company on August 6, 1923, under Captain Hamer. Two days later, he was involved in an automobile pursuit in San Antonio which ended in the arrest of Joseph Carter. The prisoner was charged with possession and transportation of liquor and arraigned before Commissioner Edwards. He was held under a bond of five hundred dollars. On the fifteenth, Miller, and Rangers Molesworth and Joseph "Joe" Orberg, staged a raid on an alleged gambling and bootlegging den on Pecan Street. They discovered only two bottles of liquor but seized gambling paraphernalia and a ledger of names; the latter was turned over to the grand jury. Frank Cassiano, former city auditor, and Ben F. Ruby, a man well known to the authorities, were arrested for possession, and their bonds were fixed at five hundred dollars each. The state officers were only beginning their drive to free the Alamo City of gambling and bootlegging. They daily received information and tips by the score, all of which were acted upon. Armed with twelve search warrants, Miller, Molesworth, and Ranger William T. Miles raided two residences by August 22 and discovered liquor and distilling equipment in both locations. Two men were taken into custody and turned over to federal authorities, although one of the warrants was later found to have been improperly issued. A third search was staged on a farm near Martinez, but no alcohol was located. The property's owner, Albert Tessman, swore out a complaint in Bexar County Criminal Court the next day charging Miller with aggravated assault. Tessman alleged he had exchanged words with the Ranger, whereupon Miller pulled his pistol and struck the farmer over the head. When he became aware of the charge, Miller voluntarily surrendered and posted a two-hundred-dollar appearance bond on the twenty-fourth. He denied the accusation as stated in the complaint and informed the *San Antonio Express*: "I slapped him. I did not strike him with my gun, nor draw my gun." Two additional charges were filed against Miller on August 25, one for aggravated assault and the other for simple assault. The latter complainant was service car driver Joseph Carter, who had been present during a raid earlier in the month. Miller was arrested by a deputy sheriff and posted bonds totaling $250. After four postponements, the trial for the Tessman case finally convened on September 17, before Judge Nelson Lytle in Bexar County Criminal Court. Miller was found not guilty after fifty minutes of jury deliberation.[21]

Even while he was awaiting his court date, Miller transferred to Company E under Captain Berkhead Clarence Baldwin on September 1, 1923. The new outfit had been specifically formed to combat the rampant speakeasies, gambling, prostitution, and cockfighting occurring in San Antonio. The mayor, sheriff's department, police, prosecutors, and judges had permitted or encouraged lax enforcement of the law, and they protested the stationing of Rangers in the city. Several weeks before Miller's arrival, the grand jury had returned twenty-four indictments for violations of the gambling laws. However, Baldwin and his men encountered resistance from the local courts, and the subsequent trials ended without a single conviction, or in instructed verdicts of not guilty. Even the newspapers opposed the state's campaign. The federal courts were more cooperative. On September 8, Baldwin assembled his entire command at their headquarters in a two-story residence at 331 Garden Street before they embarked on three raids. The first occurred at a black resort north of town that resulted in six prisoners and the seizure of 250 bottles of beer and a gallon of whiskey. On September 15, for the first time in their two-month stay in town, the state officers worked with local authorities when they were joined by three sheriff's deputies in a trio of raids on homes in East End. The next day, Miller, Baldwin, Miles, Taylor, Darlington, and Ranger Robert Abraham "Abe" Boyd cooperated with Customs inspector Charles Stevens in raiding a house and barn near the power station on the South Loop. Two hundred gallons of rye whiskey, ten or twelve bottles of Scotch whiskey, five hundred gallons of mash, and a ninety-gallon copper still were seized. Complaints were subsequently filed with Commissioner Edwards. Baldwin and his men scored a substantial coup on September 29 when they raided a distilling plant on the banks of the Medina River, four miles from Castroville. They seized a one-hundred-gallon copper still, one hundred feet of copper coil, a two-thousand-gallon cypress vat containing one thousand gallons of mash, 5,500 pounds of sugar, and twenty gallons of finished product. Four men were arrested. The following month, the Rangers seized twenty-six stills, destroyed over one thousand gallons of liquor, and apprehended thirty-two suspects.[22]

The Rangers' contentious cleanup of San Antonio did not only include local bootleggers and gamblers. Group Head Harry Whitten Hamilton, the agent in charge of the Prohibition enforcement unit in San Antonio, was charged with conspiracy to violate the Volstead Act on October 9. In the complaint filed by Baldwin, he was accused of selling two confiscated stills and a fifteen-foot-length of copper coil back to bootleggers for twenty-four dollars. Along with three other men, Hamilton was arraigned before

Commissioner Edwards, waived preliminary examination, and posted a one-thousand-dollar bond. The following day, with Adjutant General Thomas Dickson Barton's full support, Baldwin brought charges for misapplication of public funds against Mayor John Wallace Tobin, County Clerk Jack R. Burke, District Clerk Osceola Archer, County Attorney Tom J. Newton, and County Collector John A. Bitter. Bond was fixed at five hundred dollars each. District Judge W. W. McCrory charged the Ninety-fourth District grand jury with investigating the Ranger's complaints and determining whether the collection of *ex officio* funds by county officers constituted intent to defraud. In a "stinging rebuke" of Barton, the grand jury no-billed the five defendants on October 12, and did the same for many of the people arrested in the recent raids.[23]

State and federal laws differed on the disposition of seized liquor. The Dean Law required state officers to transfer custody to county sheriffs, while the Volstead Act provided that only a sample was needed as evidence and the remainder could be poured out in front of witnesses. As liquor confiscated in Bexar County was invariably returned to its original owners, Baldwin chose to act under federal statutes. For this and other reasons, the captain's enemies grew to include District Attorney Duncan Alexander McAskill, who was not the pious public servant commonly believed. Indeed, Baldwin gathered evidence that McAskill was similarly returning seized gaming paraphernalia to gamblers, and the prosecutor decided to target the captain and several of his men. Baldwin was indicted twice by the grand jury on October 25 for illegally disposing confiscated liquor and for failure to properly document the seized material. Additionally, even though Miller had been earlier exonerated in the killing of Zaragosa De Leon and honorably discharged from Company E on the last day of October, he was indicted for murder on December 17. Perhaps to give him a measure of legal protection, Miller received a warrant of Special Ranger the same day. N. G. Williams, now a practicing attorney, was likewise charged in De Leon's death, although witnesses at the *habeas corpus* hearing stated he had taken no part in the altercation. The pair were released on five-hundred-dollar bonds. The trial was set for April 4, 1924, in Thirty-seventh District Court. Furthermore, Ranger Yantis Halbert "Buck" Taylor was indicted for killing a street merchant. He obtained a change of venue to DeWitt County.[24]

Berkhead Clarence Baldwin, ca. 1930. *Courtesy Texas Ranger Hall of Fame and Museum, Waco, TX.*

Even though he was under indictment, Miller reenlisted in Company E in San Antonio on December 23, 1923, under Captain Baldwin. He was granted a severance so Williams could be tried first and, upon his inevitable acquittal, be available to testify on Miller's behalf. By order of Judge Duval West, the former Prohibition agent's case was transferred to U.S. district court on January 23, 1924. Williams was tried in state court and given an instructed verdict of not guilty on April 4. Miller's case would receive a similar resolution.[25]

In the first two months of 1924, delegations of mothers appealed to Baldwin to close pool halls where the youth were squandering their time and money. The captain observed over forty such establishments operating in the city were in violation of the state law that had gone into effect on May 1, 1919, outlawing these types of ventures. The Continental Club in the Continental Hotel on Commerce Street, the Oriental Club across the street, the Pastime Club on Houston Street, and another three halls were closed on April 18, 1924, and complaints were filed against two individuals. On June 21, Rangers under Baldwin and Hamer swept through town searching for pool halls and speakeasies. Four individuals were charged with violating the Volstead Act, and the state officers seized several bottles of beer and a sizable supply of whiskey. Twenty Chinese men were arrested and booked at the city jail on gambling charges. The prisoners were arraigned before Justice of the Peace Benjamin Sappington Fisk. The Rangers' drive occurred at the same time city detectives and federal agents were targeting "dope heads, boozers, and vagabonds." Given the number of cases on the county courts' dockets, Commissioner of Fire and Police Phil Lee Wright ordered future complaints would be made out to the corporation court. Working with Customs inspectors, Baldwin announced on July 11 that his Rangers had broken a vast liquor smuggling ring operating from New Orleans to North Texas and beyond. Three suspects were arrested in Victoria that same day, and two more ringleaders were taken into custody in San Antonio two days later. The latter pair appeared before Commissioner Edwards and were remanded to federal custody. Over five hundred quarts of bonded liquor linked to the gang were seized in San Antonio. In addition, the fishing schooner *Olga* and three liquor-laden automobiles were confiscated at Port Lavaca.[26]

Even while enforcing the law, the Rangers of Company E were running afoul of local and federal authorities in San Antonio. The difficulty began when Miller executed a search warrant on a homeowner on August 23, 1923. Although the authorization had been issued by Judge McCrory, Justice Campbell ruled that, according to the state statutes, Rangers could not serve process without the presence of a sheriff, a constable, or their deputies. The justice quashed the warrant, suppressed the evidence, and ordered the seized liquor returned to the defendant. Campbell went on to dismiss several more cases on the basis that illegal search warrants had been used to obtain evidence. Given this development and the difficulty of securing indictments from the grand jury, General Barton ordered that the Rangers file their liquor cases in federal court rather than state court. During an arraignment before the U.S. commissioner, a defendant testified state officers had entered his home without a search warrant and turned the confiscated twenty-five gallons of liquor over to Prohibition agents. Further investigation revealed this was an ongoing trend. The U.S. Supreme Court had held that a federal officer receiving evidence from a state officer could not inquire as to how the evidence was obtained. The decision allowed the Rangers to take full advantage of a legal loophole to present their cases into federal court. Further, according to an opinion of the Ninth Circuit Court of Appeals, the Fourth Amendment was intended to only restrain the federal government.[27]

Captain Baldwin and state Prohibition Director Frank Cole fell into a brief dispute when, on April 22, 1924, the latter's agents refused to accept any more liquor cases that did not conform to state law regarding search warrants, despite having accepted some 240 complaints in the past. The war of words intensified when Cole claimed in a speech to the Anti-Saloon League that Company E Rangers were illegally entering homes and holding residents at gunpoint while searching for liquor. Baldwin categorically denied the allegation and challenged Cole to name a single specific example. The Ninety-fourth District grand jury was charged on May 9 with investigating the entire matter. Five days later, Federal Judge West ruled that Rangers were not subject to the search warrant provision of the Volstead Act.[28]

Baldwin reported to the adjutant general in early September that, in the past year, his Rangers had closed forty gambling dens and thirty pool halls;

arrested 442 individuals for liquor violations, thirty for other felonies, and 543 for misdemeanors; and captured 203 stills, 37,720 gallons of whiskey mash, 41,000 gallons of beer, 3,190 gallons of corn whiskey, six thousand pounds of sugar, and fourteen automobiles. The captain asserted these actions had been taken without the assistance of local officials, and he and his Rangers had been harassed in the courts by the county and district attorneys. On October 9, Baldwin and Rangers James W. Cawthon and John Alexander Gillon raided the University Club, where Mayor Tobin and several current and former city officials were playing bridge. The participants later acknowledged the three Rangers "acted like perfect gentlemen," but arresting the mayor and thirteen other prominent men likely did not make the state officers' presence in San Antonino any less problematic. Charged with misdemeanors, Tobin and the other defendants appeared in the court of Justice Fisk on the fourteenth, and their cases were dismissed due to lack of evidence. Baldwin and his men then halted gambling occurring at the Gonzales County fair and arrested forty-six men. The Thirty-seventh District grand jury subpoenaed every Ranger in Company E, except for the captain, to appear on October 30. The following day, four indictments were returned against Baldwin for unlawfully disposing of confiscated liquor, and another against Richard Ross Bledsoe for assault to murder. The captain requested a speedy trial, and Judge William Sneed Anderson ended the matter with instructed verdicts of not guilty.[29]

The obstruction and legal harassment Baldwin and his men had faced during their seventeen months in San Antonio was about to grow worse. After Rangers searched his San Antonio home, Captain John Edward Elgin filed through his attorney a petition for an injunction in Fifty-seventh District Court that argued the statutes establishing the Ranger Force as an organization on March 31, 1919, had violated the state constitution. In addition to flouting the will of the public, the claimant specifically argued the Rangers' presence in San Antonio directly defied the enacting clause in the legislation, as they were not "protecting the frontier against marauding or thieving parties" in the Alamo City. Ruling the 1919 law to be unconstitutional on January 15, 1925, Judge Robert Berkeley Minor issued an injunction suspending the Rangers' activities and wages. The Rangers of Company E remained idle at their headquarters at 430 Madison Street while awaiting orders from Austin. On January 27, Baldwin closed headquarters three days before the lease expired, and most of the company was summoned to Cuero to appear as witnesses in the murder trial of Ranger Yantis Taylor. The charge was another obvious ploy to discredit the company, and the judge directed a verdict of not guilty due to insufficient evidence. Company E's stint in San Antonio contributed to another alteration in the Ranger Force's employment. Henceforth, they were to be sent only to jurisdictions where their presence had been requested by local authorities. In accordance with the Ferguson administration's cost-cutting policy, Miller and the rest of the company were honorably discharged on February 21. Four days later, Chief Justice William Seat Fly of the Fourth Court of Civil Appeals ruled the law creating the Ranger Force was "constitutional, and infringes no provision of the Constitution expressed or implied."[30]

While awaiting the courts' decisions, Miller was employed by the Galveston, Harrisburg & San Antonio Railroad (a line of the Southern Pacific Company) in San Antonio as a sergeant in the Special Agents' Department. Railroads throughout the country had organized official detective bureaus over the previous thirty-plus years, and their duties were generally to protect company property against negligence, "malicious mischief," or depredations; passengers from gamblers, pickpockets, and robbers; and freight and baggage from theft, loss, or damage. The Southern Pacific had established its own force in 1901 to keep order at depots and railyards, and aboard trains. Miller and Special Agent J. L. Martin were searching the railyards on the night of January 23 for one T. E. Everson. The suspect was alleged to have shot and wounded Policeman Antonio Valdez the previous evening. At eleven o'clock, the agents spotted a man sneaking through the east yards and followed him to a spur track beyond Menger Creek. Identifying him as Everson, Miller and Martin approached the subject with leveled pistols and took him into custody.[31]

Miller experienced a close call on March 24. He and J. L. Seale, a fellow railroad detective, had crept to a position on Menger Creek, near the east railyards. There they observed two men stripping an automobile. The operatives approached the duo with the intention of making an arrest. Suddenly, one of the individuals produced a handgun and pointed it at Miller. Before anyone could react, Seale pulled his own sidearm and covered the pair of suspects. "Drop it, quick," he ordered. His command was promptly obeyed. The vehicle was later found to be stolen, and the two thieves were jailed on charges of felony theft. On November 13, Miller and Agent A. C. Street arrested a trio of young "bummers" from Fort Worth, as they scrambled off a freight train in the Southern Pacific railyards. The three "knights of the road" appeared before Judge John Franklin "Pete" Onion in corporation court. Since the day was Friday the thirteenth, one of the young men requested the case be continued. "Nothing doing," the judge replied. "This is my lucky day." He fined the youths ten dollars each. After the Southern Pacific westbound limited slowed for the Houston Street crossing on October 9, 1926, Miller arrested a seventeen-year-old boy who had been riding atop the dining car. The youth admitted he and a companion had committed a daytime burglary of the Clodine depot the previous day. However, the accomplice had jumped from the train a few blocks before Houston Street with the loot in a gripsack.[32] While engaged in protecting the rail line, Miller received a warrant of Special Ranger on March 7, 1927, which expired one year later. His state authority was renewed on May 9, 1928, for another twelve-month term.[33]

Miller married Eva Augusta Meyer on June 3, 1928, at her parents' home in La Grange. She had been born on October 29, 1900. Remembered as a devout, gracious woman, she worked at the Collins Garden School in San Antonio as a teacher. The couple made their home at 1203 Hammond Avenue. Returning to work, Miller found an intoxicated man asleep on the railroad tracks near the Seguin road on the morning of June 11. The special agent removed the drunk from the rails and arrested him minutes before a freight train passed through. Miller subsequently went to work for the Texas & New Orleans Railroad, another subsidiary of the Southern Pacific, as a sergeant, then the Texas Sheep & Goat Raisers Association as an inspector. He received a warrant of Special Ranger on June 3, 1929, at the request of the association's president Thomas Albert Kincaid of Ozona and attorney Clifton Copenhaver Belcher of Del Rio. Miller's authorization expired June 3, 1930. He received a new warrant on June 14, which was renewed on June 14, 1931.[34]

On January 31 of the latter year, Miller completed a three-day investigation by arresting Clarence and Marvin Ernst for the theft of forty head of goats from the Robert Nabers ranch near Harper. Nineteen head had been re-marked prior to the apprehension. The two brothers underwent a preliminary hearing in Fredericksburg and posted a bond of one thousand dollars each. The case was scheduled for trial in district court, which was to convene on February 9.[35]

Uvalde Police Chief John Frank Connor had been killed in the line of duty on December 20, 1930. Bert Homer Hunter and his three sons, Lester Floyd "Skeet," Bert Franklin, and James, were charged with premeditated murder, and the case was transferred to the Thirty-eighth District Court in Kerrville on a change of venue. Testimony began on April 14, 1931, in Judge Lee Wallace's courtroom, and Miller was among the seven Rangers called as prosecution witnesses. The case attracted a great deal of attention, and more than one hundred state and defense witnesses were present. Following more than three hours of deliberation on April 21, the jury voted for an acquittal.[36]

Miller was employed by the Texas Game and Fish Commission as a game warden. He was patrolling the Live Oak Ranch, thirty-five miles west of Kerrville, on January 10, 1933, when he encountered three men who were unable to produce a hunting license. Upon further questioning, Miller's suspicions were aroused, and he relieved one of the suspects of a pistol. Placing the trio under arrest, he searched their Essex sedan and discovered an arsenal of sawed-off shotguns, rifles, and handguns. He also found cigarettes, tobacco, and dry goods stolen from an Eola drug store the previous night. Miller transported his prisoners to the county jail, where they were discovered to be wanted in Bexar County. Although Concho County wanted the three for the Eola heist, the prisoners were held awaiting the arrival of two San Antonio police officers. His warrant as Special Ranger expired on January 20, 1933, but Miller continued to work for the Game Commission. On February 20, he, Officer Emil Habecker, and Constable Jeff Duncan were called to Point Rock to appear as witnesses in a criminal trial. The First National Bank of San Marcos was robbed of seven thousand dollars on the afternoon of May 22. Abducting two bank officials and a patron, the three thieves escaped in a large black sedan. The hostages were released a few miles outside town;

the robbers disappeared into the hills northwest of San Marcos. Barely two hours later, they were spotted on the Cyprus Creek road. Kerr County Sheriff Moore, Miller, Officer Habecker, and Constable Duncan drove the Fredericksburg and Cyprus Creek roads, but the robbers had already passed through. When not chasing desperados, Miller and the five other game wardens in Kerr County kept active, as fifty charges of game and fish law violations were filed between September 1, 1932, and August 31, 1933, costing defendants $734 in fines.[37]

Plagued by increasing livestock thefts, thirty Kerr County stock raisers established the Kerr County Ranchmen's Protective Association on July 6, and elected Robert Real as the body's president. The ranchers were able to secure the posting of a Texas Ranger to the area for the express purpose of halting stock thieves. Moreover, a reward of $250 was offered by the organization for the conviction of persons accused of theft by any association member. Having received a warrant of Special Ranger on June 16, 1933, and carrying an additional commission of deputy sheriff, Miller was employed by the association as an inspector. He made his residence in Mountain Home. For several weeks, Miller had been investigating livestock thefts when he stopped an automobile operating without headlights on the Harper Road, four miles north of town, on August 1. He discovered the carcass of a female deer and arrested two individuals for violating the game laws. He signed a complaint in Edgar Hugh Turner's justice court, and one of the men was assessed $114 in fines; the heavy penalty being enacted as this was his second offense. Eva arrived from San Antonio on October 13, and the couple made their home in Kerrville. The next day, Miller was on Arthur Real's sheep ranch, ten or twelve miles south of town, when he heard two gunshots. Going to the wild turkey preserve from whence the sounds had come, the special ranger encountered twenty-two-year-old Rayburn Pearson, a Camp Verde dairyman, who was carrying two dead turkeys. According to Miller's testimony, he ordered Pearson to halt, whereupon the suspected poacher opened fire with a rifle, but missed. Responding to the clear provocation, Miller shot him once through the heart from a distance of one hundred yards. Voluntarily surrendering to Kerr County authorities, the special ranger was charged in justice court with murder, and released on a fifteen-hundred-dollar bond.

When the Thirty-eighth District Court opened its next session, the grand jury returned a no-bill in the case.[38]

Miller was discharged as a Special Ranger on October 18, but his warrant was renewed on November 3, 1933. The authorization was to become void on November 2, 1934, but he received an extension to November 2, 1935. However, he was discharged on January 22, 1935.[39]

Eva gave Miller another son when Robert Albert was born on January 27, 1934, in Kerrville. They made their home at 1611 McKinley Avenue in San Antonio.[40]

With a growing family, Miller needed to find steady, well-paying work. He was hired by the Charles Schreiner Bank (Unincorporated) in Kerrville as a "bank inspector," or security officer. The repository was a private institution and the eighth oldest in the state. In addition to his new position, Miller had befriended rancher and former game commissioner Gustave Frederick "Fritz" Schreiner and banker Louis Albert Schreiner. While still employed in a private capacity, he retained his authority as a lawman. Indeed, Miller received a warrant of Special Ranger on June 21, 1935, at the request of the Schreiner brothers.[41]

In 1936, Miller accompanied Rangers Alfred Young Allee and Joe H. Bridge into Mexico in search of seventy-three sheep stolen from a rancher south of Del Rio. With the assistance of local law officers in Piedras Negras, the Americans were able to identify the livestock, arrange for the thieves' and the buyers' arrest, and return the animals north of the border.[42]

On January 24, 1937, Miller signed a complaint that was filed in Justice of the Peace Joseph Washington "Joe" Burkett, Jr.'s court accusing Bandera County rancher Claude Black with swindling the bank. On October 27, 1936, while obtaining a loan of $350, Black had allegedly given a chattel mortgage on livestock he did not own. The ranchman waived a hearing and, being unable to meet the one-thousand-dollar bond, was remanded to jail to await the Thirty-ninth District Court's grand jury, which convened on March 29. Black was indicted and entered a plea of guilty at his trial on April 5. He was sentenced to four years in the state penitentiary.[43]

A third son, Frost Woodhull Miller, was born on September 18, 1937, in Kerrville. By August 1938, Eva and the children were living in San Antonio where she taught school. Miller continued to reside in their six-room rock house at 1306 Main Street in Kerrville. This domestic arrangement continued for some ten years, but both husband and wife often made short visits to one another. Tragedy struck when Frost was diagnosed with Vincent's Stomatitis (Trench mouth) that resulted in acute suppression of the urine. The doctors at the Physicians' and Surgeons' Hospital in San Antonio performed a spinal puncture, but the medical science of the day was not enough. Young Frost died on June 22, 1939. He was buried in the La Grange cemetery. With time, heartbreak receded, and the Millers resumed their lives. Indeed, a fourth son, Charles Schreiner Miller, was born on August 31, 1942, at Kerrville General Hospital.[44]

On September 16, 1941, Miller attended a law enforcement conference at the Kerrville City Hall, presided over by Acting Special Agent-in-Charge Maurice Wilson Acers of the Federal Bureau of Investigation's San Antonio office. The meeting gathered together forty peace officers from throughout the Hill Country to foster cooperation in curbing potential sabotage and fifth column activities. Judge Kenneth Koch Woodley of the Thirty-eighth District Court spoke on "The Citizen's Duty in National Defense" and pledged the support of Texas law enforcement agencies to the FBI's mission.[45]

On June 21, 1942, Miller was involved in a record-breaking apprehension when a Chrysler sedan was reported stolen in front of the Comfort Community Theater at 9:53 p.m. Exactly seven minutes later, Miller and Police Chief Walter Moss arrested a Chicago man wanted for federal parole violation, and safely secured the purloined automobile. In early June of 1947, Miller and five other Kerr County peace officers attended another meeting with the FBI in Rocksprings.[46]

Miller has been largely remembered as a gunslinger, yet during his time in Kerr County, he shrewdly built a substantial investment portfolio. He acquired a town lot from Richard Wood in July 1937 for $4,693, which he sold to Otto D. Miller in July 1943. In July 1938, he advertised the house on Main Street as a rental. By 1940, the Millers had purchased a two-story home at 857 Estes Avenue in Alamo Heights. One of his sons remembered the Sunday family feasts at this house, and Miller's well-cooked Beefmaster steaks. In May of 1942, Miller purchased fifty-two acres of land along Johnson

Creek for $3,116, then sold the tract to Louis Schreiner for the same amount. The following December, he purchased eighty-two acres from Schreiner for $1,647. He sold five town lots in Kerrville to Frank M. Boushall in March 1946, and a total of eighty-seven acres to The Church in the Hills and the City of Kerrville in September. In partnership with Gus Young, he shipped 1,880 lambs to market in June 1947.[47]

On December 16, 1944, Whitfield Scott Schreiner and Aime Charles Schreiner, Jr., trustees of the A. C. Schreiner Trust Estate, deeded the Millers, for the sum of one dollar and "other good and valuable consideration," four tracts totaling 424 acres of land situated along Quinlan Street and Stadium Drive. In early 1948, he built a two-story house on Remschel Hill near the stadium that commanded a "broad sweep of scenic loveliness toward the west." Several months later, Eva and the children returned to Kerrville, and the reunited family moved into their new home. Miller established a horse ranch on his property and hired a manager and various Mexican families to work the spread. He raised Quarter Horses that were registered with the Quarter Horse Performance Association. Some of his stock went to Ruidoso Downs, New Mexico, to participate in horse racing. As a member of the Kerrville Group of the Kerr County Soil Conservation District, he constructed nineteen thousand feet of channel type terraces to retain more water on the field and halt erosion.[48]

Miller's real estate holdings expanded into Edwards County on August 9, 1937, where he purchased a one-half interest in the oil and gas royalties derived from a tract of 1,920 acres. On June 26, 1941, he purchased two town lots in Rocksprings. He sold the properties to the previous owners on February 26, 1942.[49]

Through Miller's employment with the Schreiners and his own commercial enterprises, he became well acquainted with lawyer and future governor John Bowden Connally, Jr. and U.S. Congressman Lyndon Baines Johnson, who was destined for the highest office in the land. However, not all his professional and personal relations were so cordial. Louis Schreiner's daughter, Mae Louise, had married Edward Bennett Carruth, Jr. on April 5, 1926. In addition to being a Schreiner son-in-law, Ed was also vice president and general manager of the bank. He and Miller reportedly hated each other.[50]

Whether Carruth was the reason for Miller's decision to leave the Schreiners' employ is unknown, but he was again appointed to the Texas Rangers on January 1, 1951. He reentered the service as a junior grade Ranger and was assigned to Company D in Carrizo Springs. Alfred Y. Allee was Miller's new captain. Eight months later, Miller assisted in moving Eva and the children to San Antonio.[51]

On March 12, 1951, Judge Samuel Gaither Reams of the Seventy-ninth District Court signed a temporary restraining order prohibiting the operation of El Ranchito Bar in Duval County. District Attorney Homer Ernest Dean, Jr. and County Attorney Reynaldo F. Luna filed a complaint asserting proprietors Raul and Juan Barrera and eight women were permitting gambling and prostitution on the premises. A hearing for the court order was scheduled for March 21, and Miller and Ranger Bennie C. Krueger were instructed to serve the papers. Dean sought a permanent injunction on April 23, and Captain Allee testified in court concerning a raid conducted on the night of January 20. Six women had been arrested and charged with prostitution, and Raul paid their fines. The lawmen also broke up a craps game and apprehended five men, as well as a poker game that ended in eleven arrests. Ranger Tully Elwyn Seay later described, on the stand, the January 24 raid he and Miller had made in which five women were arrested for vagrancy. The defendants pled guilty in justice court and were fined ten dollars each and costs. Exactly one month later, Seay had arrested another five women for prostitution, "some of them for the third offense." The first defendant in the case had been found not guilty by a six-member jury in Justice Sylvestre Gonzalez's court, and Allee requested the other four complaints be dismissed. Instead, he planned to permanently station two Rangers in the county. During a recess in the April 23 proceedings, Duval County Judge George Berham Parr argued with Reams over the mention of his ex-wife in the questioning of Raul. She was the owner of record for the property El Ranchito occupied, and the county judge was indignant over her inclusion. When Parr angrily cursed, Reams ordered him out of the courtroom. Reams then proceeded to issue a temporary injunction prohibiting gambling and prostitution on the grounds of El Ranchito. He further ordered the club padlocked for one year as a public nuisance on April 26. Barrera's attorney immediately announced they would appeal the decision to the Fourth Court of Civil Appeals. Even as this particular case was adjudicated, the bad blood between Parr and Reams worsened, and soon drew Miller and the Rangers into the dispute.[52]

Since 1908, the Democratic Party machine initiated by Archer "Archie" Parr had reigned supreme in Duval and Jim Wells Counties. Inheriting his father's empire in 1942, George Parr enforced his iron-handed rule through coercion, violence, corruption, fraud, and forgery. As historian Evan Anders observed:

> He regularly used the threat of violence to intimidate voters. The bloodshed that claimed the lives of several political dissenters after Archie Parr's death has its roots in the attitudes and the actions of the man who consolidated Democratic dominance. He set the precedents for disregarding the law and relying on armed force.[53]

George Parr, the second "Duke of Duval," had learned his lessons well and, indeed, surpassed his sire in the application of violence. Radio commentator and Parr critic William Lovejoy Heywood "Bill" Mason was murdered by Jim Wells County Deputy Sheriff Sam Smithwick, a Parr loyalist, on July 29, 1949. U.S. Border Patrol Inspector Edwin Hodges Wheeler, also antagonistic to the Duke's machine, was discovered in his burning vehicle on July 6, 1952, with a fatal gunshot wound to the head. They would not be the last to die by Parr's order.[54]

Additionally, Parr's successful usurping of the 1948 U.S. Senate race had won him the status of kingmaker. By the early 1950s, he politically controlled eighteen South Texas counties. The electorate of Duval County routinely gave his candidates 99 percent of its votes, while voters in the other counties overwhelmingly backed Parr.[55] Indeed, he owned every judge in Duval and Jim Wells Counties, except for Sam Reams. Governor Robert Allan Shivers had appointed Reams, a former district attorney and state representative, to fill an expired term in the Seventy-ninth District, which encompassed Brooks, Duval, Jim Wells, and Starr Counties. Parr engineered Reams's defeat in the November 1950 general elections, but the purported winner, Anthony Joseph Vale, Sr., declined the judgeship, publicly choosing instead

George Berham Parr. *Courtesy Corpus Christi Caller-Times.*

to retain the legislative seat to which he had been simultaneously reelected. Furthermore, the state canvassing board, acting on evidence of fraud, refused to certify the Duval County returns. Reams remained on the bench and, as the next election season drew near, impaneled a Jim Wells County grand jury on March 3, 1952, to investigate voting irregularities. Reams issued a statement critical of Parr on March 18, and the grand jury declared that the members would use their authority under the Texas Election Code to ensure free and fair elections. Publicly opposed to Parr's dominance, Reams impaneled a Duval County grand jury on April 7 for the same purpose.[56]

The Duke, by then the county sheriff, was also challenged by the newly organized Freedom Party in the 1952 primaries. In response, he used his authority to harass and intimidate his opponents. His badge-wearing thugs enforced his suppression of dissent with physical violence. Supplemented by a plea from Judge Reams, seven members of the Duval County grand jury signed a petition requesting state assistance. After grand jurors were threatened, the governor turned to Allee and Company D. The captain, who personally loathed George Parr, dispatched Miller and Ranger Joe Bridge to San Diego on May 7. The two Rangers parked their state vehicle in front of the Duval County courthouse and went inside to be sworn in as bailiffs. Convening on the morning of May 12, the grand jury, assisted by a pair of assistant attorneys general, studied the evidence of voter fraud accumulated by Reams, while Miller and Bridge sat outside the closed jury room. The lawmen had no need to overtly impose their will; instead, their formidable presence as they quietly rested in their chairs with their wide-brimmed hats, high-heeled boots, and holstered sidearms spoke volumes. In interviews with newsmen, Parr claimed the grand jury had been packed with men opposed to him personally and predicted the ploy would lead to the defeat of Reams and the Freedom Party at the polls. The grand jurors recessed on the evening of May 13 in preparation for their report to Reams on the sixteenth. During the two-day session, they had failed to subpoena a single witness, and seven of nine individuals voluntarily waiting to be heard were ignored. Delivering two reports to the court, the bitterly divided grand jury adjourned until July 28, two days after the completion of the primary election.[57]

Miller resigned on June 30, but withdrew the resignation the next day and transferred to Company C in Paducah. The company was commanded by Captain Raymond Waters. Even though he was a member of another outfit, Miller remained in Duval County in the weeks leading up to the July 26 primary. Renting an apartment in San Diego, he and Bridge were seemingly everywhere throughout the county's small towns, and kept Parr and his minions on their best behavior. The *New York Times* later emphasized the Texas Ranger legend in its reportage by noting the state officers "never numbered more than two or three men at a time, one Texas Ranger traditionally being the equivalent of a brigade of ordinary peace officers." The election was peaceful, but Parr's candidates proved victorious. In particular, Judge Reams lost his contest to Charles Woodrow Laughlin. As the voting ended, District Judge Arthur Anthony Klein of Harlingen issued a court order instructing Duval County election judges to remove the ballot boxes to Alice. Miller and Bridge left to pursue other cases, but the Rangers would return.[58]

Miller was transferred to Headquarters Company under Captain Clint Peoples and was stationed in Luling on September 1, 1953.[59] The charred remains of a man were discovered in a burned barn on the Jack Capp ranch near Wimberly on April 4, 1954. Miller, Hays County Sheriff Jack Gary, and San Antonio homicide detectives worked the case. Amid the ruins of the structure, investigators retrieved a scrap of brown cloth that was identified as being part of a tailored suit for vacuum cleaner salesman Raymond L. Rotter. The victim had been missing since the third, and his station wagon was found abandoned in a downtown San Antonio parking lot. Bloodstains on the vehicle and a spent .32-caliber shell casing located under the seat suggested Rotter had been shot before being burned in the barn. Muddy caliche stuck to the undercarriage was similar to that at the crime scene, as were the tire tracks. Rotter had been last seen in the company of his employee Marion R. Palomera of San Marcos. Additionally, Palomera had recently cashed a check written by Rotter for $1,950. Based on the evidence, a pickup order for the man, already on parole for murder from the prison at Terre Haute, Indiana, was broadcast statewide on April 8. Fleeing Texas, he traveled to Mexico City and Nogales, Mexico, to Tucson, Arizona, to California and Dallas, and to Tucson once more before arriving in Chicago. He was arrested in the latter place on June 3 while operating an automobile for which he could not produce registration papers. Alerted by the local authorities, Miller, along with Sheriff Gary, traveled to the Windy City to extradite the fugitive. The Ranger later testified Palomera gave a verbal confession while the trio drove back to Texas. Jailed in Hays County on June 19, the suspect signed a seven-page written statement confessing to the killing. The same day, Palomera was charged with murder with malice and taken to San Antonio for fingerprinting.[60]

Described as a "ladies' man," Miller initiated an extramarital affair with Irene Marie Hall at some point in time. Whether the years he and Eva spent living separately had any bearing on the situation is unknown. Regardless, they divorced on July 21, 1955, in Bastrop County. In the midst of the legal proceedings, Eva was able to freeze Miller's assets and acquire 124 acres of their tract, along with house and improvements, in Kerr County. She also received the Alamo Heights house in the settlement. However, a resurvey revealed the Kerrville property consisted of 406 acres rather than the 377 originally believed. Eva filed a civil suit in the Second Thirty-eighth District Court on June 28, 1958, to determine the property's true boundary line. Her attorneys argued she was entitled to an additional fourteen acres. The case was scheduled for a civil jury trial on January 25, 1960, then the attorneys agreed on delays to October 12, 1961. The case was then continued indefinitely, and Judge Marvin Blackburn later granted an extension until January 26, 1963. When the case finally came to trial, Miller argued the Kerr court did not have jurisdiction, as the property settlement had been decided in Bastrop County. Judge Blackburn sustained the motion and dismissed the case in April 1963. Two months later, Eva appealed the decision to the Fourth Court of Civil Appeals in San Antonio, which ruled in a suit involving title to land, as the divorce decree was a final judgment, the Bastrop County court had no standing. Miller filed an application for a writ of error to the Texas Supreme Court on April 16, 1964. Without written opinion, the state's high court declined to hear his appeal, and the case was remanded to the Thirty-eighth District. *Miller v. Miller* was heard once more in Blackburn's courtroom on January 18, 1965, and finally went to the jury on the twenty-fifth. However, two days into their deliberations, the members were dismissed as Miller and Eva had reached a settlement agreement.[61]

Even while engaged in the lengthy court battle, Miller married Irene in 1956 or 1957. She had been born on May 2, 1914, in Gonzales. Having grown up on the family farm, this was her first wedding.[62]

Miller had been promoted to senior grade Ranger on September 1, 1955. As part of the Department of Public Safety's restructuring, Headquarters Company was reorganized as Company F, and Miller established a duty station in Mason on September 1, 1957. Captain Peoples remained in command. Ranger Louis Hardy Purvis was being shifted from Kerrville to Alpine, and Kerr County was added to Miller's district.[63]

Rollie White Ledbetter, a stock raiser in McCulloch County, was charged on May 15, 1958, with murdering his wife by putting strychnine in her whiskey. Gladys Ray Ledbetter, the victim, had been poisoned on April 15, and died five days later in the hospital. Miller and Sheriff Luke Vogel took the suspect to Waco on May 14 for a lie detector test. Returning to Brady the next day, the rancher signed his confession. Arraigned before Justice of the Peace Joseph Clinton Myrick, Ledbetter waived an examining trial and was held in the county jail without bail. The grand jury for the Thirty-fifth District met on the nineteenth and indicted Ledbetter. He was freed on a twenty-thousand-dollar bond. The case was transferred to Mason County on a change of venue. After a postponement and a second transfer to Travis County, Ledbetter was found by the jury to be insane. He was committed to a state mental institution.[64]

On July 30, 1961, a scuffle on the banks of the San Saba River between two fishing parties from Brownwood and San Saba ended in a killing. The following day, Edmon Nolan Robertson, twenty-four, was charged with murder in Ward Ellis, Jr.'s justice court, and bail was set at five thousand dollars. Miller, Sheriff Brantley Barker, and Highway Patrolman Jess Askey investigated the incident. The lawmen discovered the shooting had resulted from a two-hour argument between the fishermen. The victim was eighteen-year-old Lewis Warren Woods, who had been fatally struck in the left side by a .22-caliber bullet. Woods was pronounced dead on arrival at the San Saba hospital, while another youth, Davis Harris, was treated for a concussion. Fleeing the scene, the Brownwood group was stopped at a roadblock near town and taken into custody. Robertson provided a signed statement to District Attorney Carlos Ashley.[65]

In addition to homicides, Rangers were often called upon to assist local departments when needed. Miller and Police Chief George Calder took two suspects into custody near Brownwood. The pair, a husband and wife team, were wanted on felony warrants from Phenix City, Alabama, for second-degree burglary. The man was also wanted for a parole violation, having been released from the Alabama state prison just three months prior.[66]

The George Walker grocery and service station at Algerita, eight miles west of San Saba, was burglarized on the night of November 28, 1962. Miller and the San Saba County Sheriff's office investigated the crime. Entry into the store was gained by removing a screen on a rear window. The number of thieves was unknown, but ten cartons of cigarettes and a cash register containing $350 was taken.[67]

At 2:00 a.m. on June 23, 1965, Joe Casual Bierschwale, twenty-one years old, arrived at the home of Gillespie County Deputy Sheriff Lawrence Burrer and confessed to the murder of his missing wife. Sheriff Hugo Klaerner was notified, and local and state officers traveled to the Bierschwales' former home on U.S. Highway 87, three-quarters of a mile south of Fredericksburg. The decomposing body of nineteen-year-old Shirley Ruth Bierschwale was discovered in a shallow grave inside a nearby tool shed. Miller assisted the sheriff in the case, as did County Attorney Richard Hoerster, Ranger Edgar Dalton "Ed" Gooding, Highway Patrolman Walter Werner, DPS fingerprint technician Billy Rafield Wier, and DPS crime scene photographer Milburn Lloyd DeGlandon. Investigators determined the victim had been murdered and buried on May 8, and an autopsy ruled the cause of death to have been blunt force trauma to the back of the head. Joe Bierschwale was charged in Justice of the Peace George Bryant Worley's court with murder with malice. The suspect was convicted on April 25, 1966, and sentenced to twenty years in prison.[68]

Nineteen-year-old Ronald Lee Barlow entered a guilty plea on September 10, 1965, to slaying Constable Oda Hyatt in San Saba. The constable had been shot with his own pistol after stopping a pickup truck south of town on June 7. Barlow was arrested the next day and ultimately sentenced in Judge Jack B. Miller's district courtroom to life imprisonment at Huntsville. Two years later, he petitioned the federal courts for a writ of *habeas corpus*. Appearing before Judge Jack Roberts on June 2, he swore under oath that he had lied in his earlier signed confession, and declared he had been coerced by law officers. "I had no choice but to plead guilty," Barlow testified.

"I was threatened with the death penalty." He further claimed that, while being interrogated by Rangers and other law officers in Dallas, he had been knocked out of his chair with a book. While lying handcuffed on the floor, the lawmen had allegedly kicked Barlow until he gave a statement. Miller was summoned to appear as a witness, as was Judge Miller, Sheriff Barker, District Attorney Carlos Ashley, and Vivian Reavis, a former clerk in the county tax office. Ranger Miller and Reavis each testified Barlow had been given the required statutory warnings and made his statement in his own words. Ashley confirmed he had made a deal with Barlow's attorney to take the death penalty off the table in exchange for a guilty plea. Judge Miller testified he had been convinced Barlow had truthfully confessed to the crime. Judge Roberts denied the writ and dismissed the petition. Barlow was remanded to the state penitentiary to serve out the remainder of his sentence.[69]

As he grew older, Miller became, among other Rangers, a legend in his own time. Captain Allee suspected the salty Ranger had likely killed seven or eight men in the course of his career, but Miller had been justified in each incident. Captain Robert Kenneth "Bob" Mitchell said, "He was a tough old man, involved in lots of violence himself. But he was one of the few that could change with the times and he typed his own reports, he handled all his correspondence and he was one of the old-time Rangers who came into the next century and excelled."[70]

Miller liked to tease new Rangers. When he first met a novice private, he would say, "Now let me tell you something Ranger. If you ever get anybody that needs killing, if you don't want to do it, just call me and I'll do it for you." Given Miller's reputation, not all the rookies were sure whether he was joking.[71]

He transferred to Company E in Comanche in December 1967, and Captain James E. Riddles became his commanding officer. Miller became a good friend to the Riddles family. The captain respected the older Ranger, and worked with Miller every chance he could. Jim Riddles's son said in an interview, "A lot of the companies didn't mess with Charlie. Charlie's history was rough, he had been in gunfights … he was the Ranger who had a gunfight down there, and when they got there, he was pouring a cup of coffee out of an urn that had a bullet hole in it."[72]

This popular tale has a slight variation. In the alternate story, Miller and another Ranger were assigned to a rowdy town. While there, they entered the local café for a cup of coffee, but all the seats in the establishment were taken. Miller asked the proprietor to give them coffee, and they would drink it standing. "We don't serve people standing," the café owner asserted. The Rangers waited patiently for two seats to open, but the customers pointedly settled back and ordered additional coffee. Responding to the "freeze out," Miller whipped out two pistols and shot the coffee urn twice. He then calmly held two cups under the jetting streams, handed one to his partner, and the two lawmen drank their coffee in a suddenly emptied café. Miller supposedly drew a stiff suspension, but little verification could be found to support the legend.[73]

Rather than thrilling gunplay, however, the work of the Rangers is mostly routine. Miller was called upon to assist in the investigation of a break-in at Sloan Super Save in San Saba on April 7, 1968. Working with Sheriff Barker once more, Miller learned the burglars had gained access to the grocery store by breaking the lock on the back door. Sixty dollars was taken from the cash register, as was an estimated one thousand dollars' worth of inventory.[74]

The Rangers and, indeed, all of Texas lost a giant on May 7, 1968, when Colonel Homer Garrison, Jr. succumbed to bronchial cancer at M. D. Anderson Hospital and Tumor Institute in Houston. Holding the top spot in the DPS for thirty years, the director's creed was to "pick good men, train them properly, work as a team, and shoot square with everybody."[75]

Miller retired from the Texas Rangers on June 30, 1968. That same day, a party was held in his honor at the YO Ranch, with former Rangers Leo Henderson Bishop, Manuel T. Gonzaullas, Walter Everette "Ebb" Riggs, Walter Arthur Russell, and Robert A. Crowder, and retired game warden Captain Robert J. "Bob" Snow, in attendance. Continuing to call Mason home, Miller went to work for the James River Ranch as a game warden and manager. He was a member of Las Moras Masonic Lodge No. 444 in Brackettville, the Scottish Rite in San Antonio, and the First Presbyterian Church in Mason. He continued to raise horses and gifted the racing steed, Concord, to jockey Henry Uriegas.[76]

As Ranger Robert Charles "Bob" Favor discovered, retirement had not sapped Miller's toughness or, indeed, his pain threshold. When the latter was kicked by a horse in the summer of 1970, his leg was broken as were three lower teeth at the gumline. He crawled into his house and called Doctor Steve King, a large animal veterinarian in Brady, and Ranger Favor. Miller requested the doctor bring a portable X-ray machine to Mason. Arriving at the same time, King and Favor found the former lawman in bed, having already set his own leg. The X-ray device proved the self-treatment was sufficient. Miller then took up a pair of pliers and, with Favor holding a small mirror, proceeded to extract each of his smashed teeth without the benefit of painkillers.[77]

Described as "the last of the crusty old-time lawmen," Miller died at 4:00 p.m. on December 8, 1971, from an acute cerebrovascular accident at St. John's Hospital in San Angelo. Other causes contributing to his death included arteriosclerotic heart disease and diabetes mellitus. His funeral service was held in the Mason Funeral Home Chapel on the morning of December 11, which was followed by his burial in the State Cemetery in Austin the following afternoon. The pallbearers were Colonel Wilson Edward "Pat" Speir, Colonel Leo Earl Gossett, Jr., Captain James L. Rogers, Jim Riddles, Elmer Birk De Glandon, Captain Edwin George "Butch" Albers, Jr., Captain William Delpard "Bill" Wilson, and Tom Henderson. Speir praised Miller for "a highly distinguished career of service … [whose] example and dedication stands as an inspiration to all law enforcement officers." He was buried at Garrison's right hand.[78]

After divorcing Miller, Marie married James Astuto, an Italian-born U.S. Army warrant officer. Among other duty stations, they were in the Panama Canal Zone and at Fort Sam Houston. At some point in time, she operated a lake-side vacation camp that Hattie liked to visit. James died on December 4, 1963, and Marie died on February 26, 1969, in Tarrant County. She was buried next to James at Fort Sam Houston National Cemetery.[79]

Myrtle, Miller's stepdaughter for only a few years, married Jim Davis Green. She died in Fort Worth on September 10, 1960, and was buried in East Greenwood Cemetery in Weatherford.[80]

Thomas, his stepson, worked at Kelly Air Force Base in aircraft maintenance. He died of a coronary occlusion on January 24, 1978. He was interred in Mission Burial Park.[81]

After the divorce, Le Ray married train engineer Glenn A. Collins. They moved to Indianapolis, Indiana, where she gave birth to another son in 1930. Collins proved to be an abusive man, so she divorced him, moved back to San Antonio in 1935, and opened a boarding house. She married Robert Charles Reischling, a civil service employee at Kelly Air Force Base, on December 17, 1938. She died on November 28, 1996, and was buried in Mission Burial Park North.[82]

Roger was a topographical draftsman in the 36th Division of the Texas National Guard at age eighteen. He was close to his discharge date when Japanese naval forces attacked Pearl Harbor. Joining the war effort, he was a mechanized cavalry platoon sergeant in the Salerno and Cannes invasions. Returning to the States, he built his own house and attended junior college in San Antonio. He married Doris Lanell Steinert on August 14, 1948, which resulted in one son. Roger attended the University of Texas at Austin, and graduated with an architectural engineering degree. He worked as a structural engineer, and retired as president of an engineering consulting firm in 1987. Doris died on May 22, 1998, of lung cancer, and Roger followed her on August 31, 2016.[83]

Eva retired after thirty years as a teacher. She continued to live in Alamo Heights until she moved to Austin to be closer to Robert. She spent the last few years of her life in a nursing home. Eva died on March 19, 1994, in Austin, and was buried in the La Grange Cemetery.[84]

Robert was known in the family as a “renegade” who enjoyed angering his father. He attended the University of Texas at Austin, and served in the Air Force ROTC. He graduated with an art degree and established an advertising company in Austin. He married Ina Marie (Maris) Lincecum on October 10, 1959, in Seguin. She had two daughters from a previous marriage. Ina died on February 6, 2015.[85]

“Little Charles” was described as the “golden child” in that he loved to please his father. He attended Texas Military Institute and finished second in his class. He then attended the U.S. Military Academy and graduated on

June 3, 1964. His nomination and acceptance into West Point were personally aided by President Johnson. Although commissioned into the Infantry branch, as well as being Airborne- and Ranger-qualified, Charles transferred to the Finance Corps and served as a paymaster in Vietnam. He married Dale Kenny Gentry at the Rice University chapel on March 5, 1966. They had two sons and one daughter. Charles worked for a home construction company in Houston before going into business for himself building apartment complexes in Austin. After the housing market crash in the early 1980s, he went to work for University Savings Association in Houston as a commercial loan executive. Charles died on August 29, 1988, of leukemia.[86]

Irene moved from Mason to Odessa in 1980 to be closer to her three sisters. She died at Medical Center Hospital in Odessa on August 10, 1992. One week later, she was buried next to Miller in the State Cemetery.[87]

Charlie Miller was a man whose exploits provoked tall tales, although they sometimes contain a kernel of truth. However, his record of a half-century of duty to Texas is entirely real and reflects the pride he felt being associated with the Rangers. The shootings in which he was involved early in his service created a legend not always welcomed in the more bureaucratic organization of his later career. To those who knew him, though, he was a tough peace officer yet a generous and loyal friend.

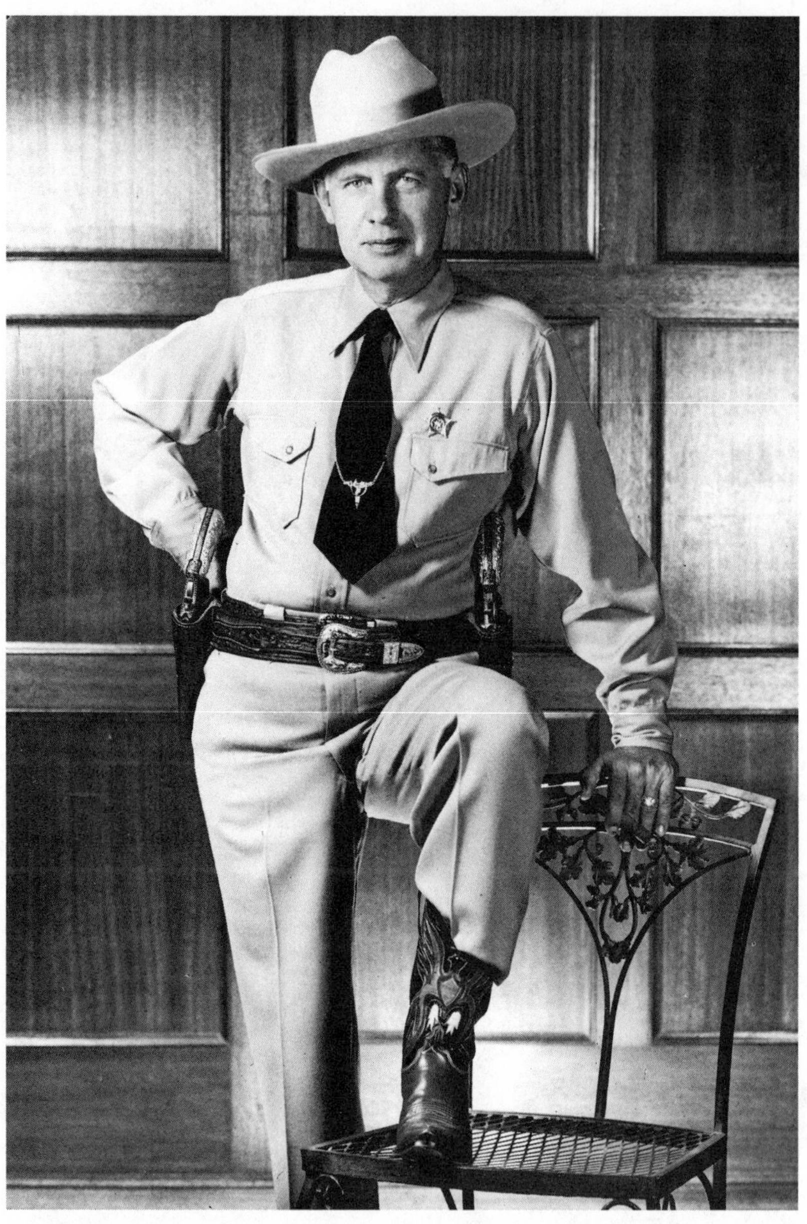

Captain M. T. Gonzaullas, October 16, 1951. #1983/112-R-374-1a.
Courtesy Texas State Library and Archives Commission, Austin, TX.

Chapter 5

Manuel T. Gonzaullas: "Meaningful Accomplishments"

Manuel Terrazas Gonzaullas had a past shrouded in mystery. His personnel record disclosed no personal history prior to his joining the Ranger service. As a result, his biographers have had to rely on the contradictory information he himself provided about his early life. Ranger Lewis Calvin Rigler observed: "No one ever got really close to 'Lone Wolf' unless it was his wife Laura. No one knew exactly where he was born or anything much about his life before he enlisted in the Ranger service about [1920]." Despite this reticence, he enjoyed his name being in the headlines, and was exceedingly proud of his service to Texas. His meaningful accomplishments included an untold number of felony arrests of gamblers, bootleggers, thieves, and killers. Perhaps, most important was his presence on the forefront of the changes affecting the Rangers, as the service embraced modern crime-fighting technologies.

He claimed to have been born in Spain on July 4, 1891. His parents were Ramon Diaz Gonzaullas, a native of either Spain or Portugal, and Helen Josephine (von Druff) Gonzaullas, a Canadian of German descent. They were either naturalized American citizens visiting Europe when their son came into the world, or they emigrated to the U.S. in 1893 and obtained citizenship. Regularly accompanied by his family, Ramon was a mining engineer who traveled extensively through Mexico, Cuba, and Central and South America. As a result, Manuel was unsure of his exact place of birth, and accounts of him being born in Cádiz or Port du Trinidad (which does not exist) were based solely on statements to reporters. According to the tale told to Robert W. Stephens, Gonzaullas's parents were killed by the hurricane that struck Galveston on September 8, 1900, and their bodies were never recovered. Court records were similarly swept out to sea, so their names absent from the incomplete list of recorded deaths presents yet another ambiguity. In another version related by Brownson Malsch, Manuel was brought up in El Paso, where two brothers were killed in a 1906 bandit attack that also wounded his parents. This account was earlier told to a women's club meeting in Longview in February 1935. He also informed his audience that he thereafter joined the "Vigilants," a band of foreigners formed to suppress major crime. While living in the border town, Gonzaullas was said to have idolized the "Border Boss," Captain John R. Hughes, and dreamed of becoming a lawman himself.[1]

The folklore that has surrounded Gonzaullas maintains he fought in the Mexican Revolution as a major at the age of twenty. Which insurgent faction held his allegiance has never been made clear. He likewise allegedly soldiered in China, and claimed employment of five years as a U.S. Treasury Department special agent. According to a *San Antonio Express* article written in 1935, Gonzaullas's service as a federal officer occurred in the eastern and midwestern states during and after World War I. He had purportedly worked on bribery and conspiracy cases, one of which involved 350 defendants. However, none of these claims has been supported by the primary source material. Indeed, a Statement of Federal Employment within his Official Personnel Folder at the National Personnel Records Center in St. Louis, Missouri, specifically states, "no record of employment prior to 12-1-1921." An employee information document in the same file, which was signed by Gonzaullas and dated June 19, 1922, offered him a chance to record his supposed earlier stint in Treasury, but he did not disclose any such service.[2]

Undeniably, the confusion inherent in Gonzaullas's conflicting stories is matched by other official records. The enumerator for the 1920 federal census cataloged the future Ranger captain as Manuel T. Gonzales, a native of Spain. His father shared the same birth country, and his mother hailed from Canada. The date his parents emigrated to the U.S. was recorded as 1893, matching one particular assertion. Ten years later, the census spelled his last name as "Gonzalellas," although misspellings were not unusual. In this survey, Texas was listed as his and his father's birthplace, while his mother was born in New York.[3]

However, other possibilities exist in the census records. For example, an eighteen-year-old Mexican named Manuel Gonzales was living in San Antonio in 1910 as an unemployed recent emigrant. While not an uncommon name, the notion that this young man could be the Manuel Gonzaullas of Texas Ranger lore is a reasonable hypothesis. In the racially charged atmosphere of South Texas in the early twentieth century, an ambitious individual might have wished to shed the negative connotations attached to *metizos*, and rebrand himself as a European and again later as a native-born Texan.[4]

The same census noted another Manuel Gonzales, who was born in Spain in 1890 and maintained a permanent residence in Galveston. Unfortunately, this individual had been convicted of theft on May 8, 1909, and was incarcerated at the Eastham convict camp at Huntsville. He entered the prison farm on June 10, 1909, and was released two months early on March 15, 1911. While perhaps a blasphemous question, might Gonzaullas have changed the spelling of his name and revised his background in order to conceal a criminal past? In fairness, his time behind bars could have been arguably the result of a youthful indiscretion, one he never repeated. Indeed, his entire adult life was spent in the completely opposite direction as he devoted himself to the cause of law and order. The zeal with which he pursued evildoers might have been based on a solemn vow to atone for his early lapse in judgment. This is naturally mere speculation, but nevertheless within the realm of possibility.[5]

In their 2019 book, *Texas Rangers in Transition*, Professors Charles H. Harris III and Louis R. Sadler may have added groundbreaking new information to the Gonzaullas legend. Sponsored by the Arizona State Fair, the cross-country El Paso–Phoenix Road Race was held in the fall of 1919. Among the forty-two entrants was "Manuel T. Gonzaullas," who brought his Locomobile No. 3 from Atlantic City, New Jersey, to participate. He was described in the *El Paso Herald* as having "won many honors on the track, both in Europe and in the United States … he has won 37 first places and 92 second places." Gonzaullas and his codriver, Fred Kyle, were situated in the third starting position when the race began on November 2. However, the racecar's speedometer soon broke, and, twenty-five miles from El Paso, they hit a rut that smashed the right front wheel, damaged the left front, bent the axle, and broke the steering rod. Gonzaullas was thrown ten feet from the vehicle and ruptured a blood vessel in his stomach. Despite the injury, he and Kyle fixed the damage and were in second place upon entering Deming, New Mexico. Unfortunately, another accident near Lordsburg put the car out of commission, and the pair failed to cross the finish line the next day. Whether the racer in question was the future Texas Ranger or someone who shared a surname of unusual spelling remains undetermined.[6]

The first confirmed fact in Gonzaullas' personal history is his marriage to the vivacious Laura Isabel Scherer in Riverside, California, on April 12, 1920. She had been born in Brooklyn, New York, on July 24, 1898. According to both of Gonzaullas's previous biographers, the two had earlier met in New York City, while Gonzaullas was there on a Treasury Department case. The couple lived at the Jewel Apartments in El Paso in early 1920, where Manuel worked as a mining engineer. However, the enumerator for the Fourteenth Census obtained the information for their precinct on January 15 and 16, three months before their wedding in California. More questions arise from this detail: did Manuel and Laura have an earlier ceremony, and the trip to California was a combination of second wedding and honeymoon? Or were they living as man and wife without the benefit of clergy or justice of the peace when visited by the census taker, and the trip to the West Coast was their first ceremony?[7]

The second verifiable occurrence is his application for the Ranger Force, which bears the date of July 13, 1920. Writing to the adjutant general, Gonzaullas noted he spoke three languages, had traveled the world, and was "very familiar with conditions along the border and [knew] the Mexican people thoroughly." He declared of a potential law enforcement career, "I would tackle anything in this line regardless of risk." Enlisting on October 1, he was assigned to Company A, which was headquartered at Del Rio under the command of Captain Jerry Gray. However, on the same day he joined the service, Gonzaullas was assigned to accompany Captain Roy Wilkinson Aldrich to Wichita Falls and report to District Attorney Fletcher Samuel Jones. Privates Hubert Patrick "Red" Brady, William Lee Lesueur, James Walter McCormick, William Edward Powers, and Caleb Thomas Williams comprised the rest of the detachment. The first three Rangers arrived in Wichita Falls on October 2.[8]

The Rangers had been summoned to the North Texas oil fields because lawlessness was rampant. Lacking the resources to hire staff investigators, District Attorney Jones had first requested assistance in late August. He informed Governor William Pettus Hobby that local law enforcement officials were corrupt. He also warned that unless the situation changed, citizens would take matters into their own hands with "lynch law and mob violence." Four men were killed in the first two weeks of October, including an elderly night watchman at the Waggoner building. Five men were being held by county authorities on charges of murder. Houston Columbus "Doc" Snow, a nefarious gambler and gunman, was lodged in the Fort Worth jail awaiting indictment for the killing of tire dealer William Sherrod Toney and real estate agent William Marvin Caple in Kemp City on September 30. At the time of their deaths, the two murder victims had been special deputies assisting officers in a raid on a gambling house. Jones and Wichita County Attorney John Davenport proposed the Thirtieth, Seventy-eighth, and Eighty-ninth District Courts set aside all civil matters on the docket in order to concentrate on the backlog of criminal cases.[9]

In the first six months of Burkburnett's stint as a boomtown, the population had grown from one thousand residents to eight thousand. Dance halls were full, and some had been closed on account of immoral behaviors. Substance abuse thrived, and local law officers had seized $42,000 in morphine. Judge Phlete Augustus Martin of the Eighty-ninth District impaneled a special grand jury on October 11, 1920, to investigate the origins of this most recent crime wave. The next day, Aldrich arrested three deputy sheriffs assigned to the northwest Burkburnett field and charged them with accepting bribes from gambling house operators. The trio was indicted by the grand jury, one for suborning perjury and the other two for taking bribes. Additionally, the grand jurors returned two true bills against Doc Snow for murder. As the Rangers and local law enforcement began to make gains, the county's criminal element seemed to grow desperate. In the last two weeks of the month, four officers were shot, three fatally, while attempting to arrest gamblers and hijackers. Following a gun battle between a businessman and two alleged robbers, six more Rangers were dispatched to Wichita County on the eighteenth. The next day, Aldrich led Rangers Gonzaullas, Brady, and G. W. Jackson, Wichita Falls Police Chief Lee Huff, Deputy U.S. Marshal James Marion "Jim" Allen, Constables William Harrison "Bill" Lay and William Warren Belcher, and Special Agent Patrick Floyd "Young Pat" Garrett, Jr. of the Missouri, Kansas & Texas (Katy) Railroad in raids on every known gambling hall, speakeasy, and still from Burkburnett to the Red River. Seven stills were seized, and three men and a fourteen-year-old boy were arrested. Two more bootleggers were arrested by McCormick and Lesueur the following day.[10]

After the crime wave in Wichita County had been subdued, the Rangers began working the oil towns of Eastland and Stephens Counties. The area had grown uncontrollably from a land of peanut, corn, and cotton farming into a restless morass of hijackers, bootleggers, and murderers. During the month of November, two hundred lawbreakers were placed in the Eastland County jail, and the monthly average stayed at that number for the remainder of the year. Gonzaullas was able to report to Aldrich that two suspects were in jail, another had been indicted, and a fourth received a four-year prison sentence. Less welcome news was the individual tried and acquitted, and the other who jumped bail and fled to Mexico. In Desdemona, the self-important town marshal, a deputy sheriff, and the justice of the peace, all corrupt members of the vice ring, ran afoul of the American Legion's Peavy-Price Post and were given twenty-four hours to leave town. Conversely, the Rangers were welcomed by the Law and Order League, which had petitioned the governor for assistance with allegedly corrupt city administrators. On November 27, the Rangers made raids on gambling halls that resulted in 125 arrests. The prostitutes picked up in the sweep were not detained, but they were ordered to leave town.[11]

Later the same evening, the Baptist Church in Desdemona was doused in kerosene and set ablaze. The arson was aimed at intimidating the congregation, particularly Reverend James Arthur Kidd, a prominent leader in the League. Even though the alarm was turned in, and the fire extinguished before significant damage occurred, the act enraged the local citizens, who now wholeheartedly supported the Rangers. Two days later, the state officers captured a large quantity of gambling equipment and liquor.[12]

Also on the night of November 29, two bandits robbed the players of a poker game on Brook Street in Wichita Falls of ten thousand dollars in jewelry and cash. Gonzaullas and Patrolman Homer Palmer were searching an alley near the scene of the holdup when a man shot at the Ranger from the darkness. Aiming at the unknown assailant's white shirt, Gonzaullas returned fire and was rewarded with a cry of pain. The wounded man escaped through a gateway at the rear of a house, and a bloody handkerchief was found in the yard through which he ran. The discarded bag of stolen jewels was found the next morning.[13]

The citizens of Ranger and the chamber of commerce protested the sending of state officers to their city, fearing such an act would give it a bad name. The townspeople's hard feelings were manifested when Gonzaullas, Brady, Ranger Martin Nickolas Koonsman, and Deputy Sheriff James Becton Ames raided a grocery store on Marsten Street on December 4. Fifteen gallons of whiskey were discovered, and the law officers arrested the owner, Frank Watkins. During the trip to the jail, the prisoner resisted, and Gonzaullas shot him in the scuffle. The wounded man was taken to a nearby hospital, and the prognosis for his recovery was favorable. Mirroring the resentment of the local citizenry, Eastland County Sheriff Samuel Elijah Nolley promptly arrested Gonzaullas and Koonsman on a charge of assault with intent to kill. However, the sheriff perhaps wanted to hinder interference into his own gambling house rackets, and Koonsman later opined Nolley would have killed the Rangers on the slightest excuse.[14]

Stunned by the town's response, the two lawmen were quickly released on bonds of fifteen hundred dollars each. Captain Charles Jourdan Blackwell and nine Rangers arrived on the morning of December 7, while Assistant Attorney General Clifford L. Stone set up his headquarters in Breckenridge in neighboring Stephens County. Eastland County Judge Calvin Rhea Starnes, Sr. sent a telegram to Acting Adjutant General Timothy Jones Powers that explained the reason for the hostility in the county. The judge claimed Rangers were searching individuals and homes without the benefit of warrants and had failed to offer cooperation to the sheriff. Powers replied he had received no evidence to corroborate the accusation, and departmental policy was to support the Ranger Force until such verification was produced. Reading the judge's comments in the Dallas and Fort Worth papers, Robert Benjamin Waggoman, publisher of the *Ranger Daily Times*, took exception to the statement, and detailed the multiple hinderances placed upon the state officers by corrupt county lawmen. Adjutant General William Dade Cope later reviewed the operations in the oil field and approved of the Rangers' actions. He further stated they would remain until local law enforcement could adequately handle the situation. The Eighty-eighth District grand jury met on December 14 and returned twenty indictments, but the panel members refused to hand down any against Gonzaullas and Koonsman. Additionally, the members endorsed the work performed by the Rangers. Gonzaullas was grateful to the grand jurors, Captain Aldrich, Stone, and other officials of the adjutant and attorney general's departments. However, he felt only disgust for the actions of Eastland County lawmen.[15]

With their two colleagues free, the state officers turned their attentions to Breckenridge. Working with a citizens' vigilance committee, a reorganized sheriff's department, and Prohibition Agent Rudolph Daniel Shumate, Aldrich, Gonzaullas, Koonsman, and Lesueur arrested five men for bootlegging and peddling morphine , four for manufacturing illegal liquor, three for hijacking, and one for assault with intent to commit murder. One thousand dollars' worth of morphine, assorted drug paraphernalia, and a quantity of alcohol were recovered. By the second day, thirty-nine people had been lodged in the county jail. The raiders located a still on the Graham road, approximately two miles north of the city, and confiscated two fifty-gallon casks of liquor. In town, they discovered a sizeable hoard of stolen automobile accessories. On December 16, Gonzaullas and Lesueur captured a still mounted in a canvas-covered wagon and three gallons of moonshine three miles north of Breckenridge. In the same area, they found another still of "considerable capacity," seven gallons of liquor, and one hundred gallons of mash. The two Rangers arrested four individuals in total and charged them with manufacturing, selling, possessing, and transporting illegal spirits. Two days later, Gonzaullas arrested a man for unlawfully carrying a concealed weapon and another for possessing intoxicating liquors. On the nineteenth, the sergeant and Koonsman apprehended six men holding an illegal poker game in the woods three miles north of town. The prisoners were transported to the courthouse where they pled guilty and paid a fine of $3,160 each. Ranger Drew Kirksey Taylor, a member of Aldrich's detachment, estimated that 60 percent of the local underworld had been apprehended in the first twenty days.[16]

In late December, Gonzaullas was sent back to Wichita County to continue restraining the criminal element. On a personal level, he was glad for the transfer, as Laura had come to Wichita Falls on November 8 to be near her husband. Unfortunately, the Ranger had spent the entire time working and could give little attention to his bride. During this time, he began studying the Bertillon fingerprint system and graduated as a credentialed expert six months later. Furthermore, he secured his lasting reputation by contending with lawbreakers who were determined to resist efforts to clean up the oil fields.[17]

Gonzaullas was of medium build, although he was muscular and strong. He grew into a flashy, dapper dresser with a well-developed fondness for diamonds, and a love for fancy firearms and automobiles. He was noted for his courtesy to everyone except lawbreakers. Like Captain John H. Rogers, Gonzaullas was a fervent Presbyterian and carried a small Bible in his pocket. Author Robert W. Stephens, a personal friend, described the Ranger: "He was personable but secretive, unwaveringly loyal and was motivated throughout his life by a high degree of principle … He was vain, occasionally profane and once observed that he had been called cocky, which he did not dispute."[18]

Already becoming acknowledged for his work in 1920, the *Wichita Daily Times* reported:

> Ranger Gonzaullas, who is known throughout the oilfields where he has been on duty as "Lone Wolf," was recognized by at least a dozen

> characters in the field, who approached him and said they were leaving for other places immediately. Proper warning was issued to all of them. Mr. Gonzaullas stated Wednesday morning that the cleanup raids would be conducted periodically, and with a few words was away for another trip.[19]

Contrary to his extroverted nature, Gonzaullas kept his own counsel and preferred to work alone. "I went into a lot of fights by myself," he reminisced, "and I came out by myself too."[20]

Gonzaullas and Ranger Sergeant McCormick raided a gambling house in Newtown on April 1, 1921. Ten men attempted to flee when Gonzaullas broke through the front door, but McCormick was stationed at the rear and stopped the getaway with several warning shots. Brought before Justice of the Peace Joseph Franklin Maxwell, nine of the suspects pled guilty to charges of gambling, while the house's operator was given a preliminary hearing, and bound over for the grand jury; he was released on a bond of one thousand dollars. On April 16 and 17, the two Rangers seized two stills and apprehended three men in Newtown. The captured haul included a half-gallon of corn whiskey, a quantity of apple and raisin wine, three barrels of mash, and a supply of corn and sugar. Gonzaullas, McCormick, and Private Roy Wesley Hardesty swept through Archer County, searched five locations, and located and destroyed an abandoned still before conducting a raid on a farmhouse on May 4. Sheriff Joe Armor McDonald, County Attorney Reuben S. Morrison, Justice of the Peace Murray Archer Lea, Sr., and Mayor Eugene Marion Hooper accompanied the state lawmen. The raiders arrested one man and seized a twenty-gallon still, cooling vats, three barrels of mash, and fifty gallons of Choctaw beer. The confiscated materials were destroyed, and the suspect was taken to the county jail on a charge of violating the Dean Law. Gonzaullas and McCormick raided a rooming house in Bridgetown on July 31. They were forced to contend with a guard at the front door and the sheer size of the building, which contained thirty-two rooms. Finding poker games taking place in the office and on the second floor, the state officers arrested thirteen men. The suspects pled guilty and paid the fines, while the establishment's owner was held on a charge of operating a gambling house.

The building was mysteriously burned to the ground later in the night. On the night of August 10, Gonzaullas and his partner observed a porter deliver a pint bottle of whiskey to an individual waiting in an automobile. The bottle was recovered from the vehicle, and complaints were filed against both men. Nine days later, the Rangers raided a private residence on Mill Street and seized 183 gallons of wine, including two fifty-gallon barrels, one twenty-five-gallon keg, and numerous smaller containers. No arrests were made as the house's owners were out of town. Gonzaullas's busy first year seasoned him as a peace officer, and oil and real estate entrepreneur Neal Orville Monroe commented, "I do not think from my observation of him while here that I ever saw a man that really grew as he did here … as he grew from day to day to be a bigger man in the work."[21]

Gonzaullas transferred to Company C on September 1 in Del Rio where he was ordered to report to Captain Frank Hamer.[22] On November 21, he resigned from the Ranger service to become a federal Prohibition agent under David H. Morris, Prohibition director for Texas. Taking up his new duties on December 1, Gonzaullas was sent to the Texarkana district. On January 7, 1922, he led a special "flying squad" of agents in Mexia and conducted a raid, in cooperation with General Barton and thirteen Rangers. Complaints against eleven men were filed with U.S. Commissioner Andrew Phelps McCormick in Waco two days later. Due to long hours and fraying tempers, Gonzaullas had occasion to exchange heated words with Ranger Jerome B. Wheatley, and the two men nearly came to blows. In time, though, they put the matter behind them and became close friends. Gonzaullas and his men went on to bedevil bootleggers in Beaumont, Port Arthur, Galveston, and San Antonio. Returning to Austin in late March to make his report, Gonzaullas reviewed his team's activities in Limestone County. They had seized 3,800 gallons of mash, eight complete stills, one wagon load of sugar, another of chops (ground corn), an undetermined amount of copper coils and barrels, and a sizeable quantity of corn whiskey. The agents destroyed their seized material, except for the small portions needed as evidence for trial. Nineteen people were arrested, and complaints were filed against four or five of them.[23]

Gonzaullas retuned to Galveston in late spring for two more sweeps through the city. On April 29, he, Agent Elmer Birdie McClure of the flying squad, Assistant Prohibition Director for Texas Bassett Richard Miles, Houston division chief Louis B. Manss, and Agent William Ware Edwards raided ten suspected downtown locations and seized a large quantity of liquor. The targeted places were all in close proximity to the police station. Sixteen men were arrested and taken to the county jail to await the filing of charges before U.S. Commissioner Charles Grainger Dibrell.[24]

In May, the federal prohibition commissioner ordered the bureau to reorganize into eighteen districts. District 14 was established to encompass the state of Texas, except for El Paso, Jeff Davis, Hudspeth, Culberson, and Presidio Counties. Twenty-five additional men were appointed to the prohibition force, bringing the total number of agents in Texas to sixty-five. Morris continued to oversee all agents in the state, while William Anthony Nitzer, Jr. was to manage district 14 with the title of division chief general. Making his headquarters in Dallas, he proved to be a hands-on leader. On June 2, Gonzaullas came under the supervision of the Chief of the General Prohibition Agents in Washington, with a raise of three hundred dollars in his annual salary. He transferred to Nitzer's office later the same month.[25]

Having returned to Beaumont, Gonzaullas, accompanied by Nitzer, was on Fannin Street on July 22, 1922, to execute a search warrant on the automobile of Justice of the Peace Herbert Edwin Showers, a long-time invalid who had been nominated for reelection that very day. According to the agents' statements, Gonzaullas removed two 1-quart bottles of whiskey from the vehicle, and the magistrate threatened Nitzer with bodily harm and attempted to pull his pistol. At the time of this episode, federal agents were not required to be armed, and, thus, Nitzer was not carrying a weapon. Gonzaullas, on the other hand, routinely packed a handgun, which, on this occasion, was tucked into his waistband. Eyewitnesses later testified Showers's pistol was halfway out of concealment when Gonzaullas shot the justice and inflicted a mortal wound.[26]

The Prohibition agent surrendered himself to local authorities and appeared before Justice of the Peace Andrew Jackson "Jack" Ward. Charged with murder on July 24, he was refused bail and lodged in the Jefferson County jail pending a meeting of the Fifty-eighth District grand jury. The panel swiftly returned an indictment. Astonishingly, Nitzer was likewise indicted on the twenty-sixth, and jailed. Director Morris came to the aid of his men by personally leading a delegation of federal attorneys, Prohibition agents, and a U.S. marshal to Beaumont. The officials had the case transferred to federal district court on account of Gonzaullas and Nitzer's status as federal officers at the time of the shooting. Thus, the U.S. attorney was placed in the position of defending the two indicted men, while the state's attorney was to prosecute. Gonzaullas and Nitzer were remanded to the custody of Deputy U.S. Marshal John Clinton Abernathy on July 27 under a writ of *habeas corpus*. Four days later, following a day-long hearing before Federal District Judge William Lee Estes, the two agents were released on one-thousand-dollar bonds each.[27]

Free to continue their duties pending trial, Gonzaullas and Nitzer went to Dallas for a series of raids before heading to Pioneer in Eastland County. District Judge Walter Raleigh Ely, Sr. of Abilene related to Taylor County grand jurors how a federal Prohibition agent had told him Pioneer was a "wide-open town." The jurist further claimed the local officers had been bribed, and urged the governor to respond with martial law. Sweeping through Pioneer on September 8 and 9, fifteen federal agents, including Gonzaullas and Nitzer, closed drug stores and soft drink stands where liquor was found; discovered two large distilleries and one brewery; seized several thousand gallons of whiskey, whiskey mash, brandy, beer, and corn whiskey; and destroyed thousands of liquor bottles. Prior to the raid, Edith Zutler, an undercover federal agent, was instrumental in securing evidence that formed the basis for twenty-one federal search warrants. Seven men were arrested and charged with violations of the Volstead Act. The defendants were arraigned before U.S. Commissioner Wilberforce Dunlap Girand in Abilene, and waived examination. Two of the men submitted bonds of $750 and one thousand dollars respectively, while the others were remanded to custody.[28]

On October 13, state and federal authorities initiated a "general clean-up drive" on Dallas and the surrounding area. Over a three-day period, raids netted five thousand gallons of mash, hundreds of gallons of bonded and corn whiskey, and three automobiles. Gonzaullas filed complaints of unlawful manufacture and possession of liquor and the illegal possession of a still on at least ten individuals. Working with Police Chief Linton Prentice Archer and Officer James Edward Bevil of Groesbeck, Gonzaullas next seized a 350-gallon still hidden in the "No Man's Land" along the Navasota River between McKenzie and Democratic Crossing. Beginning on October 24, the three lawmen had kept a watch on the camouflaged bootlegging operation. On the twenty-seventh, Gonzaullas and his companions crawled toward the still through dense brush for more than two miles. As the trio neared their goal, they made a sudden rush, but the noise the officers made crashing through the last fifty yards of underbrush alerted the bootleggers. Some escaped by swimming across the river, while others fled into the brush. The agent and the two policemen were able to console themselves with the seizure of four thousand gallons of corn mash, one hundred gallons of corn liquor, and six hundred 1-quart bottles.[29]

In the meantime, Gonzaullas and Nitzer applied for a writ of *habeas corpus* on the charge of murdering Justice Showers. On November 21, 1922, Judge Estes ruled the two federal agents would stand trial. The case was transferred to Sherman on a change of venue. Grayson County Attorney Hubert Bookout acted for the state, and Assistant U.S. Attorney Randolph Bryant defended the agents, both of whom pled self-defense.[30]

Meanwhile, Nitzer directed Prohibition agents, including Gonzaullas, in raiding one of the largest distilleries in the Southwest. On December 22, the federal lawmen swooped down on a farmhouse located seven miles northeast of Dallas. Faced with eight vicious dogs in the yard, Gonzaullas and J. C. "Jack" Harwell pulled their pistols and instructed a man standing nearby to put the canines in the house or they would be shot. The individual complied, and the agents continued with the raid. In an adjacent barn, they seized one hundred gallons of corn whiskey and a number of fifty-gallon barrels of corn mash. Gonzaullas removed his shoes and rolled up his pant legs, then knocked in the ends of the barrels. Nearly 7,500 gallons of mash was poured out onto the ground, and Gonzaullas was soon wading through four inches of liquid. Additionally, two 150-gallon copper stills were destroyed. Two men, one of them a former prohibition agent, were arrested and arraigned the same afternoon before U.S. Commissioner Robert Vance Davidson, Jr. Gonzaullas signed the complaint charging the pair with possession, manufacturing, and transporting intoxicating liquor.

The suspects waived a preliminary hearing and were each released on bonds of one thousand dollars.[31]

Following an extended conference in Washington, Gonzaullas was assigned to the Dallas district on February 24, 1923. Within the Lone Wolf's jurisdiction, Titus County held the reputation of being a particularly hazardous locale for Prohibition agents. Disguised as an oil lease hound, Gonzaullas infiltrated the county alone to gather evidence on bootleggers and a rumrunning ring suspected of using fast cars to transport liquor shipments to Central and North Texas. His cover allowed him to travel throughout the county and meet a wide variety of people. Once his investigation was complete, Gonzaullas obtained search warrants, and single-handedly arrested 150 violators and confiscated sixty-six stills without incident.[32]

His efforts not restricted to Texas, Gonzaullas was loaned in June 1923 to a "special intelligence unit" of the Commission of Internal Revenue, which was investigating a large bootlegging ring in Mobile, Alabama. The tentacles of the criminal enterprise reached into Charleston, South Carolina, and Galveston. Working undercover with Special Agent A. R. Butler, Gonzaullas was instrumental in securing evidence for the case. Due to his performance, he was promoted to general prohibition agent on August 25. However, Gonzaullas was not the only rising star present in Mobile. The newspapers noted the presence of famous New York agent Isidor "Izzy" Einstein and his partner, Peter Reagan. Additionally, acting in a sting operation, government men accepted several thousand dollars in bribe money from bootleggers for supposed protection. Fifty-two federal agents swept through Mobile on November 12 and seized ten thousand quarts of imported liquor valued at $100,000. Truckloads of illegal alcohol were transported to the federal building the next day, and scores of warrants were served by U.S. marshals on leading citizens of Mobile. Twenty-five of the arrests were made for conspiracy to bribe a government official, and sixty for trafficking and illegally selling liquor. The suspects were brought before U.S. Commissioners John Irwin Burgett and John Blocker Thornton for arraignment and the setting of bonds.[33]

Impaneled on November 26, the grand jury examined 135 cases and handed down 117 indictments on December 15. Seventy-one defendants were named under a blanket indictment of conspiracy to violate the national prohibition act and bribe government officials. However, guilty pleas, a mistrial, and dismissals soon reduced the total to fifty-two, including former Police Chief Patrick J. O'Shaughnessy, Sheriff Paul Gillen Cazalas, businessman Robert Lawrence Holcombe, Sr., ex-sheriff and legislator William H. Holcombe, Jr., prominent attorney Percy Henry Kearns, U.S. Attorney Aubrey Boyles, and politician William Joseph Hanlon. The subsequent trial began on April 28, 1924, in Judge Robert Irvin's federal district court. Agent William R. Harvey, who called himself Gonzaullas's "silent partner," testified on May 5 on the large amounts of graft they feigned pocketing from bootleggers seeking protection from government raids. Gonzaullas took the stand on the seventh and described the specifics of the months-long investigation. On May 9, he underwent cross-examination by the defense. The prosecution rested, and the defendants' counsels began presenting their cases. Kearns, the first defense witness called to the stand, claimed that he and Boyles had not attempted to bribe Gonzaullas, but had instead sought to ensnare someone they believed to be a corrupt lawman. The trial ended on May 22, and forty-four cases went to the jury. The results were mixed with eleven convictions and thirty-three acquittals. All but one of those found guilty were considered ringleaders, including Representative Holcombe, O'Shaughnessy, and Kearns.[34]

While justice was being served in Mobile, Gonzaullas traveled to New Orleans where he made a survey of the potential liquor providers. His presence in the city sent the bootleggers and rumrunners scurrying for cover. He then returned to Texas for his own stint as a defendant. On June 10, numerous influential Texans, including General Barton, appeared on Gonzaullas's behalf as character witnesses. Nitzer was acquitted the following day on an instructed verdict from Judge Estes. Gonzaullas was found not guilty on the twelfth.[35]

Gonzaullas resigned from the prohibition service on August 31, effective immediately. The previous month, the press reported Gonzaullas was retiring from law enforcement to engage in real estate. However, this new career path does not seem to have been seriously pursued, as he rejoined the Treasury Department on September 1 without the loss of any seniority. He continued to serve fourteen more days, then resigned once more. He was reenlisted in the Ranger Force with an effective date of July 2.[36]

On November 13, 1924, Governor Neff ordered Gonzaullas to investigate the mysterious death of prominent merchant Cerf Cohn in Waxahachie. The victim had been murdered in the rear of his home on the fifth, and Ellis County Sheriff Henry Forbes was stymied as to a motive or suspect. The murdered man's father offered a one-thousand-dollar reward on November 9, and the William J. Burns International Detective Agency sent C. H. Wilson, a Dallas-based operative, to assist county authorities. Upon his arrival on the fourteenth, Gonzaullas promptly received cooperation from Sheriff Forbes, Wilson, and City Marshal James Richard Toone. Additionally, District Attorney Tom J. Ball recalled the Ellis County grand jury into session to hear witnesses. The Ranger began by conducting preliminary examinations and interviews and reviewing the various phases of the investigation. Beginning on November 15, Gonzaullas traveled to Dallas and Corsicana to follow new lines of inquiry. Even after the grand jury adjourned on November 25, the Ranger continued to work up the case. Over two hundred people were interviewed, and numerous suspects eliminated, but ultimately Cohn's murder remained unsolved. Gonzaullas's involvement in the case ended with the inauguration of Miriam Amanda "Ma" Ferguson, as he was honorably discharged on February 21, 1925. Captain Aldrich reopened the probe on April 25, but his efforts to unravel the "web of secrecy that [had] pervaded the case" were also in vain.[37]

In July, George Clem Gray, a former Prohibition agent and Titus County deputy sheriff, was residing on death row at Huntsville for the murder of Ottice Stanley Ballard. Gonzaullas had arrested the condemned man several years earlier for a liquor violation, and Gray openly expressed animosity for his one-time colleague. Nevertheless, Gonzaullas worked to obtain a commutation of the death sentence from Governor Ferguson. Gray wrote a cordial letter of thanks, although he ultimately met his end in the electric chair on August 7.[38]

Having received a commission of special deputy sheriff, Gonzaullas was standing with Deputy W. E. Perkins outside the Wareham-Buick plant in downtown Dallas on August 13. There on business, they encountered

John Baptiste Johnson, a known forger who was passing bad checks. When called on to halt, the man turned a pistol on Gonzaullas. The ex-Ranger shot the forger six times "loose-like" from the hip; Johnson miraculously survived his wounds. The grand jury met the next day, questioned witnesses, and found no cause to charge either Gonzaullas or Perkins. Captain Hickman removed Johnson from the hospital to the county jail on the nineteenth, so he could answer questions concerning the Engler family murders.[39]

Gonzaullas was reinstated into the Prohibition Unit on September 26, 1925, and took his oath on October 1. After working undercover for over a month, he and fellow Prohibition officer Bryant Clark Skeen mounted three raids in Dallas County. Gonzaullas and agents Lon Hollis Tyson, Alsey Howard Miller, and Walter John Knight struck popular roadhouses and speakeasies in "Little Mexico."[40]

His federal appointment made public in March, Gonzaullas was placed in charge of the Dallas district. He supervised five agents, including Skeen and Lee Shannon, from an office at 307 Postoffice Building. On April 18, the Lone Wolf led a raid on a roadhouse north of town, and arrested four men who were later arraigned before Commissioner Lee R. Smith. More importantly, though, the agents obtained the names of fifty prominent Dallas residents for further investigation.[41]

Gonzaullas was appointed agent-in-charge of the neighboring Fort Worth district on September 26, 1926. Operating in Borger the following month, Gonzaullas and Agent Walter Knight led five Prohibition officers in working undercover to identify liquor dealers. On October 11, they coordinated with the county sheriff in securing evidence of illegal activity. Four days later, U.S. Marshal Samuel Levi Gross of the Northern District led ten deputy marshals and Prohibition agents, including Gonzaullas, Knight, Rufus Clark Van Zandt, and William Leonard Zent, Sr., in a sweep through the hamlet of Dixon Creek and the lower end of Borger's three-mile-long Main Street. Armed with shotguns and search warrants, they arrested more than a score of lawbreakers, destroyed three hundred gallons of liquor and eight thousand bottles of beer, and closed (with padlocks and federal injunctions) a dozen rooming houses, domino halls, confectionaries, and soft drink stands. Gonzaullas was noted for the enthusiasm with which he applied a sledgehammer to some of the two or three dozen confiscated slot machines. The prisoners were herded into a domino parlor and kept under armed guard. Only ten men and three women of those apprehended were held, while the rest were released. The remaining detainees were transported to the Potter County jail, arraigned before U.S. Commissioner Rollie Scales, and given the option to plead guilty in U.S. District Judge William H. Atwell's courtroom. Immediately afterward, the federal officers left town, and Ranger Captain Roy Carlisle Nichols, Sergeant J. B. Wheatley, and Rangers Henry Doyle Glasscock and Clarence Marvin Ezell arrived on October 16 and 17 to assume full responsibility for policing Borger.[42]

With the boomtown pacified, albeit temporarily, Gonzaullas returned to the Dallas office; he was appointed a special investigator in November by Commissioner Frank V. Wright, the Prohibition administrator in Fort Worth. The Lone Wolf continued to supervise enforcement in Dallas, except when his new commission required him to travel out of town. Some months later, he was named the agent-in-charge of the Wichita Falls district, which encompassed twelve counties. Working with Inspector John E. Hamilton from Fort Worth and Deputy Sheriff William Pearl "Wiley" Timmons, Gonzaullas raided nine drug stores and one garage on January 4, 1927. Charges were filed against twelve suspects before U.S. Commissioner John Albert Lantz the following day. Gonzaullas and fellow agent Robert S. Hubbard raided a farmhouse on the Scotland–Henrietta road on the evening of February 4. As the occupants attempted to flee, one brandished a firearm while exiting the rear door only to be shot in the hand. Five men in total were arrested and fifteen gallons of whiskey seized. Two of the suspects were lodged in the Clay County jail, another pair was taken to the Wichita Falls lockup, and the wounded individual was treated at the hospital and placed under house arrest. Seven horses were stolen from the premises of a Breckenridge contractor on the night of February 22. A complaint of horse theft was filed, and Gonzaullas, like the Rangers of old, tracked the culprits to a ranch near Burkburnett on Saturday morning. He recovered the stolen equines and arrested two men who were placed in the county jail.[43]

Accompanying Hickman, Gonzaullas left Fort Worth for Borger on the night of June 13 to assist the state government in once more clamping down on the troubled boomtown. The dry agent's instructions were to secure statements and evidence that would justify federal prosecutions on a conspiracy charge. Conducted in conjunction with Hickman and Hamer, Gonzaullas' investigation revealed the cleanup efforts of the two captains in April had dismantled a criminal conspiracy between local officials and an underworld syndicate dealing in illegal liquor, gambling, narcotics, and prostitution. Unfortunately, witnesses vital to a successful prosecution had fled and, Gonzaullas warned, the fragmented elements of the scheme might well reorganize and resume business. Once the Lone Wolf filed his report, Commissioner Wright closed the case. Gonzaullas resigned from the Treasury Department on June 15 and reenlisted in Company B the following day.[44]

Several fights in Childress between blacks and whites on August 13 threatened to become a full-blown race riot. Mayor William Palmer Jones appealed to Austin for assistance, and Gonzaullas and Chesley Omer Moore were dispatched to the scene on August 15. However, the trouble was over almost as soon as they arrived. Twenty-five men were arrested for unlawful assembly or assault, and convicted of the charges in County Judge William Bradley Howard's court. Reports reached the governor that additional Rangers would not be needed.[45]

Returning to Borger for several months, Gonzaullas was reassigned to Lubbock, where he became ill and spent ten days in bed. He was diagnosed with poisoning by hydrogen sulfide gas from the oil fields. He was later moved to a Dallas hospital to complete his recovery.[46]

Constable Leroy Franklin "Lee" Stegall was murdered in Flomot, Motley County, on November 28, 1927. As he drove through the town's main street, his assailants had leaped onto his vehicle's running board and shot him to death. Calvin Barnes, Adolphus and Harmon Moseley, Paul Landry, and William Franklin Allen, all hailing from Flomot, were arrested, charged with murder, and held in the county jail. Sheriff Claude Warren requested state assistance, and Gonzaullas, Hickman, and Ranger William Hale Kirby were sent to Lubbock on December 1. The Rangers arrived at noon on the second and met with Motley County deputies. Promoted to sergeant by this time, Gonzaullas left for Matador and Flomot in midafternoon to further investigate. Hickman and Kirby stayed at the jail to await developments. On December 3, the captain left town to testify in the Yancy Storey trial in Sherman, while Gonzaullas and Kirby remained. Two days later, the suspects waived a *habeas corpus* hearing in Seventy-second District Court after prosecutors and defense attorneys agreed on bail totaling eighteen thousand dollars. With the trial pending in the Fiftieth District Court at Matador, Gonzaullas and Kirby moved to trouble spots in Sherman and Borger respectively. Allen was the only suspect to be convicted, and he received a sentence of five years in prison. However, the verdict was reversed on appeal three years later.[47]

Per the instructions of Adjutant General Robert Lamar Robertson, Gonzaullas and Ranger Samuel Cloud "Sam" Mayes interviewed James W. Wayman, attorney for the American National Insurance Company, in Galveston on December 21, 1927. During the conversation, Wayman pointed to George Mussey, who owned three gambling houses in town: George's Place at 2108 Market Street; Roseland, 59th Street; and Piccadilly on the corner of 61st Street and Beach. Wayman had hired private investigators to visit the establishments while they were in full operation. One troubling piece of information was Wayman's assertion that Galveston County Sheriff Robert Edgar Kirk was dealing cards in George's Place. The attorney recommended the state launch an investigation after the holidays and send not less than two undercover Rangers. He warned the state officers that gambling was occurring under city and county protection and that the local authorities were not to be trusted. Gonzaullas made a report to the adjutant general and ended his letter with," Advise if I'm to return to Galveston and continue investigations." While Mayes and Kirby examined pool and gambling halls in January 1928, the vice trades in Galveston would continue for another thirty-odd years before their end. The Rangers were involved in that endeavor as well.[48]

Eddie Vernon "Buddy" Hall, an "oil scout" for Gulf Oil Company, was driving northwest along the Sweetwater–Lubbock highway on the night of January 10, 1928, en route to the town of Post. By eight o'clock in the evening, he was three hundred yards south of Justiceburg when he spotted two cars parked facing him on either side of the road. The cars flashed their lights, and in the brightness, he saw an array of armed men clustered around

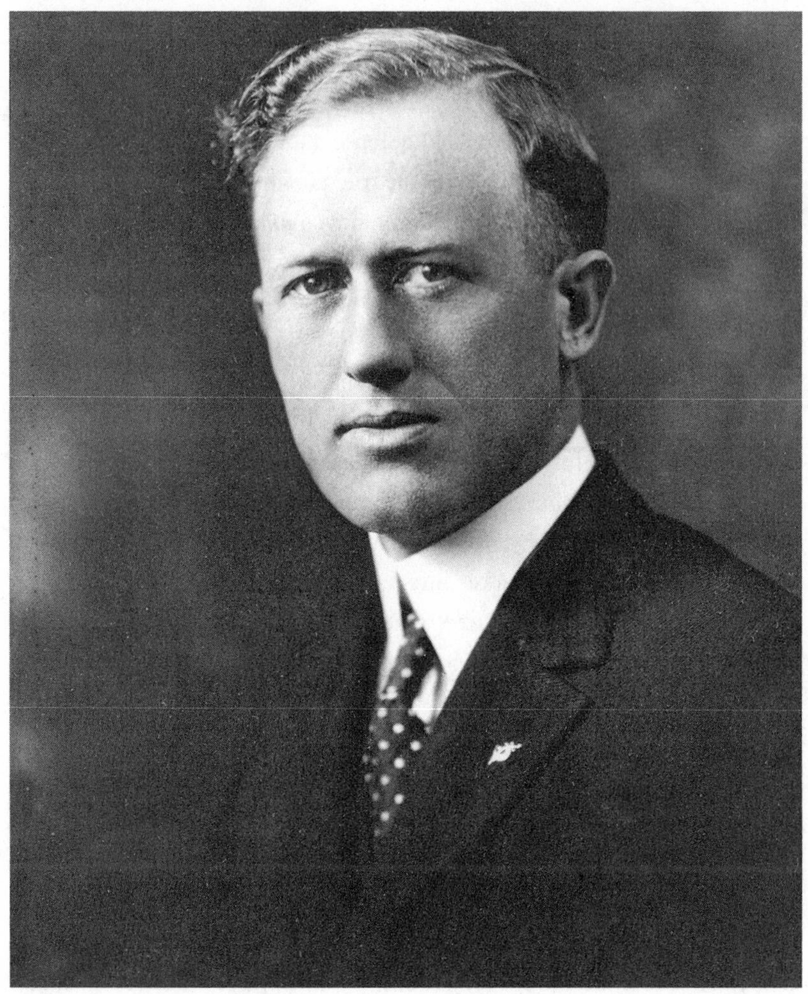

Dan Moody, Governor of Texas during launching of USS *Houston* (CA-30). HCA30.P3. *Courtesy Special Collections, University of Houston Libraries, Houston, TX.*

the cars. Thinking he was being waylaid by hijackers, Hall threw himself flat on the seat and stomped on the accelerator of his Buick roadster. As Hall roared through the gauntlet, gunfire tore into his car, blew out the windshield, and ripped off the lower part of the steering wheel. He was hit in the leg by thirty-seven buckshot pellets. He drove into Justiceburg to find a doctor.

Suddenly, an automobile carrying Constable John George Key, Deputy Constable Perry Crowley, and several possemen pulled up and demanded to know why Hall had not stopped at the roadblock when ordered. The oil scout replied they had not identified themselves as lawmen. A posse member, who lived in Post, offered to drive Hall there to seek medical attention. Hall was forced to pay for his treatment since the constables contended his refusal to stop for officers made the injury his responsibility.[49]

Three days after the incident, Grover Cleveland Phillips, president of the West Texas Oil Scouts Association, sent a telegram to Governor Daniel James Moody. In his message, Phillips observed the bank at Sylvester had been robbed earlier that day and submitted that the posse members were desirous of the five-thousand-dollar reward the Texas Bankers' Association were offering for *dead* robbers. They had not tried to confirm Hall's identity before opening fire, and indeed had sought to kill him rather than arrest him. Phillips asked the governor to order an investigation.[50]

On January 15, Moody assigned the task to Captain Hickman, the service's bank robbery expert, who delegated it to Gonzaullas. The sergeant traveled to San Angelo and Justiceburg, arriving on the seventeenth, where he conducted interviews of all participants and witnesses. He meticulously examined Hall's riddled Buick and noted three hundred bullet holes; 90 percent of which were found in the upper portion of the vehicle. If Hall had not ducked down, the Lone Wolf determined, he would have been shot some two hundred times in the head and torso. The Ranger further concluded the officers were guilty of assault with intent to kill, and advocated their prosecution. Gonzaullas met with Garza County Sheriff William Felix Cato and County Attorney Leon Oliver Moses, and the officials assured him the matter would be presented to the next grand jury.[51]

An indictment was unlikely at the local level, but the Hall episode was only one example of numerous incidents spawned by the stipulation the bankers' association had placed on earning rewards. Such practices would finally be stopped through the actions of another Texas Ranger.

On February 9, Gonzaullas was sent to Nacogdoches to report to Judge Charles Albert Hodges of the Second Judicial District and assist in an officer-involved shooting investigation. According to Deputy Carl Butler's initial statement to the press, he and Sheriff Thomas Garrett Vaught had been attempting to make an arrest on January 3 at Egg Nogg ranch when the sheriff, his closest friend, received a mortal gunshot wound to the abdomen. Butler was struck in the right forearm by the same assailant. However, from his hospital bed, Vaught gave a surprising oral statement to his attorney that Butler had shot him. Charged with assault to murder in justice court on the fourth, the deputy remained under guard at his home pending the sheriff's recovery. He refused to make any statements to the county attorney or to the media. Vaught died of his wounds on January 6, and Butler was arrested by Constable George William Stone, charged with murder, and released on a five-thousand-dollar bond after waiving a preliminary hearing. On the ninth, the commissioners court appointed Chief Deputy Thomas Fuller "Tom" Lambert to fill the vacant office of sheriff. Gonzaullas examined the characters of the participants in the shooting and found both possessed excellent reputations. However, while interviewing the sheriff's widow, the Ranger learned Vaught was ill and prone to drink to excess. Butler, in his own conversation with Gonzaullas, claimed Vaught was suicidal. Wrapping up his investigation, Gonzaullas gave the results of his probe to the grand jury. On March 3, Butler was exonerated by the grand jury, which returned a no-bill against him. Going public for the first time, Butler spoke on the matter of Vaught's death. "It was a very regrettable affair," the former deputy said. "I fired in self-defense that morning."[52]

On May 1, 1928, Adjutant General Robertson directed a raid on Loma Linda, the clubhouse of the Harris-Fort Bend County Association that stood near the line between the two counties. Earlier described as resembling a "high class gambler and all around sport," Gonzaullas had entered the building without being required to possess a membership card and spent the evening watching a "good show." Once the full complement of seven Rangers—Hamer, Hickman, Roy Aldrich, Mayes, Moore, Asa Light Townsend, and James Edward "Jim" McCoy—arrived after midnight, they and Gonzaullas arrested sixteen officials and members of the organization on gaming charges. Although the lawmen had anticipated resistance, the raid proceeded without incident. While the club was searched, one hundred wealthy guests were temporarily detained. The state officers seized three large dicing tables, one blackjack table, two roulette wheels, a box of dice, twelve packs of playing cards, five packs of chips, over two thousand dollars in cash, and forty dollars in express money orders. At the examining trial before Justice Charles Holmans in Richmond, Charles Frederick "Fred" Browning and Bert Cowan Wakefield were charged with operating a gambling establishment and released on a three-thousand-dollar bond, while bail for the other fourteen was set at one thousand dollars.[53]

Gonzaullas undertook an undercover assignment to investigate bootlegging and gambling in Fort Worth. He discovered eight vice dens, and provided the information to deputy Prohibition administrator George Appsalom Hammons. The dry agent replied that the operators had moved to their current locations after having other saloons closed through federal raids. Similarly, Gonzaullas found an unchastened Fred Browning and Bert Wakefield running craps and poker games in the basement of the old Worth Building. The Ranger noted: "We had arrested them as the operators of the Harris-Fort Bend Association, formerly known as the Loma Linda on the south side of the Houston–San Antonio highway, three miles in Fort Bend County."[54]

Working undercover on October 7, Gonzaullas, accompanied by Ranger Sam Mayes, was standing in the lobby of the Metropole Hotel in Waco when they were approached by the establishment's manager. The latter suggested they might like to visit an upstairs room where a certain craps game was in progress. Led to Room 77, the Rangers observed several craps games with eleven enthusiastic players clustered around the tables. Before the state officers could place their bets, someone recognized Gonzaullas. With their cover blown, the Rangers identified themselves, arrested the gamblers, and seized $768 and assorted gaming equipment. Leaving Mayes to watch the prisoners, Gonzaullas went to Room 30 where he had seen a poker game the previous night. The game had just ended, but the chips remained on the table. All the participants were taken into custody, and Gonzaullas confiscated the cards and chips.[55]

Appearing before Justice of the Peace J. H. Hall in Gainesville on October 14, Silas Jorman, a black youth, was charged with criminal assault upon Mrs. LaDelle Hassenpflug, a frail twenty-three-year-old white woman.

The following day, Jorman was transferred to Fort Worth and lodged in the Tarrant County jail for safekeeping. Judge Alvin Clark Owsley of the Sixteenth District Court convened a special session of the Cooke County grand jury on October 16. Jorman was quickly indicted for criminal assault, attempted criminal assault, and robbery with a deadly weapon. The same day, the badly beaten victim identified the suspect from a packet of six photographs. Judge Owsley ordered a change of venue to Sherman, and the case went to trial before Judge Silas Hare in Fifteenth District Court on November 12. Gonzaullas, Hickman, and Ranger Dott Edward Smith, Sr. assisted local officers in searching every spectator who entered the courtroom for weapons, including women. Despite earlier threats of violence from Klan members, the proceedings transpired peacefully. Given the case on the fourteenth, the jury deliberated for six minutes, then sentenced Jorman to death by electrocution.[56]

Based on a request from Motley County Judge John Floyd Jordan, Gonzaullas was assigned to combat bootleggers in Matador. On November 22, Gonzaullas and Special Ranger John Edward Russell, Sr., former sheriff of Motley County, raided a filling station on the Lee highway, nine miles east of Matador, and a still one mile further to the north on the U. L. Wilie ranch. The following day, the officers struck a residence east of Roaring Springs. In total, they arrested two individuals and confiscated eight hundred gallons of whiskey, nine thousand gallons of mash, 3,500 pounds of sugar, eighteen hundred half-gallon fruit jars, four hundred whiskey bottles, three hundred pounds of yeast, three hundred pints of beer, and a five hundred-gallon copper still with numerous pieces of distilling paraphernalia. As a result of the raid, eleven criminal cases were opened. Charges were filed against the two apprehended men, and their bonds were set at two thousand and one thousand dollars respectively.[57]

Gonzaullas attended the trial of Browning and Wakefield in Richmond on December 5. The two defendants claimed they had merely rented Loma Linda as a clubhouse and know nothing of any gambling equipment found inside. The next day, the court issued an injunction that ordered the roadhouse be closed for one year, and Browning and Wakefield were acquitted in December 1929.[58]

Gonzaullas and Ranger James Porter "J. P." Huddleston traveled to Hillsboro and reported to Sheriff George Payton Simons and County Attorney William Chalfont Morrow. Their presence had been requested to assist in the homicide investigation of Austin Irving Rice, who had been killed on July 15, 1929. On that day, a constable had found a Ford in a ditch two miles north of Grandview, with a large quantity of fresh blood on the seat and floorboards. The constable took the car to his home for safekeeping, and Rice's body was later discovered under a culvert on the Hillsboro highway two miles north of Itasca. A bundle of bloody clothing was recovered at Island Creek, one mile south of Grandview. The cause of death was blunt force trauma and a gunshot wound to the head, and the murder weapon was believed to have been a handgun of unknown caliber. Alerted by the constable, Hill County authorities organized a posse, but the search proved fruitless. Information supplied on the sixteenth by a Hillsboro filling station operator led authorities to believe Rice's killer was black. Additionally, a man bearing the same description was seen "skulking" through fields above Alvarado. Upon their arrival, the Rangers questioned eighty-six suspects, and Gonzaullas concurred in his report that the motive of the killing was robbery. The victim was known to have been carrying twelve dollars and a two-dollar Ingersoll watch while en route from Houston to Fort Worth. In the vicinity of Marlin, he apparently gave a ride to an unknown black man, who later killed him and stole his belongings. Unclaimed by friends or family, Rice was buried on July 25 in the Itasca cemetery. Investigators had few clues and virtually no leads to pursue, and the case ultimately went unsolved.[59]

On October 31, Gonzaullas went to the new oil town of Van and conferred with Van Zandt County Sheriff William Pittman "Pitt" Nixon, County Attorney James Marion Shields, Sr., and Smith County Sheriff Thomas Carlton "Tom" Sikes. The local officials desired to keep their jurisdictions free of a criminal element and requested the Ranger's assistance. Gonzaullas took part in searching thirty questionable locations, seizing five caches of liquor and one still, and recovering stolen property. Fifty-one suspects were ordered to leave town. Following his departure, Gonzaullas opined: "Van is the most law-abiding and self-respecting oil town I was ever in." He returned on November 20 and assisted in eight searches. The officers made three arrests and confiscated one load of liquor. Another eight questionable characters were given "sundown orders."[60]

Gonzaullas, in cooperation with Sheriff Nixon and four deputies, launched a series of raids in Van on February 17, 1930. Thirty-five men and fifteen women were arrested and charged with vagrancy, bootlegging, prostitution, narcotics peddling, forgery, and assault with intent to murder. Forty-nine dance halls and other establishments were closed. Undesirables were instructed to depart, and those who could not make bond were transported to the county jail at Canton.[61]

On July 11, Jesse Lee Washington, a black man, was accused of beating Mrs. Ruth Vaughan, a white woman, with a metal pipe near Aberdeen, Collingsworth County; she died several hours later at Shamrock General Hospital. Washington was working on the adjacent Lynn Sparlin farm, and his guilt was assumed almost from the beginning. He was arrested by Sheriff Claude McKinney and driven, first, to Hollis, Oklahoma, to pick up Harmon County Sheriff Edward Thornton Smith. The two lawmen then took the prisoner to the Childress County Attorney's office. Once there, the alleged killer was interrogated for over twelve hours before making a 3:00 a.m. confession to raping and killing Ruth. Present in the room were McKinney, Smith, Collingsworth County Attorney Luther Edna Gribble, District Attorney James Claude Mahan of the One-Hundredth District, and Childress County Attorney Clyde C. Broughton. Washington was secretly taken to the Oklahoma State Reformatory in Granite for safekeeping. As news of the murder spread along both sides of the state line, angry mobs of white men threatened to eradicate the black residents of Erick and Shamrock and their respective environs. Taking a heroic stand that would lead to his defeat in the next election, Wheeler County Sheriff Walter Keton McLemore stood between the mob in Shamrock and their intended victims for two entire days. The threat of widespread racial violence prompted him to request Ranger assistance. Gonzaullas and Rangers Huddleston, W. H. Kirby, and Robert Gray "Bob" Goss were sent from Austin on July 15. Once arrived, the Rangers informed the citizens of Shamrock that Washington and every black person in town were now under their protection.[62]

A letter of protest signed by forty white Shamrock women was telegrammed to the governor:

> Big newspaper display of your instructions to Texas Rangers to kill our fathers, husbands and brothers in order to protect confessed Negro rapist and murderer who so brutally attacked and killed Ruth Vaughan, one of the sweetest characters of our community, horrified us … we protest such instructions in behalf of all the white women of Texas.[63]

On July 16, Sheriff McKinney, dressed as an oil field worker, pulled up to the Gray County courthouse in Pampa and escorted Washington to a jail cell. Immediately behind the sheriff's car were Gonzaullas and his three fellow Rangers, all of whom climbed out of their vehicle and proceeded to unload an impressive arsenal of two machine guns, 150 grenades, ten thousand rounds of ammunition, and assorted rifles, shotguns, and pistols. The sight of the grim-faced Rangers and their intimidating firepower sent a message to would-be vigilantes that there would be no repeat of the Sherman riot of three months before.[64]

The following day, the heavily armed Rangers and three Pampa detectives delivered Washington, clad in steel body armor, to a prearranged arraignment before Judge William Rees Ewing in Shamrock. They arrived in the Thirty-first District courtroom at precisely 6:00 p.m. The defendant pled not guilty and was ordered held without bail. The judge convened a special grand jury, which immediately indicted Washington for first-degree murder; the entire hearing lasted five minutes. The case was then transferred to Miami in Roberts County on a change of venue. A crowd of nearly one hundred watched the lawmen and their prisoner arrive and depart from the opposite side of the town square. Two mobs were ready to take the prisoner from the Rangers, but the state officers distracted them while Sheriff McKinney, again disguised, took Washington back to Pampa. The alleged murderer would remain safely in his cell, guarded by the Rangers, until his trial. Gonzaullas vowed he would "protect the prisoner at any cost." Indeed, during Washington's day in court on July 28, he was surrounded in his chair by Rangers intent on shielding him from would-be assassins. Although his physical safety was assured, the defendant's rights under the law were not as well protected. His court-appointed attorney, Judge Edward F. Ritchey, failed to meet with Washington until the day of the trial. The defendant entered a plea of guilty, although he might not have understood the ramifications. Several newspapers described him as possessing low intelligence. Six witnesses testified for the prosecution and none for the defense. The evidence was entirely circumstantial and rested mainly on Washington's admission. Following a twelve-hour trial, which included time spent on jury selection, the defendant was convicted after ten minutes of deliberation. Judge Ewing sentenced him to death.[65]

The following evening, Gonzaullas and Goss were transporting Washington to Huntsville along Highway 5, four miles northwest of Vernon and east of the filling station operated by Clifton and Minnie Barrett. Twelve-year-old Ewell Laverne Barrett was riding his wooden toy scooter when he darted into the highway directly in the path of the Rangers' high-powered roadster. Gonzaullas was at the wheel, and he vainly attempted to swerve to the left, but the boy was struck by the auto's right front fender. Screeching to a halt, the Rangers left their prisoner in the car and rushed to the injured youth. Wasting no time, they placed Ewell, who was still breathing, in the roadster and raced to the Vernon hospital. Tragically, the boy died before reaching medical care. Following an investigation, the district and county attorneys announced on the thirtieth that no charges would be filed as the accident had been unavoidable. Gonzaullas and Goss departed with Washington for Dallas, en route to the state penitentiary. The convicted murderer died in the electric chair on September 12. The final disposition of the case was never in doubt, but Gonzaullas and his companions insured that the rule of law, and not mob violence, decided the issue. Whether true justice was administered in the case is less certain.[66]

The largest oil boom in the state's history began on October 3, 1930. On that day, the Daisy Bradford No. 3 well owned by Columbus Marion "Dad" Joiner brought in the initial strike in the Woodbine sands beneath Rusk County. Upon testing, Joiner's discovery yielded over fifty-two barrels in seventeen minutes with an estimated daily production of 5,600 barrels. The significance of the find went virtually unrealized until the Lou Della

Crim No. 1 in Gregg County produced a 22,000-barrel per day gusher on December 27. Oilmen, investors, and landowners began to realize the extent of the vast oil reservoir two-thirds of a mile under the ground. In time, the oil field, which became one of the world's largest, would cover six hundred square miles in Rusk, Smith, Upshur, and Gregg Counties and boast approximately 25,000 wells. Becoming the center of the oil boom, Kilgore grew in several weeks from a rural business center in a region numbering a few hundred drought-afflicted cotton and pea farmers to a tent and shanty town of ten thousand souls. As more wells tapped into the oil pool, land prices rose steeply from ten dollars per acre to one thousand dollars.[67]

Following the normal pattern of boomtowns elsewhere, the legitimate speculators, land agents, oil scouts, and roughnecks who rushed to the fields were quickly joined by conmen, bootleggers, gamblers, prostitutes and pimps, and thieves intent on separating the oilmen from their money. Dance halls, gambling parlors, and taverns flourished along Highway 80 between Longview and Gladewater. Deputy Sheriff Albert Adams, later the Longview police chief, noted in an interview the rush had attracted "some of the worst criminals in the United States." While admitting much of the crime was petty in nature, he also described offenses ranging from armed robbery to murder.[68]

On January 28, 1931, Gregg County Sheriff Martin Hays requested newly inaugurated Governor Ross Shaw Sterling send Rangers to police the entire 120-acre oil field. Captain Hickman dispatched Gonzaullas and Privates Goss and Huddleston to support the local constable in arresting lawbreakers, including corrupt officials, or inducing them to leave the area. Arriving on February 3, Gonzaullas roamed the crowded streets of Kilgore, Pistol Hill, Newton, Gladewater, and Longview for several days while sporting dirty work clothes and an unshaven face. His understanding of the situation complete, the Ranger reappeared in immaculate whipcord breeches and coat, intricately carved silver belt buckle, a diamond pinky ring, and a diamond-studded Shriner's pin on his lapel. With his presence noted, Gonzaullas flamboyantly declared, "Crime may expect no quarter. Gambling houses, slot machines, whiskey rings, and dope peddlers might as well save the trouble of opening, because they will not be tolerated in any degree. Drifters and transients have their choice of three things: engaging in a legitimate business, getting out of town, or going to jail!"[69]

Gonzaullas used a technique that, while not admissible in court, had proved effective in boomtowns of the previous decade. He inspected hands. The Ranger reasoned that a man with dirty, work-hardened hands was likely honest and a good citizen. In contrast, men with clean, soft hands were apt to be "pimps or gamblers or thugs or some other kind of outlaw."[70]

The three Rangers also employed a long "trotline," purchased from Mayor Malcolm Crim's hardware store, and housed their prisoners in the unoccupied First Baptist Church building. The guests of the improvised jail received one meal every day and utilized a bucket that was passed around for a urinal. The church's pulpit was used to fingerprint incoming detainees. Gonzaullas reminisced years later that he had approximately one hundred prisoners on a busy night. The suspects were interrogated, and every week some were transported to the Gregg County jail in Longview on such charges as murder, bank robbery, gambling, and rumrunning. Other shady characters were instructed to promptly leave town. Once the number of prisoners decreased, the lockup was moved to an abandoned feed store, and the construction of a permanent jail was completed on March 25.[71]

Temporary assistance arrived on March 11 in the form of Captain Albert Mace, Sergeant J. B. Wheatley, and Ranger Benjamin Maney Gault. Less than two hours after they stepped off the train from Dallas, the trio, accompanied by Gregg County deputies, arrested twenty-two men in two separate hotels on gambling charges. Shortly after the suspects were released on bond, the three Rangers departed for Austin. Gonzaullas, Goss, and sheriff's deputies raided the Hilltop Garage in Longview on March 28. Seizing twenty-five gallons of liquor cleverly hidden in an air pressure tank, they apprehended three men and charged them with violations of the Dean Law. One man was arrested for carrying a concealed weapon, and numerous others for vagrancy. Three men were arrested, fingerprinted, and photographed on April 9 on charges of violating the Dean Law at Overton. When taken into custody, they had a large number of firearms in their possession. From Austin, Hamer expressed interest in talking to the trio, as he suspected them of involvement in armed robberies in Texas, Louisiana, and elsewhere.

Bob Goss standing, Tom Hickman, and Tom L. Heard on horseback.
Courtesy Texas Ranger Hall of Fame and Museum, Waco, TX.

Their particulars, photographs, and fingerprints were forwarded to the senior captain. On April 17, Gonzaullas and Goss raided a roadhouse three miles outside Longview on the Kilgore highway and arrested three men and two women. The state officers confiscated five firearms and several gallons of whiskey. The same day, the Rangers raided a domino parlor in Longview and apprehended forty suspects, including an escaped convict, three alleged drug addicts, and five who were held for further investigation. The prisoners were marched down the main street to the county jail. With the Reverend George W. Wilburn presiding, a meeting of Kilgore residents was held at the schoolhouse, and the assembly unanimously adopted a resolution expressing "appreciation of the work done by these officers and commend their service in behalf of public safety and welfare."[72]

The fire at the Sinclair Oil Company's No. 1 Cole well near Gladewater was the most disastrous oil field blaze in Texas history. Nine workers were killed on April 28 when a spark ignited the oil gusher. On May 1, Gonzaullas was present as Myron Macy Kinley, a Tulsa-based pioneer in oil well control and firefighting, fell and broke his leg while approaching the conflagration. The Ranger immediately dropped his ornate gun belt and braved the flames to pull the incapacitated man to safety. Myron went to the hospital, while his younger brother, Floyd Tipton "Harry" Kinley, took over suppression operations. With his leg set and encased in a cast, the elder Kinley returned to the well to observe. Hickman and Goss were on scene to assist in keeping the 2,200-acre Cole tract free of the hundreds of curious onlookers swarming into the area. Harry extinguished the fire two weeks later using a nitroglycerine charge.[73]

Gonzaullas effected another thirty arrests in Kilgore and Longview before being ordered by Hamer to Malakoff on May 20. The town was the scene of a labor dispute as Mexican laborers were being threatened into leaving the Malakoff Fuel Company lignite mines. A dance hall in a Mexican settlement one mile northeast of town had already been dynamited, and a placard bearing the demand "leave pronto" was found near the ruins. General Sterling assured Luis Lupián G., Mexican consul general at San Antonio, that his countrymen would receive protection from the Ranger Force. Henderson County Sheriff Joel Baker, the county attorney, and Goss assisted in the investigation. On May 23, the officers discovered A. L. Tubbleville, a discharged employee of the Malakoff company, had purchased fifty-three sticks of dynamite. They arrested the suspect, jailed him at Athens, and filed a complaint charging him with white capping and arson by explosives.[74]

On June 10, the Rangers and city constables raided honky-tonks in Longview and took fifty individuals into custody. Later that night, Gonzaullas and Goss teamed with Police Chief Pike K. McIntosh, Constable Aaron Patterson "A. P." Farrar, and five policemen and swooped down on Pistol Hill in search of a particularly troublesome gang of hijackers. They found, instead, one of the most complete gambling establishments encountered in the oil fields. One hundred and twenty-three people were arrested in the raid, and guns, knives, gaming paraphernalia, and a large quantity of liquor were confiscated. Twenty-five questionable characters were instructed to leave the area. Picked out of a lineup of thirty suspects, Thomas H. Ashburn was arrested on a charge of robbery with firearms. Farrar took the suspect to the county jail where he was held without bail pending action by the grand jury.[75]

Going into the Old Field section of Longview, Gonzaullas and Goss dressed themselves as oil field workers on June 26 and gained entry to the Palace Royal Dance Hall on the south side of Ware Street at eleven o'clock. The Rangers overpowered the guards before the alarm could be sounded. Seventy-three men were placed under arrest, and the gambling equipment inside the casino was destroyed. Axes were likewise applied against the establishment's tables, chairs, and other furniture. The prisoners were transported to the jail in a convoy of commandeered vehicles. Gregg County deputies began processing them at 1:30 a.m., and the activity lasted through the night. Two men were charged with operating a gambling house.[76]

Captain Hickman placed Gonzaullas in overall charge of the detachment in the oil field, with Goss stationed at Kilgore, Hardy Burl Purvis at Henderson, and Dan Lafayette McDuffie at Gladewater. On July 7, 1931, McDuffie, Police Chief William Angelo Dial, and two other officers were responding to a call that Jeff F. Johnson, an intoxicated ex-jailer, was firing his .30-30 rifle recklessly inside the city limits. The officers drove to Johnson's location near the business district of town and, upon their arrival, the suspect opened fire with his long gun from a doorway. The bullet ricocheted off the steering wheel, struck McDuffie in the right hip, glanced off the edge of his watch, and tore a quarter-sized hole in his abdomen. Chief Dial, who had served in Company D under Captain William L. Wright, fatally shot the assailant seven times through the body. Thirty minutes after being wounded, McDuffie died of blood loss while en route to the hospital in Longview. The chief was found the next day to have fired in self-defense. Upon hearing of the incident, Hickman, Gonzaullas, and Goss raced to Gladewater, but there was little they could do except escort their fallen comrade's body home to New Boston for his funeral. The entire Gladewater Police Department and seven Rangers—Hickman, C. O. Moore, Gonzaullas, Maney Gault, Kirby, Goss, and George Allen—were among the mourners. Even while in the midst of a capital case, the district court adjourned, and the judge and court officials attended as a group.[77]

Following an armed robbery at a Kilgore movie theater on December 15, Gonzaullas searched nearby boardinghouses for anyone matching the description of the thief. Finding such an individual, the Ranger examined the suspect's room and uncovered a cache of five handguns and ammunition. He also discovered a bundle of cash and some jewelry secreted in the toilet tank. The ill-gotten gain was wrapped in a handkerchief that had two eyeholes cut into it. Completing his search, Gonzaullas, Night Police Chief Marvin Wootan, and Officer Ulysses S. Huntsman took the suspect, Calvin A. Spencer, and his brother William J. Spencer, who had been present in the room, into custody. The Ranger ushered the alleged thieves to the scene of the crime where the box office cashier identified William as the armed robber. Due to the evidence he collected in the boardinghouse, Gonzaullas put both men in jail.[78]

The Ranger conducted a search of the suspects' car and found a Louisiana Highway Patrol badge. The following day, he discovered the badge's owner was a trooper who had been overwhelmed by two men near Nachitoches and relieved of his badge, sidearm, and vehicle. The officer had been left alive on the side of the road. The Spencers were extradited to Caddo Parish to answer for the charge.[79]

On January 12, 1932, Gonzaullas and three Rangers employed bloodhounds in the manhunt for the killer of San Augustine County Deputy Sheriff Henry Isom Chandler. The lawman had been murdered the previous day at the Camp Worth logging camp, twenty-five miles east of Nacogdoches. The state officers and posses from Shelby, San Augustine, and Nacogdoches Counties combed the area. Despite their best efforts, though, the unidentified fugitive was never found.[80]

Continuing his investigation into the Spencer brothers, Gonzaullas and Wootan were able, by January 19, to link the two suspects to a series of robberies, seven rapes, and an aggravated assault in Texas and Louisiana. A nineteen-year-old victim traveled with Gonzaullas to Shreveport to identify the brothers as those who had robbed her and a male companion before pistol-whipping the man and assaulting her. The Gregg County grand jury returned indictments on the pair for criminal assault and burglary, and County Attorney John E. Taylor announced he would seek the death penalty. Gonzaullas returned the brothers to Marshall on February 5 for trial.[81]

The successful completion of the case led an automobile dealer in Shreveport to present Gonzaullas with a brand-new, eight-cylinder Chrysler coupe. The car had been customized with armor plating, bulletproof windows, and a Thompson submachine gun mounted on a swivel in the front passenger seat. On February 21, the Lone Wolf posed for pictures with his new vehicle, then returned to work.[82]

Oilman Harold Lafayette "H. L." Hunt, Jr. was threatened with the kidnapping of two of his children in early March 1932. The communication that arrived at his Tyler home instructed Hunt to proceed to the Blue Moon Night Club, located between Gladewater and Longview, and meet with the extortionists. As aviator hero Charles Augustus Lindbergh's son had been abducted only a week prior, the family took the matter seriously. They contacted the sheriff, who brought in the Rangers. James Garfield Hunt, H. L.'s brother, and Sherman McLean Hunt, Jr., the oil tycoon's nephew, drove to Kilgore and met with Gonzaullas. Belting on a pair of pistols and secreting a small handgun, a knife, and a derringer about his person, the Ranger followed the two Hunts to the rendezvous in his Chrysler. Upon arriving, they watched as four tough-looking men were led out of the club in handcuffs by a "great big Ranger." Described as *mafioso* from Chicago, the quartet were put on the express train bound for the Windy City and told, "Don't ever come back to the state of Texas. If you do you're dead." The mobsters were not known to have returned.[83]

Gonzaullas's vehicle made another contribution when Clyde Barrow's gang arrived in Denton on April 11 to reconnoiter for a planned robbery of two banks. As Ralph Fults walked around the old courthouse, he noticed all the automobiles were parked nose to the curb on the north side of the town square except for one. That particular Chrysler seemed oddly heavy, and when he peered closer Fults was shocked to see Hickman and Gonzaullas sitting in the front seat. As nonchalantly as possible, the outlaw walked away, rendezvoused with the rest of the gang, and they beat a hasty retreat from town.[84]

Captain Albert Mace led Gonzaullas, Huddleston, Kirby, and Ranger Warren Elmer Lowe in conducting raids on six establishments in Sweetwater on May 20, 1932. They were joined by Police Chief Normal Bernard Hall, policemen Jack Yarbrough and Rufus Arp, and Constable (and former Special Ranger) William Wilson "Wilse" Hudson. Nine individuals were arrested for liquor law violations and two more for vagrancy. The lawmen seized several hundred bottles of beer, approximately 250 quarts of whiskey, several cases of empty flasks, bottles labelled as gin, and assorted equipment. Two of the suspects waived examining trials in Justice of the Peace Isaac Walker Brashear's courtroom. Bond was set at one thousand dollars each.[85]

Captain Alfred F. Dion, a reserve army air corps officer and flying circus performer, was also the leader of a notorious gang of extortionists and hijackers. On April 6, he had threatened to dynamite the Taylor Refinery Company plant near Tyler unless he was paid $2,500. When his demands were refused, Dion promised to murder two oil company employees, which convinced Taylor officials to pay the money. He remained at large until he was arrested by Gonzaullas in Houston in late August. The Ranger took Dion back to Tyler and filed charges of robbery by threat.[86]

Gonzaullas was fired by Governor Miriam Ferguson on January 18, 1933. The previous three gubernatorial elections had created a biannual turnover in the Ranger service, which offered private industries a plethora of experienced law officers needing employment. Similar to other discharged Rangers, Gonzaullas gravitated to the troubled East Texas oil fields. He became chief special agent for the Atlas Pipeline Company and the Spartan Refining Company. He recruited eighteen unemployed former Rangers, including Walter Everette "Ebb" Riggs, to guard the pipelines. On April 7, 1934, Gonzaullas announced his candidacy for the office of Gregg County sheriff. Bob Goss, now the Kilgore police chief, was vying for the same position. However, both ex-Rangers were unsuccessful when the incumbent, William Henry Hayes, was victorious in the polls.[87]

The nature of American law enforcement changed for many officers on December 15, 1933. On that date, the Twenty-first Amendment of the U.S. Constitution became effective and repealed the nation's failed prohibition experiment. However, Texas maintained its dry laws until voters rescinded them on August 24, 1935. The reformists were not entirely defeated, though, as new legislation passed into law prohibited the sale of liquor by the drink in public establishments, and permitted local option.[88]

On December 18, 1934, Gonzaullas accepted an appointment from the Gregg County Criminal District Attorney's Office to be the new chief investigator. District Attorney-elect Claude Allen Williams had made the suppression of vice and other criminal activity a major issue of his campaign. Once he assumed office on January 1, 1935, Williams and his hard-charging investigator proved to be a formidable team. In one of his first acts, Gonzaullas amassed data on illegal beer and liquor sales in the vicinity of Kilgore in preparation for the first grand jury of the year. Williams initiated injunctive proceedings and obtained temporary restraining orders against two suspected gambling houses in Longview. Additionally, the district attorney announced all persons receiving suspended sentences would be fingerprinted, with the records preserved in Longview, and copies sent to the FBI in Washington. Gonzaullas was designated the office's fingerprint expert and equipped with a complete laboratory. Their pro-active stance was put to use in clearing a vicious homicide. Emma Marie Sage was shot to death on April 11 in the Pickwick Hotel coffee shop in Gladewater. Don E. Covin, who had committed the murder in full view of eyewitnesses, was arrested a half-hour later and charged with her death. Held without bond, the suspect had been recently paroled from Huntsville after serving four years for the killing of a young woman in a Houston hotel. The twenty-seven-year-old mother of two children, Sage had been in a relationship with Covin. Gonzaullas informed the media that Covin had confessed to pressuring the victim into accompanying him to St. Louis. She had refused, a decision that led to her murder.[89]

Gonzaullas then returned to his raiding practices on June 11 when he struck a house near the Railroad Commission office in Kilgore. The investigator seized 458 half-gallon jars of bootleg whiskey, and Gonzaullas believed the house was used for storing the contraband. On July 31, he confiscated nine slot machines and applied for a court order authorizing him to destroy them. He seized another nine machines on the fourteenth.[90]

Once the Texas Department of Public Safety was established, the Headquarters Division was created to maintain and administer the Bureaus of Identification and Records, Communications, Intelligence, and Education. Acting Director Louis Graham Phares named Gonzaullas superintendent of the Bureau of Intelligence on September 1. Under the guidance of the senior

Ranger captain, Gonzaullas served as the commission's chief of detectives and oversaw the department's undercover officers. As director of the state's Crime Detection Laboratory, he was "to accumulate and analyze information of crime activities" and "aid in the detection and apprehension of violators of the law." Despite the ambitious goals, Gonzaullas was hampered by a lack of money. In the first year of operations, the legislature only appropriated $5,660 for his entire bureau. The second fiscal year saw a reduction of four hundred dollars in his budget. Due to these restrictions, the Bureau of Intelligence relied on borrowed personnel, including Rangers Quincy Lowman, Alva Loran Barr, and Joe N. Thompson. Additionally, before the funding situation improved, Gonzaullas was forced to obtain surplus equipment from other departments.[91]

Gonzaullas was the perfect choice, not only because of his practical experience in the field, but also his earlier criminalistics training. A firearms enthusiast, he amassed a remarkable collection of rifles and pistols, bullets, and spent cartridge casings. Under his stewardship, the laboratory became a leader in the science of ballistic analysis. The lab also specialized in moulage casting of footprints and tire treads, the evaluation of trace evidence (fingerprints, hair, and fibers), and the examination of blood, handwriting, and documents. Gonzaullas and his staff began their work, sharing cramped quarters downtown with the Bureau of Identification before moving to Camp Mabry.[92]

In 1936, the science of ballistics was used for the first time on record to convict a hunter of illegally killing a deer. On December 8, 1935, game wardens Ray Williams and Curtis McElroy had been informed eight deer carcasses were on a ranch near Fort Davis. The legal hunting season was scheduled from November 16 to 30. The two wardens spent four days locating the remains in a hidden cache. They extracted from the one complete body a .25-35 caliber bullet and reviewed a list of 265 hunters known to have worked the area. Williams and McElroy interviewed Jesse Earl Good of Kermit, who owned a rifle of the relevant bore, and borrowed from him the long gun. Test-firing a bullet through the rifle, they sent the slug to Gonzaullas for examination. The bullet was microscopically compared to that taken from the deer carcass and found to be a match. Good was arrested, and Gonzaullas sent a representative to testify at the subsequent trial the following April, with photographic blowups of the two bullets. The defendant was found guilty on the basis of this indisputable evidence and fined one hundred dollars.[93]

The DPS's leadership underwent changes when Colonel Horace Henry Carmichael was appointed director on May 13. While no longer in the top spot, Phares continued to head the Highway Patrol. James McCormick was relieved of his position as senior Ranger captain on July 30, and Carmichael assumed the duties on a permanent basis. While steadily organizing his bureau, Gonzaullas was assigned in June 1936 to special duty during President Franklin Delano Roosevelt's tour of Texas. Together with Phares and Ranger Captain Hardy Purvis of Company A, he reinforced the Secret Service's presidential protection detail and acted as an honor escort for the chief executive. Roosevelt's visit coincided with the centennial celebration of the state's independence from Mexico. Governor and Mrs. James Burr V. Allred and U.S. Senator and Mrs. Morris Sheppard accompanied the tour. The three DPS officers met the president's train in Texarkana, and remained until the party departed for Oklahoma.[94]

Gonzaullas and Bee County Sheriff James Brennon Arnold departed Beeville on July 13 to search for Bryan Black, a county civil engineer, who was believed to be wandering through the brush near Round Rock in a daze. Black had disappeared four days previously, and eyewitness testimony and physical evidence consisting of hair, blood, a hat, and a pair of shoes led the officers to theorize he had been beaten with a rock and left for dead. On July 14, the missing man appeared at a ranch house more than a mile from the crime scene. Weak from loss of blood and lack of food, he was taken to Seton Infirmary in Austin. The blow to Black's head had left him unable to remember the incident, and investigators had few leads. Twice more in the next year, Black disappeared from his Skidmore home and was found partially clothed miles away, hinting at a possible neurological disorder rather than an assault.[95]

By August 31, 1936, Gonzaullas's staff of lab technicians and undercover detectives closed 140 out of 142 cases, including fifty-six murders. Modern audio equipment helped to solve eleven cases, and electrical equipment another four. The lab analyzed physical evidence such as twenty-three explosives,

122 bullets, fifty-seven powder burns, twenty-one bloodstains, and 125 photographs, drawings, and descriptions of crime scene data. On December 26, Gonzaullas and Carmichael departed the state for a two-month tour of police crime labs in the Northeast and Canada. When they returned to Texas, the two law officers brought back an increased knowledge of the means needed to modernize the department's forensic assets. Gonzaullas also requested, from corporations and researchers, scientific data and journal articles. With this newfound wealth of information, he taught the forty-five students of the department's first peace officer training course. Once more serving as an instructor on February 7, 1939, he presented a lecture to three hundred military policemen in the post theater at Fort Sam Houston on ballistics and other crime-detection methods.[96]

Passed on April 29, 1937, and approved five days later, House Bill No. 975 finally authorized appropriations that allowed the bureau to add ten criminal investigators to the staff. Walter Estes "Dub" Naylor, Carroll Grover Rush, and Zeno A. Smith were among those who joined. More changes occurred on September 24 of the following year when Carmichael suffered a fatal heart attack while driving his vehicle along Barton Springs Road. He was succeeded by Homer Garrison, Jr. three days later.[97]

As chief of the state crime lab, Gonzaullas frequently found himself in court offering expert testimony for the prosecution. The trial of twenty-year-old Joe Polanco began in San Antonio's Criminal District Court on September 29, 1936, for the robbery-murder of bus driver George Forbes the previous May. The defendant was also facing robbery by assault charges for the holdups of two other bus drivers, and three accomplices had been similarly indicted. One of them, a juvenile, turned state's evidence and accused Polanco of being the trigger man in the slaying. Gonzaullas was the prosecution's fourth witness and described, on the thirtieth, how he had connected the fatal bullet to Polanco's .38-caliber handgun then in evidence. Once the state rested, Polanco took the witness stand and claimed he had been beaten in order to force his signed confession. Nevertheless, he was convicted on October 2 and sentenced to death in the electric chair. The other three participants in Forbes's murder entered guilty pleas on the fifth and were given long stretches in prison.[98]

Gonzaullas's lab conducted tests on the bullets that killed Police Officer Agnal Aubray "Bill" Edwards in San Antonio on January 16, 1937. During the subsequent trial, the ballistics expert took to the stand on February 17, and linked the slugs and ejected shell casings to the recovered murder weapon. Based in part on this testimony, the defendant was found guilty and executed by electrocution. In another case, twenty-five-year-old farmer Philip Pair was on trial for the shotgun slaying of his wife, Agnes, at their McAdoo home on October 3, 1936. Testimony began on April 6, 1937, in Judge Alfred Jennings Folley's courtroom in Dickens. Gonzaullas testified on the mechanical nature of the murder weapon and the near impossibility of an accidental discharge. The Pair case was not the only instance of uxoricide that involved the intelligence bureau chief. On January 27, 1939, Guadalupe Cantu, a wealthy McAllen merchant, went on trial for the January 1937 killing of his wife. Gonzaullas was called to the stand on the first day of testimony, and recounted how a bullet taken from the victim's body was matched to a .45-caliber Colt revolver owned by the defendant.[99]

Taking the stand on May 25, 1939, Gonzaullas testified in the murder trial of state liquor inspector William Hanson "Bill" Strickland in Ballinger. The defendant was charged in the death of filling station owner Dan Ira Liverman on October 21 of the previous year. The state officers had come to Liverman's business with search and arrest warrants, but the suspect had refused to comply. While Liverman, known as a "dangerous man," ran for his adjacent house shouting threats, Strickland and Robert Henry "Bob" Gambell, another agent, shot him twice in the chest. Questioned by state and defense attorneys, Gonzaullas spent an hour informing the jurors on steel-jacketed and lead bullets, the science of ballistics, and bullet wounds in relation to Liverman's fatal injuries.[100]

During the biennium that ended on August 31, 1940, the Scientific Crime Detection Laboratory conducted 2,235 examinations that resulted in 1,782 positive identifications of blood, flesh, viscera, narcotics, fibers, paper, fingernail scrapings, and various other substances. George Washington Gambell's Ballistics Section made 1,177 examinations of firearms, bullets, cartridge casings, powder burns, and explosives, with 1,039 positive results. However, on September 1, 1939, the lab was transferred from Gonzaullas's purview to the Bureau of Identification to comply with the 1935 law that had created the DPS.[101]

Despite his success in creating a superlative unit, the Lone Wolf yearned to return to the challenges of fieldwork. On February 26, 1940, Gonzaullas's request to transfer back to the Rangers was granted. Exchanging responsibilities with Captain Royal George Phillips, he was named captain of Company B in Dallas. Although the transfer essentially represented a demotion, Gonzaullas was eager to embark on what became the most satisfying period of his career.[102]

The DPS publicly defined the modern Texas Ranger later in the year. Captain Gonzaullas may well have served as the example for the official description:

> He's a strange combination of the old and the new, this present-day Ranger. He has of necessity clung to the traditions and methods of a vanishing age, yet at the same time he is a modern-day scientific criminal investigator, fully schooled in the utilization of ballistics, chemistry, fingerprinting, and all other scientific devices through which up-to-date law enforcement agencies bring criminals to justice.[103]

Although long illegal in Texas, gambling enjoyed popularity in the state's urban centers, especially the largest in Gonzaullas's district: Dallas, Fort Worth, Waco, and Wichita Falls. Most Rangers viewed the issue as a matter for local law enforcement and a distraction from their mission to investigate major crimes. Still, crusading clergymen or ambitious politicians used the lawbreaking for their own ends, and invariably the Rangers were sent to deal with the ongoing problem. On January 4, 1940, Gonzaullas, accompanied by two Rangers and a pair of Dallas vice squad detectives, pounced on a bookie joint located on Commerce. The officers arrested every individual in the establishment and seized all the equipment, except the tables and chairs. Justice of the Peace Walter Lewis "Lew" Sterrett presided over the examining trials, and the bookmaker paid fines totaling $275 for himself, two assistants, and twenty patrons. Other city vice officers struck another establishment on South Field, and found at least ten more had been hastily closed. Following a conference the next day with District Attorney

Andrew Patton, Gonzaullas announced he and his men would assist local officers with more raids.[104]

On September 11, after Rangers informed them of illegal activity involving their equipment, the Postal Telegraph Company closed down wire service to several bookies involved in horse race betting. Meeting with company officials were the district attorney, Gonzaullas, Rangers Robert A. "Bob" Crowder and Ernest Daniel, and vice squad officers Tracey Boyd Griffin and Joseph Macon Sides. Patton later announced, "the backbone of horse race bookmaking in Dallas had been broken."[105]

The body of Lamar County Chief Deputy Sheriff George Richardson Robertson was discovered on September 11, hidden in a wooded area four miles east of Powderly. Lying in the back seat of an automobile, the fallen officer had been brutally beaten, slashed, and shot four times. More than twenty-four hours prior, he had been kidnapped by Charles Morton "Buddy" Acker and Turner Ross Fowler, Jr., both of whom the deputy and Sheriff James Harvey Ratliff had arrested at Carpenter's Service Station on suspicion of attempting to sell a stolen tire and wheel. Robertson transported the two desperadoes in their own dark green 1939 Ford sedan, but the vehicle vanished while en route to the county jail. The car was reportedly spotted the next day in Terrel, Oklahoma. The possible crossing of state lines made the case an offense under the Federal Kidnapping Act of 1932 (the "Lindbergh Law"). As such, special agents of the Federal Bureau of Investigation became involved in the massive manhunt that encompassed the woods and sideroads of North and East Texas and southeast Oklahoma. Once their identities were established, Acker and Fowler were connected to armed robberies in Huntsville and Buffalo, Texas. After the deputy was discovered, scores of local, state, and federal officers and three hundred civilian volunteers searched the Red River bottoms for the killers. Lamar County offered a reward of $250 for information leading to the arrest of the killers. Gonzaullas was placed in charge of the pursuit and the homicide investigation. Working with Sheriff Ratliff, the captain coordinated parties of lawmen and bloodhounds in patrolling designated zones. He, Bob Crowder, and Ernest Daniel examined the Ford in detail for fingerprints and other trace evidence. The captain informed newspaper reporters that the material gathered proved conclusively Acker and Fowler were the perpetrators. Gonzaullas swore to remain on the case until the suspects were in custody. Formerly of Clarksville, Stewart Stanley was reassigned from the border country to assist in the investigation.[106]

The fugitives were charged with murder with malice aforethought on the thirteenth, and indicted by the Sixth Judicial District grand jury four days later. On October 11, Acker was captured in the dense woods near Oakhurst, and Fowler was taken while walking along the railroad tracks in New Waverly on the thirteenth. To avoid the chance for mob violence in Paris, the two suspects were lodged in the Dallas County jail. Their confessions confirmed Fowler had shot Robertson with a revolver hidden in the Ford sedan. When the killers crossed over into Oklahoma, they threw the murder weapon into the Red River. The handgun was recovered by Paris police officers from a clump of weeds. The fugitives had stayed on the move and traveled through Oklahoma, Texas, New Mexico, Arizona, and Mexico. After being deported from Mexico due to a lack of passports, they returned to Texas approximately one week before their captures.[107]

Judge Albert Sidney Broadfoot of the Sixth District Court granted the accused a charge of venue to the Fifteenth District in Sherman. Jury selection began on March 11, 1941, and Judge Robert Cleveland Slagle, Jr. granted a defense motion for a severance. Acker's trial opened March 14, and Judge Slagle heard defense arguments challenging the legality of Acker and Fowler's apprehension at the filling station. Asserting all evidence was predicated on inadmissible testimony, the defendants' two attorneys moved for a mistrial and an instructed verdict of not guilty. However, the judge dismissed their motions. Acker was found guilty on the fifteenth and sentenced to two to ninety-nine years in prison. After a continuance, Fowler's trial opened on June 11. He was convicted four days later and received the same sentence as his accomplice.[108]

In the early months of 1941, Gonzaullas worked an eleven-week labor strike at the Rodgers-Wade Furniture Factory in Paris. Beginning on December 16, 1940, the members of Local No. 137, Upholsterers' International Union, which was affiliated with the American Federation of Labor, demanded a 25 percent wage increase, a forty-hour workweek, and a closed shop agreement. The walkout was marred by violence in the initial stages, and company executives called for the presence of Rangers. Along with Privates Bob Crowder, Ernest Daniel, and Alva Barr, the captain arrived on January 22 and opened an investigation. After six weeks of forced idleness, Rodgers-Wade resumed operations on the twenty-seventh with forty willing employees. In the meantime, the state officers erected a small frame building near the furniture factory from which to keep watch. They maintained strict neutrality toward picketers and strikebreakers alike. Gonzaullas commented, "the rights of the strikers to peaceful picketing and all other legal means will be upheld just as firmly as the legal rights of the company." Three factory employees were physically attacked on February 19, and seven strikers were arrested by the following morning. Criminal complaints were filed in Lamar County Court ranging from use of abusive language, to simple assault, to aggravated assault, to rioting. Management and union officials finally reached a compromise agreement on March 1, but Gonzaullas remained in Paris for more than a week to guarantee peace.[109]

On August 25, 1942, Gonzaullas led five Rangers in raids on Denison establishments. Fifty slot machines were confiscated, and thirty-six persons were arrested. The perpetrators were brought before Judge Carlisle Barton Carroll's municipal court. The seized machines were slated for the salvage drive in support of the war effort.[110]

Gonzaullas would be repeatedly asked throughout his career how many men he killed in the line of duty. Seventy-five has proven to be the number most frequently cited by others, no matter how improbable that total. The captain himself categorically denied the figure, but he also never answered the question. Instead, he told one reporter, "Just write that I found it necessary to kill several … But I will say this: I would rather be tried for killing six outlaws, than to have one of them tried for killing me."[111]

One such confirmed incident occurred after Robert Lacy Cash and Cleo Andrews absconded from the Retrieve Prison Farm in Brazoria County on January 21, 1943. Cash had received a life sentence for the 1937 murder of a traveling salesman in Dallas. Andrews was imprisoned on robbery and burglary convictions in Harrison and Upshur Counties. Five days after the escape, Gonzaullas learned from an informant that the fugitives were en route to Gladewater. The captain and Upshur County Sheriff James Gordon Anderson, Gregg County Sheriff Lonnie Ray Smith, three deputies, a constable, a Gregg County District Attorney's investigator, and Rangers Robert Logan "Bob" Badgett and Richard "Dick" Oldham spotted the escapees' stolen automobile in front of a nightclub on the Gladewater–Gilmer highway. The law officers blocked the car with their own three vehicles and called on the fugitives to surrender. Skidding to a halt, the wanted men instead opened fire, and the lawmen responded. Lacy was struck thirty times, and Andrews was apparently also disabled. Gonzaullas and Sheriff Smith approached the bullet-riddled getaway car, and the captain opened the front passenger door with his right hand. He held his pistol in the other.[112]

"Look out. Cap, I believe he's playing 'possum!" Sheriff Anderson warned from the other side of the vehicle.[113] Gonzaullas automatically stepped back as Andrews shot at him at point-blank range. The bullet pierced the Ranger's suit coat and grazed his shoulder, but "Lone Wolf's left-handed shooting with a 1911 Colt .45 was dead on and dead right, an empty magazine and Cleo's cold-eyed vacant stare mute validation."[114]

Another encounter with escaped felons occurred when Collins Monroe Mershon and Walter Henry LeMay bolted from the Retrieve farm on April 18 and embarked on a seven-week-long crime spree. The fugitives committed a string of robberies, car thefts, safecracking, burglaries, and assaults across a dozen counties. Believing the pair would target stores in Dallas, Gonzaullas and Police Inspector John Will Fritz made plans to trap them. Through an informant, the authorities learned Mershon and LeMay were staying in a house on Michigan Avenue in Trinity Heights. Gonzaullas, Fritz, and other officers surveilled the residence for two days before a maroon sedan stopped in front of the house on June 5. Mershon and LeMay, and a companion later identified as Steve Roberts, were observed in the vehicle. Fritz and Detectives John Taylor Luther and Leon Marsh began to approach when suddenly the car roared away.[115]

With the policemen in hot pursuit, the convicts' automobile flew across Michigan, Alaska, and Lancaster Streets at speeds nearing one hundred miles per hour. Fritz and Luther shot at the rear tires of the fleeing car, which failed to make a turn onto Ledbetter Drive, careened over a ditch, and came to rest in a clump of neck-high Johnson grass. The city detectives opened fire, and Mershon and Roberts surrendered. LeMay disappeared into the woods and grass around Five-Mile Creek. Summoned by police radio, some twenty squad cars responded to the scene, and officers fanned out to secure the perimeter. Three Luscombe monoplanes were called from nearby Curry Field to circle overhead and search for the fugitive. Soon arriving with Crowder and Rangers Tully Elwyn Seay and Norman Kemp "Dick" Dixon, Gonzaullas quickly discovered LeMay's trail.[116]

Evading the search parties for three hours, the convict broke into the garage of a residence on Burnside Avenue and hid in a large storage closet. The Lone Wolf approached the garage, entered, and made his way to the cabinet. He opened the door and found a disappointed LeMay. After being taken into custody, LeMay was questioned by lawmen from six different counties, and assisted them in clearing approximately forty-five robberies and burglaries. The thief, Mershon, and Roberts were indicted on forty-eight counts.[117]

Worsening socioeconomic conditions and wartime shortages mixed with Jim Crow Era prejudices in 1943 to exacerbate racial divisions throughout the country. That year, Los Angeles, Detroit, New York, Mobile, Philadelphia, Baltimore, Newark, St. Louis, and Washington, DC were scenes of racial violence. The port city of Beaumont, Texas, was torn by strife when Mae Yelton, a white twenty-three-year-old mother, accused an unnamed black man of sexual assault on June 15. The alleged victim's husband was employed at the Pennsylvania Shipyards. Later that night, more than two thousand of his fellow workers and another one thousand outraged townspeople marched on City Hall. Although the victim could not identify her attacker, the increasingly frenzied mob dispersed into smaller packs and vandalized the black downtown district in what became known as the "Night of Terror." The rioters moved into black neighborhoods in the central and north sections of Beaumont. Stores and restaurants were pillaged, several buildings were torched, and more than one hundred residences were ransacked. Fifty people were injured, and Ellis Brown, a white man, and John Johnson, an African American, were killed. Several months later, Alex Mouton, another black man, died of the vicious injuries he had received.[118]

Beaumont Mayor George "Red" Gary mobilized the Eighteenth Battalion of the Texas State Guard, and Police Chief Ross Dickey and Sheriff William Wallace Richardson, Jr. readied their officers. Adjutant General Arthur Balfour Knickerbocker dispatched additional units from Port Arthur, Houston, Liberty, Conroe, Livingston, Nacogdoches, Lufkin, and Baytown. Eighteen hundred guardsmen, one hundred highway patrolmen, and seventy-five Rangers, including Gonzaullas, arrived in town that night. Hardy Purvis, John J. Klevenhagen, and Edward Lee "Eddie" Oliver came from Houston, and the Company A captain took charge of the situation. The Highway Patrol quickly closed all roads leading into and out of town, and a curfew of 8:30 p.m. was imposed. On the sixteenth, State Senator Alexander Mack Aikin, Jr., acting as governor in the absences of Governor Coke Robert Stevenson and Lieutenant Governor John Lee Smith, declared martial law. Production at shipyards, steel mills, and refineries was halted. Mayor Gary closed all liquor dispensaries, parks, and playgrounds, cancelled every public gathering, and ordered black workers to stay home. Purvis led several hundred persons in searching the woods three miles northwest of town for Mrs. Yelton's alleged attacker; no arrest was made. Rangers, highway patrolmen, and guardsmen patrolled the city, and more than three hundred rioters were apprehended. Due to the large numbers of prisoners, the overflow from the city and county jails were transferred to an impromptu barbed-wire stockade at the Jefferson County fairgrounds. Lieutenant Colonel Sidney Caldwell Mason, commanding the enforcement of martial law, convened a military tribunal on June 17, and Lieutenant Colonel Royal Phillips, acting in his wartime role as assistant chief of staff for intelligence, heard the cases of those arrested. By the twentieth, twenty-nine were charged with assault and battery, unlawful assembly, and arson, and remanded to the custody of the civil authorities. The remainder were released due to a lack of evidence. Aikin cancelled martial law on the same day. Phillips closed his inquiry on June 22, and only 206 out of thousands of rioters were brought to trial. None received serious sentences, and those responsible for the three deaths went unpunished. Moreover, Mrs. Yelton, the alleged rape victim, had received a physical examination on the seventeenth, and Doctor Barker Daniel Chunn, Sr. determined she had neither been assaulted nor recently engaged in intercourse.[119]

Doctor Roy Elwin Hunt and his wife, Mattie Mae, were murdered in their Littlefield home on October 26. The couple's bound and blood-soaked bodies were found by their five-year-old daughter, Jo Ann, in the master bedroom. After being incapacitated by an anesthetic, the doctor had died instantly from a gunshot wound to the head, while Mrs. Hunt suffered a fatal blow to her skull. Jo Ann reported seeing her parents' killer before he forced her into a closet and rendered her unconscious with chloroform. James Clyde "Jim" Thomas, a sometime enforcer for Dallas gambling czar Lester Ben "Benny" Binion, quickly became the prime suspect in the murder. When arrested for a parole violation on October 27, he had one hundred dollars on his person and admitted he had possessed $720 a few days previously. However, Thomas claimed he had borrowed the money from a friend in Amarillo and lost most of it in a poker game. Fortuitously, the investigation benefitted from a spirit of cooperation that ran across jurisdictional lines. On October 31, Lamb County Sheriff Samuel Evin "Sam" Hutson followed a trail of clues through Waco, Temple, Houston, and Galveston. During his stay in Central Texas, Hutson conferred with Detective Captain Marvin Burton and McLennan County Sheriff Homer Casey. Captain Benjamin Maney Gault planned a trip to Waco and Cameron to follow a lead, while Gonzaullas and his Rangers questioned several people in Dallas.[120]

Sheriff Hutson announced to the press on November 2 that a telephone call from Galveston to the Panhandle on the morning of the Hunt homicide had been traced to Thomas, an ex-convict. The call was made to a lady friend of the felon in order to establish an alibi that he was with a married woman in the Oleander City. The knots used to bind the Hunts were thought to be the same that had trussed Lenro and Laurine Keeton in a March 1940 robbery of their Lubbock residence. Furthermore, the Keetons had been left under the influence of an anesthetic, which led investigators to connect the two crimes. Thomas had been arrested and questioned but not charged.[121]

Thomas was indicted for the Hunt murders on April 10, 1944, by the Lamb County grand jury. Bond was set at $25,000. Thomas was tried in Sixty-fourth District Court in Plainview and convicted on August 30; he received the death penalty. As his previous criminal record was discussed in the jury room, Judge Clarence Dallas Russell declared a mistrial and granted Thomas a new trial. Given a change of venue, the defendant faced the jury once more on January 8, 1945, as the 106th District Court convened in Lemesa. The effort availed him nothing, though, as he was found guilty and sentenced to death.[122]

For some time, the gamblers of Dallas had been allowed to operate freely provided they paid a weekly fine; the system had garnered the city coffers thousands of dollars every year. However, the policy was abruptly reversed; Gonzaullas and his company cooperated with Dallas police on November 10, 1944, in closing gambling operations. A number of Rangers were brought to town to participate in the sweep, and identical actions were conducted in Fort Worth, San Antonio, and Houston. In Dallas, Gonzaullas's raiders found only empty rooms in buildings where gambling had previously flourished. The captain believed gaming operators had been warned of the raids, and refused to comment on how long the shutdown would last.[123]

One year later, a series of murders occurred that would prove to be Gonzaullas's most famous and confounding case. On February 22, 1946, a young couple, parked along a lover's lane on the outskirts of Texarkana, was attacked by a tall, possibly masked, man. The pistol-armed assailant beat the male victim, twenty-five-year-old James Mack "Jimmy" Hollis, unconscious with his weapon, then vaginally violated nineteen-year-old Mary Jeanne Larey with a foreign object (likely the barrel of his handgun). The savage attack left Hollis with a fractured skull, and both suffered severe emotional trauma, but they survived. Two more victims—twenty-nine-year-old Richard Lanier Griffin and seventeen-year-old Polly Ann Moore—were not so lucky. They were found on March 24, each shot in the back of the head with a .32-caliber pistol while in a parked car off Highway 67, south of the previous crime scene. Significantly, there was no indication on the bodies of an antemortem beating, but contradictory reports seem to indicate Moore was the victim of a sexual assault. Likewise notable, the crime scene was contaminated by sloppy local law enforcement personnel and curious bystanders, which may have led to the obliteration of usable physical evidence. Ranger James Newton "Jim" Geer arrived in Texarkana the following day to lend his assistance to Bowie County Sheriff William Hardy "Bill" Presley. Joined by Dick Oldham on March 26, Geer followed more than two hundred leads, but none of them panned out.[124]

On April 14, officers discovered the body of seventeen-year-old Paul James Martin in a ditch in Spring Lake Park, two miles from his abandoned vehicle. Investigators established Martin's identity and ascertained he had been with Betty Jo Booker, age fifteen, when last seen. The lawmen organized a search for the missing girl, and, six hours later, she was found a mile away under a pine tree where she had been raped and murdered. Both victims had struggled with their assailant before being gunned down with a .32 pistol.[125]

With this second double homicide, Gonzaullas departed for Texarkana to assume personal command of the Rangers' investigation. He directed all six men of Company B to follow him to the town. Several highway patrolmen in four radio-equipped patrol cars, and four technicians from the state crime lab were also dispatched to the scene. The resident FBI agent in Texarkana was requested to photograph the scene and dust Martin's vehicle for latent fingerprints. Even as the state officers arrived in town, so too did the media. While cooperating with Sheriff Presley, Gonzaullas's sheer force of personality made him the prominent figure in the investigation, although newspaper editors and other law officers would criticize his courting of the press. "We're up against a clever, intelligent killer," the captain told reporters. "We have information, but I can't give it to the public. We are working day and night on every possible lead." Suspects were brought in for questioning from over a hundred miles away, and authorities requested a voluntary midnight curfew on April 16. Reportedly missing from Martin's car was Betty Jo's alto saxophone, and one early person of interest was taken into custody after he attempted to sell a similar instrument to a Corpus Christi music store on April 20. However, he was eliminated from the investigation. In an effort to be as thorough as possible, one bullet and one shell casing recovered from the Martin-Booker crime scene were sent to the FBI's world-famous laboratory in Washington, DC. Analysis of the ammunition confirmed the same type of weapon was used to kill the four victims. Citizens and local lawmen raised the reward for information to $5,965. With a shadowy killer in their midst, the forty thousand citizens of Texarkana were virtually in a state of panic.[126]

The "Phantom Slayer," as he was dubbed by the *Texarkana Daily News*, possibly struck again on May 3, this time at a farmhouse ten miles from

Texarkana, on U.S. Highway 67 in Miller County, Arkansas. Walter Virgil Starks, an area farmer, was sitting in his parlor listening to the radio when he was fatally shot in the back of the head. The assailant, who was outside, fired several more .22-caliber bullets through the window, hitting Katherine Ila "Katie" Starks twice in the face, then attempted to enter the house. The seriously wounded and horrified woman raced to a neighbor's home across the road. Investigators later determined the murderer had broken in through the back door as Mrs. Starks exited the front. For whatever reason, he did not follow her.[127]

Gonzaullas and other investigators rushed to the scene. Having walked through Stark's blood on the floor, the killer left a trail leading outside where the muddy ground, thanks to a recent rain, allowed the lawmen to follow his footprints to the road. Presumably, the suspect climbed into an automobile and escaped, but a .22 bullet and a red metal flashlight were recovered from where they had been dropped. Shell casings collected outside the house indicated the murder weapon was likely a Colt Woodsman semiautomatic pistol. The items did not provide any clues, and no physical evidence was located that pointed to the killer's identity. Whether the Starks murder was committed by the same perpetrator as those credited to the Phantom Slayer was a subject of debate for the investigating officers. The reason the killer used a different caliber weapon in this instance, some theorized, was because the media had reported his ammunition of choice, and he disposed of the gun. Gonzaullas personally believed Starks had been murdered by a second individual.[128]

In the midst of the homicide investigation, a five-year-old girl was assaulted in town, but the attacker fled her screams before he could complete his repugnant act. Sheriff Presley arrested Homer Lee King, aged twenty, within a short time of receiving the report, and deposited him in an undisclosed jail. After Gonzaullas and District Attorney Weldon Glass interviewed the suspect, King was charged with assault with intent to commit rape. County officials cautioned the public against connecting the attack with the five unsolved murders. The following month, Gonzaullas spoke to assembled peace officers during the semiannual training conference hosted by the FBI at the Dreyfuss Club on White Rock Lake. He outlined the progress made in the case to that point and requested the attendees' assistance.[129]

Elsewhere, following a seven-week shutdown in Corsicana marked by two instances of violence, the Corsicana Cotton Mills reopened on July 16 under police supervision. Eighty-four employees entered the gates, while picketers continued to march in protest. District Judge Augustus Pace Mays had issued an injunction against members of Local 77, United Textile Workers of America, and set a hearing on the restraining order for July 25. Taking a respite from the Texarkana case, Gonzaullas and Ernest Daniel were on hand. The captain signed a felony complaint on union worker Johnnie Williams for preventing a nonunion employee from entering the plant. After appearing before Justice of the Peace William Henson Johnson, Williams was released from jail on a three-thousand-dollar bond. The following day, the scene was calm, as each party went about their business. The captain predicted law enforcement officers would not be further needed.[130]

Returning to Texarkana, Gonzaullas announced on October 30 he was investigating whether Martin Stover Tuley, an ex-convict and Van Alystyne farmer, had any connection to the recent murders. The suspect had been charged with the rape of a sixteen-year-old girl in Wylie on the twenty-seventh. District Attorney Dwight Whitewell pressed for an early trial and signaled his intention to ask for the death penalty. Gonzaullas was not convinced of the man's guilt and directed Ranger Dixon to interrogate Tuley. They concluded the suspect was not the Phantom Slayer, although Tuley was convicted of rape and sentenced to fifty years in the penitentiary. Another, perhaps more promising, suspect surfaced in June 1947 with the arrest of Youell Lee Swinney and his wife, Peggy Lois, on a charge of auto theft. Youell made seven incriminating statements that led investigators to consider him a person of interest. Under questioning, Peggy confessed that Swinney was the Texarkana Phantom, although the details of her story changed over time. While certain portions of her accounts were confirmed, Peggy was determined to be an unreliable witness, and she refused to testify against her husband in court. Authorities were divided on whether Swinney was the killer they had sought for months. The Rangers and Sheriff Presley were not convinced, as the evidence they had was only circumstantial. Instead,

Swinney was convicted of auto theft as a habitual offender, and received a sentence of life imprisonment.[131]

Remaining skeptical of Swinney's guilt in the five murders, Gonzaullas ordered his men to unobtrusively return to their home stations in August. He hoped their quiet departure would keep the killer from realizing the Rangers had gone and resuming his murderous endeavors. The captain had attempted every investigative tactic at his command but, devoid of any new leads, the Phantom murders would remain unsolved.[132]

Seaman Irving Goodspeed was charged with the murder of *Dallas Morning News* contract carrier Martin Camp on October 31, 1946. The victim's body had been discovered on the roadside five miles east of Bowie. His blood-stained and fire-damaged automobile was found in an alley in Alvord. Fleeing the country to Brazil, Goodspeed was arrested by local police aboard the oiler SS *Denison Victory* on December 6. The United States and Brazil had no extradition treaty, and months were spent in negotiating the fugitive's return to face justice. Ranger Bob Badgett and Montague County Sheriff John Leland "Buck" Jameson flew to Santos, Brazil, and escorted their prisoner home aboard the SS *Murray M. Blum*. While in port in Victoria, Brazil, on March 9, Goodspeed was able to escape the ship for less than twenty-fours before being recaptured. He then spent the remainder of the twenty-four-day voyage in irons. Landing in New Orleans on March 31, the lawmen and the fugitive were greeted by Gonzaullas and Denton newsman William T. "Bill" Rives, both of whom escorted the party to Dallas. Goodspeed was placed in the Dallas County jail on April 1, 1947, and held until his trial in Bowie.[133]

In April 1947, two Liberty ships, the SS *Grandcamp* and the SS *High Flyer*, were moored six hundred feet apart at the Port of Texas City. On the sixteenth, at 8:00 a.m., the *Grandcamp's* cargo, 2,100 metric tons of ammonium nitrate fertilizer, caught fire and exploded more than an hour later. The blast destroyed the Monsanto Chemical Corporation plant, nearly one thousand buildings in town were leveled, and the detonation's heat ignited spilled benzol, propane, and ethylbenzene. People 250 miles away in Louisiana felt the shockwave. Firefighters from neighboring jurisdictions, military personnel, and medical staff from the University of Texas at Galveston rushed to the scene. Ignited by the blast, the 872 metric tons of ammonium nitrate and sixteen hundred metric tons of sulfur aboard the *High Flyer* detonated at 1:10 a.m. The two explosions and numerous secondary fires that burned for a week killed approximately 581 people, including thirty volunteer firefighters. Eight hundred and forty-four dependents, many without resources, were forced to struggle for basic survival. Captain Fred Olsen initially led the Rangers dispatched to the devastated town, and eight more Rangers, including Bob Crowder, were ordered on April 17 to reinforce the state police presence. Governor Beauford Halbert Jester declared a state of emergency the same day. On the twentieth, the shell-shocked citizens of Texas City were alarmed to discover a naphtha tank, which had been blown two miles by the explosion into the Republic Oil refinery, was leaking fumes. Officials calmed the public, as workers pumped the tank dry. In anticipation of curious onlookers rushing to the scene, the DPS deployed sixteen additional officers and placed Gonzaullas in overall charge.[134]

Fresh from the worst disaster in the state's history since the 1900 Galveston hurricane, Gonzaullas next worked another labor strike. On June 19, the captain, some of his Rangers, and local law officers rushed to Clarksville to keep the peace when tomato growers protested processors enacting a price drop on their product. The decrease from eight cents per pound to four cents resulted in some farmers threatening others with violence if the latter should agree to the reduction. Once Gonzaullas and the other peace officers arrived, the price rose to five cents. While tomato markets at Avery, DeKalb, and Boxelder were disturbed, Red River County Sheriff Taylor Franklin McCoy observed growers peacefully frequenting the packing sheds the next day.[135]

As the members of the Greatest Generation returned home from foreign battlefields, they sought to realize the American Dream through higher education and homeownership. Across the nation, veterans wanted to block memories of bombed-out towns, jungle firefights, and sinking ships with a peaceful suburbia and upward social and economic mobility. Many in the South decided to take part in the democratic process for which they fought, and campaigned as reform candidates against organized crime, entrenched political machines, and public corruption. In Dallas County, William Reid Wilson and Steve Guthrie, both former army officers, were swept into office during this wave of local "GI revolts." On January 1, 1947, the day Wilson was sworn-in as district attorney, Benny Binion left for Las Vegas, although he kept his policy racket under the management of trusted subordinate Harry Urban, Sr. Even with the gambling boss's departure, vice rings nevertheless continued to run rampant in West Dallas and Deep Ellum. Reported widely in the newspapers, Chicago racketeers failed to induce Sheriff Guthrie into tacitly allowing gambling in the county. In response, Gonzaullas led a dogged effort in fifty-eight northeast Texas counties beginning in early January 1947 to enforce gaming laws. During the first night of the drive, the Rangers found all known gambling establishments closed in Dallas and Fort Worth. Thus, no arrests were made, and no gaming paraphernalia was seized.[136]

Top O'Hill Terrace, owned by Fred Browning, had continued to operate since Tom Hickman's ill-starred 1935 raid. At the behest of a Fort Worth pastor, Gonzaullas raided the notorious gaming club shortly before midnight on August 11, 1947. The Lone Wolf, Rangers Crowder and Badgett, and Special Investigator Dub Naylor from Austin crawled through the woods behind the mansion for several hundred yards until they reached the back of the establishment. They surreptitiously waited until the attendant opened the rear exit for some patrons. Before the door could close, the lawmen were inside, and they surprised everyone at the tables in the subterranean casino. Browning, his eight attendants, and fifty of his clientele were arrested, and all the high-priced gaming equipment was confiscated. The defendants appeared before Justice of the Peace Frank Hurley the following morning, and Browning personally paid the fines of his employees and patrons—$2,267 in total. Gonzaullas had to be content with destroying the equipment, which was valued at $25,000. The captain declined to file felony charges, as the court actions would "embarrass prominent Fort Worth and Dallas citizens." Receiving protests from citizens who objected to a person's prominence being a factor in filing cases, Tarrant County District Attorney Alfred Milton Clyde, Sr. requested the grand juror subpoena Gonzaullas and the rest of the raiding party for questioning. Ultimately, despite periodic raids, Top O'Hill remained in business until Browning's death on October 30, 1953.[137]

Gonzaullas, Oldham, Stanley, Geer, Daniel, Selwyn Hodge Denson, and Lewis C. Rigler traveled to Marshall to investigate unrest at Wiley

College, a historically black institution. On January 5, 1948, students gathered to oppose the expulsion of twenty-five undergraduates involved in a strike the previous autumn. Two days later, the demonstrators stood in front of the administration building and issued a statement announcing they would continue to protest until the ousted members were reinstated. The college reported only 10 percent of the student body was attending classes. On January 8, as the seven Rangers remained ready to protect property and lives on campus, Sheriff Barry Rosborough served temporary restraining orders on the twenty-five students.[138]

The Citizens State Bank of Buffalo in Leon County was robbed on February 27 by a lone bandit. The gunman escaped with two thousand dollars, and his getaway car, stolen in Corsicana three days prior, was later discovered on a dead-end road off Highway 75. Investigators believed he had been picked up by an unknown accomplice. Gonzaullas took charge of the three hundred federal, state, and local officers conducting the search, including Leon County Sheriff Benjamin Guy Lee, Anderson County Sheriff Leroy Paul Stanford, and Freestone County Sheriff James Rogers "Jim" Sessions, Sr. An analysis of fingerprints recovered from the vehicle revealed the suspect was ex-convict Bernice Lee Franklin. He was apprehended in a Texarkana, Arkansas, dance hall on March 16 and transported to Waco to face federal charges. At the time of his arrest, Franklin had $867 on his person, money that was subsequently confirmed to have come from the Buffalo bank.[139]

Missing since July 1948, the body of Dallas salesman George Samuel "Jack" Rose was found on September 15 in a shallow grave on the bank of Kentucky Lake one mile from Highway 70 near Camden, Tennessee. An autopsy determined the cause of death was a single gunshot to the skull under the left ear. Working under the coordination of Gonzaullas, investigators determined Rose had been killed on Highway 6 in Bosque County during a hunting trip. An argument over a planned robbery of the First National Bank of Dallas had culminated in the murder. Jim Harvey "Red" Corbett was charged in his death, and Frederick E. Miller and Stanley Arthur Tousant were named as accessories. The three were extradited from Florida where they had been held on warrants for armed robbery in Ohio. Corbett and Miller attempted to pin the blame on each other, and the former led police to the victim's grave. Rose's widow made a positive identification through his clothing and dental work. Corbett was held in the Cleburne jail without bond, while the other two were each released on $2,500 bail.[140]

Corbett was indicted by the Bosque County grand jury and tried in Fifty-second District Court in Meridian in November. Gonzaullas testified, and Corbett was convicted and sentenced to twenty-five years. Miller and Tousant waived jury trials, and Judge Robert Bates Cross immediately sentenced the pair to two years.[141]

The Phantom Killer case returned to the public consciousness when Gonzaullas questioned a man who had admitted to killing a couple in Waco. The suspect had reportedly arrived from Texarkana three years before the most recent murders. Ranger Stewart traveled to Bowie County to investigate and concluded the man had been in California during the five murders in 1946. Indeed, he moved to Waco directly from the Golden State rather than stopping in Texarkana.[142]

Gonzaullas and Rangers Badgett, Daniel, Rigler, and E. J. "Jay" Banks raided the Hi-Lite Club in Sherman on July 30, 1949. Local authorities were not involved, and the state lawmen arrested thirty prominent Grayson County citizens. The patrons pled guilty to misdemeanor charges in Ralph Oliver's justice court, paid their fines, and were released. The club's owner and eight employees were charged with operating a gaming establishment and released on $750 bond. Judge Slagle called the Fifteenth District Court's grand jury into special session on August 9 and empowered the members to investigate gambling. [143]

As the decade neared its end, Dallas was threatened with a gangland war between rival gambling rings. Mildred Noble, the wife of gambler Herbert "The Cat" Noble, was killed on November 29 in front of their Oak Cliff home by a car bomb meant for her husband. The widower believed the murder had been orchestrated from Las Vegas by Benny Binion. With Noble's chief nemesis out of reach, Hollis Delois "Lois" Green, a Binion associate who had likely carried out the killing, was slain on December 23 after leaving a Christmas party at the Sky-Vu Club. In retaliation, Noble was shot in front of his house on New Year's Eve, but he recovered. Gonzaullas and his men observed the situation, although neither the city nor county law enforcement agencies requested assistance.[144]

The Rangers were welcome in Mexia where games of chance were common, and Gonzaullas, Joe Thompson, and other members of Company B raided night clubs in town on December 17 and 18. Three trailer loads of slot machines were seized and transported to Dallas. Additionally, complaints were filed against eleven club owners in Justice of the Peace Roy Kirton's court.[145]

Dallas and Mexia were not alone in their rampant vice problems. The *Morning News* ran a piece on October 8, 1950, that alleged Tarrant County was rife with illegal gambling. The unnamed journalist informed his readers he had personally placed bets in several gambling houses in the Fort Worth area. District Attorney Stewart Walton Hellman acknowledged gambling occurred in the county, but insisted it had not reached the proportions experienced in Dallas and other locales. He called for a grand jury investigation to examine the reporter's assertions but subsequently proved reluctant in prosecuting the thirty-two indicted gamblers and one law officer. Gonzaullas allegedly commented to the *Fort Worth Press* that gambling had once occurred but was now a thing of the past. Several days later, though, he denied making the assertion and proclaimed he had been misquoted: "It's a ridiculous statement. You could not make such a statement about any city. There is gambling in Fort Worth and Dallas and almost every American city."[146]

On May 3, 1951, Gonzaullas submitted his retirement letter to Colonel Homer Garrison, effective July 31. He cited his sixtieth birthday and his desire to enter a new field of endeavor that would allow him to spend more time with Laura. In summarizing his thirty-one-year career, Gonzaullas said:

> When I first joined the Texas Rangers and took the oath … it was the fulfillment of all my boyish hopes and dreams. At times, the long road was rough and rugged, and the life dangerous, but regardless of the nature of my assignments, I have always endeavored, to the best of my ability, to meticulously obey and carry out orders in the true traditional Ranger form. Now, as I am about to come to the close of my long Ranger career, it is indeed gratifying to know that I have contributed in some small way to the success and progress of one of the finest world renowned Law Enforcement Organizations, and I shall

> always cherish the fond memories of the many years that I have served in same, and been associated with the wonderful personnel that makes up this magnificent body.[147]

His plans to leave the Rangers were publicly announced the following month. On July 10, Henderson County Sheriff Jess Sweeten, an old friend and a staunch supporter of the DPS, organized a large retirement party for the Ranger captain. The function was held at the Koon Kreek Club near Athens. Colonel Garrison and his headquarters staff, fifteen Rangers, and numerous peace officers from across Texas assembled to pay tribute to the legendary lawman. On behalf of Company B, Bob Crowder, his successor, presented Gonzaullas with an engraved leather briefcase, while another well-wisher gave him a pen and pencil set. The Lone Wolf, "one of the last of the old-time, quick-drawing Texas Rangers," spoke well of the Rangers of the 1950s, praising their embracement of education and modern equipment. He commended Garrison as a leader, "I was never given a bad order or told to pull a punch. I was just told to be fair to everybody and I've tried to do it."[148]

By the time of his retirement, Gonzaullas had amassed a collection of 580 firearms, as well as an assortment of knives, clubs, and other weapons taken off the criminals he put behind bars. Several of his handguns were extravagant weapons presented to him by admirers, including a matched set he carried in the early 1930s. Given to the Ranger as a birthday present, they were Colt Single Action Army .45-caliber revolvers elaborately engraved and inlaid with gold. The grips were ivory and decorated with the head of a longhorn steer and embossed with gold. At the time he wore them, the pistols were valued at eight hundred dollars. In his final month as a Ranger, Gonzaullas parted with the vast majority of his collection and only retained three matched pairs of handguns—two 1911 .45 semiautomatics, two .44 revolvers, and two Smith & Wesson .38s. These six were inscribed with his famous axiom: "Never draw me without cause nor shield me with dishonor."[149]

While keeping his Dallas home, Gonzaullas commuted to Los Angles to work as a technical advisor for Columbia Studios. His major efforts were first spent on the radio program "Tales of the Texas Rangers" starring Joel McCrea. Bob Goss once sardonically said of his former partner, "The most dangerous place in Texas is between Gonzaullas and a camera." However, according to Lewis Rigler, he was slated to make an introductory statement for the show in front of a film crew. Unfortunately, even after twenty takes, Gonzaullas was unable to overcome a severe case of stage fright, and another opening needed to be made. Despite the former Ranger's case of nerves, the broadcast later spawned a successful television series produced by Stacy Keach, Sr. through Columbia's subsidiary, Screen Gems. Gonzaullas acted as a consultant for fifty-two episodes of the television version, and several of the show's story lines were drawn from the captain's real-life experiences. He also worked for Universal-International in advising on *The Lawless Breed* directed by Raoul Walsh and starring Rock Hudson as John Wesley Hardin. After five years in Tinsel Town, though, Gonzaullas and Laura permanently returned to Texas, where they both served on the board of directors at Gaston Episcopal Hospital. Manuel also acted as president of the hospital.[150]

Even while he worked with Hollywood producers and directors, Gonzaullas did not lose his interest in Texas law enforcement. The former captain appeared before the federal grand jury in Fort Worth on March 18, 1952, and testified on crime in the state. Convening the day before, the twenty-three panel members also met with six police chiefs, two senior police officers, two district attorneys, and an Episcopal minister.[151]

On June 25, 1957, Gonzaullas was subpoenaed to appear before the Travis County grand jury to answer questions concerning businessman Ben Jack Cage's operations. The former Ranger had been employed by a Cage subsidiary, the Atlas Alarm Corporation, three years prior to the summons. Atlas had existed as a corporate entity from December 1, 1953, to July 26, 1954. The grand jury was investigating the collapse of ICT Insurance Company, another Cage business, earlier in the year. The panel members were also inquiring into the alleged bribery of several Texas lawmakers. Gonzaullas was asked by reporters if he was once more working for the state. He replied, "I have no connection directly or indirectly with the investigation of the Ben Jack Cage corporation." He testified on the stand he did not work for ICT, although the two companies shared the same office building. In his only personal interaction with Cage, Gonzaullas had signed a contract to serve six months as vice president, and another six on retainer.[152]

In retirement, Gonzaullas became interested in preserving the history of the Texas Rangers. On October 15, 1968, he attended the ceremony dedicating the Homer Garrison, Jr. Museum at Fort Fisher in Waco. Gonzaullas was the guest of honor at a function on December 15 at the museum. As part of the ceremony, an oil portrait of the retired captain created by artist Holmes Ed Jones and donated to the City of Waco was put on permanent display. Also in attendance were Colonel Wilson Edward "Pat" Speir, Doctor Henry Jackson Flanders, Jr. of Waco's First Baptist Church, Roger Norman Conger, and Father Mark Deering of the St. Louis Catholic Church. The Texas Legislature created the Texas Ranger Commemorative Commission to celebrate the approaching 150th anniversary of the Ranger service. Gonzaullas had meanwhile become interested in the Texas Rangers Association, and Captain Clint Peoples appointed him to the Commemorative Commission in 1972. The organization was intent on raising one million dollars in donations to construct a hall of fame next to Fort Fisher. Ground was broken for the new Texas Ranger Hall of Fame on August 4, 1973, but Gonzaullas, visiting California at the time, was forced to send his regrets.[153]

Captain Gonzaullas died of pancreatic cancer and arteriosclerotic heart disease at Gaston Hospital in Dallas on February 13, 1977. His remains were cremated at the Restland Crematory, and the ashes were dispersed in Restland's Urn Scattering Garden on February 15.[154]

Colonel Garrison once disclosed the reason for Gonzaullas' success: he was a "master of planning and he was always ready for any eventuality. When he went on a case he figured that anything might happen and he planned for it. He also gave thought to what he would do if he were in the other fellow's place."[155] "In my opinion," the director asserted, "Captain Gonzaullas will go down in history as one of the great Rangers of all time."[156]

On May 26, the House of Representatives adopted a resolution that paid tribute to Gonzaullas and extended its sympathies to his widow. When the legislature adjourned for the day, the body did so in his memory. The Senate concurred and adopted the resolution the following day.[157]

Laura died on arrival at Presbyterian Hospital on August 15, 1978, of arteriosclerotic cardiac disease. She too was cremated at Restland Crematory and, while Restland has no record of the event, likely her ashes were also scattered in the garden.[158]

Following Laura's death, the executor of her estate traveled to Waco on March 1, 1980, to present a collection of memorabilia Gonzaullas had bequeathed the Texas Ranger Hall of Fame and Museum. The material included the captain's personal papers, five hundred photographs, a dozen books, and five scrapbooks containing thirteen hundred newspaper and magazine clippings.[159]

The life story of Manuel T. Gonzaullas reads like a great Western novel worthy of Owen Wister or Jack Schaefer. He arrived in Texas from an uncertain past, he served the cause of law and order with courage and distinction, he faced foes in mortal combat and prevailed, and he loved only one woman. Then, with no gravestone to mark his passing, he disappeared back into the mists of legend.

Marvin Burton. *Courtesy Janith Johnson.*

Chapter 6

Marvin Burton: "He Would Not Be Stampeded"

Marvin "Red" Burton was cut from the same cloth as frontier lawmen and earlier Texas Rangers. Whether his foe was the Ku Klux Klan, or a bootlegging ring, or any other villain, he would not be stampeded. He lived his life with a firm conviction in the ideals of justice and the law, although the aggressiveness with which he pursued wrongdoers sometimes led to pugnaciousness. Adjutant General William Warren Sterling remarked: "Tall, strong, and intelligent, Burton was more than a match for the shrewdest or toughest lawbreaker. He [had] the blue-gray eyes and soft voice of the natural fighting man." Furthermore, his work ethic, straightforward demeanor, and high standards inspired loyalty and respect among his colleagues.

He was born on August 10, 1885, on the family farm near Riesel, McLennan County, Texas. His father, John Fletcher Burton, was born in Mississippi on January 15, 1854, while his mother, Mary Alice (Cubley) Burton, was born on July 27, 1856. The elder Burton worked as a farmer, banker, and businessman, and served as a county commissioner. In addition to Marvin, John and Mary raised William Robert Burton, born in 1874; twins Laura Pearl Burton and John Carl Burton, born June 14, 1878; Luther Milton Burton, born January 28, 1880; and Travis Henson Burton, born May 18, 1883. Mary died on June 26, 1886, and was buried in Fletcher Cemetery south of Robinson. John married Mary Elizabeth "Mollie" Hudgins on December 20, 1888. She had been born in Scottsboro, Alabama, on August 17, 1857. They brought into the world Marvin's half-sisters Augusta Burton, born on August 1, 1891; Ellen Burton, on October 6, 1893; and Ruby Burton, on January 15, 1896.[1]

Marvin married Florence Mae Dill on August 19, 1903. She had been born on May 19, 1884, in Mountain Home, Arkansas. Following the wedding, he managed a ranch near Wortham that belonged to an aunt. They raised two daughters: Laura Mae, born on July 17, 1904, and Lula Alice, born on June 27, 1908.[2]

The family moved to Waco in 1913, where, using money saved over the previous eight years, Burton purchased a town lot and built a house at 2021 Proctor Street. He became a charter member of Herring Avenue Methodist Episcopal Church, South. After a brief time as a day laborer, he was employed by the Cleveland Construction Company as a foreman at the Texas Power & Light Company plant work site. Later, he was a foreman in a project at the old Sanger Brothers Department Store in downtown Waco. By August 1917, he was working for the Grace Construction Company and overseeing building projects at Rich Field.[3]

That same year would see the start of Burton's law enforcement career. The city of Waco, and McLennan County, were both having trouble retaining good officers. The political climate, low wages, and racial violence contributed to the problem. Indeed, the chief of police, Guy James McNamara, had calmly watched the extralegal execution of Jesse Washington from the mayor's office window in May 1916. The convicted man's torture-murder at the hands of vigilantes, in complete disregard for his life and Fifth Amendment rights, cast a pall over the city for years. In the first of many such occasions, the county commissioners drafted the tall, slender, and freckle-faced Burton to pin on a city policeman's badge in October 1917. Respecting the notion of public service, he reluctantly accepted on the condition he would do so for six months only. After a brief period of training, Burton's first assignment was to direct traffic at the intersection of Fourth Street and Austin Avenue using a manual stop/go sign. Eventually, he was transferred to night patrol, and rode a motorcycle through residential neighborhoods and the environs of the city. As time passed, and Burton grew more experienced, he began to reconsider his earlier decision to leave the police department after the half-year limit.[4]

Despite the newfound fascination with his occupation, Burton would soon be forced to make an important choice. On October 20, 1917, McLennan County residents voted in a local option election to ban the sale of intoxicating liquors. The resulting order, passed by the commissioners' court, drove many law officers into difficult ethical dilemmas. While some policemen across the country supplemented their meager salaries with payoffs and graft from rumrunners, the plain-spoken and moral Burton refused to take a bribe or otherwise cease in enforcing the law. Along with two other officers, he arrested five soldiers and a taxi driver on June 10, 1918, for possession of whiskey near Camp McArthur. When offers of money, promotions, and favors failed to move him, he was transferred to the daytime watch for "the good of the department." Disgusted with being punished for merely doing his sworn duty, Burton resigned and joined the sheriff's office in late 1919. He was soon chief deputy for Sheriff Robert Caldwell "Bob" Buchanan.[5]

Newspaper reports indicate Burton's duties as a deputy were mainly of a routine nature. He made arrests for a wide variety of offenses, including burglary, armed robbery, forgery, illegal gambling, running a "disorderly house," stolen automobiles, spousal abuse, assault, and murder. On March 29, 1920, under orders from Sheriff Buchanan and County Attorney Frank Burton Tirey, Sr., Burton, two other deputies, and an assistant county attorney visited the E. B. Reed Greater Show carnival and closed the games of chance that were in violation of the state's gaming laws. In the late spring, Buchanan announced a war on illegal bootleggers, and filed complaints in James Jefferson Padgett, Sr.'s justice court. The sheriff began his drive on May 22 when he and Burton made two separate raids, arrested one suspect each, and confiscated a pair of whiskey distilleries. The lawmen also seized a large quantity of liquor in various stages of manufacture. Sheriff Chesley Omer Moore of Falls County brought murder suspect Jesse Flores to the McLennan County lockup on November 4 for safekeeping. Flores was alleged to have killed Deputy Sheriff Oscar Bryant Sharp during a failed jailbreak in Marlin, and Moore had decided to move his prisoner as a precaution against possible mob violence. Coincidentally, Burton had been a member of the posse that previously arrested Flores on a robbery charge, which landed him in the Falls County jail. The prisoner remained in Waco only a short time before Burton took him to Hillsboro for a few days. Flores was brought back to Waco, then returned to Marlin for his trial and subsequent conviction. Burton was present with other Waco-McLennan lawmen in Marlin to witness Flores hang. In December 1920, Robert J. Riddle was charged with the murder of Ida Sorley. The defendant was tried in Judge Richard Irby Munroe, Sr.'s Fifty-fourth District Court, and Burton, who had arrested Riddle, testified on his investigation into the homicide. Riddle had written a confession after his arrest, which the prosecutor read into the record. The defense strategy rested on a plea of not guilty by reason of insanity. The case went to the jury on April 1, 1921, and they convicted him. Riddle received a sentence of ninety-nine years in prison.[6]

The following day, Burton and Assistant County Attorney Chester H. Machen searched a city lot located on the corner of Nineteenth Street and Dunton Avenue. In a barn behind the house, the law officers found two stills with paraphernalia, five gallons of corn whiskey, and approximately sixty gallons of mash. A complaint was filed charging the homeowner with violating the Dean Law, the state's prohibition statute that was more stringent than the national Volstead Act. Appearing in Justice Padgett's court, the defendant was released on a bond of $750. Burton was transporting Arthur Erath from the city lockup to the county jail on April 15, 1921, when the prisoner leaped from the deputy's car at the intersection of Third Street and Austin Avenue. Erath raced north along Third, but Burton, not relishing a foot chase, called on the fleeing man to halt. When the order was ignored, Burton shot him in the arm, whereupon Erath promptly surrendered. In another episode, two complete stills were found on the east side of the county by Burton and Constable William David Thompson of Axtell on April 23. No alcohol was discovered, but Burton took charge of the equipment. Later in the summer, on July 4, Burton and Deputy Carey Blake Stanford seized a still hidden in a cottage on Gurley Street along the Brazos River. The equipment had been in full operation at the time of capture with forty gallons distilling in the sixty-gallon boiler. A husband and wife were arrested for violation of state prohibition laws and placed in the county jail. The law officers filed a complaint in Justice of the Peace James R. Jenkins's court. Burton set a new record for the speediest arrest when, on July 19, he received a telegram from police officers in Mariana, Florida, requesting a suspect wanted on felony charges be apprehended. Within the hour, the deputy found the fugitive in Leroy, placed him under arrest, and lodged him in the county jail to await extradition. Five days later, Burton and Stanford raided a residence on South Third Street and arrested nineteen persons engaged in a craps game. Complaints were filed in county court charging illegal gambling. The deputies raided a house near Axtell on July 25, and discovered six gallons of corn whiskey. A search for a still proved fruitless. One man was arrested and charged with violation of the Dean Law. In an examining trial before Justice Padgett, the defendant's bond was fixed at $750.[7]

After Marvin's brother, John, passed away on July 13, 1912, his widow, Adeline "Addie" (House) Burton, moved with their five children to Red River County, where she worked as a farm laborer. Addie died in 1921, and Burton and Florence fostered their nephew, Raymond Matthew Burton, who had been born on April 23, 1912.[8]

Maude Brazell Aven died on July 2, 1921, of an apparent illness. Her six-month-old daughter, Fannie Elbert Aven, passed away on July 20. Evidence subsequently surfaced indicating Maude and Fannie may have been victims of foul play. Buchanan and Burton were also investigating the suspicious August 6 death of Charles Leslie Keyes, which they believed was connected to the Avens. Burton was present when Maude's body was exhumed at White Rock Cemetery on the morning of August 19. Doctor Wilby T. Gooch, Sr., chair of the Baylor University Chemistry Department, examined her stomach and liver for traces of poison. Based on sufficient probable cause, a complaint of murder was filed the same day against Dessie Bell Keyes and William Truman Aven, the spouses of the two deceased adults. Additionally, Aven was the uncle of Leslie Keyes (as he was known). That evening, the suspects were taken into custody, and Mrs. Keyes was questioned by Buchanan, Burton, Tirey, and Machen. She steadfastly denied any knowledge of Maude's death. Burton questioned Aven, who freely admitted to poisoning his wife. On the twentieth, he also confessed to leaving his incapacitated nephew sprawled across railroad tracks near Elm Mott to die under the wheels of a passing freight train. His motive was an illicit love affair with Mrs. Keyes, but she continued to deny a role in the murders and claimed she had been forced into the relationship. The results of Gooch's examination were revealed at an inquest held by Justice Jenkins on August 24, in which the doctor testified Mrs. Aven had died from a massive ingestion of arsenic. Dessie was freed on a bond of three thousand dollars while William remained in custody. The following day, Fannie's body was exhumed and likewise tested. Arsenic in sufficient quantities to cause death was found, and Gooch stated that, in his expert opinion, the poison would not have passed to the baby during nursing. Additional murder charges were filed against Aven and Keyes, and they were formally arraigned on August 31. The grand jury indicted the two suspects separately for the murders of Leslie and Fannie. The indictment against Dessie for Fannie's death was later dismissed.[9]

Aven was tried in Judge Munroe's district courtroom on September 22. Burton was among those examined before the court, with the jury excused, regarding the admissibility of the defendant's confession. After Munroe allowed the statement to be entered into evidence, and the jury returned, Tirey took the stand and read aloud Aven's written words. The effect on the jury and spectators was chilling, and the prosecution rested shortly before five o'clock. Surprisingly, the defense did the same without calling any witnesses. Aven was convicted of his wife's murder in September and given the death penalty. His attorneys made a motion for a new trial on November 3. Judge Munroe denied the defendant his request, and the defense legal team gave notice of appeal. Dessie was found not guilty of Maude's murder. William's case in the death of Leslie was continued and granted a change of venue to Falls County, but never brought to trial. Dessie's trial for the murder of her husband began with jury selection on December 12. Despite the signed confession, she was acquitted three days later. The verdict in Aven's murder case was reversed and remanded to the lower court. On December 6, 1923, during his new trial, Aven denied on the stand he had written a statement confessing to his wife's murder and claimed Dessie had poisoned Maude. The jury did not believe his story and convicted him for the death of his wife for the second time. Once more appealing the decision, Aven's conviction was upheld by the Court of Criminal Appeals on April 1, 1925. He was sentenced to die in the electric chair on February 27, 1926. Believing Aven was facing his final days, Burton, no longer with the sheriff's department, visited the condemned man on January 30. However, following numerous petitions and a thirty-day reprieve, Governor Miriam Ferguson commuted his death sentence to life imprisonment on March 27.[10]

Meanwhile, in early October 1920, Z. R. Upchurch, a high-ranking Ku Klux Klan "kleagle" in Atlanta, attended a United Confederate Veterans reunion in Houston. While there, he exploited romantic notions of Southern heroism and the "Lost Cause" to recruit members into the state's first chapter of the KKK. The Klan subsequently expanded its insidious reach throughout Texas, including the cities of Dallas, Fort Worth, San Antonio, and Waco. Decrying urban crime and immorality, the Klan not only directed its violent and racist attentions toward black people but also targeted white "moral transgressors" and bootleggers. Their presence in McLennan County was doubtless strengthened by the membership of Mayor Ben C. Richards and the entire Board of Police Commissioners, including, possibly, Police Chief Lee C. Jenkins.[11]

However, the Klan's support was not universal. An editorial denouncing the group later appeared in the *Dallas Morning News*, and described locales such as McLennan County:

> Have you not noticed where they claim to have their greatest membership? It is among people who believe in lynchings and mob law. They claim to have the best citizens of the country in their klan—and I have no doubt there are some good citizens among them, being led off by the high ideals they claim to stand for—but by their acts they prove they do not stand for good.[12]

On October 1, 1921, the Klan of McLennan County decided to hold a parade through the black neighborhood of Lorena, a small village south of Waco, before going to the local Baptist church for an ice cream social. Burton and Sheriff Buchanan visited the Klansmen at their camp, and told them while they had a Constitutional right to assemble, they would have to demonstrate with their faces revealed. Article 446 of the state penal code specified that assemblies in which the participants sought to intimidate others while disguised were illegal. Buchanan was well within his lawful authority to demand the Klansmen march unmasked. Nevertheless, several county residents pleaded with the sheriff not to interfere, but Buchanan, an unbending enforcer of the Law, refused to waver. Burton was similarly approached, and he firmly replied, "I have not deserted the sheriff when he was not in trouble, and I do not intend to leave him in a pinch now." The Klan defied the sheriff's legal order and began to march down Highway 81 with their heads completely covered by hoods. More than three thousand people had gathered to witness the parade. Buchanan assembled approximately twenty men and led them toward the fifty to one hundred white supremacists. By the time, the posse reached the head of the parade under the streetlight, only Buchanan, Burton, and Deputy Ira Mack Wood remained. The sheriff approached two Klan leaders, one of whom was holding the American flag and the other a flaming cross. Whipping back the first individual's hood, the lawman promised he would recognize the Klansman in the future. Buchanan moved to the second leader when another robed figure, later discovered to be a Waco policeman, came up behind the sheriff and clubbed him over the head. Outraged Klansmen swarmed over the fallen Buchanan, seized his sidearm, and began to mercilessly beat him. Burton was similarly being assailed by six white supremacists when the sheriff was struck by a bullet. Fifteen to twenty shots were fired in quick succession. Buchanan managed to pull his pocketknife and begin to slash at his attackers until an enraged Burton snatched a small pistol from his pants pocket and shot the sheriff's assailant. Emptying his gun into the crowd, the battered and bloodied deputy pulled his holstered .41-caliber single-action Colt and shot a Klansman leveling a handgun at the sheriff. He fired at another robed figure, forcing the man to flee. With the rest of the mob following suit, Burton discovered citizens unaffiliated with the Klan had dragged his boss into a nearby drug store. Besides the injuries suffered by the law officers in the chaotic melee, area businessman Louis Crow had been mortally wounded, and eight other locals bore knife or bullet wounds of varying severity.[13]

Besieged by bloodthirsty Klansmen, Burton got the sheriff out of the building through a coal chute and into a waiting ambulance. The deputy directed the driver to take the road west for MacGregor, then to Waco, instead of taking the direct route that was blocked by the white supremacists. The sheriff was admitted to Colgin Hospital with gunshot wounds to the right side of his chest and right leg, and eventually recovered. The attorney general issued a legal opinion supporting Buchanan's interpretation of the law concerning intimidating activities while masked. However, public sentiment favored the Klan, and Buchanan and Burton were publicly rebuked by the Seventy-fourth District Court grand jury on November 5. In a subsequent session, the jurors indicted the sheriff for Crow's death. Inez L. Crow, widow of the dead man, and Carl West, shot in the throat during the street battle, each filed a lawsuit against Buchanan and his bondsmen demanding fifty thousand dollars in damages. The sheriff continued to oppose the Klan and announced his intentions for re-election. Although eighty-odd citizens stood surety for his bond of five thousand dollars, Buchanan's political career was effectively finished.[14]

Samuel Liken Connally, a night watchman at the railyards, was making his rounds on December 1 when he was accosted by three black men, one of whom produced a handgun. They demanded his money, and the armed robber became enraged when he revealed he had none. Connally was shot several times and laid across the tracks where he stayed until his son Bernard found him twenty minutes later. He lingered in the hospital for several weeks battling pneumonia before finally succumbing to his wounds on December 21. While Connally lay dying, George Killough and brothers Elijah and Jake Graves were arrested for the crime. Killough confessed to Police Chief Lee Jenkins and Assistant County Attorney Frank Minnock Fitzpatrick, Sr. At 10 p.m., on December 5, a mob of two hundred white men, described as "orderly and quiet," gathered in front of the jail, but the suspects had already been taken to Dallas for their safety. Burton was managing the sheriff's department while Buchanan was still convalescing. Having waited for them on the courthouse lawn, the chief deputy allowed three members of the assembly to enter the jail and verify the prisoners were no longer in residence. Burton spoke to the crowd afterward and complimented them on their orderly conduct. With their would-be victims gone, and the situation diffused, the mob peacefully dispersed.[15]

On January 4, 1922, Burton led a raid on a moonshining operation in the backyard of a candy factory in Edgefield. He arrested three men and captured a still, one gallon of whiskey, and 150 gallons of mash. A charge of violating the prohibition laws was filed in Justice Padgett's court. After the examination trial, two of the suspects were released. Eight days later, Burton and Deputy Lee Shannon raided a rooming house on Third Street and arrested nine men. Charges of gambling were filed in county court.[16]

Guarded by Burton and four Texas Rangers, the Graves brothers and Killough were transported by automobile from Dallas to Waco on January 15 for their court date. The move was kept secret until the suspects were safely in the McLennan County jail. Having been charged with murder and highway robbery, their trial opened the next morning in Fifty-fourth District Court. Their defense attorneys immediately filed a motion requesting a severance, which the court granted. When Burton, Buchanan, Ranger Sergeant Edgar B. "Ed" McMordie, and Rangers James Lemuel "Lem" Lamkin, Lon B. "Jack" Barnett, and Martin Nickolas Koonsman escorted Killough from the jail for the afternoon session, a mob of approximately six hundred surged across the courthouse yard. Captain Tom R. Hickman, leading the Ranger detachment, brandished a "'baby' machine gun" and forced the crowd back to the sidewalk. Within thirty seconds, the yard and alley were cleared. During his trial, Killough pled not guilty and recanted his confession, claiming he had been intimidated into making it. The case went to the jury on the seventeenth, and the defendant was found guilty. He was sentenced to death by hanging, but later died in jail of tuberculosis while awaiting an appeal. In their own trials, the brothers were likewise convicted, although they were given ninety-nine-year prison sentences.[17]

Farmer Joseph Leon Turk discovered the bodies of merchant William H. Barker and his wife, Lula Mae, on the morning of February 11, 1922, at their farmhouse near Concord. The husband had been shot in the head, while Mrs. Barker's cranium was split by an ax. Turk also found in the house his thirteen-year-old son, Homer Leon, who had gone to the Barker's house the previous evening to play dominoes. The boy was suffering from a crushed skull and remained in critical condition. Neighbors found a bullet embedded in the wall of the general store on the property, and a double-bladed ax stained with blood in the backyard; the handle had been broken off a foot from the head.[18]

Notified of the double homicide, Burton, Mack Wood, Deputy Sheriff Bailey Philips "Phil" Hobbs, and Constable John Leslie Stegall left for the crime scene. The only witness to the horrific crime was Willie Lou Barker, the murdered couple's four-year-old daughter. Under Stegall and Hobbs's gentle questioning, she described how her father had been shot down in the yard near his store on the tenth at 10 p.m., then the murderers entered the house, demanded money from Lula, and killed her in the kitchen. Willie told investigators, "The men looked like Mexicans, but talked like negroes." Late the following day, Burton took seven black men employed by neighboring farms into custody. Two of the prisoners were identified as having been seen walking along the Waco–Corsicana road in front of the Barker farm at the time of the murders. However, interrogations that lasted into the night failed to elicit any confessions. Three white men and eight Mexican woodcutters were subsequently held for questioning, but no evidence was produced to justify the filing of charges. Tragically, Homer died on the fourteenth at Baptist Sanitarium in Waco without ever regaining consciousness. Over the next several days, those who had been detained were released after being cleared. Cooper Johnson and Bennie Young became prime suspects. The pair had been apprehended while wearing bloody overalls, which they claimed were soiled while butchering hogs. They allegedly confessed after vigorous interrogation, although some details were inconsistent with the known facts. The pair were indicted and placed in the Ellis County jail for safekeeping.[19]

Burton was acting as a bailiff for Judge Munroe's courtroom on February 24, 1922. Called to the witness stand, seventeen-year-old Marcine Matthews turned and calmly shot the defendant, John Stephen Crosslin, Sr., three times. Burton was unable to reach the teenager in time to prevent Crosslin's murder. Instead, he disarmed Marcine and carried her to the sheriff's office, where she was locked in a room for a time. Two years previously, the dead man had been convicted of sexually assaulting Marcine and sentenced to nine years in prison, but the case was later reversed and remanded for retrial. "He disgraced me, ruined my health and deprived me of school privileges. But he will never ruin another girl," she stated. Captain Hickman had been on duty in Judge Harvey MacGaughey Richey, Sr.'s courtroom across the hall, and he rushed to the scene moments after the shots were fired. Finding Burton and other deputies had control of the situation, he returned to his post. Burton filed a criminal complaint against Marcine charging her with murder. She was released under a bond of four thousand dollars. An examining trial before Padgett was scheduled for the twenty-eighth.[20]

On March 8, the body of an unidentified man was discovered half-submerged in Tehuacana Creek, seven miles from Waco on the Mexia road. The victim had been shot in the back of the head. Notified of the homicide, Burton, Justice Jenkins, and other sheriff's deputies arrived at the scene. The investigators determined the deceased had likely been killed in the previous forty-eight hours on the bridge crossing the creek, and pushed into the water. A *News-Tribune* reporter found a printed receipt downstream and turned the evidence over to Jenkins. However, little headway could be made until the victim was identified. On March 23, Stegall and Hobbs were able to confirm the dead man was Carl J. Brenna of Florence, Kansas, but that was the last breakthrough in the case.[21]

William Walter Shropshire, an independent wood hauler, was found dead on the night of March 16 atop a wagon load of wood. Sitting in an upright position, Shropshire had been shot seven times at close range, while his team grazed along the Marlin Road near the East Waco compress on Spring Street. Passersby notified the police department, and Justice Padgett ruled the victim had met his end at the hands of an unknown assailant. Burton took J. W. Clyde and Will Miles into custody for investigation, and one bullet was extracted from the body as evidence. Burton, Mack Wood, Stegall, Officer William L. "Bill" Parker, Chief Jenkins, and County Attorney Tirey questioned several persons of interest throughout the seventeenth. An empty wallet was found in Miles's possession, but he denied any knowledge of the item. Under firm questioning, he confessed the pocketbook belonged to Shropshire and to destroying several of the victim's receipts and memoranda. Investigators uncovered a recently used twelve-gauge shotgun and a large copper still in the Miles residence. Witness interviews revealed Shropshire and the suspect had fallen into a disagreement over four hundred gallons of whiskey the victim had contracted to produce. A complaint of murder was filed against Clyde and Miles, and the latter waived an examining trial on March 22.[22]

On March 23, Captain Hamer and a detachment of Rangers arrived in Waco to guard Johnson and Young during their trial. The city was on edge as the memory of the "Waco Horror"—the immolation and lynching of convicted murderer Jesse Washington—was still fresh. Sending four Rangers to Waco, Hamer and Private Elmer Birdie McClure went to the Waxahachie jail to transport the prisoners to their court hearing. Both the captain and Sheriff Buchanan were determined vigilante justice would not prevail. The next day, before the prisoners were brought into the courtroom, every spectator was searched for weapons. With Hamer, Ed McMordie, McClure, and Rangers William Mackinnon Molesworth, Jerome B. Wheatley, Charles E. Miller, Claude Darlington, and Joseph "Joe" Orberg in attendance, the trials lasted one week. Young was allotted ninety-nine years in prison on March 28, while, two days later, Johnson was condemned to hang. Employing Hamer's preferred practice of overwhelming force, the assembled Rangers, one of them armed with a Thompson submachine gun, kept the crowd from attempting to lynch the defendants. Regrettably, as will be revealed, the two convicted men had been accorded an injustice.[23]

Eula Ausley, a seventeen-year-old white girl, was brutally raped and murdered on May 4, approximately one mile from Kirven in Freestone County. After she failed to return home from school, her grandfather and several neighbors went out to search for her. They found the girl's horse tied to a fence near the public road and discovered her body a quarter-mile further off the lane. Eula's head had been crushed, her throat was slashed from ear to ear, and her body bore twenty-eight knife and ax wounds in the head, neck, and chest. Burton received a telephone call from the authorities in Wortham requesting his assistance in the case. He contacted Freestone County Sheriff Horace Milton Mayo, who was in Waco on business, while lawmen and volunteers from Kirven, Wortham, Mexia, and other towns combed the countryside for clues. Burton opted not to go to Wortham immediately, as the roads were in terrible condition. Tragically, events then unfolded at breakneck speed, and the deputy's presence quickly became moot.[24]

Three black men—McKinley "Snap" Curry, Moses Jones, and John Cornish—were taken into custody by Mayo on the fifth. The suspects had been field hands working on the homestead of Eula's uncle, Kirven City Marshal Otis Clifton King. Curry reportedly confessed to the murder and implicated the other two. At 3:00 a.m., on the sixth, an unmasked lynch mob of three hundred whites marched to the county jail at Fairfield and took the prisoners from Mayo after a brief struggle on the front porch. Transporting the doomed trio to a vacant lot near Kirven's business district, the heavily armed crowd castrated and disemboweled Curry and bound him to a turning plow situated in the middle of a pile of cordwood. The timber was drenched in gasoline, kerosene, and crude oil and set ablaze. Even as they screamed their innocence, Jones and Cornish were likewise hurled into the flames. Wood was continually added to the pyre until the following noon when the bodies had been completely reduced to ash. The general consensus was that the grand jury would not look into the matter.[25] The memorial service for the murdered trio drew three hundred members of the county's black community, which alarmed the white residents. Approximately one thousand armed men gathered in Kirven throughout the seventh amid rumors of racial strife, but the day ended peacefully.[26]

However, the naked body of Shadrack Green, a twenty-five-year-old black man, was discovered on the morning of May 8, riddled with bullets, and hanging from a tree limb in the Caney bottoms between Fairfield and Kirven. Attached to the corpse was a sign that read, "Don't cut me down. I committed suicide." Green was rumored to have been named in Curry's confessions, and no clues pointed to the identity of the former's killers. Sheriff Mayo, who had been embarrassed by the martial law declaration in his jurisdiction four months prior, immediately contacted District Attorney Daniel James Moody and requested the presence of Rangers. Mayo feared an "uprising of negros," and the governor prepared to send two detachments under Hamer from Austin and Hickman from Wichita Falls. News of their impending arrival seems to have somewhat calmed tensions, and the Rangers' movement orders were canceled.[27]

However, the community would experience more death when Marshal Otis King and his brother, Deputy Sheriff John T. King, led a posse from Teague to the black settlement of Simsboro on June 2. Leroy Gibson, suspected of complicity in Eula's attack, and his brother Allie were killed in the ensuing shootout, and several posse members were wounded. The situation threatened to spiral completely out of control, but Mayo kept the factions apart until passions cooled. Although General Barton held several Rangers in readiness, he received no requests for assistance from local authorities. Investigating the troubles, Prohibition agent Manuel T. Gonzaullas noted many of the hamlet's residents were hiding in fear. Additionally, Tom Barry, another black man under suspicion, went missing on May 20, and his fate remains unknown. Circumstantial yet compelling evidence developed by attorney Monte Akers points to Andrew Thomas Prowell and his two sons, Charles Audey and Andrew Claude, as Eula's actual killers. The motive was said to have been a family feud, of which the young high schooler's death was the final horrific act.[28]

Five weeks after Bennie Young and Cooper Johnson were found guilty, Waco became the scene of a series of murders, attempted murders, and two sexual assaults. The first to die was cotton buyer and sometime deputy constable William Parks Driskell, Sr., who was shot in his garage on May 8. An attack on William Cottrell and Ina Sheffield, parked in a lover's lane in Cameron Park, occurred ten days later; both victims survived. Harrell Thomas Bolton and Margaret Hays were not as fortunate. On May 26, the two were attacked on the Corsicana Road, and Bolton was shot to death. The assailant dragged Margaret into the woods where she was brutally raped over a three-hour period. The perpetrator then caught a passing freight train bound for Fort Worth. Burton was the first officer on scene, and Margaret described her attacker as a light-skinned black man with a gold tooth. In the heated atmosphere, the emotionally traumatized victim identified twenty-three-year-old Jesse Thomas, who fit the description, as her rapist. Her enraged father promptly shot and killed the accused man on the spot, then a mob dragged the corpse to the town square behind a truck and tossed it onto a bonfire. Tragically, evidence was soon collected that confirmed Thomas's innocence. When other suspects were threatened with similar violence, the prosecutor appealed to Adjutant General Thomas Dickson Barton for assistance. Hamer, McMordie, Miller, Wheatley, and William Molesworth rushed to the scene on the same day. Once arrived at the county jail, Hamer mounted the front steps with a Thompson submachine gun and simply waited for the gathering crowd to act. Intimidated by the captain's implacable stare and steady resolve, the mob dispersed, and the heavily armed Rangers took up positions around the lockup. Two days later, with Waco practically back to normal, all but two Rangers were recalled to Austin. However, Constable Stegall began establishing connections between the recent attacks, and, in anticipation of further racial strife, Captain Tom R. Hickman and the Company B headquarters were transferred from Wichita Falls to Waco on June 5.[29]

The following month, Burton was invited to meet with Governor Pat Morris Neff, who offered him an appointment to the Rangers. Ironically, Burton was one of the few law officers in the state who had no ambition to become a Texas Ranger. Although the sheriff had been defeated by Leslie Stegall in the recent election, and the deputy was likely to lose his own job on the first of January, Burton was still reluctant to be away from his family for extended assignments. Additionally, as Buchanan was still recovering, Burton was effectively in charge of the office. The governor pointed out Burton's pending employment situation and reflected on the difficulty of finding a new job. "Governor, I can still dig ditches," Burton told him. "Well," the executive replied, "you think of this 'til September the first and if you decide you want the job you send me a telegram and I'll send you a commission." Ultimately Burton concluded since Neff had personally requested his services, he could not turn the governor down. On the last day of August, Burton sent a message to Neff and accepted the offer. The next day, he received his warrant of authority in the mail, and Richard Harding "Bob" Hall succeeded him in the sheriff's department. Burton was assigned to Company B under Captain Hickman, but he was left in Waco for a time to assist Buchanan, then transferred to Smithville for three months to keep the peace during a railroad strike. Accompanied by Crawford Constable Scott Lewis, Burton was placed in charge of thirty-six "Railroad Rangers."[30]

After the horrific murders of six months prior, Waco remained seemingly serene until another couple was attacked on November 21, 1922. At Lover's

Governor Pat M. Neff. George Grantham Bain Collection. *Courtesy Prints and Photographs Division, Library of Congress, Washington, DC.*

Leap in Cameron Park, near the Bosque River, Grady Skipworth was shot and killed while Naomi Boucher, his female companion, was raped, then pushed off a precipice. Although injured, she survived the fall and was able to alert the authorities. Night Chief of Police Tate Shelton and Detective Wiley Wilson Stem, Sr., Constable Stegall, and Deputy Wood were called to the scene to investigate. Having recently returned to Waco, Burton had the sad duty of bringing Skipworth's father to the park for a positive identification. Naomi described her assailant as a light-skinned black man with a gold front tooth, an all-too-familiar depiction. An anonymous letter delivered to the sheriff's department on November 24 led Burton to a rooming house on Mary Street, where he discovered evidence pointing to Ford mechanic Ivory Clay. The suspect matched the well-known description, and his answers to the Ranger's questions were unsatisfactory. Burton arrested him, and Naomi identified Clay as her attacker on December 2. An examining trial was held on January 9, 1923, and the defendant was bound over to the grand jury.[31]

However, while Clay languished in the county jail, the serial killer and rapist seemingly struck on January 14. While a man and woman were driving along Twelfth Street, a black gunman leaped onto the running board of their car, but the male driver resisted and forced the attacker to flee. Fortuitously for investigators, the intruder's cap was left behind in the vehicle. Unfortunately, five days later, yet another couple was murdered. William Edwin Holt and Mrs. Ethel Jacobs Denecamp were parked on Springfield Road, two hundred yards from the Tehuacana Bridge, when an armed man burst from the shadows and gunned them down. Their bodies were found in a nearby clearing on January 21. Even with this most recent homicide, Clay's *habeas corpus* hearing opened on the twenty-fifth in Judge Munroe's court, and numerous eyewitnesses testified he had been home at the time of the Skipworth slaying. Additionally, Clay had been in jail during the time of the attack on Holt and Denecamp, murders which bore the *modus operandi* of the serial killer stalking Waco. Finally, defense counsel presented evidence that seemed to point to another individual. In light of these factors, the judge dismissed the case.[32]

On January 28, recently elected Sheriff Stegall received a letter that implicated chauffeur Roy Mitchell in the Barker-Turk murders. Additionally, three different witnesses identified the cap dropped in the Twelfth Street attack as belonging to Mitchell, who matched the description of the serial killer. City Detectives Hollis Barron and George Jackson arrested the suspect on expedient gambling charges, and, while searching his home on East Jefferson Avenue, discovered items linking Mitchell to at least three of the murders. Remembering the grisly fate of Jesse Thomas, Stegall had the prime suspect transferred to the Hill County jail on the thirtieth. Mitchell had been questioned twice before concerning the murder spree, but released after establishing alibis. This time, he confessed to numerous sexual assaults and nine murders on February 8 and 9, including the three homicides for which Cooper Johnson and Bennie Young had been convicted, and the rape for which Jesse Thomas had been murdered. Following a preliminary hearing on February 21, Mitchell was indicted on March 6 for five murders, two attempted murders, three criminal assaults, and two attempts of criminal assault. Hamer and a Ranger detachment guarded Mitchell's five trials in Fifty-fourth District Court, which began on March 15. During the proceedings, the defendant claimed his confessions had been forced. Having been an integral part of the lengthy investigation, Burton was a witness for the state on April 19. Hamer also provided testimony, and the accused was found guilty in each of the cases. After a failed appeal, the sentence of death was carried out on July 30, atop the gallows in the Waco jail yard. Although they had been proven to be innocent, Johnson had died of tuberculosis on July 26 while still at the county farm, and, in a supreme act of injustice, Young would not be pardoned and released until March 9, 1934.[33]

Burton stopped in Waco on April 7, 1923, to visit his family while traveling from Corpus Christi to Paducah in Cottle County. He had been assigned to report to Fiftieth District Judge James Henry Milam on the ninth for special service. District Attorney James Ross Bell, who was prosecuting rancher John Beal Sneed, had been marked for death, and rumors stated the attorney would be killed when he rose to address the jury. Burton was to provide protection. Sneed, already notorious for his role in the Sneed-Boyce feud, had been indicted for assault with intent to murder Claude Benjamin Berry in Paducah on March 7. The shooting had been in retaliation for the earlier killing of Wood Barton, Sneed's son-in-law, by Berry. The defendant's lawyer had requested a change of venue, and Judge Milam held a hearing on the motion. As Bell began to make his arguments to the jury, Burton perceived that two of Sneed's relatives sitting in the courtroom were armed. He approached the pair and quietly asked them to accompany him to County Judge Walter James Arrington's office next door. In the presence of Arrington, Burton instructed the two to remove their guns and lay them on the judge's desk. Carrying the weapons in a folded newspaper, the Ranger took the men to the room where the impaneled grand jury was meeting, laid the .380 pistols on the table, and explained the situation. Thirty minutes later, Sneed's kinsfolk were indicted, and Burton and Sheriff Morgan Wright escorted them to jail. Sneed was subsequently shot by relatives of Berry, which delayed further court hearings. Sneed recovered, and his case was transferred to Knox County; after several postponements, the trial opened on February 7, 1924. The defendant was acquitted, but Burton's involvement in the matter had already ended by this time.[34]

Prohibition was the top priority on Pat Neff's agenda in his second administration. Indeed, he had chaired the local option committee in 1917 that had made McLennan County dry. In addition to his oath to support the Constitution of the United States and the laws of Texas, the governor also held a deep personal conviction regarding the consumption of alcohol. In a speech to the National Association of Civil Engineers, he said: "We have but one Federal Constitution, and every part of that Constitution is binding on every state. It is binding on Texas … The bootlegger is an enemy, a poisoner, an extortioner who would any hour in the night sell the American flag for a bottle of beer." On February 14, 1921, Neff chaired a conference of Ranger captains and Clifford G. Beckham, the chief Prohibition administrator for Texas, and informed the assembled lawmen that any Ranger discovered to be imbibing intoxicating liquor would be summarily dismissed. He also ordered the state officers to cooperate fully with the U.S. government's efforts to halt distilling and bootlegging. However, he was suspicious of federal overreach into the state's affairs and, the following July, encouraged the legislature to enact more rigorous enforcement mechanisms in support of the Dean Law. Unlike the governors of Illinois, New York, or Florida, the largest difficulty Neff faced in enforcing state prohibition laws was not the smuggling of liquor across an international border, but the countless number of stills hidden in every county in the state, except those in West Texas.[35]

As a citizen and a peace officer, Burton likewise supported the prohibition laws. The Ranger believed he could enforce them in four or five counties single-handedly, but only with the cooperation of prosecutors, the courts, and law enforcement officers. Unfortunately, throughout his time fighting bootleggers, Burton would find support from local authorities to be severely lacking.[36]

The most extensive liquor ring was found in Somervell County, fifty miles southwest of Fort Worth. Hidden among the craggy, forested hills, bootleggers in the county imported tough and knowledgeable distillers from Oklahoma, Tennessee, and Kentucky to manufacture their product for thirsty customers in Fort Worth, Dallas, Waco, Wichita Falls, and Ranger. Their criminal enterprises enjoyed the protection of Sheriff Thomas Walter Davis, who took monthly payments of six dollars for every barrel of moonshine produced. Indeed, ordinary citizens of the county profited handsomely by selling corn and sugar to moonshiners and bootleggers. All resented outside interference in their affairs.[37]

In July 1923, James Aaron "Dick" Watson and Pruitt Merrill, "special prohibition enforcement officers" acting under the orders of the governor, infiltrated the moonshining syndicate. Both men were under indictment for transporting illegal alcohol, and they had agreed to work clandestinely in exchange for the charges being dropped. The pair earned the trust of the still operators to the point where Watson was conveying bribe money to county officials. While waiting for the undercover officers to gather evidence, Burton, accompanied by McLennan County Deputy Constable Kenneth Malcolm Webb, Sr. and former county jailer Scott Chaplin, impounded a thirty-gallon copper still, nine barrels of mash, and an assortment of jugs and bottles at a residence near the McGregor road eight miles west of Waco on July 21. One man was arrested, and a complaint filed in court. Four days later, at the same location, the Ranger and Constable Harvey Hill Butts found two 50-gallon stills, fourteen mash barrels, and assorted equipment hidden in an abandoned barn and a dense thicket. Burton, Webb, Chaplin, and Tom Cook seized two fully equipped stills, seven barrels of mash, and five gallons of finished corn whiskey on the China Springs road approximately one mile from the Big Bosque bridge. Burton, Chaplin, and Cook raided a still on Rogers Hill between Gholson and West on the thirtieth. They arrested four men, and confiscated a twenty-gallon still, one hundred gallons of mash, and a small quantity of finished corn. The officers destroyed the mash and submitted the remainder as evidence in federal court.[38]

By late August, Watson and Merrill were able to justify a raid and met with Burton and Ranger Rudolph Daniel Shumate at the Dallas courthouse. Plans for the move into Somervell County had been developing for most of the month, and search warrants were already in hand. Leaving for Cleburne the same evening, the four lawmen, and Rangers Lee Shannon and Joseph Wiley "Joe" McElroy, recruited officers from Johnson, Hood, and Bosque Counties. The raiders descended on Glen Rose, the county seat, on August 25 in three detachments. Shumate and Watson led one squad along the highway from Cleburne, another swept westward from Meridian, and Burton and Merrill's men drove from Granbury in a Hudson touring car. The raiders combed the rugged hills and cedar brakes for two days, and seized twenty-three stills and varied equipment, eight hundred pounds of sugar, sixty gallons of corn whiskey, eighty-four bottles of beer, several gallons of wine, and two hundred barrels of mash. Equipment and liquor that could not be carried out of the brush were destroyed. The assorted stills, cooper tubing, condensers, hose, and the whiskey, beer, and wine were piled on the courthouse lawn and turned over to the U.S. marshal. Thirty-one men, including Sheriff Davis and County Attorney Edward Lee Roark, were arrested in over forty raids. Burton personally took seventeen prisoners to Waco, single-handedly, in five automobiles, with the Ranger in the rear vehicle.[39]

On the twenty-seventh, Burton appeared before U.S. Commissioner Andrew Phelps McCormick in Waco to file complaints. Davis and Roark were immediately lodged in the McLennan County jail where the sheriff confessed to taking payoffs. Roark denied the allegations. The two county officials were charged with conspiracy to violate the Volstead Act, while the other twenty-nine suspects were charged with the manufacture, possession, and sale of intoxicating liquor. Davis and Roark were both freed on bonds of fifteen hundred dollars. The bail of those charged with possession was set at five hundred dollars each, and those charged with possession and sale made bonds of $750 each. Thirteen more suspects remained at large. However, Neff instructed Burton to request a dismissal of the federal charges and seek indictments under the state's tougher Dean Law. Shumate and Dallas County District Attorney Shelby Shepard Cox, the latter acting as legal advisor, arrived in Glen Rose on August 28 to continue the investigation and obtain affidavits. Burton, Bosque County Sheriff William Washington Wright, and Johnson County Deputy Joe David Crawford likewise returned, and they raided the farm of William Isaiah "Bill" Glass seven miles north of town the next day. Attempting to escape into a dense thicket, Alonzo Tullis Holt, a prominent leader of the ring, was killed in a shootout with the lawmen. Capturing Bill and his son William Lawrence Glass, the law officers seized a one-hundred-gallon still, ten gallons of moonshine whiskey, and over eleven hundred gallons of mash. Burton traveled to Waco once more and, in accordance with normal procedure, was arrested and charged with murder. He was released on a bond of $250.[40]

With the "rum ring" in disarray, Judge Irwin Traylor Ward of the Eighteenth District Court convened the grand jury on September 3 and charged them "as public-spirited citizens to drive bootleggers out of Somervell County." As the first witness called to testify, Burton presented to the jurors the evidence accumulated from the raids. Forty-four indictments were returned, and a change of venue to Johnson County was granted for twenty-one cases. The remainder were transferred to Bosque County.[41]

William Warren "Bill" Sterling described Burton's "manner with inoffensive people [as] a model of gentility and courtesy, but when dealing with criminals, he becomes a one man riot squad." An uncompromising opposition to lawbreakers is commendable in a peace officer, but Burton was known to carry his aggressiveness too far. He was accused of breaking a prisoner's jaw with a pistol butt while a deputy sheriff, and roughly handling a bootlegging suspect. He had been involved in an altercation with "a fellow named Smith" on July 31 in Waco, and subsequently approached City Recorder James Davis Willis to willingly plead guilty to public fighting. When Willis replied there was no complaint against him, Burton's companion, Tom Cook, volunteered to file one. With the matter entered into the record, Burton accepted responsibility and paid the one-dollar fine. Finding a reduction in the Ranger Force to be fiscally necessary, General Barton instructed Captain Aldrich, on October 1, to write their fractious subordinate and request his resignation.[42]

Burton had been instrumental in dismantling the liquor ring, and the order must have been rescinded as he continued to carry out official duties in Cleburne and Glen Rose. Unfortunately, he demonstrated a high-handed behavior. On November 9, he confiscated the automobile of John Frederick "Fred" Cleveland, Jr., a Dallas post office employee, in the same town. A friend of Cleveland's brother had borrowed the car, and was subsequently found in possession of corn whiskey. Two days later, Burton and Dick Watson stopped an auto at gunpoint on the Glen Rose–Granbury road. The vehicle was driven by J. Warren Hutt, editor of the Dallas-based *Texas 100 Per Cent American* newspaper, and his partner, Archie Goodwin. In a letter to Barton, Hutt claimed Burton and Watson made no attempt to identify themselves as peace officers, yet searched the vehicle for liquor anyway. Finding none, the lawmen climbed into their Ford and proceeded to Glen Rose. Still in possession of Cleveland's auto by November 19, Burton was accused of removing the spare wheel and generally abusing the car. Due to insufficient evidence in the case, Prohibition officials and the U.S. attorney had declined to initiate forfeiture proceedings against the postal worker. After Federal District Judge Duval West became involved, Barton ordered Burton to return the automobile in "as good condition as when seized."[43]

McLennan County Attorney Frank Tirey was appointed a special prosecutor for the Glen Rose matter, and he took cases to trial beginning in Cleburne. Sheriff Davis was convicted of accepting a bribe on November 14 and sentenced to four years' imprisonment. However, his attorneys appealed the decision. Davis resigned his office on December 10, and Joseph Dotson was appointed to fulfill the term. Burton was not impressed with the new sheriff and informed Aldrich: "He is sixty five years old, never had any experience as an officer, and is in simoothy [*sic*] with the bootleggers." The quartermaster replied the next day: "I'm sorry to hear that the new sheriff at Glen Rose is not the kind of man needed there. He may be guided by the fate of the last one however." While awaiting his next appearance in court, Burton single-handedly seized three large stills—four hundred-gallon, two hundred-gallon, and eighty-gallon, respectively—within three miles of Glen Rose on December 28 and 29 and arrested five men. He took a small measure of corn whiskey as evidence and destroyed the remainder.[44]

Meanwhile, Navarro County had seen a major oil discovery near Corsicana in January 1923. Following a predictable pattern, boomtowns leaped into sudden existence and experienced a rising tide of violence and crime.

The local authorities were unsuccessful in stemming the lawlessness in the oil fields. Paltry raids uncovered liquor stills, brothels, and gambling dens, but few arrests ended in indictments. Indeed, a bootlegging syndicate began to organize. By January 1924, uneasy county officials realized they needed outside assistance.[45]

Burton was contacted by the Navarro County district attorney and agreed to lead the subsequent crackdown. By the middle of January, undercover operatives, including Watson, were dispatched to gather evidence for the probe. After three weeks of investigation, Burton arrived in town at 7 p.m. on February 7 to organize the last great raid of the Neff administration's crusade. Within twenty minutes of the Ranger registering in a downtown Corsicana hotel, an auto loaded with whiskey parked next to Burton's car. The driver quickly found himself arrested, and his vehicle and cargo were confiscated. At nine o'clock, Burton; Watson; special officers John Francis Maloney, Hilliard Clinch Brite, Jr., and David Jesse Reese; County Attorney Ballard Wilson George; Sheriff Walter Hayes and seven county deputies; and five Corsicana police officers went into the oil field. Over the next three days, gambling dens, dance halls, and speakeasies in the towns of Navarro, Tuckertown, Whitten, and Mildred were raided. Illicit red and corn whiskey, choc beer, paregoric (anhydrous morphine), and gambling equipment were seized, stills were destroyed, and approximately 125 gamblers, prostitutes, and bootleggers were brought before Justices of the Peace Joseph L. Cox and John James Sullivan on various felony charges. Fifty had been arrested for violating liquor laws, while the remainder were charged with gaming, vagrancy, or illegal possession of a firearm. On February 8, Burton personally led raids on the Commercial, Main, and Beaton Hotels in Corsicana, confiscated sizeable quantities of liquor, and arrested prostitutes and nearly every porter and bellhop. Other businesses, mostly restaurants, were placed under surveillance and closed when arriving liquor shipments were seized. Mopping-up operations occurred on Saturday when an exclusive speakeasy in the Corsicana National Bank was closed. Four full quarts of premium Scotch whiskey were seized, as were two partially filled quart bottles, several half-gallon fruit jars that once contained corn whiskey, and a set of drinking glasses. The total number of apprehensions rose to eighty-nine. Burton departed town on February 10, having gone without sleep for three days.[46]

Although the kingpins of the bootlegging ring escaped the dragnet, the raids saw every illegal establishment in the county closed, and the area was virtually free of vice for the next six months. Two hundred and sixty-one prisoners were held in the county jail during the month of February. County Attorney George presented eighty complaints to the grand jury, and numerous witnesses were called to testify. Following ten days of closed hearings, the panel members returned fifty felony indictments for prohibition and gambling violations, and possession of concealed weapons. Robert Lee "Bob" Shoop was personally under sixteen indictments and free on a five-hundred-dollar bond for each case. However, he failed to show for his April 7 court appearance before Judge Hawkins Scarborough of the Thirteenth Judicial District. Forfeiting eight thousand dollars, Shoop was arrested in Bristow, Oklahoma, on the seventeenth and returned to Navarro County. He was convicted of all charges on May 20 and sentenced to eighteen months' imprisonment. Indeed, approximately twenty of the defendants were successfully prosecuted and incarcerated.[47]

Continuing his work in Somervell County unaided, Burton rode into a canyon on February 15 and captured two bootleggers, two barrels of mash, twenty-six gallons of whiskey, and a well-equipped two-hundred-gallon still; a third suspect escaped. Four days later, Shumate and Burton took to the witness stand in the trial of Ed Roark, and described how the ex-county attorney had admitted to taking bribes before he was placed under arrest. Mounting a legal strategy of arguing the points of law involved, defense counsel contended Roark was in the custody of the officers when he confessed. Judge Ward overruled their objections to the admissibility of the lawmen's testimony. Dick Watson, described by Burton as "the best under-cover man I ever saw," was also brought from Navarro County to Cleburne to testify as the state's principal witness. The case went to the jury on February 21.[48]

During the trials, supporters of the moonshiners grew more and more outraged and threatened those who opposed the "rum ring." The former also demanded the governor cease meddling in local affairs. Once they were dismissed by the court, Watson and Burton returned to Glen Rose to stay at the residence of Thomas Askey "Tom" Duncan. At nine-thirty that same night, Watson visited Doctor Jackson Gordon Daniel's house. While engaged in conversation with the physician and other friends, he was fatally struck in the back by a shotgun blast fired through a closed window from outside. The unknown assailant climbed into an automobile containing three other persons and made his escape. Hearing the gunshot, Burton rushed to the scene, but he could find no trace of the killer. Five Rangers and officers from Johnson, Bosque, and Hood Counties picked up fifteen suspects by the next day. Six of the men—Doctor William Burman Pruitt, Sr.; the West brothers, Albert Murray, Willis W., and Sonley; and siblings William Boone "Grandy" and Charles Culberson Moss—were arrested on charges of murder, while another six were held for questioning. Four of the latter group were released on the afternoon of February 22. Burton informed reporters, "I am confident Watson's slayer is among the prisoners." Rangers Shumate and Joseph Hamilton Leach of Company C were ordered to Glen Rose to assist Burton. Judge Charles A. Pippen ordered four of the suspects to Cleburne for *habeas corpus* proceedings. Collin Asbury Milam, Sr., wealthy bank president and merchant, became the seventh man charged in Watson's death on February 23, although he was freed after submitting bail. On February 27, Doctor Pruitt was released on a bond of seven thousand dollars. Held in the Tarrant County jail, Grady Mosswas similarly freed on a five-thousand-dollar bond. At the same time, the jury in the Roark case had become hopelessly deadlocked and was dismissed on the twenty-fifth; a new trial was scheduled for March 3. On April 29, the Somervell County grand jury adjourned without returning any indictments in the matter of Watson's death. His killer or killers never faced justice.[49]

Marvin Bishop Simpson, Sr., a Fort Worth attorney, filed a civil suit in Ninety-fifth District Court in Dallas on behalf of Willis West, Murray West, Sonley West, James West, and Charlie Moss demanding $125,000 in damages. Naming Dallas County Sheriff Daniel Simeon "Dan" Harston, Burton, Shumate, county jailer Henry W. Clark, and Doctor Robert Ernest House of Ferris, the claimants alleged a conspiracy of brutal treatment, sleep deprivation, and forcible injections of "truth serum" over a five-day period. While the suit seems to have been dismissed, House, an Ellis County obstetrician, had used scopolamine as a general birth anesthetic before discovering its properties for detecting deception. He championed the use of the drug in law enforcement circles throughout the 1920s. Shortly after the claim to the Dallas court, a charge of criminal libel was filed in Somervell County against Simpson. On the motion of Somervell County Attorney Joseph Anderson Moore, the latter case was dismissed by County Judge Cecil Curtis Collings for insufficient evidence.[50]

As the Glen Rose moonshine raids had dismantled the criminal ring in Somervell County, Burton turned his attention to Leon County. At sunrise on March 16, he, and Prohibition agents Lee Shannon and George B. Ray, raided a fortified cabin deep in the thickets north of Concord. Although the avenues of approach were covered by loopholes in the structure's walls, the lawmen gained entry into the building and arrested two men. They also seized two hundred gallons of aged red whiskey and two elaborate large-capacity stills. A small measure of liquor was kept as evidence and the rest destroyed. Complaints were filed in court in Waco the following day. The two suspects were arraigned before U.S. Commissioner McCormick, and each was released on a one-thousand-dollar bond.[51]

In Waco, Burton, Ranger Joseph Hamilton Leach, and Agents Shannon and Ray observed illegal gambling occurring in a building at 603-1/2 Franklin Avenue on April 19. The next day, they raided the game and seized a dice table, two large sacks of poker chips, and numerous decks of playing cards. Fourteen men were arrested and charged in Judge Jenkins's court. The same day, the lawmen raided a room in Mrs. Laura Carpenter's Tribune Apartments at 413-1/2 Washington Avenue. The two occupants were taken into custody for possession of liquor. Approximately a dozen bottles of corn and rye whiskies, wine, and cognac were seized.[52]

Burton next tracked the Somervell County bootlegging network's links into Bosque County. Around midnight on May 31, with Burton at the wheel, he and City Marshal Charles Andrew Barker of Meridian were engaged in a high-speed pursuit of area farmers Frank Terrell, John Pool, and Aubrey Smith along the Clifton–Meridian road. Subsequently testifying the suspects shot first from their Ford automobile, Barker returned fire from the rear seat, striking Terrell in the back of the head. The wounded man died in Meridian at three o'clock the next morning. Bottles of liquor had been thrown from the fugitive vehicle during the chase and were later found smashed on the roadside. Holding an empty magazine, a recently-fired .38-caliber semiautomatic pistol was discovered on the floor of the car between the front and back seats. Complaints on all parties were filed in Justice of the Peace Enos Jenkins's court. Surrendering to Constable William Barnett Baxter, Burton and Barker were charged with murder, and Pool and Smith with transporting liquor. The four men were each released on bonds of one thousand dollars. A veteran of the recent world war, the well-regarded Terrell was buried with full military honors. Pool and Smith pled guilty at their trials and received one-year suspended sentences, while Burton and Barker were indicted by the grand jury on December 31, 1925. The two lawmen were each freed on five-thousand-dollar bail. The case against them was scheduled on the court docket for the April 1926 term.[53]

Burton was discharged by order of the governor on May 31, 1924.[54] Despite his lack of official standing, he and Prohibition agent George Webb arrested two men near Richland on September 11, on charges of prohibition violations. The prisoners were taken to the Navarro County jail.[55]

John Hightower, a cotton picker for a farm near the town of Victoria in Limestone County, shot his wife in the shoulder following an argument on September 8. Owen Rawls Cotton, a local farmer, attempted to apprehend Hightower, only to have part of his jaw shot away. He was also wounded in the neck, and his condition reported as serious. Sheriff Whit Popejoy quickly mounted a posse of fifty men, including Burton. However, the fugitive was discovered hiding at Christmas Creek, three miles south of Prairie Hill, by farmer Pink Reed. Hightower wounded Reed with a pistol shot, who returned fire and instantly killed his assailant with a shotgun blast to the heart.[56]

The town of Mart in the southeastern corner of McLennan County was experiencing "a lawless condition" in February 1925, and the mayor, city commissioners, and local businessmen requested Burton pin on the badge of town marshal. Taking over the office from Sue Mackie "Mac" Jester, Burton dealt with burglaries, swindles, vehicular accidents, desertions from the military, and auto thefts. In addition to these routine matters, he was involved in handling a series of murders. On October 5, Clayton Briggs was fatally shot in the home of Dollie Gameson in McClanahan, Falls County. The two families had been engaged in an ongoing quarrel, and Mrs. Gameson's fourteen-year-old son, Ernest, killed Briggs with a shotgun to save his widowed mother from a beating. After the slaying, the youth ran eight miles to reach a telephone and notify Burton. Ernest then surrendered to the city marshal upon the latter's arrival. On October 31, Dollie was shot to death while traveling on the Marlin–Waco road. Dophitt Briggs, Clayton's brother, quickly became a suspect in the murder and, upon learning of this development, he surrendered at the courthouse. He made no attempt to obtain bail. Falls County Attorney Cecil Glass presented a large volume of evidence to the grand jury. On November 14, the jurors indicted Dophitt on a charge of murder.[57]

Burton announced his candidacy for the office of county sheriff at the end of January 1926. The field proved full as incumbent Leslie Stegall faced four opponents, including Burton and former police chief Guy McNamara. In time, "Burton for Sheriff" clubs were organized in Mart and West to proclaim Burton's fitness to hold the office. On the twenty-third of the same month, Burton assisted two federal agents in seizing a pair of stills in Limestone County and arresting four men. Complaints were filed the next day in Commissioner McCormick's court.[58]

Charged with murder in the death of Frank Terrell two years previously, Burton and Marshal Barker finally had their days in court. Barker was the first to be tried, and he was acquitted on April 1 after the jury deliberated for only thirty minutes. Although Burton's trial was scheduled for the twelfth, the county attorney moved on April 8 that the charge be dismissed due to insufficient evidence.[59]

Despite his poor performance as Waco's top cop a decade earlier, Guy McNamara was enjoying a commanding lead in a straw poll prior to the Democratic primary on July 24. The race drew a great deal of public interest, with 15,247 white voters registered. On Election Day, Stegall confounded the polls and won 5,170 votes, while McNamara earned 3,633. Although Burton had a respectable amount of support for his campaign, including more than ninety women voters in Mart, he placed third with 2,104 votes. Stegall secured a third term, as he triumphed over McNamara in the run-off election held on August 28. In the time leading to the second contest, Burton, on the heels of his defeat, was convalescing after a recent attack of appendicitis.[60]

Jewel Hart, pardoned by Governor Miriam Amanda Ferguson after serving seven years of a life sentence for the murder of a Mart merchant, was wanted in Trinity County on burglary charges. Along with two accomplices, Hart was alleged to have robbed a store and post office in Grovetown. On June 29, Burton arrested the suspect at his mother's home in Limestone County, eight miles east of Mart. Hart was remanded to Trinity County the next day.[61]

The First National Bank of Otto, in Falls County, was robbed by two bandits on November 7. The youthful pair entered the bank and, while one covered the room with a firearm, the other forced bank employees to gather over six thousand dollars. Exiting, the thieves escaped in a cream-colored Chrysler roadster. Burton, Night Chief Wilder Green McDonald, Sr., and Detective George Blount, the latter two from the Waco police, traveled to the scene of the crime. The city marshal found, in a pasture, a piece torn from a license plate issued in McLennan County. The lawmen ascertained the two robbers had driven to the meadow and met a third confederate with another vehicle. One auto headed to Groesbeck and the other drove through the Cedar Crest oil field toward Mexia. Burton and Mexia officers traced the second car to Teague. The following day, the marshal assisted Falls County Sheriff Henry Thomas Barton and Dallas County Deputy James Patrick "Pat" Richards in apprehending two of the suspected bank robbers at a Dallas hotel. The officers recovered approximately three thousand dollars in cash, two vehicles, and a complete set of burglary and safe-blowing tools. Three eyewitnesses from Otto identified the men as the bandits, and charges of robbery with firearms were promptly filed in Marlin.[62]

On April 11, 1928, Burton was investigating a case in Mart when he discovered Aubrey Wilhite, a young cotton mill employee in Waco, was selling stolen bolts of fabric to a local merchant. The marshal and Detective Wiley Stem took Wilhite into custody around noon, and the youth confessed to the larceny. He was brought before Judge Kyle Vick of the county court-at-law and pled guilty to theft under fifty dollars. The judge fined him one dollar and court costs. The same day, Burton helped to bring a wanted man to justice. Dan Fuller was facing charges of liquor law violations and jailbreaking. Credited as the largest still operator in Lampasas

County, he had been at large for twenty days since escaping from the county jail. His short stint of freedom came to an end when Burton and Stem discovered Fuller at approximately 7 p.m. during a search of the underbrush near Gholson. The fugitive offered no resistance. Following a telephone call to the Lampasas County sheriff, the two lawmen departed Waco with their prisoner. On May 11, Burton assisted Rangers Chesley O. Moore and Ed McMordie, Waco detectives George Blount and Wilburn Ernest Westmoreland, and Assistant McLennan County Attorney Holvey Williams in a liquor raid in Leon County. Two suspects were charged with the manufacture and sale of intoxicating liquors. The pair were arraigned before U.S. Commissioner McCormick the same day, and bond was set at one thousand dollars each. In June, George Daniels was shot in the abdomen and abandoned in a field on a Limestone County ranch. Discovered and taken to his brother's home near Mart, Daniels died of his wounds on June 17. Shortly thereafter, Sam Davis confessed to Burton, and indicated the shooting had occurred over one dollar following a dice game.[63]

Not disenchanted by his defeat in the previous election, Burton challenged Leslie Stegall for the office of county sheriff in 1928. During a Daniel James Moody rally held in Waco on July 27, all the county's candidates were welcomed to the platform, and Burton announced to the crowd, "I will close the gambling houses." However, his promise was not enough to attract the necessary number of votes in the Democratic primary the following day. Stegall triumphed by a count of 6,439 to 4,435.[64]

Burton announced his resignation from the marshal's office on February 28, 1929. The *Waco News-Tribune* noted he had been intending for some time to apply for a position with the Ranger Force. Indeed, two years prior, he had been offered the rank of private for immediate service in Borger, but Burton turned down the appointment due to the low pay. This time, rather than a regular commission, he received a warrant of Special Ranger on March 12. With that authority, he was employed by the Texas Oil Company to protect the pipeline under construction from New Mexico to Port Arthur. Later in the summer, he was detailed to guard company property in Sonora, Sutton County. During this pleasant assignment, he stayed at the McDonald Hotel, where, in September, he encountered the vacationing Governor Moody.

Over breakfast, the executive informed him martial law would be soon declared in Borger. After Moody departed for a hunting trip in Mexico, Burton told Mrs. McDonald he expected to be going to Borger soon.[65]

The reason for his prediction was the murder of John A. Holmes, the district attorney of Hutchinson County. In response, National Guardsmen and Captains Hamer and Hickman, Sergeant J. B. Wheatley, and Rangers Chesley Moore, Benjamin Maney Gault, Manuel Gonzaullas, William Hale Kirby, Dott Edward Smith, Sr., and Jules Wakeman "Tod" Aldrich were sent to restore order. The Rangers were additionally instructed to find Holmes's killer. Speaking at a luncheon in Amarillo, Federal District Judge James Clifton Wilson asserted the homicide was "the most serious crime in the history of Texas in thirty years and I believe the hand that fired the shot either was the hand of an official or had official sanction." Moody followed through on his comment to Burton and declared martial law in the county. Just back from his own one-day trip to Mexico, Burton took a long-distance call from Hickman. "You still a fighter?" the captain asked. "I'm the fightingest son of a gun in the world," Burton answered. Hickman informed him he was needed in Borger, but Burton replied, although he wanted a big case, the Texas Company was giving him twice a Ranger's salary, with an extra fifty dollar per month car allowance and an unlimited expense account. As his presence was considered vital, the Hutchinson County commissioners agreed to match Burton's earnings. The Texas Company approved a leave of absence, provided Burton return for emergencies involving the pipeline. Arriving on the last day of September, Burton was assigned to take over the Hutchinson County sheriff's office in Borger with the title of chief deputy. He lived in the Black Hotel across the street from his place of work. Ranger Moore was appointed sheriff on October 16 and headquartered in Stinnett. Albert Ramos Mace took over the office of police chief. William A. Henderson, manager of Burton's residence, replaced Glenn A. Pace as mayor. The National Guardsmen departed town on October 17, and Brigadier-General Jacob Franklin Wolters declared he was "leaving the city clean." With Borger quieted, four Rangers—Kirby, Dott Smith, Gault, and Purvis—were deemed sufficient to keep order. On October 29, the governor formally lifted martial law.[66]

John A. Holmes. *Courtesy Hutchinson County Historical Museum, Borger, TX.*

Notorious outlaw William Jennings Bryan "Whitey" Walker was under indictment for the murder of two Hutchinson County officers. Due to a lack of material witnesses, District Attorney Clem Calhoun obtained a continuance when the case was called to trial on November 4. The following day, Sheriff Fred Bowles of Pontotoc County, Oklahoma, arrived with extradition papers for Walker. The desperado was to be taken to Ada to face charges of bank robbery. According to Sheriff Moore, Walker was fearful of returning to Oklahoma where an array of felony counts awaited him, and even threw himself from a moving car in a vain attempt to escape. Together with fellow convicts Irvin Newton "Blackie" Thompson and Roy Alvin Johnson, the career criminal would make a more successful breakout from the state penitentiary at McAlester on August 30, 1933.[67]

As part of his duties, Burton was designated the lead investigator in the still-unsolved Holmes killing. During the period of martial law, a military court of inquiry had attempted to unravel the mystery without success. Burton worked up the case for over a year. He accumulated considerable evidence, including eyewitness statements, that James Hodges, a boiler works manager in Borger, and his friend Sam Jones, a former constable, had killed Holmes as a murder for hire on behalf of the old sheriff and chief of police, and other corrupt officials. Hodges was arrested at his home, while Burton traveled to Hobbs, New Mexico, and returned Jones to Borger on November 1, 1929. The pair were formally charged with homicide. Calhoun went before the grand jury, which handed down indictments on the two alleged hit men. Hodges and Jones were held for three weeks, doubtless to their lawyers' chagrin, and a *habeas corpus* hearing was threatened for November 18. On the sixteenth, Burton took the two prisoners from Stinnett to the Tarrant County jail, but Hodges managed to contact and retain local attorneys Charles and Clyde Mays, who applied for writs of *habeas corpus*. Before the court order could be served, Burton spirited his prisoners out of Fort Worth, and the three passed through Cleburne on the way to Stinnett. Borger attorney William Campbell Witcher successfully filed for a *habeas* review on November 19, and Hodges's and Jones's attorneys caught up with their clients in Wichita Falls and served the summonses. During the court proceeding, Burton, Sheriff Moore, and Calhoun were charged with illegally removing the prisoners from Hutchinson County and depriving them of their liberty. Calhoun, possessing a fiery temper, exchanged harsh words with Witcher, and they had to be separated by Deputy Sheriff W. L. Kelley. Under orders from two different courts, Burton returned his prisoners to the Hutchinson County jail. The two suspects were freed on bonds of $7,500 each. However, Calhoun insisted Hodges post an additional bond of fifteen hundred dollars for an earlier liquor indictment, and Jones a similar amount for an outstanding bribery charge. The pair had difficulty in finding bondsmen willing to file surety in district court, as Moore refused to involve himself in the matter.[68]

Using Moore's and Burton's absence to their advantage, two men robbed the First State Bank of Stinnett of six thousand dollars in cash on November 22. Entering the bank, they purportedly forced assistant cashier Reuben A. "Leo" Franks to open the vault. After taking the money, the thieves handcuffed Franks and left him inside the box, but the door failed to close. Although the cashier was able to free himself and sound the alarm, the robbers had already made their escape. Burton returned home the same day and questioned the newspaper boy who had seen the suspects enter and exit the bank. Subsequently interviewing Franks in the cashier's office, the deputy bluntly informed the bank employee that his involvement in the heist was obvious. Franks initially denied his guilt, then finally confessed to everything. W. R. "Bert" Smith, a former deputy sheriff and owner of four cotton gins in Lelia Lake, had convinced Franks and J. W. "Billy" Adams, an ex-convict and barber in Amarillo, to participate in the robbery. However, unbeknownst to Adams, Smith planned to kill him for the five-hundred-dollar reward posted by the Texas Bankers' Association. Burton took Franks to the Amarillo hotel where the loot was supposed to be split. They found Adams alone in the room, and the deputy took him into custody. Five hundred dollars was discovered under a mattress, while forty dollars were in a purse. Returning to Borger, Adams readily confessed after a moment of third-degree questioning. He offered to show Burton the location of the hidden money. Taking his prisoner to Lelia Lake, Burton found the loot under a trapdoor in the bathroom of Smith's house. Braced with the obvious evidence of his culpability, Smith attempted to gain possession of the deputy's sidearm, proclaiming "he would rather be dead than return to his family in guilt." Burton subdued the man and arrested him. Bootlegger Tarance Andrew "Lorrance" Popejoy was apprehended on the twenty-fifth as a coconspirator and placed in the county jail. Smith, Adams, and Franks were indicted on November 26; Popejoy followed suit three days later. While not an admirer of the Rangers, Asa Philip "Ace" Borger, the town's namesake, and the majority stockholder in the bank, presented Burton with a three hundred dollar check as a token of his appreciation.[69]

Granted a change of venue, the series of trials for the quartet began in the Eighty-fourth District Court in Panhandle on January 13, 1930. Claiming to have been in Clarendon at the time of the robbery, Smith was acquitted two days later. Franks pled guilty, but his jury deadlocked on the appropriate punishment. Judge Ernest Jerome Pickens dismissed the jurors and scheduled a retrial for January 27, but Franks's second hearing ended in a hung jury. Adams received a nine-year prison sentence, and Popejoy's trial was postponed until the March term of district court in Stinnett. The latter's case seems to have never been heard. Despite his earlier acquittal, Smith did not completely escape justice, as he was tried in Amarillo on December 9 for concealing stolen property and conspiracy to commit theft over fifty dollars. He was found guilty and sentenced to three years. His attorneys appealed, and Smith was granted a new trial.[70]

The trial of Jim Hodges and Sam Jones was scheduled for May 19, but Judge Pickens granted a continuance on the fifteenth. Although they had been indicted, most of the defendants' statements to officers and the district attorney were ruled inadmissible by the grand jury, and the prosecution had to rely on uncooperative witnesses. Acknowledging the weakness of the case, Calhoun declined to go to trial, and the defendants remained free under bond. Burton continued to pursue leads in Kansas, Oklahoma, and New Mexico, but ultimately the case went unsolved. Earlier in his legal career, Holmes had defended criminals, and Burton's inquiry revealed the murder victim was perhaps not the selfless crusader he was purported to be. He concluded: "My investigation convinced me personally that Holmes was not too far above the balance of the gang of officers at Borger but that he was operating as a lone wolf and he was crossed with the other faction."[71]

Although Holmes's murder consumed much of his time, Deputy Burton handled other cases for the people of Hutchinson County. Hope Larson escaped from the Nolan County jail on January 13, 1930. The fugitive was reportedly in Pampa, but he was finally apprehended in Borger by Deputy John Parks on February 5; Burton assisted in the arrest. His warrant as a Ranger was set to expire on March 12, and Burton wrote Captain Aldrich requesting a renewal. To justify the "special favor," he explained the occasional need to cross county lines, and mentioned his eventual return to the Texas Company. The entreaty seems to have been denied, but Burton continued to work for the sheriff's department. In the municipal elections held on June 24, ousted officials attempted to return to power through a new city charter. Former mayor John R. Miller, removed from office in 1927, was able to gain a city commission seat, and his colleagues appointed him to reoccupy his old office. Under the new charter's residency requirements, Police Chief Mace was obliged to resign his post. Clem Calhoun chose to serve out the remainder of his term and return to private practice. Even with the changes, the ex-Rangers who had overseen the local law enforcement agencies were successful in ensuring the old syndicate could not resume their illicit activities. The Great Depression, which would soon begin, was to play a larger role, as Borger ceased to be a major outlet of oil. With the legitimate revenue stream gone, the market for liquor, gambling, and prostitution likewise disappeared.[72]

Even as vice rackets faded in Borger, other crimes presented challenges to the county's law enforcement officers. On July 20, Burton was called to the Alamo Plant of the Phillips Petroleum Company at McGregor. An elderly man named Perry, who lived in a company camp on the Canadian River, informed him of a group of suspicious men occupying the camp house next door. As they showed up every week or two with plenty of guns and two new Fords, Perry was of the opinion they were bank robbers, but, when he returned home, the men were gone. Even though the Donley County State Bank in Clarendon had been robbed of $7,500 on June 23, Burton did not assign a great deal of importance to the tip.[73]

At one o'clock on the afternoon of July 27, Burton arose from a nap after working all night. Walking to the sheriff's office, he was informed Perry had reported the return of the mystery men. Shortly thereafter, Burton and Deputy Lex Leon Board responded to an auto accident involving an intoxicated man in front of the Phillips company school. Reaching the scene, the deputies found the impaired driver had fled up the Clemmons Highway and across the Canadian River. While in pursuit, Burton and Board spotted a car near the river matching Perry's earlier description. Burton was about to ignore the sighting and resume searching for the drunk driver when the car immediately left the road and raced across the prairie. Burton immediately followed the fleeing automobile into a canyon. Rounding a bend, Burton and Board found the car abandoned with one man running into an old pump house nearby and another climbing the side of the canyon wall. Ordering Board to stay with the car, Burton, gun in hand, pursued the second fugitive up the rim and onto the prairie for a quarter-mile. The day was extremely hot, and the sun beat down on the two running men. As Burton closed on his quarry, the man spun around and leveled two revolvers. His own pistol at the ready, the deputy walked closer to the gunman, and the two looked at each other for about fifteen seconds. Burton asked, "Why don't you shoot?" The outlaw made no reply. Burton then stated, "Drop those guns or I'm going to blow you in two." The gunman released his weapons, which Burton then secured. The lawman walked his prisoner back to the cars. Board had been unarmed, so Burton supplied the deputy with a rifle and ordered him to guard the captive. He then took the fugitive in the pump house into custody without incident.[74]

Burton chained the two prisoners together in the backseat and drove to the camp house where he found two women inside. He searched the residence and found a sack from an Alluwe, Oklahoma, bank containing cash and traveler's checks. In speaking to Perry's wife next door, Burton learned three men had recently run into a low shinnery—a dense growth usually of scrub oak—that grew along the river bottom and stood nearly as tall as a man. Leaving the women at the house, Burton, Board, and the two shackled prisoners motored down the Clemmons Highway when the chief deputy saw a man run across the road ahead of them and toward the side of a mountain. Burton ordered Board to fire a few warning shots, but the runner only sped up. Burton turned off the road and followed a draw as far as he could before leaping out of the car. He followed the fugitive into the canyon, but the man jumped into a clump of bushes and loosed two shots. Burton returned fire, and the would-be gunman threw down two guns and yielded. After the deputies' car crossed the river, Burton spotted another man hiding under a clump of bushes off the side of the road. The fugitive complied with the order to surrender, and Burton shackled him with the others.[75]

Returning to the Perry residence with Board and the four prisoners, Burton learned that a fifth individual had been in the camp house with the other wanted men. A female neighbor told him the suspect had recently emerged from the shinnery and gone into a nearby unoccupied home. The exhausted Burton went into the indicated residence and found the outlaw in the bathroom drunk and asleep, with a rifle in his hands. The deputy took him into custody. In the end, Burton and Board had captured a total of seven people and secured eight revolvers, four high-powered rifles, and two automatic shotguns. They also recovered nearly three thousand dollars stolen in a bank robbery in Alluwe on May 22, and another in Edna, Kansas, on July 27. Burton and Board transported their prisoners in two cars back to Borger, then on to the county seat. Once in Stinnett, Burton called the authorities in Alluwe and Edna and discovered the two local bankers' associations had offered a combined $2,250 reward for the capture of the robbers.[76]

Four of the suspects—identified as George Magness, Oliver Park Magness, Alvin Payton, and John Nichols—gave statements to Calhoun; the fifth was released. The thieves were then extradited on July 31 to Oswego, Kansas, where they waived a preliminary hearing. When George's mother beheld her younger son in his cell, she berated Labette County Sheriff Alfred C. Coad and reportedly declared, "Hell, sheriff, bank robbin' aint [*sic*] hardly no crime at all." Burton testified in the subsequent trial in Oswego. On September 19, Park Magness and Nichols pled guilty and were ordered to serve ten to fifty years behind bars. Maintaining their innocence for several weeks, George Magness and Payton finally pled guilty on October 14 and drew sentences of twenty to one hundred years. The heavier prison terms were due to previous convictions in Oklahoma. The following day, while he and Payton were being transported to the state penitentiary at Lansing, George produced a gun smuggled earlier into the jail, murdered Undersheriff Melvin C. Hamilton, and wounded Coad before being shot to death by the sheriff and Special Deputy Roy McClain. Payton had picked the lock of Magness's handcuffs and attempted to prevent McClain from responding to the threat. Burton arrived in Borger the same day, only to find a telegram informing him of the tragic news. Charged with murder and intent to commit murder, Payton went on trial in District Judge Charles Franklin Trinkle's courtroom in Fort Scott on January 7, 1931. The bank robber was convicted the same day and received two life sentences, one for Hamilton's murder and the second under the state's habitual criminal statute.[77]

While the four bank robbers faced justice, Amarillo attorney Alfred Day Payne, Sr. formally admitted on August 7 to planting three sticks of dynamite in his car on June 27 and killing his wife, Exa Johnson Payne, and maiming Alfred, Jr., their ten-year-old son. He also admitted to attempting murder on four previous occasions. While sitting in the courthouse and dictating his twenty-thousand-word confession, which covered sixty pages, the lawyer repeatedly smiled, sarcastically joked, and wept. He frequently turned to District Attorney Edward W. Thomerson to request waiving a trail and moving to an immediate execution. Payne claimed his extramarital affair with his secretary was not a factor, but, instead, blamed financial troubles and his fear that Mrs. Payne would discover his dalliance. He also expressed concern over the fate of his two daughters, and his sorrow that his son was alive and crippled. Burton sat in the room with the confessed murderer through the day and night, and later informed the press of the proceedings. Lottie Mae Moore, the sheriff's wife, prevented a massive jailbreak on August 21 by holding eighteen prisoners at bay with a gun until a deputy could assist her. However, four managed to escape before being recaptured shortly afterward. Amid the commotion, Payne sat in his cell and calmly ate his lunch. "I think they were fools for trying to escape at mealtime," he later commented. Eight days later, Payne was indicted by the Potter County grand jury and arraigned before District Judge Henry Sumrall Bishop the same day. Speculation at the time asserted relatives were planning to enter over the defendant's protest a plea of not guilty by reason of insanity. Burton was one of the law officers scheduled to testify in the upcoming trial. The question of Payne's mental state and guilt would never be answered, however, as he managed to blow himself up on August 30 using a vial of nitroglycerin he had smuggled into the jail.[78]

Sheriff Moore was narrowly defeated by former deputy James Lewis "Jim" Crane in the Democratic primary on August 23. The incumbent continued the campaign as a write-in candidate, but he still lost to Crane in the general election on November 5.[79] The threat of losing his job under the new administration was mitigated when Burton reenlisted as a Special Ranger on December 28, 1930, at the request of Governor Moody. On January 1, 1931, Burton was sent to Leon County to assist newly elected and inexperienced Sheriff Abb Seale in beginning his tenure. The Ranger was discharged five days later but continued to reside in the county seat of Centreville.[80]

He enlisted in Company C on March 1, 1931. Headquartered at Del Rio, Captain Asa Light Townsend was the company commander, but Burton was directed to meet Captain Hickman in Gladewater the same day. Arriving for his appointment, Burton lunched with Hickman, Captain A. R. Mace, and Privates Thomas Lee Heard, Walter Everette "Ebb" Riggs, Daniel Lafayette McDuffie, and William Kirby. Over their food, the state officers planned a general roundup of the criminal element in Kilgore. Sergeant Gonzaullas and Rangers Robert Gray "Bob" Goss and James Porter "J. P." Huddleston were already waiting in the beleaguered oil town. Hickman's detachment drove their horse trailers to a spot near Kilgore and proceeded to unload their mounts for a reconnoiter. The next day, amid cold and rainy weather, the ten Rangers descended on Kilgore and raided domino parlors, cafés, speakeasies, rooming houses, shacks, and tents. They padlocked a dozen brothels, two saloons, and a gambling house, and seized a large quantity of narcotics. Unless an individual could quickly demonstrate a legal means of support, he was likely to be taken into custody. Fortunately for the peace officers, the muddy roads kept lawbreakers from fleeing the dragnet. Overseen by Detective Captain Leonard Motier Pack of Dallas, three Dallas police automobile theft identification experts, and the local constable and his deputy, the prisoners were shackled to trace chains extending from a "trotline" running through the middle of the abandoned Baptist church. Furthermore, each was fingerprinted and photographed for comparison with neighboring police departments. However, the Rangers missed apprehending one car thief who stole a vehicle parked in front of the house where the lawmen slept. Before sundown, more than three hundred suspects had been apprehended, and the district attorney assisted in filing complaints against those believed to have committed crimes. Hickman informed the press he was just getting started.[81]

Leaving the others to manage efforts in Kilgore, Burton, Gonzaullas, Heard, and Riggs swept through the "unpainted yellow pine shacks" of Joinerville and Henderson. In the first encampment, they established a makeshift jail in an empty twenty-five by fifty-foot lot between two frame buildings. While Heard and Riggs guarded the "bull pen," as the lockup was named, Burton and Gonzaullas strode through the watering holes, gambling dens, and whorehouses. Going into the structures alone, each Ranger rounded up eight to ten individuals, searched them for guns or knives, and arrested those suspected of wrongdoing. Approximately 25 percent were armed, although others disposed of their weapons before being taken into custody. The two lawmen then escorted their prisoners back to the bullpen for Heard and Riggs to guard. Within two hours, they had gathered one hundred suspects, who were then ordered to walk to the church in Kilgore.[82]

In three days, nearly four hundred suspicious characters were arrested, but only thirty-five were held after being questioned. The remainder of "undesirables," including forty women, were ordered to leave town. Sheriff Dudley Snyder "Dud" Barker came from Fort Stockton to collect a man wanted on a murder charge. Sheriff Hayes and his office transported forty suspects to the Gregg County jail for further investigation. Four others were identified as being involved in major crimes in other states. The hard-charging Rangers continued to make numerous raids in Kilgore and Longview for gambling and liquor violations through April. Temporarily leaving town, Burton uncovered a large still west of Fort Worth on April 21.[83]

With Kilgore tamed, Burton transferred to Company B on May 1. He worked undercover in Fort Worth to locate the largest gambling houses and bootlegging joints operating in the city. He also gathered general information in advance of the Stock Show. He then assisted Kirby and McDuffie in raids in Bosque County. On July 6, Burton and Martin drove to Glen Rose and raided several dwellings. They found evidence of the recent removal of stills, but the moonshiners had left mash, barrels, and equipment to be destroyed. The following day, the pair observed where other stills had been removed and destroyed the abandoned paraphernalia. At the end of the month, Burton was stationed in Gladewater to replace the slain Dan McDuffie and dispatched to Longview and other towns situated around the oil field. He assisted the Texas National Guard during the period of martial law and performed general peacekeeping duties in the absence of the police force.[84]

Thief and killer T. J. "Speck" Buckley, alias Bucklan, first came to the attention of law enforcement when he and his partner, W. E. "Rusty" Russell, hijacked an automobile at Troup, Smith County, in the early hours of August 30, 1931. At noon the same day, Bucklan, soon to be known as the "triple threat criminal," shot and killed Russell while driving on the Gilmer road near Gladewater and rolled his body onto the highway; twelve-year-old Edith Schmoyer standing a few feet away witnessed the murder. Having only the little girl's description, Burton and Highway Patrolman John Calloway Gregory pursued the outlaw through Oklahoma, New Mexico, Arizona, and California until the trail led back to Texas. The lawmen had to take up other duties, but Bucklan was never far from their minds.[85]

On September 19, Burton assisted Gregg County officers in a weekend drive on narcotics and liquor trafficking in Longview and its environs. Five men were arrested on various sale and possession charges. The following month, Burton drove to Pistol Hill, then attended district court in Gladewater. By order of Governor Ross Shaw Sterling, on October 23, he, Ranger Lockhart Valentine Hightower, Sr., and Game Warden Hugh Ashford occupied the 4,600 acres of land along the Red River, twenty miles northwest of Texarkana, that was the subject of a boundary dispute between Texas and Arkansas. After six days of undisturbed vigilance by the state officers, the matter was settled by officials meeting in Little Rock. Burton and Hightower rejoined the company at Gladewater. Ten prisoners absconded from the Smith County jail on November 8, and two escapees under robbery charges were apprehended by Burton the following day at Gladewater.[86]

While conducting a liquor raid in Gladewater on December 21, Burton arrested five men. One of the suspects he instantly recognized: "I knew I had W. E. Russell's killer the minute I laid my eyes upon him, for the little Upshur county [*sic*] girl's description of the highway murderer fitted him perfectly." Gregory confirmed the identification, and Bucklan confessed. Amazingly, he was allowed to make bail, and once freed, embarked on a whirlwind crime spree. He struck repeatedly in the East Texas oil fields "as swiftly and silently as a gray wolf, each time apparently leaving no tell-tale mark behind by which baffled peace officers in the various counties could identify him." Bucklan joined the five-man gang led by armed robber Elbert Cole Oglesby, and they held up the Winona State Bank and Trust Company on May 25, 1932. The thieves then kidnapped three Van Zandt County deputies and carjacked a couple on July 10. Bucklan committed one hijacking at the Boone Refining Company one mile east of Arp on July 27.[87]

By this time, Burton was working in Waco. The body and wrecked auto of Nathan Washington Rhambo, a wealthy black undertaker in Austin, was found near Dawson on June 22, 1932. The following day, Carl Stewart, a black undertaker in San Antonio, was arrested by Hubbard City Marshal Lem Overton Bates and Night Watchman George Thorn for kidnapping and murdering Rhambo. Burton and Waco police detective Reuben M. McDonald took custody of the suspect and transported him to Austin. Stewart was taken to Corsicana the next day and indicted for murder. Not forgotten, Bucklan and Oglesby held up the Boone refinery on August 9, raided the Beacon refinery on August 16, kidnapped a Dallas motorcycle patrolman on August 20, and committed a second robbery at the Beacon refinery three days later. Burton and Gregory were dispatched to pursue the desperadoes.[88]

The state officers drove to Canton to question two gang members who had been recently captured. One of them was identified as "Curley" Oglesby, Cole's younger brother. Curley was transferred to the Smith County jail, and Cole's wife and mother came to the lockup in Tyler on August 19 with an attorney. Burton and Gregory placed the women under surveillance and followed them to their apartment house in Dallas. Meeting with local police detectives, they kept a close watch on the residence. At 8:30 a.m. the next morning, Burton led the law officers in storming the dwelling and arresting Bucklan, two women, and another accomplice. Even though Captain Hickman was on his trail, Cole Oglesby remained at large until he was killed by Oklahoma City police detective Charles Gerald "Jerry" Campbell on October 17.[89]

Bucklan was found guilty in four separate trials in Van Zandt, Rusk, Gregg, and Smith Counties on two counts of highway robbery, one of murder, and one of robbery with firearms. He received prison sentences totaling 109 years at hard labor and entered Huntsville on April 5, 1933.[90]

In October, Burton was working in the East Texas oil fields around Gladewater much to the chagrin of the local newspaper. Indeed, the daily's slogan read: "These rangers must go." Along with Rangers James Edward "Jim" McCoy and Maney Gault, Trooper Gregory, and Edward Andrew "Ed" Gormley of the Auto Theft Bureau in Dallas, Burton investigated an automobile theft ring that had moved forty to fifty stolen cars throughout the state. He tracked two suspects to a tourist cabin in Longview and kept them under observation for two days. Taking them into custody on November 11, he discovered a cache of money hidden in a pillowcase on the cabin's bed. The cash amounted to $132, all of them one-dollar bills, except for one 5-dollar note. The pair denied ownership of the cash, which Burton believed had been stolen in a bank robbery. Three more men were arrested on November 18 and lodged in the Tyler jail, while several cars were recovered. Burton then spent the last of November and the first several weeks of December attending district court in Tyler. On December 23, four men carjacked an individual on the 2300 block of Parrott Avenue in Waco, and Burton and Detective William Westmoreland arrested three suspects the following day.[91]

Burton was discharged from the Ranger service on January 18, 1933. Despite a lack of official credentials, he was summoned by Bosque County Sheriff Pearl Benson two days later to solve a daylight bank robbery in Cranfills Gap. On January 17, the thieves had walked out of the bank with nearly eight hundred dollars in stolen money. Since Burton was no longer on the state's payroll, the bank's officials agreed to cover his expenses for the duration of the case. By the night of the twenty-first, Burton was back in Waco with three suspects having been lodged in the Meridian jail. Two men were later convicted of the crime.[92]

Shortly after midnight on January 26, four men in a maroon sedan forced the three occupants of a Wald truck to pull over fourteen miles south of Waco on the Marlin road. Brandishing sawed-off shotguns, the robbers marched their captives to a railroad signal post and bound them together. The bandits, the truck, and the sedan drove off to the north. Freeing themselves, the three victims walked to Harrison's Switch and contacted Assistant Police Chief Wilder McDonald. The story of the hijacking was relayed at the police station to Detective Captain William Lee "Buck" Buchanan, Assistant District Attorney Francis Joseph Bauerle, Highway Patrol Captain Seabren Orville Hamm, and Burton. The truck was found ten hours later near Ennis, emptied of ten thousand dollars' worth of merchandise. Burton followed leads to Corsicana, where a suspect was deposited in the city jail, and to Ennis. He investigated in Dallas, then made a one-day visit to Waco on January 30 before returning.[93]

The investigation expanded to include Ennis and Ellis County authorities and four Texas Rangers—Captain Harry Thomas Odneal, Sergeant Albert "Bert" Whisnand, and Privates Cayce Bonds Shelton and Sidney Nolan "Sid" Kelso. Burton's unofficial role in the case seems to have ended at this point. Eight men from Ennis and Boyce were jailed on March 3 on charges of highway robbery, and receiving and disposing of stolen goods. District Attorney Archibald Duncan "Archie" Gray commented, "Ennis has been the base of operations for a ring trafficking in stolen cigarettes and other merchandise, as well as narcotics." Already wanted on burglary and jailbreak charges, Floyd "Dago" Seay and Jack Stewart were also suspected of participating in the January 26 holdup. The pair were captured, and both pled guilty to robbery with firearms. Their sentence of five years, added to other convictions, brought the total to more than a century behind bars, which led the *Waco Tribune-Herald* to ask, "what did five years more or less matter."[94]

On May 27, 1933, oil was discovered in the small town of Tomball, Harris County. Conventional wisdom held that the bonanza would follow the same pattern as other boomtowns. The rush of oil field workers and those who supplied them was sure to be quickly followed by a flood of lawlessness that would overwhelm local authorities. Sheriff Thomas Abner Binford anticipated a problem and requested Ranger assistance. While in Gregg County, Burton had been appointed a Special Ranger on April 8, and he was assigned to aid Binford. Upon arriving in town, he made his residence at the Davis Hotel, situated across Main Street from the bank, on the corner of Cherry and Main. During business hours, Burton positioned himself just inside the double doors of the bank, unless he was called away on official business. The town seemed relatively quiet: men became intoxicated and spent the night in jail, only to pay the fine before being freed to imbibe again. A man passing hot checks traveled through town. Burton broke up craps games and other minor crimes. The anticipated disorder may have been deterred due to Burton's hard-earned reputation. He remained in Tomball until he was certain the town was pacified, then returned to Waco.[95]

Burton's Ranger career came to an end on January 23, 1934, when his Special Ranger warrant expired. He briefly worked for a pipeline company in Longview before becoming a "special investigator" in Mexia. Groesbeck dairyman John L. Adams had been kidnapped and later found dead in a stock tank on May 25. Burton was employed to work the case, and he and Sheriff William Lee Adams attempted to trace the ownership of the .38-caliber revolver that had been left next to the body. A nineteen-year-old laborer was questioned in the city jail, and later led Burton to the victim's coin purse that was buried in the woods near his home. A mysterious note written to Adams's son the day after the abduction was also examined. Within thirty-six hours, three other suspects had joined the laborer in custody. County Attorney Henry Jackson filed charges against the laborer and was prepared to prosecute two others; the fourth suspect had been released.[96]

Two men robbed the First National Bank of Atlanta, Texas, on June 6 and stole ten thousand dollars. With the trail going cold, bank officials hired Burton on July 29 to act as a private detective and catch the thieves. After three weeks of investigation, the former Ranger learned of dimes that had been deposited into a bank. He traced the specie to two Little Rock natives. Burton accompanied officers in arresting the pair of suspects, who were identified by eyewitnesses.[97]

Waco Mayor Carl Mason abruptly resigned on November 22, 1934, and all his department appointees were slated for replacement. After holding several secret sessions, the town's municipal government decided to replace the current city manager with William Clifton Torrence. Attorney Woodie Moore Zachry, Sr. was chosen the new police chief, and Burton succeeded Captain George Blount as the department's chief of detectives. The former Ranger's name had been mentioned for the top position, and fifteen hundred citizens signed a petition urging his appointment. He was likewise considered for the open slot of city fire marshal, based on his record as an investigator. After an absence of seventeen years, Burton's return to the Waco Police Department brought him a monthly salary of $150. Zachry made the reorganization of the police his first priority, and dismissed eleven officers in "the best interests of the department."[98]

Although Burton was now a supervisor, he was still actively involved in investigations. Indeed, he began working with city detectives two days before his appointment was made official. Burton's first year on the job saw a rash of robberies and burglaries. In response, the captain announced a drive on thieves and pilferers, and promised to lodge them in the city jail until after the Christmas season. Two men robbed the Safeway store at Eighteenth and Washington Streets on January 19, then robbed the Piggly Wiggly at Twenty-second and Bosque ten minutes later. Based on information provided by Sheriff William Brode Mobley, Sr., the armed suspects were peacefully arrested at 9 p.m. the next day by Burton, Deputy Sheriffs Jess S. Stanfield and John W. Duncan, and Deputy Constable Irving Paul Stanford. Thieves broke into a store in Prairie Hill on March 21, 1935, but they were interrupted by the local constable. In fleeing the scene, the perpetrators abandoned a stolen Model A Ford in which was later found a water spaniel likely belonging to the car's owner. Burton attempted to return the auto and the dog to the rightful person. The automobile of George W. Pittman was stolen in early April 1935, and the car thief was found in Dallas attempting to sell the purloined vehicle. Burton was assigned to retrieve the suspect and the car and return them to Waco. Detectives arrested three people on charges of forging government checks. One of the suspects claimed a fourth individual was the guilty party, and Burton traveled to Fort Worth on June 11 to retrieve the person of interest. In August, Burton and Detective Westmoreland arrested a man wanted in Waxahachie in connection with approximately twenty burglaries. The two lawmen had been given a description of the suspect by Dallas authorities and tipped he was selling stolen property. On being notified of the apprehension, Waxahachie police officers came to Waco and took charge of the prisoner. Burton and Westmoreland accompanied Coryell County Sheriff Joseph Milton White to Orchard Lane on September 16 in search of stolen cattle. They not only found one of the cows, but also discovered two 75-gallon stills in the house of the man in possession of the animal. Two suspects were arrested, and complaints were filed in federal court in connection with the stills. Charges of cattle theft remained under consideration. On October 10, the Tenth Court of Civil Appeals ruled marble machines were illegal gaming devices and were, thus, subject to seizure and destruction. Approximately 250 machines in Waco brought $1.5 million in revenue to operators, yet city and county law enforcement agencies elected to give storeowners reasonable opportunity to comply before confiscation was undertaken. A complaint filed in the court of Justice Clint Allen on December 3 charged a man with burglarizing a Windsor Avenue home of jewelry, an overcoat, and a radio. The suspect was arrested in Denton, and the stolen items found in his possession were returned to Waco by Burton and Deputy Sheriff John Duncan.[99]

In conjunction with similar efforts throughout Texas, agents of the U.S. Narcotics Bureau initiated a drive in Waco to apprehend members of a drug ring. Rather than Mexico, the product was being shipped west from New York and other East Coast cities, and dealers in Waco were earning an average of $150 a day from their criminal enterprise. In addition to the heroin and morphine flooding the streets, other offenses were being committed, as property stolen in petty thefts was sold at cut-rate prices to pay for addicts' habits. Burton and Westmoreland cooperated with the effort, and four suspects were soon arrested; an arrest warrant was issued for a fifth. One of the alleged dealers was indicted by the federal grand jury on February 27, and the other three were released by Justice Claude Harvey Segrest, Sr. on one-thousand-dollar bonds each.[100]

Burton, Westmoreland, Detective Wiley Stem, and policemen Richard Grover McClain and Jack Lafayett Hackney aided Secret Service agents in arresting Tommy Crowson and John Latt for counterfeiting. The two appeared before U.S. Commissioner James Davis Willis for a preliminary hearing. Crowson was charged with possession and the transferring of four bogus twenty-five-cent pieces. Latta pled guilty to possessing molds to manufacture the counterfeit quarters and possession of illicit coins. Bond was fixed at $750 and $1,250, respectively.[101]

Sheriff Harry Rogers of Jasper County, Missouri, arrived in Waco on July 22 with an extradition order for Frank Hardy on a charge of bank robbery. The suspect's attorneys attempted to obtain a writ of *habeas corpus* to prevent the transfer, but they were too late. Burton and Assistant District Attorney Frank Hartley appeared at the county jail and removed the prisoner, ostensibly for a conference with the district attorney. Instead, the law officers put Hardy into a waiting coupe and drove away. The lawyers, Police Chief Clyde Curtis Maxey, and Sheriff Mobley were nonplussed in finding the prisoner gone, and Maxey radioed Burton to return with Hardy. Telephoning the sheriff two hours later, the detective chief revealed Governor James Burr V. Allred had signed the order and Hardy had been turned over to Rogers.[102]

By 1938, Burton was a substantial property owner. He operated a two-hundred-acre farm of "good black land" near Mart. The crops he grew included corn, other feed, and cotton. The *News-Tribune* noted the "comfortable houses, with barns suited to the needs of so large an acreage." In addition, Burton owned a fifteen hundred-acre stock farm straddling both sides of the Navasota River in Robertson and Leon Counties. He kept twelve hundred acres in pasture, and his herd of one hundred Hereford cattle, and twenty horses and mules, grazed on Bermuda grass and burr clover. The remaining land was utilized to farm feed and cotton.[103]

Maxey resigned from the police department to run for sheriff in the 1946 election. The city board of aldermen unanimously named Burton to succeed him as chief on June 18. Burton had not applied for nor sought the vacant position, and only reluctantly accepted the appointment. To protect his civil service status and his twelve years' service credit, he received a leave of absence from his position as detective captain. Burton graciously took out a notice in the *News-Tribune*, thanking friends and well-wishers for their support.[104]

The following month, a labor strike at the General Tire and Rubber Company plant experienced a bout of violence on the seventeenth, when a plant foreman was assaulted by a United Rubber Workers union member on the corner of Fourth Street and Austin Avenue. Chief Burton and Officer Joe Kemble arrested both men, and they were released on bonds of ten dollars each. The foreman was subsequently taken to Providence Hospital for treatment.[105]

As a city department administrator, Burton found few opportunities to be the hard-charging lawman who had harried moonshiners twenty years before. While Mayor Richard Clarence Bush and the city council met with the chamber of commerce to discuss traffic problems in town, the police department was instructed, on July 24, to diligently enforce the laws concerning double parking, failure to completely halt at stop signs, and speeding. Burton and City Engineer Manton Hannah were appointed in early August to study the practicality of making Elm, Taylor, Seventh, and Ninth Streets one-way avenues. While working on the traffic issue, Burton was able to secure positions for twelve new officers in the city's budget, effective October 3. Four of those recruits were to be motorcycle officers who would enforce parking ordinances and free beat cops for other duties. On the sixteenth, Burton announced a crackdown of traffic violations and revealed his officers had been plentifully supplied with tickets. In one day, 209 summonses were filed, which was a 400 percent increase. However, Judge Wilmer Cleburne Haley of the city court dismissed the cases involving parking in unmetered spaces in the business district. He reasoned violators had not been sufficiently notified of the increased enforcement effort and were entitled to one warning. For all other cases, he imposed a one-dollar fine. Late in the year, the police chief worked with Hannah's replacement, John Strange, to make recommendations on angle parking. The board of aldermen adopted a resolution to replace angle parking ordinances with parallel parking on the city's streets. On December 29, Burton noted motorists were observing the new rules.[106]

Police officers had seized seventeen slot machines at the New Moon dance hall on November 18. Elbert Roosevelt Erwin filed a civil suit in county court naming Burton personally, and claimed the machines were taken from his shop and not in use. The chief was directed to relinquish the gaming equipment under a sequestration order on January 11, 1947. He responded by filing a felony complaint in justice court against Erwin for "exhibiting" one of the slot machines for play. Held in the city jail, the dance hall operator was freed on the thirteenth on a $750 bond. Burton's predecessor, Woodie Zachry, was one of the attorneys representing Erwin. County Judge Douthit Young McDaniel, Sr. dismissed the plaintiff's lawsuit on January 31, and signed a court order instructing Burton to destroy the gambling devices. Additionally, he charged Erwin for the court costs involved. On May 7, the indictment against Erwin was dismissed by District Judge Drummond Webster Bartlett at the written request of eleven grand jurors. Instead, Erwin pled guilty to a misdemeanor and paid a five-hundred-dollar fine.[107]

While the slot machine case wound its way through the courts, Waco and McLennan County saw a spate of robberies. On November 22, 1946, the First National Bank of Mt. Calm was robbed by a single thief who never showed a weapon during the heist. The soft-spoken bandit, described as being approximately fifty years of age, forced a female cashier to hand over four thousand dollars, mostly in new one-dollar bills. He nonchalantly made his escape in an auto east on the Waco–Corsicana road. The alarm went out to neighboring jurisdictions, and Burton and Detectives Westmoreland and Tilley Saunders Buchanan (the son of the former sheriff) were the first law officers to respond. They were soon joined by representatives from the FBI, the Highway Patrol, and the Hill County Sheriff's office. Roadblocks were erected, but the bandit escaped the dragnet.[108]

Forcing open the rear door of the Safeway store at 2415 North Eighteenth Street on January 18, 1947, thieves chiseled from the concrete foundation a heavy steel safe containing an undisclosed amount of money. The strongbox was then loaded into the back of a pickup truck and driven away. Working with Detective Buchanan, Burton personally investigated the crime and interviewed a suspect the next day. That same evening, he, Detective Captain Stem, and Buchanan drove to Walnut Springs after being informed by a Texas Ranger based in Stephenville of a safe found in a pasture near Glen Rose. Opened and empty, the steel box, estimated to weigh six hundred pounds, fit the description of the one stolen in Waco. The investigators theorized the robbery had been perpetrated by at least three people.[109]

Clark's Grocery Store on the corner of Eleventh Street and Austin Avenue was held up on February 6 by a pistol-wielding man. Entering the premises twenty minutes before closing time, the clean-cut thief calmly held the store clerk and three customers at gunpoint, smashed a shotgun found near the rear wall, smoothly robbed the till of one thousand dollars, and escaped into the night. Due to the gloves the suspect wore, there were no usable fingerprints. With no other witnesses or evidence with which to pursue a lead, investigators were even unaware how the armed robber left the scene. Stem theorized he had parked a car in the alley behind the store. Burton commented to reporters on his belief that the crime had been committed by an experienced professional. Believed to be a simple robbery at first, the case took on more dramatic dimensions when evidence soon led investigators to Walter Glen Ransom, a twenty-three-year-old felon on parole for armed robbery from the Minnesota State Prison.[110]

A former resident of the State School for Boys at Gatesville, Ransom began a widely publicized crime spree in Mt. Pleasant on February 10, 1947. For the next four days, he committed robberies and burglaries in Henrietta,

Talco, Paris, Greenville, and Commerce, and one kidnapping in Bogata, Red River County. While engaged in his rampage of larceny, Ransom evaded more than one hundred law officers and numerous civilian possemen conducting a massive manhunt in Northern Texas. Ransom attempted to cross the state line near the town of Telephone, but Oklahoma lawmen turned him back with gunfire. The barefooted and unarmed desperado was finally cornered on Gil Goss's farm located on the forks of the Red River and Bois D'Arc Creek. Having peacefully surrendered, he was taken to the sheriff's office in Bonham and questioned by Ranger Captain Manuel T. Gonzaullas and Ranger Paul Raymond Waters in the presence of other officers and some journalists. In addition to being charged for the Waco holdup, Ransom confessed to the robbery of the Furr Food Store in Lubbock on January 28. Tragically, Dallas police officer Preston Daniel Hale, a wartime veteran of the Army Air Corps, was killed on the twelfth when the search plane he was piloting crashed. The effort to apprehend the fugitive cost the State of Texas $32,000 in salaries, equipment, and supplies. Before being transferred to Waco, Ransom was tried for car thefts committed during his crime spree and sentenced to four years' imprisonment. He was indicted by the McLennan County grand jury for the Clark's Grocery robbery. His trial was scheduled for the Fifty-fourth District Court.[111]

Burton and McLennan County Sheriff Charles Grear Alexander sponsored a two-week school for approximately 115 local, state, and federal peace officers from twenty different Central Texas counties. The special agent-in-charge of the FBI office in San Antonio was invited to head the course at the Roosevelt Hotel beginning on February 10. The course ended on the twentieth with a mock trial in the Fifty-fourth District courtroom.[112]

Fresh from a three-day goodwill trip to Mexico, President Harry S. Truman visited Waco on March 6, 1947, to receive an honorary Doctor of Laws degree from Baylor University. The chief executive's security detail was augmented by troops from Fort Hood, and by local and state law officers from Waco, Dallas, Fort Worth, Mexia, Temple, and other towns. Numbering more than five hundred men, the task force stood ready to guard the president's route from Municipal Airport through the business district along South Fifth Street to the Baylor campus. Waco's entire complement of seventy policemen was on hand, the largest number to be simultaneously on duty up to that point in time. Prior to Truman's stopover, police officers questioned building owners and occupants on the route as part of the painstaking preparations. Along with the Secret Service, Burton warned the expected thousands of bystanders to remain on the sidewalks as the presidential motorcade passed through the streets. Demonstrating the relative innocence of the times, Secret Service Agent Leo Williams informed reporters the tops of the automobiles would be down if weather permitted. "We want to give all a chance to see the President," he commented. On the appointed day, Burton rode in the lead vehicle of the motorcade with Secret Service chief James Joseph Maloney, Sheriff Alexander, and several other visiting officers. Homer Garrison, Jr., director of the Texas Department of Public Safety, and the police chiefs of Dallas and Temple were likewise present.[113]

Downtown Waco was victimized by an epidemic of arson attempts in the spring of 1947, and police detectives and Fire Chief Lee Harrington questioned numerous suspects. The Rainbow Garment Company factory, the DeWitt-Clark Lumber Company, and the Olmsted-Kirk Paper Company had all suffered a fire. On May 23, the unknown firebug tried to use a kerosene-soaked rag and a pile of kindling to burn down the Bone-Crow Company printing plant on North Sixth Street before being frightened away. Thirty minutes prior, firefighters had battled two blazes on South Fifth Street. Another effort was made behind buildings on the six hundred block of Franklin Avenue. The *modus operandi* led investigators to believe the arsons were the work of one individual. On March 29, Patrolmen Theron Joel Richey and Finley Votaw approached a young man in an alley, but the youth fled, only to be apprehended in a movie theater shortly thereafter. Another boy was arrested in the alley, and he confessed to being present when the first suspect turned in four or five false fire alarms. Burton and Stem were aware they had little to no evidence with which to charge the youth, but they did note no arsons had been attempted since the arrest.[114]

Florence's health had begun to decline in 1940. She died at Providence Hospital on October 20, 1948, of "cerebral apoplexy," a condition now recognized as a stroke. She was buried at Rosemound Cemetery.[115]

In late 1950, Burton was ensnared in the feud between City Manager Robert Cottman Hoppe and the local press. Some city commissioners spread the rumor the chief was using department vehicles and the free labor of prisoners for ranch work, although supporters steadfastly maintained he had never employed city cars for personal use. Furthermore, Burton explained the allegation concerning prisoners likely sprang from the time he had paid one volunteer for his assistance with a sick cow. Nevertheless, the board of aldermen relieved Burton of his duties as police chief on December 17, 1950, and appointed Night Captain Jesse Virgil Gunterman in his stead. Reverting to his permanent rank, Burton was assigned to his successor's old position. Hoppe opposed the ouster and briefly offered his resignation in protest. However, Burton requested vacation and was scheduled to take up his new responsibilities on February 1, 1951. Instead, he tendered his resignation, effective January 31, to City Attorney Diuguid Mim Wilson in the absence of Hoppe. Before leaving the department, though, he remained on the city's payroll until his fifty days of accumulated sick leave was paid under the provisions of the 1947 civil service law. He later moved to a one-hundred-acre ranch outside Riesel, barely two miles from where he was born. Burton felt slighted by his dismissal and, for the rest of his life, never again set foot in the City Hall building.[116]

In his final years of law enforcement work, Burton had met Gladys Audrey (Ivy) Winn. She was employed by the Waco Police Department as a secretary from October 1, 1949, until her resignation effective January 15, 1951. She was born on July 9, 1902, and served as postmistress of Newby in her father's store from April 6, 1927, to May 26, 1928. She was also involved in home building, and oversaw the construction of her mother's house in Riesel. Gladys had wed Robert Harmon "Bert" Winn, a service station manager and bus driver, on February 16, 1928, in Leon County. They had no children, and their union ended in divorce. Marvin and Gladys married in Anderson County on November 3, 1959.[117]

For many years, Burton was a benefactor of the Riesel-Hallsburg community. He was largely responsible for the H & H Water Supply Corporation financing a water supply system in the Hallsburg and Harrison area. He was also involved in homesite development along Highway 6 and Highway 164 east of the junction of the two roads. He served as lay leader for his church, and spent eight years on the board of lay activities of the district.[118]

On the evening of May 16, 1970, Burton died upon impact in a two-vehicle accident at the intersection of Gresham Street and Highway 7 in Marlin. His car had been hit broadside and slammed into a telephone pole. The other driver suffered only bruises. Described by his old friend, W. E. Westmoreland, as "one of the greatest [law officers] Texas ever had," he was buried in Riesel Cemetery three days later.[119]

Before and after her marriage to Burton, Gladys worked for the Moody Chamber of Commerce and Agriculture as the organization's collector. She also served the Golden Circle Class of the First Baptist Church of Bellmead as assistant secretary. Gladys died at a Waco hospital on September 28, 1988, and was buried in Riesel Cemetery.[120]

By April 1930, Alice was employed by the Hutchinson County tax collector as a stenographer. The following year, she gave birth to a daughter at The Cedars Sanitarium and Maternity Home in Dallas. The father was not named on the birth certificate. According to the 1940 federal census, Alice was living at her parents' home without her daughter. The whereabouts of the child are undetermined. Alice belonged to the Women's Missionary Society of Herring Avenue Methodist Church and served as treasurer. She died in Dallas on July 3, 1971, and was buried next to her mother.[121]

Laura married James Shearer Rogers on January 9, 1926. The following year, they moved to Dallas, where James worked as a representative for a pharmaceutical company. He was later a registered pharmacist. James died at University Hospital on July 12, 1976, two weeks after suffering a stroke induced by arteriosclerotic cardiovascular disease. He was buried in Rosemound Cemetery. Laura died on January 6, 1995, and she was laid to rest next to her husband.[122]

Raymond attended Weatherford Junior College and Baylor University, and graduated from Southwestern University in 1936. The same year, he married Mildred Newton Crawford, and was the father of two daughters and one son. In 1935, he became a member of the Central Texas Conference of the United Methodist Church and served numerous churches, including those in

Cleburne, Comanche, Cisco, Ennis, Stephenville, Weatherford, and Fort Worth. Raymond served as an Army Air Corps chaplain in the Pacific from 1942 to 1945. In 1967, he was appointed conference director of missions and evangelism. He also served Pleasant Mound UMC Dallas in the North Texas Conference. Dying at home in Fort Worth on November 17, 2006, he was buried at Laurel Land Memorial Park.[123]

Marvin Burton was an immovable force. For over thirty years, he faced a variety of offenders ranging from white supremacists, to bootleggers, to murderers without fear or favor. His determined stand at Lorena in opposition to popular sentiment demonstrates his moral and physical courage, and his performance at Glen Rose exhibits his resolve to fulfill a tough assignment.

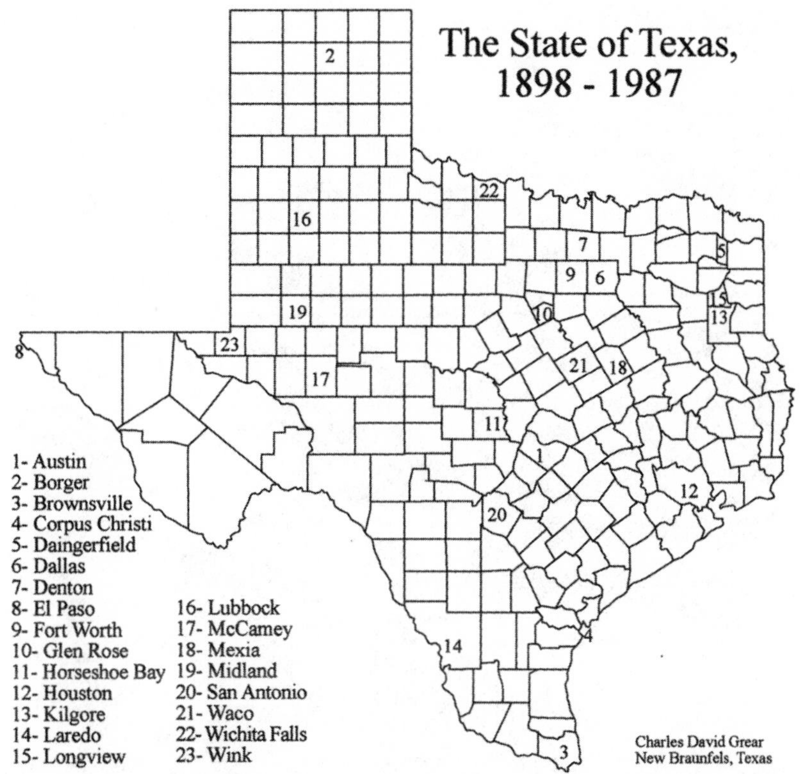

Map of Texas, 1898–1987. *Courtesy Charles David Grear.*

Captain Bob Crowder, 1948. #1983/112_R-316-1. *Courtesy Texas State Library and Archives Commission, Austin, TX.*

Chapter 7

Robert A. Crowder: "Always Faithful"

Robert Austin "Bob" Crowder often said he would not trade his Ranger position for the presidency of the United States. Indeed, his dedication to and love for the Texas Ranger service was evident in his words and his deeds. Always faithful to his sworn oath, he enforced the law as more a peacemaker than a gunfighter. His confidence, lack of conceit, and strength of character combined in a natural ability to lead others. While a widely regarded professional law officer, as a man, he was approachable and loyal to friends. To his family, he offered a firm yet steady guidance. Colonel Homer Garrison once gestured to Crowder and commented: "I have heard it said that the Texas Rangers are the Marines of law enforcement. If so, there goes my top Marine."

He was born in Minden, Rusk County, Texas, on January 29, 1901. His parents were Robert Richard Crowder and Cora L. (Anderson) Crowder. Richard, as he was known, was a farmer born in 1868 in Tippah County, Mississippi. He and Cora married on November 11, 1894, in Rusk County. Bob's brothers were Morris Gould Crowder, born on May 19, 1896, and Walter H. Crowder, born on October 22, 1897.[1] When young Bob was fifteen months old, Cora was injured in the ankle and leg when a shotgun accidentally discharged. She died soon afterward due to lead poisoning. The elder

Crowder married Sarah Lorene "Loffie" (Nix) Aiken in Panola County on December 13, 1906. She had been born on April 17, 1877, and added five sons by a previous marriage to the growing family: James Edgar, William Oscar, Charles Barnet, Robert Lee, and Edney Marvin Aiken. Additionally, Sarah gave birth to Don Doyle Crowder on October 1, 1907. However, the union proved brief, and Richard and Sarah divorced. By 1910, Bob Crowder was living on the farm belonging to Isabella Hays, his father's sister, along with his father and two older brothers.[2]

Even at the age of nine, Crowder demonstrated he was a hard worker. Due to the family's financial difficulties, he toiled on a nearby farm for eight dollars per month (seven of which he sent to his father) and room and board. He later quit and was employed on another farm with an increase in monthly pay to thirteen dollars. His early life was not filled with boyhood games, but rather with doing a "man's work" and sharecropping fifty acres of corn, sweet potatoes, peanuts, and cotton, plus an additional five acres of sugarcane. His original application to the Department of Public Safety indicated he attended high school in Minden until his fourth year.[3]

After his landlord cheated him of his fair share in the harvest's proceeds in 1914, Crowder left and went to work for a county road crew at thirty dollars a month. He spent one year building bridges and improving primitive dirt tracks and country lanes into more modern roads. He then relocated to Henderson where he hauled freight in a horse-drawn wagon from the train depot to local farms and businesses. Several years later, he and his brothers worked with wheat harvesters moving northward across the Plains states. In between seasons, they worked on cattle ranches and hay farms in eastern Colorado.[4]

Tiring of his hand-to-mouth existence, Crowder enlisted in the United States Marine Corps in Denver on September 24, 1921. He listed his occupation as "laborer." A medical examination on September 29 described him as brown-haired, brown-eyed, six feet, one inch in height, and 168 pounds in weight. He was formally sworn into service with Company B at the Recruit Depot, Marine Barracks, Mare Island, California, on October 1. He was assigned Service No. 177821.[5]

Before the establishment of the San Diego Recruit Depot in 1925, the Corps' western boot camp was found at Mare Island, a marshy peninsula in

San Pablo Bay, northeast of San Francisco. Crowder's commanding officer was Second Lieutenant Irving Ernest Odgers, but, as a brand-new recruit, he would see little of officers. Instead, his world was controlled by the noncommissioned officers of the company, especially his drill instructor, Sergeant Henry Ruskofsky. The sergeant was described as a "tough, mean-mouthed 'little Napoleon'" who seemed especially hostile toward the tall, lean Texan. Unused to the severe military regimen of the day, Crowder was extremely rebellious and often awarded punishments for his infractions. Eventually, the training, discipline, and *esprit de corps* of Marine boot camp changed Crowder's attitudes, and he graduated as a tougher and more disciplined man.[6]

Crowder was temporarily assigned to the Detached Guard Company, Western Recruiting District, Captain Cecil S. Baker and Second Lieutenant Stephen Skoda commanding, in San Francisco on November 10.[7] The company had been created days before in response to a rash of mail robberies. The losses in the previous three years had amounted to six million dollars in cash and negotiable bonds. On November 7, President Warren Gamaliel Harding sent a letter to Secretary of the Navy Edwin Denby directing him to "detail as guards for the United States Mails a sufficient number of officers and men of the United States Marine Corps to protect the mails from depredations by robbers and bandits."[8] Secretary Denby, a former Marine himself, complied and in a message to the Corps specified the rules of engagement:

> You must, when on guard duty, keep your weapons in hand and, if attacked, shoot to kill. There is no compromise in this battle with bandits. If two Marines guarding a mail car, for example, are suddenly covered by a robber, neither must hold up his hands, but both must begin shooting at once. One may be killed, but the other will get the robber and save the mail. When our Marine Corps men go as guards over the mail, that mail must be delivered or there must be a dead Marine at the point of duty.[9]

Fortunately, Crowder did not have to give his life in defense of the mail, and he transferred back to Mare Island six days later. There, he was assigned to Guard Company No. 1 under the command of Captain Baker.

On November 22, he was assigned to the Marine Detachment aboard the U.S.S. *Oklahoma*. The *Oklahoma* (BB-37), a 27,500-ton *Nevada*-class battleship, was assigned to Battleship Division Three of the Battle Fleet and homeported at the Puget Sound Navy Yard in Bremerton, Washington.[10]

On June 25, 1922, the detachment's commanding officer, Captain Charles I. Murray, certified that Crowder had qualified as an expert marksman. On July 21, Crowder was found to be absent from quarters for twenty-four hours. Although he remained on duty, he was designated a Prisoner at Large while awaiting disciplinary action. On July 24, he was sentenced to two day's confinement on bread and water. His subsequent service must have met required standards, as he was authorized by Captain Stephen V. Graham, commanding officer of the *Oklahoma*, to take a furlough from December 22 to January 21, 1923.[11]

On April 10, he was assigned to the rifle range detachment at Camp Lewis, Washington. He qualified as a sharpshooter on April 21 and three days later as an expert rifleman with an automatic rifle. On April 26, Crowder qualified as a primary marksman and an expert rifleman (noncompetitive). He was also a member of the division rifle team, which stood first in competition and was awarded a two-dollar prize.[12]

Crowder's days as a Marine were filled with annual training activities. Through the summer, he received a sharpshooter and an expert rifleman insignia. He qualified as a swimmer first class and as a director trainer on September 8. He was detailed to that role the same day. On September 17, Crowder was promoted to the probationary regular warrant of corporal, bypassing that of private first class.[13]

Crowder's name appears on the muster roll dated October 1 to October 31, 1923, for Company F at the Marine Barracks, Mare Island. His rank is given as private. He was also listed on the muster roll of the Marine Detachment on the *Oklahoma* as a corporal for the same month. On the latter roll, his status was recorded as being sick from the eighteenth to the nineteenth but present for duty. On December 21, he was given a furlough by Captain W. Pitt Scott, commanding the *Oklahoma*, lasting until January 19.[14]

On April 3, Crowder was detached to the navy's recreation camp at Kitsap Lake, Washington, for three days. He was then detached to the rifle range at Fort Lawton, Washington. On April 11, Crowder's temporary promotion to corporal was confirmed to become a permanent warrant to date from September 17, 1923. Returning to duty on April 17, he qualified as a sharpshooter and received his primary marksman badge on April 26.[15]

On June 20, he transferred to the Marine Corps Base, Naval Operating Base, San Diego, California, and the following day was assigned to the 59th Company, 7th Regiment under, first, Second Lieutenant Chesley G. Stevens, then Captain Henry L. Larsen.[16] On July 9, Crowder was posted to the Sea School Detachment at the Recruit Depot under the command of First Lieutenant John B. Neill. Prior to starting his new assignment as an instructor, he took furlough until August 7.[17]

Crowder was honorably discharged on September 30, 1924, upon the expiration of his enlistment. His various commanding officers had rated his professional conduct for military efficiency, obedience, and sobriety, and he finished with an average score of 4.9 out of five. Crowder was approved to receive the Good Conduct Medal on September 4, and awarded the decoration upon his separation.[18]

Returning once more to the civilian world, Crowder found the task of finding steady work difficult. After scant success in Henderson, he traveled to Dallas and was employed by American Express as a truck driver, then by the city as a streetcar conductor. This second job was so frustrating he felt a significant change was needed. He applied to the Dallas Police Department and was accepted on June 26, 1925. The fourth police chief in the last four years, Claude Woodson Trammell faced the violence created by Prohibition, the early stages of the forthcoming Depression, and answering citizens' demands with too few officers and limited resources. The training then practiced by the department was nonexistent, and the veteran officers were unwilling to share their knowledge; Trammell would institute regular classes in due time. When asked if he knew how to ride a motorcycle, Crowder answered affirmatively, although he had in fact no clue. He was assigned to duty as a motorcycle officer and managed only a few hours' practice at the local Harley-Davidson dealership before his first day on the job. He was later reassigned to walk a beat, and his fortune changed in the form of Officer Louis Oliver Buzan, who took the younger Crowder under his wing and instructed him in the trade of police work. The training and friendship he received from Buzan were central to Crowder's outlook as a public servant, and he was later promoted to warrant officer. His steady employment allowed him to purchase a house for $1,800 in the Clifton Place neighborhood from J. W. Ullman on June 26, 1926.[19]

While in Dallas, he met Lucile June Simmons. She had been born on June 27, 1900, in Waverly, Alabama. Lucile was an exceptionally creative and social person who delighted in talking with other people. Described as "sweet and giving," she was nevertheless resilient and exceptionally loyal to family and friends. Her children from a previous marriage were James Thomas Sturgis, born in Hope, Arkansas, on April 18, 1919, and Marcoline Harriet Sturgis, born on August 21, 1920, in Dallas. A spitfire in her youth, Lucile left James and Marcoline with her fundamentalist Christian parents, so she could go to Dallas to become a flapper. She eventually returned to Arkansas to reclaim her children, then settled down in Dallas. Married in early 1928, Crowder and Lucile purchased a home on Sunset Crest on March 10 from John W. Riley for $3,230. The Crowders were described as being very devoted to each other, and he continued to adore her to the end. Crowder came to love his step-children as if they were his own and, indeed, at some point between 1930 and 1940, he formally adopted them. The one stipulation Bob posed was that James and Marcoline had to be legally of age to decide for themselves whether he could adopt them.[20]

In the autumn of 1929, Crowder became interested in the recently formed Highway Patrol, and he decided to apply to be one of the first fifty officers. Given his educational limitations, he was surprised to be appointed to the force on January 10, 1930. He attended the first training academy at Camp Mabry, where his prior Marine and police experience proved to be a significant advantage. Following his graduation on February 20, he was granted badge number sixteen and remained as a drill instructor for the second training class. Following this duty, he was stationed at Texarkana in District No. 1 on April 1. In the enabling legislation, the Highway Patrol had been charged with enforcing vehicle and traffic regulations on the state's public thoroughfares. Because the concept of the patrol was so new, Crowder and his partner, Edwin Hilburn Bruce, spent more time explaining the role of their agency and the relevant laws to citizens than making arrests for minor violations; usually they issued warnings. The size of the patrolmen's district meant the two worked seven days a week to cover the narrow dirt and gravel roads in their territory. In order to better enforce the law and cover the state's vast expanse, the size of the force was increased in August 1931 to a total of 120 patrolmen, then 147 four years later. Crowder and Bruce's salary was $150 per month, although that was reduced by fifty dollars in 1933 due to state budget cuts caused by the Great Depression. Regardless of the long hours and the minimal pay, Crowder was successful in the Highway Patrol, earning a promotion to sergeant in November 1931. Despite his record, Crowder suddenly found himself frozen in the chain of command for reasons unknown, although office politics was a strong possibility. He was denied a promotion to lieutenant that had been all but promised at the end of the academy cycle. When the rank of sergeant was eliminated by the legislature in 1933, he lost his stripes, and was shifted to Fort Worth, then Mineral Wells, and finally to Wichita Falls in 1935. That same year, the Highway Patrol was transferred to the Department of Public Safety and granted authority and legal powers equal to those bestowed upon the Texas Rangers.[21]

In those years with the Highway Patrol, Crowder was responsible for a number of high-profile arrests. On February 24, 1934, he was one of the patrolmen searching for the desperadoes Bonnie Parker and Clyde Barrow. He never met the homicidal pair on that day or any other, but he and his partner did encounter Frank "Red" Callan, a notorious career criminal wanted for bank robbery in Kansas. The fugitive had also recently escaped from Huntsville. Callan and two other men were sitting in a car parked at a filling station in Electra. Although the trio was heavily armed, they chose not to resist arrest when Crowder walked up to the car. On January 6, 1936, Oklahoma bank robber and escaped convict Jack Brunson, and his companions J. C. Vestal and Lloyd Ward, engaged in a wild crime spree. Pursued by local and state officers through Wichita and Archer Counties, they held up three people and stole two vehicles before being captured. The arresting officers were Crowder, Highway Patrolman John Lowry, Wichita County Deputy Sheriff Dick Howard, and Inspector Lott Thomas Keffer of the state comptroller's office. Charges of robbery with firearms and auto theft were filed in Justice Ben Fly's court in Wichita Falls against the three suspects. Brunson and Ward were also identified as the pair who had kidnapped Reuben Joe Luther, a Dallas police officer, for three hours on January 3. Brunson and Ward received fifty- and twenty-five-year sentences respectively, while Vestal was given a five-year term. Even while Crowder was accumulating an impressive record of apprehensions, the rumor mill hinted by 1937 that Highway Patrol Chief Louis Graham Phares was planning to fire him.[22]

With his once-promising career seemingly at an end, Crowder was surprised when he received a telephoned invitation from Superintendent Manuel T. Gonzaullas to join the Bureau of Intelligence. Recent legislation had provided the bureau funding for ten criminal investigators, and Crowder immediately responded in the affirmative. He was formally appointed an investigator on May 5. He was stationed in Tyler on June 1 and immediately went to work. Grateful to Gonzaullas for the opportunity, Crowder performed his duties with a vengeance. "We were working day and night, honest to God, that year I lived in Tyler," he said in a 1969 interview with Doctor Ben H. Procter. "I don't believe I slept two nights all through the night. I was always called out for some reason." In addition to routine investigations, he and Ranger Norman Kemp "Dick" Dixon were instrumental in apprehending an interstate gang that had stolen oil field equipment worth millions of dollars in Gladewater, Longview, London, and other locales. Twenty-two men were being held in the Gregg County jail by April 28, 1938, and fifty thousand dollars in equipment had been recovered. Crowder next broke up a Dallas-based car theft ring whose reach extended to Houston and the Panhandle. Personnel changes in the Rangers would positively effect Crowder in time. Captain James Walter McCormick, stationed in Wichita Falls for the previous two years, submitted his resignation on May 14; Private William Harrison "Bill" Lay followed his superior in leaving the service. Rangers Benjamin Maney Gault and Lester Stewart were assigned to Wichita Falls to replace the two men. Transferred to the same city on June 11, Crowder was attached to Ranger Company B under Captain Royal George Phillips seventeen days later.[23]

On January 1, 1939, he formally transferred to the Texas Rangers, but remained in Wichita Falls. Later in the summer, as part of a cost-cutting measure, Governor Wilbert Lee "Pappy" O'Daniel reduced the number of Ranger captains by two, which required the service to reorganize. Captain Phillips closed Company B's substations and concentrated his seven men on September 1 at the rustic two-story log cabin at Fair Park in Dallas that served as company headquarters. Crowder was promoted to sergeant on the same day. His old mentor, Captain Manuel Gonzaullas, assumed command of the company the following year.[24] Procter described the professional relationship the two Rangers forged:

> The two made quite a team. One seemed to offset the other's weaknesses and complement the other's strengths. Gonzaullas, flashy yet dapper in western-style garb, catlike in his movements … brought a wealth of experience to his captaincy, dating as far back as the early 1920s when on the border with Captain Frank Hamer. A master psychologist, he tried to intimidate men with his appearance and reputation … Crowder, on the other hand, was the steady, quiet enforcer, an omnipresent, giant shadow of Gonzaullas, who took vicarious pleasure in his captain's growing fame and fanfare, much like a deputy in the Old West who protected his sheriff from "backshooters." Yet such respect was mutual, because Gonzaullas always consulted Crowder before determining a course of action. Consequently, together they fashioned an enviable record.[25]

Fiscal year 1940 brought several more changes to the Ranger's organization. Beginning on January 4, all Rangers were instructed to report directly to Colonel Garrison, although the company commanders maintained supervision. The captains were not stripped of their authority, but the colonel did desire closer oversight of the undermanned force.[26] Between 1946 and 1948, the service possessed only forty-five Rangers, including Crowder, or one Ranger for every 5,941 square miles and for every 142,000 people in the state. Yet, despite their small numbers, the Rangers conducted 6,285 fugitive apprehensions and criminal investigations for murder, robbery, rape, burglary, theft, arson, narcotics trafficking, sex crimes, and other felonies. These cases resulted in 1,753 arrests and 638 convictions and twenty death sentences. They also handled 10,661 investigations for misdemeanors such as assault, gambling, swindling, and unlawful possession of firearms By virtue of the 550,253 hours worked, the stolen property that was recovered amounted to over one million dollars.[27]

On the basis of his contributions to these statistics, and upon the death of Captain Maney Gault, Crowder was promoted to the command of Company C in Lubbock on December 9, 1947. Physically, Crowder was the epitome of the Texas Ranger captain. He was tall and lean with the long legs of a horseman. His face was angular and quick to smile. His athletic build and stamina stayed with him into his later years due in part to his active lifestyle and his favorite hobby of golf.[28] A man of few words, his powerful presence ensured he was in command of any room he entered. According to a grandson, he preferred to let his actions speak for him. The captain's towering force of personality "disarmed" many wrongdoers into submitting peacefully, so he was rarely forced to resort to pulling his sidearm. He would also counsel teenage boys who were headed for trouble by driving them around and talking to them man-to-man about their choices before letting them go.[29]

Due to be tried in Thirty-second District Court, twenty-six-year-old Cecil Chester Davis escaped from the Scurry County jail on June 22 by sawing through the bars. Stealing a car, he fled east. Highway patrolmen in the Abilene district were alerted to the jailbreak and ordered to watch the roads. City and county officers in Taylor County were similarly on the lookout. Summoned to the scene, Crowder worked with Rangers Kelly Rogers and William Erastus "Rass" Renfrow of Lubbock, Ranger James L. Rogers of Lamesa, Deputy Vernie Head, and Troopers J. R. Reed and T. T. Brady of Sweetwater to capture the fugitive.[30]

O. T. McDaniel was found dead in his car on August 3, 1948, in Parmer County, with a .22-caliber rifle near the body. The victim had been a service station operator and former commissioner for Curry County, New Mexico. Crowder and Ranger Paul Raymond Waters investigated and ascertained McDaniel had unknowingly purchased a bogus oil lease in Mills County two days before his death; the fraud had cost him $12,600. Their primary suspect, Sidney Andrew Miller of Fort Worth, surrendered to Crowder on the twelfth, and waived an examining trial in Farwell. He was arraigned in Justice of the Peace William Jess Newton's courtroom. Although Miller had been indicted on a swindling charge in Littlefield the same day and posted bail of three thousand dollars, he was released on a seven-thousand-dollar bond. Four other individuals were also charged in connection with the homicide, but one was released after questioning. Miller appeared before the Parmer County grand jury on October 11.[31]

The case turned a strange twist when Sidney's brother, Que Robert Miller, a former sheriff of Foard County and an ex-convict, was found shot to death on September 30 in his automobile near Oakland Lake. Investigators theorized the victim knew his killers, but Fort Worth and Tarrant County detectives differed over whether the deaths of McDaniel and Miller were connected. Unfortunately, both cases went unsolved.[32]

A bus strike in Lubbock turned violent when the terminal of Texas, New Mexico, & Oklahoma Motor Coaches, Inc. was devastated in a bombing on June 14, 1948. Chief Deputy Sheriff George Eubank swore out a complaint, which District Attorney Lloyd Croslin filed with the court. Armed with arrest warrants, Eubank, Croslin, and Assistant District Attorney Ernest Glenn Pharr traveled to Hobbs, New Mexico. They joined Crowder, Waters, Lubbock County Sheriff Grady Harrist, and Lea County Deputy Charles Trimble, all of whom had been working the case for the last several hours. Clyde Loma and Drew Storey, both of Hobbs, waived extradition and were escorted to Lubbock. Houston Miller, a local businessman, was likewise arrested. The three suspects were charged on October 22 with arson by explosive. Miller posted a $2,500 bond, while Loma and Storey were held in lieu of similar bail. Miller refused to give a statement to investigators. Lomax signed a confession that he had tossed a half-stick of dynamite into the offices of two bus company executives. He also described two meetings with Miller prior to the blast. Storey made only a verbal statement that he had accompanied Lomax to Lubbock from Hobbs. The latter two men waived an examining trial the next morning in the court of Justice of the Peace Cornelius Eugene Lynn. Bail was set at $2,500, and the pair were bound over for the grand jury. The Ninety-ninth District grand jury convened on November 29, and the three men were indicted.[33]

On August 30, 1950, mobster Meyer Harris "Mickey" Cohen and *Saturday Evening Post* writer Denis A. "Denny" Morrison flew from Los Angeles to Odessa. The former had made the trip at the invitation of Mayor Thomas Leo Moore of Electra to invest in both legal and illegal opportunities in the West Texas oil fields. After Cohen met with gambler and racketeer Harry Brook of Chicago, and well-known gamblers Ray West and A. Ray LeMaster of Wichita Falls, the entire party drove to Wichita Falls where they checked into the Kemp Hotel. Cohen's interest in Texas speculations had come to the attention of the Rangers, and Crowder drove from Lubbock in order to pay a visit to the gangster and his cohorts. Captain Gonzaullas and Ranger James Newton "Jim" Geer likewise traveled from Dallas to lend assistance. After holding a short meeting, the two captains went to the hotel, secured Cohen's room key from the front desk, and took Cohen and Brook into custody without the benefit of a warrant. After being fingerprinted, photographed, and questioned, the hoodlums were lodged into the county jail while the Rangers took a nap. The state lawmen then escorted their prisoners to the Fort Worth airport. Cohen and Morrison were placed on a waiting American Airlines plane, and Brook caught an eastbound flight to Cleveland. During a three-hour layover in El Paso, local officers, warned by the Rangers, took the gambler into custody, then ensured he made his flight. After returning to Los Angeles, a disheveled Cohen complained he had been physically assaulted by the Rangers and threatened to sue. However, he never took legal action.[34]

Cohen did return to El Paso on March 21, 1951, to attend the funeral of Detective Ralph Marmalejo, Jr., and was served with a subpoena to appear before the Special House Crime Investigating Committee in Austin in six days' time. Cohen neglected to show, and the committee cited him for contempt. The Travis County grand jury returned an indictment for willful failure to appear. Since the charge was a misdemeanor, the committee recommended extradition not be pursued and agreed if Cohen stayed out of Texas, the indictment would have its desired effect.[35]

On July 6, 1951, the Rangers were called upon to aid the Dallas authorities in investigating a series of ten bombings in South Dallas. Since February 1950, the homes of thirteen black families living in previously all-white neighborhoods had been destroyed by dynamite. Five other bombings occurred in other parts of the city during the same time period. By the time the Rangers were summoned, no injuries had occurred, yet no arrests were imminent in spite of the posted one-thousand-dollar reward. Crowder had been named to replace the retiring Gonzaullas as the new commander of Company B, effective August 1, 1951. Even though he was not yet officially in command, Crowder joined the company's eleven Rangers in the investigation and met with Police Chief Carl Frederick Hansson to learn details of the case. Following the conference, Crowder announced to the press: "The Rangers are in." On July 11, a bungalow at 4622 Meadows was dynamited at 8:15 p.m. The explosion demolished the back of the structure which was located in an all-black section of South Dallas. At ten o'clock that same night, the bombers struck again at 4527 Crozier, but the homeowner, a widowed black woman, drove them off with a hail of bullets. Patrolling nearby, Police Officer Stavis Ellis heard the shots and rushed to the scene. He cut the burning fuse from the two-pound dynamite stick, then dumped a bucket of water on the explosive. Crowder and Chief of Detectives Harry Taylor Riddell went to the Meadows address at dawn. The captain said, "We didn't find a thing—just a bunch of rubble. My boys and the city boys are working hard—shaking every bush."[36]

The police received a tip from a confidential source who thought the bombers had crossed a line. The officer who obtained the name of the suspect reported it to Chief Hansson, who, in turn, informed Crowder. Claude Thomas Wright, the forty-two-year-old person of interest, was a clothes presser and lived in the part of town where the bombers had struck. Crowder placed Ranger Sergeant E. J. "Jay" Banks in charge of the investigation into Wright, and the sergeant put the suspect under surveillance. By July 23, Banks believed he had sufficient probable cause to arrest Wright and an accomplice. Banks and Dallas police officers took Wright and his sixty-one-year-old half-brother, Arthur Eugene Young, into custody. Both suspects had lengthy arrest records for bootlegging. Crowder and Riddell filed charges in Justice of the Peace William E. "Bill" Richburg's court early on the twenty-fourth, alleging Wright and Young had bombed a home on 2214 Eugene on June 24. The two counts of arson by explosive and two counts of attempted arson by explosive carried sentences of two to twenty years and one to seven years, respectively.[37]

Banks personally interrogated the two suspects, who initially denied any wrongdoing, at the Dallas city jail. Since Young suffered from a kidney ailment due to diabetes, the Rangers transferred him to Parkland Hospital to receive treatment. Young was subsequently released and interviewed at Company B headquarters, where he confessed to being present while Wright planted bombs at two houses. Banks then removed Wright to DPS headquarters in Austin, and the suspect was given a polygraph test later in the afternoon. Wright confessed to participating in three successful bombings on June 24 and in two more that were failures. He claimed he was attempting to save his home from the "encroachment of Negroes." After the exam was completed, Wright showed the investigators a dynamite bomb he had hidden for use on another house. Wright was transferred to the Travis County jail and held without bail.[38]

The investigators believed neither man was a ringleader of the bombings, and they intended to keep working the case until they found the mastermind. Criminal District Judge Henry King impaneled a special grand jury of twelve influential white and black men on July 24 to investigate the case. Building upon the information they developed in interrogating Wright and Young, the Rangers, in conjunction with the police and the Dallas fire marshal's office, were able to crack the case. Former coal miner James Paz Alvarez was charged with bomb making, and labor union official Charles Otho Goff with being one of three organizers of the bombings. The grand jurors handed down thirteen indictments by the third week of September.[39]

While Dallas police and Company B were conducting this investigation, gambler Herbert "the Cat" Noble failed to survive the twelfth attempt on his life when a landmine exploded under his vehicle at his Grapevine ranch on August 7. The killers had waited in an oak thicket some seventy-five yards from the blast site to detonate the device. The only viable physical evidence from the demolished 1951 Ford sedan and the shredded victim was an automobile battery and a few strands of wire. Eyewitnesses described two or three men fleeing the scene in a blue Chevrolet pickup truck at the time of the murder. Noble had alleged he was the subject of a fifty-thousand-dollar bounty arranged by Lester Ben "Benny" Binion, a Dallas underworld figure turned Las Vegas casino owner. Lieutenant George Butler of the Dallas Police Department conveyed Noble's experiences to the U.S. Senate Subcommittee on Organized Crime ("the Kefauver Committee"), and, indeed, the gambler had testified under oath before the Texas House Crime Investigating Committee on April 2. Crowder and Ranger Lewis Calvin Rigler joined forces with Denton County Sheriff Walter Ones Hodges to close the case. Hodges, blinded by buckshot in a shooting three years before, knew of an individual who owned a vehicle matching the description, and a mysterious telephone call led the lawmen to seek four ex-convicts in Fort Worth.[40]

The investigation spread to include six former members of Hollis Delois "Lois" Green's old gang, and "nitro man" George Rennie "Jack" Nesbit of Fort Worth, who had once been arrested on a charge of assault with intent to murder Noble, was taken into custody by Crowder. However, the suspect offered an airtight alibi. Ex-convict Finley Donica was similarly arrested at his West Dallas home. A blue pickup was parked in his front yard. Gamblers Charles Frank Cates and LeRoy Randolph "Tincy" Eggleston, and gunman James Clyde "Jim" Thomas, all prominent in the Fort Worth underworld, were likewise interrogated. Crowder, Lieutenant Butler, and Dallas County Sheriff James Eric "Bill" Decker diligently worked the case. Three unexploded nitroglycerin bombs were discovered in an abandoned gravel pit near Lake Worth on September 15. Crowder theorized the nitro could be linked to the Noble murder and sent Rigler and Daniel to assist the Fort Worth authorities. The captain and Butler traveled to Las Vegas on November 12 and interviewed Binion. Naturally, the latter denied any involvement. By the following May, at least forty suspects were being considered, although not one could be conclusively tied to the murder. However, numerous other open cases were solved, including more than 150 burglaries and the firebombing of ex-sheriff Steve Guthrie's restaurant. Donica, James Nathan Gilreath, and Robert Edward "Bob" Braggins admitted to that particular crime and claimed Noble had paid them for their services.[41]

For the previous two years, the State had been endeavoring to topple political boss George Berham Parr from his throne, and Attorney General Price Daniel ordered an investigation of the Duval County records. Crowder likely looked on with interest as teams of state attorneys and accountants, and federal agents, descended on San Diego, but many of the documents had vanished. By January 1954, the daunting case against Parr was being readied for court. On February 24, IRS agents appeared before Federal Judge James Burr V. Allred in Corpus Christi and filed for an injunction to prevent the South Texas State Bank in Alice and the San Diego State Bank from destroying or concealing records. George Parr was president of both institutions.[42]

In addition to the legal actions, Rangers of Company D held personal grudges against Parr and his cronies. The political kingpin and Juan Barrera (alias Juan Canante), described as one of Parr's lieutenants, were charged in Judge Wash Storm, Jr.'s county court with unlawfully carrying pistols on January 18, 1954. They pled not guilty and each were released on a fifteen-hundred-dollar bond. Stepping into the hallway, Parr was approached by Captain Alfred Young Allee, Joe H. Bridge, and Walter Russell. Questions led to a brawl when Duval County Sheriff Archer "Archie" Parr, George's nephew and heir apparent, reached for his pistol. Allee disarmed the sheriff and clouted the elder Parr with a fist when he intervened. George suffered a torn and bloody ear while Archie had his glasses knocked off when Bridge struck him. The three Rangers appeared before the Jim Wells County grand jury on the twenty-third to answer questions concerning the fracas. Following a contentious argument over whether they should disarm while testifying, Allee and Bridge were indicted on charges of assault with intent to murder.[43]

Another scuffle took place between Allee and District Attorney Raeburn Norris outside the Windmill Café in San Diego on February 9. The elder Parr sought an injunction on February 16 in Judge Allred's federal court against Allee and Bridge, alleging they intended to kill him. Allred ordered the two Rangers to appear in Houston and show cause why he should not grant Parr's request. While Allee was otherwise occupied, Crowder was temporarily ordered to Duval to supervise the four-man Ranger detail working there. At the State's request, the indictment against Bridge was dismissed on March 29. Parr, through his attorneys, moved on April 19 for a dismissal of Allee's case "for the good of the country." The following day, Allee was cleared of the charge, and Crowder returned to Dallas. Despite the best efforts of law enforcement, the Parr regime continued to function.[44]

On Saturday, April 16, 1955, Ben Riley, a six-foot-two-inch, 220-pound inmate at Rusk State Hospital, and twenty of his fellow convicts in the segregated black section, overpowered and took as hostages attendants W. C. "Bill" Curtis, Joe Taylor, and H. B. "Hub" Taylor, trustee C. W. "Pat" Patterson, patient Robert Williams, Assistant Supervisor Clyde White, and Doctor Leslie DeWitt Hancock, beating all six men in the process. White and Hancock were making the morning rounds in the maximum-security unit when they were informed someone had been injured in a fight. The two officials rushed to Ward Six where they walked into a trap. White ordered Hancock to contact hospital superintendent Doctor Charles Whitfield Castner and request he come to the ward. Five minutes later, Castner arrived and found Hancock suffering from stab wounds and a concussion. The senior doctor insisted his subordinate be permitted to leave to seek medical treatment while Castner heroically stayed in his stead. Riley agreed and further allowed all but Curtis, Hub Taylor, and White to likewise depart. The original hostage-takers, joined by eighty other inmates, retained control of the building containing Wards Six and Seven. Riley demanded to speak to a newspaper reporter.[45]

Rusk State Hospital was situated 120 miles southeast of Dallas and housed 2,500 inmates, including six hundred judged to be criminally insane. Claiming he was the "son of God," Riley, then aged fifteen, had killed a man in Salina, Kansas, on November 5, 1952. Due to his minor status, he could not be prosecuted, but he was sent to his native Texas as a parole violator. Described as unrepentant and "cold-blooded," he was later declared insane and conveyed to Rusk. Riley and Joe Murphy, his fellow ringleader and a sex offender, related to Emmett Holman Whitehead, the twenty-seven-year-old editor of the *Rusk Cherokeean*, examples of alleged prisoner abuse on the part of trustees. Inmate Leroy Joseph Bienvenu also allowed Willey Shattuck, Whitehead's photographer, to take pictures of the "bruises" he had purportedly received as a result of ill-treatment. Among Riley's demands were improved counseling, planned exercise periods, a halt to inmate beatings, privileges equal to those extended to white prisoners, and a hearing before state officials. Riley did warn that if law enforcement personnel attempted to enter Ward Six, or if they did not comply with his demands, the hostages would die. Whitehead and his photographer left to print an extra edition of the weekly newspaper. The story detailed recent events and Riley's claims about the state of affairs at the facility. Prior to publication, though, Whitehead performed his journalistic due diligence and ascertained the marks on Bienvenu's body were actually second-degree burn scars that were noted on his admittance record in 1954. When later asked why he had displayed the scars when his story was demonstrably false, Bienvenu replied, "I thought it would help prove our point."[46]

Crowder had returned to the office from lunch at one o'clock when he received a call from Garrison informing him of recent events at Rusk. The captain told his superior he would quickly depart and ordered Richard "Dick" Oldham, Jay Banks, and Ernest Daniel to follow as soon as possible with tear gas and riot gear. Pushing his 1955 Oldsmobile to the limit, Crowder reached Rusk in ninety minutes. When he arrived at the hospital, the captain discovered that Riley desired to speak to a Ranger "if he represented the government." In a telephone conversation with the hostage-takers, Crowder ensured they understood his conditions before agreeing to meet with them. "I'm not comin' in unarmed because you've already got three people over there as hostages and I don't want to be the fourth one—and I'm not going to be … If somethin' goes amiss, I know who's going to fall first." Crowder then interviewed Whitehead and available hospital workers to discover as much as he could about the state of affairs in the two wards. With "commonsense in his brain, compassion in his heart, and ice-water in his veins," the tall Ranger captain walked through the electrically controlled gate at 3:10 p.m. toward the inmate-held building. When Crowder reached the entrance, he had his Colt 1911A-1 .45 tucked inside his waistband. Riley met him at the top of the stairs with an ice pick and a pair of scissors in his belt.[47]

The two men talked for the next twenty minutes. The captain quietly allowed that Riley had committed a serious error and that if any harm came to the hostages "it's just going to be worse for you." The inmate replied with a reiteration of his fellow prisoners' complaints. Riley again requested a hearing, to which Crowder responded, "OK, I'll see that you get a hearing." Crowder ordered Riley and his waiting accomplices to put down their weapons. He then added, "I want the superintendent and the two attendants down here unharmed." Riley dropped his makeshift weapons and called for the others to do the same. With Crowder observing, the hostage-takers all emerged from the building and surrendered. The hostages followed unhurt, and the seven-hour ordeal was over.[48]

Crowder's entry into the unit had been a brave but calculated risk. Before he began talking with Riley, he had placed Highway Patrolman (and future Ranger) Jim Ray, armed with a scoped rifle, in a position fifty yards from the convict. During the entire conversation between Crowder and Riley, the trooper had maintained a bead on the inmate's heart. If Riley had moved against Crowder, Ray was prepared to kill the ringleader.[49]

Later Garrison asked Crowder what he had said to the inmates. "Aw, boss, I just told them to cut out that stuff," Crowder replied, his eyes sparkling with humor. Garrison did not pursue the issue. Crowder was later interviewed about the incident and asked much the same question. "Well, I was pretty lucky that day," the captain observed. "I don't know how I would have come out with that many against me, had they decided to call my hand, but know this: I would have taken eight of them with me."[50]

Despite this and other episodes, in all his years as a Marine and a law officer, Crowder never shot another human being. "Oh, I've did a little shooting in my time," he said in 1969. "Been shot at several times, too. But no one ever got hurt, and I'm glad. A gunslinger's reputation isn't something a man needs, or should want."[51]

Disappointingly, Gregg County was one scene of racial animosity that turned violent. Following a successful bond election for school funding in March 1955, specifically the upgrading of an all-black school in the Rusk County town of Mayflower, a group of white supremacists began a campaign of intimidation against black residents and any supporters of the bond issue. On October 22, at 11 p.m., two white men drove by the Hughes Café, a black-owned restaurant on Highway (Tatum–Longview) 149 in Gregg County, and fired approximately nine rounds from a Mossberg .22-caliber semiautomatic rifle into the establishment. One of the bullets struck sixteen-year-old John Earl Reese in the head and mortally wounded him. Sisters Joyce Nelson, fourteen, and Johnnie Nelson, sixteen, were wounded. The two shooters went on to fire into several homes in the black neighborhood in Mayflower. Reese died the next day at Gregg Memorial Hospital.[52]

The sheriff investigated, but he apparently had no real desire to solve the crime. Driven by racism or personal associations, other local officials were either indifferent or wished to cover up the shooting. Indeed, while John Earl Reese's death certificate noted the direct cause of his demise to be a gunshot wound and the antecedent cause a fractured skull, the death was ruled "accidental."[53]

Three months later, Crowder, Jay Banks, and Dick Oldham began to look into the case. The captain arrested two suspects—Joe Reagan Simpson and Perry Dean Ross—on January 25, 1956, in Marshall and Houston, respectively. They were confined in the Longview jail, and bond was set at five thousand dollars. Both men confessed to involvement in the slaying, and Ross signed a written statement that he was the shooter at the café. Throughout much of the night. Simpson and Ross related details of the murder, including how the rifle was tied to driftwood and thrown into the Sabine River. The pair were indicted on February 2, although District Attorney Ralph Prince characterized the crime as "a case of two irresponsible boys who were attempting to have some fun by scaring Negroes." Crowder stated the case was based on "iron-clad" physical evidence. Behind the scenes maneuvering by local authorities resulted in Ross being found guilty of murder "without malice" on April 23, 1957, and given a five-year suspended sentence. Simpson, the driver during the café shooting, received the same on September 6. Neither man spent one day in prison for their crimes.[54]

The U.S. Supreme Court ruling in *Brown v. Board of Education*, issued on May 17, 1954, held that the "separate but equal" doctrine found in *Plessy v. Ferguson* (1896) was unconstitutional under the Equal Protection Clause of the Fourteenth Amendment. Jacob Dickson, president of the Topeka, Kansas, Board of Education, declared the decision was "in the finest spirit of the law and true democracy." The Court delivered a second opinion on May 31, 1955, that remanded future desegregation cases to the lower federal courts, and instructed district courts and public schools to begin the process of desegregation "with all deliberate speed." While significant victories for the cause of civil rights, the groundbreaking decisions did nothing to make the issue less volatile, and ambiguous language allowed states and local school boards to avoid desegregation for a time. To the state's credit, though, approximately one hundred school districts in Texas, mostly in the western part of the state, voluntarily integrated without incident by the end of 1956.[55]

In August 1956, Texas gubernatorial candidates U.S. Senator Price Daniel, Judge Ralph Yarborough, and "Pappy" O'Daniel (an ex-governor), as well as incumbent chief executive Robert Allan Shivers, favored excluding black children from white schools regardless of the *Brown* decision. In Mansfield, a small farming town south of Fort Worth, the school board similarly opposed for over a year the enrollment of three black students in the local high school. The teens had been previously forced to take a Trailways bus at their own expense to Fort Worth's I. M. Terrell High School. L. Clifford Davis, counsel for the area National Association for the Advancement of Colored People (NAACP) branch, had filed a class-action lawsuit in federal district court on October 7, 1955, on behalf of the town's black students. Judge Joe Ewing Estes of Fort Worth ruled for the school board, and Davis appealed the decision to the Fifth U.S. Circuit Court of Appeals. The appellate court overturned the lower court on June 28, 1956, and Judge Estes decreed on August 25 that the Mansfield school board allow the registration of the three students. The enrollment was scheduled to occur on Thursday and Friday, August 30 and 31. On the thirtieth, Judge Estes refused to sign an order delaying the integration. School Superintendent Robert Lloyd Huffman defiantly told the jurist: "[Negroes] had better not try to register today. There is a human barricade of whites on the school grounds ... There will be trouble." Indeed, an angry mob of several hundred men gathered in front of the high school, and the resident NAACP head began receiving threats. Three effigies were hung on school property. Tarrant County Sheriff Harlon Wright and four deputies moved among the crowd attempting to keep the peace. None of the hopeful students appeared, and the throng dispersed by mid-afternoon.[56]

The mob assembled again on Friday, which was the day designated for rural students to be registered. Acting under orders from Governor Shivers and Colonel Garrison, Crowder dispatched Sergeant E. J. "Jay" Banks and Ranger Ernest Daniel to Mansfield "to co-operate with local authorities in preserving the peace." Despite the Rangers' presence, the probability of bloodshed kept the teenagers away, although several news photographers and

Assistant Tarrant County District Attorney Grady Haight were manhandled. That same day, Judge John Brown of the Fifth Circuit Court in Houston denied the school board's appeal to postpone integration. The most significant moment of the entire episode was the first day of classes on September 4. Approximately two hundred people again gathered, although they appeared to be less threatening than in the previous days. Crowder, Banks, Daniel, and Rangers Lewis Rigler, George Marvin Roach, and Byron Odell Currin were on hand with weapons and riot gear in their car trunks. Additionally, three Rangers infiltrated the crowd by posing as curious bystanders. The captain sized up the crowd and positioned his men at various vantage points, then put a booted foot on a post and began to nonchalantly whittle. Although the Rangers prevented the outbreak of violence, the intimidated students once more chose not to register and continued to attend their old high school in Fort Worth. The school board's attorney filed a petition with Supreme Court Justice Hugo Black requesting a stay of Judge Estes's court order, but the request was denied.[57]

Early in the episode, Governor Shivers had instructed the Mansfield school board to transfer any student, white or black, whose attendance could "reasonably" incite violence. Obeying his own orders from the governor, Crowder told a crowd of 150 protesters on September 4 that any black students who sought to register would be immediately relocated to another school district "for safety reasons." Reverend Donald W. Clark of St. Timothy's Church in Fort Worth traveled to Mansfield to witness the mob's lack of "Christian action." Becoming visibly upset, the young Episcopal priest pointed to a hanging effigy and declared, "Man is made in the image of God, and man is the image of God, and you've got the image of man hanging on that flagpole." The cleric's comment angered the mob, and, before trouble could commence, Sergeant Banks entered the throng and quietly escorted Clark away. Mansfield was but one of several Southern communities that resisted desegregation, and President Dwight David Eisenhower was reluctant to exert federal police powers unless the states proved unable to maintain law and order. After the Rangers departed, an uneasy peace hung over the town. Seventh District Judge Otis Theodore Dunagan in Tyler issued a temporary injunction on September 28 against the NAACP that lasted until May 11, 1957. The school would remain segregated until 1965, when a threatened loss of federal funds forced the board to finally obey the law.[58]

By 1956, the Department of Public Safety was in desperate need of modernization. In the previous twenty years, the legislature had added numerous bureaus, responsibilities, and personnel to the department. Seventeen hundred people in seventeen separate divisions and sections, including the Highway Patrol and the Texas Rangers, were reporting to Director Garrison. The same year, while on-call twenty-four hours a day, the eighty-one Rangers performed average workweeks of seventy-four and one-half hours—with no overtime pay. They handled 5,832 complaints and returned $759,000 in stolen property, mostly livestock. A leader of Garrison's caliber could manage the excessive span of control, but, nevertheless, improvements to the DPS were urgently needed. In the same year, the nonprofit Texas Research League (TRL) undertook a review of the entire department for administrative inefficiencies, structural weaknesses, and financial waste. Producing a frank and concise report, the research staff cited the department's vertically organized divisions that operated independently of one another rather than in concert, inadequate inspection and evaluation of field activities, constraints on promotional opportunities and leadership development, and shortcomings in policy development and coordination. They presented draft proposals for a revised plan of organization to Garrison by the end of the year. The colonel improved the TRL's recommendations.[59]

Possibly anticipating legislative approval of the study, Garrison named Crowder to become acting chief of the Texas Rangers on October 1, 1956. The TRL's report made no mention of the position, but apparently the director intended the promotion to be a stopgap measure. Another improvement the colonel was able to provide to the Rangers' equipment inventory was the purchase of fifteen specially made Dodge Cornel pursuit cars equipped with 285-horsepower Chrysler engines. Peering under the hood of one vehicle, Garrison quipped, "Now if we can get a little horse sense in the drivers, then we've got it made."[60]

The TRL report was submitted to the Public Safety Commission on January 27, 1957. The legislature approved a new act on May 20, which authorized the DPS to reorganize as deemed necessary as long as such restructuring did not exceed the total number of divisions then in existence. With the legislation going into effect on September 1, 1957, the DPS commenced an extensive shakeup. The field structure of the department was distributed into six regional commands headquartered in Houston, Dallas, Lubbock, Corpus Christi, Midland, and Waco. Each headquarters office was commanded by a Highway Patrol major. All regional DPS employees, including the Rangers, would report to the majors, who, in turn, answered to Headquarters. For the first time, the Rangers of the DPS were not under the direct command of the director, a fact they universally disliked.[61]

On the same day, Crowder's title of acting chief expired, and he was promoted to the command of Region 5. Headquartered at 4010 Avenue R in Lubbock, the new major supervised DPS operations in a sixty-county area. Sergeant Banks had assumed acting command of Company B upon Crowder's earlier promotion; he was named captain on September 1.[62]

Noted for frequently being featured in the media, Captain Banks did not enjoy universal respect from his men, and he was forced to live in Crowder's shadow. With the approval of the Public Safety Commission, he was dismissed from the service on March 2, 1960, for neglect of duty in closing certain gaming establishments in Fort Worth. Undercover DPS agents had reportedly conducted two gambling raids in Tarrant County in recent days, and Banks apparently did not take the issue seriously. The discharged captain alleged his firing was the result of a policy dispute with Garrison. The colonel denied the charge, saying, "There has been no squabble and there has been no difference on any policy matter. Banks' dismissal was ordered solely because of his failure to carry out specific orders."[63]

Crowder was granted a transfer back to the Rangers on March 15, 1960. Surrendering his rank of major and $675 monthly salary, he resumed his post as captain of Company B, where he earned $516 per month. As part of the shakeup, Ranger G. W. Burks was transferred from Paris to Dallas.[64]

At this time, the civil rights movement came to Marshall, a bastion of Old South attitudes. Several young black men were arrested for attempting to sit at white-only lunch counters. Some seven hundred black and white college students responded by demonstrating in front of the Harrison County courthouse on March 30. Firefighters, employing hoses and high-pressure water streams, dispersed the protestors, and approximately 250 students were held in technical custody; arrest warrants were prepared for fifty-five. Doctor Doxey Alphonso Wilkerson, a teacher at all-black Bishop College, was fired by the university's president for involvement in the demonstration. The professor, a former Communist, denied any participation. The following day, Crowder and several Rangers arrived in town, locked three entrances to the courthouse as a "precautionary measure," and posted a guard at the fourth. Local officers were a visible presence on the streets, but students peaceably attended classes at Bishop and Wiley Colleges.[65]

Long-time Congressman Sam Rayburn died of cancer on November 16, 1961. His body was brought to his hometown of Bonham accompanied by President John Fitzgerald Kennedy and former chief executives Harry Truman and Dwight Eisenhower. Among the other dignitaries was Vice President Lyndon Baines Johnson, justices of the U.S. Supreme Court, members of the Joint Chiefs of Staff, and various senators and representatives. The eleven Rangers of Company B were assigned to assist the Secret Service with presidential security. The funeral was held at the First Baptist Church, with a graveside service at Willow Wild Cemetery.[66]

The Crowders experienced more personal losses when Marcoline died at St. Paul Hospital in Dallas on August 8, 1963. She had worked as a stenographer for a merchandise mail-order company and North American Aviation, then married Rae Milton Clifton, a World War II veteran and Republic National Bank of Dallas trust officer, on May 7, 1945. She was buried at Restland Memorial Park. Rae died on May 9, 1964, at Baylor Hospital in Dallas. He was laid to rest next to Marcoline. Shortly thereafter, Crowder and Lucile took their three orphaned grandchildren, seventeen-year-old Carol Ann, twelve-year-old Catherine Edell, and seven-year-old George Milton, into their home to raise.[67]

For years, Crowder had owned forty-two acres of bottomland south of Dallas and personally built a farmhouse on the property. After duty weeks of fifty and sixty hours, he would work his land, known as "Dunrovin," as a way of relaxing and spending time with his grandchildren. When the family visited the farm on Sundays, the Crowders were creatures of habit.

The captain would spend some time in the fields before allowing himself one hour of television and an evening of bridge. Lucile would cook Sunday dinner and spend the day playing games with the children. They also regularly attended the Church of Christ on Sunday mornings and Wednesday evenings. Crowder was remembered by his family as a loving man who was generous with the little time he had outside the Rangers. Carol and Catherine describe him as extremely kind and compassionate yet stern. He was a good parent to his grandchildren, and they were able to count on his support with any problem. One granddaughter appreciated that he was always fully engaged with whoever was with him and involved in their interests. A grandson noted: "He had a profound faith, iron clad principles and lived his life accordingly. Yet he let others find their own way unless he was asked to help." The former Marine taught his wife and grandchildren to shoot and handle firearms in a respectful manner. Lucile spent a great deal of time with the children, teaching them to can food and sew.[68]

Although, by current standards, Crowder held old-fashioned views regarding women in the workplace, Lucile owned a gift shop in Dallas, which sold fine china and small pieces of art. Once Crowder became Texas Ranger chief, and they moved to Austin, she sold her store. One time when Lucile was suffering from bleeding ulcers, Bob stepped in and took over the running of the household without comment. Both Lucile and Crowder offered a sense of stability to the newly orphaned youngsters.[69]

While seeing to his family's welfare, the captain still devoted significant time and energy to his duty. The pumping of "hot oil" by wells slanted to siphon from neighboring leases was estimated in June 1962 to cost the industry approximately six million dollars every thirty days. That month, sixty leases in Gregg, Upshur, and Rusk Counties were under scrutiny by the DPS, the Railroad Commission, and the state attorney general's office for illegal drilling deviations. In addition, large concerns, such as Humble Oil and Refining Company and Texaco, filed civil suits in the Fourth District Court at Henderson against twelve oil field operators and financial institutions. Attorney General William Reid Wilson, Jr. obtained temporary injunctions prohibiting the plugging of wells with cement and other materials to hinder investigators. Crowder, forty Rangers, and nearly twenty Highway

Patrolmen were dispatched on June 8 to maintain the security of suspect wells and prevent tampering. Regulations permitted only a three-degree deviation from the vertical, and inspectors began conducting around-the-clock inclination and directional surveys on 160 wells. The following day, Dallas County District Attorney Henry Wade filed charges against William Odia Davis, Jr. in Justice of the Peace Glenn Byrd's court. The defendant was the majority stockholder of the Ebro Oil Company. Wade alleged Davis had committed theft under false pretenses by swindling the Nortex Oil & Gas Corporation out of six million dollars through deviation drilling on eight leases in Gregg and Rusk Counties. Ebro had sold Nortex some twenty wells, but the positive geological reports purportedly failed to realize four or five of them were pumping oil from an adjacent Humble property. The rest were supplied by plastic feeder lines from the producers. Crowder reported to the district attorney that the suspect had fled the state to either Palm Springs or Las Vegas. Davis's lawyers later indicated he would return to Texas and surrender himself. On June 11, he took the further step of filing a $250,000 slander suit against Nortex in district court in Henderson. Meanwhile, by June 24, inclination tests confirmed the presence of illegality in the oil field. Sixty-four wells were found to have deviated, and one shaft, slanting fifty-six degrees, was discovered to have used 5,100 feet of pipe when the bottom was 3,500 feet under the ground.[70]

Accompanied by three attorneys, Davis surrendered to Gregg County Sheriff Noble Crawford on June 13, and was immediately released on a fifteen-thousand-dollar bond. An examination hearing was docketed before Justice Byrd on the twenty-seventh. Crowder, Ranger Sergeant Lester Robinson, and Jim Ray were among eleven persons summoned to testify for the prosecution. Davis's legal team subpoenaed an equal number, including three insurance executives and six Nortex managers. At the same time, the Railroad Commission's probe looked into other operators and came to involve several state and federal district courts. The number of leases under temporary restraining orders grew to fifty, and Attorney General Wilson filed three lawsuits seeking nineteen million dollars in penalties for slant drilling and violating the commission's orders concerning tampering. By the end of the year, sixty-two individuals were indicted on 358 criminal charges. Regardless of the larger picture, Byrd dismissed the theft charges against Davis on June 30, citing the state's failure to make a case sufficient for the grand jury. District Attorney Wade declared his office would drop the charges, but indicated his intention to re-file if new evidence emerged.[71]

Loving County landowner Victor Ely "Pete" Brookfield was reported missing on February 3, 1964, while in Dallas on business. Working the case, Crowder determined the potential victim had recently been involved in protracted negotiations with major oil companies. Apparently known as an eccentric man, Brookfield had refused all offers to purchase or lease the mineral rights on his property. According to the captain's investigation, Mrs. Joy Mann "Rusty" Chandler, operator of a Pecos abstract and title firm, allegedly persuaded Brookfield to dispose of his rights in exchange for a $118,000 check from the Midland oil company of Meeker and Hill. The check was divided into two deposits at the Wynnewood State Bank in Oak Cliff, with $68,000 credited to one account bearing Brookfield's name and fifty thousand dollars into another in the name of Brook-Chan Properties, a supposed partnership. Brookfield was traced to an Odessa hotel from which he disappeared on February 5, and law officers conducted an unsuccessful search for him. Crowder and Ranger James Spivey "Jim" Nance arrested Chandler on October 1, and the captain filed a complaint in a Dallas court charging her with passing a forged instrument. She was arraigned and freed on ten thousand dollars bail awaiting a grand jury indictment. Company B continued to investigate, but Ernest Daniel commented, "Frankly, we don't know whether he is alive. Some officers are convinced he was killed in Mexico." On December 16, Texas Rangers disclosed that new information indicated Brookfield had been in the El Paso area, although he was possibly prevented from alerting authorities as to his location. The following April, an Odessa private detective, hired by the missing man's mother, offered a ten-thousand-dollar reward for information leading to the recovery of Brookfield. Neither avenue of inquiry bore fruit, and Victor Brookfield was never found.[72]

Even after Crowder's subsequent retirement, though, some paltry clues as to Brookfield's whereabouts emerged from the shadows. In October 1969,

Chandler, now Mrs. William Elmo Carpenter, was indicted by a federal grand jury in Pecos on two counts of failure to pay income taxes in 1964 on $58,756, which, ironically, was part of the money involved in her forgery case. She was also indicted on four counts of perjury that had occurred in her grand jury testimony. During her trial, which opened on March 2, 1970, in U.S. District Judge Ernest Guinn's courtroom, a handwriting expert from Washington, DC, testified that a letter written by Brookfield to his mother thirteen days after his disappearance was a forgery. Enrique Montemayor, the mayor of Ojinaga, Mexico, attested that a woman he could not identify as Carpenter had in 1964 offered him one thousand dollars to arrest and detain an unnamed male. He claimed he had refused. Patricio Gomez testified he had accompanied Carpenter to Mexico and served as translator in her conversation with the mayor. The prosecution additionally brought to the stand witnesses who identified Carpenter's brother-in-law as the Victor Brookfield who had accompanied the defendant on several business transactions in 1964. In her defense, Carpenter testified she had seen Brookfield several times after his disappearance, and her claims were similarly supported by eyewitnesses. On March 7, the jury convicted Carpenter on all counts. Taken to the El Paso County jail to await sentencing, she was ordered on March 27 to serve a total of twenty-eight years in a federal penitentiary, some of the sentences to run concurrently.[73]

On October 16, 1968, twenty-five hundred members of the United Steelworkers of America took to the picket line at the Lone Star Steel plant south of Daingerfield in Morris County. The strikers were protesting working conditions and company rules. As the sheriff only employed two deputies, he requested assistance from the state. Throughout the entire 210 days of the labor dispute, nearly every Ranger would be on scene at one time or another. Crowder was given overall command, but only Rangers Robert Kenneth "Bob" Mitchell and Glenn Elliott, both of Company B, worked the entire length of the strike.[74]

The whole episode was marked by vandalism, assaults, and bombings, as well as two killings. Crowder had nails driven into his car tires on six occasions, and he was forced to avoid rocks, bottles, gunfire, and numerous threats, hurled at him. Throughout the crisis, he maintained an air of stern yet

Company B, Texas Rangers. Front (L to R): Ernest Daniel, Lewis Rigler, Bob Crowder, Lester Robertson, Bob Badgett; Rear (L to R): Charlie Moore, G. W. Burks, Glenn Elliot, Bob Mitchell, Red Arnold, Frank Kemp. *Courtesy Texas Ranger Hall of Fame and Museum, Waco, TX.*

tolerant authority. Crowder and Mitchell disguised themselves as workers on October 22, and drove out of the plant's main gate in a company pickup truck hoping to entice a response. With the captain in the driver's seat, they headed down U.S. Highway 259 toward Longview. Immediately after they departed, a pickup with three passengers began following the Rangers. Three miles later, the chase vehicle flicked its lights, and Crowder pulled over to the side of the road. The pickup drove up alongside, and the three men inside began shooting with a .22-caliber rifle. "I slid over," recounted Crowder, "and Ranger Mitchell fired three loads of buckshot into their pickup. They lit out and we chased them at 90 miles an hour until they had to stop at a dead end road [in Ore City]." Mitchell leapt out of the truck ready to shoot, but Crowder calmly said, "Robert, don't kill 'em." Approaching the stopped vehicle, the two Rangers found three middle-aged thugs, as well as firearms, a length of chain, a number of rocks, and two jars of moonshine whiskey. The shooters—William E. Montgomery, Leo White, and Archie W. Connor, Jr.—were arrested on charges of assault with intent to murder and placed under bond by Justice of the Peace Elmer Scott Simpson, although they never stood trial.[75]

Two security guards suffered gunshot wounds in the legs while patrolling the plant's grounds on November 26, although they were listed as being in satisfactory condition the following day. Lone Star Steel and the local of the United Plant Guard Workers of America offered rewards totaling six thousand dollars for the arrest and conviction of the guilty parties. The incentives were never claimed. The stakes were raised when Aubrey Smithy "Smitty" Blackburn from nearby Pittsburg crossed the picket line, which led to his roadside murder on January 16, 1969.[76]

On one particular day, Crowder told reporters for the *Houston Chronicle*:

> You've got to remember, these people—on both sides—are scared. They've been shot at, rocked, beaten, bumped into, cursed, ambushed, and spit on. Things are tense around here, and these people aren't themselves. They'll eventually kiss and make up and go back to being decent, law-abiding citizens. And some of them might even have a kind word for the Texas Rangers.[77]

The strike ended on May 11, 1969, when the union voted to resume work. Ranger Elliott wrote in his memoir: "I did not think then, or now, that a Ranger has any business working a strike. No matter what we do, we lose." He further summed up the sentiment of all Rangers: "Our job should have been working murders, bank robberies, and other major criminal cases, not trying to keep two sides apart—especially when both sides down deep wanted to fight."[78]

The Lone Star strike proved to be Crowder's last major case. On September 1, 1968, the Public Safety Commission had adopted a new policy that changed the mandatory retirement age from seventy to sixty-five. One of those affected was the sixty-seven-year-old Crowder. The commission did allow employees who applied for a one-year extension to remain in order to prepare for retirement. Crowder and twenty-seven other DPS employees requested the postponement.[79]

Ultimately, all good things come to an end. Along with the seven other Rangers who faced mandatory retirement, Crowder was honored at a banquet at the Ridgewood Country Club in Waco on August 25, 1969. The event was hosted by the Fort Fisher Committee, the Waco Chamber of Commerce, and the city's residents. Captain Clint T. Peoples, commander of Company F and advisory member of the Fort Fisher commission, invited four hundred local and state luminaries and law enforcement officials. Colonel Wilson Edward "Pat" Speir, DPS director, was the featured speaker for the occasion, and he praised the eight lawmen who had a combined 261 years of service to Texas. Crowder retired effective August 31, 1969. In an interview with Robert Nieman, Ranger Glenn Elliott asserted, "Crowder was the best Captain that I worked for … without any question." Bob Mitchell called him "one of the best men I ever knew."[80]

On September 15, Crowder was employed by Security Couriers of Dallas to head their newly formed investigation division; Badgett was named the assistant director. One week later, Governor Preston Smith appointed Crowder to the Texas Board of Private Detectives, Investigators, Patrolmen, and Watchmen. Even in retirement, the former captain maintained a connection to his beloved Ranger service. On May 30, 1971, during the annual meeting of the Former Texas Rangers Association in San Antonio, Crowder was elected to the board of directors for a three-year term. Captain Allee, retired from commanding Company D the previous year, was chosen as the organization's president. In delivering the keynote address, Colonel Speir declared to the assembled lawmen, "I believe we must have Rangers as long as we have a Texas."[81]

Captain Robert A. Crowder suffered a massive coronary occlusion at approximately five o'clock on the afternoon of November 26, 1972. He was taken to Presbyterian Hospital where he was pronounced dead on arrival. He was buried at Restland Memorial Park cemetery in Dallas on November 29.[82]

Lucile continued to live in Dallas and raise Catherine and George. She died on May 31, 1983, and was buried next to her husband.[83]

Having had to live for a time with his maternal grandfather, who was not a pleasant man, James always felt fortunate being adopted by Bob and Lucile Crowder. He loved to fly airplanes, so he entered a junior college program for the express purpose of becoming an aviation cadet. After one year of college, James enlisted in the U.S. Army Air Corps on December 19, 1941. While an aviation cadet at the Air Corps Advanced Flying School in Lubbock, he married Mary Wanda Sloan at the post chapel on September 5, 1942. Crowder acted as his son's best man. The couple would raise three sons. James served both in the States and overseas. Following the war, he remained in the service, as the Army Air Corps transitioned into the U.S. Air Force. He flew B-52 bombers for the Strategic Air Command before retiring as a major after sixteen years of service. James then became a highly regarded corporate pilot and expert on jet airplanes. Although he retired in his sixties, he continued to fly and completed his last recertification at age eighty. Mary died on October 18, 1997, in Dallas. James died in Boulder, Colorado, on June 23, 2005.[84]

Carol attended the University of Oklahoma and graduated with a master's degree in English. She married and has two children and two step-children. She has been engaged for over twenty years in public policy involving child welfare and home-care. She currently works for the New York State Department of Health in a management position.[85]

Catherine attended the University of Texas and went to work as a licensed registered nurse. She married and had one daughter and one son. She presently works as a certified nurse educator in Austin.[86]

George suffered the most from the death of his parents and grandfather and went through some hard times before he found his way. He married and adopted his wife's child before they ultimately divorced. He worked as a floor refinisher for residential and commercial property owners. George died on July 4, 2001, in Dallas.[87]

Bob Crowder was the most effective and respected Ranger captain of his time. He earned his spurs in the Marine Corps and in police work. Mentored under "Lone Wolf" Gonzaullas, he rose to become a natural, confident leader of men. While he is chiefly remembered for the Rusk State Hospital Riot, that episode, one of many in a long, illustrious career, aptly demonstrates his fidelity and courage.

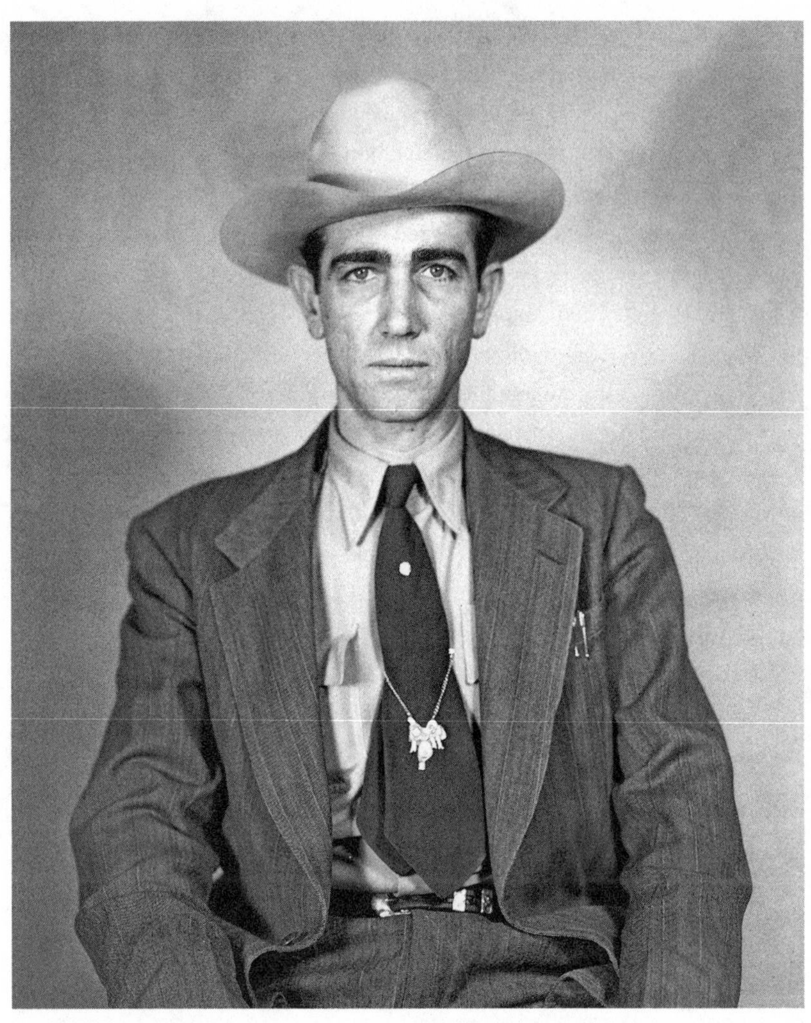

J. J. Klevenhagen. #1983/112_R-274-1. *Courtesy Texas State Library and Archives Commission, Austin, TX.*

Chapter 8

John J. Klevenhagen: "Absolute Zeal and Commitment"

John Joseph Klevenhagen, Sr. combined the manners and abilities of the frontier Ranger with those of the modern law enforcement officer. He was tall, lean, leather-faced, and completely unrelenting. He was a matchless horseman and a deadly shot, but also well-versed in the often-arcane facets of criminalistics. Unusual among those who wore the *cinco peso* badge, he was a licensed pilot, and more than once used his flying skills to bring criminals to justice. However, an absolute zeal and commitment to his duty would shorten his life. Ranger Ed Gooding commented: "I never saw a man with a fire burning inside him like the one in Captain Klevenhagen. He drove himself unmercifully. He finally drove himself into a much too early grave, but the captain would not have had it any other way."

He was born on June 2, 1912, on the family cattle ranch near New Braunfels, Comal County, Texas. His parents were Frank John and Mary Helen (Videau) Klevenhagen. His father, a former soldier born in Iowa City, Iowa, on January 27, 1890, was a car inspector for the Galveston, Houston & San Antonio Railroad and a general contractor, while his mother was a housewife born in Galveston on September 10, 1885. They were married on April 20, 1911. Young John's siblings were Frances Helen Klevenhagen, born on September 10, 1910;

twin brothers Robert Gerard and George Joseph Klevenhagen, born on February 17, 1914; and Margaret "Baby" Klevenhagen, born on November 5, 1916. According to Margaret's daughter, who lived in Frank and Mary's household until she was seven, the Klevenhagen patriarch (known to his descendants as "Pop") was "tough" on his sons. Church and a strong sense of morality were foundations of the children's upbringing, and a leather strap sometimes reinforced Frank's strict parenting.[1]

While Klevenhagen was a young boy, possibly in early June 1926, rustlers targeted several Comal County ranches, including that owned by Frank. Several Texas Rangers responded and meeting them fueled Klevenhagen's desire to join that legendary corps. "They became my heroes," he later recalled. "Every kid in Texas wanted to be a Ranger, but I made up my mind I would be one." The youth emulated the lawmen as they went about their duties, talked with them in their camps, and persuaded them to teach him how to shoot, track, and live off the land. He was eventually a proficient rider and an expert marksman.[2]

Meanwhile, Klevenhagen dropped out of the eighth grade in order to work on the family's ranch. By his sixteenth birthday, Klevenhagen considered himself ready to become a Ranger. Unfortunately, rather than eager teenagers, the service was only accepting applicants who had exhibited superior abilities in law enforcement work. Undeterred, Klevenhagen decided he would mold himself into the kind of officer worthy of the name Texas Ranger. He applied with the San Antonio Police Department and the sheriffs' and constables' offices in Bexar and Comal Counties, but all refused him on account of his young age.[3]

Klevenhagen secured a job as a lineman with the San Antonio lighting company, then assessed his future. His height of nearly six feet and weight of 150 pounds suggested adulthood, and he had bested enough bullies in fights to be confident of his ability to handle himself. He completed his transformation by growing a thick black mustache that seemingly added maturity to his features. He also purchased a poll tax, which was required for anyone twenty-one years or older, and declared his age as twenty-two. "I guess I did hedge a little on my age," he admitted months before his death.[4]

His determination was rewarded in 1930 with acceptance into the San Antonio Police Department where he was employed as a motorcycle officer. While he claimed to be of voting age, Klevenhagen was still only seventeen. Soon after starting as a policeman, he began developing a network of confidential informants. His dark skin tone and fluent Spanish enabled him to make significant inroads into the Hispanic community. He established himself as a fair-minded man of his word who never betrayed a confidence.[5]

His career with the police department proved relatively brief, however. By 1933, Klevenhagen was employed by Hal J. Ross, promoter of the Walkathon Arena on the corner of Navarro and Augusta Streets, as a special deputy sheriff. In the early morning of November 13, he and Constable William Everett Isbell of Precinct 6 were patrolling the stadium during a marathon contest when they encountered Ben Ruby, gambling house and nightclub operator. According to Klevenhagen, Ruby slapped Isbell in what the constable described as a "playful-like" manner, and the latter returned the gesture by poking the gambler in the belly. Quite possibly, the exchange was not as good-natured as Isbell related, since Ruby began to pull a gun before he was disarmed. The club owner was removed from the premises by Police Sergeant William Christoph. Following the altercation, the two lawmen approached Virgil Edward "Red" Berry, speakeasy and nightclub owner; Joe Max "Skeet" Hobrecht, convicted bandit, killer, and rumrunner; and Polk Clint Neal, slot machine operator. Isbell asked whether Hobrecht was carrying a firearm, and, while reaching toward his waistline, the desperado retorted, "What's it to you?" Swiftly, Klevenhagen removed a gun from Hobrecht's belt, and Berry and Neal were likewise disarmed. Isbell swore out charges of unlawfully carrying pistols against the latter three before Judge McCollum Burnett in County Court-at-Law No. 1. The next day, Police Chief Owen William Kilday announced the city would seek no legal action in Ruby's case. Consequently, Klevenhagen appeared in the county attorney's office on the fifteenth and filed a complaint against Ruby for the weapons possession.[6]

The charges for all four men were dismissed on January 24, 1934, on the motion of Assistant County Attorney Marion Roy McClanahan, Sr.

The prosecutor argued the search of the defendants had been illegal and a conviction would not be sustained. Klevenhagen informed the *San Antonio Light* he had not been interviewed by anyone in the county attorney's office. He reiterated that Ruby had pulled a gun, and, for the first time, publicly revealed that the hammer of the defendant's weapon had snapped down on the thumb of Police Officer Jesse Yantis during a struggle for possession. The special deputy declared himself ready to repeat his words under oath in front of the Ninety-fourth District grand jury. The impaneled members investigated the matter and subpoenaed Klevenhagen and Isbell to appear. Shortly after his own appearance before the grand jury, the county attorney filed new charges on February 7 identical to the previous ones against Ruby, Hobrecht, Berry, and Neal.[7]

For some time, career criminal Otto A. "Skeeter" Claus had been engaged in a quarrel with former police officer Alfred Clifton "Bill" Street. On February 2, Street encountered his foe at the Embassy Bar, and the two began to argue. A friend of the latter slid a pistol covered by a paper across the bar, which Claus seized and used to fatally shoot Street. William T. Mitchell, a city policeman who responded to the scene, removed a .45 pistol from Claus's belt. Special Deputy Klevenhagen and Constable Samuel Calvin Cain, Jr. of Precinct 7 also reported to the Embassy. Claus was charged with murder, and his trial was scheduled for April 23.[8]

The legal proceedings resulting from the Walkathon Arena matter had seemingly ended in Joe Hobrecht being found guilty on April 5 of the weapons charge. He was fined one hundred dollars and court costs. Red Berry had been acquitted in his hearing the day before, as Judge Burnett ruled the search for his pistol had been illegal due to lack of probable cause. Indeed, Klevenhagen had testified, "They all three came in together and I just figured they had guns." Hobrecht's admission to Isbell that he was carrying a gun was considered sufficient grounds for the search. During Ben Ruby's trial, which convened on the twelfth, Joe Clyde Musgrave, a former deputy sheriff, contradicted Klevenhagen's earlier statement and claimed he had been present at the altercation. Promised immunity from prosecution, as he had also been illegally armed, Musgrave testified he, Sergeant Christoph, and Officer Yantis had stepped between Isbell and Ruby. The ex-deputy asserted he had personally removed the gun from Ruby's belt before the racketeer could react. In light of the immunity deal, the judge instructed the jury to disregard details of the actual search, but allowed Musgrave's subsequent testimony into evidence. The former lawman related how he had followed Ruby into the parking lot and returned his pistol. Polk Neal, recently found guilty of unlawfully carrying a gun at the same incident, testified the gambler had not brandished a weapon. Former prizefighter Jack Avalon, a "stick-man" at a dice game at the International Club on East Travis Street, also backed Musgrave and Neal's statements. Ruby was acquitted by the jury.[9]

The Embassy Bar case was tried in Ninety-fourth District Court before Judge Wilton Wade McCrory. The proceedings were marred by charges of intimidation and bribery of witnesses. The prosecution's only eyewitness, a soldier from Fort Sam Houston, testified that Claus and Street had been arguing in the bar when the former produced a pistol. The witness related how Claus had shot the victim five or six times, and characterized the defendant as the aggressor in the fatal altercation. According to the coroner's inquest, Street had been hit in the chest, arms, head, and thigh. As the trial date drew near, the serviceman alleged Claus approached him on March 30 and warned him to take a furlough. Officer Mitchell described his disarming of Claus and later claimed another policeman had made an attempt to change Mitchell's testimony with the promise "If [Claus is] acquitted, you'll be taken care of." Klevenhagen and Cain confirmed Mitchell's statement as to the weapon's location. Testimony closed on June 15 without the defendant or his chief witness taking the stand. The state requested the death penalty.[10]

Based on Klevenhagen's impressive arrest record, his calmness and nerve, and his ability to be where he was most needed, Constable William Welder "Will" Wood of Precinct 1 hired him as a deputy constable in the summer of 1934.[11] Led by Chief Deputy Constable James Washington Davis, Constables Klevenhagen, Elbert James "Bob" Ginder, Joseph Harvey "Joe" Passant, Sr., and Joe M. Dominguez raided the Aztec Business Men's Club, a suspected bookmaking operation at 308 Aztec Building, on December 28. Five men were arrested, and complaints were filed before Justice of the Peace John Franklin "Pete" Onion charging gambling with cards.

Their appearance for a hearing on January 3, 1935, was guaranteed by bonds of fifty dollars each.[12]

Klevenhagen had worked for Wood for six months when the constable announced on December 1, 1934, that he would reappoint his entire staff on the first of the year. However, Klevenhagen resigned his position. Wood made an application to rehire Klevenhagen as a motorcycle officer on January 7, 1935. The commissioners' court held a public hearing the same day and denied the request. On February 1, a motion to appoint Klevenhagen a deputy for Constable Clinton D. Jones of Precinct 8 was tabled. The delay was due to disagreement among the commissioners regarding the current fee system. In the meantime, Constable Cain of Precinct 7 took a leave of absence on February 11, and Klevenhagen was named to fill the vacancy in an acting capacity. On March 1, he resigned and resumed his old position with Constable Wood.[13]

While taking a coffee break in the county courthouse two years previously, Klevenhagen had met Viola Rosabell Wolff, a courthouse telephone switchboard operator for the past five years. Their brief chat led to a romance that culminated in marriage on May 7, 1935, when they were wedded at the Selma Catholic Church. The constable's new bride was a hometown girl who had been born on December 20, 1911.[14]

With the end of Prohibition, the state legislature had enacted a new liquor control act. On December 6, 1935, Klevenhagen signed a complaint before First Assistant District Attorney William Patrick Camp charging an individual with three counts of selling whiskey in wholesale quantities without the proper permits from the Texas Liquor Control Board and the other appropriate county and state agencies. The case was heard in County Court-at-Law No. 2. Constable Wood, Klevenhagen, and Deputies Ginder and Dominguez raided a house on West Poplar Street on January 16, 1936. Described as the largest liquor seizure since Repeal, they confiscated a three hundred-gallon still and fifty 50-gallon drums of whiskey mash. One man was arrested.[15]

Defeating incumbent Albert West, Jr. in the Democratic primary, Wood was elected sheriff of Bexar County on November 3, 1936, and he chose Klevenhagen for the position of investigator. Klevenhagen campaigned actively for his employer, and the race had not been uneventful. Indeed, Chief Deputy Sheriff Alfonso Newton, Jr. wandered into the county clerk's office on the morning of July 6 and observed Klevenhagen marking a ballot for a visually impaired and elderly gentleman who had apparently left his spectacles at home. Certain to lose his job if West was defeated, Newton was naturally outraged and assigned a deputy to the clerk's office. As her role of switchboard operator was under the sheriff's purview, Viola was affected by the post-election consequences. On July 29, the commissioners' court eliminated the county highway patrol, effective August 1, as the six officers had vocally favored West. Wood had been supported by the city administration, which was allied with the commissioners. Chief Deputy Newton retaliated by threatening to discharge the courthouse's two operators and the matron. Negotiations between West and the commissioners were tense, but, in the end, the two operators stayed at their posts through the end of the year. However, Sheriff-elect Wood announced he intended to replace Viola and her coworker at the beginning of his administration. District Attorney John Read Shook questioned whether the sheriff had the power to fire courthouse employees. Regardless of the limits of Wood's authority, as her husband was slated to join the sheriff's department on January 1, 1937, Viola chose to resign the same day.[16]

The San Antonio Police Department suffered twin blows in quick succession as Patrolmen John William Stowe was killed while off-duty on December 3, 1936, and Motorcycle Officer Agnal Aubrey "Bill" Edwards was murdered on January 16, 1937. Klevenhagen worked the second case. Before he was shot to death, Edwards had halted the vehicle of two armed robbers on the 400 block of Jones Avenue near Oak Street. Abandoned at the scene, the killers' automobile was reported as stolen, and a thumbprint lifted from the car's side was analyzed for comparison. Edwin Paul Bogasch and Herbert C. "Dusty" Rhodes, the police department's dactylography experts, examined the fingerprints of more than two hundred individuals on file. Klevenhagen and Dominguez arrested a suspect in an East Crockett Street parking lot and recovered four .32-caliber pistols from his home. The deputies took two of the handguns, both of which had been recently fired, and the bullet that killed Edwards to the DPS crime lab for examination. Shell casings found at the crime scene matched a Savage .32-caliber semiautomatic pistol Chief Deputy Constable Duke Carver, Sr. recovered from the North Palmetto home of John W. Vaughn's brother. Based on information given by Vaughn, Carver took into custody Donald Richard "Donald Duck" Baker. In his trial, Vaughn claimed Baker, his partner in two gas station robberies, had fired the fatal shots. Baker was already indicted, and he claimed he was not in the car at the time of the murder. Manuel T. Gonzaullas, chief of the state crime lab, testified on the evidence that linked the bullets that killed Edwards to the murder weapon. Subsequent witnesses connected the gun to Vaughn personally. The defendant was tried on February 20, convicted, and given the death penalty. Since he had not been in possession of the murder weapon, Baker was sentenced to ninety-nine years imprisonment. However, one of the jurors was subsequently disqualified. Vaughn was given a new trial on March 8, 1938. Four days later, a jury voted to put him to death for the second time.[17]

Elderly San Antonio residents Quirino and Eusebia Ramos were found dead in their home on February 5, 1937. Known as wealthy recluses, the brother and sister had been bound, gagged, and beaten to death three days before the discovery of their bodies. Investigators quickly suspected three men, and charges were filed in Justice of the Peace Bartholomew Harrington "Bat" Corrigan's court. Uncle and nephew Jose Rendon Morin and Juan Felan Morin, two of the fugitives, crossed the border into Mexico at Laredo and hid themselves north of Monterrey. On February 7, Klevenhagen, Joe Dominguez, and Laredo Police Chief Candelario Mendiola traveled to Monterrey to enlist the assistance of Mexican authorities. They met with Captain Uvaldo Garate, police inspector general of Nuevo Leon, and Monterrey Chief of Detectives Enrique Martinez. Following a three-day search, the Morins were apprehended at their hideout. Juan "Blacksnake" Garcia, the third accomplice, had been already jailed in Nuevo Laredo on an unrelated misdemeanor charge before his identity was established. The American law officers returned to Laredo to await the deportation of their quarry. Klevenhagen and Dominguez were outspoken in praising their Mexican counterparts, as well as U.S. Consul William Preston Blocker in Monterrey and Nuevo Leon Governor Anacleto Guerrero. However, as the deputies returned to Nuevo Laredo on February 13, collected the pair of Juans, and made their way back over the international bridge, they were stopped just before the midpoint by Mexican authorities. The *federales* declared the extradition paperwork was not in order and reclaimed the two fugitives. Texas officials requested Washington intercede on the state's behalf for extradition. The lengthy process neared completion on March 30 when First Assistant District Attorney Leonard John "Buck" Gittinger, Sr. completed the legal documentation, which invoked the extradition treaty of February 22, 1899. Additionally, Governor Allred signed an executive order directing Klevenhagen and Dominguez to travel to Nuevo Leon and Tamaulipas and receive the three indicted fugitives into their custody. The governor personally named the deputies as his agents in the matter.[18]

In August 1937, Klevenhagen pursued Lawrence Rea, a notorious bandit and killer who had escaped from the California state prison at San Quentin. Once on the lam, the convict committed a series of robberies and kidnappings from California to Texas over a period of several weeks that netted him more than ninety thousand dollars. While briefly in the Alamo City, Rea and an accomplice robbed the San Antonio Public Service Company's counting room of seventeen hundred dollars, which put Klevenhagen, Chief Deputy Constable Carver, and Chief Sheriff's Investigator Cyrus Lucas Heard on his trail. After evading police officers and sheriff's deputies in Austin, the felon left behind one dead farmer and two more wounded near Govalle. Clarence Godbey McGraw, the identification expert for the Department of Public Safety, analyzed trace evidence left by the killer and confirmed Rea was the guilty party. The fugitive was also linked to seven robberies and two kidnappings in Houston and Galveston. After tracing Rea through an informant to a gambler's residence at 1918 Huldy in Houston, Klevenhagen notified Detective Lieutenant Cecil Priest, who ordered the house to be surrounded on August 15. Eight police cars, loaded with submachine guns, rifles, and shotguns, responded to the scene. One of the Houston officers was a detective named Clairville Vincent "Buster" Kern with whom Klevenhagen would develop a lifelong friendship. Priest shouted for Rea to give himself up. The outlaw did not respond, and the lieutenant ordered two tear-gas grenades be fired through the windows of the house. A muffled gunshot was heard from inside followed by the front door opening and two occupants coming out to surrender. Rea remained inside. Donning gas masks, Kern and Lieutenant Hobson McGill went inside and found Rea in a second-floor bedroom. The robber had lain down on the bed and shot himself in the heart with a shotgun. Although largely forgotten, Rea possessed a fearsome underworld reputation at the time, and he swore, "No cop will ever take me alive." His death by his own hand proved to be the largest mystery to the officers. Klevenhagen revealed to reporters, "We can't figure out why he didn't come out and fight."[19]

Late the following month, Klevenhagen and his fellow deputies were confronted with one of the most baffling murder mysteries in San Antonio history. A young woman had gone to visit her sister in the country, and the two ladies discovered what they thought was a half-full barrel of refuse thrown onto the side of the Sulphur Springs road, nine miles from town. The stench of chemicals and rotting flesh emanating from the drum led the young female to tell a friend, who passed on the information to Klevenhagen. On September 29, he and Deputy Gordon Hagen located the vessel, which, they ascertained, contained ground flesh, hair, teeth, and bones soaked in a strong chemical. When pouring some of the ghastly liquid into a quart jar to be used as a sample, Klevenhagen spilled some on his hand and suffered a yellow burn. An identical discovery had been made several days prior on a farm east of Randolph Field, and another sample was secured. The pair of jars were taken to the DPS lab in Austin for analysis by Manuel Gonzaullas.[20]

Jesus Quintero was found in his automobile outside the Red Ball Garage and Bar in Elmendorf on January 22, 1938. Accompanied by Deputies William Bernhard "Bill" Hauck, Jr. and James L. Rhodes, Klevenhagen responded to the scene. The victim had been shot in the chest around 7 p.m., but the deputies could initially find no witnesses to the crime. The officers searched the building and found five bullet holes in the wall in addition to the one in Quintero's body. Evidence was developed that George William Keilmann, a former Wilson County commissioner, had walked into the tavern and, "with malice aforethought," shot Quintero over a land dispute. The morning after the shooting, the deputies searched for Keilmann and found him in a rooming house on Martin Street. The suspect was in bed, and a pistol with six spent cartridges lay on the dresser. Klevenhagen arrested Keilmann and charged him with murdering Quintero. Justice of the Peace Oliver Lee Wiley held an inquest, and the suspect was indicted by the grand jury on March 15.[21]

Career criminal Selvie Winfield "Harry" Wells had escaped from the Arkansas State Penitentiary on January 14, 1938. He returned home to Texas and married a Kingsville college student under the alias "Harry Northcutt." A bridegroom of only three days, Wells stole nearly $2,500 from the Citizens State Bank of Luling on March 5. After lying low for a week in Kingsville, he made a desperate dash through South Texas. In his wild bid for freedom, Wells evaded three posses and wounded two Beeville officers before being cornered on the fifteenth in a two-room oil field shack two miles from Gladewater. Indeed, Klevenhagen had received the tip that led him to that location along with several Bexar County deputies, DPS Criminal Investigators Robert A. Crowder and Norman Kemp "Dick" Dixon, Bexar County highway patrolmen, and FBI Special Agent Gus Tiner "Buster" Jones and additional G-men. Tear gas bombs thrown by Klevenhagen, Crowder, and Patrolman Bill Hauck forced the desperado out of the residence and into the custody of the twenty-one law officers. As the outlaw had in his possession a sawed-off shotgun, a rifle, and several pistols, the apprehension might have ended differently. More than half of the stolen loot was recovered with the remainder being lost through gambling in Corpus Christi, Robstown, and San Diego. Following a brief jurisdictional dispute the same day, Agent Jones arranged for Wells to be taken to San Antonio to face federal charges of bank robbery. A complaint was filed before U.S. Commissioner Paul Alvin Lockhart, and the defendant was arraigned for a preliminary hearing. The thief then languished in the Bexar County jail while awaiting the federal grand jury in Del Rio. Refugio County Sheriff Ira Heard arrived in town bearing two warrants charging Wells with robbing a filling station and a citizen. Additionally, Bexar, Bee, Kleberg, and Fort Bend Counties wanted the outlaw on various charges.[22]

The new year brought resolution to an old case. John Vaughn's death sentence was affirmed by the Court of Criminal Appeals on January 12, 1938. Along with another condemned man, he rigidly stood before Judge

McCrory on March 8 and listened as he was sentenced to the electric chair for his crimes. The jurist pronounced, "It is the judgement of this court that you be sentenced to death before sunrise on the twenty-second day of April." When offered the chance to speak, Vaughn continued to maintain his innocence and blame Donald Baker for the murder. Once the district attorney composed the death warrants, the two handcuffed and chained prisoners were loaded into a vehicle with Klevenhagen and Dominguez. With an escort car containing Hauck and Deputy Nathan Rufford McRae, Sr. leading the caravan, Klevenhagen drove to Huntsville. Another vehicle with Deputies Elton Ray Cude, Sr. and James Rhodes and County Jailer Bob Ginder brought up the rear. Later that afternoon, Vaughn was delivered safely to his cell on death row.[23]

On March 23, Klevenhagen was honored for his role in apprehending Rae and Wells. The sheriff's investigator received from Assistant District Attorney Leroy Jeffers a scroll that bore the signatures of forty county officials paying tribute to his work as a peace officer. Several months later, Klevenhagen, Duke Carver, and Cyrus Head were somewhat annoyed when a blood-and-thunder radio dramatization of the Rae case reimagined the three as police lieutenants and credited the San Antonio Police Department with the bandit's demise. Unsure whether the editing of the truth was an attack on the sheriff, or the result of sloppy research and writing, Klevenhagen swore off listening to further radio shows.[24]

With Wells's case scheduled on the federal docket, U.S. District Judge Robert Johnston McMillan released the defendant into Sheriff Heard's custody. The outlaw was slated to face justice in Refugio County prior to being returned to San Antonio. Klevenhagen and Hauck were subpoenaed to appear as witnesses in Wells's trial. Jury selection began on April 6 in Judge James P. Pool's district courtroom in Refugio. In addition to Klevenhagen and Hauck, the courtroom was filled to capacity with law officers from Karnes, Wharton, Matagorda, and Refugio Counties. Wells was sentenced in federal court to ninety-nine years at Alcatraz.[25]

Klevenhagen next made the quite novel decision to obtain a passenger pilot's license and became a student at the United Hanger. According to the *San Antonio Express*, the deputy aspired to become a pilot in government service or for a private transcontinental airline. In order to accrue additional flying time, he embarked on a flight to Cleveland, Ohio, and met a United Aero Corporation official in Cincinnati. The pair flew a new Aeronca KC-A airplane from the factory and returned to Stinson Field on June 15.[26]

On June 27, 1938, the body of Jose Dorantes was found on the tracks of the Missouri, Kansas & Texas Railroad near Camp Street. The victim, a florist company bill controller, had been severed at the hips into two portions. Klevenhagen investigated the puzzling "train murder" and received a tip on July 1 that a man had been spotted splitting a large money roll. Assisted by Deputies Hubert Carl Boek, Dewey Rinearson, and Lee Rogers, Klevenhagen arrested Santiago Sainz and Martin Sepulveda for the crime. Charges of murder and robbery by assault were filed against the suspects on July 1. Two eyewitnesses who had previously made false reports to authorities were also taken into custody. Written confessions were made to Hicks Arthur Woods, criminal investigator for the district attorney. Revising their accounts, the latter pair asserted Sainz and Sepulveda struck the victim with a stick and pushed him under the wheels of a passing train.[27]

Nineteen years old at the time of the crime, Carlos Fernandez had been convicted on February 27, 1937, of Officer John Stowe's murder at the Kentucky Club on East Commerce Street, and the jury imposed the death penalty. The case was affirmed by the Court of Criminal Appeals on June 1, 1938, and Judge McCrory set the execution date as before sunrise on August 19. "The warden shall cause a current of electricity sufficient to cause to pass through your body," the judge pronounced. While not involved in the actual homicide investigation, Klevenhagen and four other deputies escorted the condemned man to Huntsville where he was placed on death row. Mexican consulate officials pleaded for the youth to receive a life sentence, but the board of pardons narrowly voted against clemency. However, eleven hours before his final appointment, Fernandez received a thirty-day stay of execution from Governor Allred. The night before the reprieve expired, the governor commuted the death sentence to one of life imprisonment.[28]

In September 1938, Klevenhagen was involved in closing one of the most shocking criminal cases in the state's history. Joseph Douglas "Joe" Ball was a tough bootlegger and owner of the Sociable Inn in Elmendorf, a small town in Bexar County. Known as the local bully, he habitually carried a gun and kept five alligators in a concrete pool behind his establishment. Sometimes, to entertain his rowdy customers, Ball threw live dogs and cats to his crocodilian pets in the tank. Klevenhagen suspected him of being a rustler who crept onto ranches, butchered cows on the range, and sold the meat to crooked shopkeepers. Unfortunately, the deputy was unable to secure enough evidence for an arrest.[29]

On September 23, Deputy Sheriff John Gray learned from an informant that Ball had been seen carrying a fifty-five-gallon gasoline drum into a shed behind his sister's house. Apparently, a vile odor was wafting from the container. The next day, Klevenhagen and Gray went to the residence in question to investigate. The two officers theorized the barrel might have contained a branded hide, which would possibly be enough to get a conviction. When they arrived, the sister told them Ball had removed the barrel after she complained of the stench. Klevenhagen and Gray decided to take Ball into custody and hold him until they could find the barrel. Finding their suspect at his business, Ball agreed to come in but asked to be allowed to close up for the day. Gray stayed outside and Klevenhagen and Ball went indoors. The deputy leaned against the door jamb while Ball went to the register, opened it, and began counting the cash. The bartender took a small metal cash box from under the counter, set it down beside the register, and opened it with a key. Suddenly, he spun around with a .45 semiautomatic in his hand.[30]

Klevenhagen pulled his pistol and ordered the bar owner to drop his weapon. Instead, Ball turned the .45 on himself and fired a bullet into his own heart. The tavern-keeper's death did not end the matter, though. The deputies searched the building and found an ax covered with blood and matted hair. A frightened employee named Clifton Wheeler took the investigators to the Cardenas Ranch and a shallow grave on the banks of the San Antonio River. Wheeler claimed that Ball had forced him to carry the fetid barrel to the site and dig a hole. Wielding shovels, the lawmen soon unearthed portions of a dismembered woman's corpse. Wheeler told investigators that Ball had used an ax and a butcher's saw for the grisly chore. The female's head and clothing had been burned approximately two hundred yards from the grave.

The unfortunate victim was identified as Hazel "Schatzie" Brown. Wheeler then led authorities to another grave on a remote beach near Ingleside, but a recent windstorm had changed the topography by dumping ten to twenty feet of sand. Spurred by Wheeler's certainty regarding the location, laborers kept digging through the shifting dunes by hand for two days before halting to obtain the proper heavy equipment. In the meantime, Klevenhagen, Hauck, and Gray escorted Mary Dolores "Buddy" Ball, the murderer's widow, from San Diego to San Antonio. Mrs. Ball professed to having important knowledge of Hazel.[31]

Using a gasoline-powered shovel to dig twelve feet down into the beach, then continuing to excavate by hand, the incomplete remains of another female were uncovered on October 13. Klevenhagen, Justice of the Peace Normal Dolton Sanford of Aransas Pass, and Ranger Captain Lee Horace Miller were among those at the scene. Indeed, the deputy, while in the hole gathering up loose bones around the corpse, was buried up to his armpits when the sides caved in. Fortunately, Ginder and Wood pulled him free. Sanford held an inquest on the beach and took a sworn statement from Wheeler. Once the body was removed from the sandy grave and taken to a local undertaker, the second woman's remains were confirmed to be those of Minnie "Big Minnie" Gotthardt. Like Hazel, she had been one of Ball's waitresses and engaged in a sexual relationship with the killer. Wheeler confessed to witnessing Ball shoot Minnie in the back of the head while the trio stood on the beach. The discoveries led investigators to inquire into the whereabouts of five women, four of them, including Julia Turner and a girl known only as Stella, were previously employed by Ball. A widespread rumor claimed the modern-day "Bluebeard" had fed his victims to the alligators kept on his premises.[32]

Fresh from a demanding homicide investigation, the indefatigable Klevenhagen led Emmett Smith and Joe Dominguez in a raid on a palatial rock house near Elmendorf. Based on information received from William Henry Williams, an Oklahoma City private detective, the deputies smashed a multi-state syndicate involved in smuggling weapons into Mexico. The deputy sheriffs recovered seventeen rifles and four pistols stolen from the Oklahoma City Hardware Company. The thieves had taken an estimated ten thousand dollars' worth of firearms and ammunition, and additional guns were believed to be either stored in a San Antonio warehouse or already transferred across the border. Grover and Ray Bates, two brothers, were arrested at the house located on the Corpus Christi road twelve miles south of San Antonio, and a third suspect was sought by authorities. Four men were charged with grand larceny in Oklahoma City. On October 23, Klevenhagen received a wire from the Los Angeles Police Department's chief of detectives that Grover was wanted in Vancouver, British Columbia, on an eighty thousand dollar swindling charge. Klevenhagen filed fugitive from justice complaints against the pair in Justice Gerhardt's court. The two brothers were held without bail in the county jail, and Gerhardt ruled a hearing for Grover would convene after ninety days, pending extradition proceedings. Two lawyers from Oklahoma City, and a local attorney, filed a writ of *habeas corpus* in Criminal District Court, seeking the Bates' release. Assistant District Attorney Gittinger consulted with Assistant U.S. Attorney James McCollum Burnett (son of the judge), and the two decided to dismiss the fugitive complaints, as they should have originated from a federal or state district court according to the extradition treaty between the United States and Great Britain. Instead, Gittinger filed charges of grand larceny and obtaining money under false pretenses against Grover in Seventy-third District Court. Ray was freed on bail, but his brother remained behind bars. Klevenhagen filed fugitive charges against Grover in the same district court on the twenty-seventh.[33]

While Klevenhagen and the rest of the sheriff's department were occupied with a serial killer and an international fugitive, they also dealt with crimes more mundane and closer to home. In early October, the Criminal District Court grand jury commenced investigating the city's assessor-collector's division. The probe had begun with the delivery of papers and photostatic copies belonging to Bonner Richard Mann, former employee of the city tax department. The documentation detailed an association between Mann and Frank Henry Bushick, Jr., son of the tax commissioner, through the Carrizo Orange Company. Accused of using his influence to reduce personal property assessments in exchange for cash payments, the younger Bushick was the subject of thirteen indictments containing forty-one counts of felony theft, accepting a bribe, and conspiracy to commit theft. Mann and four other individuals, all employees of the personal property rendition department in Commissioner Bushick's office, were also indicted on October 18. Although he was granted immunity from prosecution, Mann was named in twelve of the indictments. Armed with search and seizure warrants ordered by the grand jury and signed by Judge McCrory, Assistant District Attorney Leroy Jeffers, Grand Juror Pleasant Jackson McNeel, Jr., and Deputy Elton Cude searched Bushick, Jr.'s residence on October 20 and collected canceled checks, deposit slips, account books, correspondence, and other records. While the officers gathered a trove of documents, the sought-after account ledgers and entry books had disappeared. Bushick, Jr. was also missing, and a statewide broadcast was issued for his apprehension.[34]

The grand jury continued to investigate. The elder Bushick resigned his office, and Mayor Charles Kennon Quin engaged a certified public accounting firm to thoroughly examine the tax rolls. On January 13, 1939, Mann, known as "The Amazing Mr.," forfeited a one-thousand-dollar bond and drove to Dallas. The following day, he received $175 as a bribe to leave the state; he promptly fled by rail from Fort Worth to the West Coast. Mann's disappearance was noted when Bushick, Jr.'s trial opened on the sixteenth, and McCrory revoked his bond and ordered his arrest as a fugitive from justice. The younger Bushick filed a motion for a sanity hearing, but he was judged competent on January 19. The jury trial was rescheduled for February 20. Edwin C. Ueker, District Attorney Shook's chief investigator, traveled to Houston to determine when Mann left that city and to contact any of the latter's friends. The absconder was taken into custody in Los Angeles by the police fugitive squad on January 22. Although Mann professed a willingness to return as a witness, Shook decided to proceed with formal extradition. Klevenhagen entered the investigation when he and Roland Michel "Mike" Rule, an investigator with the DA's office, drove to Austin on the twenty-third to obtain extradition papers, then traveled with Shook to the City of Angels the next day. The officers and their prisoner returned to San Antonio on January 29. The following morning, Shook requested Mann and Alfred Royce "Sonny" Dietzmann, another tax department employee, be indicted for bribery and acceptance of bribery. Both men signed statements detailing the criminal conspiracy and were held in the county jail as material witnesses. The grand jury returned indictments against Mann and Dietzmann, and the former pled guilty in McCrory's courtroom. In a surprising move, Bushick, Jr. pled guilty on February 2 and was sentenced to two years in prison.[35]

On November 2, Doctor David Hart Carson, a Kerrville physician, was found in his car dead from a gunshot wound to the head three miles north of San Antonio. A .32-caliber pistol, an empty hypodermic needle, and a half-filled whiskey bottle lay next to the body. Officers from Kerrville and San Antonio, and the sheriff's department, investigated the suspicious death. Rather than a suicide, the deceased was suspected to be the victim of foul play. Certain his friend and colleague had been kidnapped and murdered, Doctor Louis Harward Webb, superintendent of Veterans Administration Hospital, Legion Branch (present Veterans Affairs Medical Center), requested an investigation by the FBI. Ranger Captain Miller, Rangers Alva Loran Barr and Dick Dixon, and DPS chief chemist and toxicologist Joseph Hoyland Arnette were assigned to participate as well. However, the case grew more complicated when Klevenhagen and Deputy Frank Matthews discovered the body of ex-convict Olen Calvin Ireland in a rooming house on November 3. The lawmen had been searching for the felon, as he was seen with Carson several hours before the latter's death. Doctor Carson was the part-time supervisor of the eye, ear, nose, and throat clinic at the hospital, and Ireland had been one of his patients. Eyewitnesses had placed the pair in the Charles Schreiner Bank, where the obviously harried doctor obtained a loan of one hundred dollars, then handed the cash to Ireland. They were also seen together at a filling station near the hospital. The deputies received a tip that a man matching Ireland's description took a taxicab to his lodgings at 2 a.m., five hours before Carson's body was found. Justice of the Peace Raymond Gerhardt returned a coroner's inquest verdict that Ireland had committed suicide by slashing his wrists, cutting his forehead, and hanging himself with a bedsheet. Although the second victim's room was searched, all but one of the five twenty-dollar bills were missing. The deputies did, however, discover a suicide note that did not mention Carson. Curiously, the fingerprints lifted from the whiskey bottle belonged to neither Carson nor Ireland. At the request of Kerr County Attorney Walter Petsch, Gerhardt delayed his verdict regarding Carson's demise. On December 21, the justice declared he had been unable to determine the official cause of death.[36]

On April 29, Klevenhagen and Deputies Don Dent Wallen, Vernon Curham Schneider, Frank William Matthews, and Joe Dominguez raided a gambling parlor at 709 San Pedro Avenue. Two days later, they struck the same location and found more than thirty men and women engaged in illegal gaming. In the two raids, the lawmen arrested three individuals whose fines ranged between five and twenty-five dollars. Twenty-five hundred bingo cards, one thousand poker chips, and assorted tables and chairs were confiscated. Klevenhagen and Dominguez surprised forty-odd participants and spectators of a dice game on the 500 block of Nebraska Street on May 17. After the crowd had scrambled out of the doors and windows, fifteen dollars was left on the table. The deputies confiscated the cash and arrested the two operators. On the twentieth, Klevenhagen, Schneider, and Bob Ginder raided a poker game being played in the rear of a café on Produce Row. Eight people were arrested. As part of a weekend drive to curtail vice, on August 6, Klevenhagen and Deputies Matthews, Schneider, Samuel Herschel Hale, and Elton Cude raided the Oriental Club on the corner of Commerce and Laredo Streets, the Olmos Dinner Club on San Pedro Avenue, and the International Club on Produce Row. Twenty-eight people in total were arrested, and money, dice, cards, chips, chairs, and a pool table were seized.[37]

On the night of July 3, Edward "Eddie" Daehnert, taxicab driver and musician, was found shot and stabbed to death on Mission Road near the south end of the San Antonio River bridge. A twenty-five-foot-long blood trail led from the bridge to the body. Two eyewitnesses were one block away near Pleasure Island when they heard three gunshots and a woman's scream. As they approached the bridge, they saw a car, possibly a taxicab, drive away. Daehnert's body was sprawled on the path. Klevenhagen worked up the case and discovered the victim had climbed into a car with a woman after leaving work five hours prior to his death. Ascertaining the female's identity as Ruby Mahavier, Klevenhagen visited her local residence. While searching, Klevenhagen discovered evidence Ruby shared a Houston address with her husband Benjamin Franklin "Frank" Mahavier, which led him to contact the Houston authorities and request they detain the couple. While the deputy made his call, the Mahaviers were traveling toward the Magnolia City and, upon their arrival early on July 4, police officers took them into custody. Interrogated by Homicide Captain George Peyton, the husband and wife incriminated themselves. The same day, Klevenhagen and Captain Miller drove to Houston to interview the two suspects. The two sessions revealed that, on the night in question, Ruby and Daehnert had exited Eddie's parked car at the bridge and entered a nearby clump of trees. Having concealed himself in the trunk of the vehicle hours before, Frank interrupted the tryst, shot the victim twice, stabbed him once, and spirited his wife away. The lawmen returned the Mahaviers to San Antonio on the fifth, where Klevenhagen filed charges against Frank in Ottis West's Precinct 6 justice court. Rather than being charged, Ruby was held as a material witness before she was released into her father's custody.[38]

More than a year after the crime, George Keilmann's murder trial got underway on July 24, 1939, in Criminal District Court. Judge Kenneth Koch Woodley of Hondo presided in place of the vacationing Judge McCrory. Two days later, Klevenhagen and his fellow deputies took the stand and described the course of their investigation. During defense testimony, Keilmann's wife and sixteen-year-old son each stated that an argument, which began outside the tavern, led to the shooting inside, and that both men were armed. Taking the stand on his own behalf, the defendant claimed he went into the bar to demand an apology for insults Quintero had hurled at Mrs. Keilmann. He allegedly spotted Quintero, gun in hand, and, thinking his life in danger, pulled his own weapon. The two men fired at the same time. The case was given to the jury, and, after nearly five hours of deliberation, Keilmann was acquitted. Amazingly, during the trial, two witnesses, one each for the prosecution and the defense, had been arrested and charged with perjury on the stand.[39]

San Antonio Mayor Maury Maverick, George P. Glass, former business manager of the International Ladies' Garment Workers' Union, Rebecca Taylor, education secretary of the same organization, and Richard "Dick" Jeffrey, the mayor's secretary, were each indicted on October 16 on five felony and ten misdemeanor counts of unlawfully purchasing poll tax receipts. Maverick, Taylor, and Jeffrey each posted five one-thousand-dollar bonds for the felony charges and ten for the misdemeanors. Apprehended in St. Louis after the indictments were returned, Glass posted a five-thousand-dollar bond and refused to waive extradition, and a hearing was scheduled for October 24. Governor Wilbert Lee "Pappy" O'Daniel signed an extradition requisition to Lloyd Stark, his counterpart in Jefferson City, along with an executive warrant, and Klevenhagen and Assistant District Attorney Melvin Douglas "Buck" Jones flew to Missouri on October 17. However, the Texans learned Glass had secured his release on a writ of *habeas corpus*, and the extradition hearing was postponed until November 7. Klevenhagen and Jones remained in St. Louis for a few days investigating several aspects of the poll tax buying racket; they returned to San Antonio on the twenty-first.[40]

The extradition of George Glass was finally approved after a delay of several weeks. Klevenhagen and Jones drove to St. Louis on November 6 with the intention of collecting Glass and returning him to San Antonio. They had him in their custody for a few minutes after the writ of *habeas corpus* was squashed, but the union official's attorney served a new order on the Texas officers. The next hearing was scheduled for November 16. On November 17, flanked by his lawyer, Glass surrendered to Bexar County authorities who were waiting for him as he stepped down from the St. Louis train at the Missouri Pacific station. Taken into custody by Klevenhagen, Jones, and Mike Rule, he was transported to the courthouse and appeared before Judge McCrory. Bond was set at one thousand dollars for each of the felony indictments against Glass. An additional two hundred dollars each was levied for the misdemeanors. Glass and his attorney held a closed-door conference in the district attorney's vacant office, then met with prosecutors Jones and Gittinger, and Rule. The defendant gave a lengthy statement that took a court reporter five hours to copy.[41]

The trial of Mayor Maverick opened on November 27 in Criminal District Court. Judge McCrory disqualified himself to preside over the proceedings, and Judge Bryce Ferguson served in his colleague's place. The defendant was acquitted of all charges on December 8. Glass was tried in County Court-at-Law No. 2 on March 26, 1940. The state called three witnesses, each of whom testified briefly. The defense rested the same day without putting any witnesses on the stand. Predictably, Glass was found guilty of the misdemeanor charge.[42]

Klevenhagen found himself battling a different kind of foe on May 2, 1940, when he, Deputy Lennis Brice, and county highway patrolman Nathan R. McRae responded to the report of a house fire at 119 Main Drive, adjacent to the Bandera Road. Even though the fully involved structure was three miles outside the city limits, the San Antonio Fire Department ran the call due to the relative proximity of the Woodlawn Hills School. The deputies and the firemen fought the blaze, but the home could not be saved. Fire damage was estimated to be six thousand dollars.[43]

While campaigning for Sheriff Wood's reelection on May 18, the hot-tempered Klevenhagen was drawn into an altercation with Mario Campa, a discharged city employee and son of a political club leader. Campa had declared the offices of the sheriff and Justice Gerhardt "were the headquarters of the Reds." Standing in a courthouse corridor, the political operative allegedly hurled more insulting references to Wood and his deputies, and Klevenhagen slapped the man across the face.

"That wasn't called for, Johnny," protested Campa, ignoring the provocative words he himself had just uttered.

"You are right," Klevenhagen growled, and he stomped into the nearby office of Justice Corrigan. There he swore out a complaint of simple assault against himself and was released on bond. Immediately thereafter, Deputy Frank Matthews signed a complaint against Campa for vagrancy. At the trial on May 23, Klevenhagen pled guilty and paid a fine of five dollars and court costs. Corrigan dismissed the vagrancy charge, but found Campa guilty of abusive language and assessed a similar penalty. Klevenhagen filed his appeal bond to Corrigan and perfected his appeal to the county court-at-law on June 3, while Campa did not complete his own appeal before the expiration of the required time limit. A *capias* was issued for the latter's arrest. This would not be the last time Klevenhagen would pay for losing his temper, but, in the meantime, he and Viola were delighted to welcome their only child, John Joseph, Jr., into the world on May 19.[44]

Another opportunity to advocate for his employer proved more peaceful when Klevenhagen spoke at a rally in Denver Heights Park on July 20. He noted the current staff of twenty-three deputies was the same number as twenty years previously, but praised the sheriff for the vigorous campaign to curtail vice in the county. He also called the audience's attention to the department's fingerprint and identification bureau, which had been established at the personal expense of the sheriff and his deputies. More than three hundred "mugs" had been taken locally, and the bureau had fifteen thousand statewide wanted notices on file. Although he did not inform the crowd, Klevenhagen had been particularly valuable to Emmett Smith, the sheriff's fingerprint expert, in constructing a darkroom.[45] Unfortunately, Klevenhagen's efforts could not assist Wood to electoral victory, and he lost his job once the new sheriff assumed office.

Refrigeration engineer Richard Louis Agnew was beaten to death with a blunt instrument on March 14, 1941, and his battered body was discovered two days later on the Schultz road eight miles north of San Antonio. The victim's blood-spattered luggage and briefcase were retrieved from the Mercedes canal, his Chevrolet was found burned near Brownsville, and the vehicle's spare tire was recovered in Falfurrias. As the clues continued to accumulate, the investigation expanded statewide by the eighteenth. Authorities in Fort Worth, San Antonio, Houston, and Bay City questioned numerous suspects, and Klevenhagen, described in newspaper accounts as a "private investigator," traveled to Edinburg to assist detectives in the Rio Grande Valley. The manhunt centered on Houston on March 21, where Klevenhagen and Bexar County Deputy Aubrey Davenport positively identified James Benjamin Alford of Pioneer, Louisiana, and Jack A. Rupert of Eureka, Kansas, as the culprits. The same day, Chief Deputy Sheriff Charles Peters of Bexar County signed a complaint in Justice Corrigan's court. Evidence was presented to the grand jury, and the impaneled members returned murder indictments. Klevenhagen, Sheriff's Investigators Aubrey Hopkins and Aubrey Davenport, and Highway Patrol Captain William Struwe Bouldin then traveled to Houston to follow up on several leads.[46]

At an undetermined point in time, District Attorney Shook hired Klevenhagen as a special investigator, possibly when the trail led to the West Coast.

Alford and Rupert were arrested in San Andreas. On April 4, they guided Klevenhagen, Davenport and Hopkins, and Assistant District Attorney William Patrick Camp to the original crime scene near the Longhorn Portland Cement Company plant, sixteen miles north of San Antonio. The pair were then transported to the Hidalgo County jail where they gave detailed written statements. Both claimed repeatedly they had not meant to kill Agnew and blamed the violent outcome on alcohol. The pistol used to bludgeon Agnew, a Smith & Wesson .44-caliber revolver, was later recovered from Olmos Creek, thirteen miles north of Three Rivers. Alford's trial convened in Judge McCrory's courtroom on April 28. Under Assistant District Attorney Gittinger's direction, Klevenhagen took the stand as a prosecution witness on the thirtieth, and described the trip to the killing ground, the points Alford and Rupert subsequently visited in the Valley, and the recovery of the murder weapon. Numerous eyewitnesses followed Klevenhagen and identified the pair as having sold them property connected to the victim. Deputy Davenport testified regarding Alford's voluntary statement taken in California.[47]

With the Agnew case closed, Klevenhagen moved to more routine investigative duties in the district attorney's office and worked a variety of cases, including those involving negligent homicide and bookmaking. While some sources contend Klevenhagen was Shook's chief investigator, Edwin Uecker continued to fulfill this role. During the summer, Klevenhagen and John William "Jack" Knight of the State Board of Medical Examiners investigated a criminal ring whose members were avoiding the legitimate adoption route and, instead, selling babies to the highest bidder. Gittinger declared on August 15 that his office possessed evidence seven newborns had been sold by a group of crooked midwives within the previous two months. He estimated one hundred were peddled every year for prices ranging from twenty to forty-five dollars. Furthermore, four or five deaths had occurred in illegal abortions conducted by members of the ring. On August 19, Klevenhagen filed a complaint charging nurse Roberta Jarquin with "unlawfully selling a child under 15 years of age" in Bat Corrigan's justice court. Two days later, Jarquin appeared before Corrigan for a preliminary hearing and her bond was fixed at one thousand dollars. The following day, Louisa Gonzales was similarly charged as an accomplice to the crime.[48]

Klevenhagen was appointed a Texas Ranger on September 1, 1941, in the Houston district commanded by Captain Hardy Burl Purvis. When notified he had secured the coveted position, Klevenhagen later said, "It meant a salary cut for me, but I grabbed my hat, shouted that I was quitting, and lit out for Austin." Along with five additional new officers, his first assignment was to investigate the increasing frequency of cattle rustling. Klevenhagen and others familiarized themselves with a new system of combatting stock thefts that included requiring bills of sale, inspection of livestock in transit on highways, night patrols of roads, and systematic examination of auctions and other sales outlets.[49]

On February 22, 1942, Ray J. Abbaticchio, special-agent-in-charge of the FBI's Houston office, supervised the mass arrest of seventy-five Axis aliens in the city's vital industrial center and the seizure of large quantities of contraband. Between 150 and two hundred federal agents, Texas Rangers (including Klevenhagen), sheriff's deputies, and city policemen were divided into approximately fifty squads and began the roundup at dawn. The law officers executed search warrants issued by U.S. Attorney Douglas Wear McGregor on one hundred residences. They took the Japanese, German, and Italian suspects into custody and confiscated twenty short wave radios, twelve rifles, eighteen other firearms, seventeen sets of binoculars, one telescope, thirty-four cameras, two motion picture cameras, three projectors, approximately 4,100 rounds of ammunition, chemical supplies, machetes, blackjacks and billy clubs, and assorted other items. Five days later, Klevenhagen was one of the thirty squads of Rangers, FBI agents, and city and county lawmen that searched seventy-two premises in Galveston. The officers arrested forty-four enemy aliens and seized firearms, ten pounds of gunpowder, short wave radios, photographic equipment, and other contraband. Eleven suspects were turned over to immigration officials and held on enemy alien warrants pending a hearing before the Enemy Alien Hearing Board. The remainder were released.[50]

During his years of service to the state, Klevenhagen made numerous trips to the wide-open town of Galveston on official business. Local acceptance of bootlegging and rumrunning, gambling, and prostitution had enabled Islanders to escape the ravages of the Depression. After America's entry into World War II, the city's elected leaders and their constituents, not to mention the vice lords, saw no reason to upset the status quo. Along with another Ranger, on the night of May 30, 1942, Klevenhagen raided the Treasure Island nightclub on Market Street and discovered a dice game in progress. The lawmen seized ten pairs of dice, a number of poker chips, and forty to fifty dollars in cash. Klevenhagen filed a complaint against the club's operator on a charge of maintaining a gambling establishment. On June 9, the defendant was fined fifty dollars and costs in James Albert Piperi's justice court.[51]

Klevenhagen was promoted to Senior Texas Ranger on July 1, 1943.[52] Two months later, he and Ranger Edward Lee "Eddie" Oliver raided gambling establishments in Galveston and arrested twenty men and two women. The two lawmen signed complaints in the justice courts of Orra M. Richmond and James Lawrence McKenna. The defendants were fined a total of $587 and costs.[53]

On the night of September 7, 1947, William Ayers, a twenty-two-year-old inmate at the Darrington prison farm, escaped by sawing a tank window bar and scaling a ten-foot-high wire fence. He remained at large while evading the posse that sought him. Klevenhagen and Captain John Easton, the farm manager, led the manhunt throughout the night. By morning, bloodhounds had cornered the fugitive in the Brazos River bottoms. Hiding in a field near a sulfur mine on the Long Point road, Ayers was twice ordered by officers to surrender. "Instead he got up and started running across the pasture away from us. So we fired when he ran," Easton later informed reporters. Ayers was struck on the right side of his back by a high-powered rifle bullet and a twelve-gauge shotgun blast; he died of his wounds within minutes. The following day, Easton and Klevenhagen were publicly identified as the shooters.[54]

The Democratic Party primary for Galveston County in August 1948 was the subject of a probe into voting irregularities. Klevenhagen and Ranger Mart Jones investigated events in Precinct 33 on the twenty-seventh. The two state officers visited the Gateway Club and the Showtime, both on 61st Street, to question the owners why poll tax receipts had been mailed to their establishments instead of their homes. At each nightclub, the Rangers found a dice table and several slot machines. Before the lawmen left each location, the tables were destroyed, and the machines were confiscated.[55]

Klevenhagen was once more in Galveston on assignment on April 4, 1949, when he learned of the murder of Marvin L. Clark, an area grocer and brother-in-law of Harris County Commissioner Hugh May. The victim had closed his C&M Food Town store on Broadway late that night, then walked home carrying a cashbox containing four hundred dollars. Reaching the front steps of his residence on Bayou Shore Drive, Clark was gunned down by a robber who stole the money and Clark's Colt .45 pistol. Headgear later identified as a welder's hood was found at the scene. Assigned to the investigation on the ninth, Klevenhagen and Oliver conferred with Galveston Chief of Detectives William John Burns, and the three spent several hours reviewing the details of the case. The Rangers and detectives questioned 185 suspects before apprehending James Madison Turner III of Texas City on November 24. After being given the statutory warning, the suspect signed a statement in the office of County Attorney Raymond Eugene Magee two days later. Klevenhagen, Oliver, Sheriff Buster Kern, Texas City Police Chief William Lawrence Ladish, and Captain James Davis Walters, Jr. of the Harris County Sheriff's office were in attendance. Additionally, hair samples taken from the suspect matched those recovered from the welder's hood. Brought before Justice James McKenna for an examining hearing, Turner pled guilty to the crime. However, during the trial in Tenth District Court, which opened on August 1, 1950, counsel clashed over the admissibility of the confession. Once the jury was excused, the defense claimed Turner had been subjected to "the most outrageous, inhuman, and cruel treatment" while in police custody. The prosecution countered the accusation by playing for Judge Donald Moore Markle a forty-five-minute wire recording Klevenhagen had taken of Turner's interview with investigators in the Texas City police station on November 25. Having changed his plea to not guilty, the defendant took the stand on August 3 and accused the two Rangers and several police officers of physical abuse during his interrogation. Following two days of arguments, the judge overruled the defense motion, admitted the signed confession as evidence, and reseated the jury. Turner spent nearly two days testifying on his own behalf and repeatedly

C. V. Kern. MSS0415-0359. *Courtesy Houston Metropolitan Research Center, Houston, TX.*

repudiated his written and recorded statements. Contrary to his earlier ruling, Markle did not allow the recording into evidence. On August 10, the prosecution and defense rested, and, after five hours of deliberation, the jury convicted Turner. Sentenced to thirty years' imprisonment, he was transported to Huntsville on September 29.[56]

Even while working the Clark homicide, Klevenhagen remained vigilant for lawbreaking in Galveston County. Between May 2 and June 11, he raided approximately two dozen nightclubs, including the Silver Moon, the Circus Club, and the Top Hat, and confiscated gaming equipment and cash. At least thirty men were arrested on gambling charges, and their fines ranged from twenty-five to one hundred dollars each. On June 13, the Ranger delivered to District Clerk Heiman Hugo Treaccar, Sr. seven heavy bags of coinage. The clerk's staff spent two hours counting the pennies, nickels, dimes, and quarters which totaled over nine hundred dollars. The specie was then deposited in a local bank pending a court order regarding its deposition. The following day, County Attorney Magee filed suit in Tenth District Court for an order authorizing the destruction of the seized dice boards and slot machines. On the eighteenth, Klevenhagen and Oliver raided the Imperial Athletic Association club, arrested two brothers, and smashed gambling paraphernalia. Charges of operating a gaming house, and one count of resisting arrest, were filed in McKenna's justice court. Both defendants were released on bond. Klevenhagen's early summer of raiding ultimately accounted for more than $2,800 in seized monies. District Judge Charles Grainger Dibrell signed four court orders that turned the funds over to Galveston County "for its own use and benefit." The two Rangers also assisted Galveston detectives in apprehending a Houston man who robbed a taxicab driver on June 23 of forty dollars and a wristwatch near the Texas City Wye and Highway 6.[57]

On October 20, 1949, a ten-year-old girl from La Porte was reported to have been assaulted. Thirteen hours after receiving the report, Klevenhagen and Sheriff Kern arrested Allen Conway Williams, a merchant seaman, aboard a yacht berthed at Morgan's Point. The victim positively identified the suspect as her attacker. Williams was charged with criminal assault and tried before District Judge Frank Williford, Jr.[58]

Between September 1, 1948, and August 31, 1950, the fifty-one members of the Ranger service conducted 24,879 felony and misdemeanor investigations throughout the state's 254 counties. They worked 442,000 hours and traveled nearly four million miles, three thousand of which was on horseback. In 3,049 cases, they availed themselves of the crime laboratory in Austin. The state officers made 7,563 arrests in this biennium that resulted in over six thousand convictions. They recovered stolen property with a total worth of 1.5 million dollars and executed four thousand search warrants. Additionally, the Rangers seized and attached property valued in excess of a quarter-million dollars.[59]

While the Rangers performed their duties, and Texas enjoyed the post-war economic boom, the state was attracting the attention of organized criminal syndicates wishing to expand their territories. One victim of the Mafia's attempted takeover in Houston was Vincent J. Vallone, Sr., who was murdered in his Cadillac on July 15, 1949. While en route to his mansion on Chocolate Bayou Road, a dark sedan pulled up alongside his car, and an occupant fired a shotgun blast into the side window, striking the victim in the back of the head. The sixty-five-year-old Vallone, seemingly a legitimate Galveston businessman, was actually a past associate of Salvatore "Big Sam" Maceo, gambling kingpin on the Island. Indeed, in October 1937, the pair, along with seventy-two other men, had been arrested by Federal Bureau of Narcotics agents investigating an international drug conspiracy and subsequently extradited to New York City to face trial in U.S. district court. The indictment against Vallone was dismissed in May 1939, while Maceo was acquitted of the charges in October 1942. The former was sentenced to ninety-nine years for a Harris County murder in October 1939, but pardoned after serving only five. Prior to his death, Vallone owned and operated an Italian restaurant and a horse-racing sports book, and intended to start up a casino in Houston.[60]

Klevenhagen teamed with Harris County sheriff's investigators to work the case. Informants led the Ranger and Kern to thirty-one-year-old Richard Diego "Dick" Carlino, a war veteran and Houston grocer, and Louis J. Marino, owner of a Third Ward icehouse. The two suspects were arrested on October 15. Avoiding the media, the two officers escorted their prisoners to the Texas City jail. They interrogated Carlino and obtained a typewritten confession before returning him to Houston. Mafia elements had demanded an interest in Vallone's proposed casino scheme, but he had declined. His refusal resulted in the Syndicate contracting the murder. On the seventeenth, Kern filed murder charges before Justice Wallace Chauncey "Walter" Ragan, Sr., and the pair were denied bail. Carlino retained the notorious defense attorney Percy Foreman, then claimed his confession had been extracted through third-degree methods. Nevertheless, he was indicted while Mariano was no-billed by the grand jury. The trial in Austin, convened in November 1950, ended in a mistrial. The jury had deliberated for more than seventeen hours.[61]

While the state prepared to retry Carlino, Klevenhagen was involved in investigating the July and August 1950, Democratic primaries in Montgomery County. Voting irregularities had been the cause of more than one probe in that locale, and, in October, Rangers were once more dispatched to Conroe. The county grand jury reported that certified returns for seven races in the Willis box differed from later tabulations of votes cast in the precinct. On the twenty-fourth, another report revealed that four more voting boxes had been checked with anomalies being found in those for Splendora and Conroe's North Side. Ranger Eddie Oliver informed District Judge Ernest Coker that he was under orders to remain until the investigation was complete. Klevenhagen joined Oliver later.[62]

On March 8, 1951, Bexar County roads employee Andrew J. Sendemer was shot to death while interrupting an attempted robbery at the Hilltop Garage on U.S. Highway 181, near San Antonio. The thieves escaped with only six dollars. Klevenhagen developed information that quickly led to the perpetrators' capture. Robert E. Miers, Richard Dean Thorbus, Leroy "Pegleg" Johnson and Lynnda Clark, all from Houston or Corpus Christi, were apprehended by Harris County authorities on the ninth and tenth, and interviewed by Klevenhagen, Kern, and Bexar County deputies. The three men signed statements confessing to the murder and described how they had escaped to Houston by way of Victoria. The four suspects were transported to San Antonio on the eleventh. After their booking, the males were arraigned before Justice of the Peace John Navarro Ogden. Miers and Thorbus waived a preliminary hearing, and Johnson requested an attorney. While being interviewed in the county jail by investigators, Clark, a pretty, red-haired divorcee, related how the quartet had sworn to remain silent after the murder, and each had vowed to kill anyone who talked. With honor among thieves more illusion than reality, Johnson drew a thirty-year prison sentence, Clark received five years due to her cooperation, and Thorbus and Miers, the man who had killed Sendemer, were given life imprisonment.[63]

In Galveston, "controlled" gambling and liquor sales by the drink had been managed by Sam and Rosario "Papa Rose" Maceo since the 1930s. The brothers were Sicilian-born barbers who first became involved in illegal activity in 1921. As they gradually assimilated the two extant bootlegging gangs on the Island, the Maceos ascended in prominence and began buying properties across Galveston. They were ideally suited to running a criminal enterprise, with Sam acting as the charming front man and Rose as the feared mastermind and enforcer. The pair established a restaurant called the Chop Suey Café on an existing pier at Seawall Boulevard and 21st Street in October 1922. The name was changed to Maceo's Grotto four years later, then the brothers reopened the restaurant in November 1933 as the Sui Jen Café. They renovated their eatery to become a swanky private club and changed the name to the Balinese Room in January 1942. Known for high-rolling dice and roulette games and *cordon bleu* cuisine, the notorious Balinese booked many famous acts, including Frank Sinatra, Phil Harris, the Three Stooges, Duke Ellington, and Mel Torme. "The atmosphere was so friendly that you almost enjoyed losing your money there," one Galveston gambler remembered.[64]

Sam and Rose would either own or have an interest in over sixty nightclubs in Galveston County, including the Hollywood Dinner Club in Galveston, the Silver Moon in Dickinson, and the Streamline Dinner Club in Algoa. As "private clubs," these were generally closed to the public and required a membership for entry. The brothers' betting parlors took wagers on horseraces and baseball games occurring across the country. Slot machines owned or leased by the Maceo's Galveston Novelty Company and Dickinson Equipment Company were in three hundred restaurants, barber shops, grocery and drug stores, washaterias, and bars. The Turf Athletic Club at 2214 Market Street served as the syndicate's headquarters. Their extensive investments also included legitimate real estate interests and oil and gas holdings. While the Maceos were the undisputed crime lords of Galveston, they refrained from dabbling in the sex trade. The town's fifty whorehouses and one thousand prostitutes located on Postoffice Street between Twenty-fifth and Twenty-ninth were left alone as long as the brothel owners did not engage in gambling. The brothers also had a similar, although sometimes frostier, relationship with banker and hotelier William Lewis Moody, Jr. in which each organization respected the other's sphere of influence.[65]

Gambling in the "Free State of Galveston" proved to be a challenge every bit as difficult to overcome as in San Antonio, if not more so. Although gaming and liquor by the drink were illegal, the profits derived from the enterprise flowed into every quarter of Galveston life. Insulated from past economic downturns, the general public had been willing to tolerate the Maceos. Popular support for the Maceo empire was derived from the brothers keeping 2,500 people employed, ensuring street crime was rare, generously donating to worthy civic causes, operating honest games, and taking care the average citizen did not lose too much money. Indeed, locals were discouraged from patronizing Maceo casinos unless they were self-employed. Instead, the brothers catered to Houston oil millionaires and other high-rollers from such places as St. Louis, Oklahoma City, Mexico, and Puerto Rico. Almost every local law officer, prosecutor, and judge was on the payroll of either the Maceos or the brothel owners. The periodic raids on the city's nightclubs, demanded by ministers, sporadic crusaders, or Austin politicians at election time, were regarded as a waste of time by Rangers. Over the years, they attempted to crack down on gambling, but such efforts proved short-lived due to inadequate manpower and opposition from the local community.[66]

One such attempt occurred on June 18, 1951, when Attorney General Price Daniel obtained a temporary injunction preventing the Maceo syndicate, Southwestern Bell Telephone Company, and Southwestern Associated Telephone Company from transmitting horse racing information. Ultimately, the injunction proved ineffective as bookmakers violated the court order throughout the state. Representative Fred Vancleve Meridith of Terrell, chairing the Special House Crime Investigating Committee, held public hearings on the twenty-fifth and twenty-sixth into the situation in Galveston. A notable comment transpired when Sheriff Frank Biaggne was asked why he had not raided the Balinese Room, and the law officer replied that he could not enter because he "was not a member." The hearings coincided with a general closing of the Island's gaming establishments, and the Galveston grand jury handed down twenty-three felony gambling indictments for Maceo syndicate members. Speaking to newspaper reporters on July 13, Meridith publicly remarked that gambling, including dice games, bingo parlors, roulette wheels, sports books, and baseball pools, had resumed in Galveston. He also rebuked local officials for possibly being lax in their sworn duties. The same day, Klevenhagen was in Galveston conversing with County Attorney Magee and Detective Chief Burns on an open investigation. The Ranger did not disclose the nature of his visit, but the *Galveston Daily News* noted the city was "wide-open." Attorney General Daniel encouraged the local citizens and authorities to take "prompt action," but Magee later dismissed ten of the indictments and Judge Dibrell, father of Maceo attorney Louis James Dibrell, threw out the remainder. Galveston's freewheeling character continued for a few more years.[67]

After the end of his first trial, Diego Carlino's defense was granted a change of venue, and the case was moved to Fifty-first District Court in San Angelo in February 1952. Beginning on the eighteenth, the flamboyant Foreman defended his client in court by attacking the character of Kern and Klevenhagen. He claimed the two peace officers had beaten Carlino to extract a confession. During his closing argument, Foreman thundered, "They tortured him to make him confess. Who among you can say you, too, would not have confessed to [this] killing, innocent though you may be, if these pistol-packing, blackjack-wearing, handcuff-carrying, booted and spurred officers of the so-called law had predetermined you guilty and decided you were going to confess?" Persuaded by bombastic rhetoric rather than evidence, the jury acquitted Carlino after only one hour of deliberation. Immediately following the verdict, the two publicly humiliated lawmen confronted the attorney in the hallway outside the courtroom. The altercation turned physical, and Foreman, nursing bruises, contusions, and a pair of black eyes, claimed he was struck four times. Witnesses stated the pair hit the lawyer "nine or ten times." Kern admitted to punching him once, while Klevenhagen said nothing.[68]

Less than three hours after the incident, the officers pled guilty to the misdemeanor charge of simple assault. Corporation Court Judge Jimmie Birsh Keen fined them five dollars each, which was quickly paid by a number of men in the courtroom, including additional lawmen. The whole episode proved to be bigger news than the outcome of the Carlino trial. Representative Douglas Crouch of Denton demanded Klevenhagen's suspension for his "high-handed" behavior. The chairman of the state bar association's grievance committee threatened to seek the Ranger's dismissal. Garrison responded on March 2 by stating he had received no complaint and therefore the inquiry would be handled locally. The altercation with Foreman did not seem to have any visible effect on Klevenhagen's career.[69]

On March 10, Klevenhagen and Ranger Everard Caldwell "Eddie" Campbell raided the Top Hat in Alvin and arrested nineteen customers on misdemeanor charges. Arraigned before Justice of the Peace Emil Schenck in Alta Loma, the defendants were released with one-dollar fines and court costs. The two operators of the gaming table were originally taken into custody on felony counts, but the justice reduced the charges to misdemeanors. They were assessed a total of seven hundred dollars in fines and costs of sixty-three dollars.[70]

In the final days of August, Klevenhagen and Oliver made two separate visits to the Reno Club at 2106 Market Street in Galveston. On August 27, the two Rangers broke up a card game in the establishment, smashed gaming tables and liquor bottles, and arrested operators Pasquale De Carlo, Edwin King Abbott, and Vincent Joseph Bernacchi, and nineteen patrons. Oliver signed a misdemeanor complaint in County Attorney Magee's office. The following evening, the pair of lawmen entered the nightclub, inspected the premises, and left without any official action. That same night, the twenty-two individuals earlier apprehended were assessed $776 in total fines in Justice Richmond's court. Klevenhagen followed up his raids by delving once more into voting irregularities in Galveston County. Thomas William "Buckshot" Lane, defeated in the August 23 run-off primary election for the Ninth Congressional District seat, requested an investigation and filed suit in Fifty-sixth District Court charging voter fraud in eight precincts. Upon the application of Attorney General Price Daniel, Judge Dibrell impounded the relevant records of the Galveston County Democratic Executive Committee and 120 voting machines operated by the commissioner's court, and ordered them delivered into the district court's custody. John Marion Criss, Jr., committee secretary, complied on the thirtieth. Klevenhagen was among the state and judicial officials present when the vote totals recorded on the devices were verified to match those reported by election officials.[71]

During the biennium that ended on August 31, 1952, the state's fifty-one Rangers worked 11,567 criminal investigations which resulted in nine hundred felony apprehensions and 1,355 misdemeanor arrests. Their cases resulted in four death sentences and imprisonments totaling 2,764 years. In the course of their duties, they covered two million miles by automobiles, airplanes, or horses in 154,000 regular hours and 57,000 "night duty" hours. During their travels, they wrote 2,111 reports, conducted interviews of 51,993 people, and obtained 3,014 sworn statements.[72]

Jacob Stokes "Buddy" Floyd, Jr., the college student son of a forthright attorney in Jim Wells County, was assassinated in front of his Alice home on September 8, 1952. The elder Floyd was a prominent leader in the Freedom Party that was opposing George Berham Parr's political machine in Jim Wells and Duval Counties. Rangers were assigned to San Diego and Alice on a rotating basis to investigate the homicide and maintain a continuous presence. Additionally, Klevenhagen was assigned to assist Spurgeon Bell of Houston, a special prosecutor appointed by Governor Robert Allan Shivers. The Jim Wells County grand jury was impaneled to investigate Buddy's murder, and the Ranger appeared as a witness. The lawmen established the elder Floyd, a Freedom Party leader, was the intended target, and his son's murder had been a mistake. The hitman was identified as Alfredo Cervantes, but he fled to Mexico and escaped justice. Nago L. Alaniz, law partner of District Attorney Raeburn Norris, and Mario "El Turko" Sapet, a San Antonio tavern keeper and Duval County deputy sheriff, were charged as accomplices. Arrested on December 10, Alaniz was freed under a bond of $21,000. The cases were transferred to District Judge Arthur Orin Newman, Sr.'s court in Brownwood. Sapet was convicted of murder and conspiracy and sentenced to ninety-nine years in prison. The Court of Criminal Appeals upheld the conviction on January 20, 1954. With another change of venue, Alaniz's trial convened in Waco on October 4, 1954. He was defended by Percy Foreman. Klevenhagen arranged for an entry permit to allow the appearance of Gumescindo Montez Gonzales, a Mexican national who had tended bar in San

Antonio the previous year before returning home. Testifying in Spanish, Gonzales linked Alaniz and Sapet to Cervantes, while Foreman dismissed the witness as a liar "with testimony for sale to the highest bidder." The defendant was acquitted because he warned the senior Floyd minutes before the murder, even though the alert came too late to save Buddy.[73]

James Wilson Gamble, a deputy sheriff in De Soto Parish, Louisiana, was shot down on May 16, 1954, along Highway 171, five miles north of Grand Cane. Ex-convict Jasper McDonald Self was identified as a suspect in the deputy's slaying. Self was arrested in a Houston apartment on the twenty-seventh, as he breakfasted with a nineteen-year-old blonde woman. Later that same evening, Klevenhagen, Oliver, and De Soto Parish Sheriff Harmon Thomas Burgess, Sr. whisked the murder suspect out of town, apparently before a writ of *habeas corpus* could be presented. While Self was reportedly taken to Center, Shelby County Sheriff Charlie Brown Christian claimed the accused had not been lodged in his jail. Klevenhagen, who was a guest in a Center hotel, refused to comment on Self's whereabouts. The accused was transferred to the De Soto Parish jail after he signed a waiver of extradition before Shelby County Judge Ozroe Bush.[74]

Ben Coleman was found strangled with a towel in a Galveston hotel at 2811 West Market Street on September 24. The victim's pockets were turned out, and an autopsy ruled he had been dead approximately four days. With local authorities stymied, Klevenhagen and Oliver were called into the investigation by County Attorney Marsene Johnson, Jr. Arriving in town on November 4, the Rangers worked the case with Special Investigator Carlos Wilson Van Dyke, Police Chief William J. Burns, and Chief of Detectives William John Whitburn. Their investigation pointed to eighteen-year-old Lonnie Edward Charles Taylor, who had allegedly been in a sexual relationship with the victim. According to a signed statement taken by Assistant County Attorney Archibald Albert Alexander, Jr. on November 8, the suspect confessed to throttling Coleman with a cotton towel after the latter refused to loan him money. Taylor then took thirteen dollars from the dead man's pockets. The suspect was indicted and pled not guilty at his arraignment. Taylor's murder trial opened on January 17, 1955, in Judge William Elver Stone's Fifty-sixth District Court. The two Rangers were subpoenaed to appear as witnesses. Taylor took the stand and, questioned by his attorneys, claimed Klevenhagen and Oliver had taken him to West Beach and used third-degree methods to elicit a confession. Klevenhagen denied the accusation and testified he and his partner were not present in Alexander's office when Taylor confessed to the crime. After deliberating for one hour, the jury returned a verdict of not guilty.[75]

Another officer-involved shooting occurred on November 27, 1954, when Highway Patrolmen Robert James Crosby and Doyce C. Doolin made a traffic stop for reckless driving on the Beaumont Highway (present McCarty Street) in northeast Houston. The pair were unaware the suspect car's occupants had shot and wounded Harris County Deputy Sheriff Jimmy Scarborough just a short time before. As the two patrolmen exited their state vehicle, Merle Wayne Ellisor, a convicted felon, opened fire, killing Crosby and wounding the other officer. Merle was wounded in the back during the exchange. Archie Lee Ellisor, the gunman's brother who had also been in the car, was arrested in a Liberty tourist court on the twenty-eighth. Still at large, Merle became the objects of one of Harris County's largest manhunts, as over one hundred Rangers, state policemen, local officers, and volunteers searched a wooded area near Brays Bayou. Klevenhagen had noticed a number of petty robberies involving food and clothing from tugboats on the bayou. Additionally, two housewives supplied information that a man matching Ellisor's description was in the vicinity. Thanks to Klevenhagen's hunch and the tips, two detectives captured Ellisor hiding in the brush on December 1. The killer was found guilty of capital murder and executed on April 4, 1957.[76]

Serving ten years for bank robbery, career criminal Frank Lee Morris escaped from the Louisiana State Prison at Angola in April 1955 and took refuge in Brazosport. Working from a local motel, he and two felons committed a string of robberies, including the theft of approximately eight thousand dollars from a Pasadena supermarket's safe. Klevenhagen assisted local authorities in the investigation and shared information from Lake Jackson Police Chief John Simpson "Cap" Brown, who had received a tip concerning Morris's activities. Based on Brown's report, the purloined safe was recovered from Chocolate Bayou, but Morris and his cohorts eluded their pursuers. After robbing a bank in Kansas City, they were apprehended the following year in Baton Rouge. Morris's penchant for daring breakouts did not end there, though. In January 1960, he was transferred to Alcatraz Federal Penitentiary, from which he and John and Clarence Anglin staged an escape attempt on June 11, 1962. The three were never found and considered "missing and presumed drowned."[77]

Roland Thomas Dosier of Aransas Pass was the victim of a robbery turned homicide on May 2. His decomposing body was found in brush near the Aransas County Airport, and his abandoned automobile was discovered twenty miles north of Rockport. The only clues for investigators were provided by an eyewitness who had seen a teenager target practicing with a pistol. The young man had worn a burr haircut, possessed a red bicycle, and admitted to a fear of copperhead snakes. The law officers interviewed and cleared twenty young men matching the description before settling on sixteen-year-old Donald Eugene Moore of Victoria as the prime suspect. The youth was already being held in the Victoria County jail on a charge of armed robbery. Under questioning, Moore voluntarily confessed to Klevenhagen, Aransas County Sheriff Arley Cruse Shivers, and County Attorney Weldon Burk Cabaniss on July 15. In a signed statement, the suspect described shooting Dosier in the back during a "movie inspired" crime spree. The following day, he led Shivers, Klevenhagen, Oliver, and Victoria County Deputy Sheriff Harold Eugene "Joe" Welton to a spot along Highway 35, five miles north of Rockport, where he had tossed the murder weapon. Recovering the Remington .380 semiautomatic pistol, Shivers filed a complaint charging murder with malice. Victoria County Judge Frank Crain ordered a psychiatric examination for the defendant on July 20. Declared sane, Moore was convicted in a juvenile court trial on the armed robbery charge and sent to Gatesville Reformatory School. He was indicted by the Aransas County grand jury, but his murder trial would have to wait for his seventeenth birthday, However, in the months ahead, the path to securing justice for Roland Dozier would not be smooth.[78]

The bodies of Rubye Lou McPherson, her son George Richard, and her mother Zola Dean Norman were discovered in their Dickinson home on June 25, 1955. The victims had all been shot to death with a .25-caliber pistol at close range two or three days prior. Additionally,

Mrs. McPherson's engagement and wedding rings were missing, as was her red and cream-colored 1953 Ford sedan. The triple murder sparked a nationwide manhunt and a posted reward of $1,100. The investigation quickly settled on an unidentified serviceman as the prime suspect. On the twenty-seventh, Dallas Homicide Captain John Will Fritz alerted the Rangers he was holding an airman absent without leave from Barksdale Air Force Base in Shreveport who matched the description. Klevenhagen and Oliver traveled to Dallas the following day, but the suspected individual was not the culprit. Instead, Ellis Euclid Lauhon, Jr., AWOL from Robbins Air Force Base in Houston County, Georgia, was arrested in Nogales, Mexico, while attempting to sell Mrs. McPherson's stolen automobile. Klevenhagen, Oliver, and Constable Earl Turner of League City traveled to Nogales, Arizona, and extradited Lauhon to Galveston on July 2. The defendant's legal team mounted an insanity defense. The sanity hearing convened on May 14, 1956, and Klevenhagen, Oliver, Turner, and a female eyewitness testified on the twenty-first. On the stand, the two Rangers described how Lauhon had willingly admitted to the triple homicide during the six-and-a-half-hour flight from Arizona. He also professed to shooting and robbing a service station attendant in El Paso while fleeing toward the Pacific coast. He repeated the confession in the office of Assistant County Attorney Alexander. In the combined twelve hours Klevenhagen spent with the suspect, Lauhon's speech, conduct, and appearance led the Ranger to believe he was sane and "knew the difference between right and wrong." However, three psychiatrists from the University of Texas Medical Branch testified that the accused suffered from paranoid schizophrenia. The jury verdict found Lauhon to be insane, and the defendant was removed to Rusk State Hospital on June 11.[79]

Jan David Broderick, a Texas A&M University student, was found dead on a farm road near Hempstead on December 30, 1955. Ronald Edward Menter was identified as the prime suspect, but he had absconded to New Jersey. Menter was arrested by the Newark authorities on January 2, 1956, while driving Broderick's car, and Klevenhagen flew east to collect the fugitive. The Ranger and his prisoner returned to Texas on January 5, 1956, where Menter, handcuffed to Klevenhagen, spoke to reporters at

Houston International Airport: "I killed him because we had an argument. Now I'm sorry I did it." Accompanied by Waller County Sheriff Albert Sterling Fletcher, Klevenhagen and his prisoner drove to Hempstead.[80]

Ted Thomas, an armed prison escapee from Tennessee, took hostage two young women in the Liberty County oil field on April 1, 1956. After being held for several hours, the unfortunate captives managed to elude their kidnapper and reach safety. Already searching for the convict since March 30, Klevenhagen and Sheriff Wesley Patrick "Red" Rose were leading a posse of more than one hundred lawmen from Liberty, Harris, and Chambers Counties. Their search had begun in the Lake Houston area near Crosby, and Thomas killed five pursuing bloodhounds during the chase. The women took Rose to Thomas's camp, but the surviving dogs lost the trail by two o'clock in the morning. After some coffee in town, the officers concentrated their manhunt in the Trinity River bottoms. Finally, Thomas was confronted on a creek bank on May 30 and shot by Montgomery County Constable W. F. Reeves while trying to flee. He died of his injuries at John Sealy Hospital in Galveston the same day.[81]

On July 6, Klevenhagen was chosen to supervise another manhunt, this time for Alton G. Halson, a mentally ill man who had shot and wounded Constable Milton Lewis in Somerville. Although the posse numbered at times 150 men, Halson remained hidden on a large hill in the Brazos River bottom known as Green's Mountain. On July 9, the thirty-five-year-old fugitive was cornered by prison bloodhounds in a dense thicket, and he began firing on the officers accompanying the dogs. Arriving on scene, Klevenhagen spurred his horse toward the man's hiding place in the brush with his cocked .45 in one hand, his reins in the other, and a sawed-off, double-barreled shotgun in his saddle scabbard.[82]

"This is Texas Ranger Johnny Klevenhagen," he shouted, curbing his mount. "Come out with your hands up and you won't be harmed!" The fugitive responded by appearing from concealment with his arms raised high, but his hands were holding two pistols. The deranged man wordlessly leveled his weapons and opened fire at the Ranger. The first slug whined past Klevenhagen's ear as he was forced to control his panicking horse. The two men continued to exchange fire at a range of fifteen feet, but the bullets all missed due to the pitching mount. Finally able to dismount, the lawman pulled his shotgun and blasted Halson in the face and chest with 000 buckshot. Klevenhagen's report was characteristically brief: "Searched on horseback and foot. After 275 hours, located subject in Yegua Creek bottom. Subject resisted and fired on Ranger. Subject was killed."[83]

Even as these fugitive cases were being resolved, Captain Purvis submitted his resignation on May 10, 1956, in order to begin a new career. On January 1, 1957, Klevenhagen replaced Purvis as captain of Company A. In departing, Purvis reflected on his career: "The Rangers are a splendid organization. I am proud to have served with them."[84]

On March 5, an unknown assailant threw the contents of a bottle of muriatic acid at Doctor Roy Elston McMeans, Jr., a chiropractor in Conroe, when the latter opened the door to his clinic. McMeans received burns to his face and one eyeball. Garrison personally assigned Klevenhagen to the case. Investigators followed two lines of inquiry: the assault was either the work of a deranged individual, or the attacker had meant to intimidate witnesses in the bribery case of State Representative James Edward Cox, Sr. of Conroe. McMeans had already testified before a House committee that Cox agreed to accept a bribe of five thousand dollars. The legislator had been indicted, but he denied the charge. Klevenhagen, Conroe Police Chief Edwin Adolph "Eddie" Stephan, and Ranger Hollis Milton Sillavan rushed to Austin on March 8. Reporters theorized the trip was made to take evidence to the DPS crime lab. However, the next day, Klevenhagen confessed to reporters that investigators had no specific suspect, but they were looking at eight to ten individuals. However, the case would remain unsolved.[85]

As the new captain settled into his duties, a case from the recent past returned to the forefront. The murder case against Donald Moore convened on April 15 in Judge William Glenn Gayle, Sr.'s Thirty-sixth District Court in Rockport. However, due to the defendant's alleged obsession with "movies of the bad kind," his counsel claimed he was not mentally competent to stand trial. Rather than decide on Moore's innocence or guilt, the proceedings turned into a sanity hearing. Called to the stand by District Attorney John Hobbs Miller, Klevenhagen, Sheriff Shivers, three other law enforcement officers, and County Attorney Cabaniss testified as to Moore's mental stability.

The witnesses cited his clear recollection of the murder and ability to provide precise details, and all denied there were any physical signs of impairment. The case went to the jury on the sixteenth, and, following over three hours of deliberation, the members decided Moore was competent. After being found sane, the defendant immediately waived jury trial and entered a plea of guilty. He was sentenced to ten years' imprisonment.[86]

Fresh from seeing one murderer put behind bars, Klevenhagen turned to the apprehension of a vastly more dangerous killer. Gene Paul Norris was a career desperado from Lawton, Oklahoma. Appearing on the FBI's Ten Most Wanted list, the "bandit with a quick smile and ready trigger" had a criminal history dating back to the 1930s, with at least six convictions including bank robbery and burglary. Gene Paul, who preferred his middle name, was also a suspect in more than forty contract murders, including Fort Worth gamblers LeRoy Randolph "Tincy" Eggleston and Charles Frank Cates, Fort Worth narcotics pusher Edward Eugene Townley, Dallas dope peddler Oland Ray Towers, and Oklahoma City bootlegger Orville Lindsay Chambless. The thirty-five-year-old triggerman seemed to enjoy the taking of life and exhibited a sadistic nature at the slightest excuse. Taking into account sensationalist journalism, Norris still rates as an equal to John Wesley Hardin as Texas's most notorious killer and surpassed the bloody record of Bonnie and Clyde.[87]

In March 1957, Norris began planning a quarter-million-dollar heist at the Fort Worth National Bank branch on Carswell Air Force Base. Before he put his caper into operation, though, he held up a number of Houston and Galveston gambling dens for operating capital. Klevenhagen suspected Norris and his partner, thirty-one-year-old William Carl "Silent Bill" Humphrey, of the April 17 beating deaths of gambler John "Johnnie" Brannan and his semi-invalid wife, Lillie, in Houston. The murdered man had been the star witness in the 1937 homicide trial of Thomas Nathan "Pete" Norris, Paul's older brother. Two guns were found several days later in a vacant lot. One had belonged to a gambler who admitted Norris had robbed him of the weapon and some cash, while the other had belonged to Brannan. Klevenhagen also discovered that Humphrey had been arrested in Temple for being drunk and disorderly a few days after the murder. Among the items on his person was a gold and diamond horseshoe ring known to have been Brannan's lucky charm. The ring had been wrenched from the dead man's finger following the slaying. Klevenhagen swore out John Doe arrest warrants for Norris and Humphrey and set out after the duo.[88]

As investigators learned later, Norris intended to pull the Carswell job on Tuesday, April 30, the day a $255,000 military payroll became available; this robbery promised to be the pinnacle of Norris's bloody career. He secured a diagram of the bank's floor plan from James Edward Papworth who had been imprisoned with the branch's former manager, a man doing time for embezzlement. Papworth also produced the name and address of bank cashier Elizabeth Barles. Along with Humphrey, Norris intended to kidnap the woman and her twelve-year-old son John from their Lake Worth home. He also proposed to use the base entry sticker on Barles' windshield to get past the Air Police at the gate, and her keys to gain entry to the bank. The two robbers next meant to ambush the armored car couriers when they arrived with the payroll. After the couriers were tied-up and the money stolen, Norris and Humphrey would return to Mrs. Barles's house and retrieve their getaway car. Before they took their leave, mother and son were to be murdered so as to leave no witnesses.[89]

An experienced thief and hitman, Norris had the resourcefulness, boldness, and firepower to carry off the robbery. What he did not plan for was an FBI informant (likely Papworth) who shared details of the ruthless plot with law officers. Captain E. J. "Jay" Banks, in whose Company B jurisdiction the robbery would take place, invited Klevenhagen to participate. Through the use of FBI wiretaps, the law officers knew the two robbers would be scrutinizing Mrs. Barles's house on Meandering Road and the bank before the commencement of the job.[90]

On Monday morning, April 29, Klevenhagen and Banks staked out the bank employee's home in Banks's high-powered Dodge, along with Tarrant County Sheriff Harlon Wright, Fort Worth Police Chief Cato Hightower, and city detective Captain Otha Roy Brown. Mrs. Barles and her son had been moved to a safe location the previous day. Ranger Sergeant Arthur Watts Hill, Ranger Jim Ray, and city Chief of Detectives Andre Fournier were in a second vehicle at "Casino Beach," an amusement park on Meandering Road near the Jacksboro Highway. A third car held Ranger Ernest Daniel, city detective (and future Ranger) George Brakefield, and Deputy Sheriff Robert "Bobby" Morton two miles south on the highway near the air base.[91]

Alerted by the FBI agents who followed the two hoodlums from Fort Worth to Meandering Road, the waiting lawmen observed the pair drive past the Barles residence in a rehearsal for the following day. Humphrey was behind the wheel of a souped-up 1957 Chevrolet when he and Norris spotted the surveillance. They crashed through a roadblock and roared down the Jacksboro Highway with the Rangers in hot pursuit at speeds reaching 120 miles per hour. Norris, in the passenger seat, shot at the trailing officers in Banks's Dodge, and Klevenhagen, Wright, and Hightower returned fire. The breakneck speeds never slackened even as the chase roared down the main street of Azle, leaving scattered vehicles and pedestrians in its wake. Three miles east of Springtown in Parker County, Humphrey turned right onto a muddy country road, the pursuit thus far having covered twenty-one miles. Klevenhagen and the two other officers continued to shoot into the robbers' vehicle. Three miles down the dirt road, Humphrey took a curve at too high a speed, and the getaway car careened out of control and crashed into a pair of trees at the edge of Walnut Creek.[92]

The hoodlums exited the Chevrolet and ran, shooting as they went. Moments later, Banks' Dodge shuddered to a stop crossway on the road. The five lawmen rolled from the vehicle and entered the fray. Smeared in mud and blood, Humphrey went down in a hail of twenty-three bullets as he tried to cross the rain-swollen creek. Norris kept fleeing while firing his .38 pistol at the officers. At the same time, the vehicle with Hill and Ray arrived on the scene. Ray, who was driving, stomped on his brakes, swung the car in a complete circle, and skidded to a halt three feet from Banks's automobile. Ray leaped out and Klevenhagen shouted, "I'm out of ammunition! He's getting away! Give me a gun." The Ranger threw Klevenhagen his shotgun, but Norris, fifty yards from the cars, was already falling under a sustained burst from Jay's M-2 carbine. The later autopsy detailed sixteen bullet wounds in Norris's corpse stretching from ankles to head.[93]

While shoot-outs with desperate criminals did occasionally occur, sometimes confrontations were more comical in nature. Limestone County Sheriff Jack Hamilton Bothwell received information on March 30 that two men were planning on breaking into the county tax assessor-collector's office at the courthouse. The burglars' intended goal was the money derived from the sale of vehicle license plates. Bothwell contacted the Rangers for assistance, and Klevenhagen and Captain Clint T. Peoples brought a combined seven men to Groesbeck. Three state officers and the sheriff were inside the tax office on the thirty-first when the thieves broke open a window with a hatchet. Crawling into the room, the felonious pair were surprised to find a collection of determined-looking lawmen. Bothwell later described the arrest: "We told them to throw up their hands and they broke and ran. Everybody started shooting. The men made it to their car 100 yards away but we stopped them before they got another 100 yards." Charges of burglary were filed in the court of Justice of the Peace James Jefferson Barfield.[94]

The issue of gambling in Galveston once more involved Klevenhagen. Sam and Rose Maceo had died in April 1951 and March 1954 respectively, but their nephews Anthony J. and Victor J. Fertitta assumed the syndicate's leadership. For a time, the new kingpins enjoyed the same degree of support from the courts as their uncles, which continued to hamper the eradication of gaming. Indeed, Ranger raids on the Balinese had turned into theater for the club's patrons. As the lawmen raced down the six-hundred-foot pier and burst into the establishment's dining room, the house band began playing "The Eyes of Texas," and the guests merrily serenaded the raiders. By the time the officers reached the casino secreted in a backroom, the operators had been warned by an electric signal from the front desk, and the gaming paraphernalia was concealed within thirty seconds. However, changing conditions on the Island caused cracks to appear in the Maceo empire's heretofore sturdy foundation. Neither of the Fertittas were as well-regarded as their uncles, high-rollers chose to visit Nevada where gambling had been legalized, and reform-minded World War II veterans did not support the perpetuation of Galveston as an open city. Additionally, the vastly lucrative Balinese Room was destroyed in a $200,000 fire on October 3, 1954, and the brothers lacked the liquid capital to quickly rebuild. Another blow

Balinese Room. RGD0006N-1957-1250-1-7. *Courtesy Houston Metropolitan Research Center, Houston, TX.*

occurred the following year when an article and accompanying photographs appeared in *Life* magazine that exposed nationally the failure of authorities to enforce gambling and prostitution laws in the county. Attempting to cope with diminishing profits and escalating bad press, the Fertittas made the fateful decisions to lay off 660 casino employees and cease bribing city and county officials.[95]

Early in 1957, Colonel Garrison received a call from Texas Attorney General William Reid Wilson, who had been recently sworn into office. When district attorney in Dallas, the politically ambitious Wilson had waged a vigorous campaign against illegal gambling, and he wanted Ranger assistance to do the same in Galveston. Wilson employed Assistant Attorney General Cecil Rotsch and Texas City lawyer James P. Simpson, a former combat pilot and FBI agent, to serve as his field commanders. To secure sufficient probable cause for search warrants, he also appointed trusted mainlanders Carroll Spiller Yaws and James D. "Buddy" Givens to work undercover at the refurbished Balinese Room, the Pirate Club, the Imperial Club, the Western Room, the Metropole Club, and other nightspots. To finance the operation, Wilson went to a Dallas philanthropist who had secretly bankrolled his earlier crackdown and received fifty thousand dollars.[96]

The work of Yaws and Givens yielded promising results, and the attorney general's assistants were able to obtain warrants. Cooperating together with stringent security, Garrison, Wilson, and Simpson organized raids on sixty-five of the Fertitta's venues. On the night of June 6, a convoy of Rangers, state troopers, and staffers from the attorney general's office drove down the Gulf Freeway from Houston to Galveston forty-five minutes away. When they reached their first destination, the Balinese, they found the club closed down and its parking lot empty. Although the raid had been painstakingly planned, someone had tipped off the gambling kingpins. Wilson openly speculated a bribed Ranger had been the informant, but Klevenhagen refused to accept the attorney general's slander. Bounding from his chair, the short-tempered captain thundered, "Don't you dare accuse my men of leaking information. You better clean up your own back yard before you start accusing my Rangers of anything!" Klevenhagen then pointed out how the leak likely originated among the attorney general's large secretarial pool.[97]

On June 10, Wilson countered the raid's failure by filing twenty-four cases in the Tenth District Court and twenty-three in the Fifty-sixth District based on the evidence already attained. By the fourteenth, his office secured from Judge Markle one-year injunctions on forty-seven gambling dens, brothels, and taverns as areas of "habitual public nuisance." Over the next several months, Markle and Judge William E. Stone also issued fourteen temporary restraining orders inhibiting nightclub owners from permitting gambling at their establishments. At least one operator was cited for contempt of court in violating the terms of the orders, jailed for three days, and ordered to pay a one hundred dollar fine. Twenty-one club operators formally requested jury trials and had their cases placed on the two court dockets. The lawmen still needed additional evidence and, using visitation letters, were able to access bank, telephone, and power and water records. Rangers executed search warrants based on information derived from the public. Regardless of the risks to his re-election, Sheriff Paul Hopkins offered the full resources of his department to the effort. However, in a surprising move, District Attorney Louis Flatts Benson challenged Wilson to provide evidence to his office and the grand jury regarding gambling operators. In his report, the attorney general noted a similar lack of cooperation from the city police department. Popular opinion regarding the vice trades had become evenly divided by this time, and the Galveston Ministerial Alliance praised the state and county law officers for their efforts.[98]

On June 15, the Wilson-Garrison operation delivered two crucial blows to the Maceo criminal empire. First, Klevenhagen began to assign two Rangers to Galveston on a continuous basis. The state officers paid "friendly" visits nightly to the establishments named in the various injunctions to pressure them into abandoning any illicit activities. Next, using intelligence from an informant willing to risk his life, Rotsch directed a raid on old Fort Travis, the abandoned coastal artillery installation on the Port Bolivar peninsula. The state attorney, Klevenhagen, Ranger Edgar Dalton "Ed" Gooding, and DPS intelligence officer George Reed discovered a huge cache of gaming equipment in three warehouses and a concrete gun bunker. Judging by the amount of dust covering the machines, the 375 slot machines were not among those removed from gambling houses the previous week. Klevenhagen summoned a pair of fishermen to help in breaking up the equipment with sledgehammers. The total value of the gambling paraphernalia was estimated at $375,000 (or, adjusting for inflation, approximately $3,380,000 in current dollars). The crusade to rid Galveston of illegal gambling garnered much media attention, but the campaign also shut down the city's notorious red-light district on Postoffice Street. In the course of one raid, Rangers had approximately forty prostitutes lined up on the infamous thoroughfare. At this point, the Fertittas' grip on the Galveston underworld began to fail fairly quickly.[99]

Klevenhagen, Oliver, Rotsch, eight men from the attorney general's office, Galveston Police Commissioner Walter Benjamin Rourke, Sr., and Police Chief Oscar Eugene Henson raided seven slot machine distributors on June 17. In all, they found fifty-two gambling devices worth approximately seventy thousand dollars and destroyed twenty-six of them. The next day, the captain, "working almost around the clock," supervised the seizure of more than fifty gambling devices, a box of poker chips, and 210 cases of tip books from three separate warehouses. The death blow to the Maceos occurred on June 19 when two assistant attorneys general, Gooding, and Ranger James Frank "Pete" Rogers discovered some fifteen hundred machines, roulette wheels, blackjack tables, and boxes of chips and dice at the old Hollywood Supper Club.[100]

On June 20, Klevenhagen and Wilson were at the city dump's incinerator to supervise the burning of several truckloads of gaming devices taken two days before. The value of the destroyed slot machines and roulette wheels was estimated at one million dollars. As he was going off duty, the fire marshal stopped the immolation at midnight. Also, numerous cast-iron devices could not be consumed by the funeral pyre. In the early hours of June 21, Rangers and members of Wilson's staff watched as three loads of confiscated gambling equipment were piled aboard the *Josephine* and the *Shorty Brunt* at Pier 18. The seized paraphernalia was unceremoniously pushed into the Gulf near the sunken concrete boat off Pelican Island. However, they may have violated federal law in disposing of the machines in navigable waterways instead of an industrial waste dumping ground. Apparently, the state had also failed to secure a permit from the U.S. Corps of Engineers.[101]

Klevenhagen, Rangers Gooding and Tully Elwyn Seay, Commissioner Rourke, and Chief Henson made a surprise sweep through Galveston's nightspots on August 17. They found no illegal gambling equipment, only a number of tip books, and made no arrests. In all, the Garrison-Wilson campaign had destroyed gaming paraphernalia worth an estimated $1,800,000. By September 26, the grand jury had handed down 175 indictments, with 117 of them concerning violations of state gaming laws. Anthony Fertitta was eventually found guilty of one count of keeping a gambling house and given a two-year suspended sentence. His brother was apparently acquitted of any charges. Even after Klevenhagen's death, the practice of visits to the nightclubs continued. Since the eight men of Company A had other duties in addition to the Galveston problem, Colonel Garrison regularly sent a Ranger from another company to assist them. In the end, every man on the force, except for Charles E. Miller and Louis Hardy Purvis, spent time on the Island. The routine lasted until 1960, when the gambling industry in Galveston was effectively ended.[102]

In the mid-1950s, Rangers worked an average of seventy-four hours and thirty minutes a week, with no overtime pay. Their workaholic natures were exacerbated by too many cigarettes, too much coffee, and too few healthy meals. Not one of them left the service unless they retired or died.[103]

A fitting example of this steadfastness, Klevenhagen suffered his first heart attack on December 20, 1957, while driving home from the funeral of his close friend, Houston oilman James Marion "Silver Dollar Jim" West. He was transported to Methodist Hospital in Houston and reported as being in critical condition. The captain eventually recovered and prepared to return to work. On November 15, 1958, he attended a Rice Institute–Texas A&M football game in Houston and collapsed in front of a concession stand. Klevenhagen died at 4:30 a.m. on November 26 at Methodist Hospital. His cause of death was listed as a myocardial infarction due to coronary artery disease. Funeral services were held at the Pat H. Foley Chapel at Alamo Funeral Home in San Antonio on November 27. The Reverend Ray Mayfield of Conroe Baptist Church officiated. Following the ceremony, Klevenhagen was escorted by a large motorcade to Mission Park Cemetery for burial. Colonel Garrison called him "one of the finest peace officers I have ever known."[104]

On February 4, 1959, the Fifty-sixth Legislature adopted Senate Resolution No. 46 in honor of Captain Klevenhagen, declaring he "represented the highest standards of integrity, intelligence and bravery in fulfilling the arduous duties and requirements for a period of seventeen years as a Texas Ranger." When the Senate adjourned for the day, the members did so in his memory.[105]

Following her husband's death, Viola was employed as a clerk in the civil division of Sheriff Kern's office. She married police officer Travis Lee Dickey on September 22, 1961, in Richmond, Texas. Travis died on May 30, 1993. She died on March 25, 2007. Viola's funeral services were at Forest Park Lawndale Main Chapel, and she was buried in Mission Burial Park in San Antonio.[106]

John Jr. received a bachelor's degree in police administration from the University of Houston and a master's degree from Sam Houston State University. Following in his father's footsteps, he entered the Harris County Sheriff's Department in 1961, with the sponsorship of Sheriff Kern. He married Carolyn Lawless and fathered a son and a daughter. John rose through the ranks from patrol deputy to warrant server, juvenile division investigator, patrol lieutenant, and juvenile captain. He resigned from Kern's staff in 1972 to support former Houston police chief Jack Heard in the election for sheriff. Heard won and placed Klevenhagen in charge of the patrol bureau. John went on to head the detective, law enforcement, and detention bureaus before resigning in 1981 after 20 years with the department. By 1984, Klevenhagen was co-owner of a small oil distribution company when he narrowly won election for the office of sheriff. Known as "a character" and a hard-working, honest, and professional peace officer, he oversaw the sheriff's department through a tumultuous period and dealt with issues of jail overcrowding, funding, and manpower. John was re-elected in 1988 and 1992. On June 19, 1995, Klevenhagen resigned to become co-owner of a car dealership. He died of a brain tumor on May 13, 1999, in Houston. He was buried in the city's Forest Park Cemetery.[107]

John Klevenhagen pursued his work with the Texas Rangers with an obsessive drive. Blending the best of the service's traditions with modern techniques, he amassed an unsurpassed record of courage and dedication. Indeed, he devoted himself completely to his duty, even at the cost of his own life.

Captain Peoples, July 1, 1954. #1983/112_R-398-1. *Courtesy Texas State Library and Archives Commission, Austin, TX.*

Chapter 9

Clinton T. Peoples: "A Contradictory Figure"

Clinton Thomas Peoples wore nine badges throughout his nearly sixty years in law enforcement, including those of senior Ranger captain and U.S. marshal. Over his long career, he accrued an outstanding record of achievement as a law officer, yet he was often a contradictory figure among his Ranger peers. He was charming and gracious, but his soaring ego alienated many. Devoted to promoting a steadfast public image of the Texas Rangers, he was a leader in bringing the Texas Ranger Hall of Fame and Museum into existence. However, similar to Hickman and Gonzaullas, he sought the limelight and made himself the central character in the story. As author and retired federal agent Bob Alexander commented, "Within Texas Ranger ranks, Clint Peoples's personal reputation ebbed and flowed and, more often than not, ebbed."

He was born in Bridgeport, Wise County, Texas, on August 25, 1910. William Thomas Peoples, his father, had been born in Cameron, Milam County, on May 21, 1874. He had married Emma Flora Brooks on December 22, 1895, in Milam County, and the children from his first union were Menta Myrtle Peoples, born November 22, 1898, and Raymond Bartlett Peoples, born August 8, 1899. After what appears to have been a divorce, William, or

"Tom" as he was known, then married Susie Mae (Johnson) Baugh on December 10, 1905. Susie had been born on December 17, 1884, in Rhome, Wise County. In addition to his half-brother and half-sister, Clint's siblings were Herman Allen Peoples, born on May 31, 1912, and Mae Louise Peoples, born on September 17, 1913. After working as a farmer and a café owner in Childress and Bridgeport, Tom became a foreman on the King Ranch in 1914.[1]

When the violence of the Mexican Revolution threatened his family, Tom resigned his ranch job in October 1917 and took them to the small East Texas town of Willis. There the Peopleses took over an abandoned farm two miles east of town and scratched a living from the red, gravelly soil. Tom was an enterprising man and, in addition to the family's truck farm and diary, he went into partnership with his father-in-law to purchase the shoe and harness ship in Conroe in August 1919. He also worked as an auctioneer. Similarly busy, Clint attended Spring Hill elementary school in Willis from 1917 to 1924, along with his chores and other assorted responsibilities as the eldest son. At age eight, Peoples became ill during the Spanish influenza epidemic of 1917 and 1918. In September 1922, his legs were burned in an accidental fire, and he remained confined to a bed for six weeks.[2]

Tom ran for the office of constable in Willis in 1926. During the campaign, he promised to win the race or leave the township. True to his word, after his defeat, he relocated his wife and children to land along U.S. Highway 75, six miles to the south of Conroe. Needless to say, he avoided further participation in politics. On his new thirty acres, Tom built a house and eventually a tourist court, grocery store, café, filling station, garage, and sawmill. Clint attended Conroe High School from 1924 to 1928, and played on the baseball team. He had thought of attending Texas A&M University, but a fire that destroyed the family's residence and business forced him to change his plan. By 1930, he was working as an automotive mechanic.[3]

That same year, Peoples became a deputy for the Montgomery County Sheriff's Department. Decades later, he informed a newspaperman the family's closest friend was Sheriff Hugh Benjamin "Ben" Hicks. "We wanted to grow up and be like him," he quietly recalled. "He was our hero. We idolized him." Now working for his ideal lawman, the novice deputy purchased his own duty sidearm and handcuffs in a Houston pawnshop for twenty-five dollars. His first day on the job, Peoples asked his new boss how he should perform his duties. "Enforce the law!" the laconic sheriff replied. He then offered several pieces of advice on the proper use of his legal powers: "Son, you can take this pistol that you have the authority to wear and you can make a great man of yourself, or you make the biggest fool out of yourself that ever was. Don't ever get to where you feel this pistol on your hip." For two years, Peoples learned his chosen trade in the sleepy town of Conroe. He and Constable Calvitt Bertrand "Punch" Wagers raided a craps game on April 23, 1932, and arrested several players. One notable incident occurred on May 9 when Peoples and his friend Floyd Stewart went to arrest truck driver Rodney Park and two other men for disturbing the peace. The trio had recently left Tom's tourist camp and were approximately two miles distant when confronted by Peoples and Stewart. The deputy took one of the suspects to jail and left his companion in charge of the other two. A scuffle ensued between Stewart and Park over a pistol, and the latter was killed by a bullet. Sheriff Hicks announced no charges were being filed against Stewart pending the grand jury investigation.[4]

People's relatively quiet apprenticeship came to an end on June 5, 1932, when George William Strake's No. 2 oil well blew in, and Conroe became the center of the nation's third largest oil field. The county quickly became inundated with wildcatters and roughnecks, bootleggers and hijackers, and saloons and dancehalls. The streets of Conroe were filled with tough men hungry for entertainment, even if that meant challenging the authority of the county's lawmen. On his nightly rounds, Deputy Peoples often found himself in as many as three or four fights. For the sake of his personal reputation, and that of the sheriff's department, he knew he could never let an adversary get the best of him.[5]

Although he had been in office since 1921, Sheriff Hicks was defeated in the 1932 Democratic primaries by Guy Hedick Hooper, who would triumph in the general election on November 8. Peoples stayed in the sheriff's department until February 1933, then became chief deputy for Constable George Washington Templeton of Precinct No. 7. Templeton had held his office for nearly thirty years and needed the assistance of a younger man. Much of the criminal activity in the county occurred in Peoples's new jurisdiction. Additionally, the deputy received an appointment of Special Ranger on January 24, 1933, so he could conduct investigations for oil companies and the Texas Racing Commission. He was discharged from state service on October 17.[6]

After a courtship of two years, Peoples married Donna Lee Henderson on October 20, 1934, in Conroe. She had been born in Ratcliff on September 2, 1912. The couple was overjoyed when their daughter, Donna Jean Peoples, was born at Memorial Hospital on November 21, 1935.[7]

In August 1937, Loyd Daniel "Nig" Ranels and Woodrow "Red" Wilson robbed the butcher shop of William Alexander Bucher. Ironically, Bucher's brother, John, had run a similar establishment in Hillsboro, where he was the first to fall victim to Clyde Barrow's murderous ways. Ranels and Wilson stole ten dollars and a pistol and left Bucher beaten and bleeding on the floor. Constables Peoples and Wagers responded to the call and interviewed the victim. The two officers began searching for the suspects and found them attempting to steal a car near the cemetery. Although he was covered by Peoples's shotgun and Wagers's pistol, Ranels edged a hand toward the pistol in his waistband before he decided a jail cell was preferable to certain death; Wilson had already wisely surrendered.[8]

The pair remained in custody for three months before their case came to trial. Ranels was convicted on October 22 of robbery and, as a repeat offender, sentenced to life imprisonment. Not possessing his partner's lengthy criminal record, Wilson received a five-year sentence.[9]

Grover Cleveland Mostyn had been elected sheriff on November 3, 1936. He was a genial man not particularly interested in the daily law enforcement aspects of the job, and needed an experienced, hard-charging chief deputy to ramrod the department. Having known Peoples for years, Mostyn offered him the position in October 1937. While the sheriff's department dealt with many of the undesirables who could be found in any oil strike, the majority of their calls were to handle drunks, family disputes, and saloon brawls.[10]

On July 12, 1939, Hubert Hulan, a trusty under a fifteen-year sentence for robbery, escaped from the New Unity State Prison Farm at Sugarland, stole a car, and drove to Spring. He robbed a filling station operator at knifepoint of two dollars, a bottle of whisky, and a business suit. The call went out, and Peoples spotted the fugitive racing down the highway and gave pursuit. The two vehicles' speeds reached eighty miles per hour before the convict was forced to stop between Conroe and Willis by the wreckage of an automobile accident strewn across the road. Peoples took Hulan into custody and lodged him in the Harris County jail. The convict received an additional five years for his four-hour dash at liberty.[11]

As the oil boom was fading, Peoples grew disenchanted with the routine of policing a small community, and he sold his home to move to Austin. Desiring to advance in his chosen profession, he was appointed to the Highway Patrol on November 1, 1941, and attended the Eighth Recruit Training School as part of First Platoon. Peoples's platoon commander was Sergeant John Harper Hollyfield, while his platoon monitor was Sergeant Morgan Calloway Myers. After graduating on December 24, he was assigned to Kingsville. Unfortunately, he was forced to resign on May 18, 1942, due to unavailable housing for his family during the wartime period.[12]

Doubtless disappointed, he returned to the Montgomery County Sheriff's department and his former position as chief deputy for Sheriff Mostyn. He supervised eighteen deputies and a jailer, and managed the federal prisoners in the jail.[13]

On July 25, Mostyn was defeated in the Democratic primary, and the new sheriff, Herschel Raymond Surratt, upon taking office on January 1, 1943, brought in his own picked staff. Both Mostyn and Peoples were unemployed by the shakeup, but the former sheriff took a job with Superior Oil Company in Conroe as the chief of security. Peoples accepted a position as his assistant. The following year, he was drafted to run for the office of sheriff in the upcoming election, but could not overcome the money and influence wielded by Stuart's brother-in-law, Guy Hooper. Taking his defeat in stride, Peoples worked at Sun Oil Company as a maintenance worker. His new job earned him an extra fifty dollars a month, but he still dreamed of returning to law enforcement.[14]

Peoples's wish came true when he was reinstated to the Highway Patrol on January 8, 1945, and stationed in Austin. Working around the state capitol, Peoples was assigned to a variety of tasks ranging from leading parades to patrolling the highways throughout town to keeping order at legislative sessions. One of the Patrol detachment's most important duties was to provide security for Governor Coke Stevenson.[15]

Working auto accidents involving injuries and fatalities were a common occurrence for the Texas highway patrolmen, and Peoples saw his fair share of mangled metal and flesh. Twenty-one-year-old Harold Ackerman, a University of Texas student, was killed on April 5, when he fell asleep at the wheel and overturned his vehicle at the bridge over Berry Creek, five miles north of Georgetown. On June 15, Benito and Maxima Vanquez, and their six-year-old son, Benito, Jr., were walking alongside the highway near Elgin when they were struck by an out-of-control truck. Maxima and young Benito were killed while the elder Vanquez was injured. Peoples and his partner, Doyle Oliver Curington, investigated the accident, and the truck's driver, Lee Roy Johnson, was charged with negligent homicide. Peoples and Curington handled a collision on the Dallas Highway on July 15, one-and-a-half miles outside the Austin city limits. Two cars and a truck were involved, and one man was sent to Brackenridge Hospital with a fractured arm. Rupert Seidel, twenty-four years old, died instantly on November 7 when the motorcycle he was riding slammed head-on into a truck on Highway 79, five miles east of Round Rock.[16]

Peoples's hard work was rewarded with one of Texas law enforcement's most coveted positions. On December 1, 1946, he was promoted to the Texas Rangers and assigned to the Headquarters Company at Camp Mabry under Captain Fred Olson.[17]

On April 16, 1947, the freighter SS *Grandcamp*, hauling fertilizer-grade ammonium nitrate under a French flag, exploded while docked at the Port of Texas City in Galveston County. The conflagration completely obliterated the ship and everything else within a two-thousand-foot radius, including possibly four hundred crewmen, stevedores, and curious onlookers. Refineries, chemical plants, and oil storage tanks caught in the blast zone were ignited by red-hot falling debris. The detonation was so substantial that a seismograph recorded the event in Denver, Colorado, a thousand miles distant. Shrouded in an enormous cloud of black, acrid smoke, the area resembled the aftermath of a bomb strike. The DPS dispatched state troopers, Rangers, and a mobile radio facility to the scene to handle the hundreds of dead and wounded victims.[18]

Peoples raced to Texas City several hours later to support the town's seventeen police officers in search and rescue efforts. Once there, his promising career was nearly cut short when the freighter *High Flyer*, carrying a load of fertilizer, blew up on April 17. Peoples and other responders had been searching through the debris of a nearby school when a large piece of steel shrapnel nearly struck the Ranger before burying itself twelve feet into the ground.[19]

Despite his narrow escape, Peoples assisted the department's forensic technicians in identifying the terribly mutilated and burned bodies of victims. The DPS had established a morgue at Camp Wallace, a nearby wartime army post, and the state officers were able to ascertain approximately 86 percent of the deceased. The remaining unfortunates were nearly cremated remains. According to the DPS and the Red Cross, the final death toll of the worst industrial disaster in American history was 405 identified and sixty-three unidentified people, with another 113 victims believed to be missing. An estimated 3,500 were injured, although that figure is problematic, and 852 were hospitalized. The following year, property losses were estimated at fifty million dollars.[20]

In the late fall of 1947, Austin was experiencing a rash of burglaries. City Detectives Fred Lee Estepp and Thomas Stallworth "Pete" Weaver worked up the six-week investigation in conjunction with Peoples. Their prime suspect was Charles Scott Dickerson, and he was arrested on December 1 in connection with four instances of burglary and "knob knocking." Physical evidence processed by the DPS laboratory conclusively linked the suspect to the crimes. Shortly thereafter, the Brown County grand jury indicted Dickerson, and Sheriff Owen Shaw requested the Austin authorities transport the suspect to Brownwood for questioning in three similar cases. Bond was set at $2,500. Peoples and Estepp returned Dickerson to Austin on December 9. Peoples, Estepp, Weaver, and their prisoner then traveled into the hills west of town on the eleventh to recover a cache of stolen pharmaceuticals. Police Chief Raymond D. Thorp announced to the press that the cases in Austin and Brownwood, and another in Houston, had been cleared with Dickerson's apprehension. The alleged burglar was charged in Justice of the Peace Frank

Wilkins McBee, Sr.'s court and released from custody on a three-thousand-dollar bond.[21]

Two additional men and two women were arrested in connection with Dickerson's crimes. Complaints against the three males were filed for the upcoming term of the Fifty-third District grand jury. A fourth suspect in the Brown County cases was arrested in Kilgore, and Peoples took him to the Travis County jail on January 9, 1948. Two days later, the Ranger transported the prisoner to Brownwood where he was charged with three counts of burglary. Dickerson and his two accomplices were indicted on January 15 for the four Austin burglaries. The trial for Dickerson, set for the January term, was continued, and his attorney negotiated a plea bargain in Brown County. The defendant pled guilty in exchange for a two-year sentence and entered Huntsville on February 29.[22]

In his early years as a Texas Ranger, Peoples was involved in several undercover assignments. On January 18, 1951, he was dispatched to Carrizo Springs to assist Captain Alfred Young Allee in curtailing vice in Duval County. Posing as an oil field worker, Peoples visited the Flamingo Club in San Diego and encountered the town's mayor and the "Duke of Duval" himself, George Berham Parr. The establishment possessed one table each for dice and blackjack. The next day, the Ranger gained entry into El Ranchito, a sizeable tavern on the outskirts of town that boasted two dice tables and another for poker. Behind the club was a row of ten cottages housing prostitutes who charged six dollars for every transaction. Having found the evidence needed, Peoples conferred with Allee, and a raid was organized for January 21. At 12:30 a.m., the captain, Peoples, Maro Woodley Williamson, Levi Duncan, Joe H. Bridge, Tully Elwyn Seay, Bennie Charles Krueger, and Charles E. Miller descended on the Flamingo Club and El Ranchito and arrested a total of twenty-two individuals, including six prostitutes. The lawmen also seized nineteen hundred dollars' worth of gambling paraphernalia. The two clubs' owners pled guilty in justice court, and both were fined $114.50. The housemen were penalized between fifty dollars and $64.50 each and the gamblers and women $15.50 each.[23]

In a twist on normal events, District Attorney George O'Neal Dendy of the 119th Judicial District in Tom Green County requested he be charged with murder on January 18, 1951. The matter had begun two days prior when Dendy had an altercation with his tenant Ray Elmo Canada over an eviction notice that ended in the latter's death. Surrendering to the authorities, Dendy waived an examining trial and posted a five-thousand-dollar bond. The district attorney submitted his letter of resignation on January 25, which became effective on February 1. District Attorney Ralph Logan of the Fifty-first District and Sheriff Buck Bryson called for the DPS to conduct an independent investigation. Colonel Garrison dispatched Peoples to San Angelo. While the Fifty-first District grand jury acceded to Dendy's wish for an indictment on February 1, the Ranger surveyed the scene of Canada's demise and oversaw the collection of forensic evidence. Defense witnesses' account of the incident conflicted with that of the prosecution's eyewitness: Canada's widow. Thus, the trial, which convened on February 26, revolved around People's testimony. Two days later, the jury found the defendant not guilty.[24]

On September 18, police officers in Austin received a tip that narcotics were being transported to Williamson County. Rangers, Williamson County deputies, and Taylor police officers responded, and roadblocks were erected on the applicable avenues. Peoples and Doyle Curington, having also been appointed a Ranger, spotted a suspicious pickup truck on U.S. Highway 81, and pursued the vehicle for four miles before the occupants were stopped south of Round Rock. Searching the truck, the officers discovered a suitcase containing nearly five hundred military-style morphine syrettes, two large bottles of codeine, a measure of paregoric, four 6-ounce bottles of silver alloy, and fifty punchboards. The driver of the vehicle was a man who had twice been incarcerated in Louisiana, and he was charged in justice court in Georgetown with possession and transportation of narcotics. A complaint was also filed for possession of the punchboards in violation of the state's anti-gambling law. The passenger in the truck, a young woman claiming to be a hitchhiker, was similarly arrested. Three other suspects already in police custody were believed to be accomplices of the truck driver.[25]

The October 22 murder of John Douglas Kinser, owner of the Putt & Pitch Golf Course in Austin, was to be the first link in a lengthy chain of strange events. The victim was killed inside the clubhouse by a man armed with a pistol, and eyewitnesses were able to write down the killer's Virginia license plate number. Detectives Pete Weaver and Marion Meredith Lee worked the case, and the license number was traced to Malcolm Everett "Mac" Wallace, an economist with the Department of Agriculture in Washington, DC. One hour after the killing, the suspect was arrested nine miles from Austin on Highway 29 by three DPS License and Weight inspectors. Years later, Detective Lee revealed Wallace had claimed during the subsequent interview he worked for Senator Lyndon Baines Johnson. Suspecting Sheriff Ernest Best of obstructing the investigation, District Attorney Robert John "Bob" Long called in Peoples to assist the city police. The following day, Wallace was ordered to be released from custody on a writ of *habeas corpus* issued by Ninety-eighth District Court Judge Charles Olin Betts. Ninety seconds after the judge's directive, Wallace was rearrested in the courtroom and charged with murder. The warrant was signed by Justice of the Peace Travis Blakeslee. Wallace appeared before Blakeslee on October 25 for an examining trial and pled not guilty. He was bound over for the grand jury, and released on a ten-thousand-dollar bond. Throughout the legal process, the suspect remained tight-lipped and refused to discuss the case. The grand jury heard eleven witnesses on October 30. Through testimony, the grand jurors learned Kinser had been killed with a .25 semiautomatic pistol, and three spent shell casings of the same caliber were found next to the body. While Wallace was being processed at DPS headquarters on the twenty-second, a .25 bullet had been discovered on his person. The state crime laboratory administered a paraffin test that detected nitrate particles on his hands indicating he had recently fired a gun. Blood smears on Wallace's clothes matched those recovered from the crime scene. The grand jury returned a true bill against Wallace on November 1 for murder with malice aforethought.[26]

The trial opened in Judge Bett's courtroom on February 18, 1952, with jury selection. Peoples testified for the prosecution. On February 28, the jury pronounced Wallace guilty, but, surprisingly, gave the defendant a suspended sentence of five years. Judge Betts was bound by law to accept the decision. Wallace was released on his own recognizance under a one-thousand-dollar bond. Estranged from his wife, Mary Andre, Wallace was carrying on a sexual affair with Josefa Johnson, sister of then-Senator Johnson. Additionally, both women were romantically linked to Kinser. However, a motive for the crime was never officially established. The paths of Peoples and Wallace would cross again.[27]

Sam Smithwick, a former Jim Wells County deputy sheriff imprisoned for the murder of radio broadcaster William Lovejoy Heywood "Bill" Mason, was found dead in his Huntsville cell on April 15. The prisoner had a towel knotted around his neck and the other end tied to the upper bunk. With Smithwick slumped forward, the scene suggested he had killed himself. Indeed, Justice of the Peace Mabel Sandel Franklow returned a verdict of suicide, although she did not personally view the body, and no autopsy was performed. In addition, the deceased was once part of George Parr's inner circle and claimed secret knowledge of the infamous Box 13 episode involving Coke Stevenson and Lyndon Johnson. Thus, the possibility of foul play was considered significant. As newspapers ran with this particular narrative, Garrison sent Peoples and Captain Allee to investigate. One of the men named in a letter Smithwick had written to Stevenson before his death was voluntarily taken to Austin for a lie detector test. Writing the report to the colonel, Peoples noted Smithwick's crumbling mental state and concluded the ex-lawmen had taken his own life.[28]

From September 1, 1950, to August 31, 1952, the fifty-one Rangers spent 211,000 hours completing 11,567 criminal investigations. While traveling two million miles by automobile, airplane, and horse, they effected arrests in 909 felony and 1,355 misdemeanor cases. The stolen property recovered was valued at $700,000. For his part in generating those numbers, Peoples was promoted upon Garrison's recommendation to acting captain of Headquarters Company on March 4, 1953. The appointment was confirmed by the members of the Public Safety Commission on July 1.[29]

By the fall of 1953, a six-person crew of professional safecrackers and robbers had been operating in North Texas for the past four years. Thanks to an informant, Eugene Debs Bellah, his wife, Jettie Onita Ray Bellah, Melvin Thomas Renfro, William Earl Ervin, and his son, Gerald Turner Ervin, were arrested on October 3. Over a three-week period, Captain Peoples and Rangers Doyle Curington, James Carson "Jim" Paulk, Clarence Robert Nordyke,

Homer Garrison and Six Captains. (L to R) Bob Crowder, Jay Banks, Gully Cowsert, Johnny Klevenhagen, Raymond Waters, Alfred Allee, Sr., Homer Garrison, Clint Peoples. *Courtesy Texas Ranger Hall of Fame and Museum, Waco, TX.*

and Robert Lee "Bob" Badgett joined with Brown County Sheriff Ray Masters, U.S. Post Office Inspectors George Heaburg and Guy Williams, and numerous FBI agents in unraveling 198 robberies in Texas, and one each in Oklahoma and Louisiana, and tying them to the suspects. Investigators could not be certain this amount comprised the total number, but they did compile a tentative "master list" of thirteen banks and twenty-three post offices the gang was suspected of targeting. While under interrogation, one of the six confessed to participating in more than 150 heists. The sixth member of the gang, Albert Rowe Bright, was apprehended in Fort Worth on the twenty-second, and he spent twenty-four hours admitting in written statements to eighty-three burglaries. On October 24, the sextant pled guilty in Thirty-fifth District Court to charges of burglary and theft in

Brown County and received a total of forty-seven years in prison. Once Judge Arthur Orin Newman, Sr. pronounced their sentences, the suspects were arraigned in Abilene before U.S. Commissioner Gladys Walls on multiple federal charges the same day.[30]

The Austin National Bank branch on Bergstrom Air Force Base was robbed on June 5, 1954, by a lone bandit. The thief, clad in dark glasses and military fatigues, brandished a .32 semiautomatic pistol and forced three bank employees into the vault. Stuffing $32,000 in cash into a large paper sack, the suspect made his getaway on foot. Escaping from the vault, the people working in the bank notified the Air Police, and an exhaustive search was made of the base. The FBI and the Texas Rangers, including Peoples, were brought into the investigation. The authorities were unable to obtain any useful clues, and a reward of fifteen hundred dollars was offered for evidence leading to the arrest and conviction of the perpetrator.[31]

Peoples would have no direct role, but the Parr regime in Duval County, long a bane of numerous Rangers, was destined for a reckoning. In the July 1954 primary, Rangers kept a close eye on the polling places, and Sheriff Archer "Archie" Parr and District Attorney Raeburn Norris lost their races. At the same time, two hundred Parr cronies were indicted on various charges, and state and federal cases against George Parr himself were placed on the docket of the respective district courts.[32]

With the assistance of the Rangers, including some from Headquarters Company, federal agents and prosecutors built strong cases against Parr for mail fraud, embezzlement, misappropriation of public funds, and income tax evasion. For the remainder of the decade, Dual County's *patrón grande* lost nearly every civil and criminal case in the trial courts, but the criminal convictions were always reversed on appeal. Finally, the Duke was convicted in the Southern District of income tax evasion on March 19, 1974, and assessed five years' imprisonment and $14,000 in fines. Once the federal cases were resolved, the state attorney general's office took over, and the seventy-year-old Parr empire came crashing down. After an unsuccessful appeal, George, rather than be sent to prison, committed suicide on April 1, 1975.[33]

Those momentous events lay in the future, though. Peoples was one of the panelists to speak at a Special FBI Law Enforcement Conference at the Kerr County courthouse on October 15, 1954. Sponsored by Kerrville Police Chief Walter Moss and Sheriff Oliver Moore, the gathering discussed the economic losses derived from "hot" checks and the various check passing rings at work in the state. One of approximately one hundred such events, those attending the conference in Kerrville discussed the methods needed to combat the issue, including coordination between law enforcement agencies and the business community.[34]

Peoples and Glen McLaughlin, chief of the Bureau of Intelligence, were driving to Oklahoma on the morning of May 15, 1955, for a law enforcement conference in Norman. The pair were north of Waco when they heard over the police radio that Limestone County Sheriff Harry James Dunlap had been killed near Thornton. The suspect in his shooting was a mentally unbalanced man who was barricaded inside his farmhouse. Responding to the broadcast, Peoples drove at a high rate of speed to Thornton, making the one hundred-mile trip in an hour. Reaching the scene around noon, he and McLaughlin found approximately forty officers and a hundred bystanders.[35]

Ranger James L. Rogers informed Peoples that the suspect was N. J. Tynes, a farmer who had been treated for psychosis but still suffered from sporadic violent episodes. In the grips of his illness the previous night, he had shot and wounded his neighbor, John Ray Bentley, while the man was on his tractor. Sheriff Dunlap and Deputies Ernest Hillard Pippin and Jack Hamilton Bothwell had responded and attempted to apprehend Tynes, but they were fired upon and forced to retreat. The morning of the sheriff's murder, Ranger Rogers and five state troopers joined the county officers. The lawmen again tried to arrest Tynes, but the madman shot Dunlap in the head. Rogers then contacted Ranger Trenton Horton in Belton and asked him to request an armored car from Fort Hood.[36]

Peoples took command of the scene and decided the first priority was to retrieve Sheriff Dunlap's body. With the other lawmen laying down cover fire, the captain, and Highway Patrolmen Charles A. Nichols and Leon Roberts, sprinted forward, took hold of the sheriff, and dragged him behind a shed. Tynes occasionally moved into the crosshairs of a highway patrolman's scoped rifle, but Peoples had ordered the deranged man was to be taken alive if possible. In the meantime, Captain Robert A. Crowder sped to the scene from Dallas. The requested armored half-track arrived about 1:30 p.m. Peoples and Falls County Sheriff (and former Ranger) Albert Brady Pamplin climbed in, and the army sergeant driving the vehicle approached the house. While Crowder and Rogers took up positions behind sheds in the front yard, the armored vehicle circled the house while Peoples fired approximately fifteen tear gas canisters through the windows. Some thirty minutes later, the captain instructed the army driver to pull up to the back porch. Once the sergeant did so, Peoples accidentally ignited a canister, and the half-track filled with tear gas. He and Pamplin stood up in order to breathe, and Tynes triggered his rifle. The bullet snatched People's hat from his head. The two officers leaped to the ground and returned fire as they ran to the house. At the same time, Crowder and Rogers raced to the front door. Pausing on the rear porch, Peoples shot another canister through the screen door. The projectile struck Tynes' left forearm and nearly severed his hand. Crowder and Rogers charged into the kitchen and discovered Tynes on the floor. The madman arose and smashed his head into Rogers' stomach, and the Ranger shot Tynes in the right shoulder. Even seriously wounded, he resisted the four officers until they were able to subdue and drag him into the backyard. Tynes would later die in Groesbeck's Cox Hospital from his injuries, but Bentley survived. Peoples and McLaughlin cleaned themselves and drove through the night to attend the conference.[37]

The Tynes incident sent a message that changing times necessitated new approaches. Signaling the Ranger service's continuing ability to adapt, the DPS purchased five M-8 light armored cars that were made available to all state law enforcement officers. Meant to be used for riot duty and to counter barricaded suspects, they were equipped with short-wave radios, sirens, riot guns, tear gas, and long-range rifles. The bulletproof vehicles were distributed to the Ranger company headquarters throughout the state.[38]

Mills County Sheriff Conner F. "Stub" Stubblefield was shot and critically wounded on October 10, 1957, while transporting two prisoners to Huntsville. Peoples responded to the scene and took charge of the manhunt. Probing the rough hill country west of Buffalo, a mounted posse of fifty to one hundred lawmen using bloodhounds captured one of the escapees later the same day. Roadblocks were established, and mobile parties of officers patrolled the roads during the night. While two DPS airplanes circled over the area, the search continued on the eleventh, but the fugitive remained at large.[39]

The September 1, 1957, restructuring of the DPS had proven to be universally unpopular among the Rangers. In addition to now reporting to uniformed regional commanders rather than Colonel Garrison, several captains were obliged to move their company headquarters from long-standing locations to new cities. This state of affairs included Peoples, who transformed his Headquarters Company into a freshly named Company F in Waco. The entire episode reached its apex when Region Six commander Major Walter J. Elliott informed Peoples he intended to use Rangers for highway patrol during Operation Motorcide, an augmented traffic enforcement and public relations campaign envisioned to decrease road fatalities during a busy Christmas season. Peoples later recalled his reply to Elliott's directions, "Chief, I like you very much, but as long as there is breath in my body I'll not assign a Ranger to a patrol car to work traffic."[40]

Peoples worked behind the scenes to return the Rangers to their old autonomy in the department's table of organization. The Commission reversed the decision to place the Rangers under the continuing regional structure, and Garrison transmitted a message on January 1, 1958, that directed the captains to resume reporting directly to him. On January 3, Garrison summoned all Ranger captains to Austin to discuss the new arrangement. Once the meeting concluded, Garrison remarked to Peoples, "Clint, I have to agree with you. This was one bad mistake."[41]

Ex-convicts Franklin Clovis Perkins of Houston and Allen Runo of Oklahoma City were arrested on February 12, 1958, by New Orleans police officers while driving a car stolen from photoengraver Joseph Tonglet. Although charged with aggravated kidnapping, armed robbery, and auto theft, the pair was extradited to Houston, where Peoples and Police Lieutenant Woody Stephenson questioned them. The two suspects detailed a crime spree that began on January 11 with the theft of eight shotguns from a Houston dry goods store and continued fourteen days later with a two-thousand-dollar robbery from a local supermarket. They next drove to San Antonio and kidnapped and robbed insurance agent Chris McClellan before he was left bound in a wooded area. Driving McClellan's automobile, they robbed the H & W Truck Stop in Waco of thirty dollars on February 3 and abducted and killed Ray Spencer, the station attendant. A later ballistics test linked Perkins to the murder, and he claimed he acted alone. The two drove to Fort Worth where they abandoned McClellan's vehicle and split up, agreeing to meet in New Orleans. The encounter with robbery victim Tonglet, who had been left tied to a tree in the Crescent City, led to the end of their two-man crime wave. Perkins and Runo gave written statements in Liberty on the tenth, admitting to Spencer's murder. The following day, Peoples, McClellan County Sheriff Clyde Curtis Maxey, and Chief of Police Jesse Virgil Gunterman brought the two desperadoes to Waco to confront a special session of the Fifty-fourth District grand jury scheduled for February 13. Appearing before Justice of the Peace Roy Ormino for an examining trial, Perkins and Runo pled guilty to robbery and murder without malice. They were held without bond, and both were indicted for Spencer's death. On March 10, Runo pled guilty to the charge in District Judge Drummond Webster Bartlett's court and received a sentence of ninety-nine years. Perkins followed suit on April 8, but claimed the killing had been accidental. The prosecution responded by calling its entire slate of physical evidence and witnesses, including Peoples, to refute the assertion. The defense offered no testimony. Later in the same day, after over two hours of deliberation, the jury assessed the death penalty.[42]

Perkins and convicted murderer William Howard King escaped from the McLennan County jail on the night of May 2. Perkins had vowed while Sheriff Maxey was transporting him from New Orleans that "rather than ride Old Sparky, I'll make some officer kill me." Two days after the jailbreak, the pair were discovered at a small frame house on Mann Street, which was quickly surrounded by a dozen law officers, including Peoples. While his accomplice hid in tall weeds nearby, Perkins was cornered under the residence and refused to peaceably surrender. Peoples and Deputy James William "Buddy" Kuykendall shined a light under the house, and Perkins fired a shot from a .38 revolver in response. At least eight officers unleashed a barrage of lead, killing the fugitive instantly. King was taken into custody without further incident. Peoples later related he had fired three blasts from a shotgun and Kuykendall had emptied his sidearm. On the matter of Perkins's demise, the captain said, "I don't know whether my shots killed him or a pistol bullet did. Probably, I killed him. If so, I don't cherish the thought. But I don't mind it either."[43]

Two armed individuals, a blond man and his brunette female companion, robbed the Citizens State Bank of Calvert on September 10, and escaped with over twenty thousand dollars in cash in a Buick driven by a second woman. Officers described the heist as "one of the smoothest and biggest bank robberies in Central Texas in several years." The case was broken when authorities traced a telephone call William Chrismon made on September 4 to Alta Boolukos's Houston motel room. Chrismon became a primary suspect on the eleventh and the subject of a federal arrest warrant. The female suspect's license plate number was recovered from her motel registration and traced to an address in Atlanta. FBI agents arrested Boolukos and Charlotte Harrison in Atlanta, and Chrismon in Denver. Each of the suspects had been in possession of currency taken from the bank. Arraigned by U.S. commissioners in Georgia and Colorado, Chrismon and Harrison were charged in Waco with committing the hold-up, while Boolukos was charged with conspiracy.[44]

Peoples led Ranger John Henry "Johnny" Krumnow and a party of state and county officers in a raid on a gambling house near Mexia on February 17, 1960. Eleven men were arrested inside the residence, and a sizable quantity of equipment and alcohol was seized. Charges were filed in Justice of Peace Dot Jones's court, and four of the defendants were fined $119 for operating a gaming den. Seven were assessed fines of twenty dollars for gambling.[45]

In Henderson County, the Brownsboro school board fired Superintendent Homer Bass and fourteen black teachers, which contributed to the tension surrounding a feud that had simmered for a decade. The board meeting erupted into violence on June 16, 1960, which left lumber company owner Thurman Jackson dead and six wounded. Peoples, two Rangers, and three Highway Patrolmen arrived in town the next day, and they patrolled the streets. Doctor Charles Collins Rahm, Jr., osteopath and school board secretary, was charged with Jackson's murder. District Attorney Jack Yarborough Hardee charged two other individuals with assault with intent to murder and seven with assault and battery. Rahm was granted a change of venue to Orange where he was acquitted.[46]

The First State Bank of Thornton was robbed on November 5, 1960, of $1,744. Before leaving, the thief took compromising pictures of the bank's female employees with a box camera. A silver Mexican five-peso and a bank coin wrapper were found in the robber's abandoned car north of Bryan. While pursuing leads, Peoples and other Rangers working the case discovered the robber had habitually asked for the daily record of receipts, which implied an insider's knowledge. They exhibited a composite sketch throughout the region, and one individual in West identified the suspect as Lawrence Chalmous "Larry" Pope, a bank president and former newspaper publisher from Giddings. The FBI filed a criminal complaint in San Antonio for the Thornton robbery. Similarly, the Fayette County Sheriff's Department charged the suspect with the robbery of $15,880 from the Farmers State Bank at Schulenburg on November 12. On November 17, federal agents tracked Pope to the Alamo City, where he had gone on business, and raided his motel room on the northeast edge of town. Three hundred dollars of stolen money was recovered. The banker confirmed he did possess a peso as a good luck charm, but the coin had recently become lost. Shown the peso found near Bryan, Pope said, "I guess my luck has run out."[47]

Some years later, Peoples told the story of encountering Pope at his San Antonio hotel. Once he was shown the peso, the suspect had given the coin to the Ranger captain, saying, "Maybe it will bring you more luck than it did me." One of Peoples's friends took the peso to Fort Worth and visited Haltom Jewelers, who fashioned the coin into a Texas Ranger badge based on a design dating from 1835. A second badge was given to Colonel Garrison, and the Public Safety Commission approved the adoption of the design as the official symbol of the Texas Rangers' authority. Unfortunately, this tale is apocryphal as the first authenticated badge dates from 1889.[48]

Colonel Garrison announced on February 24, 1961, that Emmett Monroe Spencer, a convicted murderer on death row in Florida, had claimed he and a female accomplice killed a young woman on December 20, 1959, in a wooded area adjacent to U.S. Highway 80 between Mineola and Grand Saline. Peoples and Bob Badgett traveled to the Florida State Prison in Raiford and interviewed Spencer. Beverly Jean Williams of Houston had been listed as missing for the past eight years, and the condemned man identified her as his victim. Seemingly corroborating the inmate's story, the Rangers went to Sandy Hook, Kentucky, where they located Mary Katherine Hampton, Spencer's alleged partner in crime. Even though no body had been recovered, Garrison affirmed he had every reason to believe the confession. Three days after the announcement, though, Beverly was discovered to be living in East Gary, Indiana, with her husband. Peoples remained convinced Spencer had been in the area of Grand Saline, as the latter could accurately describe the land features.[49]

In time, Spencer confessed to forty-eight homicides and implicated Hampton in every instance. The pair were indicted on March 17 by the grand jury of St. Mary's Parish, Louisiana, for murder. They were also linked to another murder in St. Charles Parish. The case against Hampton was based on information supplied by the smooth-talking killer. The following month, after forty-three days of interrogation, Mary Katherine, eighteen years old and emotionally unstable, entered guilty pleas for both homicides and received two concurrent life sentences. There was no actual trial, and the state never had to enter evidence of her guilt. Five years later, she claimed she had been framed by Spencer and pled guilty only because she feared going to the electric chair. Hampton had turned state's evidence in the case that put Spencer on death row, and his repeated unverifiable, often inconsistent revelations of her alleged involvement were a form of revenge. Unfortunately, law enforcement officers in ten states, including Peoples and the DPS, and the families of murder victims still awaiting justice were caught up in Spencer's twisted plot. Represented by famed criminal attorney Francis Lee Bailey, Hampton was paroled from St. Gabriel's Prison for Women on November 30, 1966, after her sentence was commuted to ten-and-a-half years.[50]

By his own admission, the Henry Harvey Marshall homicide case was Peoples's "most puzzling investigation." The victim had worked for the Agricultural Stabilization and Conservation Committee of the U.S. Department of Agriculture. On the morning of June 3, 1961, he drove to his fifteen hundred-acre ranch thirty miles north of Franklin. His body was later found with five gunshot wounds to his left abdomen. The bullets that killed Marshall were confirmed to have been fired by his own bolt-action rifle. Crime lab technicians also verified the victim's weapon ejected three spent shells recovered in the vicinity of the body. However, there was no postmortem of the body, no statements taken at the inquests, and no attempt was made to examine the rifle for fingerprints. Despite this lack of a proper investigation, Justice of the Peace Leo Farmer, acting also as the county coroner, ruled Marshall's cause of death to be suicide. A political power locally, Robertson County Sheriff Howard Stegall supported the decision.[51]

Notwithstanding the official verdict on Marshall's demise, the case would not be permanently closed. In the meantime, two seventeen-year-old inmates at the State School for Boys at Gatesville were charged on August 4 in a fatal assault on an unarmed guard. After Billie Howard Malone, Air Force veteran and father of four, had been beaten into unconsciousness with a baseball bat on July 30, nine youths escaped from their dormitory and fled the grounds on foot. The local community was alarmed as 125 boys had escaped between July 15 and 17 after the suspension of two popular guards. His skull fractured, Malone died the following morning, and the escapees were recaptured on August 1 and placed in the maximum-security unit. Sheriff Winfred "Windy" Cummings filed complaints of murder with malice against suspects Charles Evert Lowe and Robert Sorter in Justice of Peace Stoney Hammack's court. The sheriff, County Attorney Don Nugent, Peoples, and Ranger Sergeant Krumnow questioned the nine runaways and another twenty youths who had not participated in the breakout or the murder. Interviewed in the River Oaks jail, Lowe and Sorter claimed they had been beaten by guards. Allegations of wrongdoing at the reform schools would be a recurring theme throughout Peoples's career.[52]

Austin police officers arrested two men and two women while they were in the act of burglarizing a supermarket. The quartet named James Hugh Leggett as their leader, and he was apprehended on August 22 in Abilene by Ranger Gene Barker Graves and local officers. In time, investigators uncovered a prolific burglary ring that was believed to have struck one thousand businesses, including auto dealers, feed stores, packing plants, lumber yards, milk companies, office buildings, lending establishments, beauty colleges, and service stations, in eighty-five counties. Eight unsolved cases in Brownwood alone were cleared based on Leggett's confession, which also implicated four other individuals. Along with Ranger Sergeant James E. Riddles, Peoples worked the case, and estimated the gang had stolen in excess of $100,000. On January 29, 1962, Leggett led Rangers John Dudley White, Jr. and William Delpard "Bill" Wilson, and city detectives Jack Jones and Aubrey Hurley, on a tour of the twenty-six locations he had burglarized in Big Springs. Additionally, the party of thief and lawmen visited three sites outside town. The last place in Big Spring marked the five hundredth identified since the Rangers and their prisoner left Austin.[53]

Colonel Garrison, District Judge John Milton Barron, District Attorney Bryan Russ, and Peoples found the nature of Henry Marshall's demise to be more than a little suspicious. Their doubts deepened when Secretary of Agriculture Orville Lothrop Freeman announced the dead man had been a key figure in two Congressional probes into the farming and financial interests of businessman and financier Billie Sol Estes. Originally built on a pyramid scheme of government farm subsidy and surplus grain storage transactions, the collapse of Estes's paper empire left businesses in ruins, including some 564 creditors who lost millions of dollars. In his capacity with the USDA, Marshall had decided on the regulatory exemptions allowing Estes to transfer cotton acreage allotments. Indeed, Estes was already under a federal indictment for fraud and a state indictment for theft. Barron and Russ impaneled a special session of the grand jury on May 21, 1962, to reopen the case and investigate whether Marshall had actually been murdered. Fifty-five witnesses were subpoenaed to appear. The same day, the judge ordered the disinterment of Marshall. Once the body was exhumed, Doctor Joseph Alexander Jachimczyk, the Harris County Medical Examiner, and four other experts performed an autopsy and found Marshall had suffered a blow to the forehead delivered with enough force to render death, and his blood contained a 30 percent concentration of carbon monoxide at the time of his demise. On May 24, the pathologist concluded with a "possible suicide, probable homicide" finding. A major focus of Peoples's investigation was locating a man who had asked for directions to Marshall's ranch on the day of the murder. He flew to Odessa to interview a promising suspect, but the individual was cleared of any involvement. Escorted by his attorney and Peoples, Billie Estes spent two hours on June 14 testifying before the grand jury. During the forty-minute morning session, the witness invoked his protections against self-incrimination under Article I of the state constitution between fifty and one hundred times. However, after he had negotiated a compromise with Judge Barron and the jurors to answer specific questions, he was more forthcoming in the afternoon session. District Attorney Russ and the grand jury interviewed over seventy-five witnesses, but the members were only able to return an inconclusive finding before recessing on June 18. Interestingly, four of the jurors were related to Sheriff Stegall. Colonel Garrison announced Peoples would continue to investigate Marshall's death as a homicide.[54]

In the coming weeks and months, Estes's abuse of the federal farm price-support system continued to reverberate in Washington. Four Kennedy administration officials resigned or were dismissed over the scandal. Several politicians, including Senator Ralph Webster Yardborough and Congressman James Thaddeus Rutherford, were found to have used their influence on the flamboyant swindler's behalf. Under multiple federal indictments for alleged fraud and theft, Estes continued to be the subject of numerous investigations conducted by the Justice and Agriculture Departments, and the House Government Operations and the Senate Investigations subcommittees. His case was transferred from Pecos to District Judge Otis Dunagan's court in Tyler on a change of venue. Estes was convicted of swindling on November 7, 1962, and sentenced to eight years in the state penitentiary. Additionally, he was convicted of mail fraud and conspiracy in U.S. district court in El Paso on March 29, 1963, and assessed a fifteen-year sentence at Leavenworth.[55]

While staging a bold daylight escape from the McLennan County jail on June 15, 1963, Ernest Rose, Jr., a convicted robber with a revoked parole, wounded Deputy Sheriff Oscar Davis Jackson. The prisoner and the deputy entered a carport at the side of the jail, where Rose's wife waited for them to ostensibly sign the papers for a recently purchased automobile. Instead, Lucille Rose passed her husband a .357 Magnum revolver, which he turned upon Jackson. In the resulting scuffle, the deputy was shot through the left hand, and the bullet lodged in his right shoulder. The Roses fled in their new 1963 Pontiac, which was later found abandoned on Rock Creek Road north of China Spring. Two .22 rifles were still inside the vehicle. Five hours after the break, Lucille was apprehended and charged with assault with intent to kill and aiding a prisoner to escape. Peoples and available Rangers were called in, and the captain received a tip the following day that the escapee wanted to surrender himself. Going to the indicted location at the entrance to Ridgewood Country Club, Peoples discovered Rose laying in a clump of weeds with a self-inflicted gunshot wound to the chest. Critically injured, the convict whispered he had shot himself because he believed he had killed Deputy Jackson. Rose was taken to Hillcrest Hospital where he further confessed to his crimes. Once doctors deemed he was safe to travel, Rose was transferred by ambulance to the state penitentiary to finish his original sentence.[56]

In the fallout from the successful escape, the Fifty-fourth District grand jury probed the activities of the sheriff's department, with Peoples and several of his Rangers acting as investigators. Sheriff Maxey and eight of his deputies submitted to lie detector tests. Deputy Wayne Moore was indicted on three separate complaints of accepting bribes from Lucille Rose in exchange for allowing her to visit her husband at all hours. Deputy Jesse Stamper was similarly charged. The grand jury's full report to District Judge Vic Hall, released on November 1, reprimanded Maxey for failing to enforce vice and gambling laws, although this criticism was mild in comparison to that directed at the district attorney. The jurors asserted District Attorney Donald Orell Hall's office had illegally dismissed felony charges, failed to forward felony complaints from the justice courts to the grand jury, requested sentences thought to be overly lenient, and pressed for the dismissal of too many indictments. Hall rebuffed the allegations and claimed they were rooted in politics.[57]

After a Garland osteopath claimed youths in the state reformatory schools near Gatesville were being abused by guards, Peoples worked with the FBI in a joint investigation. The captain toured the facilities with the physician, then delivered a one-inch thick report that found the allegations to be unfounded and complimented the school administrators for a "job well done."[58]

Peoples, Ben Krueger, two other Rangers, five FBI agents, and six DPS men investigated a robbery of the First State Bank of Eustace on September 21, 1964. A lone bandit, armed with a pistol, took an estimated thirteen thousand dollars from the vault and the cash drawers before fleeing in a green compact car driven by a waiting accomplice. Roadblocks were established immediately after the first report. Following an intensive search, the automobile, stolen in Mineola, was found abandoned and burned on a country road between Payne Springs and Houston. Tracks indicated the two thieves fled in a waiting vehicle. A hat abandoned at the scene was sent to the DPS lab for analysis, and a paroled Kaufman County burglar was arrested. He was ruled out as a suspect, but Peoples believed he had pertinent information, nevertheless. Thomas Norton Briggs, a former Henderson County resident, was arrested the following month and placed in a line-up. Eyewitnesses failed to make a positive identification, but Krueger and Sheriff Joseph William Brownlow considered Briggs a prime suspect. By the spring of 1965, Briggs, Billy Rex Pickett, and Bill Joe Wade had been indicted for bank robbery and conspiracy in connection with the Eustace heist.[59]

On July 30, 1965, the bodies of Susan Rigsby and Shirley Ann Stark, Chi Omega sorority sisters at the University of Texas, were discovered in a weedy vacant lot on the north side of Austin. The victims were identified through dental records. Due to the decomposed state of their remains, the medical examiner could only determine the victims had been strangled, although the disarrayed state of their clothing suggested rape had been committed. Investigators interviewed hundreds of people, but James Claud Cross, Jr. of Fort Worth became the primary suspect. On August 6, he contacted Police Lieutenant George Phifer and asked to meet at DPS headquarters. At the meeting, Justice of the Peace Frank McBee warned Cross of his legal rights. In the presence of Phifer and Peoples, the suspect made a voluntary statement detailing the crimes. The two coeds had been in town to enroll in summer classes. He had dated Shirley two months prior and had not known Susan at all. They were killed in Cross's apartment twelve days before the discovery of their remains. Following his confession, the suspect led Peoples, Jim Riddles, Bill Wilson, and Phifer to the location on the expressway where he had hidden the victim's suitcases. Cross was held in the Travis County jail without bail. The defendant pled guilty to both homicides at trial, but was tried only for Rigsby's murder. Cross was found sane and guilty after the jury deliberated for two hours and thirty-four minutes. He was sentenced to life imprisonment. However, the U.S. Supreme Court ruled later in the year that separate juries must hear issues of guilt and sanity. The decision would remain unused by Cross or his attorneys for twenty-one years.[60]

In mid-June 1966, the Seventy-seventh District grand jury opened a probe into the Mexia State School. Approximately sixty witnesses were interviewed, and the grand jurors reviewed an extensive quantity of transcripts, audit reports, statements, and other evidence. Peoples and Ranger Billy Joe Gunn had conducted an investigation two months previously and presented their findings on April 28 to County Attorney Holloway Martin, who released a larger report to the grand jury. The inquiry revealed wrongdoing in the school, including numerous felonies, had been occurring for the past fifteen to twenty years. Unfortunately, insufficient investigation at the time and the statute of limitations had rendered some of the offenses, such as fraud and improprieties toward female students, not subject to prosecution. The grand jurors completed their investigation on June 20 and submitted their own report to District Judge Clarence Ferguson. They returned one indictment.[61]

The Limestone County grand jury was impaneled on July 18 to investigate alleged irregularities in Mexia's city government. Peoples was one of the witnesses who testified in the proceedings. The following day, the grand jurors no-billed City Manager Dan Mize.[62]

The Donie State Bank in Freestone County was robbed on the night of August 18, 1967. This incident marked the second time the institution had been burglarized in the past three months. In the previous heist, which occurred on May 29, the perpetrators stole over nine hundred dollars. This time, prying open the rear door, the thieves failed to break into the vault. Instead, they took $675 in coinage, including fourteen dollars in pennies. Peoples and Ranger Johnny Krumnow, Deputy Sheriff James Gregory, and FBI Special Agent Lee Golden investigated. The trail led into Company B's territory, and Ranger Glenn Elliott and Harrison County Constable William Lynwood "Buck" Little took up the hunt. Billy Joe Suel, Larry Wayne Grammar, and Larry

Dean Grammar were arrested in Leesville, Louisiana, on September 2 and arraigned in Lake Charles. Extradited to Marshall, they were charged in federal court with the May 29 burglary of the Donie bank. Together with a fourth man, they were also indicted with similar heists in Elysian Fields, Talco, and Windom.[63]

From the time he took up residence, Peoples found Company F's headquarters in Waco to be insufficient. The office was a pair of shabby rooms filled with cast-off furniture in a building on Franklin Street shared with other DPS units. In 1963, realizing the bureaucracy would not solve the problem, Peoples enlisted the aid of Roger Norman Conger, a prominent area businessman and former mayor, and real estate broker James Riffle LeBlond in constructing a new headquarters building and a museum dedicated to the Texas Rangers. Approaching the Chamber of Commerce, the three men convinced them to establish a special planning committee, which would present a proposal to Garrison. The Fort Fisher Committee, named for the 1837 Texas Ranger outpost that had been located along the Brazos River, campaigned for local support while Peoples endeavored to convince the director of the proposal's feasibility. The captain worked with the committee in adopting a formal plan and finally gained Garrison's approval in early 1964. The Public Safety Commission members, including retired Ranger Captain Tom Hickman, were equally enthusiastic. Harry Mayo Provence, editor-in-chief of the *Waco News-Tribune*, and Harlon Morse "The Hookin' Bull" Fentress, the newspaper's dynamic owner, also pledged their assistance. Over the next three years, Peoples and the Fort Fisher Committee worked to secure the land and raise the necessary funds. Per the project agreements, the City of Waco was chosen to own and operate the museum. On December 12, 1967, ground was broken at the designated site located next to the Brazos and along Interstate 35. Speaking to the assembled crowd, Colonel Garrison recounted the history of the service and concluded by asserting, "I can tell you as surely as I stand on this platform that as long as there is a State of Texas there will be a Ranger force in spite of their enemies." Following the ceremony, three hundred dignitaries, including James Arness, war veteran and star of the landmark television series *Gunsmoke*, adjourned to Baylor University's Student Union for a luncheon honoring the DPS's

Dedication Ceremony, October 25, 1968. *Courtesy Texas Ranger Hall of Fame and Museum, Waco, TX.*

longtime director. Sadly, the colonel succumbed to cancer on May 7, 1968, and was only present in spirit when the new Company F headquarters, along with the Homer Garrison Texas Ranger Museum, was dedicated on October 25. The Rangers moved into their new quarters four days prior, and, reminiscing on the origins of the Texas Ranger Hall of Fame and Museum, Peoples concluded: "And that's exactly the way Fort Fisher became a reality over a selfish thing on my part."[64]

Shortly before Garrison's death, the DPS underwent a major reorganization. The largest changes introduced a new level of supervision to the department: a Traffic Enforcement Division oversaw the Highway Patrol, License and Weights, and other offices concerned with traffic; while a Criminal Law Enforcement Division coordinated the Texas Rangers and the Narcotics, Intelligence, and Motor Vehicle Theft services. All Ranger captains were directed to report to the division chief rather than the director.[65]

On January 4, 1969, the Texas House Committee on Juvenile Delinquency, which was studying allegations of abuse at state reform schools, made an unannounced visit to Mountain View, the maximum-security unit at the Gatesville School for Boys. The next day, Speaker Ben Frank Barnes and a group of state officials and legislators conducted a second surprise inspection of the facility. The results of the legislators' findings were turned over to the DPS and the FBI. Peoples was placed in charge of the state investigation. School supervisors and five youths who claimed to have been beaten by guards were given polygraph tests in Waco. In the course of the interrogations, Peoples learned the guards had disarmed three inmates during an escape attempt, but used only the necessary force to subdue them. Representatives Vernon Stewart of Wichita Falls and Claud Graves of Houston, two members of the committee, flatly refuted the Ranger's conclusions and stated their intention to investigate other allegations. Graves told reporters, "This same Capt. Peoples has investigated all Gatesville complaints and never finds anything wrong with Gatesville." Senator James Powell Word of Meridian blasted his legislative colleagues, charging them with maligning Texas Youth Council members, school employees, and Peoples "with a total and utter disregard for the truth." He particularly mentioned his disgust with the committee as they "impugned and questioned the honesty, ability and sincerity of Captain Clint Peoples of the Texas Rangers without any basis in fact whatsoever."[66]

Thirty-two-year-old Janice Dean Plentl was found dead in the bathtub of her Gatesville home on March 13. At first, her death was thought to have been caused by head injuries sustained in an accidental fall. However, an autopsy revealed she had been beaten and strangled. Peoples was called in to investigate. Shockingly, her killer was quickly identified as her husband, Highway Patrolman Wallace Bedford Plentl. The suspect was arrested by Sheriff Winfred Cummings and Highway Patrol Sergeant Leonard Marion Hancock on March 15. The Ranger captain filed a complaint charging Plentl with murder with malice aforethought in Clinton Winford Turner's justice court, and the suspect was held in the Coryell County jail without bond. Understandably, the sheriff and Plentl's partner, Patrolman James K. Hamilton, were reluctant to speak with reporters, although they referred to him as a "good officer." The following day, the patrolman agreed to make a written statement in the presence of his lawyer. District Attorney Byron McClellan presented the case to the Fifty-second District grand jury on April 14.[67]

More changes to the DPS structure occurred effective September 1, 1969, when, at the behest of Public Safety Commission chairman Clifton Wilson Cassidy, Jr., the legislature restored the inactive title of senior captain. Henceforth, the new commander held supervisory responsibility for the service's sixty-two Rangers, and he, in turn, answered to the law enforcement chief. The commission chose Peoples to fill the position beginning on November 1, and Edwin George "Butch" Albers, Jr. succeeded him as captain of Company F. Additionally, on September 1, 1970, the legislature authorized an increase in the service's strength to eighty men.[68]

Among Senior Captain Peoples's first acts was to defend against allegations of Rangers engaging in physical and verbal abuse against striking Hispanic farmworkers in South Texas. In March 1970, the Texas Advisory Committee to the U.S. Commission on Civil Rights recommended the Rangers be disbanded. "The people of Texas would never vote to abolish the Rangers and no legislature would stand for it," Peoples said from his office in Austin. "Abolish the Rangers? Why, that would be like tearing down the Alamo."[69]

One day after the Kent State confrontation on May 4, 1970, several thousand students from the University of Texas gathered on the Austin campus, then marched on the Capitol. Apprehensive the anti-war protest would turn into a riot, the DPS summoned the nearest Rangers and state troopers to assemble in Austin. Peoples instructed the law officers, "If any of those long-haired hippies get inside the Capitol, it better be over dead men." In spite of the senior captain's belligerence, brick-throwing demonstrators were able to enter the large red granite building and destroy the antique glass doors in the lobby. The state officers, reinforced by Austin policemen, used tear gas to evict the rioters from the statehouse. A bomb threat forced the evacuation of the building's occupants. Seventeen people received minor injuries, but no shots were fired and, most importantly, no one died.[70]

On July 31, 1970, Peoples used his accrued vacation time, personal funds, and some private financial assistance to embark on a goodwill tour of law enforcement agencies in eight European countries. Carrying letters of introduction from the International Association of Chiefs of Police, he also conveyed greetings from Colonel Wilson Edward "Pat" Speir, Garrison's successor as DPS director. While meeting with senior officials in London, Paris, Berlin, Stuttgart, Zurich, Rome, and Madrid, Peoples discussed issues and procedures common to law enforcement.[71]

As the sesquicentennial of the Ranger service approached, the Sixty-second Legislature created the Texas Ranger Commemorative Commission, which would begin its responsibilities on September 1, 1971. The new body was to consist of five members appointed for one year by the speaker of the house and five members selected by the lieutenant governor. Peoples served as interim chairman, and commission members included Roger Conger; Gaines DeGraffenried; Rex Cauble; James Andrew "Jimmie" Whittenburg III; Marion Bauch, Jr.; James Laurence "Larry" Sheerin; Harry Moore; Marvin Stetler; and Dan Hruska. With its first meeting scheduled for December 16, the Commission made its headquarters at Fort Fisher and the Homer Garrison Texas Ranger Museum. Its powers included the appointment of seventy-five advisory members for the planning of the commemorative year, the issuance of a special medal and firearms, and the planning and supervision of all celebratory events in connection with the anniversary. Additionally, DeGraffenried and LeBlond had long favored establishing a Texas Ranger Hall of Fame at Fort Fisher, and this concept was folded into the larger commemorative project.[72]

On December 27, 1972, the first four in a series of commemorative handguns were given to Governor Preston Smith, Governor-elect Dolph Briscoe, Peoples, and Colonel Speir. Banks throughout the state began selling 7,750 commemorative medals in either oxidized bronze or .999 fine silver on February 20, 1973. The obverse of the medal bore the likeness of Captain L. H. McNelly taken from the Joe Grandee painting that had been presented to President Richard Millhouse Nixon. On the reverse was the image of the Lone Star derived from the state seal. Proceeds from the sales were earmarked for the Texas Ranger Hall of Fame. Other celebratory objects included a sterling silver plate produced by W. N. W. Mint Industries of Amarillo; products from the Daisy Air Rifle Company,

Winchester, and Smith & Wesson; and artwork by Melvin Warren and Jack White.[73]

The Texas Ranger Sesquicentennial event occurred in Waco on August 4, 1973. Roger Conger was master of ceremonies for the groundbreaking of the Hall of Fame, and character actor Chill Wills entertained the crowd of three hundred. The entire force of eighty-two Rangers was also on hand. Later that evening, fifteen hundred individuals attended a twenty-five dollar per plate banquet, with actor Clint Walker of the TV western series *Cheyenne* serving as the master of ceremonies.[74]

In the fall of 1973, Colonel Speir and Jim Ray, chief of the Law Enforcement Division, and People's direct supervisor, began to have some concerns about misconduct on the part of the senior captain. Peoples had been contacted by a Hollywood producer who wanted to make a television series about the modern Texas Rangers. Enthusiastic about the project, Peoples promised access to case reports and his personal services as technical advisor. In return, he required a 5 percent finder's fee and a contract affording him a five hundred dollar weekly salary.[75]

The proposed business arrangement raised ethical questions, and Colonel Speir wanted answers. He detailed Chief Ray himself to investigate the senior captain's relationship with the Hollywood producers. Ray traveled to Los Angeles and met with two men involved in the negotiations on November 14. He was unable to determine whether Peoples truly intended to take the producers' money while still a state employee, or he was developing a post-retirement strategy. Regardless, the senior captain lacked the authority to unilaterally offer government documents to commercial interests.[76]

Ray reported to Colonel Speir on November 21, 1973, and detailed the conclusions of his inquiry, including a taped interview with the producers with whom Peoples had been in contact. No disciplinary action was reported to have occurred, but Peoples, on January 31, 1974, submitted his intention to retire effective May 15. He had 240 hours of unused vacation and elected to use his leave beginning March 31 rather than be compensated for the time on his final paycheck. In his letter to Speir, People commented that his stint as senior captain "has been one of the greatest honors that I think anyone could have received, to serve in the role of leadership of one of the finest and most efficient organizations in America." His record as a career peace officer had, thus far, been exemplary, but Bill Wilson, the incoming senior captain, and many of the service's members had disliked People's love of attention. The newspaper headlines and public relations campaigns irritated many Rangers who believed in an understated, practical approach to law enforcement.[77]

Meanwhile, Peoples had utilized his relationship with Senator John Tower to secure President Richard Nixon's nomination for the position of U.S. Marshal for the Northern District of Texas. The federal appointment was confirmed by the Senate on April 25. Peoples would become the fourth Texas Ranger captain in history to wear the star of a U.S. marshal. Federal District Court Judge William McLaughlin "Mac" Taylor, Jr. administered the oath of office to Peoples in Dallas on May 15. Observing the swearing-in ceremony were one hundred people, including friends, family, Texas law officers, and U.S. marshals from Arkansas and Louisiana. Also present was Wayne Colburn, director of the Marshals Service, and Captain Manuel T. Gonzaullas. "I pledge to do everything in my power to uphold the high honors of this office," Peoples remarked. "This climaxes a real fine honor for me … to reach a goal in law enforcement I've always wanted." Having noted the caseload of the federal court in Dallas was four times heavier that that of Fort Worth, Peoples was pleased that his district's headquarters office was being transferred to the former city.[78]

Despite his move to the federal government, Peoples retained his interest in the Texas Ranger Museum in Waco. The commemorative commission's executive committee awarded a nearly $350,000 contract to Hooker Construction Company to build the hall of fame. In late January 1976, the marshal announced that painter Jack White had been named an honorary life member of the Texas Ranger Hall of Fame based on his artistic and historical contributions. On February 7, standing in front of a crowd of over two thousand, the marshal was joined by entertainer Danny Thomas and State Representative Fred Head in dedicating the Texas Ranger Hall of Fame. Additionally, Senator Tower; Senator Lloyd Bentsen; Governor Briscoe; Rex Davis, director of the Bureau of Alcohol, Tobacco, and Firearms; James Green, deputy commissioner of the Immigration and Naturalization Service;

James Blackburn Adams, deputy assistant director of the FBI; William Ewing Hall, assistant director of the U.S. Marshal's Service; Stewart White, director of the Secret Service; Colonel Speir; Senior Captain Bill Wilson; and Captain Gonzaullas were among the notables who witnessed twenty Texas Rangers being immortalized in the new facility. Representing the Fourteenth District, Head stated to a *Mexia Daily News* reporter, "This Hall of Fame and Museum, which is the first in the nation dedicated to law enforcement, will be an inspiration to all Texans who believe as I do in strong law enforcement and who holds in high esteem those courageous men and women who daily protect the lives and property of everyone." Dayton Kelly assumed his duties as the director of the combined Texas Ranger Hall of Fame and Museum.[79]

In the fall of 1977, the Marshal's Service was shaken by a year-long Justice Department probe that uncovered evidence of extortion, theft, loan sharking, and narcotics trafficking by deputy marshals in several federal districts across the country. The FBI field office in Fort Worth confirmed that none of Peoples's deputies were under investigation.[80]

As Peoples's term neared its end, Senator Bentsen's office was inundated with letters and resumes from applicants for the U.S. marshal's position. In the end, Bentsen and Senator Tower agreed Peoples should be reappointed and sent their recommendation to President James Earl "Jimmy" Carter, Jr. The nation's chief executive approved a second four-year term on June 26, 1978. U.S. District Judge Halbert Owen "Hal" Woodward, chief judge of the Northern District, administered the oath of office on August 23 in Judge William Taylor's federal courtroom.[81]

More often than not Peoples's duties as marshal revolved around managing resources. During a six-day bond hearing for oilman Thomas Cullen Davis, charged in a murder-for-hire plot, the marshal was asked to provide deputies to a twenty-four-hour protection detail for Charles McCrory, the state's key witness. The request had come from the U.S. Attorney's office in Fort Worth, and, upon the approval of the federal Witness Security Program chief, Peoples assigned deputies from that city and Dallas. McCrory was named as the middleman in the conspiracy to murder State District Judge Joseph Harvey "Joe" Eidson, Jr. Prompted by alleged death threats, McCrory was moved to an unnamed location on September 3, 1978, and given a new identity. In preparation of a pretrial session on June 14, 1979, Peoples was subpoenaed by Davis's attorneys who wanted to question the marshal on federal expenditures for McCrory's protection.[82]

Occasionally, though, Peoples was able to leave the office and carry out active law enforcement work. In July 1979, Robert M. "Bobby" Johnson, a Wichita Falls grain dealer and fugitive for the previous two years, was captured in Idaho. Arraigned in federal court in Pocatello, he waived extradition. Along with Chief Deputy James Vaught and one other marshal, Peoples transported Johnson to Fort Worth to face seventeen counts of transporting stolen grain across state lines. The marshal's tenure had been positive, and, near the end of his term, he was nominated for another four-year stint.[83]

On May 29, 1979, U.S. District Court Judge John Howland Wood, Jr. was shot to death in front of his San Antonio townhouse. Hitman Charles Voyde Harrelson had been hired for the job by gambler and narcotics kingpin Jamiel "Jimmy" Chagra, who was being tried in "Maximum John" Wood's court. Peoples had a limited role in the case when Jo Ann Harrelson, the killer's second wife, was indicted for using a false name to purchase a hunting rifle two weeks before her husband murdered the judge. On September 8, the marshal took the unusual step of personally escorting Jo Ann to her hearing before U.S. Magistrate John Beirne Tolle. Peoples commented to reporters that he wanted to ensure "her rights [were] not violated. I will be with her the entire time she is here because it's a real responsibility." Following the judge's assassination, Attorney General French Smith expanded the scope of federal marshals' protection role to include entire courthouses rather than just courtrooms. Responsible for eleven judges, Peoples applauded the move and predicted he would need to increase his twenty-seven-member force to meet their new obligations.[84]

Lauriberto Ignacio, a professional soccer player who had failed to win a spot as the Dallas Cowboys' placekicker, was indicted by a federal grand jury on April 21, 1983, for conspiracy to smuggle narcotics from Brazil to Texas. The FBI, the Drug Enforcement Administration, and the U.S. Attorney's office were conducting wider investigations into six of the football team's players and their alleged connections to cocaine dealers. Peoples's role was confined to serving process as his office handled subpoenas for Tony Hill and Harvey

Martin, the Cowboys' wide receiver and defensive end respectively, to appear as witnesses in Ignacio's trial.[85]

On January 15, 1964, Billy Sol Estes had appealed his conviction before the Texas Court of Criminal Appeals, but the justices unanimously affirmed the sentence. His efforts in federal court were likewise unsuccessful. He was paroled in 1971, then indicted for tax fraud. With this latest charge, his parole was revoked. When Peoples escorted Estes to La Tuna federal penitentiary on August 26, 1979, the prisoner reportedly said, "you may be assured … that Henry Marshall very definitely did not commit suicide. He was murdered." Peoples further claimed Estes implied he should look "in the direction of Washington" for Marshall's killer.[86]

Estes was paroled from Big Spring Federal Prison Camp to Abilene on November 15, 1983. He requested immunity from the U.S. Government in exchange for information concerning at least one of "a string of murders" in the early 1960s. He also claimed he had been offered immunity by President John Fitzgerald Kennedy and his brother, Attorney General Robert Francis Kennedy, in return for revealing evidence against Vice President Lyndon Johnson. While Estes refused to divulge what crimes he would have exposed, he did say Johnson would have gone to prison.[87]

Estes and Peoples met for a two-hour lunch at an Abilene steakhouse on December 1 to discuss the Marshall case. Peoples indicated to reporters he was satisfied with Estes' part of the discussion, calling him "very cooperative." Peoples and Estes declined to comment on Estes' knowledge of the crimes and the nature of the charges for which he sought immunity. Peoples did disclose publicly for the first time the existence of a plastic bag found approximately fifty yards from Marshall's body. Peoples had located the bag about six months into his investigation. It was judged to be large enough to accommodate a man's head and a hose extending from an automobile's exhaust pipe.[88]

On March 20, 1984, Estes gave hearsay testimony before a Robertson County grand jury that Malcolm Wallace, the convicted killer of John Kinser, was the triggerman in the Marshall homicide. According to Estes, Lyndon Johnson ordered Wallace to kill Marshall because he feared the agriculture department official would link him to Estes's illegal business transactions.

The Johnson family dismissed Estes' charge as the rantings of a pathological liar, and accused him of making "scurrilous attacks" in order to promote the biography written by Pam Estes. Retired FBI agent Thomas Grace "Tommy" McWilliams, Jr., who investigated Marshall's death in 1962, characterized the twice-convicted swindler's statement as a "bunch of malarkey." The grand jury changed the official cause of death from suicide to homicide, but refused to take any action on Estes's testimony due to its unsubstantiated nature. They also called attention to the fact that all other parties in the case were dead. McWilliams believed the grand jurors would have benefitted from his investigative report, but District Attorney John Paschall had not previously known of its existence. The former agent criticized an uncooperative federal government and also charged that "Peoples couldn't testify to a thing in the world because he didn't know what was going on." McWilliams further accused the federal marshal and Estes of seeking publicity for their respective book projects. Despite the lack of credible evidence introduced into the record, Peoples believed the con artist's claims and continued to pursue that particular line of inquiry. He publicly expressed his skepticism of the accidental death rulings returned on Wallace and three other people involved in Estes's swindles.[89]

Three federal judges called Peoples into a closed-door meeting in late March to express concern that his involvement in the case could give Estes' uncorroborated statements credibility. One of the jurists was Barefoot Sanders, who, while U.S. attorney, had represented the Department of Agriculture in 1962 and attempted to block Robertson County investigators from obtaining a 175-page federal report on Estes' cotton allotment scheme in Texas. He had also served as President Johnson's legislative counsel from 1967 to 1969. Sanders was reportedly more upset than his two fellow judges.[90]

Henry Marshall's son, Donald, sued the Texas Bureau of Vital Statistics requesting a change in his father's official cause of death. The lawsuit also asked District Judge Thomas Battle Bartlett to order Doctor Jachimczyk to amend the elder Marshall's death certificate.[91] During a two-day hearing on the matter in August 1985, Peoples took the stand in 261st District Court in Austin and spoke of his certainty that Marshall had been murdered and that the guilty party had attempted to portray the crime as a suicide. Based in large part on the marshal's unshakeable testimony, Judge Peter Michael Lowry ruled on the thirteenth in the family's favor and ordered the death certificate be amended from suicide to homicide.[92]

In January 1987, the Texas Court of Criminal Appeals ruled that James Cross, murderer of Susan Rigsby and Shirley Stark, should receive a new trial since the same jury that ruled on his sanity also heard the guilt stage of his trial. After serving twenty-two years of his life sentence, James Cross was freed on May 22, while awaiting a new trial. District Judge Mace Thurman had set his bail at one million dollars, but the Third Court of Appeals reduced the amount to $150,000. Cross appeared in Judge Thurman's court on the twenty-sixth. Travis County prosecutors confirmed the confession still remained, but the majority of the evidence had been destroyed or lost. Additionally, some witnesses had since died. Cross was convicted of the lesser crime of murder with malice and sentenced to eighty years.[93]

On September 30, 1992, Cross walked out of Huntsville after having accumulated sufficient time taken off his sentence for good behavior. He had been denied parole on twenty previous occasions. Robbie Rigsby, the murdered student's mother, believed her daughter's killer "should have gotten the death penalty." Expressing a common sentiment among victims' families, she said, "You never forget. You have to live your life. It's been 25 years, but you never forget. You never forget. And she was my only child."[94]

Peoples was sworn in for his third term on September 17, 1982, by Judge Woodward. Ultimately serving for fourteen years under five separate presidential administrations, Peoples was the longest-tenured law enforcement officer in the United States. Appointed an Executive Marshal in March 1987, he was tasked with coordinating a series of commemorative events for the Marshals Service during its bicentennial celebration in 1989. When the celebrations were complete, he retired on June 3 of the same year. In an article written in the *Fort Worth Star-Telegram* days after Peoples stepped down, the reporter admitted the marshal's style and self-promotion had generated strong feelings toward him, both pro and con. One former Ranger who was not identified in the piece said, "People that like him think the world of him; others dislike him very strongly. If you were for him, he was your friend; if you were not for him or disagreed with him, well, you couldn't disagree with him without him becoming angry and think that you were his enemy." In the same article, author Mike Cox, then the DPS spokesman, said of Peoples, "If there's one word a notch below charismatic, I guess that's it. He has that special talent that makes you feel like at that particular moment that you're the most important person in his life."[95]

On November 22, 1991, Congressman Ralph Moody Hall rose before his colleagues in the U.S. House of Representatives and delivered a tribute to Marshal Clint Peoples. He extolled the lawman's long service to Texas and recounted some of his exploits. The legislator ended his remarks by extending "a sincere 'thank you' to him on behalf of all Americans for his dedication to law enforcement."[96]

Clint Peoples died on June 22, 1992, following an automobile accident. His vehicle had veered off the road and struck a utility pole. Conducted by Reverend Ron Durham, the funeral service was held at Columbus Avenue Baptist Church, with Roger Conger, Lewis Calvin Rigler, and Monsignor Mark Dearing also officiating. Peoples was buried in Waco Memorial Park.[97]

Along with Peoples, Donna Lee was active in the Sheriff's Association. Following her husband's death, she lived in Waco and attended Columbus Avenue Baptist Church. A resident at Regent Care Center of Woodway for a short time, Donna died on June 21, 2003. She was buried next to her husband.[98]

Donna Jean attended the University of Texas at Austin, where she met engineer Sam McClendon. They married in March 1958 and moved to Waco the following year. After earning a degree in elementary education from Baylor University, Donna spent twenty-eight years teaching second grade in the Midway school system. She retired in 1996. Donna Jean died on April 14, 2012, at her Waco home, and was buried in Memorial Park.[99]

Clint Peoples provoked polarizing reactions among the public and his peers. To some, he was an infallible embodiment of the Ranger mythos. To others, he was an egoist whose self-interest was paramount. Likely, the truth lies somewhere in the middle, especially when his many instances of exceptional police work are factored into the equation. Additionally, his role in the creation of the Texas Ranger of Fame and Museum should be added to the sum total of the man.

James E. Riddles. *Courtesy Texas Ranger Hall of Fame and Museum, Waco, TX.*

Chapter 10

James E. Riddles: "Quiet, Steady Professional"

James Elmer "Jim" Riddles was the type of quiet, steady professional that is the backbone of any effective law enforcement organization. Despite being involved in a number of major investigations, he did not generate the splashy headlines that others enjoyed. His understated approach was mirrored in the manner in which he behaved as a captain of Texas Rangers. He led by suggestion and respect rather than command or force of personality. His complete faith in the men under his leadership was absolute, and they returned his esteem in equal or greater measures. One of "Riddles' Rangers," Sergeant Arthur Hill publicly declared, "I don't believe that any company ever had a better captain than Jim Riddles."

He was born on the family cotton farm near Windom, Fannin County, Texas, on September 27, 1910. His parents were John Madison and Louise (Barnes) Riddles. The elder Riddles had been born in Ozark, Arkansas, on August 31, 1872, while his wife was born in Tennessee on July 6, 1876. She worked at home as a housewife. Jim's older sister was Gladys Lucile Riddles, born on August 9, 1905, and his older brothers were Thomas Leeman Riddles, born on March 1, 1907, and John Paul Riddles, born on July 29, 1909.[1]

Riddles's son commented years later: "He loved his parents, and he had three siblings … When they would go off to school in the morning, and he would try to follow, they would throw rocks at him … That was the nature of how they were." John Riddles was remembered as a harsh man but equally a generous one. Once a newly widowed neighbor asked the elder Riddles if her farmhands could borrow his mules to plow her fields, and he refused. However, the next morning, he sent his men and the mules to assist the widow.[2]

John would often travel to Galveston and hire families to work his land. One of those was headed by a black man remembered only as Terrapin. Before Riddles was old enough to attend school, he spent a great deal of time in Terrapin's home and learned a lot of life's wisdom. Later in adulthood, he would visit Terrapin and publicly talk about his enormous respect for the older man. Because of his growing up in Terrapin's house and playing with his children, Riddles developed more enlightened views on racial matters than was the norm at that time. As an adult, he came to believe in treating people fairly, regardless of skin color, but he also had to effectively work with other peace officers who did not share his lack of prejudice. The balance he had to maintain was probably the single biggest personal dilemma he faced as a peace officer.[3]

While young Riddles worked in the cotton patch, he usually carried a work of poetry or Zane Grey's classic books *Riders of the Purple Sage* and *Lone Star Ranger*. In this time, Riddles possibly decided his future career, and as his son later recounted, "I never really remember my dad setting his mind to something that he didn't do. His word was absolutely his bond." In addition to his farm work, Riddles also made extra money by driving a team of mules pulling a road grader down Windom's dirt roads.[4]

Riddles attended the red brick schoolhouse in Windom, which housed all elementary and secondary grades. The cornerstone of the building bore the name of his future father-in-law. The number of students living in town was meager, but many more came from the surrounding rural area. Riddles was a talented athlete and played baseball as a pitcher and second baseman.[5]

After graduating from high school in 1928, he attended Austin College in Sherman the following year. He was a football player and javelin thrower in school and earned a Bachelor of Science degree in Business Administration in 1933. Returning to his old high school in Windom, he taught mathematics and coached baseball and basketball. He rode a horse to school and, if a student proved unruly, Riddles would send the miscreant outside to brush the animal. When he was first hired, the school gave him the vast sum of five hundred dollars to build the gymnasium and purchase the team's uniforms. His son would later reflect that Riddles was the proudest of his time as a teacher and coach. One of his students was Glenn Elliott, later a well-regarded Texas Ranger, who would credit the coach as the reason for the baseball team's success. According to Elliott, Riddles stressed the fundamentals of the game and seemed indifferent to the idea of home runs. To supplement his income, Riddles would travel to other small towns in the summer and sign on with the local baseball teams.[6]

He first met Loneta Pearl Luttrell, his future wife, through her older brother, John Edward "J. E." Luttrell, who was a friend. She had been born on January 4, 1913, in Dodd City. Her father was the pastor of the Church of Christ in Windom, as well as the proprietor of a meat market and restaurant. Riddles saw her again after returning to Windom while she was a high school senior there, although he was never her teacher. Loneta was taken by the handsome Riddles and pursued him.[7]

While he loved teaching, Riddles decided to join the military and aid the coming war effort. He also wanted to ensure he had employment to which he could return. To that end, he applied for and was accepted into the Highway Patrol on September 1, 1941. He attended DPS Academy at Camp Mabry as a recruit patrolman. As one of the Seventh Highway Patrol School's ninety-two recruits, Riddles became close friends with Arthur Watts Hill, Frank Probst, Lewis Calvin Rigler, and Gene Graves, all of whom would serve long and distinguished careers with the Texas Rangers. On one occasion, Loneta came to visit, and Riddles decided to show her his motorcycle riding abilities. As he rode the bike between two trees, he failed to notice the width of the handlebars were about an inch greater than the space between the trunks. The cycle came to an abrupt halt, and Riddles flew over the handlebars and through the windshield. Luckily, he was not thrown out of the academy.[8]

Upon graduating on October 25, Riddles was assigned to Brownwood as a Highway Patrolman. However, the attack on Pearl Harbor and America's subsequent entry into World War II ensured his stint was brief. He enlisted in the U.S. Army on April 16, 1942, at Camp Walters near Mineral Wells. Riddles was not alone as 115 members of the DPS received leaves of absence for military service by the end of October.[9]

Riddles was assigned to the Army's Military Police Corps, which Secretary of War Henry Lewis Stimson had established as a permanent branch on September 26, 1941. The duties of this new organization included investigating crimes and offenses committed by individuals subject to military law, enforcing all police regulations relating to their area of operations, reporting violations of orders "given by them in the proper execution of their duties regardless of the grade or status of the offender," and preventing the commission of conduct prejudicial to good order and military discipline. Additionally, military policemen were engaged in controlling the movement of traffic both in active combat zones and rear areas; protecting troops from violence or accidents; recovering lost, stolen, and abandoned government property; and "relieving combat organizations of the custody of prisoners of war and operating the prisoner-of-war system—along with some new military duties, including assisting in destroying hostile airborne troops when combat troops were unavailable or inadequate to the task."[10]

Riddles's first posting was the 745th Military Police Battalion at Camp Bowie near Brownwood. The unit entrained for Camp Stoneham, California, then shipped to Honolulu aboard the S.S. *Etolin* in July 1942. Riddles returned to Fort McDowell, California, aboard the troop transport U.S.S. *Republic* (AP-33) in November and went on to Fort Oglethorp, Georgia.[11]

Even while Riddles was preparing to go to war, the straight-shooting repute of his future organization was well-known in occupied Europe. The Associated Press reported:

> Many French officials and some diplomats were excited today by mistaken reports that "Texas Rangers" had landed in Dieppe with the Allied Commando Raiders.

> The wild west touch was contributed to French speculation by London radio reports that American Rangers had participated in the action. To many Frenchmen there is only one type of Rangers—the Texas variety.[12]

Before reporting to his next duty station, Riddles and Loneta eloped to Bryan County, Oklahoma, where there was no three-day waiting period to get married. They were wed on November 25, 1942. Riddles then attended Officer Candidate School at the Provost Marshal General Training Center, Fort Custer, Michigan. Upon graduation, he was commissioned a second lieutenant on February 26, 1943. After attending the four-week occupational military police course for officers, he was assigned to Company B, 510th Military Police Battalion at Camp Maxey near Paris, Texas, as Third Platoon leader. The company commander was Captain Martin E. Francis. The battalion was officially activated on May 1, and the soldiers embarked on a fourteen-week period of rigorous instruction, which included basic infantry training and a twenty-five-mile field march with full equipment.[13]

On August 21, the entire company formed at Chapel 11 as a color guard for the wedding of First Sergeant Kenneth Harvey Kuhns. Staff Sergeant Clayton Shelley served as best man and Private First Class James E. Smith as organist, while Captain Francis gave away the bride. Another cause for celebration, although likely less joyous, was Riddles's promotion to first lieutenant in early September 1943. Despite these fleeting moments, the company spent the majority of their time preparing for war. They moved to Leesville, Louisiana, on November 10 for two weeks of maneuvers and learning the duties of road patrols, traffic control, and area guards. The company then relocated to Fort Sam Houston on December 18 and served as guards for Third Army and Fourth Army Headquarters. Captain Francis was relieved of command on January 16, 1944, and First Lieutenant Turner M. Keith became the new company commander. While in San Antonino, Riddles met Loneta at the Gunter Hotel for a brief reunion.[14]

On April 23, the company was relieved of duty at army headquarters, and the men spent several weeks in hardening exercises, sports, and furloughs. By this time, they might have grown impatient to get into the war and do their part, especially after American, British, and Canadian troops assaulted Fortress Europe through the beaches of Normandy, France. Finally, the company's overseas orders arrived, and the MPs departed San Antonio for Fort Miles Standish, Massachusetts, on June 11. After two weeks in the Bay State, they were able to enjoy a last bit of America and see the Boston Red Sox play the Chicago White Sox during a three-game series at Fenway Park. Riddles and his comrades sailed to Liverpool, England, aboard the U.S.S. *Mount Vernon* on July 1. Disembarking on the eighth, they traveled by train to Bristol. After serving as guards at the harbor and for Ninth Army Headquarters, the company entrained to Southampton where they boarded a Landing Ship, Tank bound for Normandy. They come ashore on Utah Beach on the night of August 30.[15]

The company immediately marched eight miles inland in full combat gear through rain and mud to Périers, then to St. Sauveur-Lendelin. The men bivouacked at Mi-Forêt before moving on to Beaugency on September 13, where they assisted in erecting a prisoner of war enclosure for the anticipated surrender of twenty thousand Heer, Luftwaffe, and Kriegsmarine ground troops. Major-General Botho Henning Elster, *fieldkommandantur* of Biarritz, had been rushing his "Foot March Group South" toward the Loire River, but the Germans were cut off by the U.S. Third and Seventh Armies at Poitiers by September 5. Elster met with Major-General Robert Chauncey Macon, commanding the 83rd Infantry Division, at Issoudun on the tenth. Prompted by the XIX Tactical Air Command's demonstration of airpower, the Prussian general reluctantly accepted the offered terms. The Germans began marching in three columns toward the Loire three days later. Elster formally capitulated at the Beaugency Bridge on September 16, and the disarming, searching, and processing of the prisoners was managed by the 130 to 140 MPs of Company B. The two-day endeavor went smoothly, and Elster personally gave Riddles as mementos a pistol and a boxed set of cocktail forks adorned with the German's family crest. On September 19, Riddles and Lieutenant Schwass took sixty-four men to secure German materiel south of the Loire.[16]

Company B was assigned to Arlon, Belgium, on October 1, as part of the Ninth Army Headquarters. The next day, Riddles and twenty-five men of Third Platoon were sent to Bastogne. On the fourth, while company headquarters moved into the woods outside Arlon, other detachments were posted to Longwy, Longuyon, and Sedan in France. The company marched to Maastricht, Holland, on October 19, to provide security for the army headquarters. The detachments arrived three days later, except for Riddles and Third Platoon. They were dispatched to Hasselt for two days before being posted to Wijk. As Maastricht was an island, the new camp was accessible only by two bridges across the Maas River, and a third across the Albert Canal. This presented special difficulties for the MPs who were charged with maintaining a smooth flow of military traffic. As one veteran of the company later remembered, "European streets were not designed to accommodate American vehicles—they're too narrow. Also, almost all of the towns had town squares. We could put up signs re-directing the traffic flow so that everybody could get around." The men were also worked to curtail black market activities around Tongeren, Belgium, and seized several thousand dollars' worth of stolen government property. On November 15, the battalion was inactivated, and the four officers and 155 enlisted men of Company B redesignated the 822nd Military Police Company. Assigned to XIII Corps, the company had relocated to Hoensbroek in Holland on November 9, while the 1st Platoon moved forward to Teveren, Germany, on the twenty-first. The platoon was responsible for traffic control and directing the supply convoys that conveyed rations, ammunition, fuel, and other materiel to the front. Under heavy artillery fire at times, the platoon received orders to shift to Eygelshoven, Holland, on December 6. In the meantime, Ninth Army combat units pushed toward the Roer River, with the XIII Corps protecting the left flank from Maesyck to Immendorf. The enemy was dug-in on the high ground west of the Roer in a portion of the Siegfried Line. Through tremendous sacrifice, the American drive reached the river on December 14. Throughout the autumn, the Allies had been preparing for Operation GRENADE, the anticipated push from the Roer to the Rhine. Beginning on December 16, however, the German counteroffensive into the Ardennes forced the company to redeploy to the south to provide both convoy routing and area security for Ninth Army elements moving into Belgium. The XIII Corps assumed responsibility for the entire army-sized front.[17]

The 822nd was billeted in a Catholic school in Hoensbroek, but Riddles froze his feet in the frigid temperatures. An Army surgeon showed him a fifty-five-gallon drum full of hands and feet amputated from men who had suffered severe frostbite. The doctor warned him if he did not change his socks and keep his feet dry, his appendages would be in the barrel as well. The lieutenant and his driver, Private First Class Boyd Ray McKnight, ran a wire from the firewall of Riddles's jeep to the radiator and hung socks over the running engine. Every hour, Riddles would take off his boots and change his socks. The unit moved to Herzogenrath, Germany, on December 29.[18]

At some point during that bitter winter, Riddles had gone to check on his men. A soldier brought him a sandwich wrapped in wax paper, and, once he opened it, the lieutenant tore into the food. Later he learned from the cook the lunch meat had been spam. To his future son's everlasting sorrow, spam became one of Riddles's favorite foods.[19]

The only death of an 822nd MP in overseas service occurred on February 18, 1945, in Herzogenrath. Private First Class Kary E. Prickett was electrocuted while attempting to repair a communications wire. His body was badly burned prior to being discovered by fellow soldiers.[20]

Following a devastating saturation barrage of artillery that lasted forty-five minutes, the Ninth Army began crossing the flooded Roer on February 23. The 822nd was on the east side of the river four days later and began to man traffic control points along the narrow roads around Ercklenz and search vehicles for German infiltrators. In early March, the unit supplied personnel to guard bridges during the advance east. The company also detached teams to provide escorts for convoys en route to the front lines and security for POWs being returned to the rear. On March 7, company headquarters was reassigned to Viersen, the First Platoon to Wegberg and Waldaied, the Second to Hardt and Viersen, and the Third to Vorst, Süchteln, and Oldt. Seven days later, company headquarters stayed in Viersen and the Third remained in Vorst and Süchteln, while the First Platoon went to Anrath and the Second to Dülkin. Along with the corps headquarters, the company forded the Rhine near Wessel on April 1 before the MPs billeted in Heiden. Moving once more on April 4, Riddles's outfit marched for Lette and passed through Freckenhorst, Dehine, Buckburg, Burgdorf, and Gifhorn.[21]

On April 16, the 822nd participated in the final combat operation of the Ninth Army at Klötze. Several miles to the northeast, one thousand *soldats* and thirty tanks of the Panzer-Division "von Clausewitz" had attacked an American convoy on the main supply line and captured U.S. troops. Military policemen of the company's headquarters and First Platoon established road-blocks throughout the area, while armor, infantry, and artillery elements of the XIII Corps proceeded to the pocket and destroyed the German detachment. The Second Platoon of the 822nd then marched to Gardelegen and spent the last days of the war guarding a large, ruined barn. Inside the burned-out structure were the bodies of approximately one thousand Russian, Polish, and Hungarian slave laborers evacuated from the Dora-Mittelbau concentration camp. Retreating *Schutzstaffel* (SS) troops had locked their prisoners in the barn, set fire to gasoline-soaked straw, and massacred anyone who rushed out of the flames. For the Americans, the grisly scene was confirmation that the rumors of widespread German atrocities were true. An unidentified soldier from Long Island said, "I never was so sure before of exactly what I was fighting for. Before this you would have said those stories were propaganda, but now you know they weren't. There are the bodies and all those guys are dead." Beginning on April 21 or 22, two hundred citizens of Gardelegen were forced to dig graves for the murdered victims. The burial operation was completed on the twenty-fourth.[22]

Riddles had his own small part to play in the discovery of the Holocaust. Having studied German for many years in school, he was often assigned to interrogate prisoners. He also gathered photographic evidence of German war crimes in liberated concentration camps that was later used for the Nuremberg trial.[23]

While the corps mopped up remaining pockets of resistance in its sector, the 822nd was billeted in an old beer tavern between Burgdorf and Uetze on May 3, where the First and Second Platoons patrolled the roads, guarded thousands of prisoners, and learned of the German surrender. Billeted in a 235-year-old mansion, Major General Alvan Cullum Gillem, Jr., XIII Corps commander, met with Major-General Mikhail Aleksandrovich Siiazov, commanding the Soviet LXXXIX Rifle Corps, for a military review in Klötze on May 6. The generals recognized the Allied link-up on the Elbe, and the 822nd provided escorts and guards for the event. On the eleventh, the company moved to Gifhorn for six days, then to Peine and Hocht. Captain Keith was transferred to the Provost Marshal Section at corps headquarters on May 16, and Riddles assumed command of the company.[24]

Riddles's outfit was transferred to the Seventh Army on June 13. Their new assignment was to report to Lieutenant-General Lucius Dubignon Clay in Hochst, Germany, and perform guard duties for the newly established U.S. Group Control Council. The organization had been established to form a military government that would gradually transfer control of the areas of Germany and the sector of Berlin under U.S. Army administration to civilian authority. Arriving in Hocht, Riddles sent an advance team of the First Platoon into Berlin in preparation for the July 4 ceremony. The remainder of the company arrived in the German capital on August 12. The same day, Riddles and his men were assigned to provide security for the Office of Military Government United States (OMGUS) headquarters compound on the Kronprinz-Allee. Shedding their combat posture, the personnel of the 822nd furnished guards for individual buildings and the three perimeter gates. Created on October 1, OMGUS consolidated the numerous military government offices in Germany into one administrative command.[25]

Riddles was encouraged by his superiors to remain in the military, but he had had his fill of war. He also wanted to return home and pursue his dream of becoming a Texas Ranger. Relieved of command on October 3, Riddles shipped home aboard the U.S.A.T. *Marshall Victory* and separated from service at Fort Sam Houston on November 23 with the rank of captain. In addition to reuniting with Loneta, his homecoming was possibly brightened when McKenzie Methodist Church in Honey Grove honored returning veterans, including Riddles, with a banquet on December 12. His terminal leave ended on February 4, 1946. For his wartime service, Riddles received the Bronze Star, the Good Conduct Medal, the Service Lapel Button WWII, and the World War II Victory Medal.[26]

Trading uniforms, Riddles was reinstated into the Highway Patrol. Stationed in the Lubbock district, his captain was Edwin L. Posey. Riddles and his bride settled into their share of the post-war American Dream with a house at 2206 Avenue T in Lubbock. Loneta was a parishioner of her father's church, whereas Riddles was a Methodist. He was encouraged to convert, although he never did. While not given to romantic gestures, Riddles proved to be a loyal, steadfast husband. Their son, James Boyd Riddles, was born on December 24, 1946. His middle name was derived from Riddles' wartime driver.[27]

His son later recalled, "My father did not walk around with his feelings on his sleeve, but some things were critically important to him." As a parent, Riddles demanded the best of his only child's abilities and wanted him to be a winner. Early on, James Boyd learned to live his own life and not be just James E. Riddles's son. His father encouraged him in that goal and, indeed, once threatened to block James Boyd's application to the Highway Patrol. By the late 1960s, the counterculture had spawned an atmosphere of hatred toward law enforcement, and Riddles did not want his son to have to deal with that turmoil.[28]

One event common to the careers of highway patrolmen everywhere is automobile accidents. On June 8, 1946, a married couple from Ohio was killed in the town of Sudan when the motorcycle they were both riding collided with a dump truck at the intersection of U.S. Highway 84 and Commerce Street. Riddles and his partner, Thomas Asa Rowland, investigated the accident. The driver of the truck pled guilty to not having a commercial license and was fined one dollar and court costs in justice court. He was also charged in Lamb County court with negligent homicide and posted a bond of fifteen hundred dollars.[29]

As part of their two-day Fourth of July celebration, the town of Floydada in Floyd County hosted General Jonathan Mayhew Wainwright IV, hero of Bataan and Corregidor. When the Medal of Honor recipient's C-47 landed in Lubbock, he found Riddles and Rowland waiting to escort him to the event. Gathered in Floydada's courthouse square, a crowd of fifteen thousand listened to Wainwright's address, although some expressed disappointment he did not mention his forty months in Japanese captivity. The two patrolmen accompanied the general back to Lubbock, where he caught his flight to San Antonio.[30]

On October 19, 1947, two men died in an automobile accident four miles south of Dickins on Highway 70. Seven others were injured less seriously.

Riddles and Trooper Lowndes Womack Wilhite, Jr. investigated and filed charges against one of the drivers for negligent homicide and failure to possess a driver's license.[31]

The next few years were busy ones for Riddles. The family moved into a three-bedroom home at 1926 22nd Street in Lubbock.[32] On December 9, 1948, he began attending Texas Tech University as a student and completed twelve college hours of Spanish.[33] At this time, Glenn Elliott was a young veteran living across the street from Riddles's parents in Windom. The future Ranger legend credited Riddles with encouraging him to seek a career in law enforcement.[34]

Richard McDonald, a cotton picker, was fatally shot at a farm six miles east of Lorenzo on December 20, 1949. Crosby County Sheriff Foy Addison and Assistant District Attorney Alldridge Wendell Salyars conducted an investigation and received assistance from Rangers Paul Raymond Waters and William Erastus "Rass" Renfrow, Deputies Marshall Odell Pounds and W. T. Harrington, and Riddles. Another picker, Herman Johnson, was arrested on a charge of murder with malice and placed in the county jail in Crosbyton. The sheriff filed a complaint before Justice of the Peace J. E. Richardson, who denied the suspect bond.[35]

In March 1951, Riddles was partnered with Clayton Weldon "Clay" Bednar and worked with him for the next year. Bednar would credit Riddles with teaching him "more about law enforcement during that time than I ever learned from anyone or anyplace. Jim had the maturity and wisdom which was so important to me." Ridles's influence was apparently significant as Bednar became a Ranger in 1961 and served honorably for twenty years.[36] The following year, Riddles's performance was recognized with an assignment to the Motor Vehicle Inspection Division as an inspector.[37]

Based on Captain Robert A. Crowder's recommendation, Colonel Garrison appointed Riddles to Company B, Texas Rangers on December 1, 1952. He worked briefly in Baird before being assigned to Breckenridge.[38] With his work ethic, Riddles was entering the Ranger service at an auspicious time. Working alone or with local, state, and federal authorities, the Rangers conducted 18,548 criminal investigations from September 1, 1952, to August 31, 1954.[39]

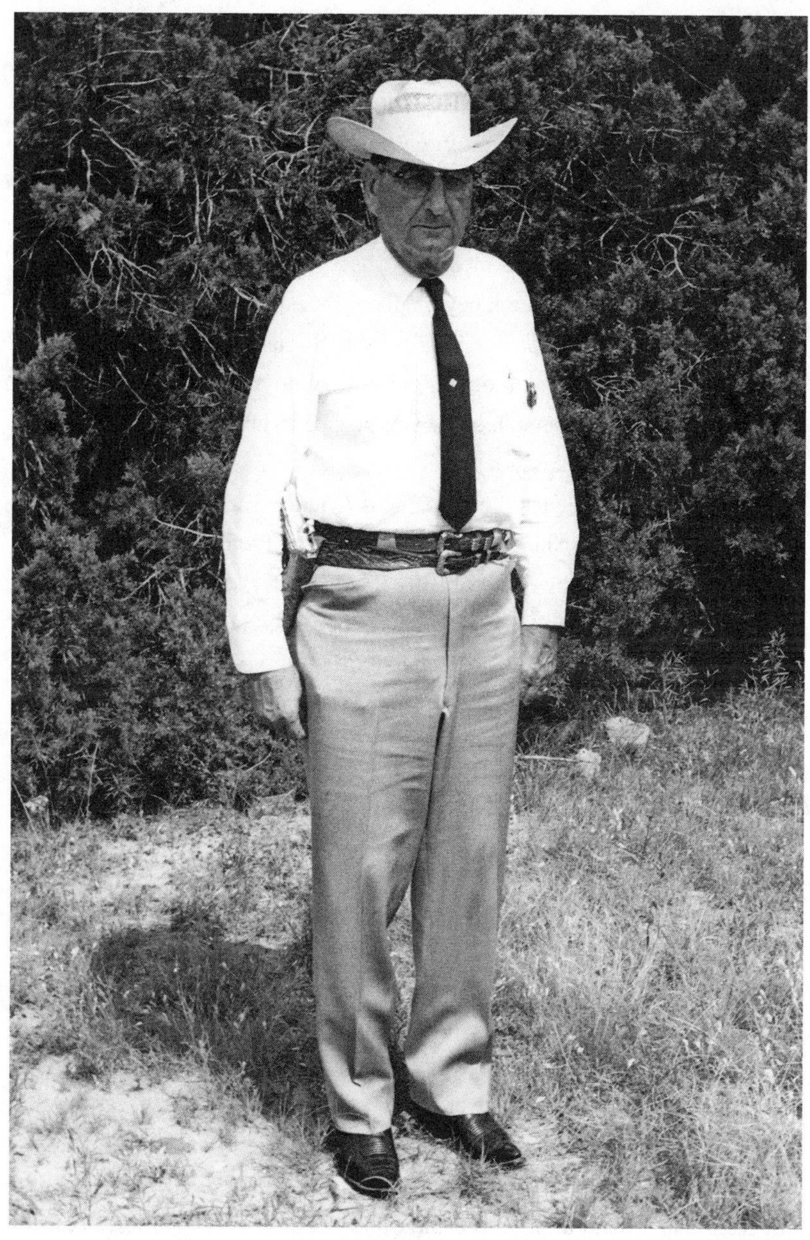

Raymond Waters. *Courtesy Texas Ranger Hall of Fame and Museum, Waco, TX.*

In describing the type of officer his father was, James Boyd summed it up in two words: "a coach." He continued, "He wasn't about telling people what to do, he could if he needed to. He was mostly about, 'okay, you're doing this, what can I do to assist you in getting out of it.' Most of the [Rangers under his command] genuinely cared about him." The same held true for the men who had served with him in the military. Despite being only ten years older than the majority of his men, "he was a father figure to a lot of them." Encouraged by Riddles to look beyond the war, a significant number returned to the States and played professional sports. Sometimes he would help the people he had sent to prison obtain gainful employment after their release. "He was a very caring person, but if you pushed it, he had a button that said, 'this was all you get,'" his son James said.[40]

On June 18, 1953, Riddles, Stephens County Sheriff Ira Tom Offield, and Callahan County Sheriff Joseph Elias "Joe" Pierce were called on to assist in investigating the death of Billy Frank West, an Odessa-based roustabout for the Standard Oil Company. West's body had been discovered earlier in the day inside his wrecked 1953 Chevrolet Bel Air on U.S. Highway 80, eight miles east of Elmdale. Ranger James Carson "Jim" Paulk and officers from the Abilene Police Department, Taylor County Sheriff's Department, and Texas Highway Patrol also worked the case. Although the victim's throat had been deeply cut, little blood was found at the scene suggesting the possible murder had taken place elsewhere. Robbery was ruled out as a motive, as nearly two hundred dollars in cash, two suitcases containing quality clothing, and several pieces of expensive fishing gear were recovered from Mathis's vehicle. The investigators eventually determined West's death may have been the result of an auto accident, and his wound was derived from contact with a chrome portion of the steering wheel.[41]

The superintendent's office at the Breckenridge high school was burglarized sometime during the night of September 11. The offenders gained entry through an exterior window. In what was termed as an "amateurish" job, the thieves escaped with almost four thousand dollars in cash. Riddles assisted Police Chief John Ollie Jackson and Deputy Sheriff Al Ramsey in investigating the case. Fingerprints were collected from crowbars, chisels, and other tools left at the scene.[42]

The following day, in an unrelated incident, Riddles was fingerprinting burglary and auto theft suspect Harvey J. Wilson, Jr. on the first floor of the Callahan County jail. As a safety measure, the Ranger had handed his .45-caliber pistol to Sheriff Pierce, who placed the sidearm in a desk drawer. While being escorted back upstairs to the jail cells, Wilson suddenly opened the drawer and seized the weapon. Doubtless to their chagrin, Riddles and Sheriff Pierce were forced by the now-armed prisoner to enter his cell. To add insult to injury, Wilson fled in the Ranger's black 1953 Ford, but not before leaving Riddles's gun in the jail. The sheriff's wife released the two officers from their confinement. Roadblocks were erected in a fifty-mile radius, but the fugitive remained at large. Even while working up the high school burglary, Riddles assisted county officers in searching the Coleman area. Later in the day, his car was found in good working order in a pasture approximately five miles south of Albany. Several firearms and ammunition were still inside the vehicle. The authorities expanded their search over the desolate ranchlands, and the escapee was apprehended by highway patrol units south of Putnam. Wilson was convicted of armed robbery in Judge Black's courtroom and sentenced to seven years in prison. The defendant also pled guilty to burglary and auto theft charges, and drew five- and two-year sentences to run concurrently.[43]

Riddles caught a break in the high school burglary case, and nineteen-year-old Bobby Ralph Lott of Fort Worth was charged in Leslie Thorpe Woodall's justice court on September 15. He had been arrested earlier in the day in Ada, Oklahoma, and Riddles and Offield transported him back to Breckenridge. Two other men were sought in connection with the crime.[44]

While escaping from the Fisher County jail on December 15, 1953, three prisoners beat Sheriff Robert Lee "Bogue" Wilkins with a length of chain and two shotguns. They then led more than thirty law officers and seventy civilians on a massive manhunt across brushy, broken terrain. In addition to Riddles and Rangers Raymond Waters, Jim Paulk, Truman Stone, and George William Burnup, the posse was comprised of Taylor County Sheriff Edwin Eugene Powell, Highway Patrolmen, two U.S. Border Patrolmen, Texas & Pacific Railroad special agents, and lawmen from Taylor, Scurry, Stonewall, Nolan, Ward, Baylor, Haskell, Shackleford, and Brown Counties. They utilized airplanes, automobiles, horses, and walkie-talkie radios to track the escapees. The chase finally ended in northeast Nolan County on December 17, when bloodhounds treed the fugitives eight miles east of Sweetwater and one mile north of U.S. Highway 80. The trio was driven by Riddles and Highway Patrol Sergeant Homer Bailey to the county jail in Abilene to await the arrival of Fisher County officers. District Attorney William Kenton "Bill" Tippen filed charges in 104th District Court against each prisoner for jailbreaking and assault to murder with malice.[45]

Burglars broke into the school tax assessor-collector's office located in Olney High School on the night of February 13, 1954, found nothing of value, and set fire to the room. The blaze consumed the assessor's records and equipment, but volunteer fire crews were able to save the rest of the building. Early the next morning, another prowler gained entry in the Carter Chevrolet dealership and stole $115 in cash. Riddles was called to assist in the investigation alongside Police Chief John Wilkins, Young County Sheriff John Edwards, and Deputy Sheriff Glenn Greer Dunaway. Few clues made themselves available to the lawmen. After two weeks of questioning, Riddles and Deputy Hugh Casey took four youths to Austin where they voluntarily submitted to lie detector tests. The suspects were cleared of involvement.[46]

Ernest Richard Windham shot and killed his brother, John, during an argument on the latter's ranch seven miles north of Clyde on February 16. While seated in his pickup, the victim was struck in the head by a .32-caliber bullet that killed him instantly. County Attorney Felix Mitchell filed a murder complaint with Justice of the Peace William Lawrence Bowlus, and Ernest was held in the Callahan County jail. The suspect did not request bail or an examining trial. Riddles, Mitchell, Sheriff Joe Pierce, and District Attorney Wiley Caffey cooperated in the investigation.[47]

On April 1, the body of Elvis Lee Beall of Mineral Wells was found floating on Possum Kingdom Lake one hundred yards from shore. Along with fellow fisherman Paul Simpson of Weatherford, the dead man had been missing since March 21. Directed by Riddles and Highway Patrolman Charles Swygert, rescue squads from Mineral Wells, Gradford, Breckenridge, and Fort Worth dragged the lake for Simpson. Searchers located the pair's overturned boat and, more than three miles distant, an oar and a felt hat believed to have belonged to Beall.[48]

Twenty-six-year-old Leah Naomi Montgomery was found dead in her Cross Plains home on February 2, 1955, the apparent victim of an accidental fall in the bathtub. Riddles, District Attorney Caffey, and Ranger Paulk were called to investigate the death, and the former interviewed the victim's husband, twenty-year-old John D. Montgomery. In a conversation at the kitchen table, the Ranger learned of the couple's troubled marriage. Additionally, each may have been involved in spouse-swapping affairs with neighbors Albert "Red" and Christine Ussery. Based on this information, Red Ussery was a suspect in the early stages of the investigation. However, after an autopsy confirmed Leah drowned, a complaint was filed in justice court charging John Montgomery with her murder. Riddles and Sheriff Homer Price took the suspect into custody the same day. Montgomery appeared before Justice Bowlus for an examining trial, and the Forty-second District Court grand jury indicted him on the homicide charge.[49]

Montgomery was tried in Baird on March 7, 1955, but the jury deadlocked. The case was transferred on a change of venue to Abilene, and the second trial opened on September 27. Doctor Jarrett Earle Williams, a pathologist at Hendrick Memorial Hospital, testified that the fatal blow to Leah's head had come from a blunt instrument rather than the edge of the tub. Mrs. Ussery alleged her husband and the victim had been engaged in a romantic relationship, and both couples were on the verge of divorce. The second of approximately forty prosecution witnesses, Riddles testified to removing two blood-stained shirts from the Montgomery home and scrapings from under the defendant's fingernails. The blood was discovered to be Type O, which was that of both Montgomerys. The defense attorneys objected to the discussion between Riddles and Montgomery being entered into evidence, as the latter had been technically under arrest yet not given statutory warning. Judge Floyd Jones allowed the kitchen table dialog, but not a later interview at the courthouse in Baird. Calling twenty-eight witnesses to the stand on the last day alone, the prosecution rested on September 28. The defendant was acquitted the following day after two hours of jury deliberation.[50]

Charlie Ray Price was engaged in an altercation with Robert Armor in a tavern near Breckenridge on March 24, 1955. The scuffle between the two began inside the bar where Price clubbed Armor over the head with a handgun. The weapon discharged, and the bullet broke a window. The quarrel spilled outside, where Price attempted to force Armor into a pickup truck. The pistol fired once more, and Armor's wife, Sue, was fatally struck. Price went to the sheriff's office and related how he had killed Mrs. Armor. Claiming the shooting had been an accident, he was released without charges being filed. Riddles investigated the incident and testified for the prosecution in the subsequent trial in Forty-second District Court. Price was found guilty of Sue's murder and received a three-year suspended sentence. The convicted man waived the statutory two-day waiting period, and District Judge James Robert Black, Sr. immediately imposed sentencing.[51]

One hundred and forty employees of the Oil City Iron Works in Corsicana went on strike on January 2, 1956. Mayor Walter Erwin requested state assistance to keep the peace. Along with Rangers Robert Lee "Bob" Badgett and Ernest Daniel, Captain Crowder was dispatched to the scene on the fourteenth. The captain advised the press, "We will stay as long as we are needed." He further emphasized that the state officers were there to assist local law enforcement in keeping the peace, and not to interfere in the strike. Ranger George Marvin Roach of Stephenville reported to Crowder the next day. Riddles and Byron Odell Currin of Vernon were assigned to the detail and arrived in town on January 16. The state officers found the town quiet, and Riddles and Currin were withdrawn after a week.[52]

Raymond Harwell, a twenty-four-year-old former mental patient, shot his stepfather, George Lafayette Reeder, on July 9 at their farmhouse near Abilene. Reeder's wound proved to be nonfatal. Fleeing, the suspect was spotted early the next morning by Riddles, as the suspect emerged from under a bridge on Highway 36, ten miles southeast of Abilene. The Ranger radioed for backup, and, joined by twelve highway patrolmen and Callahan County deputies, took Harwell into custody in a pasture south of Ray's Service Station without incident. The fugitive was not armed at the time of his arrest.[53]

When not working, Riddles hunted deer and doves and liked to take his son fishing. He collected firearms, and James Boyd was the only student in elementary school who shot pistols in a nearby quarry at the end of the day. True of many Rangers of his generation, Riddles rarely took vacations. His son recalled one that consisted of a drive from Austin to San Benito to South Padre Island. After a stay of ten minutes, they drove back to Austin.[54]

As part of the reorganization implemented by Colonel Garrison on September 1, 1957, Riddles was transferred from Breckenridge to Jacksboro.[55] He hardly had time to get settled before he was promoted to the rank of sergeant on December 28 and assigned to Company F in Waco. In his new position, he served as second-in-command to Captain Clint Peoples.[56]

On June 9, 1958, Waco authorities received information that two Houston youths suspecting of raping a woman one week prior were working in Lorena. Riddles, Captain Peoples, Detective Tilley Saunders Buchanan, and Patrolman Jesse Moring traveled to the aforementioned town. One of the suspects was arrested there, while the other was apprehended in Waco. Interviewed in the Waco city jail, the younger of the pair told investigators how he and his accomplice had run the victim off a deserted road, forced her into the back seat of their car, and sexually assaulted her at knifepoint. Houston police officers arrived in Waco on the tenth to take the two rapists back to face justice.[57]

On October 28, 1958, the Sears, Roebuck & Co. store in Corsicana was burglarized of $250 in merchandise, including a .22 semiautomatic pistol. Later in the day, Riddles arrived in town to process fingerprints found at the crime scene. The evidence pointed to L. T. Townley as the perpetrator, but he had escaped from the Navarro County jail early that morning. While making his getaway, he struck jailer Vernon Lambert with a concrete-filled sock. The fugitive's description was broadcast over the state's police radio network. The FBI entered the case on October 31 when a special agent conferred with Sheriff Rufus Pevehouse on possible charges of unlawful flight to avoid prosecution. Townley was already under indictment for burglary, and the grand jury returned two true bills on an additional charge of burglary and another for assault with intent to murder. Townley would remain at large until July 8, 1959, when he was apprehended at his parents' home in Corsicana. The next day, he pleaded guilty to all charges in district court and received a sentence of two to twelve years for the burglary plea and two to fifteen years for assault.[58]

Although the Rangers were tasked with investigating major crimes, often their cases were more mundane in nature. On January 19, 1959, Riddles, Ranger John Henry "Johnny" Krumnow, and Deputy Sheriff Ray Johnson arrested a local man on a gambling charge. The case was settled the following day with a guilty plea and a nineteen dollar fine in Justice of the Peace John Cabaniss's court. Riddles and Captain Peoples arrested an Axtell man on March 9 for running an illegal cockfighting pit seven miles east of town on the Corsicana highway. The defendant pleaded guilty before Justice Cabaniss, who fined him one hundred dollars and court costs.[59]

When Ranger John Dudley White, Jr. was relocated to Midland, Riddles moved to Austin in June 1959. Private William Delpard "Bill" Wilson assisted the sergeant in the state capital from October 9, 1961, to February 1, 1967.[60]

Jim Riddles, war veteran and professional law officer, was afraid of nothing, except his wife's wrath. One case in point concerned the time Riddles and his son were at Camp Mabry breaking a horse. The younger man was atop the animal, and the steed ran through a barn. The low doorframe swept James Boyd out of the saddle into a large pile of boulders, then the horse kicked him. The bloodied youth was on his hands and knees when Riddles ran up to him. He looked at his son, then told him, "Don't tell your mother." The two Riddles drove home and attempted to nonchalantly enter the house, but Loneta came outside instead. She took one look at her son and exclaimed, "What happened!?" James Boyd was in the hospital for two days.[61]

Riddles enjoyed lasting friendships with a number of fellow Texas Rangers, including Walter Russell, Bill Wilson, Hyman Radford "Lefty" Block, Jim Ray (a close friend of Loneta), and Glenn Elliott. Riddles would often find a reason to visit Elliott and ensure they discussed official business, so he could justify using the gasoline in his state-issued car. Charlie Miller was a good family friend. While some looked askance at Miller's old school methods, Riddles understood the veteran Ranger's value, and Miller in turn "would have walked through hell" for his sergeant.[62]

On February 16, 1962, hotel desk clerk Eddie Paul Hein walked into the office of Jackson County Sheriff Kenneth Spears in Altus, Oklahoma, and confessed to slaying William Grimes "Babe" Womack in Taylor, Texas, twenty-six years previously. Hired to commit the act in exchange for fifteen thousand dollars, the killer had fatally struck the victim on the head with an iron pipe on April 3, 1936. The sheriff later quoted Hein: "I can not [*sic*] live with it any longer." Ranger Bryan Curbin of Wichita Falls took the suspect into custody, and Riddles informed the Oklahoma authorities the confession had been confirmed by a lie detector. Hein and Charles "Bubba" Hague, Womack's nephew who had allegedly paid for the murder, were held in the Williamson County jail. Hague was not indicted, and Hein received a five-year suspended sentence at his trial.[63]

"He could be as nice as a preacher in church, and he could be as mean as a snake," Riddles's son said of his father. "I think for that reason, he was probably successful as a Ranger, because his specialty was interrogation. Most of the time, the people he interrogated wanted to get it off their conscience, and he gave them an avenue that went a little deeper than just two people talking. He could bring religion into it from the perspective of [at] some point you're going to have to own this. If you did it, you did it."[64] Local officers also respected Riddles' abilities as an interrogator. One county sheriff was quoted as saying, "I'd rather have my suspect interrogated for an hour or two by Ranger Riddles than run him on a polygraph machine."[65]

On November 11, 1963, Police Chief James Melton Mumford of Elgin, a small town east of Austin, responded to a call for assistance from State Trooper Tommy Moseley. The patrolman was in pursuit of a stolen 1962 Volkswagen on Highway 290 and subsequently forced the vehicle's driver off the road. Twenty-year-old Rudolph Grady Coffey leaped from the car and opened fire with a Walther P-38, wounding Moseley with the first shot. He continued to shoot at the trooper. Mumford arrived on the scene and emptied his .45 pistol at the assailant. Reloading, the chief stepped from his vehicle when Coffey shot him in the head. Slumping back into his car, Mumford died instantly. The youth, with the assistance of his accomplice, sixteen-year-old Joyce Ann Gordon, fired a total of seventeen shots. Moseley, although struck in the chest, managed to crawl down the side of a hill and flag a motorist driving through the underpass. Moments after killing Mumford, the suspects were subdued and captured by three passing truck drivers. Robert Owen, a DPS employee and former Elgin dispatcher, came across the two parked patrol cars, and Chief Mumford's body, and radioed the DPS dispatcher that an officer was down. Law enforcement personnel from across Central Texas raced to the scene. Riddles was one of the first to arrive and assisted in taking the two young suspects to the city jail. The subjects of a six-state alert for two gas station robberies and a pair of kidnappings in Florida and car thefts in Mississippi, Coffey and Gordon were charged in Milton John Frenzel, Sr.'s justice court with murder and assault with intent to commit murder. Mosley was taken to the Elgin hospital, then immediately transported to Brackenridge Hospital in Austin for advanced medical treatment. After emergency surgery, the patrolman eventually recovered.[66]

Riddles then stopped what would have possibly been the last lynching by vigilantes in Texas. Having heard of the shooting of the two law officers, an angry mob of approximately two hundred townspeople came to the jail with a rope for Coffey. "Hang him," the crowd chanted. Riddles went outside and ordered them to disband. When the mob refused, the Ranger told them it would be a shame to kill any of them over such a worthless SOB, but he would shoot the first man to step onto the porch. The crowd dispersed, and Coffey was transported to the Travis County jail for his own protection. Gordon was placed in the Garden House juvenile hall in Austin.[67]

The couple was transferred to the Bastrop County jail on November 18. Confessing to the crime, Coffey was indicted eleven days later. As a juvenile, Gordon was not charged at that time, but Judge Henry Warren Sebesta ordered her transferred to the State School for Girls at Gatesville. The jurist ruled she would remain until her eighteenth birthday when she would be charged with accessory to murder as an adult.[68]

District Judge Leslie D. Williams of the Twenty-first District Court granted a change of venue in Coffey's case to La Grange. The following month, Coffey's lawyers argued the case should be removed from Central Texas entirely, but Judge J. Lee Dittert overruled the motion and set the trial for April 27, 1964. However, on May 4, Judge Dittert reversed himself and sent the case back to Bastrop County. The murder trial was then transferred to the Eighty-fifth District Court in Bryan on December 31.[69]

As the Coffey case was progressing, Raymond Earl "Blackie" Hawkins died in the parking lot of the Longhorn service station in Luling on November 17, 1964, when his truck cab was destroyed by nitrate-based explosives. The blast resulted in portions of his lower extremities being scattered over a one-hundred-foot radius. Riddles and Ranger Bill Wilson investigated, and the evidence quickly pointed to Walter Jones, Hawkins's coworker at the Westwood Furniture Company in San Marcos. Riddles drove to the Veterans Administration Hospital in Kerrville where Jones had admitted himself on the sixteenth. "He was the best suspect we had," the Ranger later testified. Jones talked freely and admitted to knowing Hawkins's vehicle would be left unattended for two days. He also confessed to having experience with dynamite. After apprising the suspect of his rights, Wilson took a sworn statement from Jones. Lorene was indicted for conspiracy to commit murder and released on $2,500 bail. The case was subject to several hindrances, including one mistrial and several continuances.[70]

While the wheels of justice slowly ground forward, skeletal remains were discovered on February 2, 1965, by a Highway Department employee near Interstate 35 three miles south of Belton. An autopsy confirmed the victim had been killed by two .22-caliber bullets. Two days later, through laundry marks and the widow's positive identification, authorities ascertained the dead man to be James B. Taylor, a former soldier stationed at Fort Hood. Working up the case, investigators determined Taylor had left his residence on November 4, 1964, and traveled to San Antonio to make arrangements concerning his retirement pay. The next day, his vehicle was found abandoned on the street. On February 8, Harold Lee Rohloff was arrested at his San Antonio apartment on a warrant from Bell County charging him with Taylor's murder. That same evening, Riddles and Bill Wilson escorted the suspect to Austin. The Rangers questioned Rohloff, who denied any involvement. The suspect was given a lie detector test, but because he had been drinking the results were inconclusive. Rohloff was taken to Belton and placed in jail.[71]

The Coffey trial finally began with jury selection on February 15. On the fourth day, defense attorneys challenged the admissibility of Coffey's sixteen-page confession. Riddles and the other officers present during the interview testified that no force or coercion had been used. District Judge John M. Barron ruled the defendant's statement was allowable. The case went to the jury on the twentieth, and they returned a verdict of guilty; Coffey was given a life sentence.[72]

Victoria County Sheriff Montie William Marshall, Captain Alfred Young Allee, and DPS intelligence chief Otis Newton "Newt" Humphreys, Sr. led twelve state officers in simultaneous raids on the local Veterans of Foreign Wars post, the Elks Club, and the American Legion post on June 23. Riddles, Bill Wilson, Frank Horger, Jack Van Cleve, and Toliver Henry "Tol" Dawson comprised the Rangers on the team, and they were joined by five of Humphreys's agents. Thirty-one slot machines, one marble table, thirteen dollars in quarters, and record books were seized, and two club officers and managers were charged with felonious violation of the state's anti-gambling laws. Justice of the Peace Alfred Charles Baass set bonds at one thousand dollars each. However, despite its relative success, the operation did not begin on a positive note. While reconnoitering their intended targets earlier in the day, Riddles and some of his colleagues were sitting in a parked car at the intersection of Goliad Highway and the Upper Valley Mission Road. Their vehicle was suddenly struck on the left rear bumper by a truck turning onto the highway from the farm road. The accident resulted in no injuries, and the lawmen were able to complete their assignment.[73]

The body of Harold Brooks Flory was found on September 3 in the San Marcos River near Luling. Before being dumped in the water, he had been bludgeoned to death. The dead man's pockets were turned out, and his killer subsequently stole his pickup. Cardwell County Sheriff Desmond Reed was unable to find witnesses to the homicide. Riddles was placed in charge of the investigation, and he issued a statewide alert for the missing truck. The vehicle was quickly located in Sayre, Oklahoma, and Riddles traveled to the Sooner State to recover the truck and attempt to determine who had driven it there. Based on fingerprint evidence, murder charges were filed against Donald Melvin Boggs, and a nationwide bulletin was issued for his arrest. Texas authorities consulted with Arizona officials concerning a possible connection between Flory's murder and that of two men who were shot to death near U.S. 66 and Ashfork. Boggs was picked up in Flagstaff on September 9 driving one of the Arizona victim's car, and he gave a full confession.[74]

After a stern warning from Judge Leslie Williams to the officers of the court about speaking to the press, the trial of Joyce Gordon opened on January 19, 1966. Patrolman Mosley and two of the truck drivers were the first of six prosecution witnesses to take the stand. After two days of testimony, the case went to the jury. However, the members deadlocked, and Judge Williams declared a mistrial.[75]

Beginning on May 10, 1967, Walter Jones was finally tried for the murder of Blackie Hawkins in Twenty-second District Judge Diaz Bromfield Wood's courtroom in New Braunfels. Among the state's witnesses, Lorene Hawkins testified that her husband had beat her, but denied she had asked Jones to tamper with the victim's truck. The trial ended in a hung jury. In his second trial the next year, Jones read his statement into evidence that he and Lorene Hawkins, the victim's widow, had been sexually intimate and discussed "getting rid" of her husband. Riddles testified that Jones had confessed to planning with Lorene to provoke an argument with Hawkins and kill him in "self-defense." He also described finding a suicide note written by Lorene to Jones. However, District Judge Paul Huser Schulenburg tossed out some physical evidence admitted in the previous trial. On April 26, Jones was found not guilty.[76]

Turning to another homicide case, Riddles worked with the Georgetown Police Department, the Williamson County Sheriff's Department, and other DPS officers to solve the shocking crime. Fifteen-year-old James Gordon Wolcott was charged with murdering his parents, Gordon and Elizabeth (Libby), and his seventeen-year-old sister, also named Elizabeth, in Georgetown on August 5, 1967. Investigators determined Wolcott had fired seven "well-aimed" shots into the victims with a .22 rifle, and there were no signs of struggle. The underage suspect was taken before County Judge Sam V. Stone, who ordered him held pending a juvenile delinquency hearing. In the meantime, Wolcott, who turned sixteen in the county jail, underwent psychiatric tests to determine his mental competency. The hearing opened on September 13 in Williamson County Court, and Judge Stone waived juvenile jurisdiction over Wolcott and certified him as an adult. Riddles appeared before Twenty-second District Court Judge Kirby Vance on September 26 during the subsequent examining trial. The defendant was bound over to the grand jury, which indicted him on three counts of murder with malice.[77]

Following the death of Jim Paulk on September 20, 1967, Riddles was promoted captain of Company E in Midland on December 1. Jim Ray was promoted to sergeant of the company on the same day.[78] Captain Riddles quickly became confident that every Ranger in his company was capable of handling any investigation or situation that arose. He was often heard to declare, "my Rangers don't need supervision in the field. If they needed field supervision they wouldn't be Rangers. Occasionally they may need some help and that's my job."[79] If the captain needed to issue a reprimand, he did so in private and in a manner that left the culprit ashamed of disappointing his superior. As a result of his command style, Company E developed such a strong *espirit de corps* that the members began calling themselves "Riddles' Rangers."[80]

As previously noted, one of Riddles's greatest passions was sports. He held season passes to the Midland baseball teams. One time a key player for the San Marcos high school football team got into trouble with the law; alcohol was involved. The sheriff arrested the player one day before a game. Riddles visited the jail and convinced the sheriff to release the youth into his custody. The captain then took the football athlete to the game, where he played one of his best performances. Afterward, Riddles took the teenager back to jail.[81]

The trial of James Wolcott for only his father's murder opened in Georgetown on January 29, 1968, with jury selection. In pretrial hearings, the defendant had entered a plea of not guilty due to temporary insanity. Once the jury was seated, defense attorneys argued he suffered from paranoid schizophrenia and delusions of persecution, and had regularly sniffed glue in the seven months prior to the murders. The prosecution countered that Wolcott was in full possession of his faculties. Riddles took the witness stand and, over defense objections, testified the teenager had confessed he killed his parents because he hated them. While recounting the sequence of events to the Ranger, Wolcott also revealed where he had hidden the rifle. The case was given to the jury, which accepted the insanity plea and acquitted the remorseless Wolcott on February 1. Judge Vance committed the youth to Rusk State Hospital.[82]

The Texas Rangers took the lead in a series of coordinated raids on suspected gambling houses in key cities. Working in conjunction with local departments, Riddles supervised his company's activities in Lubbock, Midland, and Odessa, while Captain Peoples handled Mexia and Austin. Rangers Dudley White, John Wood, and Robert Charles "Bob" Favor of Company D struck houses in Victoria and San Antonio. Other Rangers were active in Dallas and Houston. The targeted residence in Odessa contained no evidence of gaming, but one of two in Midland did hold signs of a bookmaking operation. Altogether, the raids resulted in a total of twenty arrests.[83]

Sixty thousand members of the Oil, Chemical, and Atomic Workers Union went on a nationwide strike on January 4, 1969, against major oil companies. While the walk-out affected mostly facilities on the Gulf Coast, the Sinclair Oil

Arthur Watts Hill, Max Westerman, Ralph Rohatch, and Bob Crowder (L to R). *Courtesy Texas Ranger Hall of Fame and Museum, Waco, TX.*

switch stations and pipelines in the Permian Basin also witnessed some unrest. Riddles, Rangers Arthur Hill, Alfred Allee, Jr., and Ralph Rohatsch worked with Schleicher County Sheriff Orval Edmiston and Deputy Jack Jones to keep order at Sinclair's Hulldale Plant and nearby booster stations.[84]

Twenty-seven-year-old Nancy Lee Mitchell disappeared from her Kermit home on September 16, 1970. Her two children were found asleep when their father returned from work, and there were no signs of struggle in the house. However, slashed clothing identified as belonging to the missing housewife was discovered scattered along Highway 302, some five miles east of town. Local authorities conducted an "intensive search" for Nancy, and a statewide all-points bulletin was issued. Riddles assisted Winkler County Sheriff Lynn Bates "Bill" Eddins in the investigation, and both suspected foul play. The captain reported his office was working on several leads, mostly by process of elimination. Regrettably, within two weeks, the case came to a standstill.[85]

On May 22, 1971, the $18.6 million LBJ Library was dedicated on the University of Texas campus as the official repository of the former president's papers. President Richard Nixon, Vice President Spiro Agnew, and various congressmen were on hand for the event; so was about half of the entire Ranger service, including some from Company E. As the dignitaries spoke, war protestors gathered on 26th and Red River Streets. The Rangers arrayed themselves across Red River to keep the demonstrators from approaching the library. Rangers avoided the bags filled with human excrement and urine that the activists hurled.[86]

Before his men had left West Texas for Austin, Riddles had counseled them, "Boys, just do the needful." With the autonomy the captain's guidance gave them, the Rangers selected targets in case the protestors charged the lawmen's line. Fortunately for the unruly demonstrators, they dispersed and moved to another area of town. Twenty-seven activists would be arrested by the end of the day, mostly by Austin police officers.[87]

In the months since Nancy Mitchell's disappearance, Riddles had continued to work up the case. Tragically, her skeletal remains were found on June 4, 1971, on a sandy, mesquite-covered oil lease east of Kermit. The coroner's inquest noted the cause of death was unknown, but Nancy was "probably murdered." Ranger Tol Dawson and Chief Deputy William H. Sage escorted the bones to the DPS laboratory for testing, then to the Dallas County medical examiner. The Dallas authorities were interested due to a number of similar deaths in their jurisdiction.[88]

Michael Ray Mathis of Midland drove to the Thrifty Lodge on West Fourth Street in Big Spring on June 13, 1971, and shot to death used car salesman Bobby Ray Johnson. Following the murder, Mathis placed Johnson's body in the trunk of his car and returned home. That same day, Riddles received a telephoned tip from Mathis's wife in San Angelo regarding the location of the victim. The captain contacted Midland Police Chief E. J. "Jay" Banks, who subsequently found blood, four spent cartridge casings from a .30-30 rifle, and "evidence of extensive use of pills" in Johnson's motel room. Riddles and eighteen Rangers, Midland police officers, and sheriff's deputies surrounded Mathis's home after quietly evacuating nearby residents. The suspect was already under indictment in Tom Green County for assault with intent to murder. When Mathis was ordered to surrender, he answered with gunshots. Riddles and the others returned fire. Tear gas canisters were lobbed into the residence, one of which accidentally started a fire. The officers entered the burning structure and found Mathis, gun in hand, dead on a bed in the back of the house. He had suffered a single gunshot wound to the chest and massive facial injuries from being struck by a gas canister. Johnson's riddled body was discovered in the car trunk, as Mrs. Mathis had described. No motive for the murder was immediately apparent, and an extensive investigation was opened. The lawmen soon learned Mathis had called his wife, claimed the killing had been accidental, and swore he would not be taken alive. However, the multiple bullet wounds in Johnson's body refuted the assertion. Kay Haney of Lubbock and her three-year-old son were in the house at the time of Mathis's death, but they escaped injury by leaving through the backdoor when the shooting began. She was determined to have been present in Johnson's motel room and later signed a statement alleging the victim's death was unintentional. As a matter of standard procedure, District Attorney James Albert "Jim" Mashburn presented the case to the Midland County grand jury, but publicly doubted the peace officers' actions had violated the law. Concurring with

Mashburn, the grand jurors formally ruled Mathis's death to be a justifiable homicide and cleared the lawmen of any criminal responsibility.[89]

In addition to Nancy Mitchell in Kermit, a number of females in Fort Worth, Dallas, and several West Texas towns, especially Odessa, were victims in a series of potentially related homicides during this time. Among these unfortunate women were Dorothy Ann Smith, murdered on November 5, 1968; Linda Ann Cougat, last seen alive on October 19, 1969; Ruth Maynard, on January 9, 1971; and Gloria Sue Green, on June 17, 1971. In mid-January 1972, Ector County Sheriff Alfred Marlin "Slim" Gabrel traveled to Aztec, New Mexico, to question ex-convict Johnny Emanuel Meadows concerning Green's disappearance. Meadows directed investigators to a vacant lot in South Odessa on the nineteenth, where they found Green's body hidden under a mattress. The formal murder complaint was filed against Meadows in Justice of the Peace Otis Moore's court in Odessa on January 21. The suspect was granted a change of venue to Fort Worth, where Riddles visited him in the Tarrant County jail on August 10. The nature of their conversation was not initially disclosed, but later it was learned Meadows admitted to killing Cougat. Meadows pled guilty to Green's murder and received a sentence of life imprisonment. He was returned to Odessa and confessed to the deaths of Cougat, Maynard, and Smith. After the case was transferred to Dallas, Meadows recanted his statements, claiming they were made under duress. District Court Judge John Vance disqualified the confessions on April 28, 1973, on the basis the prosecution could not prove they were made voluntarily. The murder indictments were dismissed, then Meadows claimed he had been branded while in the Ector County jail. An investigation by Riddles and Ranger Ashby Lige "Al" Mitchell proved the claim was bogus. Following a failed appeal, Meadows began serving his life sentence at Huntsville.[90]

On April 27, 1973, Presidio County Sheriff Ernest Daniel "Hank" Hamilton and Deputy William Massey responded to a call from the Ralston Ranch concerning a 1965 Oldsmobile sedan mysteriously parked in a pasture next to U.S. Highway 90, ten miles west of Marfa. The two lawmen questioned the driver. Abruptly, the individual, later identified as George Sylvester Duckworth, pulled a .22 Beretta and opened fire, killing the sheriff and wounding the deputy in the left arm. Massey managed to reach his vehicle and radio for backup. Duckworth, a retired Air Force major, was taken into custody by U.S. Border Patrol officers. Sergeant Hill investigated the homicide. The following day, District Attorney Aubrey Edwards filed murder charges with Justice of the Peace Narisco Sanchez, Jr. in Marfa, and Riddles and Sergeant John Perry "J. P." Lynch II transported the suspect to the Ector County jail. On May 9, Lynch returned the prisoner to Marfa for an appearance before the grand jury.[91]

Riddles and four of his Rangers, Texas Highway Patrolmen, and local police officers conducted a crackdown on drug dealers in Big Spring on May 12. As the result of a two-month undercover investigation, ten adult suspects and one juvenile were arrested in the northern part of town on nineteen counts of selling heroin or marijuana. Additionally, a fifteen-year-old girl, reported as a runaway, was taken into custody. District Attorney Robert H. "Bob" Moore III and Justice of the Peace Gustavo Ochotorena, Jr. were present when the prisoners were brought into the police station. Moore immediately filed complaints, and the jurist continued to hear cases into the early morning hours. The bonds set totaled more than $200,000.[92]

On August 30, 1973, Riddles returned to college as a student at Sul Ross State University in Alpine. On December 21, 1974, he completed his Bachelor of Arts degree in Law Enforcement Administration. The family would receive his degree four days after his funeral.[93]

While the investigation into Nancy Mitchell's death had continued with no real leads, a suspect unexpectedly emerged on May 7, 1974. Carpet layer and youth minister Tommy Ray Kneeland had been arrested for kidnapping sixteen-year-old Danita Ann Cash on April 23 in Arlington. The victim was able to escape unharmed. While being interviewed by Fort Worth police, Kneeland suddenly confessed to raping and murdering Nancy and to killing teenagers Mary Jane Handy and Robert Gholson near the Greater Southwest International Airport on July 1, 1972. Kneeland and his family had lived across the street from the Mitchells at the time of Nancy's disappearance, and the oil lease where she was found belonged to Kneeland's father. Kneeland was charged with murder with malice in Clovis Odell Jones's justice court in Kermit on May 8. Two charges of murder with malice and one of aggravated kidnapping were filed on the ninth before Justice of the

Peace William Woodson Matthews of Fort Worth. Bail was denied for each case. Kneeland was transferred the same night to Winkler County to be arraigned for Nancy's death.[94]

The Winkler County grand jury returned a true bill for murder on June 3. The consequence to Kneeland's swathe of death and anguish came relatively swiftly. He was convicted of Handy and Gholson's murders by a Fort Worth jury on November 8 and received two life sentences. On May 23, 1975, he was granted a change of venue from Kermit to Fort Stockton. He was found guilty of Nancy's slaying on June 26 and sentenced to 550 years in prison.[95]

Riddles was not present to see the result of boundless perseverance and countless manhours. On January 22, 1975, he came home from work as usual, wound his gun belt around his holstered pistol in the bedroom, and laid down on the bed. Almost immediately, he began exhibiting signs of a medical emergency. Sergeant Lynch was called to the house to help the captain to the car. He temporarily lost consciousness on the way to Parkview Hospital. Although his condition is treatable by modern standards, the medical science of the time was insufficient to save him. He died at 11:30 p.m. of an acute myocardial infarction brought on by arteriosclerotic heart disease. His death certificate also revealed he had suffered from gout (probably as a result of freezing his feet in the war) and diabetes mellitus (which likely contributed to his heart disease). Following funeral services at Newnie W. Ellis Chapel in Midland, he was buried at Oakwood Cemetery in Honey Grove.[96]

Loneta, known as "Bigmama" to her grandchildren, never remarried and continued to love her late husband as much she ever had when he was alive. She remained in Midland until 1987 when she moved next door to her son in Abilene. In 1996, she moved with her son's family to Elgin. She later relocated to Taylor where she died on February 21, 2007, of natural causes. She was buried next to her husband at Oakwood Cemetery.[97]

While attending Southwest Texas State University, James Boyd married Carolyn Sue Cooksey, his high school sweetheart, in Bastrop on August 17, 1968. He graduated with a bachelor's degree in industrial arts in 1971, and went to work for the Texas Department of Mental Health and Mental Retardation. He was drafted into the army the following year. The captain's son recalled his father only ever having cried twice, once on the way to the cemetery where his parents were buried, and the second when James Boyd told him he was likely going to war. Fortunately, he remained out of a combat zone and was discharged in 1973. Carolyn worked as a mathematics teacher, and, in time, they brought two children into the world. James continued as a qualified mental retardation professional and a facilities manager at MHMR until 1995. The next year, he moved his family to Elgin where he managed a family farm and taught industrial technology at Elgin Middle School. Carolyn died on May 19, 1998, and was buried in Oakwood Cemetery in Honey Grove. James remarried on January 18, 2007, to an insurance specialist. He retired in 2010, and died on August 1, 2012, in Round Rock. He was buried next to Carolyn.[98]

In April 1996, retired Rangers Glenn Elliott and A. L. Mitchell nominated Jim Riddles to the Texas Ranger Hall of Fame. Submitted alongside this letter were others from Rangers Clay Bednar, George Cole Frasier, Charlie Mack Hodges, Pedro Gonzalez "Pete" Montemayor, Clayton McKinney, Sidney Clement "Sid" Merchant, and William Troy "Bud" Newberry, as well as DPS Senior Pilot Investigator Bill Ray McCoy, Mrs. Ellen Mitchell, retired Ector County District Attorney John H. Green, and former Jones County Sheriff Woodrow Simmons. Jim Riddles was inducted into the Texas Ranger Hall of Fame in June 1997. There was a formal ceremony with the family following the Memorial Service held during the annual reunion.[99]

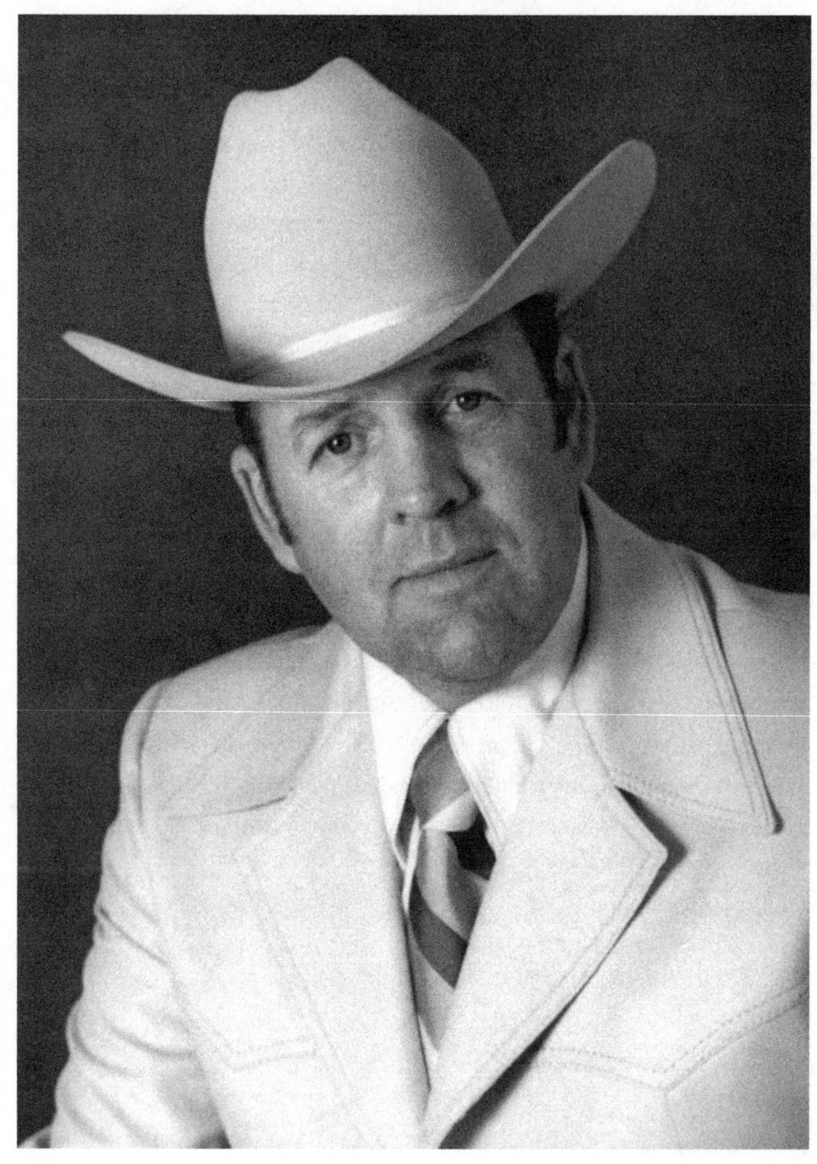

Bobby Paul Doherty. *Courtesy Texas Ranger Hall of Fame and Museum, Waco, TX.*

Chapter 11

Bobby Paul Doherty: "Knew the Risks Well"

Bobby Paul Doherty was cut down at the beginning of a promising career in the Texas Rangers. By all accounts, he was an honorable public servant who loved his family, his occupation, and his life. His senseless death serves as a stark reminder of the dangers law enforcement personnel face on a daily basis. Doherty knew the risks well. Every morning, he donned his badge and his gun and left his home to ensure the residents of his district could exist in peace and safety. His loss would rip a hole in the lives of family and friends that has never fully healed. Retired Ranger John Dudley White, Jr., who lost his father to violent lawbreakers, said of Doherty's death: "This same thing could have happened to me and any other Ranger who has served this state. God has been with us. All I can do now is weep for this fallen officer and pray for his soul."

He was born in Mount Calm, Hill County, Texas, on July 29, 1936. His parents were Paul Edward and Doris (Scruggs) Doherty. Born on July 14, 1907, in Franklin, Paul was an oil field and cotton field worker. His wife was born on June 1, 1914, in Cleburne and worked as a homemaker. Later, they owned an antique store in Beaumont. Bob, as he preferred to be called, was an only child. He attended Effie Morris Elementary School in Lake Worth and Lake Worth High School. In school, he was an average to above-average student. Despite his mother's fears he would be hurt, he played tackle on the Bullfrogs football team, catcher on the baseball team, and guard on the basketball team.[1]

In 1952, while a sophomore, he met freshman Martha Carolyn Walter in study hall, the last period of the day. Doherty sat at the desk behind her, and his first encounter with his future wife was when she looked over her shoulder and saw him copying an English paper belonging to someone else. As time passed, they began to speak to one another in class. The study hall teacher happened to be Frank Kring, Bob's football coach. The instructor stopped the two teenagers from talking in class, so they began to pass notes. Kring tried to curtail this activity as well. One day as the coach was watching the pair, Doherty wrote a note and passed it to Carolyn. Kring bellowed, "Doherty! Bring that note to me!" Doherty handed the note to King, who read it: "Dear Mr. Kring—I sure hope we win the game tonight!"[2]

Every Friday night, the high school football team would gather to ride a school bus to the away games. As a member of the pep squad, Carolyn rode the bus set aside for that group. One evening, while the two buses were loading, Doherty poked his head out the window and called to Carolyn, "I'll meet you here after the game." What followed was their first date. Years later, Carolyn reminded him he had never formally asked her for a date. He replied, "Well, I thought about it so much, I thought I did."[3]

Doherty attended Lamar State College of Technology (present Lamar University) in September 1954 on a football scholarship. The records do not indicate a specific major, only an entry noted as "Sciences."[4] His father had a job at the shipyard in Beaumont at the same time. Doherty left college after the end of the spring semester in May 1955 because he missed Carolyn. She graduated from high school the same year and trained to become a registered x-ray technician.[5]

Doherty went to work for General Dynamics' Convair aircraft manufacturing plant in Fort Worth. He also served as a volunteer firefighter in Lake Worth.[6] While working at the plant, a sizeable amount of sheet metal fell on Doherty. He went to the clinic where Carolyn was working and, while x-raying his lower leg and foot, she discovered several broken bones. Shortly before the accident, Doherty had received a letter from the draft board that he was being called to military service. The doctor for whom Carolyn worked wrote to the board and explained Doherty's injuries. As a result, he received an exemption.[7]

They married on October 25, 1957, and lived in a one-bedroom rented house in Lake Worth. By all accounts, the union was loving and stable, and their son would later state that he never saw his parents argue.[8]

Carolyn's uncle, Burrel Glenn Robb, was a Highway Patrol trooper in Llano who influenced Doherty to apply to the Department of Public Safety in 1958. Doherty entered the DPS Academy in Austin as a student patrolman on December 3. Future Ranger Robert Charles "Bob" Favor was one of his classmates. Graduating from School No. 4 on January 31, 1959, Doherty was commissioned a Highway Patrolman on March 13 and assigned to the Wharton office in Region 2.[9] His first partner was Reeves C. Jungkind, who was well known for his pistol shooting prowess. Jungkind would later become the academy's firearms training officer and pistolsmith. Inspired by his partner, Doherty was a member of the department's competitive pistol team and served as a firearms instructor to various small local police departments.[10]

While they were stationed in Wharton, Bob and Carolyn were patients of a clinic in El Campo, approximately twelve miles away. The doctors there were supportive of Highway Patrol families and never charged them for services.[11] A daughter, Kelly Lyn, was born on August 16, 1960, and a son, Buster Wayne, on October 17, 1961.[12] Bob and Carolyn would later joke they had their children fourteen months apart so as to take advantage of the free medical care.[13]

After Patrolman Kenneth Harrison was killed in the line of duty in Cooke County, Doherty transferred to the Gainesville office in Region 1 on September 1, 1963. The Doherty family lived in a four-room rented house.[14] In Gainesville, Doherty was paired with George Charles Jeff "Big Daddy" King, who would retire in August 1996 as Chief of Traffic Law Enforcement. At one point in their partnership, the troopers received the "Hook'n Bulls" award. Sheriff's deputies had gone to serve a mental warrant on a dangerous individual. The suspect was holding the officers at bay with a shotgun, and threatening to kill them if they came onto his property. Doherty and King drove up, and the deputies stepped back while the two troopers walked up to the deranged man's fence. The suspect, a religious fanatic, refused to go peacefully, again threatening to kill the lawmen. Doherty said, "Before you make a decision like that, we need to have a word of prayer." The man reverently closed his eyes, and the officers quickly subdued him and took him into custody.[15]

On a Sunday morning in 1964 or 1965, while Carolyn and the children were attending Grand Avenue Baptist Church, Doherty and King were on patrol duty. The two troopers were passing by the Sunday school building when Doherty, who was driving, saw his family come out. He pulled over to the curb, exited the patrol car, and walked over. Holding his children, Doherty stood on the sidewalk and talked to them and his wife. Carolyn looked at King sitting in the passenger seat of the patrol unit and noticed he was rocking back and forth with his arms crossed over his chest. She asked what was wrong with George. Bob replied, "Oh, George broke his hand [in a fight] and I'm taking him to the hospital." Earlier, the two patrolmen had arrested a man and were taking him to the jail, which was located in the county courthouse. As they were walking up to the building, the prisoner started to run, but George tackled him. The would-be fugitive resisted, and George attempted to subdue him. At one point in the scuffle, the man turned his head, and George hit the sidewalk with his fist.[16]

Finally, on September 1, 1968, Doherty transferred to the Fort Worth office.[17] He worked around the Lake Worth, Blue Mound, and Watauga communities. The following year, he partnered with Bob G. Prince, who would retire from the Texas Rangers as Captain of Company F in Waco. As Prince recalled, "We weren't just partners, we were best friends."[18]

With the assistance of Dave Teague, a family friend, Doherty built a white brick house on a three-and-a-half-acre parcel that had been part of Carolyn's father's dairy farm. The home had three bedrooms, two baths, and a double garage. It was also entirely heated by wood-burning fireplaces. The center of family life was the den. There Doherty kept his collection of handguns and a rifle thought to have been carried by one of George Custer's troopers.[19]

In order to provide for his family, Doherty worked numerous nights and weekends for the overtime and second-shift pay differentials. Buster hated for his father to take vacations because Bob moonlighted as a carpenter for Teague during those times, which meant Buster also had to work for Teague.[20]

Life was good for the Dohertys in those years. The family attended the First Baptist Church of Lakeside, where Bob was ordained as a deacon.[21] He played in DPS softball teams in Gainesville and later in Saginaw with Buster, and enjoyed varmint hunting along the Red River. Carolyn would later tell Buster more than once, "God was preparing us for his death all our lives because we had such a good life." Buster would add, "He built a good foundation for us."[22]

As a reward for his hard work and dedication, Doherty was promoted to the rank of Patrolman II on September 1, 1973. "An officer's primary responsibility is lives," he observed. "If you ever get to where you don't consider people ... and their feelings, you're in the wrong business."[23] He was a serious professional, but also not above the occasional practical joke. A classic example occurred about one week before his promotion to Ranger. Bob Prince, who was working as a Ranger in Palestine, had to drive to Miami, Florida, to extradite a prisoner and asked Doherty to join him. The Highway Patrol released Doherty to work with his friend. At that time, Prince had a pronounced phobia of drawbridges, which he had mistakenly once confided to Doherty. After they arrived in Miami, the officers had to travel across a drawbridge with Prince at the wheel and Doherty in the passenger seat. As Prince drove white-knuckled across the span, Doherty slapped the dashboard and yelled "Drawbridge!" Prince stomped on the brakes while Doherty laughed, enjoying his joke. They took custody of the prisoner from the Miami authorities and began the return trip. They were driving north through Florida when Doherty fell asleep. Suddenly Prince slammed on the brakes, turned on the siren, and yelled "Drawbridge!" Prince got his revenge when Doherty was startled awake, but unfortunately the prisoner was equally surprised and injured his back. The three travelers arrived home, and the prisoner was brought before the judge so he could be warned of his Miranda rights. The judge read the defendant his rights, then asked if he understood. The prisoner replied, "Yeah, but" so the judge read them again. The judge again asked whether the prisoner understood and again

Bob Prince. *Courtesy Texas Ranger Hall of Fame and Museum, Waco, TX.*

the latter hesitated. The judge read them a third time and once more asked if he comprehended. The prisoner said, "Yes, Judge, I understand but what I don't understand is what this drawbridge was."[24]

As mentioned, Bob Prince was already serving as a Ranger and talked Doherty into applying for the prestigious service. Doherty scored well on the written test and the oral interview board but not high enough to get the vacancy. He retook the test the following year and this time placed second on the eligibility list. Tragically, on December 14, 1975, the day his impending promotion was announced, Bob's father, Paul, passed away after a heart attack at church.[25] Doherty officially promoted to the Texas Rangers on July 1, 1976.[26] Normally upon advancement, DPS officers transfer to another part of the state, but a new position in Company B opened up at that same time. Because of his familiarity with the region, Doherty was assigned to the vacant slot. In contrast to her earlier concerns that he would become injured in sports, his mother, Doris, could not have been prouder of her son when he made Ranger.[27]

Doherty came to the Rangers with the reputation of being "a very serious and very effective trooper." He arose to be a highly successful and well-respected Ranger. Wherever he went in his duties, he drew other officers to him. Many of his close friends in the DPS, such as Reeves Jungkind, George King, and Bob Prince, went on to hold important positions in the department. "When he did something, it was virtually always right," Captain Prince remembered.[28]

Much as he had been in the Highway Patrol, Bob was a workaholic Ranger. During his time in Company B, he never took a full day off, and the family had not taken a vacation since 1974. In spite of his relentless work ethic, Bob never missed one of Buster's high school football games where he played as a capable middle guard.[29]

One of the first cases he handled in his brief Ranger career involved accused forger William Schoengarth. A $185 counterfeit check had been traced to the suspect, and Doherty was involved in a raid at the former's self-storage warehouse on the south side of Fort Worth on July 23. Schoengarth was arrested, and investigators seized a plate used to print counterfeit state treasury checks, as well as 879 fake driver's licenses, 158 credit cards, and 320 Social Security cards. The perpetrator was charged with passing a forged instrument and with forgery of a government document. Doherty appeared before Justice of the Peace Robert Earl "Bob" Ashmore for the examining trial on October 1 and testified concerning the arrest and the items confiscated.[30]

Doherty was on the periphery of the Thomas Cullen Davis episode. The wealthy oilman was accused of attempting to murder his estranged wife, Priscilla Lee, at their Fort Worth mansion on August 2, 1976, and killing her lover Stanford A. T. "Stan" Farr. One of Priscilla's friends was shot and paralyzed by the attacker, and her twelve-year-old daughter Andrea was found dead in the wine cellar with a single gunshot wound to the torso. While Doherty did not participate in the subsequent homicide investigation, he did serve as Priscilla's bodyguard during the resulting murder trial in Fort Worth, which began on February 22, 1977, and ended in a mistrial on April 13. The case was transferred to Amarillo, but Doherty's involvement by then was finished.[31]

On February 9, 1978, Captain Dwight Crawford, chief of criminal investigations for the Denton County Sheriff's Office, was called to the county jail cell of Kenneth Ray Bunyard. The prisoner and one Jimmy Leonard Baker had been partners in the drug trade before they fell into a dispute. Bunyard was subsequently arrested on a charge of theft from a local pharmacy. Bunyard identified Baker as a major dealer of marijuana, cocaine, and amphetamine in the Gainesville-Denton area. Bunyard and his girlfriend, Mary Lea Nosser, offered to show Crawford and Deputy Bailey Gilliland the location of Baker's residence in Gainesville. The officers and the informants drove to the town and met with Justice of the Peace Tom Crawford. The party then went to a residence north of the city near the interstate that was identified as belonging to Baker and his wife, Linda.[32]

Since the investigation into the various drug connections would cross county lines, Captain Crawford called upon Doherty for support. Sometime between February 13 and 17, Nosser agreed to assist the law officers in brokering a sting operation. Doherty also called in DPS narcotics agent Ben A. Neel to act as "Sam McCloud," the buyer from St. Louis. Nosser, an actual street dealer from St. Louis, was able to convince Baker and Linda that "McCloud" was to be trusted. Baker agreed to sell fifty pounds of marijuana from an anticipated shipment to the undercover agent.[33]

The last clear memory Buster has of his father took place on Sunday, February 19, 1978. Carolyn had told her son to wake Doherty, who had worked late the previous night, so the family could get ready for church. Buster went to his parents' bedroom door and called for his father to get up, but Doherty continued to sleep. Twice more Carolyn told Buster to wake

Doherty, so the final time Buster decided to leap on top of his dad. The two wrestled for a time before going to services.[34]

Church was followed by a deacon's meeting, then a telephone call from Captain Crawford about the drug raid that Nosser had tried to arrange for three-thirty that afternoon. The operation failed to come about that day as the sheriff's investigators had not been given a sufficient amount of time to organize. The buy-bust was instead scheduled for the next day.[35]

Monday, February 20 was the official state holiday for George Washington's birthday, but the lawmen were nevertheless hard at work. At three-thirty in the afternoon, Doherty, along with Crawford and Neel, was interviewing Bunyard and Nosser. The shipment had arrived during the weekend, but Baker and his cronies decided to throw a party in Dallas rather than attend to business. Nosser was present at the gathering and would allege that Baker attempted to kill her with an overdose of heroin mixed in Coca-Cola. Whether Baker had guessed Nosser was working for the authorities or she had imagined the whole scenario was for Doherty and Crawford to decide. They took a gamble when Nosser left two hours later to attend a scheduled meeting with Baker. The situation resolved itself when Nosser called at six-fifteen and said, "He's ready to do the deal tonight."[36]

The law officers immediately responded. Crawford contacted the Ramada Inn in Denton and rented Room 154 for "Steve McCloud" and Room 155 for the arrest team, who arrived on the scene at seven o'clock. Agent Neel was carrying six hundred dollars in "buy" money. Almost immediately the plan began to change when Nosser called Crawford to tell him Baker was bringing only one pound of marijuana rather than the agreed-upon fifty pounds. He would tell Neel, "I thought you'd want to taste it first." All was ready when Nosser ushered Jimmy and Linda Baker into Room 154 at approximately seven-thirty. Neel was alone when he allowed the trio to enter, but waiting and listening next door was Doherty, Crawford, and Deputies Gilliland and Ronald "Tracker" Douglas. Neel feigned smoking the offered joint, presented his compliments, then Baker called his accomplice, Joe Madison Fultner, to produce the remaining shipment. While waiting, Neel provided beer, and the quartet proceeded to drink.

Neel regaled them with stories of his supposed days as a Mafia-connected heroin dealer in St. Louis.[37]

Approximately one hour later, Joe Fultner arrived bearing a sack. Once he was in the room, the lawmen burst through the door from the adjacent room and arrested the offenders. Crawford took custody of the sack and discovered only nineteen pounds of marijuana inside. When questioned, Baker told the officers a total of twenty pounds was all he could get. Neel would later testify, "I told Mr. Baker that if he would assist us in going ahead with the entire fifty pounds … in other words, by getting the remaining thirty pounds … I would advise the district attorney that he cooperated." Baker informed the officers that his connection, a friend named Greg, who lived near Argyle, was in possession of a large amount of marijuana.[38]

Baker subsequently telephoned Gregory Arthur Ott, a twenty-seven-year-old philosophy graduate student at North Texas State University (present-day University of North Texas), in order to broker a deal between Ott and "Steve McCloud." The word "marijuana" was never uttered in the brief conversation; instead the dealers used the term "bracelet." The transaction was set to take place at Ott's residence later that night.[39]

Crawford had Linda Baker and Fultner booked into the county jail on charges of delivering and selling a controlled substance, while he and Doherty secured another fourteen hundred dollars in "buy" money to combine with Neel's six hundred. Meanwhile, Neel and the two county deputies finished the beer and planned the upcoming operation. Much would be made later of the alcohol consumption, but Doherty, a man who rarely drank even off-duty, was with Crawford at the sheriff's office. DPS narcotics agent Don Piper Jones joined the group at the hotel. Evidently, Jones was not expecting to make any arrests since he did not bring his sidearm; Neel instead loaned him a .357 Magnum handgun. Crawford and Doherty returned carrying the money and driving a Chevrolet 4×4 pickup truck with a white camper shell on the back.[40]

The lawmen set out for Ott's house with Neel and dealer-turned-informant Baker in the cab, while Doherty, Crawford, Agent Jones, and deputies Gilliland and Douglas were hidden under a blanket in the back. All the officers were in plainclothes except for Crawford who wore his official-issue jacket with the sheriff's departmental patch on either shoulder. Doherty had put the identification half of his badge case in the left chest pocket of his coat so that his Ranger star hung visible on the outside. Deputy Douglas also wore his badge in full view. At approximately eleven o'clock on the night of February 20, the truck pulled off of Hickory Hill Road near Argyle and drove up the long gravel driveway of Twin Pines Ranch. Ott had lived in a small rental home on the property for about four years. Baker informed the officers that Ott stored his wares in the barn behind the frame residence. The plan was for Baker and Neel to enter the dwelling where Baker would introduce the undercover agent to Ott as "McCloud." The trio would then walk the forty to fifty yards to the barn to examine the merchandise, then return to the house with the marijuana in hand. Neel would leave the south-facing kitchen door open to signal the others outside to enter.[41]

Neel described in his report the next day how Ott acted in a cold and paranoid manner, relentlessly questioning the undercover agent as to whether he was a police officer. Ott was also carrying a .38-caliber pistol in a holster at his side. Neel convinced the drug dealer he merely wanted to complete the transaction. Once the two exchanged driver's licenses, Ott was mollified and invited Neel and Baker out to the barn. Unbeknownst to Ott, Neel was carrying false identification bearing his "Steve McCloud" alias.[42]

Events went as planned until the sign was given and the raid team exited the camper. The raised overhead door dropped and hit Bob in the back with a loud crash. He seized his Remington Model 870 shotgun and raced to the west kitchen window of the house, with Crawford on his heels. Crawford later testified that he shouted, "Police officers!" as they ran to the house. Doherty continued north along the west side of the house. Looking in the window, Crawford saw a long-haired, bearded man inside moving east through the residence, and he rushed down the south side to cut the suspect off on the east. The sheriff's captain again shouted, "Police officers!" Agent Jones, the third man out of the camper, ran to the open kitchen door. The two deputies got tangled in the blanket and were slow in exiting the camper. Both deputies later testified they heard unidentified voices inside the house shout, "Drop the gun or I'll kill you!" and "He's got a gun!" followed by two gunshots that were several seconds apart.[43]

Inside the back bedroom, Neel, Baker, and Ott were looking at the fifteen pounds of marijuana on the bed, when they heard the sound of the falling camper door. Ott went to look out the west kitchen window and saw the five men climbing out of the back of the truck. Gun in hand, he raced through the middle room toward the beaded curtain beyond which was the living room. Ott passed the bedroom door where Neel was standing, his Colt .45 pistol in hand. The agent recounted, "I stepped out into the doorway of the bedroom and I hollered in a real loud voice just right in his face, 'Police officer! Drop the gun!' He … started toward the doorway [leading to the living room] … Again I yelled, 'Police officer! Freeze!'"[44]

Ott turned with the right side of his body toward Neel as if to fire his gun. The agent responded by firing one shot at Ott as he was about to pass through the beaded curtain into the darkened living room, but the bullet missed. Ott moved to the living room door situated at the northwest corner of the house. Directly opposite the dealer's position outside were Doherty and Deputy Gilliland. They heard the sound of Neel's gunshot. While Gilliland tried to see inside through a window curtain, Doherty prepared to make entry. The Ranger kicked the door open hard, but, as it was rebounding off the interior wall, Ott fired through the wood and struck Bob above the right eye. Ott had time to re-cock his revolver and catch up a shotgun before he was apprehended by Agents Neel and Jones and Deputy Douglas.[45]

Unconscious yet still showing vital signs, Doherty was taken to Westgate Hospital in Denton, then rushed by ambulance to John Peter Smith Hospital in Fort Worth. The fallen officer was surrounded by an escort of approximately a dozen police cars. Ranger Thomas Edward "Tom" Arnold of Company B, stationed in Arlington, notified Carolyn that her husband had been shot. Arnold told Carolyn he was coming to take her to the hospital, but she replied there was no time. So calm she surprised even herself, Carolyn called her pastor, Reverend Jesse Leonard; her mother, who lived next door; and finally Azle Police Chief Charles Stewart. The activity had woken Kelly, by then a high school senior and honor student. Her mother said, "Your daddy's been shot. Don't wake Buster 'till we see how bad it is."[46]

In mere minutes, Carolyn, her mother, Pastor Leonard, and Chief Stewart were in a police cruiser racing toward the hospital. The brotherhood of law officers was in full force that night, as traffic at every intersection along their route was stopped by a city, county, or state police vehicle.[47]

Chief Stewart's speeding car reached the hospital in the early hours of February 21, moments before the ambulance. Carolyn and her supporters waited by the emergency room door. She prayed that her husband's wound would not be serious, but when she saw him being brought in she knew the worst. The emergency room was crowded with numerous law enforcement personnel who had come to lend Bob and Carolyn their strength. After an agonizing wait of a few minutes, G. W. Burks, captain of Company B, drew her aside and said, "Carolyn, he's gone." Pronounced dead at 1:04 a.m., Bobby Paul Doherty was the first Texas Ranger to be killed in the line of duty since 1931.[48]

Carolyn would later remark, "It's funny the things you think to say at a moment like that. I asked if Bob had ever been conscious. [Burks] said no. That's what I wanted to hear. I asked if they got the man who did it. He said yes."[49]

Appropriate for a man of Bob Doherty's character and reputation, the funeral that began at 11 a.m. on Thursday, February 23 drew a crowd of more than 2,200 family members, friends, and fellow peace officers from across Texas, Arkansas, and Oklahoma. Three hundred and fifty of those lawmen were assembled in the parking lot as an honor guard. The service was too large for the Dohertys' own house of worship, so it was held at the Rosen Heights Baptist Church, with the Reverend Jesse Leonard officiating. Some mourners had to be directed to an alternate chapel because of the lack of space. An estimated six hundred more gathered outside. Flowers, sympathy letters, and telegrams arrived from across the United States and around the world. Texas Attorney General John Hill, Colonel Wilson E. Speir, director of the DPS, and most of the ninety-two Texas Rangers were in attendance.[50]

At the funeral, Captain Prince was told by "several guys that 'Bob was my best friend.' How many people have more than one best friend? There was six or eight guys who thought Bob was their best friend. He had that unique ability to make everybody feel special." He recalled later that he too "lost the best friend I ever had in my life." After the service, Dwayne Hickman, a Highway Patrolman who joined the DPS just so he could work with Doherty, told Buster, "Your father was very respected. Even the thugs respected him." The fallen officer was buried at Azleland Cemetery, twenty miles northwest of Fort Worth.[51]

The Texas House of Representatives, with the Senate in accord, unanimously adopted House Concurrent Resolution No. 16 on July 27, 1978. The measure paid tribute to the memory of Ranger Bobby Paul Doherty and publicly extended the lawmakers' sympathy to his survivors.[52]

Meanwhile, as mourners honored the life of Bob Doherty, Greg Ott had been arraigned before Denton County Court-at-Law Judge J. Ray Martin, and was being held without bond in the county jail on a charge of capital murder. Jimmy Baker was soon sent to federal prison for violating his probation on an earlier firearms conviction. He at first confirmed the account of those law officers present at the time of the shooting, but he would change his story two months later, claiming prior Ranger intimidation. On August 21, he was sentenced to ten years in prison and fined three thousand dollars for selling marijuana to Neel on February 20; Linda was given five years' probation. Kenneth Bunyard and Mary Nosser were married in jail one day after the murder. Bunyard was a free man by the time Ott's murder trial started in May.[53]

On February 22, Ott refused to speak in his own defense at an examining trial, and he was bound over to the Denton County grand jury on capital murder charges. He continued to be held without bond. Ott was indicted by the grand jury on March 2.[54]

Up to that time, Denton County District Attorney Jerry Cobb had not prosecuted a capital case in his career. Indeed, Denton County had never tried a capital murder case to a final conclusion. The fact that the victim was a Texas Ranger made the task even more daunting for Cobb. His case had to rest on proving that the lawmen were acting in the course of their sworn duties and that Ott knew he was firing on a police officer.[55]

Ott had been provided with the court-appointed services of attorneys Robert Hal Jackson and Alan Lee Levy. The lawyers' strategy was to present the raid as a bungled mess that should be blamed on the officers involved. They also suppressed any possible testimony by Ott's friends that might prove damning by advising them to leave town.[56]

The *State of Texas v. Gregory Arthur Ott* lasted from May 30 to June 17 in 158th District Court, with Judge Robert George "Bob" Scofield presiding. Rather than capital murder, Ott was convicted of first-degree murder after the jury deliberated for ninety minutes. In the punishment phase on July 27, the defendant was formally sentenced to life imprisonment. The jury returned the lesser verdict because they believed there was reasonable doubt Ott knew he was shooting at a police officer through the door. To his credit, Cobb later wrote the Doherty family a heartfelt letter of apology for being unable to obtain a capital murder conviction.[57] Ott was remanded to the custody of the Texas Department of Criminal Justice and incarcerated in the maximum security Darrington Unit. Doris would be asked why she thought God had taken her son. She sternly replied, "God did not take my son. Sin took my son."[58]

The previous year, the Sixty-fifth Legislature had passed Senate Bill No. 152, which amended Article 42.12 of the Code of Criminal Procedure to include a deadly weapon provision. Article 42.12 Section 3f (a)(2) stated the provisions of Sections 3 and 3c (which relate to probation) did not apply to a defendant who used or exhibited a deadly weapon as defined in Section 1.07(a)(11) of the Penal Code during the commission of a felony offense. When a defendant used a deadly weapon, the trial court was to enter the affirmative finding in its judgment. If convicted, he was not to be eligible for parole until his actual calendar time served, without consideration for good conduct time, equaled one-third of the maximum sentence or twenty calendar years, whichever was less.[59]

Because District Attorney Cobb had not requested a deadly weapon finding, Ott earned credit for good behavior and became eligible for parole on January 10, 1990. His hearing on February 15 received a positive vote from the Texas Board of Pardons and Paroles. No parole official contacted the Doherty family to inform them. Captain Prince was called at his home in Houston by the warden of Huntsville Penitentiary on Thursday, February 22 and informed Ott was at the Walls Unit scheduled to be released on Tuesday.

Prince immediately contacted Glenn Heckman, the chairman of the parole board, and was told if the captain would lodge a protest, the board would order Ott held for thirty days until the process could be completed. Prince called Carolyn and every Ranger field office in the state. The board's office started receiving faxes of protest letters at nine or ten o'clock Friday morning. By one in the afternoon, they were so inundated with transmissions the board members withdrew their earlier decision and kept Ott in prison. Ott's case came up for review annually over the next nine years, and Prince; Carolyn, Buster, and Kelly; the Texas Rangers; and family and friends were compelled to submit letters to prevent his possible parole.[60]

On August 10, 1999, Ott was again recommended for parole after serving twenty-one years.[61] The approval rested on whether the state of Florida would accept him.[62] Hal Jackson and Al Levy, his former trial attorneys, and William T. "Bill" Habern, the lawyer who had represented him pro bono since 1990, declared he had paid his debt to society and had been a model prisoner. "He is as rehabilitated as anybody could ever be," Habern said.[63]

Carolyn Doherty, her family, and the Texas Rangers naturally disagreed, arguing murderers are rarely rehabilitated and once free he would pose a threat to law-abiding citizens. "I think I owe it to my husband's memory to fight Ott's release, and I owe it to all the law enforcement members," Carolyn in an interview, "I lost his wonderful companionship for the rest of my life, and my grandchildren don't have the joy of knowing their granddad."[64]

Denton County Sheriff Weldon Lucas, DPS narcotics supervisor at the time of the murder, a former Texas Ranger, and a friend of the Doherty family, concurred: "Twenty-one years ago, he was willing to shoot a police officer to protect his drug investment. This is not blind loyalty to the Rangers. I am thinking of the danger he would bring to the police officers out there today. I don't think he's changed."[65]

While the state decided on Ott's release, Carolyn was once again forced to re-experience the pain of losing her husband: "I won't quit the fight, because I know that jury intended for him to be there [in prison] longer than this," she said. "But if the day comes and he is released, I'll have a clear conscience that I didn't sit on my thumbs and let him get out. I owe it to Bob to do this."[66]

The only person Captain Prince knew in Florida happened to be Michael W. Moore, the secretary of the state Department of Corrections. Prince contacted Moore and informed him that Ott was being considered for parole if the "Sunshine State" would take him. As he told the Florida official, "y'all don't need another convicted cop-killer." Moore turned out to be the one individual who had to approve the transfer, and he refused the request without hesitation.[67] The parole board in Texas decided on September 14 to deny Ott for another year. He was once more refused parole in March of 2001, with a review scheduled to occur in three years.[68]

Beginning in 2002, *Texas Monthly* magazine and two television programs—an episode of A&E Network's *American Justice* series entitled "Don't Mess with Texas" and the Court TV daily show *Catherine Crier Live*—initiated a media campaign to set Ott free. Indeed, in order to emphasize the drama, producers of *American Justice* secured permission to film in the old 150th District courtroom. They portrayed the murder as an accident where Ott's pistol had been in the closet prior to the raid, became tangled in the bead curtain, and unintentionally went off. They referred to claims that Ott had been robbed twice before so he possessed his pistol for self-defense only. They recounted Ott's good behavior in prison.[69]

In a letter to the Victim Services Division, Prince countered the media's assertions by referring to sworn testimony that officers on the scene had observed Ott carrying a weapon before the murder; that revolvers do not discharge accidentally, instead the trigger has to be manually pulled; that such a contention was not presented at trial and if proved would likely have resulted in a conviction of negligent homicide; there were no previous police reports in Denton County of property crimes in which Ott was a victim; and, finally, although Ott may have been a perfect prisoner, "his conduct has been as we would expect from all inmates." Prince summed up his arguments: "Ott has clearly conned the media to think it is excusable and permissible to murder a peace officer to defend and protect his illegal contraband." Other written protests were sent to Victims Services, including those from TDCJ Director for Region 2 James Almon "Jim" Shaw, Jr.; Monroe County, Georgia, Sheriff James Carey Bittick; Tarrant County Commissioner J. D. Johnson; Tarrant County Sheriff Dee Anderson; Tarrant County District Attorney Timothy

Cullen "Tim" Curry, Sr.; retired DPS Director Dudley Melvin Thomas; Acting Smith County District Attorney Dillon Matt Bingham; now-retired Ranger Sergeant William Matthew "Matt" Cawthon; and Doctor John Marvin Smith III of San Antonio. Especially poignant was the letter sent by Sergeant Don Jones, who was at that time working for the North Central Texas Narcotics Task Force. In his note, he recounted his time at Doherty's side in the ambulance as the paramedics raced to the hospital.[70]

Larry Joe Doherty, Bob's first cousin and star of the syndicated courtroom program *Texas Justice*, echoed Prince's sentiments. In a letter to Governor James Richard "Rick" Perry and the parole board, he continually stressed that Ott had never expressed any contrition or remorse for Doherty's death. He took exception to moving stories the media presented about Ott's mother being too ill to visit him in prison, while ignoring Doris Doherty's greater loss.[71]

On May 25, 2004, Gregory Arthur Ott, State I.D. 01592906 and TDCJ I.D. 00282372, was paroled after twenty-six years in prison to live in Longwood, Florida, near his parents. Supervised by the Florida Department of Corrections under the Interstate Compact, he is barred from traveling to Tarrant, Parker, or Denton Counties without prior consent. Bill Habern said in an interview, "It's long overdue." Carolyn commented, "This is something we have fought for years and years. All I can say that is we tried. We tried our very best. Friends and family and law enforcement really worked hard at it for many years. It just didn't work this time."[72]

After Ott's release, Ranger Headquarters was asked for a comment, and they deferred to Bob Prince due to his close friendship with the Doherty family and his tireless fight to keep Ott in prison. Retired and living in Waco, the captain said, "He was convicted of killing a peace officer in the performance of duty and received a life sentence. Certainly any peace officer, and I think the majority of people in the state of Texas, would expect him to serve the sentence that was given to him."[73]

Reflecting on the aftermath of Ott's release, Buster said, "I'm suspicious of the media of any sort … February 21st was the day he was killed and every year that was a bad day for me. It was starting up for about a week and my wife could tell when it was getting that way. Having to go through writing the parole board and getting people to write to the parole board. It was something I felt that we had to do, and since he's been out, February 21st could come and go. It's kinda like closure. For years … it was a chore to keep him behind bars when we shouldn't have to have been doing that." Prince added, "It opened up wounds every time."[74]

Carolyn never remarried and lived in the same home her husband built in Azle. A widow for forty-three years, she taught Bible study classes at First Baptist Church of Lakeside and delighted in her grandchildren. Carolyn died on February 23, 2021.[75] Proud to be associated with the Texas Rangers, Doris attended every reunion and function possible until she died on May 11, 2007.[76]

Kelly graduated from high school a few months after her father's death and attended Texas Tech University. She received a degree in petroleum land management and went to work in the petroleum industry in Fort Worth. Bob Prince gave her away at her wedding, and she has a son and a daughter. Her family built a house next to Carolyn's.[77]

Buster attended Tarrant County College and Texas State Technical College in Waco while living with Prince. He met his future wife the first weekend after he moved away. Similar to his father, he returned to Fort Worth because he was too far away from her. He works as an engineering supervisor at a hospital in Azle. Prince again stood in for Bob at Buster's wedding. Buster and his wife were married for fifteen years before the birth of their twin sons.[78]

Without reservation, Bob Prince nominated Doherty to be enshrined in the Texas Ranger Hall of Fame. As he said, "It's not how [the inductees] died, it's how they lived." The vote of the Texas Ranger Association was unanimous, and Bobby Paul Doherty was inducted into the Hall of Fame in 1994.[79]

The Former Texas Rangers Association bestowed a Memorial Cross in Bob Doherty's honor on February 18, 2012. At the service, Bob Prince would observe: "Bob certainly put his priorities right. His priorities were the church and his God, his family, his friends, and then his job next … He was a Ranger you could ride the river with."[80]

Stanley K. Guffey. *Courtesy Texas Ranger Hall of Fame and Museum, Waco, TX.*

Chapter 12

Stanley Keith Guffey: "Sheer Grit, Raw Courage"

Stanley Keith "Stan" Guffey gave his life to save a little girl from a depraved killer. He spent a lengthy career apprehending dangerous individuals and corrupt politicians, but his one act of supreme sacrifice epitomizes the sheer grit, raw courage, and selfless commitment that Texas Rangers must possess. Like his peers in that elite organization, Guffey had willingly shouldered the risks and responsibilities that came with his oath to protect others, even at the cost of his own life. The late H. Joaquin Jackson said, "Captain Mitchell, his company, and all of us who knew Stan Guffey were devastated to hear of his death. Simple words cannot describe how much Stan Guffey's colleagues loved and respected him."

He was born in Perryton, Ochiltree County, Texas, on November 28, 1946. His father, Marsen Franklin "Happy" Guffey, had been born on August 21, 1913, in Lipscomb County. His mother, Willora (Curry) Guffey, was born on December 6, 1918, in Canadian, Hemphill County. They married on March 26, 1938. Stan's sisters were Linda Gayle, born July 9, 1942, and Brenda Kay, born November 19, 1944. Marsen and Willora divorced, and the former married LaVerda Mae (Camp) Schroeder. LaVerda had three children from a previous marriage: Donna Jo, born on December 11, 1951; Daniel Lee, on December 23, 1950; and Denise Lynn, on June 25, 1956.

Willora later worked as a bookkeeper for Adcock and Prater Grading Service. Stan attended Perryton High School through his sophomore year and graduated from Canadian High School on May 25, 1964. Guffey was a capable student who achieved good grades without much trouble. He was raised as a cowboy and inherited his father's affinity for horses. He possessed an outgoing personality who put the people around him at ease. To those in need, he was very generous. Despite his young age, he married Olivia Sue Rawlins on September 18, 1962, and fathered two sons, Michael Keith, born August 10, 1963, and Stacy Franklin, born June 6, 1967.[1]

Guffey rode in the rodeo circuit and was working for the ranch of Allen Webb in Canadian when he applied for the Texas Department of Public Safety. From childhood, Guffey had a dream to become a Texas Ranger. An uncle and three older cousins had been in law enforcement at various times, and Guffey followed in their footsteps.[2] He was accepted into the DPS on October 1, 1968, and attended School No. 31 at the Training Academy as a patrolman-trainee. After graduating on January 10, 1969, he was assigned to the Highway Patrol's Brownsville office in Region 3 as a Patrolman I.[3] While Guffey was making strides in his ambitions, all was not well on the domestic front. He and Olivia filed for divorce in 107th District Court in November 1969, due to irreconcilable differences, and the proceedings were finalized on February 4, 1970.[4]

He married Margarita "Margie" Trevino on September 14, 1970. His new bride was a nineteen-year-old student in behavioral science at Texas Southmost College. They would have no children.[5]

On the night of January 29, 1972, Guffey clocked a vehicle allegedly traveling at ninety miles per hour in Brownsville. The trooper pulled the car over, only to discover the driver was three-term state representative Enrique "Henry" Sanchez, Jr. Disregarding the man's status, Guffey placed Sanchez under arrest for driving while intoxicated, and the legislator was promptly freed on a five-hundred-dollar bond. While appearing before County Court-At-Law Judge Robert Hernandez, District Attorney Franklin Thomas "Dut" Graham, Sr. filed a motion to dismiss the case on the grounds of insufficient evidence. The judge granted the request, and Sanchez, vying to be named speaker pro-tem of the House, was released.[6]

Guffey was promoted to Patrolman II on March 1, 1974. He attended Texas Southmost College in Brownsville from the fall semester of 1974 to the spring semester of 1975, and accumulated twenty-three credit hours. He continued to patrol the highways of the Valley and handled countless automobile accidents. On January 30, 1976, Raimer Leland Daltzell of Rancho Viejo was killed when his motorcycle collided with a car at the intersection of FM 1847 and FM 511. Daltzell's wife was a passenger on the bike, and she suffered nonlife threatening fractures. The driver of the car was not injured. Guffey worked the accident, and Daltzell's death was the seventh in the region since the beginning of the year. Guffey responded to another mishap late the following month when a crash on Southwest Road, three miles outside town, sent two area women to the hospital with minor injuries.[7]

Assigned to be Guffey's partner, Raymond Leonard Coffman began his first day as a Highway Patrolmen on March 8, 1976. The two would become best friends, and each served as best man at the other's wedding. Indeed, Guffey and future Senior Captain Bruce Casteel later encouraged Coffman to apply to the Texas Rangers in 1986.[8]

Guffey and Margarita filed for divorce, which was finalized on April 13, 1976.[9] While his permanent station remained Brownsville, he was on detached duty with the South Texas Border Stepped Up Law Enforcement Program in McAllen from February 1, 1977, to April 1, 1978. The purpose of the task force was to combat organized crime and narcotics trafficking along the Texas–Mexico border from Brownsville to Del Rio. He remained on detached duty with STBSULEP and was transferred to the Spearman office, which became his new permanent station. On January 1, 1979, he was promoted to the Texas Rangers and was assigned to Company D in Laredo. Captain Jack O'Day Dean was his supervisor.[10]

Guffey married twenty-one-year-old Josefina Garza "Josie" Gonzalez on June 15, 1977, at St. Luke's Catholic Church in Brownsville. Ironically, during their honeymoon, the newlyweds visited the Texas Ranger Hall of Fame and Museum in Waco. In time, they had two sons, Christopher Brian, born on October 13, 1978, and Travis Ryan, born on September 29, 1980.[11]

Guffey worked with two Texaco investigators on a high-volume credit card fraud. An official with the oil company later wrote Colonel Adams that "the case was difficult and required investigative knowledge, skill, perseverance, and patience. Ranger Guffey obviously employed all of those requirements, and was able to bring the case to a very successful conclusion with the arrest of two suspects."[12]

His sister, Brenda, described Guffey as an extremely humorous man who loved to tell and hear a joke. He also enjoyed playing practical jokes on his friends, but he could be very serious as well. If pushed, he had a temper. Gifted with a strong sense of right and wrong, he was inclined to defend the "underdog," or someone being bullied.[13]

Called to Carrizo Springs in mid-May to investigate Dimmit County officials mishandling Middle Rio Grande Development Council funds and other charges of public malfeasance, Guffey worked with Rangers Rudolfo Flores "Rudy" Rodriguez and Morgan Louis Miller in the probe. Cooperating with Assistant Attorney General Gerald "Jerry" Carruth, Rodriguez acted as lead investigator in the case. The grand jury handed down twelve indictments against five individuals, including County Attorney Pablo V. Bustamante. Already tried for official misconduct in Forty-seventh District Court, Bustamante had received seven months' probation. In the current case, he secured a plea bargain by offering to resign in return for not being tried on four additional charges.[14]

Guffey transferred to Company F in Brady on November 1, 1982, where he replaced Ranger Robert Charles "Bob" Favor. His supervisor was the highly respected Captain Robert Kenneth "Bob" Mitchell. Josie acquired a job as a loan clerk at the Commercial Bank in town, and Guffey gained entry into a "tight-knit circle" of five police officers, sheriff's deputies, and state troopers who shared the office. Having participated in Law Enforcement Rodeo Association team roping for years, he found an able partner in Jack Davis Andrews, special ranger and livestock association inspector. Guffey served as the header, and Andrews was the heeler. When not working, the two met together frequently at the Club Café coffee shop.[15]

Among the first cases Guffey worked in his new assignment was a shooting in Llano. On the night of December 20, a local man was fatally wounded with a shotgun after being discovered inside the Lindsey Fur Company on West Grayson Street. David Cherry, the furrier company's manager,

Bob Mitchell. *Courtesy Texas Ranger Hall of Fame and Museum, Waco, TX.*

was sleeping inside the building when he heard a noise. Searching the warehouse, Cherry encountered the burglar and fired his weapon.[16]

One of Company F's secretaries observed Guffey was "our birddog … he followed every little rabbit trail in an investigation. His reports were always well-documented." In contrast to the older generations of Texas Rangers, Captain Mitchell said, "Stan had a reputation for cranking out his paperwork in a hurry, sometimes typed up a report late at night, when his fellow Rangers were beat and ready to call it a day. He even carried a typewriter around in his DPS car."[17]

On Friday morning, January 11, 1985, Mitchell was at his Fort Fisher office in Waco when he received notification by telephone of a kidnapping. All but one of the company members were in town for a staff meeting, so the captain ordered his men to assemble in Alvarado.[18]

At approximately 7:40 that morning, thirteen-year-old Amy McNeil of Alvarado was abducted from her brother's Jeep while they were going to school. Amy, a blonde junior high cheerleader, had been with Mark McNeil, her seventeen-year-old brother, and their fourteen-year-old cousin. The three were near the McNeil home, one and a half miles outside town, when a gray automobile pulled onto the main road and began following Mark's vehicle. The car's driver increased his speed, but instead of passing as Mark believed he would, the car pulled alongside the Jeep. Mark and his passengers were forced off the road, and a man pointed a sawed-off shotgun at his face. Another assailant armed with a handgun moved to the passenger side of the Jeep and dragged a terrified Amy to the gray car. The two kidnappers warned Mark not to notify the authorities and drove away with their captive.[19]

Mitchell went to the McNeil residence, where he found the FBI already on the case. At ten o'clock in the morning, Amy's father, Don McNeil, a wealthy director of the Alvarado State Bank, received a telephone call from the kidnappers. The male voice on the other end of the line ordered him to ready $100,000 in cash for the next call at noon, or McNeil would never see Amy alive again. Using the bank's parking lot as a command post, the authorities assembled the ransom money and recorded the serial numbers.[20]

The kidnappers were late with their second call, but at 1 p.m. they again contacted McNeil. When he answered the ringing phone, he heard his daughter's frightened voice. Amy assured her father she was alright. The day was frigid, and McNeil asked if she was warm. "Yes," she answered. McNeil then asked her if she knew her location, to which she replied, "No." The call was abruptly terminated. The authorities had placed a trace on the phone line, but the conversation was too brief. The tap did specify the call had originated in the Dallas/Fort Worth metroplex. Shortly afterward, one of the kidnappers called back and instructed McNeil to await another call. The Rangers spent a restless night at the bank.[21]

The captors phoned numerous times throughout the following day, but the call for which McNeil and the lawmen had been waiting came at five o'clock Saturday afternoon. The kidnapper who seemed to be in charge ordered McNeil to proceed to a particular telephone booth at the Road Runner station on Miller Road and Interstate 30 in eastern Dallas and await additional instructions.[22]

Ransom money in hand, McNeil drove his Lincoln limousine toward the location, unobtrusively followed by Mitchell and his company, several Johnson County deputies, and two FBI agents. Guffey and Ranger Ralph Jackson Wadsworth had succeeded Doherty in Company B were assigned to fly in a single-engine DPS airplane as observers. One of McNeil's taillights was disconnected to distinguish his vehicle from the chase cars.[23]

Ranger John Lee "Johnny" Waldrip later related how Guffey had earlier in the day claimed he could not fly in helicopters and airplanes on account they made him nauseous. However, this may have been an excuse to avoid a task that took him out of the action. Josie remembered: "Stan told me that he did not want to be in the aircraft knowing that there was nothing he could do, but watch … The feeling of not being able to be on the front line was not him!" Whatever the motivation, when the captain asked for volunteers for the surveillance assignment, the unsuspecting Waldrip, thinking he was playing a good prank, told Mitchell how Guffey had experience in aircraft. Most importantly, though, throughout the entire ordeal that followed, the pilot and the Rangers in the airplane never lost sight of the events below.[24]

Once at the designated spot, Amy's father was ordered to drive eighty-two miles on I-20 to another phone booth at a Texaco station in Tyler. After arriving at the third destination at about 9:30 p.m., he was directed to a closed Gulf service station on I-30, seven miles east of Mount Pleasant in Titus County. Watching from above, Guffey and Wadsworth maintained their visual contact with McNeil's car and the procession of law enforcement vehicles in his wake. Rangers John Earl "Johnnie" Aycock and Joseph Brantley Foster arrived at the drop site ahead of McNeil and selected a place of concealment where they could watch the designated phone booth at the service station. Equipped with rifles and binoculars, they stretched out on the cold ground and waited.[25]

McNeil was ten minutes late to the drop because his limousine had experienced engine trouble. After waiting for a seemingly endless amount of time, Mitchell canceled the operation around midnight and ordered everyone back to the McNeil residence. As the officers were driving away, Aycock and Foster observed a 1983 Buick driving slowly past the service station without stopping, then turning onto I-30. The Rangers suspected the kidnappers and Amy were in the vehicle, and radioed a description of the car to the other lawmen. The Rangers learned from the vehicle registration that the Buick had been reported stolen in Arlington earlier that night.[26]

Rangers Joe Frank Wilie and James Esten "Jimmy" Ray, Sr., occupying the nearest available unit, spotted the car a short while later in Mount Pleasant and moved to intercept. The fugitives turned off the road onto another, stopped, and switched off their headlights. However, the DPS aircraft, with Guffey and Wadsworth on board, kept the Buick in sight and vectored the Rangers to its location. Driving at speeds exceeding one hundred miles per hour, Wilie and Ray approached the suspect vehicle. Suddenly, its lights came on, and the car roared away. The officers gave chase through the city streets, then began taking fire.[27]

"They're shooting at us," Wilie radioed Mitchell, who was still parked near the drop site.

"Are you sure?" the captain responded.

"I'd sure welcome a second opinion," Wilie replied as bullets ricocheted off the front of the state unit and shattered the windshield. The two Rangers pulled their pistols to return fire, then one of the kidnappers dragged Amy into view. The officers refrained from shooting, and one of the captors' bullets perforated the gas line of the Rangers' unit; fuel sprayed across the hot manifold. Wilie and Ray were forced to suspend the chase as flames rolled out from under the hood of their car.[28]

By this time, Captain Mitchell realized the Rangers would not be able to rescue Amy without a confrontation. They had to stop the Buick and keep the abductors from hurting or killing her. Passing Wilie's disabled car, Rangers

Howard Burton "Slick" Alfred and Johnny Waldrip in one car, Ranger John Wallace Dendy and Johnson County Deputy Sheriff D. J. Maulder in another, and two FBI agents in a third, continued the high-speed pursuit across Titus, Franklin, and Hopkins Counties over a span of twenty minutes. The chase abruptly ended in the small town of Saltillo where the kidnappers ran out of gas in the front yard of a private house.[29]

Two of the abductors leaped out of their car, took cover behind a Dodge van parked in the driveway, and opened fire at the lawmen with shotguns. As their unit screeched to a halt in the yard, Dendy and Maulder engaged the kidnappers with a rifle, while Waldrip and Alfred laid down a ferocious fire with a shotgun and Slick's Smith & Wesson .357 Magnum from the street. From the circling DPS plane, Wadsworth radioed, "They're having a gunfight down there! They're having a hell of a gunfight!" The federal agents stopped immediately behind the van, their car's siren wailing, and, as they came under fire, they ducked down to the floor and remained there.[30]

After two or three minutes of exchanging gunshots, the gunmen began trying to surrender. Alfred and Maulder ran toward the Buick. Peering inside, Maulder spied two males and two females. He identified one of the females as Amy. Alfred asked him, "Is that Amy?" Maulder answered she was the kidnapped girl. Alfred replied, "Let me have her."[31]

The Ranger took the teenager into his arms and led her back toward his car. He drove her to the Mini Mart to meet her father, who had ridden in Mitchell's car during the pursuit. At the store, McNeil dashed to his daughter and enveloped her in a tight embrace.[32]

The kidnappers, four men and one woman, were by this time in custody, including the two gunmen who had suffered minor gunshot wounds. They were taken by ambulance to the hospital for treatment. Authorities later linked the suspects to a crime spree of car thefts and armed robberies in Dallas. Guffey later commented he had felt completely helpless as he watched the gun battle from the air, and swore he would never again be placed in that kind of situation. The officers involved in the case had not had a decent night's sleep since the three-day episode began. With the teenager safely returned to her parents and the kidnappers confined in jail, the Rangers were ready for a well-earned rest.[33]

Guffey was involved in another abduction case after New Braunfels pharmacist Eldon Thomas Calk picked up a hitchhiker later tentatively identified as Jack Kelly around 4:00 p.m. along Texas Highway 46. One mile from Boerne, Calk's passenger pulled a knife and commandeered the pickup truck. The kidnapper drove to an undeveloped subdivision on Kendalia Road where he demanded Calk's billfold. Finding no cash in the wallet, he beat his captive, inflicting damage to the right eye and bruises and abrasions to the face, arms, and back. The two then drove through Johnson City and Fredericksburg into Llano County before the vehicle run out of gas on Texas 16 outside Cherokee, between Llano and San Saba. Kelly fled on foot into a pasture while Calk used the telephone in a nearby house to report his four-hour ordeal to the authorities. Officers, including Guffey, Johnny Waldrip, San Saba County Sheriff Bill Williams, and Llano County Chief Deputy Sheriff Rod Decker, searched the area and called for bloodhounds. Shortly after nine o'clock, two shotgun-wielding ranchers chanced upon Kelly and held him at gunpoint until deputies arrived. He was transported to the San Saba County jail and charged with aggravated kidnapping. Bail was set at fifty thousand dollars.[34]

Beginning on Wednesday, January 14, 1987, the small resort community of Horseshoe Bay on the shores of Lake LBJ, forty-five miles northwest of Austin in Llano County, was rocked by a violent chain of events supposedly found only in the big cities. At approximately 2:00 p.m., Denise Johnson, the twenty-two-year-old live-in maid for the William "Bill" Whitehead family, called her employer's secretary, who was also her roommate, and reported she was being abducted from their residence at 12051 Lighthouse Drive. In addition to leasing the house for his employees' use, Whitehead, owner of Whitehead Enterprises trucking company, kept an office on the premises. Ranger Waldrip and Deputy Decker were called to respond. Waldrip interviewed the secretary, who related Johnson had said she was in the house across the street. The Ranger organized a search of the neighboring homes, but the officers found no sign of intruders or forced entry. He then canvassed all of Johnson's friends and acquaintances without any success toward finding her. No ransom demand was ever delivered, so, on January 20, the authorities requested the public's assistance in locating Johnson.[35]

At 4:00 a.m., on Thursday, January 22, Whitehead and his wife, Leigh, received a telephone call at their home at 12044 Lighthouse and were told their daughter, two-year-old Kara Leigh, had been kidnapped while the family was sleeping. The perpetrator had used Denise's key to enter the Whitehead home and even lingered to eat some of the family's food and smoke one of Whitehead's cigars. By two in the afternoon, the Whiteheads had received still more calls demanding thirty thousand dollars in twenty-dollar notes and a fully fueled automobile in exchange for Kara Leigh's safe return. The abductor also demanded a promise no one would hinder his escape. Captain Mitchell and Rangers Guffey, Waldrip, Joe B. Davis, James Louis "Jim" Miller, Fred Lee Cummings, and Johnnie Aycock had been requested to assist the investigation earlier that morning by Special Agent-in-Charge Byron Sage of the FBI's Austin field office. Sage was supervising the joint operation involving the sheriff's office and federal agents. The FBI began a series of negotiations with the kidnapper and was able to determine he had likely killed Johnson. The suspect was described as "cool, calm, in control and very businesslike in his demands. He seemed to know what he was doing." Using a telephone trace, the authorities were able to determine the calls had come from a vacant house across the street at 12036 Lighthouse. The perpetrator had been able to see the activity at the Whitehead house by peeking under the slightly raised garage door.[36]

The suspect was later identified as Brent Albert Beeler, a twenty-three-year-old Houstonian who had violated his parole for credit card fraud. The lawmen knew that, having killed Johnson, Beeler was fully capable of murdering Kara Leigh as well. The Rangers hatched a high-risk plan at their command post in the Marble Falls city hall to entice Beeler into coming out of hiding, safely recover the girl, and take the perpetrator into custody. Guffey and Aycock both volunteered for the apprehension and rescue assignment. Aycock would later comment: "We both knew we stood a chance of dying. We weren't sure how it would come out." Because of the low light, the rapid actions that would likely decide the situation, and the possibility that Beeler had accomplices, no police sharpshooters were deployed for the operation. However, the Rangers were equipped with body armor and had received extensive weapons instruction as a normal part of their training.[37]

Following instructions, at 9:29, the evening of the twenty-second, Bill Whitehead drove a 1987 Lincoln Town Car provided by Llano County District Attorney Sam Oatman into the driveway of the vacant house, left the keys in the ignition and a briefcase containing the ransom money on the front seat, and exited the running vehicle to return home. The vehicle's back seat had been removed, and Guffey and Aycock were partially hidden

John Aycock. *Courtesy Texas Ranger Hall of Fame and Museum, Waco, TX.*

under a blanket in the open space. One minute later, Beeler emerged from the house carrying Kara Leigh, placed her on the front seat, and grabbed the briefcase containing the money. When he tossed the case into the backseat, he saw the Rangers. Pistol in hand, the two lawmen rose up from the back seat. Guffey identified himself as a Texas Ranger and ordered Beeler to surrender. As he backed out of the front seat, Beeler swore and shot Guffey in the head with a Smith & Wesson Model 29 .44 Magnum handgun. The Ranger had time to get off one shot before he was struck, but the bullet missed. Aycock reached into the front seat and pulled Kara Leigh into the back, shielding her with his own body. At the same time, he fired his 9 mm pistol nine times through the windshield and driver's side door, hitting Beeler in the groin, side, chest, and shoulder. He then exited the vehicle to check the fallen men's conditions. Beeler had died instantly as a result of his wounds. Rushed to Shepperd Memorial Hospital in Burnet, Guffey was pronounced dead on arrival.[38]

Authorities were still concerned Beeler might have had an accomplice, so they cleared the house. Approximately fifteen minutes later, the body of Denise Johnson was discovered in a boathouse behind the vacant residence. She had either been bludgeoned to death or suffocated when her mouth and nose were taped over two days before. She had also been tortured and raped more than once. Inside the house itself, investigators found empty liquor bottles and a collection of pistols and rifles. Beeler had obtained his arsenal and supplies by burglarizing area homes.[39]

Colonel James Blackburn Adams, director of the DPS, commented at the scene on Friday that if Guffey and Aycock "had not acted in the unselfish, heroic manner" they did, little Kara Leigh would also have died.[40] Guffey "chose to identify himself as a Ranger. By attempting to effect the apprehension without bloodshed, he gave his life … Had Guffey, when he had the opportunity, shot and killed the kidnapper before identifying himself, before giving [Beeler] an opportunity to surrender. I don't think there is any question in anyone's mind that the Rangers would have been crucified for having executed someone without benefit of trial."[41]

Beeler "just picked us out at random," Leigh Whitehead said in an interview. "It's been just a real nightmare for the whole family."[42]

The two houses of the Seventieth Legislature unanimously adopted House Concurrent Resolution No. 23 and Senate Concurrent Resolution No. 18 on January 27, 1987, each of which paid tribute to the life of Stan Guffey and his commitment to his duty and extended sympathy to his family.[43] The Public Safety Commission adopted a resolution on January 29 that recognized and applauded Stan Guffey's dedication and courage even at the cost of his own life. Guffey and Aycock were each awarded the Department of Public Safety's highest award, the Commissioners' Medal of Valor, on February 10.[44]

Guffey's funeral was originally scheduled to be held at St. Patrick's Catholic Church in Brady, where Stan was a member, but its size was too small to accommodate the anticipated turnout. Instead, the service was held at the Sunset Ridge Church of Christ west of town. More than nineteen hundred mourners came to pay their respects on Monday, January 26, including the Whitehead family. Amy McNeil and her family also attended. Colonel Adams gave the eulogy and reflected, "His courage in doing what is right and had to be done cost him his life … It is an example of raw courage and heroism at its best." An escort of 150 police vehicles and a three-mile-long funeral procession accompanied the hearse carrying Stan Guffey's body to his final resting place at Resthaven Cemetery. He received a twenty-one-gun salute and a DPS bugler played Taps at the gravesite.[45]

The following day, services for Denise Johnson, a native of Omaha, were held at the Evangelical Covenant Church in Wauss, Nebraska. She was laid to rest at Woodlawn Cemetery.[46]

District Attorney Oatman, a close personal friend of Guffey, convened a special grand jury to investigate the facts of the case, a routine procedure when law officers are involved in shootings. After meeting for seven-and-a-half hours on February 12, the panel returned its findings. The officers involved were absolved of any blame in the deaths of Guffey and Beeler. "Beeler 'called it'," Aycock said. """We didn't call it. When a man draws a gun and shoots at you, he calls it." The grand jurors also found sufficient evidence to indict Beeler for two counts of capital murder and two counts of kidnapping, determined that the killing of Beeler by Ranger Aycock was justifiable homicide, and praised the work of Guffey, Aycock, and Waldrip, as well as Oatman and the other law enforcement agencies present.[47]

The grand jury further investigated allegations that an armed Beeler had been questioned, but not detained, by a security guard on December 27. Approximately a half-dozen sheriff's officers acted as security for the unincorporated development. The Horseshoe Bay Property Owners' Association compensated the sheriff's office for the deputies' services. Beeler was able to talk his way out of the situation by telling the guard he was living in an area home and had not wanted to leave the firearm in a car stuck in the mud nearby. Besides the handgun, there was nothing suspicious about his story or demeanor, so the guard let him go. If the officer had checked further, he would have discovered the parole violation and bench warrant on Beeler. The grand jury felt "that there has been a significant lack of cooperation and communication between law enforcement agencies within the county." The members expected "better cooperation and communication in the future."[48]

Based on his heroism and professionalism, Guffey was inducted into the Texas Ranger Hall of Fame on June 6, 1987. Three hundred and fifty people were in attendance, including Josie, Willora, Marsen and LaVerda, Brenda and her husband, and Linda and her daughter. Colonel Adams, Special Agent Sage, and Ranger Waldrip paid tribute to the fallen officer.[49] For more than fifteen years, the Curtis Stroup Arena near Brady was the venue for the Stan Guffey Memorial Junior Rodeo, which quickly became the largest competition of its type in the state. More than twelve hundred youths from Texas and six other states participated in the 1989 rodeo. The top prize for each event was a handmade trophy saddle.[50]

Two months after her husband's induction, Josie filed a wrongful-death lawsuit on behalf of her two sons against the Horseshoe Bay Property Owner's Association. The petition alleged the security guard who questioned Beeler in December 1986 and allowed him to go free had been negligent in his duties. As the guard's employer, the association was liable for Stan's subsequent death. No specific amount of compensation was requested. On January 17, 1989, the two parties settled for an undisclosed sum. The terms of the settlement were sealed per court order as the agreement concerned minor children.

The attorneys and their clients could not comment on the specifics as confidentiality was a condition of the settlement.[51]

The senseless tragedy was compounded further on June 24, 1992, when Bill, Leigh, and Kara Whitehead and three friends were killed in an airplane crash near Alamogordo, New Mexico. Whitehead's twin-engine turboprop had been flying from Oregon en route to home in Llano. "They all left there at the same time, and they just didn't get back," said a relative of one of the crash victims who did not want to be identified. "We don't know what happened. We can't say sometimes what's meant to be."[52]

On January 21, 2012, Josie, their four grown sons, grandchildren, friends and other family, and the Former Texas Rangers Association held a ceremony at Resthaven Cemetery. A Memorial Cross was placed on the late Ranger's gravesite "to honor his life and sacrifice." At the service, Josie remarked, "It's hard for people who never met Stan to grasp what he was. But for those of us who knew him, no words are needed."[53]

Josefina struggled to raise two elementary-age boys as a young widow, but she persevered. Returning to her job at the bank, she received a pension from the state, which was the equivalent of one-half of her husband's salary. A member of the Whitehead family established a trust for their sons. She married an orthopedic surgeon in November 1991. They lived in Alice before moving to San Marcos in 2009. She owns and operates a business that manages medical sharps for medical practices, surgical centers, and hospitals. Josie and her husband also manage a cattle ranch.[54]

Michael enlisted in the U.S. Air Force and served in Kuwait during Operation Desert Storm. After his discharge, he attended Lubbock Christian University, then worked with his brother Stacy as a plumber. He married in 2011 and is currently employed at a nitrogen facility in Oklahoma as a service supervisor.[55]

Stacy enlisted in the U.S. Marine Corps after graduating from high school in 1986. He was one week away from completing boot camp at Camp Pendleton, California, when he received news of his father's death. He deployed to Kuwait for Operation Desert Storm. After separating from the service, he attended Texas Tech University for one year, then became a licensed plumber. He married and fathered one son and two daughters.

He owned his own plumbing business and later became the maintenance manager for a hospital in Plano. He divorced in 2010 and remarried two years later. Stacy currently works as a building manager for a school district in the Dallas/Fort Worth metroplex.[56]

Travis is a math teacher in a Mansfield middle school. He married in June 2006, and he and his wife have two boys. He also has a daughter from a previous relationship.[57]

Through his sacrifice, Stan Guffey helped to make certain a dangerous murderer could no longer hurt innocent people, and a little girl could enjoy a few more years of her childhood. In the course of split-second decisions, who could know the final outcome? By his actions, though, Guffey and his career has become a standard by which future generations of Texas Rangers can measure themselves.

Afterword

With Stan Guffey's tragic story having been told, this trilogy comes to an end. Before closing, a few thoughts might be in order. The Texas Ranger service has been in existence since 1823, and many heroic men, and more recently some equally intrepid women, have been the custodians of that illustrious name. The Rangers traditionally, although not always in practice, prefer to focus on the teamwork that is important to effective law enforcement rather than highlight the individual. They do honor certain Rangers, though, as the best among them. So, who is the next to be inducted into the Hall of Fame? Will it be Glenn Elliott, "the Ranger's Ranger," or Bob Mitchell, "the Ranger's Captain," or some other worthy individual? No definite answer has been shared to date, but that choice will be decided by active and retired Rangers at a future annual reunion. The decision will not be a popularity contest, but, rather, a serious appraisal of a career of someone who has best demonstrated the ideals and traditions of an organization they all love. Someone who has acted with courage in the face of mortal danger, and someone who has displayed dedication to the people of the state and, indeed, to a law-abiding society in general.

Naturally, no human institution is perfect. The pages comprising this trilogy have depicted the highs and lows of the Texas Rangers, and sometimes they have been found wanting. The thirty-one men discussed in these three books are representatives of their particular time and place in history. The French phrase *autres temps, autres moeurs*, or "other times, other customs," correctly notes the cultural milieu of the past is not the same as that of the present. Some people centuries ago might have done things that leave a twenty-first-century observer aghast, but there are always reasons for an action. Usually, something more substantial than the person was merely an -ist exhibiting an -ism. Whether that motivation, in the end, was justified is the basis for historical debate. Ultimately, context is key to understanding preceding events.

Some previous authors have not taken this truth to heart. The literature concerning the Rangers exists along a spectrum with two polar opposites. One extreme posits the conviction the Indian fighters and lawmen can do nothing right. The opposite end is for those who believe Rangers can do no wrong. Américo Paredes definitely belonged to the first camp. He was bitterly opposed to the mythos of the Rangers as espoused by fellow folklorist J. Frank Dobie and historian Walter P. Webb. Paredes's work was more rooted in the popular folklore (i.e., oral history and song) of the border country rather than a balanced analysis of written primary sources. The trio of Chicano scholars Julian Samora, Joe Bërnal, and Albert Peña depicted the nineteenth-century Rangers as brutal and racist men who slaughtered Mexicans and Indians indiscriminately. As presented throughout these three books, there were undoubtedly some who did not live up to the ideal, but primary documentation fails to support the revisionist notion of a systemic pattern of murder. Despite this, modern activist historians have continued to advance the themes of Paredes, Samora, Bërnal, and Peña through a combination of misinterpretations, assumptions, confirmation bias, dismissals of any ambiguities, and the uncritical acceptance of only one version.

The most recent work at the time of this writing was produced by former *Dallas Morning News* reporter Doug Swanson. Being coincidentally released at the same time as the most recent wave of anti-police sentiment in the United States, Swanson authored a textbook example of advocacy journalism rather than a serious study of history. Although deeply flawed, the book did have repercussions. Prompted by the general threat of civil unrest, and swayed by early excerpts of Swanson's volume, the Dallas City Council summarily opted to remove the famous Ranger statue from Love Field's main terminal. Additionally, the Texas Ranger Hall of Fame and Museum found itself besieged by a wave of negative press from outlets with a common political perspective.

On the other side of the spectrum, Webb was undoubtedly biased toward the Rangers, although he did attempt to support his conclusions through good scholarly practices. Robert Utley, Mike Cox, Chuck Parsons, Bob Alexander, Harold J. Weiss, and many others have taken a more nuanced "center-Webb" position in that the pro generally outweighs the con. This author also believes the Rangers have largely been a positive, albeit imperfect, force for good in Texas and the Southwest. This viewpoint concedes problems in policy, procedure, and performance did arise, but the historical evidence shows the Ranger service underwent multiple reforms over the years in a steady march toward modernity. Building upon the efforts of those who came before, the current members of the service have more than earned the trust gifted to them by the people of Texas.

Throughout the thousands of pages that have filled these three books, it has been the intention of this author to present thirty-one men as flesh-and-blood human beings who answered the call to service in their respective eras. They were not perfect men, but they were the type who moved toward the danger in order to protect that which they held most dear. They were men who epitomized the Ranger Ideal.

Endnotes

Abbreviations

A&ISD-TSLAC: Archives and Information Services Division, Texas State Library and Archives Commission

AA: *Austin American*

AAS: *Austin American-Statesman*

AHQ: *Arkansas Historical Quarterly*

AS: *Austin Statesman*

ASU: Angelo State University

BCAH: Briscoe Center for American History

BDH: *Brownsville Daily Herald*

DMN: *Dallas Morning News*

ETHJ: *East Texas Historical Journal*

FCJ: *Floresville Chronicle-Journal*

FTRA: Former Texas Ranger Association

FWST: *Fort Worth Star-Telegram*

GDN: *Galveston Daily News*

LWT: *Laredo Weekly Times*

MR: Monthly Returns

NARA: National Archives and Records Administration

NPRC: National Personnel Records Center

RAG: *Report of the Adjutant General of the State of Texas*

ROS: Record of Scouts

RSR: Ranger Service Records

SADE: *San Antonio Daily Express*

SAE: *San Antonio Express*

SAEN: *San Antonio Evening News*

SAL: *San Antonio Light*

SALG: *San Antonio Light and Gazette*

SHQ: *Southwestern Historical Quarterly*

SR: Scout Reports

SRSU: Sul Ross State University

TRD: *Texas Ranger Dispatch*

TRF Investigation: *Proceedings of the Joint Committee of the Senate and the House in the Investigation of the State Ranger Force*, Thirty-sixth Legislature, Regular Session.

TRHF&M: Texas Ranger Hall of Fame and Museum

TSLAC: Texas State Library and Archives Commission
WNT: *Waco News-Tribune*

**Note: In order to abbreviate references for sources found in the Texas State Archives, this author has adopted, in part, Robert Utley's method of citing the record group followed by the box number: e.g., 401-178 denotes Record Group 401 (Adjutant General's office), box 178.

Notes for Chapter 1

1. Texas Death Certificate, William Lee Wright, March 20, 1942, File No. 22. Although his hometown is sometimes given as Yorktown in DeWitt County, William W. Sterling and Maude Gilliland both correctly maintained Wright was born in Lockhart. His death certificate and obituary also listed Caldwell County as his birthplace. Furthermore, the Caldwell County tax rolls for 1868 place Wright's father in that particular locale.
2. Marjorie Burnett Hyatt, "Littleberry Wright Family," *History of DeWitt County, Texas* (Dallas, TX: Curtis Media Corporation, 1991), 830; *FCJ*, December 15, 1966. Gail Shriber, Wilson County Historian, wrote a lengthy article for the paper entitled "The Life and Times of Captain Will L. Wright Texas Ranger and Law Officer." Death Certificates, Mrs. Cornelia Elizabeth Cline, January 3, 1919, File No. 5244, Milam Harper Wright, February 14, 1938, File No. 7261; Find A Grave: Zora Lee Wright Warren; D. E. Kilgore, *A Ranger Legacy: 150 Years of Service to Texas* (Austin: Madrona Press, 1973), 57; Patty Newman Turner, et al., *Joseph and Rachel Rabb Newman, An Old Three Hundred Family, and their Descendants* (Odessa, TX: P.N. Turner, 1998), 135, 145; *Seventh U.S. Census*, Panola County, Mississippi; *Eighth U.S. Census*, Karnes County, Texas.

   E. A. "Dogie" Wright mentioned, in addition to Neelie and Zora, an aunt named "Dolly" who was buried in Sutherland Springs. Transcript of Interview, Tape 16, Box 2K227, E. A. "Dogie" Wright Papers, BCAH, 1–2. Whether this was a nickname for Mary is undetermined. Mrs. Shriber referred to the third sister as "Belle (Mrs. Johnson)."

   Anne's grandfather had been John Jackson Tumlinson, Sr., the first *alcalde* of the Colorado District in Stephen F. Austin's original colony. Her father, Joseph, served in Captain Robert M. Coleman's ranger company in 1835, and he went on to fight in the Texas Revolution. He was also a leading participant in the Sutton-Taylor feud. Her two uncles,

John, Jr. and Peter, had both commanded ranger companies before the Civil War, the former in Major Robert A. Williamson's Ranger Corps, and the latter during the Cortina troubles. Samuel H. Tumlinson, *Tumlinson, A Genealogy* (Eagle Bay, BC: privately printed, n.d.), 38, 40–41, 43–44, 65–71; Kilgore, *A Ranger Legacy*, 33–38, 40, 49, 51–52, 83 n9; Steven L. Moore, *Savage Frontier: Rangers, Riflemen, and Indian Wars in Texas* (Denton: University of North Texas Press, 2002), 1: 55, 76. Milam would continue in the family tradition of law enforcement by serving as a Ranger under Captain John R. Hughes, as a mounted Customs inspector, and as sheriff of Hudspeth County. Maude T. Gilliland, *Horsebackers of the Brush Country* (Brownsville: Springman-King Co., 1968), 113. See also Lucille Latham White, "The Tumlinsons," *Old West* 18 (Winter 1981): 14–17.

3. Confederate Muster Roll Abstract Records, L. B. Wright, TSLAC.
4. *FCJ*, December 15, 1966; Tax Rolls, Caldwell County, 1868–1869; *Ninth U.S. Census*, DeWitt County, Texas; L. B. Wright, Box 2-9/910, Bonds and Oaths of County and State Officials, TSLAC; Chuck Parsons, *The Sutton-Taylor Feud: The Deadliest Blood Feud in Texas* (Denton: University of North Texas, 2009), 126, 132; Turner, et al., *Joseph and Rachel Rabb Newman*, 145–146.
5. Hyatt, "Littleberry Wright Family," 830; Interview with Zora Belle Wright Fore, December 7, 1973, Recording A1993-005.0253, South Texas Oral History & Folklore Collection, Texas A&M University at Kingsville. Hereafter cited as Zora Fore interview, 1973. *FCJ*, December 15, 1966; Maurine Liles, comp., "Texas Ranger Captain Will Wright," MS, 2009, n.p.; Richard B. McCaslin, *Sutherland Springs, Texas: Saratoga on the Cibolo* (Denton: University of North Texas Press, 2017), 89, 114–116; *SAE*, March 20, 1932, March 8, 1942 (quotation); Turner, et al., *Joseph and Rachel Rabb Newman*, 145–146. Ann died on October 19, 1923, at Captain Wright's home in Floresville. *FCJ*, October 26, 1923.
6. *FCJ*, March 13, 1942; Sammy Tise, *Texas County Sheriffs* (Albuquerque, NM: Oakwood Printing, 1989), 546; Liles, "Texas Ranger Captain Will Wright," n.p.
7. *SAE*, April 5, 1925 (quotation); *Houston Post*, June 8, 13, 15, 18, 25, 1897; *Laredo Daily Times*, June 14, 1897; *BDH*, June 17, 28, August 2, 1897; *San Antonio Daily Light*, July 7, 21, 24, 30, August 2, 1897; West C. Gilbreath, *Death on the Gallows: The Encyclopedia of Legal Executions in Texas* (Fort Worth: Wild Horse Press, 2017), 370–371.

The June 7, 1896, issue of the *Daily Light* carried a story of a Maximo Martinez, who had been accused of rape but released due to lack of evidence. It is unknown whether this man was the same individual who committed the three murders. The name was not uncommon.

8. Hyatt, "Littleberry Wright Family," 830; Turner, et al., *Joseph and Rachel Rabb Newman*, 148.
9. Liles, "Texas Ranger Captain Will Wright," n.p.; Monthly Returns, Company E, February 28, 1899; Inactive Personnel Record, William L. Wright, TDPS; H. G. DuBose, "Report of Rangers Work in Laredo," March 28, 1899, Volume 15, Box 2R289, Walter Prescott Webb Collection, BCAH. The original may be found in Box 401-450, TSLAC. Transcript of Interview, Tape 17, Box 2K227, "Dogie" Wright Papers, BCAH, 4; Bob Alexander and Donaly E. Brice, *Texas Rangers: Lives, Legend, and Legacy* (Denton: University of North Texas Press, 2017), 334–335; *Houston Post*, March 24, 1902. For more on Rogers and his distinguished career, see Darren L. Ivey, *The Ranger Ideal Volume 2* (Denton: University of North Texas Press, 2018), Ch. 12.
10. Records of Scouts, Company E, April–June 1899; Monthly Returns, Company E, May 31, 1899; *Houston Post*, June 9, 1899; Special Order No. 8, June 8, 1899, 401-1013, TSLAC; Wright to Scurry, June 9, 1899, Wright to Rogers, June 10, 1899, Volume 15, Webb Collection, BCAH; James C. Kearney, et al., *No Hope for Heaven, No Fear of Hell: The Stafford-Townsend Feud of Colorado County, Texas, 1871–1911* (Denton: University of Texas Press, 2016), 176.
11. ROS, Company E, July–August 1899; *DMN*, July 22, 1899.
12. Robert Maxwell Brown, *Strain of Violence: Historical Studies of American Violence and Vigilantism* (New York: Oxford University Press, 1975), 150–151.
13. Special Order No. 16, August 18, 1899, Special Orders No. 19, August 19, 1899, 401-1013, TSLAC; ROS, Company E, August 1899; *SAE*, August 20, 1899; *SAL*, August 20, 1899; Tise, *Texas County Sheriffs*, 400; Find A Grave: Jefferson Davis Bland.
14. ROS, Company E, September 1899.
15. MR, Company E, December 31, 1899; RSR, M. H. Wright, 401–178, TSLAC; ROS, Company E, December 1899; *San Antonio Express*, July 25, 1902.
16. ROS, Company E, February 1900; *GDN*, February 1, 1900; *Houston Daily Post*, February 8, 1900; Kearney, et al., *No Hope for Heaven, No Fear of Hell*, 107–108, 165.

17. ROS, Company E, February–April 1900 (quotation); *Bryan Morning Eagle*, February 21, 22, 1900; *SAE*, February 22, 1900; *Houston Daily Post*, February 22, 23, 1900; Tise, *Texas County Sheriffs*, 400; Find A Grave: Levie Old.
18. Special Orders No. 29, February 19, 1900, 401-1013, TSLAC; ROS, Company E, March 1900; MR, Company E. June 30–July 31, 1900.
19. RSR, W. L. Wright, 401-178, TSLAC; *Corpus Christi Caller*, June 15, 1900; ROS, Company E, August 1900.
20. MR, Company E, November 30, 1899, October 31, 1900; RAG, 1899–1900; ROS, Company E, November 1899, September–October 1900; *BDH*, October 29, 30, 1900; *Laredo Daily Times*, October 25, 26, 1900; Donald Clifton Crawford, "James Richard Devenport," unpublished MS, 1999, 1, 4, 7. Mr. Crawford is the grandson of Jim Devenport, the spelling of whose birthname was changed to "Davenport" in the printed press of the time and in subsequent documentation. Cox, *Time of the Rangers*, 22; Annette Martin Ludeman, *La Salle County: South Texas Brush County, 1856–1975* (Quanah, TX: Nortex Press, 1975), 118–120; Stanley D. Casto, *Settlement of the Cibolo-Nueces Strip: A Partial History of La Salle County* (Hillsboro, TX: Hill Junior College Press, 1969), 14–15.
21. *San Antonio Daily Light*, October 26, 1900 (first quotation); William Warren Sterling, *Trails and Trials of a Texas Ranger* (Norman: University of Oklahoma Press, 1968), 409–411 (second quotation); Find A Grave: William Merrill Burwell. For more on Devenport's earlier misdeeds, see Bob Alexander, *Whiskey River Ranger: The Old West Life of Baz Outlaw* (Denton: University of North Texas Press, 2016), 45–47.
22. ROS, Company E, November–December 1900; Special Orders No. 97, November 24, 1900, 401-1013, TSLAC (quotation); *Alpine Avalanche*, December 21, 1900; *Tenth U.S. Census*, De Witt and Karnes Counties, Texas; Death Certificate, Mathews Abner Avant, July 30, 1925, File No. 24419.
23. ROS, Company E, January 1901; Find A Grave: Samuel Vaughn "Pete" Edwards, Jr.
24. ROS, Company E, March–April 1901; MR, Company E, April 30, 1901; *RAG, 1901–1902*, 31–32; *Cuero Daily Record*, March 2, 1900; *Houston Post*, March 3, 1900; Texas Department of Criminal Justice, Convict Record Ledgers, 1998/038-155, TSLAC, 172. Named a captain

in the newspapers, Robinson had served in that rank as a chaplain with the Fourth Texas Volunteers in the Spanish-American War. United States Volunteers Service Records, William D. Robinson, 401–248, TSLAC.

25. ROS, Company E, May–June 1901; *Cuero Daily Record*, June 16, 17, 18, 21, 23, 24, 25, 1901; *SADE*, June 23, 1901; Kilgore, *A Ranger Legacy*, 68–69; Richard J. Mertz, "'No One Can Arrest Me': The Story of Gregorio Cortez," *Journal of South Texas* 1 (1974): 8–9; Lewis Smith, "Manhunt!," *The Cattleman* 63 (June 1976): 139–140; C. L. Patterson, *Sensational Texas Manhunt* (San Antonio, TX: Sid Murray & Son, 1939), 13–15; Hyatt, "Littleberry Wright Family," 830; Turner, et al., *Joseph and Rachel Rabb Newman*, 148; Transcript of Interviews, Tape 3, Box 2K227, "Dogie" Wright Papers, BCAH, 2.
26. MR, Company C, September 30–October 31, 1901, March 31–April 30, 1902; *San Antonio Light*, April 17, 1902; *Twelfth U.S. Census*, Kimble County, Texas; *Palo Pinto County Star*, April 25, 1902; *Corpus Christi Caller-Times*, April 10, 1938. In his account for the newspaper, Wright had remembered McAtee's name as Batees "or Battice, a French name." *Kerrville Mountain Sun*, April 28, 1938.
27. MR, Company E, April 30, 1902; *Palo Pinto County Star*, April 25, 1902; *Corpus Christi Caller-Times*, April 10, 1938; *Kerrville Mountain Sun*, April 28, 1938; Tise, *Texas County Sheriffs*, 307.
28. MR, Company C, April 30–June 30, 1902; *Shiner Gazette*, July 16, 1902; *Houston Daily Post*, July 21, 22, 24, 1902; *Austin Daily Statesman*, July 21, 1902.
29. *FCJ*, December 15, 1966; MR, Company C, August 31, 1902; Inactive Personnel Record, William L. Wright, TDPS; *SAE*, September 1, 4, 1902.
30. Tise, *Texas County Sheriffs*, 546; Thad Sitton, *The Texas Sheriff: Lord of the County Line* (Norman: University of Oklahoma Press, 2000), 78–79; Transcript of Interviews, Tape 3, "Dogie" Wright Papers, BCAH, 2, 14; *SAE*, January 19, 1903.
31. William Berry Wright, *Career Hunting: Texas Rangers vs. Standard Oiler* (El Cajon, CA: W. B. Wright, 1982), 2; Transcript of Interviews, Tape 3, "Dogie" Wright Papers, BCAH, 2-3; Kilgore, *A Ranger Legacy*, 69; Zora Fore interview, 1973 (quotation).
32. Jim Coffey, "Will Wright: Rangers and Prohibition," *TRD* 20 (Summer 2006): 8–9; *SAE*, November 17, 1902, March 8, 1942 (quotation); Sitton, *The Texas Sheriff*, 5–6.

33. *San Antonio Daily Light*, June 9, 1904.
34. *SAE*, July 18, 1904; Tise, *Texas County Sheriffs*, 546.
35. *San Antonio Daily Light*, July 26, 1906.
36. Tise, *Texas County Sheriffs*, 546.
37. *AS*, January 30, 1907.
38. *SADE*, July 1, 3, 1907; *AS*, July 2, 1907; *San Antonio Gazette*, July 3, 1907; *SAL*, August 3, July 3, 1907.
39. *SAL*, November 30, December 1, 2, 1907.
40. Hyatt, "Littleberry Wright Family," 830; Wright, *Career Hunting*, 1; Turner, et al., *Joseph and Rachel Rabb Newman*, 148. Wright's obituary seems to be the only source that mentions a son dying in childhood. *FCJ*, March 13, 1942. Attempts to discover a primary source that confirms this sad event were unsuccessful.
41. *San Antonio Gazette*, February 28, March 14, 1908; *LWT*, March 1, 1908; MR, Company C, March 31, 1908; *SADE*, March 20, 1908; *Houston Post*, March 16, 1908; *SAL*, May 21, 1908. Sisk was identified in newspapers as "R. S. Fisk," but Dr. Richard B. McCaslin provided this author with the accurate name.
42. *SADE*, July 4, 1908; *San Antonio Gazette*, July 4, 1908; *SAL*, July 4, 1908; McCaslin, *Sutherland Springs, Texas*, 128.
43. *San Antonio Gazette*, September 4, 5, December 19, 1908; *Houston Daily Post*, September 4, 1908; *SAL*, September 5, 1908; *SADE*, September 19, December 5, 1908; Death Certificate, J. D. Becton, December 5, 1908, Registrar No. 6680; *Twelfth U.S. Census*, Wilson County, Texas. In 1900, Toombs was a hired hand working for Dr. Becton.
44. Tise, *Texas County Sheriffs*, 546; *SAL* and *San Antonio Gazette*, both dated December 5, 1908; Find A Grave: Dave Leftwich Hemsell, CPT Benjamin Dennis Lindsey, Eli Calloway Seale.
45. *SALG*, May 16, 1909; *AS*, May 17, 1909; Find A Grave: Benjamin Sappington "Ben" Fisk, John Edgar Trainer.
46. *SALG*, June 12 (quotation), 19, 1909; *Victoria Advocate*, June 12, 1909; *SADE*, July 27, 1925; J. Will Falvella, "Capt. Wright, a Gallant Texas Ranger," *Frontier Times* 1 (September 1924): 6; Liles, "Texas Ranger Captain Will Wright," n.p.; Find A Grave: Albert Alexander Lyons, Marcus Walton Hines; Death Certificate, William Henry Adams, August 10, 1937, File No. 40182.
47. *SAE*, June 2, 4, 9, 10, July 12, 1910; *SALG*, June 5, 1910.
48. Bob Alexander, *Riding Lucifer's Line: Ranger Deaths Along the Texas-Mexico Border* (Denton: University of North Texas Press, 2013),

220–223; *BDH*, August 1, 2, 1910; *SADE*, August 1, 1910; *SAL*, May 28, 1910. Lawrence served eleven months on a two-year sentence for cattle rustling before he was pardoned on September 9, 1896. Texas Department of Criminal Justice, Convict Record Ledgers, 1998/038-154, TSLAC, 42; *Greenville News*, June 1, 1910.

49. Testimony of W. B. Hinkley, February 12, 1919, *TRF Investigation*, 1326; *BDH*, August 1, 1910.
50. *BDH*, August 1, 2, 1910; *SALG*, August 1, 1910; *SADE*, August 2, 1910; MR, Company D, August 31, 1910; *RAG, 1909–1910*, 8–9.
51. *BDH*, August 2, 5, 1910; *SADE*, August 4, 1910; *GDN*, August 5, 1910; *SALG*, August 14, 1910.
52. Harris and Sadler, *Texas Rangers and the Mexican Revolution*, 43; *BDH*, August 1, 1910; *SADE*, August 2, 1910; Find A Grave: Joseph Laulom "Jose" Crixell. Crixell was killed on August 9, 1912, by Cameron County deputy and former Ranger Paul Jerome McAlister. Even though the incident was a clear case of murder, McAlister was acquitted on a plea of self-defense. Clifford R. Caldwell and Ron DeLord, *Texas Lawmen, 1900–1940: More of the Good and the Bad* (Charleston, SC: History Press, 2012), 58.
53. Caldwell and DeLord, *Texas Lawmen*, 397–398; *SADE*, August 19, 20, 21, 23, 24, 1910; *LWT*, August 28, 1910; *SALG*, August 23, 1910; Find A Grave: Charles William McCabe.
54. Liles, "Texas Ranger Captain Will Wright," n.p.; Transcript of Interviews, Tape 3, "Dogie" Wright Papers, BCAH, 16; Doug Dukes, *Firearms of the Texas Rangers: From the Frontier Era to the Modern Age* (Denton: University of North Texas Press, 2020), 353; Tise, *Texas County Sheriffs*, 546; *SADE*, January 9, 14, 1911; *SALG*, January 9, 1911. After Wright's death, the pistol was bequeathed to Dogie. Gilliland, *Horsebackers*, 107. Presently, it is on display at the Texas Ranger Hall of Fame and Museum, Waco, Texas.
55. *GDN*, February 7, 1911; *LWT*, February 12, 1911; *Biennial Report of the Secretary of State, 1912* (Austin, TX: Von Boeckmann-Jones Co., 1913), 250.
56. *Brownsville Herald*, May 25, 26, 27, 1911; *GDN*, May 17, December 14, 1911; *SADE*, May 23, 24, 25, 1911. W. C. Linden, while a district attorney, had worked with Captain Bill McDonald in breaking up the notorious San Saba Mob. For more details, see Darren L. Ivey, *The Ranger Ideal Volume 2* (Denton: University of North Texas Press, 2018), 381–385.

57. *SAE*, December 8, 9, 11, 12, 13, 14, 15, 1911; *GDN*, December 14, 1911; *SAL*, December 17, 1911; Find A Grave: Samuel Green Tayloe, Joseph Verlinde Vandenberg, Jr., William Madden Fly. Another witness under process was folklorist J. Frank Dobie, who was living in Beeville. *SAL*, December 7, 1911.
58. *Laredo Daily Times*, October 17, 1890, *AS*, September 23, 1905, February 7, 1909; *SADL*, October 8, 1905; *Investigation of Mexican Affairs*, I, Senate Document No. 285, 66th Congress, 2nd Session, 1223; *GDN*, October 12, 1905, June 18, 1911; *FCJ*, January 22, 1914; *LWT*, February 5, June 18, June 25, July 25, 1911; August 4, 1912; March 8, 15, 1914. Some alleged his escape from the soldiers was a prearranged ploy to permit him to join the Constitutionalists as a spy and report their plans back to the Federal commanders. Others thought he had been allowed to enlist in the federal cause at some other location.

    First introduced in 1857, and enshrined in the Mexican Constitution of 1917, the judicial *amparo* (or *amparo casación*) is a process for the protection of human rights not specifically addressed in the Mexican constitution. For more details, see José María Serna de la Garza, *The Constitution of Mexico: A Contextual Analysis* (Portland, OR: Hart Publishing, 2013).
59. *GDN*, August 1, 1911; *AS*, August 2, 1911.
60. *GDN*, November 21, 1911; *SAL*, November 20, 1911; *SAE*, November 21, 22, 1911, January 6, 7, 1912; *Victoria Advocate*, November 25, 1911; Transcript of Interview, Tape 6, Box 2K227, E. A. "Dogie" Wright Papers, BCAH, 6; Find A Grave, James Henry Bain Sr., James Frank Henson, Richard Lee Edwards.
61. *FCJ*, September 27, October 1, 18, 1913.
62. Tise, *Texas County Sheriffs*, 546; *FCJ*, July 16, 1913.
63. *FCJ*, April 16, July 10, 17, 1914; *GDN*, July 9, 1914; Randolph B. Campbell, *Gone to Texas: The History of the Lone Star State* (New York: Oxford University Press, 2003), 348–352; Tise, *Texas County Sheriffs*, 546. See also Jessica Brannon-Wranosky and Bruce A. Glasrud, eds., *Impeached: The Removal of Texas Governor James E. Ferguson* (College Station: Texas A&M University Press, 2017).
64. FCJ, August 14, 1914; *GDN*, July 14, 1915; Liles, "Texas Ranger Captain Will Wright," n.p.
65. *AS*, *AA*, and *GDN*, all dated October 1, 1914; *FCJ*, December 4, 1914; Find A Grave: George Washington Parks, Norman Dudley Cone; Lonnie Leon Parks.

66. *FCJ*, December 4, 1914. According to genealogist Bonnie Parks, an unverifiable family rumor asserts that Park's widow, Lucibie Gertrude Parks, had conspired with her son in the murder in order to acquire the colonel's fortune. Parks to the author, June 14, 2018. George's property had been valued at $300,000 to $400,000, and his will provided his wife with a "substantial allowance" and divided the rest of the estate between his eight children. *Houston Post*, November 16, 1914.
67. *FCJ*, December 4, 1914; *AA*, December 1, 1914; *Houston Post*, October 21, 1914, January 12, February 11, July 24, 25, 1915.
68. *North County Times*, October 8, 1996.
69. *GDN*, September 19, 1915; RSR, John J. Edds, 401-54, TSLAC.
70. *SAL*, October 31, November 1, 1915; Find A Grave: Robert Hamilton "Robbie" Heinatz II, John Wallace Tobin, James W. Galbreath, James Cannon Wall, Horace Faulkner Pirtle.
71. *SAL*, November 30, 1915; *GDN*, December 1, 1915; *Houston Post*, December 1, 1915.
72. *LWT*, December 5, 1915.
73. *FCJ*, January 14, 1916; Transcript of Interview, Tape 5, Box 2K227, "Dogie" Wright Papers, BCAH, 7–8.
74. *SAL*, January 12, 13, 1916; *FCJ*, January 21, 1916; Transcript of Interview, Tape 5, "Dogie" Wright Papers, BCAH, 8.
75. *FCJ*, March 31, 1916; *La Prensa*, April 6, 1916.
76. *FCJ*, April 7, 1916; *La Prensa*, April 6, 1916.
77. Charles H. Harris III and Louis R. Sadler, *The Plan de San Diego: Tejano Rebellion, Mexican Intrigue* (Lincoln: University of Nebraska Press, 2013), 140–155; *SAE*, May 12, 23, 1916; *AS*, May 11, 12, 13, 15, 1916; *Houston Post*, May 12, 15, 1916; *GDN*, May 12, 1916; *Victoria Advocate*, May 12, 1916; F. Arturo Rosales, *¡Pobre* Raza*! Violence, Justice, and Mobilization among México Lindo Immigrants, 1900–1936* (Austin: University of Texas Press, 1999), 16.
78. *AA* and *AS*, both dated May 23, 1916; *SAE*, May 25, 27, 1916; John Busby McClung, "Texas Rangers Along the Rio Grande, 1910–1919" (Ph.D. dissertation, Texas Christian University, 1965), 89; Richard Ribb, "Revolution, Revenge, and the Rangers, 1910–1920," *War Along the Border: The Mexican Revolution and Tejano Communities*, ed. Arnoldo de León (College Station: Texas A&M University Press, 2012), 79; Harris and Sadler, *The Texas Rangers and the Mexican Revolution*, 307 (quotation).
79. *FCJ*, October 6, 13, November 24, 1916; *Victoria Advocate*, October 12, 1916.

80. Tise, *Texas County Sheriffs*, 546.
81. *SAL*, May 5, 1917.
82. *RAG, January 1, 1917–December 31, 1918*, 61–62.
83. Special Order No. 1, January 2, 1918, Companies Vertical File, TRHF&M; *RAG, January 1, 1917–December 31, 1918*, 59; RSR, W. L. Wright and John J. Edds, 401-65, -54, TSLAC; MR, Company D, January 1918, TSLAC; *FCJ*, January 11, 1918; *SAL*, November 29, 1917; *LWT*, December 2, 23, 1917; *Victoria Advocate*, December 27, 1917; Transcript of Interview, Tape 1, Box 2K227, "Dogie" Wright Papers, BCAH, 1. Alfred B. Carnes immediately succeeded Wright in the sheriff's office and served for twenty years. *FCJ*, January 4, 1918; Tise, *Texas County Sheriffs*, 546.
84. Wright, *Career Hunting*, 5.
85. Reprinted in ibid., 3.
86. Sterling, *Trails and Trials*, 412.
87. Hanson to Harley, February 20, 1918, 401-574, TSLAC.
88. Wright's report, March 7, 1918, Volume 20, Box 2R390, Walter Prescott Webb Collection, BCAH. The original may be found in Box 401-574, TSLAC. *Brownsville Herald*, March 8, 1918; *DMN* and *Houston Post*, both dated March 9, 1918; Tise, *Texas County Sheriffs*, 288; Charles H. Harris III, et al., *Texas Ranger Biographies: Those Who Served, 1910–1921* (Albuquerque: University of New Mexico Press, 2009), 68, 196, 305, 311, 398–399.
89. Wright's report, March 7, 1918, Volume 20, Webb Collection, BCAH; *SAE*, March 9, 1918; Harris, et al., *Texas Ranger Biographies*, 261–262.
90. Wright's report, March 7, 1918, Volume 20, Webb Collection, BCAH (quotation); *Brownsville Herald*, March 8, 1918; *DMN*, March 9, 1918; *SAL* and *AS*, both dated March 10, 1918; *SAE*, March 11, 12, 1918; *Victoria Daily Advocate*, March 12, 1918; Webb, *Texas Rangers*, 510.
91. Wright's report, March 7, 1918, Volume 20, Webb Collection, BCAH; *FCJ*, March 15, 1918; *Brownsville Herald*, March 8, 1918; *LWT*, March 17, 1918 (quotation).
92. *LWT*, March 17, 1918; Hanson to Harley, March 28, 1918, Volume 20, Webb Collection, BCAH.
93. *LWT*, April 14, 1918; *AA*, April 15, 1918 (quotation); McClung, "Texas Rangers Along the Rio Grande," 105; Harris, et al., *Texas Ranger Biographies*, 131.

94. *LWT*, August 18, 1918.
95. Hanson to Harley, October 15, 1918, Volume 20, Webb Collection, BCAH; *RAG, January 1, 1917–December 31, 1918*, 61; Harris and Sadler, *Texas Rangers and the Mexican Revolution*, 420; *Brownsville Herald*, October 14, 1918 (quotation).
96. John E. Clark, "Reflections on the Duke of Duval: The Litigation Record," *South Texas Studies* 8 (1997): 31–32; George Schendel, "Something Is Rotten in the State of Texas," *Collier's* 127 (June 9, 1951): 14.
97. Evan Anders, *Boss Rule in South Texas: The Progressive Era* (Austin: University of Texas Press, 1987), 174.
98. Anthony R. Carrozza, *Dukes of Duval: The Parr Family and Texas Politics* (Norman: University of Oklahoma Press, 2017), 18–24; *Senate Journal, Thirty-sixth Legislature, Regular Session*, 128, 837–838, 840, 867; Abney and Hester to Hanson, November 7, 1918, Ryan to Hobby, n.d., Volume 20, Webb Collection, BCAH; David Montejano, *Anglos and Mexicans in the Making of Texas, 1836–1986* (Austin: University of Texas Press, 1987), 145–147; Anders, *Boss Rule*, 257–259; *GDN*, February 14, 18, 1919; *AA*, February 14, 1919; *SAEN*, February 19, 1919; Harris, et al., *Texas Ranger Biographies*, 337.
99. Paul N. Spellman, "Dark Days of the Texas Rangers, 1915–1918," *South Texas Studies* 12 (Spring 2001): 87–88; Special Order No. 6, January 30, 1919, Wright Vertical File, TRHF&M; *GDN*, February 13, 1919; *SAEN*, February 14, 1919; Testimony of Captain William Wright, February 13, 1919, Charge No. 2, January 31, 1919, *TRF Investigation*, 1516–1531, 3–4. Monica Muñoz Martínez provides a thorough analysis of the proceedings in the fourth chapter of *The Injustice Never Leaves You: Anti-Mexican Violence in Texas* (Cambridge, MA: Harvard University Press, 2018).
100. Charge No. 3, Testimony of John Edds, February 7, 1919, Hanson to Harley, October 23, 1918, Statement of J. J. Edds, October 18, 1919, Statement of Zaragosa Sánchez, Statement of Jesús Sánchez, Statement of Federico Saldana, Statement of Monroe Wells, Testimony of Capt. William Wright, all dated February 13, 1919, *TRF Investigation*, 4, 481–484, 487–492, 780–781, 782–784, 785–786, 786–788, 882, 882, 1519–1520, 1526–1529; Hanson to Harley, October 10, 1918, Volume 20, Webb Collection, BCAH; RSR, John J. Edds, 401–54, TSLAC; *SAEN*, February 1, 7, 14, 1919; *GDN*, January 30, 1920; Richard Henry Ribb, "José Tomás Canales and the Texas Rangers: Myth, Identity,

and Power in South Texas, 1900–1920" (Ph.D. dissertation, University of Texas at Austin, 2001), 164, 206; Harris, et al., *Texas Ranger Biographies*, 229. The U.S. Supreme Court ruled in *Kurtz v. Moffitt* (1885) that civilian police agencies and private citizens had not been granted the authority through common law or congressional legislation to arrest deserters absent a military warrant. John R. Vile and David L. Hudson, Jr., *Encyclopedia of the Fourth Amendment* (Thousand Oaks, CA: CQ Press, 2013), 383.

101. Testimony of John Edds, February 7, 1919, Hanson to Harley, September 16, 1918, Statement of John Edds, September 3, 1918, Statement of Sabas Ozona, Statement of Federico Lopez, Statement of Ed. Yzaguirre [*sic*], Statement of Capt. W. L. Wright, Edds to Perkins or Thompson, Edds to Whom It May Concern, Wright to Harley, all dated September 7, 1918, Harley to Wright, September 12, 1918, Testimony of Federico Lopez, February 12, 1919, Testimony of Eduardo Izaguirre, Testimony of Captain William Wright, February 13, 1919, *TRF Investigation*, 485–487, 761–772, 1298–1308, 1308–1319, 1521; Hanson to Harley, September 16, 1918, Volume 20, Webb Collection, BCAH; Martinez, *The Injustice Never Leaves You*, 199–201. In his ninth charge, Canales criticized the internal investigations into alleged wrongdoing such as the Muñoz and Gomez killings. Charge No. 9, February 1, 1919, *TRF Investigation*, 125–126.
102. Testimony of W. T. Vann, February 7, 1919, *TRF Investigation*, 579–580; William Thomas Vann, World War I Draft Cards, M1509, RG 163, NARA.
103. Harley to Hamer, March 26, 1919, TSLAC; Special Order No. 19, March 4, 1919, Special Order No. 21, March 10, 1919, General Order No. 5, June 20, 1919, Wright Vertical File, TRHF&M; *RAG, 1919–1920*, 44; RSR, W. L. Wright, 401–65, TSLAC; *BDH*, August 22, 1919. Besides Edds, Wright's men included Harold William Adams, Samuel Patrick "Pat" Chesshir, Harrison L. Hamer, and Robert Bell Sutton. Harris, et al., *Texas Ranger Biographies*, 2, 59, 161–162, 368.
104. *FCJ*, November 28, 1919; *SAE*, November 22, 23, 1919; *AA*, November 22, 1919; *GDN*, August 14, 1919; Death Certificate, Jose Corona, November 22, 1919, Registrar's No. 31520. Later accounts identified Wright's assailant as "Davila." For an example, see *San Patricio County News*, April 30, 1925. The grave of a Santiago Davilla is in Brownsville's Old City Cemetery, but his marker bears a death date of November 27, 1919. Find A Grave: Santiago Davila.

105. Thompson to Cope, April ?, 1920, Hutchinson to Aldrich, April 24, 1920, Morton to Aldrich, March 10, 11, 1920, 401-582, TSLAC; Hanson to Harley, October 15, 1918, Volume 20, Webb Collection, BCAH; Gilliland, *Horsebackers*, 15–16, 33; John R Peavey, *Echoes from the Rio Grande* (Brownsville, TX: Springman-King Company, 1963), 182, 206–207; *RAG,* January 1, 1917–December 31, 1918, 62; Liles, "Texas Ranger Captain Will Wright," n.p.; Homero S. Vera, "Los Tequileros," *El Mesteño* 3 (February 2000): 4. See also Maude T. Gilliland, "The Remarkable Texas Rangers," *Quarterly of the National Association and Center for Outlaw and Lawman History* 5 (January 1980).
106. Webb, *Texas Rangers*, 554–557; Sterling, *Trails and Trials*, 83–84 (first quotation); Gilliland, *Horsebackers*, 17 (second quotation), 33.
107. Wright to Cope, January 20, 1920, Tape 8.1, James R. Ward Collection, ASU. Following the lockdown of the West Texas Collection during the Covid-19 crisis, Professor Charles H. Harris III and Professor McCaslin generously provided this author with copies of their respective notes. *Brownsville Herald*, January 4, 15, 1920; Wright to Aldrich, January 6, 1920, Aldrich to Wright, January 9, 1920, folder 85, Roy W. Aldrich Papers, SRSU; *SAEN*, June 24, 1919; Harris, et al., *Texas Ranger Biographies*, 261, 304–305, 306.
108. Tumlinson to Aldrich, May 20, 1020, 401–586, TSLAC; *Brownsville Herald*, January 11, 22, 1920; Louis Frank Shelton, World War I Draft Cards, M1509, RG 163, NARA; Find A Grave: Emmette Knepp Goodrich, Hugh Eugene Barnes.
109. Gilliland, *Horsebackers*, 17, 33; Hutchinson to Aldrich, May 30, 1920, 401–586, TSLAC; Cope to Wright, September 21, 1920, Tape 8.1, Ward Collection, ASU; *SAE*, September 24, 1920; James Randolph Ward, "The Texas Rangers, 1919–1935: A Study in Law Enforcement" (Ph.D. dissertation, Texas Christian University, 1972), 35.
110. *FCJ*, December 3, 1920; *GDN*, December 2, 1920; Death Certificate, Louis Clarence McDuff, October 10, 1980, File No. 90963.
111. Aldrich to Brady, April 13, 1922 (second quotation), Aldrich Papers, SRSU; Wright to Aldrich, January 23, 1921, Wright to Barton, March 19, 1921, Wright to Aldrich, April 23, 1921 (first quotation), Tape 8.1, Aldrich to Gray, March 4, 1921, Tape 5.1, Wright to Aldrich, March 6, 1922, Wright to Barton, March 6, 1922, Tape 8.2, Ward Collection, ASU; Morton to Aldrich, March 11, 1920, Aldrich to Morton, March 13, 1920, 401-582, Aldrich to Wallis, February 17, 1922, Aldrich to

Brady, February 24, 1922, -589, Aldrich to Brady, April 8, 1922, -590, TSLAC; Gilliland, *Horsebackers*, 26, 51–52; *GDN*, February 11, 16, 1921; *SAE*, February 15, 1921; Transcript of Interview, Tape 1, "Dogie" Wright Papers, BCAH, 1; Dukes, *Firearms of the Texas Rangers*, 293. Dukes clarified in an email to this author, dated October 20, 2020, that his research indicated the "Tumlinson Specials" were Model 1895s. Nonetheless, several letters included in the Ward Collection refer to a substantial expenditure of .30-30 ammunition among Wright's men. *AS*, September 21, 1924 (third quotation); Wright, *Career Hunting*, 16 (fourth and fifth quotation), 17, 20–21.

112. Wright to Barton, February 28, 1921, Wright to Aldrich, May 31, August 17, 1921, Tape 8.1, Gray to Barton, March 30, 1921 (first quotation), Tape 5.1, Ward Collection, ASU; Wright to Barton, September 13, 1921, Volume 21, Webb Collection, BCAH; *RAG*, January 1–August 31, 1922, 54; Jesse Perez, "Reminiscences, 1870–1927," TS, Box 2R134, BCAH, 77–79; Edds to Aldrich, September 19, 1921 (second quotation), 401-587, TSLAC; Harris, et al., *Texas Ranger Biographies*, 78–79, 40–41; *AS*, May 22, 1921; *LWT*, August 7, September 18, 1921; *FCJ*, August 21, 1921; *AA*, September 12, 1921; *GDN*, September 17, 1921; Walter Prescott Webb, "Veteran Ranger Protects Border," *The State Trooper* (September 1924): 13; Webb, *Texas Rangers*, 504, 554–557; Gilliland, *Horsebackers*, 36–41; Terrence J. Barragy, *Gathering Texas Gold* (Kingsville: Cayo del Grullo Press, 2003), 70 (third quotation).
113. Wright to Barton, November 19, 1921, Tape 8.2, Ward Collection, ASU; Perez, "Reminiscences," 80; *SAL*, April 6, 1922 (quotation); Harris, et al., *Texas Ranger Biographies*, 126, 255, 396; Gilliland, *Horsebackers*, 126–127; Find A Grave, Walter Frank Smith.
114. Wright to Barton, November 24, 1921, Tape 8.2, Ward Collection, ASU; Wright to Barton, November 24, 1921, Volume 21, Webb Collection, BCAH; Perez, "Reminiscences," 80–81; *AA* and *FWST*, both dated November 19, 1921; *LWT*, November 20, 27, 1921; *SAL*, November 23, 1921, April 15, 1927; *SAE*, July 27, 1924; Ward, "The Texas Rangers," 56–57; Gilliland, *Horsebackers*, 25; Webb, "Veteran Ranger Protects Border," 13.
115. *SAE*, *AA*, *Houston Post*, all dated January 15, 1922; *Mercedes Tribune* and *La Prensa*, both dated January 18, 1922; *Brownsville Herald*, January 15, 1922, May 1, 1940. Various newspaper articles describe Minner as being sixty years old, but his gravestone indicates he was forty-five or forty-six at the time of his death. Find A Grave: J. W. Minner.

116. *Laredo Times*, March 19, 1922; Wright to Aldrich, April 6 (first quotation), May 9, 1922, Tape 8.2, Ward Collection, ASU; *SAE*, May 30, 1922 (second quotation).
117. Webb to Aldrich, August 19, 1922, 401-592, TSLAC; Barton to Gray, July 24, 1922, Tape 5.1, Wright to Barton, August 30, 1922, Tape 8.2, Ward Collection, ASU; *Brownsville Herald*, July 22, 1922; *Victoria Advocate*, July 23, 1922; *SAEN*, *Fort Worth Record*, *FWST*, all dated July 25, 1922; *Brownwood Bulletin*, July 29, 1922; *GDN*, July 29, 1922; *Corsicana Daily Sun*, August 9, 1922; *Wichita Daily Times*, July 28, 1922; Harris, et al., *Texas Ranger Biographies*, 271.
118. Pat M. Neff, *The Battles of Peace* (Fort Worth, TX: Pioneer Publishing Company, 1925), 140; *SAE*, August 4, 11, 15, 1922; *Victoria Advocate*, August 9, 1922; *SAL*, August 9, 1922; *Wichita Daily Times*, August 9, 1922.
119. RSR, John J. Edds and D. C. Webb, 401-54, -65, TSLAC; Wright to Barton, August 30, 1922 (first quotation), Aldrich to Wright, n.d. (third quotation), Tape 8.2, Ward Collection, ASU; Perez, "Reminiscences," 1–2; *SAE*, August 24, 1922 (second quotation).
120. Aldrich to Darlington, October 18, 1922, TSLAC; *AS*, October 15, 1922; *GDN*, October 16, 1922; Becky Flores, "Caught in the Crossfire: A Sociohistorical Analysis of Conflict in a 'Contact Zone' in 1920s South Texas," *South Texas Studies* 12 (Spring 2001): 54–55, 64; Find A Grave: Samuel Johnson "Fred" Roberts, Gustavus Ericson "Gus" Warren, Frank Gravis Robinson, Tilford Lee Petzel, Joseph Arnold "Joe" Acebo, William James Cody.
121. Perez, "Reminiscences," 88–89; *AS*, October 15, 16, 1922, January 14, 1923; *GDN*, October 16, November 4, 1922; *Brownsville Herald*, October 16, 18, 1922; *SAE*, October 16, 17, 27, November 6, 7, 1922; *SAL*, October 16, 1922; Hamer to Crawford, October 16, 1922, Tape 5.1, Ward Collection, ASU; *Houston Post*, January 27, 1923; *Fredericksburg Standard*, January 13 1923; John Boessenecker, *Texas Ranger: The Epic Life of Frank Hamer, the Man Who Killed Bonnie and Clyde* (New York: Thomas Dunne Books, 2016), 271–272; Zora Fore interview, 1973; Harris, et al., *Texas Ranger Biographies*, 4, 174; Find A Grave: DR Peter Gray Lovenskiold, Judge William Wellington Sharp; Robert Young, "The Guns of Frank Hamer," *Quarterly of the National Association and Center for Outlaw and Lawman History* 7 (Summer 1982): 3. Wright's pistol is on display at the Texas Ranger Hall of Fame and Museum, while Hamer's weapon is in a private collection. Dukes, *Firearms of the Texas Rangers*, 355–356.

122. *SAEN*, November 24, 1922; *AS* and *Brownsville Herald*, both dated November 9, 1922; *AA*, November 20, 1922.
123. *Brownsville Herald*, November 9, 15, 18, 24, December 5, 1922, June 6, 1950, December 15, 1955; *AS*, November 15, 16, 1922; *St Louis Post-Dispatch*, November 15, 1922; *Evening Star*, November 16, 1922; *SAEN*, November 16, 1922; *Wichita Daily Eagle*, November 23, 1922 (first quotation); *AS*, November 19, 23, December 6, 1922; *New York Daily News*, November 26, 1922; Wright to Barton, December 1, 1922 (second quotation), and attached affidavits, 401-594, TSLAC; *FCJ*, December 1, 1922; Charles H. Harris III and Louis R. Sadler, *The Texas Rangers in Transition: From Gunfighters to Criminal Investigators, 1921–1935* (Norman: University of Oklahoma Press, 2019), 168–169; Carrigan and Webb, *Forgotten Dead*, 149–150; Nicholas Villanueva, Jr., *The Lynching of Mexicans in the Texas Borderlands* (Albuquerque: University of New Mexico Press, 2017), 170; *FWST*, Jun 5, 1954; Death Certificate, Thomas Jefferson Buckow, December 15, 1955, File No. 61857; Find A Grave: George Tollie Humphries.
124. Aldrich to Gray, November 1, 1922 (first two quotations), Tape 5.1, Ward Collection, ASU; Perez, Reminiscences," 91–92; Gilliland, *Horsebackers*, 26, 36–38; Charles Schreiner III, et al., comps., *A Pictorial History of the Texas Rangers: "That Special Breed of Men"* (Mountain Home, TX: YO Press, 1969), 111 (third quotation); *Brownsville Herald*, December 3, 1922; *AS*, December 19, 1922; *SAE*, December 19, 1922, April 5, 1925 (fourth quotation); *SAL*, December 22, 1929; *LWT*, December 24, 1922.
125. Wright, *Career Hunting*, 28; Webb, *Texas Rangers*, 556; *SAEN*, December 19, 1922 (first quotation); *SAE*, April 5, 1925 (second quotations). The shootout inspired the *corrido* "Los Tequileros" immortalized by the Mexican Norteño band Los Alegres de Terán. Homero S. Vera, "Corrido 'Los Tequileros'," *El Mesteño* 3 (February 2000): 18. Professor George T. Díaz has been particularly condemnatory of the Las Animas shooting, decrying it as the "stalking, ambush, and murder of the three smugglers." However, he filtered his interpretations through the *corrido*, a "song … recorded decades after the historical event" that may not be the most objective of sources. Curiously, the professor acknowledges discrepancies, such as dates, within the many versions of the *corrido* while still using it as the foundation for his criticisms. Díaz further claimed Wright and his party killed the three *tequileros* to avenge the death of Bob Rumsey. This seems unlikely as the captain

had peacefully apprehended numerous smugglers in the four months since the Customs agent's murder. *Border Contraband: A History of Smuggling Across the Rio Grande* (Austin: University of Texas Press, 2015), 100–102 (first quotation on p. 100), 216 n7 (second quotation). While writing his own full-length biography, *Texas Ranger Captain William L. Wright* (Denton: University of North Texas Press, 2021), Richard McCaslin generously shared with this author his thoughts and conclusions on the Las Animas fight.

126. Perez, "Reminiscences," 93; *SAE*, December 23, 28, 29 (quotation), 1922; *AS*, December 28, 29, 1922.
127. *SAE*, January 1, 3, 4, 5, 6, 7, 8, 9, 10, 11, 12, 1923; *AS* and *Houston Post*, both dated January 14, 1923; Find A Grave: John Francis Mullally, Champe Goodwyn Carter, Manuel John Raymond, John Adam Pope.
128. Wallis to Aldrich, April 16, 1923, Aldrich to Wheatley, May 5, 1923, 401–597, TSLAC; *SAE*, April 6, 1923; *Corpus Christi Times*, April 16, 1923.
129. Harbison to Wright, April 16, 1923, Wright to Barton, April 27, 1923, Tape 8.2, Ward Collection, ASU; Perez, "Reminiscences," 114; *SAL*, October 23, 1924; Harris, et al., *Texas Ranger Biographies*, 165–166. Aristeo has also been identified as "Severino García" and "E. Gracia." A smuggler for the previous ten years, *El Pajaro*, or the Bird, was known for his ability to evade law enforcement, but he disappeared after leaving Guerrero, Mexico, on September 15, 1924, and crossing the border at Falcon in Zapata County. The mystery deepened when a "young and pretty" woman's body was discovered floating down the Rio Grande at Las Guerras ranch near Roma the following month. She had been shot six times, and the frazzled ends of a rope were around her neck. The dead girl was thought to be Gracia's sweetheart. Certain he was dead, Gracia's relatives "tightened up their saddle-girths [and] oiled their guns" prior to a search of arroyos along the river for his remains and a pursuit for those responsible. *SAL*, October 29 (quotations), November 2, 1924. Dogie Wright asserted Gracia was lured into crossing the border and extralegally executed for his alleged role in the death of rancher Gregg Gibson. Transcript of Interview, Tape 7, Box 2K227, "Dogie" Wright Papers, BCAH, 13.
130. *SAE*, August 25, September 6, 1923; *San Patricio County News*, August 30, 1923; *FCJ*, September 7, 1923; Tise, *Texas County Sheriffs*, 39; RSR, Light Townsend, 401–64.
131. *Brownsville Herald*, November 27, 1923.

132. Barton to Wright, January 15, 1924, Tape 8.2, Ward Collection, ASU; *SAL*, January 9, 11, 16, 20, 1924; *AS*, January 14, 16, 17, 1924; *FCJ*, January 18, 1924; RSR, Duncan S. Wright, 401-65, R. R. Bledsoe, -52; *Corpus Christi Caller*, February 5, 8, 1924; Death Certificate, Duncan Sylvester Wright, November 5, 1956, File No. 54567. Acting as a Nueces County deputy constable, Bledsoe was killed in a gun battle alongside Constable Carl M. Bisbee on July 5, 1925. The fight might have been the violent result of a legitimate arrest or a political dispute, but it also took the lives of deputy game warden Paul J. McAlister and rancher George Ryder. Caldwell and DeLord, *Texas Lawmen*, 289–290, 436.
133. Wright to Aldrich, May 16 (first quotation), September 2, 1924, Tape 8.2, Ward Collection, ASU; *SAE*, July 27, 1924; *Granbury News*, August 1, 1924; Wright to Aldrich, June 14, 1925, folder 3, Box 3P157, Aldrich Papers, BCAH (second quotation); *Victoria Advocate*, September 4, 1924; *Houston Post-Dispatch*, September 7, 1924.
134. Wright to Aldrich, September 14 (quotation), 18, 1924, Tape 8.2, Ward Collection, ASU; RSR, James Warren Smith, 401-63, John W. Sadler, -62.
135. *SAE*, September 24, 1924; *FCJ*, October 3, 1924; Wright to Aldrich, October 24, 1924, Tape 8.2, Ward Collection, ASU. The seizure was the first on record in which a wagon of the type used by pioneers and a six-mule team was taken in a liquor raid.
136. Wright to Aldrich, November 17, 1924, Tape 8.2, Ward Collection, ASU; *SAE*, *AA*, and *Corpus Christi Caller*, all dated November 18, 1924; RSR, Eugene H. Tumlinson, 401-64.
137. Neff, *Battles of Peace*, 141.
138. For more on the transition from the Frontier Battalion to the Ranger Force, see Ivey, *The Ranger Ideal Volume 2*, 346–347, 348, 390–391, 431–432, 482–483.
139. Wright to McGee, January 28, 30, 1925, Tape 8.2, Ward Collection, ASU; Walter Prescott Web, "Texas Ranger Case Important," *The State Trooper* 6 (August 1925): 13–14, 20; 270 *Southwestern Reporter* 874 (1925); Arts. 6754 and 6757, *Revised Civil Statutes of the State of Texas, 1911*, 1451; *AS*, October 15, 26, 1924, February 26, 1925; *SAL*, January 16, 1925; *AA*, January 22, 30 (second quotation), 1925; *Brownsville Herald*, January 16, 22, 1925; *Paris Evening Times*, January 23, 1925; *SAE*, January 30, February 4, 1925; *Corsican Daily Sun*, January 30, 1925; *Mexia Daily News*, January 30, 1925 (first

quotation); W. P. Webb and M. F. Kennedy, "With the Texas Rangers," *The State Trooper* (October 1925): 11; Find A Grave: Robert Berkeley Minor.

140. *SAE*, February 13, March 27, 1925; *WNT*, February 10, 1925; *GDN*, February 21, 1925; *AS*, March 26, 1925; Inactive Personnel Record, William L. Wright, TDPS; Special Orders No. 9, March 25, 1925, Wright Vertical File, TRHF&M. A copy can be found in folder 85, Aldrich Papers, SRSU. RSR, W. L. Wright, 401-65, TSLAC; *Corpus Christi Times*, March 27, 1925; *FCJ*, April 10, 1925; Webb and Kennedy, "With the Texas Rangers," 11.
141. Written on March 20, Wright's letter was reprinted partially or in its entirety in *SAE*, March 28, 1925, *Corpus Christi Caller*, March 30, 1925, *FCJ*, April 3, 1925, *DMN*, April 5, 1925, and *San Patricio County News*, April 30, 1925.
142. *FCJ*, November 20, 1925; *Corpus Christi Caller*, November 15, 1925.
143. *FCJ*, November 27, 1925; *Corpus Christi Caller*, November 20, 1925.
144. *FCJ*, February 19, July 30, 1926; *Corpus Christi Times*, February 11, May 16, 17, July 6, 1926; *Corpus Christi Caller*, July 22, 1926; Find A Grave: Ben Dechard Lee, Sr.
145. *Brownsville Herald*, January 30, 1927; *SAL*, April 15, 1927; *FCJ*, May 13, 1927; RSR, W. L. Wright, 401-65, TSLAC; Wright to Robertson, May 1, 1927, Tape 3.1, Ward Collection, ASU; Hall to Wright, May 3, 1927, Wright to Moody, May 4, 1927, Valls to Moody, May 6, 1927 (quotation), Box 2007/170-52, Daniel J. Moody Papers, TSLAC; *RAG, August 31, 1927, and August 31, 1928*, 18.
146. RSR, W. W. Taylor, 401-64, J. C. Parker, -61; Davis to Moody, May 11, 1927, Box 2007/170-53, Moody Papers, TSLAC; Wright to Aldrich, September 5, 1927, Wright to Nichols, October 2, 13, 17, 24, 31, 1927, Aldrich to Wright, November 30, 1927, Wright to Aldrich, December 1, 1927, Wright to Robertson, December 8, 1927, Robertson to Wright, January 14, 1928, Wright to Robertson, January 17, 1928, Tape 3.1, Rogers to Robertson, January 18, 1928, Tape 3.2, Ward Collection, ASU; Roger M. Olien and Diana Davids Olien, *Oil Booms: Social Change in Five Texas Towns* (Lincoln: University of Nebraska Press, 1982), 133 (quotation); Special Order No. 25, December 31, 1927, Wright Vertical File, TRHF&M; *GDN*, December 8, 1927; *SAE*, January 21, 1928; *SAL*, January 20, 1928; *Corsicana Daily Sun*, January 21, 1928;.
147. Downds to Moody, Fuller to Moody, Metcalfe to Moody, Brite to Moody, Bunton to Moody, all dated January 20, 1928, Davis and

Womack to Moody, January 24, 1928, Box 2007/170-53, Moody Papers, TSLAC; Wright to Robertson, February 5, 25, 1928, Tape 3.1, Mayes to Wright, February 3, 1928, Wright report, February 24, 1928, Wright to Robertson, March 6, 1928, Tape 11.1, Ward Collection, ASU; Olien and Olien, *Oil Booms*, 133; *FCJ*, March 2, 1928; *RAG*, August 31, *1928*, 33; Ward, "The Texas Rangers," 161; Bryan Burrough, *The Big Rich: The Rise and Fall of the Greatest Texas Oil Fortunes* (New York: Penguin Books, 2009), 46.

148. *Carlsbad Current-Argus*, November 25, 1927, February 28, 1928, February 15, May 14, 1929; Jerry Sinise, *Black Gold and Red Lights* (Austin, TX: Eakin Press, 1982), 36–38; *Abilene Morning Reporter*, March 18, 1929; *El Paso Herald*, March 28 (all quotations), June 12, 1928; Wright to Aldrich, April 28, 1939, folder 5, Box 3P157, Aldrich Papers, BCAH. In an email dated December 23, 2019, Brian Norwood of the Jal Historical Society & Museum kindheartedly shared his knowledge on Herwig's stint in Lea County. Although he worked both sides of the law, Herwig was a respected businessman in Jal, and his name appears on many of the original property deeds in town.
149. *FCJ*, March 30, 1928.
150. Wright to Robertson, March 11, 24, 1928, Wright to Robertson, October 19, 1928, Tape 3.1, Ward Collection, ASU; *FCJ*, April 27, July 20, 1928; *GDN*, May 25, 1928; *Corsicana Semi-Weekly Light*, May 29, 1928; *RAG*, August 31, 1928, 33–34; Ward, "The Texas Rangers," 161–162; *El Paso Herald*, October 6, 11, 13, 1928; Olien and Olien, *Oil Booms*, 135, 137 (quotation). Wright investigated charges against the sheriff in May of the following year, and Priest resigned two months later. Wright report, May 5, 1929, Tape 9.1, Ward Collection.
151. Wright to Robertson, February 14, August 27, 1929, Tape 11.2, 19, July 28, 1929, Tape 9.1, Ward Collection, ASU; *RAG*, September 1, 1928–August 31, 1929, 20; *Laredo Times*, November 4, 1928; *Lubbock Morning Avalanche*, October 18, December 4, 7, 8, 20, 1928; *Amarillo Globe*, December 18, 19, 1928; *FWST*, December 20, 1928; *AS*, December 20, 1928.
152. Harris and Sadler, *Texas Rangers in Transition*, 367; Smith to Robertson, January 29, 1929, Tapes 11.1 and 11.2, J. E. Wright to W. D. Smith, February 7, 1929, Tape 11.2, Ward Collection, ASU; *AS*, December 21, 1928, May 3, 4, 1929; *AA*, May 3, 4, 1929; *Fort Worth Star-Telegraph*, December 21, 1928, January 14, 1929; *Lubbock Morning Avalanche*,

December 21, 1928 (quotation), May 2, 1929; *Amarillo Globe*, January 11, April 26, 1929.

153. Wright reports, January 13, 20, February 10, April 31, 1929, Tape 9.1, Wright to Robertson, January 7, February 14, 1929, Tape 11.2, Ward Collection, ASU; *El Paso Herald*, February 2, 1929.
154. J. E. Wright to W. D. Smith, February 7, 1929, Tape 11.2, Ward Collection, ASU; *FWST*, May 1, 2, 1929; *Lubbock Morning Avalanche*, May 1, 2, 3, 1929; *AS*, May 3, 4, 1929; *AA*, May 3, 4, 1929.
155. *Lubbock Morning Avalanche*, March 26, 1930; *Abilene Reporter-News*, October 9, 1932, January 7, 1933; *Big Spring Daily Herald*, October 13, 1932; *Mexia Weekly Herald*, October 14, 1932.
156. *Abilene Reporter-News*, June 7, 24, 1933; *Big Spring Daily Herald*, May 8, 12, August 8, 1933; *Odessa American*, January 20, 1933; *Lubbock Morning Avalanche*, May 9, 10, 1933, January 20, 1934.
157. *SAE*, April 24, 1931.
158. *Big Spring Daily Herald*, May 27, 1931; Harris, et al., *Texas Ranger Biographies*, 422.
159. *FWST*, April 9, 1931; *Lubbock Morning Avalanche*, April 9, 1931; *Odessa American*, June 26, 1931; *Abilene Morning News*, June 27, 1931.
160. Wright to Sterling, May 5, 1932, Tape 10.1, Ward Collection, ASU.
161. *Lubbock Morning Avalanche*, June 15, 16, 1932; *El Paso Herald-Post*, June 15, 1932.
162. *Big Spring Daily Herald*, August 31, 1932.
163. Inactive Personnel Record, William L. Wright, TDPS; *FCJ*, December 23, 1932; *Corpus Christi Caller-Times*, December 29, 1932; *SAE*, January 22, 1933.
164. *Corpus Christi Caller-Times*, March 26, 31, 1933; *SAE*, March 31, 1933.
165. *Corpus Christi Caller-Times*, July 30, 1933.
166. *Corpus Christi Caller-Times*, August 6, 10 (quotation), 1933.
167. RSR, W. L. Wright, 401-65, TSLAC; *SAE* and *Houston Chronicle*, both dated February 17, 1935; *FCJ*, February 23, 1935; Sterling, *Trails and Trials*, 183 (quotation).
168. *SAE*, March 19, 1935; *GDN*, March 19, November 5, 25, 1935; *Brownsville Herald*, March 18, 1935 (quotation); *AA*, August 28, 1935; Norman D. Brown, *Biscuits, the Dole, and Nodding Donkeys: Texas Politics, 1929–1932*, ed. Rachel Ozanne (Austin: University of Texas Press, 2019), 324; *Corpus Christi Times*, October 18, November 4,

1935; *Corpus Christi Caller-Times*, November 3, 1935; *Denton Record-Chronicle*, October 16, 1935.

169. *SAE*, December 29, 1935; David Allison Blackwell, William Wallen Musgrave, World War II Draft Cards, RG 147, NARA.
170. *Valley Morning Star*, February 23, 1936.
171. *Valley Morning Star*, November 3, 8, 1936.
172. *SAE*, November 22, December 11, 1936; *Valley Morning Star*, November 21, 22, 1936; *Corpus Christi Caller-Times*, November 25, 1936; *Laredo Times*, December 6, 1936; *GDN*, December 7, 1936; "The Battle of the Fence," *Life* 1 (December 14, 1936): 18.
173. *Brownsville Herald*, July 30, 1937 (first quotation); Joe H. Bridge, Jr., *The Life and Times of Joe H. Bridge: Texas Ranger, 1936–1956* (s. l.: Joe H. Bridge, 2003), 58 (second quotation). Ranger Ernest Best was assigned the case later in 1937 and kept chasing leads through the remainder of his career. *DMN*, May 8, 1953, Gonzaullas Scrapbook 4, TRHF&M, 316. One of Colonel Homer Garrison's chief goals was to see the Blanton case solved, but, unfortunately, no resolution was ever reached. Jack Martin, "Col. Homer Garrison, Jr., Director of the Department of Public Safety," *True Detective Mysteries* 34 (August 1940): 116. For more on the case from the Blanton family's perspective, see Mona D. Sizer, *Texas Justice, Bought and Paid For* (Plano: Republic of Texas Press, 2001), 1–65.
174. *Corpus Christi Times*, December 1, 2, 1936.
175. *Corpus Christi Times*, February 15, 1937.
176. *Corpus Christi Times*, April 26, 1937.
177. *Corpus Christi Times*, May 16, 19, July 16, 28, August 30, 1937; *Corpus Christi Caller-Times*, June 27, 1937.
178. *Corpus Christi Times*, September 16, October 13, 1937.
179. *Corpus Christi Times*, January 11, 18, 1938.
180. *Corpus Christi Times*, April 19, 24, 1938.
181. *Corpus Christi Times*, June 17, 1938. Lowman served as a Texas Ranger for thirty-two years, and, at the time of his death on December 28, 1965, was one of the oldest Rangers on active duty. *Corpus Christi Caller-Times*, December 30, 1965.
182. *FCJ*, February 15, 1913, June 27, 1919; Charles Hays Wright, World War I Draft Cards, M1509, RG 163, NARA; Charles H. Wright, World War I Service Record Cards, Texas Military Force Museum; Ben H. Chastaine, *Story of the 36th* (Oklahoma City: Harlow Publishing Company, 1920), 14, 41–43; *SAE*, May 13, 1927; *McAllen Daily Press*,

January 3, 1932; *Corpus Christi Times*, June 28, 29, 1938; *Brownsville Herald*, June 29, 1938; RSR, Charles Hays Wright, 401-65, TSLAC; Gilliland, *Horsebackers*, 114; Death Certificate, Charles Hays Wright, June 28, 1938, File No. 29151; Turner, et al., *Joseph and Rachel Rabb Newman*, 147. See also Rex F. Harlow, *Trail of the 61st: A History of the 61st Field Artillery Brigade During the World War, 1917–1919* (Oklahoma City: Harlow Publishing Company, 1919).

183. *Corpus Christi Times*, July 15, 1939.
184. *FCJ*, July 21, 1939.
185. Sterling, *Trails and Trials*, 416; Inactive Personnel Record, William L. Wright, TDPS; *Corpus Christi Times*, August 15, 1939.
186. Reprinted in *FCJ*, August 25, 1939.
187. *FCJ*, November 10, 1939.
188. *FCJ*, March 1, April 19, 1940.
189. *Corpus Christi Times*, March 7, 1942; *SAE*, March 8, 1942; *FCJ*, March 13, 1942; Death Certificate, William Lee Wright, March 20, 1942, File No. 22.
190. *FCJ*, June 22, 1967.
191. *FCJ*, June 5, 1942, July 7, 1950; *Corpus Christi Times* and *SAE*, both dated April 19, 1958; Turner, et al., *Joseph and Rachel Rabb Newman*, 147; Death Certificate, Mary Ann Wright, April 23, 1958, File No. 351.
192. Connie Rodriguez, telephone interview with the author, June 27, 2012. Hereafter cited as Connie Rodriguez interview, 2012. Maurice H. Wright, World War I Draft Cards, M1509, RG 163, NARA; *FCJ*, June 27, 1919; *Fourteenth U.S. Census*, Wilson County, Texas; *Fifteenth* and *Sixteenth U.S. Census*, Bexar County, Texas; Death Certificate, Maurice Humphrie Wright, February 29, 1960, File No. 7188; Turner, et al., *Joseph and Rachel Rabb Newman*, 147.
193. Connie Rodriguez interview, 2012; *FCJ*, March 11, 1921; *Brownsville Herald*, August 6, 1936; *Corpus Christi Times*, May 1, 1963; Turner, et al., *Joseph and Rachel Rabb Newman*, 147; *Corpus Christi Caller-Times*, June 2, 1996.
194. RSR, Emanuel A. Wright, 401–65, TSLAC; Sitton, *The Texas Sheriff*, 158; Hyatt, "Littleberry Wright Family," 830; Harris and Sadler, *Texas Rangers in Transition*, 63–64; Hudspeth County Marriage Record, 1: 212; *Sixteenth U.S. Census*, El Paso County, Texas; *FCJ*, May 18, 1951; Kilgore, *A Ranger Legacy*, 34, 69; Tise, *Texas County Sheriffs*, 270; *El Paso Times*, May 28, 1974 (first quotation); *Corpus Christi*

Caller-Times, December 15, 1929 (second quotation); *Del Rio News-Herald*, May 27, 1986 (third quotation), December 20, 1989.

195. Wright, *Career Hunting*, 9, 20; W. B. Wright to Aldrich, July 19, 1939, folder 249, Aldrich Papers, SRSU; Marriage License No. 11908, Record of Marriage Licenses Book 816, Los Angeles County Recorder's Office, Norwalk, California, 160; *Sixteenth U.S. Census*, Bernalillo County, New Mexico; *FCJ*, January 20, 1939, September 1, 1950, March 7, 1952; *Los Angeles Times*, August 6, 1962; Turner, et al., *Joseph and Rachel Rabb Newman*, 147.

196. *FCJ*, September 7, 1945, November 1, 1946, September 19, 1947; *SAE*, September 9, 1945; *Sixteenth U.S. Census*, Cochise County, Arizona; Ronald E. Marcello, "Lone Star POWs: Texas National Guardsmen and the Building of the Burma-Thailand Railroad, 1942–1944," *SHQ* 95 (January 1992): 293, 296, 298, 307; *GDN*, September 16, 1945; *San Diego Union*, July 27, September 3, 1947, March 15, 1948, April 13, 1950, April 27, 1952, December 18, 1961, April 11, 1962, March 30, April 4, 1963, April 13, 1966; *North County Times*, October 8, 1996.

For more on Tom's harrowing World War II experiences, see Interview with Houston T. Wright (OH 466), Oral History Collection, Special Collections, University of North Texas Libraries. See also Clyde Fillmore, *Prisoner of War* (Quanah, TX: Nortex Press, 1973), and Kelly E. Crager, "Texan Prisoners of the Japanese: A Study in Survival," *Texans and War: New Interpretations of the State's Military History*, ed. Alexander Mendoza and Charles David Grear (College Station: Texas A&M University Press, 2012).

Notes for Chapter 2

1. John Boessenecker, *Texas Ranger: The Epic Life of Frank Hamer, the Man Who Killed Bonnie and Clyde* (New York: Thomas Dunne Books, 2016), 6–7; H. Gordon Frost and John H. Jenkins, *"I'm Frank Hamer": The Life of a Texas Peace Officer* (Austin, TX: Pemberton Press, 1968), 5. Boessenecker's book has replaced Frost and Jenkins as the definitive work on Frank Hamer's life and times. Registers of Enlistments in the U.S. Army, M233, RG94, NARA; Charles H. Harris III, et al., *Texas Ranger Biographies: Those Who Served, 1910–1921* (Albuquerque: University of New Mexico Press, 2009), 159–162; Death Certificates, F. A. Hamer, Registrar's No. 11793, April 9, 1925, Lou Emma Hamer, August 30, 1934, Registrar's No. 38932, Alma Dell Knoll, February 11,

1975, Registrar's No. 459; *Arizona Daily Star*, April 30, 1908; *Del Rio News-Herald*, March 25, 1991; Flavious Letherage Hamer, World War I Draft Cards, RG 163, NARA. Franklin died on March 26, 1925, in Snyder, while Lou died on August 29, 1934, in Del Rio. *SAE*, March 28, 1925, August 31, 1934.

2. Joe Wreford Hipp, *The Oldest Ranch in Texas: Rancho de la Purísima Concepción, A Ranch on the Road to History* (Austin, TX: Eakin Press, 2000), 54–55; Frost and Jenkins, *"I'm Frank Hamer"*, 5; *Laredo News*, June 14, 2006; Harrison Kinney, "Frank Hamer: Texas Ranger," *American Gun* 1 (Spring 1961): 82; William Warren Sterling, *Trails and Trials of a Texas Ranger* (Norman: University of Oklahoma Press, 1968), 421 (quotation).
3. Robert Young, "The Guns of Frank Hamer," *Quarterly of the National Association and Center for Outlaw and Lawman History* 7 (Summer 1982): 1; Webb, *Texas Rangers*, 521 (first quotation); Byron C. Utecht, "Frank Hamer, Crusader," *Texas Parade* 18 (November 1957): 50 (second quotation), 52.
4. Kinney, "Frank Hamer," 82.
5. Boessenecker, *Texas Ranger*, 14–17, 466 n16; *Twelfth U.S. Census*, Mills County, Texas; Frost and Jenkins, *"I'm Frank Hamer"*, 8–15; *Tenth* and *Twelfth U.S. Census*, Kaufman County, Texas; *San Saba News*, June 10, 1954.
6. Webb, *Texas Rangers*, 525–526; Frost and Jenkins, *"I'm Frank Hamer"*, 20–21; Marsha Lea Daggett, ed., *Pecos County History* (Fort Stockton, TX: Pecos County Historical Association, 1984), 1: 417; *Twelfth U.S. Census*, Tom Green County, Texas. For more on the bandit, see Jeffrey Burton, *The Deadliest Outlaws: The Ketchum Gang and the Wild Bunch* (Denton: University of North Texas Press, 2009).
7. Daggett, ed., *Pecos County History*, 2: 313; Webb, *Texas Rangers*, 530–531; Buckley B. Paddock, *A History of Central and Western Texas* (Chicago, IL: Lewis Publishing Company, 1911), 1: 394.
8. Ernest Woodward, telephone interview with the author, June 8, 2018; Patrick Dearen, *Crossing Rio Pecos* (Fort Worth: Texas Christian University Press, 1996), 113; Record of Appointment of Postmasters 71B, roll 126, M841, RG 28, NARA, 213; Marks and Brands, Pecos County, 1: 137. This author is indebted to Kirby Franklin Warnock, editor and publisher of *Big Bend Quarterly*, and Mr. Woodward. In a series of emails, dated May 29–June 5, 2018, both gentlemen provided much-needed assistance in confirming the existence of the "Carr

Ranch." Jeff White of the UT Land System shared information on the university lands and Pecos County leases in an email dated June 7, 2018.

9. Webb, *Texas Rangers*, 525–526; Frost and Jenkins, *"I'm Frank Hamer"*, 20–21; *AAS*, July 18, 1948; Sammy Tise, *Texas County Sheriffs* (Albuquerque, NM: Oakwood Printing, 1989), 410.
10. Jaclyn Jeffrey, "Ranch Days and Indian Ways: The Early Life of Frank Hamer," *The Texas Ranger Annual* 3 (1984): 8; Boessenecker, *Texas Ranger*, 23–24; MR, Company C, April 30, 1906; RSR, Frank A. Hamer, 401–56, TSLAC.
11. *Kansas City Star*, June 3, 1934.
12. Harris, et al., *Texas Ranger Biographies*, 160; Bud Hamer, Bobbie Hamer Smith, and Harrison Hamer III interview with Robert Nieman at Waco, Texas, September 23, 2000, Oral History Project, TRHF&M, 24. Cited hereafter as Hamer family interview, 2000.
13. Harold B. Simpson, "Frank Hamer: Texas Ranger," *The Texas Ranger Annual* 3 (1984): 11; *AS*, September 29, October 3, 1906; *SADE*, October 4, 1906
14. *SADE*, December 2, 3, 4, 1906; *Houston Daily Post*, December 2, 4, 1906; *San Angelo Press*, December 6, 1906. Sheriff Robinson claimed in a telegram that he had shot Putnam in the exchange.
15. MR, Company C, May 31, 1907; SR, Company C, October 8, 1907; *San Antonio Gazette*, May 24, 1907.
16. *RAG, 1907–1908*, 12–13; MR, Company C, October 31, 1907; *Houston Daily Post*, September 7, 8, 20, October 4, 8, 1907; *SADE*, September 8, 1907; *Austin Daily Statesman*, September 28, October 5, 6, 8, 1907; Gary B. Borders, *A Hanging in Nacogdoches: Murder, Race, Politics, and Polemics in Texas's Oldest Town, 1870–1916* (Austin: University of Texas Press, 2006), 173–174.
17. *SAL*, October 26, 1907; *Houston Daily Post*, October 25, 28, 29, 30, November 6, 1907; *Austin Daily Statesman*, October 27, November 1, 7, 8, 16, 23, 1907; *GDN*, November 6, 1907; MR, Company C, November 30, 1907; RSR, J. T. Laughlin, 401–58, TSLAC.
18. *Houston Daily Post*, January 14, March 8, April 20, June 25, 26, 27, 28, 30, July 1, 3, 1908; *Austin Daily Statesman*, January 25, April 24, July 2, 1908; MR, Company C, May 30, 1908.
19. MR, Company C, June 30, 1908; *GDN* and *SAL*, both dated June 23, 1908; *Beaumont Enterprise*, June 23, 1908; *Waxahachie Daily Light*, June 23, 24, 1908; *AS*, June 24, 1908; Clifford R. Caldwell and

Ron DeLord, *Eternity at the End of a Rope: Executions, Lynchings, and Vigilante Justice in Texas, 1819-1923* (Santa Fe: Sunstone Press, 2015), 481–483.

20. MR, Company C, June 30–July 31, 1908; SR, Company C, July 15, 1908; *Austin Daily Statesman*, July 15, 17, 25, 1908, February 13, 1909; *Houston Daily Post*, July 16, 1908; West C. Gilbreath, *Death on the Gallows: The Encyclopedia of Legal Executions in Texas* (Fort Worth: Wild Horse Press, 2017), 200.
21. Navasota, Texas, City Council Minutes, November 4, December 17, 1908; Frost and Jenkins, *"I'm Frank Hamer"*, 32 (quotation); *Navasota Examiner*, December 3, 17, 1908; *AS*, December 19, 1908; *FCJ*, July 22, 1955; Young, "Guns of Frank Hamer," 3; Clarke Newlon, "Outlaw Tamer of the New West," *Startling Detective Adventures* 13 (November 1934): 38; MR, Company C, November 30, 1908; RSR, Frank A. Hamer, 401-56, TSLAC.
22. Boessenecker, *Texas Ranger*, 74–75 (quotation on p. 75).
23. Frost and Jenkins, *"I'm Frank Hamer"*, 32, 37 (quotation); Utecht, "Frank Hamer, Crusader," 53.
24. Glen Alyn, comp., *I Say Me for a Parable: The Oral Autobiography of Mance Lipscomb, Texas Bluesman* (New York: De Capo Press, 1994), 133–134, 147, 158. By the 1960s, Mance Lipscomb had become one of the country's foremost bluesmen and played with fellow legends Muddy Waters, Lightnin' Hopkins, and Howlin' Wolf. He influenced such future musicians as Bob Dylan, Janis Joplin, and Stevie Ray Vaughan. Gary Hartman, *The History of Texas Music* (College Station: Texas A&M University Press, 2008), 71–72.
25. *Navasota Examiner*, January 14, 1909.
26. Frost and Jenkins, *"I'm Frank Hamer"*, 37–38 (quotation on p. 38); *Navasota Examiner*, February 11, 1909; Webb, *Texas Rangers*, 527.
27. Boessenecker, *Texas Ranger*, 85–87; Death Certificate, Mollie Ford, August 23, 1937, Registrar No. 43853; *Thirteenth U.S. Census*, Waller County, Texas; Marriage Record No. 5380, Waller County Marriage Records, Book A, 525.
28. *Navasota Examiner*, April 29, October 7, 1909.
29. *Navasota Examiner*, April 14, 1910; Navasota, Texas, City Council Minutes, April 14, 1910; Newlon, "Outlaw Tamer," 60; Jim Wilson, "Frank Hamer, Legendary Lawman," *American Rifleman* 159 (October 2011): 60.
30. Frost and Jenkins, *"I'm Frank Hamer"*, 39–40; *Navasota Examiner*, July 21, 28, 1910; *Houston Post*, July 19, 1910.

31. *Navasota Examiner*, July 28, 1910; Alyn, *I Say Me for a Parable*, 157–158 (quotation on p. 157), 153; Sterling, *Trails and Trials of a Texas Ranger*, 421.
32. *Navasota Examiner*, March 2, 9, 1911; *Austin Daily Statesman* and *Houston Daily Post*, both dated March 3, 1911. Predating the Constitution, the "fleeing felon rule" stood for decades with gradual limitations occurring in the twentieth century. In 1985, the U.S. Supreme Court's ruling in *Tennessee v. Garner* established constitutional standards under the Fourth Amendment regarding the police use of deadly force. David C. Brody, et al, *Criminal Law* (Gaithersburg, MD: Aspen Publisher, 2001), 271–275.
33. *Navasota Examiner*, March 2, April 20, May 1, 1911; *Houston Post*, April 19, May 7, 1911; *GDN*, May 3, 1911.
34. Harold L. Platt, "Energy and Urban Growth: A Comparison of Houston and Chicago," *SHQ* 91 (July 1987): 6–8; Bartee Haile, *Texas Boomtowns: A History of Blood and Oil* (Charleston, SC: History Press, 2015), 19; Mitchel P. Roth and Tom Kennedy, *Houston Blue: The Story of the Houston Police Department* (Denton: University of North Texas Press, 2012), 53–55, 64; Louis J. Marchiafava, "The Houston Police 1878–1948," *Rice University Studies* 63 (Spring 1977): 9, 10; *Houston Post*, April 2, 10, August 2, 1910; *GDN*, April 13, 1911.
35. *GDN*, April 20, 21, 1911; Marchiafava, "Houston Police," 10; Alyn, *I Say Me For a Parable*, 162–164; *Houston Post*, November 8, 1911.
36. *Houston Post* and *Bryan Daily Eagle and Pilot*, both dated February 6, 1912; *GDN*, February 7, 15, 1912; *Austin Daily Statesman*, February 7, 1912.
37. *Houston Post*, May 18, 1912; Tise, *Texas County Sheriffs*, 243.
38. *Houston Post*, *AS*, and *GDN*, all dated February 29, 1912; General Index to Pension Files, 1861–1934, RG 15, NARA. For a sympathetic treatment of Ransom, see Pat Hill Goodrich, *Captain Ransom, Texas Ranger: An American Hero, 1874–1918* (Nappanee, IN: Evangel Publishing, 2007).
39. Boessenecker, *Texas Ranger*, 96; *Houston Post*, June 7, 8, 9, 11, 12, 13, 14, 16, 29, 30, July 23, 1912; *Bryan Daily Eagle and Pilot*, June 12, 1912; *Austin Daily Statesman*, June 22, 1912. Ransom resigned his position as a special officer on April 3, 1913. *Houston Post*, April 3, 1913.
40. *Houston Post*, June 15, 16, 18, 1911, January 6, 1913; Clifford R. Caldwell and Ron DeLord, *Texas Lawmen, 1900–1940: More of the*

Good and the Bad (Charleston, SC: History Press, 2012), 174; Tise, *Texas County Sheriffs*, 243.

41. *Houston Post*, January 4, 6, April 23, 1913; *GDN*, April 23, 1913; Texas Department of Criminal Justice, Convict Record Ledgers, 1998/038-158, TSLAC, 134.
42. *Houston Post*, February 26, 1911, January 17, 1913.
43. *Houston Post*, August 5, 1911, January 4, February 19, 1913, June 9, 1917.
44. *Houston Post*, February 20, March 5, 1913.
45. Boessenecker, *Texas Ranger*, 104; *Houston Post*, April 16, 17, 18, June 12, 1913; *Bryan Daily Eagle and Pilot*, June 12, 1913.
46. Boessenecker, *Texas Ranger*, 108; *AS*, July 11, 1913; *Bryan Daily Eagle and Pilot*, April 17, 1914; *Llano News*, September 1, 1914; Frank Hamer interview with J. Evetts Haley, Houston, Texas, December 6, 1943, J. Evetts Haley Collection, HML&HC. Hereafter cited as Frank Hamer interview, 1943. Robert A. Caro, *The Years of Lyndon Johnson: Means of Ascent* (New York: Alfred A. Knopf, 1990), 150; Lewis Nordyke, "Calculatin' Coke," *Saturday Evening Post* 217 (October 28, 1944): 41; Testimony of Dayton Moses, January 31, 1919, *TRF Investigation*, 107.
47. Hamer family interview, 2000, 12; *Fourteenth* and *Fifteenth U.S. Census*, Harris County, Texas; *Houston Post*, August 23, 1937; *Hempstead News*, August 27, 1937; Death Certificate, Mollie Ford, August 23, 1937, Registrar's No. 43853.
48. Bruce A. Glasrud and Harold J. Weiss, Jr., eds., *Tracking the Texas Rangers: The Twentieth Century* (Denton: University of North Texas Press, 2013), 74 (quotation); Acts 1915, Regular Session, 34th Legislature, Ch. 97, *General and Special Laws of Texas*; *RAG, 1915–1916*, 11.
49. Hutchings to Hamer, April 2, 1915, Hutchings to Sanders, April 6, 1915, 401-549, TSLAC; Inactive Personnel Record, Frank A. Hamer, TDPS; RSR, Frank A. Hamer, 401-56, J. D. Dunaway, -54, Winfred F. Bates, -51, E.. B. Hulen, -57, W. L. Barler, -51, Nat B. Jones, -58, TSLAC; *RAG, 1915–1916*, 11; SR, Company C, April 30, 1915; MR, Company C, May 31, 1915; John Busby McClung, "Texas Rangers Along the Rio Grande, 1910–1919" (Ph.D. dissertation, Texas Christian University, 1965), 69–70; *Comanche Chief*, October 15, 1915; *Houston Post*, April 25, 1918; *SAE*, November 7, 1918; Caro, *Means of Ascent*, 150; 208 *Southwestern Reporter* 920–921 (1919); Find A Grave:

James Dallas Dunaway, SGT Winfred Finis Bates, Pvt. Eugene B. Hulen, William Lee 'Willie Lee' Barler."

50. Boessenecker, *Texas Ranger*, 115; Mark Boardman, "No Quarter: The Texas Rangers vs. Mexican Insurgents, 1915–1919," *True West* 53 (January/February 2006): 40; John R. Peavey, *Echoes from the Rio Grande* (Brownsville, TX: Springman-King Company, 1963), 89–90; Bob Alexander, *Riding Lucifer's Line: Ranger Deaths along the Texas-Mexico Border* (Denton: University of North Texas Press, 2013), 242–243, 249–251.
51. Charles H. Sadler III and Louis R. Sadler, *The Plan de San Diego: Tejano Rebellion, Mexican Intrigue* (Lincoln: University of Nebraska Press, 2013), 84–85, 98, 252; F. Arturo Rosales, *¡Pobre* Raza*! Violence, Justice, and Mobilization among México Lindo Immigrants, 1900–1936* (Austin: University of Texas Press, 1999), 15; William M. Hager, "The Plan of San Diego: Unrest on the Texas Border in 1915," *Arizona and the West* 5 (Winter 1963): 328–329; Charles C. Cumberland, "Border Raids in the Lower Rio Grande Valley, 1915," *SHQ* 57 (January 1954): 294; Benjamin Heber Johnson, *Revolution in Texas: How a Forgotten Rebellion and Its Bloody Suppression Turned Mexicans into Americans* (New Haven, CT: Yale University Press, 2003), 1; Milo Kearney and Anthony Keith Knopp, *Border Cuates: A History of the U.S.-Mexican Twin Cities* (Austin, TX: Eakin Press, 1995), 181–182; Bob Alexander and Donaly E. Brice, *Texas Rangers: Lives, Legend, and Legacy* (Denton: University of North Texas Press, 2017), 356.
52. *SAE*, August 7, 1915; MR, Company B, August 31, 1915; McClung, "Texas Rangers Along the Rio Grande," 77–78; Peavey, *Echoes from the Rio Grande*, 103, 107–108; Boardman, "No Quarter," 42.
53. *SAE*, September 8, 1915.
54. Peavey, *Echoes from the Rio Grande*, 128–129.
55. Inactive Personnel Record, Frank A. Hamer, TDPS; RSR, Frank A. Hamer, 401–56, TSLAC; MR, Company B, October 31, 1915; Lorie Rubenser and Gloria Priddy, *Constables, Marshals, and More: Forgotten Offices in Texas Law Enforcement* (Denton: University of North Texas Press, 2011), 73; Spiller to Hutchings, November 1, 4, 1915, AG to Spiller, November 2, 1915, Hamer to AG, November 7, 19 (quotation), 1915, AG to Hamer, November 11, 1915, 401–552, TSLAC. Monica Muñoz Martínez details Ransom's transgressions in the second chapter of *The Injustice Never Leaves You: Anti-Mexican Violence in Texas* (Cambridge, MA: Harvard University Press, 2018).

On December 29, 1917, in a reprisal for an attack on the Brite Ranch in Presidio County, Fox and members of his company executed fifteen prisoners near the village of Porvenir. Paul N. Spellman, "Dark Days of the Texas Rangers, 1915–1918," *South Texas Studies* 12 (Spring 2001): 86.

56. Hamer to Hill, December 1, 1932, Harrison Hamer Collection. Copy provided to the author courtesy of John Boessenecker. Weems to Ferguson, December 21, 1916, Volume 19, Box 2R390, Walter Prescott Webb Collection, BCAH; *Snyder Signal*, December 22, 1916; *El Paso Morning Times*, December 17, 19, 1916. Ed and Gladys had married in Scurry County on August 31, 1905. Scurry County Genealogical Society, *Scurry County Marriage Record*, 1 (Snyder, TX: Scurry County Genealogical Society, 1991), 17.

57. Bill O'Neal, *The Johnson-Sims Feud: Romeo and Juliet, West Texas Style* (Denton: University of North Texas Press, 2010), 31, 51, 84–91; Hamer to Hill, December 1, 1932, Hamer Collection (quotation); Texas Department of Criminal Justice, Convict Record Ledgers, 1998/038-155, TSLAC, 178; Merrill [*sic*] to Ferguson, December 20, 1916, Wroe to Adjutant General, December 21, 1916, Spiller to Hutchings, November 1, 4, 1915, AG to Spiller, November 2, 1915, Hamer to AG, November 7, 19, 1915, AG to Hamer, November 7, 22, 1915, 401-560, TSLAC; Weems to Ferguson, December 21, 1916, Webb Collection, BCAH; Boessenecker, *Texas Ranger*, 146–147. According to the Adjutant General's office, McMeans had enlisted in Company C on November 13, 1903, and July 19, 1905. His dates of discharge were not recorded. RSR, George McMeans, 401-59, TSLAC. He was appointed tax collector on August 29, 1905. Gee McMeans, Box 2-9/854, Bonds and Oaths of County and State Officials, TSLAC. Among other newspapers, the October 2, 1917, edition of the *Galveston Daily News* incorrectly stated McMeans had served as Ector County sheriff. Tise, *Texas County Sheriffs*, 167, and the biennial reports of the Secretary of State do not support this assertion. See also Bob Alexander, *Bad Company and Burnt Powder: Justice and Injustice in the Old Southwest* (Denton: University of North Texas Press, 2014), 396 n42. "Gee McMeans" was employed as a cattle inspector in Galveston County in August 1907 and lost the election for Martin County sheriff in July 1908, while "G. McMeans" was an El Paso County deputy sheriff in November 1909. *SADE*, August 16, 1907; *Abilene Reporter*, July 31, 1908; *Houston Post*, November 27, 1909; *El Paso Herald*, May 24, 1911. Dudley

White was killed in the line of duty on July 12, 1918. *RAG, January 1, 1917–December 31, 1918*, 61.

58. Hamer to Hutchings, January 10, 1917, AG to Sam H. Hill, January 10, 1917, AG to Hamer, January 11, 1917, Hamer to Hutchings, January 13, 1917, 401–560, TSLAC; RSR, Frank A. Hamer, 401–56, TSLAC.
59. Boessenecker, *Texas Ranger*, 148; Frost and Jenkins, *"I'm Frank Hamer"*, 66–67 (quotation on p. 67); Kinney, "Frank Hamer: Texas Ranger," 83; Orleans Marriage Indices 39, Vital Records Indices, Division of Archives, Louisiana Secretary of State, 883.
60. *El Paso Herald*, February 15, 1918; *DMN*, February 15, 1918; *Snyder Signal*, February 22, 1918; Larry Lobdill, "Lone Star Hit Man," *Wild West* 28 (June 2015): 42–49. See also Ida Foster Campbell and Alice Foster Hill, *Triumph and Tragedy: A History of Thomas Lyons and the LCs* (Silver City, NM: High Lonesome Books, 2003).
61. *Snyder Signal*, June 8, September 14, 28, 1917.
62. Hamer to Hill, December 1, 1932, Hamer Collection (quotation); *Abilene Daily Reporter*, October 1, 2, 1917; *Snyder Signal*, September 14, October 5, 1917; Frost and Jenkins, "I'm Frank Hamer", 70.
63. Hamer to Hill, December 1, 1932, Hamer Collection; *Abilene Daily Reporter*, *DMN*, and *GDN*, all dated October 2, 1917; *Fort Worth Record*, October 3, 1917; *Snyder Signal*, October 5, 1917.
64. Hamer to Hill, December 1, 1932, Hamer Collection; *Aspermont Star*, October 4, 1917; *Abilene Daily Reporter*, October 2, 3, 1917; *DMN*, October 7, 1917; *SAE*, October 3, 1917; *Snyder Signal*, October 19, 1917. Lieutenant Doug Dukes, Austin Police Department (Ret.), generously shared with this author the benefit of his law enforcement and firearms expertise in analyzing the Sweetwater shootout.
65. Robert K. DeArment, *Bat Masterson: The Man and the Legend* (Norman: University of Oklahoma Press, 1989), 101–102; *Kansas City Star*, June 3, 1934 (first quotation); Frank Hamer interview, 1943 (second quotation); Webb, *Texas Rangers*, 524 (third quotation); Wilson, "Frank Hamer," 60.
66. Newlon, "Outlaw Tamer," 58.
67. *Snyder Signal*, October 19, 1917; Frost and Jenkins, *"I'm Frank Hamer"*, 74; O'Neal, *Johnson-Sims Feud*, 124; *Abilene Daily Reporter*, September 24, 25, 1918; Mike Cox, *Texas Ranger Tales: Stories That Need Telling* (Plano: Republic of Texas Press, 1997), 221.
68. Inactive Personnel Record, Frank A. Hamer, TDPS; RSR, Frank A. Hamer, 401–56, TSLAC; Hanson to Johnston, November 19, 1918,

Johnston to Hamer, November 22, 1918, 401-577, TSLAC; *RAG, January 1, 1917–December 31, 1918*, 61; Hanson to Harley, October 15, 1918, Volume 20, Webb Collection, BCAH (quotations). Taylor was the son of the family's first casualty in the old Sutton-Taylor feud. D. E. Kilgore, *A Ranger Legacy: 150 Years of Service to Texas* (Austin, TX: Madrona Press, 1973), 62.

69. Sterling, *Trails and Trials*, 423–424; Testimony of Capt. W. T. Vann, February 7, 1919, *TRF Investigation*, 563; Hanson to Harley, October 15, 1918, Volume 20, Webb Collection, BCAH; Kilgore, *A Ranger Legacy*, 63; Webb, *Texas Rangers*, 528–529.
70. *RAG, January 1, 1917–December 31, 1918*, 61; Testimony of Capt. W. T. Vann, February 7, 1919, *TRF Investigation*, 563; Hanson to Harley, October 15, 1918, Volume 20, Webb Collection, BCAH; Alexander, *Riding Lucifer's Line*, 288–290, 296–297; RSR, Frank A. Hamer, 401-56, TSLAC.
71. Testimony of José Canales, February 10, 1919, Testimony of Jesse Dennett, February 7, 1919, Cross-examination of José Canales, February 10, 1919, Testimony of E. H. Parker, February 13, 1919, *TRF Investigation*, 879–880, 885–886, 527–528, 925–927, 1416–1419; *SAEN*, February 14, 1919.
72. Testimony of José Canales, February 10, 1919, Canales to Hobby, December 12, 1919, Hobby to Canales, December 14, 1919, *TRF Investigation*, 887, 888–890, 890–891.
73. Harley to Canales, December 19, 1919, Canales to Harley, December 21, 1919, Harley to Canales, December 23, 1919, Harley to Haymer [*sic*], December 23, 1919, *TRF Investigation*, 891–895; William D. Corrigan and Clive Webb, *Forgotten Dead: Mob Violence against Mexicans in the United States,* 1848–1928 (New York: Oxford University Press, 2013), 124.
74. Harris and Sadler, *Texas Rangers and the Mexican Revolution*, 430–431. The definitive source on the Texas Rangers during the Mexican Revolution, Harris and Sadler's book is also likely the best secondary work on the 1,605 typed pages covering the joint committee's proceedings. Adopting a fair yet critical, when appropriate, approach, they provide an exhaustive analysis of the entire Canales episode.
75. Special Order No. 37, December 27, 1918, Hamer Vertical File, TRHF&M; *RAG, January 1, 1917–December 31, 1918*, 61; Testimony of José Canales, February 10, 1919, *TRF Investigation*, 900–901.

76. *Journal of the House of Representatives of the Regular Session of the Thirty-sixth Legislature* (Austin, TX: Von Boeckmann-Jones, 1919), 37, 163–164; Richard Henry Ribb, "José Tomás Canales and the Texas Rangers: Myth, Identity, and Power in South Texas, 1900–1920" (Ph.D. dissertation, University of Texas at Austin, 2001), 184–185; Corrigan and Webb, *Forgotten Dead*, 124.
77. McClung, "Texas Rangers Along the Rio Grande," 107 (first quotation); *Journal of the House of Representatives of the Regular Session of the Thirty-sixth Legislature*, 167–168, 177–179, 182, 196, 198–199, 201–202; Corrigan and Webb, *Forgotten Dead*, 124; Exceptions to Charges, February 3, 1919, Supplemental Answer of Adjutant General, February 11, 1919, *TRF Investigation*, 135, 1085–1088.
78. Acts 1919, Regular Session, 36th Legislature, House Concurrent Resolution No. 20, *General and Special Laws of Texas*; Special Order No. 7, January 30, 1919, Hamer Vertical File, TRHF&M. Another copy of the order can be found in RSR, Frank A. Hamer, 401-56, TSLAC. See also *Journal of the House of Representatives of the Regular Session of the Thirty-sixth Legislature*, 197, 211, 213, 216.
79. Charges Nos. 1–5, January 31, 1919, Charges Nos. 6–10, TRF Investigation, 3–7, 123–166; *AS*, *AA* and *DMN*, all dated January 31, 1919. The committee members were originally representatives Thomas Jefferson Tilson, Samuel Cabell Lackey, William Madison Tidwell, and Dan Scott McMillin. Tilson requested he be excused from serving on the committee, and the Speaker appointed William Harrison Bledsoe in his place to act as the chairman. The Senate appointed Senators Paul Dewitt Page, Edgar Earnest Witt, and Robert Lee Williford to the panel. Page was to act as vice-chair. *Journal of the House of Representatives of the Regular Session of the Thirty-sixth Legislature*, 238, 247.
80. Testimony of José Canales, February 10, 1919, Canales to Hobby, December 12, 1919, Hobby to Canales, December 14, 1919, *TRF Investigation*, 879–891, 900–901; Ribb, "José Tomás Canales and the Texas Rangers," 299–300. On February 7, while the hearings were taking place, Ranger Bertram Cleman Veale was killed by Captain Kinlock Faulkner Cunningham in a private quarrel. As a result, all Rangers who were in attendance upon the committee were instructed to disarm during their stay in Austin. Special Order No. 9, February 7, 1919, Hamer Vertical File, TRHF&M.
81. *Journal of the House of Representatives of the Regular Session of the Thirty-sixth Legislature*, 535–539.

82. Corrigan and Webb, *Forgotten Dead*, 125; Acts 1919, Regular Session, 36th Legislature, Ch. 144, *General and Special Laws of Texas*; Harold J. Weiss, Jr., "The Texas Rangers Revisited: Old Themes and New Viewpoints," *SHQ* 97 (April 1994): 637.
83. *AA*, January 18, 1919; Harris and Sadler, *Texas Rangers and the Mexican Revolution*, 396–397, 427; James W. Robinson, *The DPS Story: History of the Development of the Department of Public Safety in Texas* (Austin: Texas Department of Public Safety, 1975), 6; Mitchel P. Roth, "Through the Ages: Texas DPS History," *Courtesy, Service, and Protection: The History of the Texas Department of Public Safety* (Paducah, KY: Turner Publishing Company, 2003), 20; John C. Sparrow, *History of Personnel Demobilization in the United States Army* (Washington, DC: Department of the Army, 1952), 11–19; Don M. Coerver, "'Wire Me Before Shooting': Federalism in (In)Action—The Texas-Mexico Border during the Revolution, 1910–1920," *The Mexican Revolution: Conflict and Consolidation, 1910–1940*, ed. Douglas W. Richmond and Samuel W. Haynes (College Station: Texas A&M University Press, 2013), 53–54.
84. Ribb, "José Tomás Canales and the Texas Rangers," 375.
85. *Rules and Regulations Governing State Ranger Force of the State of Texas*, 401-1184, TSLAC, 1.
86. Boessenecker, *Texas Ranger*, 198; Webb, *Texas Rangers*, 532; Frost and Jenkins, *"I'm Frank Hamer"*, 61–62 (quotation on p. 62); Utecht, "Frank Hamer, Crusader," 51; *SAEN*, March 11, 1919; *Houston Post*, March 12, 1919; Special Order No. 28, March 26, 1918, Hamer Vertical File, TRHF&M; RSR, Frank A. Hamer, 401-56, TSLAC. Hanson later became chief investigator for Albert B. Falls's Congressional inquiry into Mexican affairs, then chief Immigration inspector in San Antonio. In March 1924, Ranger Captain Berkhead Clarence Baldwin testified before a Senate committee investigating corruption within the Department of Justice. He asserted that federal officials were failing to prosecute liquor smuggling, weapons trafficking, and neutrality violations on the border. The captain specifically implicated Hanson in supplying arms to the 1920 revolution of Esteban Cantú. Baldwin also alleged abuses of power by U.S. Attorneys Henry Zweifel and John D. Hartman, Prohibition Group Head Harry Hamilton, and U.S. Marshal David Walker (brother-in-law to the attorney general). Hanson, Zweifel, and Hartman publicly denied the charges. *New York Times*, March 9, 16, 1924; *AS*, March 15, 16, 1924; *Evening Star*, March 16, 1924.

87. Boessenecker, *Texas Ranger*, 202–203; Aldrich to Hamer, June 24, 1919, AG to Hamer, August 8, 1919, 401-580, TSLAC; Inactive Personnel Record, Frank A. Hamer, TDPS; RSR, Frank A. Hamer, 401-56, TSLAC.
88. Boessenecker, *Texas Ranger*, 206–207; Inactive Personnel Record, Frank A. Hamer, TDPS; Stevens to Adjutant General, December 7, 1919, Aldrich to Stevens, December 10, 1919, Stevens to Aldrich, December 12, 1919, Volume 21, Box 2R290, Webb Collection, BCAH; Special Order No. 92, December 15, 1919, Hamer Vertical File, TRHF&M; RSR, Frank A. Hamer, 401–56, TSLAC; *El Paso Herald*, January 1, 1920.
89. W. Clayton Carpenter, "The Red River Boundary Dispute," *The American Journal of International Law* 19 (July 1925): 517–519; Monroe Billington, "The Red River Boundary Controversy," *SHQ* 62 (January 1959): 356–357; *AS*, August 17, 1919. For more on the origins of the boundary dispute, see Philip Coolidge Brooks, *Diplomacy and the Borderlands: The Adams-Onís Treaty of 1819* (Berkeley: University of California Press, 1939).
90. Special Order No. 6, March 16, 1920, Hamer Vertical File, TRHF&M (quotation); Grant Foreman, "Red River and the Spanish Boundary in the Supreme Court," *Chronicles of Oklahoma* 2 (September 1924): 306; *FWST*, January 30, March 13, 1920; *Enid Daily News*, March 4, 1920; *AS*, March 10, 1920, November 22, 1940; *Oklahoma News*, March 11, 1920; *Daily Oklahoman*, March 13, 1920; Carpenter, "The Red River Boundary Dispute," 520–523; Gerald Forbes, "Oil and the Red River Boundary," *Southwestern Social Science Quarterly* 27 (September 1946): 158; James Randolph Ward, "The Texas Rangers, 1919–1935: A Study in Law Enforcement" (Ph.D. dissertation, Texas Christian University, 1972), 28–29. Youmans's permanent judicial post was the Western District of Arkansas. *Southwest American*, April 12, 1932.
91. Special Order No. 17, April 10, 1920, Special Orders No. 18, May 11, 1920, Hamer Vertical File, TRHF&M; Inactive Personnel Record, Frank A. Hamer, TDPS; RSR, Frank A. Hamer, 401–56, TSLAC; Frank A. Hamer, Internal Revenue Service, Official Personnel Folders, NPRC; *AS*, May 16, June 26, 1920; *Snyder Signal*, June 18, 1920; *AA*, July 5, 8, 1920; Boessenecker, *Texas Ranger*, 229–230.
92. *Breckenridge American*, July 2, 1920; *GDN*, June 27 (quotation), August 26, 1920; *SAE*, August 31, 1920.

93. Frost and Jenkins, *"I'm Frank Hamer"*, 95–96; *AS*, August 10, 1920; *SAEN*, August 11, 14, December 14, 1920; *SAE*, December 12, January 20, 1921; *AA*, January 20, 1921; *Leavenworth Post*, April 3, 1921; *Wichita Beacon*, April 17, 1921.
94. Jeanne Bozzell McCarty, *The Struggle for Sobriety: Protestants and Prohibition in Texas, 1919–1935* (El Paso: Texas Western Press, 1980), 11; *El Paso Herald*, September 16, 24, October 26, 1920.
95. *El Paso Herald*, January 10, 11, 1921; *El Paso Times*, January 11, 13, 1921; Frost and Jenkins, *"I'm Frank Hamer"*, 92, 95.
96. *AS*, February 24, June 18, 1921, June 13, 1922; *AA*, February 27, 1921, February 5, 1922.
97. *El Paso Herald*, February 26, 28, March 1, 1921, September 19, 1929; Frost and Jenkins, *"I'm Frank Hamer"*, 91–92; *El Paso Times*, November 18, 1962.
98. *El Paso Herald*, March 2, 3, 7, 1921; *El Paso Times*, March 3, 4, 1921; *AA*, March 3, 6, 1921.
99. Zarko Franks, "When to Say 'Manos Arriba!'," *Houston Chronicle Magazine* (June 16, 1963): 5. An undated clipping can be found in the Hamer Vertical File, TRHF&M. Caldwell and DeLord, *Texas Lawmen*, 402, 404–407, 444–445, 463, 475–476; *El Paso Times*, March 22, May 3, 1921.
100. Frank A. Hamer, Internal Revenue Service, Official Personnel Folders, NPRC.
101. *AS*, May 9, 10, 29, 30, 1921; *AA*, May 9, 13, 30, 1921; *Wichita Daily Times*, May 30, 1921; *Register of the Department of Justice and the Courts of the United States* (Washington, DC: Government Printing Office, 1922), 61.
102. *AS*, June 8, 17, 18, 1921; *AA*, June 9, 10, 14, 17, 18, 1921; *Cameron Herald*, June 9, 1921; *Taylor Daily Press*, June 10, 1921.
103. *AA*, August 25, 26, 28, 1921; *AS*, August 27, 1921.
104. *AS*, *AA*, and *El Paso Herald*, all dated August 30, 1921; *GDN*, *Houston Post*, and *El Paso Times*, all dated August 31, 1921; *RAG, January 1–August 31, 1922*, 54; Special Order No. 18, September 3, 1921, Companies Vertical File, TRHF&M; RSR, Frank A. Hamer, 401–56, TSLAC; Frank A. Hamer, Internal Revenue Service, Official Personnel Folders, NPRC.
105. Walter P. Webb, "Texas Rangers Quell Troubles," *State Trooper* 5 (August 1924): 13.
106. Hamer to Aldrich, September 9, 1921 (first quotation), Tape 5.1, James R. Ward Collection, ASU; Aldrich to Edds, September 8,

1921, 401–587, TSLAC (second quotation); Charles H. Harris III and Louis R. Sadler, *The Texas Rangers in Transition: From Gunfighters to Criminal Investigators, 1921–1935* (Norman: University of Oklahoma Press, 2019), 37–38, 538 n76.

107. *Salt Lake Tribune*, November 23, 24, 25, 28, 30, December 1, 2, 3, 1913; *Salt Lake Telegram*, November 21, 22, 28, December 2, 9, 1913; *El Paso Herald*, January 2, 8, 9, 1914; Lish to Kennard, December 2, 2002, Randy Lish Collection; [James O. Bennett], *Utah's Greatest Manhunt: The True Story of the Hunt for Lopez By An Eyewitness* (Salt Lake City, UT: F. W. Gardiner, 1913), 44–47, 101; Lynn R. Bailey, *The Search for Lopez: Utah's Greatest Manhunt* (Tucson, AZ: Westernlore Press, 1990), 11, 20, 22–24, 80–82; Laurence P. James, "The Great Underground Manhunt," *Journal of the West* 18 (April 1979): 11–20; T. A. Rickard, *The Utah Copper Enterprise* (San Francisco, CA: s. n., 1919), 42–43.

108. Frost and Jenkins, *"I'm Frank Hamer"*, 98–101; Christopher Lance Habermeyer, *Gringos' Curve: Pancho Villa's Massacre of American Miners in Mexico, 1916* (El Paso, TX: Book Publishers of El Paso, 2004), 54–69; Miguel Antonio Levario, *Militarizing the Mexican Border: When Mexicans Became the Enemy* (College Station: Texas A&M University, 2012), 44–45; *El Paso Herald*, January 13, 14, 1916; Mark Boardman, "The Myths of a Border Warrior," *True West* 61 (June 2014): 12; Daniel D. Arreola, *Postcards from the Sonora Border: Visualizing Place Through a Popular Lens, 1900s-1950s* (Tucson: University of Arizona Press, 2017), 65–67.

109. *Houston Post*, August 5, 1945; Randy Lish, interview with Frank A. Hamer, Jr., San Marcos, Texas, and affidavit of Frank A. Hamer, Jr., both dated October 26, 2002, Lish Collection.

110. *Salt Lake Tribune*, November 21, 2002, February 17, 2003; Synopsis of the Frank Hamer-Rafael Lopez Investigation, May 4, 2003, and Yocom to Kennard, January 24, 2003, Lish Collection. When Lish asked about the existence of official statements on the Lopez shooting, Frank, Jr. replied, "The rangers didn't make many reports. Except for their rifles." Lish-Hamer interview, 2002.

111. Birth Certificate, Billy Beckham Hamer, Register No. 511, December 16, 1921; Special Order No. 20, December 27, 1921, Hamer Vertical File, TRHF&M; RSR, Frank A. Hamer, 401–56, TSLAC.

112. Webb, "Texas Rangers Quell Troubles," 13.

113. *RAG, January 1–August 31, 1922*, 38, 55; Thomas D. Barton, *Report of State Ranger and Martial Law Activities of the National Guard*

of Texas, 1921 and 1922 (Austin: Von Boeckmann-Jones Company, 1923), 7–10, 14–15; E. A. Sterling to Aldrich, December 21, 1921, folder 3, Box 3P157, Roy W. Aldrich Papers, BCAH; Aldrich to Gonzaullas, January 13, 1922, Aldrich to Wells, January 19. 1922, Aldrich to Gillon, January 16, 1922, 401-588, TSLAC; Harry Krenek, *The Power Vested: The Use of Martial Law and the National Guard in Texas Domestic Crisis, 1919–1932* (Austin, TX: Presidial Press, 1980), 60–61; Haile, *Texas Boomtowns*, 59; *Mexia Evening News*, January 9, 10, February 4, 1922; *GDN*, January 9, 11, 1922; *Houston Post*, January 10, 1922; Kyle W. Shoemaker, "How Mexia Was Made a Clean City," *Owenwood Magazine* 1 (May 1922): 20–21; Robert M. Utley, *Lone Star Lawmen: The Second Century of the Texas Rangers* (New York: Berkley Books, 2007), 93; Cox, *Time of the Rangers*, 110–111; RSR, Horace Greathouse, 401-56, TSLAC.

114. *RAG, 1921–1922*, 95; Shoemaker, "How Mexia Was Made a Clean City," 25; Pat M. Neff, *The Battles of Peace* (Fort Worth, TX: Pioneer Publishing Company, 1925), 72; Diana Davids Olien and Roger M. Olien, *Oil in Texas: The Gusher Age, 1895–1945* (Austin: University of Texas Press, 2002), 122.
115. *DMN*, January 13, 1922.
116. *Mexia Evening News*, January 12, 1922.
117. *RAG, January 1–August 31, 1922*, 38; Barton, *State Ranger and Martial Law Activities*, 8, 10–12; Jacob F. Wolters, *Martial Law and Its Administration* (Austin, TX: Gammel's Book Store, 1930), 82–83; *Mexia Evening News*, January 13, 17, 18, 20, 22, February 1, 10, 15, 23, 1922; Mark Stanley, "Booze, Boomtowns, and Burning Crosses: The Turbulent Governorship of Pat M. Neff of Texas, 1921–1925" (M.A. thesis, University of North Texas), 52; *DMN*, January 13, 14, 16, 1922; *GDN*, January 14, 1922, George W. Gray, "The Watch on the Rio Grande," *The American Magazine* 101 (May 1926), 200 (quotation).
118. *Mexia Evening News*, January 21, February 25, 26, 28, 1922; *DMN*, January 18 (quotation), February 19, 27, 1922; *SAE*, January 29, 1922; *Bryan Daily Eagle*, January 30, 1922.
119. *AA*, January 14, 1922; Jenkins and Frost, *"I'm Frank Hamer"*, 113–118; E. B. Mann, "Who Was Frank Hamer," *Field and Stream* 84 (March 1980): 148. The rifle is on display at the Texas Ranger Hall of Fame and Museum in Waco.
120. Barton, *State Ranger and Martial Law Activities*, 12.
121. Hamer to Barton, September 18, 1922, [Aldrich?] to Hamer, October 5, 1922, Tape 5.1, Ward Collection, ASU; *GDN*, October 14, 1922; *SAEN*,

October 25, 1922. Jones was a former Texas Ranger who had served in Company A. For more on his life and career, see George Ellis, *A Man Named Jones* (New York: Signet Books, 1962).

122. Randolph B. Campbell, *Gone to Texas: A History of the Lone Star State* (New York: Oxford University Press, 2003), 368; Norman D. Brown, *Hood, Bonnet, and Little Brown Jug: Texas Politics, 1921–1928* (College Station: Texas A&M University Press, 1984), 51, 56, 60.
123. *DMN*, March 9, 1922.
124. Campbell, *Gone to Texas*, 368; Brown, *Hood, Bonnet, and Little Brown Jug*, 58; *SAE*, May 11, 1922.
125. *Brownwood Bulletin*, November 16, 1922; *SAE*, November 17, 18, 21, 1922; *SAEN*, November 17, 1922; *Corsicana Daily Sun*, November 17, 1922; *Houston Post*, November 18, 1922; Corrigan and Webb, *Forgotten Dead*, 148–151; Martin Guevara Urbina, et al., *Ethnic Realities of Mexican Americans: From Colonialism to 21st Century Globalization* (Springfield, IL: Charles C. Thomas, 2014), 109–110.
126. *AS*, March 17, 1923; *SAE* and *GDN*, both dated March 18, 1923.
127. *Taylor Daily Press*, April 2, 1923; Aldrich to Davidson, July 8, 1923, and attached documents, folder 60, and Nichols to Aldrich, August 7, 1923, folder 81, Roy W. Aldrich Papers, SRSU. Hinting at some factionalism within the Ranger officer ranks, Nichols's letter ends with the postscript, "keep this letter confidencial [*sic*]. dont [*sic*] let Hamer see it." *GDN*, June 7, July 4 (quotation), August 15, 1923; Barton to Crawford, July 6, 1923, Tape 5.1, Ward Collection, ASU; *AS*, July 6, 18, August 27, 1923; Brown, *Hood, Bonnet, and Little Brown Jug*, 159.
128. Aldrich to Davidson, July 8, 1923, and attached documents, folder 60, Aldrich Papers, SRSU; *AS*, July 9, 23, 24, August 17, 1923, June 12 (second quotation), 16, November 30, December 1, 1926, June 12, 1927; *AA*, July 7, 10, 18, 20, 24, 25, 1923, June 13, 14, December 4, 1926; *WNT*, July 7, 10 (first quotation), 1923; *Fort Worth Record-Telegram*, November 30, 1926; *Victoria Advocate*, December 1, 1926.
129. *SAE*, July 25, 26, August 21, 1923; *AS*, July 25, August 25, 26, 1923; *AA*, August 7, 8, 1923; Brown, *Hood, Bonnet, and Little Brown Jug*, 158.
130. *WNT*, August 6, 1923; *AS*, August 17, 19, 20, 21, 1923; *GDN*, August 17, 21, 1923; *Port Arthur News*, August 18, 1923; *AA*, August 19, 20, 21, 1923, September 25, 1962; *SAE*, August 21, 1923; Frank Hamer, interview with J. Evetts Haley, Austin, Texas, January 15, 1939, J. Evetts

Haley Collection, HML&HC; *Amarillo Daily News*, July 26, 1949; Find A Grave: Elijah Thomas McDonald.

131. *AS*, August 17, 18, 19, 21, 30, September 19, 1923, January 6, 1924; *AA*, September 13, 20, 1923; *Fort Worth Record*, September 13, October 12, 1923, January 6, 1924; *SAE*, September 16, 1923; *FWST*, October 13, 1924; *Abilene Daily Reporter*, November 22, 1923; Boessenecker, *Texas Ranger*, 180. The Texas Court of Criminal Appeals reversed Stanford's conviction on a technicality on January 21, 1925, and remanded the case to the lower court. *GDN*, January 22, 1925.
132. Charles C. Alexander, *The Ku Klux Klan in the Southwest* (Lexington: University of Kentucky Press, 1965), 81–82; Patricia Bernstein, *Ten Dollars to Hate: The Texas Man Who Fought the Klan* (College Station: Texas A&M University Press, 2017), Ch. 10; James W. Paulson, "Breaking the Back of the Texas Klan," *Texas Bar Journal* 75 (March 2012): 209; Mika Smith, "Hooded Crusaders: The Ku Klux Klan in the Panhandle and South Plains, 1921–1925" (M.A. thesis, Texas Tech University, 2008), 30–33.
133. *AS*, May 1, 1924; RSR, Walter E. Mayberry, 401-159, TSLAC.
134. Webb, "Texas Rangers Quell Trouble," 14; *Denton Record-Chronicle*, June 12, 13, 1924; *SAE*, June 13, 1924; *AA*, June 13, 14, 17, 1924; *Corpus Christi Times*, September 26, 1938; *Seguin Gazette-Enterprise*, October 10, 1968.
135. *AS*, February 20, 1925; Hans Peter Nielsen Gammel, comp., *Laws of Texas, 1923–1925* (Austin, TX: Gammel's Book Store, 1925), 1285–1286.
136. *AS*, May 1, 11, 1925; *GDN*, May 2, 13 (quotation), 1925; Special Order No. 13, April 28, 1925, Hamer Vertical File, TRHF&M.
137. Walter Prescott Webb, "Texas Rangers in Eclipse," *The State Trooper* 7 (January 1926): 13 (first quotation); Webb, *Texas Rangers*, 513 (second quotation); Inactive Personnel Record, Frank A. Hamer, TDPS; RSR, Frank A. Hamer, 401-56, TSLAC; *GDN*, June 4, 1925.
138. Boessenecker, *Texas Ranger*, 285; Inactive Personnel Record, Frank A. Hamer, TDPS; RSR, Frank A. Hamer, 401-56, TSLAC; *AA*, *Brownwood Bulletin*, and *AS*, all dated October 24, 1925. The reasons for Hamer leaving the Ranger Force, even temporarily, has been debated. Boessenecker asserted in *Texas Ranger*, 284, 298, he initially resigned out of principle. In *Lone Star Lawmen*, 112, Utley stated his return was arranged by McGee. Harris and Sadler dispute the popular notion in *Texas Rangers in Transition*, 218, and

maintain Hamer's appointment as a special investigator was due to a deal struck between himself and the Fergusons. Thus, they assert, Hamer was a "Ferguson Ranger."

139. Frost and Jenkins, *"I'm Frank Hamer"*, 126; *AA* and *GDN*, both dated Novembers 23, 1925.

140. Tod Aldrich to Aldrich, May 31, June 1, 21, July 2, 1926, folder 60, and June 11, 1926, folder 68, Aldrich Papers, SRSU; Ryan reports, June–July 1926, Tape 1.2, Ward Collection, ASU; *AA*, May 23, June 22, 25, 1926; *San Patricio County News*, May 27, June 3, 10, 24, July 1, 22, September 2, 1926; *SAL*, June 21, 1926; *GDN* and *Corpus Christi Times*, both dated June 26, 1926; Mrs. J. A. Ramsey, "When Death Rode the Spanish Trail," *Master Detective* 11 (February 1935): 6, 9, 12, 62–63.

141. Tod Aldrich to Aldrich, August 1, 24, September 6, 1926, folder 60, Aldrich Papers, SRSU; Ryan reports, June–July 1926, Tape 1.2, Ward Collection, ASU; Ramsey, "When Death Rode the Spanish Trail," 64–67; *San Patricio County News*, August 26, September 2, 9, 16, November 25, December 2, 1926, January 13, 20, 1927; *AA*, August 26, 27, September 23, 26, November 8, 12, 23, December 12, 30, 1926; *GDN*, August 27, September 4, 26, November 19, 23, 24, 27, December 12, 1926; Jerry E. Cravey, "Cracking the Red Riddle of the Rio Grande Valley," *Startling Detective Adventures* No. 37 (August 1931): 77–78; Keith Guthrie, *The History of San Patricio County* (Austin, TX: Nortex Press, 1986), 264–265.

142. *San Patricio County News*, August 8, 1929; *AA*, July 17, 21, 23, August 2, 3, 1929; *SAL*, July 22, August 29, 1929; *GDN*, August 2, 1929; Ramsey, "When Death Rode the Spanish Trail," 67 (quotation).

143. *AS*, August 20, 1926, May 11, 1927; *SAE*, August 24, 1926; *AA* and *Fort Worth Record-Telegram*, both dated November 15, 1926; *GDN*, November 15, December 4, 1926, May 12, 1927; *WNT*, December 4, 1926; Walter P. Webb, "Larger Texas Force," *The State Trooper* 8 (February 1927): 18.

144. Death Certificates, J. A. Barnes, Jr., November 18, 1923, File No. 33472, J. A. Barnes, Sr., November 15, 1923, File No. 33473; Hickman to Aldrich, November 20, 1923 (quotation), Tape 6.2, Ward Collection, ASU; *AS*, September 1, November 14, 15, 16, 18, 24, December 6, 23, 1923, December 9, 11, 12, 13, 1926, February 23, 1927, November 3, 1931; *GDN*, November 15, 16, 17, 21, 24, December 25, 1923, December 11, 14, 30, 1926, May 1, 3, 1927.

145. *El Paso Herald*, December 16, 1926; *Abilene Reporter-News*, December 16, 1926.
146. Special Order No. 2, February 2, 1927, Special Order No. 7, April 30, 1927, Hamer Vertical File, TRHF&M; Inactive Personnel Record, Frank A. Hamer, TDPS; RSR, Frank A. Hamer, 401-56, TSLAC; *RAG, August 31, 1927, and August 31, 1928*, 17–18; *GDN*, March 26, 1927; Walter Prescott Webb, "Rangers Reorganized," *The State Trooper* 8 (July 1927): 13.
147. *FWST*, October 4, 1927; R. D. Morgan, "Ace Pendleton: Oklahoma's Prince of Thieves," *OklahombreS Journal* 12 (Spring 2011): 5–6; *AS*, October 4, 7, 1927; *AA*; October 5, 6, 1927; *Daily Oklahoman*, October 9, 1927; *SAE* and *SAL*, both dated October 30, 1927; *GDN*, October 31, 1927; *Kerrville Times* and *San Saba News*, both dated November 24, 1927. Extradited to Oklahoma, Black and Walker were convicted of a bank robbery in Allen and given life sentences in McAlester. *DMN*, December 12, 20, 1928, May 12, 1931.
148. *FWST*, January 30, 1926; Hickman to Aldrich, April 2, 1926, Tape 1.1, Ward Collection, ASU; *WNT*, November 30, 1927; *Corsicana Semi-Weekly Light*, December 2, 1927; *AA*, December 16, 17, 1927; *SAE*, December 17, 1927; Death Certificate, Joe Dotson, February 13, 1931, Registrar No. 9963.
149. *Corsicana Daily Sun*, November 12, 1927 (quotation); *DMN*, November 15, 1927; Montague to Moody, February 12, 1928, Box 2007/170-53, TSLAC; *Denton Record-Chronicle*, February 25, 1928; *AS*, March 12, 13, 1928; *SAE*, March 13, 14, 1928; *San Saba News*, March 29, 1924; Webb, *Texas Rangers*, 533–534, 536–538.
150. *El Paso Herald*, December 24, 1927; *Fort Worth Record-Telegram*, December 24, 1927 (quotation), March 29, June 12, 1928; *AA*, December 24, 1927, February 11, March 27, 1928; *Abilene Morning Reporter-News*, December 25, 1927, June 10, 1928; *Corsicana Daily Sun*, February 11, 1928; *FWST*, March 19, 21, June 13, 1928; *GDN*, March 28, 1928. After his breakout, Baze settled in Washington State where he changed his name to James Sydney Calvin and raised a second family. He died a free man in April 1966. T. Lindsay Baker, *Gangster Tour of Texas* (College Station: Texas A&M University Press, 2011), 125–126. Smith's sentence was commuted by Governor Ross Sterling to twenty years in December 1932. On December 22, 1934, he assisted guards at the Retrieve prison farm during a storm and received a full pardon from Governor Miriam Ferguson. *Abilene Morning Reporter*, December 23, 1934.

151. *AS*, December 29, 1927, March 13, 14, 19, 1928; *Corsicana Daily Sun*, March 12, 28, 1928; *SAE*, March 13, 14, 1928; *AA*, March 14, 27, 1928; *New York Times*, April 8, 1928.
152. *AS*, April 11, 25, July 2, 1928, September 18, 1929; *SAE*, April 12, May 23, November 13, December 5, 1928; *AA*, April 4, 1928; *GDN*, April 8, 15, November 14, 15, 20, 1928; *Corsicana Daily Sun*, April 25, 1928; *Lubbock Morning Avalanche*, April 19, 1928, January 5, 1929; *AA*, April 12, 1929; *Pleasanton Express*, September 3, 1969, Gonzaullas Scrapbook 4, TRHF&M, 374; Webb, *Texas Rangers*, 538.
153. *AS*, October 15, 1929, June 19, 1931; *Corsicana Daily Sun*, March 3, 1930, June 19, 1931; *Amarillo Globe*, June 19, 1931; *Lubbock Morning Avalanche*, June 20, 1931, February 24, 1934. Dumas's conviction was upheld by the Court of Criminal Appeals on November 1, 1939. He received a full pardon in February 1951. *FWST*, November 2, 1939; *Lubbock Morning Avalanche*, February 23, 1951.
154. *AS*, March 19, April 20, 22, May 2, 1928; *AA*, April 26, 28, 30, June 7, 19, 1928; *Mexia Weekly Herald*, May 4, 1928.
155. *AA*, *WNT*, and *GDN*, all dated October 10, 1928; Caldwell and DeLord, *Texas Lawmen*, 25–26; Death Certificate, Joseph Blunn, October 22, 1928, File No. 45744; *Fifteenth U.S. Census*, Travis County, Texas.
156. *AS*, November 1, 2, 4, 1928; *McAllen Daily Press*, November 1, 1928; Charles Schreiner III, et al., comps., *A Pictorial History of the Texas Rangers: "That Special Breed of Men"* (Mountain Home, TX: YO Press, 1969), 83.
157. *McAllen Daily Press*, November 5, 8, 9, 1928; *AS*, November 8, 9, 1928; *Corsicana Daily Sun*, November 9, 10, 1928; *AA*, November 10, 1928.
158. Mike Gault, telephone interview with the author, March 27, 2019. Hereafter cited as Mike Gault interview, 2019. John Fusco, "The Legendary Maney Gault," *True West* 67 (April 2019): 39; *RAG, September 1, 1928–August 31, 1929*, 20.
159. Cox, *Time of the Rangers*, 139–140; *AS*, March 1, 2, 1929; *SAL*, March 1, 2, 4, 19, 22, 1929; *GDN*, March 2, 1929; *SAE*, March 3, 1929.
160. Hamer report, March 28, 1929; *AS*, March 26, 27, 1929.
161. *Abilene Morning News*, April 9, 1929.
162. *AA*, May 7, 8 (second quotation), 1929; *Corsicana Daily Sun*, May 7, 1929 (first quotation).
163. *Corsicana Daily News*, June 4, 1929.
164. ——— to Robertson, June 20, 1929, Tape 11.2, Ward Collection, ASU; *GDN*, June 20, 21, 1929; *AS*, June 20, 1929.

165. Moody to Thomerson, September 14, 1929, Box 2007/170-52, Moody to Bradham, September 17, 1929, Box 2007/170-51, Daniel J. Moody Papers, TSLAC; Gault report, September 14, 1929, Moore report, September 14, 1929, Wheatley report, September 15, 1929, Tape 11.2, Ward Collection, ASU; *Fort Worth Record-Telegram*, September 16, 1929; *Amarillo Globe-Times*, September 18, 19, 24, 1929; *Borger Daily Herald*, September 22, 1929 (first quotation); *AS*, September 24, 1929; Jerry Sinise, *Black Gold and Red Lights* (Austin, TX: Eakin Press, 1982), x, 112; Hutchinson County Historical Commission, *History of Hutchinson County, Texas: 104 Years, 1876–1980* (Dallas, TX: Taylor Publishing Company, 1980), 25.
166. Proclamation of Governor Moody, September 28, 1929, Moody to Pickens, September 17, 1929, Moody to Hamer, September 17, 1929, Box 2007/170-51, Moody Papers, TSLAC; *RAG, September 1, 1928–August 31, 1928*, 51–52, 80, 105–111; Wolters, *Martial Law*, 96–106, 117; Wheatley report, September 15, 1929, Gault report, September 29, 1929, Tape 11.2, Ward Collection, ASU; Krenek, *The Power Vested*, 90–92; *SAE*, September 15, 16, 18, 22, 24, 27, October 1, 1929; *Amarillo Globe-Times*, September 19, 24, 30, October 2, 4, 7, 1929; *Lubbock Avalanche-Journal*, September 15, 24, 29, October 1, 1929; *AS*, September 30, October 1, 1929; *Abilene Morning News*, September 24, October 4, 1929; *Abilene Morning Reporter-News*, September 22, 1929; *GDN*, September 18, 25, 1929; *Borger Daily Herald*, September 29, 30, October 1, 1929.
167. *RAG, September 1, 1928–August 31, 1928*, 52; Krenek, *The Power Vested*, 94; Sinise, *Black Gold and Red Lights*, 110; *Lubbock Morning Avalanche*, October 1, 12, 1929; *Amarillo Globe-Times*, October 3, 8, 1929.
168. *RAG, September 1, 1928–August 31, 1928*, 52, 80, 103; Wolters, *Martial Law*, 108–109; Wheatley report, October 20, 1929, Tape 11.2, Ward Collection, ASU; *Amarillo Globe-Times*, October 7, 17, 1929; *AS*, October 16, 17, 18, 1929; *GDN*, October 21, 1929. Asa Borger, who likely benefitted from the corruption occurring in his namesake, was slain on August 31, 1934, in the post office lobby by Arthur Huey, the county tax collector. The motive was attributed to a long-standing feud. Claiming self-defense at his trial, Huey was acquitted of the murder charge. *AS*, September 1, December 16, 1934.
169. *Fort Worth Press*, October 16, 1929.
170. Stephen William Schuster IV, "The Modernization of the Texas Rangers, 1930–1936" (M.A. thesis, Texas Christian University, 1965), 7–10; *AA*,

March 23, 26, 1929; Hickman to Aldrich, November 25, 1925, Folder 57, Aldrich Papers, SRSU; Acts 1929, Regular Session, 41st Legislature, Ch. 247, *General and Special Laws of Texas*.

171. *AA*, September 21, 1927, February 19, March 4, 1930; *AS*, December 30, 1927, February 22, 1930.

172. *Sherman Daily Democrat*, May 4, 5, 6, 1930; *DMN*, May 11, 1930; Donna J. Kumler, "'They Have Gone From Sherman': The Courthouse Riot of 1930 and Its Impact on the Black Professional Class" (Ph.D. dissertation, University of North Texas, 1995), 104–105, 107; Arthur F. Raper, *The Tragedy of Lynching* (Chapel Hill: University of North Carolina Press, 1933), 321–322; Moody to Robinett [*sic*], May 13, 1930, Box 2007/170-53, Daniel J. Moody Papers, TSLAC; Graham Landrum, *Grayson County: An Illustrated History of Grayson County, Texas* (Fort Worth, TX: University Supply & Equipment Company, 1960), 92–93.

173. Hamer to Moody, May 13, 1930, Box 2007/170-53, Moody Papers, TSLAC; *Sherman Daily Democrat*, May 9, 11, 1930; Edward H. Phillips, "The Sherman Courthouse Riot of 1930," *East Texas Historical Journal* 25 (October 1987): 13; Glasrud and Weiss, eds., *Tracking the Texas Rangers*, 111; *AA*, May 10, 1930; *Denton Record-Chronicle*, May 9, 1930; *Corsicana Daily Sun*, May 9, 1930 (quotation).

174. Hamer to Moody, May 13, 1930, Box 2007/170-53, Moody Papers, TSLAC (quotations); *Sherman Daily Democrat*, May 11, 1930; *AS*, May 9, 1930; Mike Cox, *Texas Ranger Tales II* (Plano: Republic of Texas Press, 1999), 195–197.

175. Hamer to Moody, May 13, 1930, Box 2007/170-53, Moody Papers, TSLAC; *RAG, September 1, 1928–August 31, 1929*, 80; "King Mob Runs Amuck in Texas," *Literary Digest* No. 105 (May 24, 1930): 11; *Sherman Daily Democrat* and *AS*, both dated May 9, 1930; *AA*, May 10, 1930; *DMN*, May 15, 1930; Kumler, "'They Have Gone From Sherman'," 126, 139–142; Raper, *Tragedy of Lynching*, 327–328 (quotation on p. 328); Phillips, "Sherman Courthouse Riot," 13–15.

176. Proclamation of Governor Moody, May 10, 1930, Moody to Pool, May 16, 1930, Box 2007/170-53, Moody Papers, TSLAC; *RAG, September 1, 1928–August 31, 1929*, 54–55, 114–122; *Sherman Daily Democrat*, May 11, 20, 1930, June 3, 4, 1931; Krenek, *The Power Vested*, 115, 117–123, 129; Phillips, "Sherman Courthouse Riot," 16; *AS*, May 10, 1930; *AA*, May 10, 15, 1930; Thomas Michael Murphy, "History of the Sherman Riot" (M.A. thesis, Austin College, 1931), 53;

Kumler, "'They Have Gone From Sherman'," 149; Trayce Darter Hudy, "The Texas Guard During Martial Law and a State of Emergency: A Select Study Focusing on Galveston, Sherman, Beaumont and Texas City" (M.A. thesis, Texas Woman's University, 2001), 91–92, 104; *Big Spring Daily Herald*, May 15, 16, 1930; *Corsicana Daily Sun*, May 14, 17, 1930; Texas Department of Criminal Justice, Convict Record Ledgers, 1998/038-143, TSLAC, 52. After leaving Huntsville, McCasland moved to Los Angeles, California, and worked as a waiter. Continuing to run afoul of the law, he served a four-year sentence at Folsom State Prison for burglary, being paroled in September 1949. Descriptive Registers, Folsom State Prison Records, California State Archives, 12.

177. Utley, *Lone Star Lawmen*, 134.
178. Roger Tuller, "Frank Hamer: Facing Down the Mob During the Sherman Riot," *Never without Honor: Studies of Courage in Tribute to Ben H. Procter*, ed. Archie P. McDonald (Nacogdoches: Stephen F. Austin State University Press, 2013), 73–74.
179. Boessenecker, *Texas Ranger*, 376.
180. Martin report, March 15, 1931, Tape 10.1, Ward Collection, ASU; *AS*, March 23, 1931; *SAE*, March 23, April 4, July 30, 1931; *Denton Record-Chronicle*, March 23, 1931; *GDN*, April 4, 1931; *Laredo Times*, August 27, 1931.
181. *AS*, November 24, 1931; *SAL*, January 12, 29, 1932.
182. Martin to Hamer, December 1, 1931, Allen to Sterling, March 16, 1932, Tape 10.1, Ward Collection, ASU; *Corsicana Daily Sun*, February 11, December 7, 1931; *SAE* and *Taylor Daily Press*, both dated December 7, 1931.
183. *Brownsville Herald*, February 21, October 17, 26, 1932, November 29, 1933; *SAL*, February 21, 1932; *Laredo Times*, March 13, 1932; Kearney and Knopp, *Border Cuates*, 210.
184. *AS*, September 9, 1932; *AA*, March 21, 1953; Find A Grave: Armistead Mason Ramsay.
185. Norman D. Brown, *Biscuits, the Dole, and Nodding Donkeys: Texas Politics, 1929–1932*, ed. Rachel Ozanne (Austin: University of Texas Press, 2019), 190–192, 203–204; Campbell, *Gone to Texas*, 387; Schuster, "The Modernization of the Texas Rangers," 19–20.
186. Webb, *Texas Rangers*, 539 (first quotation); Frost and Jenkins, *"I'm Frank Hamer"*, 185; Utley, *Lone Star Lawmen*, 152; Boessenecker, *Texas Rangers*, 385; Harris and Sadler, *Texas Rangers in Transition*,

481; *SAL*, January 15, 1933 (second quotation); *FWST*, November 19, 1932; *Cameron Herald*, December 22, 1932; *Marshall Evening Messenger*, January 9, 1933 (third quotation).

187. *SAL*, November 20, 1932.
188. Calhoun to Shepard, December 7, 1932, Hamer Vertical File, TRHF&M.
189. *DMN*, January 22, 1933.
190. *DMN*, January 15, 20, 1933; Newlon, "Outlaw Tamer," 39; Brown, *Biscuits, the Dole, and Nodding Donkeys*, 204; Hamer family interview, 2000, 28.
191. RSR, Frank A. Hamer, 401-56, TSLAC; Boessenecker, *Texas Ranger*, 385–386; *El Paso Herald-Post*, April 5, 1933.
192. *AS*, May 23, July 1, 1933.
193. Campbell, *Gone to Texas*, 387; Cox, *Time of the Rangers*, 156–157; Harris and Sadler, *Texas Rangers in Transition*, 455 (quotation).
194. Criminal Case File No. 8250, Northern District of Texas, RG 21, NARA, 7; Report of SA C. B. Winstead, January 25, 1934, FBI File No. 26-4114. As noted, one of the special agents involved in the federal investigation was Charles B. Winstead, the man later credited with killing John Dillinger. *AA*, January 28, 1934; Jeff Guinn, *Go Down Together: The True Untold Story of Bonnie and Clyde* (New York: Simon and Schuster, 2009), 247–248; Sid Underwood, *Depression Desperado: The Chronicle of Raymond Hamilton* (Austin, TX: Eakin Press, 1995), 42–43. Alleging prison officials had covered up the true details to conceal their guards' incompetence, Mullen claimed credit for masterminding the escape and asserted Barrow only drove the getaway car. James Mullen, "I Framed Ray Hamilton's Prison Break," *Startling Detective Adventures* 15 (November 1935): 10–17, 75–76.

    At that time, the Texas prison system was considered one of the worst in the country. For more on this neglected topic, see Bob Alexander and Richard K. Alford, *Tall Walls and High Fences: Officers and Offenders, The Texas Prison Story* (Denton: University of North Texas Press, 2020).
195. Mitchel Roth, "Bonnie and Clyde in Texas: The End of the Texas Outlaw Tradition," *East Texas Historical Journal* 35 (October 1997): 32, 33; Reports of SA C. B. Winstead, March 6, 1933, May 25, 1933, FBI File No. 26-3068, Report of SA W. F. Trainor, May 27, 1933, FBI File No. 26-4397, Report of SA F. S. Dunn, May 15, 1933, SAC F. J. Blake to Kansas City SAC, June 21, 1933, Report of SA J. R. Calhoun, November 6, 1933, FBI File No. 26-4114, Report of SA W. C. Jamison,

November 22, 1933, FBI File No. 26-5301; William Cx Hancock, "It's Death to Bonnie and Clyde," *True West* 16 (May–June 1968): 15–17, 56. As bank robbery was not yet a federal crime, the FBI wanted the Barrow Gang for violations of the National Motor Vehicle Theft Act and for theft of government property.

For more on the gang's first two years, see W. D. Jones and Clarke Newlon, "I Saw Clyde Barrow Kill Five Men," *Startling Detective Adventures* 12 (May–June 1934); Edward Portley and C. F. Waers, "The Inside Story of 'Bonnie' Parker and 'The Bloody Barrows'," *True Detective Mysteries* 22 (June–October 1934); W. D. Jones, "Riding with Bonnie and Clyde," *Playboy* 25 (November 1968); Blanche Caldwell Barrow, *My Life with Bonnie and Clyde*, ed. John Neal Phillips (Norman: University of Oklahoma Press, 2004); Brad Chisholm, "Okabena: A Bank Robbery Revisited," *Minnesota History* 62 (Winter 2010): 124–135; and James R. Knight, "Incident at Alma, Arkansas: The Barrow Gang in Northwest Arkansas," *AHQ* 56 (Winter 1997): 399–426.

196. Lee Simmons, *Assignment Huntsville: Memoirs of a Texas Prison Official* (Austin: University of Texas Press, 1957), 126–128; Newlon, "Outlaw Tamer," 58; Guinn, *Do Down Together*, 254–255. In 1948, Tom Hickman related how he and Manuel Gonzaullas had been approached by Simmons and offered the assignment to hunt down Barrow and Parker. Both refused saying, "We don't ambush people and we don't shoot women." Captain Fred McDaniel told a similar story in 1935. John Neal Phillips, *Running with Bonnie and Clyde: The Ten Fast Years of Ralph Fults* (Norman: University of Oklahoma Press, 1996), 354 n3.

Nieman theorized Frank was not given a Ranger commission for the manhunt because of his ongoing feud with Estill. Perhaps, Nieman conjectured, either one or the other Hamer brother, or possibly both, refused to work in the same organization as his sibling. Robert Nieman, "On the Trail of Bonnie and Clyde: Why Frank Hamer Wasn't Serving as a Texas Ranger, A New Theory," *TRD* 13 (Spring 2004): 37–38.

Frank Hamer, Jr. confirmed in an interview his father carried a .38 Super during the chase. Jim Wilson, "Frank Hamer's 'Mystery' Pistol," *Handguns for Sport and Defense* 6 (March 1992): 63. Rick Cartledge, "The Guns of Frank Hamer," *OklahombreS Journal* 4 (Spring 1993): 12. The provenance of Hamer's Remington Model 8F, which is owned by the Sam Houston Sanders Corps of Cadets Center at

Texas A&M University and loaned to the Texas Ranger Hall of Fame, has been conclusively verified. However, no evidence is known to exist that proves this particular weapon was used at Gibsland. See n204 for further discussion on the firearms employed in the ambush.

197. *AA*, February 3, 4, 7, June 19, 1934; *FWST*, February 3, 5, 6, June 18, 1934. One wonders whether the tension between the Hamer brothers was palpable to the other people in the room.

198. Frank Hamer interview, 1943; Webb, *Texas Rangers*, 540; Henderson Jordan and C. F. Waers, "The Inside Story of the Killing of 'Bonnie' Parker and Clyde Barrow," *True Detective Mysteries* 23 (November 1934): 44–45; John Reddy, "The Man Who Trapped Bonnie and Clyde," *Reader's Digest* (May 1968): 122–123; Clarke Newlon and Bob Alcorn, "I Killed Clyde Barrow," *Startling Detective Adventures* 13 (August 1934): 6, 9; Hancock, "It's Death to Bonnie and Clyde," 58.

199. Guinn, *Go Down Together*, 269; Bryan Burrough, *Public Enemies: America's Greatest Crime Wave and the Birth of the FBI, 1933–34* (New York: Penguin Books, 2004), 230; Jordan and Waers, "The Inside Story," 74; Boessenecker, *Texas Ranger*, 405 (quotation).

200. Report of SA E. J. Dowd, March 29, 1934, Memorandum of SA E. J. Dowd, March 17, 1934, FBI File No. 26-4114. The U.S. Bureau of Investigation became the Division of Investigation on June 10, 1933. The agency would be renamed the Federal Bureau of Investigation on July 1, 1935. Athan G. Theoharis, ed., *The FBI: A Comprehensive Reference Guide* (Phoenix, AZ: Oryx Press, 1999), 364.

201. Report of SA F. S. Dunn, May 9, 1934, FBI File No. 26-4114, 1–2; Guinn, *Go Down Together*, 264; Underwood, *Depression Desperado*, 48–49, 73–74; Hancock, "It's Death to Bonnie and Clyde," 17.

202. Criminal Case File No. 8250, Northern District of Texas, NARA, 9–10; Report of SA C. B. Winstead, April 14, 1934, Report of SA H. E. Hollis, April 19, 1934, FBI File No. 26-4114, 1, 3–6; *DMN*, February 24, 1935, May 19, 1934; *Dallas Daily Times-Herald*, September 6, 1934; Baker, *Gangster Tour of Texas*, 57–58. Whether Bonnie or Methvin killed Wheeler and Murphy has been a bone of contention, and the current conventional wisdom points to the latter. Labeled a fraud in recent years, farmer and eyewitness William Schieffer consistently claimed for the two months he was in the news that a man and a woman were the shooters. *FWST*, April 2, May 27, 31, 1934. The major weakness in his account is his courtroom identification of Billie Jean (Parker) Mace, not her sister. However, both women were described as auburn-haired

and small in stature, and a mistake in distinguishing them is plausible. Furthermore, neither Raymond Hamilton's brother Floyd, to whom Schieffer also pointed, nor Billie were the subject of rewards, so he had no apparent financial incentive to perjure himself on the stand. *SAE*, May 25, 27, 1934; *AS*, May 31, 1934. His filmed description of the murders, *Fox Movietone News Story 21–705: Hunt for Bonnie and Clyde* (1934), can be viewed at the University of South Carolina's Moving Images Research Collections website. While on a Sunday drive, Fred and Edith Giggal witnessed the immediate aftermath of the double homicide and asserted they saw "two men" standing over the slain patrolmen. On the other hand, the short-haired Bonnie was described as wearing riding breeches rather than a dress and may have looked mannish from a distance. *DMN* and *Dallas Evening Journal*, both dated April 2, 1934. Emma Parker claimed Methvin later confessed to shooting the two lawmen. Jan Fortune, ed., *Fugitives: The True Story of Clyde Barrow and Bonnie Parker* (Dallas, TX: Ranger Press, 1934), 236. Her statement should be regarded with much skepticism due to obvious desires to both protect her daughter's memory and finger the man who played a part in Bonnie's death. Additionally, Emma's allegations are called into question by the other eyewitness accounts and the ballistics testing on the arsenal later recovered from Clyde and Bonnie's car. Recent authors have treated the members of the Barrow and Parker clans as unimpeachable witnesses when, in actuality, they had every reason to blame Methvin for the twin murders. Hamer was convinced "that Clyde Barrow and Bonnie Parker did it." He stated to the United Press, "They talked to people about the killing and described it." *El Paso Herald-Post*, May 26, 1934.

203. *Dallas Daily Times-Herald*, May 23, 1934; Simmons, *Assignment Huntsville*, 131; Fusco, "The Legendary Maney Gault," 38. With the two families so close, Gladys may have suggested her husband take Maney on the manhunt. Mike Gault interview, 2019. Judge Williams had served as a Ranger from September 1 to October 1, 1923. During that month, he was undercover in Richmond and Blue Ridge investigating conditions in the oil fields. Harris and Sadler, *Texas Rangers in Transition*, 123–124.

204. Jordan and Waers, "The Inside Story," 74; Simmons, *Assignment Huntsville*, 132; Webb, *Texas Rangers*, 542; SAC R. Whitley to J. E. Hoover, April 24, 1934, SAC R. Whitley to J. E. Hoover, April 30, 1934, FBI File No. 26-4114; *Kansas City Star* and *Paris Evening*

News, both dated May 23, 1934; Cartledge, "Guns of Frank Hamer," 12–13; David Snell, "The Day the Real Bonnie and Clyde Were Gunned Down," *Life* 64 (February 16, 1968): 21 (quotation); Wilson, "Frank Hamer," 63. For a compilation of the three principal eyewitness accounts, see James R. Knight, *Three Ambushes* (Dallas, TX: Southwestern Historical Publications, 2006), 2, 6, 11. For an interview with Hinton, see Grover Ellis, "The Man Who Killed Bonnie and Clyde," *Texas Monthly* 1 (August 1973): 34, 86. Reprinted as "Death of Bonnie and Clyde: Eyewitness Story," *True* 55 (May 1974): 25, 36, 39.

The rifle used by Oakley (serial no. 48990) had been borrowed from Dr. Henry Daniel Shehee, an Arcadia dentist. James R. Knight, *Bonnie and Clyde: A Twenty-first-Century Update* (Austin, TX: Eakin Press, 2003), 166. In a rare display of accord, the narratives of Hamer, Jordan, and Hinton all agree the later wielded a BAR. Unfortunately, a great deal of speculation and error has gone into determining the types of firearms the rest of the posse carried at Gibsland. For example, interviewed two or three months after the shooting, Alcorn made the unlikely claim they were armed with shotguns and four BARs. Newlon and Alcorn, "I Killed Clyde Barrow," 9. The reenactment depicted in the short film *The Retribution of Bonnie and Clyde* (1934) produced by the Jamieson Film Company features Hinton with his BAR and Alcorn firing a Remington Model 8. The likelihood they used the same weapons in the ambush and in the movie seems high. The greatest debate rests on Hamer's choice of weapons. Some sources have maintained he used a Remington Model 8 modified with a twenty-round magazine from the Peace Officer Equipment Company of St. Joseph, Missouri. The first mention of this claim appeared in Larry Buchanan's documentary *The Other Side of Bonnie and Clyde* (1968). In the film, Frank Hamer, Jr. displayed a rifle (serial no. 10045) purportedly carried by the captain in the ambush. However, that particular weapon was a Remington Model 81 "Special Police," which was first produced in 1940. Additionally, Remington's extended magazines for the Model 8 were the fifteen-round variety. Sandy Jones and Bob Fischer state Hamer used a Colt R-80 Monitor Machine Rifle, which was the civilian equivalent of a BAR. "It's Death to Bonnie and Clyde," *OklahombreS Journal* 10 (Winter 1999): 4, 7. Yet the pair offer no evidence to support their assertion. Citing the Jones and Fischer article, Guinn, in *Go Down Together*, 335, and Knight, in *Bonnie and Clyde*, 165, each echo this contention, even though Hamer was known to have disliked full-automatic weapons.

In an email dated July 29, 2019, Shelly Crittendon, Collections Manager at the Texas Ranger Hall of Fame, informed this author that the Colt Monitor (serial no. C-103168) in the museum was donated by the late Joaquin Jackson. According to available information, the rifle belonged to Hamer, and the captain loaned it to Hinton for the ambush. However, she cautioned there was no conclusive proof for this claim. James L. Ballou repeats the unverified anecdote in his otherwise authoritative *Rock in a Hard Place: The Browning Automatic Rifle* (Cobourg, Ontario: Collector Grade Publications, 2000), 84–85. Photographs taken the day of the shooting depict a standard Model 8, three shotguns, and a BAR on top of the bullet-riddled Ford. The sharp-eyed observer can note the Remington did not have the heavily checkered forearm that appears on Hamer's engraved .30 rifle. Since a Remington Model 8 did not appear among the outlaws' arsenal, one could logically assume these were among the weapons carried by the posse. In a series of emails dated July 30, 2019, Cameron Woodall of The Great Model 8 website (thegreatmodel8.remingtonsociety.com) generously shared with the author his expertise on the rifle and his conclusions regarding this puzzle.

205. Guinn, *Go Down Together*, 269; Boessenecker, *Texas Ranger*, 424–425.

206. Jordan and Waers, "The Inside Story," 75–76; *GDN*, May 23, 24, 1934; *Shreveport Times*, *AS*, *Paris Evening News*, and *Kansas City Star*, all dated May 23, 1934; *Dallas Daily Times-Herald*, May 23, 1934 (second quotation); *DMN*, May 24, 1934; Newlon and Alcorn, "I Killed Clyde Barrow," 9, 72; Knight, *Three Ambushes*, 6–7; Snell, "The Day the Real Bonnie and Clyde Were Gunned Down," 21; Zarko Franks, "Bonnie and Clyde," *Houston Chronicle Magazine* (July 31, 1977): 12; Robert Nieman, "What Were You Thinking?: Ted Hinton and Bonnie and Clyde," *TRD* 18 (Fall 2005): 22 (first quotation); Carroll Y. Rich, "The Autopsy of Bonnie and Clyde," *Western Folklore* 29 (January 1970): 29–31; William M. Simpson, "A Bienville Parish Saga: The Ambush and Killing of Bonnie and Clyde," *Louisiana History: The Journal of the Louisiana Historical Association* 41 (Winter 2000): 17–18. Minutes after the two desperadoes were killed, Hinton used his 16 mm movie camera to film the scene. The two minute clip is available on Youtube.com. The Ford had been stolen from Jesse and Ruth Warren of Topeka, Kansas, on April 29. *Manhattan Mercury*, May 24, 1934. Based on amateur forensic analysis, Jones and Fischer claim in "It's Death to Bonnie and Clyde," 7, the ambush took sixteen seconds from start to finish.

207. Jordan and Waers, "The Inside Story," 76; *GDN*, May 23 (first quotation), August 14, 1934; Simpson, "A Bienville Parish Saga," 18; *St. Louis Post-Dispatch*, May 23, 1934 (second quotation); *Kansas City Star*, May 23, 1934; *Lubbock Morning Avalanche*, August 14, 1934; Franks, "Bonnie and Clyde," 16; Knight, *Bonnie and Clyde*, 169; *Beaumont Journal*, May 24, 1934; *Houston Chronicle*, September 22, 1935.
208. *Mexia Weekly Herald*, May 25, 1934 (first quotation); *GDN*, May 24, 1934 (second quotation); *Kansas City Star*, June 3, 1934 (third quotation). Among other papers, MacDonald's article was reprinted in the *Hartford Courant*, June 6, 7, 1934; the *Des Moines Tribune*, June 6, 7, 8, 1934; the *Milwaukee Journal*, June 9, 11, 12, 1934; and the *Baltimore Sun*, June 17, 1934. He received his Pulitzer in 1931 for solving the murder of a Texas woman by her husband. *Amarillo Daily News*, April 10, 1942. For more on Bailey, see J. Evetts Haley, *Robbing Banks Was My Business: The Story of J. Harvey Bailey, America's Most Successful Bank Robber* (Canyon, TX: Palo Duro Press, 1973). There exist a plethora of Dillinger books. For one of the better choices, see Elliott J. Gorn, *Dillinger's Wild Ride: The Year That Made America's Public Enemy Number One* (New York: Oxford University Press, 2011).
209. Webb, *Texas Rangers*, 544; Simmons, *Assignment Huntsville*, 176–177; *Pampa Daily Times*, June 22, 1934; *Corsicana Daily News*, July 5, 1934; Clarke, "Outlaw Tamer," 36 (quotation). Gault considered the shooting to be a necessary duty for which he was neither proud nor ashamed. His great-grandson said, "fate put him in a position where society had to step up." Mike Gault interview, 2019. Reserved and humble, the Ranger refused to give any interviews, and one reporter described him as "cold-eyed, mysterious, and he doesn't talk." Fusco, "The Legendary Maney Gault," 40.
210. Knight, *Three Ambushes*, 3; Young, "Guns of Frank Hamer," 4; Simpson, "A Bienville Parish Saga," 18; Mrs. Barrow to Hamer, July 28, 1934, Mrs. Parker to Hamer, October 16, 1934, Hamer Vertical File, TRHF&M. The letters were reproduced in Roger Conger, "Frank Hamer and the Barrow-Parker Era," *The Texas Ranger Annual* 3 (1984): 32, 34. Mann, "Who Was Frank Hamer," 150.
211. *AS*, May 25, 1934; *Victoria Daily Advocate*, June 5, 1934; Boessenecker, *Texas Ranger*, 445–447 (quotation on p. 447). Hoover's lust for power and publicity, and his need to eliminate perceived rivals, has been thoroughly documented in a number of works, including

Richard Gid Powers, *Secrecy and Power: The Life of J. Edgar Hoover* (New York: Free Press, 1987); Curt Gentry, *J. Edgar Hoover: The Man and the Secrets* (New York: W. W. Norton & Company, 2001); and Matthew Cecil, *Branding Hoover's FBI: How the Boss's PR Men Sold the Bureau to America* (Lawrence: University Press of Kansas, 2016).

For more on Jones, Winstead, White, and the rest of Hoover's "hired guns," see Burroughs, *Public Enemies*, 12 *ff.*

Chaplain P. B. Hill allegedly stated that Hoover had rated Hamer as "one of the greatest law officers in American history." Frost and Jenkins, *"I'm Frank Hamer"*, 280. No mention of this implausible claim could be found before 1968, the year the Frost and Jenkins book was published.

212. Minutes of the Texas Prison Board, July 24, 1934, Box 1998/038-8, TSLAC; *Lubbock Morning Avalanche*, July 24, 1934; Underwood, *Depression Desperado*, 124–125, 197; *SAE*, August 9, 1934 (quotation); *Paducah Sun-Democrat*, August 13, 1934; *AS*, December 7, 31, 1934, March 13, May 10, 1935; *Bastrop Advertiser*, January 3, 24, 31, 1935; *AA*, April 2, 10, 1935. For more on the ill-fated breakout, see Patrick M. McConal, *Over the Wall: The Men Behind the 1934 Death House Escape* (Austin, TX: Eakin Press, 2000).
213. *AS*, *WNT*, and *El Paso Times*, all dated April 25, 1935; *FWST*, April 25, 1935, November 16, 1963; *AAS*, November 16, 1963; Susan P. Baker, *Murdered Judges: Of the 20th Century and Other Mysterious Deaths* (Austin, TX: Sunbelt Eakin, 2004), 65–70.
214. *GDN*, October 26, 1935, May 4, 1945; *Houston Chronicle*, October 12, 13, 14, 1935, December 30, 1937, September 1, 2, 1938, May 4, 5, 1939; *Abilene Reporter-News*, August 6, 1941; *Sixteenth U.S. Census*, Travis County, Texas; Frost and Jenkins, *"I'm Frank Hamer"*, 262–263, 264; Roth and Kennedy, *Houston Blue*, 100; *AA*, May 4, 1945.
215. Boessenecker, *Texas Ranger*, 451; Utecht, "Frank Hamer, Crusader," 50; *AS*, March 29, 30, 1941; *Sweetwater Reporter*, March 30, 1941; *Lubbock Avalanche-Journal*, April 20, 1941; Frank Hamer interview, 1943. According to Frost and Jenkins, in *"I'm Frank Hamer"*, 268–269, Hamer had purportedly written to King George VI of England in 1939, and offered the services of forty-nine former Texas Rangers to address the Nazi threat. The Roosevelt administration was said to have halted the proposal in accordance with the United States' stated policy of neutrality. While an example of Hamer's patriotism, the story is not supported by independent evidence.

216. Hamer family interview, 2000, 13; *AA*, May 20, 1938, April 4, June 17, 1945, January 19, 1949.
217. Anthony R. Carrozza, *Dukes of Duval: The Parr Family and Texas Politics* (Norman: University of Oklahoma Press, 2017), 55–57; Boessenecker, *Texas Ranger*, 454; Caro, *Means of Ascent*, 325, 327–328; John E. Clark, "Reflections on the Duke of Duval: The Litigation Record," *South Texas Studies* 8 (1997): 36; *Corpus Christi Times*, September 10, 1948; Inactive Personnel Record, Frank A. Hamer, TDPS.
218. Frost and Jenkins, *"I'm Frank Hamer"*, 277; Caro, *Means of Ascent*, 328–329, 334; Ginger McGoldrick-Spradlin, "The Crucible of Texas Politics: An Analysis of the United States Senatorial Primaries of 1941 and 1948" (M.A. thesis, East Tennessee State University, 2011), 126, 128–129, 131–132, 134; *Corpus Christi Times*, September 10, 1948; Robert Dallek, *Lone Star Rising: Lyndon Johnson and His Times, 1908–1960* (New York: Oxford University Press, 1991), 328, 331; Edward B. Foley, *Ballot Battles: The History of Disputed Elections in the United States* (New York: Oxford University Press, 2016), 208; Dale Baum and James L. Hailey, "Lyndon Johnson's Victory in the 1948 Texas Senate Race: A Reappraisal," *Political Science Quarterly* 109 (Autumn 1994): 610–611.
219. Caro, *Means of Ascent*, 330–331, 334; Carrozza, *Dukes of Duval*, 66; *Corpus Christi Times*, September 10, 1948.
220. *Corpus Christi Times*, September 11, 1948; *AS*, September 11, 14, 22, October 6, 1948; *AA*, September 12, 14, 22, 29, 1948; Caro, *Means of Ascent*, 335, 348, 353, 363–364, 380–381, 384; June R. Welch, "The Texas Senatorial Election of 1948" (M.A. thesis, Texas Technological College, 1953), 163–164, 179–180; Ken Wise, "Lyndon B. Johnson vs. Coke R. Stevenson, et al.," *Texas Bar Journal* 75 (March 2012): 217.
221. *AS*, October 20, 21, 1949; *AAS*, July 31, 1977; Dallek, *Lone Star Rising*, 332; Clark, "Reflections on the Duke of Duval," 36.
222. Boessenecker, *Texas Ranger*, 458–459; *AAS*, March 11, 1951.
223. Inactive Personnel Record, Frank A. Hamer, TDPS; Death Certificate, Frank A. Hamer, July 15, 1955, File No. 36604; *Brownsville Herald*, July 11, 1955; *SAE* and *AA*, both dated July 12, 1955; Mann, "Who Was Frank Hamer," 150.
224. Karen Blumenthal, *Bonnie and Clyde: The Making of a Legend* (New York: Viking, 2017), 200–206; Burrough, *Public Enemies*,

360–361 (quotation on p. 361). Declared by *Forbes* in 2015 to be the wealthiest practicing attorney in the United States, Jamail became known as the "King of Torts." *AAS*, December 24, 2015. The 2019 crime drama *The Highwaymen*, directed by John Lee Hancock and written by John Fusco, was purportedly made as a direct refutation of the earlier film. Although Kevin Costner and Woody Harrelson ably portrayed Hamer and Gault, the movie suffered from too many historical inaccuracies and contrived events.

225. Death Certificate, Gladys Hamer, May 21, 1976, File No. 46069; *AAS*, May 18, 1976; *Brownville Herald*, May 19, 1976.
226. *AA*, September 18, 1924; *Fifteenth* and *Sixteenth U.S. Census*, Scurry County, Texas; Marriage Record No. 874, Mitchell County Marriage Records; *Abilene Reporter-News*, March 1, 1950, April 13, 1966.
227. *AA*, January 4, 1927, July 29, 1928, July 18, 1948; *AS*, May 28, 1926, June 18, 1968; *Baldwin Times*, January 13, 1955.
228. *AA*, November 5, 1939, June 25, 1943; *SAL*, April 8, 1973; *San Marcos Daily Record*, November 14, 1996, September 28, 2006.

Notes for Chapter 3

1. Charles H. Harris III, et al., *Texas Ranger Biographies: Those Who Served, 1910–1921* (Albuquerque: University of New Mexico Press, 2009), 176–177; *Seventh and Eighth U.S. Census*, Nelson County, Kentucky; *Twelfth U.S. Census*, Cooke County, Texas; Marriage License and Certificate, Nelson County, Kentucky; Cooke County Tax Rolls, 1885; Death Certificate, Willett J. Hickman, June 6, 1965, Registrar's No. 3116, Nannie H. Conley, August 31, 1973, File No. 60750; Cooke County Deed Records, 82: 451, 84: 345, 86–550–552, 87: 235–236, 103: 282, 104: 84–85, 105: 473–474, 111: 279, 112: 538, 121: 537, 135: 547, 144: 566; Will of Mollie Hickman, No. 2208, Box 174, Cooke County Probate Records. Mollie died on May 21, 1914, of intestinal poisoning. She was buried in Fairview Cemetery. Death Certificates, Mary McCormick Hickman, n.d., Registrar's No. 9545.
2. Mike Cox, *Texas Ranger Tales II* (Plano: Republic of Texas Press, 1999), 178; Ellsworth Collings, *The 101 Ranch* (Norman: University of Oklahoma Press, 1971), 119, 154, 166, 216, 218; David B. Hickman, telephone interview with the author, May 10, 2012. Hereafter cited as David Hickman interview, 2012.
3. Roger Conger, et al., "Mexican Buttons and Bandoliers: The Oral Memoirs of Captain Tom Hickman," *The Texas Ranger Annual* 2

(1983): 37, 40; Cox, *Texas Ranger Tales II*, 178; *Abilene Reporter-News*, June 28, 1952.

4. *DMN*, August 25, 1918.
5. Shickman [*sic*] to Parley [*sic*], April 2, 1918, Woodul to Shickman [*sic*], April 3, 1918, 401-574, TSLAC.
6. RSR, Tom R. Hickman, 401-57, TSLAC; *FWST*, June 12, 1919; Conger, et al., "Mexican Buttons and Bandoliers," 38.
7. Acts 1919, 2nd Called Session, 36th Legislature, Ch. 42, *General and Special Laws of Texas*.
8. Special Order No. 47, August 8, 1919, Hickman Vertical File, TRHF&M; *AS*, September 3, 1919. Brooks was promoted to captain of Headquarters Company on September 1. RSR, Joe B. Brooks, 401–52, TSLAC; *Houston Post*, September 28, 1919.
9. Special Order No. 63, September 16, 1919, Hickman Vertical File, TRHF&M.
10. Special Orders No. 77, October 21, 1919, Hickman Vertical File, TRHF&M.
11. W. Clayton Carpenter, "The Red River Boundary Dispute," *The American Journal of International Law* 19 (July 1925): 519–520; *GDN*, October 8, 1919; *AS*, October 9, 17, 19, 21, 23, November 13, 1919; *Lawton Constitution*, November 14, 1919; *FWST*, November 15, 20, 1919; Special Order No. 85, November 13, 1919, Hickman Vertical File, TRHF&M.
12. Bartee Haile, *Texas Boomtowns: A History of Blood and Oil* (Charleston, SC: History Press, 2015), 36–37; *El Paso Herald*, March 6, 1919; Special Order No. 88, December 5, 1919, Hickman Vertical File, TRHF&M.
13. Special Order No. 91, December 16, 1919, Hickman Vertical File, TRHF&M.
14. Special Order No. 93, December 19, 1919, Hickman Vertical File, TRHF&M; Hill to Hobby, December 19, 1919, McKenzie to Cope, December 22, 1919, 401–581, Cope to Hill, December 23, 1919, Hill to Pope [*sic*], December 24, 1919, Brooks to McKenzie, December 24, 1919, -582, TSLAC; *AA*, December 20, 21, 23, 24, 1919; Find A Grave: Edward Alvin Hill.
15. *AS*, January 10, 20, 21, 1920; *FWST*, January 20, 21, 1920; Gerald Forbes, "Oil and the Red River Boundary," *Southwestern Social Science Quarterly* 27 (September 1946): 153, 157.
16. *FWST*, January 21, 25, 27, 29, 1920; Sparks to Cope, January 30, 1920, Tape 5.2, James R. Ward Collection, ASU; *AS*, February 10, 1920

(quotation); John Boessenecker, *Texas Ranger: The Epic Life of Frank Hamer, the Man Who Killed Bonnie and Clyde* (New York: Thomas Dunne Books, 2016), 212–213; Joseph F. Zimmerman, *Interstate Disputes: The Supreme Court's Original Jurisdiction* (Albany: State University of New York, 2006), 69–70; Stevens to Hobby, February 3, 1920, Volume 21, Webb Collection, BCAH; *AS*, February 10, 1920 (quotation).

17. Randolph B. Campbell, *Gone to Texas: A History of the Lone Star State* (New York: Oxford University Press, 2003), 358; *RAG, January 1, 1919–December 31, 1920*, 68; Joseph Abel, "Opening the Closed Shop: The Galveston Longshoremen's Strike of 1920–1921," *SHQ* 110 (January 2007): 318; William D. Angel, Jr., "Controlling the Workers: The Galveston Dock Workers' Strike of 1920 and Its Impact on Labor Relations in Texas," *East Texas Historical Journal* 23 (October 1985): 15, 17; Virginia Duncan, "The Life of Captain Roy W. Aldrich" (M.A. thesis, Sul Ross State Teachers College, 1942): 56.
18. *RAG, January 1, 1919–December 31, 1920*, 69–71, 73; Jacob F. Wolters, *Martial Law and Its Administration* (Austin, TX: Gammel's Book Store, 1930), 57–58; Harry Krenek, *The Power Vested: The Use of Martial Law and the National Guard in Texas Domestic Crisis, 1919–1932* (Austin, TX: Presidial Press, 1980), 15; *GDN*, June 3, 4, 8, 1920; Angel, "Controlling the Workers," 18, 22; James C. Maroney, "The Galveston Longshoremen's Strike of 1920," *East Texas Historical Journal* 16 (March 1978): 35; Abel, "Opening the Closed Shop," 320, 325, 328.
19. Special Order No. 21, June 5, 1920, Hickman Vertical File, TRHF&M.
20. *AS*, July 2, 22, 1920; *SAEN*, July 3, 23, August 28, 31, 1920; Special Order No. 32, July 13, 1920, Hickman Vertical File, TRHF&M.
21. *RAG, January 1, 1919–December 31, 1920*, 74–75; Wolters, *Martial Law*, 71–73, 77–78; Krenek, *The Power Vested*, 17, 19, 27; *GDN*, June 20, October 1, 1920; Maroney, "Galveston Longshoremen's Strike," 36; Abel, "Opening the Closed Shop," 323, 336–338, 340.
22. Special Order No. 41, September 11, 1920, Hickman Vertical File, TRHF&M.
23. Special Orders No. 52, September 25, 1920, Companies Vertical File, and Special Orders No. 54, September 29, 1920, Special Orders No. 62, October 27, 1920, Hickman Vertical File, TRHF&M; RSR, Charles Blackwell, 401–52, Tom R. Hickman, -57, TSLAC; James Randolph Ward, "The Texas Rangers, 1919–1935: A Study in Law Enforcement"

(Ph.D. dissertation, Texas Christian University, 1972), 34; Cope to Brooks, January 15, 1921, 401–584, TSLAC; *GDN*, September 19, 20, 25, 27, 30, October 1, 2, 27, November 1, 1920; David G. McComb, *Galveston: A History* (Austin: University of Texas Press, 1986), 167. The National Guard still performed valuable service on September 29 by fighting a fire for two days on Pier 35 which threatened the entire waterfront. On October 2, they again fought a dangerous blaze, this time on Pier 41. *RAG, January 1, 1919–December 31, 1920*, 77–80.

24. Angel, "Controlling the Workers," 24.
25. RSR, Tom R. Hickman, 401–57, TSLAC; Aldrich to Brady, November 26, 1920, 401–584, TSLAC; Hickman to Aldrich, December 1, 1920, folder 76, Roy W. Aldrich Papers, SRSU; *Breckenridge American*, December 1, 1920; *Fort Worth Record*, December 1, 1920; *FWST*, December 1, 2, 1920, February 20, 1921; Death Certificate, A. E. Lockhart, December 4, 1920, File No. 35956; *DMN*, December 18, 1920. Ellis had enlisted in June 5, 1920, in Ranger Company D and served for fifteen days. RSR, Jim M. Ellis, 401–54.
26. Hickman to Aldrich, December 19, 1920, folder 76, Aldrich Papers, SRSU; *AS*, January 4, 1921; *Fort Worth Record*, January 4, 6, 1921; *FWST*, January 5, 6, 7, February 7, 10, 11 (quotation), 1921. Following his acquittal, Ellis served as a Travis County deputy sheriff. *Fort Worth Record*, February 11, 1921.
27. Whitworth to Aldrich, January 20, 1921, 401-584, TSLAC; Hickman to Barton, January 25, 1921 (quotation), Barton to Hickman, January 27, 1921, Tape 6.2, Ward Collection, ASU; AS, January 22, 1921; *FWST*, January 28, 1921; Charles H. Harris III and Louis R. Sadler, *The Texas Rangers in Transition: From Gunfighters to Criminal Investigators, 1921–1935* (Norman: University of Oklahoma Press, 2019), 78–79; Find A Grave: William Henry Whitworth.
28. *FWST*, February 25, 27 (quotation), 1921; *AA*, February 24, 27, 1921.
29. *RAG, January 1–August 31, 1921*, 53; *FWST*, February 12, March 2, April 26, 1921; *AA*, February 25, March 3, April 27, 1921; *DMN* and *GDN*, both February 26, 1921; Harris and Sadler, *Texas Rangers in Transition*, 73.
30. *Paris Morning News*, January 23, February 15, 1920; *Fourteenth U.S. Census*, Lamar County, Texas; *Bonham Daily Favorite*, April 13, 14, 20, 25, 29, May 27, 1921; *FWST*, April 14, 15, 16, 17, 21, 26, 28, May 27, 1921; *WNT*, April 18, 26, 1921; Hickman to Barton, April 21, 1921, Tape 6.2, Ward Collection, ASU; *AA*, April 27, 28, 1921; West

C. Gilbreath, *Death on the Gallows: The Encyclopedia of Legal Executions in Texas* (Fort Worth: Wild Horse Press, 2017), 227–228.

31. Adjutant General to Hickman, April 25, 1921, Warfield to Adjutant General, June 6, 1922 (quotation), Aldrich to Hickman, August 19, 26, 1921, Hickman to Barton, September 9, 1921, Tape 6.2, Ward Collection, ASU; Aldrich to Fulton, September 19, 1921, Aldrich to Monroe, September 22, 1921, Monroe to Aldrich, September 29, 1921, Fulton to Barton, September 30, 1921, Box 401-587, TSLAC; *Wichita Daily Times*, December 2, 5, 14, 21, 1921.
32. *WNT*, February 22, 23, 28, March 1, 2, 7 (quotation), 1922; *FWST*, February 23, 28, March 2, 7, 1922; *Corsica Daily Sun*, February 23, 1922; *Mexia Evening News*, March 2, 1922; Harris, et al., *Texas Ranger Biographies*, 19, 222.
33. *FWST*, March 10, 1922; *Wichita Daily Times*, April 6, 14, 1922.
34. RSR, Tom R. Hickman, 401–57, TSLAC.
35. *Mexia Evening News*, June 4, 1922; *SAE*, June 5, 1922; Conger, et al., "Mexican Buttons and Bandoliers," 43.
36. Thomas D. Barton, *Report of State Ranger and Martial Law Activities of the National Guard of Texas, 1921 and 1922* (Austin: Von Boeckmann-Jones Company, 1923), 22; Brown, *Hood, Bonnet, and Little Brown Jug*, 83; Mark Stanley, "Booze, Boomtowns, and Burning Crosses: The Turbulent Governorship of Pat M. Neff of Texas, 1921–1925" (M.A. thesis, University of North Texas), 74; *Denton Record-Chronicle*, July 7, 12, 1922; Paul Douglas Casdorph, "The Texas National Guard and the 1922 Railroad Strike at Denison," *Texas Military History* 3 (Winter 1963): 211.
37. Barton to Nitzer, July 14, 1922, 401–591, TSLAC; Barton to Gray, July 14, 1922, Hamer to Barton, August 6, 1922, Tape 5.1, Ward Collection, ASU; Aldrich to Harkey, August 23, 1922, TSLAC; *RAG, January 1–August 31, 1922*, 40, 55–56; Pat M. Neff, *The Battles of Peace* (Fort Worth, TX: Pioneer Publishing Company, 1925), 74–75; Barton, *State Ranger and Martial Law Activities*, 22; Wolters, *Martial Law*, 89; Harris and Sadler, *Texas Rangers in Transition*, 100; *Denton Record-Chronicle*, July 13, 14, 15, 17, 18 (quotation), 20, 21, 23, 24, 25, 26, 29, 1922; *FWST*, July 14, 19, 28, 1922; *SAEN*, July 15, 25, 1922; *Wichita Daily Times* and *Mexia Daily News*, both dated July 18, 1922; *SAE*, July 19, 26, 29, 1922; *GDN*, July 21, 25, 26, 27, 1922; *DMN*, July 24, 25, 1922; *AS*, July 25, 28, 1922; *Meridian Tribune*, August 18, 1922.

38. Neff, *Battles of Peace*, 76; Barton, *State Ranger and Martial Law Activities*, 22; Krenek, *The Power Vested*, 54–55; Brown, *Hood, Bonnet, and Little Brown Jug*, 86; Hickman to Barton, October 24, 1922, Aldrich to Hickman, October 28, 1922, Hickman to Barton, December 12, 19, 1922, Tape 6.2, Ward Collection, ASU; Ward, "The Texas Rangers," 81; Casdorph, "The Texas National Guard and the 1922 Railroad Strike," 217; *DMN*, July 24, 1922; *Denton Record-Chronicle*, August 2, 3, September 22, October 9, 10, 19, 1922; *Meridian Tribune*, August 18, 1922; *FWST*, October 19, 1922; *GDN*, October 1, December 1, 1922, January 2, 1923; *Brownwood Bulletin*, December 7, 1922.
39. *AA*, June 6, 1923; Hickman to Barton, June 14, 23, 1923, Tape 6.2, Ward Collection, ASU.
40. *Brownwood Bulletin*, January 7, 1924; *AA*, January 8, 1924; Death Certificate, Mamie Hickman, April 19, 1924, Registrar's No. 14608; Special Order No. 5, February 18, 1924, Hickman Vertical File, TRHF&M; Hickman to Aldrich, March 5, 1924, Tape 6.2, Ward Collection, ASU; Ward, "The Texas Rangers," 116.
41. Texas Death Certificate, Mamie Hickman, April 19, 1924, Registrar's No. 14608; *AA*, April 19; *SAE*, April 19,1924; *GDN*, April 19, 1924; *Houston Post*, April 19 (quotation), 1924.
42. *AA*, April 21, June 16, July 8, 1924, October 12, 1925; *Mexia Daily News*, April 21, 1924; *FWST*, May 18, June 16, 17, July 1, 1924; *Houston Post*, April 20, 1924; Hickman to Aldrich, July 1, 1924, folder 3, Box 3P157, Roy W. Aldrich Papers, BCAH; *New York Times*, June 15, 17, 18, 19, 20, 1924; *Fort Worth Record*, July 9, 1924; Cox, *Texas Ranger Tales II*, 180.
43. Hickman to Barton, August 16, November 3, 13, 1924, Hickman to Aldrich, January 30, February 2, 1925, Tape 6.2, Ward Collection, ASU; *SAE*, October 8, 1924; Sammy Tise, *Texas County Sheriffs* (Albuquerque, NM: Oakwood Printing, 1989), 307, 176; *FWST*, January 20, 1947; *Fort Worth Record*, February 9, 1925.
44. D. J. Taylor, "The Story-Martin Gang Brought the Era of Organized Crime to Denton County," *Denton County Historical Commission Retrospect* (Fall 2015): 6; Walter Prescott Webb, "Lone Ranger Gets Bandit," *The State Trooper* 7 (March 1926) ; *Denton Record-Chronicle*, January 31, February 3, 1925: 9; Tise, *Texas County Sheriffs*, 155.
45. *SAL*, February 3, 1925; *AA*, February 3, 4, 1925; *GDN*, February 3, 4, 1925; *SAE* and *WNT*, both dated February 4, 1925; Taylor, "The Story-Martin Gang," 6.

46. Hickman report, March 30, 1925, Hickman to Aldrich, February 2, 1925, Hickman to Adjutant General, February 16, 1925, Tape 6.2, Hickman to McGee, February 16, 1925, Hickman to McGee, March 30, 1925, Hickman to McGee, April 16, 1925, Hickman to McGee, June 15, 1925, Hickman to Aldrich, June 22, 1925, Hickman report, July 28, 1925, Hickman report, August 24, 1925, Hickman report, September 13, 1925, Tape 1.1, Ward Collection, ASU; *Brownwood Bulletin*, March 11, August 29, September 11, 12, 1925; *Taylor Daily Press*, March 19, 1925; *Corsicana Daily Sun*, June 10, August 25, 1925; *DMN*, August 25, 1925; *GDN*, August 25, 26, 1925; *Denton Record-Chronicle*, August 13, 25, 26, 27, 28, September 2, 5, 7, 15, 25, 28, October 3, 1925; *AS*, August 25, 26, 1925; *Laredo Times*, August 25, 27, 1925; *Fort Worth Record*, August 25, 1925, and *Dallas Journal*, August 28, 1925, Gonzaullas Scrapbook 2, TRHF&M, 118, 116; *FWST*, September 23, 1925; *SAE*, October 14, 1925; Webb, "Lone Ranger Gets Bandit," 10.
47. Hickman to Aldrich, January 30, 1926, Hickman to Matthews, January 31, 1926, Hickman to Aldrich, May 24, 1926, Tape 1.1, Hickman to Nichols, October 23, 1927, Tape 3.2, Ward Collection, ASU; *Denton Record-Chronicle*, October 12, November 15, 18, 23, December 7, 1925, May 28, 29, 30, 1928, January 12, 1929, January 28, June 30, 1930; *Brownwood Bulletin*, January 15, 1926; *SAE*, October 14, 1925, May 19, 1927. See also Mike Cochran, "W. A. Martin and the Story Gang: The Shootout on Oakland Street," MS, n.d., available at www.dentonhistory.net.
48. *AA*, May 16, 17, 20, 1925; *WNT*, May 16, 17, 20, 1925.
49. *AA*, May 21, June 1, 1925, April 15, 17, 1926; *Corsicana Daily Sun*, May 21, 1925; *AS*, May 22, 1925; *WNT*, May 23, June 1, 2, 1925, April 15, 17, 1926; Hickman to Aldrich, May 25, 1925, Tape 1.1, Ward Collection, ASU; Aldrich to Tod Aldrich, May 25, 1925, folder 68, Aldrich Papers, SRSU; *FWST*, May 29, 1925.
50. Boessenecker, *Texas Ranger*, 283–284; *Brownwood Bulletin*, May 21, 22, 1925; *DMN*, May 22, 1925; *WNT*, May 23, 1925; *GDN*, May 31, July 3, 1925; Hickman to Aldrich, June 2, 1925, Hickman to McGee, July 5, 1925, Tape 1.1, Hickman to McGee, July 11, 1925, Tape 6.2, Ward Collection, ASU. An associate of gambler Lester Ben "Benny" Binion, Marshall was charged on November 27, 1931, in Ellis County with burglary and robbery with firearms. *SAE*, November 28, 1931.
51. RSR, Tom R. Hickman, 401–57, TSLAC; Cox, *Time of the Rangers*, 127; Ward, "The Texas Rangers," 125–126; *AA*, October 13, 1925.

52. Hickman report, August 19, 1925, Tape 1.1, Ward Collection, ASU; *AS*, August 10, 11, 12, 13, 14, 17, 20, October 4, 1925, September 9, 1926, January 2, 1927; *AA*, October 14, November 29, 1925; R. D. Thorp and M. Harris, "$1,000 for the Murderer of the Three Englers," *True Detective Mysteries* 30 (April 1938): 5–6, 7, 9, 110, 112; Find A Grave: James Elmer McClain. Thorp later served thirty years as Austin chief of police and two years as assistant DPS director. *AAS*, February 2, 1975. Webb claimed Hamer solved the murder. Webb, *Texas Rangers*, 530.
53. *Laredo Times*, November 16, 1925 (first quotation); *SAE*, December 9, 1925; Matthews to Wilhoit, March 8, 1926, TSLAC (second quotation).
54. Hickman to Matthews, December 14, 1925, and Deposition to D.A. at Fort Worth, December 13, 1925, Tape 1.1, Ward Collection, ASU; Stewart Stanley as told to Violet Short, "Texas' House of Horror," *Master Detective* 8 (May 1933): 34–37, 54–55; James Pylant, *Blood Legacy: The True Story of the Snow Axe Murders* (Stephenville, TX: Jacobus Books, 2008), 15, 74–76; *Fort Worth Record-Telegram*, December 12, 14, 18, 21, 1925.
55. *WNT*, December 15, 19, 1925; *DMN*, January 22, 24, 28, 29, 1926, August 12, 1927; Pylant, *Blood Legacy*, 91, 102, 109; Stanley and Short, "Texas' House of Horror," 56.
56. Conger, et al., "Mexican Buttons and Bandoliers," 43; Hickman to Aldrich, January 30, 1926, Hickman to Matthews, January 31, 1926, Hickman to Aldrich, February 11, 1926, Hickman to Matthews, April 11, 1926, Hickman to Aldrich, May 1, 1926, Hickman to Matthews, May 16, 1926, Hickman to Matthews, June 27, 1926, Tape 1.1, Ward Collection, ASU; *AA*, January 9, 1926; *Brownwood Bulletin*, August 26, 1926.
57. Harris and Sadler, *Texas Rangers in Transition*, 259; *AA*, September 10, 1926; *Clarksville Times*, September 13, 1926; Walter P. Webb, "Bank Robbers Slain: Texas Ranger Captain Takes No Chances on Escape of Two Desperadoes Taken in Crime," *State Trooper* 8 (November 1926): 7; *SAL*, September 9, 1926; *Corsicana Daily Sun*, September 9, 11, 1926; *GDN*, September 11, 1926; *Abilene Morning News*, September 12, 14, 1926.
58. *Brownwood Bulletin*, September 17, 1926.
59. Simple Resolution No. 3, *Journal of the Senate of Texas, Being the First Called Session of the Thirty-ninth Legislature* (Austin, TX: A. C. Baldwin & Sons, 1926), 14; *AA* and *Brownwood Bulletin*, both dated September 14, 1926; *AS*, November 10, 1927; *SAL*, December 9, 1927.

60. *House Journal*, Fortieth Legislature, Regular Session, 441–445; H. Gordon Frost and John H. Jenkins, *"I'm Frank Hamer": The Life of a Texas Peace Officer* (Austin: Pemberton Press, 1968), 161–162; *AA*, February 3, 1927.
61. Frost and Jenkins, *"I'm Frank Hamer"*, 162; *AA*, 4, 1927; *DMN*, February 3, 1927; *GDN*, February 3, 1927; Brown, *Hood, Bonnet, and Little Brown Jug*, 346.
62. Frost and Jenkins, *"I'm Frank Hamer"*, 162–163; Walter P. Webb, "Rangers Arrest Lawmakers," *The State Trooper* 8 (April 1927): 11; *AA*, February 3, 4, 6, 7, 1927; *GDN*, February 3, 1927; *AS*, February 5, 6, 7, 1927.
63. *Mexia Daily News*, February 24, 1927; *Abilene Morning News*, February 24, April 21, 1927; *SAE*, April 21, 28, November 8, 1927; *GDN*, July 12, 1927; *Denton Record-Chronicle*, April 18, 1928.
64. Hutchinson County Historical Commission, *History of Hutchinson County, Texas: 104 Years, 1876–1980* (Dallas, TX: Taylor Publishing Company, 1980), 19, 24–25; Hickman to Robertson, March 2, 3, 1927, Tape 3.1, Ward Collection, ASU; Diana Davids Olien and Roger M. Olien, *Oil in Texas: The Gusher Age, 1895–1945* (Austin: University of Texas Press, 2002), 146; Jerry Sinise, *Black Gold and Red Lights* (Austin, TX: Eakin Press, 1982), 32, 35–36; Norman Crockett, "Crime on the Petroleum Frontier: Borger, Texas, in the Late 1920s," *Panhandle-Plains Historical Review* 64 (1991): 53–55; Mike Cox, *Texas Ranger Tales: Stories That Need Telling* (Plano: Republic of Texas Press, 1997), 201–202.
65. Davis to Robertson, April 1, 1927, Tape 3.1, Ward Collection, ASU; *FWST*, April 2, 1927; *Borger Daily Herald*, April 6, 10, 1927; *AS*, April 6, 1927 (quotation); *Abilene Morning News*, April 2, 1927; *SAL*, April 2, 1927, September 14, 1929; *Laredo Daily Times*, April 2, 1927; *GDN*, February 27, April 3, 1927; *Abilene Morning Reporter-News*, February 27, April 3, 1927; *WNT*, April 8, 1927. Although Terrill and Kimes are often portrayed as partners, the latter asserted they never worked together. For more on these outlaws, see Michael Koch, *The Kimes Gang* (Bloomington, IN: AuthorHouse, 2005). Taylor was the same individual who had commanded Company F in 1918. Harris, et al., *Texas Ranger Biographies*, 375.
66. *DMN*, November 28, 1954.
67. Hickman to Robertson, April 18, 1927, Tape 3.1, Sterling to Robertson, April 27, 1927, Tape 3.2, Ward Collection, ASU; *RAG, August 31,*

1927, and August 31, 1928, 19; *AS*, April 7, 8, 1927; *Borger Daily Herald*, April 8, 1927; Sinise, *Black Gold and Red Lights*, 80–81; Cox, *Texas Ranger Tales*, 205.

68. Aldrich to Robertson, July 20, 1927, and attachments, folder 61, Aldrich Papers, SRSU; *RAG, August 31, 1927, and August 31, 1928*, 19; Miller to Moody, April 8, 9, 1927, Gatewood to Moody, April 9, 1927, Spencer to Commissioners' Court, April 19, 1927, Box 2007/170-52, Daniel J. Moody Papers, TSLAC; Miller to police department, April 9, 1927, Tape 11.1, Ward Collection, ASU; Norman D. Brown, *Biscuits, the Dole, and Nodding Donkeys: Texas Politics, 1929–1932*, ed. Rachel Ozanne (Austin: University of Texas Press, 2019), 58; Crockett, "Crime on the Petroleum Frontier," 58; *Borger Daily Herald*, April 6, 13, 18, 24, May 3, 4, July 25, 27, August 7, 1927; Robert M. Utley, *Lone Star Lawmen: The Second Century of the Texas Rangers* (New York: Berkley Books, 2007), 122–123; *Abilene Reporter-News*, April 3, 1927; *GDN* and *WNT*, both dated April 10, 1927; Haile, *Texas Boomtowns*, 85; *SAE*, April 23, May 4, August 7, 1927; Harris and Sadler, *Texas Rangers in Transition*, 311. The indictment against Miller was quashed in July due to the fact that city ordinances had not defined the duties of the mayor and the police department at the time of the alleged bribe. As an *ex officio* figure without a legal police force, the court ruled, Miller could not provide the protection indicated in the charge. *Borger Daily Herald*, July 28, 1927.

    Charles H. Jenkins, ed., *Revised Civil Statutes of Texas, 1925* (Austin, TX: Gammel's Book Store, 1926), 2386: "The usual method of ascertaining whether an individual is holding an office contrary to law is by an information in the nature of the common law writ of *quo warranto*."

69. Biggs to Moody, May 11, 1927, Nichols to Hickman, May 11, 1927, Tape 3.1, Ward Collection, ASU; Olien and Olien, *Oil in Texas*, 147; General Order No. 1, April 29, 1927, Companies Vertical File, TRHF&M. A copy resides in folder 61, Aldrich Papers, SRSU. RSR, Tom R. Hickman, 401-57, TSLAC; *Abilene Morning Reporter-News* and *Mexia Daily News*, both dated May 15, 1927; *RAG, August 31, 1927, and August 31, 1928*, 18; *FWST*, May 29, 1927; *Tulsa Daily Register*, May 20, 1927.

70. *Laredo Daily Times*, 25, 1927; *Amarillo Globe-News*, June 6, 1928; *SAE*, July 12, 1929.

71. *FWST*, June 10, November 10, 1927.

72. *AA*, August 23 (quotation), 24, September 4, 1927; *AS*, August 23, September 3, 1927; *GDN*, August 23, 1927.
73. *AA*, November 18, 1927; January 2, 1928; *FWST*, November 18, 1927, 1928; *DMN*, November 19, 30, 1927; *Fort Worth Record-Telegram*, November 19, 23, 29, 30, 1927; Hickman to Aldrich, September 19, 1927, Tape 3.2, Ward Collection, ASU.
74. *Amarillo Globe-News*, January 16, 1961; *Denton Record-Chronicle*, December 23, 1927; A. C. Greene, *The Santa Claus Bank Robbery* (Denton: University of North Texas Press, 1999), 35.
75. *Amarillo Globe-News*, January 16, 1961; Greene, *Santa Claus Bank Robbery*, 37–38; Boyce House, "The Santa Claus Bank Robbery," *Startling Detective Adventures* 4 (March 1930): 15; T. Lindsay Baker, *Gangster Tour of Texas* (College Station: Texas A&M University Press, 2011), 133.
76. *Denton Record-Chronicle*, December 23, 24, 1927; *GDN*, December 26, 1927; Cox, *Texas Ranger Tales II*, 178; Caldwell and DeLord, *Texas Lawmen*, 77–81.
77. *Denton Record-Chronicle*, December 24, 27, 29, 1927; *AA*, December 28, 1927; *SAL*, December 28, 1927; Hickman to Robertson, January 2, 1928 (quotation), Tape 3.2, Ward Collection, ASU; *Lubbock Morning Avalanche*, January 19, 1928; Greene, *Santa Claus Bank Robbery*, 88, 110; House, "The Santa Claus Bank Robbery," 16. Bradford served as a peace officer for fifty years, mostly as a constable and police chief in Palo Pinto County. *Stephenville Empire-Tribune*, November 25, 1949.
78. Hickman to Aldrich, January 1, 1928 (quotation), Hickman to Robertson, January 2, 1928, Tape 3.2, Ward Collection, ASU; Greene, *Santa Claus Bank Robbery*, 120–122; *SAL*, December 28, 30, 1927; *Denton Record-Chronicle*, December 28, 30, 1927; *AA*, December 31, 1927; Baker, *Gangster Tour of Texas*, 139; Robert W. Stephens, *Lone Wolf: The Story of Texas Ranger Captain M. T. Gonzaullas* (Dallas, TX: Taylor Publishing Company, 1979), 35–37.
79. Utley, *Lone Star Lawmen*, 127–128; Greene, *Santa Claus Bank Robbery*, 129–130, 155–156; *Denton Record-Chronicle*, December 31, 1927, January 3, 18, 20, 23, 26, 28, February 1, March 21, 22, 24, 29, 1928, August 23, 27, 30, 31, October 25, November 19, 20, 1929; *AA*, February 21, 27, 1928; *AS*, August 31, September 1, 6, 1929; *Corsicana Daily Sun*, February 27, 1928, August 30, 1929; Baker, *Gangster Tour of Texas*, 142.

80. Hickman to Robertson, August 7, 1928, Tape 11.1, Ward Collection, ASU; *Abilene Reporter-News*, April 8, 1928; *Corsicana Daily Sun*, April 24, 1928; *GDN*, April 25, 1928; *FWST*, April 7, 8, 25, 1928. Despite Hickman's conclusion, Justice of the Peace J. H. McDonald recorded Jackson's cause of death as "murdered by unknown party." Death Certificate, Boss Jackson, May 8, 1928, File No. 125953.
81. *DMN*, May 7, 9, 10, 13, 1928; *FWST*, May 9, 11, 1928; *Fort Worth Record-Telegram*, May 11, 1928; *AA*, May 19, 1928.
82. *AS*, June 20, 21, 22, 23, 24, 1928; *AA*, June 21, 22, 23, 24, 28, August 2, 1928; *GDN*, June 21, 1928; *FWST*, December 24, 1929; Clifford R. Caldwell and Ron DeLord, *Texas Lawmen, 1900–1940: More of the Good and the Bad* (Charleston, SC: History Press, 2012), 210; Dwight Watson, "In the Name of Progress and Decency: The Response of Houston's Civic Leaders to the Lynching of Robert Powell in 1928," *The Houston Review of History and Culture* 1 (2005): 26–29.
83. *AS*, June 26, 1928; *DMN*, June 27, 1928.
84. *Laredo Times*, October 9, 1928.
85. *GDN*, December 20, 1928; *Belton Journal*, December 20, 1928.
86. *Abilene Morning News*, April 23, August 31, 1929; *Corsicana Daily Sun*, May 31, August 26, 31, September 6, 1929; *Lubbock Morning Avalanche*, June 1, 1929; *AS*, June 2, 1929; *FWST*, August 21, September 8, 1929; *Denton Record-Chronicle*, August 30, 1929.
87. Harris and Sadler, *Texas Rangers in Transition*, 311–313; Holmes to Moody, March 5, 1929, Aldrich to D. E. Smith, March 14, 1929, D. E. Smith to Robertson, April 24, 1929, Tape 11.2, Ward Collection, ASU; Moody to Callum, July 10, 1928, White to Wiginton, August 1, 1929, Box 2007/170-52, Hamer to Robertson, August 9, 1928, TSLAC; *Borger Daily Herald*, August 10, 12, 15, 26, 29, 1928, September 29, 1965; *Amarillo Globe*, July 30, 1928; *Brown Biscuits, the Dole, and Nodding Donkeys*, 58; Utley, *Lone Star Lawmen*, 129; Wolters, *Martial Law*, 91.
88. Holmes to Moody, April 20, 1929, Box 2007/170-52, Moody Papers, TSLAC.
89. *GDN*, June 29, 1929; *Lubbock Avalanche-Journal*, June 30, 1929; Utley, *Lone Star Lawmen*, 130; Ward, "The Texas Rangers," 166–167.
90. Hickman to J. W. Aldrich, March 13, 1930, with attached statement, folder 5, Box 3P157, Aldrich Papers, BCAH; RSR, J. T. DeGraftenreid, 401–75, W. P. McConnell, -59, TSLAC.

91. *FWST*, June 5, 1930; *Fifteenth U.S. Census*, Tarrant County, Texas; David Hickman interview, 2012.
92. *Abilene Reporter-News*, May 11, 1930; *Abilene Morning News*, May 23, June 4, 1930; *SAL*, June 13, 1930; Hickman to Robertson, n.d. [June 28, 1930?], Hickman to Aldrich, n.d. [June 30, 1930?], folder 5, Box 3P157, Aldrich Papers, BCAH; *AA*, July 30, 1930; *SAE*, August 20, 1930 (quotations); *Laredo Times*, October 8, 1930; *Fifteenth U.S. Census*, Tarrant County, Texas.
93. *GDN*, December 3, 1930; Hickman to Sterling, January 28, 31, 1931, Gonzaullas to Hickman, January 27, March 15, 1931, Tape 10.2, Ward Collection, ASU; RSR, Albert R. Mace, 401–59; *FWST*, November 16, 1930, February 23, 1971. Mace succeeded the recently deceased John H. Rogers.
94. Stephen William Schuster IV, "The Modernization of the Texas Rangers, 1930–1936" (M.A. thesis, Texas Christian University, 1965), 11–13; *AS*, January 16, 1931; RSR, C. O. Moore, 401–60, TSLAC.
95. Hickman to Robertson, January 10, 1931, Hickman to Sterling, February 7, 21, March 6, 26, April 1, 8, 15, November 28, 1931, May 7, 14, June 4, July 23, September 7, October 1, November 21, December 7, 1932, Tape 10.2, Ward Collection, ASU.
96. *Big Spring Daily Herald* and *Corsicana Daily Sun*, both dated March 19, 1931.
97. *AS*, April 1, 1931; *Corsicana Daily Sun*, April 10, 1931; Hickman to Sterling, April 18, 1931, Tape 10.2, Ward Collection, ASU.
98. *Denton Record-Chronicle* and *Laredo Times*, both dated December 17, 1925; *SAL*, July 21, 1926; Acts 1931, Regular Session, 46th Legislature, Ch. 259, *General and Special Laws of Texas*; *SAE*, February 9, 1934.
99. "Red River War," *Time Magazine* 18 (August 3, 1931): 17; Rusty Williams, *The Red River Bridge War: A Texas-Oklahoma Border Battle* (College Station: Texas A&M University Press, 2016), 1, 51, 59, 86–87; *AS*, July 17, 1931; *AA*, July 17, 1931; *Corsicana Daily Sun*, July 24, 1931.
100. Robert L. Dorman, *Alfalfa Bill: A Life in Politics* (Norman: University of Oklahoma Press, 2018), 265; *SAE*, July 25, 1931; William Warren Sterling, *Trails and Trials of a Texas Ranger* (Norman: University of Oklahoma Press, 1968), 221 (quotation); Hickman to Sterling, July 18, 1931, Tape 10.2, Ward Collection, ASU.

101. "Red River War," 17; Dorman, *Alfalfa Bill*, 266–267; Williams, *The Red River Bridge War*, 136–137, 149, 165; Sterling, *Trails and Trials*, 222–223; Brown, *Biscuits, the Dole, and Nodding Donkeys*, 138; Huddleston to Hickman, July 20, 1931, Hickman to Sterling, July 25, 1931, Tape 10.2, Ward Collection, ASU; *AS*, July 23, 24, 1931; *Corsicana Daily Sun*, July 24, 1931; "Tom Hickman's Shooting," *Time Magazine* 18 (August 31, 1931): 2 (quotation).
102. Williams, *The Red River Bridge War*, 181–182, 197; "Red River War," 17; *Laredo Times* and *Corsicana Daily Sun*, both dated July 24, 1931; *AS*, July 25, 26, 1931; *SAE*, *GDN*, and *Big Springs Daily Herald*, all dated July 26, 1931; *Mexia Weekly Herald*, July 31, 1931.
103. *RAG, August 31, 1931–August 31, 1932*, 14–16; *AS*, August 17, 1931; *GDN*, August 17, 31, 1931; Krenek, *The Power Vested*, 141–144; Warner E. Mills, Jr., *Martial Law in East Texas* (Tuscaloosa: University of Alabama Press, 1960), 1, 26, 28; Page S. Foshee, "'Someone Get the Governor An Aspirin': Ross Sterling and Martial Law in East Texas," *East Texas Historical Journal* 41 (October 2003): 6, 10; Robert D. Boyle, "Chaos in the East Oilfield, 1930–1935," *SHQ* 69 (January 1966): 349; Gonzaullas to Hickman, August 23, 1931, Tape 10.2, Ward Collection, ASU.
104. Gonzaullas to Hickman, August 23, 1931, February 9, 1932, Goss to Hickman, August 16, 1931, Hickman to Sterling, August 22, September 5, 1931, October 30, 1931, Burton to Hickman, August 22, 1931, Tape 10.2, Ward Collection, ASU; Krenek, *The Power Vested*, 147–149; *AS*, August 17, 24, 25, 1931; *GDN*, August 17, 1931; *Big Spring Daily Herald*, August 21, 1931; *Kilgore Daily News*, August 24, 1931; Mills, *Martial Law in East Texas*, 30.
105. Hickman to Sterling, August 29, September 5, 1931, Tape 10.2, Ward Collection, ASU; *Kilgore Daily News*, *GDN*, and *FWST*, both dated August 31, 1931; *DMN*, August 31, 1931 (quotation).
106. *AS*, September 4, 5, 6, 1931; *Mexia Weekly Herald*, September 4, 1931; East Texas Chamber of Commerce, *A Book of Facts: Martial Law in East Texas* (Longview: East Texas Chamber of Commerce, 1932), 6, 8; Olien and Olien, *Oil in Texas*, 186; Brown, *Biscuits, the Dole, and Nodding Donkeys*, 154; Bryan Burrough, *The Big Rich: The Rise and Fall of the Greatest Texas Oil Fortunes* (New York: Penguin Books, 2009), 78; Foshee, "'Someone Get the Governor An Aspirin'," 11.
107. Hickman to Sterling, September 5, October 10, 24, 1931, Gonzaullas to Hickman, September 20, 1931, Tape 10.2, Ward Collection, ASU;

Longview Morning Journal, September 3, 1931; Ward, "The Texas Rangers," 200; *AA*, October 15, 20, November 10, December 12 (quotation), 1931; *Corsicana Daily Sun*, November 10, 1931; Caldwell and DeLord, *Texas Lawmen*, 151–152. Williams was both an ex-chief of police in Wink and a former convict in Oklahoma.

108. Hickman to Sterling, January 17, 1932, Tape 10.2, Ward Collection, ASU; *GDN*, January 17, 1932.
109. *Laredo Times* and *FWST*, both dated February 11, 1932; Hickman to Sterling, February 13, 1932, Tape 10.2, Ward Collection, ASU; Harris, et al., *Texas Ranger Biographies*, 249; Find A Grave: Fred Egbert Edwards. Chaplain P. B. Hill assisted in the raids.
110. Gonzaullas to Hickman, May 1, 1932, Hickman to Sterling, February 20, July 9, August 27, 1932, Gonzaullas to Hickman, August 28, September 4, 11, 1932, Tape 10.2, Ward Collection, ASU; Brown, *Biscuits, the Dole, and Nodding Donkeys*, 158; David F. Prindle, *Petroleum Politics and the Texas Railroad Commission* (Austin: University of Texas Press, 1981), 31; Cox, *Time of the Rangers*, 150–153; Krenek, *The Power Vested*, 165; Ruel McDaniel, *Some Ran Hot* (Dallas, TX: Regional Press, 1939), 112 (quotation), 115, 192, 198; *GDN*, May 2, 1931; *SAE*, May 2, September 5, 1932; *Laredo Times*, August 23, 24, 1932; *Lubbock Morning Avalanche*, August 23, 1932; *Corsicana Daily Sun*, October 28, 1932.
111. Hans Peter Nielsen Gammel, comp., *Laws of Texas, 1931–1933* (Austin, TX: Gammel's Book Store, 1933), 852–857; Prindle, *Petroleum Politics and the Texas Railroad Commission*, 31. The issue was further addressed by the Hot Oil Act of 1935 sponsored by U.S. Senator Thomas Terry Connally, but operators and the public looked on quotas and regulations with "amused tolerance." The new federal law and subsequent indictments did little to halt the situation. "Again, Hot Oil," *Time Magazine* 31 (April 4, 1938): 71.
112. *Fort Worth Press*, March 12, 1932, Gonzaullas Scrapbook 2, TRHF&M, 152; Hickman to Sterling, March 12, 13, 1932, Gonzaullas to Hickman, March 13, 1932, Tape 10.2, Ward Collection, ASU.
113. *SAL*, August 23, 1932.
114. *RAG, January 18, 1933–December 31, 1934*, 46; RSR, Tom R. Hickman, 401–57, TSLAC; *AS*, January 1, 1933; *SAE*, January 15, 1933; *El Paso Herald-Post*, January 25, 1933.
115. *RAG, January 18, 1933–December 31, 1934*, 46, 51–52; *Report and Recommendations of the Senate Committee Investigating Crime*, 43rd

Legislature, 1933–1934, (Austin: 1934), 294–295; Karl Ashburn, "Crime in Texas," *Southwest Review* 19 (July 1934): 364; Schuster, "The Modernization of the Texas Rangers," 21–25, 28–30; Harris and Sadler, *Texas Rangers in Transition*, 435, 444. Schuster stated the number of Special Ranger commissions was 2,344, while Harris and Sadler gives the figure as the aforementioned 2,245.

116. Schuster, "The Modernization of the Texas Rangers," 38–39; *Lubbock Avalanche-Journal*, April 15, 1934; *SAE*, September 24, 1930, May 10, 1934; *DMN*, December 9, 10, 11, 12, 13, 14, 15, 1934.

117. James W. Robinson, *The DPS Story: History of the Development of the Department of Public Safety in Texas* (Austin: Texas Department of Public Safety, 1975), 8; Brown, *Biscuits, the Dole, and Nodding Donkeys*, 299–300; The Joint Legislative Committee on Organization and Economy and Griffenhagen Associates, *The Government of the State of Texas*, Pt. 3: 54–70.

118. Schuster, "The Modernization of the Texas Rangers," 37; RSR, Tom R. Hickman, 401–57, TSLAC; *Lubbock Morning Avalanche*, January 24, 1935; *Denton Record-Chronicle*, February 7, 1935.

119. *SAE*, January 29, March 18, September 21, 1935; *Paris Evening News*, January 30, 1935; *Lubbock Avalanche-Journal*, January 30, April 12, 1935; *Mexia Weekly Herald*, February 1, 1935; *DMN*, March 18, 1935; *AS*, March 19, 1935; *SAL*, April 10, 1935.

120. Thomas Lee Charlton, "The Texas Department of Public Safety, 1935–1957" (M.A. thesis, University of Texas at Austin, 1961), 27; *Senate Journal, Regular Session, 44th Legislature*, 163, 194, 263, 377, 383; *House Journal, Regular Session, 44th Legislature*, 119, 400, 404, 451, 1282–1283; *Report and Recommendations of the Senate Committee Investigating Crime*, 43rd Legislature, 298; *Abilene Daily Reporter*, December 12, 1934.

121. *Report and Recommendations of the Senate Committee Investigating Crime*, 43rd Legislature, 292.

122. *DMN*, May 4, 1935; *House Journal, Regular Session, 44th Legislature*, 2284; *Senate Journal, Regular Session, 44th Legislature*, 454; Acts 1935, 44th Legislature, Regular Session, Ch. 181, Acts 1937, Regular Session, 45th Legislature, Ch. 373, *General and Special Laws of Texas*; Harold J. Weiss, Jr., "The Texas Rangers Revisited: Old Themes and New Viewpoints," *SHQ* 97 (April 1994): 638.

123. Schuster, "The Modernization of the Texas Rangers," 71–73; *AS*, August 12, 1935; Cox, *Time of the Rangers*, 165–170; *Big Spring*

Daily Herald, May 20, 26, 1935; Charlton, "The Texas Department of Public Safety," 40; *DMN*, May 4, 1935; *Denton Record-Chronicle*, May 14, June 1, 1935; *Senate Report*, 1933–1934; *DPS Annual Report, August 10, 1935–December 1, 1936*, 9; RSR, Tom R. Hickman, 401–57, TSLAC. Webb prophesized in *Texas Rangers*, 567, the "functions of the un-uniformed Texas Rangers will gradually slip away and … those of the Highway Patrol will increase." He further warned the Department of Public Safety meant "a practical abolishment of the [Ranger] force." Happily, time has proven the professor incorrect on this point.

124. *AA*, December 14, 1935; *SAL*, December 3, 1933; *SAE*, December 4, 1935. Browning's World War I and World War II draft registration cards confirm his little-seen full name.
125. Cox, *Time of the Rangers*, 173; *AA*, December 14, 1935; *Sixteenth U.S. Census*, Travis County, Texas.
126. *AS*, November 10, 13, 1935; *AA*, December 14, 1935; *Corsicana Daily Sun*, December 14, 1935 Baker, *Gangster Tour of Texas*, 277.
127. *GDN*, November 7, 1935; *Corsicana Daily Sun*, November 19, 1935; *DMN*, November 20, 1935.
128. *AS*, November 11, 1935; *DMN*, November 11, 1935.
129. *SAE*, December 4, 1935.
130. *AS*, November 11, 1935; *Paris Evening News*, November 11, 13, 1935; *DMN*, November 12, 13, 1935; *SAE*, November 12, 14, 1935; *San Augustine Tribune*, December 19, 1935; Charlton, "The Texas Department of Public Safety," 54; *Corsicana Semi-Weekly Light*, November 15, 1935; RSR, Tom R. Hickman, 401-57, TSLAC; *AA*, November 13, 1935; *Longview News-Journal*, August 17, 1937.
131. *House Journal, 2nd Called Session, 44th Legislature*, 476, 546; *SAE*, November 15, December 1, 4, 12, 1935; *SAL*, December 4, 1935; *Denton Record-Chronicle* and *Laredo Times*, both dated December 3, 1935; *Paris Evening News*, November 14, 1935; *Big Spring Daily Herald*, November 14, December 3, 1935; Schuster, "The Modernization of the Texas Rangers," 63; James M. Day, *Captain Clint Peoples, Texas Ranger: Fifty Years A Lawman* (Waco, TX: Texian Press, 1980), 69 (second quotation); *AA*, December 4 (first quotation), December 14, 1935; *DMN*, December 4, 1935. Kelso was dismissed from the service on December 31, 1935. RSR, Sid Kelso, 401–58, TSLAC. On November 25, 1938, he was arrested on a charge of armed robbery. Two years later, he was exonerated by a Williamson County grand jury

for a November 10, 1939, hijacking. Peoples arrested him on gambling charges on July 6, 1949, to which Kelso pled guilty. *AA*, November 26, 1938; *AS*, January 6, 1940, July 6, 7, 1949.

132. *Corsicana Daily Sun*, December 4, 14, 1935; *SAL*, December 12, 13, 15, 1935, April 1, 1936; *GDN*, December 13, 1935; *SAE*, December 12, 14, 1935; *DMN* and *Abilene Morning Reporter-News*, both dated December 15, 1935; Schuster, "The Modernization of the Texas Rangers," 64. The probe proved inconsequential in the long run, and the findings were never recorded in the *House Journal*.
133. Cox, *Texas Ranger Tales II*, 190; *Sixteenth U.S. Census*, Cooke County, Texas; Tise, *Texas County Sheriffs*, 130; *SAE*, December 12, 1935; *Denton Record-Chronicle*, December 11, 1935; *Lubbock Morning Avalanche*, December 13, 1935; *Abilene Reporter-News*, July 1, 1945, June 28, 1952.
134. David Hickman interview, 2012; *DMN*, November 28, 1954; *Abilene Reporter-News*, June 25, 1944, July 4, 1948, July 4, 1950, April 12, July 3, December 30, 1951, July 3, 1952; *SAL*, September 2, 1936; *Lubbock Avalanche-Journal*, May 8, 1936; *Corsicana Daily Sun*, February 4, 1955 (quotation), June 25, 1931.
135. *Denton Record-Chronicle*, January 18, 22, 27 (quotation), 1956; *Brownwood Bulletin*, September 16, 1956.
136. *Amarillo News-Globe*, September 1, 1946; *SAL*, September 11, 1946.
137. *SAL*, May 1, 1952 (quotation); Texas Death Certificate, Thomas W. Doswell, August 22, 1951, Registrar's No. 3190.
138. *FWST*, January 1, 1957; *AA*, January 3, 1957, February 18, 1961; *El Paso Herald-Post*, February 18, 1961; *GDN*, February 19, 1961; *Big Spring Daily Herald*, January 23, 1958; *Cuero Record*, January 29, 1962.
139. Cox, *Texas Ranger Tales II*, 191.
140. Death Certificate, Thomas Rufus Hickman, February 5, 1962, File No. 17; *AS*, January 29, 1962.
141. David Hickman interview, 2012; Death Certificate, Tina M. Hickman, January 7, 1980, File No. 101518.
142. David Hickman interview, 2012; California Marriage Records, 1960–1985, California Department of Health Services, 16624; California Divorce Index, 1966–1984, California Department of Health Services, 10132.
143. David Hickman interview, 2012; Marriage License, Grayson County Marriage Records; *FWST*, May 6, 1979. For more on David and his art, see http://davidbhickman.com/.

Notes for Chapter 4

1. Humphries to Robinson, December 9, 1971, Miller Vertical File, TRHF&M. Confirming Miller's date of birth proved to be a challenge. Some accounts assert he falsified his actual age late in his career, so as to avoid retirement. However, various documents dating from his younger days when he had no reason to alter his birth year indicate the event did indeed occur in 1898. Miller Family Tree, MS, n.d.; Death Certificates, Charles E. Miller, November 30, 1951, File No. 55530, and Hattie Miller, May 18, 1950, File No. 21562; Bexar County Marriage Registers, Book N, 415; Roger H. Miller, telephone interview with the author, July 3, 2012. Cited hereafter as Roger Miller interview, 2012.
2. *Twelfth U.S. Census*, Atascosa County, Texas, and Colorado County, Texas; Texas Department of Criminal Justice, Convict Record Ledgers, 1998/038-155, TSLAC, 13; *Thirteenth U.S. Census*, Bexar County, Texas.
3. SAGHS files; *SAE*, May 26, 1914, July 21, 1918; Bexar County Marriage Registers, Book 7, 222; Miller Family Tree, MS, n.d.; Birth Certificates, Henry Herman Miller, July 13, 1942, File No. 116, and Wilhelmina Anna Miller, January 11, 1978, File No. 391.

   For ten years prior to her death, Hattie had suffered from diabetes mellitus. Slipping into a diabetic coma on May 13, 1950, she died at Baptist Memorial Hospital four days later. She was buried in Mission Burial Park on May 19. Death Certificate, Hattie Miller, May 18, 1950, File No. 21562; *SAE*, May 19, 1950; *Kerrville Mountain Sun*, May 25, 1950.

   Katie died at home on October 26, 1951. She was buried at Sunset Memorial Park on October 29. SAE, October 27, 1951.

   On November 29, 1951, while at home, Miller's father shot himself in the heart with a .22-caliber rifle. He was pronounced dead on arrival at Robert B. Green Hospital and buried at Sunset Memorial Park. Death Certificate, Charles E. Miller, November 30, 1951, File No. 55530; *SAE*, November 30, 1951.
4. *SAL*, March 19, 1917; Marriage License No. 43050, Bexar County Marriage Registers, Book 10, 599. In the marriage information, Marie Minica's name is misspelled as "Maria Menicia." *Fourteenth U.S. Census*, Bexar County, Texas; Death Certificate, Mrs. Jim D. Green, September 13, 1960, File No. 56265, Thomas Louis Minica, January 27, 1978,

Registrar's No. 443; Charles Edward Miller, Jr., World War I Draft Cards, M1509, RG 163, NARA; *Worley's San Antonio Directory, 1918*, 526. Several secondary sources have claimed Miller served as a mercenary with Pancho Villa in the waning days of the Mexican Revolution. For one example, see Pamela Colloff, "Law of the Land," *Texas Monthly* 35 (April 2007): 117. This contention is not supported by primary sources. The tale might have its origins in the experiences of Dr. Charles H. Miller, a surgeon with the Cananea Consolidated Copper Company who volunteered to treat wounded *villaistas* at Agua Prieta in November 1915. For more, see Thomas H. Naylor, "Massacre at San Pedro de la Cueva: The Significance of Pancho Villa's Disastrous Sonora Campaign," *Western Historical Quarterly* 8 (April 1977): 125–150.

5. Special Order No. 99, December 10, 1919, Miller Vertical File, TRHF&M; RSR, Charles E. Miller, 401–60, TSLAC; *RAG, 1919–1920*, 44.
6. *RAG, 1919–1920*, 44.
7. Special Order No. 7, March 17, 1920, Miller Vertical File, TRHF&M; Charles H. Harris III, et al., *Texas Ranger Biographies: Those Who Served, 1910–1921* (Albuquerque: University of New Mexico Press, 2009), 114, 159, 255, 209, 311, 125, 344, 275, 89, 239, 327, 103.
8. Special Order No. 10, March 23, 1920, Miller Vertical File, TRHF&M; Davis to Cope, April 10, 1920, Volume 21, Box 2R290, Walter Prescott Webb Collection, BCAH; Charles Schreiner III, et al, comps., *A Pictorial History of the Texas Rangers: "That Special Breed of Men"* (Mountain Home, TX: YO Press, 1969), 113.
9. Special Order No. 13, April 10, 1920, Miller Vertical File, TRHF&M.
10. *Galveston Tribune*, December 6, 1920; *El Paso Herald*, December 14, 1920; *San Antonio Light*, December 15, 1920; *Houston Post*, December 17, 1920; *Del Rio News-Herald*, May 5, 1942; *GDN*, November 13, December 22, 1920; Harris, et al., *Texas Ranger Biographies*, 36, 83, 77, 383, 233, 246, 199.
11. Roger Miller interview, 2012; *Fourteenth U.S. Census*, Kinney County, Texas; Birth Certificate, Roger Hamer Miller, January 9, 1923, File No. 194. Lora often went by her middle name which was sometimes spelled "Leray." Find A Grave: La Ray Clark Reischling.
12. Transcript of Interview, Tape 1, Box 2K227, E. A. Wright "Dogie" Papers, BCAH, 10; *GDN*, June 22, 25, November 15, 17, 1921; *Houston Post*, June 22, 26, 1921; *DMN*, November 20, 1921; Death

Certificate, William Tompkins Ochiltree Holman, August 3, 1921, File No. 18005.

13. RSR, Charles E. Miller, 401–60, TSLAC; *SAE*, May 15, 1922; Sammy Tise, *Texas County Sheriffs* (Albuquerque, NM: Oakwood Printing, 1989), 481; Death Certificate, Jesse Lott Cook, April 13, 1938, File No. 20280.
14. Special Orders No. 22, May 11, 1922, Miller Vertical File, TRHF&M; RSR, Charles E. Miller, 401–60, TSLAC; *SAEN*, May 14, 20, 1922; *Fort Worth Record-Telegram*, May 16, 1922.
15. *SAEN*, May 24, 1922; *AA*, May 27, June 5, 1922, March 27, 1940.
16. RSR, Charles E. Miller, 401-60, TSLAC; Charles E. Miller, Internal Revenue Service, Official Personnel File, NARA; *SAEN*, October 5, November 3, 9, 1922; *SAL*, November 18, 1922.
17. *SAEN*, January 11, 1923; *SAE*, March 16, 1923.
18. *SAL*, May 6, 10 (both quotations), 1923.
19. *SAL*, May 16, 17, 21, 23, 1923; *SAE*, May 17, 18, 1923; Death Certificate, Zaragosa De Leon, May 17, 1923, File No. 013896. Miller was known to have wrapped a piece of rawhide around his pistol's grips, which deactivated the safety. He also carried the gun tucked in his waistband with a round in the chamber and the hammer on half-cock. Years later, a young firearms instructor noted the blatant safety violation, and Miller reportedly replied, "Son, if the damned old thing wasn't dangerous, I wouldn't be wearing it." Jim Wilson, "Life with the 1911," *Shooting Illustrated* 10 (July 2011): 46.
20. *Brownsville Herald*, June 16, 1923; *SAE*, June 17, 20, 1923; *SAL*, June 19, 22, 1923; *AS*, June 19, 1923.
21. RSR, Charles E. Miller, 401-60, TSLAC; *SAE*, August 9, 18, 23 (quotation), 26, 29, September 5, 6, 12, 13, 1923, February 23, 1924; *SAL*, August 16, 17, 22, 24, 26, September 4, 17, 19, October 26, 1923; *AS*, August 23, 1923.
22. Berkhead Clarence Baldwin, "Biography of Baldwin," MS62 1A-172, TRHF&M, 88; RSR, Charles E. Miller, 401-60, TSLAC; *SAE*, September 9, 1923; Walter Prescott Webb, "Lawless Town Gets Ranger Justice," *The State Trooper* 5 (April 1924): 13–14; *SAL*, September 16, 17, 30, 1923; Pat M. Neff, *The Battles of Peace* (Fort Worth, TX: Pioneer Publishing Company, 1925), 138–139.
23. *SAL*, October 10, 11, 12, 27, 1923, January 7, 1931.
24. Charles H. Harris III and Louis R. Sadler, *The Texas Rangers in Transition: From Gunfighters to Criminal Investigators, 1921–1935*

(Norman: University of Oklahoma Press, 2019), 192; Baldwin, "Biography of Baldwin," 89, 90–91; Aldrich to Davis & Ridgeway, October 11, 1923, 401-600, TSLAC; RSR, Charles E. Miller, 401–60, Noland G. Williams, -65, TSLAC. Miller's Special Ranger warrant expired on December 23, 1924. *AS*, October 25, 26, 1923; *SAL*, October 26, December 17, 27, 28, January 11, 24, 1923, June 17. 1924; *AA*, December 18, 1923; *SAE*, March 23, 1924. For further details on Taylor's case, see Cox, *Time of the Rangers*, 118.

25. RSR, Charles E. Miller, 401–60, TSLAC; *SAL*, January 16, 24, April 4, 1924; Harris and Sadler, *Texas Rangers in Transition*, 192.
26. *SAE*, April 19, June 22, 26, July 12, 14, 1924; *AS*, April 19, 1924; *Houston Post*, July 12, 14, 1924. In another example of the unverifiable legends that surround Charlie Miller, he was supposedly awarded a "lifetime commission" in 1924 by Plutarco Elías Calles, interior minister and later *presidente* of Mexico, that allowed him to legally pursue Texas fugitives into Mexico. DPS Public Statement, December 9, 1971, Miller Vertical File, TRHF&M; *Brownsville Herald*, December 12, 1971.
27. Baldwin, "Biography of Baldwin," 90; *SAL*, August 28, 1923; *GDN*, September 2, 1923; *AS*, October 26, 28, 1923; *Houston Post*, October 27, 1923.
28. *SAE*, May 8, 10, 24, 1924; *AA*, May 17, 1924; *AS*, June 5, 1924; *GDN*, May 15, 1924.
29. *SAE*, September 5, October 10, 15, 31, 1924; *SAL*, September 4, November 21, 22, 1924; *GDN*, October 11, 1924; Walter Prescott Webb, "Rangers Called in To Clean Up Austin," *The State Trooper* 6 (November 1924): 21; *Houston Post*, October 20, November 10, 1924; *AS*, November 2, 1924; Find A Grave: Judge William Sneed Anderson.
30. *AS*, January 15, 1925; *AA*, January 16, 1925; *SAE*, August 2, 1924, January 15, 28, February 21, 1925; *SAL*, February 1, 1925; Walter Prescott Webb, "Fight Against Texas Rangers," *The State Trooper* 6 (July 1925): 11; Hans Peter Nielsen Gammel, comp., *Laws of Texas, 1919* (Austin, TX: Gammel's Book Store, 1919), 263 (first quotation); *GDN*, February 21, 26, 1925; Harris and Sadler, *Texas Rangers in Transition*, 194; Special Orders No. 1, February 20, 1925, Miller Vertical File, TRHF&M; 270 *Southwestern Reporter* 874, 879 (second quotation) (1925). A prominent figure in Republican Party circles, Elgin was an old Indian fighter, surveyor, and newspaperman. Grace

Miller White, "Captain John E. Elgin," *Frontier Times* 21 (May 1944): 337–340. Upon his enlistment in Company E, Yantis Taylor had recorded his occupation as "aviator." Indeed, he had served as a flying cadet in 1918 and, after his state service, entered the Army Air Corps in 1926. He served in North Africa and Europe during World War II and retired as an Air Force brigadier general in 1949. *New York Times*, October 24, 1956.

31. *SAL*, January 24, 1925; H. S. Dewhurst, *The Railroad Police* (Springfield, IL: Charles C. Thomas, 1955), 24–25.
32. *SAL*, March 25, November 13, 1925, October 9, 1926.
33. RSR, Charles E. Miller, 401–121, TSLAC.
34. Roger Miller interview, 2012; *La Grange Journal*, June 7, 1928; *Fifteenth U.S. Census*, Bexar County, Texas. The 1930 federal census listed Eva as a Bible school teacher. Andrew Miller, telephone interview with the author, January 10, 2013. Cited hereafter as Andrew Miller interview, 2013; *Worley's San Antonio City Directory, 1929–1930*, 305; Miller to Aldrich, May 22, 1929, folder 61, Roy W. Aldrich Papers, SRSU; RSR, Charles E. Miller, 401–92, TSLAC.
35. *Kerrville Mountain Sun*, February 5, 1931. Miller's S&GRA service should not be confused with that of Charles Richard Miller (1875–1933), who was employed by the Texas and Southwestern Cattle Raisers Association as an inspector based in Dilley. *SAE*, April 17, September 10, 1924; *SAL*, February 3, March 7, 1928, November 12, 1929, September 3, 1930; *Laredo Times*, September 28, 1930; *Fifteenth U.S. Census*, Frio County.
36. *Kerrville Mountain Sun*, April 16, 30, 1931; Clifford R. Caldwell and Ron DeLord, *Texas Lawmen, 1900–1940: More of the Good and the Bad* (Charleston, SC: History Press, 2012), 356–357.
37. RSR, Charles E. Miller, 401–92, TSLAC; *Kerrville Times*, January 12, May 25, 1933; *Kerrville Mountain Sun*, February 23, September 14, 1933.
38. RSR, Charles E. Miller, 401–92, TSLAC; *Kerrville Mountain Sun*, July 13, August 3, October 19, 1933, April 5, 1934, January 27, 1944; *Kerrville Times*, October 19, 1933; *SAL*, October 16, 1933, April 5, 1934; *Brownsville Herald*, October 16, 1933; *Big Spring Daily Herald*, October 17, 1933.
39. RSR, Charles E. Miller, 401–92, TSLAC.
40. Birth Certificate, Robert Albert Miller, File No. 5743, March 12, 1934; *Worley's San Antonio City Directory, 1934–1935*, 706.

41. Schreiner, et al., comp., *A Pictorial History of the Texas Rangers*, 113; Sixteenth U.S. Census, Bexar County, Texas; Roger Miller interview, 2012; *AA*, September 27, 1929; RSR, Charles E. Miller, 401–92, TSLAC.
42. Joe H. Bridge, Jr., *The Life and Times of Joe H. Bridge: Texas Ranger, 1936–1956* (s. l.: Joe H. Bridge, 2003), 26.
43. *Kerrville Times*, January 28, April 8, 1937; Find A Grave: Joseph Washington Burkett, Jr.
44. *Kerrville Mountain Sun*, August 25, December 8, 2, 1938, June 29, December 28, 1939, May 29, 1941, July 9, September 3, 1942, July 15, 1943, October 19, 1944; Death Certificate, Frost Woodhull Miller, June 23, 1939, File No. 26659; *Kerrville Times*, September 3, 1942. Frost was likely the namesake of the county judge who had served on the bench from 1932 to 1937. In ill health, the former jurist took his own life on March 7, 1939. *SAE*, March 8, 1939.
45. *Kerrville Mountain Sun*, September 18, 1941.
46. *Kerrville Mountain Sun*, June 25, 1942, August 31, 1944, June 12, 1947.
47. *Kerrville Times*, July 22, 1937, July 28, 1938, May 21, December 17, 1942, July 8, 1943; *Worley's San Antonio City Directory, 1940*, 1090; Roger Miller interview, 2012; *Kerrville Mountain Sun*, May 21, 1942, January 4, 1945, March 28, September 19, 1946, June 19, July 3, 1947.
48. Kerr County Deed Records, 74: 419–421; Roger Miller interview, 2012; *Kerrville Mountain Sun*, January 4, 1945, January 8 (quotation), March 4, August 12, 1948
49. Edwards County Deed Record 33: 559–560, 34: 90–91, C: 331–332.
50. Roger Miller interview, 2012; Charles A. Schreiner III, interview with Don Hedgpeth and William G. Stacy, Kerrville, Texas, February 19 and April 21, 1998, Oral History Project, Kerr County Historical Commission, 9.
51. Inactive Personnel Record, Charles E. Miller, TDPS; Special Order No. 10, January 15, 1951, Miller Vertical File, TRHF&M. The order confirmed verbal orders issued on January 1, 1951, effective at 7:45 a.m. *Kerrville Mountain Sun*, August 30, 1951.
52. *Corpus Christi Times*, January 25, March 13, 14, 22, April 19, 25 (quotation), 27, 1951; *Valley Morning Star*, January 26, 1951; Find A Grave: Tully Elwyn Seay.
53. Evan Anders, *Boss Rule in South Texas: The Progressive Era* (Austin: University of Texas Press, 1987), 193.

54. John E. Clark, "Reflections on the Duke of Duval: The Litigation Record," *South Texas Studies* 8 (1997): 33, 37.
55. George Schendel, "Something Is Rotten in the State of Texas," *Collier's* 127 (June 9, 1951): 15.
56. "The Duke Delivers," *Time Magazine* 52 (September 27, 1948): 26; "Triggers and Tension in a Texas Dukedom," *Life* 36 (April 5, 1954): 33; Schendel, "Something Is Rotten in the State of Texas," 71; *Corpus Christi Times*, November 8, 9, 10, 11, 14, 20, 22, 1950, March 4, 20, April 8, 9, 1952.
57. *Corpus Christi Times*, March 28, April 15, May 6, 8, 9, 12, 13, 14, 16, 1952; Bridge, *Life and Times of Joe H. Bridge*, 74, 79; *AS*, May 13, 14, 16, 1952; *AA*, May 13, 14, 1952; *Kerrville Times*, May 13, 1952; John E. Clark, *The Fall of the Duke of Duval: A Prosecutor's Journal* (Austin, TX: Eakin Press, 1999), 70.
58. Pribble to Wilson, March 30, 1982, Miller Vertical File, TRHF&M; Inactive Personnel Record, Charles E. Miller, TDPS; *Lubbock Evening Journal*, July 11, 1952; *Corpus Christi Times*, May 27, July 28, 1952; *AS*, July 25, 1952; Bridge, *Life and Times of Joe H. Bridge*, 74; *New York Times*, February 4, 1954; Carrozza, *Dukes of Duval*, 97.
59. Inactive Personnel Record, Charles E. Miller, TDPS.
60. *AS*, June 4, 7, 195; *SAE*, June 7, 20, 19544; *Lubbock Morning Avalanche*, April 8, 1954; *Big Spring Herald*, June 7, 1954; *Mexia Daily News*, June 10, 1954.
61. Roger Miller interview, 2012 (quotation); Kerr County Deed Records, 120: 321–325; C. E. Miller v. E. M. Miller A-10112, Texas Supreme Court Records, Box 201-2109, TSLAC; 376 *Southwestern Reporter 2nd Series* (1964) 80–82; *Kerrville Times*, July 26, 1955; *Kerrville Mountain Sun*, July 28, 1955, January 21, August 18, 25, 1960, October 5, 12, 19, 1961, August 1, 1962, January 23, April 24, 1963, May 27, 1964, January 13, 20, 27, 1965; *Corpus Christi Times*, June 26, 1963; *SAE*, June 27, 1963, January 16, 30, February 6, May 21, 1964.
62. *Odessa American*, August 12, 1992; *Fourteenth*, *Fifteenth*, and *Sixteenth U.S. Census*, Gonzales County, Texas.
63. Inactive Personnel Record, Charles E. Miller, TDPS; *Kerrville Times*, August 13, 1957.
64. *WNT* and *Brownwood Bulletin*, both dated May 16, 1958; *FWST*, May 20, August 29, October 22, 1958, January 20, 1959; *AS*, December 18, 1959, April 28, 1960.

65. *Brownwood Bulletin*, July 31, 1961.
66. *Brownwood Bulletin*, December 2, 1961.
67. *Brownwood Bulletin*, November 29, 1962.
68. *AS*, June 23, 1965; *Fredericksburg Standard*, June 23, 1965, April 27, 1966; *SAE*, June 24, 1965; Ed Gooding with Robert Nieman, *Ed Gooding: Soldier, Texas Ranger* (Longview, TX: Ranger Publishing, 2001), 187–190.
69. *San Saba News*, June 29, 1967
70. Jim Wilson, "Charlie Miller: A Unique Ranger," *Shooting Times* 41 (October 2000): 96; Robert Mitchell, interview with Robert Nieman, Windom, Texas, October 29, 1996, Oral History Project, TRHF&M, 57.
71. Jim Ray, interview with Robert Neiman, Bullard, Texas, October 18, 1997, Oral History Project, TRHF&M, 81.
72. Inactive Personnel Record, Charles E. Miller, TDPS; James B. Riddles, James E. Riddles, and Carolyn Ann Riddles, interview with the author, Elgin, Texas, May 10, 2012.
73. *Denton Record-Chronicle*, December 10, 1971; *Brownsville Herald*, December 12, 1971; Wilson, "Charlie Miller," 96.
74. *San Saba News*, April 11, 1968.
75. *Dallas Times-Herald*, May 7, 8, 1968, Gonzaullas Scrapbook 4, TRHF&M, 345, 349.
76. Inactive Personnel Record, Charles E. Miller, TDPS; Schreiner, et al., comp., *A Pictorial History of the Texas Rangers*, 112–113; *SAE*, December 10, 1971; *Brownsville Herald*, December 12, 1971; *SAL*, July 31, 1972.
77. Bob Favor, *My Rangering Days* (s. l.: s. n., 2006), 238. See also Bob Favor, interview with Nancy and Eddie Ray, Clyde, Texas, September 5, 2008, Oral History Project, TRHF&M.
78. *Denton Record-Chronicle*, December 10, 1971; Death Certificate, Charles Edward Miller, December 16, 1971, File No. 92340; *AA*, December 10, 1971; *SAL*, December 10, 197; *San Angelo Standard-Times*, December 10, 1971; *Brownsville Herald*, December 12, 1971 (quotation).
79. *Fifteenth U.S. Census*, Balboa District, Panama Canal Zone; *Sixteenth U.S. Census*, Bexar County, Texas; Roger Miller interview, 2012; *SAE*, December 6, 1963, February 28, 1969.
80. Death Certificate, Mrs. Jim D. Green, September 13, 1960, File No. 56265.

81. Death Certificate, Thomas Louis Minica, January 27, 1978, Registrar's No. 443; *SAL*, January 26, 1978.
82. Roger Miller interview, 2012; Comal County Marriage Record Book R, 304; *Fifteenth U.S. Census*, Marion County, Indiana; *SAEN*, November 30, 1996, September 25, 1998.
83. Roger Miller interview, 2012; *SAL*, August 16, 1948; Find A Grave: Roger Hamer Miller, Doris L. Miller.
84. Andrew Miller interview, 2013; *AAS*, March 17, 1994.
85. Roger Miller interview, 2012; Marriage License No. 1308, Guadalupe County Marriage Records 28, 619; *AAS*, February 9, 2015.
86. Andrew Miller interview, 2013; *New York Times*, May 31, 1964; *SAEN*, January 30, March 6, 1966; *SAL*, March 7, 1966. Charles's West Point classmates include General Barry Richard McCaffrey and Judge Eugene R. Sullivan.
87. *Odessa American*, December 8, 1985, November 22, 1989, August 12, 1992.

Notes for Chapter 5

1. Robert W. Stephens, *Lone Wolf: The Story of Texas Ranger Captain M. T. Gonzaullas* (Dallas: Taylor Publishing Company, 1979), 8, 10–12; Brownson Malsch, *"Lone Wolf" Gonzaullas, Texas Ranger* (Norman: University of Oklahoma Press, 1998), 1–2; *Longview Daily News*, February 5, 1935; Death Certificate, Manuel T. Gonzaullas, February 16, 1977, File No. 08344; *DMN*, February 15, 1977. At least six thousand people—approximately one-fifth of the population—died in the Galveston hurricane. Paul Burka, "Grand Dame of the Gulf," *Texas Monthly* 11 (December 1983): 164. The Rosenberg Library in Galveston maintains a roll of the storm's confirmed victims. For more details, see www.gthcenter.org. U.S. Marshal Charles William Geers, Jr. of the Western District of Oklahoma, a personal friend of Gonzaullas, asserted the Lone Wolf was "born and reared in the Mexican border country." *Mineral Wells Index*, July 1, 1935, Gonzaullas Scrapbook 2, TRHF&M, 168.
2. Malsch, *"Lone Wolf" Gonzaullas*, 9; Stephens, *Lone Wolf*, 7, 9–10, 13; *SAE*, September 7, 1935; Manual T. Gonzaullas, Internal Revenue Service, Official Personnel Folders, NPRC.
3. *Fourteenth U.S. Census*, El Paso County, Texas; *Fifteenth U.S. Census*, Dallas County, Texas.

4. *Thirteenth U.S. Census*, Bexar County, Texas.
5. *Thirteenth U.S. Census*, Bexar County, Texas; Texas Department of Criminal Justice, Convict Record Ledgers, 1998/038-157, TSLAC, 132.
6. Charles H. Harris III and Louis R. Sadler, *Texas Rangers in Transition: From Gunfighters to Criminal Investigators, 1921–1935* (Norman: University of Oklahoma Press, 2019), 14; *Arizona Republic*, October 21, 24, 1919; *El Paso Herald*, October 16, November 2 (quotation), 6, 1919.
7. Malsch, *"Lone Wolf" Gonzaullas*, 7; Marriage License, Riverside County, California; *Twelfth U.S. Census*, Kings County, New York; Death Certificate, Laura Isabell Gonzaullas, August 18, 1978, File No. 59719; *Fourteenth U.S. Census*, El Paso County, Texas; *El Paso Herald*, May 20, 1920.
8. Gonzaullas to Adjutant General, July 13, 1920, 401-583, TSLAC; Malsch, *"Lone Wolf" Gonzaullas*, 7; Stephens, *Lone Wolf*, 14; Special Orders No. 56, October 1, 1920, Gonzaullas Vertical File, TRHF&M; James Randolph Ward, "The Texas Rangers, 1919–1935: A Study in Law Enforcement" (Ph.D. dissertation, Texas Christian University, 1972), 41; *Wichita Daily Times*, October 3, 1920; Virginia Duncan, "The Life of Captain Roy W. Aldrich" (M.A. thesis, Sul Ross State Teachers College, 1942): 57; Charles H. Harris III, et al., *Texas Ranger Biographies: Those Who Served, 1910–1921* (Albuquerque: University of New Mexico Press, 2009), 225, 309, 406. When he applied for a Ranger position, Gonzaullas was employed at John W. Swansen's merchandise brokerage company in the First National Bank building. Stephens, *Lone Wolf*, 14; *El Paso City Directory*, 1920 (El Paso: Hudspeth Directory Company, 1920) 839.
9. Jones to Hobby, August 27, 1920 (quotation), 401-583, TSLAC; *Wichita Daily Times*, October 3, 4, 1920; *GDN*, October 8, 10, 1920; *SAEN*, October 15, 1920; *San Saba News*, October 21, 1920.
10. Rick Ruddell, *Oil, Gas, and Crime: The Dark Side of the Boomtown* (New York: Palgrave Macmillan, 2017), 23; Aldrich to Matthews, October 28, 1920, 401–583, TSLAC; *Wichita Daily Times*, October 4, 11, 13, 14, 20, 21, 1920; *GDN*, October 13, 15, 1920; *Denton Record-Chronicle*, October 14, 1920; *SAEN*, October 15, 1920; *SAE*, October 19, 1920; *AA*, October 20, 1920; *AS*, October 26, 1920; *Texas Oil Ledger*, October 30, 1920; Harris, et al., *Texas Ranger Biographies*, 222, 27; Find A Grave: James Marion Allen. On July 21, 1923, Ranger Martin N. Koonsman killed Snow during a raid in the Freeman-Hampton oil fields in Archer County. *AS*, July 22, 1923. As one would expect

from his name, Garrett was the son of the famed New Mexico lawman who had killed Billy the Kid. *Santa Fe New Mexican*, June 4, 1927.

11. Carl Coke Rister, *Oil! Titan of the Southwest* (Norman: University of Oklahoma Press, 1949), 167–168; Bartee Haile, *Texas Boomtowns: A History of Blood and Oil* (Charleston, SC: History Press, 2015), 43; *GDN*, October 10, 12, 1920; Gonzaullas to Aldrich, November 12, 1920, folder 74, Roy W. Aldrich Papers, SRSU; David Frisbie, "Desdemona's Reign of Terror," *American Legion Weekly* 2 (August 27, 1920): 3–4; newspaper clipping dated November 30, 1920, Gonzaullas Scrapbook 1, TRHF&M, 3.
12. *Waxahachie Daily Light*, November 29, 1920; *Galveston Tribune*, November 30, 1920.
13. newspaper clipping dated December 1, 1920, Gonzaullas Scrapbook 1, TRHF&M, 3.
14. Stephen, *Lone Wolf*, 17; Malsch, *"Lone Wolf" Gonzaullas*, 13; Aldrich to Attorney General, Aldrich to Cope, n.d., folder 74, Aldrich Papers, SRSU; Aldrich to Gray, December 7, 1920, Tape 5.1, James R. Ward Collection, ASU; *Galveston Tribune*, December 3, 1920; newspaper clipping dated December 4, 1920, Gonzaullas Scrapbook 1, TRHF&M, 4; *Fort Worth Record*, *Breckenridge American*, and *Brownwood Bulletin*, all dated December 6, 1920; *GDN*, December 7, 1920; *AA*, December 7, 1920; Ward, "The Texas Rangers," 46.
15. Aldrich to Bracewell, n.d., Gonzaullas to Aldrich, December 29, 1920, folder 74, Aldrich Papers, SRSU; Stephens, *Lone Wolf*, 18–19; Malsch, *"Lone Wolf" Gonzaullas*, 13–14; Sterns [*sic*] to Powers, December 6, 1920, Waggoman to Acting Adjutant General, December 9, 1920, Tape 5.2, Ward Collection, ASU; *Galveston Tribune*, December 6, 8, 11, 1920; *SAL*, December 7, 11, 14, 17, 1920; *Breckenridge American*, December 7, 15, 1920; *GDN*, December 8, 10, 11, 1920; *AS*, December 14, 1920.
16. Malsch, *"Lone Wolf" Gonzaullas*, 17–18; *Breckenridge American*, December 10, 16, 21, 1920; *SAEN*, December 9, 1920; newspaper clipping dated December 11, 1920, Gonzaullas Scrapbook 1, TRHF&M, 5; *AA*, December 22, 1920.
17. Gonzaullas to Aldrich, November 12, December 29, 1920, folder 74, Aldrich Papers, SRSU; Gonzaullas to Aldrich, July 20, 1921, 401-586, TSLAC.
18. Malsch, *"Lone Wolf" Gonzaullas*, 5–6; Stephens, *Lone Wolf*, 8.
19. *Wichita Daily Times*, December 29, 1920.

20. Malsch, *"Lone Wolf" Gonzaullas*, 1.
21. *Wichita Daily Times*, April 2, 3, 17, May 5, July 31, August 1, 11, 20, 1921; Monroe to Aldrich, September 9, 1921, Volume 21, Box 2R290, Walter Prescott Webb Collection, BCAH (quotation).
22. Special Orders No. 12, September 1, 1921, Special Orders No. 14, September 9, 1921, Gonzaullas Vertical File, TRHF&M.
23. Aldrich to Gonzaullas, November 25, 1921, 401-588, TSLAC; Manuel T. Gonzaullas, Internal Revenue Service, Official Personnel Folders, NPRC; Malsch, *"Lone Wolf" Gonzaullas*, 37–41; Stephens, *Lone Wolf*, 31; *DMN*, November 22, 1921; *AS*, November 22, 1921, January 10, 1922; *AA*, December 6, 1921, January 9, 11, March 26, 1922; *SAE*, April 22, 1922.
24. *GDN*, April 30, 1922; *Fourteenth U.S. Census*, Harris County, Texas.
25. *AA*, May 9, July 11, 1922; *AS* and *GDN*, both dated May 13, 1922; Manuel T. Gonzaullas, Internal Revenue Service, Official Personnel Folders, NPRC.
26. *GDN*, July 23, 24, August 1, 1922; *AS*, *AA*, and *Port Arthur News*, all dated July 23, 1922. Secondary descriptions of the events that instigated the shooting differ. Malsch wrote in *"Lone Wolf" Gonzaullas*, 42, that Gonzaullas and Nitzer had searched a Fannin Street recreation hall that was suspected of selling liquor. While performing this duty, they saw two men on the street taking a drink out of a pint bottle. Upon approaching, the altercation with Showers ensued. Stephens described in *Lone Wolf*, 32, how the dry agents were investigating a liquor ring, of which Showers was a member, and approached the justice on the street. Showers assaulted Gonzaullas and produced a weapon.
27. *Marshall Messenger*, July 24, 1922; *AS*, July 25, 26, 1922; *Houston Post*, July 27, 28, 1922; *GDN*, July 28, August 1, 1922, January 30, 1924; *AA*, July 28, August 1, 1922; John Clinton Abernathy, World War II Draft Cards, RG 147, NARA.
28. *Dallas Dispatch*, September 1, 1922, *Dallas Times-Herald*, September 9, 1922, and *Pioneer Oil Herald*, September 12, 1922, Gonzaullas Scrapbook 1, TRHF&M, 20; *AS* and *Abilene Daily Reporter*, both dated September 10, 1922; *Comanche Chief*, September 15, 1922.
29. *Dallas Journal*, October 16, 1922, and *Dallas Daily Times-Herald*, October 29, 1922, Gonzaullas Scrapbook 1, TRHF&M, 21.
30. Stephens, *Lone Wolf*, 32–33; *AA*, November 19, 1922; *GDN*, November 22, 1922, January 30, February 5, 1924.

31. *DMN*, December 23, 1922; *Dallas Dispatch*, March 6, 1923, Gonzaullas Scrapbook 1, TRHF&M, 23.
32. *DMN*, February 25, 1923; *Dallas Dispatch*, March 16, 1923, Gonzaullas Scrapbook 1, TRHF&M, 25.
33. Stephens, *Lone Wolf*, 33; *Mobile Register*, September 2, November 14, 1923, and *Mobile News-Item*, n.d., November 14, 1923, Gonzaullas Scrapbook 1, TRHF&M, 29, 39, 35, 38; *Selma Times-Journal*, November 13, 1923; Manuel T. Gonzaullas, Internal Revenue Service, Official Personnel Folders, NPRC. Working together for five years in the Big Apple, Izzy Einstein and his equally unimposing partner, Moe W. Smith, achieved an incredible record of nearly five thousand arrests, with a 95 percent conviction rate. In that time, they confiscated five million bottles of illegal liquor. Lucy Moore, *Anything Goes: A Biography of the Roaring Twenties* (New York: Overlook Press, 2010), 16–17. Their exploits inspired the 1985 television movie, *Izzy and Moe*, starring Jackie Gleason and Art Carney. For more on these improbable crime busters, see Isidor Einstein, *Prohibition Agent No. 1* (New York: Frederick A. Stokes Company, 1932).
34. *Mobile News-Item*, November 24, December 7, 14, 19, 1923, April 4, 14, May 7, 9, 1924, and *Mobile Register*, December 16, 17, 1923, May 6, 8, 13, 23, 1924, Gonzaullas Scrapbook 1, TRHF&M, 41, 44–45, 50, 56, 55, 77, 84, 49, 46, 68–69, 78–80, 99–100; Gonzaullas to Aldrich, April 16, 1924, folder 74, Aldrich Papers, SRSU; *Selma Times-Journal*, May 5, 6, 9, 12, 21, 22, August 27, 1924, February 18, 22, 1925.
35. *New Orleans Times-Picayune*, December 5, 1923, Gonzaullas Scrapbook 1, TRHF&M, 35; *DMN*, June 9, 10, 11, 1924; *GDN*, June 12, 1924.
36. Manuel T. Gonzaullas, Internal Revenue Service, Official Personnel Folders, NPRC; Malsch, *"Lone Wolf" Gonzaullas*, 57, 58; Stephens, *Lone Wolf*, 33; *Dallas Journal*, July 1, 1924, Gonzaullas Scrapbook 1, TRHF&M, 100; *DMN*, July 2, 1924; Harris and Sadler, *Texas Rangers in Transition*, 17.
37. *Waxahachie Daily Light*, November 6, 7, 8, 10, 11, 13, 14, 15, 17, 18, 20, 22, 24, 25, December 9, 11, 1924, April 25, 1925 (quotation); *DMN* and *GDN*, both dated November 15, 1924; Special Order No. 1, February 20, 1925, 401-1184, TSLAC.
38. *AA*, June 1, 1923; *DMN*, July 2, August 8, 1925; *Dallas Journal*, July 7, 1925, Gonzaullas Scrapbook 2, TRHF&M, 111; *GDN*, July 8, 1925. Four years previously, Gray had been acquitted of assault to murder.

By 1923, he was under indictment for bank robberies in Titus and Upshur Counties. *AS*, February 5, 1921; *GDN*, July 12, 1923. Most newspapers spelled the murder victim's first name as "Otis," but his headstone is inscribed with "Ottice." For more on the Ballard murder, see Harris and Sadler, *Texas Rangers in Transition*, 116.

39. *Dallas Dispatch*, August 13, 1925, Gonzaullas Scrapbook 2, TRHF&M, 112; *DMN*, August 14, 15, 1925.
40. Manuel T. Gonzaullas, Internal Revenue Service, Official Personnel Folders, NPRC; Stephens, *Lone Wolf*, 34; *AA*, November 5, 1925.
41. *Dallas Dispatch*, March 23, 1926, and *Dallas Journal*, April 19, 1926, Gonzaullas Scrapbook 2, TRHF&M, 121.
42. Manuel T. Gonzaullas, Internal Revenue Service, Official Personnel Folders, NPRC; Stephens, *Lone Wolf*, 34; Matthews to M. A. Ferguson, October 13, 1926, Matthews to Nichols, October 13, 1926, Nichols to Matthews, October 17, 1926, Tape 1.2, Ward Collection, ASU; *Fort Worth Press*, October 16, 1926, Gonzaullas Scrapbook 2, TRHF&M, 122; *Fort Worth Star-Telegraph*, October 14, 26, 1926; *Amarillo Daily News* and *GDN*, both dated October 16, 1926; Robert M. Utley, *Lone Star Lawmen: The Second Century of the Texas Rangers* (New York: Berkley Books, 2007), 116; T. Lindsay Baker, *More Ghost Towns of Texas* (Norman: University of Oklahoma Press, 2003), 46. After the accidental shooting death of sixteen-year-old Mildred Toothman, Captain Nichols and Company C were assigned to the Panhandle oil field district from mid-October to early November. *AA*, October 14, 1926; Special Order No. 14, October 13, 1926, Special Order No. 15, November 6, 1926, Hickman Vertical File, TRHF&M. While Gonzaullas and his companions were conducting their raid, Justice Department agents arrested three alleged automobile thieves and took them to Amarillo. Two federal narcotics agents patrolled the streets securing evidence for future cases against drug dealers in town.
43. Gonzaullas to Aldrich, March 6, 1927, folder 74, Aldrich Papers, SRSU; *DMN*, November 12, 15, 1926, January 6, 1927, April 16, 1956; *Wichita Daily News*, February 5, 27, 1927; *Wichita Falls Record News*, February 5, 1927, Gonzaullas Scrapbook 2, TRHF&M, 123; *Fifteenth U.S. Census*, Wichita County, Texas; *Sixteenth U.S. Census*, Tarrant County, Texas.
44. Hickman to Robertson, June 13, 1927, Tape 3.1, Ward Collection, ASU; Wright to Moody, May 23, 1927, Gonzaullas to Butler, June 15, 1927, Wright to Moody, June 24, 1927, Box 2007/170-52, TSLAC; Utley,

Lone Star Lawmen, 123; Stephens, *Lone Wolf*, 34, 39–40; Manuel T. Gonzaullas, Internal Revenue Service, Official Personnel Folders, NPRC.

45. *DMN*, August 16, 1927; Newspaper clipping, dated August 19, 1927, Gonzaullas Scrapbook 2, TRHF&M, 124; *Borger Daily Herald*, August 15, 16, 1927; *AS*, August 16, 1927; *AA*, August 16, 1927; Find A Grave: William Bradley Howard, Will Palmer Jones.
46. *Amarillo Daily News*, September 8, 1927.
47. Clifford R. Caldwell and Ron DeLord, *Texas Lawmen, 1900–1940: More of the Good and the Bad* (Charleston, SC: History Press, 2012), 275–276; *AS*, December 2, 4, 5, 1927; *AA*, December 2, 3, 1927; *Fort Worth Record-Telegram*, December 3, 1927; *Abilene Reporter-News*, December 4, 1927; *Fort Worth Record-Telegram*, April 3, 1930.
48. Gonzaullas and Mayes report, December 21, 1927, Mayes report, n.d., Tape 11.1, Ward Collection, ASU; Find A Grave: Robert Edgar Kirk.
49. Gonzaullas to Robertson, January 21, 1928, Gonzaullas Scrapbook 5, TRHF&M, n.p.; *SAE*, January 15, 1928; Find A Grave: Eddie Vernon "Buddy" Hall.
50. Phillips to Moody, January 13, 1928, Gonzaullas Scrapbook 5, TRHF&M, n.p.; *SAE*, January 15, 1928.
51. Gonzaullas to Robertson, January 21, 1928, and Moody to Hall, January 31, 1929, Gonzaullas Scrapbook 5, TRHF&M, n.p.; Utley, *Lone Star Lawmen*, 125–126; *Lubbock Morning Avalanche*, January 19, 1928.
52. Gonzaullas to Robertson, February 9, 1928, Tape 11.1, Ward Collection, ASU; *AS*, January 4, 5, 7, 9, 1928; *Beaumont Enterprise*, January 5, 7, March 4, 1928; Find A Grave: Charles Albert Hodges, Thomas Fuller Lambert.
53. Pitman to Robertson, April 19, 1928 (first quotation), Tape 11.1, Ward Collection, ASU; *GDN*, May 2, 1928 (second quotation); *Fort Worth Record-Telegram*, May 2, 1928. Browning and Wakefield had a lengthy business partnership in illegal gaming that stretched from Houston to Fort Worth. For examples, see *FWST*, January 8, 1929, March 31, 1951, *Houston Chronicle*, December 4, 1935.
54. Gonzaullas to Robertson, July 15, November 3 (quotation), 1928, Tape 11.1, Ward Collection, ASU; *FWST*, December 20, 1959; Find A Grave: George Appsalom Hammons.
55. Gonzaullas report, January 25, 1929, Tape 11.1, Ward Collection, ASU.

56. *FWST*, October 15, 16, 17, 18, 22, November 13, 14, 1928; *AS*, October 17, November 12, 14, 1928.
57. Jordan to Robertson, November 25, 1928, Tape 11.1, Ward Collection, ASU; Harris and Sadler, *Texas Rangers in Transition*, 329; Jordan to Moody, November 25, 1928, [Moody] to Jordan, November 27, 1928, Box 2007/170-52, Daniel J. Moody Papers, TSLAC; *Lubbock Morning Avalanche*, November 27, 1928; Find A Grave: John Edward Russell, Sr.
58. Gonzaullas to Robertson, December 9, 1928, Tape 3.2, Ward Collection, ASU; *Brownsville Herald*, December 4, 1929.
59. Gonzaullas to Robertson, July 27, 1929, Tape 11.2, Ward Collection, ASU; *FWST*, July 15, 16, 17 (quotation), 25, 1929; *DMN* and *Houston Post*, both dated July 16, 1929; Death Certificate, Austin Irving Rice, August 6, 1929, File No. 36906.
60. Gonzaullas to Robertson, November 16, 21, 1929, Tape 11.2, Ward Collection, ASU; *FWST*, November 13, 1929; *Tyler Journal*, November 22, 1929.
61. *Dallas Daily Times-Herald*, February 18, 1930, and *DMN*, February 19, 1930, Gonzaullas Scrapbook 2, TRHF&M, 128.
62. *Shamrock Texan*, July 13, 16, 1930; July 16, 1930; *Pampa Daily News*, July 29, 1930; Arthur F. Raper, *The Tragedy of Lynching* (Chapel Hill: University of North Carolina Press, 1933), 451–452; Dougherty to Moody, July 13, 1930, Marshall to Moody, July 15, 1930, Secretary to Marshall, July 16, 1930, Box 2007/170-53, Moody Papers; Donald E. Green, "Son of the Hundredth Meridian: Collingsworth County During the Great Depression," 14–16, 19. Dr. Green, retired history professor at the University of Central Oklahoma, graciously shared a rough draft excerpt from a forthcoming book discussing both his boyhood in Collingsworth County and a more general history of the southeast Texas Panhandle.
63. Morgan, et al. to Moody, July 16, 1930, Box 2007/170-53, Moody Papers, TSLAC. Reprinted in *Shamrock Texan*, July 16, 1930.
64. *Pampa Daily News*, July 16, 1930; *Shamrock Texan*, July 16, 20, 1930; *AA*, July 17, 1930.
65. *Pampa Daily News*, July 18, 28, 29, 1930; *AS*, July 17, 18, 28, 29, 1930; *AA*, July 18, 28, 29, 1930; *Vernon Daily Record*, July 16, 1930 (quotation); Utley, *Lone Star Lawmen*, 133–134; *Shamrock Texan*, July 16, 20, 30, 1930; *Abilene Reporter-News*, August 1, 1930; Green, "Son of the Hundredth Meridian," 17, 19, 21.

66. *AS*, July 30, 1930; *AA*, July 31, 1930; *DMN*, July 31, August 1, 1930; *Vernon Daily Record*, July 30, 31, 1930; *Shamrock Texan*, July 30, 1930; *Dallas Journal*, September 12, 1930, Gonzaullas Scrapbook 2, TRHF&M, 135. In spite of the confession and subsequent execution, some residents of Collingsworth County believed Henry Hugh Vaughan, Ruth's husband, had actually killed her and framed Washington. However, no evidence supports the notion, which amounts to little more than rumor. Green, "Son of the Hundredth Meridian," 23. Two years after the murder, Henry committed suicide by cyanide poisoning in a San Antonio alley. *SAL*, September 13, 1932.
67. Diana Davids Olien and Roger M. Olien, *Oil in Texas: The Gusher Age, 1895–1945* (Austin: University of Texas Press, 2002), 170; Randolph B. Campbell, *Gone to Texas: A History of the Lone Star State* (New York: Oxford University Press, 2003), 377; William T. Chambers, "Kilgore, Texas: An Oil Boom Town," *Economic Geography* 9 (January 1933): 73–75; Bobby H. Johnson, "Oil in the Pea Patch: The East Texas Oil Boom," *East Texas Historical Journal* 13 (March 1975): 34, 38; Robert D. Boyle, "Chaos in the East Oilfield, 1930–1935," *SHQ* 69 (January 1966): 340.
68. Carl Coke Rister, *Oil! Titan of the Southwest* (Norman: University of Oklahoma Press, 1949), 312; Johnson, "Oil in the Pea Patch," 38; Boyle, "Chaos in the East Oilfield," 345; Bryan Burrough, *The Big Rich: The Rise and Fall of the Greatest Texas Oil Fortunes* (New York: Penguin Books, 2009), 75.
69. Hays to Sterling, January 28, 1931, Hickman to Hamer, February 2, 1931, Gonzaullas to Hickman, February 9, 1931, Tape 10.2, Ward Collection, ASU; Robert Nieman, "In Their Own Words: 'They Just Passed the Bucket'," *TRD* 3 (Spring 2001): 4; Stephens, *Lone Wolf*, 49; *St. Louis Post-Dispatch*, May 17, 1931, Gonzaullas Scrapbook 5, TRHF&M, 416; *Gregg County Oil News*, February 6, 1931 (quotation), Gonzaullas Scrapbook 2, TRHF&M, 136; John A. Clark and Michel T. Halbouty, *The Last Boom* (New York: Random House, 1972), 135; Margaret Hunt Hill, *H.L. and Lyda* (Little Rock, AR: August House Publishers, 1994), 74.
70. M. T. Gonzaullas interview with Stacy Keach, Sr., New Boston, Texas, July 1957, Oral History Project, TRHF&M, 6. Cited hereafter as Gonzaullas interview, 1957. *SAE*, March 2, 1931.
71. *St. Louis Post-Dispatch*, May 17, 1931, Gonzaullas Scrapbook 5, TRHF&M, 416; Stephens, *Lone Wolf*, 51; Hill, *H.L. and Lyda*, 75; Cox, *Time of the Rangers*, 146–147; Ward, "The Texas Rangers," 192.

72. Gonzaullas to Hickman, February 9, March 22, 31, June 28, 1931, Tape 10.2, Ward Collection, ASU; *Kilgore Daily News*, March 30, 1931, Gonzaullas Scrapbook 2, TRHF&M, 140; *Corsicana Daily Sun*, March 12, April 18, 1931; *St. Louis Post-Dispatch*, May 17, 1931, Gonzaullas Scrapbook 5, TRHF&M, 416; *Kilgore Daily News*, April 2, 1931 (quotation); Clark and Halbouty, *The Last Boom*, 137.
73. Hickman to Sterling, May 9, 1931, Tape 10.2, Ward Collection, ASU; *Longview Daily News* and *Corsicana Daily Sun*, both dated May 1, 1931; *FWST*, May 2, 4, 1931; *Kansas City Star*, May 10, 1931. Myron Kinley mentored legendary firefighters Paul Neal "Red" Adair (played by John Wayne in *The Hellfighters*), Asger "Boots" Hansen, and Edward Owen "Coots" Matthews. For more on his exciting career, see Jesse D. Kinley, Call Kinley (Tulsa, OK: Cock a Hoop Publications, 1996).
74. *FWST*, May 20, 21, 22, 1931; Gonzaullas to Hickman, May 24, 1931, Tape 10.2, Ward Collection, ASU; *La Prensa*, May 21, 22, 1931; *Kilgore Daily News*, May 28, 1931.
75. Gonzaullas to Hickman, June 14, 1931, Tape 10.2, Ward Collection, ASU; *Longview Morning Journal*, June 10, 11, 1931; *Kilgore Daily News*, June 11, 1931; *AA*, June 12, 1931; *Kilgore News Herald*, April 5, 1968.; Find A Grave: Aaron Patterson "A. P." Farrar.
76. Gonzaullas to Hickman, June 28, 1931, Tape 10.2, Ward Collection, ASU; *Longview Morning Journal*, June 27, 1931; Longview Daily News, June 28, 1931.
77. Hickman to Sterling, July 10, 1931, Tape 11.2, Ward Collection, ASU; *AS*, July 8, 1931; *SAE*, July 8, 9, 10, 1931; *DMN*, July 9, 10, 1931; *GDN*, July 9, 1931; Utley, *Lone Star Lawmen*, 145; Caldwell and DeLord, *Texas Lawman*, 413–414; RSR, Dan McDuffie, 401-59, William Dial, -54, TSLAC.
78. *Longview Morning Journal*, January 20, 1932, Gonzaullas Scrapbook 2, TRHF&M, 151; *Abilene Reporter-News*, April 14, 1973.
79. *Marshall News Messenger*, December 17, 1931
80. *Corsicana Daily Sun*, January 12, 1932; Caldwell and DeLord, *Texas Lawmen*, 328.
81. *Longview Morning Journal*, January 20, February 4, 1932, Gonzaullas Scrapbook 2, TRHF&M, 151.
82. *Shreveport Times*, February 21, 1932.
83. Hill, *H.L. and Lyda*, 86.
84. John Neal Phillips, *Running with Bonnie and Clyde: The Ten Fast Years of Ralph Fults* (Norman: University of Oklahoma Press, 1996), 73–74; Jeff Guinn, *Go Down Together: The True Untold Story of Bonnie and*

Clyde (New York: Simon and Schuster, 2009), 97–98. The simultaneous robbery of two banks has been an aspiration for American bank robbers since the Dalton brothers tried and failed at Coffeyville, Kansas, on October 5, 1892. Henry Starr made another similar unsuccessful effort in Stroud, Oklahoma, in 1915. For more, see L. R. Kirchner, *Robbing Banks: An American History, 1831–1999* (Edison, NJ: Castle Books, 2003).

85. *Abilene Morning News*, May 13, 1932; *Big Spring Daily Herald*, May 20, 1932; Harris, et al., *Texas Ranger Biographies*, 190.
86. Gonzaullas to Hickman, September 4, 1932, Tape 10.2, Ward Collection, ASU; *McAllen Daily Press*, November 30, 1933; *AS* and *DMN*, both dated September 1, 1932.
87. *Longview Daily News*, April 8, 1934, Gonzaullas Scrapbook 2, TRHF&M, 162–163; *DMN*, April 8, 1934; *El Paso Herald-Post*, September 22, 1933; Charles Schreiner III, et al., comps., *A Pictorial History of the Texas Rangers: "That Special Breed of Men"* (Mountain Home, TX: YO Press, 1969), 123.
88. Jeanne Bozzell McCarty, *The Struggle for Sobriety: Protestants and Prohibition in Texas, 1919–1935* (El Paso: Texas Western Press, 1980), 49–50.
89. *Longview Ledger and Greggton Gauger*, December 19, 1934, *Kilgore Daily News*, January 9, 1935, *Longview Daily News*, January 9, February 21, 1935, April 11, 1935, n.d., *Dallas Daily Herald*, n.d., Gonzaullas Scrapbook 2, TRHF&M, 164, 166, 167, 170.
90. *Longview Daily News*, June 13, August 1, 15, 1935, Gonzaullas Scrapbook 2, TRHF&M, 166.
91. Acts 1935, Regular Session, 44th Legislature, Ch. 181, *General and Special Laws of Texas*; *DMN*, October 1, 1935, Gonzaullas Scrapbook 2, TRHF&M, 168; Inactive Personnel Record, Manuel T. Gonzaullas, TDPS; *DPS Annual Report, August 10, 1935–December 1, 1936*, 5; *Laredo Times* and *Abilene Daily Reporter*, both dated September 6, 1935; Hans Peter Nielsen Gammel, comp., *The Laws of Texas, 1934–1935* (Austin: Gammel's Book Store, 1935), 1093; Thomas Lee Charlton, "The Department of Public Safety, 1935–1957" (M.A. thesis, University of Texas at Austin, 1961), 73; Stephens, *Lone Wolf*, 64.
92. Malsch, *"Lone Wolf" Gonzaullas*, 125; *DPS Annual Report, August 10, 1935–December 1, 1936*, 7; *AA*, September 7, 1935; Charlton, "The Department of Public Safety," 48–50; Mitchel P. Roth, "Through the Ages: Texas DPS History," *Courtesy, Service, and Protection:*

The History of the Texas Department of Public Safety (Paducah, KY: Turner Publishing Company, 2003), 27.

93. *FWST* and *Abilene Daily Reporter*, both dated April 24, 1936; Bruce A. Glasrud and Harold J. Weiss, Jr., eds., *Tracking the Texas Rangers: The Twentieth Century* (Denton: University of North Texas Press, 2013), 147.
94. *DPS Annual Report, August 10, 1935–December 1, 1936*, 5–6; *AA*, July 31, 1936; Malsch, *"Lone Wolf" Gonzaullas*, 135; *SAL*, June 10, 1936.
95. *SAE*, July 13, 16, 1936; *AA*, July 14, 15, 16, 18, 21, 24, August 20, 21, 1936; *AS*, April 18, 1937.
96. *Austin Dispatch*, September 24, 1936, Gonzaullas Scrapbook 2, TRHF&M, 183; *SAE*, December 17, 1936, February 8, 1939; *GDN*, December 25, 1937.
97. Charlton, "The Texas Department of Public Safety," 86, 89; Robinson, *The DPS Story*, 18; Jack Martin, "Col. Homer Garrison, Jr., Director of the Department of Public Safety," *True Detective Mysteries* 34 (August 1940): 67. Charlton asserted that "A. L. Ford" became the assistant chief of the Bureau of Intelligence on May 5, 1937. This is inaccurate. Augdil Lee Ford, a former Fort Worth policeman and an ex-Ranger, was the number two man at the Bureau of Identification. *Fort Worth Star-Telegram*, November 22, 1978. Firearms expert George W. Gambill was Gonzaullas's chief deputy.
98. *SAE*, September 29, 30, October 1, 2, 1936, *SAL*, September 30, October 1, 2, 1936, and *SAEN*, September 30, October 1, 2, 1936, Gonzaullas Scrapbook 2, TRHF&M, 188–191; Elton R. Cude, *The Wild and Free Dukedom of Bexar* (San Antonio, TX: Munguia Printers, 1978), 274–275. Gonzaullas's ballistics testimony was the first from the DPS to be introduced in a Bexar County court. *SAL*, October 8, 1936. Despite his limited role, Gonzaullas was apparently fascinated with the case as he devoted six entire pages of his scrapbook to the trial.
99. Caldwell and DeLord, *Texas Lawmen*, 324; *SAL*, February 3, 17, 18, March 11, 1937; Texas Death Certificate, Agnal Aubrey Edwards, January 19, 1937, Registrar's No. 430; *Lubbock Morning Avalanche*, April 7, 1937; *Valley Star-Monitor-Herald*, January 30, 1938; *Laredo Times* and *Abilene Reporter-News*, both dated January 27, 1939.
100. *Abilene Reporter-News*, May 25, 26 (quotation), 1939; William Hanson Strickland, World War II Draft Cards, RG 147, NARA; Death Certificate, Dore [*sic*] Ira Liverman, November 4, 1938, File No. 47556.
101. *DPS Biennial Report, 1938–1940*, 25, 38.

102. *DPS Biennial Report, 1938–1940*, 25; Charlton, "The Texas Department of Public Safety," 115; *AS*, February 14, 1940, Gonzaullas Scrapbook 3, TRHF&M, 220; Stephens, *Lone Wolf*, 66.
103. *DPS Biennial Report, 1938–1940*, 15. Reprinted in *Victoria Advocate*, February 5, 1941.
104. *DMN*, June 5, 6, 1940; Death Certificate, Walter Lewis Sterrett, July 27, 1981, File No. 52293.
105. *DMN*, September 12, 1940; Tracey Boyd Griffin, Joseph Macon Sides, World War II Draft Cards, RG 147, NARA.
106. *Paris News*, September 10, 11, 12, 13, 16, 1940; James Allen, "Robertson's Ride with Death," *Master Detective* 25 (November 1941): 78–79; Athan G. Theoharis, ed., *The FBI: A Comprehensive Reference Guide* (Phoenix, AZ: Oryx Press, 1999), 53; *Dallas Times-Herald*, September 12, 1940, *Lamar County Echo*, September 13, 1940, and *Paris News*, September 15, 1940, Gonzaullas Scrapbook 3, TRHF&M, 221–222; *Denton Record-Chronicle*, September 13, 1940.
107. *Paris News*, September 13, 15, 17, October 14, 1940; Allen, "Robertson's Ride with Death," 80; *DMN*, October 12, 16, 19, 1940, Gonzaullas Scrapbook 3, TRHF&M, 223; Caldwell and Clifford, *Texas Lawmen*, 243.
108. *Paris News*, March 10, 13, 14, 15, 16, 21, May 18, June 10, 16, 20, 1941; Texas Department of Criminal Justice, Convict Record Ledgers, 1998/038-170, TSLAC, n.p.
109. *Paris News*, January 23, 24 (quotation), 26, 27, 30, February 6, 20, March 2, 3, 1941.
110. *Denison Press*, August 25, 1942, Gonzaullas Scrapbook 3, TRHF&M, 233; *Abilene Reporter-News*, August 25, 1942; Death Certificate, Carlisle B. Carroll, February 5, 1958, File No. 2445.
111. Stephens, *Lone Wolf*, 9; *DMN*, February 15, 1977; *Longview Morning Journal*, February 15, 1977; Utley, *Lone Star Lawmen*, 202 (quotation).
112. *AA* and *Paris News*, both dated January 26, 1943; *DMN*, January 26, 27, 1943; *Dallas Times-Herald*, January 26, 1943, Gonzaullas Scrapbook 3, TRHF&M, 234; James Gordon Anderson, Lonnie Ray Smith, World War II Draft Cards, RG 147, NARA.
113. *Gladewater News*, January 29, 1943, Gonzaullas Scrapbook 3, TRHF&M, 234.
114. *Paris News*, January 26, 1943; *DMN*, January 26, 27, 1943; Bob Alexander and Donaly E. Brice, *Texas Rangers: Lives, Legend, and Legacy* (Denton: University of North Texas Press, 2017), 368 (quotation).

115. *Dallas Times-Herald*, June 4, 1943, and *DMN*, June 6, 1943, Gonzaullas Scrapbook 3, TRHF&M, 237.
116. *Dallas Times-Herald*, June 4, 1943, and *DMN*, June 6, 1943, Gonzaullas Scrapbook 3, TRHF&M, 237–238; Kemp Dixon, *Chasing Thugs, Nazis, and Reds: Texas Ranger Norman K. Dixon* (College Station: Texas A&M University Press, 2015), 116.
117. *Dallas Times-Herald*, June 4, 7, 10, 1943, Gonzaullas Scrapbook 3, TRHF&M, 237–239; Dixon, *Chasing Thugs, Nazis, and Reds*, 116–117.
118. *DMN*, June 17, 1943; James S. Olson and Susan Phair, "Anatomy of a Race Riot: Beaumont, Texas, 1943," *Texana* 11 (Winter 1973): 64–65, 68; James A. Burran, "Violence in an 'Arsenal of Democracy': The Beaumont Race Riot, 1943," *East Texas Historical Journal* 14 (March 1976): 42–44; Pamela Lippold, "Recollections: Revisiting the Beaumont Race Riot of 1943," *Touchstone* 25 (2006): 55, 57, 59.
119. *SAL*, June 16, 1943; *Beaumont Journal*, June 17, 1943; Olson and Phair, "Anatomy of a Race Riot," 65–66, 70; Burran, "Violence in an 'Arsenal of Democracy'," 44–47; Lippold, "Recollections," 55–57; Dixon, *Chasing Thugs, Nazis, and Reds*, 94–95; Trayce Darter Hudy, "The Texas Guard During Martial Law and a State of Emergency: A Select Study Focusing on Galveston, Sherman, Beaumont and Texas City" (M.A. thesis, Texas Woman's University, 2001), 122, 136.
120. Death Certificates, Roy Elwin Hunt, Registrar's No. 47652, Matty May Hunt, Registrar's No. 47651, both dated November 5, 1943; *DMN*, October 30, 1943, and *Dallas Times-Herald*, November 1, 1943, Gonzaullas Scrapbook 3, TRHF&M, 243; *GDN*, November 1, 1943; Dana Middlebrooks Samuelson and Robert Samuelson, *Clovis Road: The Dr. Roy Hunt Murder, Littlefield, Texas, 1942–1943* (Dallas, TX: Highgate Publishing, 2009), 78–79, 85, 88–89; *Lubbock Morning Avalanche*, November 3, 1943; Tise, *Texas County Sheriffs*, 318.
121. *DMN*, November 1, 3, 1943, Gonzaullas Scrapbook 3, TRHF&M, 243; *GDN*, November 1, 1943; *Lubbock Morning Avalanche*, November 3, 1943.
122. *DMN*, April 11, August 31, 1944, January 8, 10, 1945, and *Dallas Times-Herald*, August 30, September 23, 1944, Gonzaullas Scrapbook 3, TRHF&M, 243–244; Samuelson and Samuelson, *Clovis Road*, 91–92, 98–99.
123. *DMN* and *SAL*, both dated November 10, 1944; Gary W. Sleeper, *I'll Do My Own Damn Killin': Benny Binion, Herbert Noble, and the Texas Gambling War* (Fort Lee, NJ: Barricade Books, 2006), 77.

124. Michael Newton, *The Texarkana Moonlight Murders: The Unsolved Case of the 1946 Phantom Killer* (Jefferson, NC: McFarland & Company, 2013), 3–5, 18–21, 23; James Presley, *The Phantom Killer: Unlocking the Mystery of the Texarkana Serial Murders: The Story of a Town in Terror* (New York: Pegasus Crime, 2014), 3–5, 25–26, 32, 36, 39; *Texarkana Gazette*, March 25, 26, 1946; Cox, *Texas Ranger Tales*, 246–248; "Phantom Killer Terrorizes Texarkana," *Life* 20 (June 10, 1946): 40.
125. *Texarkana Gazette* and *FWST*, both dated April 15, 1946; *Arkansas Gazette*, April 15, 16, 1946; Wyly to Director, April 20, 1946, FBI File No. 62-80864; *DMN*, April 16, 1946.
126. Malsch, *"Lone Wolf" Gonzaullas*, 164; Dixon, *Chasing Thugs, Nazis, and Reds*, 126; *Texarkana Gazette*, April 16, 17, 18, 25, 1946; *DMN*, April 17, 18 (quotation), May 1, 1946. Although the United Press reported the Bureau was active in the investigation, Director J. Edgar Hoover limited the Dallas field office to laboratory and identification services unless the unknown subject crossed state lines in an unlawful flight to avoid prosecution. Olsen to Rosen, April 15, 1946, Hoover to Dallas SAC, April 16, 1946, Garrison to Hoover, April 19, 1946, Hoover to Garrison, April 26, 1946, FBI File No. 62-80864; Newton, *The Texarkana Moonlight Murders*, 40, 44–45, 46; "Phantom Killer Terrorizes Texarkana," 40.
127. *Texarkana Gazette*, May 4, 5, 1946; Presley, *The Phantom Killer*, 89, 93–96.
128. Dixon, *Chasing Thugs, Nazis, and Reds*, 127; Captain M. T. Gonzaullas, interview with Captain Bob Mitchell and Alva Stem, Dallas, Texas, January 26, 1977, Oral History Project, TRHF&M, n.p.; *DMN*, May 4, 1946; *Texarkana Gazette*, May 5, 6, 1946; Hoover to Davis, May 10, 1946, FBI File No. 62-80864; Presley, *The Phantom Killer*, 100–101.
129. *FWST*, May 21, 1946; *DMN*, June 22, 1946.
130. *Corsicana Daily Sun*, July 17, 1946.
131. *DMN*, October 31, 1946; Dixon, *Chasing Thugs, Nazis, and Reds*, 130; Presley, *The Phantom Killer*, 156, 162; Newton, *The Texarkana Moonlight Murders*, 91, 95–96, 101. Presley unequivocally asserted Swinney was the killer, while Newton examined the likelihood of several possible killers. For more, see Jereme Kennington and Dr. John Tennison, "Phantom Killer: Suspects Swinney and Tennison," presented at the Museum of Regional History in Texarkana on January 14, 2017, and accessible at YouTube.com.

132. Cox, *Time of the Rangers*, 204–206; Newton, *The Texarkana Moonlight Murders*, 116–117. Malsch, *"Lone Wolf" Gonzaullas*, 166–168: "The 'Lone Wolf' had his opinion in the matter. Years after the series of events, he commented that the officers had a good idea who the perpetrator was, but could not move in because of lack of conclusive evidence."

133. *Dallas Times-Herald*, March 10, April 1, 1947, *DMN*, March 12, April 1, 1947, Gonzaullas Scrapbook 3, TRHF&M, 260; *DMN*, April 2, 1947; *Brownsville Herald*, April 1, 1947; *Denton Record-Chronicle*, July 7, 1967.

134. Chuck Lyons, "The 1947 Texas City Explosion," *History Magazine* 17 (June/July 2016): 9–10; Milton MacKaye, "Death on the Water Front," *Saturday Evening Post* 230 (October 26, 1957): 96; *DMN*, April 18, 1947; *GDN*, April 21, 1947.

135. *DMN*, June 21, 22, 1947; Find A Grave: Taylor Franklin McCoy.

136. James C. Cobb, *Redefining Southern Culture: Mind and Identity in the Modern South* (Athens: University of Georgia Press, 1999), 30; Sleeper, *I'll Do My Own Damned Killin'*, 79, 82–85; Alan B. Govenar and Jay F. Brakefield, *Deep Ellum: The Other Side of Dallas* (College Station: Texas A&M University Press, 2013), 200; *SAL*, January 8, 1947; *DMN*, January 9, 1947; *GDN*, January 9, 1947. In addition to its establishments that offered alcohol, gambling, and sex, Deep Ellum was a center for early jazz and blues musicians such as Lemon Henry "Blind Lemon" Jefferson, Huddie William "Leadbelly" Ledbetter, and Sam "Lightin'" Hopkins. David G. McComb, *Spare Time in Texas: Recreation and History in the Lone Star State* (Austin: University of Texas Press, 2008), 32

137. Malsch, *"Lone Wolf" Gonzaullas*, 179; Utley, *Lone Star Lawmen*, 216–217; *DMN*, August 11, 15, 1947; *Paris News*, August 15, 1947; T. Lindsay Baker, *Gangster Tour of Texas* (College Station: Texas A&M University Press, 2011), 280; *Corpus Christi Times*, October 30, 1953.

138. *Marshall News Messenger*, January 8, 1948; *FWST*, January 8, 9, 1948.

139. Malsch, *"Lone Wolf" Gonzaullas*, 183; *SAL*, February 28, 1948; *Paris News*, March 16, 1948.

140. *DMN*, September 7, 11, 16, 18, 1948, *Dallas Times-Herald*, September 8, 18, 1948, *Nashville Tennessean*, September 15, 18, 1948, *Memphis Press Scimitar*, September 16, 1948, *Memphis Commercial Appeal*,

September 16, 1948, Gonzaullas Scrapbook 3, TRHF&M, 278–280; *FWST*, October 3, 1948.

141. *FWST* and *Denton Record-Chronicle*, both dated November 9, 1948.
142. *DMN*, January 5, 7, 1949.
143. *DMN*, August 2, 7, 1949.
144. *GDN*, January 4, 1950; "The Last Days of 'The Cat'," *Time Magazine* 58 (August 20, 1951): 19; Gary Cartwright, "Benny and the Boys," *Texas Monthly* 19 (October 1991): 194; Sleeper, *I'll Do My Own Damn Killin'*, 131.
145. *DMN*, December 20, 1949.
146. *DMN*, October 8, 11 (quotation), 1950; *FWST*, March 31, August 23, 1951; Ann Arnold, *Gamblers and Gangsters: Fort Worth's Jacksboro Highway in the 1940s and 1950s* (Austin, TX: Eakin Press, 1998), 142.
147. Gonzaullas to Garrison, May 3, 1951, Gonzaullas Scrapbook 4, TRHF&M, BB.
148. *DMN*, June 21, July 11 (first quotation), 1951, *Dallas Times-Herald*, June 21, 1951, *Athens Review*, June 21, 1951, and *Houston Chronicle*, July 10, Gonzaullas Scrapbook 3, TRHF&M, 294–295; *St. Louis Post-Dispatch*, July 22, 1951, Gonzaullas Scrapbook 4, TRHF&M, 301; *SAE* and *Brownsville Herald*, both dated June 21, 1951; *Abilene Reporter-News*, July 10, 1951; *Corpus Christi Times*, July 11, 1951; *Amarillo Globe-News*, July 29, 1951; *Paris News*, August 2, 1951 (second quotation); Inactive Personnel Record, Manuel T. Gonzaullas, TDPS.
149. *DMN*, June 21, 1951, and *Houston Chronicle*, July 10, 1951, Gonzaullas Scrapbook 3, TRHF&M, 294; *Pampa Daily News*, July 20, 1930; *Abilene Reporter-News*, July 29, 1951.
150. Cox, *Texas Ranger Tales II*, 252; "End of a Texas Ranger," *Newsweek* 38 (August 6, 1951): 54; *DMN*, July 29, 1951, July 13, 1969, February 15, 1977; *El Paso Times*, December 7, 1952; *Fort Worth Press*, December 10, 13, 1952, Gonzaullas Scrapbook 4, TRHF&M, 315; *Denton Record-Chronicle*, July 2, 1967; *Del Rio News-Herald*, July 6, 1969; *Corsicana Daily Sun*, September 8, 1974; Robert Nieman, "The Lone Wolf was Camera Shy," *TRD* 4 (Summer 2001): 36.
151. *FWST*, March 15, 19, 1952.
152. *DMN*, June 22, 1957; *AA*, June 22, 26, 1957; "Lone Wolf Gonzaullas Becomes Vice-President of Atlas Alarm," *Sheriff's Association of Texas Magazine* (February 1954), Gonzaullas Scrapbook 4, TRHF&M, 319.

153. *FWST*, October 16, 1968, and *WNT*, December 11, 13, 16, 1968, Gonzaullas Scrapbook 4, TRHF&M, 347, 337; *DMN*, July 28, 30, 1973, Gonzaullas Scrapbook 5, TRHF&M, 411–412.
154. Death Certificate, Manuel T. Gonzaullas, February 16, 1977, File No. 03844; *Dallas Times-Herald*, February 14, 1977; *DMN*, February 15, 1977; Wilfong to the author, December 10, 2018.
155. *DMN*, May 25, 1963.
156. *DMN*, February 15, 1977.
157. Acts 1977, Regular Session, 65th Legislature, House Concurrent Resolution No. 58, *General and Special Laws of Texas*.
158. Death Certificate, Laura Isabell Gonzaullas, August 18, 1978, State File No. 59719; *DMN*, August 19, 1978; Wilfong to the author, December 10, 2018.
159. *Waco Times-Herald*, March 2, 1980.

Notes for Chapter 6

1. Red Burton, interview with Fred A. Carpenter, Mart, Texas, 1969, Southwest Collection, Texas Tech University Libraries. Hereafter cited as Red Burton interview, 1969. Ben H. Procter, *Just One Riot: Episodes of the Texas Rangers in the 20th Century* (Austin: Eakin Press, 1991), 46; Twelfth U.S. Census, McLennan County, Texas; *Arkansas Gazette*, August 15, 1910; Find a Grave: Mary A. Burton, Luther Milton Burton, Augusta Burton Johnson, Ellen Burton, Ruby Burton Robertson. Red's father died on May 26, 1932, of a coronary occlusion brought on by high blood pressure. Mollie died on July 8, 1943, due to "senility" and "malnutrition." Texas Death Certificates, John F. Burton, June 6, 1932, Registrar's No. 2, Mollie Elizabeth Burton, July 9, 1943, File No. 36.
2. *DMN*, February 6, 1965; Red Burton interview, 1969; Death Certificates, Mrs. Florence Mae Burton, October 25, 1948, File No. 772, Alice Burton, July 8, 1971, File No. 46807; Birth Certificate, Laura Mae Rogers, n.d., File No. 8127.
3. Procter, *Just One Riot*, 46–47; Red Burton interview, 1969; *Riesel Rustler*, May 22, 1970; *DMN*, February 6, 1965.
4. Procter, *Just One Riot*, 47–48; DMN, February 6, 1965; Patricia Bernstein, *The First Waco Horror: The Lynching of Jesse Washington and the Rise of the NAACP* (College Station: Texas A&M University Press, 2005), 110; *Waco Citizen*, May 28, 1970. See also James M.

SoRelle, "The 'Waco Horror': The Lynching of Jesse Washington," *Southern Historical Quarterly* 86 (April 1983).

5. James B. Seymour, Jr., "Evils More Deadly Than the Carnage of the Battlefield: The Fight for Prohibition in McLennan County in 1917," *East Texas Historical Journal* 40 (March 2002): 64; Procter, *Just One Riot*, 48; *Waco Morning News*, June 11, 1918; Sammy Tise, *Texas County Sheriffs* (Albuquerque, NM: Oakwood Printing, 1989), 365.
6. *WNT*, April 1, May 23, June 4, 10, July 6, 10, August 17, September 19, 1920, April 1, 2, 7, 27, 28, May 7, 25, July 9, 16, 20, 22, August 1, 12, September 2, 4, November 19, 26, December 7, 1921, February 4, 5, 11, March 11, May 26, 31, June 29, July 20, 1922; *GDN*, November 5, 1920; Clifford R. Caldwell and Ron DeLord, *Texas Lawmen, 1900–1940: More of the Good and the Bad* (Charleston, SC: History Press, 2012), 131; Find A Grave: James Jefferson Padgett, Sr.
7. *WNT*, April 3, 16, 23, July 5, 20, 25, 27, 1921; Jeanne Bozzell McCarty, *The Struggle for Sobriety: Protestants and Prohibition in Texas: 1919–1935* (El Paso: Texas Western Press, 1980), 7.
8. Find A Grave: John C. Burton, Sr.; *Fourteenth U.S. Census*, Red River County, Texas; *WNT*, August 20, 1921; *Fifteenth U.S. Census*, McLennan County, Texas; *FWST*, November 19, 2006.
9. *WNT*, August 20, 21, 22, 23, 24, 25, 26, 28, 31, 1921; Death Certificate, Leslie Keyes, August 8, 1921, Registrar's No. 23284. William was the informant on Leslie's death certificate. 253 *Southwestern Reporter* (1923) 521-525. An oddity noted during research into this case was that William and Maude's surviving daughter, born in March 1909, was named Dessie. Whether this is a coincidence or an indication of something further insidious on the part of William is unknown.
10. *WNT*, September 23, November 1, 27, December 11, 12, 1921, October 20, 1922, July 1, 1923, April 2, 1925, February 2, 3, 7, 15, 28, March 27, 1926; *GDN*, November 5, 1921; *Daily Courier-Gazette*, November 28, December 16, 1921, October 12, 1922, December 6, 7, 8, 1923, February 23, 1926; *AS*, December 11, 13, 14, 16, 1921; Texas Department of Criminal Justice, Convict Record Ledgers, 1998/038-162, TSLAC, 121.
11. Charles C. Alexander, *The Ku Klux Klan in the Southwest* (Lexington: University of Kentucky Press, 1965), 36–37; Richard H. Fair, "'The Good Angel of Practical Fraternity:' The Ku Klux Klan in

McLennan County, 1915-1924" (M.A. thesis, Baylor University, 2009), 37, 44; Robert Maxwell Brown, *Strain of Violence: Historical Studies of American Violence and Vigilantism* (New York: Oxford University Press, 1975), 284.

12. *DMN*, March 9, 1922. The *Dallas Morning News* publicly opposed the Klan, while the *Waco News-Tribune* adopted a more supporting editorial slant.
13. *WNT*, October 2 (quotation), 3, 1921; *AS* and *AA*, both dated October 3, 1921; *Penal Code of the State of Texas, Regular Session, 32nd Legislature*, 112.
14. Procter, *Just One Riot*, 49-52; Lewis Rigler, interview with Robert Nieman, Gainesville, Texas, July 16, 1994, Oral History Project, TRHF&M, 4; *WNT*, October 2, 3, 4, 11, 16, November 6, 23, 1921, January 20, 21, 1922; *DMN*, January 8, 20, 1922. In an early example of media bias, the *News-Tribune* failed to print statements from the sheriff's office or editorials from citizens supporting Buchanan's actions. More balanced reportage on anti-Klan sentiment in McLennan County was presented by the *Austin Statesman* and *Dallas Morning News*. Fair, "The Ku Klux Klan in McLennan County," 71–72.
15. *WNT*, December 2, 6 (quotation), 7, 1921, January 17, 1922. Bernard Connally was murdered in Erath County four years after his father's death. The case was closed with the assistance of Captain Tom Hickman and Ranger Stewart Stanley. See Ch. 3 for more details.
16. *WNT*, January 5, 13, 1922.
17. *WNT*, January 16, 17, 19, 20, 22, 29, 1922; *DMN*, January 11, 17, 19, 20, 21, 1922; Death Certificate, George Kellough, September 7, 1922, Registrar's No. 1610.
18. *WNT*, February 13, 1922; Ella Marie Farmer, "The Phantom Killer of the Brazos," Pt. 1, *True Detective Mysteries* 23 (November 1934): 56.
19. *WNT*, February 13, 15, 16, 1922; Farmer, "Phantom Killer of the Brazos," Pt. 1: 57–59, 77–78.
20. *FWST* and *Brownwood Bulletin*, both dated February 24, 1922; *WNT*, February 25, 1922; *San Saba News*, March 2, 1922 (quotation).
21. *WNT*, March 9, 10, 11, 23, 24, 1922.
22. *WNT*, March 17, 18, 19, 23, 1922.
23. *WNT*, March 23, 1922; *Wichita Daily Times*, March 23, 1922; *GDN*, May 27, 1922; William D. Carrigan, *The Making of a Lynching Culture: Violence and Vigilantism in Central Texas, 1836–1916* (Urbana:

University of Illinois Press, 2004), 1–2, 189–190; Farmer, "Phantom Killer of the Brazos," Pt. 1: 78.

24. *WNT*, May 5, 1922; *SAE*, May 6, 1922; Monte Akers, *Flames After Midnight: Murder, Vengeance, and the Desolation of a Texas Community* (Austin: University of Texas Press, 1999), 13–14, 36–37, 50.
25. *SAE*, May 6, 7, 1922; Akers, *Flames After Midnight*, 57, 62–63; Clifford R. Caldwell and Ron DeLord, *Eternity at the End of a Rope: Executions, Lynchings, and Vigilante Justice in Texas, 1819–1923* (Santa Fe: Sunstone Press, 2015), 575–576.
26. *WNT*, May 8, 1922.
27. *Mexia Evening News* (quotation) and *Corsicana Daily Sun*, both dated May 8, 1922; *SAE*, May 8, 9, 10, June 3, 4, 1922; Akers, *Flames After Midnight*, 45.
28. *AA*, June 3, 4, 1922; *WNT*, June 3, 1922; Akers, *Flames After Midnight*, 45, 108, 116–121, 159, 161. From May 8 to the twentieth, an additional four black men were lynched at Plantersville, Texarkana, Conroe, and Alleyton for various alleged crimes. *SAE*, May 21, 1922.
29. *WNT*, May 20, 26, 27, 1922; *Corsicana Daily Sun*, May 26, 1922; *GDN*, May 27, 30, 1922; Farmer, "Phantom Killer of the Brazos," Pt. 1: 78; Ella Marie Farmer, "The Phantom Killer of the Brazos," Pt. 2, *True Detective Mysteries* 23 (December 1934): 39–41, 73–74; Clarke Newlon, "Outlaw Tamer of the New West," *Startling Detective Adventures* 13 (November 1934): 35–36; *AS*, May 28, June 4, 1922.
30. M. "Red" Burton, interview with Roger N. Conger, Waco, Texas, May 1, 1956, Marvin Burton Vertical File, TRHF&M, n.p. Cited hereafter as Marvin Burton interview, 1956. Red Burton interview, 1969; RSR, Marvin Burton, 401-53, TSLAC; *WNT*, July 23, September 2, 1922, February 3, 1929; *GDN*, September 30, 1922.
31. *AS*, November 21, 1922; *Corsicana Daily Sun*, November 21, 1922; Ella Marie Farmer, "The Phantom Killer of the Brazos," Pt. 3, *True Detective Mysteries* 23 (January 1935): 39–41, 72–73. Ranger R. D. Shumate believed Boucher and her two brothers had killed Skipworth and arrested the trio on January 12. Taking his prisoners to Dallas, he evaded a *habeas corpus* writ and drew the ire of the issuing judge, resulting in a bench warrant. For a brief candid description of Shumate's investigation, see Charles H. Harris III and Louis R. Sadler, *The Texas Rangers in Transition: From Gunfighters to Criminal Investigators, 1921–1935* (Norman: University of Oklahoma Press, 2019), 158. Former police officer and practicing attorney John Boessenecker

was far less complimentary in *Texas Ranger: The Epic Life of Frank Hamer, the Man Who Killed Bonnie and Clyde* (New York: Thomas Dunne Books, 2016), 269–270.

32. Death Certificate, William Edwin Holt, January 30, 1923, File No. 2517; Farmer, "Phantom Killer of the Brazos," Pt. 1: 77, 79, Pt. 2: 39, 76, Pt. 3: 73–76.
33. *SAE*, March 15, 1923; *WNT*, April 19, 1923, March 10, 1934; 254 *Southwestern Reporter* 804-805 (1924); Farmer, "Phantom Killer of the Brazos," Pt. 3: 76–79. Fresh from his unsuccessful investigation of the Bouchers, Shumate believed Stegall's case was faulty and reported to Barton: "The sheriff's department seems to be altogether wedded to the theory that a negro is bound to have committed all of these murders and nobody but a negro seems to satisfy them." Shumate to Barton, January 31, 1923, 401-595, TSLAC. Aldrich replied, "The General has received your report on the Skipworth matter. We think you are right in your view of the murder. Don't believe it is a [Negro] job." Aldrich to Shumate, February 2, 1923, 401–595, TSLAC. Mitchell's family remained convinced he had been framed for the crimes with planted evidence. *Waco Tribune-Herald*, April 23, 1978.
34. Red Burton interview, 1969; *WNT*, March 9, April 8, 18, 1923; *Paducah Post*, March 8, May 10, August 2, 23, 1923; *AA*, November 12, 1922. In the midst of the quarrel, Sneed had murdered Colonel Albert Gallatian Boyce, Sr, former general manager of the XIT Ranch and kin to ex-Ranger Ira Aten's wife. For more on the affray, see Bill Neal, *Vengeance Is Mine: The Scandalous Love Triangle That Triggered the Boyce-Sneed Feud* (Denton: University of North Texas Press, 2011).
35. Seymour, "Evils More Deadly," 59; Pat M. Neff, *The Battles of Peace* (Fort Worth, TX: Pioneer Publishing Company, 1925), 90 (quotation); *AA*, February 16, 1921; *WNT*, July 9, 1921.
36. Marvin Burton, "The Story of the Glen Rose Liquor War in 1923," MS26, Series 1, Red Burton Collection, TRHF&M, 1.
37. Red Burton interview, 1969; McCauley to Aldrich, August 9, 1923, 401–599, TSLAC; Robert M. Utley, *Lone Star Lawmen: The Second Century of the Texas Rangers* (New York: Berkley Books, 2007), 104; James Randolph Ward, "The Texas Rangers, 1919–1935: A Study in Law Enforcement" (Ph.D. dissertation, Texas Christian University, 1972), 103.
38. *WNT*, July 22, 25, 31, August 2, 1923; Martin Brown, *The Glen Rose Moonshine Raid* (Charleston, SC: History Press, 2017), 46–47.

39. Burton, "Glen Rose Liquor War," 3–6; McCauley to Aldrich, August 6, 9, 13, 16, 1923, Aldrich to McCauley, August 13 (letter and telegram), 17, 24, 1923, 401-599, TSLAC; *AS*, August 26, 1923; Aldrich to Nichols, August 27, 1923, Tape 5.2, James R. Ward Collection, ASU; *WNT*, August 31, 1923, February 3, 1929; RSR, R. D. Shumate, 401-63, TSLAC. Writing in his unpublished manuscript, Burton noted that Shumate often purposefully identified himself to the press as a captain. He had served as an "acting captain" during the 1922 railroad strike but never with the permanent rank. While praising the Ranger as a good friend and an excellent officer, Burton disapproved of Shumate's misleading claims to the newspapers.
40. Burton, "Glen Rose Liquor War," 6; Neff, *Battles of Peace*, 140; *WNT*, August 2, 26, 27, 30, 31, 1923; *AS*, August 27, 28, 1923; *Brownwood Bulletin*, August 27, 1923; *AA*, August 29, 1923; *GDN*, September 1, 1923; Brown, *Glen Rose Moonshine Raid*, 59; Death Certificates, William Washington Wright, n.d., File No. 52922, Joe David Crawford, September 23, 1941, File No. 42486, Alonzo Tullis Holt, September 4, 1923, File No. 25157; *Fourteenth U.S. Census*, Bosque County, Texas. Bill Glass was convicted of murder with malice in January 1942 and served four years in Huntsville. Texas Department of Criminal Justice, Convict Record Ledgers, 1998/038-170, TSLAC, n.p.
41. *SAE*, September 4 (quotation), 1923.
42. William Warren Sterling, *Trails and Trials of a Texas Ranger* (Norman: University of Oklahoma Press, 1968), 225; Friend to Barton, December 27, 1922, 401-594, Tirey to Neff, February 6, 1923, Neff to Tirey, February 8, 1923, -595, Aldrich to Shumate, September 20, 1923, -599, October 1, 1923, -600, TSLAC; Affidavit of J. D. Willis, July 31, 1923, Folder 57, Aldrich Papers, SRSU (quotation); RSR, M. Burton, 401–53, TSLAC.
43. Cleveland to Federal Judge, November 19, 1923, Hutt to Barton, November 14, 1923, Shumate to Barton, November 22, 1923, Hutt to Shumate, November 22, 1923, West to Barton, November 24, 1923, Barton to West, November 30, 1923, Barton to Burton, November 30, 1923 (quotation), 401-600, TSLAC; *DMN*, May 13, 1948; Find a Grave: John Frederick "Fred" Cleveland, Jr.
44. *Brownwood Bulletin*, November 15, 1923; *GDN*, November 18, 1923; *FWST*, December 11, 1923; Burton to Aldrich, December 25, 1923, Aldrich to Burton, December 26, 1923, 401-601, TSLAC; *WNT*, January 3, 1924.

45. James R. Ward, "Establishing Law and Order in the Oilfields: The 1924 Ranger Raids in Navarro County, Texas," *Texana* 8 (1970), 38–40.
46. Marvin Burton interview, 1956; *Corsicana Daily Sun*, February 8, 9, 11, 1924; Ward, "Establishing Law and Order," 40–44; *WNT*, February 9, 10, 11, 1924; *DMN*, February 10, 1924.
47. Ward, "Establishing Law and Order," 44; *Corsicana Daily Sun*, March 1, April 8, 17, May 7, 1924; Texas Department of Criminal Justice, Convict Record Ledgers, 1998/038-161, TSLAC, 204. Expanding on Burton's coordinated campaign, county and city law officers kept the remnants of the bootlegging ring from regaining their former stature. *Corsicana Daily Sun*, May 9, 29, 1924.
48. *SAE*, February 20, 22, 1924; *WNT*, February 17, 21, 1924, February 3, 1929 (quotation).
49. Shumate to Aldrich, February 22, 1924, Aldrich to Shumate, February 26, 1924, 401–601, TSLAC; *WNT*, February 22, 1924; *GDN*, February 22, 23, 24, 27, 1924; *Brownwood Bulletin*, February 22, March 1, 1924; *Corsicana Daily Sun*, February 22, 23, 29, 1924; *AS*, February 22, 23, 24, 1924; *Denton Record-Chronicle*, February 22, 1924; *SAE*, February 23, April 30, 1924; *Mexia Daily News*, February 25, 1924; *FWST*, March 1, 1924; *Clifton Record*, March 7, May 2, 1924. In the years since his death, Watson has been identified as a Corsicana police officer. According to Acting Police Chief Allen Calloway, the deceased was never on the city's payroll.
50. *Clifton Record*, May 2, 1924; *WNT*, June 4, 1924; *Odessa American*, September 19, 1955. For more on House's argument, see Robert E. House, "The Use of Scopolamine in Criminology," *The American Journal of Police Science* 2 (July–August 1931): 328–336. By the 1930s, the drug was replaced in scientific studies by sodium amytal or sodium pentothal.
51. *WNT*, March 17, 19, 1924.
52. *WNT*, April 21, 1923; *Morrison and Fourmy's Waco City Directory, 1921–1922* (Houston: Morrison & Fourmy's Directory Co., 1922), 539.
53. *WNT*, June 2, 1924, January 5, April 2, 1926; *Daily News Telegram*, June 3, 1924; *Lockhart Register*, June 5, 1924; *Victoria Advocate*, June 6, 1924; *Clifton Record*, June 6, October 3, 1924.
54. RSR, M. Burton, 401-53, TSLAC.
55. *Corsicana Daily Sun*, September 12, 1924.
56. *SAE* and *Mexia Daily News*, both dated September 9, 1924.

57. *WNT*, June 27, October 5, November 3, 4, 5, 15, December 14, 1925, March 18, 1926, July 23, September 16, November 9, 1927, November 17, December 22, 1928.
58. *WNT*, January 31, February 4, 25, March 7, May 23, July 15, 1926.
59. *WNT*, April 2, 1926; *FWST*, April 9, 1926.
60. *WNT*, July 18, 20, 21, 24, 26, August 8, 31, 1926; Tise, *Texas County Sheriffs*, 366.
61. *WNT*, July 1, 1927.
62. *WNT* and *AS*, both dated November 8, 1927; *Fort Worth Record-Telegram*, November 9, 1927; *San Saba News*, August 12, 1948; *FWST*, January 27, 1948.
63. *WNT*, April 12, May 12, June 18, 1928.
64. *WNT*, April 21, July 27, 28, 29, 1928; Tise, *Texas County Sheriffs*, 366.
65. Red Burton interview, 1969; Marvin Burton, "The Johnny Holmes Murder Case," MS26, Series 1, Red Burton Collection, TRHF&M, 1–2; *WNT*, March 2, 15, June 11, 1929; Moody to Burton, April 8, 1927, Burton to Moody, April 9, 1927, Box 2007/170-52, Daniel J. Moody Papers, TSLAC; RSR, Marvin Burton, 401–53.
66. *AS*, September 14, 15, 26, 27, 1929; Utley, *Lone Star Lawmen*, 130, 132; Jacob F. Wolters, *Martial Law and Its Administration* (Austin: Gammel's Book Store, 1930), 17, 118; Red Burton interview, 1969 (second and third quotation); *DMN*, September 21, 1929 (first quotation); Hickman to Robertson, October 26, 1929, Gault report, November 3, 1929, Tape 11.2, Ward Collection, ASU; *Corsicana Daily Sun*, October 16, 17, 1929; *Lubbock Morning Avalanche*, October 17, 1929; *WNT*, October 19, 1929; *Borger Daily News*, December 14, 1928.
67. *Denton Record-Chronicle*, November 5, 1929; *SAE*, November 6, 1929; Jerry Sinise, *Black Gold and Red Lights* (Austin, TX: Eakin Press, 1982), 86; *Daily Oklahoman*, September 2, 1933. On March 11, 1923, Thompson was released from McAlester so he could work as an informant for the federal investigation into the Osage Indian homicides. Appallingly, while Thompson did provide evidence to the prosecution, he also robbed the First State Bank of Avery and killed Drumright policeman Ulysses Sterling Lenox on July 2, 1924. For more on the thief and the federal agents in Osage County, Oklahoma, see David Grann, *Killers of the Flower Moon: The Osage Murders and the Birth of the FBI* (New York: Doubleday, 2017).
68. Burton, "Johnny Holmes Murder Case," 6–13; Marvin Burton interview, 1956; Red Burton interview, 1969; Hutchinson County

Historical Commission, *History of Hutchinson County, Texas: 104 Years, 1876–1980* (Dallas: Taylor Publishing Company, 1980), 25; Sinise, *Black Gold and Red Lights*, 135–136; Bartee Haile, *Texas Boomtowns: A History of Blood and Oil* (Charleston, SC: History Press, 2015), 94; Utley, *Lone Star Lawmen*, 133; *AS*, November 3, 4, 1929; *GDN*, November 4, 23, 30, 1929; *SAE*, November 18, 22, 1929; *FWST*, November 20, 21, 22, 23, 24, 25, 26, 1929; *Denton Record-Chronicle*, November 21, 22, 23, 1929.

69. Red Burton interview, 1969; *Amarillo Globe*, November 22, 25, 1929; *GDN*, November 23, 27, 1929; *El Paso Herald*, November 23, 1929; *Lubbock Morning Avalanche*, November 27, 30, 1929, January 14 (quotation), 1930; Find A Grave: Tarance Andrew "Lorrance" Popejoy. Tarance's older brother was John W. "Shine" Popejoy, a notorious Borger hoodlum. Ironically, the elder Popejoy was arrested for robbing the Stinnett bank on March 15, 1932. He was killed while attempting to escape the Hutchinson County jail on January 16, 1933. *FWST*, March 16, 1932, January 16, 1933.
70. Red Burton interview, 1969; *Amarillo Globe*, January 13, 14, 15, 29, December 9, 12, 1930; *Lubbock Morning Avalanche*, January 14, 16, 1930; *Pampa Daily News*, January 13, 16, December 8, 10, 1930; Texas Department of Criminal Justice, Convict Record Ledgers, 1998/038-164, TSLAC, 75; *FWST*, February 19, 1931.
71. *Pampa Daily News*, April 2, May 20, 1930; *Lubbock Morning Avalanche*, April 4, 1930; *GDN*, April 5, 1930; *Denton Record-Chronicle*, May 15, 1930; *Corsicana Daily Sun*, May 15, 1930; Burton, "Johnny Holmes Murder Case," 14–18 (quotation on p. 18). On October 26, 1945, District Attorney William Lewis McConnell filed a motion to dismiss Jones's murder indictment "because in the opinion of the State's Attorney, the evidence is insufficient to warrant the probability of a conviction." Eighty-fourth District Court Judge Jack Rice Allen approved the request. Sinise, *Black Gold and Red Lights*, 140.
72. *Abilene Morning News*, February 6, 1930; RSR, Marvin Burton, 401-53, TSLAC; Burton to Aldrich, March 10, 1930, folder 15, Roy W. Aldrich Papers, SRSU; *Fifteenth U.S. Census*, McLennan County, Texas; *Amarillo Daily Globe*, June 25, 1930; *Pampa Daily News*, June 24, 25, 26, July 9, 1930; Utley, *Lone Star Lawmen*, 130, 132; Norman Crockett, "Crime on the Petroleum Frontier: Borger, Texas, in the Late 1920s," *Panhandle-Plains Historical Review* 64 (1991): 60–61.
73. Marvin Burton interview, 1956; *GDN*, June 24, 1930.

74. Marvin Burton interview, 1956; Red Burton interview, 1969; *Amarillo Globe-Times*, July 28, 1930; *Iola Daily Register*, July 28, 1930; *Miami Daily News-Record*, July 28, 1930; *Lubbock Morning Avalanche*, July 29, 1930; *SAE*, July 29, 1930.
75. Marvin Burton interview, 1956; Red Burton interview, 1969; *Amarillo Globe-Times*, July 28, 1930; *SAE*, July 29, 1930.
76. Marvin Burton interview, 1956; Red Burton interview, 1969; *Miami Daily News-Record*, July 25, 1930; *Iola Daily Register*, July 28, 1930; *SAE*, July 29, 1930; *Lubbock Morning Avalanche*, July 29, 1930.
77. Marvin Burton interview, 1956; *Miami Daily News-Record*, July 28, October 15, 16, 1930; *Iola Daily Register*, July 29, 31, August 1, September 20, October 15, 16, 18, 1930, January 7, 8, 1931; Rod Beemer, *Notorious Kansas Bank Heists: Gunslingers to Gangsters* (Charleston, SC: History Press, 2015), 12–13 (quotation on p. 13); *Corsicana Daily Sun*, October 15, 16, 1930; *Lubbock Morning Avalanche*, October 16, 1930; Daniel D. Holt, comp., "Law Enforcement Officers Who Have Died in the Line of Duty," *Kansas History* 10 (Summer 1987): 150.
78. *Abilene Morning News*, August 8, 1930; *GDN*, August 22, 1930; *Lubbock Morning Avalanche*, August 30, 1930.
79. *Pampa Daily News*, August 24, November 5, 1930.
80. RSR, M. Burton, 401-70, TSLAC; Marvin Burton, "The Kilgore Raid, 1931," MS26, Section 1, Red Burton Collection, TRHF&M, 1; *SAE*, February 15, 1931; Tise, *Texas County Sheriffs*, 333.
81. RSR, Marvin Burton, 401-53, TSLAC; Hickman to Sterling, March 7, 1931, Gonzaullas to Hickman, February 8, 1931, Tape 10.2, Ward Collection, ASU; Burton, "The Kilgore Raid," 1–2, 4; John Anthony Clark, *The Last Boom* (New York: Random House, 1972), 137; *SAE*, February 15, March 2, 4, 1931; *DMN*, March 3, 1931; *Corpus Christi Times*, March 4, 1931 (quotation); *Corsicana Daily Sun*, March 4, 19, 1931; *Mexia Weekly Herald*, March 8, 1931; Ruel McDaniel, *Some Ran Hot* (Dallas, TX: Regional Press, 1939), 155–156.
82. Gonzaullas to Hickman, February 15, 21 (quotation), March 22, 31, July 12, 1931, Tape 10.2, Ward Collection, ASU; Burton, "The Kilgore Raid," 3.
83. Burton, "The Kilgore Raid," 5; Gonzaullas to Hickman, March 8, 31, April 5, 1931, Tape 10.2, Ward Collection, ASU.
84. RSR, Marvin Burton, 401-53, TSLAC; Burton, "The Kilgore Raid," 5; Burton to Hickman, June 14, 1931, Kirby to Hickman, July 13, 1931,

Burton to Hickman, August ?, 23, 1931, Tape 10.2, Ward Collection, ASU; *Kilgore Daily News*, July 31, 1931.

85. *Longview Daily News*, September 2, 1931; *Tyler Morning Telegraph*, October 11, 1932; Death Certificate, W. E. Russell, August 30, 1931, Registrar's No. 38422.
86. *Longview Daily News*, September 21, 1931; *AS*, October 23, 1931; *FWST*, October 25, November 9, 1931; *Tyler Morning Telegraph*, October 30, 1931; *WNT*, August 30, 1946.
87. *AA*, December 22, 1931, October 20, 1932; *FWST*, December 22, 1931, May 25, 1932; *Tyler Morning Telegraph*, October 11 (quotation), 19, 1932.
88. *FWST*, June 23, 24, 25, 1932; *Corsicana Daily Sun*, June 25, 1932; *AA*, August 17, 1932; *Tyler Morning Telegraph*, August 10, October 19, 1932.
89. *Tyler Morning Telegraph*, October 11, 1932; *Tyler Courier-Times*, October 16, 1932; *DMN*, August 24, October 18, 1932; Hickman to Sterling, October 15, 18, 1932, Tape 10.2, Ward Collection, ASU. Campbell served as an FBI agent from 1934 to 1965 and was a member of the team that brought down John Dillinger. *Los Angeles Times*, January 3, 1991. Oglesby had four living brothers at the time of his death. Which one of them was nicknamed "Curley" remains unclear.
90. *Tyler Morning Telegraph*, October 11, 28, 1932, April 6, 1933; *Tyler Courier-Times*, October 16, 1932; Texas Department of Criminal Justice, Convict Record Ledgers, 1998/038-165, TSLAC, 275.
91. *WNT*, October 25, 28 (quotation), November 16, December 25, 1932; *Tyler Morning Telegraph*, November 19, December 1, 13, 1932; DMN, May 23, 1950.
92. RSR, Marvin Burton, 401-53, TSLAC; *WNT*, January 22, April 2, 1933.
93. *WNT*, January 27, February 1, 1933; *Corsicana Daily Sun*, January 27, 1933. One of J. Edgar Hoover's "hired guns," William Buchanan served as an FBI special agent from September 1934 to his death in July 1947. *WNT*, July 16, 1947.
94. *Waxahachie Daily Light*, March 4, 1933 (first quotation), January 19, 1971; *FWST*, April 9, 1933; AS, October 25, 1933; *Waco Tribune-Herald*, July 9, 1933 (second quotation); Find A Grave: Harry Thomas Odneal, Albert "Bert" Whisnand, Cayce Bonds Shelton.
95. Charles B. Mahaffey, "A Segment of Law Enforcement," unpublished MS, n.d., Archives Files, FTRA; RSR, M. Burton, 401–70, TSLAC.

96. RSR, M. Burton, 401–70, TSLAC; *WNT*, May 27, 28, 1934; *Mexia Daily News*, May 24, 1950.
97. *Waco Tribune-Herald*, September 9, 1934.
98. *Dallas Evening News*, February 6, 1965; *Sixteenth U.S. Census*, McLennan County, Texas; *WNT*, June 6, 24, November 23, 28, December 18, 21, 29 (quotation), 1934, January 1, 1947.
99. *WNT*, December 9, January 21, April 5, 9, June 12, September 17, October 11, December 4, 6, 13, 1935.
100. *WNT*, March 1, 1936.
101. *WNT*, February 16, 1937.
102. *WNT*, July 23, 1937.
103. *WNT*, May 10, 1938 (quotation).
104. *WNT*, June 20, 23, 1946.
105. *WNT*, July 18, 19, 1946.
106. *WNT*, July 18, 21, August 8, September 28, October 2, 16, December 5, 23, 31, 1946, January 1, 8, 1947.
107. *WNT*, January 12, 14, 25, February 1, 21, May 8, 1947.
108. *WNT*, November 23, 1946.
109. *WNT*, January 20, 21, 1947.
110. *WNT*, February 8, 22, 1947.
111. *DMN*, February 14, 1947; *WNT*, February 20, 22, March 13, 25, 1947; *Dallas Times-Herald*, February 14, 15, March 12, 1947, Gonzaullas Scrapbook 3, TRHF&M, 264, 266.
112. *WNT*, February 1, 2, 9, 11, 20, 1947.
113. *WNT*, February 16, March 2, 4, 5, 1947.
114. *WNT*, March 25, 27, April 2, 1947.
115. Death Certificate, Florence Mae Burton, October 25, 1948, File No. 772.
116. *Waco News-Citizen*, August 30, 1960; *WNT*, February 1, 1951; July 29, 1948; *Waco Times Herald*, June 6, 1951; *Dallas Evening News*, February 6, 1965; *Waco Citizen*, May 21, 1970; Death Certificate, Jesse Virgil Gunterman, September 14, 1968, File No. 71600.
117. *WNT*, January 4, 1951; *Record of Appointment of Postmasters, 1832–1971*, M841, RG 28, NARA; *Fifteenth and Sixteenth U.S. Census*, McLennan County, Texas; Leon County Marriage Records, Book H: 300; Anderson County Marriage Records, 33: 151A.
118. *Waco Citizen*, August 22, 1958; *Riesel Rustler*, May 22, 1970.
119. Death Certificate, Marvin Burton, May 20, 1970, File No. 33695; *Waco Tribune-Herald*, May 17, 1970, Gonzaullas Scrapbook 4, TRHF&M, 381.

120. *Waco News-Citizen*, May 5, 1959; *Waco Citizen*, April 2, 1976, June 14, 1977, April 17, 1979; *Riesel Rustler*, October 7, 1988.
121. *Fifteenth U.S. Census*, Hutchinson County, Texas; Birth Certificate, Eunice Howard Burton, April 25, 1931, Registrar's No. 30640; *Sixteenth U.S. Census*, McLennan County, Texas; *WNT*, December 5, 8, 1935; *Waco Tribune-Herald*, April 25, 1974; Death Certificate, Alice Burton, July 8, 1971, File No. 46807.
122. *Waco Tribune-Herald*, January 8, 1995; McLennan County Marriage Records 16, 498A; *Fifteenth U.S. Census*, McLennan County, Texas; *Sixteenth U.S. Census*, Dallas County, Texas; Death Certificate, James Shearer Rogers, July 14, 1976, File No. 51286.
123. *FWST*, November 19, 2006.

Notes for Chapter 7

1. Death Certificates, Robert A Crowder, November 29, 1972, File No. 89850, Morris Gould Crowder, June 4, 1932, Registrar's No. 23, Walter H. Crowder, August 3, 1934, Registrar's No. 32359; Texas County Marriage Index, 1837–1977; *Ninth U.S. Census*, Tippah County, Mississippi. Bob Crowder has been described by several people as a quiet man who never talked, much less bragged, about himself. For whatever reason, he was also reticent in sharing much of his personal history with family members.
2. Ben H. Procter, *Just One Riot: Episodes of the Texas Rangers in the 20th Century* (Austin: Eakin Press, 1991), 85. Procter interviewed Crowder in Dallas in February and October of 1969 where he was apparently more forthcoming. Robert Nieman, "20th Century Shining Star: Capt. Bob Crowder," *TRD* 14 (Summer 2004): 12; Panola County Marriage Record Book H, 368; *Panola Watchman*, December 12, 1906; Death Certificate, Don Doyle Crowder, March 4, 1942, Registrar's No. 9590; *Thirteenth U.S. Census*, Rusk County, Texas. The 1910 census listed Sarah as a window, which was often a genteel practice of referring to divorced women. *Thirteenth U.S. Census*, Panola County, Texas. She died on February 27, 1965, in New London of arteriosclerotic heart disease and congestive heart failure. Death Certificate, Sarah Lorene Brown, March 2, 1965, File No. 19074.
3. Procter, *Just One Riot*, 85–86; Pribble to Wilson, March 30, 1982, Crowder Vertical File, TRHF&M.
4. Procter, *Just One Riot*, 86.

5. Robert A. Crowder, Military Personnel File, RG 127, NARA.
6. Marine Corps Muster Roll, October 1–31, 1921, RG 127, NARA, 125, 131; Ed and Catherine Gilbert, *U.S. Marine in World War I* (London: Osprey Publishing, 2016), 14; Procter, *Just One Riot*, 87–88.
7. Marine Corps Muster Roll, November 1–30, November 9–30, 1921.
8. Robert W. Tallent, "The Great Mail Call," *Leatherneck* 38 (February 1955): 45.
9. George Corney, "Crime and Postal History: Bring in the Marines!" *Marine Corps Gazette* 77 (October 1993): 50.
10. Marine Corps Muster Roll, November 9–30, 1921; November 1–30, 1921; *Navy Directory, 1923*, 221.
11. Marine Corps Muster Roll, June 1–30, December 1–31, 1922, January 1–31, 1923; Jeff Phister, et al., *Battleship Oklahoma BB-37* (Norman: University of Oklahoma Press, 2008), 175.
12. Marine Corps Muster Roll, April 1–30, 1923; Crowder, Military Personnel File, NARA; Marine Corps Muster Roll, May 1–31, 1923.
13. Marine Corps Muster Roll, June 1–30, July 1–31, August 1–31, 1923; Crowder, Military Personnel File, NARA.
14. Marine Corps Muster Roll, October 1–31, December 1–31, 1923; January 1–31, 1924; Phister, et al., *Battleship Oklahoma*, 175.
15. Marine Corps Muster Roll, April 1–30, 1924.
16. Marine Corps Muster Roll, June 1–30, 1924.
17. Marine Corps Muster Roll, July 1–31, August 1–31, 1924.
18. Crowder, Military Personnel File, NARA.
19. Procter, *Just One Riot*, 89–90; *DMN*, July 26, 1925, July 7, 1926; Carlton Stowers, *Partners in Blue: The History of the Dallas Police Department* (Dallas, TX: Taylor Publishing Company, 1983), 64; Lewis C. Rigler and Judyth W. Rigler, *In the Line of Duty: Reflections of a Texas Ranger Private* (Denton: University of North Texas Press, 1995), 153.
20. Catherine McGuire, telephone interview with the author, April 18, 2013. Cited hereafter as Catherine McGuire interview, 2013. Birth Certificate, Marcoline Harriet Sturgis, September 8, 1920, Registrar's No. 2191. While living in Arkansas, Lucile had married James Henry Sturgis, a Detroit-born mechanic and veteran of the First World War. The date of their divorce is undetermined. Carol Rodat interview, telephone interview with the author, April 27, 2013. Hereafter cited as Carol Rodat interview, 2013. *DMN*, March 11, 1928; *Fifteenth U.S. Census*, Bowie County, Texas; *Sixteenth U.S. Census*, Dallas County.

The relevant adoption records remain sealed, and the surviving family members have no knowledge of the exact date.

21. Procter, *Just One Riot*, 90–93; Roster of students, 1st Recruit Training School, TDPS Training Academy Records, Box 2005/128-1, TSLAC; Acts 1929, 2nd Called Session, 41st Legislature, Ch, 42, Acts 1931, Regular Session, 42nd Legislature, Ch. 164, Acts 1935, Regular Session, 44th Legislature, Ch. 181, *General and Special Laws of Texas*; James W. Robinson, *The DPS Story: History of the Development of the Department of Public Safety in Texas* (Austin: Texas Department of Public Safety, 1975), 6; *DPS Annual Report, August 10, 1935–December 1, 1936*, 5; Inactive Personnel Record, Robert A. Crowder, TDPS; *DMN*, March 1, 5, 1930; *Fifteenth U.S. Census*, Bowie County, Texas.
22. *DMN*, September 30, 1956, Gonzaullas Scrapbook 4, TRHF&M, 366; *AS*, February 24, 1934; *DMN*, January 7, 8, 1936; *FWST*, January 24, 1936; Texas Department of Criminal Justice, Convict Record Ledgers, 1998/038-167, TSLAC, 121–122. Phares was himself dismissed on July 1, 1938. In a newspaper interview, he alleged Governor Allred had repeatedly interfered in departmental affairs and stripped Phares of his authority "bit by bit." *SAL*, July 3, 1938.
23. Procter, *Just One Riot*, 93; *Corpus Christi Times*, April 28, 1938; Kemp Dixon, *Chasing Thugs, Nazis, and Reds: Texas Ranger Norman K. Dixon* (College Station: Texas A&M University Press, 2015), 31–35; Thomas Lee Charlton, "The Texas Department of Public Safety, 1935–1957" (M.A. thesis, University of Texas at Austin, 1961), 86; Inactive Personnel Record, Robert A. Crowder, TDPS; *Lubbock Avalanche-Journal*, May 15, 1938; *AS*, May 27, 1938.
24. Inactive Personnel Record, Robert A. Crowder, TDPS; *DMN*, September 2, 1939; *Sixteenth U.S. Census*, Dallas County, Texas.
25. Procter, *Just One Riot*, 94.
26. Charlton, "The Texas Department of Public Safety," 114; Robinson, *The DPS Story*, 21.
27. *DPS Biennial Report, 1947–1948*, 8, 17.
28. Inactive Personnel Record, Robert A. Crowder, TDPS; *Big Spring Daily Herald*, December 10, 1947; *DMN*, December 11, 1947; *Houston Chronicle*, February 9, 1969. Gault died on December 4 of heart disease. Garrison praised the late captain: "Gault was, above all things, a loyal officer. He was cool headed and didn't know the meaning of fear. He was typical of the Ranger service and a credit to the service." *Lubbock Morning Avalanche*, December 5, 1947.

29. Carol Rodat interview, 2013; James T. Crowder, Jr., telephone interview with the author, January 26, 2013. Cited hereafter as James Crowder interview, 2013.
30. *Abilene Reporter-News*, June 23, 1948.
31. *Amarillo Globe*, August 4, 5, 6, 1948; *Lubbock Evening Journal*, August 5, 12, 13, 18, 1948; Find A Grave: Sidney Andrew Miller.
32. *FWST*, October 2, 1948, August 8, 1951.
33. *Lubbock Morning Avalanche*, October 23, 1948; *Lubbock Evening Journal*, December 1, 1948.
34. "Investigation into the Activities of Mickey Cohen in Texas," Folder 8, Box 1, Texas Crime Investigating Committee Records, Southwest Collection, Texas Tech, 1–5; *Wichita Falls Record-News*, *Lubbock Morning Avalanche* and *El Paso Herald-Post*, all dated August 31, 1950; *Amarillo Daily News* and *Lubbock Evening Journal*, both dated September 1, 1950; *DMN*, August 3, 1950, Gonzaullas Scrapbook 3, TRHF&M, 293; Tere Tereba, *Mickey Cohen: The Life and Crimes of L.A.'s Notorious Mobster* (Toronto: ECW Press, 2012), 151.
35. *El Paso Times*, March 22, 1951; *Final Report*, Folder 6, Box 1, Texas Crime Investigating Committee Records, Texas Tech, v-vi; *Vernon Daily Record*, December 30, 1965. Husband of *Los Angeles Mirror* gossip columnist Florabel Muir, Morrison was labeled Cohen's "publicity agent" in newspaper reports.
36. Cox, *Time of the Rangers*, 222; *DMN*, July 7 (first quotation), 12, 13 (second quotation), 1951; *GDN*, July 10, 1951. Raymond Waters succeeded Crowder as captain of Company C.
37. Cox, *Time of the Rangers*, 222; *DMN*, July 24, 25, 1951; Susie Mills, *Legend in Bronze: A Biography of Jay Banks* (Dallas: Ussery Printing Company, 1982), 180.
38. *DMN*, July 25 (quotation), 1951; Linda Jay Puckett, *Cast a Long Shadow: A Casebook of the Law Enforcement Career of Texas Ranger Captain E. J. (Jay) Banks* (Dallas: Ussery Printing Company, 1984), 60.
39. Cox, *Time of the Rangers*, 222–223; *DMN*, July 24, 25, August 9, 11, 14, 16, 18, 31, September 9, 23, December 9, 1951; Find A Grave: Charles Otho Goff.
40. *DMN*, *FWST*, and *AA*, all dated August 8, 1951; "The 11th Attempt to Kill Herb Noble," *Life* 31 (August 20, 1951): 40; Rigler and Rigler, *In the Line of Duty*, 121; Gary W. Sleeper, *I'll Do My Own Damn Killin': Benny Binion, Herbert Noble, and the Texas Gambling War* (Fort Lee,

NJ: Barricade Books, 2006), 164; Gary Cartwright, "Benny and the Boys," *Texas Monthly* 19 (October 1991): 193; *Final Report*, Folder 6, Box 1, Texas Crime Investigating Committee Records, Texas Tech, vii.

41. *DMN*, August 10, 11, 12, 27, November 7, 1951, April 25, 26, 27, May 3, 1952; *FWST*, August 9, 1951; Sleeper, *I'll Do My Own Damn Killin'*, 209, 235–243. During the sweep of early 1952, numerous suspects were subjected to the notorious "East Texas Merry-Go-Round."
42. "Texas Dukedom," 33–34; *Corpus Christi Times*, February 23, 1954; *New York Times*, February 4, 6, 1954; John E. Clark, *The Fall of the Duke of Duval: A Prosecutor's Journal* (Austin: Eakin Press, 1999), 71.
43. *Corpus Christi Times*, January 18, 21, 23, 24, February 23, 1954; *GDN*, January 24, 1954; Joe H. Bridge, Jr., *The Life and Times of Joe H. Bridge: Texas Ranger, 1936–1956* (s. l.: Joe H. Bridge, 2003), 80–81; John E. Clark, "Reflections on the Duke of Duval: The Litigation Record," *South Texas Studies* 8 (1997): 38; Find A Grave: Charles Woodrow Laughlin.
44. *Corpus Christi Times*, February 23, 1954; Bridge, *Life and Times of Joe H. Bridge*, 81; *New York Times*, February 10, 17, March 4, 30, April 21 (quotation), 1954.
45. Procter, *Just One Riot*, 96–97; *Rusk Cherokeean*, April 21, 1955, January 9, 1975; Cox, *Time of the Rangers*, 230; *DMN*, April 17, 1955.
46. Procter, *Just One Riot*, 97–98; *Rusk Cherokeean*, April 21, 1955 (second quotation), January 9, 1975; *DMN*, April 17, 1955; *Salina Journal*, April 18, 1955 (first quotation).
47. Procter, *Just One Riot*, 98–99; *Rusk Cherokeean*, January 9, 1975; Bob Alexander and Donaly E. Brice, *Texas Rangers: Lives, Legend, and Legacy* (Denton: University of North Texas Press, 2017), 370 (quotation).
48. Procter, *Just One Riot*, 100; *Rusk Cherokeean*, January 9, 1975; Cox, *Time of the Rangers*, 230–232.
49. Jim Ray, interview with Robert Neiman, Bullard, Texas, October 18, 1997, Oral History Project, TRHF&M, 33. Cited hereafter as Jim Ray interview, 1997.
50. *Houston Chronicle*, February 9, 1969.
51. *Houston Chronicle*, February 9, 1969.
52. Kaylie Simon, "Lost Life, a Miscarriage of Justice: The Death of John Earl Reese," Northeastern University: Civil Rights and Restorative Justice Project, MS, 3, 4–6; *Longview Daily News*, January 26, 1956; "Bad Day in Longview," *Time Magazine* 69 (May 6, 1957): 29.

53. Death Certificate, John Earl Reese, October 25, 1955, File No. 49373.
54. Simon, "Lost Life," 9–12; *Longview Daily News*, January 26 (both quotations), 27, 29, February 2, 3, 1956, April 24, September 6, 1957; "Bad Day in Longview," 29.
55. James T. Patterson, *Brown v. Board of Education: A Civil Rights Milestone and Its Troubling Legacy* (New York: Oxford University Press, 2001), 65–69, 83–85 (second quotation on p. 84), 89; *Manhattan Mercury*, May 17, 1954 (first quotation); *AS*, May 17, 1954. In overturning *Plessy* and *de jure* racial discrimination in public schools, the Supreme Court's decision provided legal precedent for the Civil Rights Act of 1964, the Voting Rights Act of 1965, and the Fair Housing Act of 1968. Charles J. Ogletree, Jr., *All Deliberate Speed: Reflections on the First Half-Century of Brown v. Board of Education* (New York: W. W. Norton & Company, 2004), 131–132, 139, 141, 230.
56. Randolph B. Campbell, *Gone to Texas: A History of the Lone Star State* (New York: Oxford University Press, 2003), 427; L. Clifford Davis, interview with Callie Millier, Fort Worth, Texas, April 11, 2014, Oral History Collection 1818, University of North Texas, 31–33, 34; Charles Waite, "Price Daniel, Texas Democrats, and School Segregation, 1956–1957," *East Texas Historical Journal* 48 (Fall 2010): 110–111; Robyn Duff Ladino, *Desegregating Texas Schools: Eisenhower, Shivers, and the Crisis at Mansfield High* (Austin: University of Texas Press, 1996), 77–78, 105; Anna Victoria Wilson and William E. Segall, *Oh, Do I Remember: Experiences of Teachers During the Desegregation of Austin's Schools, 1964–1971* (New York: State University of New York Press, 2001), 49–50; Patterson, *Brown v. Board of Education*, 104; *Corsicana Daily Sun*, August 30 (quotation), September 5, 1956.
57. Robert M. Utley, *Lone Star Lawmen: The Second Century of the Texas Rangers* (New York: Berkley Books, 2007), 226–228; *FWST*, August 31, September 1, 3, 4, 5, 1956; *DMN*, September 30, 1956, Gonzaullas Scrapbook 4, TRHF&M, 366; Puckett, *Cast a Long Shadow*, 93; Ladino, *Desegregating Texas Schools*, 111.
58. Ladino, *Desegregating Texas Schools*, 103, 111–112; *FWST*, August 31, September 1, 4 (all quotations), 5, 9, 11, 1956; Wilson and Segall, *Oh, Do I Remember*, 50; Martin Herman Kuhlman, "The Civil Rights Movement in Texas: Desegregation of Public Accommodations, 1950–1964" (Ph.D. dissertation, Texas Tech University, 1994), 120; Mills, *Legend in Bronze*, 194. In 1957, the legislature passed almost a dozen pro-segregation bills, one of which authorized Attorney

General John Ben Shepperd to prosecute individuals or groups advocating for desegregation. Brian D. Behnken, *Fighting Their Own Battles: Mexican Americans, African Americans, and the Struggle for Civil Rights in Texas* (Chapel Hill: University of North Carolina Press, 2011), 95.

59. Charlton, "The Texas Department of Public Safety," 185–187; Robinson, *The DPS Story*, 29–30; Karl Detzer, "Texas Rangers Still Ride the Trail," *Reader's Digest* 71 (September 1957): 139, 140, 142; Texas Research League, *The Texas Department of Public Safety: Its Services and Organization* (Austin: Texas Research League, 1957), v, 1–5, 10, 16–24.
60. Inactive Personnel Record, Robert A. Crowder, TDPS; *DMN*, September 23, October 27 (quotation), 1956.
61. Texas Research League, *Texas Department of Public Safety*, vii–viii, 25–27, 66; Acts 1957, Regular Session, 55th Legislature, Ch. 261, *General and Special Laws of Texas*; Charlton, "The Texas Department of Public Safety," 187–188; Robinson, *The DPS Story*, 30–33.
62. Inactive Personnel Record, Robert A. Crowder, TDPS; *Lubbock Avalanche-Journal*, September 1, 1957; *Lubbock Morning-Avalanche*, November 27, 1972. Crowder had thoroughly enjoyed living in Lubbock and continued to own his home there. Even while living in Dallas, he rented the house to other Rangers who were assigned to Company C. Glenn Elliott, interview with Robert Nieman, Longview, Texas, January–October 1995, Oral History Project, TRHF&M, 245. Cited hereafter as Glenn Elliott interview, 1995.
63. Cox, *Time of the Rangers*, 253; *FWST*, March 4, 5 (quotation), 1960; *DMN*, March 5, 9, 1960; Puckett, *Cast a Long Shadow*, 136–137. Banks was clearly a dedicated and redoubtable lawman, but Mills's and Puckett's works both reveal, perhaps inadvertently, his hubris and his passionate hatred for Captain Crowder, Colonel Garrison, Assistant Director Joe Fletcher, and Public Safety Commission Chairman C. T. McLaughlin. Robert Utley hinted at personal misconduct on the part of the ousted Ranger in "Terminating Oklahoma's Smiling Killer," *TRD* 17 (Summer 2005): 64, but noted, "the theories never became public." Banks was appointed chief of police in Big Spring later in 1960, and removed from office by the city commission in June 1971. Despite his ignominious departure from the Rangers, former DPS colleagues, including James Riddles, wrote letters of endorsement for Banks. *Big Spring Daily Herald*, June 17, 1971.

64. Inactive Personnel Record, Robert A. Crowder, TDPS; *Paris News*, April 3, 1960. Patrol Captain Harry Weldon Hutchison was promoted to take Crowder's place as commander of Region 5. *GDN*, March 10, 1960.
65. *DMN*, April 1, 2, 1960; *AS*, March 31, 1960 (quotation).
66. Glenn Elliott with Robert Nieman, *Glen Elliott: A Ranger's Ranger* (Longview, TX: Robert Nieman, 1999), 86–87.
67. *Sixteenth U.S. Census*, Dallas County, Texas; Death Certificates, Marcoline Harriett Clifton, August 12, 1963, File No. 4566, Rae Milton Clifton, May 12, 1964, File No. 28467; *DMN*, May 8, 1945, August 10, 1963, May 11, 1964; Glenn Elliott interview, 1995, 1209; Carol Rodat interview, 2013.
68. James Crowder interview, 2013; Catherine McGuire interview, 2013; James Crowder to the author, January 22, 2021 (quotation); Radot to the author, January 24, 2021.
69. Catherine McGuire interview, 2013; *New York Mirror*, n.d., Gonzaullas Scrapbook 4, TRHF&M, 366.
70. Texas Attorney General's Office, *Biennial Report of Will Wilson,* December 14, 1962, 37, 40; David F. Prindle, *Petroleum Politics and the Texas Railroad Commission* (Austin: University of Texas Press, 1981), 92; *DMN*, June 3, 10, 12, 1962; *Longview Daily News*, June 4, 6, 10, 12, 13, 14, 1962.
71. Texas Attorney General's Office, *Biennial Report of Will Wilson,* December 14, 1962, 42–44; *Longview Daily News*, June 11, 17, 21, 26, 27, 28, 29, 1962; *Longview News-Journal*, July 1, 1962; *DMN*, June 20, 1962; "Texas Counts 33 Illegally Slanted Holes," *Oil and Gas Journal* 62 (July 2, 1962): 59.
72. *DMN*, October 2, November 19 (quotation), 1964; *Abilene Reporter-News*, October 2, 1964; *Amarillo Globe-Times*, November 18, 1964; *El Paso Herald-Post*, December 16, 1964; *Odessa American*, April 2, 1965. Brookfield's headstone in Fairview Cemetery in Pecos does not display a death date. Find a Grave: Victor Ely Brookfield.
73. *El Paso Herald-Post*, October 8, 1969; *Odessa American*, March 1, 4, 6, 8, 1970; *Lubbock Morning Avalanche*, March 5, 28, 1970.
74. Cox, *Time of the Rangers*, 276–277; Robert Mitchell, interview with Robert Nieman, Windom, Texas, October 29, 1996, Oral History Project, TRHF&M, 29–30. Cited hereafter as Bob Mitchell interview, 1996. Elliott with Nieman, *Glen Elliott*, 104–105.
75. Bob Mitchell interview, 1996, 30–31; Rigler and Rigler, *In the Line of Duty*, 63; *DMN*, November 23, 1968, May 12, 1969, January 21, 1972; *Gilmer Mirror*, November 7, 14, 1968.

76. *DMN*, November 27, 1968; Elliott with Nieman, *Glen Elliott*, 108.
77. Stan Redding, "Trouble at Daingerfield," *Houston Chronicle Magazine* (February 9, 1969), 12
78. *DMN*, May 12, 1969; Elliott with Nieman, *Glen Elliott*, 103, 108 (quotations).
79. *DMN*, October 4, 1968.
80. *DMN*, July 23, 1969; Waco *Herald-Tribune*, July 25, 1969; Inactive Personnel Record, Robert A. Crowder, TDPS; Glenn Elliott interview, 1994, 16; Bob Mitchell interview, 1996, 14. R. L Badgett and Ernest Daniel of Company B, Mart Jones of Company A, "Rass" Renfrow of Company C, Jim Nance of Company E, and Ben Kreuger of Company F retired on September 1. Zeno Smith of Company D retired on December 1. *GDN*, July 17, 1969.
81. *DMN*, August 27, September 23, 1969, August 2, 1970, April 1, 1971; *SAE*, May 31, 1971.
82. Death Certificate, Robert A Crowder, November 29, 1972, File No. 89850; *DMN*, November 27, 1972, and *Dallas Times-Herald*, November 27, 1972, Gonzaullas Scrapbook 5, TRHF&M, 403; *DMN*, November 28, 1972.
83. *DMN*, June 4, 1983; Catherine McGuire interview, 2013.
84. James Crowder interview, 2013; Electronic Army Serial Number Merged File, 1938–1946; *Lubbock Morning Avalanche*, August 11, 1942; Lubbock County Marriage Record, 10: 379; *DMN*, September 13, 1942; *Boulder Daily Camera*, June 27, 2005. In what seems to be a family tradition, James and Mary took in their youngest son's children after he fell on hard times.
85. Carol Rodat interview, 2013.
86. Catherine McGuire interview, 2013.
87. Catherine McGuire interview, 2013.

Notes for Chapter 8

1. Birth Certificates, John Joseph Klevenhagen, June 2, 1912, File No. 19581, Frances Helen Klevenhagen, September 23, 1957, File No. 30935, Robert G. Klevenhagen, February 17, 1914, File No. 4349, and George Joseph Klevenhagen, December 2, 1939, Registrar's No. 84; Bexar County Marriage Record, 1: 327; Barbara Gann to the author, May 2, 2019; Barbara Gann, telephone interview with the author, May 13, 2019. Hereafter cited as Barbara Gann interview, 2019. Mary died on April 19, 1944, of a cerebral hemorrhage brought on by hypertension.

She was buried in San Fernando Archdiocesan Cemetery No. 2 in San Antonio. *SAL*, April 20, 1944; Death Certificate, Mary Videau Klevenhagen, April 20, 1944, File No. 709. Frank married Jennie Colton on April 22, 1950. Dying on January 24, 1960, of arteriosclerosis, he was laid to rest next to his first wife. Guadalupe County Marriage Record, 19: 381; *SAE*, January 25, 1960; Death Certificate, Frank John Klevenhagen, January 25, 1960, File No. 547.

2. *AS*, June 3, 1926; Robert Nieman, "20th Century Shining Star: Capt. Johnny Klevenhagen," *TRD* 10 (Spring 2003): 5; Stan Redding, "Top Gun of the Texas Rangers," *True Detective* 78 (February 1963): 54; *Corpus Christi Times*, November 26, 1958.
3. Nieman, "Capt. Johnny Klevenhagen," 6; *Corpus Christi Times*, November 26, 1958.
4. Redding, "Top Gun," 54–55; *AS*, November 26, 1958 (quotation).
5. Douglas V. Meed, *Texas Ranger Johnny Klevenhagen* (Plano, TX: Republic of Texas Press, 2000), 3, 7.
6. *SAL*, November 15, 1933, February 8, April 15 (quotation), 1934. Hobrecht was a particularly dangerous career criminal. Four years earlier, he had been convicted for the ambush slaying of federal Prohibition agent (and former Ranger captain) Charles F. Stevens on September 25, 1929. Hobrecht was sentenced to seven years' imprisonment, but the case was reversed before he ever went behind bars. He was never retried. T. Lindsay Baker, *Gangster Tour of Texas* (College Station: Texas A&M University Press, 2011), Ch. 7.
7. *SAL*, January 28, 30, 1934.
8. *SAE*, April 18, June 16, 1934; Death Certificate, Alfred Clifton Street, Registrar's No. 5805, February 3, 1934; Elton R. Cude, *The Wild and Free Dukedom of Bexar* (San Antonio, TX: Munguia Printers, 1978), 274.
9. *SAE*, February 20, 22, April 5 (quotation), 1934; *SAL*, April 5, 12, 1934.
10. *SAE*, June 16, 1934.
11. Meed, *Texas Ranger Johnny Klevenhagen*, 7.
12. *SAE*, December 29, 1934.
13. *SAL*, December 2, 1934, January 25, 1935; *SAE*, January 8, February 1, 2, 10, March 2, 19, 1935.
14. Meed, *Texas Ranger Johnny Klevenhagen*, 7; *SAL*, May 7, 1935; *Houston Chronicle*, March 28, 2007.
15. *SAE*, December 7, 1935; *SAL*, January 16, 1936.
16. *SAL*, July 6, 30, 31, December 27, 30, 1936, January 10, 1937; *SAE*, July 30, November 29, December 31, 1936; Sammy Tise,

Texas County Sheriffs (Albuquerque, NM: Oakwood Printing, 1989), 44. The county highway patrol had been established on August 1, 1935, and personnel was chosen under agreements between the commissioners, the county judge, and the sheriff. Patrolmen operated under Sheriff West's direction, but their salaries came from the road and bridge fund.

17. *SAL*, January 19, 20, February 20, 1937, March 13, 1938; *SAEN*, February 10, 20, 1937, Gonzaullas Scrapbook 3, TRHF&M, 209–210; Death Certificate, Agnal Aubrey Edwards, January 1, 1937, File No. 430; Cude, *The Wild and Free Dukedom*, 278-281.

    Redding states in "Top Gun," 55, that Klevenhagen apprehended Selanes Canedo for the November 24, 1936, murder of Joseph W. Daly. However, Klevenhagen was still a deputy constable at the time of the homicide, and San Antonio Police Detective Fred Phelps Littlepage was the lead investigator. Sheriff's deputies did arrest Canedo on December 3 while searching for the murderer of Officer Stowe, but Klevenhagen was not among them. He did, however, have a minor role in the case of Evelyn Guckian May, Daly's niece, who was briefly a suspect during Canedo's trial. During those same proceedings, Gonzaullas testified on the prosecution's ballistics evidence. For more on the Daly and Stowe cases, see *SAL*, November 26, December 3, 4, 16, 1936, February 1, 2, 3, 4, 5, 15, March 27, July 31, 1937, March 13, 1938; *SAE*, December 17, 1936; *SAEN*, February 3, 1937; Death Certificates, John W. Daly, November 5, 1936, File No. 52773, and John W. Stowe, December 8, 1936, File No. 58181.
18. *SAL*, February 5, 6, 7, 12, 14, March 31, 1937; *Laredo Times*, February 11, 1937; Charles I. Bevans, comp., *Treaties and Other International Agreements of the United States, 1776–1949*, 9 (Department of State Publication No. 8615): 900-907.
19. Duke Carver, with J. J. Klevenhagen and Cyrus Heard, as told to W. Boyd Gatewood, "'They'll Never Take Me Alive,'" *Official Detective Stories* 5 (January 15, 1938): 2, 4 (first quotation), 6; Owen W. Kilday, as told to Lawrence Topperwein, "Man Trap!: The Red Riddle of Lawrence Rea," *True Detective Mysteries* 29 (February 1938): 37, 103–104; *SAL*, August 17, 1937 (second quotation); Redding, "Top Gun," 56–57; *GDN*, August 17, 1937.
20. *SAL*, September 29, 1937.
21. *SAL*, January 23, 1938, July 25 (quotation), 1939; *SAE*, July 27, 1939; Redding, "Top Gun," 55; Find A Grave: William Bernhard Hauck, Jr., Oliver Lee Wiley.

22. *SAL*, March 15, 16, 1938; *SAE*, March 16, 1938; Kemp Dixon, *Chasing Thugs, Nazis, and Reds: Texas Ranger Norman K. Dixon* (College Station: Texas A&M University Press, 2015), 24.
23. *SAL*, March 8, 9, May 21, 1938; Cude, *The Wild and Free Dukedom*, 282; Nathan Rufford McRae, World War II Draft Cards, RG 147, NARA. Selanes Canedo, convicted killer of John W. Daly, was at Vaughn's side when they were both sentenced to death. Upon the request of the Mexican consul in San Antonio, and the board of pardons and paroles, Canedo received two stays of execution from Governor Allred.
24. *SAL*, March 23, May 26, 1938; *SAE*, March 24, 1938.
25. *SAL*, April 5, 8, 1938.
26. *SAL*, June 12, 13, 1938; *SAE*, June 16, 1938.
27. *SAL*, July 1, 1938; Death Certificate, Jose Dorantes, June 30, 1938, File No. 26143.
28. *SAE*, December 6, 1936, July 2, August 16, 18, 19, September 16, 17, 1938; *SAL*, April 6, 7, July 1 (quotation), August 18, 1938; Cude, *The Wild and Free Dukedom*, 263–266.
29. Cude, *The Wild and Free Dukedom*, 301; Michael Hall, "Two Bar-Maids, Five Alligators, and the Butcher of Elmendorf," *Texas Monthly* 30 (July 2002): 118.
30. *SAE*, September 25, 1938; *GDN*, September 25, 1938; *SAL*, November 13, 1938; Cude, *The Wild and Free Dukedom*, 299, 301–302.
31. *SAE*, September 25, 1938; *SAL*, September 25, 27, 29, October 3, 7, 8, 9, 1938; *GDN*, September 25, 26, October 8, 1938; *Brownsville Herald*, September 26, 1938; Hall, "Two Bar-Maids," 125.
32. *SAE*, October 14, 1938; *SAL*, October 11, 14, November 13, 1938; Cude, *The Wild and Free Dukedom*, 307. Klevenhagen and Miller appeared before Justices Gerhardt and Sanford, respectively, and filed complaints charging Wheeler with the murders of Brown and Gotthardt. The defendant was indicted by the grand jury in Sinton. The following year, Wheeler pled guilty to a charge of accessory to murder and was sentenced to two years' imprisonment. *SAL*, October 10, 16, 1938; *SAE*, April 26, 1939.
33. *SAL*, October 23, 24, 25, 26, 31, 1938; *Daily Oklahoman*, October 24, 1938.
34. *SAE*, October 11, 21, 1938; Find A Grave: Pleasant Jackson McNeel, Sr.
35. *SAL*, November 2, 28, 1938, January 23, 24, 26, 28, 29, 31, February 2, 1939; *SAE*, January 25, 1939.

36. *Kerrville Mountain Sun*, November 3, 10, December 29, 1938; *Kerrville Times*, November 3, 10, 17, 1938; *AA*, December 22, 1938; *AS*, December 23, 1938; Death Certificate, David H. Carson, December 23, 1938, Registrar's No. 48627; Kemp Dixon, *Chasing Thugs, Nazis, and Reds: Texas Ranger Norman K. Dixon* (College Station: Texas A&M University Press, 2015), 41–42; Find A Grave: Dr. David Hart Carson. Navy veteran Ireland had been sentenced to life imprisonment in the Kansas State Prison at Lansing for murder in January 1925. He was paroled in February 1938 for hospitalization and treatment of tuberculosis. *Marshall County News*, November 18, 1938.
37. *SAE*, May 2, 21, August 7, 1939; *SAL*, May 17, August 7, 1939; Death Certificates, Frank William Matthews, File No. 16304, April 25, 1950, Samuel Herschel Hale, File No. 31764, August 2, 1954.
38. *SAL*, July 4, 5, 1939.
39. *SAL*, July 16, 24, 25, 28, 29, 30, 1939; *SAE*, July 27,1939; Redding, "Top Gun," 55.
40. *SAE*, October 18, 19, 23, 1939; *SAL*, October 17, 18, 25, 1939.
41. *SAE*, October November 18, 1939; *SAL*, November 6, 9, 1939.
42. *SAE*, October 23, 1939, March 26, 1940; *SAL*, November 27, December 8, 1939.
43. *SAE*, May 3, 1940.
44. *SAE*, May 19 (first quotation), 24, June 4, 1940; *SAL*, May 19, 24, June 4, 1940; Meed, *Texas Ranger Johnny Klevenhagen*, 51 (second quotation).
45. *SAL*, May 26, July 20, 1940.
46. *SAE*, March 22, 23, May 1, 1941; *SAL*, March 22, 1941; *Brownsville Herald*, March 18, 1941; William Struwe Bouldin, World War II Draft Cards, RG 147, NARA.
47. *SAE*, March 23, April 5, May 1, 1941; *Valley Morning Star*, April 5, May 1, 1941.
48. *SAE*, August 9, 16, 20 (quotation), 22, 1941; *SAL*, January 24, August 9, 22, December 30, 1941. Uecker was employed as chief investigator from December 5, 1934, to January 1, 1947. *SAL*, December 9, 1934, December 26, 1946.
49. Inactive Personnel Record, John J. Klevenhagen, TDPS; *DMN*, September 14, 1941; *GDN*, September 14, 1941; *Corpus Christi Times*, November 28, 1958 (quotation).
50. *DMN*, February 23, 28, 1942; *AA*, February 28, 1942; *AAS*, December 30, 1986.

51. Gary Cartwright, *Galveston: A History of the Island* (Fort Worth: Texas Christian University, 1991), 208–209, 241; *GDN*, June 10, 1942.
52. Inactive Personnel Record, John J. Klevenhagen, TDPS.
53. *GDN*, September 16, 1943.
54. *SAL*, September 9, 1947; *Valley Morning Star*, September 9, 10, 1947; *Victoria Advocate*, September 9, 1947.
55. *GDN*, August 28, 1973.
56. *GDN*, May 1, September 23, 24, November 27, 28, 29, 1949, March 5, May 5, August 3, 4 (quotation), 5, 8, 9, 10, 11, September 27, 1950, April 18, 1974; *Baytown Sun*, November 29, 1949; Hugh V. Haddock, "Killer from Mars," *Inside Detective* 28 (April 1950): 21, 46.
57. *GDN*, May 4, 13, 17, June 15, 20, 25, September 22, 27, October 12 (quotation), 1949.
58. *Baytown Sun*, December 9, 1949.
59. *DPS Biennial Report, 1949–1950*, 13–14.
60. *AS*, October 5, 1937, April 15, May 13, 25, 1938, May 16, October 21, 1939, September 22, 23, October 24, 1942, July 16, 1949; *Corpus Christi Times*, October 5, 1937; *AA*, May 4, 1938, February 6, 1941; *New York Times*, May 26, 1938, October 25, 1942; *GDN*, July 17, 1949; Death Certificate, Vincent Vallone, Sr., July 31, 1949, File No. 33863. Maceo family members firmly asserted Sam Rose, a teetotaler, was framed and the drugs found in his vehicle were planted by a prostitute on the orders of William L. Moody, Jr. Allan Waldman, "Isle of Illicit Pleasures: Big Sam and Papa Rose," *In Between*, no. 164 (November 1983): 10–11. For more on the heroin and marijuana trade in Texas, New York, and elsewhere in the 1930s, see Heloise Cabot, "Marijuana—Weed of Sin," *American Detective* 9 (August 1938): 4–13. One of the few existing copies of this issue can be found at the Rosenberg Library in Galveston. According to the late Elizabeth Fontaine "Lise" Darst, onetime museum curator at the library, its rarity stems from Sam Maceo's attempts to purchase every copy from Galveston to New Orleans.
61. *Baytown Sun*, October 17, 18, 1949; *GDN*, October 18, 1949; *DMN*, October 31, 1950; Meed, *Texas Ranger Johnny Klevenhagen*, 88, 95. Regarding Foreman's criminal defense practice, a common belief in Texas was expressed as "If you hire Foreman, you're guilty as hell." Marshall Smith, "His Lifetime Record—Won: 700, Lost 1," *Life* 60 (April 1, 1966): 94.
62. *Corpus Christi Times*, October 25, 1950.

63. *SAE*, March 11, 1951; Meed, *Texas Ranger Johnny Klevenhagen*, 135, 144, 146.
64. *GDN*, October 15, 1922, November 9, 1933, July 27, 1977; Robert Neiman, "Galveston's Balinese Room," *TRD* 27 (Fall 2008): 6–9; Cartwright, *Galveston*, 214; Henry David, "A Time Past: Gambling in Galveston," *In Between*, no. 29 (August 1978): 23; Tabitha Nicole Boatman, et al., *Galveston's Maceo Family Empire: Bootlegging and the Balinese Room* (Charleston, SC: History Press, 2014), 27–28, 54, 57, 60, 90; Allan Waldman, "Isle of Illicit Pleasures: The Gamblers," *In Between*, no. 163 (October 1983): 23 (quotation). See also Baker, *Gangster Tour of Texas*, Ch. 16.
65. Neiman, "Galveston's Balinese Room," 6–9; Frank E. Chalfant, *Galveston: Island of Chance* (Houston: Treasures of Nostalgia, 1997), 29–30, 32; Paul Burka, "Grand Dame of the Gulf," *Texas Monthly* 11 (December 1983): 168; *GDN*, July 27, 1977; Steven Long, "Shutdown, June 10, 1957: The Day the Wheels Stopped Turning," *In Between*, no. 166 (December 1983): 17; Gary Cartwright, "One Last Shot," *Texas Monthly* 21 (June 1993): 162; Waldman, "Big Sam and Papa Rose," 10. For more on the Island's sex trade, see Kimber Fountain, *Galveston's Red Light District: A History of The Line* (Charleston, SC: History Press, 2018). According to legend, when Sam Maceo built twenty luxury apartments on the corner of Twenty-third Street and Avenue Q, Moody informed him, "I stayed out of the gambling business, and I expect you to stay out of the hotel business." Honoring the unofficial truce, the Maceos promptly demolished the building. David G. McComb, *Galveston: A History* (Austin: University of Texas Press, 1986), 174.
66. Cartwright, *Galveston*, 215; Neiman, "Galveston's Balinese Room," 9; *AS*, June 4, 11, 1951; Burka, "Grand Dame," 216; Boatman, et al., *Galveston's Maceo Family Empire*, 74–75; Waldman, "The Gamblers," 23; McComb, *Galveston*, 177. The Maceos have been credited with keeping Alphonse Capone's Chicago gangsters and Albert Anastasia's New York *mafiaso* from gaining a foothold on the Island. Chalfant, *Galveston*, 34.
67. *AS*, June 18, 1951; *AA*, June 19, 24, 1951; *Final Report*, Folder 6, Box 1, Texas Crime Investigating Committee Records, Southwest Collection, Texas Tech, 6-7 (first quotation on p. 6); *GDN*, July 14, 1951 (second and third quotations); McComb, *Galveston*, 186; Cartwright, *Galveston*, 252.

68. *GDN*, March 5, 1952; *Baytown Sun*, March 1, 1952; *Kerrville Daily Times*, February 26, 1989 (quotation). Foreman's standard defense strategy was to put people other than his client on trial: "The best defense in a murder case is the fact that the deceased should have been killed, regardless of how it happened." Smith, "His Lifetime Record," 96.
69. *GDN*, March 5, 1952; *SAE*, March 3, 1952 (quotation); *Baytown Sun*, March 1, 1952; Cox, *Time of the Rangers*, 223–224; Find A Grave: Jimmie Birsh Keen.
70. *GDN*, March 18, 19, 1952; Death Certificate, Eveard Caldwell Campbell, October 15, 1982, File No. 83115.
71. *GDN*, August 29, 31, September 4, 1952.
72. *Department of Public Safety Biennial Report Fiscal Years, 1951–1952*, 12–13.
73. *AS*, September 9, 11, 1952; *Brownsville Herald*, March 18, 1953, October 4, 1954; *SAL*, October 8, 1954; *Corpus Christi Caller-Times*, September 14, 21, October 23, 1952; *SAE*, October 11, 1952; *Corpus Christi Times*, January 20, 21, 1954; *New York Times*, February 6, 1954; Bridge, *Life and Times of Joe H. Bridge*, 74, 79; John E. Clark, *The Fall of the Duke of Duval: A Prosecutor's Journal* (Austin: Eakin Press, 1999), 67–68. Although indicted, Alaniz became an assistant county attorney in San Diego. *Corpus Christi Times*, February 23, 1954. The other Rangers assigned to Duval County included Wiley Williamson, Truemon Stone, Walter Russell, John Dudley White, Ben Krueger, Levi Duncan, Tulley Seay, Clint Peoples, L. H. Purvis, Ernest Daniel, and E. J. "Jay" Banks.
74. *Shreveport Times*, May 28, 29, 1954, July 17, 1982.
75. *GDN*, November 6, 9, 1954, January 16, 20, 1955.
76. *GDN*, December 2, 1954; Meed, *Texas Ranger Johnny Klevenhagen*, 169.
77. *San Francisco Examiner* and *Brazosport Facts*, both dated June 13, 1962; *Oakland Tribune*, June 12, 1962; J. Campbell Bruce, *Escape from Alcatraz: A Farewell to the Rock* (New York: McGraw-Hill, 1963), 8, 148–149. The FBI closed its case file in 1979, while the U.S. Marshals Service's investigation remains open. In recent years, members of the Anglin family have advanced the claim that the escape was successful, and the prisoners were able to settle into ordinary lives at least through the 1970s, if not beyond. For more on these theories, see Michael Esslinger and David Widner, *Escaping Alcatraz: The Untold Story of the Greatest Prison Break in American History* (San Francisco: Ocean View Publishing, 2017).

78. *SAL*, July 15, 1955; *Corpus Christi Caller-Times*, July 17, 1955; *Corpus Christi Times*, July 21, 1955, April 15, 1957.
79. *Brownsville Herald*, June 28, 1955, May 22, 1956; *SAE*, July 6, 1955; *GDN*, May 22 (quotation), June 8, 1956.
80. *Corpus Christi Times* and *GDN*, both dated January 6, 1956.
81. *AS*, March 31, April 2, 1956; *Corpus Christi Times*, April 2, 6, 1956; *GDN*, May 21, 1956.
82. *Corpus Christi Times*, July 8, 9, 10, 1956; Randy Sillavan, "Remembrances of My Dad: Hollis Milton Sillavan," *TRD* 5 (Fall 2001): 40; Redding, "Top Gun," 71. Several newspapers misidentified the disturbed man as "Tillson Hanson, Jr."
83. Meed, *Texas Ranger Johnny Klevenhagen*, 195 (first quotation); Death Certificate, Alton G. Halson, July 12, 1956, File No. 39522; *Corpus Christi Times*, November 25, 1958 (second quotation).
84. *AA*, May 11, 1956; Inactive Personnel Record, John J. Klevenhagen, TDPS; Charles Schreiner III, et al., comps., *A Pictorial History of the Texas Rangers: "That Special Breed of Men"* (Mountain Home, TX: YO Press, 1969), 133 (quotation).
85. *GDN*, March 6, 1957; *Corpus Christi Times*, March 8, 1957; *SAL*, March 10, 1957; *House Journal, Fifty-fifth Legislature, Regular Session*, 601–602, 938-939, 3441–3673; Death Certificate, Edwin Adolph Stephan, March 30, 1964, File No. 45450; *AA*, October 11, 1957.
86. *Victoria Advocate*, February 15, 1957; *Corpus Christi Times*, April 15 (quotation), 16, 1957.
87. *Lawton Constitution*, October 10, 1957; *DMN*, April 30, 1957 (quotation); *Corpus Christi Times*, April 30, 1957; Robert M. Utley, "Terminating Oklahoma's Smiling Killer," *TRD* 17 (Summer 2005): 59; Ann Arnold, *Gamblers and Gangsters: Fort Worth's Jacksboro Highway in the 1940s and 1950s* (Austin: Eakin Press, 1998), 155, 159. Gary Cartwright, "Talking to Killers," *Texas Monthly* 30 (July 2002): 61: "Norris was an angular, rawboned man, taller than his mug shots suggested, more cordial than I had expected, and far less menacing. His cat-gray eyes had a soothing effect, and he talked with such apparent sincerity that I ran out of paper before I could ask a question."
88. Redding, "Top Gun," 72–73; *DMN*, May 1, 1957; Jim Ray, interview with Robert Neiman, Bullard, Texas, October 18, 1997, Oral History Project, TRHF&M, 42; *Lawton Constitution*, October 11, 1957; Meed, *Texas Ranger Johnny Klevenhagen*, 180–182; Corpus *Christi Times*, May 1, 1947. The Brannans' cause of death was identical: "cerebral

hemorrhage, laceration of brain, and severance of spinal cord." Death Certificates, Mrs. Lillie Brannan, April 19, 1957, File No. 20253, Johnnie Brannan, April 19, 1957, File No. 20254.

89. *DMN*, April 30, May 1, 1957; *Lawton Constitution*, October 11, 1957; *Corpus Christi Times*, April 30, 1957; Arnold, *Gamblers and Gangsters*, 160.
90. *Lawton Constitution*, October 11, 1957; S. E. Spinks, *Law on the Last Frontier: Texas Ranger Arthur Hill* (Lubbock: Texas Tech University Press, 2007), 132–133; Nieman, "Capt. Johnny Klevenhagen," 8; Linda Jay Puckett, *Cast a Long Shadow: A Casebook of the Law Enforcement Career of Texas Ranger Captain E. J. (Jay) Banks* (Dallas: Ussery Printing Company, 1984), 116.
91. *DMN*, April 30, May 1, 1957; Spinks, *Law on the Last Frontier*, 134–135; Utley, "Terminating Oklahoma's Smiling Killer," 60; Robert Nieman, "Jim Ray," *TRD* 2 (Winter 2000): 24; Puckett, *Cast a Long Shadow*, 117.
92. *DMN*, April 30, 1957; *Lawton Constitution*, October 11, 1957; Spinks, *Law on the Last Frontier*, 135–136; Meed, *Texas Ranger Johnny Klevenhagen*, 184–185; Puckett, *Cast a Long Shadow*, 117–119.
93. *Corpus Christi Times*, April 30, 1957; *Lawton Constitution*, October 11, 1957; Spinks, *Law on the Last Frontier*, 136; Puckett, *Cast a Long Shadow*, 119; Death Certificates, William Carl Humphrey, May 4, 1957, Registrar's No. 257, Gene Paul Norris, May 4, 1957, Registrar's No. 258. Meed credits Klevenhagen in *Texas Ranger Johnny Klevenhagen*, 185–186, with killing Norris, but the other participants in the gun battle attributed the deed to Banks.
94. *Corpus Christi Times*, April 1, 1957 (quotation).
95. *AS*, April 17, 1951, March 15, October 4, 1954; Burka, "Grande Dame," 169; Boatman, et al., *Galveston's Maceo Family Empire*, 105–106; "Wide-Open Galveston Mocks Texas Laws," *Life* 39 (August 15, 1955): 26–27; Jean M. Brown, "Free Rein: Galveston Island's Alcohol, Gambling, and Prostitution Era, 1839–1957" (M.A. thesis, Lamar University, 1998), 118; David G. McComb, *Spare Time in Texas: Recreation and History in the Lone Star State* (Austin: University of Texas Press, 2008), 33, 170.
96. Texas Attorney General's Office, *Biennial Report of Will Wilson,* December 14, 1962, 1–2; *GDN*, June 11, 1957; Long, "Shutdown, July 10, 1957," 20–21.
97. Texas Attorney General's Office, *Biennial Report of Will Wilson*, 2; Ed Gooding with Robert Nieman, *Ed Gooding: Soldier, Texas Ranger*

(Longview, TX: Ranger Publishing, 2001), 108 (quotation); *GDN*, June 11, 1957.

98. Texas Attorney General's Office, *Biennial Report of Will Wilson*, 2–3; *GDN*, June 11, 12, 13, 14, July 2, 3, 9, 12, 19, 24, 31, August 21, 29, 1957; *Brownsville Herald*, June 18, 1957; Long, "Shutdown, July 10, 1957," 21.
99. Gooding with Nieman, *Ed Gooding*, 110–111; *GDN*, June 15, August 14, 1957; McComb, *Galveston*, 187; McComb, *Spare Time in Texas*, 16.
100. *GDN*, June 18, 19 (quotation), 1957; *Brownsville Herald*, June 18, 1957; Texas Attorney General's Office, *Biennial Report of Will Wilson*, 4; Gooding with Nieman, *Ed Gooding*, 114.
101. GDN, June 21, 22, 23, 1957; *Brownsville Herald*, June 21, 1957.
102. *GDN*, August 18, 29, September 27, 1957, April 17, 1959; Gooding with Nieman, *Ed Gooding*, 107, 178. Sam T. "Little Sam" Maceo, first cousin of the gambling kingpins, remembered: "After the island shut down (by Atty. Gen. Will Wilson), lots of our people moved to Vegas. I tell you all they had to say is that they were from Galveston and worked for Sam and Rose. They were hired. Automatic. No questions." *GDN*, July 27, 1977.
103. Detzer, "Texas Rangers Still Ride the Trail," 140.
104. *Corpus Christi Times*, December 21, 1957, November 28, 1958; Meed, *Texas Ranger Johnny Klevenhagen*, 215; *Houston Chronicle*, November 18, 26, 27, 1958; *Brownsville Herald*, November 26 (first quotation), 27, 1958; *SAL*, November 26, 1958; *SAE*, November 27, 1958; *GDN*, November 27, 1958; Death Certificate, John J. Klevenhagen, December 1, 1958, File No. 62796; Barbara Gann interview, 2019.
105. Acts 1959, Regular Session, 56th Legislature, Senate Resolution No. 46, *General and Special Laws of Texas*.
106. *Victoria Advocate*, May 2, 1958; Marriage License No. 45976, Harris County, Texas; *Houston Chronicle*, March 28, 2007.
107. *Houston Chronicle*, May 14, 1999.

Notes for Chapter 9

1. James M. Day, *Captain Clint Peoples: Texas Ranger* (Waco: Texian Press, 1980), 1; Milam County Marriage Record, 6: 481; Find A Grave: Menta M. Peoples Moore, Herman Allen Peoples; Birth Certificates, Clinton Thomas Peoples, May 22, 1970, File No. 30601, Raymond B. Peoples, March 25, 1925, Registrar's No. 636, and Mae Louise Peoples, June 2, 1975, File No. 30767; *Fourteenth* and *Fifteenth U.S. Census*,

Montgomery County, Texas. Emma was living in her father's El Paso household in 1910, and reported her marital status as single. *Thirteenth U.S. Census*, El Paso County, Texas. Tom died at his residence in Whitney on February 18, 1953. The primary cause of death was listed as carcinoma of the lung. He was buried in Mt. Olivet Cemetery. Death Certificate, William Thomas Peoples, February 27, 1953, File No. 8935. Susie died at Johnson County Memorial Hospital on December 18, 1964. She was interred next to her husband. Death Certificate, Susie Mae Peoples, December 22, 1964, File No. 78766.

2. Ben H. Procter, *Just One Riot: Episodes of the Texas Rangers in the 20th Century* (Austin: Eakin Press, 1991), 75–76; *Conroe Courier*, August 15, 1919, November 3, December 29, 1922; Resume, Peoples Vertical File, TRHF&M; *SAL*, April 25, 1982.
3. Procter, *Just One Riot*, 76; Resume, Peoples Vertical File, TRHF&M; *Fifteenth U.S. Census*, Montgomery County, Texas; *Conroe Courier*, June 24, 1992.
4. Resume, Peoples Vertical File, TRHF&M; *Conroe Courier*, April 29, 1932, June 24, 1992; *Houston Chronicle*, May 10, 1932; Procter, *Just One Riot*, 77; *Mexia Daily News*, July 25, 1969 (first quotation); Sammy Tise, *Texas County Sheriffs* (Albuquerque, NM: Oakwood Printing, 1989), 382; Thad Sitton, *The Texas Sheriff: Lord of the County Line* (Norman: University of Oklahoma Press, 2000), 46 (second quotation); *Victoria Advocate*, May 12, 1932.
5. Bryan Burrough, *The Big Rich: The Rise and Fall of the Greatest Texas Oil Fortunes* (New York: Penguin Books, 2009), 93; Procter, *Just One Riot*, 78.
6. Day, *Captain Clint Peoples*, 18, 19; *Conroe Courier*, September 2, 1932; Tise, *Texas County Sheriffs*, 382; RSR, Clint Peoples, 401-96, TSLAC.
7. *Waco Tribune-Herald*, June 24, 1992; Birth Certificate, Donna Lee Henderson, n.d., Registrar's No. 32223; Resume, Peoples Vertical File, TRHF&M; Birth Certificate, Donna Jean Peoples, December 7, 1935, Registrar's No. 93886.
8. Day, *Captain Clint Peoples*, 41–42.
9. 237 *Southwestern Reporter* 317–319 (1951); Texas Department of Criminal Justice, Convict Record Ledgers, 1998/038-168, TSLAC, 93.
10. Tise, *Texas County Sheriffs*, 382; Day, *Captain Clint Peoples*, 24; Henry Mostyn, "Grover Cleveland Mostyn," *Magnolia Memories*, ed. Celeste Graves (Bloomington, IN: AuthorHouse, 2004), 531–532.

11. *Houston Chronicle*, July 12, August 11, 1939; *Conroe Courier* and *AA*, both dated July 13, 1939.
12. Procter, *Just One Riot*, 79; Roster of students, 8th Recruit Training School, TDPS Training Academy Records, Box 2005/128-1 TSLAC; Inactive Personnel Record, Clinton T. Peoples, TDPS; Resume, Peoples Vertical File, TRHF&M.
13. Day, *Captain Clint Peoples*, 25, 59; Resume, Peoples Vertical File, TRHF&M.
14. Day, *Captain Clint Peoples*, 59–61; Tise, *Texas County Sheriffs*, 382; Resume, Peoples Vertical File, TRHF&M.
15. Inactive Personnel Record, Clinton T. Peoples, TDPS; Resume, Peoples Vertical File, TRHF&M.
16. *AS*, April 5, July 14, November 7, 1946; *AA*, June 16, November 8, 1946.
17. Procter, *Just One Riot*, 79.
18. Hugh W. Stephens, *The Texas City Disaster, 1947* (Austin: University of Texas Press, 1997), 1–4, 30; John Ferling, "Texas City Disaster," *American History* 30 (January/February 1996): 51–53.
19. Stephens, *Texas City Disaster*, 5; Day, *Captain Clint Peoples*, 73.
20. James W. Robinson, *The DPS Story: History of the Development of the Department of Public Safety in Texas* (Austin: Texas Department of Public Safety, 1975), 24–25; Stephens, *Texas City Disaster*, 5, 100; Ferling, "Texas City Disaster," 61; American National Red Cross, *Texas City Explosion, April 16, 1947* (Washington, DC: s. n., 1948), 2.
21. *AS*, December 11, 12, 1947; *AA*, December 11, 12, 29, 1947, January 12, 1948; Find A Grave: Frank Wilkins McBee, Sr.
22. *AS*, December 12, 1947, January 16, 1948; *AA*, January 12, 13, 16, 27, February 26, 1948; Day, *Captain Clint Peoples*, 75.
23. Day, *Captain Clint Peoples*, 95; *Corpus Christi Times*, January 22, 1951; Find A Grave: Maro Woodley Williamson.
24. *Lubbock Morning Avalanche*, January 16, February 26, 1951; *Odessa American*, January 17, February 8, 27, March 1, 1951; *AS*, January 17, 1951; *Abilene Reporter-News*, January 18, 26, February 1, 28, March 1, 1951.
25. *Mexia Daily News*, September 19, 1951; *SAE*, September 20, 1951.
26. *AA*, October 23, 24, 25, 26, 31, November 1, 2, 1951; *Dallas Times-Herald*, April 6, 1984; Joan Mellen, *Faustian Bargains: Lyndon Johnson and Mac Wallace in the Robber Baron Culture of Texas* (New York: Bloomsbury, 2016), 86, 88.

27. *AA*, February 18, 23, 24, 28, 1951; Mellen, *Faustian Bargains*, 81–82, 84.
28. Day, *Captain Clint Peoples*, 96; *Corpus Christi Times*, April 16, May 25, 26, 28, 29, July 7, 1952; *AA*, April 17, May 25, 26, 27, 29, 30, July 8, 1952.
29. *DPS Biennial Report, 1951–1952*, 12–13; Procter, *Just One Riot*, 79; *AS*, July 3, 1953.
30. *Abilene Reporter-News*, October 25, 1953.
31. *SAE*, June 6, 17, 1954.
32. *New York Times*, March 18, August 1, 1954.
33. John E. Clark, *The Fall of the Duke of Duval: A Prosecutor's Journal* (Austin: Eakin Press, 1999), 2, 77–85, 96, 101–104, 304–311, 315, 323–329.
34. *Kerrville Times*, October 13, 1954.
35. Day, *Captain Clint Peoples*, 108; Procter, *Just One Riot*, 82.
36. Procter, *Just One Riot*, 80–81; *WNT*, May 16, 1955; *Cuero Record*, May 16, 1955.
37. Day, *Captain Clint Peoples*, 109–110; *WNT*, May 16, 1955; Procter, *Just One Riot*, 82–84. Sergeant Jim Mraz and Private First Class David Wychiskally, both of the 720th Military Police Battalion, operated the armored car during the standoff.
38. *Corpus Christi Times*, October 18, 1955.
39. *Brownwood Bulletin*, October 11, 1957.
40. Day, *Captain Clint Peoples*, 123 (quotation).
41. *DMN*, December 31, 1957, Gonzaullas Scrapbook 4, TRHF&M, 368; Day, *Captain Clint Peoples*, 123 (quotation).
42. *WNT*, February 4, 10, 12, April 9, 1958; *Commerce Daily Journal*, February 6, 11, 1958; *SAEN*, February 9, 1958; *GDN*, February 12, 1958.
43. *SAL*, May 4, 1958; *Cuero Record*, May 4, 1958; *Waco Citizen*, May 8, 1958 (first quotation); Day, *Captain Clint Peoples*, 129 (second quotation).
44. *WNT*, September 11, 1958 (quotation); *Abilene Reporter-News*, September 15, 1958.
45. *Mexia Daily News*, February 18, 1960.
46. *Big Spring Daily Herald*, June 19, 1960.
47. *WNT*, November 16, 17, 19, 1960; *GDN*, November 16, 19, 1960; *Mexia Daily News*, November 17, 18, 1960, August 4 (quote), 1969.
48. Mexia Daily News, August 4 (quote), 1969; Darren L. Ivey, *The Texas Rangers: A Registry and History* (Jefferson, NC: McFarland & Co., 2010), 308–311.

49. *SAEN*, February 25, 1961; *Corpus Christi Times*, February 27, 1961.
50. *Corpus Christi Times*, March 17, April 14, 1961; *Lake Charles American Press*, March 17, April 12, 18, 19, 1961, March 8, August 26, 27, 30, October 1, December 1, 1966; Michael L. Radelet, et al., *In Spite of Evidence: Erroneous Convictions in Capital Cases* (Boston: Northeastern University Press, 1992), 163–170. Two decades later, serial killers Henry Lee Lucas and Ottis Toole would confess to over two hundred unsolved homicides and erect a warren of contradictions and lies that wasted the resources and time of dozens of law enforcement agencies, including the Rangers. For more on these ghoulish predators, see H. Joaquin Jackson with James L. Haley, *One Ranger Returns* (Austin: University of Texas Press, 2008), 87–100.
51. Day, *Captain Clint Peoples*, 131; *Abilene Reporter-News*, June 3, 1962, December 29, 1969; *GDN*, June 4, 1962; Mellen, *Faustian Bargains*, 144.
52. *Gatesville Messenger and Star-Forum*, July 21, August 4, 1961.
53. *Brownwood Bulletin*, January 26, 1962; *Abilene Reporter-News*, January 26, 1962; *Big Spring Daily Herald*, January 30, 1962.
54. *AS*, May 9, 1962; *Abilene Reporter-News*, May 21, 22, June 4, 7, 1962; *GDN*, May 26, June 2, 4, 10, 14, July 14, 1962; "Decline and Fall," *Time Magazine* 79 (May 25, 1962): 24–29; "A Scandal Hot As a Pistol," "A Man Mired in the Incredible Estes Mess," and Richard Oulahan, "The Bumpkin Who Turned into a Warped Wizard," *Life* (June 1, 1962): 77–81, 86, 88, 90, 93; *Hearne Democrat*, June 8, 1962; *SAL*, May 25, June 21, 1962; *Grand Prairie Daily News-Texan*, July 19, 1962; "Still Digging," *Time Magazine* 79 (June 1, 1962): 18–19; Mellen, *Faustian Bargains*, 151–152.
55. *GDN*, May 26, 1962; *Abilene Reporter-News*, June 4, 1962; *El Paso Times*, March 29, April 16, 1963.
56. *WNT*, June 17, 18, 20, 25, 1963; *GDN*, June 17, 1963; Oscar Davis Jackson, World War II Draft Cards, RG 147, NARA.
57. *AA*, August 14, 15, 1963; *AS*, August 14, 1963; *WNT*, November 2, 1963.
58. *Gatesville Messenger and Star-Forum*, August 7, 1964.
59. *Corsicana Daily Sun*, September 21, 22, 1964; *Tyler Morning Telegraph*, September 22, 23, October 17, 19, 1964, April 10, 1965; Joseph William Brownlow, World War II Draft Cards, RG 147, NARA.
60. *GDN*, August 8, 1965; "Focus on the Forty Acres," *Alcalde* 54 (April 1966): 24; *SAEN*, July 31, August 8, 1965.
61. *Mexia Daily News*, April 13, 14, 26, 29, June 20, 1966.

62. *Mexia Daily News*, July 20, 1966.
63. *Mexia Daily News*, August 18, 1967; *Marshall News Messenger*, September 21, 29, November 30, 1967; Find A Grave: William Lynwood "Buck" Little.
64. James M. Day, *One Man's Dream: Fort Fisher and the Texas Ranger Hall of Fame* (Waco: Texian Press, 1976), 5–17; *WNT*, December 13, 1967 (quotation); Bob Alexander and Donaly E. Brice, *Texas Rangers: Lives, Legend, and Legacy* (Denton: University of North Texas Press, 2017), 375. The year before, Garrison had made Arness an honorary Texas Ranger in recognition of his positive portrayal of an American lawman.
65. Robinson, *The DPS Story*, 37–38; Mitchel P. Roth, "Through the Ages: Texas DPS History," *Courtesy, Service, and Protection: The History of the Texas Department of Public Safety* (Paducah, KY: Turner Publishing Company, 2003), 45.
66. *GDN*, January 6, 1969; *Gatesville Messenger and Star-Forum*, January 10, 1969 (quotations).
67. *Gatesville Messenger and Star-Forum*, March 21, 1969; *Abilene Reporter-News*, 16, 1969.
68. Inactive Personnel Record, Clinton T. Peoples, TDPS; Robinson, *The DPS Story*, 43; *SAL*, October 22, 1969; *SAE*, November 5, 1969.
69. *Victoria Advocate*, March 14, 1970; *SAE*, March 24, 1970 (quotation).
70. Cox, *Time of the Rangers*, 283 (quotation); *AA*, May 5, 6, 1970.
71. *SAE*, July 31, 1970.
72. Acts 1971, Regular Session, 62nd Legislature, Ch. 614, *General and Special Laws of Texas*; *SAE*, December 14, 1971; *Waco Tribune-Herald*, November 16, 1969; Day, *One Man's Dream*, 25.
73. *SAL*, December 28, 1972; *La Marque Times*, February 22, 1973; W. N. W. Mint Industries to Members of Texas Ranger Commemorative Commission, December 31, 1973, Gonzaullas Scrapbook 5, TRHF&M, 447, 449.
74. Day, *One Man's Dream*, 32–36; *FWST*, August 4, 1973; *Waco Tribune-Herald* and *AAS*, both dated August 5, 1973.
75. Ray to Speir, November 21, 1973, "Clint Peoples Investigation file," Box 1998/097-11, TSLAC; Robert M. Utley, *Lone Star Lawmen: The Second Century of the Texas Rangers* (New York: Berkley Books, 2007), 257–258.
76. Ray to Speir, November 21, 1973, Box 1998/097-11, TSLAC; Cox, *Time of the Rangers*, 294.

77. Inactive Personnel Record, Clinton T. Peoples, TDPS; *AAS*, February 14, 1974 (quotation); *DMN*, February 26, 1974, Gonzaullas Scrapbook 5, TRHF&M, 442. Day, in his biography of Clint Peoples, avoided any mention of the controversary.
78. Peoples to Tower, November 12, 1968, Peoples Vertical File, TRHF&M; *Dallas Times-Herald*, December 23, 1973, *DMN*, April 26, May 16, 1974, and *FWST*, May 16, 1974 (quotation), Gonzaullas Scrapbook 5, TRHF&M, 443–444; *AAS*, April 26, 1974; *Waco Tribune-Herald*, May 16, 1974.
79. Day, *One Man's Dream*, 36; *Waco Tribune-Herald*, August 3, 1974, October 12, 1975; *Victoria Advocate*, January 28, 1976; *Waco Citizen*, February 10, 1976; *Mexia Daily News*, February 10, 1976 (quotation); *DMN*, February 8, 1976, and *AAS*, February 8, 1976, Gonzaullas Scrapbook 5, TRHF&M, 456.
80. *FWST*, September 13, 1977.
81. *FWST*, March 13, 1977, June 27, 1978; *DMN*, August 24, 1978.
82. *FWST*, August 29, September 6, 7, 1978, June 9, 1979; *DMN*, August 29, September 7, October 1, 1978.
83. *FWST*, July 17, 18, 20, 1979, May 21, 1981.
84. *DMN*, September 2, 9 (quotation), 1981; *FWST*, September 29, 1982; "Texas Sniper," *Time* 120 (October 25, 1982): 40. For more on the assassination, the assassin, and the Ranger who caught him, see Bob Alexander, *Old Riot, New Ranger: Captain Jack Dean: Texas Ranger and U.S. Marshal* (Denton: University of North Texas Press, 2018), 182 *ff*.
85. *DMN*, April 22, July 9, 1983.
86. *SAE*, January 16, 1964; *AAS*, August 17, 1979; Mellen, *Faustian Bargains*, 230; Day, *Captain Clint Peoples*, 135 (quotation).
87. *FWST*, November 18, 1983; *AAS*, December 2, 1983.
88. Abilene *Reporter-News* and *DMN*, both December 2, 1983.
89. *DMN*, March 22, 1984; *FWST*, March 21, 23, 24, 25, 1984; *AAS*, March 23, April 1 (first quotation), 1984; *GDN*, April 1, 1984 (second quotation). Well outside the scope of this work, the theory of a criminal conspiracy involving political corruption and assassination that was masterminded by Lyndon Johnson and Mac Wallace continues to thrive. The thirty-sixth president was an incongruous figure responsible for pivotal deeds, such as the Civil Rights Acts, even if his motives were not entirely pure, and the intentional escalation of the Vietnam War. He was indeed a ruthless political animal capable of unprincipled acts

in the service of his own power. Whether that includes serial murder remains unproven.

90. *AAS*, March 29, 1984; *FWST*, March 30, 1984.
91. *FWST*, December 27, 1984.
92. *AAS*, August 13, 1985; *FWST*, August 14, 1985.
93. *FWST*, January 14, 1987.
94. *AAS* September 30, 1992 (quotations).
95. *DMN*, September 18, 1982; *FWST*, March 12, 1987, June 11, 1989.
96. Honorable Ralph M. Hall (TX), *Congressional Record*, 137: 174 (November 22, 1991).
97. *Conroe Courier* and *Waco Tribune-Herald*, both dated June 24, 1992. The Monroe County Sheriff's Department Training Academy was named in honor of the former lawman.
98. *Waco Tribune-Herald*, June 23, 2003.
99. Day, *Captain Clint Peoples*, 172; *AA*, March 16, 1958; *Waco Herald-Tribune*, April 15, 2012.

Notes for Chapter 10

1. Sheryn R. Jones, ed., *Fannin County Folks and Facts: A History of Fannin County, Texas* (Dallas, TX: Taylor Publishing Company, 1977), 305; Birth Certificates, James Elmer Riddles, March 9, 1942, File No. 32058, Gladys Lucile Riddles, March 12, 1942, File No. 3562, Thomas Leeman Riddles, March 17, 1942, File No. 62340; *Paris News*, June 16, 1977.

   Having suffered from chronic fibroid phthisis for twenty-five years, John Riddles died on January 6, 1948, of pneumothorax and bronchopleural fistula. He was buried in Oakwood Cemetery in Honey Grove. Death Certificate, John M. Riddles, January 14, 1948, Registrar's No. 1847; *Lubbock Evening Journal*, January 9, 1948. Louise died at home on October 10, 1949, of hypertensive cardiovascular disease. She was buried next to her husband at Oakwood Cemetery the following day. Death Certificate, Louise Riddles, October 24, 1949, File No. 48181.
2. James B. Riddles, James E. Riddles, and Carolyn Ann Riddles, interview with the author, Elgin, Texas, May 10, 2012. Hereafter cited as James Riddles interview, 2012.
3. James Riddles interview, 2012.
4. James Riddles interview, 2012.

5. James Riddles interview, 2012.
6. James Riddles interview, 2012; Glenn Elliott with Robert Nieman, *Glenn Elliott: A Ranger's Ranger* (Longview, TX: Robert Nieman, 1999), 9.
7. James Riddles interview, 2012; Amendment to Birth Certificate, Loneta Pearl Luttrell, May 24, 1974, File No. 1174-A.
8. James Riddles interview, 2012; Roster of students, 7th Recruit Training School, TDPS Training Academy Records, Box 2005/128-1, TSLAC; S. E. Spinks, *Law on the Last Frontier: Texas Ranger Arthur Hill* (Lubbock: Texas Tech University Press, 2007), 25.
9. Roster of students, 7th Recruit Training School, TDPS Training Academy Records, Box 2005/128-1, TSLAC; Elliott and Mitchell to members of the Active & Retired Ranger Association, April 1, 1996, James E. Riddles, Army Separation Qualification Record, both in Archives Files, FTRA; James Riddles interview, 2012; Thomas Lee Charlton, "The Texas Department of Public Safety, 1935–1957" (M.A. thesis, University of Texas at Austin, 1961), 130.
10. Robert K. Wright, Jr., *Military Police* (Washington, DC: Center of Military History, 1992), 9 (quotations). For more on the regulations Riddles would have enforced, see *Articles of War, Approved June 4, 1920* (Washington, DC: Government Printing Office, 1920).
11. "As per Family Bible" and "From Another Bible," typescript, Archives Files, FTRA. For more on the two ships, see Roland W. Charles, *Troopships of World War II* (Washington, DC: Army Transportation Association, 1947).
12. *El Paso Times*, August 20, 1942.
13. Bryan County, Oklahoma, Marriage Records 51, 638; Elliott and Mitchell to members of the Active & Retired Ranger Association, April 1, 1996, James E. Riddles, Army Separation Qualification Record, both in Archives Files, FTRA; "PMG Graduates 2nd Lts.," *Army and Navy Journal* 80 (March 13, 1943): 802; Certification of Military Service, NA Form 13038, NPRC; "822nd Military Police Company, Memories" (Berlin, DE: privately printed, 1945), 11; Jane Lawson Hammonds, "822nd Military Police Company: The Forgotten 'Supporting Cast' of the Ninth Army," MS, 2001, n.p.
14. *Paris News*, August 23, September 8, 1943; T. M. Keith, January 10, 1945, 822nd Military Police Company: Historical Reports, 1943–1946, Box 4930, RG 338, NARA, 2; "822nd Military Police Company, Memories," 11; Hammonds, "822nd Military Police Company," n.p.; James Riddles interview, 2012.

15. T. M. Keith, January 10, 1945, 822nd Military Police Company: Historical Reports, 1; "822nd Military Police Company, Memories," 11; *Boston Globe*, June 29, 30, July 1, 1944; Elliott and Mitchell to members of the Active & Retired Ranger Association, April 1, 1996, James E. Riddles, Army Separation Qualification Record, both in Archives Files, FTRA; Robert L. Gunnarsson, Sr., *American Military Police in Europe, 1945–1991* (Jefferson, NC: McFarland & Co., 2011), 77; Hammonds, "822nd Military Police Company," n.p.
16. James Riddles interview, 2012; "822nd Military Police Company, Memories," 12; Hammonds, "822nd Military Police Company," n.p.; Samuel Wallace Magill, "We Took 20,000 Germans," *Life* 17 (October 2, 1944): 17–18; *Stars and Stripes*, September 19, 22, 1944; *Conquer: The Story of Ninth Army* (Washington, DC: Infantry Journal Press, 1947), 49–50; T. M. Keith, October 2, 1944, 822nd Military Police Company: Historical Reports, 2. Some sources identify the German general as Erich Elster. Photographs of the keepsakes were provided to the author by James E. Riddles.
17. T. M. Keith, November 3, 1944, January 10, 1945, 822nd Military Police Company: Historical Reports, 1–2, 4, n.p.; "822nd Military Police Company, Memories," 12; Hammonds, "822nd Military Police Company," n.p.; Gunnarsson, *American Military Police in Europe*, 77; *Aiken Standard*, November 11, 1987 (quotation); Gardner A. Dean, *One Hundred and Eighty Days: XIII Corps* (Peine, DE: Corps Public Relations Section, 1945), 7.
18. T. M. Keith, January 10, 1945, 822nd Military Police Company: Historical Reports, n.p.; "822nd Military Police Company, Memories," 11–12; James Riddles interview, 2012. A native of Landis, North Carolina, McKnight enlisted on May 29, 1943, and received his discharge on March 13, 1946. Following the war, he spent thirty-six years as a police officer in neighboring Salisbury and served fifteen years as police chief at W. G. Hefner VA Medical Center. He died on September 21, 2009. *Salisbury Post*, September 22, 2009.
19. James Riddles interview, 2012.
20. Hammonds, "822nd Military Police Company," n.p.
21. Dean, *One Hundred and Eighty Days*, 13–14; A, H. Levine, January 10, 1946, 822nd Military Police Company: Historical Reports, n.p.; "822nd Military Police Company, Memories," 13; Hammonds, "822nd Military Police Company," n.p.; Gunnarsson, *American Military Police in Europe*, 77.

22. A. H. Levine, January 10, 1946, 822nd Military Police Company: Historical Reports, n.p.; "822nd Military Police Company, Memories," 13; Hammonds, "822nd Military Police Company," n.p.; Steven J. Zaloga, *Downfall 1945: The Fall of Hitler's Third Reich* (Oxford, UK: Osprey Publishing, 2016), 46; Gunnarsson, *American Military Police in Europe*, 77; *New York Times*, April 19, 1945 (quotation); Christopher E. Mauriello, *Forced Confrontation: The Politics of Dead Bodies in Germany at the End of World War II* (Lanham, MD: Lexington Books, 2017), 44–46.
23. James Riddles interview, 2012.
24. Dean, *One Hundred and Eighty Days*, 29, 37; A. H. Levine, January 10, 1946, 822nd Military Police Company: Historical Reports, n.p.; "822nd Military Police Company, Memories," 13; Boris Shub, *The Choice* (New York: Duell, Sloan and Pearce, 1950), 14; Gunnarsson, *American Military Police in Europe*, 77.
25. "822nd Military Police Company, Memories," 13; Earl F. Ziemke, *The U.S. Army in the Occupation of Germany, 1944–1946* (Washington, DC: Center of Military History, 1975), 401–402; Gunnarsson, *American Military Police in Europe*, 77.
26. James Riddles interview, 2012; A, H. Levine, January 10, 1946, 822nd Military Police Company: Historical Reports, n.p.; Army Separation Qualification Record, James E. Riddles; "As per Family Bible" and "From Another Bible," Archives Files, FTRA; Certification of Military Service, NA Form 13038, NPRC; *Paris News*, December 16, 1945.
27. *Lubbock Morning Avalanche*, December 25, 1946; James Riddles interview, 2012.
28. James Riddles interview, 2012.
29. *Lubbock Avalanche-Journal*, June 9, 1946. A Coast Guard veteran of World War II, Rowland served over thirty-seven years with the DPS, retiring as a Trooper II in 1976. He died in 2002. *The DPS Chaparral* (March 2002): 3.
30. *Lubbock Morning Avalanche*, July 5, 1946.
31. *Lubbock Evening Journal*, October 20, 1947.
32. *Hudspeth's Lubbock City Directory, 1948*, 540.
33. Transcript, SRSU, April 26, 1974.
34. Glenn Elliott, interview with Robert Nieman, Longview, Texas, February 14, 1994, Oral History Project, TRHF&M, 3.
35. *Lubbock Evening Journal*, December 21, 1949; Death Certificate, Paul Raymond Waters, November 4, 1970, File No. 82001; Find A Grave: William Erastus Renfrow.

36. Rednar to members of the Active & Retired Ranger Association, n.d., Archives Files, FTRA; San Angelo Standard Times, January 21, 2004.
37. *Lubbock Morning Avalanche*, June 13, 1952; *Lubbock Evening Journal*, July 2, 3, 1952.
38. Robert Nieman, "20th Century Shining Star: Capt. Jim Riddles," *TRD* 18 (Fall 2005): 16.
39. *DPS Biennial Report, 1952–1954*, 26.
40. James Riddles interview, 2012.
41. *Abilene Reporter-News*, June 18, 19, 1953.
42. *Abilene Reporter-News*, September 12, 13, 1953; *FWST*, September 16, 1953.
43. *Big Spring Daily Herald*, September 13, 1953; *Brownwood Bulletin*, September 13, 1953; *Lubbock Morning Avalanche* and *Lubbock Evening Journal*, both dated September 14, 1953; *Abilene Reporter-News*, September 15, 21, November 18, 1953.
44. *FWST*, September 16, 17, 1953; *Abilene Reporter-News*, September 19, 1953.
45. *Abilene Reporter-News*, December 18, 1953; Find A Grave: Edwin Eugene Powell.
46. *Olney Enterprise*, February 18, March 11, 1954; Death Certificate, Glenn Greer Dunaway, January 11, 1967, File No. 06616.
47. *Abilene Reporter-News*, February 17, 1954.
48. *Abilene Reporter-News*, March 23, April 2, 1954.
49. *Abilene Reporter-News*, February 6, 8, 9, March 9, September 28, 1955; Death Certificate, Leah Naomi Montgomery, February 8, 1955, State File No. 5905.
50. *Abilene Reporter-News*, March 9, September 28, 29, 30, 1955.
51. *Abilene Reporter-News*, June 15, 1956.
52. *Corsicana Daily Sun*, January 2, 13, 14, 16, 24, 1956 (quotation).
53. *Abilene Reporter-News*, July 10, 1956.
54. James Riddles interview, 2012.
55. *Abilene Reporter-News*, September 8, 1957.
56. James M. Day, *Captain Clint Peoples, Texas Ranger: Fifty Years A Lawman* (Waco: Texian Press, 1980), 120–121.
57. *WNT*, June 10, 1958.
58. *Corsicana Daily Sun*, October 29, 30, 31, November 4, 1958, July 9, 1959.
59. *WNT*, January 21, March 10, 1959.

60. Day, *Captain Clint Peoples*, 121.
61. James Riddles interview, 2012.
62. James Riddles interview, 2012.
63. *Abilene Reporter-News*, February 16, 1962 (quotation); *FWST* and *GDN*, both dated February 16, 1962; *AA*, April 17, 1962.
64. James Riddles interview, 2012.
65. Elliott and Mitchell to members of the Active & Retired Ranger Association, April 1, 1996, Archives Files, FTRA.
66. Robert Owen, "In the Line of Duty," *Elgin, Etc: Stories of Elgin, Texas* (Elgin: Elgin Historical Association, 2008), 190; *AAS*, November 16, 19, 1963; *Bastrop Advertiser*, November 21, 1963; Phil Marquette, "Twisted Trail of Terror," *Master Detective* 67 (March 1964): 57–58; *GDN*, March 18, 1978.
67. James Riddles interview, 2012; Owen, "In the Line of Duty," 190; *Bastrop Advertiser*, November 21, 1963.
68. *AAS*, November 28, 1963; *FWST*, November 30, 1963; Marquette, "Twisted Trail of Terror," 58; Find A Grave: Henry Warren Sebesta.
69. *AS*, February 25, April 10, May 5, 1964.
70. *SAE*, May 11, 1967.
71. *FWST*, February 4, 5, 10, 1965; *SAE*, February 9, 1965.
72. AS, February 15, 1965; *AA*, February 19, 1965; *AAS*, February 20, 1965.
73. *Victoria Advocate*, June 25, 1965.
74. *SAE*, September 5, 6, 7, 1965; *SAL*, September 6, 1965; *AA*, September 8, 9, 10, 1965.
75. *AS*, January 19, 20, 1966; *AA*, January 21, 1966.
76. *SAE*, May 10, 11, 1967, April 26, 27, 1968.
77. *AAS*, August 6, 1967; *FWST*, August 7, 17, 1967; *AA*, September 7, 14, 29, 1967; *AS*, September 13, 27, 1967.
78. Inactive Personnel Record, James B. Riddles, TDPS; *AS*, November 29, 1967.
79. Nieman, "Capt. Jim Riddles," 16.
80. Elliott and Mitchell to members of the Active & Retired Ranger Association, April 1, 1996, Archives Files, FTRA; Spinks, *Law on the Last Frontier*, 162. Elliott with Nieman, *Glenn Elliott*, 9: "To this day, if you meet a Ranger who served under Jim Riddle [*sic*] he will proudly tell you that he was a 'Riddle Ranger.'" Sid Merchant indelicately commented: "My captain, Jim Riddles, has balls as big as two brass bathtubs." Robert M. Utley, *Lone Star Lawmen: The Second Century of the Texas Rangers* (New York: Berkley Books, 2007), 260.

81. James Riddles interview, 2012.
82. *AS*, January 29, 30, 1968, October 10, 1967; *FWST*, December 8, 1967, January 31, February 1, 1968. Wolcott was declared legally sane on July 8, 1974. Due to the earlier verdict, he did not stand trial for his mother and sister's deaths. *AAS*, July 9, 1974.
83. *AAS*, *SAE*, and *DMN*, all dated December 29, 1968; *Odessa American* and *Mexia Daily News*, both dated December 30, 1968; *Victoria Advocate*, December 31, 1968.
84. Spinks, *Law on the Last Frontier*, 184–186; *Odessa American*, January 6, 1969.
85. *Odessa American*, September 18 (quotation), 19, 20, 21, 30, November 25, 1970; Find A Grave: Lynn Bates "Bill" Eddins.
86. *AAS*, May 22, 1971.
87. Cox, *Time of the Rangers*, 283–284.
88. *Odessa American*, June 13, 1971; *Lubbock Avalanche-Journal*, June 5, July 9, 1971; Death Certificate, Nancy Lee Mitchell, June 23, 1971, File No. 95720 (quotation); *Del Rio News-Herald*, January 16, 1998; Find A Grave: William H. Sage.
89. *Abilene Reporter-News*, June 14, 16, 1971; *Big Spring Daily Herald*, June 14, 1971; *Odessa American*, June 14, 1971; *Lubbock Avalanche-Journal*, June 14, 15 (quotation), 16, 17, 1971; Death Certificate, Michael Ray Mathis, June 18, 1971, File No. 43498.
90. *Odessa American*, January 20, 21, October 4, 5, 12, 13, 1972, February 23, May 9, July 17, September 26, 1973; *AS*, January 20, 1972; *Lubbock Avalanche-Journal*, April 21, October 7, 1972; *FWST*, October 5, 1972; *DMN*, April 29, 1973; Al Mitchell, interview with Nancy and Eddie Ray, Midland, Texas, September 7, 2008, Oral History Project, TRHF&M, 2. Other unfortunate victims include Eula Mae Miller, last seen on July 12, 1970; Oleta Fuller, on February 10, 1971; and Carolyn Montgomery, on August 9, 1971. Their cases remain unsolved. *Odessa American*, February 17, July 4, 1971; *DMN*, August 10, 1971.
91. *Odessa American*, April 29, May 9, 1973; Spinks, *Law on the Last Frontier*, 202–205.
92. *Big Spring Daily Herald*, May 13, 1973.
93. College Transcript, SRSU, James Elmer Riddles; James Riddles interview, 2012.
94. *Lubbock Avalanche-Journal*, June 19, 1971; *Odessa American*, May 10, 16, 1974; Death Certificate, Clovis Odell Jones, February 12, 1979, File No. 22266; Find A Grave: Judge William Woodson Matthews. Kneeland was for a time a suspect in the rape and murder of Fort Worth

high school student Carla Walker on February 20, 1974. At the time of this writing, that open case may be headed toward a resolution. On November 12, 2020, a Tarrant County grand jury returned a capital murder indictment against a seventy-seven-year-old man on the basis of a positive DNA match. *FWST*, November 12, 2020.

95. *Odessa American*, November 9, 1974, May 24, June 26, 1975. Kneeland was paroled after serving twelve years and nine months of his multiple life sentences. *Tyler Morning Telegraph*, October 15, 1987. He was arrested on a parole violation on July 29, 1994, and returned to prison. *McAllen Monitor*, August 28, 1994.
96. James Riddles interview, 2012; *Midland Reporter-Telegram*, January 23, 24, 1975; *Paris News*, January 24, 1975; Death Certificate, James Elmer Riddles, January 27, 1975, File No. 04744. Captain Riddles shares the cemetery with Ranger Robert Gray "Bob" Goss and Ranger Captain Charles Albert "Charlie" Moore, Jr.
97. James Riddles interview, 2012; *AAS*, February 22, 2007; *Taylor Daily Press*, February 22, 2007.
98. James Riddles interview, 2012; *Elgin Courier*, August 1, 2012
99. Elliott and Mitchell to members of the Active & Retired Ranger Association, April 1, 1996, and assorted letters, Archives Files, FTRA; James Riddles interview, 2012.

Notes for Chapter 11

1. Inactive Personnel Record, Bobby Paul Doherty, TDPS; *Sixteenth U.S. Census*, Hill County, Texas; Birth Certificate, Doris Scruggs, June 1, 1914, File No. 1043; Death Certificate, Paul Edward Doherty, December 19, 1975, File No. 91934; Bob Prince and Buster Doherty, interview with the author, Fort Worth, Texas, August 25, 2011. Cited hereafter as Prince and Doherty interview, 2011. *FWST*, November 14, 1950, September 13, 1952.
2. Prince and Doherty interview, 2011; Memorial Cross ceremony organized by the Former Texas Rangers Association, Azle, Texas, February 19, 2012. Cited hereafter as Memorial Cross ceremony, 2012.
3. Memorial Cross ceremony, 2012.
4. Short to the author, August 21, 2011; Gary Cartwright, "The Death of a Texas Ranger," *Texas Monthly* 6 (August 1978): 104.
5. Memorial Cross ceremony, 2012.
6. Prince and Doherty interview, 2011.

7. Memorial Cross ceremony, 2012.
8. Prince and Doherty interview, 2011; *FWST*, October 27, 1957.
9. Doherty to the author, January 21, 2021; Inactive Personnel Record, Bobby Paul Doherty, TDPS; Roster of students, Recruit Training School No. 4, TDPS Training Academy Records, Box 2005/128-10, TSLAC; Favor to the author, July 17, 2020.
10. Prince and Doherty interview, 2011; *AAS*, October 11, 2013. Jungkind was inducted into the Texas Highway Patrol Hall of Fame on November 5, 2005.
11. Memorial Cross ceremony, 2012.
12. Prince and Doherty interview, 2011.
13. Memorial Cross ceremony, 2012.
14. Memorial Cross ceremony, 2012; Inactive Personnel Record, Bobby Paul Doherty, TDPS.
15. "DPS News From Around the State," *The DPS Chaparral* (April 2005): 1; Prince and Doherty interview, 2011; *AAS*, March 1, 2005.
16. Memorial Cross ceremony, 2012.
17. Inactive Personnel Record, Bobby Paul Doherty, TDPS.
18. Prince and Doherty interview, 2011.
19. Memorial Cross ceremony, 2012; Cartwright, "Death of a Texas Ranger," 99.
20. Prince and Doherty interview, 2011.
21. Cartwright, "Death of a Texas Ranger," 105.
22. Prince and Doherty interview, 2011.
23. Inactive Personnel Record, Bobby Paul Doherty, TDPS; *FWST*, October 31, 1973 (quotation).
24. Prince and Doherty interview, 2011.
25. Prince and Doherty interview, 2011; Memorial Cross ceremony, 2012; Death Certificate, Paul Edwards Doherty, December 19, 1975, File No. 91934.
26. Inactive Personnel Record, Bobby Paul Doherty, TDPS.
27. Prince and Doherty interview, 2011; *FWST*, February 23, 1978.
28. Prince and Doherty interview, 2011.
29. Prince and Doherty interview, 2011; Cartwright, "Death of a Texas Ranger," 100.
30. *FWST*, October 2, 1976.
31. Prince and Doherty interview, 2011; Gini Graham Scott, *Homicide by the Rich and Famous: A Century of Prominent Killers* (Westport, CT: Praeger, 2005), 101–107.

32. Report of Captain D. Crawford, February 22, 1978, Denton County Sheriff's Office, 1.
33. Report of Captain D. Crawford, February 22, 1978, 1.
34. Prince and Doherty interview, 2011.
35. Report of Captain D. Crawford, February 22, 1978, 2.
36. Report of Captain D. Crawford, February 22, 1978, 3; Cartwright, "Death of a Texas Ranger," 99–101.
37. Report of Captain D. Crawford, February 22, 1978, 4, 6; Cartwright, "Death of a Texas Ranger," 101.
38. Cartwright, "Death of a Texas Ranger," 101; Report of Captain D. Crawford, February 22, 1978, 5; *FWST*, March 8, 1978.
39. Report of Captain D. Crawford, February 22, 1978, 6; Cartwright, "Death of a Texas Ranger," 101.
40. Report of Captain D. Crawford, February 22, 1978, 6; Prince and Doherty interview, 2011; *FWST*, October 1, 2000.
41. Report of Captain D. Crawford, February 22, 1978, 6, 8, 9; *FWST*, February 21, 1978; Cartwright, "Death of a Texas Ranger," 101–102.
42. Report of Agent B. A. Neel, February 21, 1978, DPS, 2.
43. Report of Captain D. Crawford, February 22, 1978, 9; *FWST*, March 7, 1978; *DMN*, June 14, 1978; Cartwright, "Death of a Texas Ranger," 102–104.
44. Report of Agent B. A. Neel, February 21, 1978, 3; Cartwright, "Death of a Texas Ranger," 104; *FWST*, March 8, 1978.
45. Report of Agent B. A. Neel, February 21, 1978, 3; Cartwright, "Death of a Texas Ranger," 104. Bob Alexander and Donaly E. Brice, *Texas Rangers: Lives, Legend, and Legacy* (Denton: University of North Texas Press, 2017), 380: "The law-enforcing brotherhood collectively cried: But for the grace of God or Lady Luck there go I."
46. *Waco Tribune-Herald*, February 21, 1978; Cartwright, "Death of a Texas Ranger," 104 (quotation); *FWST*, November 5, 2013.
47. Cartwright, "Death of a Texas Ranger," 104.
48. Cartwright, "Death of a Texas Ranger," , 105 (quotation); Report of Agent B. A. Neel, February 21, 1978, 3. Doherty was succeeded in Company B by Ralph J. Wadsworth, formerly of Houston. *FWST*, March 9, 1978.
49. Cartwright, "Death of a Texas Ranger," 105.
50. *FWST* and *AAS*, both dated February 24, 1978; Richard Grimmett, "Texas Ranger Killed in Narcotics Raid," *DPS Chaparral* 20 (April 1978): 1, 4; Cartwright, "Death of a Texas Ranger," 105.

51. Prince and Doherty interview, 2011; Grimmett, "Texas Ranger Killed," 4.
52. Acts 1978, 2nd Called Session, 65th Legislature, House Concurrent Resolution No. 16, *General and Special Laws of Texas*.
53. Report of Agent B. A. Neel, February 21, 1978, DPS, 5; *FWST*, February 21, 22, April 26, August 23, September 1, 1978; Cartwright, "Death of a Texas Ranger," 172.
54. *AAS*, February 23, 1978; *FWST*, March 3, 1978.
55. Cartwright, "Death of a Texas Ranger," 171.
56. Cartwright, "Death of a Texas Ranger," 173–174.
57. Cartwright, "Death of a Texas Ranger," 176; *FWST*, May 30, 31, June 17, 1978, August 27, 2017; Clark to the author, August 24, 2012; *DMN*, September 11, 1999; Cobb to Doherty family, June 22, 1978, Doherty Vertical File, TRHF&M.
58. *AAS*, July 29, 1978; Prince and Doherty interview, 2011.
59. Acts 1977, Regular Session, 65th Legislature, Ch. 347, *General and Special Laws of Texas*. Section 3f (a)(2) has since been recodified as 3g (a)(2). Acts 1991, 72nd Legislature, Regular Session, Ch. 541, *General and Special Laws of Texas*.
60. Prince and Doherty interview, 2011; Board of Pardons and Paroles Minutes, n.d.; Battson to the author, August 15, 2012.
61. Board of Pardons and Paroles Minutes, n.d.; Battson to the author, August 15, 2012.
62. Prince and Doherty interview, 2011.
63. Gary Cartwright, "Greg Ott, Free," *Texas Monthly* 32 (July 2004): 48; *DMN*, September 11, 1999 (quotation).
64. *DMN*, September 11, 1999.
65. *DMN*, September 11, 1999.
66. *DMN*, September 11, 1999.
67. Prince and Doherty interview, 2011.
68. Board of Pardons and Paroles Minutes, n.d.; Battson to the author, August 15, 2012.
69. Gary Cartwright, "Free Greg Ott," *Texas Monthly* 28 (August 2000): 134–135, 143–146; *FWST*, January 30, December 23, 2003; *Montana Standard* and *Salisbury Daily Times*, both dated August 23, 2003; *Tampa Tribune* and *Salt Lake City Tribune*, both dated August 24, 2003; *New York Daily News*, December 23, 2003.
70. Price to Kazen, January 19, 2004, Jones to Kazen, January 21, 2004, and assorted letters, all from Doherty Vertical File, TRHF&M; Find A Grave: James Almon "Jim" Shaw, Jr., Timothy Cullen "Tim" Curry, Sr.

71. Doherty to Perry, et. al., January 13, 2004, Doherty Vertical File, TRHF&M.
72. Clark to the author, August 24, 2012; *FWST* and *Denton Record-Chronicle*, both dated May 26, 2004.
73. Prince and Doherty interview, 2011; *Houston Chronicle*, May 26, 2004 (quotation).
74. Prince and Doherty interview, 2011.
75. *Azle News*, March 3, 2021.
76. *FWST*, May 13, 2007.
77. Prince and Doherty interview, 2011.
78. Prince and Doherty interview, 2011.
79. Prince and Doherty interview, 2011.
80. *Azle News*, February 23, 2012; Memorial Cross ceremony, 2012.

Notes for Chapter 12

1. Perrin to the author, November 1, 2012; Jennings to the author, January 10, 2021; *Pampa News*, June 25, 1967; *Canadian Record*, May 30, 2002. Marsen died on July 8, 1988, in Wheeler. *Canadian Record*, July 14, 1988. Willora died on May 25, 2002, in Canadian. *Amarillo Globe-News*, May 27, 2002. LaVerda died on June 13, 2015, in Canyon. Find A Grave: LaVerda Mae Camp Guffey, Daniel Lee Schroeder.
2. *Borger News-Herald*, January 25, 1987; Perrin to the author, November 1, 2012.
3. Martinez to the author, June 19, 2012; Roster of students, Recruit Training School No. 31, TDPS Training Academy Records, Box 2005/128-19, TSLAC.
4. *Brownsville Herald*, November 6, 1969; Cameron County Divorce Records, File No. 3491, February 4, 1970.
5. Marriage License No. 093584, September 14, 1970, Cameron County Marriage Records; *Brownsville Herald*, September 20, 1970, July 20, 1975; Stacy Guffey, telephone interview with the author, January 25, 2021.
6. *Brownsville Herald*, December 1, 1972.
7. Martinez to the author, June 19, 2012; *Brownsville Herald*, February 1, 26, 1976.
8. Robert Nieman, "21st Century Shining Star: Ray Coffman," *TRD* 11 (Summer 2003): 27.
9. Cameron County Divorce Records, File No. 179000, April 13, 1976.

10. Martinez to the author, June 19, 2012; Bob Alexander, *Old Riot, New Ranger: Captain Jack Dean: Texas Ranger and U.S. Marshal* (Denton: University of North Texas Press, 2018), 277, 366.
11. Marriage License No. 056610, June 15, 1977, Cameron County Marriage Records; Travis Guffey to the author, October 30, 2012; Jennings to the author, January 10, 2021; *San Angelo Standard-Times*, January 22, 2012.
12. Stan Guffey eulogy, Guffey Archives File, FTRA.
13. Perrin to the author, November 1, 2012.
14. *Del Rio News*, July 2, August 13, 1981.
15. Inactive Personnel Record, Stanley K. Guffey, TDPS; Mitchel P. Roth, "Through the Ages: Texas DPS History," *Courtesy, Service, and Protection: The History of the Texas Department of Public Safety* (Paducah, KY: Turner Publishing Company, 2003), 52; Martinez to the author, June 19, 2012; Favor to the author, July 17, 2020; Jennings to the author, January 10, 2021; *AAS*, January 24, 1987 (quotation).
16. *Llano News*, December 23, 1982.
17. Stan Guffey eulogy, Guffey Archives File, FTRA.
18. Howard "Slick" Alfred, interview with Robert Nieman, Athens, Texas, June 30, 2005, Oral History Project, TRHF&M, 54. Cited hereafter as Howard Alfred interview, 2005. In his autobiography, retired Ranger Edgar Dalton "Ed' Gooding praised Mitchell as a "Captain's Captain." Ed Gooding with Robert Nieman, *Ed Gooding: Soldier, Texas Ranger* (Longview, TX: Ranger Publications, 2001), 253.
19. Robert Nieman, "Howard 'Slick' Alfred and the Amy McNeil Kidnapping," *TRD* 25 (Winter 2005): 14; *Paris News*, January 14, 1985.
20. Howard Alfred interview, 2005, 55; *GDN*, January 14, 1985. McNeil had also been a forerunner in the development of the hand-held calculator. *Paris News*, January 14, 1985.
21. Cox, *Time of the Rangers*, 310–311.
22. Howard Alfred interview, 2005, 56.
23. Ralph Wadsworth, interview with Robert Nieman, Kaufman, Texas, January 29, 2006, Oral History Project, TRHF&M, 53. Cited hereafter as Ralph Wadsworth interview, 2006.
24. Ralph Wadsworth interview, 2006, 53; Johnny Waldrip, interview with Nancy Ray and Eddie Ray, Sherman, Texas, October 20, 2008, Oral History Project, TRHF&M, 35. Cited hereafter as Johnny Waldrip interview, 2008. Jennings to the author, January 10, 2021.

25. Howard Alfred interview, 2005, 56; *GDN*, January 14, 1985.
26. Johnny Waldrip interview, 2008, 33–34; Howard Alfred interview, 2005, 57; *GDN*, January 14, 1985.
27. Howard Alfred interview, 2005, 58–60; *GDN*, January 14, 1985. James Ray was the nephew of retired Ranger and DPS executive Jim Ray.
28. Cox, *Time of the Rangers*, 312; Johnny Waldrip interview, 2008, 34.
29. Howard Alfred interview, 2005, 59–60; *GDN*, January 14, 1985. John Dendy served as a Ranger from 1973 to 1992. His son, Kirby, was also a Ranger, and served as captain of Company F from 1995 to 2011. The younger Dendy capped his forty-three-year career in law enforcement as chief of the service from 2012 to 2014. Kirby's son, Travis, promoted to the Rangers in July 2019, making the Dendy family the first three uninterrupted generations of Texas Rangers. *Texas Ranger Association Foundation Newsletter* 8 (July 2014), 1; *Texas Ranger Hall of Fame and Museum Newsletter*, July 2019.
30. Howard Alfred interview, 2005, 60–62; Nieman, "Howard 'Slick' Alfred," 16.
31. Howard Alfred interview, 2005, 62; *Paris News*, January 14, 1985.
32. Howard Alfred interview, 2005, 62.
33. *GDN*, January 14, 1985; *Paris News*, January 14, 15, 1985; *AAS*, January 27, 1987; Jennings to the author, January 10, 2021.
34. *AAS*, May 21, 1985; *New Braunfels Herald-Zeitung* and *Llano News*, both dated May 23, 1985.
35. *AAS*, January 23, 24, 1987; Cox, *Time of the Rangers*, 331; Bob Mitchell interview, 1996, 50–51.
36. Bob Mitchell interview, 1996, 51; *AAS*, January 23, 24, 1987; *GDN*, January 24, 1987; Bill Johnston, "The Day the Last Texas Ranger Died," interview with Robert Riggs, *Justice Facts*, podcast audio, November 24, 2020, https://www.justicefactspodcast.com/2020/11/24/the-day-the-last-texas-ranger-died-e7/; Bob Alexander and Donaly E. Brice, *Texas Rangers: Lives, Legend, and Legacy* (Denton: University of North Texas Press, 2017), 384.
37. Bob Mitchell interview, 1996, 52; *Llano News*, January 29, 1987; AAS, January 17, 1988 (quotation).
38. *AAS*, January 23, 24, 1987; *GDN*, *DMN*, and *Houston Chronicle*, all dated January 24, 1987; H. Joaquin Jackson and David Marion Wilkinson, *One Ranger* (Austin: University of Texas Press, 2005), 178.
39. *AAS*, January 24, February 14, 1987; *Llano News*, January 29, 1987.

40. *AAS*, January 24, 1987.
41. *Waco Tribune-Herald*, January 27, 1987. Byron Johnson informed this author that the now-retired Aycock has in recent years refused to discuss the events of January 22, 1987. Honoring the Ranger's wishes, no attempt was made to contact him.
42. *Dallas Times-Herald*, January 24, 1987.
43. Acts 1987, Regular Session, 70th Legislature, House Concurrent Resolution No. 23 and Senate Concurrent Resolution No. 18, *General and Special Laws of Texas*; *AAS*, January 28, 1987.
44. Guffey Vertical File, TRHF&M; Mitchel P. Roth, "Through the Ages: Texas DPS History," *Courtesy, Service, and Protection: The History of the Texas Department of Public Safety* (Paducah, KY: Turner Publishing Company, 2003), 97. Aycock received a second Medal of Valor in January 1995. Joaquin Jackson, in *One Ranger*, 185, called him "the greatest Ranger of his generation."
45. *AAS*, January 26, 27, 1987; *FWST*, January 27, 1987; Jennings to the author, January 10, 2021. Author Mike Cox, the DPS spokesman at the time, wrote the eulogy for Colonel Adams. A copy is in the Guffey Archives File, FTRA.
46. *AAS*, January 27, 1987.
47. *Llano News*, January 29, 1987; *GDN*, February 15, 1987; *AAS*, January 17, 1988 (quotation). A copy of the minutes for the Llano County grand jury, November 1986 term, is in the possession of the author.
48. *Houston Chronicle*, January 24, 1987; *AAS*, February 14, 1987; *Waco Tribune-Herald*, February 15, 1987 (quotations).
49. *Canadian Record*, June 11, 1987.
50. Jennings to the author, January 10, 21, 2021; *Hood County News*, September 3, 1988; *Kerrville Times*, September 3, 1989; *Waco Citizen*, July 20, 1990; *AAS*, July 16, 1994.
51. *AAS*, January 17, 1988; *Odessa American*, January 18, 1989.
52. *AAS*, June 26, 1992 (quotation); Jennings to the author, January 10, 2021.
53. *San Marcos Daily Record*, January 15, 2012 (quotation); *San Angelo Standard-Times*, January 22, 2012.
54. *AAS*, January 17, 1988; Travis Guffey to the author, October 30, 2012.
55. Stacy Guffey, telephone interview with the author, January 25, 2021.
56. Stacy Guffey interview, 2021
57. Travis Guffey to the author, October 30, 2012.

Bibliography

Archives and Manuscript Collections

822nd Military Police Company: Historical Reports, 1943–1946. Box 4930. Record Group 338: Records of U.S. Army Operational, Tactical, and Support Organizations (World War II and Thereafter), 1917–1999. NARA, College Park, Maryland. Copy in the possession of the author.

Aldrich, Roy W., Papers. Archives of the Big Bend, SRSU, Alpine, Texas.

———. Box 3P157. BCAH, University of Texas at Austin.

Archives Files. FTRA, Fredericksburg, Texas.

Baldwin, Berkhead Clarence. "Biography of Baldwin." MS62 1A–172. Texas Ranger Research Center, TRHF&M, Waco, Texas.

Bexar County, Texas. Marriage Registers. Book N: June 24, 1896–November 16, 1897. Bexar County Clerk's Office, San Antonio, Texas. Copies in the possession of the author.

Burton, Marvin. Interview with Fred A. Carpenter. Mart, Texas. 1969. Tape recording. Southwest Collection/Special Collections Library. Texas Tech University, Lubbock, Texas.

———. Interview with Roger N. Conger. Waco, Texas. May 1, 1956. Typescript. Texas Ranger Research Center, TRHF&M, Waco, Texas. A condensed version was published as "No Bashful Item: The Reminiscences of Red Burton." *The Texas Ranger Annual* 2 (1983).

———. "The Johnny Holmes Murder Case." Typescript. MS26, Series 1. Red Burton Collection. TRHF&M, Waco, Texas.

———. "The Kilgore Raid, 1931." Typescript. MS26, Series 1. Red Burton Collection. TRHF&M, Waco, Texas.

———. "The Story of the Glen Rose Liquor War in 1923." Typescript. MS26, Series 1. Red Burton Collection. TRHF&M, Waco, Texas.

California Department of Corrections. Folsom State Prison Records, 1879–1949. ID #R136. California State Archives, Office of the Secretary of State, Sacramento, California.

Certification of Military Service. NA Form 13038. NPRC, St. Louis, Missouri. Copy in the possession of the author.

Confederate Muster Roll Abstract Records. A&ISD-TSLAC, Austin, Texas.

Department of Public Safety. Training Academy Records. A&ISD-TSLAC, Austin, Texas.

Electronic Army Serial Number Merged File, 1938–1946. World War II Army Enlistment Records. Record Group 64: Records of the National

Archives and Records Administration. NARA, College Park, Maryland. Online at www.archives.gov.

Federal Bureau of Investigation. "Bonnie and Clyde." File Nos. 26-3068, 26-4114, 26-4397, 26-5301. Online at vault.fbi.gov.

———. "Texarkana Phantom Moonlight Murders." File No. 62-80864. Online at vault.fbi.gov.

Fore, Zora Belle Wright. Interview. Corpus Christi, Texas. December 7, 1973. Recording A1993-005.0253. South Texas Oral History & Folklore Collection. South Texas Archives, Texas A&M University at Kingsville.

Gonzaullas, Manuel T., Scrapbooks. Five volumes. MS4. MTG Collection. Texas Ranger Research Center, TRHF&M, Waco, Texas.

Governors' Papers and Records. Record Group 301. A&ISD-TSLAC, Austin, Texas.

Hamer, Frank. Interview with J. Evetts Haley. Austin, Texas. January 15, 1939. Note cards. J. Evetts Haley Collection, HML&HC.

———. Interview with J. Evetts Haley. Houston, Texas. December 6, 1943. Note cards. J. Evetts Haley Collection, HML&HC.

Hamer, Harrison, Collection. Bastrop, Texas.

Internal Revenue Service. Official Personnel Folders. NPRC, St. Louis, Missouri.

Los Angeles County, California. Record of Marriage Licenses Book 816. Recorder's Office, Norwalk, California. Copy in the possession of the author.

McLennan County, Texas. Marriage Records Book 16. McLennan County Clerk's Office. Waco, Texas. Copy in the possession of the author.

Mitchell County, Texas. Marriage Records. County Clerk's Office, Colorado City, Texas. Copy in the possession of the author.

Perez, Jesse. "Reminiscences, 1870–1927." Typescript. Box 2R134. BCAH, University of Texas at Austin.

Texas Adjutant General's Department. Record Group 401. A&ISD-TSLAC, Austin, Texas.

———. World War I Service Record Cards. Texas Military Force Museum, Camp Mabry, Texas.

Texas Attorney General's Office. Biennial Report of Attorney General Will Wilson. Austin, December 4, 1962.

Texas Crime Investigating Committee Records, 1950–1953 and undated. Box 1. Southwest Collection/Special Collections Library. Texas Tech University, Lubbock, Texas.

Texas Department of Criminal Justice. Convict Record Ledgers, 1849–1954. Twenty-nine ledgers. A&ISD-TSLAC, Austin, Texas.

Texas Department of Criminal Justice. Texas Prison Board Minutes, 1927–1957. A&ISD-TSLAC, Austin, Texas.

Twelfth–Fifteenth Census of the United States. Record Group 29: Records of the Bureau of the Census, National Archives Publications T623, 624, 625, T626. NARA, Washington, DC. Online at Ancestry.com.

United States Army. Registers of Enlistments in the U.S. Army, 1789–1914. Record Group 94: Records of the Adjutant General's Office, Microfilm Publication 233. NARA, Washington, DC. Online at fold3.com.

United States Department of Veterans Affairs. *General Index to Pension Files, 1861–1934*. Record Group 15: Records of the Department of Veterans Affairs, 1773–2007, Microfilm Publication T288. NARA, Washington, DC.

United States District Court, Northern District of Texas (Dallas Division). Criminal Case File No 8250. Record Group 21: Records of District Courts of the United States. NARA, Fort Worth, Texas.

United States Marine Corps. Official Military Personnel Files, 1905–1998. Record Group 127: Records of the U.S. Marine Corps. NPRC, St. Louis, Missouri.

———. U.S. Marine Corps Muster Rolls, 1893–1940. Record Group 127: Records of the U.S. Marine Corps, Microfilm Publication T977. NPRC, St. Louis, Missouri. Material accessed at Ancestry.com.

United States Post Office Department. Record of Appointment of Postmaster, 1832–1971. Record Group 28: Records of the Post Office Department, Microfilm Publication M841. NARA, Washington, DC. Online at Ancestry.com.

United States Selective Service. World War I Draft Registration Cards. Record Group 163: Records of the Selective Service System, 1917–1939, Microfilm Publication 1509. NARA, Washington, DC. Material accessed at Ancestry.com.

———. World War II Draft Registration Cards. Record Group 147: Records of the Selective Service System, 1926–1975. NARA, St. Louis, Missouri. Material accessed at Ancestry.com.

Vertical Files. Texas Ranger Research Center, TRHF&M, Waco, Texas.

Ward, James R., Collection. Digitized audio recordings. West Texas Collection. Angelo State University, San Angelo, Texas. Copies of notes provided to the author by Dr. Charles H. Harris III and Dr. Richard B. McCaslin.

Webb, Walter Prescott, Collection. BCAH, University of Texas at Austin.

Wright, E. A. "Dogie," Papers. BCAH, University of Texas at Austin.

Articles

"The 11th Attempt to Kill Herb Noble." *Life* 31, no. 8 (August 20, 1951).

Abel, Joseph. "Opening the Closed Shop: The Galveston Longshoremen's Strike of 1920–1921." *SHQ* 110, no. 3 (January 2007).

"Again, Hot Oil." *Time Magazine* 31, no. 14 (April 4, 1938).

Allen, James. "Robertson's Ride with Death." *Master Detective* 25, no. 3 (November 1941).

Angel, William D., Jr. "Controlling the Workers: The Galveston Dock Workers' Strike of 1920 and Its Impact on Labor Relations in Texas." *ETHJ* 23, no. 2 (October 1985).

Ashburn, Karl. "Crime in Texas." *Southwest Review* 19, no. 4 (July 1934).

"The Battle of the Fence." *Life* 1, no. 4 (December 14, 1936).

Baum, Dale, and James L. Hailey. "Lyndon Johnson's Victory in the 1948 Texas Senate Race: A Reappraisal." *Political Science Quarterly* 109, no. 4 (Autumn 1994).

Billington, Monroe. "The Red River Boundary Controversy." *SHQ* 62, no. 3 (January 1959).

Boardman, Mark. "The Myths of a Border Warrior." *True West* 61, no. 6 (June 2014).

Boyle, Robert D. "Chaos in the East Oilfield, 1930–1935." *SHQ* 69, no. 3 (January 1966).

Burka, Paul. "Grand Dame of the Gulf." *Texas Monthly* 11, no. 12 (December 1983).

———. "The Law West of the Trinity." *Texas Monthly* 8, no. 3 (March 1980).

Burran, James A. "Violence in an 'Arsenal of Democracy': The Beaumont Race Riot, 1943." *ETHJ* 14, no. 1 (March 1976).

Carpenter, W. Clayton. "The Red River Boundary Dispute." *The American Journal of International Law* 19, no. 3 (July 1925).

Cartledge, Rick. "The Guns of Frank Hamer." *OklahombreS Journal* 4, no. 3 (Spring 1993).

Cartwright, Gary. "Benny and the Boys." *Texas Monthly* 19, no. 10 (October 1991).

———. "The Death of a Texas Ranger." *Texas Monthly* 6, no. 8 (August 1978).

———. "Free Greg Ott." *Texas Monthly* 28, no. 8 (August 2000).

———. "Greg Ott, Free." *Texas Monthly* 32, no. 7 (July 2004).

———. "One Last Shot." *Texas Monthly* 21, no. 6 (June 1993).

———. "Talking to Killers," *Texas Monthly* 30, no. 7 (July 2002).

Carver, Duke, with J. J. Klevenhagen and Cyrus Heard, as told to W. Boyd Gatewood. "'They'll Never Take Me Alive'." *Official Detective Stories* 5, no. 5 (January 15, 1938).

Casdorph, Paul Douglas. "The Texas National Guard and the 1922 Railroad Strike at Denison." *Texas Military History* 3, no. 4 (Winter 1963).

Chambers, William T. "Kilgore, Texas: An Oil Boom Town." *Economic Geography* 9, no. 1 (January 1933).

Clark, John E. "Reflections on the Duke of Duval: The Litigation Record." *South Texas Studies* 8 (1997).

Coffey, Jim. "Will Wright: Rangers and Prohibition." *TRD* 20 (Summer 2006). Online at texasrangers.org.

Conger, Roger, Gaines de Graffenreid, and Tom Hickman. "Mexican Buttons and Bandoliers: The Oral Memoirs of Captain Tom Hickman." *The Texas Ranger Annual* 2 (1983).

Corney, George. "Crime and Postal History: Bring in the Marines." *Marine Corps Gazette* 77, no. 10 (October 1993).

Cravey, Jerry E. "Cracking the Red Riddle of the Rio Grande Valley." *Startling Detective Adventures* 7, no. 37 (August 1931).

Crockett, Norman. "Crime on the Petroleum Frontier: Borger, Texas, in the Late 1920s." *Panhandle-Plains Historical Review* 64 (1991).

Cumberland, Charles C. "Border Raids in the Lower Rio Grande Valley, 1915." *SHQ* 57, no. 3 (January 1954).

David, Henry. "A Time Past: Gambling in Galveston." *In Between*, no. 29 (August 1978).

"Decline and Fall." *Time Magazine* 79, no. 21 (May 25, 1962).

Detzer, Karl. "Texas Rangers Still Ride the Trail." *Reader's Digest* 71, no. 425 (September 1957).

"DPS News from Around the State." *The DPS Chaparral* (April 2005).

Draper, Robert. "Twilight of the Texas Rangers." *Texas Monthly* 22, no. 2 (February 1994).

"The Duke Delivers." *Time Magazine* 52, no. 13 (September 27, 1948).

"End of a Texas Ranger." *Newsweek* 38, no. 6 (August 6, 1951).

Farmer, Ella Marie. "The Phantom Killer of the Brazos." Three parts. *True Detective Mysteries* 23, no. 2 (November 1934), no. 3 (December 1934), no. 4 (January 1935).

Ferling, John. "Texas City Disaster." *American History* 30, no. 6 (January/February 1996).

Flores, Becky. "Caught in the Crossfire: A Sociohistorical Analysis of Conflict in a 'Contact Zone' in 1920s South Texas." *South Texas Studies* 12 (Spring 2001).

"Focus on the Forty Acres." *Alcalde* 54, no. 8 (April 1966).

Forbes, Gerald. "Oil and the Red River Boundary." *Southwestern Social Science Quarterly* 27, no. 2 (September 1946).

Foreman, Grant. "Red River and the Spanish Boundary in the Supreme Court." *Chronicles of Oklahoma* 2, no. 3 (September 1924).

Foshee, Page S. "'Someone Get the Governor an Aspirin': Ross Sterling and Martial Law in East Texas." *ETHJ* 41, no. 2 (October 2003).

Franks, Zarko. "Bonnie and Clyde." *Houston Chronicle Magazine* (July 31, 1977).

Frisbie, David. "Desdemona's Reign of Terror." *American Legion Weekly* 2, no. 31 (August 27, 1920).

Fusco, John. "The Legendary Maney Gault." *True West* 67, no. 4 (April 2019).

Gray, George W. "The Watch on the Rio Grande." *The American Magazine* 101, no. 5 (May 1926).

Grimmett, Richard. "Texas Ranger Killed in Narcotics Raid." *The DPS Chaparral* 20, no. 4 (April 1978).

Haddock, Hugh V. "Killer from Mars." *Inside Detective* 28, no. 4 (April 1950).

Hager, William M. "The Plan of San Diego: Unrest on the Texas Border in 1915." *Arizona and the West* 5, no. 4 (Winter 1963).

Hall, Michael. "Two Bar-Maids, Five Alligators, and the Butcher of Elmendorf." *Texas Monthly* 30, no. 7 (July 2002).

Hancock, William Cx. "It's Death to Bonnie and Clyde." *True West* 16, no. 5 (May–June 1968).

House, Boyce. "The Santa Claus Bank Robbery." *Startling Detective Adventures* 4, no. 22 (March 1930).

Hunter, J. Marvin. "The Outstanding Texas Ranger." *Frontier Times* 22, no. 3 (December 1944).

"In Memory … A Tribute to Texas Ranger Stan Guffey." *Texas DPSOA Monthly* (March 1987).

James, Laurence P. "The Great Underground Manhunt." *Journal of the West* 18, no. 2 (April 1979).

Jeffrey, Jaclyn. "Ranch Days and Indian Ways: The Early Life of Frank Hamer." *The Texas Ranger Annual* 3 (1984).

Johnson, Bobby H. "Oil in the Pea Patch: The East Texas Oil Boom." *ETHJ* 13, no. 1 (March 1975).

Jordan, Henderson, and C. F. Waers. "The Inside Story of the Killing of 'Bonnie' Parker and Clyde Barrow." *True Detective Mysteries* 23, no. 2 (November 1934).

Kilday, Owen W., as told to Lawrence Topperwein. "Man Trap!: The Red Riddle of Lawrence Rea." *True Detective Mysteries* 29, no. 5 (February 1938).

Kinney, Harrison. "Frank Hamer: Texas Ranger." *American Gun* 1, no. 2 (Spring 1961).

"The Last Days of 'The Cat'." *Time Magazine* 58, no. 8 (August 20, 1951).

Lippold, Pamela. "Recollections: Revisiting the Beaumont Race Riot of 1943." *Touchstone* 25 (2006).

Long, Steven. "Shutdown, June 10, 1957: The Day the Wheels Stopped Turning." *In Between*, no. 166 (December 1983).

Lyons, Chuck. "The 1947 Texas City Explosion." *History Magazine* 17, no. 5 (June/July 2016).

MacKaye, Milton. "Death on the Water Front." *Saturday Evening Post* 230, no. 17 (October 26, 1957).

Magill, Samuel Wallace. "We Took 20,000 Germans." *Life* 17, no. 14 (October 2, 1944).

"A Man Mired in the Incredible Estes Mess." *Life* 52, no. 22 (June 1, 1962).

Mann, E. B. "Who Was Frank Hamer?" *Field and Stream* 84, no. 11 (March 1980).

Marcello, Ronald E. "Lone Star POWs: Texas National Guardsmen and the Building of the Burma-Thailand Railroad, 1942–1944." *SHQ* 95, no. 3 (January 1992).

Marchiafava, Louis J. "The Houston Police 1878–1948." *Rice University Studies* 63, no. 2 (Spring 1977).

Maroney, James C. "The Galveston Longshoremen's Strike of 1920." *ETHJ* 16, no. 1 (March 1978).

Marquette, Phil. "Twisted Trail of Terror." *Master Detective* 67, no. 6 (March 1964).

Martin, Jack. "Col. Homer Garrison, Jr., Director of the Department of Public Safety." *True Detective Mysteries* 34, no. 5 (August 1940).

Morgan, R. D. "Ace Pendleton: Oklahoma's Prince of Thieves." *OklahombreS Journal* 12, no. 3 (Spring 2011).

Mullen, James. "I Framed Ray Hamilton's Prison Break." *Startling Detective Adventures* 15, no. 88 (November 1935).

Newlon, Clarke. "Outlaw Tamer of the New West." *Startling Detective Adventures* 13, no. 76 (November 1934).

———, and Bob Alcorn. "I Killed Clyde Barrow." *Startling Detective Adventures* 13, no. 73 (August 1934).

Nieman, Robert. "20th Century Shining Star: Capt. Bob Crowder." *TRD* 14 (Summer 2004). Online at texasrangers.org.

———. "20th Century Shining Star: Capt. Johnny Klevenhagen." *TRD* 10 (Spring 2003). Online at texasrangers.org.

———. "21st Century Shining Star: Ray Coffman." *TRD* 11 (Summer 2003). Online at texasrangers.org.

———. "Galveston's Balinese Room." *TRD* 27 (Fall 2008). Online at texasrangers.org.

———. "Howard 'Slick' Alfred and the Amy McNeil Kidnapping." *TRD* 25 (Winter 2005). Online at texasrangers.org.

———. "In Their Own Words: 'They Just Passed the Bucket'." *TRD* 3 (Spring 2001). Online at texasrangers.org.

———. "Jim Ray." *TRD* 2 (Winter 2000). Online at texasrangers.org.

———. "On the Trail of Bonnie and Clyde: Why Frank Hamer Wasn't Serving as a Texas Ranger, A New Theory." *TRD* 13 (Spring 2004). Online at texasrangers.org.

Nordyke, Lewis. "Calculatin' Coke." *Saturday Evening Post* 217, no. 18 (October 28, 1944).

Olson, James S., and Susan Phair. "Anatomy of a Race Riot: Beaumont, *Texas*, 1943." Texana 11, no. 1 (Winter 1973).

Oulahan, Richard. "The Bumpkin Who Turned into a Warped Wizard." *Life* 52, no. 22 (June 1, 1962).

Paulson, James W. "Breaking the Back of the Texas Klan." *Texas Bar Journal* 75, no. 3 (March 2012).

"Phantom Killer Terrorizes Texarkana." *Life* 20, no. 23 (June 10, 1946).

Phillips, Edward H. "The Sherman Courthouse Riot of 1930." *ETHJ* 25, no. 2 (October 1987).

Platt, Harold L. "Energy and Urban Growth: A Comparison of Houston and Chicago." *SHQ* 91, no. 1 (July 1987).

"PMG Graduates 2nd Lts." *Army and Navy Journal* 80, no. 28 (March 13, 1943).

Ramsey, Mrs. J. A. "When Death Rode the Spanish Trail." *Master Detective* 11, no. 6 (February 1935).

"Red River War." *Time Magazine* 18, no. 5 (August 3, 1931).

Redding, Stan. "Top Gun of the Texas Rangers." *True Detective* 78, no. 5 (February 1963).

Reddy, John. "The Man Who Trapped Bonnie and Clyde." *Reader's Digest* (May 1968).

Rich, Carroll Y. "The Autopsy of Bonnie and Clyde." *Western Folklore* 29, no. 1 (January 1970).

Roth, Mitchel P. "Bonnie and Clyde in Texas: The End of the Texas Outlaw Tradition." *ETHJ* 35, no. 2 (October 1997).

"A Scandal Hot as a Pistol." *Life* 52, no. 22 (June 1, 1962).
Schendel, George. "Something Is Rotten in the State of Texas." *Collier's* 127, no. 23 (June 9, 1951).
Schuster, Simon W., IV. "The Modernization of the Texas Rangers, 1933–1936." *West Texas Historical Association Yearbook* 43 (1967).
Seymour, James B., Jr. "Evils More Deadly Than the Carnage of the Battlefield: The Fight for Prohibition in McLennan County in 1917." *ETHJ* 40, no. 1 (March 2002).
Shoemaker, Kyle W. "How Mexia Was Made a Clean City." *Owenwood Magazine* 1, no. 6 (May 1922).
Sillavan, Randy. "Remembrances of My Dad: Hollis Milton Sillavan." *TRD* 5 (Fall 2001). Online at texasrangers.org.
Simpson, William M. "A Bienville Parish Saga: The Ambush and Killing of Bonnie and Clyde." *Louisiana History: The Journal of the Louisiana Historical Association* 41, no. 1 (Winter 2000).
Smith, Lewis. "Manhunt!" *The Cattleman* 63, no. 1 (June 1976).
Smith, Marshall. "His Lifetime Record—Won: 700, Lost 1." *Life* 60, no. 13 (April 1, 1966).
Snell, David. "The Day the Real Bonnie and Clyde Were Gunned Down." *Life* 64, no. 7 (February 16, 1968).
Spellman, Paul N. "Dark Days of the Texas Rangers, 1915–1918." *South Texas Studies* 12 (Spring 2001).
Stanley, Stewart, as told to Violet Short. "Texas' House of Horror." *Master Detective* 8, no. 3 (May 1933).
"Still Digging." *Time Magazine* 79, no. 22 (June 1, 1962).
Tallent, Robert W. "The Great Mail Call." *Leatherneck* 38, no. 2 (February 1955).
Taylor, D. J. "The Story-Martin Gang Brought the Era of Organized Crime to Denton County." *Denton County Historical Commission Retrospect* (Fall 2015).
"Texas Counts 33 Illegally Slanted Holes." *Oil and Gas Journal* 62, no. 27 (July 2, 1962).
Texas Ranger Association Foundation Newsletter 8 (July 2014).
Texas Ranger Hall of Fame and Museum Newsletter (July 2019).
"Texas Sniper." *Time* 120, no. 17 (October 25, 1982).
Thorp, R. D., and M. Harris. "$1,000 for the Murderer of the Three Englers." *True Detective Mysteries* 30, no. 1 (April 1938).
"Tom Hickman's Shooting." *Time Magazine* 18, no. 9 (August 31, 1931).
"Triggers and Tension in a Texas Dukedom." *Life* 36, no. 14 (April 5, 1954).

Utecht, Byron C. "Frank Hamer, Crusader." *Texas Parade* 18, no. 6 (November 1957).

Utley, Robert M. "Terminating Oklahoma's Smiling Killer." *TRD* 17 (Summer 2005). Online at texasrangers.org.

Vera, Homero S. "Corrido 'Los Tequileros'." *El Mesteño* 3, no. 29 (February 2000).

———. "Los Tequileros." *El Mesteño* 3, no. 29 (February 2000).

Waite, Charles. "Price Daniel, Texas Democrats, and School Segregation, 1956–1957." *ETHJ* 48, no. 2 (Fall 2010).

Waldman, Allan. "Isle of Illicit Pleasures: Big Sam and Papa Rose." *In Between*, no. 164 (November 1983).

———. "Isle of Illicit Pleasures: The Gamblers." *In Between*, no. 163 (October 1983).

Watson, Dwight. "In the Name of Progress and Decency: The Response of Houston's Civic Leaders to the Lynching of Robert Powell in 1928." *The Houston Review of History and Culture* 1, no. 2 (2005).

Webb, Walter Prescott. "Bank Robbers Slain." *The State Trooper* 8, no. 3 (November 1926).

———. "Fight Against Texas Rangers." *The State Trooper* 6, no. 11 (July 1925).

———. "Larger Texas Force." *The State Trooper* 8, no. 6 (February 1927).

———. "Lawless Town Gets Ranger Justice." *The State Trooper* 5, no. 8 (April 1924).

———. "Lone Ranger Gets Bandits." *The State Trooper* 7, no. 7 (March 1926).

———. "Rangers Arrest Lawmakers." *The State Trooper* 8, no. 8 (April 1927).

———. "Rangers Called in To Clean Up Austin." *The State Trooper* 6, no. 3 (November 1924).

———. "Rangers Reorganized." *The State Trooper* 8, no. 11 (July 1927).

———. "Texas Ranger Case Important." *The State Trooper* 6, no. 12 (August 1925).

———. "Texas Rangers in Eclipse." *The State Trooper* 7, no. 5 (January 1926).

———. "Texas Rangers Quell Troubles." *The State Trooper* 5, no. 12 (August 1924).

———. "Veteran Ranger Protects Border." *The State Trooper* 6, no. 1 (September 1924).

———, and M. F. Kennedy. "With the Texas Rangers." *The State Trooper* 7, no. 2 (October 1925).

Weiss, Harold J., Jr. "The Texas Rangers Revisited: Old Themes and New Viewpoints." *SHQ* 97, no. 4 (April 1994).

White, Grace Miller. "Captain John E. Elgin." *Frontier Times* 21, no. 8 (May 1944).

"Wide-Open Galveston Mocks Texas Laws." *Life* 39, no. 7 (August 15, 1955).

Wilson, Jim. "Charlie Miller: A Unique Ranger." *Shooting Times* 41, no. 10 (October 2000).

———. "Frank Hamer, Legendary Lawman." *American Rifleman* 159, no. 10 (October 2011).

———. "Frank Hamer's 'Mystery' Pistol." *Handguns for Sport and Defense* 6, no. 3 (March 1992).

———. "Life with the 1911." *Shooting Illustrated* 10, no. 7 (July 2011).

Wise, Ken. "Lyndon B. Johnson vs. Coke R. Stevenson, et al." *Texas Bar Journal* 75, no. 3 (March 2012).

Young, Robert. "The Guns of Frank Hamer." *Quarterly of the National Association and Center for Outlaw and Lawman History* 7, no. 2 (Summer 1982).

Books

208 *Southwestern Reporter*. St. Paul, MN: West Publishing Company, 1919.

237 *Southwestern Reporter*. *Second Series*. St. Paul, MN: West Publishing Company, 1951.

253 *Southwestern Reporter*. St. Paul, MN: West Publishing Company, 1923.

254 *Southwestern Reporter*. St. Paul, MN: West Publishing Company, 1924.

270 *Southwestern Reporter.* St. Paul, MN: West Publishing Company, 1925.

376 *Southwestern Reporter. Second Series*. St. Paul, MN: West Publishing Company, 1964.

Alexander, Bob. *Old Riot, New Ranger: Captain Jack Dean: Texas Ranger and U.S. Marshal*. Denton: University of North Texas Press, 2018.

———. *Riding Lucifer's Line: Ranger Deaths Along the Texas-Mexico Border*. Denton: University of North Texas Press, 2013.

———, and Donaly E. Brice. *Texas Rangers: Lives, Legend, and Legacy*. Denton: University of North Texas Press, 2017.

Alexander, Charles C. *The Ku Klux Klan in the Southwest*. Lexington: University of Kentucky Press, 1965.

Alyn, Glen, compiler, *I Say Me for a Parable: The Oral Autobiography of Mance Lipscomb, Texas Bluesman*. New York: De Capo Press, 1994.

Akers, Monte. *Flames After Midnight: Murder, Vengeance, and the Desolation of a Texas Community*. Austin: University of Texas Press, 1999.

American National Red Cross. *Texas City Explosion, April 16, 1947*. Washington, DC: s. n., 1948.

Anders, Evan. *Boss Rule in South Texas: The Progressive Era*. Austin: University of Texas Press, 1987.

Arnold, Ann. *Gamblers and Gangsters: Fort Worth's Jacksboro Highway in the 1940s and 1950s*. Austin: Eakin Press, 1998.

Arreola, Daniel D. *Postcards from the Sonora Border: Visualizing Place Through a Popular Lens, 1900s–1950s*. Tucson: University of Arizona Press, 2017.

Bailey, Lynn R. *The Search for Lopez: Utah's Greatest Manhunt*. Tucson, AZ: Westernlore Press, 1990.

Baker, Susan P. *Murdered Judges: Of the 20th Century and Other Mysterious Deaths*. Austin, TX: Sunbelt Eakin, 2004.

Baker, T. Lindsay. *Gangster Tour of Texas*. College Station: Texas A&M University Press, 2011.

———. *More Ghost Towns of Texas*. Norman: University of Oklahoma Press, 2003.

Ballou, James L. *Rock in a Hard Place: The Browning Automatic Rifle*. Cobourg, Ontario: Collector Grade Publications, 2000.

Barragy, Terrence J. *Gathering Texas Gold*. Kingsville, TX: Cayo del Grullo Press, 2003.

Barton, Thomas D. *Report of State Ranger and Martial Law Activities of the National Guard of Texas, 1921 and 1922*. Austin: Von Boeckmann-Jones Company, 1923.

Beemer, Rod. *Notorious Kansas Bank Heists: Gunslingers to Gangsters*. Charleston, SC: History Press, 2015.

Behnken, Brian D. *Fighting Their Own Battles: Mexican Americans, African Americans, and the Struggle for Civil Rights in Texas*. Chapel Hill: University of North Carolina Press, 2011.

Bennett, James O. *Utah's Greatest Manhunt: The True Story of the Hunt for Lopez By an Eyewitness*. Salt Lake City: F. W. Gardiner, 1913.

Bernstein, Patricia. *The First Waco Horror: The Lynching of Jesse Washington and the Rise of the NAACP*. College Station: Texas A&M University Press, 2005.

———. *Ten Dollars to Hate: The Texas Man Who Fought the Klan*. College Station: Texas A&M University Press, 2017.

Bevans, Charles I., compiler. *Treaties and Other International Agreements of the United States, 1776–1949*. Volume Nine. Department of State Publication No. 8615.

Blumenthal, Karen. *Bonnie and Clyde: The Making of a Legend*. New York: Viking, 2017.

Boatman, Tabitha Nicole, Scott H. Belshaw, and Richard B. McCaslin. *Galveston's Maceo Family Empire: Bootlegging and the Balinese Room*. Charleston, SC: History Press, 2014.

Boessenecker, John. *Texas Ranger: The Epic Life of Frank Hamer, the Man Who Killed Bonnie and Clyde*. New York: Thomas Dunne Books, 2016.

Borders, Gary B. *A Hanging in Nacogdoches: Murder, Race, Politics, and Polemics in Texas's Oldest Town, 1870–1916*. Austin: University of Texas Press, 2006.

Bridge, Joe H., Jr. *The Life and Times of Joe H. Bridge: Texas Ranger, 1936–1956*. s. l.: Joe H. Bridge, 2003.

Brody, David C., and James R. Acker. *Criminal Law*. Third Edition. Burlington, MA: Jones & Bartlett Learning, 2015.

Brown, Martin. *The Glen Rose Moonshine Raid*. Charleston, SC: History Press, 2017.

Brown, Norman D. *Biscuits, the Dole, and Nodding Donkeys: Texas Politics, 1929–1932*. Edited by Rachel Ozanne. Austin: University of Texas Press, 2019.

———. *Hood, Bonnet, and Little Brown Jug: Texas Politics, 1921–1928*. College Station: Texas A&M University Press, 1984.

Brown, Robert Maxwell. *Strain of Violence: Historical Studies of American Violence and Vigilantism*. New York: Oxford University Press, 1975.

Bruce, J. Campbell. *Escape from Alcatraz: A Farewell to the Rock*. New York: McGraw-Hill, 1963.

Burrough, Bryan. *The Big Rich: The Rise and Fall of the Greatest Texas Oil Fortunes*. New York: Penguin Books, 2009.

———. *Public Enemies: America's Greatest Crime Wave and the Birth of the FBI, 1933–34*. New York: Penguin Books, 2004.

Caldwell, Clifford R., and Ron DeLord. *Eternity at the End of a Rope: Executions, Lynchings, and Vigilante Justice in Texas, 1819–1923*. Santa Fe: Sunstone Press, 2015.

———. *Texas Lawmen, 1900–1940: More of the Good and the Bad*. Charleston, SC: History Press, 2012.

Campbell, Randolph B. *Gone to Texas: The History of the Lone Star State*. New York: Oxford University Press, 2003.

Caro, Robert A. *The Years of Lyndon Johnson: Means of Ascent*. New York: Alfred A. Knopf, 1990.

Carrigan, William D. *The Making of a Lynching Culture: Violence and Vigilantism in Central Texas, 1836–1916*. Urbana: University of Illinois Press, 2004.

Cartwright, Gary. *Galveston: A History of the Island*. Fort Worth: Texas Christian University Press, 1991.

Casto, Stanley D. *Settlement of the Cibolo-Nueces Strip: A Partial History of La Salle County*. Hillsboro, TX: Hill Junior College Press, 1969.

Chalfant, Frank E. *Galveston: Island of Chance*. Houston: Treasures of Nostalgia, 1997.

Clark, John A., and Michel T. Halbouty. *The Last Boom*. New York: Random House, 1972.

Clark, John E. *The Fall of the Duke of Duval: A Prosecutor's Journal*. Austin: Eakin Press, 1999.

Cobb, James C. *Redefining Southern Culture: Mind and Identity in the Modern South*. Athens: University of Georgia Press, 1999.

Coerver, Don M. "'Wire Me Before Shooting': Federalism in (In)Action—The Texas-Mexico Border during the Revolution, 1910–1920." *The Mexican Revolution: Conflict and Consolidation, 1910–1940*. Edited by Douglas W. Richmond and Samuel W. Haynes. College Station: Texas A&M University Press, 2013.

Collings, Ellsworth. *The 101 Ranch*. Norman: University of Oklahoma Press, 1971.

Conquer: The Story of Ninth Army. Washington, DC: Infantry Journal Press, 1947.

Cox, Mike. *Texas Ranger Tales: Stories That Need Telling*. Plano: Republic of Texas Press, 1997.

———. *Texas Ranger Tales II*. Plano: Republic of Texas Press, 1999.

———. *Time of the Rangers: From 1900 to the Present*. New York: Tom Doherty Associates, 2009.

Cude, Elton R. *The Wild and Free Dukedom of Bexar*. San Antonio, TX: Munguia Printers, 1978.

Daggett, Marsha Lea, editor. *Pecos County History*. Two volumes. Fort Stockton: Pecos County Historical Association, 1984.

Dallek, Robert. *Lone Star Rising: Lyndon Johnson and His Times, 1908–1960*. New York: Oxford University Press, 1991.

Day, James M. *Captain Clint Peoples, Texas Ranger: Fifty Years A Lawman*. Waco: Texian Press, 1980.

———. *One Man's Dream: Fort Fisher and the Texas Ranger Hall of Fame*. Waco: Texian Press, 1976.

Dean, Gardner A. *One Hundred and Eighty Days: XIII Corps*. Peine, Germany: Corps Public Relations Section, 1945.

Dearen, Patrick. *Crossing Rio Pecos*. Fort Worth: Texas Christian University Press, 1996.

DeArment, Robert K. *Bat Masterson: The Man and the Legend*. Norman: University of Oklahoma Press, 1989.

Dewhurst, H. S. *The Railroad Police*. Springfield, IL: Charles C. Thomas, 1955.

Díaz, George T. *Border Contraband: A History of Smuggling Across the Rio Grande*. Austin: University of Texas Press, 2015.

Dixon, Kemp. *Chasing Thugs, Nazis, and Reds: Texas Ranger Norman K. Dixon*. College Station: Texas A&M University Press, 2015.

Dorman, Robert L. *Alfalfa Bill: A Life in Politics*. Norman: University of Oklahoma Press, 2018.

Douglas, C. L. *The Gentlemen in the White Hats: Dramatic Episodes in the History of the Texas Rangers*. Dallas: South-West Press, 1934.

Dukes, Doug. *Firearms of the Texas Rangers: From the Frontier Era to the Modern Age*. Denton: University of North Texas Press, 2020.

East Texas Chamber of Commerce. *A Book of Facts: Martial Law in East* Texas. Longview: East Texas Chamber of Commerce, 1932.

El Paso City Directory, 1920. El Paso: Hudspeth Directory Company, 1920.

Elliott, Glenn, with Robert Nieman. *Glen Elliott: A Ranger's Ranger*. Longview, TX: Robert Nieman, 1999.

Favor, Bob. *My Rangering Days*. s. l.: s. n., 2006.

Foley, Edward B. *Ballot Battles: The History of Disputed Elections in the United States*. New York: Oxford University Press, 2016.

Fortune, Jan, editor. *Fugitives: The True Story of Clyde Barrow and Bonnie Parker*. Dallas, TX: Ranger Press, 1934.

Frost, H. Gordon, and John H. Jenkins. *"I'm Frank Hamer": The Life of a Texas Peace Officer*. Austin: Pemberton Press, 1968.

Gammel, Hans Peter Nielsen, compiler. *Laws of Texas*, 1919. Austin: Gammel's Book Store, 1919.

———. *Laws of Texas, 1923–1925*. Austin: Gammel's Book Store, 1925.

———. *Laws of Texas, 1931–1933*. Austin: Gammel's Book Store, 1933.

———. *The Laws of Texas, 1934–1935*. Austin: Gammel's Book Store, 1935.

Gilbreath, West C. *Death on the Gallows: The Encyclopedia of Legal Executions in Texas*. Fort Worth: Wild Horse Press, 2017.

Gilliland, Maude T. *Horsebackers of the Brush Country: A Story of the Texas Rangers and Mexican Liquor Smugglers*. Brownsville: Springman-King Co., 1968.

Glasrud, Bruce A., and Harold J. Weiss, Jr., editors. *Tracking the Texas Rangers: The Twentieth Century*. Denton: University of North Texas Press, 2013.

Gooding, Ed, with Robert Nieman. *Ed Gooding: Soldier, Texas Ranger*. Longview, TX: Ranger Publishing, 2001.

Govenar, Alan B., and Jay F. Brakefield. *Deep Ellum: The Other Side of Dallas*. College Station: Texas A&M University Press, 2013.

Greene, A. C. *The Santa Claus Bank Robbery*. Revised Edition. New York: Alfred A. Knopf, 1972; rpt. Denton: University of North Texas Press, 1999.

Guinn, Jeff. *Go Down Together: The True Untold Story of Bonnie and Clyde*. New York: Simon and Schuster, 2009.

Gunnarsson, Robert L., Sr. *American Military Police in Europe, 1945–1991: Unit Histories*. Jefferson, NC: McFarland & Co., 2011.

Guthrie, Keith. *The History of San Patricio County*. Austin, TX: Nortex Press, 1986.

Habermeyer, Christopher Lance. *Gringos' Curve: Pancho Villa's Massacre of American Miners in Mexico*, 1916. El Paso, TX: Book Publishers of El Paso, 2004.

Haile, Bartee. *Texas Boomtowns: A History of Blood and Oil*. Charleston, SC: History Press, 2015.

Harris, Charles H., III, Frances E. Harris, and Louis R. Sadler. *Texas Ranger Biographies: Those Who Served, 1910–1921*. Albuquerque: University of New Mexico Press, 2009.

Harris, Charles H., III, and Louis R. Sadler. *The Plan de San Diego: Tejano Rebellion, Mexican Intrigue*. Lincoln: University of Nebraska Press, 2013.

———. *The Texas Rangers and the Mexican Revolution*. Albuquerque: University of New Mexico Press, 2004.

———. *Texas Rangers in Transition: From Gunfighters to Criminal Investigators, 1921–1935*. Norman: University of Oklahoma Press, 2019.

Hipp, Joe Wreford. *The Oldest Ranch in Texas: Rancho de la Purísima Concepción, A Ranch on the Road to History*. Austin: Eakin Press, 2000.

Hudspeth's Lubbock City Directory, 1948. s. l.: Hudspeth Directory Company, 1948.

Hutchinson County Historical Commission. *History of Hutchinson County, Texas: 104 Years, 1876–1980*. Dallas: Taylor Publishing Company, 1980.

Hyatt, Marjorie Burnett. "Littleberry Wright Family." *History of DeWitt County, Texas*. Dallas: Curtis Media Corporation, 1991.

Ivey, Darren L. *The Ranger Ideal: The Texas Rangers in the Hall of Fame*. Two volumes. Denton: University of North Texas Press, 2017–2018.

———. *The Texas Rangers: A Registry and History*. Jefferson, NC: McFarland & Co., 2010.

Jackson, H. Joaquin, with James L. Haley. *One Ranger Returns*. Austin: University of Texas Press, 2008.

Jenkins, Charles H., editor. *Revised Civil Statutes of Texas, 1925*. Austin: Gammel's Book Store, 1926.

Johnson, Benjamin Heber. *Revolution in Texas: How a Forgotten Rebellion and Its Bloody Suppression Turned Mexicans into Americans*. New Haven, CT: Yale University Press, 2003.

Jones, Sheryn R., editor. *Fannin County Folks and Facts: A History of Fannin County, Texas*. Dallas, TX: Taylor Publishing Company, 1977.

Kearney, James C., Bill Stein, and James Smallwood. *No Hope for Heaven, No Fear of Hell: The Stafford-Townsend Feud of Colorado County, Texas, 1871–1911*. Denton: University of Texas Press, 2016.

Kearney, Milo, and Anthony Keith Knopp. *Border Cuates: A History of the U.S.-Mexican Twin Cities*. Austin: Eakin Press, 1995.

Kilgore, D. E. *A Ranger Legacy: 150 Years of Service to Texas*. Austin: Madrona Press, 1973.

Knight, James R. *Three Ambushes*. Dallas, TX: Southwestern Historical Publications, 2006.

Krenek, Harry. *The Power Vested: The Use of Martial Law and the National Guard in Texas Domestic Crisis, 1919–1932*. Austin: Presidial Press, 1980.

Ladino, Robyn Duff. *Desegregating Texas Schools: Eisenhower, Shivers, and the Crisis at Mansfield High*. Austin: University of Texas Press, 1996.

Landrum, Graham. *Grayson County: An Illustrated History of Grayson County, Texas*. Fort Worth, TX: University Supply & Equipment Company, 1960.

Levario, Miguel Antonio. *Militarizing the Mexican Border: When Mexicans Became the Enemy*. College Station: Texas A&M University, 2012.

Ludeman, Annette Martin. *La Salle County: South Texas Brush County, 1856-1975*. Quanah, TX: Nortex Press, 1975.

Malsch, Brownson. *"Lone Wolf" Gonzaullas, Texas Ranger*. Norman: University of Oklahoma Press, 1998.

Martínez, Monica Muñoz. *The Injustice Never Leaves You: Anti-Mexican Violence in Texas*. Cambridge: Harvard University Press, 2018.

Mauriello, Christopher E. *Forced Confrontation: The Politics of Dead Bodies in Germany at the End of World War II*. Lanham, MD: Lexington Books, 2017.

McCarty, Jeanne Bozzell. *The Struggle for Sobriety: Protestants and Prohibition in Texas: 1919–1935*. Southwestern Studies Monograph No. 62. El Paso: Texas Western Press, 1980.

McCaslin, Richard B. *Sutherland Springs, Texas: Saratoga on the Cibolo*. Denton: University of North Texas Press, 2017.

McComb, David G. *Galveston: A History*. Austin: University of Texas Press, 1986.

———. *Spare Time in Texas: Recreation and History in the Lone Star State*. Austin: University of Texas Press, 2008.

McDaniel, Ruel. *Some Ran Hot*. Dallas, TX: Regional Press, 1939.

Meed, Douglas V. *Texas Ranger Johnny Klevenhagen*. Plano, TX: Republic of Texas Press, 2000.

Mellen, Joan. *Faustian Bargains: Lyndon Johnson and Mac Wallace in the Robber Baron Culture of Texas*. New York: Bloomsbury, 2016.

Mills, Susie. *Legend in Bronze: A Biography of Jay Banks*. Dallas: Ussery Printing Company, 1982.

Mills, Warner E., Jr. *Martial Law in East Texas*. Inter-University Case Program No. 53. [Tuscaloosa]: University of Alabama Press, 1960.

Montejano, David. *Anglos and Mexicans in the Making of Texas, 1836–1986*. Austin: University of Texas Press, 1987.

Moore, Lucy. *Anything Goes: A Biography of the Roaring Twenties*. New York: Overlook Press, 2010.

Moore, Steven L. *Savage Frontier: Rangers, Riflemen, and Indian Wars in Texas*. Volume 1. Denton: University of North Texas Press, 2002.

Mostyn, Henry. "Grover Cleveland Mostyn." *Magnolia Memories*. Edited by Celeste Graves. Bloomington, IN: AuthorHouse, 2004.

Neff, Pat M. *The Battles of Peace*. Fort Worth, TX: Pioneer Publishing Company, 1925.

Newton, Michael. *The Texarkana Moonlight Murders: The Unsolved Case of the 1946 Phantom Killer*. Jefferson, NC: McFarland & Company, 2013.

Ogletree, Charles J., Jr. *All Deliberate Speed: Reflections on the First Half-Century of Brown v. Board of Education*. New York: W. W. Norton & Company, 2004.

Olien, Diana Davids, and Roger M. Olien. *Oil in Texas: The Gusher Age, 1895–1945*. Austin: University of Texas Press, 2002.

Olien, Roger M., and Diana Davids Olien. *Oil Booms: Social Change in Five Texas Towns*. Lincoln: University of Nebraska Press, 1982.

O'Neal, Bill. *The Johnson-Sims Feud: Romeo and Juliet, West Texas Style*. Denton: University of North Texas Press, 2010.

Owen, Robert, Jr. "In the Line of Duty." *Elgin, Etc: Stories of Elgin, Texas*. Elgin: Elgin Historical Association, 2008.

Paddock, Buckley B. *A History of Central and Western Texas*. Chicago: Lewis Publishing Company, 1911.

Parsons, Chuck. *The Sutton-Taylor Feud: The Deadliest Blood Feud in Texas*. Denton: University of North Texas, 2009.

Patterson, C. L. *Sensational Texas Manhunt*. San Antonio, TX: Sid Murray & Son, 1939.

Patterson, James T. *Brown v. Board of Education: A Civil Rights Milestone and Its Troubling Legacy*. New York: Oxford University Press, 2001.

Peavey, John R. *Echoes from the Rio Grande*. Brownsville, TX: Springman-King Company, 1963.

Phillips, John Neal. *Running with Bonnie and Clyde: The Ten Fast Years of Ralph Fults*. Norman: University of Oklahoma Press, 1996.

Phister, Jeff, with Thomas Hone and Paul Goodyear. *Battleship Oklahoma BB–37*. Norman: University of Oklahoma Press, 2008.

Presley, James. *The Phantom Killer: Unlocking the Mystery of the Texarkana Serial Murders: The Story of a Town in Terror*. New York: Pegasus Crime, 2014.

Prindle, David F. *Petroleum Politics and the Texas Railroad Commission*. Austin: University of Texas Press, 1981.

Procter, Ben H. *Just One Riot: Episodes of the Texas Rangers in the 20th Century*. Austin: Eakin Press, 1991.

Puckett, Linda Jay. *Cast a Long Shadow: A Casebook of the Law Enforcement Career of Texas Ranger Captain E. J. (Jay) Banks*. Dallas: Ussery Printing Company, 1984.

Pylant, James. *Blood Legacy: The True Story of the Snow Axe Murders*. Stephenville, TX: Jacobus Books, 2008.

Radelet, Michael L., et al. *In Spite of Evidence: Erroneous Convictions in Capital Cases*. Boston: Northeastern University Press, 1992.

Raper, Arthur F. *The Tragedy of Lynching*. Chapel Hill: University of North Carolina Press, 1933.

Ribb, Richard. "Revolution, Revenge, and the Rangers, 1910–1920." *War Along the Border: The Mexican Revolution and Tejano Communities*. Edited by Arnoldo de León. College Station: Texas A&M University Press, 2012.

Rickard, T. A. *The Utah Copper Enterprise*. San Francisco, CA: s. n., 1919.

Rigler, Lewis C., and Judyth W. Rigler. *In the Line of Duty: Reflections of a Texas Ranger Private*. Denton: University of North Texas Press, 1995.

Rister, Carl Coke. *Oil! Titan of the Southwest*. Norman: University of Oklahoma Press, 1949.

Robinson, James W. *The DPS Story: History of the Development of the Department of Public Safety in Texas*. Second Edition. Austin: Texas Department of Public Safety, 1975.

Roth, Mitchel P. "Through the Ages: Texas DPS History." *Courtesy, Service, and Protection: The History of the Texas Department of Public Safety*. 65th Anniversary Edition. Paducah, KY: Turner Publishing Company, 2003.

———, and Tom Kennedy. *Houston Blue: The Story of the Houston Police Department*. Denton: University of North Texas Press, 2012.

Rubenser, Lorie, and Gloria Priddy. *Constables, Marshals, and More: Forgotten Offices in Teas Law Enforcement*. Denton: University of North Texas Press, 2011.

Ruddell, Rick. *Oil, Gas, and Crime: The Dark Side of the Boomtown*. New York: Palgrave Macmillan, 2017.

Samuelson, Dana Middlebrooks, and Robert Samuelson. *Clovis Road: The Dr. Roy Hunt Murder, Littlefield, Texas, 1942–1943*. Dallas, TX: Highgate Publishing, 2009.

Schreiner, Charles, III, Audrey Schreiner, Robert Berryman, and Hal F. Matheny, compilers. *A Pictorial History of the Texas Rangers: "That Special Breed of Men*." Mountain Home, TX: YO Press, 1969.

Scott, Gini Graham. *Homicide by the Rich and Famous: A Century of Prominent Killers*. Westport, CT: Praeger, 2005.

Scurry County Genealogical Society. *Scurry County Marriage Record*. Book 1 (1884–1907). Snyder: Scurry County Genealogical Society, 1991.

Shub, Boris. *The Choice*. New York: Duell, Sloan and Pearce, 1950.

Simmons, Lee. *Assignment Huntsville: Memoirs of a Texas Prison Official*. Austin: University of Texas Press, 1957.

Sinise, Jerry. *Black Gold and Red Lights*. Austin, TX: Eakin Press, 1982.

Sitton, Thad. *The Texas Sheriff: Lord of the County Line*. Norman: University of Oklahoma Press, 2000.

Sleeper, Gary W. *I'll Do My Own Damn Killin': Benny Binion, Herbert Noble, and the Texas Gambling War*. Fort Lee, NJ: Barricade Books, 2006.

Sparrow, John C. *History of Personnel Demobilization in the United States Army*. Washington, DC: Department of the Army, 1952.

Spinks, S. E. *Law on the Last Frontier: Texas Ranger Arthur Hill*. Lubbock: Texas Tech University Press, 2007.

Stephens, Hugh W. *The Texas City Disaster, 1947*. Austin: University of Texas Press, 1997.

Stephens, Robert W. *Lone Wolf: The Story of Texas Ranger Captain M. T. Gonzaullas*. Dallas, TX: Taylor Publishing Company, 1979.

Sterling, William Warren. *Trails and Trials of a Texas Ranger*. Norman: University of Oklahoma Press, 1968.

Stowers, Carlton. *Partners in Blue: The History of the Dallas Police Department*. Dallas, TX: Taylor Publishing Company, 1983.

Tereba, Tere. *Mickey Cohen: The Life and Crimes of L.A.'s Notorious Mobster*. Toronto: ECW Press, 2012.

Texas Research League. *The Texas Department of Public Safety: Its Services and Organization*. Austin: Texas Research League, 1957.

Theoharis, Athan G., editor. *The FBI: A Comprehensive Reference Guide*. Phoenix, AZ: Oryx Press, 1999.

Tise, Sammy. *Texas County Sheriffs*. Albuquerque, NM: Oakwood Printing, 1989.

Tuller, Roger. "Frank Hamer: Facing Down the Mob During the Sherman Riot." *Never Without Honor: Studies of Courage in Tribute to Ben H. Procter*. Edited by Archie P. McDonald. Nacogdoches: Stephen F. Austin State University Press, 2013.

Tumlinson, Samuel H. *Tumlinson, A Genealogy*. Eagle Bay, BC: privately printed, n.d.

Turner, Patty Newman, George Newman, and Betty Newman Wauer. *Joseph and Rachel Rabb Newman, An Old Three Hundred Family, and their Descendants*. Odessa, TX: P. N. Turner, 1998.

Underwood, Sid. *Depression Desperado: The Chronicle of Raymond Hamilton*. Austin, TX: Eakin Press, 1995.

Urbina, Martin Guevara, et al. *Ethnic Realities of Mexican Americans: From Colonialism to 21st Century Globalization*. Springfield, IL: Charles C. Thomas, 2014.

Utley, Robert M. *Lone Star Lawmen: The Second Century of the Texas Rangers*. New York: Oxford University Press, 2007.

Villanueva, Nicholas, Jr. *The Lynching of Mexicans in the Texas Borderlands*. Albuquerque: University of New Mexico Press, 2017.

Webb, Walter Prescott. *The Texas Rangers: A Century of Frontier Defense*. 2nd Edition. Austin: University of Texas Press, 1965.

Williams, Rusty. *The Red River Bridge War: A Texas-Oklahoma Border Battle*. College Station: Texas A&M University Press, 2016.

Wilson, Anna Victoria, and William E. Segall. *Oh, Do I Remember: Experiences of Teachers During the Desegregation of Austin's Schools, 1964–1971.* New York: State University of New York Press, 2001.

Wolters, Jacob F. *Martial Law and Its Administration.* Austin, TX: Gammel's Book Store, 1930.

Wright, Robert K., Jr. *Military Police.* Washington, DC: Center of Military History, 1992.

Wright, William Berry. *Career Hunting: Texas Rangers vs. Standard Oiler.* El Cajon, CA: W. B. Wright, 1982.

Zaloga, Steven J. *Downfall 1945: The Fall of Hitler's Third Reich.* Oxford, UK: Osprey Publishing, 2016.

Ziemke, Earl F. *The U.S. Army in the Occupation of Germany, 1944–1946.* Washington, DC: Center of Military History, 1975.

Zimmerman, Joseph F. *Interstate Disputes: The Supreme Court's Original Jurisdiction.* Albany: State University of New York, 2006.

Correspondence

Battson, Harry. Email to the author. August 15, 2012.

Clark, Jason. Email to the author. August 24, 2012.

Crittendon, Shelly. Email to the author. July 29, 2019.

Crowder, James T., Jr. Email to the author. January 22, 2021.

Doherty, Buster. Email to the author. January 22, 2021.

Dukes, Doug. Email to the author. October 20, 2020.

Favor, Robert C. "Bob." Email to the author. July 17, 2020.

Gann, Barbara. Email to the author. May 2, 2019.

Guffey, Travis. Email to the author. October 30, 2012.

Jennings, Josie. Email to the author. January 10–21, 2021.

Martinez, Rosemary R. Email to the author. June 19, 2012.

Norwood, Brian. Email to the author. December 23, 2019.

Parks, Bonnie. Email to the author. June 14, 2018.

Perrin, Brenda. Email to the author. November 1, 2012.

Pribble, Jim. "Resume of Captain Robert Austin Crowder, Texas Ranger Service." Interoffice memorandum to Senior Captain W. D. Wilson. March 30, 1982.

Prince, Captain Bob G. Letter to Raven Kazen, Victim Services Division. January 19, 2004.

Short, William D. Email to the author. August 31, 2011.

Warnock, Kirby Franklin. Email to the author. May 29–June 5, 2018.

White, Jeff. Email to the author. June 7, 2018.

Woodall, Cameron. Email to the author. July 30, 2019.

Woodward, Ernest. Email to the author. May 29–June 5, 2018.

Internet Sources

Find a Grave.

Johnston, Bill. "The Day the Last Texas Ranger Died." Interview with Robert Riggs. *Justice Facts*. Podcast audio. https://www.justicefactspodcast.com/2020/11/24/the-day-the-last-texas-ranger-died-e7/ (accessed November 24, 2020).

Interviews

Alfred, Howard "Slick." Interview with Robert Nieman. Athens, Texas. June 30, 2005. Online at www.texasranger.org.

Crowder, James T., Jr. Telephone interview with the author. January 26, 2013.

Davis, L. Clifford. Interview with Callie Millier. Fort Worth, Texas. April 11, 2014. Oral History Collection No. 1818, University of North Texas. Online at omeka.library.unt.edu.

Elliott, Glenn. Interview with Robert Nieman. Longview, Texas. February 14, 1994. Online at www.texasranger.org.

———. Interview with Robert Nieman. Longview, Texas. January–October 1995. Online at www.texasranger.org.

Gann, Barbara. Telephone interview with the author. May 13, 2019.

Gault, Mike. Telephone interview with the author. March 27, 2019.

Gonzaullas, Manuel T. Interview with Captain Bob Mitchell and Alva Stem. Dallas, Texas. January 26, 1977. Online at www.texasranger.org.

———. Interview with Stacy Keach, Sr. New Boston, Texas. July 1957. Online at www.texasranger.org.

Guffey, Stacy. Telephone interview with the author. January 25, 2021.

Hamer, Flavus "Bud," Bobbie Merle Hamer Smith, and Harrison Hamer III. Interview with Robert Nieman. Waco, Texas. September 23, 2000. Online at www.texasranger.org.

Hickman, David B. Telephone interview with the author. March 15, 2012.

McGuire, Catherine. Telephone interview with the author. April 18, 2013.

Miller, Andrew. Telephone interview with the author. January 10, 2013.

Miller, Rex A. Telephone interview with the author. June 29, 2012.

Miller, Roger H. Telephone interview with the author. July 3, 2012.

Mitchell, Robert K. Interview with Robert Nieman. Windom, Texas. October 29, 1996. Online at www.texasranger.org.

Prince, Captain Bob G., and Buster Doherty. Interview with the author. Fort Worth, Texas. August 25, 2011. Digital recording in the possession of the author.

Ray, Jim. Interview with Robert Nieman. Bullard, Texas. October 18, 1997. Online at www.texasranger.org.

Riddles, James B., James E. Riddles, and Carolyn Anne Riddles. Interview with the author. Elgin, Texas. May 10, 2012. Digital recording in the possession of the author.

Rigler, Lewis. Interview with Robert Nieman. Gainesville, Texas. July 16, 1994. Online at www.texasranger.org.

Rodat, Carol. Telephone interview with the author. April 27, 2013.

Rodriguez, Connie. Telephone interview with the author. June 27, 2012.

Wadsworth, Ralph. Interview with Robert Nieman. Kaufman, Texas. January 7, 2006. Online at www.texasranger.org.

Waldrip, Johnny. Interview with Nancy Ray and Eddie Ray. Sherman, Texas. October 20, 2008. Online at www.texasranger.org.

Woodward, Ernest. Telephone interview with the author. June 8, 2018.

Newspapers

Abilene Daily Reporter
Abilene Morning News
Abilene Morning Reporter
Abilene Morning Reporter-News
Abilene Reporter
Abilene Reporter-News
Aiken Standard (SC)
Alpine Avalanche
Amarillo Daily News
Amarillo Globe
Amarillo Globe-News
Amarillo Globe-Times
Arizona Daily Star (Tucson)
Arizona Republic (Phoenix)
Arkansas Gazette (Little Rock)
Aspermont Star
Austin American
Austin American Herald

Austin American-Statesman
Austin Daily Statesman
Austin Dispatch
Austin Statesman
Azle News
Baldwin Times
Bastrop Advertiser
Baytown Sun
Beaumont Enterprise
Big Spring Daily Herald
Bonham Daily Favorite
Borger Daily Herald
Brazosport Facts
Breckenridge American
Brownwood Bulletin
Brownsville Daily Herald
Brownsville Herald
Bryan Daily Eagle
Bryan Daily Eagle and Pilot
Cameron Herald
Carlsbad Current-Argus
Clifton Record
Comanche Chief
Commerce Daily Journal
Conroe Courier
Corpus Christi Caller
Corpus Christi Caller-Times
Corpus Christi Times
Corsicana Daily Sun
Corsicana Semi-Weekly Light
Cuero Daily Record
Daily Courier-Gazette (McKinney)
Daily News Telegram (Sulphur Springs)
Daily Oklahoman (Oklahoma City)
Dallas Daily Times-Herald
Dallas Dispatch
Dallas Evening Journal
Dallas Evening News
Dallas Journal

Dallas Morning News
Dallas Times-Herald
Del Rio News-Herald
Denison Press
Denton Record-Chronicle
Elgin Courier
El Paso Herald
El Paso Herald-Post
El Paso Times
Enid Daily News
Evening Star (Washington, DC)
Floresville Chronicle-Journal
Fort Worth Record
Fort Worth Record-Telegram
Fort Worth Star-Telegram
Fredericksburg Standard
Galveston Daily News
Galveston Tribune
Gatesville Messenger and Star-Forum
Gilmer Mirror
Gladewater News
Grand Prairie Daily News-Texan
Greenville News (SC)
Gregg County Oil News
Hearne Democrat
Hempstead News
Houston Chronicle
Houston Daily Post
Houston Post
Houston Post-Dispatch
Hutchinson News (KS)
Kansas City Star
Kerrville Mountain Sun
Kerrville Times
Kilgore Daily News
Kilgore News Herald
La Grange Journal
Lake Charles American Press (LA)
Lamar County Echo (Paris)

La Marque Times
La Prensa (San Antonio, TX)
Laredo Daily Times
Laredo Weekly Times
Lawton Constitution (OK)
Leavenworth Post (KS)
Llano News
Lockhart Register
Longview Daily News
Longview Ledger and Greggton Gauger
Longview News-Journal
Los Angeles Times
Lubbock Avalanche-Journal
Lubbock Morning Avalanche
Manhattan Mercury (KS)
Marshall County News
Marshall Evening Messenger
Marshall Messenger
Marshall News Messenger
McAllen Daily Press
Meridian Tribune
Mexia Daily News
Mexia Evening News
Mexia Weekly Herald
Midland Reporter-Telegram
Mineral Wells Index
Mobile Register (AL)
Mobile News-Item (AL)
Navasota Examiner
New Orleans Times-Picayune
New York Daily News
New York Times
North County Times (Escondido, CA)
Oakland Tribune
Odessa American
Oklahoma News (Oklahoma City)
Olney Enterprise
Paducah Sun-Democrat (KY)
Palo Pinto County Star

Pampa Daily News
Panola Watchman
Paris Evening News
Pioneer Oil Herald
Pleasanton Express
Port Arthur News
Riesel Rustler
Rusk Cherokeean
Salina Journal (KS)
Salt Lake Telegram
Salt Lake Tribune
San Angelo Press
San Angelo Standard
San Angelo Standard-Times
San Antonio Daily Express
San Antonio Daily Light
San Antonio Evening News
San Antonio Express
San Antonio Express and News
San Antonio Gazette
San Antonio Light
San Antonio Light and Gazette
San Augustine Tribune
San Diego Union (CA)
San Francisco Examiner
San Marcos Daily Record
San Patricio County News
San Saba News
Santa Fe New Mexican
Seguin Gazette-Enterprise
Selma Times-Journal (AL)
Shamrock Texan
Sherman Daily Democrat
Shiner Gazette
Shreveport Times
Snyder Signal
Southwest American (Fort Smith, AR)
St. Louis Post-Dispatch
Stars and Stripes (Rome and Naples)

Sweetwater Reporter
Taylor Daily Press
Texarkana Gazette
Texas Oil Ledger (Fort Worth)
Tulsa Daily Register
Tyler Courier-Times
Tyler Morning Telegraph
Valley Morning Star (Harlingen, TX)
Valley Star-Monitor-Herald (Harlingen, TX)
Vernon Daily Record
Victoria Advocate
Waco Citizen
Waco News-Tribune
Waco Tribune-Herald
Waxahachie Daily Light
Wichita Beacon (KS)
Wichita Daily Eagle (KS)
Wichita Daily Times (Wichita Falls, TX)
Wichita Falls Record News

Public and Official Documents

Birth Certificates. Bureau of Vital Statistics, Texas Department of Health. Austin, Texas. Copies in the possession of the author.

Bryan County, Oklahoma. Marriage Records 51 (June 17–November 26, 1942). Bryan County Clerk's Office. Durant, Oklahoma. Material accessed at FamilySearch.org.

California Death Index, 1940–1997. Center for Health Statistics, California Department of Health Services. Sacramento, California. Material accessed at Ancestry.com.

California Divorce Index, 1966–1984. Center for Health Statistics, California Department of Health Services. Sacramento, California. Material accessed at Ancestry.com.

California Marriage Records, 1960–1985. Center for Health Statistics, California Department of Health Services. Sacramento, California. Material accessed at Ancestry.com.

Crawford, Captain Dwight. Supplementary Investigation Report, February 22, 1978. Denton County Sheriff's Office. Denton, Texas. Copy in the possession of the author.

Fainter, John W., Ruben R. Cardenas, and Calvin R. Guest. Resolution. Public Safety Commission. January 29, 1987. Copy in the possession of the author.

Grayson County, Texas. Marriage Records. Grayson County Clerk's Office. Sherman, Texas. Material accessed at Ancestry.com.

Inactive Personnel Records. Texas Department of Public Safety. Austin, Texas.

Neel, Agent Ben A. Report of Investigation, February 21, 1978. File No. 1B-760016. Narcotics Service, Texas Department of Public Safety. Austin, Texas. Copy in the possession of the author.

Oregon Death Index, 1903–1998. Oregon State Archives and Records Center. Salem, Oregon. Material accessed at Ancestry.com.

Panola County, Texas. Marriage Record Book H (1903–1908). Panola County Clerk's Office. Carthage, Texas. Material accessed at FamilySearch.org.

Texas Death Certificates. Bureau of Vital Statistics, Texas Department of Health. Austin, Texas. Copies in the possession of the author.

Texas Legislature. *General and Special Laws of Texas*, 1884–1997.

———. *Penal Code of the State of Texas Adopted at the Regular Session of the Thirty-second Legislature, 1911*. Austin: Austin Printing Company, 1911.

———. *Revised Civil Statutes of the State of Texas Adopted at the Regular Session of the Thirty-second Legislature, 1911*. Austin: Austin Printing Company, 1912.

———. House. *Journal of the House of Representatives of the Regular Session of the Fiftieth Legislature of the State of Texas*. Austin: A. C. Baldwin & Sons, 1947.

———. *Journal of the House of Representatives of the Regular Session of the Thirty-first Legislature of Texas*. Austin: Von Boeckmann-Jones Co., 1909.

———. *Journal of the House of Representatives of the Regular Session of the Thirty-sixth Legislature*. Austin: Von Boeckmann-Jones, 1919.

———. Senate. *Journal of the Senate of Texas, Being the First Called Session of the Thirty-ninth Legislature*. Austin: A. C. Baldwin & Sons, 1926.

———. *Journal of the Senate of the State of Texas, Regular Session of the Fiftieth Legislature*. Austin: Von Boeckmann-Jones Co., 1947.

———. *Journal of the Senate of Texas, Twenty-seventh Legislature*. Austin: n.p., 1901.

———. *Report and Recommendations of the Senate Committee Investigating Crime*. Forty-third Legislature, 1933–1934. Austin: 1934.

Texas Secretary of State. *Biennial Report of the Secretary of State, 1912.* Austin: Von Boeckmann-Jones Co., 1913.

United States. Department of Justice. *Register of the Department of Justice and the Courts of the United States.* Washington, DC: Government Printing Office, 1922.

Waller County Marriage Records. Book A, 2-6 (1873–1917). Waller County Clerk's Office, Hempstead, Texas. Copy in the possession of the author.

Public Events

Bobby Paul Doherty Memorial Cross service. Organized by the Former Texas Rangers Association. Azleland Memorial Park, Azle, Texas. February 19, 2012. Digital recording in the possession of the author.

Theses and Dissertations

Brown, Jean M. "Free Rein: Galveston Island's Alcohol, Gambling, and Prostitution Era, 1839–1957." M.A. thesis, Lamar University, 1998.

Charlton, Thomas Lee. "The Texas Department of Public Safety, 1935–1957." M.A. thesis, University of Texas at Austin, 1961.

Duncan, Virginia. "The Life of Captain Roy W. Aldrich." M.A. thesis, Sul Ross State Teachers College, 1942.

Fair, Richard H. "'The Good Angel of Practical Fraternity': The Ku Klux Klan in McLennan County, 1915–1924." M.A. thesis, Baylor University, 2009.

Hudy, Trayce Darter. "The Texas Guard During Martial Law and a State of Emergency: A Select Study Focusing on Galveston, Sherman, Beaumont and Texas City." M.A. thesis, Texas Woman's University, 2001.

Kuhlman, Martin Herman. "The Civil Rights Movement in Texas: Desegregation of Public Accommodations, 1950–1964." Ph.D. dissertation, Texas Tech University, 1994.

Kumler, Donna J. "'They Have Gone from Sherman': The Courthouse Riot of 1930 and Its Impact on the Black Professional Class." Ph.D. dissertation, University of North Texas, 1995.

McClung, John Busby. "Texas Rangers Along the Rio Grande, 1910–1919." Ph.D. dissertation, Texas Christian University, 1965.

McGoldrick-Spradlin, Ginger. "The Crucible of Texas Politics: An Analysis of the United States Senatorial Primaries of 1941 and 1948." M.A. thesis, East Tennessee State University, 2011.

Murphy, Thomas Michael. "History of the Sherman Riot." M.A. thesis, Austin College, 1931.

Ribb, Richard Henry. "José Tomás Canales and the Texas Rangers: Myth, Identity, and Power in South Texas, 1900–1920." Ph.D. dissertation, University of Texas at Austin, 2001.

Schuster, Stephen William, IV. "The Modernization of the Texas Rangers, 1930–1936." M.A. thesis, Texas Christian University, 1965.

Smith, Mika. "Hooded Crusaders: The Ku Klux Klan in the Panhandle and South Plains, 1921–1925." M.A. thesis, Texas Tech University, 2008.

Stanley, Mark. "Booze, Boomtowns, and Burning Crosses: The Turbulent Governorship of Pat M. Neff of Texas, 1921–1925." M.A. thesis, University of North Texas, 2005.

Ward, James Randolph. "The Texas Rangers, 1919–1935: A Study in Law Enforcement." Ph.D. dissertation, Texas Christian University, 1972.

Welch, June R. "The Texas Senatorial Election of 1948." M.A. thesis, Texas Technological College, 1953.

Unpublished Material

"822nd Military Police Company, Memories." Berlin, Germany: privately printed, 1945.

Cox, Mike, and Colonel James B. Adams. Stan Guffey eulogy, MS, n.d. Archives Files, FTRA, Fredericksburg, Texas.

Crawford, Donald Clifton. "James Richard Davenport." MS, 1999. Copy provided to the author by Chuck Parsons.

Green, Donald E. "Son of the Hundredth Meridian: Collingsworth County During the Great Depression." Chapter Four. Rough draft excerpt, n.d. Copy in the possession of the author.

Hammonds, Jane Lawson. "822nd Military Police Company: The Forgotten 'Supporting Cast' of the Ninth Army." MS, 2001. Retrieved from http://www.janesgenealogy.info/army822nd.htm.

Liles, Maurine, compiler. "Texas Ranger Captain Will Wright." MS, 2009. Wilson County Historical Society Archives, Floresville, Texas.

Mahaffey, Charles B. "A Segment of Law Enforcement." MS, n.d. Archives Files, FTRA, Fredericksburg, Texas.

Miller Family Tree, MS, n.d. Copy provided to the author by Roger H. Miller.

Riddles, James Elmer. Unofficial College Transcript. Copy provided to the author by Sul Ross University, Alpine, Texas.

Index

A

B

C

E

F

G

H

I

J

K

L

M

S

T

Z